The beauty of diamond jewellery
Award-winning designs by Hisako Takagiwa
(necklace, worn here as a tiara) and Horst Sattler (ring)
(By courtesy of De Beers Consolidated Mines Ltd.)

GEMS

Their Sources, Descriptions and

Identification

ROBERT WEBSTER, F.G.A.

ARCHON BOOKS

LONDON
BUTTERWORTHS

Published in the United States of America
by
Archon Books
The Shoe String Press, Inc.
995 Sherman Avenue
Hamden, Connecticut 06514

SBN 208 00973 6
Suggested U.D.C. number: 549.091 + 671.15

Made and printed in Great Britain by
William Clowes and Sons, Limited, London and Beccles

FOREWORD

Most of us are familiar with the chairman who, when saddled with the task of introducing some distinguished lecturer hitherto quite unknown to him, opens his preamble: 'I am sure that Mr. So-and-so is too well known to you to need any introduction from me . . .'. He then surreptitiously fumbles the notes with which he has just been armed to find out what precisely are Mr. So-and-so's qualifications as a lecturer on the subject in hand.

Having known Mr. Webster for nearly 30 years, first as a student and later as colleague and friend, I have no need to consult any notes in recommending him and his new book to the public. Indeed, were this foreword addressed to gemmologists only, the cliché—needs no introduction from me—would strictly be true, since Mr. Webster's books, his lectures, and his very numerous articles in the specialized journals have given him a more than national reputation.

However, his latest and greatest book is intended not merely for the student and jeweller, but for those of the general public who wish to learn something, or more than something, about precious stones and ornamental materials. To such let it be said that Mr. Webster is supremely well fitted for his task. In 1934 he passed the diploma examination of the Gemmological Association with distinction, and even in his student days was engaged in original research. Soon this bore fruit when he was awarded the coveted Research Diploma of the Association for his work on ivory and its substitutes.

Webster's *Gemmologists Compendium* first appeared in 1937, and this useful compilation of essential data at once endeared itself to students, and has continued, in revised form, to be a most popular work of reference. This was followed, in 1941, by *Practical Gemmology*—essentially a short course in gemmology for the student—which has also achieved a continuing success.

Soon after World War II Mr. Webster joined the staff of the Precious Stone Laboratory of the London Chamber of Commerce in Hatton Garden. Having the resources of a well equipped laboratory at his disposal naturally enlarged the range and depth of Mr. Webster's fields of research, and our knowledge of numerous aspects of gem behaviour has been increased as a consequence of his thorough investigations.

In the past, almost all major works on gemstones have been written by mineralogists who, despite their erudition and scientific knowledge of minerals, have approached the study of gemstones as it were from the outside. We owe these early authors a great debt for laying the solid foundations on which subsequent developments have been built, but gemmology has evolved its own techniques and its own specialized approach, and is now entitled to be treated as a subject in its own right. Here for the first time we have a complete book on precious stones written by a professional gemmologist who knows gems and all their characters from the inside, and is able to describe both the materials and the instruments by which they are studied from first-hand experience.

For all types of reader this book should provide the most comprehensive, accurate, and readable account of gemstones at present available, and I feel privileged to be asked to commend it.

B. W. ANDERSON

CONTENTS

		Page
Foreword	. . . .	v
List of colour plates	. . . .	ix
Preface to the Second Edition.	. . . . . .	xi
Preface to the First Edition	. . . . . .	xiii
Introduction	. . . .	xv

Chapter

1	The Origin and Recovery of Gemstones	. . . .	1
2	Diamond	13
3	Ruby and Sapphire	54
4	Emerald, Aquamarine and Other Beryls	. . . .	76
5	Chrysoberyl and Spinel	. . . . . .	96
6	Topaz and Tourmaline	. . . . . .	107
7	Zircon, Peridot and Spodumene	. . . . .	120
8	The Garnets	. . . .	134
9	Moonstone and Other Feldspar Gemstones	. . .	149
10	Gems of the Silica Group including Amethyst, Agate and Opal	.	160
11	Turquoise and Lapis-Lazuli .	. . . . .	197
12	The Jades	210
13	Marcasite and Hematite	. . . . . .	221
14	The Natural Glasses	227
15	Marble	235
16	Lesser Known Ornamental and Gem Materials	. .	247
17	Synthetic Gemstones	. . . . . .	309
18	Imitation Gemstones	. . . . . .	345
19	Composite and Artificially Coloured Stones	. . .	361
20	The Fashioning of Gemstones	. . . . .	369
21	Pearl—its Cultivation and Imitation	. . . .	398
22	Coral, Shell and Operculum .	. . . . .	455
23	Amber and Jet	466

CONTENTS

Page

24 Ivory and Tortoise-shell 475

25 How Gemstones are Identified 492

26 Crystals 494

27 Hardness, Cleavage and Fracture 514

28 Specific Gravity 522

29 Light and Optical Effects 539

30 Colour in Gemstones 555

31 The Measurement of Refractive Index 573

32 Colour in Gem-testing 598

33 The Microscope 622

34 Inclusions in Gemstones 672

35 Luminescence 681

36 X-rays in Gem-testing 698

37 Electrical and Magnetic Phenomena of Gemstones . . . 716

38 Chemistry and Gemstones 724

   Identification Tables 733

   Appendices 775

   Index 805

LIST OF COLOUR PLATES

Plate   Facing page

FRONTISPIECE   The Beauty of Diamond Jewellery

I   Rough Diamond Crystals 16

II   Uncut Diamond Crystals 22

III   Diamond Fringe Necklace 34

IV   Diamonds—Some colours and styles in which they are cut   42

V   Necklace and Ear Pendants in Diamond and Ruby . . 54

VI   Suite of Diamond and Sapphire Jewellery . . . 62

VII   The Sapphire Group 72

VIII   Suite of Diamond and Emerald Jewellery . . . 84

IX   The Beryl Group 94

X   Chrysoberyl and Spinel 98

XI   Sinhalite, Topaz and Peridot 108

XII   The Tourmaline Group 114

XIII   The Zircon Group 122

XIV   Some Rare Stones 130

XV   The Garnet Group 140

XVI   The Quartz Group 168

XVII   Nephrite. Massive Spinach-green Jade Brushpot . . 212

XVIII   Various Colours of Jadeite 218

XIX   Cabochons of Ornamental Stones 268

XX   Gemstones in Their Natural Form 500

XXI   Absorption Spectra 618

XXII   Absorption Spectra 620

PREFACE TO THE SECOND EDITION

Experience with the two volumes of the first edition has shown that a single volume would be more convenient to the user. Despite the production of a book having a greater weight, *Gems: their Sources, Descriptions and Identification* is now produced complete within a single cover.

The arrangement of the text has not been altered except that additions have been made to various chapters so that newer information could be incorporated, in particular that on synthetic stones. New tables on plastics and their identification, drawn up by Mr. H. Lee, will provide more help in dealing with the identification of these difficult materials, and separate tables on refractive indices and specific gravities have been included to supplement the comprehensive main table of constants. The new blue zoisite gemstone, Tanzanite, has called for an alteration in the text. The section 'Thulite', which was previously the only gem material of the zoisite species, has now been entitled 'Zoisite' in order to more conveniently cover the new variety.

My thanks go to the many friends all over the world who have sent me items of information, or pointed out errors or omissions in the first edition. Dr. Kurt Nassau has been most helpful in advising on the newer synthetic stones and Mr. Craig C. Smith gave valuable information on the new chrome chalcedony found in Rhodesia. The staff of both western and eastern head-quarters of the Gemological Institute of America gave helpful advice, and I must give my thanks to Mr. B. W. Anderson for his ever-ready assistance, advice and criticism. I thank Mr. H. Lee and Mr. Dennis Smith for their help in proof reading this second edition.

New coloured plates, with a somewhat different outlook, replace those of Hallwag used in the first edition, as these earlier plates are no longer available. The new plates have been provided by the courtesy of De Beers Consolidated Mines Ltd.; Messrs. Garrards Ltd. (The Crown Jewellers); Messrs. Christie Manson, and Woods; and The Institute of Geological Sciences through the staff of the Geological and Survey Museum, who prepared the coloured plates of the stones specially for this edition.

ROBERT WEBSTER

PREFACE TO THE FIRST EDITION

For two decades, an earlier work of mine—*Practical Gemmology*—has proved a useful elementary textbook on the subject of gem materials and their testing, a study now known as 'gemmology'. During this period, new materials have been found and testing methods greatly improved, so that the simple expositions given in *Practical Gemmology* do not now cover the subject adequately and a new book has become a necessity.

The majority of books written on the subject of gems start with a detailed account of the physical and optical properties of gem materials. They then go on to the theory and use of instruments used in gem-testing before describing the gems themselves. In this work, the usual scheme is reversed and a more practical approach is made. A short introduction to the formation of such minerals in the earth leads to descriptions of the various gem materials.

Following this, there are chapters on synthetic stones, composite and imitation stones, and how gemstones are fashioned for the market. The first volume concludes with descriptions of pearl, coral, jet and amber, and other materials used in ornamentation which owe their genesis to organic processes. The second volume deals with the technical aspects of gem materials and is followed by descriptions of the various methods used in gem identification. The book is completed by a section containing tables and useful data.

The arrangement of describing the gemstones themselves before their technical aspects may be considered open to objection as some technical data must be included in the descriptions of the stones. This is a minor point against the value of an arrangement which introduces the subject in the logical sequence of the finding in the rough state of the natural gems, the production of synthetic and imitation stones, and the fashioning of these various natural and man-made materials into a finished gemstone. Where possible, some simple explanation of the meaning of the technical references is brought out as the gem story unfolds.

One problem which besets any writer on gemstones is to select the order in which the gem materials are discussed. Whatever method is used, some criticism is inevitable. In this work the better-known jewellery stones are placed first, and are followed by the lesser known stones in alphabetical order, unless, for some reason, the stones are better placed in a group forming a small subchapter.

In the technical section an endeavour is made to tell something of the history of gem-testing which has led to the present high standard of what has with some truth become known as 'scientific gemmology'. In this section, too, are details of the use and working of a number of special instruments not usually included in such books.

Throughout the compilation of this work considerable assistance has been received from many members of the Gemmological Association and of the jewellery trade. A special debt of gratitude is owed to Mr. G. F. Andrews and Mr. H. Lee, who read and criticized the original typescript manuscript.

I owe much to my colleagues Mr. B. W. Anderson and Mr. C. J. Payne for their encouragement and for unstintingly supplying me with much of the data accumulated in the archives of the Laboratory of the London Chamber of Commerce. Further, Mr. Anderson freely handed over to me much of his unpublished work on the causes of colour, the hardness and the methods of determining the density of gemstones. These notes have been duly incorporated in the text. Likewise, Mr. Payne allowed the incorporation of his articles on the method of refractive index determination by minimum deviation, and that on interference figures, both of which were published in *The Gemmologist*.

Mr. Lee, with his technical knowledge of chemistry, gave considerable help on the chemical aspects of plastics, and the chapter on chemistry is based mainly on his information.

My thanks go to Dr. W. E. Smith of Chelsea College of Science and Technology for his help with the chapter on the geology and the formation of minerals which forms the first part of the book. Dr. W. Stern advised on the part dealing with the marketing and industrial uses of diamonds, and Herr G. O. Wild of Idar-Oberstein gave information on a number of topics, particularly on the quartz gems.

Mr. J. Asscher, Jnr., of Amsterdam checked the notes on diamond polishing, and Mr. C. L. Arnold and Mr. G. E. Bull-Diamond likewise checked the part on lapidary working of gemstones.

A number of line drawings, particularly of crystals, were kindly prepared for me by Mr. G. A. White of Norwich. Dr. E. Gübelin allowed the use of some of his excellent photomicrographs to illustrate the chapter on gemstone inclusions, which was mainly compiled from his published researches. It is appropriate here to mention that Plates I–XVI appeared in Dr. E. Gübelin's *Edelsteine*, and are reproduced by courtesy of Hallwag, Berne. Mrs. V. G. Hinton kindly took the pearl surface photomicrograph specially for me, and Dr. E. H. Rutland, Mr. B. W. Anderson, Mr. R. K. Mitchell and Mr. H. Lee assisted in the task of reading the proofs.

The Gemmological Association kindly allowed the incorporation in this work of my articles on emerald, ruby and sapphire, and marble, as well as a number of illustrations which had previously been published in the *Journal of Gemmology*. The chapters on the microscope, x-rays and luminescence are largely made up from my articles published in *The Gemmologist* and are reprinted, together with the illustrations, by courtesy of N.A.G. Press Ltd. Finally, the pictures of the pearl cultivation in Japan were supplied by Shell Photographic Unit and the Cultured Pearl Company, and those of diamond mining by the Anglo-American Corporation.

ROBERT WEBSTER

INTRODUCTION

The study of gems is of absorbing interest, not only to the connoisseur and to those whose business is to buy and sell jewellery but to the ordinary man in the street and his wife, for it is they who appreciate gems for their beauty and for their power of adornment.

With the exception of pearl, coral and a few other organically produced materials, most gems are lustrous or brightly coloured minerals found in the rocks of the earth's surface. Many such minerals have been used for personal decoration, as charms or amulets, or for the embellishment of objects of virtu or utility, from times which predate written history.

The first of the three cardinal virtues of a gem is undoubtedly beauty— beauty through transparency and depth of colour as in the ruby or the emerald; through colour alone as in the turquoise; or through the splitting up of the white light into the spectral colours, the so-called 'fire', which is so well seen in the diamond. The 'play of colour' due to interference of transmitted light rays gives to the opal its unique appearance. Reflections from regularly arranged inclusions within the stone give rise to the cat's-eye and star-stone effects. However, much of the beauty of gemstones is latent until brought out by the work of the lapidary who cuts and polishes the stones in symmetrical forms.

For use in ornaments, a gemstone should be able to resist abrasive and chemical attacks which would tend to mar the polish and thus destroy the lustre. Durability is thus the second virtue and depends upon the hardness of the mineral. In general, gem minerals are hard minerals. Glass imitation stones are not durable: they are too soft to resist the abrasion by the sand and dust particles and the chemical action of the sulphur in the atmosphere.

Often of far greater influence than either beauty or durability is rarity. A mineral may be fairly common, yet really fine pieces suitable for fashioning into gemstones may be quite scarce. This is so in the case of the emerald. A flawless emerald of fine colour is exceedingly rare and may well command a higher price than a diamond of comparable size and quality. The law of supply and demand, often influenced by the caprice of fashion, governs to a great extent the rarity of gemstones. There are many stones which undeniably possess the qualifications of beauty and durability but are in little demand.

It used to be quite common practice to divide gemstones into two classes —precious stones and semi-precious stones—but the division was quite arbitrary. Precious stones are usually understood to be diamond, ruby emerald, sapphire and pearl, with perhaps black opal and alexandrite. All of these are stones in fairly constant demand with a high value for fine specimens. Semi-precious stones are the peridot, aquamarine, topaz, tourmaline, zircon and amethyst in company with all other stones which do not command such high prices and for which the demand is more prone to the whims of fashion. Use of the term 'semi-precious' is now discouraged.

It may surprise the uninitiated to know that ruby with its crimson colour and the lovely blue sapphire belong to the same mineral species. This is a species known as corundum, an impure form of which is the abrasive emery. The striking difference in colour of ruby and sapphire is solely due to a trace of a metallic oxide as an impurity. Similarly emerald, aquamarine and the blushing rose-coloured morganite are all colour varieties of the species beryl.

Changing the colour of gemstones by heat, by irradiation and by staining, has become commonplace in species susceptible to such changes.

The turn of the century brought further problems for the jeweller. Extensive experiments carried out by scientists throughout the world began to produce results, and synthetic stones started to enter the field of commerce. At first only the ruby was so produced, then the sapphire, to be followed by synthetic sapphires of fancy colours. Later, gems of the spinel species were made synthetically in a galaxy of lovely colours. The 1930s saw the beginning of the synthetic emerald and after the end of World War II new stones which had little or no counterpart in nature were synthetically produced by the scientist. Finally, the successful synthesis of the diamond was announced (although the product was only of grain size and its use that of an abrasive).

CHAPTER 1

THE ORIGIN AND RECOVERY
OF GEMSTONES

SHELLS OF THE EARTH

Gem materials, except for those which are of organic origin or due to man's artifice, are found in the rocks forming the upper or accessible levels of the earth's crust.

There are various theories as to the nature and structure of the earth's interior. The most important suggests that there is a heavy central core, probably of nickel-iron, termed the barysphere, which is about half the diameter of the earth. This core has a density about 8 times heavier than water and is surrounded by a less dense homogenous layer which may be metallic sulphides or oxides and has a density of 5–6. Overlying this is a shell of heavy compressed silicates having a density of 3·6–4, which is surrounded by a crustal layer some 30–40 miles thick, composed of a complex series of consolidated rocks. These outer layers are termed the lithosphere and have a density of 2·8–3·2 (*Figure 1.1*).

The innermost layer of the lithosphere consists mainly of rocks which are silicates containing magnesium (for example olivine) and is known as the SIMA layer. The rocks of the outer layer are silicates containing aluminium (for example feldspar): this layer is known as SIAL, and is most important in the genesis of gemstones.

ROCK COMPOSITION

All rocks are mineral aggregates, each mineral being a distinct inorganic chemical compound possessing a definite chemical composition and internal atomic structure. In most cases, rocks are composed of several different minerals although one mineral may predominate over the others. Indeed, in the case of the white ornamental marble only one mineral—calcite—is present. Since the relative abundance of minerals in any one rock mass is subject to variation, the bulk chemical composition of a rock is also subject to variation and is not fixed as rigidly as is the chemical composition of an individual mineral.

Rocks are usually classified under three broad headings: (*a*) igneous, (*b*) sedimentary, and (*c*) metamorphic. Igneous rocks are those which were produced by the solidification of hot molten matter (magma) which was pushed into (intruded into) fissures in the earth's crust, or was extruded on the surface as lava flowing from a volcano (*Figure 1.2*). Pyroclastic rocks, that is those which consist of large or small rock fragments blown out of volcanoes, are also usually classified as igneous rocks.

Figure 1.1. The shells of the earth. (1) The lithosphere (crustal layers) with a density of 2·8–3·2. (2) Shell of eclogite (dense silicates) with a density of 3·6–4. (3) Shell of sulphides and oxides with a density of 5–6. (4) Nickel-iron core with a density of 8

Igneous Rocks

During the cooling of magma, the individual minerals crystallize out around local centres. Some minerals do so at an early stage and were able to develop good crystal outlines except when they came into contact with something during growth. On the other hand, the last minerals to crystallize out rarely show good crystal outlines since they were forced to occupy the irregular spaces between the crystals which were already in existence.

Slow cooling of magma in major intrusions below the earth's surface usually produces coarse-grained rocks in which the individual crystals are readily visible to the naked eye. Such a rock is granite. Although best known as a building stone, this has at times been used as a decorative stone

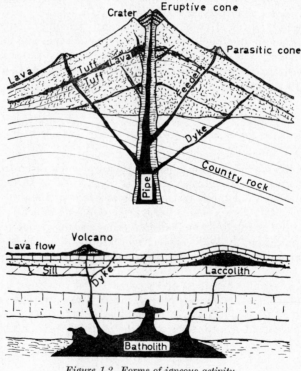

Figure 1.2. Forms of igneous activity

2

mounted in jewellery. Typical granite is composed mainly of feldspar, glassy-looking quartz (rock crystal) and mica, which are essential minerals of such a rock, although a dark coloured ferro-magnesian mineral, such as biotite or hornblende, is usually present. In granite, the feldspar crystallized at an earlier stage than quartz so that the feldspar crystals are more likely to show external form than the quartz (*Figure 1.3*).

The more rapid cooling of the magma which filled fissures generally produces medium-grained rocks. A hand lens is needed to distinguish the individual grains in these. However, the still liquid part of the magma may have solidified around large crystals of certain minerals so that the rock contains large crystals embedded in a fine-grained groundmass. This is called a porphyritic structure and such rocks are termed porphyries. Well-known porphyries are the 'Perfido serpentino' of Greece and the 'por-

Figure 1.3. Granite (Aberdeen), a typical igneous rock. The dark areas are mica; the intermediate coloured areas are pink feldspar and the white areas are rock crystal

phyrites leptosephos' of upper Egypt, rocks which had a considerable vogue for ornamentation in the heydays of the Greek and Roman Empires.

Pegmatites are exceptions to the general rule that minor intrusions are medium to fine-grained. They are a fruitful source of gem minerals. Pegmatites are of very coarse texture so that the crystals may be measured by inches, or even by feet. The extremely coarse texture is said to be due to the presence of considerable quantities of water and other fluxing agents which kept the solution in a very mobile state, and thus favoured the formation of large crystals by free diffusion of molecules with fewer centres of crystallization.

One pegmatite rock which could be mentioned here, for it has been used for ornamental purposes, is graphic granite, which consists of intergrowths of quartz and feldspar which interlock in an angular pattern resembling the cuneiform writing of ancient times.

Cavities caused by gases and fluids trapped in the solidifying magma produce cavities lined with free growing crystals of such high-temperature minerals as topaz and beryl. From these so-called miarolitic cavities, gem crystals are often recovered.

The cooling of certain minor intrusions and the lava flows extruded out at the earth's surface was so rapid that there was no time for crystallization to take place. The rock became so fine-grained that the minerals can only be determined under the high powers of a microscope. In this manner the natural glass known as obsidian was formed. It is a rock which has been fashioned for use in jewellery.

Sedimentary Rocks

The second group of rocks, the sedimentary rocks, result from the breaking down (denudation) of earlier formed rock masses. There are three stages in the formation of typical sedimentary rocks. First, the chemical and mechanical 'weathering' of source rocks by the action of rain, wind or ice; by changing temperatures of day and night or winter and summer; by the chemical breakdown of unstable minerals; or by chemical action of the atmosphere.

The second stage is the transportation of the products of weathering by moving water or wind. Rocks formed by sedimentary deposits which have

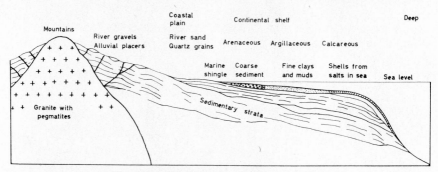

Figure 1.4. The formation of sedimentary rocks

been airborne are described as aeolian, as opposed to aqueous when the sediments are carried by water.

Thirdly comes the deposition of the debris. The insoluble weathering products are separated into coarse and finer particles, for the smaller and lighter particles are carried farther away from the primary source than the larger and heavier particles. When the pebbles, sands or silts fall to the ground or the sea bed, they—especially the smaller grain sizes—form sediments in layers. Owing to the subsequent deposition of other layers, these become consolidated and cemented together to form the stratified (layered) rocks. They are sometimes called secondary rocks.

The soluble products of weathering may be deposited by precipitation from water by the action of organisms living in it, or by simple evaporation of mineralized water in places favouring rapid evaporation. The massive gypsum, well known as the ornamental material alabaster, is often produced in this manner. *Figure 1.4* illustrates the formation of sedimentary rocks.

Examples are the limestones and sandstones. The limestones produce many of the ornamental 'marbles' used in architecture and for small objets d'art. Coal and lignite, and this includes jet, are formed by the accumulation of plant remains and are classed as sedimentary rocks. The larger fragments of rocks, either as water-worn pebbles or as angular fragments, may be cemented together by secondary mineralization. When pebbles are so cemented together the resulting rock is termed a conglomerate, an example being the so-called 'Hertfordshire pudding-stone' which may occasionally be met as polished pieces (*Figure 1.5*). Should the fragments be angular, the material is termed a breccia, and fragments of agate or jasper so cemented form 'brecciated agate' or 'brecciated jasper'. Such rocks have been cut and polished for ornamental purposes (*Figure 1.6*).

The sorting of the detritus (gravel, sand, silt and so forth) of broken-down rocks, is commonly carried out by the action of streams and rivers.

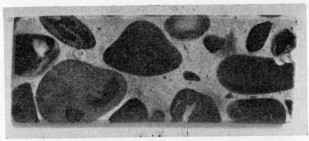

Figure 1.5. Hertfordshire pudding-stone—a conglomerate

Figure 1.6. Brecciated agate

The rocks need not be primary rocks, for during the vast ages of geological time sedimentary rocks formed earlier can suffer similar disintegration. Such sorting by water may depend greatly upon the density of the mineral being carried along. The more important gem minerals, being relatively heavy, tend to fall into any depression in the river bed forming placer deposits. The river beds may be ancient, having long since ceased to carry water and are now covered and obliterated by more recent soils. It is in such old river courses that the water-worn pebbles of many gemstones are found. Such deposits are known as alluvials. *Figure 1.7* shows a heap of water-worn pebbles from the Ceylon gem gravels.

Sedimentary rocks may accumulate in regions where life is possible,

Figure 1.7. Water-worn pebbles from the Ceylon gem gravels

consequently they may contain the remains of once living organisms. A few fossils are of importance as gem materials; for example, wood opal or silicified wood, produced by the replacement and impregnation of the woody tissues of trees by silica while the wood is entombed in sedimentary rocks such as sandstone. Fossil shells, corals, or crinoids (sea lilies) in limestones give attractive marbles. *Figures 1.8* and *1.9* show respectively a 'shell marble' and an encrinital limestone.

Metamorphic Rocks

Heat and pressure from intrusions of igneous rocks, or from the folding of rock masses during deep-seated disturbances in the earth's crust during the birth of mountains, may alter the surrounding country rocks, whether they be igneous or sedimentary, so that a new type of rock is produced. Such an alteration is termed metamorphism. When extensive areas—some hundreds or thousands of square miles—are affected by deep-seated igneous activity regional or dynamothermal metamorphism (*Figures 1.10a* and *b*) is said to occur, and under these conditions rocks such as schists,

Figure 1.8. Fossil shell limestone. A limestone containing masses of a freshwater snail shell. The so-called Purbeck marble

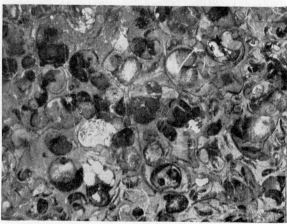

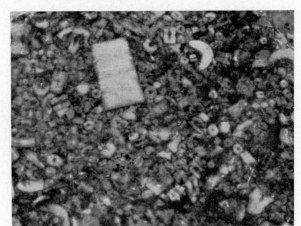

Figure 1.9. Fossil lime-stone containing masses of crinoids (sea lilies). Encrinital marble from Derbyshire

gneisses, granulites, and some crystalline limestones and quartzites are produced.

Often the metamorphic alteration of an earlier rock takes place locally around igneous intrusions, which may be of no great size, and may occur at the edges of small dikes and veins. This type of metamorphism is called contact or thermal metamorphism (*Figure 1.10c*). High temperature is the main cause of the alteration, but gases given off during the closing stages of the crystallization of the igneous intrusion may have an influence. A feature of contact metamorphism is an aureole of successive zones around the intrusion. The alteration of the original rock is most marked near the edge of the intrusion.

The metamorphism of a pure limestone will produce a white marble, such as the marble of Carrara in Tuscany, Italy. In this case the metamorphism causes a recrystallization of the calcium carbonate of the limestone, producing interlocking crystals of calcite. Owing to the cramped space for crystal growth, the new calcite crystals show no regular outlines. Similarly a sandstone metamorphoses to a quartzite, a much harder rock than marble. It can be seen that each irregular grain is one individual crystal of calcite or of quartz, in marble or quartzite respectively, if a thin section of such a rock is observed in polarized light (*Figure 1.11*).

During alteration by metamorphism, any impurities in the original rock, the so-called accessory minerals, may crystallize out as separate minerals which are disseminated through the newly formed rock. Thus green fuchsite mica may form crystals throughout quartzite, producing the green aventurine quartz so often met with as beads and rounded shaped stones in jewellery. The ruby and sapphire of Burma have been similarly produced by metamorphic action on the limestone country rock, and garnet is found in mica schist, a rock with an abundance of flaky minerals having a parallel orientation.

Rocks Formed by Vapour Action

By the action of chemically active vapours (pneumatolysis), or fluids, often assisted by the heat from the intrusion of molten matter, new rocks

7

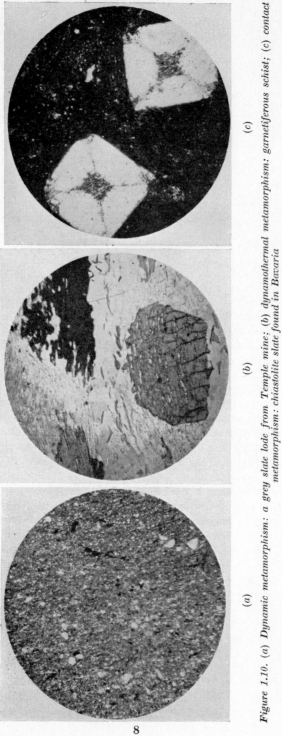

(a)

(b)

(c)

Figure 1.10. (a) Dynamic metamorphism: a grey slate lode from Temple mine; (b) dynamothermal metamorphism: garnetiferous schist; (c) contact metamorphism: chiastolite slate found in Bavaria

may be produced from old ones. New minerals are formed by the action of the vapours, particularly boron and fluorine, which produces such minerals as tourmaline and topaz in granitic rocks. Reactive rocks such as limestones near large granite intrusions may be affected by vapours to give rocks such

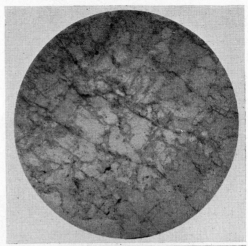

(a)

Figure 1.11. Photomicrographs of a thin section of quartzite (a) in ordinary light and (b) in polarized light showing the individual grains

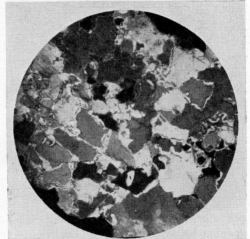

(b)

as the skarns, rich in iron or magnesium minerals, for example andradite garnet. Rocks which owe their alteration to vapour are termed pneumatolytic rocks.

Mineral-rich Water

Much mineral-rich water travels through cracks and fissures in the country rock and deposits low-temperature minerals in them. Such veins or lodes, the latter term being used for metallic veins, may open out into cavities, called vughs (vugs). The vughs may be lined with crystals deposited from the water. Many of the deposited minerals have gem significance.

1*

9

In a vugh, the minerals deposited are of a different nature from the surrounding rock. When a cavity formed in a primary rock has no secondary mineralization from percolating waters, any crystals projecting into the cavity will only be those which comprise the surrounding rock mass. Such a cavity is correctly called a drusy cavity, but this term is often erroneously used interchangeably with vugh and with geode.

Geodes are hollow cavities lined with crystals deposited from mineral-rich waters which have percolated into steam cavities in lavas, or into cavities in sedimentary rocks, and even into fossils. Such geodes are a common source of gem crystals, particularly rock crystal and amethyst, although the latter is often found in vughs. Owing to their likeness to

Figure 1.12. Quartz crystals in a geode. A typical 'potato stone'

potatoes when removed from the rock formation, geodes are often called 'potato stones' (*Figure 1.12*). The original shape of the gas vesicles in lava is often lenticular or almond-shaped—they are termed amygdaloidal. Such cavities may be completely filled with minerals, commonly agate, and they are then called amygdales or nodules.

In caves, the mineral-rich water dripping from the roof forms hanging rock masses called stalagtites. Similar but upstanding masses may form on the floor of the cave and are stalagmites. A stalagmite may grow upwards to such an extent that it joins the stalagtite above it to form a complete pillar between roof and floor. Further deposition of minerals may well occur in irregular sheets over the floor of the cave and this is often banded in structure. It is from such formations that the banded calcites, the so-called 'onyx marbles', and rhodochrosite are obtained.

Rock Systems

The geologist divides the rocks of the earth's surface into groups which are then subdivided into smaller divisions called systems. Such systems are noted in Table 1.1 and with them their approximate ages. Some knowledge of these systems may be necessary in order to understand them clearly when they are referred to later.

TABLE 1.1

Rocks of the Earth's Surface

Group	System	Estimated age in millions of years
Quaternary	Pleistocene	1
Cainozoic (recent life) also	Pliocene	12
known as Tertiary	Miocene	23
	Oligocene	35
	Eocene	70
Mesozoic (middle life) also	Cretaceous	135
known as Secondary	Jurassic	180
	Triassic	220
Palaeozoic (ancient life)	Permian	270
also known as Primary	Carboniferous	350
	Devonian	400
	Silurian	430
	Ordovician	490
	Cambrian	600
Archaean or pre-Cambrian	—	> 3,000

GEM BELTS

The foregoing description of rock and mineral formation tells something of how our gemstones have been formed by nature. The survey given is generalized and greatly condensed. It may truthfully be said that gem minerals are abnormal minerals found in abnormal rocks. This is the reason, in many cases, for the rarity of gemstones and may also account for their localization in definite areas.

Thus there are the gem-rich metamorphosed limestones of upper Burma which supply the world's finest rubies, sapphires and spinels, and with them a great number of other and rarer gemstones. The Mogok Stone Tract, as this area is called after the town of Mogok, is one of the most prolific gem areas of the world—but not for diamonds, which are found only in specialized rock formations which do not occur in Burma. The alluvial deposits of Ceylon, from which so many gem minerals are obtained, are the result of the erosion of schistosic and gneissic rocks and crystalline limestones which were the result of metamorphism of older rocks. Ruby, sapphire and zircon are found in similar alluvial deposits which stretch from Vietnam to Thailand.

The pegmatites of Madagascar provide an interesting suite of gem minerals, such as beryl, tourmaline, garnet, topaz, spinel, kunzite, iolite, amazonstone and a transparent golden-yellow feldspar. They form a typical area

11

for gemstone recovery. The same may be said for the gem and lithium-bearing pegmatites of the Pala district of San Diego County, California, from which much of the beautiful kunzite, pink beryl, and similarly coloured tourmaline comes. Pegmatite veins are the source of the beryl and tourmaline and many other rarer gem minerals found in the Minas Gerais and Minas Novas districts of Brazil. Other types of rocks provide other gem minerals, including diamond, in Brazil.

Many smaller, or less important, gem belts could be cited. Some reference is made to them where individual gem species are described.

MINING METHODS

The methods used in the mining of gem materials are usually simple and often crude. Deep shaft mines, so common in coal mining, are used only for the 'pipe' diamond deposits of Africa. Other gems are not mined in depth but are won by driving short tunnels (adits) into the hillsides, as in the recovery of some ruby and sapphire in Burma and some emeralds in Colombia.

An opencast type of mining by digging away the overburden is another method used in getting at the gem-bearing rocks. In special cases, where a suitable supply of water is available, powerful jets of water (monitor jets) are used to break down the subsoil and loose rock from the side of hills. 'Terrace mining' is used for some conditions of rock formation, particularly on hillsides, by cutting away the earth and rock, in steps or terraces. Emerald is recovered from the Chivor mine in Colombia by such a method.

The method of recovering gem gravel from the dry beds of ancient rivers, as practised in Burma, Ceylon and Thailand particularly, is to dig a small pit down to the gravel and, if conditions are right, drive short horizontal galleries from the base of the pit. Usually the broken-down ground containing the gemstones needs to be treated by washing in sluices, which floats away the lighter 'gangue' material and leaves the heavier 'gemmy' concentrate.

In the running water of streams and rivers, the gem pebbles are recovered by 'panning'. A shallow dish is used into which some of the gravel is placed with water and by a gentle movement of the pan, the water is swirled over the edge carrying with it the lighter gangue.

CHAPTER 2

DIAMOND

COMPOSITION AND SHAPE

Reputed to endow the wearer with purity, love and joy, the diamond—the 'Adamas' of the Greeks—is traditionally the emblem of fearlessness. Romantic in history and symbolic of love, diamond is the hardest of natural substances. It is crystalline carbon, akin in chemistry to graphite, which is one of the softest minerals known. What forces nature to marshal the carbon atoms to form the close-packed cubic arrangement which gives the diamond structure rather than the more open hexagonal packing of graphite is one of the many mysteries which diamond poses.

Diamond crystals belong to the cubic system of crystal architecture. When showing a perfection of form, they habitually take that of the octa-hedron, a form which may be described as two equilateral four-sided pyramids base to base. Such crystals usually have bright shining faces pitted with triangular markings called 'trigons'. *Figure 2.1* shows a number of octahedral diamond crystals, some of which show 'trigons'. The natural 'trigons' have their points directed to the edge of the octahedral face of the crystal. Similar markings, called 'etch pits', follow the orientation of the face of the crystal.

A star-shaped form of crystal often occurs; this is due to twinning. These platy crystals may be described as octahedra in which half of the crystal has been rotated through 180 degrees. Such crystals are termed macles. Many diamond crystals assume nearly round forms owing in part to the curved form of the faces, this being particularly so in the case of crystals having 24 or 48 faces. The stepping of the octahedral faces also produces a tendency to roundness of form and to give curved edges to the crystal. It is common to find these rounded crystals with a gum-like skin, called nyf. Stones showing a corrugated, grooved, or scaly appearance owing to this stepping are known as 'crinkles'.

Cube and dodecahedral forms which have six square and twelve rhomb-shaped faces respectively are other habits assumed by diamond crystals. Many diamond crystals as found, particularly those of industrial grade used for purposes other than as gems, are so distorted in form that they may appear as irregular lumps like washing soda. However, except to the in-experienced, the adamantine lustre is characteristic of diamond (*Figure 2.2*).

INDIA

Diamond first became known from India and it was from old Indian mines that the historically large diamonds such as the Koh-i-nûr and the Jehangir (*Figure 2.3*) were found. Of the very early days of diamond mining in India

Figure 2.1. Diamond crystals showing 'trigons'

little is known. From statements made in an old Indian manuscript of the first century B.C. it is thought that diamond was known in India during the Buddhist period of about 400 B.C. The first authentic mention of the Indian diamond fields was by J. B. Tavernier, a French jeweller and traveller, who visited the East between A.D. 1630 and A.D. 1668. Tavernier was not the first European to visit the mines, but he was the first to chronicle them.

The ancient Indian mines were situated in three main groups, the most important being those of the southern district. Although so important in the past they are now virtually abandoned. They stretched from the Godivari river in Hyderabad in the north to the Pennar river in Madras as the southern limit. It was along the Kristna river, which like the Godivari and

Figure 2.2. A large diamond ($426\frac{1}{2}$ carats) recovered from the Premier mine in the Transvaal. This shows how irregular a rough diamond can be
(By courtesy of the Anglo-American Corporation of South Africa Ltd.)

14

Pennar discharges into the Bay of Bengal, that the more historical stones were found. This area, usually referred to as Golconda, was one of the five mediaeval states formed by the disintegration of the Kingdom of the Deccan. Golconda existed as a State from A.D. 1347 to A.D. 1687 and the city of Golconda, now just ruins a few miles from Hyderabad, was the capital of the state. Golconda was not a mining area itself but was most probably a mart for the stones which were found in the many mines in the state and also from adjacent mines.

Particular mention must be made of the mines of Kollur, on the Kristna, for this is reputed to be the source of the Koh-i-nûr (Mountain of Light) diamond which now reposes in the front crosspatée of the Queen's State Crown, and also of the superb Hope blue diamond. Many Indian stones were cut as flat tablets, probably from cleavage pieces, which are called lasques. Maybe it is from this name that the term 'laxey diamond' applied to rather shallow brilliants originated.

Figure 2.3. The Jehangir diamond; an 83-carat Indian diamond
(By courtesy of Sotheby and Co.)

In the Bundelkhand district of Central Provinces, between the rivers Ken and Son, lie the northern group of workings. These have been mined to a limited extent in recent times. There are three types of deposits in this locality. They are (1) alluvial terraces of some of the river valleys; (2) in a conglomerate rock; and (3) in a volcanic 'pipe' situated at Majgawan, which lies some 12 miles south-west of Panna, in which well-shaped octahedral crystals of a light green colour are found. In 1955 the 'Panna Diamond Mining Syndicate' was instrumental in the further working of this area and the Majgawan pipe. This syndicate invited Russian technicians to investigate the mines and to see to the supplying of equipment. It was also proposed that Russian technicians and geologists should survey the Golconda area of Hyderabad and Andhra States.

The eastern group, the third of the groups of Indian mines, lies around the Mahanadi valley in Central Provinces and in the neighbouring Sambalpur district of Orissa. These mines have, in general, been abandoned. Further to these main groups, Mohum Tagore mentions the districts of Himalayas, Surat, Chota Nagpur, and Berar as diamond-bearing localities. The truth of these assertions is debatable.

Apart from the Majgawan pipe, the Indian diamonds are found in sandstone or conglomerate, or in the sands and gravels of old river beds. The associated minerals are usually confined to quartz pebbles and variously coloured jaspers. Panna diamonds have been known for 200 years.

BORNEO AND INDONESIA

That diamonds occur in Borneo and Indonesia (formerly the Netherlands East Indies), has been known since, it is said, about A.D. 600, and certainly since before the fourteenth century. The small stones, rarely exceeding one carat in weight, are found in the extreme west of the island. The principal deposits are in the vicinity of the Landek river near Pontianak and in the tributaries of the upper reaches of the river. Other deposits are along the upper reaches of the Sekajam river and near Sanggau on the Kapuas river. Another diamondiferous district lies in the south-east of the island in the area around Martapura near Banjarmasin. This is more important and stones up to 20 or more carats have been found in the swampy mining district. The principal workings are near Tjampaka on the Banjoe Irang river, and there are numerous occurrences along the Riam Kanan and Riam Kiwa rivers, and also along the coast rivers. Scattered finds have been made along the Pembuang (Serujan) and Kotawaringin rivers which lie to the south of the island.

The Borneo diamonds are won from alluvial deposits made up from the detritus from ancient rivers. The mining is carried out by Indonesian natives and some Chinese. It declined after 1930, but since the formation of the Indonesian Republic a fresh impetus to mining by the natives has been given. Some miners work alone while some work in family groups, yet others formed co-operatives of from 4 or 5 to 20 men in what are called kongsies, but the methods used are primitive. The production is absorbed by Eastern markets and many of the stones are native cut at Martapura. Diamonds from Borneo are said to be harder than diamonds from other localities, excepting perhaps Australia, but this hardness may be due more to the variation of grain caused by twinning of the crystals than to an actual greater hardness.

A most curious and seemingly irrational superstition regarding certain diamonds prevails among the Malay and Chinese workers in the Borneo diamond mines. Certain well crystallized diamonds enclosing a grey or black core occur and these are regarded as harbingers of personal good luck by the workers and are worn by them as an amulet. However when one of these stones is found in a mine they are looked upon as the greatest sign of ill luck, and the mine, no matter how profitable, is abandoned. The mine owner may himself not be superstitious, but nothing will induce the workmen to work that mine again and a new site has to be chosen. The Malays know such stones by a name which means 'the soul of the diamond' and they say that once the soul has left the mine, it is dead.

BRAZIL

The discovery of diamonds in Brazil occurred at a place now called Diamantina, but which was formerly known as Tejuco. The pioneer explorers,

Plate I
Rough diamond crystals
with stone shovel and hand lens

(By courtesy of De Beers Consolidated Mines Ltd.)

the bandeirantes, when panning for gold along the Jequitinhona river, frequently found bright pebbles at the bottom of their pans, or bateas as they are called. The larger ones they saved and used as chips in their card games and the smaller ones were discarded. These pebbles were diamonds, but their nature was unknown at the time.

Authorities differ as to the date these pieces were identified as diamonds and how this identification came about. Most give the date as 1725, although 11 years earlier has been mentioned as the true date. Who first spotted the white pebbles as diamond is again not certainly known. One version suggests that it may have been a priest who had been to India and had seen diamonds, or, according to H. Emmanuel, by an inhabitant of the State of Minas Gerais named Bernando Fonseca Lobo who had seen rough diamonds in a previous visit to the East Indies.

The influx of Brazilian diamonds to Europe during 1727 so shook the Dutch diamond merchants that they feared for their market. To counteract this they spread a report that the stones were only poor quality Indian stones exported from Goa, in Portuguese India, to Brazil and then to Europe. The Portuguese merchants subsequently sent Brazilian diamonds to Goa and sold them as Indian stones, so turning the tables on the Dutch merchants.

Diamond is widespread in Brazil. Besides the initial find at Diamantina in Minas Gerais and at other places in this State, stones have been found in Matto Grosso and Bahia, where in 1754, a slave who had been transferred to the area saw the similarity of the soil to the diamondiferous earth of Minas Gerais. Goyaz, Amazonas, Maranhão, Paraná, Piauhy, and São Paulo are other Brazilian States in which diamonds have been found.

Brazilian diamonds are won from a number of diverse types of rocks. In the so-called high level plateau, the rocks comprise three series, all of which are probably pre-Cambrian in age. The lowest stratum of these rocks is the Minas series, a metamorphosed rock which contains no diamonds. This series is overlaid by the much folded and faulted Itacolomy series, which is crossed by pegmatites and dikes and intrusions of a much altered rock in which diamond occurs. This is generally known as the diamond matrix. The Itacolomy series is again overlain by the Lavras series which consist of conglomerates, phyllites, and sandstones in which diamonds are found.

Although diamond is mined on the plateau at 4,000–5,000 ft. above sea level, the greatest diamond recovery is from the detritus formed on the spot, known as grupiáras, and from the water-borne deposits from the plateau rocks. Diamond may also be mined from the alluvial deposits, either from the river beds or from the banks and terraces.

Most of the Brazilian diamond mining is carried out in a primitive manner. The miner stakes his claim and works it by stripping the overburden to reach the diamond-bearing gravel, called cascalho. He carries away the overburden, if it needs to be taken away, by laboriously carrying it on his head in a wooden platter some 15 in. in diameter, called a corrombe. When the diamondiferous gravel is reached, this also has to be similarly carried to the nearest water where it is washed on screens of different mesh in order to recover the diamonds. Mechanical dredges are now being used.

In river mining, the river bed is uncovered by diverting the river, or by building wing dams, so as to allow sections to dry out. The overburden is then stripped from the dried sections to get down to the diamond-bearing cascalho. Diving suits are often used if the river is deep. The material may, however, be brought up in sacks by unassisted divers. Either way the soil is put into the boat carrying the divers and panned by batea or screened in order to recover the diamonds.

The majority of the Brazilian diamonds are of small size but of good quality. Large stones, as in other fields, are occasionally found. Indeed,what is probably the sixth largest diamond found, the 'Presidente Vargas' of 726 carats (a carat is a fifth of a gramme), is a Brazilian stone. Associated with the diamonds are many bean-shaped pebbles which the miners call favas and consider to be indicators of the presence of diamonds. These favas are water-worn pebbles of tourmaline, kyanite, perovskite, rutile, chrysoberyl and anatase, among others.

In the State of Bahia an unusual type of diamond is found. This is carbonado (also called carbon) which is a black microcrystalline diamond mass, which owing to its lack of cleavage and consequent toughness was formerly used in the crowns of rock drills. Carbonado is obtained from the gravels of the Paraguaçu river and its tributaries, chiefly around Lençoes and Morro do Chapéu—the area lying some 200 miles (320 km) west of Salvador (Bahia), the state capital. The largest carbon ever found in South America weighed 3,078 carats, nearly as much as the Cullinan diamond. Splinters of carbonado are often used for drilling beads.

NORTH AMERICA

As early as 1849, a straw-yellow crystal the size of a pea, which had been found in one of the gold mining placer deposits in California, was identified as a diamond. Five years later a number of other diamonds were found while panning for gold at Cherokee, Butte County, in the same state. Some 500 stones have been recovered whilst gold mining in California. Diamonds have been found in almost every state of the United States. The largest of these alluvial stones were discovered in Virginia; they are the 'Dewey', found in 1885 weighing 23·75 carats, and the 'Punch Jones', which turned the scale at 34·46 carats. Geologists presume that these alluvial diamonds had been carried south from Canada by the sweeping action of ice-age glaciers, the probable source being, according to W. H. Hobbs, in the vicinity of James Bay, Canada.

During March 1948, great difficulty was found in drilling for water at Vassave Township, County of Abitibe in the Province of Quebec, and investigation showed that diamond grains were present. On this information the James Bay Diamond Syndicate was formed to work an area of some 2,000 acres in the Vassau-La Cornu-Pressiac area of north-western Quebec Province, Canada. Nothing further seems to have been heard of this enterprise. Diamonds have never been confirmed in Canada.

The most interesting and important locality for diamonds in North America is at Murfreesboro, Pikes County, Arkansas. Here a peridotite pipe was studied by J. C. Branner and R. N. Brackett in 1889, but they found no diamonds and from certain geological formations surrounding it concluded the pipe to be barren. In 1906, a farmer who had a hunch that he would be lucky, found diamonds in this same pipe. Since that time many diamonds have been recovered at Murfreesboro, among them the largest diamond found in North America, a crystal weighing 40·23 carats. The mine was operated by different companies until 1919 when the plant was burned down. It is now a tourist centre where amateurs may tour the diamond area and are allowed to keep any stone weighing under 5 carats they may find. A royalty must be paid on stones over that size.

In 1891, minute diamonds were found in the remains of an iron meteorite which fell at Cañon Diablo in Arizona. This led Henri Moissan to carry out experiments on diamond synthesis. Except, however, for the problems they pose, North American diamonds have little economic importance.

AUSTRALIA

Diamond was first found in Australia at Sutter's Bar on the Macquarie river near Bathurst, New South Wales, in 1851. Later discoveries were made, during 1867, at Two Mile Flat on the Cudgegong river north-west of Mudgee. At the Bingara-Tingha district near the Queensland border an important diamond field was discovered in 1872. There are a number of other locations where diamonds have been found in New South Wales, and particularly at Copeton, which lies about 15 miles from Inverell.

Small diamonds have been found in southern, central, and north Queensland. In the south at Stanthorpe and in the central district, diamonds have been recovered while washing for sapphire in the Ruby Vale district. In the far north of Queensland diamonds have turned up during panning for gold and tin in the wild and rugged country at the source of the Gilbert river.

The Australian diamonds are small in size and are usually yellow or off-coloured, but white and many fancy coloured stones have been reported from the alluvial deposits. The stones are recovered as a rule during gold mining operations. They are rarely cut as gems, but are mainly used for industrial purposes. The diamonds found in Australia are said to be, like those of Borneo, harder than the diamonds from other sources, but this apparent superior hardness may be due to twinning. Twinning may also occur locally within the crystal producing 'hard' spots which are frequently called 'naats' or 'knots'.

Diamond in Australia is usually accompanied by water-worn pebbles of topaz, quartz, zircon, black tourmaline, garnet, spinel, but rarely, except in the neighbourhood of Ruby Vale, by sapphire. Australian diamonds are commercially unimportant although it was said that during 1957 Dr. Williamson, of the famed Tanganyika mine, had turned an appraisive eye on the Australian fields. Williamson died in 1958 and nothing came of it.

SOUTH AFRICA

The known diamond fields of the world paled into insignificance when diamond was found in such profusion in South Africa. In the year 1866, the young son of Jacobs, a Dutch farmer of Hopetown which lies near the Orange river, found a shining pebble by the riverside. This pretty stone he showed to his mother, who in turn showed it, and indeed gave it, to a neighbouring Boer named Schalk van Niekerk. Van Niekerk puzzled over the stone and consulted his friend, the trader John Robert O'Reilly, who agreed to take the stone along to Lorenzo Boyes, the Civil Commissioner at Cape Town. Boyes sent it to Dr. Guybon Atherston of Grahamstown, who determined it to be a diamond, the first diamond to be found on African soil. The stone weighed 21 carats and was exhibited at the first Universal Exhibition in Paris. It was later sold for £500.

In 1869 a diamond crystal weighing 83½ carats was found by a Hottentot. This stone was cut into a pear-shaped brilliant of 47·7 carats and given the name 'Star of South Africa'. It was bought by the Countess of Dudley to which fact the alternative name 'The Dudley Diamond' is due.

The identification of the glistening pebble found by young Jacobs as diamond sparked off, during 1867, a frenzied rush of diggers to the Vaal and Orange rivers. It was estimated that some 4,000 of them and their hangers-on were at the diggings in 1869; but easy riches were for the few, disappointment was the lot of many. The best of these so-called 'wet diggings' were found during 1870 at a place called Klipdrift. This is now known as Barkly West on the Vaal river.

In 1870 an observant overseer, De Klerk, noticed garnets in the ground of a farm called Jagersfontein, near Fauresmith in the Orange Free State. Knowing that garnets are associated with diamonds, De Klerk searched the ground and soon found a fine crystal of some 50 carats. This farm became the noted Jagersfontein mine. Within weeks similar diamondiferous areas were found at Dorstfontein farm at Dutoitspan, at Bultfontein nearby and at Koffyfontein. All these were in arid surroundings and hence were known as the 'dry diggings'.

During 1871 a further find of diamond was made at another nearby farm, called Vooruitzigt, owned by a farmer named De Beers. This became the De Beers mine, or, as it was earlier known, as the Old De Beers mine.

Nearby, at a place called Colesberg Kopje—a name given to it by a band of prospectors who had come from Colesberg, a town on the Orange river—was found during the same year the celebrated 'New Rush' mine, which was later renamed the Kimberley mine. The town of Kimberley, named after the Secretary of State for the Colony, lies alongside the mine. It is the centre of the diamond mines.

The year 1890 marked a discovery on the Wesselton farm, which became the Wesselton mine, famous for its cube-shaped diamonds—which being cross-grained are very tough and well suited for industrial purposes—apart from gem quality stones. This mine was originally called the Premier mine after the Premier Cecil Rhodes.

What is known today as the Premier mine is a mine which was discovered in 1902 and lies some 20 miles north-north-east of Pretoria in the Transvaal. In this mine was found the largest diamond so far recovered from the earth's surface, the famed 'Cullinan', which in the rough weighed 3,106 carats. The Premier is the largest mine in South Africa and is an elliptical kimberlite pipe measuring 3,000 ft. by 1,500 ft. The kimberlite of the pipe is surrounded by a red microgranite (felsite). Until 1932 when it was closed, the mine was worked by open-cast methods. It was reconditioned in 1949 and is now operated by shaft mining. *Figure 2.4* shows a day's output from the Premier mine.

During 1960 A. L. Fincham discovered a diamond-bearing pipe some 40 miles east of Postmasburg in Northern Cape Province, and developed the mine called the Finsch, after Fincham and his partner Schwabel. In 1956 there were reports of a pipe south-west of Mont-aux-Sources in Lesotho (formerly Basutoland), and in 1967 a crystal of 601·25 carats was recovered from this area. In the same year there was a recovery of diamond from a pipe situated near Letlakane some 120 miles west of Francistown in the Republic of Botswana (formerly Bechuanaland).

Figure 2.4. This parcel represents a day's production at the Premier mine. It consists of gems and a large proportion of industrial diamonds
(By courtesy of the Anglo-American Corporation of South Africa Ltd.)

Diamondiferous Formations

The dry diggings consist of a typically yellowish coloured soil in which the diamonds are found. At first this soil was thought to be parts of earlier river beds or the result of patches of river soil brought up by floods in earlier times which had settled in shallow areas. The diamondiferous yellow ground had a depth of some 60 ft. and lay on the top of a harder slate-grey earth called 'blue ground'. When this blue ground was reached, the miners considered the claim to be worked out and therefore abandoned it. However, one more inquisitive than his fellows, it has been said that it was Barney Barnato, did dig down into the blue ground and did find diamonds. It is believed that Barney Barnato kept quiet about his find and bought up the abandoned claims cheaply.

Later geological study produced a better understanding of these diamondiferous formations. It was found that the surface outlines of the diamond mines were elliptical or roughly circular and were in fact the mouths of pipes which reach down through the earth's crust to unknown depths. These pipes are filled with an iron-rich basic brecciated igneous rock to which the name kimberlite has been given. Kimberlite, or blue ground, is a peridotite rich in olivine (the jewellers' peridot) and is greenish-blue in colour. At the surface, owing to the alteration by weathering, the ground takes on a yellow colour due to the oxidation of the iron content of the rock. Yellow ground is therefore simply oxidized blue ground.

Diamond Genesis

What is the origin of diamond? All diamond fields, except the pipe mines, are alluvial deposits. That is, the diamonds are not found in the rocks in which they were formed, so these water-borne deposits give little help to the problem of diamond genesis.

The diamond pipes pose many questions but give no conclusive answer as to how carbon, for that is what diamond really is, crystallizes in the cubic form, rather than in the more common hexagonal form which is graphite.

There have been many theories to account for the formation of diamond, the most common being that it occurred under intense heat and pressure. This theory is to some extent substantiated by the successful synthesis of minute diamonds by the General Electric Company. However conclusive this may seem, research workers point out that crystallization of a substance can often occur under very different conditions when in the presence of a catalyst. (A catalyst is a substance which alters the rate at which a chemical reaction proceeds but is itself unchanged at the end of the reaction.)

It is debatable whether diamonds were crystallized in the bowels of the earth and were later brought up with the rock in the pipes, which are presumed to have been formed by super-heated steam forcing up the rock (probably in a plastic condition) through the overlying rock masses; or whether they were actually formed in the pipes. The genesis of diamond still remains a mystery.

The alluvial deposits are undoubtedly derived from some undisclosed pipes whose mouths are now covered by more recent strata, or which have been buried by geological upheavals in past ages. The alluvial deposits are usually mined by panning; by washing and screening the diamond-bearing earth and finally by recovering the diamonds by sorting the concentrate on tables.

Dry Diggings

The dry diggings called for different mining methods. At first the pipe mines were worked as open pits, each claim being worked downwards

PLATE II

Uncut diamond crystals

(By courtesy of De Beers Consolidated Mines Ltd.)

independently with retaining walls between the claims acting as roadways. As the claims were dug deeper, and not always at the same speed, the walls were weakened by undercutting and mostly fell in, causing the abandonment of many claims.

When the roadways were finally demolished it became necessary to bring the blue ground up in a different manner. This was accomplished, particularly in the Kimberley mine, by constructing a vast system of wire ropes up which the buckets of blue ground were drawn from all parts of the rapidly deepening pit by means of windlasses surrounding the rim of the crater (*Figure 2.5*).

Figure 2.5. Early stages in South African diamond mining

The Combines and Personalities

As the workings went deeper they became more difficult to work, owing to falls of rock, the abandonment of claims, and flood water. To counter this, individual workings gave way to amalgamations, creating fewer and larger holdings. Even so, work from above soon became impossible and open pit mining had to be abandoned. Up to 1896 no miner in Kimberley was allowed by law to own more than ten claims, but with the necessity to combine in order to work a mine, this law had to be rescinded thus leading to the disappearance of the individual and to the beginning of the combines.

The story of the combines brings in the personalities to which the South African diamond industry owes its origin, and among which the names of Cecil Rhodes and Barney Barnato are the most colourful. Rhodes, a shrewd businessman, a scholar, and a visionary, arrived in South Africa in 1870, at the age of 17 years, in order to join his elder brother as a cotton planter in Natal. Rhodes and his brother left Natal in 1871 for Colesberg Kopje, and with another brother, Colonel Frank Rhodes, secured three valuable claims. Cecil Rhodes was not content to leave his further education unfinished, and, leaving his brothers to run the claims, returned to England and studied at Oxford for a short time. In 1880, at the age of 26, he founded the De Beers Mining Company and was subsequently elected Member of the Cape Parliament for Barkly West. The next year he again returned to England and took a Master of Arts degree at Oxford. At the age of 31 he became Treasurer of Cape Colony.

Born in 1852, the son of a small shopkeeper in Whitechapel, Barnet Isaacs in 1873 followed his brother Henry to the diamond fields. Henry Isaacs had been a bartender and a music hall performer and took for his stage name the euphonious title of Barnato. His younger brother also liked the euphony of the new name and became Barnet Barnato, or more usually Barney Barnato. Barney did not do much digging but joined forces with Louis Cohen, the pair operating as field diamond buyers, 'kopje walloping' as it was then called. Cohen made his fortune, returned to Liverpool and departed from the picture.

Barney, with his brother Henry, founded the firm of Barnato Brothers and, in 1876, bought a claim; this was at a time when the Kimberley mine was becoming more difficult and dangerous to work and when fierce price cutting was rampant. Like Rhodes, Barney foresaw that the future of the diamond mines would depend upon centralized control of mining and selling. When Barney was 27 years old, and his brother two years older, the brothers floated the Kimberley Central Diamond Mining Company.

Thus began the epic struggle for financial control between Cecil Rhodes and Barney Barnato. For Barnato the fight was pure business, but the urge which gave so much power to Rhodes was his dream of the British flag from the south to the north of the African continent.

Cecil Rhodes and his friends, who included Julius Wernher, an ex-Uhlan, and Alfred Beit, approached the bankers Rothschild for financial backing, and this they obtained.

Barney's group could not resist the heavy backing ranged against them by the Rhodes group, who finally bought the controlling interest of Barney's remaining company, the Kimberley Central, for nearly 5½ million pounds. In 1888, with the merger accomplished, the new company, under the title of De Beers Consolidated Mines Limited, put most of the South African diamond mines under unified control.

Cecil Rhodes never forgot his dream of a British Africa and stipulated that the surplus funds of the diamond industry should be used for the further development of Africa and the expansion into and colonization of the country to the north, now known as Rhodesia. Barney at first objected to this and considered that the shareholders had first claim to all profits, but finally agreed under the scholarly and forceful arguments of Rhodes, as, indeed, he was bound to, as he had no controlling influence in the new company.

Subsequently, De Beers Consolidated Mines Limited completed the unification of the mines by buying control of the Griqualand West, Dutoitspan, and the Bultfontein mines.

Mining Methods

At all mines, the limit of opencast working was soon reached and underground mining by shaft became universal for the pipe mines. The mining methods are in general the same and vary only in local peculiarities. A main shaft is driven down through the hard surrounding rocks parallel to the pipe. From this shaft sublevels are driven horizontally across the pipe, tunnels being between 25 and 50 ft. below each other. At the end of each level a slot or chamber, 10–14 ft. wide and extending vertically to the level above, is cut from the one side of the pipe to the other. The blue ground is worked backwards, working first a second slot, then a third, and so on through the width of the pipe. Each slot is worked one slot ahead of the level below it. By this stoping method of mining (*Figure 2.6*), the whole of the blue ground is removed. *Figure 2.7* shows a stage in underground mining.

More recently a system of 'block caving' has been used. Cone-shaped

Figure 2.6. Blasting hard rock projecting into open mine at Bulfontein

excavations are cut beneath a large volume of blue ground, 400 to 600 feet thick, and this is then undercut above the cones. The unsupported overhanging blue ground then slowly settles into the cones, breaks up and is drawn through the cones into 'scraper drifts' where it is pulled out by mechanical scrapers.

The broken down blue ground is loaded into trucks by hand and these are taken to ore passes and thence to the shaft bin by conveyor belts or endless rope buckets. Kimberlite is raised to the surface through the main shaft.

When freely exposed to the air, the blue ground disintegrates rapidly. Advantage was taken of this in the earlier method of treatment for the recovery of the diamond content. The blue ground was spread to a depth of some two feet over floors—levelled areas of the open veldt—and left for some months with periodical ploughing, and if necessary watering. When sufficiently decomposed, the ground was carted to washing and concentrating tables, the diamonds being picked out by hand from the concentrate.

More modern methods are now universally used. The blue ground on reaching the surface is passed through crushers where it is reduced to pieces of one inch or less in size and is fed to rotary pans fitted with revolving radial rakes. This mud puddle separates the heavy minerals including the diamonds, from the lighter kimberlite gangue.

The tailings (the heavier minerals) from the pans, of which there may be a battery working with reduced sizes of crushed rock, are then brought to a

Figure 2.7. A mechanical scraper pulling broken down blue ground along a scraper drift in the block caving method of mining

(By courtesy of the Anglo-American Corporation of South Africa Ltd.)

dump by a belt conveyor. From this dump the diamondiferous concentrate is taken by truck to the pulsators which further concentrate the ore. The final concentrate is then passed over side-shaking grease tables. A modern innovation is a method of concentration by a heavy media separation plant which eliminates the pulsators (*Figure 2.8*).

It was discovered by F. Kirsten that as diamond is water-repellent, unlike most of the other heavy concentrates, it adheres to grease. This factor is made use of in the covered, sloping side-shaking grease tables. These tables are covered by a thick layer of petroleum jelly (Vaseline) and the concentrate passed in at the top, being washed down by a gentle flow of water. The diamonds stick to the grease while the other minerals pass out at the lower end as tailings.

Periodically the grease and the diamonds adhering to it are scraped off the table. The grease is boiled off and the larger diamonds picked out by hand from any stray zircon or corundum which have a tendency to be caught by the grease. *Figure 2.9* shows a grease table. Some diamonds do not adhere to grease and for these 'non-stickers' other methods are used for recovery, such as electrostatic separation. The diamonds recovered by these processes are all sent to a central sorting office for grading.

To provide a continuous check on the efficiency of grease tables an optical separator is used which is based on the opacity of rock and the reflection and transmission characteristics of diamond.

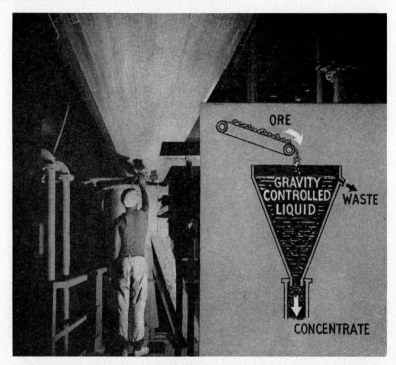

Figure 2.8. *The bottom of a cone in the heavy media separation plant at the Premier diamond mine in which diamonds and associated heavy materials are separated from the lighter materials in the blue ground. The diagram shows the operation of such a plant*
(By courtesy of the Anglo-American Corporation of South Africa Ltd.)

RHODESIA

The discovery of the diamond deposits of South Africa was the beginning of diamond finds over the greater part of the west and south-western part of the African continent.

Alluvial diamonds were discovered during 1903 in the Somabula Forest west of Gwelo in Matabeleland, Rhodesia. A little farther north of this locality there occur several pipes, but in most cases these are barren of diamond. The Rhodesian deposits have as yet little commercial importance, but prospecting is still proceeding.

SOUTH-WEST AFRICA

In 1908 diamond was detected near Lüderitz on the Atlantic coast of South-West Africa. These marine beach deposits were later found in discrete areas stretching some 60 miles along the coast north of the mouth of the Orange river. Diamonds may be found northwards along the South-West African coast as far as the Kaokoveldt, but the area is not mined. Some diamonds have been found in the small Possession Island, which lies some 2 miles off Elizabeth Bay. The area is mainly operated by the Consolidated Diamond Mines of South-West Africa, a branch of the De Beers group. The main recovery plant is at Oranjemund at the mouth of the Orange river.

Figure 2.9. Removing diamonds from the grease table at Kimberley
(By courtesy of the Anglo-American Corporation of South Africa Ltd.)

In 1927 extensive marine beach deposits were found in Namaqualand, south of the Orange river. Rich deposits were located some 80 feet above sea level on a terraced beach in which the goatshorn oyster (*Ostrea prismatica*) is present in quantity. A minor diamond field was discovered in 1956 on the 'Skeleton Coast' of South-West Africa. This area lies in the Kaokoveldt, south of the Kunene river, which forms the border of Angola.

These coastal fields are worked by the aid of mechanical excavators. The overburden, often 100 ft. in thickness, needs to be first removed. When uncovered, the diamondiferous gravel is removed by hand or by excavator and brought to a central treatment plant. *Figure 2.10* shows the overburden being removed by a mechanical shovel, and *Figure 2.11* shows a native miner digging into the diamondiferous conglomerate at Mittag, which lies

Figure 2.10. One of the big rotary scoops at the Consolidated Diamond Mines of South-West Africa. This giant which removes sand at the rate of 400 tons an hour is in a trench which is being prepared for mining in the east extension at Gemsbok Terrace
(By courtesy of the Anglo-American Corporation of South Africa Ltd.)

Figure 2.11. A native miner drills a hole into diamondiferous conglomerate in a mining face at Mittag preparatory to blasting
(By courtesy of the Anglo-American Corporation of South Africa Ltd.)

just north of Oranjemund. The diamonds from these beach deposits are not water-repellent as they are coated with a microscopic film of salts. They are therefore treated by immersion and light milling in fish oil and caustic soda to enable them to adhere to the grease on the grease table (or belt). Alternatively, an electrostatic method is used to recover the stones. *Figure 2.12* shows some of the plant at the central recovery plant of the Consolidated Diamond Mines Ltd. at Oranjemund.

Figure 2.12. Screens at the central plant of Consolidated Diamond Mines
(By courtesy of the Anglo-American Corporation of South Africa Ltd.)

The origin of these marine alluvial diamonds is open to debate. Was the original source inland, or did the parent rocks lie submerged under the Atlantic Ocean? The size of the stones diminishes as the distance from the mouth of the Orange river increases. It is therefore thought that the source is inland, the stones having been carried by rivers of former geological ages to the sea to be later cast up on the beaches near the river mouths by ocean currents.

About 1964 Marine Diamond Corporation commenced diamond recovery from the seabed off the South-West African mainland, and in 1967 the 'Pomona', a specially equipped barge, operated about a mile off the mouth of the Orange river. The sand of the seabed, up to 100 feet below, is raised by airlift and suction dredge. The diamondiferous sand is then screened, washed, concentrated by heavy media separation, and finally sorted by hand.

THE CONGO AND ANGOLA

In 1910 diamonds were found in the south-western part of the Congo in alluvial gravels in the valleys of the tributaries of the Kasai river. Farther west, diamond deposits have been located in the Kwilu basin. A more productive area was discovered around the Bushimaie river, which lies to the east of the Kasai river and some 600 miles north-west of Elisabethville in the district of Katanga, where uranium minerals vie with diamonds as a major export from the Congo. Near the Kundelungu plateau, just north of Elisabethville, a number of kimberlite masses occur, a few of which have proved to contain diamonds. The town of Tshikapa is the centre of the diamond mining operations in the Congo, which is the world's largest producer of diamond in terms of quantity, but only second (to South Africa) in terms of value. Before the West African production came on the market, the Congo produced at least three-quarters of the crushing boart so widely used in industry.

Figure 2.13. Open-cast working in the Congo diamond fields

During 1916 the Congo diamond fields were found to extend into the north-eastern part of Malange in Angola, particularly along the western bank of the Chuimbe river and both banks of the Luembe and Luana rivers. The Angola deposits are alluvial and are derived from an ancient drainage system which no longer exists.

Mining is carried out, both in Angola and the Congo, by removing the overburden to expose the diamondiferous gravel. This gravel is then excavated (*Figure 2.13*), taken to washing plants, and then treated in a heavy media separator. The concentrates are processed in a recovery section for the extraction of the diamonds.

GHANA

The discovery, in 1919, of diamond at Abomoso near the Birim river opened up diamond mining in the Gold Coast, now called Ghana. Later prospecting disclosed diamond in the district south-east of Kade and about 65 miles north-west of Accra, the capital. Diamonds from Ghana are mostly of industrial quality, although gem crystals are also recovered in some quantity.

The Ghana deposits consist of gravels from 2 to 5 ft. thick and are interesting in that the rock formations in the area are steeply dipping metamorphosed igneous and sedimentary rocks of pre-Cambrian age. The mining for diamond is carried out by removing the overburden and depositing it in previously mined sections. The exposed diamond-bearing gravel is mechanically loaded into one ton trucks and taken to the washing and recovery plants where, for the smaller diamonds, a method of 'skin flotation' is used. Much Ghana diamond gravel is worked by African leaseholders, but the main fields are operated by Consolidated African Selection Trust Ltd., though there are now American interests. Much illicit diamond mining and buying occurs which is detrimental to both the mining company and the leaseholders. Diamonds are also found in the Ivory Coast.

SIERRA LEONE

The diamond fields of Sierra Leone were not discovered until 1930, when a small diamond was found by geologist J. D. Pollet in the gravels of the Gboboro stream near the village of Fotingaia in the Nimi Koro chiefdom. Next day another stone was recovered from the same site and, later, further finds were made in the gravel of a tributary of the river Moa in the Kennema district.

On hearing of these finds, the Consolidated African Selection Trust Ltd. sent a prospecting party from the Gold Coast to Sierra Leone. They were well equipped with shaker trays and joplin jigs and with native personnel skilled in diamond mining. During 1932 the prospecting party found diamonds north of the Bandafayi watershed in the Shongbo stream near Tongoma village. Small-scale mining operations showed the deposit to exceed expectations and, further, that the diamonds tended to gather in clusters on the bedrock. The company was granted the exclusive right to prospect for diamond over an area of 4,170 square miles of the eastern district of Sierra Leone.

Further exploration showed that diamond was present in the gravels of the Sewa river, an area not included in the licence granted the Gold Coast company, and in 1934 a new subsidiary company, The Sierra Leone Selection Trust, was floated and was granted the sole right to prospect for diamond in the colony. Owing to the vast expanse of diamond bearing gravels, policing the area was almost an impossibility and illicit mining and buying was rife. During the early 1950s it was estimated that more diamonds passed out illicitly from Sierra Leone than were mined by the operating company. Much of the illicit buying is operated through the Republic of Liberia. In 1955, to alleviate this situation, a new agreement was entered into between the Sierra Leone Government and the Sierra Leone Selection Trust, enabling diamond mining to be practised legally by private persons under licence. A subsidiary company formed by the Diamond Corporation was granted the exclusive right to purchase diamonds from licensed diamond buyers and dealers in the territory.

It is interesting to note that the rock formations in Sierra Leone, unlike those of Ghana, are of cretaceous age. The diamonds produced in Sierra

Leone are in the main of good quality and are often of large size. Many of the crystals show excellent octahedral form with bright faces. Such crystals are called 'glassies' (*Figure 2.14*). Crystals of 100 carats or more are occasionally found; the 'Woyie River Diamond', recovered in 1945 weighed 770 carats. Natural bottle-green coloured diamonds are often found and such diamonds will turn light brown on heating, in a similar manner to those stones which owe their colour to artificial treatment by particle bombardment (cyclotroned and neutroned diamonds). It is from this effect that it is

Figure 2.14. A 'glassy' diamond crystal from the Sierra Leone diamond fields

suggested that uranium compounds might exist near the place where the diamonds were found.

The mining is carried on in a similar manner as in the other alluvial fields of Angola and Ghana. The Sierra Leone diamond fields are situated some 140 miles east of Freetown, and in the mining area itself the Diamond Mining Company have constructed most up-to-date mining camps on the principle of a garden city.

WEST AND EQUATORIAL AFRICA

Among the first diamonds to be discovered in the old French West Africa were those in the Région Forestière of French Guinea (now the Republic of Guinea). A minute diamond found by J. Goor, in 1933, in a river in the N'Zérékoré district on the border of Liberia was probably the first. A year later, several workable deposits of diamond were found in the Makona river district and in the rivers of Haute Guinée.

The main workings of this diamond field are located some 47 miles (75 km) north-north-east of Macenta. The diamonds are mostly found in alluvial deposits in the upper courses of the smaller streams and in old terraces associated with such minerals as ilmenite, magnetite, zircon, rutile, corundum, monazite, epidote, topaz, spinel, staurolite, tourmaline and almandine garnet. The diamond crystals are usually octahedra or dodecahedra and are frequently of a brown colour, or a clear yellow or blue colour. The stones often contain black inclusions making them unfit for gemstones. The great preponderance of the diamonds from these fields are boart.

Diamonds have been recovered from ancient river terraces along the

Figure 2.15. Diamondiferous gravel being washed in joplin jigs. The jigs are shaken by the long handles which causes the heavy density minerals to settle on the bottom of the jig screens

region of the Mambere river which runs through the western part of Oubangui-Chari district of the Central African Republic. The diamonds—production is small in amount—are recovered by clearing the thick tropical underbush of jungle and forest and removing some 5–15 ft. of overburden or top soil to reach the diamond-bearing gravel, which is then removed and passed through old-fashioned joplin jigs to concentrate the heavy minerals for final sorting (*Figures 2.15* and *2.16*). Preliminary prospecting to gauge the depth of the overburden is carried out by natives

PLATE III

Diamond fringe necklace

(By courtesy of Garrard & Co. Ltd.)

(*Figure 2.17*) and dredging machines are used to test the gravel bed of the Mambere river. In Moyen Congo and Gabon districts of the Central African Republic, a few diamonds have been recovered, but mining in these territories has practically ceased.

TANZANIA (Tanganyika)

In the area between Shinyanga and the southern shore of Lake Victoria in Tanzania, diamondiferous gravels from 3 to 6 ft. thick exist over a large area underlain by granite. Claims in this locality were pegged as early as

Figure 2.16. Natives grading the diamond-bearing gravel after it has been through the joplin jigs preparatory to the pebbles being searched for diamonds

1910, but mining did not begin until 1925. The workings were mainly at Mabuki, which lies on the railroad from Tabora through Shinyanga to the town and airport of Mwanza. The diamond deposits consist of diamond-bearing gravels on a kimberlite pipe, these outcrops being the most northerly kimberlite pipes in Africa.

Dr. John Thorburn Williamson, a Canadian of Irish descent and one time geologist to the Quebec Geological Survey, came to Mwanza in 1934. After a period on the Rand, where he became interested in diamonds and where he first formed his theory that the Tanzania diamond deposits must be derived from an original pipe somewhere in the area, he came to Tanganyika. Williamson thought that the pipe could be located by scientific study of the area and proceeded to work on these lines.

Sitting in the shade of a baobab tree at Mwadui, some 90 miles from Lake Victoria, Williamson found a diamond which was the clue to the finding of the Williamson pipe the next year. Thus successfully ended Williamson's hunch, and years of scientific prospecting, during which he never lost

Figure 2.17. Manpower is used to operate the drill used in testing the depth of the overburden in the Central African Republic diamond fields

faith in his own convictions. The Williamson mine is the largest pipe mine in Africa. The main pipe at Mwadui is said to be eight times larger than the Premier mine in the Transvaal.

So far as is known, the Williamson mine is still being operated as an open mine, mechanical excavators scooping up the gravel and emptying their grabs into 5-ton trucks. The trucks take the gravel to the concentrating pans to undergo the initial processing. Diluted to a mud-like consistency with water, the gravel and black soil is scoured by rotating rakes in wide and shallow pans. This causes the diamonds to sink to the bottom with the other heavier concentrates, but floats off the lighter materials which are drained from the top. Periodically the concentrate is shovelled out and taken in coco-pans to the jigs, where the final extraction of diamonds is carried out. The jigs in the sorting shed are manned by natives watched over by uniformed Askaris. The final tailings of concentrate are then hand-picked over by natives for any diamonds which have passed the jig. These native workers wear only an overall which has one sleeve closed at the cuff allowing only the right hand to be free for picking out the diamonds. The free hands are carefully watched by Askari guards. This primitive and outmoded method is being replaced by modern diamond recovery equipment.

The Williamson mine has supplied a number of large diamonds, including one of 240 carats, and small green and pink crystals; the largest pink weighed 54 carats in the rough and gave a stone of 23·60 carats. This stone was given to Queen Elizabeth II when she was Princess Elizabeth. In 1958 a shaft was sunk alongside the pipe to a depth of 1,260 feet from which exploratory tunnels were driven into the pipe to see if payable diamond exists.

OTHER AFRICAN MINING AREAS

Presumed to be of detrital origin and derived from the pre-existing Witwaters formation farther to the north, a number of small greenish diamonds have been recovered during the mining operations for gold in the Rand banket. During 1957 French uranium prospectors found six diamonds in the Hoggar area of the south-east Sahara, and in 1958 diamonds were discovered some 9,000 ft. up in a valley surrounded by mountains in the Makhotlong area of Basutoland (now Lesotho).

GUYANA (formerly British Guiana)

Diamonds were discovered in the gold washings of the Puruni and Mazaruni basins of British Guiana during 1887. The diamonds, small in size, are found in a gravel of ferruginous clayey or sandy nature which is overgrown with tropical jungle. The nature of the terrain makes transport difficult and recovery of the stones uneconomic. Diamonds are also found in the Cuyuni, Potaro and Berbice rivers and their tributaries.

The diamonds of Guyana are usually worn and pitted octahedra, these worn and pitted crystals being most common in the Meamu-Apiqua district and in the Potaro deposits. The finest quality and the best shapes come from the Kurupung and Eping districts. The commonest colour of Guyana diamonds is white with a slight yellow tinge, followed by 'Capes', and light and dark browns. Unusual colours are rare as are 'blue-white' stones, but occasionally a small aquamarine blue or deep green stone is encountered, mainly from the Potaro district.

The mining in Guyana is carried out in a primitive manner by West Indian natives, who are known locally as 'Pork-knockers'. These miners work on their own behalf and trade the stones they find with shops which supply them with their tools and necessities of life. The largest stone said to have been found in Guyana was a crystal of 56 carats and was recovered in the Potaro district in 1926.

During 1948 a diamond deposit was found along the Ireng river which lies along the Guyana–Brazilian frontier which led to a miniature 'rush' by miners from both sides of the frontier.

BOLIVIA

Diamonds have been found in the foothills of the Andes in Bolivia. The diamonds were discovered in the river gravels of the Rio Tuichi and have been reported from the Rio Tequeje, Rio Unduma and some other tributaries of the Upper Rio Beni. The diamonds are found in gravel beds of from 1 to 3 m (3–9 ft.) thick overlying a bed-rock of Permian age.

VENEZUELA

The finding of diamonds along the Cuyuni and Paragua rivers in the area known as Gran Sabana of the State of Bolivar in Venezuela may be said to be an extension of the diamondiferous fields of Guyana. The exploitation of these deposits is hindered by their inaccessibility but some mining and marketing of Venezuelan stones is carried out. Diamonds from the Paragua river are coated with iron oxide, but fine quality stones can be cut from them. Green diamonds are frequently encountered at Icabaru. Fancy colours, such as yellow-green, brown, reddish-brown, pink, light blue and black, are common in Venezuelan diamond deposits.

RUSSIA

The first recorded discovery of diamond in Russia was in July 1829 when a German mineralogist from Freiburg, who was at the gold-bearing and platinum-bearing deposits in the Ural mountains, identified as a diamond a stone found by a 14-year-old Russian boy named Paul Popoff of Kalinskoje. A few other small diamonds were found in the gold and platinum washings and in the recovery plant for these metals. The find had no commercial significance.

It is said that since 1941 scientific methods have been applied to diamond recovery in the Soviet Union, but the literature is not clear. However, industrial diamonds are said to come from Molotov Ablast which is situated on the confluence of the Kama and Chusovaya rivers at the foothills of the Ural Mountains and on the European side of the range. The Uralian diamonds are described as being of the 'Brazilian type' and in this supports the view expressed by Alexander von Humboldt more than a century ago.

As long ago as 1898 it was known that there were diamonds on the mid Siberian plateau located between the Lena and the Yenisei rivers, and in 1936 Professor W. S. Sobelew recognized that the geology of the area bore some resemblance to that of the dolerites of the Karoo formation of South Africa. Further research awaited the end of World War II, but a few diamonds were recovered in 1945. Russia, needing diamonds for industrial purposes, then sent out expeditions to trace the diamond sources. The first useful diamond placers were found in 1949. In 1954 a young woman mineralogist attached to one of the survey teams found the first kimberlite pipe, and by 1958 some 120 pipes had been found in Yakutia. The most reported is the Mir pipe, but it is said that the Aichal pipe, found in 1960, may surpass it in diamond content. The diamond area, mainly along the Vilyui river and its tributaries, is covered by marshy primeval woods known as Taiga, and this makes transportation difficult. At present it seems that only open-cast mining is carried out. The broken rock is taken to the treatment centre at Mirny, a town which has developed since the finding of diamonds in the neighbourhood, it being linked to the Lena river by a 180-mile motorway. At the recovery plant the rock is washed by water jets which removes the gangue material leaving mainly pyrope, garnet and diamond. The concentrate used to be hand-picked for diamond but the sorting is now done mechanically, grease tables being used. An interesting method of recovery which has been reported from Russia is by the Krassov and Finne's automatic sorter in which the diamondiferous concentrate is passed down a hopper where it passes an x-ray beam. The beam makes the diamonds 'glitter' so that they are 'seen' by a subsidiary apparatus which separates the diamonds from the gravel.

TABLE 2.1
World Production of Gem Diamonds in 1966

Africa	Carats
Angola	964,000
Central African Republic	270,000
Congo (Brazzaville)	318,000
Congo (Kinshasa)	15,000
Ghana	282,000
Guinea	21,000
Ivory Coast	110,000
Liberia	343,000
Sierra Leone	629,000
South Africa Republic	2,485,000
South-West Africa	1,583,000
Tanzania	473,000
Total African production	7,493,000
Other Lands	
Brazil	150,000
Guyana	37,000
U.S.S.R.	300,000
India	2,000
Venezuela	42,000
World production	8,024,000

CHINA

According to reliable sources, an item published in a Chinese newspaper at Pekin, on May 31, 1955, reported that diamond-bearing deposits have been discovered in northern Hunan Province in Central China, and that prospecting in the area is proceeding.

SORTING AND GRADING

When diamonds have been recovered from the mines they are sent to centres for sorting into grades. More than 90 per cent of the world's diamonds are mined in the continent of Africa, if the new Russian reports are discounted, and are sent to London to be sold through the Diamond Trading Company. Very few of the diamond mines of the world are not under the care of the Corporation which was first conceived by those great names in Kimberley in the 1890s. This Corporation ensures that supply and price is maintained at an economic level.

The work of sorting is a specialized process that is now, and has been ever since mining started, carried out by hand and eye. The first sorting may be simply into two groups, that of cuttable goods (crystals which can be fashioned into gemstones), and industrials, stones which are suitable only for industrial uses (these will be discussed later). Some 80 per cent by weight of all mined stones are of too poor a quality for cutting and are classed as industrial quality. There is no distinct division between gem and industrial grades in respect to the marginal qualities, for they may be classed as either depending on the demand.

The sorting and subsequent valuation of gem diamond depends upon four factors: size, colour, shape and purity. Stones of good weight, acceptable colour and normally of octahedral shape are termed 'stones' to which may be added 'shapes' which have many desirable features such as colour and size but which may not be quite so useful from a point of view of cutting. Macles and flats (thinner macles) form another category. Farther down the scale are mêlée which are crystals less than 1 carat in weight, and finally 'sand' which includes stones which can total as many as 120 to the carat. Cleavages are stones irrespective of weight which have been broken and therefore are of a highly irregular shape. Coated stones are crystals which have a dark coating on the surface (hard graphite?). Frosted or eroded crystals are those in which the coating has worn away leaving a dull or pitted surface.

The grading of diamonds for colour is carried out by trained personnel who have gained their knowledge purely by experience. In the case of diamonds, and in fact all gemstones, colour grading must be done by the eye alone, for no mechanical aids have been found which will function so well. There are many divisions and subdivisions into which diamonds may be colour-graded. Generally the grouping used is as follows: extra collection colour (blue-white); collection colour; finest white; fine white; browns and greens (varying from light brown to light green); top Capes; Capes (stones having a yellowish tinge); and yellows.

The above classification refers to white diamonds, for the colours mentioned are just tinges and not a strong colour. Diamonds may be found having pronounced colours, and these are called fancy stones and may be highly prized. Brown is not an uncommon shade, canary yellow less so, while pink, red, blue, and green shades are rare. Except for the pink stones, whose colour is attributed to a trace of manganese, the colour is thought to be due to lattice defects and not to trace elements as in most other gemstones.

The term blue-white is not so often used as formerly, it indicates stones which tended to show an indefinable bluish tint. This has been explained as not being a colour in the usual sense but is due to a fluorescence induced by the ultra-violet component of daylight. It is usually the best diamonds which show this effect well. Stones which are flawless and limpid are said to be 'first water', a term the origin of which is not understood.

Consideration of the internal cleanness, that is freedom from flaws or inclusions, adds a further complexity to the sorter's task. There are so many ways of classifying diamonds into groups, differing in England as well as abroad, that enumeration of them would confuse the reader rather than assist. Anyway such grouping is the job of the diamond sorter.

The actual selling of the diamond rough, as the mined crystals are called, is, in London, carried out by the Diamond Trading Company holding 'sights' once a month. The graded and valued diamonds are made up into parcels of shapes, sizes and other grades, ready for the sights. The procedure at the sights is something of a ritual. Clients are shown into the buying rooms and the buyer, or his broker, will then be offered in accordance with his application, 'a parcel of goods' as it is termed. Generally the parcel will consist of a collection of white papers (folded stone papers) each containing one or more of a particular category of stones—the whole being contained in a blue envelope. The buyer considers the parcel offered by selecting and examining several of the stones in a north light (which is best for colour appreciation). It must be appreciated that north light is only applicable to the northern hemisphere, for if the buyer is in a location south of the equator then south light is needed. The buyer must purchase the whole parcel and cannot pick and choose.

The rough crystals so purchased from the Diamond Trading Company are then fashioned into faceted stones suitable for mounting into jewellery, the brilliant cut being the best for showing to perfection the fire and lustre of a diamond. The trap cut, usually in the so-called emerald cut modification, is favoured for some diamonds, though such a style does not show the diamond's fire to the best advantage (*Figure 2.18*). The styles and methods of cutting diamonds are discussed in a later chapter.

The cut diamonds are then graded and valued, a slightly different scheme of classification being used for cut stones from that outlined above for the rough crystals. The classifications and values of cut diamonds are based upon the colour, cleanness from flaws and inclusions, the perfection of the cutting, and lastly the size of the finished stone. Again such grading and valuation is the work of the expert. The Gemological Institute of America has devised a lamp in a special housing for the colour grading of diamonds. In this lamp the stone to be graded is matched against a set of diamonds whose colour rating is known. More recently the Gemological Institute of America has devised an electronic colorimeter for diamonds. The diamond is examined by a special microscope to ascertain what flaws and inclusions mar the stone, and by the use of a spot-light the reflections from the facets of a cut stone may be used to check the symmetry of the cutting. A diamond proportion gauge, based on the optical profilometer, has also been developed by the Institute in recent years to check and measure the depth and angles of cut diamonds. The commercial ruling for the cleanness of a cut diamond is that no flaws or included marks, or surface blemishes, can be observed when the stone is thoroughly examined with the aid of a hand lens magnifying ten times. Breathing on the stone will often allow a better view of the colour.

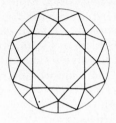

Figure 2.18. The brilliant cut and the trap cut (emerald cut) used for diamonds

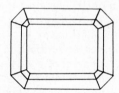

INDUSTRIAL AND SCIENTIFIC USES

The use of diamond for industrial and scientific purposes is increasing year by year as newer and often unusual needs for this hard material become available. The earliest use of diamond in industry was as an abrasive powder, and in many ways this is still the most important. Small and badly coloured diamonds and those of low grade structurally, collectively called bort (boort, boart or bortz) are crushed in a steel mortar to produce a powder which is used to charge the saws and laps used in the polishing of gem diamonds and other hard materials. The powder is produced in a variety of grades from coarse (80–120 mesh per linear inch); medium (150–200 mesh), and fine (300–400 mesh). Finer 'diamond dust' is graded into 'subsieve' sizes of 20 microns (a micron is one thousandth of a millimetre) down to as small as two or even one micron. Sets of phosphor-bronze wire sieves are used for grading the diamond powder, the finest sieve retaining particles of over about 400 mesh. Subsieve sizes are prepared either by air sifting, centrifuging, elutriating (grading particles by means of an upward current in a liquid), or by settling in oil (sedimentation). The diamond powder may be used as a paste in oil, rolled into metal, or bonded by sintering into metal or carbide wheels or shaped pieces.

The use of diamonds for rock drilling, which has so improved geological prospecting and mining, is said to date from 1863 when the diamond drill was first used by Professor Leschot. The cutting head of these tube drills by which a core is drilled out from the rock is set with suitable diamonds.

PLATE IV

Diamonds
showing some colours and styles
in which they are cut

(By courtesy of De Beers Consolidated Mines Ltd.)

Carbonado, or 'carbons' as they are called, were formerly used for rock drills but as they have become very scarce suitable industrial grade diamonds are now used. Ballas, a multicrystalline diamond with the crystallites arranged radially producing a rounded form (shot ballas) has, like carbonado, no cleavage and therefore has a great resistance to abrasion and thus is suitable for rock drills. Ballas is an exceedingly scarce form of diamond and is found in Brazil and in the Jagersfontein and Premier mines of South Africa.

The diamond-set glass cutters, called vitriers, used by glaziers incorporate octahedral-shaped crystals, from 10 to 60 per carat in size, set into the face of the working end of the tool at a correct angle so that the edge and tip of the octahedron performs the cutting action. Small diamond crystals, chips from the fashioning of larger diamonds, called splints, or small diamonds ground to the shape of a cone and mounted in a suitable pen-holder shaped metal grip are used to 'etch' on glass or metal. Such tools are termed 'writing' or 'pencil' diamonds. Fine metal wires, such as those used for the filaments of electric lamps, are drawn to small diameter by pulling the wire through diamond drawing dies. Industrial type diamonds are set staggered fashion across the cutting edge of circular or reciprocating saws used in the cutting of building stones.

A diamond set in a suitable steel holder is used for the truing of abrasive wheels used in the metal industries. Diamond-tipped turning tools, using a single shaped and polished diamond, are used in lathes for the turning of non-ferrous metals and plastic materials, and suitably shaped and polished diamonds are used in many of the modern indenter hardness testers. A diamond of similar type to that used for wire-drawing is made use of as the orifice of pressure-type oil burners of boiler furnaces. The resistance of diamond to abrasion and the action of acid avoids the increase in diameter leading to wasteful consumption of fuel, through the grit and acid contained in the oil. Ordinary orifices of metal will not stand up to such abrasion and chemical action as does the diamond. Some diamonds behave as a radiation counter—like a Geiger counter—and the suggestion is made that this type of counter might be of exceptional advantage in certain types of medicine.

CHEMICAL AND PHYSICAL PROPERTIES

The atomic structure of diamond is of considerable interest for each carbon atom lies at the centre of a regular tetrahedron and is joined to four other carbon atoms which lie at the corners of the tetrahedron. The structure is therefore a system of interlacing hexagons with each atom linked (covalently) to four others (*Figure 2.19*). It is owing to the nearness of the atoms, 1·54 Ångströms (1 Å equals 10^{-7} mm), and the fact that the whole crystal is in effect one molecule that any breakdown of the structure involves the breaking of the strong atomic bonds. Hence the chemical stability and the hardness of diamond, the hardest mineral known, with the symbol 10 on Mohs's scale of hardness. The new synthetic material borazon is said to be as hard as diamond.

Despite its hardness diamond has four directions of weakness along which the crystal will split fairly easily leaving smooth surfaces. The

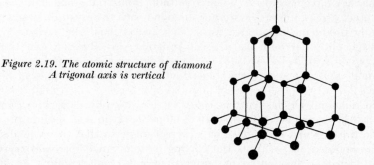

Figure 2.19. The atomic structure of diamond
A trigonal axis is vertical

cleavage, as this effect is termed, is, in the case of diamond, parallel to the faces of the octahedron. In such a direction the atomic bonds are fewer than in other directions, hence the cohesion is weaker along these planes. *Figure 2.20* illustrates the cleavage of diamond. Cleavage is of value in the fashioning of diamonds for it enables large crystals to be divided easily by splitting them along the cleavage direction. On the other hand, cleavage may be a disadvantage in that a cut stone if inadvertently knocked along a cleavage direction may develop flaws or even split in two. Such a mishap, however, is rare.

The density of diamond is 3·52 and owing to the purity of the crystals it varies little from this value. The exception is in the case of the crypto-crystalline variety known as carbonado which can have much lower values of density; values from 3·5 to as low as 2·9 having been recorded for this material.

EFFECTS OF LIGHT ON DIAMOND

Optical Properties

What causes the estimable brilliancy of a diamond? The answer lies in certain optical properties inherent in diamond, the first of which is the adamantine lustre due to the combined effect of the high polish the gem will take and the quality of the light reflected from its surface. The second cause is the ability of a well-cut diamond to return back a ray of light which enters it from the front. A ray of light entering a diamond is bent—refraction as it is called. The measure of this bending is known as the refractive index,

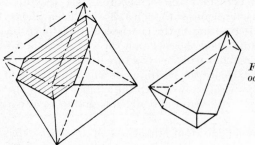

Figure 2.20. Cleavage of a diamond octahedron showing the cleaved piece removed

and is for diamond 2·417 (for yellow light) as against air–unity. Further, owing to the relatively high refractive index the rays are 'totally reflected' from the surfaces of the rear facets and returned out through the front of the diamond. *Figure 2.21* illustrates this effect.

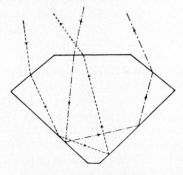

Figure 2.21. The paths of a ray of light passing through a diamond. This shows the returning of those rays which enter at the front by total internal reflection at the back facets

The third optical effect which makes diamond so attractive lies in the 'fire' exhibited by the stone. Fire, scientifically known as dispersion, is the breaking up of white light entering the stone into the spectrum colours, and in the case of diamond this is pronounced. The effect is caused by the differing amount of bending suffered by each different coloured light ray which collectively make up the white light entering the stone. Hence, diamond will have a different refractive index for each coloured ray, each of which must, of course, take a slightly different path through the stone. In diamond the red ray (with a wavelength of 6870 Å) has a refractive index of 2·407; the violet ray (wavelength of 3970 Å) an index of 2·465. The violet ray is always bent more than the other colours of the spectrum when entering an optically denser substance. A measure of the dispersion is the difference between the refractive indices of the red and the violet rays, and for diamond this is 0·058. In general the dispersion of gemstones is measured by the difference in refractive index of the stone for the red ray (6870 Å), which is the B line of Fraunhofer's solar spectrum, and the Fraunhofer G line in the blue at 4308 Å. This gives the dispersion of diamond as B to G 0·044. The dispersion of the light rays through a well-proportioned brilliant is illustrated in *Figure 2.22*. It is this play of spectrum colours flashing out which makes diamond such a beautiful gemstone.

Figure 2.22. The paths of different coloured rays of white light through a diamond. This shows the splitting up of the light by dispersion which gives the 'fire' to a stone

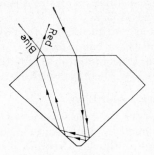

Absorption Spectra

Visible light which has passed through a diamond, if examined carefully with a spectroscope (an instrument which analyses light into the spectrum colours), will often show dark lines obliterating certain parts of the spectrum. As will be explained in the technical section, such absorption bands are distinctive for many coloured varieties of other gemstones and provide a means of testing them. This is so in the case of diamond, but a diamond, unlike other gems where the absorption spectra are due to chemical elements in the stone, either fundamentally as in the chemical composition or as an adventitious impurity, owes these absorption lines to the crystalline structure, or to faults in the structure of the crystal.

Before enumerating the absorption spectra of diamond it may be an advantage to describe another phenomenon, that of photoluminescence (fluorescence), for this effect and the absorption lines have some definite relationship. Photoluminescence may be explained as the emission of a visible glow of light when the stone is bathed in a beam of invisible ultra-violet light, cathode rays, or x-rays. It is the effects seen when diamonds are bathed in the so-called long-wave ultra-violet light that have the greatest interest with regard to the 'tie-up' with the absorption spectra.

The absorption spectra of diamond, according to B. W. Anderson, may be divided into two main groups. These are, first, diamonds of the Cape series, stones which fluoresce with a blue light and have body colours which vary from colourless to yellow. In this group the strongest absorption line is one at 4155 Å in the violet part of the spectrum, a line first observed by B. Walter in 1891. This line varies in strength with the depth of the body colour but is nearly always present even in colourless diamonds. When this line is strong other lines may be associated with it. Such lines are at 4785, 4650, 4520, 4350 and 4230 Å, all of which are in the blue and violet parts of the spectrum. Of these only that at 4785 Å is readily visible.

The second group consists of those diamonds which have a brown, greenish-yellow or green body colour, and which exhibit a green glow under ultra-violet light. Such stones show an absorption spectrum whose prominent line is a narrow one at 5040 Å in the green of the spectrum. Other weak lines at 5370 and 4980 Å may be present. Diamonds showing both blue and green fluorescence are not uncommon and in such cases the 4155 Å line will also be seen.

There are also certain colourless, bright yellow and brownish-yellow diamonds which show a yellow fluorescent glow under ultra-violet light. In these stones no discrete bands are observed except for, maybe, a weak line at 4155 Å.

It is not uncommon to observe the fluorescent glow in diamond to be localized in bands or zones, generally with some reference to the crystal form. It is of interest to note that when a strong blue fluorescence is shown, this glow when examined by a spectroscope is found to be banded.

Ultra-violet Rays

Under the long-wave ultra-violet rays (emission at 3650 Å) the glows exhibited by diamond, as mentioned above, may be a blue, or green or a yellow, although a reddish glow may occasionally be observed. The blue fluorescence may vary widely in intensity and in shade of hue from a very weak, practically indiscernible, mauve glow to a particularly bright sky blue fluorescence, and likewise the strength of the glows of other colours can vary also. This unpredictable response of diamond to excitation by long-wave ultra-violet light has been found to have a practical application as a means of identifying a multi-stone piece of diamond jewellery. If the glows of the stones are photographed the pattern of differential lumino-sities forms an identity certificate for the piece (*Figure 2.23*), for even if a facsimile piece of jewellery was made up it would be outside the bounds of probability that the stones in the new piece would fluoresce similarly.

Many diamonds show an afterglow (phosphorescence) after exposure to ultra-violet light or sunlight, but what a given stone will do is unpredictable.

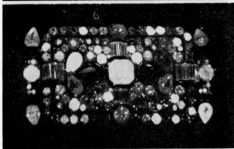

Figure 2.23. A diamond ornament in ordinary light (top), and the same piece taken when the diamonds were fluorescing under ultra-violet light. The differential effect may be used as an identity certificate

Under the short-wave ultra-violet light (emission 2537 Å) the fluores-cent effects are in general similar to those observed when the long-wave lamp is used, but the glows are very much weaker and in many cases not observable especially in the case of mauve fluorescing stones. Under x-rays most diamonds show a rather uniform bluish-white glow; the excep-tion being those diamonds which show a yellow glow under ultra-violet light and show a similar glow under x-rays, but this is not always so. If a yellow and a blue glow be present simultaneously the result will be a green glow.

It was found by R. Robertson, J. J. Fox and A. E. Martin that certain diamonds were more transparent to ultra-violet light than others. They therefore classified diamonds into two types—Type I and Type II. Type I are transparent down to about 3000 Å while Type II are much more trans-parent and pass ultra-violet light down to about 2250 Å. More recently the Type II diamonds have been subdivided into Type IIa and Type IIb. The Type IIa are said not to phosphoresce when irradiated with short-wave ultra-violet light, whilst the Type IIb when similarly irradiated show a bluish phosphorescence and will also conduct electricity. The reason for the difference in absorption of ultra-violet light, and also of infra-red, has been shown by Kaiser and Bond to be due to free nitrogen in Type I diamonds.

X-rays

The transparency of a substance to x-rays is a function of the atomic weight of the elements which make it up. The higher the atomic weight of the elements the less transparent is it to x-rays. Diamond is pure carbon (atomic weight 12) and is remarkably transparent to x-rays, whilst zircon which has the heavier zirconium atom (atomic weight 91) and silicon (atomic weight 28) and indeed all colourless stones and glass which simulate diamond are much more opaque to x-rays (*Figure 2.24*).

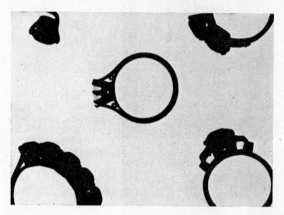

Figure 2.24. A radiograph of a diamond ring (centre), two zircon rings, a tie pin and a 5-stone synthetic rutile ring showing the difference in transparency of the diamond

Flaws and Light

Diamond to be of the best quality must be clean, that is free from flaws and spots—inclusions the gemmologist calls them. These imperfections may, however, be so small as to be undetectable under a lens magnifying ten diameters (the stone is then said to be eye clean or loupe clean) or the flaws may be so obvious as to mar severely the beauty of the stone. Further, if just one large imperfection is in the wrong place in a cut diamond it may suffer reflection from all the back facets so that to the eye the stone may appear full of flaws.

A most important study of the internal features of diamond has been made by E. Gübelin who has identified in diamond inclusions of graphite, haematite, magnetite, garnet, enstatite and zircon among others. Diamond itself is a common imperfection in diamond, and included crystals of quartz seem to be found only in Brazilian diamonds. Cleavage cracks and feathery marks often mar the transparency of diamonds, and both these, and other otherwise clear inclusions may appear as black spots when seen at such an angle that light is totally reflected at their surfaces.

48

ARTIFICIAL COLORATION

The artificial coloration of diamond has attained some commercial importance owing to the colouring effect produced when the stone is bombarded
with particles of atomic size. The production of a green colour in diamond
by bombardment with radioactive particles from radium compounds has
been known since early in the present century. Owing to the expense of the
method and the ease with which such artificial coloration can be detected—
for the stones themselves become radioactive from the treatment—'radium-
greened' diamonds are not commonly encountered. With the advance of
atomic science since World War II other methods of colouring diamonds
by particle bombardment, using modern high-voltage particle accelerators,
have led to some commercialization of artificially coloured diamonds.

Cyclotrons using protons (a particle in the nucleus of all atoms) and
deuterons (the nucleus of the heavy hydrogen atom) produce in diamond a
green colour, provided the heat generated by the impact of the particles is
dissipated (usually by the use of a jet of liquid helium), otherwise a brown
colour is produced. In any case a brown or yellow colour may be produced
by subsequently heating the greened stones at a controlled temperature.

More recently a similar type of coloration has been produced by using
neutrons (uncharged particles in the nucleus of most atoms) generated in an
atomic reactor (atomic pile) and such artificial coloration of diamond is now
carried out commercially both in Great Britain and in the United States of
America. The diamonds come from the pile green in colour and can be
altered to brown or yellow by subsequent heating under controlled conditions. Unlike 'cyclotroned' diamonds in which the colour is little more than
skin deep, the 'piled' diamonds are coloured throughout.

By the use of electrons (the unit negatively charged particles planetary
around the nucleus of all atoms) an aquamarine blue colour has been induced in gem diamonds. More scientific information on bombarded diamonds will be given in the chapter on colour.

A type of colour alteration sometimes practised, usually for fraudulent
purposes, is to paint the rear facets of off-coloured yellowish diamonds in
order to make them appear whiter. Scientifically it is well known that when
two complementary colours mingle white is produced; it is this effect which
is used in the whitening of diamonds. Off-coloured Cape diamonds are those
usually experimented with. A film of blue or violet dye is put on the back
facets of the stone, the blue (or violet) and the yellow colour of the stone
combine to give a whiter effect. The film is so thin as not to be readily seen
except where it has caught up on the raw edge (the unpolished girdle or
setting edge of the stone). As the treatment is usually carried out by using
a water-soluble dye, a thorough washing in hot water will dissolve the colour
and unmask the fake. Should a coloured lacquer be used solvents such as
acetone or amyl acetate, or even acid, may be needed to remove the colour.

SYNTHESIS AND SIMULATION

The constant handling of diamond jewellery—his most important com-
modity—gives to the jeweller such an experience of the appearance of
diamond that he rarely finds difficulty in spotting stones which are not

diamonds but which simulate them, at least under normal conditions of lighting. Rarely, through some unusual colour or imperfection of cutting, a real diamond may puzzle the jeweller. That such a stone is indeed a diamond may often be proved by examination of the unfinished edge of the girdle which may show 'naturals', part of the natural surface of the original crystal (*Figure 2.25*); the presence of these will surely identify the stone as diamond.

The synthesis of diamond has been accomplished in America but the product is of grain (powder) size only and is useful solely for industrial purposes. The subject of synthetic diamonds is told more fully in the pages on synthetic stones. It may be reiterated that there are no synthetic diamonds as far as gemstones are concerned.

If the jeweller is ever deceived with fake diamonds it is either because the light is bad at the time of the examination coupled with a too hasty decision

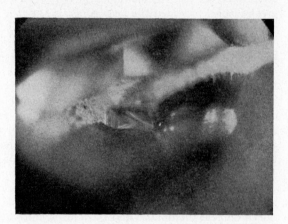

Figure 2.25. Naturals on the girdle of a cut diamond

being made, or by the encountering of some type of synthetic stone with which he is not familiar.

An unusual 'fake' in diamond is the so-called 'Piggy-back diamond' where a rather flat diamond with a large culet (facet at the back point of the stone) is set on the top of another smaller diamond so that the culet of the top stone rests on the table facet of the lower one; the whole giving the appearance of a much larger stone.

The more important stones which have some similarity to diamond in appearance are white zircon, and the synthetically produced strontium titanate, rutile, white sapphire, white spinel and the very new and effective yttrium aluminium garnet, to which may be added some highly refractive and lustrous glass imitation stones—the so-called pastes—and the diamond doublet, a composite stone. The stone most used to simulate diamond, both legitimately and, unfortunately, fraudulently is the white zircon which owes its colourless nature to heat treatment. The strong fire shown by zircon gives the stone some resemblance, when viewed in artificial light, to diamond itself, and can be most deceptive to the inexperienced person.

However, there is one feature which enables white zircon easily to be

Figure 2.26. Doubling of the back facets seen in a zircon. This is due to double refraction

detected from diamond. In diamond, as in all transparent materials crystallizing in the cubic system, a ray of light passes through as one ray, as it does in glass. Such a stone is said to be singly refractive or, scientifically, isotropic. On the other hand, zircon, which belongs to the tetragonal crystal system, has only one direction in which light passes through as one ray; in all other directions the light is split up into two rays and will produce a double image of the facet edges at the back of a stone when looked through from the front. Thus, careful examination of the stone through different directions may, if the stone be a zircon, show the opposite edges to be doubled (*Figure 2.26*).

This double effect is termed double refraction, and such stones possessing it are termed anisotropic. Double refraction cannot occur in diamond, although a spurious doubling has been encountered in diamond due to an internal reflective effect, but this is rare and only occurs in certain badly proportioned cut stones (*Figure 2.27*).

Synthetic rutile, often called 'Titania', does not present such a problem, for the fire shown by this manufactured stone is over six times that of diamond, and this unnatural fire is coupled with a very great double refraction.

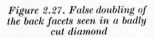

Figure 2.27. False doubling of the back facets seen in a badly cut diamond

The stones, too, are typically yellowish in colour, and these facts preclude synthetic rutile being mistaken for diamond.

The new synthetic strontium titanate is less easy to detect, for the stone has a water-white colour, single refraction and a refractive index near to that of diamond. The fire, some four times greater than for diamond, is again too much and indicates the nature of the stone, and if the stone be unset the high density (5·13) would be sufficient to identify it.

Synthetic white sapphire and synthetic white spinel have too little fire to make convincing diamond simulants. Synthetic white sapphire is doubly refracting but the birefringence, as it is called, is rather too weak for the doubling of the back facet edges to be seen easily.

The synthetic white spinel, although only slightly exceeding the white sapphire in fire, does, owing to its remarkable lustre, tend to be more deceptive, especially when trap-cut.

Figure 2.28. Reflection of the edges of the table facet on the cement layer seen in a diamond doublet

Colourless pastes are also singly refractive and can show considerable fire, but they are easily detected by their softness which may be well evident by the wear shown at the facet edges. Indeed all the stones mentioned are much softer than diamond so that if a stone is suspected it should be tested by scratching it against a test plate of synthetic sapphire (or a cut stone of this mineral). If the stone scratches the test plate then the stone must be a diamond, for the only materials harder than sapphire are the artificial products—carborundum and boron carbide—or the new synthetic compound borazon, but this has not yet been made in sizes large enough from which to cut stones. Further, all the simulants named are relatively opaque to x-rays while diamond is remarkably transparent to these rays (*see Figure 2.24*).

The diamond doublet can be the most deceptive of diamond fakes. This composite stone is constructed with a crown (top half of the stone) of real diamond which is cemented on to a pavilion (lower part of the stone) of some inferior colourless material. Such stones when looked at obliquely down the face of the stone project a shadow of the edges of the table facet (the large central facet) on to the cement layer and thus may readily be recognized (*Figure 2.28*).

The very many notable diamonds important for their historical associations or for their large size are listed in the appendices at the end of the book.

A RECENT ADVANCE IN DIAMOND RECOVERY AND SORTING

Much of the colour sorting of diamond crystals received from the mines is now carried out by optical separators which use photoelectric cells to sort the diamonds into colour grades. Such a machine, made by Gunson's Sortex Limited of Bow, London, has now been modified to operate by x-rays for use in diamond recovery at the mines. This machine (*Figure 2.29*) works on a similar principle to that devised by the Russians Krassov and Finne (see page 39) and depends upon the fluorescence of diamonds when in an x-ray beam.

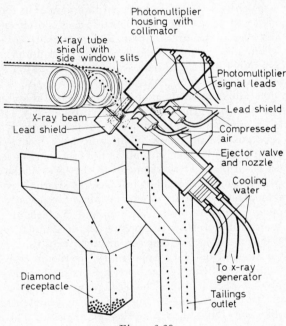

Figure 2.29

CHAPTER 3

RUBY AND SAPPHIRE

COMPOSITION AND SHAPE

It is difficult for the ordinary layman to believe that ruby, with its intense red colour, and the royal blue sapphire are one and the same mineral, a mineral composed of the gas oxygen and the light metal aluminium. Corundum, as this mineral is called, would, if pure, be perfectly colourless, and indeed some stones found in nature are practically colourless, but pure water-white stones are rare, a tinge of colour nearly always being present. The marvellous colours of ruby and sapphire are due to traces of a metallic oxide incorporated in the stone as an impurity, indicating a case where purity is not necessarily a virtue. Indeed, corundum may be found in many colours beside red and blue. Colourless, or white as it is often called, yellow, violet, green and even brown are common, and an attractive, though rather rare, orange colour may be met. Such a colour of corundum produces the stones which are sometimes called padparadscha, named after the Sinhalese word for 'lotus flower', and they make appealing gemstones.

Corundum crystallizes in the trigonal system of crystal architecture, but the habit, that is the shape the crystals take, varies greatly not only in the different varieties but also from the different localities from which they are found; ruby crystals usually show a different form from that of most sapphires. The ruby from Burma is usually a hexagonal prism terminated at both ends by a basal plane at right angles to the faces of the prism, with more or less well-developed rhombohedral faces at alternate corners. These rhombohedral faces may be partly or entirely absent, especially in the large, and usually opaque, crystals from Tanzania and Madagascar (*Figures 3.1 and 3.2*). In many ruby crystals the prisms are very much flattened, and although they may be of large diameter, are relatively thin. Such crystals often exhibit a stepped or platy appearance, as though the crystal was composed of a number of thin plates, each a little smaller in certain directions, superimposed on each other. The basal planes of many of the crystals are traversed in three directions by fine parallel striations, which take the form of hair-like lines crossing each other at angles of 120 degrees and dividing the area into small equilateral triangles.

Sapphire, usually, and in some cases ruby, takes the form of a hexagonal bipyramid of twelve triangular faces, six above and six below, meeting at a girdle. This general habit may occur in different combinations of bipyramids of different inclinations, with sometimes the girdle formed by a narrow hexagonal prism. The ends of many bipyramidal crystals are capped by the flat basal face and such forms are aptly described as having a barrel-shaped habit. The hexagonal bipyramidal habit is common in the sapphire crystals from Ceylon, and in this form the faces are often deeply

PLATE V

Necklace and ear pendants
in diamond and ruby

(By courtesy of Garrard & Co. Ltd.)

striated horizontally, due to repeated oscillation between different pyramids or between the pyramid and the basal pinacoid. The sapphires from Montana in the United States of America tend to take a rhombohedral and tabular habit. *Figure 3.3* shows some habits of corundum crystals and *Figure 3.4* shows a number of ruby and sapphire crystals.

Figure 3.1. A group of ruby crystals
from Tanzania

Figure 3.2. Crystal of sapphire from Ceylon (parallel group)

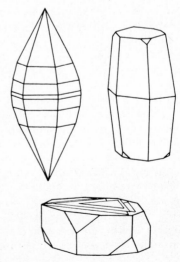

Figure 3.3. Some habits of corundum crystals

Figure 3.4. Corundum crystals. The group in the centre are Montana stones

LEGEND AND LORE

The legend and lore of ruby and sapphire are quaint. The lucky owner of a fine ruby was said to be assured of a life lived in peace and concord with all men—neither his land nor his rank would be taken from him, and his house and garden would be saved from damage by tempests.

Ruby has been claimed to be the most precious of the twelve stones God created when he created all creatures, and this 'Lord of Gems' was placed on Aaron's neck by God's command. The high esteem placed on ruby is further indicated by the names applied to ruby in Sanskrit. These were *ratnaraj*, which may be translated as 'King of Precious Stones' and *ratnanâyaka*—'Leader of Precious Stones'. The Hindu peoples described the glowing hue of the ruby as an inextinguishable fire which burned within the stone, and asserted that this inner fire could not be hidden and would shine through the clothing or through any material wrapped round the stone. If placed in water the inner heat was communicated to it causing the liquid to boil.

Ruby was said to preserve the mental and bodily health of the wearer, for it removed evil thoughts, and, although considered to be associated with passion, it was also thought to control amorous desires, to dispel pestilential vapours and reconcile disputes.

Some Indian beliefs were that he who made offerings of rubies to the images or gods in the worship of Krishna would be reborn as a powerful emperor; or if with a small ruby he would be reborn a king. Rubies, and other red stones whose colour suggests that of blood, were thought to be a remedy for haemorrhage and inflammatory diseases. Such stones were believed to confer invulnerability from wounds, but the Burmese said that it was not alone sufficient to wear the stones, but that they must be inserted into the flesh and thus become, so to speak, part of the wearer's body. Those who in this way bear a ruby about with them believe they cannot be wounded by spear, sword or gun. Ruby is the natal stone for July.

The gem of the soul, and of autumn, sapphire, the natal stone for September, was said to preserve the wearer from envy and to attract divine favour. Fraud was banished from its presence and necromancers honoured it more than any other stone, for it enabled them to hear and understand the obscurest oracles. The ancients thought sapphire to be endowed with the power to influence spirits, to be a charm against unchastity and capable of making peace between foes and protecting its owner against captivity. The Sinhalese respect the star-sapphire as protection against witchcraft.

Tradition is that the law given to Moses on the Mount was engraved on tablets of sapphire, but from Pliny's description the tablets were more probably made from the stone we now know as lapis-lazuli. The religious significance of sapphire was further enhanced in the twelfth century, when the Bishop of Rennes lavished encomiums upon the sapphire and began the use of this stone in ecclesiastical rings.

The names ruby and sapphire mean red and blue respectively; the first is derived from the Latin *ruber* and the second from *sapphirus*, the latter being derived from a Greek word of similar spelling. Similar words are found in Persian and Hebrew, and the primary derivation, though uncertain, may have been Sanskrit.

BURMA

Historical Events

The most famous locality, and maybe the only locality for fine rubies, and much sapphire, is the district around Mogok in Upper Burma. This so-called Mogok Stone Tract is an area of some 400 square miles, but the area now being spasmodically worked is some 25 miles from the town of Mogok itself.

When the Burma ruby mines were first discovered is quite unknown. The earliest that is heard of them is in a Burmese legend of untold age, which relates of an inaccessible fever-stricken valley in the Chinese country, into which human beings could not descend, but into which lumps of raw meat were flung from the surrounding hills, to be retrieved by the vultures, and from which the adhering rubies were picked off. This legend corresponds with the writings of Marco Polo (1245–1323), and he must have picked this up during his wanderings in Cathay (China). On this legend is based the story of 'Sinbad the Sailor'. A further proof of the great age of the mines is the comparative abundance of prehistoric implements, both of stone and bronze age, found amongst the detritus of the mining.

The first real record of the mines is that early Burmese history records that they were taken over from the Shan in 1597 in exchange for Mong Mit (Momeit) and that mines were then in full operation in the valley. The country, covered with dense forest, was so notoriously unhealthy that there was a shortage of labour, and to alleviate this King Bodawgyi sent thousands of captives from Manipur to work in the mines. This was about 1780, and subsequently the place became the place of exile for those who had incurred the king's displeasure. Shortly afterwards the district was placed in charge of Governors or So-Thuygis (So's) who allowed mining on payment of a tax, with a stipulation that all stones mined of an individual value of two thousand rupees and over were the property of the king without payment. This went on for some years and the So's enriched themselves greatly by oppressing the miners and forcing them to sell their stones for little or nothing to themselves. As they held absolute powers of life and death, the So's were very well placed to terrorize the unfortunate miners. Things went from bad to worse, and the miners deserted their villages and left the district.

King Mindoon Min then took over the district and control of the mines but made such a bad job that in 1863 another Governor was appointed with the responsibility of collecting a tax of some £5,000 a year from the miners, to be paid directly to the king, beside what the So could collect for himself. Under this arrangement matters became much worse and a rebellion took place, the whole Stone Tract being beset by gangs of fierce robbers and practically deserted by peaceful miners. As the king was getting no revenue he made mining free to everybody, and the miner had the right to sell all stones under 2,000 rupees in value—the king taking all stones above this value—to anyone within the Stone Tract, but not outside it. All stones not sold in the Stone Tract had to be sent under seal to a central ruby mart in Mandalay. Here they were offered for sale, and if sold the purchaser paid 10 per cent and the owner 5 per cent on the price by way of tax. If no sale took place the owner paid 10 per cent on the valuation and was then free to sell the stones anywhere. This restored prosperity for a time, but abuses again became apparent, mainly on account of the king's demand for more revenue, not only from the mines but from the Governors, which they obtained by again oppressing the miners and swindling the traders who came to the mines to buy. These demands for more money grew apace and in 1885 King Thebaw appointed a Governor whose business it was to find no less a sum than £16,000 per annum. This was the last straw, and the district again entered a state of chaos. The villages were raided daily by gangs of robbers forcing the villagers to go about in armed bands for self-protection. The road from Mogok to the river was infested with robbers, three local bandits establishing a convoy system down the road, demanding as much as 10 rupees a head for a safe passage; if travellers did not pay they were simply robbed or murdered. At this time King Thebaw was negotiating with a French syndicate for a lease of the mines, and this was one of the deciding factors which led to the annexation of Upper Burma by the British in 1886.

The Burma Ruby Mines Company

After the annexation, Streeter, the Bond Street jeweller, who was said to have been negotiating with Thebaw, obtained a concession from the British Government to work the mines. The Burma Ruby Mines Limited was immediately floated and the issue was oversubscribed in a few minutes and double the amount, £300,000, could easily have been raised.

The British Government's annual rental for the mines was fixed at the tremendous sum of £30,000 plus 30 per cent of any profits, in return for which the Company were to have the right to work any unoccupied land with use of machinery. The native miners were to be allowed to continue working by purely native methods, on payment to the Company of 30 per cent of the value of their declared finds. It was thus considered that the Company would have a monopoly of rubies and would be able to control the price of them. This was a mistaken idea as was soon evident; for the native miner naturally concealed the greater part of his finds and produced absurdly small parcels for valuation. The smuggling of the concealed stones was a simple matter and quite impossible to check, and these stones coming on the market stopped any regulation of the price of rubies. Subsequently new arrangements were made whereby the native miner paid a fixed monthly fee of 20 rupees a month for each workman he employed. This fee went to the Government but was collected by the Company, who received 10 per cent of the total for their services. The annual rent for the mines was reduced by 50 per cent, and was subsequently abolished altogether in view of the open market created by the native miners selling their stones.

At the beginning the Company's engineers were confronted with a task of great magnitude. The ruby-bearing alluvials were found to lie deep down under heavily waterlogged valleys, and a considerable portion of the ruby-bearing ground was under the town of Mogok itself. This entailed purchasing the buildings and re-erecting the town on another site. Heavy machinery and pumping plant had to be brought for 60 miles over a rough mule track through dense fever-stricken jungle infested with wild animals, ranging from tiger to elephant, and passing over mountains 5,000 ft. high. It took over a year to make a road passable by very light bullock carts, which took 3 weeks to make the journey and could not travel at all for 7 months of the year. Rinderpest was a scourge, and machinery lay abandoned on the roadside for months owing to lack of transport. These difficulties were eventually overcome and a good road constructed. At the mines a 400 kilowatt hydroelectric power station was opened, a low-level drainage tunnel constructed for a mile through a mountain range at a cost of £40,000 and five large washing mills, each dealing with some thousands of tons of earth per day, put into operation. Subsequently, three more mills were erected 8 miles away near Kyatpyin, and the mines entered on a period of prosperity.

The mines were worked by the open-cast method, there being no underground working at all. The first process was to take all the earth from grass level to bedrock and truck it away to large washing mills by hand labour and rope haulages. This method was subsequently superseded by a system of washing the earth down by large jets of water (monitor jets) under high pressure and passing the earth through a series of sluice-boxes, to which it was elevated by large gravel pumps, making a great saving in mining costs.

All went well with the mines and the Company was paying dividends until 1908, when the synthetic ruby was placed on the market, causing an immediate panic and making rubies difficult to sell. At the same time America was passing through a depression and the prices of fine rubies fell, while the depreciation in lower grades was much greater. It was the beginning of the end for the company, although all through the lean years of World War I Burma Ruby Mines Limited struggled on. The Company fought a losing fight until 1925, when it went into voluntary liquidation, only to struggle on further until 1931, when it finally surrendered its lease to the Government.

Native Mining

On the cessation of activities by the Burma Ruby Mines Limited the mining was carried on by native miners working by their primitive method. Up to the commencement of World War II these miners paid a monthly fee of 10 rupees per workman to the Government, but for an enhanced fee they were allowed to use water and explosives. In order to obtain a licence to mine in Burma it is necessary that one's name should be on a very arbitrary list of Registered Miners, but those on the list are often willing to lend their names to the less fortunate for a consideration. A licensee usually employs three workmen, who receive as payment 50 per cent of the total profits of the mine for the month to share among them. Every market day they draw a very small advance for the purchase of food, and if the month's work shows a loss that amount is wiped out, and they receive no further payment. If the mine shows a profit this sum is deducted from the 50 per cent of the total profits of the mine.

In the dry season these men mine by sinking a shaft on to the layer of byon (the name applied to the gem-bearing alluvial gravel); if there is little or no subsoil water these pits are merely small round holes just large enough to allow a man to descend into them. They are sunk very rapidly and contain no timbering. The pits are called twinlon and are usually from 20 to 40 ft. deep. After this depth they are often unsafe, but in very favourable ground may go down to 100 ft. At this depth a second shaft is sunk parallel to the first, and is connected with it by openings at intervals for the purposes of ventilation.

One workman simply squats at the bottom of the shaft and loosens the earth with a tiny spade, and then presses it into a small bamboo basket with his hands. This basket is hauled to the surface by the second workman by means of a balance crane constructed of three bamboos, and a basket of heavy stones, or other weight known as a maungdaing. Light is reflected to the workman below by means of a piece of tin set at an angle above the hole. Until the byon is reached the earth removed is thrown away, after which side tunnels are driven by two workmen along the byon in every direction for about 40 ft. Every scrap of byon is carefully removed from the entire area. The tunnels are allowed to fall in when finished with, but are consolidated so as to provide support for the top whilst the other galleries are being driven (*Figure 3.6*).

If the ground contains water a twinlon would not stand, so a square pit known as a lebin is put down. This has sides 2 ft. each way and is lightly timbered with brushwood and leaves held in place by thin sticks to keep the wet earth in place. Such pits may go down for over 200 ft. Larger pits with sides of 4½ ft. are known as kobin, while still larger ones with sides of 20–30 ft. are known as imbye. These large heavily timbered pits need a number of men to operate them and are expensive to work.

Water is removed from the wet pits by bailing with fuel-oil cans tied to the maungdaing or by the use of an ingenious bamboo pump, which is best explained by reference to *Figure 3.7*. Effective down to a depth of 20 ft., the pumps are arranged in relays for greater depths.

In the rainy season when the pits cannot be worked the hillside deposits are tackled. The miner makes a cutting into the hillside washing the loose

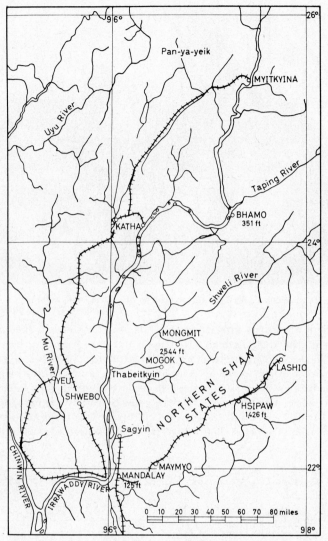

Figure 3.5. Sketch map of Upper Burma to show ruby localities
(after J. Coggin Brown)

earth away by means of sprays of water falling from bamboo pipes placed at
a height above the working. The light earth is allowed to wash away to waste
while the heavier sands and gravels are led away to narrow water courses,
where the heavier portion, containing the gems, is trapped in holes made
in the channels and is sorted by hand. This method of mining is known as
hmyawdwin and may be of any size from an insignificant cut to an
enormous opening. The water to work the mines is often brought from long
distances by channels cut in the rock, and even through tunnels, being carried over valleys on high bamboo aqueducts in bamboo mats luted with
clay.

61

Figure 3.6. Washing the byon in the Burma ruby mines
(By courtesy of the Editor, *Journal of Gemmology*)

The deposits in the interior of the hills are contained in the cracks and crevices in the rocks, which often open out into large caverns of great beauty. These caverns are reached by long tortuous passages, so small that a man can scarcely worm his way along them, and such mines are called loodwins or loos. Some of the finest stones are found in such loos.

The local streams are worked for the gems by rudely damming them with logs and brush wood and the gravel held up by this being dredged out by hand and small baskets. The return from this source is usually poor.

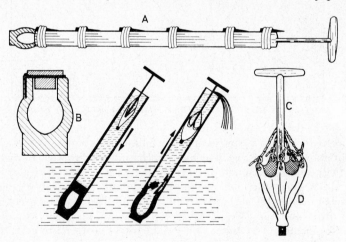

Figure 3.7. Details of the bamboo pump used by the Burmese miner for pumping out the pits: (A) complete pump, (B) detail of the end valve, (C and D) details of the plunger

PLATE VI

Suite of diamond and sapphire jewellery

(By courtesy of Garrard & Co. Ltd.)

The byon removed from the mines is placed in a pear-shaped washing place called a yebangwet and is then broken up with water by men using hoses. The slurry formed is allowed to fall into a channel from the narrow end of the yebangwet where the heavy gravels are trapped in a series of holes dug in the floor of the channel. This heavy concentrate is removed and more highly concentrated by hand in small round bamboo trays. This residue is then sorted by hand for the gems.

In all the streams poor women armed with round bamboo trays may be seen scraping up the gravel from the bed, and sorting it for rubies. This is a hereditary right for women only and is known as kanase. It is free of all fee and licence and their work must not be interfered with. Usually their finds are small.

Geology

The Burmese ruby occurs embedded in a mother rock of white dolomitic granular limestone, or marble. This is a common rock of the district and is said to be originally a sedimentary limestone, which has suffered meta-morphism by contact with intrusions of igneous rock causing the calcium carbonate to recrystallize out as marble, and its contained impurities to crystallize out as other minerals including corundum. The sapphire from the Burmese locality is, however, not found *in situ* in the marble, but in a feldspathic rock. It is in the alluvial deposits derived from the weathering of the parent rocks that the gem corundums are mostly found; this is the byon. Rubies predominate around Mogok, whilst sapphires are more common at a site some 8 miles away, near the village of Kathe, which is some 100 ft. higher than the Mogok valley. At Bernardmyo, at an elevation of some 300 ft. above Mogok, rather dark-coloured stones are found in a hard black iron-cemented conglomerate.

Burma Today

What goes on in Burma today is to some extent conjecture, for the Mogok Stone Tract became part of the battleground of the 14th Army and the Japanese invader. As Burma is no longer a British possession, it is not known what fine sapphires and rubies now emanate from Burma.

THAILAND (SIAM)

The next most important occurrence for rubies and sapphires is Siam, where the rubies are rather a brownish-red and somewhat dark in colour, while the sapphires are of excellent quality. The main occurrence covers a considerable area in the neighbourhood of Chantabun, where rubies pre-dominate, and Battambang which is important for sapphires, and the de-posits spread over the border at Phailin in Cambodia. The stones are found in a coarse yellow or brown sand, overlaying a bed of clay or basaltic rock. The beds are mostly within 6–8 ft. or less from the surface, but some of the mines are over 20 ft. deep. The Siam deposits have only been worked to any extent in comparatively modern times and at one period were worked under a concession by a British company. The mining is by native methods and the miners are mostly Burmese.

KASHMIR

Sapphires of a magnificent colour, possessing a fine milky lustre, often of a fine cornflower-blue with a slight milky appearance, are found in the Zanskar district of Kashmir. The mines are near the village of Soomjam (Sumsan) in the Pader District. The deposits were said to have been first discovered by an avalanche laying them bare in 1881, but there is reason to believe that the local inhabitants knew of them much earlier. The deposits lie in a small valley about half a mile long by a quarter mile wide in the Kanskar Range of the north-western Himalayas. The valley, on a tributary of the Chenab, lies approximately midway between Srinagar and Jammu at an elevation of 14,950 ft., and except for a few months of the year is under deep snow. The stones occur in a pegmatite vein in association with tourmaline, garnet, kyanite and euclase. The pegmatite veins penetrate lenses of actinolite-tremolite rock in crystalline limestone; the sapphires are often found in pockets of kaolin derived from the pegmatite. When first discovered the sapphires were extracted from the face of a precipice at the head of the valley, and it was not until some years afterwards that the whole floor of the valley was found to be covered with a thin layer of white pegmatite, overlain by a few feet of ordinary earth, which carried sapphires in immense quantities. Mainly due to the severity of the climatic conditions the work was carried on in a desultory way until 1924, when the mines were re-opened after the deposits came under the notice of the Kashmir Mineral Survey. The crystals are well formed and often of large size when found in the rock, but the stones found in the valley are water-worn and rarely show crystal form. The crystals are said frequently to enclose green tourmaline. Cut stones, which make excellent night stones, often contain 'silk', and according to some reports also contain inclusions of green mica. Little is known of the mining methods. The mining must be primitive, for the stones are picked out by hand, a very crude form of ground sluice being used.

CEYLON

In the south-west part of the island of Ceylon are found corundums of many colours—blue (rather pale), violet, yellow, white, green and a pink, which often attains a quality comparable to that of ruby and is, if a rich enough rose-red, called a Ceylon ruby. Star-stones, too, are plentiful in this island but as a rule do not have a colour which can be said to be fine. Pit mining is carried on in Ceylon in a similar manner to the Burmese system. The miner searches for the small and scattered localities by observing the surface for signs of rolled pebbles. These localities are often in the rice fields, and having found what he hopes will be a good spot, the miner sinks a pit which goes down maybe 50 ft. to reach the gem-bearing stratum known as illam, which is a blue and yellow mud. Sometimes the gems are found embedded in boulders of semi-decomposed gneissic rock. If the miner is not successful with his first pit he must fill it in and start another somewhere else. If he strikes gem gravel, then it is brought to the surface and panned by the use of a finely woven basket. The gravel is washed by placing it in the bottom of the basket and being broken up by water, the light mud separating off through the fine meshes of the basket and the heavy concentrate sinking to the bottom. This concentration is known as dullam and is searched for gems, which are then sold by auction. Much of the gem material won from the illam is cut and polished by native craftsmen on the island. Squatting outside his cottage, or in a back alley, the cutter fashions the corundum gems on a small wooden wheel mounted at the end of a horizontal shaft which is rotated by a drawstring bow which he saws back and forth. For polishing, a chamois leather pad is fixed over the vertical lap, and the stone is usually held in the hand while being cut and polished. The Sinhalese cutter aims at getting the most weight out of a stone, so the proportions are wrong by European standards, the base being overweight and often not symmetrical. Much blue sapphire from Ceylon is parti-coloured and the wily native cutters cut such stones with the blue colour at the bottom of the pavilion, so that by total internal reflection the stone when viewed from the top appears a good blue colour; such stones looked at sideways are found to be colourless at the top with a patch of blue near the culet. Some blue sapphires from the island contain a trace of ruby and although they are a good blue colour in daylight they tend to turn purple when seen in artificial light. In common with many stones of other species that are found in Ceylon, the corundums from this locality often show as inclusions small crystals of zircon surrounded with circular dark areas where stresses from the zircon have affected the surrounding host mineral. These inclusions are usually known as 'zircon haloes'.

AUSTRALIA

Corundum, mainly of blue, green and yellow colours, and some ruby, is found in Queensland and New South Wales. The Queensland sapphire fields are located around Anakie and extend for some 200 square miles. Ruby Vale is a prominent locality for Queensland corundum and at Willows, some 212 miles west of Rockhampton, a $217\frac{1}{2}$ carat yellow sapphire was found in 1946. The Anakie deposits, discovered in 1870, are along the banks of creeks and not in the beds of the present streams, the stones being found in a clayey, or loose and friable, alluvium. Owing to the arid nature of the area, sluice-boxes are not often used and the mining is carried on by hand-picking and by the use of hand-sieves. The New South Wales deposits, which are centred around Inverell, west of the New England Range, lie in the north-east part of the state. The sapphires are found in an alluvial deposit of recent age, and here the mining is carried on by dredging and the sapphires reclaimed by the use of sluice-boxes and pulsators. Australian sapphires are usually rather dark blue and somewhat inky, the yellows are of an attractive greenish-yellow; Australia produces probably the best of the green stones. The greenish tinge of the stones is due to iron, and this is shown by the strong 4500 Å complex seen in the absorption spectrum, by the slightly higher constants and by the lack of luminescence when under a beam of ultra-violet light. Australian corundums usually show dark 'feathers', but also show strong colour-zoning. Some sapphire is found, too, in the north-east part of the island of Tasmania.

UNITED STATES OF AMERICA

The only important locality for gem corundum in the United States of America is in Montana, where it is found as water-worn pebbles in the gravel bars of the Missouri river, and at Yogo Gulch, near Utica, where flat gemmy crystals, pale in colour but with a curious metallic lustre, are found in nearly vertical and much weathered dark-coloured fine-grained igneous dykes. Although the crystals are usually small, Montana sapphires, which may be yellow, greenish-blue or a fine blue, often show pronounced hexagonal zoning and a moderately strong 4,500 Å complex in the absorption spectrum. The blue stones have a decided greenish tint and a bright metallic lustre; ruby is not common, and the same may be said for starstones. Montana sapphires make attractive night stones. Small rubies of fair quality have been found in Macon County, North Carolina, the stones being found in the sands of Cowee Creek. Blue sapphire is said to occur in Colorado and Idaho.

OTHER OCCURRENCES

Corundum is of widespread occurrence, but the above-mentioned occurrences are the important gem localities. There are a few minor sources of gem material which have little commercial significance. There is a small deposit of ruby at Jagdalak in Afghanistan, some 30 miles east of Kabul, and small corundums of various colours are found in the Somabula Forest in Rhodesia. About 1952 a number of large ruby crystals of excellent colour but rather opaque were found by A. G. Clough in the Matabatu Mountains of the Northern Province of Tanzania. The short prismatic ruby crystals are found, sometimes as aggregates, in a bright apple-green zoisite rock. At the same period, possibly in the local alluvium, small water-worn pieces of ruby were found which were transparent enough to cut; and some of these stones were cut and, it is believed, marketed. These cut specimens were a rich colour, as good as much Burma material, but the stones were not so transparent and were extremely chrome-rich. Similar red crystals are found in Madagascar at Gogogogo, east of the Linta river in the south-western part of the island. The matrix here is said to be a green mica schist. Sapphire is also reported to have been found in Madagascar. Gemmy corundum has been mentioned as occurring in Czechoslovakia, the U.S.S.R. (Ural mountains), Romania and Borneo, and in 1969 good quality sapphires of fair size, and rubies of poorer quality, have been found in Malawi (formerly Nyasaland). Brazil and Norway also supply gem corundum.

Ruby and sapphire have been found in Mysore, India. The stones are rather like those found in the Ceylon gem gravels, but occasionally there are stones which approach the hue of the Burmese rubies. Star rubies of rather poor colour and star effect are also found in the Mysore deposits. They are rather impure and have a low density near to 3·97. Ruby and sapphire are found in the Rio Mayo, a tributary of the Patia, and in the sands of the Platayaco, in the Caqueta territory of the South American Republic of Colombia. Poor quality star corundums have been found in northern Finland, and during 1960 gemmy crystals of ruby and sapphire were found in the Gilewy Hills, and near Morogoro in Tanzania.

FACETING

Rubies and sapphires may be faceted in many different styles; mostly the mixed-cut is used, the brilliant-cut crown being backed with a step-cut pavilion. For fine stones the step-cut or trap-cut is often employed, and if the material is poor in quality or much flawed it may be cut into beads or even carved. Star-stones are cut cabochon in order to exhibit the attractive optical effect of asterism. Pale stones are often mounted with a closed setting and the back of the stone sometimes foiled with a suitable colour. W. Bingley states that it was formerly the practice, in the case of blue sapphires, to place under the stone the blue part of a peacock's feather instead of foil.

CHEMICAL AND PHYSICAL PROPERTIES

The mineral corundum is a crystallized form of aluminium oxide (Al_2O_3), traces of impurities modifying the water-white colour of the pure mineral. Ruby varies in shade from a pale rose pink through all shades of red to a deep crimson sometimes known in the jewellery trade as 'black'. The pink coloured corundum may be considered as a pale ruby but a pure pink coloured stone is known as a pink sapphire, all fancy coloured corundums being termed sapphire with the colour as prefix. The decision whether a stone is a pink sapphire or a pale ruby may often lead to debate. The colour of ruby is due to a trace of chromic oxide (Cr_2O_3), which enters the crystal structure by a small scale replacement of some of the aluminium atoms. This is known as isomorphous replacement. The amount, about 4 per cent, determines the depth of colour, but the presence of iron in the ferric state (Fe_2O_3) also modifies the tint, giving to the rubies from Siam the brownish tinge so typical of them. The so-called and one may say indefinable 'pigeon's blood', a red inclining to purple, is the prized colour of the best Burmese rubies.

Coloration of Sapphire

The colour of the blue sapphire is due to traces of iron oxide and titanium oxide, although some authorities consider that a trace of chromic oxide can take part in the coloration, a theory which has some credence because a greenish-blue glass can be obtained by the use of the oxides of chromium and iron. There is some reason for assuming that two types of coloration may be encountered in blue sapphire, for some blue sapphires decolorize on heating and some do not. Titanium and iron are known to be present in the form of ilmenite ($TiFeO_3$), a mineral found in nature, and this compound is not isomorphous with alumina, that is replaceable in the crystal lattice, so that the colouring agents are in the form of colloidal particles. That this is so has been proved by the ultra-microscope. The colloidal nature of the coloration also provides an explanation of the irregular distribution of colour in sapphire. The production of a blue colour in synthetic sapphire by the addition of the oxides of iron and titanium gives added confirmation. There is, however, an added complexity in the fact that the synthetic blue sapphire shows no iron bands in the absorption spectrum. Iron is most certainly included in the powder used to make the sapphire but appears to volatilize off in the heat of the oxyhydrogen blowpipe flame. Thus the part that iron plays in the coloration is not clearly defined, and, further, benitoite, a mineral which has a colour like sapphire, seems to have the colour due to titania alone.

Density

The density of the purest corundum, the synthetic colourless sapphire, is 3·989, but the natural ruby and sapphire usually have densities approximating to 3·997, there being little variation for specimens from different localities. An exception is the green and blue-green sapphires from Australia, which may have densities as high as 4·00.

CLEAVAGE

Corundum is a hard stone, indeed the impure material is used as an abrasive, and is rated 9 on the scale of hardness devised by F. Mohs. Despite the hardness of the mineral, however, ruby and sapphire need to be handled with some care, for they are to a slight extent brittle and if dropped on a hard surface or given a sharp blow tend to develop internal flaws and cracks. The type of fracture seen when corundum is broken is usually that termed uneven, or may be shell-like (conchoidal). There is no true cleavage in corundum, but a false cleavage or parting may be present. These are directions of weakness which are parallel to the basal plane or to the rhombohedral faces of the crystal. These directions of weakness are usually ascribed to pressure due to lamellar twinning on these faces, or to weakness caused by incipient decomposition along these planes. There are, however, some authorities who contend that they are true cleavages.

EFFECTS OF LIGHT

Refraction

Unlike minerals which crystallize in the cubic system, and amorphous (non-crystalline) materials, such as glass, a ray of light entering stones of the trigonal system such as ruby and sapphire, breaks up into two rays. This double refraction as it is called causes anything viewed through the stone to appear slightly doubled, thus the edges of the rear facets appear slightly doubled. Further, these two rays are plane polarized, at right angles to one another; that is the rays vibrate in one plane only perpendicular to the direction of travel of the ray. Thus, in corundum there will be two indices of refraction which, in the pure material, are for the fixed (ordinary) ray 1·7687 and for the movable ray (extraordinary ray), which moves from the value of the ordinary ray to the limiting value of separation, 1·7606. The natural stones do not vary very much from these values except in the case of the iron-rich green stones which may reach values of 1·78 and 1·77. As it is the lower value which is the extraordinary ray, stones of the corundum family are said to be negative in sign.

The amount of the difference between the value of the ordinary ray and that of the extraordinary ray—termed the birefringence, is 0·008 (a fuller explanation of the optics of gem materials will be given in Chapter 31).

The fact that there are two rays in these stones has an effect on the colour, for each of these rays may absorb light differently and as the stone is turned it may show a slightly different shade of colour. This effect is termed dichroism, and this differential colour effect is seen moderately well in all rubies and sapphires, except in the colourless and yellow stones. The most attractive colour in both ruby and sapphire is that due to the ordinary ray; this being a deep purplish-red in ruby and a deep royal blue in sapphire. Therefore, in order that the stone will show the best colour it is necessary for the stone to be cut with the large central facet, the table facet, at right angles to the vertical axis of the crystal.

Lustre

The lustre of ruby and sapphire is glass-like, or as it is scientifically termed vitreous, but it may approach adamantine, that is getting on towards that of diamond. The velvety sheen seen in some fine blue sapphires is said to be due to the colloidal coloration. The dispersion of the stones is only 0·018 (between the B to G range), hence corundums show little fire and the beauty of the stones lies in their colour nuances alone.

Absorption Spectrum

The absorption spectrum of ruby is characterized by fine lines in the red; the stronger being a close doublet at wavelengths 6942 and 6928 Å. Other weaker lines are at 6680 and 6592 Å which lie in the orange part of the spectrum.

There is a broad absorption area cutting out the yellow and most of the green of the spectrum, the violet too being absorbed. Therefore there is a transmission of blue light and in this window there are three narrow lines; a close doublet with wavelengths of 4765 and 4750 Å and another line at 4685 Å. The doublet in the red, with a mean wavelength of 6935 Å, is characterized by its reversibility, for under certain conditions it will show as a bright fluorescence line, and, indeed, to it are due the fluorescence effects shown by ruby under blue and violet light, and those invisible rays of shorter wavelength. This fluorescent line is best seen when light is scattered from the surface and may be viewed in a spectacular manner when the incident white light is filtered with a flask of a saturated solution of copper sulphate (which only passes blue light) and the light scattered from the ruby examined with a hand spectroscope—the bright line then being seen on a black background. Alternatively, the ruby bathed in the blue light may be viewed with a filter (gelatine or glass) which only passes red light, when the stone will be seen like a glowing coal on a black background.

The absorption spectrum of sapphire shows bands due to iron in the ferric state, and the spectrum shows considerable difference in intensity with decrease of iron content. In the iron-rich green and blue-green stones there are three evenly spaced absorption bands in the blue region. These are centred at 4710, 4600 and 4500 Å, of which the 4500 Å band is the strongest and most persistent. This 4500 Å band is sometimes so wide that it merges with the 4600 Å band giving a two-band aspect, one narrow (the 4710 Å line) and a very broad band composed of the two others. With decrease of iron content these bands, usually known as the 4500 complex, decrease in intensity till in the case of the rich blue sapphires only the 4500 Å line may be seen as a fine line and then only with difficulty, even with the aid of the copper sulphate filter which filters out the brighter light from the longer-wave end of the spectrum. Many Ceylon blue sapphires show the bright red fluorescent line at 6935 Å due to a trace of ruby, and the 4500 Å sapphire line is seen only with the greatest of difficulty.

The other colours of sapphire have absorption spectra reminiscent of the colour nearest to them. Thus the pink and violet stones show chromium spectra, but in these cases the lines in the blue window may barely be seen. Colourless and brown corundums do not show an absorption spectrum which may be observed by the use of a direct-vision spectroscope. Unlike stones from other localities the yellow sapphires from Ceylon do not show the 4500 Å complex due to iron. The absence of iron in the Ceylon sapphires is further borne out by the unusual fluorescence of Ceylon yellow sapphires. In only one case, that of an orange-red stone from Burma, has the vanadium line at 4750 Å been observed in a natural stone. Apart from this one case the 4750 Å line is diagnostic for the change-colour synthetic sapphires made to imitate the alexandrite.

Luminescence

The luminescence of chromium-coloured corundums (rubies, pink and violet sapphires) is a strong crimson light which is the same whatever radiation is used. This is due to the excitation of the chromium ion (an atom carrying an electric charge), the glow being mainly due to the intense emission from the doublet at 6935 Å. This red glow can be seen spectacularly when viewed between 'crossed filters'—that is, by placing the stone in a beam of blue light which has been passed by a copper sulphate filter and viewing the stone through a filter which passes only the red rays. The stone then appears glowing red on a black background. This is because blue light will also excite the chromium ion. If this fluorescent light be examined with a spectroscope the bright lines are the same wavelength as in the absorption spectrum. This discrete spectrum only occurs when electronic shifts, to which the luminescence is due, are sufficiently screened by an outer electron shell so as not to be too greatly interfered with by the surrounding atomic field. This effect appears to occur only with chromium, rare earths, and diamond; in the latter case, however, the mechanism is somewhat different. When rubies are viewed through the Chelsea colour filter this fluorescent red may be seen and this is a convenient method to adopt when picking out rubies from a mixed parcel of rubies and garnets, the latter not fluorescing.

The fluorescence of ruby has been suggested as a test for distinguishing between rubies from Burma and those from Siam—and for distinguishing synthetic stones from natural rubies. Experiment has shown that it is impossible to pick out the synthetics with any degree of certainty from a mixed parcel of synthetic and Burma stones. Owing to the damping of the fluorescence by iron content, rubies from Siam show a much weaker fluorescent glow than those from Burma, which glow brightly. This effect has been suggested, and used, as a distinction between the two sources of ruby. While this usually operates in typical cases it is apt to fail in precisely those cases where it is most needed, such as in the case of a deep-coloured Burma ruby and an exceptionally fine Siam stone. It should be mentioned at this stage that the gem trade refers to Burma rubies as stones of a typical red colour, and to Siam rubies as all those stones which are darker, or show a slight brownish or violet tinge, and do not approach the 'ideal' red. Ceylon rubies to the trade are those lighter coloured rubies approaching the pink sapphire. True localities may not necessarily be meant, although the designation may be correct in most cases.

In the case of the blue sapphires the luminescent glow is practically non-existent. An exception, however, is the Ceylon sapphire which contains a trace of chromium. These show a red or orange glow under long-wave ultra-violet light. Under short-wave ultra-violet light some blue sapphires show a weak blue glow, an interesting observation in view of the bright blue glow shown by the titanium mineral—benitoite—under the short-wave lamp, while it is practically inert under the long-wave rays. Most sapphires are inert under x-rays, except the Ceylon, Montana and some Indian (Kashmir) stones which may show a dull red or yellowish-orange glow. It has been reported that under bombardment by cathode rays (fast moving electrons) Kashmir sapphires show a greenish-blue glow, Burma stones a strong dark purple, Siam stones a weak dull red, and sapphires from Ceylon a vivid red fluorescence.

The iron-rich green and yellow sapphires show no luminescence under any of the aforementioned radiations, but the yellow stones from Ceylon show a strong apricot-yellow glow under ultra-violet light and x-rays. The cause of this particular luminescence does not appear to be known. Such stones when bombarded by x-rays turn to a rich topaz-colour, however weakly yellow they were originally. This colour is not permanent for the colour reverts on exposure to about $3\frac{1}{2}$ hours' sunlight or quickly when the stone is heated to a temperature of about 230°C. Colourless sapphires may also suffer this change of hue by x-ray bombardment, but the shade of yellow attained is usually lighter; and further some blue sapphires will change to a dirty amber colour.

INCLUSIONS

Much work has been carried out, particularly by E. Gübelin in Switzerland, on the nature of the inclusions in corundum, with a view to identifying the locality from which the stone emanates. It is the writer's opinion that while in some cases the evidence so obtained is sufficient to give an indication, in many cases there are insufficient grounds to formulate a satisfactory conclusion, and, apart from other factors, this is the primary reason why most gem-testing laboratories refuse to certify the locality of a stone.

Burma stones, especially rubies, show a system of short rutile needles arranged in three directions parallel to the faces of the hexagonal prism, that are crossing each other at angles of 60 degrees and 120 degrees, and these lie in planes at right angles to the principal axis of the crystal. To these needles, which may in some cases have decomposed, leaving canal-like cavities, is due the shimmering whitish sheen popularly known as 'silk' (*Figure 3.8*). Stones from Burma may show included well-formed crystals of rutile,

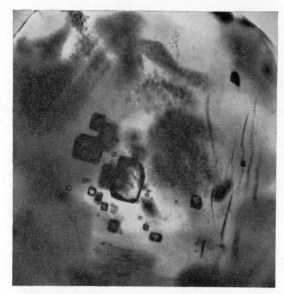

Figure 3.8. 'Silk' and inclusions in a Burma ruby

octahedra of spinel and mica platelets. Rounded crystals (*Figure 3.9*) of corundum, zircon and garnet make up the general picture of corundums from this source. The rich, bright red colour of Burma rubies is often to be seen in swirls, rather like the effect seen when treacle is stirred, hence this colour swirling is sometimes known as 'treacle.'

Siam stones usually show 'feathers' consisting of large loop-like systems of a reticulation of fine canals which often enclose swarms of hexagonal shaped 'slabs'. Quite commonly these feather systems contain a conspicuous black inclusion. Siam stones often contain tubes or tube-like liquid inclusions in cross-joined parallel arrangement producing a script-like design. Other common features are flat cavities of brownish colour and twin planes, the latter often in two sets approximately at right angles producing a checkered design. These are more pronounced when the stone is viewed between crossed nicols.

Figure 3.9. Rounded crystals in a Burma ruby

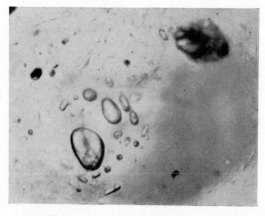

PLATE VII

The Sapphire group

Pink
7·62 carats

Green
5·10 carats

Purple
5·18 carats

Blue
18·6 carats

Orange
57·30 carats

Star sapphire
33·25 carats

Yellow
36·39 carats

Figure 3.10. Feather in a sapphire

Corundums from Ceylon show rutile needles which are characterized by being longer and more widely spaced than in the stones from Burma. They often traverse the whole stone. Very characteristic of Ceylon stones are inclusions of zircon crystals, each of which is surrounded by a halo of brown colour due to stresses caused in the host mineral. The well-defined feathers seen in stones from this island consist of large networks of irregular liquid-filled cavities. Clearly defined colour-zoning is common in Ceylon stones.

The sapphires from Kashmir owe their attractive milky or hazy appearance to a fine veil-like formation of hazy lines oriented at 120 degrees to each other. The feathers in such stones usually consist of thin films of yellow or brown colour with the edges terminated by an irregular system of liquid-filled canals. The stones from Montana, U.S.A., contain negative crystals

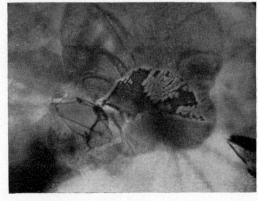

Figure 3.11. Feathers in a sapphire

surrounded by, or in near proximity to, extremely flat liquid films. Typical inclusions in such stones are long rods or tubes with projections making them appear rather like feather quills. The many accessory minerals seen in corundums from oriental localities do not appear in Montana stones. In Australian stones the feathers are liquid-filled cavities and dark flat cavities, and zonal structure is most pronounced.

STAR-STONES

Bound up with the internal features of corundums are the star-stones, or asterias, which to many have such a fascinating appeal. Much consideration has been given to the reasons for the production of the star-like effect seen in these attractive stones, and the theories have been summed-up, and added proof deduced by the work of Alice S. Tait. The 'silk' which has been previously mentioned may so impregnate the stone that the tubes or fine needle-like crystals running in three directions parallel to each pair of prism faces completely fill the crystal. If a stone be cut in the cabochon form from such material, so that the base of the cabochon is at right angles to the vertical crystal axis, that is parallel to the basal plane, three rays of white light cross the stone at right angles to the direction of the needles, thus producing a six-pointed star. This light is by reflection from the fibres and is termed epiasterism. If only one set of needles be present, as occasionally may happen, just one ray of light will be seen in a suitably cut stone, therefore under these conditions a corundum cat's-eye will be produced. Rarely, a six-rayed (12-pointed) star is seen in asteriated corundums. This effect is understood to be due to oriented needles not only conforming to the prism faces of the first order prism, but to the addition of a second set of three parallel to the faces of the second order prism which lie at 30 degrees from those of the first order. Thus, there will be not only the three rays of light from the needles parallel to the first order prism faces, but a second set of three rays due to the needles parallel to the faces of the second order, thus producing a six-rayed, or twelve-pointed star. Tait has found, from the shape of the needles and by spectroscopic examination of the material of the needles, that they are rutile crystals. It should be mentioned that in order to see the star effect (called asterism) to the best advantage, the stone should be viewed by light reflected from a single overhead light; a room with a multiple number of lights destroys the effect. Starstones may be of any colour, but the red-coloured material (star-ruby) is the most prized, with the fine blue (star-sapphire) next in value, but much depends upon the brightness and symmetry of the star and the body colour of the stone. Pink, violet and brown colours are common, but a stone with a nearly black body colour makes a most lovely asteria.

RUBIES AND SAPPHIRES OF INDIVIDUALITY

There are few true rubies with an individuality, and except for the Chhatrapati Manick so charmingly described by V. Clarke, the 43-carat Peace ruby, a crystal found in 1919, another crystal, but not of true gem quality, the 167-carat Edwardes ruby in the British Museum (Natural History section), and the 100 carat De Long star ruby in the American Museum of Natural History, there are no rubies to which names have been applied. The historical Black Prince's ruby, which graces the front of the Imperial State Crown, and the Timur ruby which is also part of the Crown Jewels, are both red spinels.

Among sapphires there are a number of fine stones, among them the St. Edward's sapphire and the Stuart, or Charles II's sapphire, both of which are companions to the Black Prince's ruby in the Imperial State Crown. The American gem dealer, Harry Winston, has, or had, in his possession several lovely large sapphires, one the so-called Catherine the Great's sapphire and another gorgeous stone weighing 337·10 carats. In the American Museum of Natural History is a 536 carat star-sapphire known as the Star of India and a smaller black star called the Midnight Star, weighing 116 carats. That sapphires can attain a large size is amply illustrated by the work of Norman Maness, who spent 1,800 hours carving a 2,302 carat sapphire into the form of the head of Abraham Lincoln.

SYNTHESIS AND SIMULATION

Corundums are made synthetically, even with the star effect, by the use of an inverted oxyhydrogen blowpipe. Such stones may be distinguished from the natural rubies and sapphires by characteristic growth lines and included gas bubbles. The full and fascinating story of gemstone synthesis is told in a later chapter.

Apart from the synthetic stones, rubies are simulated by natural red spinels, some garnets and are imitated by garnet-topped composite stones (stones having a crown of red garnet and a base of red glass), and by suitably coloured glass. Blue sapphires may be simulated by natural blue spinel and by the rare gem benitoite among others, and imitated by the garnet-topped doublet with a blue glass base and by a blue glass. Most of the blue doublets and blue glasses show a strong red through the colour filter (Chelsea colour filter) whereas real sapphires do not.

Star-corundum may be imitated by an ingenious composite stone using star rose-quartz with a coloured reflector on the base of the cabochon, or simply by engraving lines in three directions at 60 degrees on the base of cabochons cut from synthetic corundum or glass.

CHAPTER 4

EMERALD, AQUAMARINE AND OTHER BERYLS

CHEMICAL AND PHYSICAL PROPERTIES

Emeralds and aquamarines are colour varieties of the mineral known as beryl, which, besides these well-known gemstones, may be found in other colours to give such attractive, if lesser known gems, as the lovely rose-pink morganite, the rich yellow heliodor and the colourless goshenite.

Beryl is a silicate mineral in which the silicate molecule combines with the metals aluminium and beryllium. The chemical formula is $Be_3Al_2(SiO_3)_6$, but considerable replacement of the beryllia by the oxides of the alkali metals and the alumina by chromic or ferric oxides occurs. Beryl of non-gem quality is mined as the raw material for beryllium which is now increasingly used in industry.

Beryl crystallizes as six-sided prisms which belong to the hexagonal crystal system. The terminations, in the case of emerald, are usually flat faces joining the prism faces, producing the hexagonal prism of solid geometry. With the other colour varieties, and in a few cases emerald also, small pyramidal faces bevel the junction of the flat (basal) face and the prism faces. The atomic structure is formed by Si_6O_{18} groupings as independent sixfold rings formed by six SiO_4 tetrahedral groups linking through oxygen atoms. These rings are further bonded with the fairly small aluminium and beryllium atoms which serve to bind the rings tightly together, both laterally and vertically. This strength of bonding cancels out the possibility of prismatic cleavage and allows only an ill-defined and poor cleavage parallel to the basal plane. The hardness of beryl is $7\frac{1}{2}$ on Mohs's scale. In view of the importance of the beryl gems, and for the reason that the different varieties have slightly different physical properties, the varieties will be discussed individually.

EMERALD

Lore and History

The name emerald is derived from a Persian word, which later appeared in the Greek as *smaragdos* and then as *smaragdus*. From this derivative the altered forms esmeraude, émeraude and esmeralde were derived, the present form not making its appearance until the sixteenth century. The name emerald has always been used for a green-coloured mineral, but often not for the emerald we now know.

A stone that was offered nearly 4,000 years B.C. in Babylon, the earliest known gem market, emerald was dedicated by the ancients to the Goddess Venus. The birthstone for May, emerald is steeped in superstition and lore.

It is the symbol of immortality and the symbolization of faith, and by changing its colour is said to reveal the inconstancy of lovers. Emerald is said to be beneficial to the eyes.

Historically the earliest known locality for emerald was the group of mines by the Red Sea in Egypt, the so-called Cleopatra's emerald mines. These mines were probably worked some 2,000 years B.C. and from them came most of the emeralds used in the ancient jewellery. The location of these mines was completely lost during the middle ages and was not rediscovered until 1818 when Cailliaud, who had been sent by the Viceroy of Egypt to search for them, at last found the ancient workings. The mines are in the hillsides of Jebel Sikait and Jebel Zubara in northern Etbai, the hills lie parallel, and some 16 miles inland, from the Red Sea and about 100 miles north-east of Aswan, the ancient Syene. There are hundreds of shafts of the ancient mines, some of which had workings extending to a depth of some 800 ft., and in which tools and appliances dating back to the times of Sesostris (1650 B.C.) were found. Sporadic attempts have been made since the rediscovery to work the mines, but owing to the poor quality of the flawed crystals found in the micaceous and talcose schists which form the mother rock, the workings have been found unprofitable. Little data are extant concerning the properties of these light-coloured and cloudy emeralds.

Colorization

Emerald owes its verdant green colour to a trace of the chromium ion (Cr_2O_3), although a trace of vanadium may have some influence on the shade of colour. It may be recalled that chromic oxide gives to ruby its magnificent red colour. The mechanism of this change of colour is considered to be due to the difference in intensity, and in the wavelength position of the broad absorption band which is such a characteristic feature of the absorption spectra of chromium-coloured minerals. The sharp bright lines in the red shown by the fluorescence spectrum of emerald tends to prove the small-scale isomorphous replacement by the chromium atom, as it does in ruby. Traces of iron are usually present in emerald and this again may have some bearing on the final shade of colour, as indeed it may have on certain other properties.

Austria

Said to have been known since the time of the Romans there is an occurrence of emerald in a very inaccessible spot, some 7,500 ft. above sea-level, on the east side of the Legbach ravine, a branch of the Habach-thal, in Salzburg, Austria. The occurrence is of little importance, but mining by irregular methods has been carried on intermittently through the years, and in 1937 the mine was reopened on a small scale. Since World War II some crystals have been seen but whether these are from the 1937 working or from a resumption of mining since the war is not certain. The simple hexagonal crystals are found in a mica and chlorite schist, a type of mother rock similar to that of the Uralian source. Thus the inclusions seen in the Habachthal emeralds are in general similar in type to those seen in the Russian emeralds, that is actinolite rods and mica plates with rounded outline. The density of the Salzburg emeralds approximates to 2·74 and the indices of refraction are $\omega - 1\cdot591$ and $\epsilon - 1\cdot584$ showing a double refraction of 0·0068.

Colombia

Who first discovered the lovely green crystals found in the Andes of Colombia, which give to this South American country the honour of being the source of the world's finest emeralds, will never be known. It is quite evident that the native Indians realized something of the value of the emeralds which they had used for barter with other neighbouring tribes, and which probably extended to those as far north as Mexico, and south to Bolivia and Peru. Despite three hundred years' diligent search no other emerald-bearing areas outside Colombia have been found in the Andean ranges, or in Central America or Mexico. The so-called 'Peruvian' or 'Mexican' emeralds were in all probability products of the ancient Colombian mines.

Europe first knew of the fabulous emeralds from South America when Pizarro ruthlessly conquered and despoiled Peru, taking from the Incas an immense quantity of emeralds, many of incredible size being sent to the Queen of Spain. Subsequently the old native workings in Colombia were found by the Spanish invaders and worked by them, sending the stones, both those mined and those taken from the Indians, to Spain where they were later sent to Paris for sale.

The mines of Colombia are situated in the Cordillera Oriental, the eastern range of the Andes, and are principally in the Departments of Boyaca and Cundinamarca and lie to the north of Bogatá, the Colombian capital. The only workings of importance are those of Muzo and Cosquez, and those of El Chivor, sometimes known as Somondoco, a word which means 'God of the green stones'. Some other small deposits are known, but, like those near Nemoncón, are of little more than scientific interest.

The Chivor Mines

The first indication of the source of the South American emeralds came in 1537 when Gonzalo Jiménez de Quesada conquered Colombia, and was presented with nine green stones by the inhabitants of the town of Guachetá. Although the Indians carefully guarded the whereabouts of the mines, a youngster gave the invading forces the information that the emerald mines were at Somondoco, the mines now best known as El Chivor, so Chivor should be the first to be told of the famous South American emerald mines.

The Chibcha Indians of the high plateau of Colombia mined emeralds from Chivor before the Spanish conquest; the stones recovered being traded for gold from the Indian tribes across the Magdalena river. Some time after the Spanish subjugation of Colombia the conquistadores worked the mines of Somondoco. In 1592 Francisco Maldonaldo de Mendoza built an extensive viaduct, remnants of which still exist, in order to supply the water necessary to wash the mining debris away. Within one hundred years the mines were abandoned, either because of the lack of a successful yield or because of the discovery of the fruitful mines at Muzo some 150 miles to the north-west. Chivor died out as a mine and the prolific growth of tropical vegetation effectively hid the workings for over 200 years.

After a long search the Somondoco–Chivor mines were rediscovered by Don Francisco Restrepo in 1896. Restrepo had nothing to go on except a note in a chronicle written by a friar on the Spanish Conquest, which said 'The mines of Chivor are situated on the point of a ridge from which the llanos of the Orinoco can be seen'. A company, the Chivor Mining Company, was formed by Restrepo, but, although the State tax was paid for 20 years, the mine was not successfully worked. The rights to the emerald mining at Chivor passed to a German commercial group just before World War I and they, after having the report of R. Scheibe, sent, during 1911 and 1912, Fritz Klein to test the mine workings. The outbreak of war in 1914 stopped further exploitation by the company. In 1919 the mines passed to an American company—the Colombian Emerald Syndicate Ltd., which was converted in 1926 into the Colombia Emerald Development Corporation of New York, and in 1927 P. W. Rainier took over the management of the mine for the lessors. The mine had many vicissitudes with periods of inactivity and bursts of frenzied activity. It was being worked in 1937, but little is known about the war years; indeed there was little knowledge at all concerning the mine until 1950 when R. W. Alderton became manager. At the end of 1951, owing to litigation and depredations by the local banditry, Chivor ceased working and was for all intents and purposes closed. A report of 1961 states that the mine was then being operated by a Trustee in Receivership by order of the Colombian courts.

The emeralds of Chivor are found near the summit of the mountain overlooking the headwaters of the mighty Orinoco river. When the Spaniards mined for emeralds they chose the western slopes; recent mining, however, is carried out on the slopes facing the east. Until some twelve years ago when tunnel mining was commenced, the mining was of the traditional terrace-type, in which the emerald-bearing veins were exposed by digging horizontal terraces in step-like formation along gullies, and washing the debris away with water released from a lake-like reservoir above the cuttings.

The emeralds are found in vein-shaped cracks some 20 cm wide and varying in length up to 70 m. The crystals are usually in 'strings' or in 'nests' (pockets) containing anything from a few to over a hundred crystals. As the emerald pockets are approached there are showings of moralla, an uncrystallized form of green beryl, and this gives an indication that the miner may soon find a pocket of 'canutillos', the Colombian miners' name for good quality emerald crystals.

The crystals, usually of a good blue-green colour are unfortunately often shattered owing to the force of earlier geologic cataclysms. The crystals take the usual hexagonal prismatic form but often show small pyramidal faces. Often they are found loose in the pockets owing to their having been weathered out from the parent rock and such emerald crystals are covered with a tenacious coating of limonitic red iron oxide. This coating needs to be cleaned off by acid in order to see the quality of the emeralds, which are then sorted into five qualities or grades.

The emeralds of Chivor have a density of 2·69 and refractive indices of

$\omega - 1.577$ and $\epsilon - 1.571$, with a birefringence of 0·006. Chivor stones usually show a fairly strong red under the colour filter and a red fluorescence when bathed in ultra-violet light and therefore behave somewhat like the synthetic stones. The inclusions seen in Chivor emeralds (*Figure 4.1*) are the three-phase types common to South American emeralds, but most typical of Chivor stones are inclusions of well-formed crystals of pyrites (*Figure 4.2*).

Figure 4.1. Three-phase inclusions in a Chivor mine emerald

The Muzo and Cosquez Mines

The world's most beautiful emeralds are said to come from the mine at Muzo which, with the mine at Cosquez, is operated by the Colombian Government; the stones which are recovered are deposited in the Banca de la Republica for marketing. They are sold as the market warrants and when the stock of emeralds in the bank are surplus to market needs the mines are shut down; therefore mining is carried on very sporadically.

The geology of the area is fundamentally similar to that of Chivor, but the emerald-bearing veins, containing calcite, quartz, dolomite and pyrites, run through a black carbonaceous limestone and shale which form the

Figure 4.2. Pyrites crystals in a Chivor mine emerald

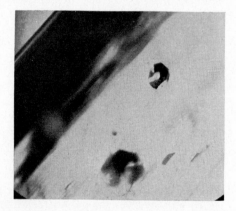

country rock. The crystals, embedded in the vein material, have the simple forms of the hexagonal prism closed with basal pinacoids. The Spaniards mined Muzo by driving adits, but the method of terracing and washing away the debris is now employed.

The yellowish-green stones from the Muzo district have a warm velvety appearance which is most prized. The density of the Muzo emeralds is generally slightly higher than for the Chivor stones; the values of the constants being, for the density 2·71 and the indices of refraction, for the

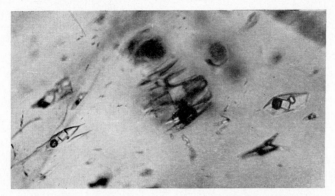

Figure 4.3. Three-phase inclusions in a Colombian emerald

ordinary ray 1·584 and for the extraordinary ray 1·578, the double refraction being 0·006. Muzo stones usually show the typical three-phase inclusions (*Figure 4.3*) of a bubble of gas in a liquid and a cubic crystal which is probably sodium chloride (common salt), contained in a flat cavity having spiky or jagged outlines with tail-like appendages (*Figure 4.4*). Pyrites crystals, so common in Chivor stones, are not seen as an inclusion in the emeralds from Muzo and Cosquez, but occasionally there is seen in Muzo emeralds yellowish-brown prismatic crystals of the rare-earth mineral called parisite, a fluocarbonate of the cerium metals, a species whose type-locality is the emerald mines of Muzo.

It has been said that the emeralds of Cosquez were the best quality, but other reports suggest that the Cosquez stones are more comparable to those of Chivor and are poorer in colour than the Muzo emeralds. Little is

Figure 4.4. Spiky flat cavities in a Colombian emerald

known of Cosquez, the last news heard of it was that in 1951 Russell W. Anderton was negotiating for the lease of the mine from the Colombian Government; what transpired and whether the mine is now being worked is not certain.

During 1964 a new type of emerald crystal was encountered (*Figure 4.5*). Originating from Colombia it consists of a central hexagonal prism of green colour from the prism faces of which six prisms of similar colour appear to have grown outward. The interstices between these 'radial' prisms are filled with fine-grained colourless beryl. The whole forms a complete hexagonal prism. The crystals are called 'Trapiche emeralds' from the Spanish word for cane-crushing gears. The green sections of the crystals are cut into small stones which characteristically have a cloudy appearance and show fine straight striations internally.

Figure 4.5. End and side views of two Trapiche emeralds from Colombia

Legal Movement of Emeralds

Early in 1934 a law was passed in Colombia requiring all persons engaged in cutting or selling emeralds to register with the Government. Emeralds that are found in the possession of unregistered persons are liable to forfeiture. A report of 1951 states that it is illegal to transport rough emeralds anywhere in Colombia without their first having been appraised and sealed by the officials of the Ministry of Mines; export being permitted on a reintegration basis, with the official peso valued at approximately two to an American dollar.

Brazil

The belief in mediaeval times that there was a fabulous source of emeralds in Brazil contributed in no small degree to the opening up of the interior of this vast country. The first expedition set off in 1554 under the leadership of one Bruzo Espinoso and a Jesuit priest. This expedition, and also a second under Martin Carvalho in 1567, failed to find the source of the coveted gem. The name of Sebastiao Fernandes Tourinho brings interest to the stories of the search for emerald in Brazil, for he made three journeys into the interior; the first in 1555 and the third and most important in 1572. Taking his followers into the 'barbarous forests of the Rio Doce' he eventually reached the watershed dividing the rivers flowing east from the tributaries of the Jequitinhonha and the Arassuahy. There he was said to have found many stones of divers colours, and finally emeralds themselves. On his return to Porto Seguro the stones were sent to Portugal where they were pronounced to be 'emeralds from the surface baked by the sun, and stones that the earth had rejected as refuse'. It was suggested that better stones would be found by digging deeper.

This 'digging deeper' suggestion led to more expeditions which were in the main organized by the Governor of Bahia. In 1574 Antonio Dias Adorno left with 650 followers and many slaves but failed to find anything but 'baked emeralds'. Twelve years later Martin Cao searched along the Rio Doce das Esmeraldas but found no emeralds; however, he made a name for himself by his inhuman treatment of the Indians he took as slaves. Marcos de Azeredo Coutinho took out an expedition in 1612 and he did find green stones which were reported by Portugal to be emeralds. Coutinho died without revealing the secret of the locality. Five more expeditions, two led by the sons of Coutinho, failed to find the emerald area; but in 1674 a sixth expedition under Fernao Dias Paes Leme from São Paulo did find Coutinho's locality of the green stones. Leme died without suffering the disappointment of knowing that the stones never were emeralds but only green tourmalines. The last expedition was organized in 1713, but its only claim to success was the discovery of the alluvial gold of the Rio das Contas.

Eventually the source of the Brazilian emerald was found at Brumadinho in Bahia, and emeralds were later located in the Rio Doce area. Therefore, were Coutinho's emeralds genuine or were they misidentified in Portugal? More recently deposits of emeralds have been found at Conquista in Bahia, at Itaberai in Goyaz and Ferros in Minas Gerais. In 1913 a find was made at Bom Jesus dos Meiros in Bahia where the crystals were found in cavities in an altered marble capping a mountain. The crystals, often much flawed, are hexagonal prisms with basal pinacoids, and with the edges truncated with small pyramidal faces. The yield is small and the mining primitive.

The density of the Brazilian emerald is 2·69 and the refractive indices are $\omega - 1·571$ and $\epsilon - 1·566$, with a birefringence of 0·005. Brazilian emerald which appeared on the market about 1900, is a pale yellowish-green and so resembles ordinary green beryl that at first they were rejected as imitations. The stones are fairly free from inclusions which further tends to give the impression that the stones are just green beryl rather than true emerald, but the existence of a chromium absorption spectrum effectively proves that the stones are true emeralds. When internal features can be seen in the Brazilian stones they are usually two-phase inclusions or tubes, or both.

Green beryl crystals which seemed to have been first found about 1962 and later came on the market emanate from the district of Salininha, Bahia. These crystals posed a problem in nomenclature for they were found to be coloured (?) by vanadium for there was only the merest trace of chromium present. It is considered that these crystals cannot be called emerald and should be known as green beryl, despite their pale emerald colour.

Russia

The source of the Uralian emerald was found quite accidentally when in 1830, a peasant noticed some green stones at the foot of a tree torn out by a storm. After the discovery large Government mines were sunk in the dense forest amid marshes some 70 km north-east of the town of Sverdlovsk, which in the heyday of the Russian Empire was known as Ekaterinburg. The mines are on the Asiatic side of the Ural Mountains and on the Tako-vaya river. The crystals—which are generally large, cloudy and of poor colour, although smaller stones of good colour form valuable stones—are found in a mica schist which is interfoliated with talc and chlorite schists. The crystals are found in this locality in association with the other beryllium minerals chrysoberyl and phenacite, and with common beryl.

Figure 4.6. Large acti-nolite crystal in a Russian emerald

Russian emeralds have a density rather higher than the emeralds from the sources previously discussed, being 2·74, and the refractive indices are 1·588 for the ordinary ray and 1·581 for the extraordinary ray; the double refraction being 0·007. The characteristic inclusions seen in Siberian emeralds are mica plates and actinolite needles in single individuals or as dishevelled groups (*Figure 4.6*). Three-phase inclusions are said to have been seen in Siberian emeralds, but in these emeralds the solid phase is rhombic in form. The observation is now considered erroneous. For a number of years during the inter-war period the mines were worked by an American company, but how they are operated today is another secret hidden behind the Iron Curtain.

Australia

The first discovery of emerald in Australia was in 1890 when W. A. Porter, while prospecting for tin, found green crystals in a dyke offshoot from a griesen granite where it had taken on the form of pegmatite. The locality is some 9 miles north by east of Emmaville in New South Wales. Professor David inspected the site in 1891 and found the crystals to have the density of 2·67, and to be intercrystallized with topaz frequently penetrating fluorite as delicately acicular prisms, or sometimes embedded in a kaolinized rock and occasionally surrounded by mispickel. In that year a crystal weighing 23 carats was found completely embedded in mispickel. In 1891 and 1892 the mine was worked by the Emerald Pro-

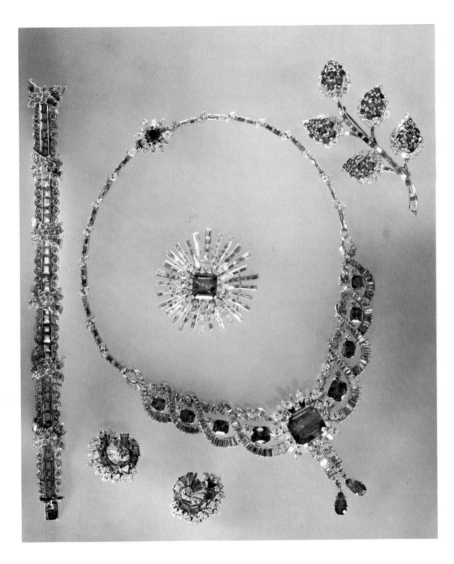

PLATE VIII
Suite of diamond and emerald jewellery
(By courtesy of Garrard & Co. Ltd.)

prietary Mines, who mined some 25,000 carats of emerald each year. Since then the mines have closed down and have only been worked sporadically by prospectors.

In 1909, a tin prospector named Ryan found in a biotite schist and in pegmatite dykes another source of emerald at Poona, a place some 40 miles north-west of Cue in Western Australia. In 1912 the State Mining Engineer made an independent discovery in the area. He secured several promising stones that were cut in Sydney and in London.

In the same year J. Pearl opened up one of the deposits but found them nearly worthless, but two fine stones were sent to Paris for cutting, one of which weighed 5 carats and was sold for £100 to the Montana Sapphire Syndicate, who resold it for £170. This Montana Sapphire Syndicate then took over the mine and spent £5,000 on equipment but the outbreak of World War I stopped the project. After this war the mines at Poona remained more or less dormant until the Star Emerald Syndicate commenced development. Little is heard of this now.

The Poona emeralds are associated with quartz, albite, oligoclase, topaz, tourmaline and fluorite, and with the micas biotite, muscovite, lepidolite and zinnwaldite. The stones are mostly pale in colour and badly flawed, but some are found which are a fine colour, including one embedded in a small quartz leader in the dark biotite schist. Batchelor reports one fine stone of 30 carats from the same locality.

A few small crystals of emerald which reached some 10 mm in length were found in the Wodgina district of Western Australia, but they were too turbid and flawed to be worth cutting. In South Australia a few poor emeralds have been found near Mt. Crawford near Williamstown, where they occur with aquamarine and heliodor in pegmatite. The occurrence at Mt. Remarkable in the same state, which was mentioned by Bauer, seems debatable, for there appears to be no record of it in the South Australian Department of Mines publications.

South Africa

In the year 1927 beryl crystals, many of which had the colour and other qualities of true emerald, were found some 12 miles east-north-east of Gravelotte station in the Leydsdorp district of the Letaba area of north-eastern Transvaal. The deposits are associated with acid pegmatite inclusions in biotite, chlorite and actinolite schists belonging to the Swaziland system. The gemmy crystals occur almost invariably in the biotite schists at or near contact with the pegmatite bodies. Associated with the emeralds are such minerals as quartz, apatite, schorl, molybdenite, pyrite and feldspar.

The crystals have the usual prismatic form and range in size up to 2 in. or more in length, but most often they are variable in colour, cloudy, cracked and flawed. Some clear pieces, however, have been sold for £100 per carat for cut stones. The flawed material is usually cut into cabochons.

In 1929 some five companies operated in the area, including the Beryl Mining Company's Somerset mine which was worked by a shaft and by open-cast mining. This mine was installed with mechanical treatment plant capable of treating up to 200 tons of emerald-bearing schist per day.

This recovery plant used a modified form of tube mill to separate the emerald crystals from the enveloping mica schist. During the period before World War II the only consistent producers were the Somerset mine and a mine operated by Cobra Emeralds Ltd., and in 1930 some 12 pounds weight of emerald crystals were being sent to London cutters each week.

During the slump of 1930 and 1931 most of the workings were abandoned, or at least ceased working, and this included the Somerset mine. In 1934 increased demand opened a new interest, but the only consistent producer was the Cobra Emerald Mining Company. Mining during the war years for all intents and purposes ceased, except perhaps for the winning of crude beryl for beryllium. After the war the mine restarted, but productivity has been marred by the trade boycott with India which took much of the poorer flawed material for cutting into cabochons to be used in native jewellery.

At one time an emerald cutting project was started in Johannesburg but the endeavour did not bear fruit. In 1947 there was talk of reopening the Somerset mine by the Beryl Mining Company, which, it seems, is still in existence, as is the Cobra Emerald Mining Company with their New Chivor mine. Other groups are also registered, including the operator of the Green Pigeon Emerald Mine.

It is said that emeralds have been recovered from biotite schist at Uitvalskop in the Schweizer Reneke district of Transvaal, and near Baviaanskop in biotite and in lenses of quartz. There is, too, a report of emeralds being found in the Kalahari desert, but no details are forthcoming.

Transvaal emeralds have a somewhat higher refractive index than for most other emeralds, typical values being 1·593 for the ordinary ray and 1·586 for the extraordinary ray; the birefringence being 0·007 and the density is near 2·75. The inclusions are typically brownish mica plates and if these are profuse they tend to make the stones dark or even brownish. The South African emeralds rarely show red through the Chelsea colour filter and hence have at times been rejected as imitations.

Rhodesia

In 1956 two geologists discovered emeralds in a schist bordering a pegmatite in the Belingwe Native Reserve country of Rhodesia. It is reported that the emerald crystals are distributed over a fairly wide area but that the occurrence, except for one small spot where stones of a superb quality are found, is either worthless or of poor quality. The colour of this best quality material is a fine deep emerald green, but owing to the flawed nature of the crystals cut stones over a quarter of a carat in weight are rare. The emeralds from this locality in Rhodesia are marketed under the name Sandawana emeralds. Emerald is also found in the Filabusi district of Rhodesia.

India

The emerald has been held in high esteem in India from ancient times, but until the find in 1943, a source of true emerald in India was not known. A number of references are extant as to Indian emerald sources, but despite careful investigation no proof of an emerald locality in India was forthcoming. The locality called Canjargum or Cangagam, given as a source of

Indian emeralds seems to refer to the aquamarine mines of Padyur near Kangayam in the Coimbatore district of Madras. It is interesting to note that some small green rolled pebbles, which the natives had regarded as emeralds, had been found at Ajmere, Rajasthan, which is perhaps better known as the old State of Rajputana. Although these stones were officially understood to be ordinary green beryls, in the light of the 1943 discovery, there must always be doubt whether or not emerald has been mined in days long past.

Even if emerald was mined in India in the past it would not account for the vast quantities of emerald used in native jewellery for some 1,500 years. J. Coggin Brown refers to old Sanskrit writings which tell of emeralds from 'a mountain situated on the edge of the desert near the sea coast', a description which could well apply to the mines of Jebel Sikait and Jebel Zubara alongside the Red Sea. In more recent times the emeralds from the mines in Siberia were the source of the emeralds used in Indian jewellery, and in the nineteenth century much poor quality emerald was exported to Asiatic countries from the stone markets of London and Paris. Much of the emerald mined in the Transvaal was sent to India, but since the trade boycott between the two countries the sale of South African rough has stopped, with the consequential pile up of emerald stocks in the Transvaal while new markets are sought.

The finding of emerald in the Arawalli mountain range of Rajasthan in 1943, was the result of the war-time search for beryl and mica as strategic minerals. During the search some small green crystals were found in the Kaliguman area of Udaipur, and these were identified as emeralds. A mining lease over the Kaliguman area was granted by the Udaipur authorities, then the independent State of Rajputana, to Sir Bhagchand Soni and his partner Seth Banjilal Thulia, the latter an emerald merchant of Jaipur. The first mining efforts in 1954 met with immediate success and crystals up to 4 in. in length were recovered. The emeralds are found in bands of biotite (mica) schist. Further searches followed this first successful attempt at emerald mining in India and other finds have been made both in Udaipur and Ajmere-Merwara. In 1947 quarrying was begun at the Rajgarh mine, which is some 15 miles south of Ajmere, in which the emeralds are found in a soft talcose-biotite schist. Another source is near Bhilwara. Emeralds are also found east of Chitral in West Pakistan. The density and refractive indices of these Pakistan emeralds lie in the region about 2·76 for the density and 1·594–1·588 for the indices of refraction.

The Indian emeralds vary greatly in quality; the stones from the Rajgarh mines, and other sources in Ajmere-Merwara, having, in general, a better quality than those from the Kaliguman mines, although good stones of large size have been recovered from the first discovered locality. The density of Indian emeralds is commonly 2·73–2·74 and the refractive indices are $\omega - 1·593$ and $\epsilon - 1·585$; the double refraction being 0·007. The inclusions seen in Indian emeralds are typically characteristic and are of a type not reported from the stones of any other locality. These inclusions consist of two sets usually running at right angles to each other. Oriented parallel to the vertical axis of the crystal are oblong cavities containing a

87

liquid and a bubble of gas. These cavities are characterized by having a shorter columnar projection on the edge of one end, giving them the appearance of 'commas' (*Figure 4.7*). E. Gübelin has shown that these cavities are groups of negative hexagonal crystals, one being remarkably longer than the other. The second type of inclusion Gübelin found to be biotite tablets and these are oriented parallel to the basal plane. Like the South African emeralds the Indian stones may not exhibit a red residual colour through the colour filter. The Indian stones are marketed mainly in Jaipur.

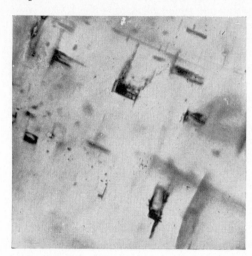

Figure 4.7. Comma-like two-phase inclusions in an Indian emerald

Norway

Emeralds have been found at Eidsvoll, at the southern end of Mjøsa lake some 35 miles north-north-east of Oslo. The crystals are found embedded in granite, and are nearly always turbid. The density of a specimen of Norwegian emerald, cabochon cut, of good colour but very turbid, was found to be 2·68. The dichroism of this specimen was found to be distinct and the absorption spectrum strong, and under the filter the stone showed a bright red. Observation by microscope of the internal features of this stone showed that it was filled with masses of inclusions, mostly 'mossy' in character, but combined with a vast number of interconnecting cavities rather like vesicles. To these masses of inclusions is due the turbidity of the stone, which would preclude such a stone being successfully cut with facets, although as a cabochon it was quite attractive.

Other Occurrences

Occasionally crystals have been reported from Stony Point, Alexander County, North Carolina and at Haddam, Connecticut, of the United States of America. Attractive cabochons of emeralds in the feldspar matrix are made from American emeralds. Reports of occurrences of emerald in the Harrach and Bouman rivers of Algeria, and also *in situ* in the neighbourhood, have not been substantiated. It may be tourmaline. Moçambique and Kenya may supply emerald.

Effects of Light

It will be noted from the values of refractive indices given for emeralds from different localities that the species beryl shows double refraction, and since the index for the extraordinary ray is less than for the ordinary ray the sign of the refraction is negative. The dichroism of emerald is distinct, with the 'twin-colours' blue-green for the extraordinary ray and yellowish-green for the ordinary ray.

Absorption Spectra

The absorption spectrum is that typical for chromium-coloured minerals; showing fine lines in the red part of the spectrum, a weak diffuse central absorption with absorption of the violet, and rather weak lines in the blue. In emerald there is a distinct difference between the absorption spectrum for the ordinary ray and for the extraordinary ray. In that of the ordinary ray only two narrow lines can be seen in the red and they are of almost equal strength. These two lines consist of the main doublet (6830 and 6800 Å) and a clear-cut line at 6370 Å; the central weak absorption patch covers from about 6250 Å to 5800 Å, and there is a narrow line in the blue at 4775 Å which may only be seen in very chrome-rich stones when another line at 4725 Å may also be noticed. The absorption of the violet commences at about 4600 Å. In the spectrum of the extraordinary ray the doublet is rather stronger, particularly the 6830 Å line of the pair; the 6370 Å line is missing and in its place are two rather diffuse lines at 6620 and 6460 Å, these being bordered on the short-wave side by characteristic transparency patches. The broad absorption region is now nearer to the red and is much weaker, and there are no lines in the blue.

Fluorescence

Emerald, although a green stone, transmits a considerable quantity of deep red, which is also a region of fluorescence, and it is this fluorescent red light which mainly gives the red colour seen when emeralds are viewed through the Chelsea colour filter. Should this fluorescence be suppressed or dimmed by a fluorescence 'poison', for example iron, such emeralds may not show red through the filter; this may well be the reason for most South African and Indian emeralds remaining green when viewed through such a filter. The majority of the emerald imitations and simulating minerals show green through the filter, but there are exceptions, such as the older type of soudé emerald, and certain varieties of natural minerals, particularly the emerald green fluorite, the demantoid garnet, and green zircons, which show reddish through the filter. The true synthetic emeralds, owing to their chrome-richness and freedom from those impurities such as iron, show a fiery red appearance through the filter. Although this strong red residual colour can betoken a synthetic emerald it must not be taken too literally, for some natural emeralds from the Chivor mines of the Bogatá region of Colombia behave similarly.

Cutting of Emerald

The cutting of emerald is usually performed on a copper lap charged with diamond dust and the polishing carried out on a similar lap with rottenstone as the agent. The best quality emeralds are almost universally fashioned in the trap-cut style with the corners truncated, giving an elongated octagonal outline, a style which has, owing to the common use for emerald, become known as the emerald cut.

It is the style of cutting which, owing to its few plane facets, shows the saturated deep velvety-green of emerald to best advantage. Although the mixed-cut, with a brilliant cut top and a step cut pavilion has been used for emerald such a fashioning is rare and is said to give a glassy look. Poor quality and badly flawed emeralds are cut *en-cabochon* or as beads, and much Indian jewellery is set with such stones, which are usually of poor quality emerald imported from Russia or the Transvaal. Native-cut stones are often 'doctored' by boiling in fat which has been suitably coloured. Such treated emeralds tend to show spots at a later date, so if any suspicion is aroused it is best to soak the stones for some time in warm alcohol when some of the false material will dissolve and unmask the trick, and, incidently, show the true colour of the stone.

An emerald cut with the table facet at right angles to the optic axis, that is at right angles to the length of the prism, will give a yellowish-green colour due to the ordinary ray. At right angles to this direction, that is with the table facet cut parallel to the prism (and of course the optic axis also) the colour is more bluish-green due to about 50 per cent of the extraordinary ray. This latter colour is often less pleasing to many than the shade paler in colour due to the ordinary ray. Emeralds are often carved, especially if the material is of good colour, but marred by many fissures and flaws.

Synthesis and Simulation

Emerald is synthetically produced and marketed as a gemstone. The methods of the production and the characters of the synthetic product are fully described in the chapter on synthetic gemstones. The more common imitations of emeralds are the composite stones, such as the garnet-topped doublets which consist of a slice of red garnet forming the crown of the stone fused to a base of green glass. The more important, however, of these composite stones are the so-called soudé emeralds in which two pieces of colourless quartz (or beryl) form the top and bottom of the stone and are cemented together with a green-coloured layer. In the earlier types this was a layer of green gelatine, but in later types a sintered layer of some copper compound is used. More recently the rock crystal has been replaced by two pieces of synthetic colourless spinel. These soudées readily give themselves away if they be immersed in water or other liquid and viewed sideways, when the clear colourless top and bottom with the dark line of the coloured layer between will show. The earlier type with the coloured gelatine layer shows red under the Chelsea colour filter. Glass imitations of emerald can be very effective and of good colour and appearance, and they are often embellished with 'flaws' and 'feathers' produced by layers of bubbles or by included extraneous matter. The so-called Ferros emerald is of glass.

Pale natural emeralds are often painted on the back with a green pigment in order to enhance the colour. This, when the stones are set with open backs, is easily detected and easily removed. When, however, the stones are set in closed settings the problem is not so easy and examination by microscope may be necessary in order to see the patchiness of the blobs of colour below the stone. Some paints used for this treatment fluoresce under ultra-violet light and so indicate a painted stone. Further, the strength of the absorption spectrum may indicate the true colour of such backed stones, for the backing may not be paint but a coloured metal foil. Rock crystal as well as pale emeralds are so treated in order to give an 'emerald' stone. The so-called 'Indian emeralds' are simply green-dyed crackled quartz.

AQUAMARINE

The most acceptable colour for aquamarine (a name which means sea water) is a clear sky-blue, which even in the darkest shades rarely reaches the hue of sapphire. Much aquamarine has a bluish-green colour, which, while not so prized today as it was formerly, does have a charm of its own. Under this group may be described also the clear green beryls which owe their colour to iron and do not have the verdant green of the chromium-coloured emerald. The other is the colourless variety, to which the name goshenite (after Goshen in Hampshire County, Massachusetts) has been applied. This name is fast becoming redundant, and the name colourless, or white, beryl is now more commonly used.

The hexagonal crystals of aquamarine are often of large size and, due to oscillation between the first and second order prisms, are often striated parallel to the prism edge. At times this striation is so pronounced that the hexagonal outline is obscured and the crystal assumes a ribbed cylindrical form. Further, due to erosion, many aquamarine crystals exhibit a tapering form.

Aquamarines, unlike emeralds, are found in large crystals of flawless clarity from which large water-clear stones can be cut. Indeed, cut aquamarines need to be of some size for the colour to be sufficiently intense to produce a good-coloured stone, small stones rarely having a depth of colour sufficient to be attractive. Practically all the lovely blue aquamarines seen in jewellery are the result of heat treatment of greenish-yellow stones, or even certain stones of a brownish-yellow colour. The blue colour is induced by heating to a temperature between 400° and 450°C, and the resulting colour is permanent. Some aquamarines and heliodors show chatoyancy.

The density of aquamarine lies between the range 2·68 and 2·71, although some Madagascan stones have been found to reach as high as 2·73, a rise probably due to a trace of alkali metal in the composition. The refractive indices for aquamarine vary from 1·570 to 1·580 for the extraordinary ray and 1·575 to 1·586 for the ordinary ray, the birefringence, negative in sign, being 0·005 for the lower indices and increasing to 0·006 for the stones with the higher refractive indices. The 'fire' (dispersion) of the beryls (including emerald) is 0·014 (B to G).

Aquamarine has, like all the beryls, a weak basal cleavage and a tendency to brittleness. The lustre is vitreous and aquamarines exhibit a distinct dichroism, the 'twin colours', the strength of which depends on the depth of the colour of the stone, are deep blue and colourless, the extraordinary ray giving the attractive blue colour. The absorption spectrum, which is ascribed to iron, is not very pronounced. There is a somewhat broad band in the violet at 4270 Å and a feeble diffuse band in the blue-violet at

91

4560 Å. Further, the extraordinary ray, which can be isolated by the use of a polaroid disc, shows these bands more strongly, and, in such conditions, there may be detected a narrow and delicate absorption line in the middle green at 5370 Å. Such a line may also be seen not only in the blue and greenish aquamarines but also in the yellow and colourless beryls. Aquamarine does not exhibit luminescence.

True colourless beryl is not common, nearly all the so-called colourless beryls have a trace of green, pink or yellow. Indeed, all the colourless beryls, like the blue and sea-green stones, show, when viewed through the Chelsea colour filter, a strong greenish-blue colour. In such a way aquamarines may be picked out from a parcel of similar-looking stones.

Occurrences

Aquamarines, with other colours of beryl, are found at Marambaia on the Mucuri river near Teófilo Otoni, and along the Jequitinhonha river near Minas Novas, both localities being in the State of Minas Gerais, Brazil. A blue beryl from the Maxixe mine, in Minas Gerais, which is seldom used for jewellery as the colour is said to fade, is unique among the blue beryls, for its high density 2·80 and its refractive indices are 1·584 and 1·592; the high values being ascribed to the alkali metal caesium. The absorption spectrum of the Maxixe beryls is also unique in that there is a rather narrow band in the red at 6950 Å, a strong band at 6540 Å and weaker bands at 6280, 6150 and 5810 Å and a very weak band in the green at 5500 Å.

The Ural mountains area which is such a prolific source of gem minerals supplies aquamarines. These are principally found at Mursinsk near Sverdlovsk. Other Russian sources are in the Adul-Chalon mountains of Transbaikalia; near the Urulga river in Siberia; near Miask in Orenburg and the Sanaka river at the southern end of the Urals. Good gem-quality aquamarines are found at over fifty different localities in the island of Madagascar.

Of the many localities in the United States of America mention may be made of the following: Stoneham, Albany and Paris, Oxford County, Maine; Haddam Neck, Middlesex County and New Milford, Litchfield County, Connecticut; Pala, San Diego County, California; Mount Antero, Chaffee County, Colorado; Hurricane mountain, Yancy County, and Grassy Creek, Mitchell County in North Carolina.

Aquamarine is found in Burma but is not common in Ceylon.

Gem aquamarine is found at Rössing in South-West Africa and recently aquamarine of rather weak colour has been found in Rhodesia. The Coimbatore district of Madras, India, as well as Rajasthan (Rajputana) and Kashmir are Indian localities where aquamarine has been found. Unimportant sources, not necessarily of gem quality are the Shinyanga district of Tanzania, the San Luis mountains of Argentina, several localities in China and at Fykanvatu at the head of the Glåmfjord, Norway, and in the Mourne mountains of Northern Ireland.

Simulants

Aquamarines are imitated by suitably coloured synthetic spinel; by garnet-topped doublets and by a fine paste (glass). The difference in their properties allows easy distinction.

BERYLS

Pink Beryls

The lovely pink, rose and peach-coloured beryl is called morganite, after the American banker and gem lover, J. P. Morgan. K. Nassau states the colour is due to manganese, not lithium as thought. The alkali metals, caesium and rubidium are often, by small-scale replacement, impurities in pink beryl and tend to raise the density and refractive indices. Most, but not all, pink beryls have a density of from 2·80 to 2·90 although some may be as low as 2·71. The refractive indices lie between 1·580 and 1·590 for the extraordinary ray and between 1·590 and 1·600 for the ordinary ray, the double refraction varying between 0·008 and 0·009. A few pink beryls (those with low density) have refractive indices only a little higher than for aquamarine. Some colourless beryls (rich in caesium) also have this higher density and indices of refraction. Morganite is heat-treated to drive off the yellow tinge.

The dichroism of morganite is distinct, the twin colours being a pale pink and a deeper bluish-pink, the stronger colour being that for the extraordinary ray. There is no characteristic absorption spectrum and the luminescence under ultra-violet light is a weak lilac, but under x-rays there is an intense, but not bright, crimson glow.

A pure pink-coloured beryl is found in the State of Minas Gerais in Brazil, and in fine large crystals from Tsilaizina, Anjanabonoina and Ampangabe in Madagascar where the stones are found in pegmatite dykes and alluvial deposits derived from them. The best known source of gem morganite in the United States of America lies in San Diego County, California, where pink beryl of a pale rose to a peach colour is found in the Stewart, Katerina, Pala Chief, San Pedro, White Queen and mines of the Pala district. Other deposits are those of the Himalaya, San Diego and Esmeralda mines in the Mesa Grande district. Morganite crystals usually assume rather short prisms, and are thus tabular in habit.

A red variety of beryl, called bixbite, which owes its colour to manganese, is found in the Thomas mountains in Utah. The small, badly flawed, hexagonal crystals have no gemmological importance.

Pink beryl is simulated by pink topaz, kunzite, natural and synthetic pink sapphire and spinel. Garnet-topped doublets and pastes are also made in a pink colour.

Yellow Beryls

The yellow beryls, to which in the case of the rich golden-coloured stones the name heliodor (from the Greek meaning sun and gift) has been applied, have a colour varying from a pale lemon yellow to a rich golden colour. The yellow colour is said to be due to iron. The physical and optical constants of the yellow beryls differ little, if at all, from those of the aquamarine. There is an unconvincing absorption band in the blue to be seen in deep yellow beryls; and, most probably due to the iron content, no luminescence is exhibited.

Yellow beryls are obtained from practically all the localities mentioned for aquamarine. Particular localities are Madagascar, Brazil and South-West Africa, where heliodor is found in association with aquamarine and a yellowish-green variety, at Klein Spitzkopje near Rössing on the Otavi railway east of Swakopmund; and also between Aiais and Gaibes on the Fish river. Some yellow beryls have been reported to show radioactivity due to their containing a trace of uranium oxide. A deep yellowish-red variety of beryl, called 'berilo bocade fogo' (fire-mouth beryl) comes from Santa Maria do Suassui in Minas Gerais.

Many localities in the United States of America produce yellow beryl but the only one of importance is the Merryall or Roebling mine at New Milford, Connecticut.

Dark Brown Beryl

An unusual dark brown beryl with a star-effect (asterism) and a bronzy schiller was said to have been first discovered in the Governador Valadares area of Minas Gerais about 1950. The weak asterism is said to be due to oriented ilmenite, and these and other coarser agglomerates cause the dark brown colour, for clear patches show that the body colour is that of pale green aquamarine. The schiller appears to be due to the structure of thin layers parallel to the basal plane, and these seem to act as mirrors. These

Figure 4.8. A type of inclusion, probably ilmenite, seen in aquamarine

Figure 4.9. Various inclusions seen in a yellow beryl from Madagascar

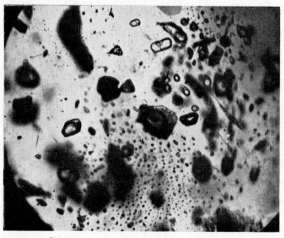

94

PLATE IX

The Beryl group

White
26·54 carats

Green
aquamarine
60·90 carats

Heliodor
82·25 carats

Blue
aquamarine
67·35 carats

Morganite
(Teofilo Oboni,
Minas Gerais)
55·71 carats

(Crown Copyright Geological Survey photograph. Reproduced by permission of the Controller of H.M.
Stationery Office)

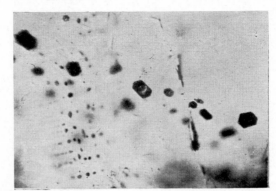

Figure 4.10. Negative crystal cavities with a gas bubble in an aquamarine

Figure 4.11. Tube inclusions in a Rhodesian aquamarine

star-beryls show neither fluorescence nor exhibit any typical absorption spectrum. Black star-beryl is reported from Alto Ligonha, Moçambique.

Inclusions

The inclusions seen in beryls (*Figures 4.8–4.11*), other than emerald which have already been discussed, are various and the colour varieties do not seem to favour any particular type of inclusion. The most common inclusions seen in beryl are long straight tubes in parallel arrangement, and which lie parallel to the prism faces. These tubes are either hollow or filled with liquid which may give to them a brownish colour. Some beryls show 'feathers' of 'negative crystal' cavities, some of which may contain a bubble of gas. An intriguing object sometimes seen in aquamarines is a flat inclusion, which under low-power magnification looks like a snowflake and when viewed by oblique illumination looks like a metallic disc. These inclusions have been aptly described as 'chrysanthemum' inclusions.

Cutting of Beryls

Aquamarines, morganites and yellow beryls need to be cut as stones of some size if the colour is to be strong enough for the stones to be attractive. In modern practice it is usual to cut beryls into the trap-cut style (the emerald cut) and such stones are mounted as important centre stones in rings, brooches, pendants and earrings.

CHAPTER 5

CHRYSOBERYL AND SPINEL

CHRYSOBERYL

Chemical and Physical Properties

The mineral chrysoberyl produces gemstones which are predominantly green, greenish-yellow or brown in colour, but two varieties of chrysoberyl, the alexandrite and the cat's-eye, have, owing to their peculiar optical properties and rarity, a prized position in jewellery. The most common colour of chrysoberyl is a transparent greenish-yellow which in Victorian and Edwardian periods had a vogue in jewellery. Such stones were often called 'chrysolite', a name, which owing to its use as a specific term for the mineral olivine in certain fields of mineralogy, leads to confusion. Therefore, in present day gemmological nomenclature the term is discontinued. The brown stones are sometimes faceted and a colourless chrysoberyl is occasionally encountered.

The most important and interesting of the chrysoberyls are the alexandrites, stones which exhibit a colour change, for the stone appears a grass-green colour in daylight, but under artificial light the hue of the stone is a raspberry red. The other important chrysoberyls are the honey-yellow to greenish or brownish-yellow stones which, when cut with a domed surface (cabochon), show a mobile streak of light. This is the cat's-eye effect, or chatoyancy as it is called. Fine specimens of both alexandrite or cat's-eye are valuable gemstones.

Chrysoberyl crystallizes in the orthorhombic system, and is found, especially in the clear yellow stones, as prismatic crystals which are usually flattened parallel to one pair of faces (the macropinacoid faces). Some crystals, particularly those of the variety alexandrite from the Ural mountains, are twinned as 'trillings', the three intergrown crystals giving an appearance of hexagonal symmetry. Such an alexandrite crystal is illustrated in the Plate XX. Much gem chrysoberyl is found as water-worn pebbles, and this is usually so in the case of the chrysoberyls found in the Ceylon gem gravels.

The chemical composition of chrysoberyl is a double oxide of beryllium and aluminium ($BeAl_2O_4$) and therefore has some similarity to spinel. It is in the small scale replacement of the alumina by chromic oxide which gives the green colour to alexandrite, and, as will be explained later, accounts for the intriguing change of colour of this variety of chrysoberyl when it is viewed in artificial light.

The density of chrysoberyl varies little from a value of between 3·71 and 3·72. The hardness is $8\frac{1}{2}$ on the scale of Mohs, and until the discovery of bromellite (beryllium oxide) was the third hardest of all known natural minerals. Chrysoberyl has three directions of cleavage, but they are weak and have little consequence. The fractured surfaces show either an uneven surface or shell-like markings, a type of fracture commonly termed conchoidal.

Effects of Light

Refraction

The optical characters of rhombic crystals, such as those of chrysoberyl, and indeed in all minerals crystallizing in systems other than the cubic—the tetragonal and the hexagonal and rhombohedral—differ in many ways from those of the species already discussed. In chrysoberyl the double refraction is biaxial, that is there are two directions of single refraction and three major optical directions. Thus there are three indices of refraction, usually denoted by the symbols α, β and γ, but for general purposes only the least and greatest (α and γ respectively) need be considered. These refractive indices vary little from the values 1·75–1·76, with a double refraction varying between 0·008 and 0·010. Some typical values for chrysoberyl are

Yellow stone	γ 1·753, β 1·747, α 1·744
	γ–α 0·0094, density 3·709
Yellow stone	γ 1·755, β 1·746, α 1·744
	γ–α 0·011, density 3·72
Alexandrite (Urals)	γ 1·759, β 1·753, α 1·749
	γ–α 0·0094
Alexandrite (Ceylon)	γ 1·755, β 1·749, α 1·745
	γ–α 0·010
Alexandrite (Burma)	γ 1·755, β 1·748, α 1·746
	γ–α 0·0085, density 3·706

Rarely are these values exceeded, but a specimen of brown chrysoberyl did give the surprisingly high index values of γ 1·770, β 1·764, α 1·759, the density of this unusual stone being 3·755. A small colourless chrysoberyl had a density, low as would be expected, of 3·703. The optical sign of chrysoberyl is positive, for the refractive index of β is nearer to α than to γ. The fire shown by chrysoberyl is small for the dispersion is only 0·015 (B to G).

Absorption Spectrum

The three optical directions of biaxial stones may show a different selective absorption to light and hence be differently coloured. This dichroism, or more correctly trichroism, as there are three rays, is particularly apparent in the case of the alexandrite variety. Alexandrites show a deep red colour with the α-ray, an orange-yellow for the β-ray, and a green colour for the γ-ray. A specimen of alexandrite from Mogok, Burma, did, however, exhibit an anomalous pleochroism (trichroism) in that the α-ray was purple, the β-ray grass-green, and the γ-ray a blue-green. The yellow and brown chrysoberyls show pleochroism more in depth of hue rather than in change of colour, the effect varying from weak in the pale greenish-yellow stones to strong in those of brown colour.

The absorption spectrum shown by yellow and brown chrysoberyls consists of a strong band at 4440 Å, a band which is due to ferric iron to which the colour of the stone is due. The absorption spectrum of alexandrite is more complex and, further, varies slightly with the optical direction within the stone. It is to the nature of the absorption of light that the remarkable colour change shown by alexandrite is due.

As in the case of ruby and emerald, which also owe their colour and their absorption spectrum to chromic oxide (Cr_2O_3) in trace amounts replacing the atoms of alumina, the absorption spectrum of alexandrite shows a broad absorption in the yellow-green and in the violet, and narrow lines in the red and the blue parts of the spectrum. The centre of the broad absorption band in the yellow-green in alexandrite lies between the centres of the similar absorption areas in ruby and in emerald. In alexandrite the transmission of the red part of the spectrum and by the green-blue part are more or less in balance and any change in the nature of the incident light will either throw emphasis on either the red or the green-blue. Daylight, which is richer in blue light, therefore tends to throw the balance to the blue-green and the stone appears green, whereas in artificial light (tungsten lamps, not the mercury vapour fluorescence lamps which are much bluer), which is richer in red rays, causes the stone to appear red in colour. The change of colour is further enhanced by the remarkable pleochroism of the alexandrite.

The full spectrum of alexandrite shown by the green (γ or slow) ray consists of a narrow doublet at 6805 and 6785 Å, of which the 6805 Å is the stronger. Weak narrow lines may be seen at 6650, 6550 and 6490 Å. The broad absorption band absorbs light from about 6400 to 5550 Å and there is an absorption of the blue and violet below 4700 Å.

The red or purple (α fast) ray shows the doublet weaker and it is the 6785 Å component which is the stronger. Only two other lines are seen in the red, at 6550 and 6450 Å, and 'transparency patches' may sometimes be seen in this region as in the case of emerald. The broad absorption now lies between 6050 and 5400 Å, and, further, in favourable conditions a line may be seen in the blue at 4720 Å. The absorption of the violet commences at 4600 Å. In the usual practice of observing absorption spectra, when 'polaroids' are not normally used to separate the rays, only a 'mixed' spectrum may be seen which will anyway vary slightly when the stone is viewed in different directions.

Luminescence

The iron-rich yellow, brown and dull green chrysoberyls, as would be expected, exhibit no luminescence when irradiated by ultra-violet light or x-rays, although some pale greenish-yellow stones have been seen to glow with a faint greenish light when under a short-wave ultra-violet lamp. Alexandrite shows a weak red glow under both long and short-wave ultra-violet light, a very dim red under x-rays, and, as reported by H. Michel, an orange glow under cathode rays. The red fluorescence of alexandrite can be well seen by the 'crossed filter' method (this will be explained in the

PLATE X

Chrysoberyl and Spinel

Purple spinel
4·43 carats

Blue spinel
5·54 carats

Red spinel
(Mogok, Burma)
3·89 carats

Alexandrite
57·08 carats
(artificial light)

Yellow
chrysoberyl
(Brazil)
7·90 carats

Green
chrysoberyl
7·66 carats

Cat's-eye
11·65 carats

(Crown Copyright Geological Survey photograph. Reproduced by permission of the Controller of H.M.
Stationery Office)

technical section), and it has been inferred that in border-line cases the presence of a red glow and a faint chromium absorption spectrum would prove the stone to be an alexandrite and not a green chrysoberyl. Such a supposition would not be acceptable to the stone merchant who would not accept a green chrysoberyl as an alexandrite unless a very definite colour change was present.

Inclusions

The internal features of chrysoberyl are particularly interesting in that when the crystal is penetrated by a series of microscopic tubes or, according to W. F. Eppler, a multitude of relatively short needles, running in a direction parallel to the vertical axis of the crystal, stones cut cabochon show a single ray of light crossing the gem (Plate XIX). Such stones are popularly

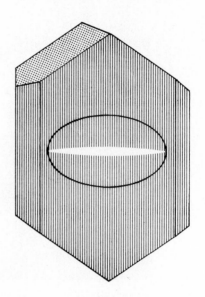

Figure 5.1. Crystal of chrysoberyl showing the needles or tubes running the length of the crystal and a cabochon stone cut from it giving the cat's-eye effect

called cat's-eyes and the name cymophane has been applied to the cat's-eye chrysoberyls. It is essential that the stone is cut from the crystal in such a way that the canals, or needles, are running parallel to the base of the stone in order to have a stone with a well-centred ray (*Figure 5.1*). The chatoyant effect is due to the reflection of light from the fine canals or needles and may be likened to the streak of light seen on a reel of silk.

A number of other species, such as quartz, tourmaline, apatite, scapolite and diopside, exhibit chatoyancy, but the term cat's-eye used alone is, in the jewellery trade, restricted to the chrysoberyl cat's-eye. In the other species which have stones showing chatoyant effect the name cat's-eye is prefixed by the name of the species, for example quartz cat's-eyes, indeed it is the quartz cat's-eyes which are most similar to the true cat's-eyes in colour even if not in sharpness of ray.

The colour of chrysoberyl cat's-eyes varies from a dark yellowish-brown to a pale yellow, a honey-yellow colour being the most prized shade. Occasionally the alexandrite variety is found which shows chatoyancy and such stones are highly desired.

The internal features seen in the alexandrite variety of chrysoberyl usually consist of 'feathers' and other inclusions which have a similarity to those seen in some rubies, this being particularly so in the case of the stones which come from Russia. The yellow and brown chrysoberyls show various types of internal imperfections, the most common being cavities filled with liquid and a bubble of gas—the so-called 'two-phase' inclusions. Flat liquid-filled cavities and long tubes are other types of inclusions. An unusual type of structure seen internally in the yellow and brown chryso-beryls are what may be called 'stepped twin-planes'. These planes which appear to lie parallel to the brachydome (one of the dome-shaped facets which cap the prisms of the crystal) are not always easy to see and oblique lighting conditions (controlled by the microscope mirror) may be needed to see them (*Figure 5.2*).

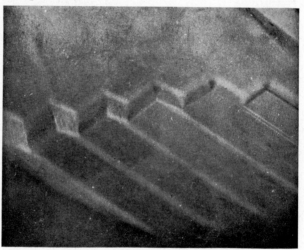

Figure 5.2. 'Stepped twin-planes' seen in a yellow chrysoberyl

Occurrences

The finest alexandrites were first found near the Takovaya river in the Ural mountains some distance north-east of Sverdlovsk (Ekaterinburg) during the year 1830. The stones, small in size and blue-green in colour, are found associated with emerald and phenakite in a mica schist. A further source of alexandrite was discovered later in the southern Urals. The two strongest dichroic colours shown by alexandrite are red and green which are the colours of the old Imperial Russia and the gem was named after Czar Alexander II, who came of age on the day alexandrites were first found in Russia.

Much larger specimens of alexandrite are found as rolled pebbles in the gem gravels of Ceylon. The hue of these Ceylon stones compares less favourably with the Uralian alexandrites, being a rich green in contra-distinction to the bluer green of the Russian stones. In artificial light the

Ceylon stones are a browner red as against the violet-red of the stones from the Urals. Despite the larger sizes the Ceylon stones are less prized than the stones from Russia. Recently alexandrite has been found at two different places in the Mogok Stone Tract of Burma. The gem gravels of Ceylon are also the most important locality for cat's-eyes, although this variety is also obtained from Brazil. Other gem varieties of chrysoberyl are found at Minas Novas in Minas Gerais, in the States of São Paulo and Espirito Santo in Brazil, in Ceylon, the Somabula forest in Rhodesia, Madagascar and Burma, where colourless chrysoberyl has also been found. Rhodesia is another source of alexandrite.

Cutting of Chrysoberyls

The usual cut for chrysoberyls is the mixed cut, in which the crown of the stone has the facets of the brilliant cut as used for diamond, while the pavilion or base of the stone conforms to the trap cut, that is the facets are rectangular. The trap cut, so favoured today for important stones, does not seem to be so often used for chrysoberyls. In order to bring out the ray of the cat's-eye such chrysoberyls must be cut *en-cabochon*, that is with a domed top. For the ray of the cat's-eye to be seen in all its glory the stone must be viewed by one light source only, such as the direct rays from the sun or from a single tungsten electric lamp; many lights confuse the ray as also do the fluorescent tube lights.

Synthesis and Simulation

There is no synthetic chrysoberyl on the market, but both synthetic corundum and synthetic spinel are made in shades of colour, complete with colour change, to imitate the true alexandrite. Such synthetic stones besides having the features of their synthetic origin have different refractive indices, density and absorption spectra to those of the true alexandrite. Spinel being singly refractive does not show dichroism, and corundum— the most common imitation—although showing fairly strong dichroism never shows the intense green ray as seen in the genuine alexandrite. The synthetic 'alexandrite type' corundum has rather a greyish-green colour in daylight and a more purple colour in artificial light.

An unusual type of imitation of alexandrite is a composite stone in which two pieces of rock crystal (colourless quartz) are cut to form the top (crown) of the stone and the base (pavilion) and are joined together with a gelatine filter suitably dyed so as to produce a colour change in artificial light. Some pastes may be encountered which have apparently been intended to imitate the alexandrite, but these stones do not necessarily change colour and owe their peculiar appearance to swirls of different coloured glass.

The only gemstone similar to cat's-eye is the quartz cat's-eye, a stone which has similar colour nuances to the chatoyant chrysoberyl. The density of the quartz cat's-eyes (2·65) is much lower than for the chrysoberyl, thus, the quartz gem will float in bromoform, a liquid with a density of 2·86, while chrysoberyl will sink rapidly in such a liquid. If the stone is mounted the density test cannot be carried out and recourse must then be made to the refractometer. It is now possible to obtain a refractive index measurement for stones having curved surfaces (cabochon cut stones) using the special method devised by Lester Benson (this method will be fully explained in the chapter on refractive index measurement).

The only other cat's-eyes which have in any way the appearance of a chrysoberyl cat's-eye, are the somewhat uncommon prehnite cat's-eye and the yellow tourmaline cat's-eye. Both of these stones will float on methylene iodide, a liquid with a density of 3·3. Chrysoberyl will sink in this liquid. A doublet with a transparent cat's-eye top and a more opaque base has been reported. Decolorized crocidolite and a special glass are other chrysoberyl cat's-eye imitations.

The yellow transparent chrysoberyl is not imitated although pastes are made with a similar colour. The greenish-yellow synthetic spinels coloured by manganese which show such a brilliant fluorescence, might be mistaken for yellow chrysoberyl if the examination was cursory.

SPINEL

Lore and Unique Stones

The derivation of the name spinel is obscure, but it probably originated from the Latin *spina* meaning a thorn. Another possible derivation is from the Greek word meaning a spark, alluding perhaps to its fiery colour. In olden times red spinel was often known under the name 'Balas ruby', a name derived most probably from Balascia (or Badakshan) in northern India, whence the earliest stones were said to have come.

The historic 'Black Prince's ruby' which is set in the front of the Imperial State Crown, is an uncut red spinel, as is the 'Timur ruby', another historical stone in the possession of the British Royal Family. This latter stone is unique in that it has engraved upon it inscriptions which give the names and dates of six owners, from Shah Jahangir (1612) to Shah Durr-i-Dauran (1754).

Chemical and Physical Properties

The mineral spinel produces a lovely suite of gemstones which, unfortunately, are overshadowed by their more opulent cousins the ruby and sapphire. Spinels are found in carmine-red, blood-red and rose-red colours, but more commonly are brownish or yellowish-red shades. Pale to deep blue, violet-blue, purple and mauve are important shades of colour, and some blue stones tend to appear more purplish when seen in artificial light.

Despite references in literature, a pure colourless natural spinel seems to be most rare, or to be non-existent; the natural white spinels always showing a trace of pink which is clearly evident when such stones are viewed side-by-side with the water-white synthetic spinel. A true green-coloured spinel is also a rarity, the so-called green spinels are iron-rich and far too dark to make attractive gemstones. Such stones, called ceylonite or pleonaste, are to all intents and purposes black in colour, but true black spinels have been found in the ejected masses from the crater of Monte Somma, Vesuvius. In rare instances spinel has been found with a star-effect, such asteriated spinels exhibiting a four-rayed star when correctly cut.

Spinel is an aluminate of magnesium, $MgO\ Al_2O_3$, or as it is sometimes written $MgAl_2O_4$, in which the magnesium may be replaced by ferrous iron or by manganese; and the aluminium by ferric iron or by chromium. Indeed gem spinel is just one of an isomorphous series in which the magnesium may be wholly replaced by ferrous iron (hercynite $FeAl_2O_4$), by zinc (gahnite $ZnAl_2O_4$), or partly by manganese and ferrous iron (galaxite). Others members of the spinel group are magnetite (FeF_2O_4) and chromite ($FeCr_2O_4$), and there are a number of other minerals which are replacements of the double oxides. Thus, even in the more restricted gem material some variation is to be expected in the chemical, physical and optical properties.

Spinel is a cubic mineral and when found as crystals they are invariably of octahedral form and often have brilliant faces (*Figure 5.3*). Some crystals

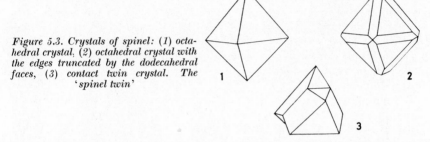

Figure 5.3. Crystals of spinel: (1) octahedral crystal, (2) octahedral crystal with the edges truncated by the dodecahedral faces, (3) contact twin crystal. The 'spinel twin'

have the edges of the octahedral faces truncated with the faces of the dodecahedron, and many crystals are twinned on the plane of the octahedral face producing flattened triangular forms. This is a type of 'contact twinning' and is called the 'spinel twin' owing to its common occurrence in spinel. The highly lustrous and often perfect octahedral crystals of spinel which are found in the Mogok Stone Tract are called by the Burmans 'Anyan nat thwe', which means 'spinels which have been cut and polished by the spirits'. Much spinel is found as water-worn pebbles in the alluvial gravels.

The mineral is comparatively hard; it is 8 on the scale of Mohs. Spinels show a very imperfect cleavage, a conchoidal fracture and have a brittle nature. The specific gravity varies from 3·58 to 3·98, but the gem spinels have a much closer range from 3·58 to 3·61, the pale pink stones having the lower values. The iron-rich ceylonites have a density varying from 3·63 to 3·90, 3·80 being a usual value. In 1937 B. W. Anderson and C. J. Payne reported the existence of a zinc-rich type of gem spinel to which the name gahnospinel was suggested. These spinels varied in colour from a pale to a dark blue and ranged in density from 3·58 to 4·06 with R.I. 1·753.

Effects of Light

Refraction

Spinels display a vitreous lustre and take a brilliant polish. The mineral has a single index of refraction. This lies between the range 1·712 and 1·80. The normal gem material being fairly constant at 1·718, but red stones which are rich in chromium may rise to 1·74. The ceylonites have the highest values at 1·77 to 1·80. The gahnospinels vary in refractive index between the limits of 1·715 and 1·753.

Absorption Spectrum

The absorption spectrum of the red and pink spinels, the colour of which is due to a trace of chromium oxide, is that typically shown by stones which owe their colouring to chromium. The spectrum is characterized by a broad absorption in the yellow-green, centred at 5400 Å and an absorption of the violet. There seems to be an absence of lines in the blue 'window' and any lines in the red are, except in rich coloured specimens, so very weak as to be seen only with difficulty. Under optimum conditions the lines in the red may be seen as bright fluorescence lines and these differ from those shown by ruby in that they are a 'group' of fine lines. These fluorescence lines have been aptly described by B. W. Anderson as the typical 'organ-pipe' fluorescent lines of red spinel. These lines, of which ten may be seen in some stones, are further characterized by two which are stronger than the others. These two have measurements of 6860 and 6750 Å and are separated from each other by a dark gap. The group is made up with a further three weak lines on the long-wave side of the strong pair, and five on the short-wave side.

The blue spinel owes its colour to ferrous iron and shows an absorption spectrum having the most important lines in the blue region, particularly a strong band centered at 4580 Å. There is a much narrower band at 4780 Å, together making a pattern quite distinctive from that of blue and green sapphire. Other weaker and less easily seen lines are at 4430 and 4330 Å, and in the orange, yellow and green at 6350, 5850, 5550 and 5080 Å. The complete spectrum of blue spinel is characteristically different from the spectrum shown by the blue synthetic spinels which owe their colour to cobalt and not to iron, thus the absorption spectrum will clearly differentiate the blue spinel of nature from that made by man. In the case of the pale blue and mauve spinels, and the zinc-rich gahnospinels, a similar type of spectrum to the deep blue stones is seen, but is very much weaker.

Luminescence

The luminescence of spinel shows considerable variation. The natural red and pink spinels show a crimson glow under ultra-violet light and this glow is very much stronger under the long-wave lamp than under the short-wave lamp; the red glow is moderately strong under x-rays. In no case is phosphorescence (an afterglow) seen. The dark blue spinels were found to be completely inert when bombarded with either of the three radiations.

The natural spinels of pale blue or violet-blue colour exhibit a green glow under long-wave ultra-violet light and x-rays, but are practically inert under the short-wave ultra-violet lamp. The purple and mauve coloured spinels appear to fall into three classes:

(1) Those stones, generally of deeper purple colour, which glow with a red colour under long-wave ultra-violet light, are practically inert under the short-wave lamp and glow with a lilac-rose to plum-red colour under x-rays.

(2) Stones which fluoresce with an orange to dull red glow under the long-wave lamp, are practically inert under the short-wave radiations and exhibit a green glow under x-rays.

(3) Stones, usually the paler mauves, which luminesce with a green light in a similar manner to the pale blue stones.

Inclusions

Spinels of gem quality are remarkably free from flaws, cracks and other imperfections. Very often they contain a few angular inclusions which are often of an appreciable size when they are liable to give rise to bright iridescent spots in the stone. These are known as 'spangles' and are particularly noticeable in artificial light: they spoil the appearance of an otherwise good stone. Unlike ruby, 'silk' does not often occur in spinel. There is, however, one form of inclusion which is distinctive to spinel. It consists of four-sided single pyramids (tetrahedra) which are often arranged in columns and partly nesting into each other. More commonly small negative (hollow cavities having a crystal outline) or solid inclusions of octahedral form, which may be spinel crystals or crystals of the other member of the spinel family—magnetite. These octahedral crystals may be grouped in densely parallel rows which are often oriented to definite crystallographic directions in the host crystal (*Figure 5.4*).

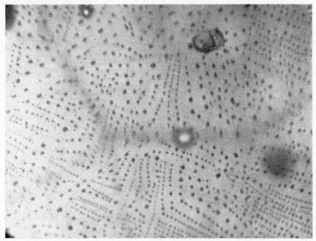

Figure 5.4. Octahedral inclusions arranged according to the crystal directions of the host mineral, seen in a blue spinel

Thin films, often containing iron staining and commonly associated with fairly large octahedral crystals, are a common spinel inclusion. The spinels from Ceylon usually show 'zircon haloes', a central inclusion surrounded with brown stain markings which may appear like wings. The cause of these surrounding brown markings was usually ascribed to staining by radioactivity from the zircon crystal which forms the centre, but more recently they have been ascribed to stress cracks caused by the unequal thermal expansion of the central inclusion and the host mineral.

A spinel showing asterism is a rarity but such stones have been encountered. Star-spinels are usually greyish-blue to black in colour and the star is generally four-pointed for the needle-like inclusions, which may be needles of rutile or needle-like sphene crystals, are oriented parallel to the cube axes. When oriented parallel to the edges of the octahedral faces a six-pointed star is produced.

Occurrences

Spinel is commonly found in association with gneiss, serpentine and allied rocks, and is generally found with corundum. Much gem spinel is found in alluvial gravels and not so often *in situ*. In the Mogok district of Burma the mineral occurs in the alluvial deposits and in streams, and in the crystalline limestone rocks. In the Burmese alluvial gravels spinel is found as remarkably perfect octahedral crystals of all sizes, or as very badly water-worn grains or pebbles; sometimes it is found in large massive lumps and broken fragments without any outward sign of crystal form. The reason given by Halford Watkins for the fine well-formed spinel crystals being found side-by-side with the far harder ruby which is in a water-worn condition, is that the spinel crystals are very localized in certain parts of the deposits and only occur in any quantity in isolated patches and have not had to travel so far as the rubies.

Spinel is found in some quantity as water-worn pebbles in the Ceylon gem gravels. In this locality a greater variety of colours, particularly blues and the very dark ceylonites, are found. The species is found, again in association with ruby and sapphire, in Afghanistan, while other localities for spinel are Siam, Australia, Sweden, Brazil and the United States of America, but spinel does not occur with the ruby and sapphire which is mined in Montana.

Cutting of Spinels

Small spinels are usually cut in the mixed-cut style, but important stones, unless in older jewellery, are more often fashioned in the trap-cut style. The terms 'ruby spinel' or 'spinel ruby' are ambiguous and should not be used in trading.

Synthesis and Simulation

Spinel is made synthetically, but except for red stones, the synthetic product is made in colours which simulate stones of other species, such as the aquamarine and the blue zircon. Pinks and yellow colours are also made, and a water-white synthetic spinel is most lustrous, so much so that when they were first placed on the British market the stones were thought to have much greater 'fire' than the natural spinel. Careful measurements proved that this was not so and the dispersion was the same as for the natural spinel. This is 0·020 (B to G).

CHAPTER 6

TOPAZ AND TOURMALINE

TOPAZ

One of the more universal canards is that all yellow stones are topaz and that all topaz is yellow. Even in present day enlightenment much yellow quartz is sold under the misnomer 'topaz', or 'quartz topaz', and the term precious topaz reserved for the true topaz. This confusion of names is ancient history, for in olden days all yellow stones were called topaz.

There are two theories as to the origin of the name topaz. The Roman writer Pliny in the first century A.D. suggests that the name was derived from the Greek word *topazos*, meaning to seek, and was apparently derived from the name for a somewhat illusive island in the Red Sea. This island is probably the one now known as the Island of St. John (or Zeberget) from which the green or yellowish-green peridot is found. It seems, therefore, that our modern peridot was in earlier days called topaz. Another and more likely derivation is that the old Sanskrit word *tapas*, meaning fire, was the root from which the modern name has sprung.

The first use of the name topaz for the precious topaz of the jeweller appears to have been made by Henckel in 1737 when he described the Saxon deposits. In the light of present confusion it seems a pity that Henckel did not select another and newer name for the mineral.

Chemical and Physical Properties

Topaz crystallizes in the orthorhombic system as prismatic crystals with the faces of the prisms often deeply striated parallel to their length. In the terminal faces considerable differences in habit occur. The brown crystals from Brazil are simply terminated with four low-angled triangular faces forming a pyramid (*see* Plate XX). In the crystals from Utah these pyramidal faces are steep, and in the Japanese and African crystals and those from a number of other localities, which are usually white or blue, a number of pyramidal and dome-shaped faces occur, with two of the dome faces often so enlarged that they meet at the top of the crystal to form a ridge, thus giving a chisel-shaped appearance to the crystal. In some cases the basal pinacoid is present producing a flat-topped crystal. *Figure 6.1* shows some topaz crystals.

Topaz crystals are usually terminated at one end only, the other being the cleaved basal plane where the crystal has been broken from the rock on which it had grown. Doubly terminated crystals are rare but not unknown. On looking down the length of a topaz crystal the outline is seen to be lozenge-shaped (diamond-shaped), but, if as sometimes occurs, the second order prism is predominant a pseudo-tetragonal or square outline is seen.

Topaz crystals occur in cavities in highly acid igneous rocks, such as granite or rhyolite; the supposition is that topaz is deposited by the action of hot fluoriferous gases after solidification of the magma. Topaz is also a common occurrence in zones of contact metamorphism and in pegmatite dykes. Much topaz is found as water-worn rolled pebbles in river gravels.

Most topaz is colourless, the blue colours being next in abundance and may be chatoyant. Stones of a green colour, resembling the sea-green aquamarine, are said to emanate from Russia. Brownish crystals are found in a number of localities, but the highly prized sherry-yellow crystals which cut into such fine jewel stones are found only in Brazil. Natural pink coloured crystals are rare and the pink topazes used in jewellery are all without doubt Brazilian yellow stones which have been altered to pink by heat treatment.

Although topaz is a hard mineral, it is 8 on the scale of hardness devised by Mohs, it will break easily in a direction at right angles to the length of

Figure 6.1. Topaz crystals from New Hampshire, United States of America

the crystal, for topaz has an extremely easy basal cleavage. This cleavage in topaz is a danger in that the least knock or blow given to the stone may start internal fissures or flaws. As many topazes are fashioned into long oval or drop shapes (pendeloques) owing to the prismatic shape of the crystals, there is a great tendency for such stones to develop flaws across them, or even to break into two parts (*Figure 6.2*). Topazes need to be treated with great care.

Topaz is in composition a fluosilicate of aluminium; the chemical formula is expressed as $Al_2(F,OH)_2SiO_4$, that is the fluorine and the hydroxyl (the OH group) can replace each other by any amount by a small-scale isomorphous replacement. In theory, therefore, there could be a pure hydroxyl

Plate XI

Sinhalite, Topaz and Peridot

Sinhalite
8·10 carats

Blue topaz
16·78 carats

Peridot
27·17 carats

Pink topaz
33·46 carats

Brown topaz
21·92 carats

White topaz
57·86 carats

topaz with the formula $Al_2(OH)_2SiO_4$, or a pure fluorine topaz ($Al_2F_2SiO_4$), but in fact there is always some hydroxyl and fluorine in the chemical make-up. Fluorine has the tendency to raise the density and to lower the refractive index of a mineral, while hydroxyl operates in the reverse way.

Effects of Light

Refraction

The sherry-brown coloured topazes from Brazil, and the heat-treated pink stones derived from them, have a density near 3·53 and refractive indices of 1·63 and 1·64 with a birefringence of 0·008. The blue and colourless stones, and the yellow stones from Russia, Saxony, the United States of America and elsewhere, have a higher density—near 3·56—and refractive indices of 1·61 and 1·62. The birefringence for these stones being greater at 0·010. These values indicate a richness in hydroxyl for the Brazilian stones and a richness in fluorine for the topazes from elsewhere. In all cases the

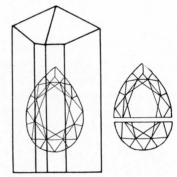

Figure 6.2. Stylized topaz crystal showing a drop-shaped stone cut from it and the liability of the stone to break in two owing to the strong basal cleavage of topaz

refraction is biaxial and positive in sign. Although these two groups of topaz are fairly well defined there have been cases where intermediate values of refractive indices have been measured. Stones with such properties, that is with a refractive index measurement of 1·62–1·63, are rare. With a birefringence of 0·010 the doubling of the rear facet edges of topaz should be well seen. This is not always so, for the doubling, although parallel, may be superimposed and thus not obvious.

Translucency and Pleochroism

Topazes are usually transparent, except in cases where abundant inclusions produce a cloudy effect. The limpid transparency of the water-clear stones is aptly described by the Brazilian and French names used for them; these are *Pingo d'agoa* and *Goutte d'eau*, both meaning drops of water. Topaz has a vitreous lustre, a characteristic slippery feel, but little fire (0·014 B to G). The stones take a fine polish and are thus very brilliant.

The pleochroism of topaz is distinct but not strong, except in the case of the 'fired' pink-coloured stones when the effect is pronounced; one ray being colourless and the others two shades of pink. The sherry-coloured stones exhibit honey-yellow, straw-yellow and pinkish-yellow for the three optical directions. The blue stones show colourless, pale pink and blue. When viewed through the Chelsea colour filter the blue stones show a greenish-blue, but this is nowhere near the strong blue effect exhibited under similar conditions by the aquamarines.

Absorption Spectra

The topazes, except for the sherry-brown types, show no observable absorption spectra which can be used in their identification. The sherry-coloured crystals from Ouro Preto in Brazil are said to contain a trace of chromium, but this element does not appear to show in the absorption spectrum of such stones. When, however, such stones are heat-treated—producing the pink-coloured topaz—the chromium takes its place in the crystal lattice and then gives rise to a chromium fluorescence and absorption spectrum. The main characteristic of this very weak spectrum is a feeble doublet about 6820 Å, which can be seen as a faint absorption line, or more readily as a fluorescent line by scattered light. It can be seen better if the incident light is filtered with a flask of copper sulphate solution.

Luminescence

The luminescence of topaz appears to vary in some accordance with the two types, the hydroxyl rich and the fluorine rich. The blue and colourless stones show a weak yellowish or greenish glow under long-wave ultra-violet light. Under the short-wave lamp the glow is very much weaker. H. Leiper has found in some colourless and bluish topazes a lemon-yellow fluorescence under the short-wave lamp and that the glow tended to show a definite orientation, three main types of orientation of the glows being noted. The effect is suggested as being a useful guide for ascertaining the best cutting directions in order to obtain the best blue colour from bluish crystals. Under x-rays the blue and colourless topazes show a greenish-white to a violet-blue fluorescence. Under x-ray bombardment the stones are found to assume a brownish-yellow colour.

The sherry-brown and pink stones, which are those most commonly found in jewellery, show a strong orange-yellow glow under long-wave ultra-violet light, and a similar but much weaker glow is seen under short-wave ultra-violet light. Under x-rays the glow is brownish-yellow to orange in colour. This is an entirely different effect to that seen when the colourless and blue stones are so irradiated.

Effects of Heat

Topaz becomes strongly electrified by either heat or friction and retains this charge for several hours. Some specimens will become highly electrified by gently stroking with the fingers. In some Brazilian crystals quite a gentle pressure between the finger and thumb in the direction of the principal axis is quite sufficient to electrify them.

It was recorded by the Greeks that yellow topaz when strongly heated decolorized, but as the yellow quartz known as citrine behaves similarly, it is difficult to be sure whether the material was the true topaz or quartz. If the reddish-brown crystals from Ouro Preto, Brazil, are slowly heated to about 450°C the crystals first become colourless but on cooling develop a colour which may vary from a salmon pink to a purple red, depending on the intensity of the original colour and on the strength of the heating.

It was said that the process was first discovered by a Paris jeweller, Dumelle by name, who communicated his discovery to the Academy of Sciences. Dumelle's process consisted in heating a topaz in a sand bath to a temperature of 500°C and leaving it to cool in the sand. Another method is to enclose the crystal in many wrappings of tinder which are then fired, the heat from the burning tinder being sufficient to 'pink' the topaz. Slow heating and slow cooling are essential to prevent the crystal from being fissured and made cloudy; too much heat or too rapid a heating will cause the stone to become completely decolorized, this occurring at over 600°C. The cause of the change of colour from brown to pink is due, as mentioned earlier, to the trace of the element chromium present in the brown stones entering the crystal lattice under the influence of the heating. Many of the paler brown topazes from other localities, probably all of the fluorine-rich

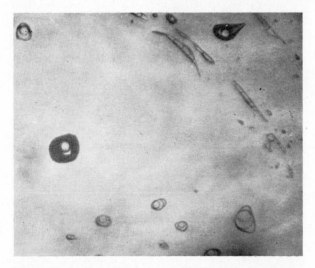

Figure 6.3. Cavities with two immiscible liquids in a white topaz

type, tend to fade in sunlight. This is particularly so with such crystals from the Urulga river in Soviet Russia and those from Japan and the Thomas mountains in Utah, United States of America.

Inclusions

The internal features seen in topaz are, in the colourless, blue and brown fluorine-rich types, usually cavities containing two or even three immiscible liquids. These cavities are often drop-shaped and the bubbles, one of which could possibly be carbonic acid gas, may be inside one another (*Figure 6.3*). Occasionally these cavities may be flattened out into thin films of liquid. A rare type of inclusion which has been observed in topaz from Nigeria is cubic crystals either singly or as groups (*Figure 6.4*). These may be fluorite crystals. The hydroxyl-rich sherry-coloured topazes and the pink stones usually show long tube-like cavities.

Occurrences

The earliest known source of topaz was probably that of Schneckenstein,

111

near Auerbach in Saxon Voightland, where the crystals, of pale wine-yellow colour or completely devoid of colour, are found in drusy cavities in association with quartz and tourmaline. Undoubtedly the best topaz for jewellery purposes is the sherry-brown material from Brazil which makes such attractive pink stones when heat-treated. The locality for these crystals is in the neighbourhood of Ouro Preto in the State of Minas Gerais. The topaz is found as nests of detached crystals embedded in clay or scaly kaolin in cavities all along a range of hills extending for about 6 miles in a south-westerly direction from Ouro Preto.

Figure 6.4. Cubic crystals in a white topaz from Nigeria

Blue and white topazes, as crystals and rolled pebbles, are abundant in many places in Brazil. It is found with diamond in the district of Diamantina, and with beryl and chrysoberyl in the Minas Novas district and elsewhere. Yellow and colourless topaz is found at La Paz, San Luis Potosi and Durango in Mexico. Colourless, pale blue, reddish and wine-yellow crystals are found in the Pikes Peak region of Colorado, in California, Texas and in New Hampshire and in the rhyolite of the Thomas mountains of Utah.

Blue, colourless and pale brown topazes are found in Tasmania, and, with tin, in the Gilbert Ranges of northern Queensland. Here the crystals are commonly flawed but the rolled pebbles are found flawless. New South Wales also produces topaz. Well-formed crystals occur in pegmatite veins and as pebbles in the river gravels near Takayama, Naegi and Hosokute in the Mino Province, Tanokamiyama in Omi Province, and Ishigure in Ise Province of Japan. The gem gravels of Ceylon produce a fair amount of good quality topaz; as do the ordinary alluvial deposits of the ruby mines of Mogok in Upper Burma. A considerable occurrence of fine yellow, blue and (mostly) colourless topaz of magnificent gem quality and large size takes place in a large pegmatite dyke at Sakangyi some 20 miles west of Mogok. The pegmatites at Mahabe and Soarano, and the alluvial deposits of the Saka river of Madagascar supply topaz. Of interest, but scarcely of gem importance, is the topaz found in the Mourne mountains of Northern Ireland, the Cairngorm mountains of Scotland, and St. Michael's Mount and Lundy Island off the Cornish and Devon coasts.

Topazes of many colours are found in Russia. Blue and green crystals are found on the eastern slope of the Urals at Alabashka near Sverdlovsk, the gem centre formerly known as Ekaterinburg, and beautiful magenta-coloured crystals are found near the Sanarka river in the Ilmen mountains. Pale brown crystals, which like those from Japan and Utah fade on exposure to sunlight, are found near the Urulga river north of the Borshchovochnoi mountains in the Nerchinsk district of Eastern Siberia. In the Adun-Chalon mountains of the same Siberian district topaz is found in good crystals. Kamchatka, in the extreme east of Siberia, also produces topaz of yellow, blue and greenish colour.

In the African continent topaz is abundant, but except for the blue coloured material has little gem importance. Well formed colourless and blue crystals are found near Klein Spitzkopje in South-West Africa; the crystals are obtained from pegmatite dykes, and topaz is also obtained from the gem gravels of the Somabula forest in Rhodesia. Blue and white topazes, as crystals and as rolled pebbles, are found around the tin workings of northern Nigeria. The workings lie around the town of Jos in the Bauchi district. The crystals are here found in veins and fissures in the contact metamorphosed aureoles caused by the younger of the granitic intrusions of the plateau. The water-worn rolled pebbles are found in streams and alluvial gravel, and the wily indigenes in the northern part of the territory place colourless pebbles of topaz in the indigo dye pots which are such a feature of Nigeria. This superficially colours the pebbles a blue shade and they are then sold to the unwary European who thinks he has a fine blue topaz. Topaz crystals have also been found near Tamanrasset (Fort Laperrine) in the Hoggar district of south-eastern Sahara. Prospectors have reported the finding of a few small diamonds in this locality.

Cutting of Topaz

The mixed cut is the style of cutting most used for topaz, and, owing to the long prismatic shape of the crystals, the stones are cut as rather longish oval or as pendeloque (drop-shaped) stones. It is characteristic of the brown topaz that it shows a darker colour at each end of the long axis of the stone. Moderately rich-coloured topazes are cut in the trap-cut style (the so-called 'emerald cut'). Many pale pink topazes are set, particularly in old jewellery, in a closed setting with the back of the stone painted with red colour, or with the settings containing a red coloured foil. It has been recorded that topaz, despite its strong cleavage, has been cut as a cameo.

Synthesis and Simulation

Topaz has been made synthetically for academic interest, but not for commercial exploitation. The process was carried out by the action of hydrofluosilicic acid on silica and alumina in the presence of water at a temperature of 500°C. The so-called synthetic topaz is a synthetic corundum of suitable colour. Except for the natural and synthetic corundum having colours similar to those of topaz, the only other natural stones which simulate topaz are tourmaline, danburite, aquamarine and quartz, all of which will float on methylene iodide (density 3·3) whereas topaz will sink.

TOURMALINE

Tourmaline is one of the more scientifically interesting minerals, and as a gemstone surpasses all others by its range of colour. Some crystals of tourmaline exhibit two, or more, colours in the one crystal and stones cut from them show this 'parti-coloration'. Some crystals are fibrous, in that they have fine fibres or canals running up through the crystal, and these crystals when cut *en-cabochon* show a cat's-eye effect.

The derivation of the name tourmaline is obscure but is generally believed to have originated from the Sinhalese 'turmali', a name applied by the local jewellers to the yellow zircon. The use of this name for tourmaline was said to have come about owing to a parcel of tourmaline being sent by mistake under this name to stone dealers in Amsterdam in 1703, and the name may well have stuck. The red and pink colours of tourmaline are sometimes known as rubellite, the blue indicolite, the colourless achroite, the brown dravite, and a peculiar reddish-violet variety is called siberite. The yellow and green tourmalines are simply called tourmaline with the colour as prefix, and, indeed, this preferable type of nomenclature is now used extensively; the fancy varietal names mentioned are now less used. There is an opaque black tourmaline which the miners call schorl; rarely have they been cut except for mourning jewellery.

Chemical and Physical Properties

Tourmaline crystallizes in the trigonal system of crystal structure. The crystals are usually of a long prismatic form and are vertically striated, an effect probably due to oscillation between the first and second order prisms. In some tourmalines the prism tends to be short and the habit is then tabular. The crystals usually show a characteristic rounded triangular section when viewed down their length. The prisms are capped by rhombo-hedral or scalenohedral faces which may differ in their angle with the prism at opposite ends of the crystal; thus one end appears flatter than the other. This feature is known as hemimorphism and is an outward sign of polarity in the crystal (*Figure 6.5*).

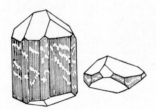

Figure 6.5. Tourmaline crystals

This polarity of tourmaline crystals is also shown by the phenomenon of pyroelectricity shown by some crystals, which, when heated to about 100°C develop positive electricity at one end of the crystal and negative at the other. This electrical charge enables the crystal to attract to itself small pieces of paper or wood ashes. Indeed, it was owing to this property that the Dutch merchants applied the name 'aschentrekker' to such crystals brought from Ceylon. It is also the cause of cut tourmalines collecting dust, when in a heated shop window, to a much greater extent than other gemstones. It must be mentioned that the iron-rich tourmalines, such as the black variety schorl, do not exhibit this pyroelectricity to any extent.

114

PLATE XII

The Tourmaline group

Parti-coloured stone
13·70 carats

Yellow tourmaline
12·38 carats

Blue tourmaline
9·58 carats

Tourmaline with coloured
stripes
(Madagascar)
57·10 carats

Green tourmaline
14·45 carats

Red tourmaline
12·12 carats

Pale brown tourmaline
22·67 carats

Another property, also due to the polarity of tourmaline crystals, is that a charge of electricity may be induced when pressure is applied in the direction of the vertical crystal axis. This effect is termed piezoelectricity and is made use of in certain depth-recording apparatus for underwater craft, specially cut tourmaline plates being used for the purpose.

The chemical composition of tourmaline is extremely complex. It may be best described as a borosilicate of aluminium and alkalies with iron, magnesium, calcium, manganese, lithium, potassium, fluorine and water. No formula can be suggested adequately to cover all the variations of the chemistry of the mineral, but a grouping into three main types is to some degree possible. They are the alkali-rich tourmalines which contain sodium, lithium and potassium and are either colourless, red or green. The iron-rich types are either dark blue, bluish-green or black in colour, while the magnesium group may be colourless, yellow-brown to brownish-black. A chromium-coloured green tourmaline and others containing venadium have been found in Tanzania.

The mineral has no distinct cleavage and the fracture is subconchoidal to uneven. The hardness varies to some extent and may be given as 7 to $7\frac{1}{2}$ on Mohs's scale, $7\frac{1}{4}$ being a good mean value. Owing to the complex nature of the chemical composition the density of tourmaline suffers some variation and has a range from 3·02 to 3·26. The various colours, however, fall into fairly well-defined groups. The best values for the various colours are as follows: pink 3·03, red 3·05, pale green 3·05, brown 3·06, dark green 3·08, blue 3·10, yellow 3·10, and black 3·15 but this may go to over 3·2.

Tourmaline is of common occurrence in crystalline schists and more siliceous igneous rocks, in pegmatites, gneiss, granulites and similar rocks. The mineral is common in zones of contact metamorphism as a result of fumarole action by the mineralizing effect of hot gases in the fluid magma. It is freely associated with quartz, mica, corundum, apatite, spodumene, scapolite, topaz, albite feldspar, beryl, garnet and cassiterite. Tourmaline is found in cavities, frequently attached by the base, and growing freely in groups, and tourmaline crystals may be found interpenetrating quartz crystals. It is quite commonly found in alluvials and as water-worn pebbles in streams.

Effects of Light

Lustre

The lustre of tourmaline is vitreous and the transparency varies from perfectly transparent through all stages of translucency to opaque, as in the black schorl. Much of the clear material is marred by many cracks and flaws and such tourmaline is usually cut into beads or even carved into figurines.

Refraction

The refractive indices of tourmaline are approximately 1·62–1·64, but vary somewhat with stones of different colours. The birefringence, too, is variable and may be as low as 0·014 or as high as 0·021; a common value is 0·018. The double refraction is strong enough for a clear doubling of the rear facet edges to be seen when viewed by a hand-lens through the thickness of the stone. Tourmaline is uniaxial and therefore only one shadow edge moves on rotation of the stone on the dense glass of the refractometer; this edge is that of the lower index for the optical sign of tourmaline is negative. The fire shown by tourmaline is small for the dispersion is only 0·017 (B to G).

The dichroism of tourmaline is one of its most outstanding features. It is specially marked in the dark brown and dark green stones, when the ordinary ray is so strongly absorbed that it does not penetrate the stone at all, so that sections cut parallel to the vertical crystal axis can be used for the production of plane polarized light. Indeed, they were so used in the early polarizers known as the 'tourmaline tongs'. In some cases the ordinary ray is so strongly absorbed that only a single edge due to the extraordinary ray is visible on the refractometer and may well give the impression that the mineral is singly refractive. Also such absorption may mask the doubling of the back facet edges when the edges are viewed through the stone.

The paler-coloured tourmalines such as the pale pinks, and particularly the yellow stones, show only a weak dichroism. The variation in dichroic effect shown by different tourmalines requires that the stones be cut with it in mind. Light travelling through a tourmaline in the direction of the vertical crystallographic axis is always deeper in colour than light travelling at right angles to this axis. Therefore dark stones need to have the table facet cut parallel to the vertical axis (to lighten the colour), and pale stones with the table facet at right angles to this, that is at right angles to the vertical axis, in order to get the most promising colour out of the stone.

Absorption Spectra

The absorption spectra shown by tourmalines are usually so weak that they lack value as a means of identification. In the green tourmalines the red part of the spectrum is almost completely absorbed up to about 6400 Å, and the yellow and green are freely transmitted except for a faint absorption region near 5600 Å. In the green part there is a fairly strong and narrow band centred at 4980 Å (attributed to ferrous iron). These are accompanied by a weaker and vaguer band at 4680 Å. A strong band in the violet at 4150 Å has been observed in some green and particularly in blue tourmalines. The red and pink tourmalines show a broad absorption region in the green, usually centred near 5250 Å, within the long-wave end of which may be seen a narrow line at 5370 Å. There are also two bands in the blue, almost as narrow as the lines in the blue of the spectrum seen in ruby. In tourmaline these lines are at 4580 and 4500 Å. Such a spectrum is seen most completely in the 'siberite' variety.

Luminescence

The luminescence effects shown by tourmaline are indeterminate as, except for the yellow stones which show an extremely weak glow too indistinct to recognize the colour, and the red and pink stones which sometimes show a lavender glow under ultra-violet light and x-rays (when they may even show slight phosphorescence), tourmalines are inert.

Effects of Heat

The influence of heat on tourmaline is variable, the result is usually to lighten the colour. Experiment has shown that at about 700°C pink tourmaline decolorizes completely and the green coloured stones lighten in colour. An interesting application of heat treatment is that certain dark green stones from South-West Africa lighten to an attractive emerald-green colour.

Inclusions

The inclusions seen in tourmalines are in general thread-like cavities which under high magnification are resolved into tubes filled with liquid and often containing a bubble of gas (two-phase inclusions). The tubes usually run parallel to the length of the crystal and if profuse are the cause of the chatoyant effect seen in tourmaline cat's-eyes. W. F. Eppler, however, takes the view that the inclusions causing the chatoyancy in tourmaline are crystal fibres. Flat films are another common inclusion and if these happen to be viewed at such an angle that the incident light is totally reflected from them they appear as black patches (*Figure 6.6*).

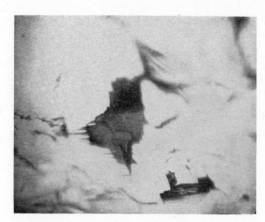

Figure 6.6. Inclusions in tourmaline

Occurrences

A principal locality for gem tourmaline is near Mursinka in the Ural mountains of Soviet Russia where good quality crystals, usually blue, red or violet-red in colour, are found in the yellow clay disintegration product of the granite in which they had formed. The village of Shaitanka, some 45 miles north of Sverdlovsk produces red crystals; these are found in druses in a coarse-grained granite. Another Russian locality is Nerchinsk in Transbaikalia where tourmaline is found near the Urulga river.

Ceylon, probably the original source of tourmaline as a gemstone, supplies stones of a yellow and brown colour from the alluvial deposits in the south-east of the island. About 20 miles south-east of Mogok in Upper Burma there is an extensive alluvial deposit of decomposed gneiss and granite carrying fine red tourmaline. The deposit lies on the banks of the Nampai river near the town of Mainglon and is worked spasmodically, often by Chinese miners, for in olden times this red tourmaline was much esteemed in China where it was used for making the distinctive button for a certain grade of Mandarin.

Brazil produces tourmalines of many colours, particularly green, blue and red crystals, and many which show zonally arranged colours (parti-coloration). The crystals are found around the basins of the Rio Doce, the Rio Jequitinhona and the lower Arassuahy rivers in the north-east of the State of Minas Gerais.

Much gem tourmaline is found, in a wide range of colours including the dark green which lightens to an emerald-green shade on heating, in the pegmatites at Klein Spitzkopje near Rössing on the Otavi railway east of Swakopmund. Crystals of emerald-green colour are found at Usakos in South-West Africa. The gem gravels of the Somabula forest in Rhodesia, and Alto Lighona in Moçambique, are other sources. In Tanzania there are found green and brown tourmalines which contain chromium and vanadium. The green chromium/vanadium tourmalines from here show, unlike normal green tourmalines, a strong red residual colour when viewed through the colour filter.

The island of Madagascar supplied much gem quality tourmaline. The crystals are mostly obtained from the pegmatite at Anjanabonoina and include all colours, the red being the most prized; the colourless crystals are the rarest. Blue, amethyst colour, rose-pink, yellow, brown and green coloured material are found in the Madagascan deposits.

The Pala district of San Diego County, California, produced much tourmaline from the pegmatites of the district. The colours found vary from jet-black 'schorl', through the deep blue, to greens and pink to pale red. Colourless material is also found at Pala. It can be said that nearly all the colours assumed by tourmaline are found in the San Diego deposits, with only brown coloured material not well represented. Two or more colours are commonly present in a single crystal, and some are characterized by concentric or layer-like zoning parallel to the vertical axis of the prismatic crystals. Some of these mixed-coloured tourmalines are of deep blue to black cores surrounded with single or multi-layers that may be colourless, blue, green or pink, or any combination of these colours, such as a colourless central portion surrounded by a rim of green-coloured material, a type called 'water melon' tourmaline.

Another type of parti-coloration is where the colours vary in layers parallel to the basal plane of the crystals, which may be green at one end and pink at the other, with perhaps a zone of colourless material in the centre or other variations of this theme. The colours in some of the zoned (parti-coloured) crystals are sharply bounded from one another, whereas in other crystals the colours appear to merge gradually and intergrade within distances of about 2 mm or less.

During the early years of the twentieth century Pala tourmaline was principally marketed in China. This was particularly so with the pink and red varieties which were highly prized by the Chinese who carved and polished it into many different forms. With the collapse of the Manchu dynasty in 1912 the oriental market was eliminated, and much of the mining for gem tourmaline curtailed.

Much gemmy tourmaline has been found in Maine, U.S.A., mainly at

Hebron and Paris (Mount Mica) where tourmaline of a bluish-green colour is abundant and pink crystals rare. At Auburn in the same state is found an attractive lilac-coloured tourmaline, as is also the deep blue, green and parti-coloured crystals. Haddam in Connecticut is another American locality for tourmaline.

Cutting of Tourmaline

Probably the best style of cutting for tourmaline is the mixed cut—a step cut back with a brilliant cut front—but today, especially for specimen stones, the trap cut is used to a great extent. Much flawed tourmaline (and the crystals may be of considerable size) is fashioned into beads or carved into small figurines.

CHAPTER 7

ZIRCON, PERIDOT AND SPODUMENE

ZIRCON

The mineral species known as zircon furnishes a suite of gemstones with a range of colour varying from colourless, through yellow, red, orange and brown, yellowish-green, a bright leaf-green to a dark green, and a sky-blue. The colourless, golden-brown and sky-blue stones, which as will be told later, owe their colour to heat treatment, are the most important in jewellery, and show off to the best advantage the adamantine lustre of zircon.

The name zircon is said to have been derived from the word zargoon, which in Arabic means vermilion and in Persian gold-coloured. Hitherto, zircons have been variously known as 'jargoon' or 'cerkonier'; the first name is said to have been derived from the Italian word gaicone, which is probably a corruption of zargoon. Yellowish-red and orange-red stones have had the names hyacinth and jacinth applied to them, but as these names have been used for any aurora-red stones whatever be their species they are better discontinued; indeed they are fast dying out. The colourless stones from material found at Matara in Ceylon were, in the eighteenth century, regarded as inferior diamonds and were called by the misnomer 'Matara diamonds', a term which should now be forgotten.

Chemical and Physical Properties

Zircon has evoked great interest to gemmologists owing to the great variation of density and refractive indices exhibited by the species, and it was not until the work of K. F. Chudoba *et al.* during 1937 that the mystery of these variations was finally solved.

The composition of the mineral is a silicate of zirconium ($ZrSiO_4$). Usually there is a little iron present as an impurity replacing part of the zirconium, a variable amount, some 0·5–4 per cent, of the rare metal hafnium, and traces of thorium and uranium, to which latter metal the striking absorption spectrum of zircon is due.

Zircon crystallizes in the tetragonal system and the crystals take the form of a combination of a square prism terminated at either end by a square pyramid, or a combination of pyramids of different inclinations. Rarely is the end of the crystal terminated by a small basal face. The crystals may, if the prism zone be small, assume a pseudo-octahedral habit, but usually the prism is elongated and the habit of the crystal is prismatic. Twinning according to the rutile law, giving knee-shaped (geniculate) forms, is occasionally seen in zircon crystals. The forms of zircon crystals are shown in *Figure 7.1*.

The hardness of zircon varies from 7 to $7\frac{1}{2}$ on Mohs's scale and may not be consistent throughout the entire stone, a factor which sometimes leads to difficulty in polishing. The cleavage is very imperfect and negligible; the fracture is markedly conchoidal and the stones by nature are brittle. This brittleness is well shown by the abrasion of the facet edges when zircons have been kept loose in a stone packet for some time, an effect termed 'paper wearing'. To avoid this the zircons sent from Bangkok are wrapped in 'strings' of tissue paper, each stone in a little twist of paper so that it cannot rub against another.

As has already been mentioned the density of zircons shows considerable variation, and for many years the reason for this was only conjecture. The answer has now been found and lies in the fact that there is not one but two zircons. Some writers mention three types of zircon but the intermediate type mentioned by them is just one phase in the alteration of one to the other of the two main types.

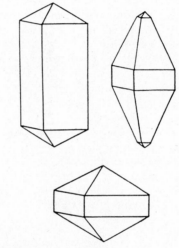

Figure 7.1. Zircon crystals

The first type of zircon, and the most important so far as jewellery stones are concerned, is the fully crystallized zirconium silicate which has a range of density from 4·67 to 4·70. The second type of zircon is the so-called 'low type' which has a density of about 4·00 (3·95–4·10). It has been established that these stones were originally the 'high type' zircons in which the crystal lattice had internally broken down so that they consist of more or less amorphous silica and zirconia. This breakdown is said to be due to the destructive effect of *alpha* particles (the nuclei of the helium atom) emanating from atoms of a radioactive element in the zircon. This element may be uranium or thorium, traces of which are isomorphously included in the zircon. That radioactive elements are present in zircon may be demonstrated by the self-photograph (autoradiograph) given by many zircons when they are placed on a bare photographic film for some hours. Minerals which are broken down by radioactivity in this manner are termed 'metamict', so that the low type of zircon can also be called metamict zircon.

It can readily be understood that this breakdown of the crystal lattice is not instantaneous and therefore there must be stones in which the decomposition is not complete, only partly complete or has only just started. Thus, there may be zircons having any density between that of the high type and that of the low type. It is these partially decomposed stones which are the 'intermediate type' of earlier writers.

Effects of Light

Refraction

The refractive indices of zircon vary considerably. The high type has refractive indices of 1·92 for the ordinary ray and 1·98 for the extraordinary ray, the birefringence, which is uniaxial and positive in sign, is 0·059. From the high type the values decrease, both in the indices and the birefringence, until the low type is reached, and this has a refractive index of 1·78. Such stones are practically isotropic, that is they are singly refractive. They have a hardness of $6\frac{1}{2}$ on Mohs's scale.

The zircon, despite its pronounced double refraction, in general shows practically no dichroism. Exceptions are the blue stones which owe their colour to heat treatment, for such stones show a particularly strong dichroism, the twin colours of which are deep sky-blue for the ordinary ray and practically colourless for the extraordinary ray. The dispersion, or fire, of zircon is approximately 0·039 (B to G), and is appreciably higher for the extraordinary ray than for the ordinary ray. Further, the amount of fire does not decrease from the high type to the low type, an effect for which it is difficult to account. Zircon approaches diamond in fire, hence well-cut colourless zircons may be mistaken for diamond if care is not taken. The strong double refraction shown by zircon will provide a sure test for zircon as against diamond, for the back facet edges will appear doubled when looked at through the stone with the aid of a hand lens. Diamond is singly refractive and cannot show a true doubling. The doubling of the back facets of zircon has been referred to and illustrated (*see Figure 2.26*) in the chapter on diamond.

Absorption Spectrum

A characteristic of zircon is the remarkable absorption spectrum exhibited by the mineral, a spectrum which was first observed by A. Church in 1866. This absorption spectrum shows at its best many strong narrow bands and fine lines throughout the spectrum, but the spectrum, which is due to uranous uranium, varies considerably in the number of bands which may be seen. The greenish-brown zircons found in Burma exhibit the richest spectrum, over forty lines having been recorded in one such stone. Ceylon zircons show a smaller number of bands, fourteen being about the usual number which can be seen; while the orange stones from Uralla, New South Wales, show only a few bands. The red stones from Auvergne, France, appear to be devoid of bands. The heat-treated colourless, sky-blue and golden-brown zircons from Indo-China show the zircon spectrum extremely weakly, usually only the strong persistent line at 6535 Å may be seen, and that only as a fine 'pencil' line, which affords clear indication of the species.

The main bands in the spectrum of zircon are at 6910, 6830, 6625, 6605, 6535 (the strongest and most persistent), 6210, 6150, 5895, 5625, 5375, 5160, 4840, 4600 and 4327 Å. It can readily be understood that

PLATE XIII

The Zircon group

White zircon
21·32 carats

Green zircon   Blue zircon   Red zircon
9·86 carats   44·27 carats   12·34 carats

Golden zircon
22·67 carats

the spectrum of the low-type zircons, which are practically amorphous, should be less sharply defined, and, indeed, this is so. The absorption spectrum of the metamict zircons shows a woolly band at the 'persistent' line wavelength of 6535 Å. Heating such low-type zircons will cause the band to sharpen and other lines to appear. There are some rare variations of the low-type absorption spectrum, one of which is notable in showing three broad strong bands in the red at 6910, 6690 and 6535 Å, the centre band being the strongest. Another type, which curiously has been found only in zircons which have a refractive index of 1·82 and a density of 3·98, shows a vague band at 6550 Å and another at 5200 Å.

Fluorescence

The fluorescence of zircon under ultra-violet light of either long or short wavelength is variable. Some stones are practically inert and some fluoresce most strongly; the colour of the glow is always a mustard yellow of varying intensity. Under x-rays the glow emitted by zircons varies not only in intensity but also in colour. Most stones show a whitish or violet-blue glow but some show a greenish or a yellowish light. It must be emphasized that great care must be taken in exposing the heat-treated types of zircons to radiations of any kind, for prolonged exposure will cause such zircons to revert to their original brown colour.

Effects of Heat

Most interesting is the influence of heat on the different types of zircons. Both the low type and those intermediate between them and the high type, if heated to about 1,450°C, tend to increase in density to the normal value near 4·7 with normal refractive indices and with a sharpening of the absorption lines. This heating causes the dissociated silica and zirconia to recombine as crystalline zircon, the amount of heating needed to bring the low type back to the high type depends upon the completeness of the original dissociation. It is said that in some cases heating will never cause the stone to return to the completely high type. This may only be due to the lack of a continuous and long heating.

The Ceylonese zircons are mostly some shade of green. On heating to a dull red heat for about an hour they become much paler, while the rarer reddish-brown stones from this locality may turn colourless under such heat treatment. The most important heat treatment of zircons is that carried out on the reddish-brown crystals found in Indo-China for it is the rough material from this locality which produces, after heat-treatment, the colourless, blue and golden stones which are so popular in jewellery.

The heating of the zircon rough is carried out by natives using crude clay stoves burning charcoal as a fuel. The stoves are provided with grates and suitable apertures to maintain the draught, which may be further increased by the addition of a tall iron chimney. The zircon rough (crystals and rolled pebbles) is placed in a fire-clay crucible which holds about one kilogram of rough zircon (*Figure 7.2*). The crucible is closed so as to produce a reducing atmosphere and the 'cooking' is carried out for between one and a half and two hours at a temperature between 900°C and 1,000°C, but these figures may be varied somewhat by the operator from his own personal experience of the behaviour of the type of rough being treated. From this treatment only about 30 per cent of the stones are suitable for fashioning into gemstones.

The poor colour, but clean, blue stones from the first heating are then subjected to a further heating in the closed crucible, and this tends to turn them colourless. Such treatment is critical for underheating tends to produce colourless stones which have a great tendency to revert to a brown colour; while overheating produces a cloudy effect. From the above description it

Figure 7.2. Heating rough zircon. Left, a tall funnel filled with coal. Right, one kilogram of rough zircon being heated
(By courtesy of George Lindley & Co. (London) Ltd.)

is seen that a heating in a reducing atmosphere may produce the sky-blue or colourless zircons.

Heating the zircon rough in a perforated crucible which allows free access of air—that is, in an oxidizing atmosphere—to a temperature of about 900°C, produces golden-yellow and colourless stones with sometimes stones of a red colour. The residue of 'off-colours' from the primary firings in a reducing atmosphere are often again heated in the oxidizing crucible, when some of the stones assume the water-white or golden-yellow colours.

Although many of the heat-treated blue stones are fairly permanent in colour, a number tend to revert in part to their original brownish hue. Such partially reverted stones have an unpleasant greenish-blue or brownish-blue colour. Reverted stones may sometimes be returned to their blue colour by judicious heating, but this may not occur in every case. A successful result was obtained on a completely reverted blue zircon (which had been, while set in a ring, thrown into an open fire) by heating to about 800°–900°C after it was packed in a crucible with wood charcoal.

Inclusions

Many zircons, particularly the natural coloured stones of low type appear 'smoky looking' when a collection of such stones are examined in a stone packet. The majority of zircons show very little in the way of inclusions characteristic of the species, except, perhaps, in the low type which exhibit

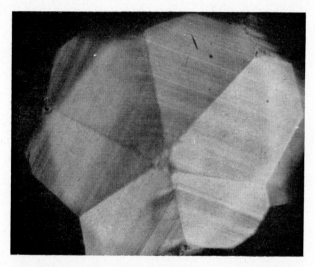

Figure 7.3. Zonal lines typical of 'low type' zircons

straight streaks and angular zoning—something, but not quite, like the zoning seen in some sapphires (*Figure 7.3*). Zircon sometimes shows chatoyancy.

Occurrences

The sources of zircon are world wide, the mineral being a common accessory constituent of igneous rocks, but the gem quality zircons are found in more localized areas. Zircon is prolific in the gem gravels of Ceylon, and the mineral is found in gem quality in the Mogok Stone Tract of Upper Burma. Red zircon is found in Espaly-Saint-Marcel near Le Puy, Haute Loire, in France, which has been long noted for the red crystals found there, and well-formed brown crystals are obtained from Arendal in Norway. Gem quality material has been found at Uralla, Sapphire, Inverell and other places in New England, New South Wales, Australia.

The most important localities for gem zircon are those of Indo-China;

the mining areas of which in some cases pass into the neighbouring territory of Thailand (Siam). The most important localities for the Indo-China and Thailand zircons, which are generally cut and marketed at Bangkok in Thailand, are the Kha, Champasak and Pailin districts (*Figure 7.4*). The Kha districts are the only areas where mined rough produces blue, golden and colourless stones after suitable heat treatment.

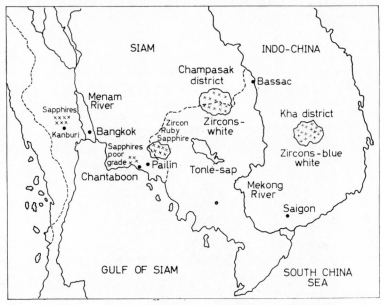

Figure 7.4. Location of zircon mines
(By courtesy of George Lindley & Co. (London) Ltd.)

Cutting of Zircon

In order to obtain the best optical effect with zircon, the stones are usually cut into a modified brilliant-cut which has a second set of pavilion facets. The octagonal and four-sided trap-cuts are now extensively used for specimen zircons of the blue and golden colours, for some of the greens and yellows, and also the browns of natural colour. The natural coloured stones are, however, more usually cut in the mixed-cut style.

Simulation

Apart from suitably coloured glass, the only stone which simulates zircon, and it is the sky-blue zircon which is imitated, is the synthetic blue spinel. The lack of double refraction and the orange residual colour shown by the synthetic stone when viewed through the Chelsea colour filter easily distinguishes it from the natural 'heat-treated' blue zircon, which shows a greenish colour through the filter.

PERIDOT

The attractive green gemstone known to jewellers as peridot belongs to the mineral species which English and American mineralogists call olivine, and

126

which German mineralogists call chrysolite. Unfortunately both these mineralogical names have been employed by jewellers for gems of other species—chrysolite for the yellow chrysoberyl and other stones of yellow colour; olivine, usually spelt olivene, for the green demantoid garnet from the Ural mountains. The name peridot suffers from no such confusion.

In ancient times the stone we now call peridot was known as topaz, a name perhaps derived from the island of Topazios in the Red Sea, an island so named because it was so often hidden by fogs that sailors found difficulty in finding it. This island, now known as Zeberget (Zebirged) or the Island of Saint John, was the only ancient source of peridot, then known as topaz but now the proper name of an entirely different species. It is said that the discovery of peridot on Zeberget was made by pirates but the location was lost for centuries. Peridot was not obtained from Zeberget again until the rediscovery of the mines in the 1900s.

The peridot used in jewellery has a rather oily bottle-green colour which is characteristic for the gem. Much peridot has a tinge of brown and such stones are less highly prized. Very rarely a brown coloured peridot is found and cut stones of this material may be said to be collectors' pieces. Before 1952 there were many 'brown peridots' but in that year it was discovered that the vast majority of the known 'brown peridots' were an entirely different and new mineral species to which the name sinhalite was applied, and sinhalites are far more common than the true brown peridots.

Peridot may attain quite large size; there is a cut stone of 319 carats in the Smithsonian Museum at Washington, U.S.A.; one of 192 carats in the Diamond Treasury at Moscow, and another of 136 carats is exhibited in the Geological Museum at South Kensington in London.

Chemical and Physical Properties

Peridot is a magnesium iron silicate derived from ortho-silicic acid and accords to the formula $(Mg,Fe)_2SiO_4$. The mineral is one of an isomorphous series of which one end member is the magnesium silicate (Mg_2SiO_4), known as forsterite; and the other is the iron silicate (Fe_2SiO_4), which is fayalite. Peridot is idiochromatic, that is the colour is due to iron in the ferrous state which is an inherent part of the composition, but only about one part of iron to eight parts of magnesium is present in the lovely green gem quality stones. Iron produces a rather sad colour of green and the rather brighter green of peridot may be due to the trace of nickel which is usually present in the stones.

Peridot is a comparatively soft stone, the hardness approximating to $6\frac{1}{2}$ on Mohs's scale, hence, while peridots are eminently suitable for setting into brooches, pendants and earrings, their use for ring stones and for setting into bracelets is not always satisfactory, as they are then subject to a greater risk of abrasion with consequent loss of polish. There is also a distinct cleavage parallel to the vertical axis of the crystal and cases have been known of stones breaking along this, admittedly weak, cleavage direction.

The crystals of peridot belong to the orthorhombic system of crystal architecture and are found as flattened prisms vertically striated (a peridot crystal is shown in Plate XX). In the minor localities they are found as rolled pebbles.

127

Effects of Light

The density of peridot approximates to 3·34 and typical figures for refractive indices are α 1·654, β 1·671 and γ 1·689. The stones are biaxial and the sign of the refraction is positive. The amount of double refraction is usually 0·036, which is large enough for the doubling of the back facet edges to be seen easily when they are viewed through the thickness of the stone by a low-power hand lens. Peridot shows little fire, the dispersion between the B and G lines of the solar spectrum being 0·020, and the lustre of the stones may best be described as oily and vitreous. The dichroism (actually the stones are trichroic as there are three optical directions) is weak, one ray being more yellowish than the others.

Absorption Spectrum

The absorption spectrum of peridot, which is due to ferrous iron, consists of three main bands in the blue. They are well separated and evenly spaced and are centred at 4930, 4730 and 4530 Å, the band at 4930 Å having a distinct narrow 'core' at 4970 Å. The 4730 Å band is also fairly

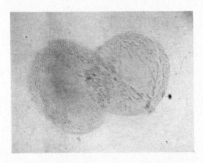

Figure 7.5. ' Water-lily leaves', an inclusion seen in peridot

narrow while the 4530 Å band is broader and less well defined. In large specimens weak and vague bands may sometimes be seen at 6530 Å in the orange and at 5290 Å in the green. It is probably due to the iron content of the stones that peridot shows no luminescence under ultra-violet light or x-rays.

Inclusions

The internal features of peridot vary greatly; those found in the Island of Saint John often show inclusions of biotite mica flakes, which if numerous impart a brownish tinge to the stone. An inclusion rather like water-lily leaves, due to the recrystallization of included liquid in flat cavities, may be found in peridots (*Figure 7.5*), and the pebbles from Hawaii show what appear at first sight to be 'gas' bubbles, but which are actually oval or pear-shaped glass drops (*Figure 7.6*). These bubbles cannot be confused with the bubbles seen in glass because the inclusions in peridot will show double owing to the strong double refraction of the stone.

Occurrences

The most important source of gem peridot was, as mentioned earlier, Zeberget, some 34 miles off the east coast of Egypt and opposite the port of Berenice. Here the crystals are found in a vein of nickel ore in a meta-morphosed peridotite rock, or dunite, much altered to serpentine. Excellent stones, but not in good crystal forms, have been obtained on the northern slope of the 6,220 ft. Kyaukpon near Pyanggaung in the Mogok district of Upper Burma.

As crystals or rolled pebbles, peridot has been found at such places as Söndmöre, Norway; Aubigny County, Queensland, Australia; Minas Gerais, Brazil; and in New Mexico and Arizona in the United States of America. In these American localities the pebbles of peridot have been eroded out from the parent rock and are found in sand-dunes and ant-hills. Some peridot is found in the Congo; in the diamondiferous 'pipes' of South Africa and in the beaches of the Pacific islands of Hawaii where the pebbles have probably been eroded from the volcanic rocks. Peridot, said to be of a

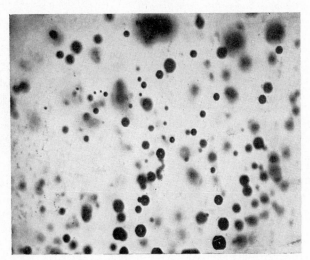

Figure 7.6. 'Gas bubble' inclusions seen in an Hawaiian peri-dot. These bubbles are actually glassy drops

sufficient size and quality to be suitable for cutting into gemstones, has been found in meteorites.

Cutting of Peridot

Peridot is best cut in the trap-cut (step) style, although oval, round and pendeloque-shaped mixed-cut stones are common. In some peridots the large table facet is not cut flat but cut with a slight doming. It may be re-marked that peridot may lose its polish after contact with hydrochloric or sulphuric acids.

Simulation

The characteristic oily lustre and strong double refraction of peridot serve to identify the stone from its counterfeits, although there are con-vincing imitations (to the eye) made in glass and in the composite stone made with a garnet top on a suitably coloured glass. In recent years a peridot-coloured synthetic corundum (a fancy-coloured synthetic sapphire) has been produced, and also a peridot imitation based on the soudé emerald type of composite stone, the top and base being synthetic colourless spinel and the join across the girdle containing a suitable green colouring matter.

SPODUMENE

A gem which has a greater vogue in the North American continent, kunzite is an attractive stone of lilac-pink colour and was so named in honour of G. F. Kunz the American gem expert. Kunzite is one variety of the mineral species called spodumene, a mineral which also supplies gem material of yellow, yellowish-green and emerald-green colours.

The name spodumene is derived from the Greek meaning 'burnt to ashes', in allusion to the appearance of the crude non-gem crystals which often reach gigantic size. Such crystals are of value only as the source of lithium metal and its compounds.

The transparent gem crystals comprise the bluish or lilac-pink variety kunzite, the yellow and yellowish-green material for which no varietal name has been coined, and the rare emerald green coloured crystals which owe their hue to chromium. These are called hiddenite, after A. E. Hidden, the one-time superintendent of the mining company which operated the mine at North Carolina, U.S.A., where the bright green crystals are found. Unfortunately, the pale yellowish-green material found at other localities has been sold as hiddenite, but the colour of this material is nowhere near the lovely green of the true chromium-coloured hiddenite.

Chemical and Physical Properties

Spodumene crystallizes in the monoclinic system as flattened prisms characterized by vertical striations, and having an irregular capping reminiscent of mountain ranges (*Figure 7.7*). The crystals exhibit strong cleavage in two directions parallel to the prism faces making the cleavages nearly at right angles to one another. In composition spodumene is a lithium aluminium silicate and accords to the formula $LiAl(SiO_3)_2$. It is one of the few gemstones which contain lithium and on this account the green hiddenite has been called 'lithia emerald'.

The hardness of the gem is 7 on Mohs's scale and the density values lie between 3·17 and 3·19.

Effects of Light

The refractive indices approximate to 1·660 and 1·675 with a fairly constant double refraction of 0·015. The refraction is biaxial and positive in sign. The stones have a vitreous lustre and exhibit little fire, the dispersion between the B and G range being only 0·017. In kunzite and hiddenite the dichroism is marked, the trichroic colours being violet, deep violet and colourless, and bluish-green, emerald green and yellowish-green respectively. Pleochroism in the yellow and yellowish-green stones is weak.

In kunzite there is no absorption spectrum that can be seen clearly and used for identification; hiddenite, however, shows the typical absorption spectrum due to chromium. In the hiddenite spectrum the close doublet characteristic of the chromium spectrum is at 6905 and 6860 Å. Weaker lines in the red and orange are positioned at 6690 and 6460 Å, while the

PLATE XIV

Some rare stones

Fibrolite
(Mogok, Burma)
19·85 carats

Danburite
26·91 carats

Kunzite
(Pe de Espirito,
Governador Valadares,
Brazil)
50 carats

Orthoclase
feldspar

Zoisite
(Tanzanite)
21·34 carats

Brazilianite
(Mendes Pimental,
Conseilhero Pena,
Minas Gerais, Brazil)
25·93 carats

broad absorption is centred near **6200 Å**. There are no lines in the blue but a general absorption of the violet is present. The yellow and yellow-green spodumenes show in the spectrum a well-defined band in the blue at 4375 Å, which is in the same position as in another pyroxene mineral, jadeite. There is a weaker narrow band at 4330 Å. Both these bands are due to iron.

The behaviour of spodumene under invisible short-wave radiations is most striking. Kunzite shows a golden-pink or orange glow under long-wave ultra-violet light, and a similar but much weaker effect is seen under the short-wave ultra-violet lamp. Under an x-ray beam kunzite shows a very strong orange fluorescence with a strong and persistent afterglow. When the phosphorescence has died away the stone is found to have changed its

Figure 7.7. A typical crystal of kunzite from Madagascar

colour to a bluish-green; this remains stable provided that the stone is kept away from a strong light. This induced colour is discharged, with emission of luminescence (orange light), if the stone is exposed for some hours to strong sunlight, or to heating at about 200°C. The yellowish-green spodumene shows a weak orange-yellow fluorescent glow under the ultra-violet light, but this is extremely weak under the short-wave lamp. The glow is fairly strong under x-rays but, unlike kunzite, no phosphorescence seems to be present and there is no change of colour. The chromium-coloured hiddenite variety does not respond to ultra-violet light to any extent, but under x-rays a slight orange glow with some phosphorescence is seen.

Occurrences

The major localities for gem spodumene are in North and South America,

Madagascar and Burma. Non-gem spodumene has been known to mineralogists for over two hundred years, but gem quality material does not appear to have been discovered until about 1877, when it was reported that transparent yellow spodumene had been found in Minas Gerais, Brazil, and that this material had been sold as chrysoberyl.

About 1879 green and yellowish green crystals were found at Stony Point, Alexander County, North Carolina in the United States of America. First thought to be diopside, the crystals were later found to be spodumene, and as mentioned earlier, named hiddenite. The crystals range in colour from a rarely found colourless variety, through a light yellow to an emerald-green. They were first found, in a pitted condition, in association with true emerald, loose in the soil, but later perfect crystals were found attached to the veins of the wall rock. The deposit is said to be now completely worked out and the few stones cut from the crystals rarely exceed two carats in weight. A true hiddenite of pale colour but in large sizes has recently emanated from Brazil.

The first discovery of a lilac-coloured spodumene was at Branchville, Connecticut, U.S.A. during 1879, where much-altered crystals of spodumene were found to have transparent spots of amethystine-coloured material. The material from this deposit had no gem significance and was of mineralogical importance only. Over two decades went by before the finding of the lovely gemmy lilac-pink crystals of kunzite in California. This was during 1902 when kunzite was found in the White Queen mine on Heriart mountain in the Pala district of San Diego County, California. Since then much gem quality kunzite has been obtained from other mines on Heriart mountain and adjacent Chief mountain. The deposit spreads north-east into the adjacent Riverside County where kunzite has been found on Coahuila mountain. The crystals found in these localities are in pegmatite and are often much altered to clay pseudomorphs. Yellow and yellowish-green spodumene accompanies the bluish-pink kunzite. Magnificent kunzite is found in the Vanderberg, Katerina, San Pedro and Pala Chief mines in the Pala district of San Diego County, California.

Spodumene, in the varieties kunzite and greenish and yellowish colours, has been known in the island of Madagascar since the second decade of the present century. The crystals occur in pegmatite veins intersecting the archaean rocks, and in the alluvial derived from them, in the western part of the island. Kunzite, the most important of the varieties, is obtained from Anjanabonoina.

Since the earlier find of yellow spodumene in the State of Minas Gerais further pockets of gem quality spodumene have been discovered in the pegmatite veins of the gem-bearing localities of this Brazilian state. The material is mainly light yellow or pale green in colour. The main source of the bluish-pink kunzite, which was found some time before 1926, lies on the outskirts of Cuieté, a town alongside the Rio Doce river, not far from Governador Valadares. Yellow and green crystals, the latter classified locally as hiddenite—it is not the true hiddenite for it is not coloured by chromium— have been found in this same locality. Several of the pegmatites north of Governador Valadares have been worked for kunzite which is found with tourmaline, beryl and mica. An unusual two-colour material, in pleasing lilac and green, has been found at a mine located near Santa Maria de Suassui, and another pegmatite a few miles from Governador Valadares is said to have produced both light green and light blue spodumene. Spodumene has been reported from the Mogok Stone Tract of Upper Burma.

Cutting of Kunzite

Owing to the strong cleavage spodumene is a difficult stone to facet, and, further, owing to the thin nature of some of the crystals it is not possible to cut good coloured stones, for to get stones of good colour advantage should be taken of the strongest of the pleochroic colours. The deepest colour is seen approximately parallel to the length of the crystal, so for the best result the stones should be cut with the table facet at right angles to this direction. This is, of course, more important in the case of kunzite, which is usually cut very deep in order to further enhance the colour. Some kunzites have a tendency to fade on exposure to strong sunlight. Some yellowish-brown spodumenes turn purple after heat treatment.

Simulation

Kunzite is simulated by synthetic pink spinel and by a suitably coloured glass, but distinction is easy as both of these stones are singly refractive as against kunzite, in which the double refraction is strong enough for the doubling of the rear facet edges to be seen with a hand lens. Further, glass and spinel are not dichroic. What may be a more convincing simulator of kunzite is a bluish-pink amethyst, but even here, apart from the differences in the indices of refraction and density, the lustre of the amethyst is not nearly that of kunzite.

CHAPTER 8

THE GARNETS

To the average layman garnet is the name for a low-priced red gemstone, a gemstone which is cut as small stones fashioned as 'roses', as the Bohemian garnets which were so prominently used in Victorian jewellery; or stones cut with dome-shaped forms as in the so-called 'carbuncles'. Garnet is, however, a much more important gemstone than this; indeed, it may not be red in colour; orange and green coloured varieties supply important and valuable stones.

Garnet is really the name for a group of minerals all of which have a common crystal habit and some similarity of chemical composition. In fact there are six members of the family, only five of which have been used in jewellery. These are the iron-aluminium silicate garnet known as almandine (almandite); pyrope in which the iron is replaced by magnesium, and grossular which has calcium with the aluminium. The rare rich orange-coloured spessartite is a manganese-aluminium silicate, and andradite, which has the lovely green demantoid as a variety, is a calcium-iron silicate. The garnet group is completed by the calcium-chromium garnet uvarovite, the emerald-green crystals of which would make attractive gemstones if they were ever found in sufficient size to cut.

CHEMICAL AND PHYSICAL PROPERTIES

Garnets crystallize in the cubic system, the forms being the twelve-faced rhombic-dodecahedron and the twenty-four-faced icositetrahedron (trapezo-hedron), and combinations of these two forms (*Figure 8.1*). The hexoc-tahedral form is sometimes found in combination, but cubic and octahedral forms are rare. The crystals show no cleavage, but there is sometimes a rather distinct parting parallel to the dodecahedral face; the fracture is subconchoidal to uneven.

The general formula given for the chemical composition of the garnets accords to $R_3''R_2'''(SiO_4)_3$, or may be written as $3R''O,R_2'''O_3,3SiO_2$, where the divalent metal (R'') may be calcium, magnesium, ferrous iron or manganese; and the trivalent metal (R''') aluminium, ferric iron or chromium. The atoms (ions) of the metals in each group have relatively similar size and thus may interchange in any amount producing a series—an isomorphous series. Garnet may be considered as consisting of two such series: (*a*) pyrope-almandine-spessartite, often called the 'pyralspite series'; and (*b*) uvarovite-grossularite-andradite, called the 'ugrandite series', but even these two system may have slight miscibility with one another.

This intermixture of the chemical composition of the garnets is the reason for the wide variation encountered in the constants of the various types of garnet, and this may be expressed more fully by the schematic diagram devised by Marie-Therese Mackowsky (*Figure 8.2*).

This diagram shows the complicated connections between the pure end members grossular, andradite (melanite), almandine, pyrope, spessartite and uvarovite. To understand the diagram it should be explained that where the arrows extend the whole distance, as, for example, between pyrope and almandine, a so-called unbroken series of mixed crystals exists, and both the exchangeable groups (here FeO and MgO) can be present in any proportions. Such isomorphous mixed series are found first between

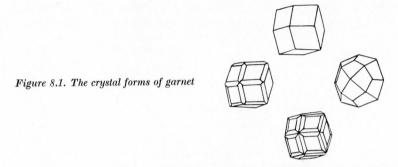

Figure 8.1. The crystal forms of garnet

pyrope and almandine, and secondly between almandine and spessartite, making these form a group in which it is always the divalent constituent which is interchangeable. In a similar manner grossular and andradite (melanite) can interchange, but in this case it is the trivalent constituents of the molecule which are miscible with one another in all proportions.

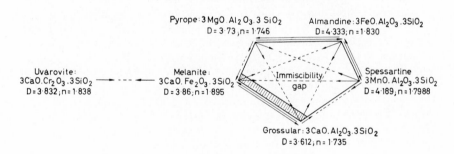

Pyrope: $3MgO.Al_2O_3.3SiO_2$
$D = 3.73; n = 1.746$

Almandine: $3FeO.Al_2O_3.3SiO_2$
$D = 4.333; n = 1.830$

Uvarovite:
$3CaO.Cr_2O_3.3SiO_2$
$D = 3.832; n = 1.838$

Melanite:
$3CaO.Fe_2O_3.3SiO_2$
$D = 3.86; n = 1.895$

Immiscibility gap

Spessartine
$3MnO.Al_2O_3.3SiO_2$
$D = 4.189; n = 1.7988$

Grossular: $3CaO.Al_2O_3.3SiO_2$
$D = 3.612; n = 1.735$

Figure 8.2. Schematic diagram of garnet families (after Mackowsky)

It is otherwise with the only partly extended arrows which link each type of garnet (with the exception of uvarovite which occupies a somewhat separate position) with all the others: that is, apart from the exceptional case where a variety occurs quite pure, a certain percentage of the other constituents is included. Even here an unbroken series is not possible, for after a certain percentage (about 10 per cent) the miscibility comes to an end, and there is the so-called immiscibility gap. A garnet which, for example, was located in the shaded portion of the diagram, would, in addition to its main components grossular and andradite (melanite), contain also a mixture of pyrope, almandine and spessartite, and under certain conditions even uvarovite. The same can be deduced for all garnets from the diagram.

The diagram is marked with the appropriate indices of refraction and densities, and the chemical composition of each of the end members. It will readily be understood that the refractive index and density of a given garnet will depend upon the proportions of the isomorphous mixture. It cannot be said with certainty, therefore, that a red garnet having a refractive index of 1·771 and a density of 3·911 will consist exactly of 30 per cent almandine and 70 per cent pyrope, since the presence of a small percentage of andradite will shift the proportions in favour of almandine, and the presence of grossular would produce a lowering effect on the values of the physical data.

Although garnets are, from their crystal structure, singly refractive, many garnets display local double refraction when examined between crossed 'polars' in a polarizing microscope. Usually this anomalous double refraction is confined to dark streaks, often in two directions at right angles, but some garnets show a convincing 'four times light and four times dark' during a complete revolution of the microscope stage carrying the stone. This optical anomaly is ascribed to stress due to the isomorphism, but as idocrase, a tetragonal mineral, has an atomic configuration similar to garnet, it might well be that at least some garnets are tetragonal in structure.

PYROPE GARNET

The pyrope garnet is usually blood-red in colour but this hue may be tinged with yellow or purple. The pyrope, if pure, would be colourless and have the formula $Mg_3Al_2(SiO_4)_3$, but the stones always have some iron and usually some chromium to which the red colour of the stones is due.

The theoretical values of density and refractive index for pure pyrope garnet are 3·51 and 1·705 respectively, but the lowest refractive index for pyrope as found in nature—and as a gemstone—is 1·730 and the density 3·65. From these limits the values rise with the increasing content of the almandine molecule, until what may be called almandine is reached. Thus there is a continuous series from pyrope to almandine, going through an intermediate series which for the sake of convenience is, in this book, made a separate group. The highest refractive index for the pyrope garnet may be said to be 1·75 and the density 3·80, but this division is quite arbitrary.

The fear that there may be difficulty in distinguishing between some low value pyrope garnets and the high value red spinels, not only on account of the overlap of refractive index, but for the reason that many bright red pyropes show a chromium absorption spectrum not very dissimilar to that of red spinel is not real. In practice no such difficulty arises as the red spinel fluoresces under ultra-violet light and pyrope garnet, owing to the iron it contains, does not. Further the absorption spectrum of red spinel shows the group of chromium emission lines in the deep red which are not seen in pyrope. The lowest density of pyrope is higher than the highest density for red spinel—3·65 as against 3·61 for red spinel.

The hardness of the pyrope variety of garnet is $7\frac{1}{4}$ on Mohs's scale and the dispersion (fire) is, for the B to G interval, 0·022.

The absorption spectrum of pyrope garnet which normally contains some, and often a considerable amount, of the almandine molecule which gives a red colour to the stone, may show the typical almandine garnet spectrum characterized by its three main bands centred at 5750, 5270 and 5050 Å. However, in the rich crimson stones, such as those from Czechoslovakia, Arizona, and Kimberley, there is a profound difference in the spectrum due to the trace of chromic oxide which gives to these pyropes their brighter colour. In such stones the chromium absorption spectrum becomes prominent and masks that of the ferrous iron, the almandine spectrum. This chromium absorption spectrum consists of a narrow and very weak doublet in the deep red at 6870 and 6850 Å. Other lines at 6710 and 6500 Å may be seen in exceptional stones. There is a broad absorption centred near 5700 Å which is nearly 1000 Ångströms wide and which covers two of the most prominent almandine bands, but allows the remaining almandine band at 5050 Å to be seen. It will be recalled that the centre of the broad absorption in the spectrum of red spinel is at 5400 Å. In common with all chromium spectra the violet end is absorbed beyond about 4400 Å.

Pyrope garnets are comparatively free from internal imperfections. Any inclusions are usually small rounded irregular crystals with a very low relief. E. Gübelin states that Bohemian garnets frequently contain quartz crystals, or crystals—possibly of augite—arranged in a circular pattern. Such a circular arrangement of inclusions is common in the 'snowball' garnets of Glen Calvie, Ross-shire, Scotland, where the phenomenon is said to indicate that the garnets have been rolled along by differential movement of the matrix of the rock during dynamothermal metamorphism, whilst the crystals were still in active growth. Some Arizona pyrope garnets have included needles and octahedral-shaped crystals.

Occurrences

The best known occurrence of pyrope garnet was in an area of some 27 square miles near Trebnitz in the north-eastern part of the old kingdom of Bohemia, now Czechoslovakia. The crystals, which are found in conglomerates, volcanic breccias and tuffs and in various alluvials derived from them, are fairly free from flaws but seldom show crystalline faces. These Bohemian pyropes gave rise to a considerable local cutting industry during the nineteenth century and this industry lasted until the finding of even better quality material in the diamond mines of South Africa. The stones are found in the kimberlite of the pipes and in the river gravels, the best pyrope being found in the De Beer's and Kimberley mines.

Pyrope garnet is found in many places in the United States of America, particularly in Arizona where the pebbles are excavated by ants digging their burrows and deposited by these small insects on their refuse mounds. Such a location is in the Navajo Reservation, Apache County.

Magnificent pyrope is said to have been found in Transbaikalia, Russia. Stones from this locality were brought to the market at old Ekaterinburg by an unknown Mongolian, but the actual source of the deposit is not known with any degree of certainty. Among the many other localities, world-wide in extent, where pyrope has been found, mention must be made of the Australian stones found some 12 miles from Bingara in the New

England district of New South Wales and Anakie and Ruby Vale in central Queensland. Other localities for pyrope garnet are the Shinyanga district of Tanzania; Burma; Rio Mina, Clavers in Cordoba and San Martin and Quines in San Luis, Argentina. In Brazil pyrope is found at Gravata and in the Mucuje and Utinga rivers.

PYROPE-ALMANDINE INTERMEDIATE SERIES

There is a range of garnets, blood-red, brownish-red to violet-red in colour, which can neither be termed pyrope nor almandine, but are intermediate between what can be called pyrope and the stones known as almandines. The index of refraction of this group may be said to range from 1·75 to 1·78 and the density between 3·80 and 3·95, but these limits are quite arbitrary.

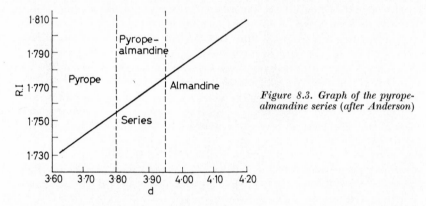

Figure 8.3. Graph of the pyrope-almandine series (after Anderson)

Attempts have been made to give a name to this intermediate group of garnets, but neither pyralmandite, proposed by L. Fermor, nor pyrandine, as suggested by B. W. Anderson, have met with universal acceptance—anyway these stones are quite correctly and unambiguously known as garnets to the jeweller. The graph (*Figure 8.3*) shows the relation to density of the refractive index of the pyrope-almandine isomorphous series and illustrates the suggested division between the groups.

In this group lies the lovely rhododendron-red garnet which has a density of 3·84 and an index of refraction of 1·76. Such stones are called rhodolite, after the colour, but the choice of name is not a happy one, for there could be confusion between it and the name rhodonite used for the manganese-silicate mineral which is used as an ornamental stone. It is usually stated that rhodolite garnet is found only at Cowee Creek, Mason Mount, Macon County, North Carolina in the United States of America, but stones of similar colour and physical and optical properties have been found in the Ceylon gem gravels.

The absorption spectrum shown by these intermediate garnets is the almandine type and due to ferrous iron, and it is because of this iron content that the red garnets do not respond with fluorescence when bathed in ultra-violet light. The stones show no dichroism, for in keeping with the crystal symmetry they are singly refractive, but anomalous double refraction is commonly seen when the stones are examined with polarized light.

The localities where these intermediate-type garnets are found are world-wide and conform to the geographical locations given for the almandine garnets.

ALMANDINE GARNET

Theoretically pure almandine, $Fe_3Al_2(SiO_4)_3$, should have a refractive index of 1·83 and a density of 4·25, but all the almandines of jewellery contain some of the pyrope molecule, and in addition grossular and spessartite are also present. So in practice garnets may be called almandine if they have a density higher than 3·95 and a refractive index greater than 1·78; that is over the values given for the intermediate group into which they merge.

The colour of almandine garnets is usually a darker and a more intense red and usually inclines more to a violet-red than is the case of the preceding groups. It is on account of their dark colour that many almandine garnets are fashioned in the cabochon form with the back hollowed out in order to decrease the thickness of the stone and hence lighten the colour. Such cabochon-cut stones are known as 'carbuncles', but the name has little significance for in olden days all red stones were termed 'carbuncles'.

The hardness of almandine is $7\frac{1}{2}$ on Mohs's scale and is therefore one of the hardest of the garnets. Of the optical properties which have so far not been given, the dispersion (fire) equals that of pyrope in having a value of 0·027 for the B to G interval. There is no dichroism, but again these garnets tend to exhibit an anomalous double refraction when viewed between crossed 'polars'.

The striking absorption spectrum of almandine garnet, which was first described by A. Church in 1866, provides a ready test for the almandine garnet. Ascribed to ferrous iron the spectrum consists of three main absorption bands centred at 5760 Å (in the yellow) and some 200 Ångströms broad, and two bands in the green at 5260 and 5050 Å which are near enough to each other to merge with one another in the case of deeply coloured almandines. There are several other bands in the complete spectrum but a weak broad band in the orange at 6170 Å and another in the blue at 4620 Å are usually clearly seen as 'outriders' to the main group of three bands. Other bands which have been measured in almandine garnet are at 4760, 4380, 4280, 4040 and 3930 Å, some of which can only be seen photographically, and all of which are too weak to affect the general appearances of the so-characteristic three (or five) band spectrum of the almandine garnet. These bands to a greater or lesser degree may be seen in all stones of the pyrope-almandine series.

Inclusions

The inclusions seen in almandine and garnets of the pyrope-almandine series consist of the following types. 'Zircon haloes', like those seen in Ceylon sapphires, occur in the Ceylon garnets (*Figure 8.4*). Another type consists of a number of dot-like crystals dispersed all over the stone. Some stones show a large number of lumpy crystals, many of which show crystal form (*Figure 8.5*) or as irregularly shaped 'lumps', the latter often in conjunction with the most common type of garnet inclusion, that of crossed needles (*Figure 8.6*). These needles which are usually in two directions with

139

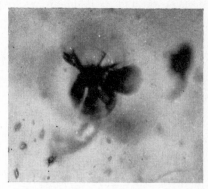

Figure 8.4. 'Zircon halo' in a Ceylon almandine garnet

mutual angles of about 110 degrees and 70 degrees may be likened to a coarse 'silk' as seen in ruby or sapphire (*Figure 8.7*). The almandines from Trincomalee in Ceylon, which are rather dull and lifeless stones, are seen to be densely packed with coarse hornblende rods.

The needle-like inclusions so common in almandine garnet are said, according to R. Brauns, to be an asbestos-like augite, and by E. J. Gübelin to be hornblende needles, and they usually run parallel to the edges of the dodecahedron. When such needle-like inclusions are thickly disseminated throughout the stone they may show a four-pointed star-effect when the stone is cabochon-cut. The asteria effect is weak and the star is never so pronounced as the six-rayed star seen in star-sapphires.

Occurrences

Almandine garnet is a mineral formed during the metamorphism of rocks and is commonly found in schists. The localities for almandine are world wide but gem quality material is more restricted in its location. India is one of the best known producers of almandine garnet, where it is obtained from the mica schist of Rajmahal in Jaipur State, the Sarwar district of Kishangarh State and the Ajmer-Merwara, all of which are in what used to be known as Rajputana; now there are no Indian States and Rajputana has

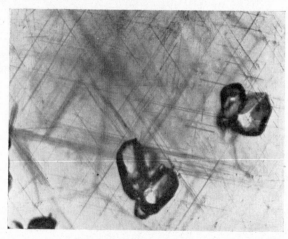

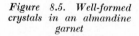

Figure 8.5. Well-formed crystals in an almandine garnet

PLATE XV

The Garnet group

Spessartite
(Pecos de Caballos,
Brazil)
8·00 carats

Demantoid,   Hessonite
3·80 carats   5·27 carats

Hessonite
15·44 carats

Almandine   Pyrope
10·08 carats   (Burma)
                                              8·80 carats

Almandine
(carbuncle)
11·07 carats

(Crown Copyright Geological Survey photograph. Reproduced by permission of the Controller of H.M.
Stationery Office)

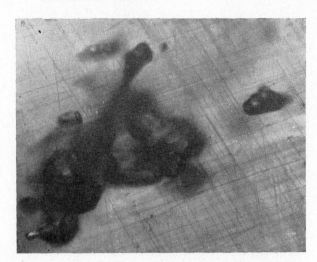

*Figure 8.6. Large ir-
regular lumpy crystals
and crossed needles in
an almandine garnet*

been renamed Rajasthan. Another Indian source is in the Warangal district
of Hyderabad. Some of the Indian garnet is asteriated and is the source of
most of the star-garnet. Almandine garnet is found at Trincomalee on the
north-east coast of Ceylon.

An almandine-pyrope garnet is found in the hornblende gneiss and the
gravels derived from it near Namaputa in the Lindi Province of Tanzania
and from Mazabika river in Zambia. In the island of Madagascar almandine-pyrope garnet is found at Fianarantsoa, Betroka, Ihosy, Fort-Dauphin,
Marolambo and near Ambositra.

In Central and South America almandine is found at Triunfo in Baja
(lower) California, and in Brazil at Sumaré and elsewhere in the State of
Rio de Janeiro; near Minas Novas in Minas Gerais; Gravata and the
Andarahy, Piabas and São Antonio rivers of Bahia; Santa Rita and Canta-
gallo in Rio Grande do Sul, and the Mucujé and Utinga rivers.

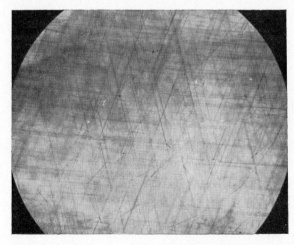

*Figure 8.7. Hornblende
needles are a common in-
clusion in almandine gar-
net and when thickly dis-
seminated through the stone
may produce asterism (star-
effect)*

Almandine and almandine-pyrope garnets are found in many states of the North American continent, particularly at Emerald Creek, Latah County, and Lewiston, Nez Perce County in Idaho, in which localities some of the garnet exhibits asterism (star-effect). Almadine, some of gem quality, is found in the mica schist and the gravels derived from it on the Skeena and Stickeen of British Columbia, and at Alert Harbour and Garnet Island in Baffin Island, Canada.

Gem quality almandine has been obtained from the Zillerthal in the Austrian Tyrol, and much garnet is found in Scotland, but it is rarely fit for cutting into gems, indeed, the non-gem almandines are opaque black or brown in colour.

Cutting of Almandine Garnet

Almandine garnet is usually faceted in the mixed-cut style, or, for important stones, in the trap-cut style (emerald cut); the older cabochon cut is now rarely used except in the case of star-garnets. Much poorly transparent or flawed material, particularly in the U.S.A. (Idaho garnets), is polished by the tumbling process as baroque (irregular) stones. This type of poor garnet is occasionally polished and drilled as beads and strung as necklets. Indeed some of the more lustrous garnet crystals are drilled without any polishing being done to them.

SPESSARTITE

The colour of this rather rare garnet ranges from yellowish-orange to aurora-red or brownish-red. Many of the stones have a somewhat similar appearance and colour to hessonite garnets, which is the transparent gem variety of the grossular garnet group, and thus spessartite garnets may be mistaken for them.

The formula for pure spessartite is $Mn_3Al_2(SiO_4)_3$, but usually some of the manganese is replaced by ferrous oxide (FeO), and some of the aluminium by ferric oxide (Fe_2O_3). To illustrate this replacement the spessartite garnet formula (as it could for any garnet if the appropriate symbols are used) may be written as $3MnO,Al_2O_3,3SiO_2$, when the replacement may be better understood. The hardness of spessartite is $7\frac{1}{4}$ on Mohs's scale; the density having the small range from 4·12 to 4·20, and the refractive index lies between 1·79 and 1·81. The dispersion is 0·027 for the B to G interval.

The absorption spectrum of spessartite has a practical value in identifying the stone. The spectrum, due to manganese in the manganous, or divalent, state, consists of weak bands at 4950, 4890 and 4620 Å. These are followed by a very strong band at 4320 Å and others at 4240 and 4120 Å which is very intense, but these last two bands may be somewhat masked by the general gloom of the violet end of the spectrum which is to some extent absorbed. The 'key' bands of the spectrum are the 4320 Å line and the intense, 4120 Å line if it can be seen. These two bands are important for the other bands may well be masked, or confused, by the bands of the almandine garnet spectrum which is universally present.

Manganese, at least in traces, in many minerals acts as an activator of luminescence, but despite the manganese in spessartite garnet there is no fluorescence shown by the stones when under a beam of ultra-violet light or x-rays. This is most probably due to either the manganese being in too great a concentration or, perhaps more likely, to the poisoning of the luminescence by the iron of the almandine molecule which always replaces some of the manganese.

The inclusions seen in spessartite garnet are to some extent typical of the variety. They consist of wavy feathers, formed by minute liquid drops, and have a peculiar 'shredded' appearance which has been likened to a Mantilla shawl.

Spessartite, and it is often known under the French form spessartine, was first found at Aschaffenburg in the Spessart district of Bavaria, hence the name, but the occurrence appears to have had no gem significance. The Italian localities San Piero in Campo, Alba, and St. Marcel in Piedmont are not known as gem producers, indeed most of the localities given for spessartite supply crystals which are too small for stones to be cut from them. Gem spessartite has been obtained from that prodigious source the Ceylon and Burma gem gravels, and clear orange crystals of a size suitable for cutting are found at Tsilaizina, near Antsirabe in Madagascar. This garnet is found, too, in New South Wales, and in Norway.

Gemmy spessartite is found at Arassuahy and Registo and in the gravels of the Santa Maria and Abaete rivers of Brazil. The mineral is found in large masses, though rather too dark to cut any but small stones, at Ceara in the north of Brazil. There are a number of sources of spessartite in the United States of America, the most prominent and best known being the Rutherford mines at Amelia, Amelia County, Virginia, and several mines near Ramona, San Diego County, California. According to R. M. Pearl, tiny perfect crystals of spessartite have been found in cavities in three volcanic hills at Nathrop, Colorado. An interesting occurrence was found during the diggings for the foundations of West 179th Street, Manhattan Island, New York City. A few small stones were cut from the material recovered from this site.

GROSSULAR GARNET

The name grossular is little known in the jewellery trade for the title is the mineralogical name for the calcium-aluminium group of garnets, which, if pure, would have the formula $Ca_3Al_2(SiO_4)_3$. Most of the grossular garnet is found as opaque pale green or rose-red crystals which have no importance in jewellery. There are, however, three varieties of grossular which take a place in ornamentation. The most important of these are the yellow and orange stones which to jewellers go under the name hessonite, or as it is sometimes mis-spelled 'essonite'.

Hessonite Garnet

The hessonite garnets, which in colour vie with spessartite, vary from a brownish-yellow, through a brownish-orange to aurora-red. The stones have a hardness of about $7\frac{1}{4}$ on Mohs's scale and a density approximating to 3·65. The single refractive index varies from 1·742 to 1·748, and the stones have a dispersion of 0·027 between the B to G interval. Hessonite garnet does not

143

show a characteristic absorption spectrum, but may show, due to the inclusion of some of the almandine molecule, a slight trace of the almandine spectrum. Hessonites, which are sometimes known as 'cinnamon stones' and are said to appear more fiery in artificial light than in daylight, do not exhibit luminescence when under the excitation of ultra-violet light or x-rays.

The internal structures shown by hessonites when they are examined microscopically, or even by a hand lens, are so pronounced as to be characteristic for the gem. The stones show a granular appearance due to the inclusion of many small transparent crystals having rounded outlines or a fused appearance, and which are often accompanied by peculiar treacly streaks which give to the stone's interior an oily appearance (*Figure 8.8*). The included shapeless crystals are said, by E. Gübelin, to be either diopside or zircon, the latter showing well-marked relief while the diopside crystals, which have an index of refraction near to the garnet, show only low relief.

Hessonite garnet is common in the gem gravels of Ceylon and practically all the gem material is obtained from this locality. Some hessonite is found in the Minas Gerais district of Brazil, and a brownish-green grossular garnet is found in fine crystals in the Vilui river, a tributary of the great Lena river of Siberia, but it is doubtful if these crystals are cut as gemstones. Hessonite is found at a number of places in the United States of America, and at Asbestos, Quebec, Canada.

An unusual clear yellow grossular garnet was found to have a refractive index of 1·734 and a density of 3·604. It had an orange fluorescence and phosphorescence under x-rays and a much weaker but similar fluorescence under ultra-violet light.

Massive Hydrogrossular Garnet

The second variety of grossular garnet which needs to be mentioned is the massive variety. The most important of the massive grossular is the green coloured material which is found in the Transvaal, and which has been marketed under the erroneous name 'Transvaal jade' (Plate XIX). The material is found on Buffelsfontein and the adjoining farm of Turffontein, which are some 40 miles west of Pretoria in almost featureless country belonging to the norite margin of the Bushveld. While the best and most commonly used material is a bright green in colour, some of the material is greyish or bluish, and some pink. It differs from true grossular in having an OH group in its chemical composition.

In general appearance the material is a homogeneous compact rock in which no minerals are recognizable. The texture is horny and the fracture somewhat conchoidal or splintery with a waxy lustre. The rock contains black specks which have been identified as magnetite although some chromite may be present. The colour of the green material is reported as due to chromium and the pink to manganese.

In a study of these garnet rocks, A. L. Hall mentions that the green and pure pink material are nearly pure garnet, but that the grey-coloured rock contains up to 25 per cent of zoisite. Hall states that the origin of the rock is not certain, but that there is some ground for regarding the rock as xenoliths of garnet hornstone derived from an original aluminous calcareous sediment by contact metamorphism combined with metasomatism.

The refractive index of the massive material, for only a diffuse shadow edge can be seen on the refractometer, approximates to 1·72, a value lower than for the hessonites. The density ranges from 3·36 to 3·55, the pink material varying from 3·36 to 3·41 and the green 'Transvaal jade' from 3·42 to 3·55. Except for the possibility of a weak chromium spectrum showing in the case of the green material, the absorption spectra of the massive grossularites show little that would aid in their identification. While the material does not exhibit any luminescent glow when irradiated with ultra-violet light, a strong orange-yellow light is seen when the material is placed

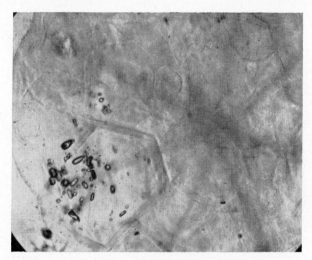

Figure 8.8. Characteristic 'eroded' crystals, probably in this case of zircon, and the peculiar oily streaks often called 'treacle' seen in a hessonite garnet

in a beam of x-rays. This x-ray luminescence is, in the case of the green material, most useful, for neither jadeite nor nephrite, nor any other jade simulant, exhibits this glow which is thus diagnostic.

A crystalline, massive form of grossularite—probably similar to the so-called 'Transvaal jade' of South Africa—occurs in the Whitehorse Copper Belt, Yukon, Canada, and a number of occurrences of massive green grossularite are reported from California and other states of the North American continent. Massive white grossularite has been found with jadeite in Burma, and has been carved by the Chinese.

Grossular garnet has a great similarity in its chemistry and structure with the mineral idocrase and a mixture of these two minerals can, and does, occur. This does pose problems in nomenclature, but if it can be shown by density and absorption spectrum that it is mainly grossular or mainly idocrase, then the specimen can fairly be called the name of the main constituent. Intermediate types should be described as grossular-idocrase integrowths. Such material has emanated from Pakistan and California; and probably Southern Africa.

145

During 1965/66 several transparent green stones, presumably from Pakistan, were identified as being a green grossular garnet. One stone was found to have a density of 3·62 and refractive index of 1·742, whilst three others had values of 3·63 and 1·738. The absorption spectrum showed lines at 6970 Å with weaker lines in the orange; a pronounced line at 6300 Å and diffuse lines at 6050 Å and 5050 Å. Similar material seems to have been reported from Zambia.

Marble Type of Grossular Garnet

The third type of grossular garnet to be mentioned might well have been discussed with the marbles, for strictly that is what it is. The material consists of dodecahedral crystals of pink grossular garnet in a matrix of white marble (*Figure 8.9*). The rock comes from Xalostoc, Morelos, Mexico,

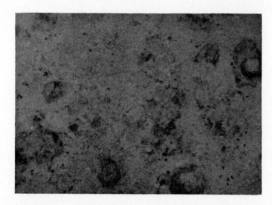

Figure 8.9. Xalostocite: dodeca-hedra of pink grossularite in white marble

and has been variously called landerite (after Carlos F. de Landers), xalostocite (after the locality), or rosolite (after its colour). The irregular disposition of the large size garnets in the calcite matrix precludes any value in suggesting constants for this material, for they would be far too variable for diagnostic purposes. The very appearance of the marble would identify the specimen for what it is.

ANDRADITE GARNET

Usually called the common garnet, andradite has two varieties which have been used in jewellery. They are the opaque black melanite which has been cut for mourning jewellery, and the lovely transparent green demantoid which is one of the rarest and most highly prized of all the garnets.

In composition pure andradite is a calcium-iron-silicate with the formula $Ca_3Fe_2(SiO_4)_3$, but partial replacement of the calcium by magnesium and manganese, and the iron by aluminium is universal. The beautiful demantoid garnet owes its attractive green colour to replacement by a trace of chromic oxide.

The black melanite crystals are usually well-formed combinations of the rhombic dodecahedron and the icositetrahedron; they may have a density rising to 3·90, and a refractive index of 1·89. The high density and the negative reading shown when the stones are tested on a standard refractometer will distinguish such black garnets from black tourmaline, black-stained chalcedony, or black glass, all of which have been used for mourning jewellery. Black andradite garnet is found on Monte Somma, Vesuvius and the Trentino in Italy. It is also found near Barèges in the Hautes-Pyrénées of France, and in many other localities.

The important green andradite garnet called demantoid, so named from its adamantine lustre, suffers from the defect of the low hardness of andradite, which is only $6\frac{1}{2}$ on Mohs's scale. The density varies from 3·82 to 3·85, and the single refractive index from 1·888 to 1·889. The colour dispersion of demantoid is 0·057 for the B to G interval, thus the stones have a greater fire than diamonds, but the effect is to some extent masked by the body colour of the stone. It was first found, in Russia, in 1868.

Demantoid garnets show reddish when viewed through the Chelsea colour filter, and the stones are characterized by an absorption spectrum consisting of a strong band at 4430 Å, which generally appears as a cut-off owing to the general obscurity of the violet end of the spectrum and only in the paler stones can any violet light be seen beyond this band. This band is due to iron (ferric oxide) which to some extent gives the green colour to the stone, but iron greens are dull greens and the bright green of demantoid is caused, as mentioned earlier, by the trace of chromium. Therefore, in fine demantoids a chromium absorption spectrum may be seen, the lines being the strong doublet near 7010 Å, a weak but sharp line at 6930 Å and two bands in the orange at 6400 and 6220 Å which are vaguer and broader than usual in chromium spectra. Demantoid does not exhibit any luminescence under ultra-violet light or x-rays.

The internal features of demantoid are characteristic inclusions of byssolite (asbestos) fibres with a radiating arrangement or as 'horse-tails' (*Figure 8.10*). Such inclusions are diagnostic for demantoid for they are not seen in any other green stone.

The Ural mountains of Russia are the main source of gem demantoid, the

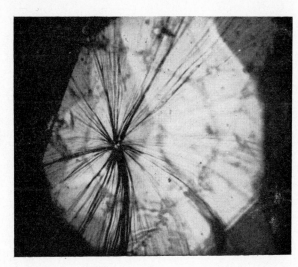

Figure 8.10. Radiating or 'horse-tail' inclusions which consist of asbestos fibres are a characteristic of demantoid garnet

(By courtesy of V. G. Hinton)

stones being found on both the European and the Asiatic sides of the range. The finest examples are found in the gold washings of Nizhne-Tagilsk in the Sissertsk district and in serpentine beside the Bobrovka tributary of the Chusovaya river. Demantoid has been found in the Congo.

A yellow andradite garnet, to which the name topazolite has been applied, is found in crystals too small for faceting into gems in the Ala valley, Piedmont, Italy, and at Zermatt, Switzerland. The use of the name topazolite for this colour variety is open to objection and it is suggested that the name be forgotten, and that if any cut gems do turn up they should be called yellow demantoid.

An andradite of an unattractive yellowish-green colour is obtained from Stanley Buttes, Arizona, and has sometimes been cut as cabochon stones.

UVAROVITE GARNET

The chromium-calcium garnet, $Ca_3Cr_2(SiO_4)_3$, would provide a valuable addition to the green gemstones were there available crystals sufficiently large to cut. Coloured by chromium which is an inherent part of the composition, the stone has the fine bright green colour which chromium gives to a mineral. The hardness of the crystals is $7\frac{1}{2}$ on Mohs's scale and the density is 3·77. The refractive index is 1·87 which is near to that of demantoid. The small crystals are found in association with chromite in serpentine, or occurring in granular limestone, in the Ural mountains, particularly at Saranovskaya near Bisersk and in the vicinity of Kyshtymsk, north-east of Zlatoust. Jordansmühl in Silesia, the Himalayas and the Pyrenees are other localities where the uvarovite garnet is found and there is considerable uvarovite found with chromite in California.

An emerald-green chrome garnet near uvarovite in composition is found at Orford, Sherbrooke County, Quebec, but again the crystals are far too small to be of value as gemstones.

CHAPTER 9

MOONSTONE AND OTHER FELDSPAR GEMSTONES

CHEMICAL AND PHYSICAL PROPERTIES

The feldspar, sometimes written as felspar, group of minerals are important for the place they take in the formation of rocks, but several varieties of the various groups supply gem materials, the most important of which is the lovely moonstone.

The feldspars, which are all closely allied in form and habit as well as in the mode of their occurrence, are aluminous silicates of potassium, sodium, calcium, or barium, but are practically without magnesium or iron. They are usually divided into four subgroups. (1) orthoclase and microcline (potassium aluminium silicate); (2) albite (sodium aluminium silicate); (3) anorthite (calcium aluminium silicate); and (4) celsian (barium aluminium silicate), this last having no interest to the student of gemmology.

Orthoclase and microcline give the gemstones moonstone and amazonite respectively, while the albite and anorthite produces by isomorphous replacement a series—the plagioclase series—in which occur a number of gem or ornamental minerals. The hardness of the mineral is about 6 on Mohs's scale, and the crystals, which are monoclinic in orthoclase and celsian and triclinic in the plagioclases, have two directions of easy cleavage which are nearly at right angles to one another. The angle does, however, vary somewhat in the different varieties. The measurement of these angles aids the petrographer and the mineralogist in their work of identification of the feldspars, but these 'cleavage angles' are of less importance to the gemmologist who approaches the problems of identity in a different manner. For a clearer understanding of the feldspars the different groups of the family which have varieties useful as gem minerals need to be discussed separately.

ORTHOCLASE

The monoclinic potash feldspar, $KAlSi_3O_8$, known as orthoclase, is transparent and colourless in its purest form and such material, called adularia, is found in small crystals in the locality of the St. Gotthard in Switzerland, but is of no gem significance. The crystals of orthoclase often exhibit, in the opaque non-gem material, one of three types of twinning, but as the gemmy material is so rarely found as euhedral (well formed) crystals, their discussion is not warranted here. Green, orange and yellow stones are found.

The important orthoclase gem is moonstone (Plate XIX), a gem which is characterized by the beautiful blue schiller shown by the better quality specimens. This lovely sheen, termed adularescence, is due to a peculiarity

in the structure whereby an intimate combination of orthoclase and albite
—one end member of the plagioclase series—are arranged in layers. Light
reflected from these layers, if they are not too thick, produces by interference effects the blue schiller. If the layers are thick the sheen is white and the
stone far less attractive. It must be pointed out that in order to obtain the
best effect it is necessary for the stone to be cut so that the plane of the base
of the cabochon lies parallel to the plane of the layers.

The density of moonstone varies from 2·56 to 2·59. Indian stones give the
higher values between 2·58 and 2·59 while the stones from other localities,
particularly those of Ceylon, give values below 2·58 and are generally
nearer to 2·56. The hardness of orthoclase is 6, orthoclase having been
selected by Mohs for the standard 6 on his scale. The refractive indices are,
for the greatest and least indices, 1·525 and 1·520 respectively. The double
refraction is 0·005 and is negative in sign. Orthoclase has a vitreous lustre
which may be pearly on cleavage surfaces, and the fire is small, the dispersion measured between the B to G interval being only 0·012. There is no
characteristic absorption spectrum to be observed in moonstone, but the
luminescent glows shown by the gem—under long-wave ultra-violet light
there is generally a bluish glow of weak intensity, or may be no glow; under
the short-wave lamp there is a weak orange glow; and under x-rays a whitish
to violet glow—may have some value in distinguishing moonstone from its
simulants.

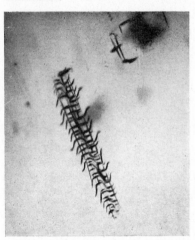

Figure 9.1. Stress cracks producing a pseudo-
insect seen in a moonstone
(By courtesy of the Journal of Gemmology)

Inclusions

The inclusions seen in moonstone are often characteristic and usually
consist, especially in Ceylon stones, of peculiar straight lath-like cracks
which run parallel to the vertical axis of the crystal. From these cracks,
which are most often in pairs or multiple, numerous branching cracks extend for a short distance in the direction of the 'b' axis, after which they
taper off in an oblique direction. Such 'stress cracks' may appear like
grotesque insects of the centipede type (*Figures 9.1* and *9.2*).

Another kind of inclusion, which may be just a modification of the
stress crack type, appears to have the main body of the crack in the form

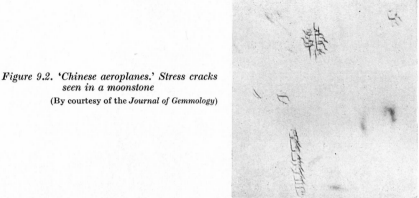

*Figure 9.2. 'Chinese aeroplanes.' Stress cracks
seen in a moonstone*
(By courtesy of the *Journal of Gemmology*)

of a cavity or negative crystal (*Figure 9.3*), while some Burma stones may show oriented needles (*Figure 9.4*); a profusion of such needles may well be the cause of the cat's-eye effect seen in some moonstones.

Occurrences

The most important source of moonstone is Ceylon, where the mineral with either a white or blue 'flash' occurs in peculiar adularia-leptynite dykes at Weeragoda near Ambalangoda in the Southern Province; and in the Dumbara and Kandy districts of Central Province. Water-worn pebbles, probably derived from the dykes, are found in the gem gravels in the southern part of the island. The mineral is also found in the Coimbatore district of Madras, India, and the material from this locality is characterized by variations in body colour from white to reddish-brown or plum-blue. Other localities are Madagascar, Burma, Tanzania and at a number of

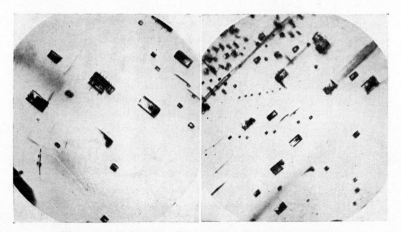

Figure 9.3. Stress cracks like negative cavities in a moonstone
(By courtesy of the *Journal of Gemmology*)

places in North America, particularly in the States of Colorado, Indiana, New Mexico, New York, North Carolina, Pennsylvania, Virginia and Wisconsin. A green moonstone comes from India.

Synthesis and Simulation

The major imitations of moonstone, apart from a very unconvincing glass, are the synthetic white spinels which have been schillerized by secondary heating, and by a similarly heat-treated amethyst. A white

Figure 9.4. Oriented needles in a moonstone
(By courtesy of the *Journal of Gemmology*)

chalcedony which shows a pale blue-moon effect when cut cabochon has been miscalled 'moonstone'.

Yellow Variety of Orthoclase

A transparent clear pale yellow to golden yellow variety of orthoclase, which is rich in iron, emanates from the pegmatites at Itrongay, Madagascar. The crystals are found loose in the soil surmounting the weathered part of the pegmatite and they are usually broken or with their faces corroded and dull. The stones faceted from this yellow orthoclase have a vogue with collectors. The density of this type of orthoclase, the colour of which is due to the iron it contains, is 2·56, which is quite a normal value, but the indices of refraction are slightly higher, the least and the greatest indices being 1·522 and 1·527 respectively. The double refraction of 0·005 is, the same as that for the normal type of orthoclase.

The yellow orthoclase shows an absorption spectrum, due to iron, which consists of two broad and diffuse bands in the blue and violet. These are a weak band at 4480 Å and a stronger band centred at 4200 Å. There is a further strong band in the near ultra-violet at 3750 Å, but this can only be observed photographically. The Madagascan yellow orthoclase shows a weak reddish-orange glow under both long-wave and short-wave ultra-violet light, and a similar and stronger glow under x-rays. An unusual yellow orthoclase from Burma, which showed a cat's-eye effect, behaved similarly except that the glow under x-rays was more yellow in hue.

The glassy straw yellow variety of orthoclase called sanidine has been cut for the whim of collectors.

MICROCLINE

The only gem variety of microcline feldspar is the verdigris-green to blue-green coloured material to which the name amazonite or amazonstone is applied (Plate XIX). Microcline has the same chemical composition as orthoclase, namely, potassium aluminium silicate and accords to the formula $KAlSi_3O_8$. The mineral differs from orthoclase in forming triclinic crystals, but the inclination of the third axis is very small and thus the crystals of amazonite strongly resemble those of orthoclase. Indeed, it is from this very small change of angle to the triclinic system of crystallization that the mineralogical name microcline is derived.

Microcline occurs in translucent to opaque well-formed crystals (*see* Plate XX), or as massive material of greyish-white, flesh to brown-red or green in colour. It is the bright verdigris-green to blue-green material that is alone used as a gem material for beads and cabochon-cut stones, but the material is not suitable for carving owing to the easy cleavages.

Like all feldspars, microcline has two directions of good cleavage and this constitutes a danger in fashioned material which may break with some facility along these directions if the stones be carelessly handled. Incipient cleavage cracks give polished surfaces a shimmering effect due to reflections from these cracks, and this is very evident when the stone is rotated. This effect and the mottled texture readily differentiates amazonstone from other green ornamental minerals.

Amazonstone is usually slightly harder than orthoclase and may reach nearly $6\frac{1}{2}$ on Mohs's scale. The density varies from 2·56 to 2·58, and the material, which is optically negative in sign, has for the greatest and least indices of refraction values of 1·522 and 1·530, values which are slightly higher than for orthoclase. The birefringence is 0·008. Microcline, or rather the amazonite variety, shows no distinctive absorption spectrum. The material usually shows a yellowish-green glow under long-wave ultra-violet light, is inert under the short-wave lamp, and exhibits a weak green glow with a fairly long afterglow when irradiated with x-rays.

The green microcline feldspar owes its varietal name, amazonstone, to the Amazon river, but although the mineral is found in Brazil it is not known to come from the vicinity of the Amazon. Green microcline is found in the pegmatite veins of Sao Miguel de Piracicaba and from Joahyma and in the region of Ferros in the State of Minas Gerais.

The most important sources of the mineral at present are the Kashmir district and elsewhere in India. In the United States of America a good quality amazonite was at one time mined at Amelia Court House, Virginia, but the mine is now closed as the best quality material has been worked out. The most important North American locality is in Colorado where the mineral is found in well-formed crystals in scattered pegmatite pockets in a schist near Crystal Peak and at Pikes Peak. The green mineral is found in the Renfrew and Parry Sound districts of Ontario, Canada, and one of the earlier sources, and probably mined today, is near Miask on the eastern side of Lake Ilmen and in the Ural mountains of Russia. It is found in these localities mainly in the form of compact masses. Amazonstone is also found in several of the pegmatites of Madagascar, notably around Anjanabonoina, Andina, Imody and Mahabe. Recently amazonite of good green colour has been found in the Sahara desert and in Tanzania; Kipewa, Quebec and southern Africa.

PERTHITE

Perthite, which owes its name to the town of Perth, Ontario, Canada, where it was first found, consists of an intergrowth of albite or oligoclase in orthoclase or microcline. The component minerals are miscible at high temperatures but on cooling are thrown out of solution producing an inter-laminated intergrowth of different feldspars.

Suitably cut this material makes a handsome ornamental stone exhibiting a rich golden labradorescence against a flesh-red to reddish-brown, or white background. Perthite is found in large masses at Dungannon, Hastings County and in the Nipissing district of Ontario, and also in a number of localities in Quebec.

PLAGIOCLASE FELDSPARS

It has already been mentioned that the plagioclase feldspars, known also as the soda-lime feldspars, constitute an isomorphous series between albite, the sodium aluminium silicate, $NaAlSi_3O_8$, and anorthite, the calcium aluminium silicate, $CaAl_2Si_2O_8$. The mineralogist has applied various names to minerals falling into certain positions in the series and in Table 9.1 is shown these subvarieties and the range of composition of each.

TABLE 9.1

The Plagioclase Feldspars—Range and Composition

Albite	90 to 100 per cent albite with 0 to 10 per cent anorthite
Oligoclase	70 to 90 per cent albite with 10 to 30 per cent anorthite
Andesine	50 to 70 per cent albite with 30 to 50 per cent anorthite
Labradorite	30 to 50 per cent albite with 50 to 70 per cent anorthite
Bytownite	10 to 30 per cent albite with 70 to 90 per cent anorthite
Anorthite	0 to 10 per cent albite with 90 to 100 per cent anorthite

In these groups are certain feldspars which have a value as gem materials, and for convenience these particular minerals will be discussed separately. However, the characters of this feldspar series—all members of which crystallize in the triclinic system not necessarily as good crystals but usually as crystalline masses—must first be given. The plagioclases, especially the oligoclase (sunstone) and labradorite, exhibit repeated twinning giving fine lamellae which appear on the basal cleavage surfaces as fine striations

Figure 9.5. The striations seen on the basal cleavage face of sunstone due to repeated twinning

(*Figure 9.5*). The refractive indices and density increase from albite with a density of 2·605 and refractive indices α 1·525, β 1·529 and γ 1·536 to anorthite which has a density of 2·765 and indices of refraction α 1·576, β 1·584 and γ 1·588. The optical orientation of the plagioclases also changes with composition and this affects the optical sign which alters in different subvarieties. The variation in density, refractive indices and optical sign are shown in the graph (*Figure 9.6*).

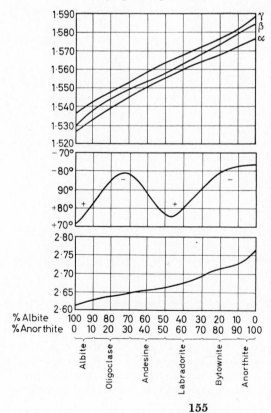

Figure 9.6. Graph showing the relation of optical sign, refractive indices and density for the various percentage compositions of the plagioclase feldspar series

155

Albite

The albite variety of feldspar also produces a moonstone, the so-called albite moonstone, but the variety is not at all common. One type is called peristerite, sometimes known as 'pigeon stone'. Peristerite is an ornamental feldspar with a white, cream, fawn or brownish-pink body colour showing a celestial-blue flash of iridescence or play of colour. A sample of this variety gave a density of 2·617 and an index of refraction near 1·54. The mineral showed a very weak brownish glow under both ranges of ultra-violet light, and a weak glow of indeterminate colour with a persistent afterglow when the stone was irradiated by x-rays.

The most beautiful peristerite is said to be found at Monteagle, Hastings County, Ontario, and this material has been fashioned into beads and cabochon stones. An ivory-white peristerite is found in some quantity in the Villeneuve mine, Labelle County and at Buckingham, Quebec. Other Canadian sources are at Bathurst, Lanark County, near the mouth of Eel Creek, on the north shore of Stony Lake, Burleigh, and at Bromley, Renfrew County, Ontario.

A transparent feldspar, nearly colourless with a tinge of blue or yellow, has been cut from material found in Kenya. The mineral is an albite/oligoclase and a specimen gave values of refractive indices of α 1·535, β 1·539 and γ 1·544, the density being 2·63. The material showed a faint whitish glow under long-wave ultra-violet light, was inert under the short-wave lamp and under x-rays exhibited a bright lime-green glow with a persistent phosphorescence of similar hue.

Oligoclase

The gem mineral of the oligoclase variety of feldspar is sunstone, or as it is sometimes known aventurine feldspar (Plate XIX), a mineral which owes its attractiveness to the inclusions of red and orange, and occasionally green, microscopically thin platy crystals of goethite or hematite or both which are disseminated in parallel orientation through the near colourless oligoclase matrix (*Figure 9.7*), and which gives to the mineral a rich golden or reddish-brown colour and specular reflections.

The density of sunstone varies from 2·62 to 2·65, the most common value being near 2·64, and the least and greatest indices of refraction are near 1·54 and 1·55. The mineral is for practical purposes inert under ultra-violet light but shows a whitish glow when irradiated with x-rays.

The source of the best sunstone is at Tvedestrand and Hiterö on the south coast of Norway, where the mineral is found as irregular masses in veins of white quartz traversing gneiss. Another locality is at Verkhne Udinsk on the Selenga river near Lake Baikal in Russia. Sunstone is found in several places near the contact of the Bancroft sodalite and nephelene syenite in Hastings County, Ontario, and there are other Canadian localities in Lanark, Renfrew and Haliburton Counties of Ontario. Sunstone of a brownish-pink colour is found in a pegmatite dyke east of the French river on the north-east side of Lake Huron, and from Kangayam, southern India.

In the United States of America sunstone is found in the States of Maine,

New Mexico, New York, North Carolina, Pennsylvania and Virginia, but the localities are relatively unimportant.

Figure 9.7. Platy crystals of hematite or goethite are responsible for the golden colour and reflective iridescence of sunstone

Some aventurine feldspar or sunstone may be adularia (orthoclase) with included platelets of hematite, and the so-called spangled sunstone from Modoc County, California, is now stated to be labradorite with coppery inclusions of goethite.

About 1887 a clear colourless to pale green variety of oligoclase was found at the Hawk mica mine near Bakersville, North Carolina, and from this material some faceted stones were cut. No information as to the properties have been given but from the description of the mineral it may well be similar to the Kenya albite/oligoclase which was mentioned under albite.

Andesine

During 1967 a massive green material, somewhat resembling jade, was determined as andesine feldspar by American workers.

Labradorite

The member of the plagioclase group known as labradorite is noted for the brilliant play of colour which flashes out over large areas of the grey-coloured mineral (Plate XIX). This play of colour, or schiller, is only seen on the more easy of the two cleavage surfaces, or on polished surfaces nearly parallel to this plane. The most beautiful colours which flash out from the grey-coloured labradorite are blues and greens which rival the iridescence seen on the wings of some tropical butterflies. Yellows, gold, reds, and purple are some of the other colours shown by specimens of labradorite.

The optical effect which produces these brilliant colours on the otherwise grey material is mostly due to interference of light from the fine lamellae of the repeated twinning, to which must be added some colour effects produced by the platy inclusions which probably give to labradorite the grey colour. These platelets, which are said to be the iron oxide magnetite, are accompanied by profuse needle-like inclusions (*Figure 9.8*). Like the hematite inclusions in sunstone these magnetite platelets may also produce flashes of coloured light due, like the schiller, to interference effects. Some labradorite does, indeed, have hematite inclusions like sunstone and thus produce an aventurescent labradorite. A colourless labradorite darkened by

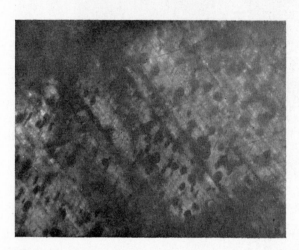

Figure 9.8. Magnetite platelets and needle inclusions which give to labradorite its grey colour, and sometimes chatoyancy

needle-like inclusions, and which has a pronounced blue flash and some degree of chatoyancy when cut in the correct direction, is called 'black moonstone'.

The density of labradorite approximates to 2·69 and the greatest and least refractive indices are near 1·568 and 1·560, the birefringence being 0·008. No characteristic absorption spectrum is observed in the material, nor does it exhibit any luminescence. While the flashes of colour show best in flat polished plates, an effect like opal is shown by carved labradorite, the carving breaking up the broad flashes into more pin-point gleams which in such work, carved despite the strong cleavage of the feldspars, is most effective. A labradorite from Finland has been called 'Spectrolite'.

A clear near-colourless to yellow transparent labradorite which does not show a play of colour is found at Millard County, Utah, U.S.A. This variety has a density near 2·68 and refractive indices for the greatest and least shadow edges of 1·572 and 1·565 respectively. A similar material comes from Mexico. A transparent type of labradorite from Madagascar shows the blue flash and needle-like inclusions as found in 'black moonstone' (Plate XIX). These types of labradorite show little in the way of luminescence under ultra-violet light, but under x-rays a bright greenish glow is seen.

The normal rock-like labradorite is found as extensive rock masses in the vicinity of Nairn on the coast of Labrador, hence the name applied to this variety of feldspar. Other sources are in Newfoundland, along the shore of Lake Huron, at Cape Mahul, at Abercrombie and at Morin in Quebec,

Canada. There are sources of the mineral in the Ukraine, especially at Gorodishch in the Zhitomir district, and in the Ural mountains, in Soviet Russia. Labradorite is found in small quantity in Arkansas, New Mexico and Vermont in the United States of America.

Bytownite and Anorthite

A reddish faceted stone has been identified as bytownite. The stone had a density of 2·739 and refractive indices of 1·56–1·57; there was observed an absorption band at 5730 Å. Anorthite has been cut for collectors.

Laurvikite (Larvikite)

The Norwegian rock known as laurvikite, so named from Laurvik in southern Norway, is a material extensively used for building façades. It is often referred to as labradorite, but is actually a rock chiefly characterized by its rhomb-shaped feldspars which give a pearl-grey iridescence. The material actually consists of crypto-perthite or anorthoclase or both, plagioclase being absent, with biotite and aegirine-augite.

CHAPTER 10

GEMS OF THE SILICA GROUP INCLUDING AMETHYST, AGATE AND OPAL

The quartz gems comprise several different groups. They are the fully crystalline quartz, to which belong the lovely amethyst and the ubiquitous rock crystal; the quartzites which supply the green aventurine and other types which are used for the carving of small ornaments; the crypto-crystalline quartz or chalcedonies, the best known of which are the agates; the impure but colourful jaspers to which are allied the hornstone, chert and flint, materials which have no gem significance despite the use of flint by early man. Lastly, but first in importance, is the opal. Strictly speaking, opal is not quartz, which is a crystalline material, but a hardened gel. However, as the chemical composition, except for some included water, is the same as that for quartz, inclusion in this group is to some extent justi-fied and is certainly convenient.

CHEMICAL AND PHYSICAL PROPERTIES OF QUARTZ

Quartz is crystalline silicon dioxide (silica) which has the formula SiO_2. Quartz has two different modifications, α quartz which forms at tempera-tures below 573°C and which is the usual type found in vein quartz and in gem crystals. Above 573°C but below 870°C is the β modification, a type which forms the quartz of granite. Above 870°C another silica mineral forms. This is tridymite, which is also silicon dioxide and also has two, or maybe three, modifications. The first of these, the α modification, is inferred to have trigonal crystallization and the β modification to be hexagonal. Then at 1,470°C the tridymite changes into cristobalite, a cubic mineral which again has two modifications. Thus these quartz minerals act as a geological thermometer. Tridymite and cristobalite have no gem significance except that the white globules sometimes found in obsidian are considered to be cristobalite. At 1,710°C the quartz (or cristobalite) melts and the molten material usually solidifies as a glass—silica glass—with a high softening point and an extremely small co-efficient of expansion.

The well-formed quartz crystals which make such beautiful mineral specimens supply such gemstones as rock crystal, amethyst, citrine and cairngorm. The forms shown by the crystals and the nature of their atomic structure have certain exceptional characteristics which are not found in other gem minerals.

Quartz crystallizes in the trigonal (rhombohedral) system. Ideally quartz forms doubly terminated crystals consisting of a hexagonal prism capped at each end by, what may be assumed to be from their appearance, hexagonal pyramids (*Figure 10.1a*). These twelve triangular-shaped faces are not, however, pyramidal faces but equal development of the faces of two rhombohedra of opposite hands, or more correctly positive and negative rhombohedra. Usually one of the rhombohedra predominates (*Figure 10.1b*) and the crystal shows clearly the trigonal nature of the crystallization. Occasionally the predominating rhombohedral faces are so large as to obscure entirely the other rhombohedron and the prism faces, the crystal then assumes the form of a rhombohedron and an aspect nearly that of a cube (*Figure 10.1c*). Some crystals may have equal development of the rhombohedral faces but with a complete absence of the hexagonal prism, thus giving a bi-pyramidal form which is called a quartzoid (*Figure 10.1d*).

Quartz crystals are characterized by the horizontal striations which appear on the prism faces. These striations are due to oscillation between the faces of the prism and the different rhombohedra, and it is to this oscillatory effect that the tapering of some quartz crystals is due.

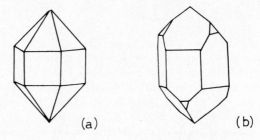

(a)   (b)

Figure 10.1. The forms of quartz crystals

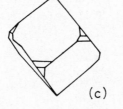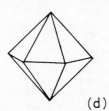

(c)   (d)

Twinning is frequent in quartz, but except in the type in which the twin crystals are in contact with their long axes at 84° 33″, that is nearly a right angle, the twinning is so intergrown that it is not readily detected by mere observation.

Other factors cause distortion in crystals and, indeed, it is rare for a crystal to show ideal form; this may be readily understood when the conditions under which crystals are forced to grow are considered. Crystals which form in rock cavities usually commence their growth from any nucleus which may be present on the rock wall, hence, as the crystals grow from the wall they will have only one termination. Further, the silica-bearing solution which feeds the crystal is always in more or less rapid movement and may be richer in silica in some flow directions than in others. This tends to cause some faces to grow faster than others. The latter, growing less fast, become the larger faces. However, whatever the irregularity of the faces, the angles between any two like faces is the same

6+G.   161

as in the perfect crystal (*Figure 10.2*). Owing to pauses in the growth of the crystal by lack of mineral charged mother-liquid, or to a change in the constitution of that liquid, ghost-like outlines may be seen in some quartz crystals; such crystals are called phantoms.

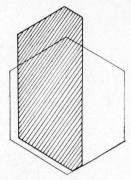

Figure 10.2. Deformed quartz crystal showing its relation to the hexagonal form and that the angles between like faces are the same

X-ray study has shown that the atomic structure of quartz, unique among the gem minerals, is helical, and that this spiral arrangement of the atoms can be either right-handed or left-handed. This right-hand or left-hand nature of quartz, termed enantiomorphism, is occasionally manifest in crystals by the position of the small trigonal pyramidal faces, if present. This is shown in *Figure 10.3*, from which it will be clear that the left-handed crystal is an exact counterpart of the right-handed one, but that each is a mirror-image of the other. Such a spiral structure causes a crystal to rotate the plane of polarization of light, and this circular polarization, as it is termed, is made manifest by the peculiarity of the optic figure seen in convergent polarized light. This figure differs from the normal uniaxial

Figure 10.3. Left-handed and right-handed quartz crystals

interference figure in that the arms of the black cross do not pass within the inner ring (*Figure 10.4*). This figure is conclusive for quartz which is the only gemstone showing the effect. A discussion of the production and interpretation of interference figures is given in the technical section.

Quartz has a hardness of 7 and is the Mohs standard for this number. Thus quartz is hard enough to take a good polish and to resist the abrasive action of dust particles in the atmosphere. The mineral shows no distinct cleavage and the fractured surface shows conchoidal or subconchoidal markings. Quartz has a density of 2·651 in rock crystal, which is the purest form, and even in the coloured varieties of crystal quartz the density only varies in the third place of decimals from this value. The refractive indices are again very constant and have the values of 1·544 for the ordinary ray and 1·553 for the extraordinary ray. The sign of refraction is, therefore, positive and the birefringence is 0·009. Quartz has a vitreous lustre and shows little fire. The value of the dispersion between the B to G interval is only 0·013, and quartz does not luminesce under ultra-violet light, to which it is transparent.

As has been mentioned earlier due to the circular polarization of quartz the uniaxial interference figure seen in convergent polarized light shows that the arms of the cross do not enter the central ring. This is specific for most quartz, but not so for amethyst, which owing to its usual 'twinned' nature shows a normal uniaxial interference figure. Owing to the bead itself acting as a converging lens, bead necklets of rock crystal can be readily proved if they are placed between two 'polaroid' discs with their vibration directions 'crossed', on turning the bead to the correct position the typical figure is shown.

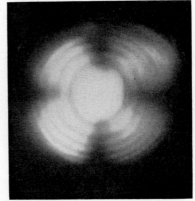

Figure 10.4. Interference figure of quartz showing the effect of circular polarization

ROCK CRYSTAL

The colourless water-clear quartz is known as rock crystal and receives its name from the hardy mountain climbers of Ancient Greece who first came upon it gleaming in hidden caves near Mount Olympus. They called it 'krustallos' meaning ice, for they believed it to be water so frozen by the Gods as to be forever solid. Crystals of colourless quartz are abundant and show considerable variation in size, from crystals so minute that it would take a hundred thousand to make an ounce to gigantic crystals weighing more than a thousand pounds.

Cutting of Rock Crystal

Rock crystal is cut into faceted stones and as beads, but the material is worth little more than the cost of cutting. The large crystals provide a suitable medium for large carved and engraved pieces (*Figure 10.5*) and many exquisite works of the glyptic art made in rock crystal are extant from Grecian and Mycenaean times, and from the Middle Ages. The peoples of China and Japan excel in the carving of this material and some fine engraving on rock crystal has been carried out during the present century by German and Bohemian artists.

The rondells, the small flat beads sometimes used for separating coloured

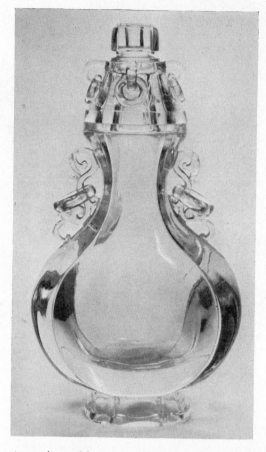

Figure 10.5. A vase and cover with loose ring handles carved in rock crystal, 14½ inches in height—Chinese: Chia Ch'ing period

(By courtesy of Sotheby and Co.)

stones in necklaces, are usually made of rock crystal, and the halves of the composite stone known as soudé emerald are usually pieces of rock crystal, often selected for the natural flaws they contain.

Rock crystal is ground and polished, mostly by Japanese workers, into crystal-gazing balls, although most of the crystal-gazing balls are moulded and polished glass. Quartz spheres over 3 in. across are rare, but there is an exceptional specimen in the United States National Museum which has a diameter of 12¾ in. and weighs 107 pounds. The distinction of quartz spheres from those made of glass, apart from the much colder feel of the quartz ball, may be made by looking through the ball at a dot or pin hole in a sheet of paper. Quartz, except for one position along the optic axis, will, owing to double refraction, show the dot doubled, whereas glass will not do this. The ball must be turned and viewed in different positions 90 degrees removed, to ensure not going down the optic axis, before condemning the ball as glass.

Piezoelectric Effect of Quartz

Untwinned rock crystal has, owing to its atomic configuration, a unique

164

technical application. During 1880 Jacques and Pierre Curie discovered that a plate of quartz cut parallel to the direction of the prism faces exhibited electric charges when stressed, as when pressure was applied in a certain way. Further they found that such a plate would expand or contract on the application of electric charges to faces normal to the so-called electric axes of the crystal, and that the crystal plate oscillated if the applied current was alternating. This is the effect termed piezoelectricity and is a phenomenon allied to pyroelectricity, in which electric charges are produced in quartz and tourmaline, and some other non-gem crystals, when they are heated.

It was not until 1922 that the piezoelectric effect of quartz was put to use. In that year W. G. Cady found methods whereby the electrically vibrating crystal could be used as a means of measuring and controlling the frequencies of radio waves, and today quartz crystal oscillators, as they are called, are not only used for the control of broadcasting wavelengths but for the control of accurate clocks, for underwater signalling and for submarine detection. The transparency to ultra-violet rays makes quartz eminently suitable for the lens systems of microscopes which use ultra-violet light instead of ordinary light in order to obtain great resolution, and in the lenses and prisms of the spectrographs used for spectrum analysis.

Inclusions

Rock crystal is often remarkably clear from internal imperfections, and any inclusions are usually crystal-shaped cavities containing a liquid and a bubble of gas—the so-called two-phase inclusions. Other crystals are often found enclosed in quartz, which forming later has grown round and enveloped them. In this category come the sagenitic quartzes, so named from the Greek for a net, for the criss-crossing needles seem like a net. When the enclosed crystals are long hair-like needles of red or golden-coloured rutile the material is called rutilated quartz (*Figure 10.6*). Other more popular names such as 'Venus hair stone', 'Cupid's darts' and 'Flêches d'amour' are applied to the material. A similar type of quartz may have included crystals of black tourmaline, or green actinolite fibres, to which the name 'Thetis hair stone' has been applied. If the actinolite crystals are so dense as to colour the quartz green it forms a variety called prase. However, such dense actinolite crystals can be enveloped in the cryptocrystalline type of quartz and produce a similar prase. A clear distinction cannot readily be accomplished without petrological investigation.

It has been reported that some forty different minerals have been found to be included in quartz but only a few have gem importance, among which are green chlorite which shows as mossy-like inclusions in quartz crystals and the orange to red goethite and hematite. The bluish-green and brown copper mineral called chrysocolla is often enclosed by colourless quartz and when such a mineral with botryoidal form is so enclosed the copper mineral appears as blue-green and brown 'hills' in a colourless matrix. Often the chrysocolla is disseminated throughout the quartz giving it a green or brown colour. Blue or violet dumortierite is another mineral which

Figure 10.6. Rutile needles in quartz as in rutilated quartz (Venus hair stone)

is often found impregnating quartz. These types of quartz are sometimes met as cabochon-cut stones. The golden yellow tufted crystals of cacoxenite are found embedded in rock crystal and such material when polished produces an attractive stone.

When clear colourless quartz is permeated by cracks, these, if thin enough, produce rainbow colours by interference of light at the thin films of air in the crack. Such stones are called 'rainbow quartz' or 'iris quartz'. A similar effect can be artificially produced by suddenly cooling a heated rock crystal, and if this cooling is carried out in water coloured with red or green dyes, this colour dries in the cracks producing the so-called firestones.

Occurrences

Rock crystal is found the world over and only some of the more important localities are mentioned here. Fine specimens, usually crystal groups, come from the Swiss and French Alps and from Hot Springs, Arkansas, U.S.A. Doubly terminated crystals, often containing black inclusions of petroleum, are found in Herkimer County in the State of New York. The most important source for rock crystal is in Brazil, where the best technical quartz is obtained in Goyaz, Minas Gerais and Bahia. Madagascar is another source of large crystals, as is the area around Mount Kimpu in the Kai Province and elsewhere in Japan. Large crystals are found in New South Wales and rutilated quartz is found at Tingha in the same Australian state. Very large quartz crystals are found at Sakangyi in the Kathe district of Upper Burma.

WHITE QUARTZ

White quartz, the so-called milky quartz, owes its milkiness to the presence of a multitude of very small cavities containing water or carbon dioxide in liquid condition. Sometimes the milkiness is only skin deep on the crystal and such crystals are called 'quartz en chemise'. Much vein quartz is white quartz and this type is often gold-bearing. Such material with included gold grains has been cut as plates or cabochons, perhaps as souvenirs of the mining camps. Milky quartz is little used as a gemstone.

BROWN QUARTZ

Quartz crystals of a clear brown colour and varying in hue from a light brown to so dark a brown as to appear black—then known as morion—are fairly common but do not have a great appeal as cut stones. Brown quartz crystals have been found in the debris of a weathered granite in the Cairngorm mountains of the Scottish Highlands. Faceted stones of this brown quartz are known as cairngorms and were traditionally used to embellish the accoutrements of the picturesque Highland dress. The supply from the Cairngorm mountains is now virtually exhausted and much of the cairngorm used for Scottish jewellery today is amethyst from Brazil which has had the colour altered to brownish-yellow by heat treatment. Some brown quartz has a smoky tinge and is then known as smoky quartz.

The usual inclusions seen in brown quartz are the two-phase negative crystal cavities in which the liquid phase is usually carbon dioxide, as is shown by the disappearance of the bubble when the quartz is heated to between 30°C and 31°C, which is the critical temperature for carbon dioxide and above which it cannot exist in the liquid state. Brown quartz shows quite a distinct dichroism, one ray being brown and the other pinkish-brown. The stone shows no absorption spectrum of diagnostic value nor does it luminesce under ultra-violet rays or x-rays.

The cause of the colour of the brown and smoky quartz is not fully understood and divers theories have been advanced to account for it. One is that the colour may be due to a colloidal distribution of silicon atoms in the structure, and another ascribes the cause to the presence of organic and carbonaceous matter. What is probably the most plausible theory is that the colour has been induced in colourless crystals by long continued bombardment by radium emanations from surrounding radioactive rocks, and this is to some extent substantiated by the fact that rock crystals tends to turn brown after intense radiation from powerful x-rays. There may be some difference, too, in the colouring of the clear brown quartz and the smoky variety. On heating brown quartz a lightening of the colour is usual, but the locality from which the crystal came, and whether it be clear brown or smoky brown, may influence the shade of colour produced by the treatment. A clear brown stone heated for one hour at 200°C turned a lovely citrine colour and another brown stone treated at 300°C for one hour completely decolorized.

The most important sources for brown quartz are in the Swiss Alps where, in 1868, in the Canton Uri, a single cavity yielded some 3,000 pounds weight of crystals. Very fine crystals of smoky quartz are found at Pike's Peak, Colorado; other North American localities are in Auburn County, Maine and Alexander County, North Carolina. Butte, Inyo, Kern, Riverside and San Diego Counties of California also supply brown quartz. Japan,

Manchuria, and Hinojosa in the province of Cordoba, Spain, have produced smoky quartz; there are some localities in New South Wales, Australia.

YELLOW QUARTZ

The yellow quartz, called citrine, varies in colour from a light golden yellow to a reddish-yellow and probably owes its colour to a trace of iron in the ferric state (Fe_2O_3). Natural yellow quartz is somewhat rare and the best material comes from Brazil. Citrine shows perceptible dichroism, does not fluoresce and exhibits nothing in the way of a characteristic absorption spectrum. Most of the yellow and brownish-yellow quartz often sold under the misnomer 'topaz' is heat-treated amethyst.

AMETHYST

The violet and purple varieties of quartz provide the most prized, and in many respects the most interesting of the large family of quartz minerals. Amethyst, the name by which this variety of quartz is known, is of ancient derivation. Pliny stated that the gem was so-called from the colour being near to, but not quite reaching, that of wine. The name is said to have been derived from the Greek word 'Amethustos', which is translated as not drunken, and was given to the stone from the curious belief that a wearer would not suffer from excess consumption of alcoholic liquors. As an amulet amethyst was believed to dispel sleep, sharpen the intellect, to be an antidote against poison, and to preserve the wearer against harm in battle.

In ecclesiastical circles amethyst has always been held in high esteem and many of the finest specimens of this beautiful variety of quartz are set in the finger rings of bishops. There are two fine amethysts in the British Regalia; a large faceted orb set below the cross and surmounting the great Star of Africa in the Royal Sceptre, and another fine stone set below the cross which surmounts the Orb.

In 1954 C. V. Raman and A. Jayaraman from their researches into amethyst postulated that it was biaxial and monoclinic but closely related to quartz. This view is not universally accepted.

Amethyst crystals are found lining vughs or the inside of hollow cavities. It is characteristic of amethyst crystals found in these drusy masses to show only the rhombohedral tops, the prism faces being absent, and it not infrequently happens, especially with South American stones, that the three alternate rhombohedral faces are the only ones developed giving crystals with a cubic aspect. Further, in these druses the faces of the rhombohedra are often arranged in parallel position. It is also characteristic of amethyst that quite often only the tips of the crystals are deep coloured, the remainder grading into milky quartz or rock crystal. Thus, although amethyst is always violet in hue, the range of colour is very wide and may vary from nearly colourless with a faint mauve tint to a glorious purple.

Coloration

Owing to a remarkable twinning of the crystal much amethyst is parti-coloured and sections cut at right angles to the vertical crystal axis are

PLATE XVI

The Quartz group

Orange-brown
quartz
22·77 carats

Citrine
22·84 carats

Green quartz
5·28 carats

Citrine
87 carats

Rose quartz
18·0 carats

Smoky quartz
25·56 carats

Amethyst
16·10 carats

often seen to have alternate triangular sectors coloured a strong violet with other alternate sectors almost colourless, thus in a cut stone colour breaks with an angle of about 60 degrees, or straight banding, are common.

The cause of the colour of amethyst is not known with any degree of accuracy and opinions as to the cause are still at variance. It was generally believed that the colour of amethyst was due to the presence of manganese, especially as manganese will produce a violet colour in some glasses, but chemical and spectroscopic analyses failed to disclose the presence of this element, except where inclusions of another mineral containing manganese gave rise to its presence. Coloration by potassium ferrocyanide, by ferric cyanide and by an organic substance have at different times been suggested as the cause of the violet hue. Another theory is that the colour is due to the concentration of molecules of different minerals along the contact zones of twinned lamellae.

Effects of Heat

The matter is complicated still further by the change of colour noted when amethyst is heated at various temperatures. When the temperature is brought up to between 400°C and 500°C the usual colour change is to a brownish-yellow or a garnet-red, but stones from different localities show different colour change, and in some cases a green colour is induced. Above 575°C the stones become colourless and a schillerization sets in. Amethyst so heated produces a simulation of moonstone. Further, there is the effect shown by these heat-treated quartzes when irradiated by emanations from radium, or by x-rays. When so treated the original colour is restored but with a superimposed smoky hue which could be driven off by reheating leaving the stone again with an amethyst colour. These effects gave rise to speculation that a disturbance of the internal molecular structure due to radiation from adjacent radioactive rock masses near where the amethyst was found might be the cause of the colour. The latest theory to find favour is that the violet colour is due to iron in a colloidal state, or to titanium.

The heat treatment of amethyst to a golden-yellow colour is extensively carried out, and nearly all the yellow quartzes marketed today are heat-treated amethyst. Most of this treated yellow quartz is sold under the misnomer 'topaz', although many attempts have been made to limit the name topaz to the true topaz of mineralogy. In an endeavour to get over the difficulty such hybrid names as 'quartz topaz' or 'topaz quartz' have been coined. What is probably the best alternative would be 'golden quartz'.

The colours of the heat-treated amethyst may vary from a yellowish-brown to a reddish-brown and in the gemstone trade the lighter hues are known as 'Palmyra topaz' and the reddish-brown stones as 'Madeira topaz', although the reddish stones have also had the name 'Spanish topaz' applied to them. These names are unsatisfactory but are unfortunately still used by some sections of the gem trade.

About 1953 it was accidentally discovered that the amethyst found at Montezuma, about 37 miles from the Rio Pardo in Minas Gerais, Brazil, would, when heated, produce a green coloured quartz, and from such

6*   169

treated material stones have been cut and sold under the name 'Prasiolita' or 'Prasiolite'. Greenish quartz has been met before this time but the origin of the material is unknown. Some greenish crystals, often parti-coloured amethyst and green, have been found in the top soil in Rhodesia, and it is surmised that the heat of the sun may well have caused the change of colour. Amethyst which 'greens' on heating has also been found at the Four Peaks region of central Arizona.

The change of colour of amethyst on heating is not always predictable, and further, stones from different sources may behave differently. Even without treatment the violet colour of amethyst may not in all stones be completely stable, for it is not unknown for unaccountable fading to occur, and not all the heat-treated green quartzes are free from the liability to fade. It must be stressed, therefore, that amethysts should be treated with care and should be kept from excessive heat; this especially applies to the working jeweller.

Effects of Light

Amethyst shows distinct dichroism, the twin-colours being bluish-violet and reddish-violet. On the contrary the brown heat-treated amethyst does not show dichroism and, thus, treated stones may be detected from those of natural brown or yellow colour by their lack of dichroism. Under the Chelsea colour filter amethysts appear a reddish colour, the stronger the more pronounced the body colour of the stone. There is a wide absorption of varying intensity in the yellow-green region of the spectrum from about 5200 to 5500 Å, but the spectrum of amethyst cannot be called distinctive and is of little aid in identification. The amethyst is practically inert as regards any luminescence, but a blue glow has been seen with some amethyst when bathed in short-wave ultra-violet light.

Inclusions

The inclusions which may be seen in violet quartz are most commonly feathers made up of negative cavities. Groups of prismatic crystals (*Figure 10.7*) or a type which looks rather like flower heads on stalks (*Figure 10.8*)

Figure 10.7. Prismatic crystals in amethyst

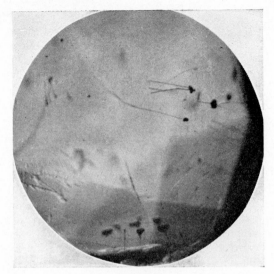

Figure 10.8. Flower bud and stalk inclusions in amethyst

may be seen. A quite common imperfection in amethyst is a mark like a thumb print (*Figure 10.9*) which is ascribed as due to the twinning so common in amethyst, hence this type of inclusion is often called a rippled fracture inclusion. Very few amethysts are free from parti-coloration with angular zones of colour, and even in the heat-treated brown stones this zonal colour marking is seen.

Occurrences

The most important source of amethyst in earlier times was Russia, where crystals of a lovely rich colour were found in cavities just beneath the turf and in association with beryl and topaz. The location is Reshev

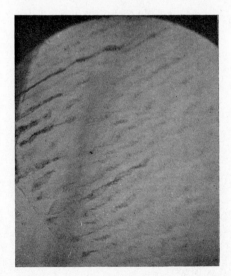

Figure 10.9. Rippled fracture inclusion in amethyst

171

and Alapayev in the neighbourhood of Sverdlovsk in the Division of Perm along the western borders of the Ural mountains. Beautiful as they are the Russian amethyst usually tends to take on a more crimson tint when viewed by electric light. Amethyst was also found in the neighbourhood of Idar-Oberstein on the Nahe in the German Rhineland but the deposits are now worked out. A lovely coloured amethyst is found in the Kaokoveldt 40 miles inland from Cape Frio in South-West Africa; and in the Osborn district of Western Australia.

Because of the discovery in the latter part of the nineteenth century of a vast amount of mauve quartz in Brazil and in neighbouring Uruguay the value of amethyst fell greatly. The most important area for this South American amethyst is in the Serra do Mar which stretches from Rio Grande do Sul, the southernmost state of Brazil, into northern Uruguay around Rivera and Artigas. The crystals are here found in amygdaloidal cavities in a black igneous rock called melaphyre. Other Brazilian localities are Campos dos Cristaes near Diamantina, Ribeirão da Paciencia at Itabarava near Ouro Preto, and at Bom Jesus dos Meiras, in the State of Minas Gerais. Rolled pebbles which have weathered out from the geodes are found in the Minas Novas district and another source is at Coimbra on the head-waters of the river Negro, a tributary of the river Parana in the State of Matto Grosso. Amethyst is also found in the State of Guanajuato in central Mexico and many fine amethysts are found in the Aztec graves.

In the United States of America amethyst has been found in a number of localities. On Rader Creek, east of Butte in Jefferson County, Montana, large groups and single crystals are found in a dyke, and a limited number of fine crystals have been found in North Carolina and in Oxford County, Maine. In the State of California there are a number of deposits in Amador, Mono, Lake and San Benito Counties. Amethyst is also found in Texas, Virginia and Pennsylvania, and in the Yellowstone National Park. The source in the Keweenaw Peninsula of Michigan on the south shore of Lake Superior may be classed as a link with Canada, for across the lake on the north and Dominion side there is a fine deposit of good quality violet quartz at Thunder Bay. Amethyst is found on the shores of Lake Nipigon and along the shores of the Bay of Fundy in Nova Scotia and some amethyst is found in the trap rock of Dubawnt lake in the North-West Territory.

In India geodes containing amethyst are worked from the deposits of the Deccan trap-rocks. Other Indian localities are the Sutlej valley in Bashahr and in the bed of the Narbada stream near Jubbulpore, but Indian sources are not important. Good quality amethyst is found in the gem gravels of Ceylon, but little material is found in Burma. Excellent amethyst of a dark violet-red colour is found in the pegmatites at Ambatomanga, Ampangabe and Tongafeno in Madagascar. A deposit of good amethyst has been reported from near Pretoria in South Africa and in Rhodesia. Fine crystals of amethyst are obtained from an occurrence at Tsunagi, Echigo Province and Fujiya in Hoki Province, Japan. Unimportant are the deposits of amethyst which are found in Cornwall, England and in Cork and the Achill island off County Mayo, Eire (Ireland). Amethyst was formerly obtained in the island of Sark in the Channel Islands and was sold as 'Sark stones'. The deposit is now exhausted and the 'Sark stones' sold to tourists is material from Brazil. Amethyst is also found in New South Wales, Australia, and has been reported from China.

Much massive quartz of an amethystine colour is used for carving. It is usually heavily flawed and very patchy in colour. The transparent crystals are usually cut in the mixed-cut style or for important stones the trap-cut style is used. Amethyst is often fashioned into beads.

Simulation

Amethyst is imitated in glass, and often in a glass which has a low refractive index containing pronounced swirl marks. Synthetic corundum is made in a colour to imitate the amethyst and a soudé type composite stone is made which can be very deceptive, for the top, if not the base as well, is made of quartz and will thus give a refractometer reading for amethyst. Pale amethyst is often mounted in a closed setting with paint or foil below in order to enhance the colour.

ROSE QUARTZ

Less common than the other varieties of crystal quartz is the pink coloured rose-quartz. It varies in colour from a strong rose-pink to a nearly white, and nearly always cloudy with fissures and never entirely clean, although some material has been found which is sufficiently clear and transparent to cut into faceted stones. The material is mainly used, however, for the production of figurines, ash trays and other small carved objects.

Rose-quartz is found as cores in large pegmatite dykes as solid masses of rose-coloured rock made up of large crystal units which do not show good boundaries but with occasional contact faces between the individual crystals. In some localities, such as Govenader Valedares in Brazil, well-formed crystals of rose-quartz have been found; they have no gem significance but make attractive mineral specimens. The cause of the pink colour, which may vary greatly in its intensity and which is said to fade in some cases, is most probably due to titanium oxide, although manganese has also been suggested as the cause.

Much rose-quartz contains microscopic needles of rutile oriented in definite crystal directions in the host crystal. These needles produce a star-effect when the stone is looked through in the correct direction at a source of light. This effect is termed diasterism and differs from the epiasterism of the star-sapphire in which the star is produced by reflection of light which is directed from above. Use is made of this diasterism of rose-quartz in the production of an ingenious imitation star-sapphire. A description of these objects is given in a later chapter. Star-rose-quartz is sometimes cut as round beads each of which reveals a star when seen in a bright light.

Despite the fact that much of the material may be marred by cracks the density of rose-quartz does not vary very much from rock crystal. Rose-quartz shows a fairly strong dichroism in the deeper hued material, but the effect falls off greatly the paler the material and in the very pale material little or no dichroism can be observed. There is no distinctive absorption spectrum and rose-quartz shows very little luminescence or none at all under ultra-violet light. A faint bluish glow is usually visible when the stone is irradiated with x-rays and an appreciable darkening of the colour of the stone may be observed at the irradiated spot.

The best rose-quartz comes from the Alto Feio in the Rio Grande do Norte and other places in the valley of the Jequitinhona of Brazil. Other localities are at Tsileo, Amparikaolo and south of Mania in Madagascar, and at Warangal, Hyderabad and Chhindwara of the Central Provinces of India. The material is also found at Goto in Iwaki Province, Japan, in South-West Africa, Bavaria in Germany, the Ural mountains in Russia and in Maine and South Dakota in the United States of America.

QUARTZ CAT'S-EYES AND CROCIDOLITE

Quartz cat's-eyes, which in the best specimens may closely resemble the chrysoberyl cat's-eyes, owe their chatoyancy to a multitude of fibres of a fine asbestos which are oriented parallel to the principal axis of the host quartz. Such stones, which are cabochon-cut in order to show the cat's-eye streak of light, may be honey-yellow, brownish to grey-green in colour, and the sharpness of the ray varies considerably with different specimens. Quartz cat's-eyes are found in the Ceylon gem gravels, in India, and the poorer greenish specimens come from the Fichtelgeberge in Bavaria.

When cut correctly the silicified asbestos called tiger's-eye or crocidolite shows a cat's-eye effect, but most of the material is cut into flat plates, beads, cabochons or carved as cameos. The surface of this subtranslucent to opaque yellow to golden-brown stone with a golden silky lustre shows a series of lustrous yellow bands alternating with brown banding which reverse in colours as the stone is turned. A tiger's-eye cabochon is illustrated in Plate XIX.

The original mineral of the veins was a blue variety of asbestos called crocidolite, and this has altered by decomposition into silica (quartz). The mineral is therefore a quartz pseudomorph after crocidolite, changing its composition but not its form, and the new mineral is known under the name pseudocrocidolite. The residual fibrous structure, now welded into a solid mass by silica is usually stained by hydrous iron oxide (limonite) which gives to the mineral its delightful golden-brown colour. If some of the original blue asbestos is present a variegated blue silicified crocidolite is produced giving a parti-coloured effect which is very pleasing. Such stones are sometimes known under the name 'Zebra', and if the mineral has not changed at all the blue stone is then known as 'Hawk's-eye'. The 'Tiger's-eye' is cut from the lovely golden-brown stone produced by oxidation of the iron content of the original asbestos. This oxidation can take place either before or after silicification occurs.

Heating the golden-coloured crocidolite will turn the brown limonite into reddish hematite and produce a red stone. The material is sometimes dyed but such treated stones are readily distinguished by their unnatural colour. The major source is Griqualand West, South Africa. Crocidolite is oriented silky fibres ('cross-fibre' veins) of riebeckite asbestos, but riebeckite is the name usually applied to the mineral when it is in disoriented masses. Such material, with limonite, is found in the neighbourhood of

174

Outjo in South-West Africa and has been cut and polished into cabochons by the mineral dealer S. Pieters of Windhoek who sells the stones under the name 'Pietersite'.

QUARTZITES

When quartz has been formed from pre-existing rocks by the metamorphic process, as detailed in Chapter 1, the rock quartzite is produced, although some quartzites are formed by silica cementation of quartz grains (sand or sandstone). Quartzite, which is used for ornamental purposes, is a rock consisting of a granular interlocking mass of quartz crystals with irregular boundaries. Often the quartzite rock contains small crystals of mica or an iron mineral, and such a rock may exhibit a schiller and is then known as aventurine quartz. One variety of aventurine quartz has included platy crystals of a green chrome mica (fuchsite mica) and this green aventurine quartz is often used for beads and other small articles of jewellery. The amount of green mica present in the quartzite can vary quite a lot and one type is so impregnated with fuchsite mica that it is practically opaque and may be said to be a quartz-schist. This type is often banded with lighter and darker green zones and may readily be mistaken for the green copper mineral called malachite.

The iron-coloured types of aventurine quartz vary from a creamy-white to a reddish-brown in colour, and a grey quartzite with mica inclusions comes from Chile. A fine reddish-brown type is found at Cap de Gata near Almeira on the south coast of Spain. Much of the white to brownish quartzite comes from Russia, particularly from the Korgon mountains in the Tomsk Division. A close-grained quartzite of bluish-white colour with veins or splotches of brownish-red, and containing small cubic crystals of pyrites is used for the carving of small ornaments, particularly at Idar in West Germany. The material is known as eosite.

India supplies most of the green aventurine quartz. Some Indian localities are Belvadi in the Hassan district of Mysore and at nearby Sindagere, the first named place producing a rich bluish-green coloured material and the other a banded type. Other sources in India are the Coimbatore and Nellore districts of Madras, where, in the latter locality is found a large-grained quartzite of delicate pale aquamarine-green colour banded with deep purple. Some green aventurine is found in Siberia and in Tanzania.

The refractive indices of quartzite correspond to those of crystal quartz, but owing to the confused mass of disoriented crystals with which the rock is composed, only a vague shadow edge at $1 \cdot 55$ will normally be seen on the refractometer. Again, owing to the inhomogeneity of the material and to the presence of impurities the density may be as low as $2 \cdot 64$ and as high as $2 \cdot 69$. The green aventurine quartz shows a red residual glow when viewed through the Chelsea colour filter, and thus may be distinguished from malachite which appears green. A chromium type absorption spectrum is shown by green aventurine quartz, but the lines in the red are rather vague and the broad absorption in the yellow-green region is not pronounced. This type of aventurine quartz shows a greyish-green glow under ultra-violet light, whereas the other types of aventurine quartz are inert.

CHEMICAL AND PHYSICAL PROPERTIES OF CRYPTOCRYSTALLINE QUARTZ

The quartz mineral called chalcedony or agate, the latter term being more used for the banded varieties, is a microcrystalline (cryptocrystalline) quartz in which fibrous crystals of quartz are embedded in an amorphous opal (hydrated silica). In most cases the agate is built up by a structure in which the fibres of the quartz run parallel to each other with their length perpendicular to the layers. These crystallites of quartz cannot readily be resolved by microscopic examination in ordinary light, but in thin section and by the use of polarized light the general structure can be seen (*Figure 10.10*). There is no distinct division between the banded agates and the chalcedony which shows no banding, except, perhaps, that the fibres may be of various sizes and be entwined, although running in the same general direction.

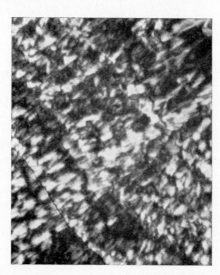

Figure 10.10. A thin section of striped agate seen in polarized light

Agate can be stained to different colours and this is commercially done on a large scale. According to W. F. Eppler the ability of an agate to take colour depends upon the water content, and agate with proportionally more opal will take colour better than the type with less opal. If the quartz fibres are long and tapering there is more space for opal, and hence more water, and such material is the best for taking colour, while the agate in which the fibres are entwined leave less space for opal and therefore does not take the colour so well. Other authorities do not agree with this conception and suggest that chalcedony is cryptocrystalline quartz displaying certain anomalous properties due to the presence of minute fluid-filled cryptopores. The stained banded agates, which are so well known, show clearly that the staining capacity of the material can, and most often does, vary in the different bands or layers and they are thus strongly thrown into relief by the staining. The non-stainable, or weakly stainable material with the structure of entwined fibres is usually tougher and is used for technical and industrial purposes, such as for the knife edges of balances, agate pivots for bearings, agate pestles and mortars, and even for the rings used to carry the line in fishing rods.

Chalcedony has a hardness of about 7 on Mohs's scale and, as would be expected in the case of a material which is a mixture of quartz and opal, the density is less than for rock crystal. The value of density approximates to 2·60, but according to impurities present may vary from 2·58 to 2·64. W. F. Eppler found that the type of agate best for staining, that is with more opal, had a density of 2·594 and the technical agate 2·600, plus or minus 0·002 in each case.

The refractive index may vary from 1·530 to 1·539 and a small amount of birefringence amounting to no more than 0·004 may be observed. This may be due to an effect known as form birefringence which is often shown by materials of one refractive index which are embedded in another of different index. Indeed, here it must be pointed out that the nature of the quartz fibres in chalcedony are not accurately known, for unlike rock crystal they are optically biaxial. Nor is it sure that the other component is pure opal or a mixture of opal and another quartz variant of which there are several rare types.

The luminescent response of chalcedony to ultra-violet light varies considerably. Mostly the glow seen is bluish-white, but in some varieties, particularly those from Wyoming in North America which contain traces of a uranium mineral, the glow is bright yellowish-green. The short-wave lamp (2537 Å) is usually best for exciting fluorescence in chalcedony, for many agates do not glow at all under the long-wave lamp. The banded agates will often show the fluorescent light in bands or in patches.

Chalcedony is a mineral of secondary origin and is deposited from solution in cavities and veins in which the mineral takes various forms. It often lines geodes or may even completely fill the cavity forming nodules which occur in both igneous and sedimentary rocks. Much chalcedony forms as botryoidal masses (*Figure 10.11*) or as stalactites.

The name chalcedony is usually applied to the material which is greyish-white to brown in colour and in which the banded structure is not usually

Figure 10.11. Botryoidal chalcedony

apparent as it is concealed by the uniform colouring and by cloudy patches (cloud chalcedony). Such material is extensively used by Oriental carvers for the production of figurines and vases and for the small ornamental articles carved in West Germany.

CHRYSOPRASE

The most prized of the chalcedonies is the green-coloured material called chrysoprase (Plate XIX). This variety which varies in colour from a lovely apple-green to a dingy greenish-yellow owes its hue to the presence of nickel, either as oxide or as silicate. Chrysoprase is usually cut into cabochons, or as beads, and for intaglios (seal stones) and cameos. The material was popular in the Victorian era and the stones were often cut as low cabochons with a narrow rim of facets around the edge.

Although intaglios and cameos in chrysoprase are said to date from Greek and Roman times, where the material used came from does not seem to be known, or even if the material was truly chrysoprase. In 1740 chrysoprase was found in several places in the vicinity of Zabkowice (Frankenstein) in Silesia and this locality supplied the bulk of the mineral, but the Silesian deposits are apparently no longer productive. A small quantity of chrysoprase is obtained from the Ural mountains. In 1878, and in later years, four occurrences of good quality chrysoprase were discovered near Visalia in Tulare County, California. The material was found in narrow veins irregularly distributed in serpentine and varied from an opaque green material to that of a beautiful translucent emerald green. There was active mining for this chrysoprase at Visalia until about 1911 after which the mines closed down as the gem had waned in popularity and the demand was insufficient to warrant mining, especially as more easily recovered material had been mined. Water-worn pebbles of good colour have been found near Nickel mountain in western Oregon.

The State of Goias, Brazil, supplies chrysoprase, and a deep green, but somewhat more opaque material was found in 1965 in the Marlborough district some 90 miles from Rockhampton in Queensland, Australia.

Although it cannot be strictly called chrysoprase, which is coloured by nickel, a chromium green chalcedony very much like chrysoprase was found in 1955, but only in recent years has it been marketed. This material, which shows red under the colour filter, is found in the Great Dyke of Rhodesia just north of Mtoroshanga.

Simulation

The dearth of the material led to the imitation of chrysoprase by staining agate green, either by the precipitation of nickel salts or by using chromium salts. The latter is more common, and such stained chalcedony may be detected readily by the brownish-red residual colour shown when the stone is viewed through the Chelsea colour filter (true chrysoprase shows green) and by the vague lines in the red part of the spectrum due to chromium which are seen when the absorption spectrum of the stone is examined. Nickel staining is more difficult to determine, but whatever type of staining is used, it is sometimes possible to see a mosaic-like veining which has been brought up by the staining. This effect is due to the sheaf-like nature of

178

the crystal fibres which lie at right angles to the layers of the chalcedony. In order to get the best penetration of the dye solutions in staining agate, it is necessary to slab the mineral parallel to the layers and then the outlines of these aggregates of crystals tend to show up. This is illustrated in *Figure 10.12*. Chrysoprase is imitated by a suitably coloured glass which, however, usually shows profuse bubbles.

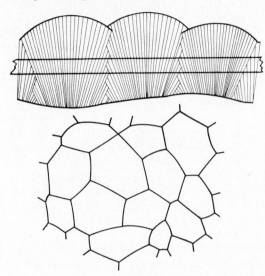

Figure 10.12. The upper part of the illustration depicts the sheaf-like micro-crystals in chalcedony showing how the material is 'slabbed' for staining. In the lower portion are shown the mosaic-like markings which are seen by transmitted light after staining

CORNELIAN AND ONYX

The flesh-red to deep clear red-coloured chalcedony is known as cornelian (carnelian) and the yellowish and brownish-red colours go under the name of sard, but the latter term is less commonly used than formerly. The cause of the colour of red chalcedony is iron, which may be in the form of hematite in the true cornelian and limonite in sard. This coloration has some interesting aspects, for it is known that nearly colourless chalcedony can be altered to a reddish colour by moderate heating in an oven, owing, it is thought, to the trace of iron, which is nearly always present in chalcedony, altering its chemical state. From this it is inferred that the natural reddish chalcedony may have derived its colour from the heating effects and the ultra-violet radiations from sunlight, coupled with exposure to moisture over long periods of time.

The chief sources of cornelian, which is most often found as pebbles lying loose on the surface or in gravel deposits, were the Arabian and Egyptian deserts. The mineral is of world-wide occurrence but the major commercial sources are in the Rio Grande do Sul of Brazil and Uruguay. India is an important source of cornelian which is also found in China, Colombia, Saxony, Scotland, the Nahe valley in West Germany and in a number of states of North America, particularly in California. Cornelian pebbles are also found in Japan.

Most commercial cornelian is artificially stained chalcedony. When the material is banded with red and white layers the stone is called sardonyx, or if the colours are black and white it is known as onyx. Such layered material is used for the carving of cameos (and intaglios) so that the raised relief will be of one colour and the background the other. A black chalcedony has been reported to occur in nature, but the black onyx of jewellery is stained chalcedony.

SOME COLOURFUL AND TRANSLUCENT CHALCEDONIES

Chalcedony containing a multitude of hair-like crystals of actinolite produces the dull green stone called prase. Masses of the green mineral chlorite included in chalcedony produces the dark green stone known as plasma, but the material is usually so coarse that the stone is practically a jasper. Plasma is found in India and China and in a number of places in the United States of America, including a source near Durkee in Oregon which has been misnamed 'Oregon jade'. Plasma often contains small white or yellow spots. When plasma contains bright red spots of jasper the stone is the popular seal stone called bloodstone (Plate XIX). Bloodstone is also known as heliotrope but this latter name is now seldom used. Some confusion is caused owing to the use of the name bloodstone (blutstein) by the Germans for the iron oxide mineral known in England as hematite. The best bloodstone is obtained from the Deccan trap-rocks of the Kathiawar peninsula in India. The United States of America, Brazil and Australia are other sources of bloodstone. A bright green chalcedony, often with white veins, which comes from southern Africa, has been called 'buddstone'. This stone, which is usually fashioned by tumbling, is a chlorite-rich chalcedony.

The red mineral cinnabar (mercuric sulphide) is an occasional inclusion in chalcedony (and in common white opal). Such a material can be a translucent white chalcedony with streaks and clouds of bright red or pink cinnabar, or it can be so impregnated with the mercury mineral as to be completely red. This variety of chalcedony is known as myrickite. Blue and green chrysocolla is another mineral which impregnates chalcedony to give a stone of intense sky-blue colour which is called chrysocolla quartz. Most of these colourful impregnated chalcedonies come from the United States of America.

Some translucent chalcedony when cut in the cabochon form has a schiller which resembles to some extent the true moonstone. A translucent chalcedony of lovely blue colour is found about 80 miles north-east of Okahandja in South-West Africa. A blue chalcedony has also been found in Cornwall, England. Chalcedonic pebbles abound along the Vaal and Orange rivers in South Africa.

AGATE

Moss Agates

Agate often contains inclusions of other minerals which assume tree-like (dendritic) forms. Such stones are known as moss agates (Plate XIX), and the included 'vegetation' may be black (probably manganese dioxide), green (possibly chlorite) and red (an iron mineral). Sometimes two or even three coloured 'trees' are in the same stone. In England and America the term mocha stone is used synonymously with moss agate, but in European countries the green moss agate alone is known as moss agate while the black and red coloured dendritic agate is termed mocha stone (*Figure 10.13*). Some dendritic agates show the dendrites so arranged as to resemble landscapes, and such agates are termed landscape or scenic agate.

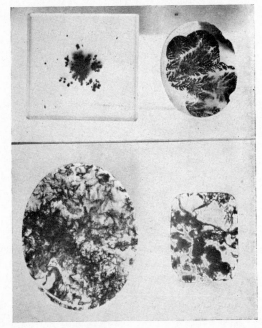

Figure 10.13. Dendritic agates: (top left) brown mocha stone; (top right) black mocha stone; (bottom) green moss agates

The best known locality for green moss agate is the Deccan trap of India. Dendritic agates are found in a number of localities in North America, particularly in Montana, Oregon, Idaho and in the Sweetwater agate beds near Granite mountain in Wyoming where the local agate contains traces of a uranium mineral and in consequence fluoresces a strong green colour under ultra-violet light. Moss agate is found in many places and some of the 'Scotch pebbles' from the Ochil mountains of Scotland show red and green moss. Moss agate is imitated by placing some chemical, like manganese dioxide, with a thin gelatine on one surface of a glass plate. When a chemical 'tree' has grown on the gel the excess water is driven off by gentle heat and a second plate of glass to act as a coverglass is cemented on. The whole may then be ground and polished in cabochon form. The readily seen join between the two pieces of glass exposes the fake.

Agate as a Fossilizing Agent

Chalcedony often replaces other materials and thus acts as a fossilizing agent. Agatized wood is a chalcedony pseudomorph after wood and this fossil wood is cut and polished for ornamental purposes (*Figure 10.14*). Bone has also been fossilized with agate, and at Tampa Bay, Florida, there is much chalcedony pseudomorphous after coral, and attractive cabochons

Figure 10.14. Fossil wood: chalce-dony pseudomorph after wood

are cut from this agatized coral, which is often artificially dyed blue and pink. Algae (seaweed) and small mollusc shells may be fossilized by silica, and like the fossil marbles, such material is cut and polished for ornamentation. The process of replacement by silica, as in the case of the petrified wood, is that the original substance is replaced particle by particle with silica so slowly that the original form remains. In the case of fossil wood this is done so that even the tree rings are still visible.

Banded Agates

The genesis of the banded agates which form geodes or nodules poses many problems. One theory of this agate formation is that a silica-rich

Figure 10.15. Section of an agate nodule showing the centre filled with crystalline quartz, from Montrose, Scotland

solution entered a cavity in the rock through ducts in the wall, and that this solution deposited the agate layer upon layer until in some cases the cavity became completely filled. Sometimes a central cavity was left open, the inner surface of which may be lined with small quartz crystals, or in others the centre may be filled with crystalline quartz (*Figure 10.15*). Ducts leading into the cavity have been found to be present in many agate nodules, but in others there is no sign of them, and it is to the absence of 'feeding canals' in many agates that the main objection to the theory lies.

An alternative theory is the silica gel theory, which postulates the cavity to contain a liquid mass of silica in the colloidal state, and which also contains a solution of some metallic salt. At a later period the silica is acted upon by a percolating acidulated water which enters the cavity from the surrounding rock and this alters the colloidal solution of silica into a semi-solid gel. The subsequent solution may contain some chemical agent which is capable of reacting with the metallic salt in the silica and by a process of periodic precipitation produce bands of colour. That such a process can occur was ably demonstrated by R. E. Liesegang, who placed on a glass slide a drop of some gel containing a colourless chemical compound; around the edge of this drop of gel was placed another colourless compound which was known to act on the first compound to produce a coloured precipitate. By rhythmic precipitation coloured rings are seen to form in the gel, rings very much like those seen in agate.

None of the theories given for the formation of agate has been completely proved and it is now generally considered that there is not one cause of agate formation. Both the theories mentioned may be the cause under certain conditions, but there may well be other causes as yet unknown.

The bands in agate may be broad, white or coloured (*Figure 10.16*), or they may be so fine as to have thousands of distinct layers to an inch. So fine and so close packed are the bands in some agate that they act upon light as a diffraction grating producing, in the iris agates, a rainbow effect when light is viewed through them.

The names given to the different types of agate are legion and many

Figure 10.16. An agate showing the banding

have local significance only. Fortification agate has the banding reminiscent of the outline of a fortress, and eye agate has the bands as concentric circles or as ovals. Sagenitic agate contains inclusions of another mineral which has needle-like form. Some amygdules are found in Burma which consist of bands of pure white opaque chalcedony embedded in a matrix of highly translucent semi-opal which may be either colourless or have a slight bluish or yellowish tinge. Certain of these stones when slit across the bands may show the figure of a more or less perfect Burmese pagoda in opaque white bands which appear to float in the almost colourless body of the stone. Such stones are called 'pagoda stones'.

Occurrences

Agate nodules are of world-wide occurrence. Agate was collected in the desert regions around Jebel Abu Diyeiba in Egypt over 3,000 years ago. From ancient times India has supplied agate, and the material was also found along the Achates river in Sicily, a river now known as the Drillo. The name agate was derived from the earlier name for this river. The agate cutting industry of Idar-Oberstein in the valley of the Nahe in the German Rhineland was said to have commenced in the fifteenth century, and the agate used was obtained from the hills around the twin towns. The Brazilian and Uruguayan deposits of the Rio Grande do Sul are the most important source of agates. Much colourful agate is found in the United States of America, particularly in the western states of the country, and the 'Scotch pebbles' from Montrose, the Ochil mountains and elsewhere in Scotland are well known.

Remarkable types of agate-filled nodules are the so-called 'thunder eggs', a legendary name given them by the American Indians, which are found in California, Nevada and Oregon in the United States of America. These nodules often contain colourful agate (and opal) and when the nodules are cut across show the agate filling to have a stellate formation (*Figure 10.17*). These nodules are found as spherical masses of silicified claystone and rhyolite and the star-shaped outline of the agate is considered to be due to the shrinkage of the mud which once filled the interior of the cavity of the

Figure 10.17. A section through a 'thunder egg'

184

rock. Subsequent flows of silica-bearing solutions silicified the shrunken mud and filled the cavity with agate.

The chalcedony enhydros or water-agate, although having no gem significance, do have a unique interest. They are masses which consist of a shell of cloudy-white chalcedony within which is sealed a quantity of water, which can often be heard splashing about when the pebble is shaken. These enhydros are found in Brazil and in the western states of America. In Oregon they are found as pseudomorphs of small shell fish.

JASPER

The variety of quartz known as jasper is a heterogeneous mass of micro-crystallized quartz which is heavily pigmented with colourful minerals. It is to this strong pigmentation that jasper owes its appeal as an ornamental stone. The colours of jasper are mainly due to iron, and are usually yellow, brown, red or green; the red when of a bright shade is quite rare and has been prized as a material for inlay and mosaics. The green jaspers when of a uniform dark shade are often known as prase, and the lighter greens as plasma. This latter type is often spotted with white. Pebbles of variegated yellow and brown colour are the so-called 'Egyptian pebbles'. Jasper takes a good polish and is often used for small objects and carvings.

The usual theory of the origin of jasper is one which ascribes the formation to igneous activity which increases the capacity of underground waters to carry silica in solution. Under favourable conditions, such as a drop in temperature, the dissolved silica is deposited along with the local impurities, of which there may be as much as 20 per cent, in the form of jasper.

Chemical and Physical Properties

Owing to the impurities present the density of the jaspers varies some-what widely and any value between 2·58 and 2·91 may be found. Most of the jaspers have a density value which is just below that of crystallized quartz (2·65) but a few specimens have shown densities which are higher. Specimens of the red and green ribbon jasper from Russia were found to have a density between 2·7 and 2·8 and a piece of heavily pigmented brown material from Siberia gave the high value of just over 2·9. The hardness of jasper is very little below that of quartz and as a rule the material is tough although it may break easily along veins or laminations. The refractive

Figure 10.18. An orbicular jasper

185

index is approximately 1·54 and the material shows no characteristic absorption spectrum or typical luminescence.

An unusual and attractive type of jasper has white or coloured 'eyes' in the matrix which may be coloured or white. Such material may have white and grey-coloured circular areas in a bright red matrix, or the matrix may be white or yellow and the circles white and red, or black and red. There are many varieties of the orbicular jaspers and the spherulites may vary in size from small dots to circles an inch or more across (*Figure 10.18*). Jasp-agate is, as the name implies, a mixture of agate and jasper and the patterning shown by polished pieces of such material can be very pleasing. Basanite is a velvety-black type of jasper with a fine grain, and unpolished plates of this material are used by jewellers for testing precious metals by their streak. It is the Lydian stone of the ancients. A brecciated jasper is found and this material takes a good polish and is used for ornaments.

Much petrified (fossil) wood is jasper, the previously existing wood fibre having been replaced molecule by molecule by silica in the form of jasper. In many cases the replacement was so slow and so perfect that every detail of the original wood structure has been preserved. Such fossil wood has been cut and polished as cabochons and for small articles. Petrified dinosaur bone from Colorado, Utah and Wyoming in the United States of America is used for ornamental purposes. Fossil 'dinny bone' is used in West Germany for such carvings as small tortoises where the markings of the fossil bone give some realism to the carving. Turritella agate (*Figure 10.19*), often used for ornamental purposes, consists of shells of the turritella which have been agatized. Generally called jasper—but which is more correctly a chert—is the light red stone often showing small portions filled with clear transparent quartz, and which is used in Germany for the production of the dyed so-called 'Swiss lapis'.

Occurrences

Jasper is of world-wide occurrence. Ribbon (riband) jasper is said to occur at Okhotsk in eastern Siberia and other varieties are found in the vicinity of Troitsk and Verkhne Uralsk in the southern Urals. India and Venezuela supply a red jasper but the most varied types of this impure quartz are found in the United States of America. Of the many American localities

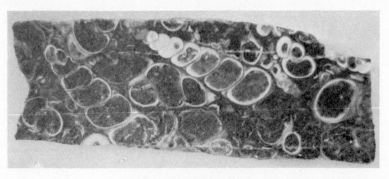

Figure 10.19. Turritella agate

mention may be made of the Morgan Hill district of Santa Clara County, California, where orbicular jasper is found in quantity; other jaspers are also found in California. Arizona, Idaho, Nevada, Oregon and Washington produce much jasper, and jasp-agate is found in the gravels of the Pecos river in Texas. The most famous locality for jasperized wood is the Arizona Petrified Forest.

OPAL

The most highly prized of the silica gemstones is the opal, but not all opal exhibits the beautiful play of colour seen in the specimens mounted in jewellery. Without these colour nuances opal is quite a common mineral and, except in certain cases, has no value in ornamentation. Four types of opal are highly prized and met with in jewellery. They are the white opal which has a light or white body colour with a fine play of colour; black opal which has a black or dark blue, green or grey body colour with vivid flashes of colour springing from the dark stone; fire opal which is transparent to translucent stone with an orange-red to red body colour which may or may not show a play of colour; and lastly, there is the water opal which shows brilliant flashes of colour in a clear colourless (water-white) stone. Other types of opal are occasionally encountered in ornamental pieces and these relatively unimportant types will be mentioned in appropriate places.

Opal has met with many vicissitudes during its long history. From Roman times until the early seventeenth century it was held in high esteem, but during the eighteenth and nineteenth centuries it fell into disfavour in the belief that the stone was a bearer of ill-fortune, a belief which was probably based on a Teutonic superstition. Others say that this disfavour came from the influence of Sir Walter Scott's novel 'Anne of Geierstein' in which opal played such a malignant part. It seems more probable, however, that Scott conceived the idea of an opal of evil influence from an already existing belief.

Chemical and Physical Properties

Opal is unlike the quartz minerals just discussed in that it is not, in the broad sense, crystalline. It is considered as a hardened jelly—a gel— which has the formula $SiO_2\,n\,H_2O$, that is silica with chemically combined water which may vary from 1 to 21 per cent, but about 6–10 per cent in precious opal. The mineral does not crystallize in any regular form as do most other gemstones but is found filling nodules, as veins or seams in rock, as botryoidal masses in cavities or as stalagmitic forms. The hardness of the gemmy varieties varies from $5\frac{1}{2}$ to $6\frac{1}{2}$ in the Mohs's scale and the fractured surface may be conchoidal or irregular.

Effects of Light

Opal has one index of refraction which varies from 1·44 to 1·46, and the density varies from 1·98 to 2·20; the black and white opals have a value near 2·10 and the fire opals are slightly lower at 2·00. The material, being singly refractive, can show no dichroism, and the absorption spectrum has little value. In the case of the fire opal the absorption spectrum is just a colour filter cutting off all the colours except the red and orange. Under both long and short-wave ultra-violet light opals showing a play of colour exhibit a luminescent response which may vary from white, to bluish, brownish or greenish with often a persistent green phosphorescence. The black opals are, however, generally inert, and the fire opals usually show a greenish-brown response. Much common opal shows a green fluorescence, and often phosphorescence, which is due to the inclusion of some secondary uranium mineral. Such uraniferous opal is common in the United States of America. The green opal from Silesia, which is coloured by nickel, is inert.

What causes the vivid coloured flashes which spring out from a piece of coloured opal? When opal is looked through at a source of light no iridescent colours are seen, the stone appearing a uniform colour which is generally creamy-white or dingy yellow, and it is only when the light impinges down on the stone that the beautiful colours are seen. The usual explanation of the cause of the iridescence is that it is due to interference of white light at thin films of material having a dissimilar refractive index to that of the main mass of the opal. Such an interference effect is the cause of the colours seen in a soap bubble or on an oily puddle of water. (The interference effects will be more fully explained in the technical section.) The thin films in opal are variously suggested as being secondary opal filling fine cracks, cracks which it is suggested were formed by contraction of the opal gel during the setting and drying. Minute calcite crystals and just air-filled cracks are other suggestions.

Recently different ideas as to the nature of the thin films have been put forward. In this the films are considered to be mesh-like layers of giant molecules of silica which have been formed by polymerization in the gel. These films are lamellar in structure, parallel and spaced at a distance from each other comparable with the wavelengths of visible light. Reflections from these equidistant layers reinforce the light and cause the brilliant flashes of colour seen in opal.

About 1964 experiments carried out by a group of Australian scientists using electron microscopy showed that the fine structure of opal consists of a regular stacking of uniform spheres of amorphous silica with regularly arranged 'voids' between. The arrangement of these spheres and voids forms a three-dimensional cubic lattice producing a three-dimensional diffraction grating. Under such conditions, Bragg diffraction of light occurs causing pure spectral colours to appear at different angles. The size of the spheres decides the longest wavelength of light which can be diffracted (*Figure 10.20*); thus, regular sheets of small size spheres may only diffract blue light and no green, yellow, orange or red. Larger spheres may diffract green, blue and violet light, while still larger spheres may give red light and all the other colours of shorter wavelength. In all cases the size of the spheres in gem opal are of a suitable size to diffract light through 180°. Opals are best viewed on a black background which would absorb any light transmitted through the stone which otherwise may be reflected or scattered back diluting the coloured flashes. Thus the effectiveness of black-based opal doublets and black dyed opal is explained.

The play of colour of opal is an iridescent effect, and the term opalescence so often applied to the colours seen in opal is strictly incorrect. Opalescence is correctly applied to the milky effect seen in common opal, some moonstone and in the so-called opal-glass. It is due to the scattering of light from small particles in the stone.

Varieties of Opal

Several of the common opals, mainly those with pronounced colour, have been cut as gems. Apart from the fire opal already mentioned there is a green opal, not unlike chrysoprase in appearance, which owes its colour to nickel. An attractive cherry-red-coloured opal, a rose-coloured opal and much yellow opal is found and occasionally cut. Opal is a common petrifying agent and much opal is pseudomorphous after wood. An opalized

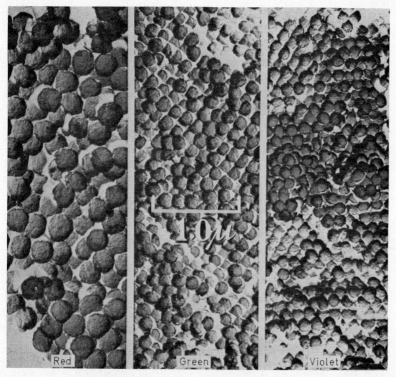

Figure 10.20. Electron micrographs of precious opal illustrating the maximum colours produced by spheres of different sizes

wood, yellow in colour with black markings, is found at Washoe County, Nevada, and attractive cabochons have been cut from it. This material is noted for its green fluorescence under ultra-violet light, a fluorescence activated by the presence in the opal of traces of a uranium mineral. The most interesting pseudomorphs in opal are the opalized freshwater and marine shells, belemnites and bones from prehistoric animals which are found in Australia. Opal is often found as pseudomorphs after gypsum,

189

glauberite, calcite and other minerals. Opalized crystal aggregates of such minerals, particularly glauberite, are known as 'pineapple opal' and form attractive mineral specimens.

Hyalite is a colourless transparent variety of opal that closely resembles melted glass; it is sometimes called Müller's glass. When this type of material shows a play of colour it is then the prized water opal. Common opal is translucent to opaque and of various hues. When milk-white, yellowish or greenish it is called milk opal. Hydrophane is a curious type of light coloured but opaque opal that becomes transparent and exhibits iridescence when soaked in water. Cacholong is an opal with either a porcelain-like or mother-of-pearl-like lustre which is so porous that it will adhere to the tongue. Menilite is an opaque greyish to brownish concretionary type, and tabasheer is an opal-like silica found within the joints of bamboo. Jasper opal is red, reddish-brown or yellow-brown and closely resembles ordinary jasper. A violet-coloured opal is found in Mexico.

Backgrounds for Opals

Thin seams of opal in dark or light-coloured sandstone are often cut so that the top of the stone is brilliant precious opal on the sandstone which forms a strong backing for the opal. Likewise, a thin piece of good opal on potch may be cut so that the potch acts as a backing. Such opals might well be mistaken for opal doublets but careful examination of the edge of the stone by a lens will show the slight irregularity of the matrix and opal and the absence of a distinctive join as seen in opal doublets. Such stones are rightly termed true opal. Opal when in small areas in the mother rock may be cut complete with the matrix and such stones are known as opal matrix. Sometimes opal forms in ironstone and the opal matrix cut from this shows patches of iridescent opal in a chocolate-brown matrix, and a similarly appearing type of opal occurs where the ironstone and opal have impregnated roots of the gidgee tree (an acacia). The stones cut from this material are called gidgee opals. Such iron-impregnated stones have a higher density than true opal and may range in density from 2·65 to 3·00.

In order to make use of thin films of opal, which are often brightly iridescent, they are made into the so-called opal doublets by backing them with pieces of potch, black onyx or a black glass called 'opalite', which is obtained from Belgium. The cement used to join the pieces has a high melting point so that it will not be affected by such heat as boiling water. An ingenious triplet is made where an ordinary opal doublet is completed with a coverglass of rock crystal which fits over the top of the iridescent opal. Water opals always show their play of colour better when they are on a dark background, so it is common to mount such opals in a closed setting with a piece of black, or preferably purple, silk below. An imitation opal made of small fragments of real opal set in a black resin has been encountered.

Occurrences

Czechoslovakia

There is little doubt that the opal known in Roman times came from the mines near Červenica (Czerwenitza), or in Hungarian as Vörösvágás, now in Czechoslovakia but formerly in Hungary. These mines lie some 6 miles north of Prešov (Eperjes), a town some 20 miles north of the important centre of Košice (Kassa or Kaschau) in the eastern part of Slovakia. The mines are in the Libánka and Simonka mountains, and at the foot of the latter is the small settlement of Dubnik (Opalbanya) which may be said to be the opal centre. There is a further mine lying to the east of Košice at Nagy-Mihály.

The Hungarian opal, for the opal from Czechoslovakia is still better known under the old name, is found in nests in a greyish-brown andesitic lava. The mining in this area is known with certainty to have been carried on since the fourteenth century and in the former times was worked by open cuttings. Today, however, a perfect network of levels has been tunnelled into the mountains. The Czechoslovakian stones have a milk-white background upon which small points of red, blue and green form a mosaic of changing hues, the so-called harlequin opal. The stones from this locality supplied the world before the discovery of the Australian opal fields.

The mining in the then Hungarian opal deposits was, until 1788, carried on successfully by the peasants of Červenica, but in that year the Hungarian Government claimed a monopoly of the mines and instituted underground working. The government endeavour was unsuccessful and was soon abandoned and for several decades the mines were unworked. They were then farmed out to individuals and successfully operated until the rich Australian fields were discovered.

Mexico

Opal, especially the fire opal, was probably known to the Aztecs (A.D. 1200–1519). The Mexican occurrences are in the States of Queretaro, Hidalgo, Guerrero, Michoacan, Jalisco, Chihuahua and San Luis Potosi, the mineral being found in cavities of volcanic lavas rich in silica (*Figure 10.21*). The yellow and hyacinth-red-coloured fire opal is found in a trachytic porphyry at Zimapan in the State of Hidalgo, and hyalite (with probably the iridescent water opal) comes from San Luis Potosi. The mines of Queretaro, which were first discovered in 1835 and have been systematically worked since 1870, are the most important. The centre of the opal trade and for the cutting of opal is the town of Queretaro; the lapidaries there use home constructed apparatus and turn out quite good specimens of polished opal. Opals of many different types are found in Mexico, but except for the fire opal, the stones do not have the quality of the opals from Australia. A non-iridescent cherry-red and a yellow-coloured opal is found in Mexico and is sometimes cut.

Honduras

The opal was found in Honduras prior to 1843, for in that year the deposits of Gracios o Dios were first described. It is considered highly probable that the pre-Colombian Quiche procured the opals used in their jewellery from the sources in Honduras. The mines are near the town of Gracias in the western part of Honduras and the opal is found in veins and bands in a dark reddish-coloured trachyte. Another source is near the town of Erandique some 25 miles south of Gracias. The opal from Honduras is unimportant commercially. Some opal is found in Guatemala and Brazil.

Australia

The credit for the first, but unrecorded, discovery of opal in the Australian continent is generally considered to belong to Mingaye, a German

Figure 10.21. An opal mine in Mexico

geologist, who in 1849 found opal near Angaston in South Australia. It was in 1872, however, that the first recorded discovery of opal was made in Australia. This was the boulder opal, thin veins of opal ramifying through hard jaspideous brown-coloured greasy boulders, and was found at Listowel Downs in central Queensland; in 1878 a company was floated to market

192

this opal. The boulders occur at various depths and are very hard and difficult to break, but the thin veins of opal are usually brilliant. The material is principally used for cameo carving.

Two sub-varieties of the boulder opal are the sandstone boulder and the yowah nut. The first of these consists of concretions made up of shells of coarse sandstone and hard siliceous clay with layers of opal between them or filling the centre. The yowah nuts—which are found not far from Yowah Homestead, hence the name—are small boulders about the size of a walnut and are found in a unique formation consisting of a regular band containing the nuts packed in like a conglomerate. The opal, like the larger boulder opal, is found either as a central kernel or as thin veils surrounding an iron stone centre or traversing the nut, but never reaching to the outer edge.

Opal may be found in a free sandstone in the form of veins or pipes varying in thickness up to an inch or more. This type is known as sandstone opal and seems to have been first found in Queensland in 1889. In this same year four prospectors, travelling in the semi-desert country nearly 700 miles inland from Sydney, wounded a kangaroo and while following the tracks of the wounded animal came upon loose opal on the ground. This find was the beginning of the famous White Cliffs opal field in Yungnulgra country about 65 miles north-west from the town of Wilcannia and some 130 miles from Broken Hill in New South Wales. Although S. R. Wilkinson in 1877 reported upon a find of opal in a soft vesicular basalt on Rocky Bridge Creek, a tributary of the Abercrombie river, the White Cliffs find was the first important opal discovery in New South Wales. The 'float' opal (loose opal on the surface) first encountered at White Cliffs indicated the presence of opal *in situ*. Examination revealed that a fine-grained siliceous sandstone occurring at depths of 25–40 ft. below the surface, called the 'bandstone', was a marker horizon for opal. Above and below this bandstone, which generally contains no opal, are fine-grained clayey sandstones and in the underlying bed opal is most abundantly found. The colourful precious opal is found in irregular patches in the thin veins of potch—the miners' term for opal which may be colourful but not showing the play of colour, or as they say 'not alive'—which fills the joints and bedding planes of the sandstone. This opal is called seam opal. It is in the opal from this district that the fossil molluscs, crinoids, belemnites and the bones of ancient vertebrate animals are found completely petrified with opal.

Originally known as Wallangulla, Lightning Ridge, just beyond the town of Walgett in north-west New South Wales and about 40 miles south of the Queensland border, is the famed locality for the black opal first found here in 1903. The rock formation is here similar to that of White Cliffs, except that there are four levels of bandstone, beneath each of which there is the white opal-rich clayey sandstone which the miners call the 'opal dirt'. The opal itself is usually found at Lightning Ridge in the form of isolated nodules to which the miners have given the name 'nobbies'. These nobbies may be opal replacement after sponges or corals.

Other opal fields in Queensland, situated mostly in desert country and suffering from lack of water supply, are the Hayricks opal mine which lies north-north-west of Quilpie, some 700 miles from Brisbane, and isolated occurrences throughout the desert area of south-central Queensland. The

Hayricks opal mine, so-called because it is situated amidst a striking group of sandstone mesas, supplies opal which is found in cracks in ironstone boulders, and is won by driving tunnels into the hillside. In New South Wales, apart from White Cliffs and Lightning Ridge which are the only two important localities in the state, mention must be made of the find at Tintenbar 5 miles north of Ballina. Opal was found here during 1901 but was not considered as a commercial possibility until 1919. The opal occurs in cavities in a decomposed basalt or is weathered out from the cavities and lies loose in the soil. The Tintenbar opal has a transparent matrix upon which the play of colours flash out, but the stones have a marked tendency to craze and for that reason the mine soon ceased operation. Other New South Wales sources are at Purnanga and Grawin, which must be considered as extensions of the White Cliffs and Lightning Ridge deposits respectively, and at Tooraweanah, Warrumbungle mountains where opal is found filling vesicles in a trachyte. Milparinka and Brindingabba near Hungerford on the Queensland border are other locations.

Seam opal, similar to that found at White Cliffs, was discovered during 1915 at Coober Pedy (Stuarts Range) in the Stuarts Range mountains of South Australia. Coober Pedy is an aboriginal name meaning 'a man in a hole' which is literally true, for all the miners' homes are underground excavations in the hillside. The precious white opal is associated with gypsum in the sandstone. Coober Pedy opal has a slight tendency to crack if it is brought up into the hot atmosphere from depths greater than 80 ft., for in summer the temperature gets up to as high as 130°F.

In 1930 opal was found at Andamooka (an aborigine word meaning 'no name') which lies some 375 miles from Adelaide and 270 miles south-east of Coober Pedy. This field, which covers only a small area, is comparatively easily worked, for the opal lies close to the surface of the band which is itself not far from the surface. Andamooka has become quite famous, not only for the type of black opal which is mined there, but for the lovely 'Andamooka opal', which when found in 1949 weighed, before cutting, no less than 6 ounces and which was eventually cut into a cabochon $2\frac{3}{4}$ in. long and weighing 203 carats. This lovely opal was set into a necklet which was presented to Her Majesty Queen Elizabeth II. In 1945 a new opal locality at Amberooka 300 miles north of Coober Pedy was discovered, where opal very different in appearance to most other Australian opal was reported found. This opal is semi-transparent with a blue body colour and a strong play of colour in green. In the same year there was reported the discovery of another opal deposit 9 miles north-west of Coober Pedy.

The 1960's brought the problem of the 'treated' opal. Certain unsaleable and previously discarded opal from the Andamooka diggings of South Australia was found to be susceptible to treatment giving it a dark background which brought out the small patches of colour. The principle used was similar to that carried out in the colouring of chalcedony to produce black onyx. One version states that the treatment is by soaking preformed stones in sugar solution, or glucose, and then 'carbonizing' with sulphuric acid followed by low heating. The darkened stones are then lightly polished. Another method mentioned is by burying the stones in cinders, covering the whole with motor car sump oil and setting fire to it. The fact that a given opal is treated cannot be surely proved, but the peculiar mosaic-like patches of colour indicate this type of opal. Unfortunately there is a natural opal with an oolitic structure which can appear similar to the treated opal.

Mining methods—In Australia the mining of opal is carried out by the sinking of a shaft, usually 5 ft. by $2\frac{1}{2}$ ft., down to below the steel-like band of hard rock, which is known as 'shincracker' as the pick is liable to cause fragments to fly off and strike the miners' shins. Penetrating the band the miner, who is known as a 'gouger', comes to the layer of opal dirt and works into this layer. Above the shaft a windlass is fixed and by a rope and crude bullock-hide or metal bucket removes the earth, or as the miner calls it the mullock, to the dumps on the surface (*Figure 10.22*). At the bottom of the mine, which may go down to 80 ft. or more, the opal is gouged out with

Figure 10.22. Opal mining at Andamooka. The miner turning the windlass is hauling up a bucket which a miner below ground has filled. In the background is an empty bucket

knives or small gougers, or with the 'spider', a steel spike or twisted piece of fencing wire made primarily to hold the candle used to light the workings and which is just jabbed into the sandstone wall by the side of the miner. The miners mostly sell all the opal they find in the rough, just nipping off a piece from the edge to see its quality, or in the case of boulders splitting with a 'tomahawk' is often carried out. Much Australian opal is now cut at the fields, particularly at Lightning Ridge. The practice of picking over old mine dumps for overlooked opal is another form of 'mining'. Such procedure is termed 'noodling'.

Other Occurrences

Fine quality precious opal is found at Virgin Valley, Humboldt County, Nevada, in the United States, where it is found in cracks and seams in opalized wood. Opal from this deposit, which was discovered about 1906, often tends to suffer from cracking or surface crazing. A dendritic opal, white and multi-coloured, occurs in many places in the United States, in Rhodesia and South Africa. The non-iridescent green opal called prase opal which is coloured by nickel is found at Kosemutz and Zabkowice (Frankenstein) in Silesia, Poland.

CHAPTER 11

TURQUOISE AND LAPIS-LAZULI

TURQUOISE

The gem turquoise, which owes its beauty entirely to its superb colour, has been used for ornamentation from remote antiquity. It was certainly known at 3000 B.C. and possibly prior to the first Dynasty of Ancient Egypt. Turquoise was also a prized gem of the lost civilizations of ancient Mexico.

The derivation of the name turquoise, by which the stone has been known since antiquity, is clouded in mystery. Turquoise (Turquois in the U.S.A.) is reputed to have been derived from the French pierre turquoise, or in old French tourques, which means 'Turkey stone', not because the stone came from Turkey, but because the Persian material, and perhaps that from Sinai Peninsula, entered Europe by way of Turkey. That is one version of the derivation of the name turquoise, another is that the name Turkey implies coming from the Orient, as it was a term of uncertain value indicating strange or foreign. That the Turkish people were conversant with turquoise is certain, particularly the material from Persia which they called by the Persian name firuse. Pliny, that great Roman recorder, mentions callais (callaina or callaica) as being a pale blue stone which may have been turquoise.

Chemical and Physical Properties

Turquoise, which is mostly found in arid regions, occurs as incrustations, nodules, botryoidal groups and as veins. The mineral has only been found in distinct crystals, of the triclinic system, at one place, that is at Lynch in Virginia, U.S.A., in 1912. The usual formation consists of a crypto-crystalline aggregate with the crystallites so fine that the material may be considered to be practically amorphous, and the mass is to some extent porous. The chemical composition of turquoise is that of a hydrous copper aluminium phosphate with some iron, but the composition is to some extent variable. The formula is given as $CuAl_6(PO_4)_4(OH)_85H_2O$, with some alumina replaced by ferric oxide. The cause of the beautiful blue colour of turquoise is not known for certainty. The sky-blue perfection colour, known in America as 'robin's egg blue' (the American robin is a red-breasted thrush), has been ascribed to copper and to copper and iron in the more bluish-green varieties, the copper being in the mineral as copper phosphate or as copper aluminate.

A convincing theory is that a complex ammino-copper ion, which might have originated from an animal source, may be responsible for the blue colour of turquoise, and that the alteration of the blue colour to green might well be due to dehydration. The colour of American turquoise is said to fade more readily than does the Persian material owing to the greater porosity of the former, due perhaps to the greater readiness to dry in the case of porous material. A story is told that merchants in order to find out whether a stone is likely to fade, carry them against the skin underneath the armpit; this does not seem to be a satisfactory test if the loss of colour is due, as is most likely, to loss of water. It has been recorded that miners bury turquoise in moist earth before offering them for sale, and that some stones regain their colour if soaked in water or in weak uric acid.

The hardness of turquoise is slightly less than 6 on Mohs's scale, and the density varies from 2·60 to 2·90, the lower ranges from 2·60 to 2·70 being usual for the more porous American stones, and from 2·75 to 2·85 for the fine compact Persian material.

The mean refractive index of turquoise approximates to 1·62. Actual determinations on the Virginian crystals (by W. T. Schaller) gave the principal indices as 1·61 and 1·65, biaxial and positive in sign. Turquoise shows an absorption spectrum consisting of a vague band at 4600 Å and a line at 4320 Å, which together form a distinctive pattern. The line at 4200 Å is too far in the violet to be seen. At best turquoise is only feebly translucent and the spectrum must usually be seen by reflected light. Turquoise shows a variable response to long-wave ultra-violet light, the glows seen varying from a dim greenish-yellow to a bright blue. With the short-wave lamp turquoise is practically inert and no glow is observed when x-rays are the exciting rays. The so-called synthetic turquoises do not fluoresce under ultra-violet rays but some pastes of turquoise colour show a strong blue under the short-wave lamp in contradistinction to the real turquoise.

Although somewhat soft, turquoise takes a good polish and being practically opaque with a wax-like lustre scratches on the surface are scarcely noticeable. There is no advantage in faceting turquoise, so that the cabochon-cut is nearly always used except for the small flat pieces so commonly used for inlay work which is a feature of some Oriental and Mexican work. Turquoise is used for carvings and for the panel-like pieces which are produced. Turquoise is so often disseminated throughout the limonite matrix that no stone large enough to cut can be got from the rough material. The stone is then cut complete with the matrix, which may be brown limonite or fawn sandstone. Such pieces are termed turquoise matrix and a stone containing patches of matrix is shown in Plate XIX. Blue turquoise is often engraved with Persian or Arabic inscriptions and the incised design inlaid with gold.

Occurrences

Persia

The finest turquoises come from the district of Nishapur, 15 miles west of Meshed in the province of Khorassan in Iran (Persia). The chain of mountains which extend from west to east between Kotshan and Nishapur consist of nummulitic limestone and sandstone associated with clay slates and interbedded with large masses of rock salt and gypsum. These rock masses have been broken through by volcanic rocks of tertiary age. The turquoise is confined to the 6,600 ft. peak called the Ali-mersai where the gem material is found in the mother rock, a porphyritic much weathered trachyte, and is cemented together by the brown iron-ore known as limonite, the turquoise being found between the layers of limonite and also in the debris (scree) at the foot of the mountain. Many hundreds of mines, which have a long history, have been worked in this area. In many cases Persian turquoise is found as a pseudomorph after feldspar and the cut stones are often characterized by small patches and veins of whitish material. Good quality Persian turquoise has a fairly constant density of 2·79. The stones are marketed at Meshed and usually exported to Russia and India.

Tibet

Much has been written of the turquoise as the national stone of Tibet where turquoise of a green colour is the more highly prized. There appears to be some doubt whether the stone is found in Tibet. Berthold Laufer states that the first European author to report the indigenous occurrence of turquoise in Tibet proper, as far as he could ascertain, was the Capuchin friar Francesco Orazio della Penna di Billi (1730). Laufer also states that according to Sarat Chandra Das the finest turquoises are obtained from a mine in the Gangs-chan mountains (Chang Chenmo range?) of Nagari-Khorsum in west Tibet. It is further recorded that turquoise occurs in several mountains of the great state of Derge in eastern Tibet, but the exact locations were not given. The material from the latter locality is said to be green in colour, the most prized shade in Tibet where the material is known by the name gyu, which is pronounced yu; whether this word was derived from the Sanskrit or the Chinese is not clear (yu is the name for jade in China).

India and China

Neither the peoples of ancient India nor of old China seem to have been acquainted with turquoise, which does not appear to have entered either of these countries until the Mogul period of the fourteenth century, although there has been the suggestion that the gem entered both India and China through the agency of the Arabs after the conquest of Persia in A.D. 642. The Mogul name for turquoise is said to have been kiris.

The existence of true turquoise in India is doubtful. From the presence of blue streaks in the copper ores of Ajmir it was earlier thought that turquoise could be found in India, but later work suggests that these blue streaks are a secondary copper ore. Marco Polo speaks of the existence of turquoise in the province of Caindu, which has been identified with the present Chinese province of Sze-Ch'uan, a territory then largely inhabited by Tibetan tribes. Turquoise is said to come from the Hopeh province of China.

Egypt

The Egyptain turquoise from the Sinai peninsula is historically the most important source, if not commercially important, for there is little doubt that the mines of Maghârah and Serâbît el Khâdim were the source of the turquoise used in Egypt over 3,000 years ago. True there is little proof that the mines were worked for turquoise or for the copper ores, for malachite, azurite and chrysocolla were also found in the mines although little now remains. Turquoise was undoubtedly used for ornamentation, not only in the Old and Middle Kingdoms, but as early as the Baderian period. The ancient name for turquoise was majkat, which in early translations was transcribed as malachite and thus accounts for the absence of the name turquoise in old records. It is interesting to note that the site of the port through which the Egyptians brought the turquoise, with which the Pharaohs and their ladies were adorned, was found in 1947. This is a low mound on the edge of the Merkhah plain about 100 yards from the Gulf from which the mines of Serâbît el Khâdim are but 17 miles inland.

The turquoise district of Sinai lies along the south-western coastlines of the peninsula bordering on the Gulf of Suez and is some 250 square miles in area. The deposits are in country which is rugged and bare and remarkable for the pronounced faulting which produces canyon-like wadis or valleys. Although the rainfall is only one inch a year, a heavy shower converts these wadis into raging torrents. There are six mines in the area, Wadi Maghârah (or Egma), Wadi Shellal, Jebel Ham'd, Um Bogma, in which area extensive mining for manganese has recently been carried on, Abu Hamad and Serâbît el Khâdim. Abu Hamad, some 16 miles in extent, Wadi Shellal and Um Bogma are poor deposits. Jebel Ham'd has not been worked for many years because the spirits of seven Bedouin who were buried by a fall of roof which had been undercut are said to haunt the place. Wadi Maghârah, the valley of the cave or grotto, is the site of ancient workings which were believed to have been worked out about 2000 B.C. Spasmodic working is carried out by destitute Bedouin who break up the sandstone at promising points by the use of home-made gunpowder, made from sulphur, saltpetre and charcoal locally obtained. A yellow seam of sandstone, consisting mainly of coarse grains of yellow quartz cemented by an iron-red clay is believed locally to indicate the presence of turquoise. This sandstone is called Al'erg Safra and directly below it is the 'baloota', a bed of paler sandstone often dirty white in colour. There is a number of stopes at this mine, the larger ones having names, the largest 'Al Yahoodiah' (the Jewess) is of immense size and the next largest, called 'El Higgigah' (the Pilgrimage), with 'Al Gâneyn' (the two rich ones, or brothers) have produced pieces of turquoise of large size even in recent years. Equally important in ancient times was the mine at Serâbît el Khâdim, $2\frac{1}{2}$ miles north of an ancient ruined temple dedicated to Hathor, Goddess of Turquoise; this mine is also spasmodically worked at present times.

Formation of turquoise in sandstone—The probable cause of the formation of turquoise in the fissured sandstone, the fissures being due to local faulting or to intrusions, is that meteoric waters, bearing in solution carbon dioxide and sulphur (by decomposition of H_2S) derived from organic matter existing on the basalts, decomposed some of the soluble constituents of the volcanic rock. Since the decomposition of any rock is accomplished by the removal of the more soluble bases and a concentration of the relatively insoluble oxides of iron, aluminium and silicon, some of these minerals descend in suspension, or in solution, and as they descend they dissolve out other constituents in the sandstone, and the limestone—such as phosphorus—in the fossil remains. Copper is also known to exist in the shales and plant remains and was also carried down in solution.

Having passed through fissures in the superincumbent layers of strata, the solutions descend still further into the sandstone until they become super-saturated, forming a zone of cementation. Pressure due to minor earth movements, such as earthquakes, causing hardening, drying and concentration until the chemical form of turquoise is assumed. These earth movements no doubt account for the presence of the much brecciated fragments of sandstone included in the gem veins and in the turquoise itself. It happens that the highly ferruginous sandstone contains the best turquoise owing to the sandstone containing considerable clay and shale at this level thus forming a much more compact stratum. The minerals in solution are held up here, the stratum being impervious, and considerable lateral extension occurs at some points giving rise to horizontal seams of turquoise parallel to the bedding planes of the sandstone.

Colour range—The Egyptian turquoise is more often greeny-blue rather than the sky-blue colour of the material from Persia, but some fine blue material is obtained from Sinai and this is characterized by the polished surface showing small circular areas of deeper blue colour. The density of Egyptian turquoise varies between 2·7 and 2·9, the purer blue-coloured material having the higher density which is usually not far removed from a value of 2·81. Some of the Egyptian turquoise is said to suffer from fading, but as a rule the material is fairly stable. The wily Bedouin are said to have a trick of colouring poor colour or greenish turquoise by soaking it in oil and polishing with an oily rag, and it is said that local lapidaries even paint the stones.

United States of America

In the western hemisphere turquoise is found in some profusion in the south-western states of the North American continent, and these were probably the sources which supplied the turquoise used by the Aztecs of Mexico, and perhaps even by the Toltecs who preceded them. The Aztec use of turquoise for decoration was mainly by inlaying, often on a wooden base with a wax or gum as a cement. Superb examples of such work are in the British Museum, one gruesome piece being the front of a human skull, completely covered with a mosaic of turquoise and lignite with the eyes of polished pyrites and the teeth of white shell. The Pueblo Indians of the American south-west also featured the inlaying of turquoise, and this may be a survival of the ancient Mexican art. The Apache Indian, who called the turquoise by the name duklij, highly prized the gem for its talismanic value, one of its supposed powers was to aid the warrior or hunter by assuring the accuracy of his aim, for if a turquoise be affixed to a gun or bow the missile sped from the weapon would go straight to its mark.

The turquoise used by the Aztecs is supposed to have been obtained mostly from the mines in New Mexico, probably from a trachyte rock in the Los Cerrilos mountains near Santa Fé, and from Nevada, Arizona and California. The sources in Lower California (Baja California) are not too well described but there is a source some 20 miles south of Rosalia on the west coast of the peninsula. In Nevada turquoise is found at a number of places, particularly in the Toiyabe range near Austin and at Colombus east of Tonapah.

In California the turquoise is found mainly in the Mohave (Mojave) desert in San Bernardino County, where the mines were worked in ancient times, not by the Californian natives but by the Pueblo people from Arizona and New Mexico who probably entered California and worked the mines seasonally. These miners worked exposed turquoise veins to a depth of about 12 ft. as open pits, by breaking and crushing the waste mass with hafted stone axes and hammers and throwing the muck out with a hand scoop made from a tortoise carapace or the shoulder blade of an animal. Heavy stone-pointed picks weighing up to eight pounds were used to break out the rock and there is some evidence that wedges were also used. No signs of the fire and water method of breaking rocks were found in the Californian mines, although there is ample evidence that such a method was used in Arizona and New Mexico. The mines of California are in the area of the Turquoise mountain, 10 miles north-east of Silver Lake. Turquoise is not now mined in California.

Turquoise has been found in the State of Colorado, particularly at the Hall mine near Villa Grove and the King mine near Manassa, where it is found in a felsite porphyry; at the Turquoise Chief mine near Leadville in Lake County, where it is found in Algonkian granite; and lastly in a stream bed near Creede, Mineral County. The material from Colorado varies considerably in quality from a firm compact turquoise of good colour to a soft semi-compact material useless for high class gems.

The turquoise is said to have been formed by meteoric waters leaching the constituents from alkali feldspars, neighbouring copper ores and apatite and depositing them in fractures. A characteristic of American turquoise is that it is lighter in colour, is more porous and chalky, and has a density which lies between 2·6 and 2·7. The find of turquoise in triclinic crystals in Virginia has already been mentioned.

Other Occurrences

A number of occurrences of turquoise are known in the Uzbek Republic of the U.S.S.R., particularly near the Kansaisk lead mines near Kuraminsk and in the Karatube mountains. Turquoise has been said to have been found at Oelnitz in Saxony and in Silesia, but little is known about these sources. A specimen of 'turquoise' from the Bunny mine at St. Austell, Cornwall and a similar specimen from Castle-an-Dinas wolfram mine at St. Columb Major has been found to be a new mineral intermediate between chalcosiderite and andrewsite and forms the middle member of what is probably an isomorphous series. This new mineral was given the name rashleighite, after Philip Rashleigh, one of the earliest of Cornish mineralogists. The turquoise-blue mineral from Liskeard, Cornwall, which was known under the name 'henwoodite' has from recent x-ray crystal analysis now found to be true turquoise. Vugs of small crystals are found in Cornwall.

Turquoise has also been reported from the Chuquicamata mine in northern Chile, some of which is said to equal in colour the best Persian turquoise. The mineral has been found near Bodalla on the south coast where it occurs in black cherts in the Wagonga series. Occurrences have also been reported from Victoria and Queensland. A 'turquoise' from a mountain near the town of Dayboro, about 40 miles north-west of Brisbane was found to have properties similar to variscite. The material has a density near to 2·5 and a refractive index of 1·58. There is an unconfirmed report of a turquoise deposit in South-West Africa.

Simulation

The material found exclusively in an ancient Celtic grave at Mane-er H'rock near Lockmariaquer in Brittany, so often mentioned in literature under the name callainite, is probably a variety of variscite having a better transparency and a bluer colour than is usual for this mineral. Naturally occurring minerals which have a strong resemblance to turquoise are lazulite and wardite, and mention must be made of the so-called 'bone turquoise' or odontolite, which is a fossil tooth or bone coloured blue with vivianite. These will be mentioned later.

It is not surprising that turquoise, so highly prized by the peoples of ancient Egypt, should have been one of the first gems to be imitated in base material. One of these early types consisted of an artificial frit composed of a crystalline compound of silica, a copper compound, which may be malachite, calcium carbonate and soda (natron). This frit, called by Vitruvius caeruleum and by Theophrastus kyanos, was, in addition to its use as a pigment, carved into small objects. Faience, perhaps better expressed as a glazed siliceous ware, was used for making beads, necklace pendants, rings, amulets and small animal figures. The material was known from pre-dynastic times (pre 4777 B.C.) and was still being produced as late as the Roman period about 51 B.C. The broken surface of faience consists of two, sometimes three, layers. There is always an inner core with an outer coating of coloured vitreous glaze, which, when present, is very marked on account of the difference in colour and density. The core consists of a fine gritty material and the glaze is a thin coating of true glass, and the special layer is probably used to enhance the glass.

Although glass has been reported to have been used prior to the eighteenth dynasty (1567–1328 B.C.), no clear confirmation is forthcoming on this point and in some quarters it has been disputed. Of these ancient blue glasses imitating turquoise most were found to be coloured by copper compounds, one, from the tomb of Tutankhamen, was coloured by cobalt and two of the Ptolemaic period by iron.

Imitations of turquoise are made in glass, enamel, stained chalcedony and rarely, porcelain. The stained chalcedonies are considerably more translucent than true turquoise and have a density of 2·63, a refractive index of 1·53 and a hardness of $6\frac{1}{2}$ in Mohs's scale. Glass imitation turquoises usually have a density near to 3·3, although lower values have been recorded. Glass imitations usually show small bubbles just below the surface or as pit marks on the surface. Porcelain imitations are not common but have a typical china lustre, are usually glazed, and have a fairly constant density of between 2·3 and 2·4.

Many artificial products made to imitate turquoise have been marketed. The so-called 'Viennese turquoise' is made by pressing together a precipitate of aluminium phosphate coloured blue by copper oleate. Another type is composed of malachite, aluminium hydroxide and phosphoric acid carefully mixed and ground to a fine powder, which, after heating to over 100°C, is compressed with great force. A new German product, produced in 1957, was found to be a mixture of bayerite and copper phosphate with the dark veinings of the 'matrix' due to some amorphous iron compound. This material is marketed under the name neolith. Some turquoise imitations from the United States of America were found to consist of grains of some natural minerals, including a copper mineral bonded with a styrenated alkyd type of plastic. It is reported that a suitably dyed jasper is another imitation of turquoise (*cf.* 'Swiss lapis').

The density of these 'pressed' and 'bonded' pieces is always lower than for natural turquoise. The pressed types give, when a 'snap' density is taken, a value of about 2·4, but on soaking the value reached may be near 2·6. The plastic bonded types vary considerably in density and range from as low as 1·85 to as great as 2·5, but are usually between 2·0 and 2·4. The refractive index of the Viennese turquoise is shown by a vague shadow edge at 1·45, that of the German types about 1·55, and the plastic bonded types near 1·56.

The easiest test for these pressed and bonded imitations is to place a spot of hydrochloric acid on an inconspicuous part of the specimen. The acid turns to a yellow-green colour which will stain a piece of filter paper (blotting paper) when the acid is soaked up by it. Such an effect does not occur with true turquoise, nor with the resin-bonded true turquoise mentioned below. Carefully applied the test does not damage the stone except for the possibility of taking away the polish at the spot where the acid was applied. These imitations blacken or fuse to a black glass when heated and do not decrepitate like true turquoise does. Further they do not show the turquoise spectrum.

An extension of the bonded types is the resin-bonded true turquoise which is produced in Arizona from local material got from the Turquoise mountain in Cochise County and near Morenci. Some of these pieces may have faked cracks suitably coloured to imitate true turquoise matrix. This bonded real turquoise does show weakly the turquoise absorption spectrum of the two bands in the blue-violet. Such bonded turquoise may be readily identified by the lower density which may vary from 2·18 to 2·55 and also by a simple chemical test which can be carried out on a very small scraping removed from some inconspicuous part of the specimen. To do this the scraping from the specimen is placed in a micro-test tube which is then strongly heated. If the material is resin-bonded a liquid, probably yellowish in colour, will condense in droplets on the walls of the cooler part of the tube, and, usually in a position between the hot part and the liquid condensate there will appear a narrow ring of sublimate consisting of feathery crystals of phthalic anhydride (see *Figure 11.1*). Further, an unmistakable odour is given off, which, although not unduly strong can best be described as 'itchy'.

The phthalic anhydride is best confirmed by rubbing in the sublimate, by means of a glass rod, a very small quantity of resorcinol and one drop of concentrated sulphuric acid and gently reheating *in situ*. Wash out with water into a small beaker and make this alkaline with sodium hydroxide or sodium carbonate when the characteristic yellow solution with a strong green fluorescence is produced. This procedure is in fact always the safest when testing for alkyds, as when these occur in a heavily polymerized molecule direct heating of the original substance with resorcinol will often lead to a negative result.

Figure 11.1. Feathery crystals of phthalic anhydride produced when alkyd resins are heated in a test tube
(Photo: G. Wild)

The colour of some turquoise tends to bleach on exposure to the sun, or to turn greenish with time. Soaking the stones in ammonia is said to improve the colour, but the effect is rarely permanent. Poor coloured stones are occasionally stained with Prussian blue, but such staining may be detected by the loss of colour at the place where a spot of ammonia has been applied. Specimens of turquoise are sometimes oiled or waxed and are considered commercially acceptable, and, presumably the method of hardening the soft friable American turquoise by impregnating with colloidal silica is also acceptable. Some turquoise which has lost its colour may sometimes be brought back to a good blue by treatment with solvents, but the results cannot be predicted.

Clever fakes of turquoise have been made of coloured clay, and a 're-constructed turquoise' is said to have been made from finely powdered ivory with copper stain and cement. Doublets have been made with a low cabochon of turquoise-coloured opacified glass with a back of blue-stained chalcedony. Cabochons cut from bone and suitably coloured, usually with phosphate of iron, are easily detected by their low density (about 2), by their effervescence with acid and by their organic structure. Other imitations of turquoise are blue-dyed howlite; surface-stained limestone; blue-dyed and plastic-treated marble beads, and recently there has been produced a completely plastic turquoise imitation which can be easily detected by its low density.

LAPIS-LAZULI

The beautiful blue stone called lapis-lazuli, has been known from ancient times. The mineral owes its name, as do several other blue minerals, to the Persian word lazhward, meaning blue. The colour of lapis-lazuli varies from a blue tending to a greenish-blue to a rich purple blue, the perfection colour being a dark blue of extraordinary depth and intensity. Owing to the inclusion of iron pyrites within the stone most specimens show bright brassy specks, which, if not too prominent, are valued as a sign that the stone is genuine. In olden days the stone was known as sapphirus, a name which is now applied to our sapphire, the blue corundum.

Chemical and Physical Properties

Unlike most of the gem materials lapis-lazuli is a complex aggregate of several minerals, particularly hauynite $(NaCa)_{4-8}(S_3SO_2)_{1-2}(Al_6Si_6O_{24})$, to which the stone owes its beautiful colour, sodalite, $Na_8Cl_2(Al_6Si_6O_{24})$, noselite, $Na_8(SO_2)(Al_6Si_6O_{24})$, and lazurite, which is an isomorphous combination of hauynite and sodalite. These four minerals all belong to the cubic system; are members of a group of rock-forming minerals known as feldspathoids which are produced when the silica content of the rock is insufficient to form completely true feldspar. There is always calcite present which produces the whitish parts of the poorer quality material, and, as previously mentioned, the iron pyrites. A small amount of diopside, augite, mica and hornblende are generally present. Lapis-lazuli is therefore a rock and not a true mineral.

The indefinite nature of the mineral's composition naturally affects the physical properties. The refractive index is generally shown as a somewhat vague shadow-edge at about 1·50 on the refractometer scale. The constant of specific gravity, although having a rather wide range, has a diagnostic value. The commercial type of lapis-lazuli has a density which varies from 2·7 to 2·9; this figure may even be higher if much pyrites is present. The hardness is $5\frac{1}{2}$ on Mohs's scale. The material is decomposed by hydrochloric acid giving off the obnoxious smell of rotten eggs (hydrogen sulphide). Under the long-wave ultra-violet lamp lapis-lazuli generally shows spots or streaks of an orange or copper-coloured glow, stronger and more pronounced in the material from Chile than in that from Afghanistan. The fluorescence is less pronounced and more pinkish when the short-wave lamp is used, and shows as ill-defined yellowish streaks when irradiated with x-rays.

Before the nineteenth century powdered lapis-lazuli produced the pigment ultramarine, but since 1828 this pigment has been synthetically produced by calcining a mixture of china clay, sodium carbonate, charcoal and sulphur in the absence of air.

Lapis-lazuli is formed by metamorphic action on impure limestone through contact with intruded masses of molten granite, causing a recrystallization to marble with the separation of a number of new minerals including lapis-lazuli.

Occurrences

The most famous locality for lapis-lazuli is in the Badakshan district of the mountainous north-eastern part of Afghanistan, the mines having been intermittently worked for 6,000 years. They were visited and described by Marco Polo in 1271, but owing to their remoteness and inaccessibility little is known of them. The mines are near a place called Firgamu on the upper reaches of the Kokcha river, which is a tributary of the Oxus, the lapis being found in a black and white limestone.

What are probably the same mines or a part of them were described by the Russian academician A. E. Fersman, who was one of an expedition in 1930 to find 'the lazurit, which legend said existed in the Pamirs. The expedition found the route exceedingly difficult and after reaching some 3,500 m (11,400 ft.) the party had to leave its horses and continue on foot along one of the rivers which had the name Liadjuar-Dara, which means "River of Lazurit". On reaching the height of 5,000 m (16,500 ft.) they found a great glacier field covered by immense stone falls from the adjacent steep wall of marble and gneiss. In this snow-white marble were veins and nests of lapis-lazuli, some bright blue, some delicately blue with beautiful passages into violet and green tints. That the natives knew of this place was given credence when one of the guides said that he had heard of it from his father and that he, with others, had previously tried to reach the place but all had contracted mountain sickness and turned back'.

The Afghanistan mines are worked in a primitive manner. The rock is heated and then quenched in order to obtain pieces of such size, about 10 pounds each, convenient for bringing out of the inhospitable locality. A quantity of this material reaches West Pakistan and is made up into jewellery at Lahore.

Amidst the wild and uninviting Sayan mountains light blue boulders of lapis-lazuli are found in the rapid Slyudyanka rivulet which flows into the southern end of Lake Baikal bordering on Mongolia. This deposit, scattered in irregular accumulations of crystalline limestone, was extracted in the Bystraya river valley during the middle of the nineteenth century, but towards the end of the century the mines were neglected and the place became overgrown with dense woods. Whether the mines have again been opened is not known.

A paler coloured lapis-lazuli is mined in the Chilean Andes, the most important localities being those at Ovalle Cordillera, Coquimbo Province and farther north near Antofagasta. On Italian mountain, high in the Sawatch range of the Colorado Rockies is found lapis-lazuli in stringers in limestone rock measuring up to 8 in. wide and outcropping for a distance of 300 ft. along the face of the mountain. As in the case of the Afghanistan lapis-lazuli the formation is due to contact metamorphic action. Folding and faulting of the mountain occurred in Cretaceous times with the intrusion of igneous rock—a diorite porphyry. The deposit was discovered in 1939, but the rock is only worked spasmodically owing to the short season, high altitude and the necessity of moving badly fractured overburden to ensure safety in working. The material is almost black to an intense blue, contains narrow veins and spots of calcite, and is heavily charged with pyrites. It lacks the texture and hardness of good quality lapis, has a waxy to sub-vitreous lustre and a density varying from 2·82 to 2·85.

An occurrence of lapis-lazuli has been found near the summit of Antonio Peak in the San Gabriel mountains in southern California about 40 miles east of Los Angeles, and also in Cascade Canyon, San Bernardino mountains. Material of a blue-grey splotched with bright blue and white, and containing pyrites inclusions is found in Baffin Island north of the Labrador peninsula, Canada. It has little merit as a gem material for it is somewhat porous and does not take a good polish. Lapis-lazuli is also found in the Mogok region of Upper Burma, the actual locality is the Dattaw valley. Lobito Bay in Angola and Pakistan (density 2·81–2·84) are other sources.

Cutting of Lapis-lazuli

An opaque stone valued for its colour only, lapis-lazuli is rarely faceted, but the material is fashioned into seal stones, beads and small carved objects, and is used as inlay material, often with a lighter coloured mineral such as the stalagtitic marble best known as 'onyx marble'.

Simulation

Lapis-lazuli is imitated by the so-called 'Swiss lapis', or 'German lapis' which is a type of jasper stained blue by the action of potassium ferro-cyanide and ferrous sulphate which produces Prussian blue, or Berlin blue. This imitation does not show the brassy specks of pyrites, but often shows glistening flakes of transparent quartz. The material which has a density varying between 2·38 and 2·60 is generally harder than true lapis and has an inferior colour to the real material.

A sintered synthetic spinel coloured blue by cobalt has been produced in Germany. The imitation, of good lapis colour, has an index of refraction of 1·725 and a density near to 3·52. Many specimens of this imitation are complete with brassy specks, but these are in fact gold pieces incorporated in the powder before the sintering.

Paste imitations of lapis-lazuli are not often seen. There have been cases of an opacified blue glass which contained spangles of copper crystals, as in goldstone, and these glass imitations purport to be imitation lapis-lazuli, but the gaudy nature of these glasses is sufficient to identify them. It has been recorded that pale coloured lapis-lazuli has had the colour enhanced by staining, but such treated stones never show the glorious colour of the best lapis-lazuli.

Some lapis lazuli has been dyed and it has been found that this dye will come off and stain a swab moistened with nail-varnish remover (amyl acetate).

Unlike its imitations, lapis lazuli will show a fairly bright whitish glow when under a beam of short-wave ultra-violet light (2537 Å). A further test for lapis which has been suggested is that the rock gives off hydrogen sulphide when moistened with hydrochloric acid.

CHAPTER 12

THE JADES

HISTORY AND LORE

About 1000 B.C. the ancient Chinese worked a tough green mineral which they prized above all else, and which they called yu, a mineral which today we know as jade. The name jade does not signify one mineral but may refer to either of two mineral species, nephrite and jadeite, which have no relation to one another except that of appearance. Jadeite, known generally as Chinese jade, is found in Burma and not in China; it did not enter China before the eighteenth century and therefore was not the chen yu, or true jade, which was so cleverly carved by Chinese craftsmen of ancient dynasties. Their jade was probably the mineral nephrite which most likely came from Khotan in central Asia, for nephrite is not known to exist with any certainty in any of the provinces of China proper, although the material has been reported from Shen-si, Kwang-tung, Kwei-chow and Yunnan, and also in Manchuria.

The nephrite variety of jade, owing to its toughness has been used for tools and weapons, and for ritual ornaments, not only by the Chinese but by the early inhabitants of the Swiss lake dwellings, by the North American Indians, by the Aztecs of central America and by the Maoris of New Zealand, who used the nephrite found in such profusion in the South Island.

The name jade was apparently first derived from the end word of piedra de hijada, the Spanish name for jade. The Spanish adventurers in the time of Cortes brought back the jade pieces which they found to be so widely distributed among the Indians. It was they who brought back the name piedra de hijada, which means stone of the flank or loins, or by another derivation colic stone. It is suggested that the flat polished pebbles with rounded edges resembled the kidneys, and would, therefore, be efficacious in disorders of that organ. Howard Hansford states that the Spaniards knew the stone as piedra de los riñones ('kidney stone'), a name which was translated into Latin as lapis nephriticus and this gives the word nephrite.

NEPHRITE

Chemical and Physical Properties

Often known as greenstone, nephrite consists of an interlocking mass of fibrous crystals having monoclinic symmetry, the felting of the crystals giving to the mineral its toughness (*Figure 12.1*). The mineral is a silicate of magnesium and calcium with some iron in the ferrous state, the composition corresponding to the formula $Ca_2(Mg,Fe)_5(OH)_2(Si_4O_{11})_2$, the colour deepening to deep green with the increase of iron to magnesium content, and with less iron and more magnesium the colour lightens to greenish-grey, the so-called 'mutton fat' jade. The mineral is in fact a member of the tremolite-actinolite series of the amphibole family, the lighter coloured varieties being nearer to tremolite and the darker to actinolite.

Nephrite often assumes a brown colour, caused, presumably, by oxidation of the iron content. Indeed many pebbles and boulders of nephrite are covered with a brown skin where the material has weathered on the outside. This weathering is often apparent along cracks penetrating the interior and producing a brown coloration along their margins. The Chinese carvers (*Figure 12.2*), so adroit at getting the most out of any material, often used the brown weathered zones to incorporate colour schemes into their carvings. Thus they may choose a small weathered pebble for carving into a snuff bottle, and, cameo fashion, incise into the brown skin to produce a two-colour effect.

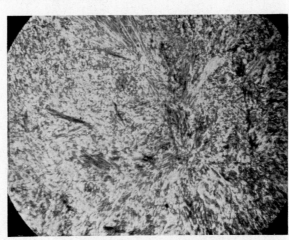

Figure 12.1. A photomicrograph of a thin section of nephrite showing the felted mass of fibrous crystals

The hardness of nephrite is $6\frac{1}{2}$ on Mohs's scale, but owing to the felted nature of the crystal aggregate the mineral is extremely tough. The density is near to 3·00 (2·90–3·02), a value considerably lower than for jadeite (3·3). The refractive indices of the individual crystal fibres have been found to vary between 1·600–1·627 and 1·614–1·641, thus giving a bi-refringence of 0·027. In practice, owing to the aggregate nature of the crystals, only a vague reading at about 1·62 can be seen on the refractometer, and for the same reason the marked dichroism of the individual fibres is masked. Nephrite shows a very indistinct absorption spectrum of a doublet in the red at about 6890 Å; however, two vague bands at about 4900 and 4600 Å and a fairly sharp line at 5090 Å are often seen. The mineral shows no luminescence under ultra-violet light, and through the colour filter the stone appears green.

There is one type of nephrite, of a yellowish or greyish-brown colour, which deserves mention. This is the so-called 'buried' jade which has so much importance from an archaeological angle. These ancient jades from neolithic and early historical times, which have been buried through the

211

intervening ages, are supposedly from indigenous sources of nephrite. The material has, after the long burial in the yellow loess of China, altered in colour and perhaps in composition from the original material. Little is known of the physical and optical properties of this buried jade, which is

Figure 12.2. Chinese carving in nephrite. White translucent jade hanging vase, with carved handle depicting dragons. The cover is suspended from the top with a seven linked chain. From the bottom is suspended a parrot on a ring perch. The vase and all its linked parts are carved from one piece of jade

so often found in a friable condition, as the material has so much more value from an archaeological standpoint than a mineralogical one.

Occurrences

The occurrences of nephrite are wide, the material being found in many parts of the world, either *in situ* or as alluvial boulders and pebbles with a

PLATE XVII
Nephrite
Massive spinach-green jade brushpot
(By courtesy of Christie Manson and Woods, Ltd.)

brown skin due to weathering. Probably the earliest known and most important source of nephrite from the Chinese carvers' point of view, is along the northern slopes of the Kuen Lun mountains near Khotan in eastern Turkestan, where it is found *in situ* as a layer some 20–40 ft. thick between hornblende-schist and gneiss, or as alluvial boulders in the beds of the Keriya, Yurungkash and Karakash rivers. An occurrence of dark green nephrite in the Lake Baikal district of eastern Siberia was discovered by J. P. Alibert in 1850, where boulders of large size are found in the rivers Onot, Bistraya, Bielaya, Kitoi and Slyudyanka, south of Irkutsk, the primary source probably being in the Sayan mountains. The jade from this locality is often marked with small black spots of graphite, a mineral mined nearby. Nephrite has been reported from the Pamir district which lies south of the Kirghiz steppes and north of Chitral.

The nephrite found in New Zealand which is variously termed 'New Zealand Greenstone', 'Maori Stone or Jade' or 'Axestone', and by the Maoris pounamu, is found *in situ* in talc and talc-serpentine rocks in the Griffin range; west of Lake Wakatipu in the Province of Otago; at Mount Cook in the Southern Alps, and in the small island of D'Urville which lies in Cook Strait separating the North and South Islands. Much boulder material is found in the glacial debris of the river valleys of north Westland. These alluvial pebbles are often flattened in form and admirably suit the fashioning of the Maoris' grotesque ornaments called Hei tiki, and for the flattened club known as the mere. New Zealand nephrite is mostly of a dark green colour and the pale greenish-grey 'mutton fat' nephrite is rarely, if ever, found there.

The finding of worked pieces of nephrite in the Swiss lake dwellings led to speculation as to the source of the material which at the time was only known from distant lands. In 1884 nephrite was rediscovered in Europe at Jordansmühl (now known as Jordanow) in lower Silesia which is now part of Poland. Nearby Reichenstein, a place which is the one now known as Dzierzoniów, also supplies nephrite which is a lighter and greyish green in colour, but some Silesian nephrite is a creamy-white to a sand colour with green patches. Occurrences of nephrite have been reported from southern Liguria in north Italy and in the Harz mountains of Germany.

North of the Arctic Circle in north-western Alaska nephrite is found at Jade mountain, 150 miles from the mouth of the Kobuk river, and in the basins of the Noatak and Kobuk rivers. The small amount of jade which is taken out from this inhospitable region is sent via Kotzebue Sound or by air. The nephrite of this region occurs in a series of outcrops of ultra-basic rocks introduced mainly in schists and limestones, but the jade from this locality has also been won from gravel deposits of the Kobuk river some 10 miles below Shungnak village. Boulders of nephrite occur in the Upper Lewis and Fraser rivers of British Columbia, and much is marketed.

In recent years the nephrite variety of jade has been found just north of Wind River range of the Rocky mountains at Lander, Wyoming in the United States of America. This jade is found as large boulders of alluvial deposition and is exposed by natural erosion as the terrain, isolated and with few habitations, is situated at high elevation and subjected to severe storms and blizzards during much of the year. This jade varied much in colour and only a small quantity is the prized green. Some Wyoming jade is chatoyant. Alluvial nephrite is also found in California, particularly at Placer County, where the Chinese miners panning for gold also found jade boulders in the river; it is thought that many of these boulders were taken back to China. Nephrite pebbles are found on the coast of Monterey County, Marin County and San Luis Obispo County. The last named is said to have a deposit of nephrite *in situ*. Nephrite, with jadeite, has been reported from a location 6 miles east of Mount Vernon in Washington, and the mineral is said to occur in the Amazon valley.

Some alluvial nephrite has been found in Mexico, which may, in part, explain the source of jade used by the Aztec and Inca civilizations, although some of the artifacts from these periods are made from jadeite. That the alluvial nephrite found at Amargoza, Bahia, Brazil, was worked by native Indians seems probable from the abundance of artifacts made from this material found in the region. An occurrence of dark green nephrite of good quality has been reported from the Mashaba district of Rhodesia and a poor quality comes from New South Wales, Australia. Nephrite is also found in Taiwan (Formosa).

Transparent actinolite crystals have been cut producing green stones which have refractive indices of 1·618–1·641 with a positive birefringence of 0·023. The density is about 3·1 and the colour is due to ferrous iron.

Since 1965 there has been marketed, usually under the name 'Wyoming jade' or 'Snowflake jade' a 'jade' which is really a mixture of the tremolite variety of amphibole and albite feldspar. The values of density determined on these intergrowths varied from 2·80 to 2·95, but were fairly constant at 2·84. The refractive index, as far as could be measured on a refractometer, was about 1·56. It is suggested that these pieces should be called 'jade matrix'.

JADEITE

Chemical and Physical Properties

Jadeite consists of an aggregate of interlocking crystals of the monoclinic system, which unlike nephrite are more granular than fibrous, and, owing to slight differences in hardness of the grains, shows on the polished surface a 'shagreened' or dimpled effect (*Figure 12.3*). Jadeite is one of the pyroxene group of minerals and is thus allied to spodumene, diopside and enstatite.

The composition of jadeite is a sodium aluminium silicate and accords to the formula $NaAl(SiO_3)_2$, but a varying percentage of the diopside molecule $CaMg(SiO_3)_2$ is often present. Jadeite has a hardness equal to quartz, that is 7 on Mohs's scale, the density lies between 3·30 and 3·36, and the refractive indices for the single crystals are near 1·654 and 1·667, but on the refractometer only a vague shadow edge will be seen at about 1·66.

Absorption Spectrum

The absorption spectrum of jadeite is characterized by the presence of a strong line in the blue-violet at 4375 Å. Accompanying this strong absorption band are similar but much weaker bands at 4500 and 4330 Å, and occasionally a vague band at 4950 Å may be seen. This band at 4375 Å is diagnostic for jadeite, but in the rich emerald-green material which is coloured by chromium this band, owing to the absorption of the violet due to the chromium spectrum, may not clearly be seen. However, the emerald-green jadeite will show lines in the red which are so characteristic of chromium coloration. These lines are at 6915 Å, which is probably an unresolved doublet with lines at 6940 and 6890 Å. This main band is accompanied by weaker bands at 6550 and 6300 Å. Under long-wave ultra-violet light the paler coloured green and the yellow, mauve and white

Figure 12.3. Photomicrograph of a thin section of jadeite showing the granular nature of this jade

jadeite shows a whitish glow of low intensity, the darker coloured jadeite being unresponsive. Very little is seen under the short-wave lamp. Under x-rays the paler shades show a white or yellowish-white glow, but it has been noticed that the colourless, pale yellow and mauve coloured stone often exhibits a strong violet or blue-violet coloured glow. Green jadeite shows green under the Chelsea colour filter.

Colour Range

Jadeite is found in all colours from pure white, through pink, brown, red, orange, yellow, mauve, blue, violet and black, an extensive range of shades of green, and mottled green and white. The most highly prized colour is a rich emerald-green of great translucency. Jadeite, therefore, has a much greater range than has nephrite. A jadeite containing a considerable amount of the oxides of iron is called chloromelanite; it is dark green to black in colour. The mauve colour in jadeite is ascribed to the presence of manganese and the duller greens to iron.

Occurrences

The only important commercial source of jadeite is Upper Burma where it is found *in situ* in dykes of metamorphosed rock of the Uru valley (a tributary of the Chindwin river). Tawmaw, Mainmaw, Pangmaw and Namshamaw are the chief dykes; the primary deposit at Tawmaw outcrops for a distance of 300 yards, and other outcrops are known along a distance of about 4 miles. The tough mineral is difficult to mine and the Chinese formerly used fire to break up the deposits. This is now superseded by modern methods of drilling and blasting. Alluvial jadeite boulders and pebbles are also mined from the Uru and other rivers of the Myitkyina district, particularly at Pakhan, Hweka and Mamon. The boulders are generally covered by a brownish skin due to weathering, and like nephrite weathered boulders, this brown overlay is often made use of by the Chinese carvers in order to obtain a two-colour effect. Both the rock and the boulders are marketed through China, the blocks being 'mawed' before sale, that is a flat of about 1 in. by 1½ in. is polished on the piece in order to show something of the colour of the material, but as the colour may not, and rarely is, uniform throughout, there is speculation as to how the piece will turn out.

Jadeite was discovered in the south-western part of San Benito County, California in the mid-1930s. The mineral is found near Clear Creek as boulders and nodules in serpentine with pumpellyite and lawsonite. Stream boulders of jadeite are found at Williams Creek and on the north fork of the Eel river, Mendocino County and Trinity County, and a similar occurrence has been found near Paso Robles in San Luis Obispo County. Jadeite has been found in a glaucophane schist at Valley Ford, Sonoma County. There is a report of the finding of doubly terminated jadeite crystals along Russian river near Cloverdale in Sonoma County but this occurrence can have no gem significance. The occurrence of jade at Leach Lake mountain, which is sawn into slabs and exported to Germany for carving into art objects, is a nephrite-jadeite mixture found in placer and bedrock deposits. The jade from California ranges in colour from white through pale green to dark greyish-green to dark bluish-green and is generally semi-opaque.

Jadeite has been reported from China and Tibet but the occurrences have not been confirmed. There is, however, a well authenticated report of the finding of jadeite near the village of Kotaki in Niigata Prefecture, Japan, but the material, owing to its inferior tone of green, does not yield a high quality gemstone. A source of jadeite is thought to exist in central America, either in Mexico or in Guatemala or both.

Whilst on a visit to Burma during 1963 Dr. E. Gübelin became interested in some bright green 'jades' nicely patterned by dark green to black spots and veins. He ascertained that the material apparently came from a place called Maw-sit-sit near Namshamaw in Upper Burma, and that the Burmese called the stone 'maw-sit-sit' after the place name. Subsequent investigation proved the material to be an albite rock containing in intimate association a chrome-rich jadeite. The refractive indices recorded varied from 1·52 to 1·54 and the densities from 2·46 to 3·15. The name 'Jade-albite' has been proposed for this material.

Cutting of Jade

The jades are fashioned mainly as carvings (*Figure 12.4*), as beads or as cabochons, the smaller carved pieces being used for ring stones, brooches or for drop earrings. The modern method of jade carving is that the rough jade piece is sawn into slab form of the requisite size, the design marked out in pencil and the carving carried out by the use of carborundum tipped grinding tools (or diamond tools) driven from an electric motor, either through a fixed head, or through a flexible drive in a similar fashion to a dentist's drill.

Figure 12.4. A large vase and cover in Imperial sodden snow jade (nephrite), 15 inches in height—Chinese: Ch'ien Lung period. Recently sold for £2,800

(By courtesy of Sotheby and Co.)

Far different and more exacting were the methods used by the Maori and Chinese craftsmen, who cut their jade by the use of thin laminae of sandstone or a slate charged with sand and water and carved with wooden or stone pencils using the same abrasive. The Maoris used a pointed stick with sand and water or a flint splinter in the end of a cleft stick and rotated by crossed strings. The Chinese had access to a most perfect drill in the hollow bamboo rod charged with sand and water. Gradually metal tools took the place of stone and bamboo until today the methods of carving are mechanized, but it must be said that modern workmanship, with all its aids, does not surpass the beauty of the work of the ancient craftsman; it may be faster, but the real beauty of jade carving was when time stood still.

Simulation

Many different minerals may simulate jade to a remarkable degree and a note of these minerals needs to be given, for example, the *bowenite* variety of serpentine which is found in Kashmir, Afghanistan and China. From the latter country many specimens of carved light yellowish-green bowenite have been exported to Western countries under the name or rather misnomer, 'new jade'. It is thought that the mineral comes from Tuoyuan in Hunan Province. Bowenite is also found at Milford Sound on the west coast of Otago County, New Zealand, near to where the true nephrite occurs. It is a translucent deep green material with a pronounced similarity to jade and this New Zealand material was worked by the Maoris who called the stone tangiwaite. The bowenite variety of serpentine has more translucency and a greater hardness than is usual for serpentine; the hardness being near to $5\frac{1}{2}$ on Mohs's scale. The refractive indices have a mean about 1·52 and the density is consistently near to 2·58 for the pale apple green material and up to 2·62 for the darker green stone. The lower hardness—bowenite can be scratched with a knife blade—distinguishes this material from the true jades. The so-called 'Korea jade' is bowenite.

The massive *prehnite* of green colour can be a most convincing jade imitation. The material has a density varying between 2·80 and 2·95 and is thus only a little less than nephrite. The hardness is 6 on Mohs's scale and the mean refractive index is 1·63, which are again not far different from nephrite. However, prehnite shows a distinctly reddish tinge when viewed through the colour filter, whereas the jades show green.

The so-called 'Transvaal jade', a massive *grossular garnet* is easily distinguished from the true jades by its higher density (3·48) and the refractive index (1·73), even if its somewhat different appearance to the jades did not give a clue to its identity. Under x-rays the green grossular garnet shows an orange fluorescent glow and is alone among the jade-like minerals to do so.

The particular sheen seen in the green variety of *microcline feldspar*, sometimes miscalled 'Amazon jade' is completely different from the lustre of jadeite or nephrite, the lower density (2·56) and refractive index (1·55) is sufficient to identify such pieces.

The massive green variety of idocrase known as *californite* has a jade-like character and may pass for the genuine material, especially as the density is a little lower than for the crystal idocrase and varies between 3·25 and 3·35 thus overlapping the values for jadeite. The refractive index at 1·72 is, however, distinctly higher than for jadeite and will distinguish the material if the refractive index can be obtained.

The bluish-green *smithsonite*, which has been sold under the trade name 'Bonamite' is generally too translucent to be readily mistaken for jade. It is a zinc carbonate and thus will effervesce with acid, and, moreover,

PLATE XVIII

Various colours of jadeite

All from Uyu River, Upper Burma

has the high density of between 4·30 and 4·35; this 'heaviness' should be apparent even in a small specimen.

The green *aventurine quartz* miscalled 'Indian jade' is so manifestly different in appearance to the true jades that no confusion should arise, but the green chalcedony known as *chrysoprase*, or even the chalcedony artificially stained green, can approach jade in appearance. The lower density (2·6) and the refractive index (1·55) readily separates this quartz mineral from the true jades. In this connexion it is interesting to mention that some years ago there was a discovery of so-called 'jade' in Baker County, Oregon, which turned out to be the quartz known as plasma.

A decomposition product of the plagioclase feldspars, *saussurite*, is often of a grey-green colour and may then resemble jade. The material has a hardness of $6\frac{1}{2}$ on Mohs's scale and a density of between 3·0 and 3·4 and is thus intermediate between the density of nephrite and jadeite, but the mean index of refraction will separate the saussurite, which has a value of 1·70, from the jades.

Agalmatolite or 'figure stone' is a massive variety of the mineral pinite, an alteration product of iolite. The lower density, about 2·80, confirmed by the low hardness of $2\frac{1}{2}$ on Mohs's scale precludes any confusion with the jades. Some agalmatolite may be steatite (soapstone), which is even less hard. 'Styrian jade' or pseudophite, does not have the typical colour of jade and moreover cannot be confused with it as the Mohs's scale hardness is only $2\frac{1}{2}$, the density about 2·7 and the refractive index 1·57.

Smaragdite, a foliated variety of amphibole often derived from diallage, has an emerald-green colour of considerable depth. The material is with difficulty distinguished from true jadeite, indeed chloromelanite may be a form of smaragdite, and it has been suggested that the material is so near jadeite that distinction is unnecessary. The density of the material is 3·25.

There has been reported from New Guinea the finding of a chrome-rich precious stone said to be of a dark green colour with lighter coloured veins and to be a chrome-rich jadeite intergrown with picotite, quartz, opal and limonite, and to have been derived from an olivine rock. The material has a density of 3·35, and is named *astridite* after Queen Astrid of Belgium.

A beautiful green rock from the Barberton district of Transvaal is *verdite*, which is a massive muscovite rock coloured green by the chromiferous variety of mica called fuchsite. It often exhibits yellow and red spots, has a refractive index near 1·58 and a density about 2·9.

The serpentinous calcite known as *Verd-antique*, or Connemara marble, could, to the uninitiated, be mistaken for a jade. This serpentine marble is quite distinctive with its green patches veined with white streaks and is easily distinguished from jade by the effervescence produced when the specimen is touched with a spot of acid. Further, the strong absorption band in the blue part of the spectrum at 4650 Å may assist identification.

White jadeite has been artificially stained a green colour, which is a fine 'Imperial jade' colour. The colour is seen to be concentrated along veins in the stone and the absorption spectrum shows two broadish bands in the red part of the spectrum which are diagnostic. Such green-stained jadeite is prone to fade. A mauve colour is produced by staining, and in this case the stones are said not to fade, but the mauve colour is rather too pronounced and the stones look unreal.

An ingenious jadeite triplet has been made. In these stones a cabochon core is cemented into a hollow-cabochon top by the aid of a green-coloured cement, and the base closed in by a third piece of jadeite, white jadeite being used for the three component pieces. Such stones are very effective and are less easily spotted than the green-stained cabochons, providing that the seam of the joining is masked by the setting. The absorption spectrum shown by these triplets is similar to that shown by the green-stained jadeite, that is one or two broadish bands in the red part of the spectrum. The chance of such stones fading is less likely.

Serpentine, probably a type of the bowenite variety, is also stained an 'Imperial jade' green colour, and quite large carved pieces as well as bead necklets have been encountered in this stained serpentine. The material is much softer than jadeite and the broad bands seen in the red part of the absorption spectrum clearly indicate that the material has been stained.

A suitably coloured and opacified lead glass makes a convincing imitation of jade. The density of these pieces is generally higher than for jadeite —it is usually about 3·7—but the nature of the pieces is obvious when the surface is examined by a lens for such a glass will show pit marks where included gas bubbles have been cut across. Some of the plastics are made to simulate jade by their colouring, and as far as that is concerned are quite effective. The exceptionally low density and the ready sectility quickly distinguishes them.

CHAPTER 13

MARCASITE AND HEMATITE

MARCASITE

The marcasite of jewellery, then usually pronounced as 'marcazeet', is, so far as the stone by this name used in jewellery is concerned, a misnomer, for the true marcasite of the mineralogist rarely ever appears in jewellery, the mineral pyrites being used almost exclusively. The confusion over the name is due to the fact that in the early eighteenth century, when minerals were not accurately determined, marcasite and pyrites were habitually taken for one another.

Chemical and Physical Properties

Marcasite and pyrites have the same composition, iron sulphide (FeS_2), but are dimorphous, that is they crystallize in different systems, marcasite in the orthorhombic system and pyrites in the cubic system.

The marcasite of the mineralogist is the unstable form of iron disulphide and crystallizes in rhombic crystals which are often twinned and with spear-shaped habit, or are aggregates of flattened twin crystals in crest-like forms to which the name 'cockscomb pyrites' is given. The colour of the mineral is bronze yellow and the density lies between 4·85 and 4·90. Marcasite is of world-wide occurrence, and many specimens of the spear-shaped habit are found in the chalk between Dover and Folkestone and in the corresponding rocks on the Pas de Calais side of the English Channel.

Pyrites, the jeweller's 'marcasite', has been used in jewellery for hundreds of years. It was apparently first used in ancient Greek jewellery and has been found in the tombs of the Incas, often as large polished pieces which were probably used as mirrors. Hence pyrites has been called 'Pierre des Incas'. Marcasite, as the jewellery trade knows the mineral, has had many vicissitudes; its first real vogue in recent times was during the middle of the eighteenth century and its popularity was said to be due to the Comtesse du Barry. The material again became fashionable during the middle of Queen Victoria's reign. Marcasites are usually set in silver for the stone does not harmonize with gold, and today the stone is much used in inexpensive jewellery.

Pyrites forms crystals which may be cubes and which have striations on each face running in a direction at right angles to those of the adjacent faces; this proves that the crystal does not have the full symmetry of the cubic system (*Figure 13.1*). Another common form of crystallization is that known as the pyritohedron which consists of twelve five-sided faces (*Figure 13.2*). Many of the crystals of pyrites possess brilliantly lustrous faces and this is particularly so with the crystals which come from the Island of Elba and some other localities. Frequently pyrites is found massive or radially fibrous and in fibrous nodular forms with a botryoidal surface. Such nodules can be picked up from the chalk of the South Downs in Sussex, England, and are often thought by the finder to be 'thunderbolts' (meteorites), which of course they are not. Such pyrites nodules are occasionally brought in to jewellers by their customers asking whether they are gold, or contain gold. It is true that some pyrites does contain a small quantity of gold but, excepting the so-called 'auriferous pyrites', the gold content has no commercial value and would not pay to refine. It is owing to the brassy appear-

Figure 13.1. Striated cube of pyrites

Figure 13.2. A double pyritohedral crystal of pyrites

ance of much pyrites that the name 'Fool's gold' has been applied to the mineral.

Pyrites has a brass or bronze-yellow colour and a high metallic lustre when polished. The hardness of the mineral is 6 to $6\frac{1}{2}$ on Mohs's scale, and the material is somewhat brittle. The density varies between 4·95 and 5·10, and the 'streak' or mark made by pyrites when rubbed across an unglazed porcelain plate (a streak plate) is greenish-black or brownish-black.

Cutting and Setting

The marcasites used in jewellery are pyrites cut and polished to a circular outline with a low pyramid of six faces on top and with a flat base, in fact a flattened rose-cut. These marcasites are, in the best jewellery pieces, hand-set, the stones being held in place by small grains turned over from the setting on to the edge of the stone. In cheaper pieces they may be simply cemented in. The mineral is cut and distributed mainly from the Jura Alps in France.

Marcasite (pyrites) is a durable stone which does not rust like cut steel, but owing to the fibrous nature of the mineral a sharp knock may crack the stone which may then loosen it from the setting so that it may readily fall out, but with normal use and care such accidents should not occur. Much modern marcasite-set jewellery is mounted in silver which has been rhodium-plated to prevent the silver tarnishing.

Simulation

Imitations of marcasite are few. In some old jewellery roses of cut steel have been used, the mounting being ordinary white metal and not silver. These earlier steel pieces were produced in Birmingham and Wolverhampton in England and the jewellery pieces were of fine workmanship and of good design. During the early part of the nineteenth century a Frenchman invented a process for the making of these steel pieces. The French type can be distinguished from the older English type by the steel studs on the base whereby they were fixed to the mount.

The modern imitations of marcasite are almost invariably mounted glass (paste) which are usually only cemented in the mount and not set by rolling over the mounting metal. The vitreous lustre, the moulded look of the facet edges and the pit marks of cut-through glass bubbles are certain indication of their nature.

HEMATITE

Chemical and Physical Properties

The compact type of iron oxide (Fe_2O_3) called hematite, or by the older spelling haematite, owes its name to the red colour of the powdered mineral which resembles dried blood. The German name for this iron oxide is blutstein (bloodstone) and has a similar derivation, but this term is confusing, for the English bloodstone is a variety of green quartz flecked with red spots.

Hematite is found in various states of compactness and varies from a soft red paint ore which was used by early American Indians to deck their faces before battle, and today as a pigment, through various degrees of compaction, most of which are used as an ore of iron for smelting, to a hard compact form which may be cut for jewellery.

The compact forms of hematite are found in large nodular masses made up of radially fibrous crystals producing a reniform nodule. Such nodular masses, from their shape, are often known as kidney ore (*Figure 13.3*). Hematite is occasionally found in the form of lustrous rhombohedral crystals, the faces of which are often tarnished, giving a colourful iridescent surface. Beautiful groups of such crystals are found in the Isle of Elba. As a point of interest there are found in the Ticino and Grison regions of Switzerland beautiful crystallized specimens of hematite composed of a rosette of platy crystals. These are known as iron roses. Around Cleator Moor in Cumberland, England, are found masses of kidney ore which breaks up into pointed fibrous crystalline fragments from which the term 'pencil ore', sometimes given to hematite, is derived.

Hematite crystallizes in the trigonal system and the colour of the compact material used in jewellery is blue-black. The hardness of these purer types may be as high as $6\frac{1}{2}$ on Mohs's scale and the density varies from 4·95 to 5·16. The refractive index, according to a determination made by special methods, is 2·94 for the extraordinary ray and 3·22 for the ordinary ray, but the refractive index is too high to allow the constant to be tested by normal methods, and has, therefore, academic interest only. The easiest test for hematite, although in the case of one imitation there is a chance of misidentification, is to rub the edge of the stone on a streak plate (white unglazed porcelain) which, if the stone be hematite, results in a red streak on the plate, indeed, powdered and purified hematite is the red polishing powder known as rouge.

Figure 13.3. Mass of kidney ore hematite

Cutting and Fashioning

The uses to which cut and polished hematite is put in jewellery are as modified trap-cut stones or as brilliant-cut stones, at least so far as the crown of the stone is concerned, for the bases of such stones are usually flat and left unpolished. To the unwary the brilliant-cut hematite when set may have the appearance of black diamond. Beads have also been produced and in this connexion such forms have been used to imitate black pearl. The most common use of hematite is for the production of seal stones, and these are most commonly cut as intaglios. Cameos in hematite are also produced and are often cut as curvettes, that is the raised carving lies in the centre of a bowl-shaped depression in the stone, the outer edge being raised, probably in order to protect the carving to some extent. Such a style of fashioning is known as chevee in North America. Most of the fashioning of hematite is carried out at Idar-Oberstein in Germany from material imported from Cumberland, England.

Simulation

Hematite is cunningly imitated by an artificial material which has the colour and appearance very like that of the true material. The composition of such imitation hematite is not surely known and may consist of a number of different types. The streak given by such imitations does not differ considerably from the red mark given by hematite, but unlike hematite such imitations are usually attracted by a magnet.

Psilomelane

Resembling hematite, for which stone it has recently been used as a simulant on account of the scarcity of hematite itself, is the mineral psilomelane. Usually found in botryoidal or stalagmitic forms the mineral is regarded as a colloidal manganese oxide with the oxides of barium, potassium and sodium, and some water. The hardness can vary from $5\frac{1}{2}$ to $6\frac{1}{2}$ on Mohs's scale and the density varies greatly, but specimens of gem material have been found to average about 4·35. Detection from hematite is by its more silvery lustre; its brownish-black streak (that of hematite is red), and that a drop of hydrochloric acid placed on an inconspicuous part of the specimen will dissolve the area and release chlorine gas which has an irritating and suffocating smell. The writer has found that this material seems to form a perfect conductor for an electric current and this provides a test against the true hematite which, although variably conductive, is at best weakly so as against that of psilomelane.

OTHER METALLIC ORES

Other metallic ores which have been cut and polished, usually for the whim of collectors, are chalcopyrite, cobaltite and smaltite, chromite and niccolite and columbite, samarskite and euxenite, etc.

Chalcopyrite

Chalcopyrite, or as it is better known copper pyrites, is more important as an ore of copper than as a gem material. The mineral is brass yellow in colour and is usually found massive and less commonly as crystals which belong to the tetragonal system. Chalcopyrite is a sulphide of copper and iron ($CuFeS_2$) and has a hardness of $3\frac{1}{2} - 4$ on Mohs's scale. The density of the mineral is near to 4·2 and the mineral is distinguished from pyrites by its deeper yellow colour and lower hardness. The occurrences are world wide.

Cobaltite and Smaltite

Cobaltite is a sulphide of arsenic and cobalt, $CoAsS$, which crystallizes in the cubic system and may be found as cubic or pyritohedral crystals, or in massive form. The mineral is opaque, has a silver-white colour tinged with pink and the lustre is metallic. The hardness is $5\frac{1}{2}$ on Mohs's scale, and with a density of between 6·0 and 6·3. Cobaltite is found in well-formed crystals at Tunaberg in Sweden and Skutterud in Norway. Other sources are Cobalt, Ontario, Canada; Dashkesan in Transcaucasia; and the Botallack mine, St. Just, Cornwall, England. Another mineral, smaltite, the cobalt arsenide, $CoAs_3$, has been cut. The mineral forms cubic crystals but is usually found massive, has a tin-white to steel-grey colour and a metallic lustre. The hardness is $5\frac{1}{2}$ on Mohs's scale and the density lies between 6 and 6·3. It is mainly found at Cobalt, Ontario, Canada, and to a lesser extent in Germany, France, Spain, Morocco and Chile.

Breithauptite; Chromite; Niccolite and Pentlandite

Chromite is an oxide of chromium and iron ($FeCr_2O_4$) and is iron-black to brownish-black in colour. The mineral crystallizes in the cubic system but the material is usually found massive. The refractive index is 2·1 and the density lies between 4·1 and 4·9. The hardness is $5\frac{1}{2}$ on Mohs's scale. Chromite is found in the United States of America, Asia Minor, Silesia, Austria, France, New Caledonia and in Southern Rhodesia. Chromite is feebly magnetic. Niccolite, the nickel arsenide, NiAs, is also known as kupfernickel, and is a pale red-coloured mineral with a metallic lustre. The hardness is $5 - 5\frac{1}{2}$ on Mohs's scale and the density varies from 7·33 to 7·67. The crystal structure is hexagonal but crystals are rare and the mineral is nearly always found massive. Niccolite is found in central Europe, France, Canada and in the United States of America. The bronze-yellow nickel iron sulphide mineral called pentlandite has been cut for the whim of collectors. It has a hardness of $3\frac{1}{2}$ to 4 on Mohs's scale and a density of 5. It is not magnetic. Another nickel ore which has similarly been cut is breithauptite. Copperred in colour, the mineral is a nickel antimonide and has a density of 7·54.

Columbite, Samarskite and Euxenite

Columbite and samarskite are two related minerals of a black colour and with a semi-metallic lustre. Columbite is a niobate and tantalate of iron and manganese and has a hardness of 6 on Mohs's scale and a density varying from 5·2 to 8·0, with an increase of tantalum when the mineral merges into the pure tantalate of iron and manganese. Samarskite is an extremely complex mixture of the oxides of niobium and tantalum with rare earth oxides. Velvet-black in colour the mineral has a hardness of 5–6 on Mohs's scale and a density varying from 4·1 to 6·2. The third of these gemmologically unimportant minerals is euxenite, a niobate and titanite of yttrium erbium, cerium and uranium. The mineral is brownish-black in colour, has a hardness of $6\frac{1}{2}$ on Mohs's scale and a density varying from 4·7 to 5·0. Euxenite is found in Madagascar, Norway, Brazil, Finland, Canada and the United States of America. A tantaliferous variety is found in Australia.

Domeykite, Algodonite and Bornite

Specimens of these copper minerals have been cut for collectors. Both domeykite and algodonite are copper arsenites found as irregular lumps in the copper mines of Michigan. The colour is tin-white to steel grey but quickly tarnishes on exposure to the air. The hardness on Mohs's scale is $3\frac{1}{2}$ to 4, and the density for domeykite is 7·2 to 7·9, and for algodonite about 8. Bornite, sometimes known as 'peacock ore' owing to the surface tarnishing with the production of iridescent colours, is a sulphide of copper and iron. The colour is usually copper-red, and the hardness 3 on Mohs's scale. The density varies between 4·9 and 5·4.

CHAPTER 14

THE NATURAL GLASSES

Of lowly importance as material for gemstones, the so-called natural glasses provide considerable interest for the many uses to which they have been put by aboriginal man, and by the problems of their genesis.

OBSIDIAN

The best known of these glasses is obsidian, a material formed by the rapid cooling of volcanic lava, which, had it been allowed to cool slowly, would have developed a crystalline structure and assumed the character of granitic rocks—acid rocks rich in silica. There can be no exact chemical composition given for obsidian, for it may vary greatly, but all obsidians have from 66 to 72 per cent of silica and are an extreme modification of rhyolite and dacite rocks.

Obsidian is normally black or grey in colour and owes any attraction it may have to an iridescent sheen caused by reflections from minute bubbles or inclusions. Such materials are the silver and golden obsidians, and these are often polished into beads for necklaces. In the United States of America a variety of obsidian having spherulitic inclusions of a white mineral on the black groundmass is cut and polished. This material is called 'flowering obsidian'. A variety banded black and red is termed 'mountain mahogany' and is sometimes used for ornamental objects and for carvings. A transparent leaf-green obsidian has been mentioned, but green is a very rare colour and most transparent green obsidians are usually found to be moldavites or merely green glass. Red and blue obsidian has been reported.

Marekanite is the name applied to smoky-brown, grey or black decomposing perlitic obsidian found along the banks of the Marekanka river at Okhotsk in Siberia. It is a variety of perlitic rhyolite glass from which large perlitic masses of clear glass readily separate. The same name, however, has been applied to material from Mexico. Glassy pebble-like solid cores of unaltered glass, about an inch or more across, from the decomposed obsidian of the American south-west, are known as 'Apache tears'. The transparent ones when cut produce stones of a grey or light grey colour and may show fine silky striations which give to the stone a cat's-eye effect. A brown-black obsidian from Hungary is known by the peoples of the nearby countries as 'Tokay lux-sapphire'.

Chemical and Physical Properties

Obsidian is a natural glass and can have no crystal structure in the general sense of the term, and can thus have no cleavage. The hardness of obsidian is near to 5 on Mohs's scale. The fracture of obsidian is eminently conchoidal and it is due to the facility with which the material can be broken into sharp-edged flakes that obsidian was so valued by Stone Age people who lived in areas where obsidian was common, the easily controlled flaking allowing the production of keen-edged spear points, knives and tools.

The lustre of obsidian is vitreous; the index of refraction lies between the limits of 1·48 and 1·51, but is most commonly near 1·49. Thin fragments viewed between crossed nicols (crossed polaroids) show the ground mass of the material to be isotropic but to have the field speckled with bright points of light due to very small crystalline particles. These 'crystallites', due to incipient crystallization, are always present in volcanic glass. The density of obsidian varies between 2·33 and 2·42, at least for the types used in jewellery.

When a thin sliver of obsidian is examined under the microscope the texture is seen to consist of a clear glassy ground containing many small crystallites. These may be round bodies which are called globulites, they may be rod-shaped when they are called belonites, or they may be coiled or twisted hair-like bodies termed trichites. When the small globulites are

Figure 14.1. Long torpedo-shaped bubbles in a golden obsidian

fused into chains the term margarites is used, probably in fanciful analogy to a string of pearls. It may take a fairly high magnification to resolve these bodies. Round or torpedo-shaped bubbles are present in some obsidian. These, which can generally be seen clearly with low-power magnification, are often in parallel arrangement, and it is this parallelization of the bubbles and the crystallites which give to some obsidian the prized sheen (*Figures 14.1* and *14.2*).

Occurrences

Obsidian is widespread in occurrence, but most of the material used in jewellery is obtained from the North American continent. Important localities are the Glass Buttes, Lake County, where iridescent obsidian is found, and at Hampton, Deschutes County, both of which are in the State of Oregon. Obsidian Cliff, Yellowstone National Park in Wyoming is a place where obsidian has been quarried since the days of the North American Indians, who used it for arrowhead material. Arizona, Colorado and Nevada have deposits of obsidian, while California has many sites where the material has been quarried from ancient times. The best known of these Californian sources are Glass Mountain, Modoc County; Little Lake, Inyo County, and Obsidian Butte on the south-west side of Salton Sea in Imperial County. 'Apache tears' are usually found in New Mexico.

Obsidian was used by the Aztecs and their predecessors for the sharp points of their weapons, for mirrors and masks, and for dainty ear ornaments. They called the material iztli and surnamed it teotetl (divine stone) because of its manifold uses. The ancient Aztec obsidian pits were rediscovered by Humbolt during the opening years of the nineteenth century at Sierra de las Navagas in the State of Hidalgo, Mexico. Obsidian is found at several other places in Hidalgo, and in the other Mexican States of Jalisco, Queretaro, Michoacan and Vera Cruz. The Maya obtained their obsidian from ancient quarries at La Joya, some 18 miles east of Guatemala City, and the Indians of Equador had a quarry at Guamani.

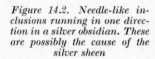

Figure 14.2. Needle-like inclusions running in one direction in a silver obsidian. These are possibly the cause of the silver sheen

Obsidian occurs throughout the world at those places where volcanic activity occurs or has occurred in the past. Such places are the Lipari Islands, Hawaii, Japan and Iceland—where the greyish obsidian which is cut and sold under the misnomer 'Iceland agate' is obtained—apart from the localities already mentioned.

BASALT GLASS

Basalt glass or tachylyte, which is found mainly on the chilled margins of basaltic intrusions, or lining or filling vesicles or cavities in basalt, is semi-translucent to opaque and usually black or brown in colour. It contains about 50 per cent of silica. Basalt glass which has a hardness about 6 on Mohs's scale, does not afford large flakes or show extensive conchoidal fracture when struck with a hammer, but breaks up into small irregular fragments and splinters. These glasses have a refractive index between 1·58 and 1·65 and a range of density between 2·70 and 3·00. Under low-power magnification the texture is seen to be uniform and the structure cannot be resolved except under high power. Basalt glasses are not normally cut as gem material but some experimental cabochons have been cut from the light grey, navy-blue, bluish-green and brown pieces found near the head-waters of the Flinders river in northern Queensland. The pieces are often attractively mottled and spotted.

METEORITES

Those extraterrestrial objects called meteorites are hardly expected to enter the field of gems, but, as will be explained, one such type of suspected meteorite has been used for ornamentation.

A meteorite is understood to be part of a disintegrated stellar body which, travelling through space, has entered the gravitational field of the earth and crashed on to its surface; thus it may be said to have cosmic origin. There are two general types of meteorites, those whose constitution is mainly iron and nickel known as siderites, and those which consist of olivine, pyroxene and a little feldspar and thus approach the basaltic rocks in composition. These are termed aerolites.

TEKTITES

It is not the metallic or stony objects from the skies which interests those who study gems, but a type having a glass-like constitution rich in silica, and which can be likened to the volcanic glass obsidian. These pieces, which are only suspected as being of meteoric origin, have, by F. E. Suess, been given the name tektites.

Figure 14.3. Surface structure of a moldavite pebble

Moldavites

The first noted occurrence of these glassy pieces was in 1787 in western Moravia and around České Budějovice (Budweis) near the Bohemian river Moldau, a river of which the Czech name is Vltava. Derived from the former name of the river the pieces were called moldavites. These lumps of glass, often peculiarly fissured on the surface—either reminiscent of alpine topography with craggy mountain tops, or with rounded crests having a botryoidal surface (*Figure 14.3*)—are transparent green, greenish-brown or brown in colour. The material has been cut as gemstones producing bottle-green stones which may have some resemblance to peridot, but are nearer in hue to green diopside. Cut moldavite has been sold under a variety of fancy and completely misleading names, such as 'Bottle stone', 'Obsidian', 'Water chrysolite' and 'Pseudo-chrysolite'. The stone has also been known under the name Bouteillenstein.

Moldavite consists of about 75 per cent silica with 10 per cent alumina and smaller quantities of iron oxides, lime, soda, potash, magnesia, titania and manganese oxide. It has the low hardness of $5\frac{1}{2}$ on Mohs's scale, a density ranging between 2·34 and 2·39 and an index of refraction of between 1·488 and 1·503. The absorption spectrum shows two ill-defined bands in the blue and a vague band in the orange, but the absorption spectrum is insufficient to be of value in identification. Moldavite does not luminesce under ultra-violet light but gives a dim yellowish-green glow under x-rays. Examination of the internal structure reveals that moldavites contain profuse round or torpedo-shaped bubbles and pronounced and peculiar swirl striae, as though a stick had been used to stir treacle (*Figure 14.4*). These bubbles and swirls are characteristic for moldavite and they are completely unlike the swirl striae seen in paste (glass), and there are no crystallites such as are seen in the volcanic glass obsidian.

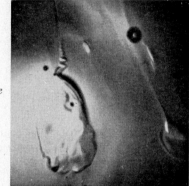

Figure 14.4. Internal structure of a moldavite

Billitonites and Australites

When first discovered moldavite was considered to be the remains of an early glassworks, a theory which held sway until other similar pieces were found in parts of the world which were not centres of ancient civilizations, particularly in Borneo, Sumatra and the Belitung island (formerly Billiton island) of Indonesia. The pieces from the last locality are called billitonites, from the former name of the island. Glassy pieces have also been found in other parts of the Malay archipelago, in the Philippines, Indo-China, the Ivory Coast of Africa and in the States of Colombia and Peru in South America.

Tektites are prominent in Australia and have been found in New South Wales, Victoria, South Australia, and Western and Central Australia, besides the island of Tasmania. Known as australites, some of these pieces are of singular form, being shaped rather like a button complete with a flange around the edge. The hypothesis that these button-shaped objects, popularly known as 'Blackfellow's buttons', were blebs of volcanic bubbles has now been more or less disproved and an extraterrestrial origin proposed for them.

The colour of these tektites varies from colourless, particularly those from Colombia, to brown, but the majority are black and opaque. They have a lower silica content than do the moldavites, a density varying between 2·36 and 2·51 and a refractive index between 1·49 and 1·53. The hardness is similar to that of the moldavites ($5\frac{1}{2}$) and they are often peculiarly marked on their surfaces, due, it is suggested, to their whirling through the air during their descent from outer space (*Figure 14.5*). It is doubtful whether these pieces have ever been cut for ornamental purposes. Quite recently some attempt was made to market the billitonites and some rough ball-like pieces were faceted. Examination of a trap-cut stone cut

Figure 14.5. A billitonite showing the surface structure

from one of the billitonites showed that the material was black and nearly opaque except in the thinner parts when the transmitted light was a greenish-black in colour. The refractive index was 1·51 and the density 2·455. The stone had a number of small round bubbles and these were similar to those seen in artificial glass.

Pit Glass

A. Church mentions that moldavite is an occasional occurrence in the gem gravels of Ceylon and cites this as added evidence of the natural source of the material. There has been no clear confirmation of this report, but a number of pieces of so-called 'pit glass' which is mostly brown or green have been credibly reported. These pieces seem to have the characters of ordinary artificial glass. They do not have the strong swirls and profuse bubbles of moldavite, but they may have an internal pattern like the billitonites, and therefore the matter must so far be considered unproven.

CRATER GLASS

It is necessary to mention certain other types of natural glasses, which, although not of meteoric origin have had their genesis in meteoric action, or in which the origin is completely a matter of conjecture. The first of these two types is obtained from meteoric craters, the glass being formed by the intense heat generated by the impact of a meteor on to the earth's surface where the surface soil is siliceous, such as in a sandy desert.

Such glass, white, greenish-yellow or black in colour, is in general simply a fused quartz, about 90 per cent silica with some impurities, of which the most common is iron. The material is slaggy and contains numerous vesicles. The specific gravity of these glasses varies from 2·10 to 2·31, a range which is sensibly lower than for the previously mentioned moldavites and tektites. The value is in many cases lower than that for pure fused quartz (silica glass, 2·203), probably owing to the included vesicles. The refractive index varies from 1·46 to 1·54, the high values probably being due to a richness in iron. This crater glass has been found in many widely different places, mostly in localities known for their sandy deserts, such as Waber in Arabia, Henbury in Central Australia, and at Meteor Crater, Arizona, in the United States of America, to which material the name lechatelierite has been given.

Small pieces of glass varying from colourless, through yellowish-green and olive green to black, slaggy and full of vesicles have been found in the Jukes-Darwin mining fields near Queenstown in western Tasmania. Known as Darwin glass, or Queenstownite, the material was first thought to be a tektite of meteoric origin, but on subsequent examination the material has been grouped with the glasses from meteoric craters which it so closely resembles. The density and refractive index of this glass is given as 2·27–2·29 and 1·47–1·50 respectively.

FUSED SAND GLASS

Analogous to these crater glasses are the fulgurites or lightning tubes which are thin tubes of fused sand caused by the intense heat set up when a lightning flash strikes and enters the sand of the desert. Scarcely a natural glass, but certainly a crater glass, is the fused sand formed by the first experimental atomic bomb which was exploded in New Mexico during 1945. This material, which has been named trinitite, is vesicular and greenish in colour, and the constants for the material are similar to those for ordinary crater glass. Even after many years much of this fused sand is still radioactive. It may appear unlikely that such material would be used for ornament, but it is on record that some has been fashioned into gems—mainly as publicity for film stars. In view of the radioactivity present it would certainly be a risk to wear such objects for too long at any one period.

SILICA GLASS

A nearly pure silica glass of mysterious origin found in 1932 in the wastes of the Libyan desert is known simply as silica glass. The material is found as sand blasted lumps up to 16 pounds in weight. It is of a greenish-yellow colour and is usually cloudy rather than clear due to the inclusion of vast numbers of irregularly shaped vesicles (*Figure 14.6*).

Silica glass consists of nearly pure silica (98 per cent SiO_2), has a refractive index of 1·46 and a density of 2·21, a hardness of 6 on Mohs's scale and a vitreous lustre. The stones cut from this material lack brilliancy and have a very small amount of fire, for the dispersion is 0·10 for the B to G interval. Occasionally there are found included in such glass, either as strings, clusters,

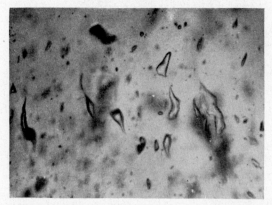

Figure 14.6. Internal structure of silica glass showing the irregularly shaped vesicles

or single individuals, spherulites of the cubic modification of quartz known as cristobalite. A little of the material has been cut and polished for collectors, but its insipid tint and poor brilliancy does not allow the stones cut from silica glass to be at all attractive.

Lumps of a glassy material, usually striped with greyish-blue and dark brown or black, are occasionally encountered. The material looks like an obsidian but it is actually a furnace slag and has a density near to 2·82.

CHAPTER 15

MARBLE

Marble, which gets its name from the Latin word marmor, which means a shining stone, may be defined as a crystalline aggregate of calcite which often has a saccharoidal texture. From the commercial point of view the term marble includes quite a number of ornamental stones, which cannot all be covered by the above definition, and may even include such soft minerals as alabaster. The marbles dealt with in this chapter will be the true marbles, the often colourful compact limestones, and the stalagmitic calcites often called onyxes, so important as media for some of the more handsome clock cases, cigarette boxes and other small objets d'art.

TRUE MARBLES

Metamorphic Occurrences

True marbles are the product of the alteration of an existing calcareous rock by the agency of heat, and possibly pressure, which occurred through geologic upheavals in past ages by contact metamorphism, as has been explained in Chapter 1. When the country rock which suffers this metamorphic change is a very pure limestone, the resulting metamorphic rock is a pure white granular marble, such as the Marmor Pentelicum, or Pentelikon marble which is quarried on Pentelikon mountain some 8 miles northeast of Athens. Another of the Greek white subtranslucent statuary marbles was mined as early as the sixth century on the Island of Paros in the Aegean Sea, one of the largest of the group of the Cyclades.

Another important group of white marbles are those found in the Apuan Alps around Carrara in Tuscany, Italy. The purest white marble from this locality is quarried on Monte Altissimo about 8 miles from Seravessa. When the marbles of the Apuan Alps are less pure they become clouded with greyish veins; such a marble is often called 'Sicilian marble', a misnomer for which various reasons have been given. Hundreds of marble quarries are dotted about the 25 miles between Pisa and Spezia on the west coast of northern Italy. These quarries, generally in groups, are mainly in the valleys of the Rayaccione and Sagro near Carrarra, and around Massa and Seravessa.

The limestones which have suffered metamorphism may have contained impurities and such impure rocks will produce attractively coloured marbles. A marble rock may be shattered by subsequent earth movements and the fissures so produced in the marble may be reconsolidated by other, often coloured, mineralization, thus producing the lovely veined marbles. If the fissures are very numerous and are filled with secondary minerals of many colours the product is then a variegated marble. A marble which suffers great stresses subsequent to its formation may break up into angular fragments which are subsequently recemented together by infiltration or by pressure. Such a rock is a brecciated marble, and such marbles can be most attractive.

Many limestones contain more or less magnesia and when silica is also present the two combine to form magnesium silicate, and these magnesium silicates, which frequently contain traces of iron, become readily altered by later chemical action into green serpentine. The resulting serpentinous marbles are known as ophicalcite, and examples of such rocks are the well-known Connemara marble, or Irish green marble which is found in County Galway, Eire. Iona stone found near the Bay of Portna-Carrack on the small Inner Hebridean island of Iona is a similar serpentine marble, and another source of ophicalcite is at Glen Tilt in Perthshire, Scotland.

The metamorphism of impure limestones may produce a marble which has comparatively large euhedral crystals embedded in the calcite ground-mass. The ruby found at the Mogok Stone Tract of Upper Burma has crystallized in white marble, and the white marble quarried at the Sagyin

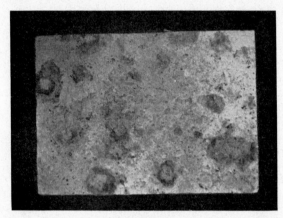

Figure 15.1. Xalostocite, a marble containing pink crystals of grossular garnet

quarries, north of Mandalay, occasionally has rubies embedded in it. At Xalostoc, Morelos, Mexico, is found an ornamental marble which consists of large crystals of pink grossular garnet in a creamy-white marble. This marble is called xalostocite, or alternatively, landerite or roselite (*Figure 15.1*). A similar material is said to have been found at Juarez, Lower California. The so-called Tiree marble which is found on the small island of Tiree which lies off the island of Mull, Argyllshire on the west Scottish coast, is another such marble which contains visible crystals of diopside in a pink groundmass (*Figure 15.2*).

Nomenclature

The names applied to the various types of marbles are legion and there would be little value in repeating what may well be local quarry names. In general there are two main types of nomenclature, one consisting of the name of the quarry and one which infers in some manner the colour of the marble, and these may often be combined. Thus, cipollino is the name applied to marbles which have alternate bands of white and green. The name is particularly applied to the marble from the quarries on the Greek island of

Euboea (Negroponte), a marble which was known as the 'Marble of Carystus'. The modern name, cipollino, relates to the well-defined layers resembling an onion (cipolla). The name pavonazzo which is applied to a group of white or pale yellow marbles traversed with coloured veins, is said to have originated from the supposed resemblance between the colour of the purple veins and the plumage of a peacock (pavone).

When the marble is brecciated the term breccia or breche may be incorporated in the title, and Griottes are red marbles whose colour resembles the Griotte cherry. The impossibility of attempting to identify a marble by the name is illustrated by the so-called Molina rosa, a reddish marble from the Garfagnana quarries of Tuscany, which owes its name to the Spanish marble quarried near the town of Molina.

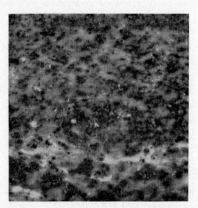

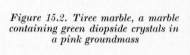

Figure 15.2. Tiree marble, a marble containing green diopside crystals in a pink groundmass

STALAGMITIC CALCITES OR 'ONYXES'

Chemical and Physical Properties

The second type of marble to consider is the massive crystalline calcium carbonate deposits which form from waters charged with calcium bicarbonate. These are the so-called travertines and stalagmitic deposits. Although calcium carbonate is almost insoluble in pure water, when the water contains carbon dioxide, as all natural waters do, the calcium carbonate from the limestone rocks, over which the water flows, will be acted upon, producing the more water-soluble calcium bicarbonate. Pressure increases and heat, by driving off the carbon dioxide, decreases the solubility of the carbonate which will, on decrease of pressure or on heating the water, or by its evaporation—all processes which lead to the loss of the gas carbon dioxide—result in the precipitation of crystalline calcium carbonate producing beds of travertine or stalactites and stalagmites, which in general have a layered structure. This physico-chemical description of the deposition may not, however, tell all the story, for organisms such as algae and bacteria may assist in the deposition and it is not always possible to separate the purely inorganic deposition from the biochemical processes.

Nomenclature

The travertines and stalagmitic calcites are often banded; they are commercially known as the 'onyx marbles' or 'oriental alabaster'; both terms are misnomers for onyx usually implies a banded chalcedony (agate) while the name alabaster is, in correct mineralogical nomenclature, a massive gypsum—a hydrous calcium sulphate. The origin of the use of these mineralogically incorrect names is a matter of some conjecture. That the names alabaster and onyx were applied to the stalagmitic calcites in Biblical times seems clear, and that at different epochs the material was successively known as 'oriental alabaster', 'alabaster onyx' and 'onyx marble', the latter name being current at the present time.

There seems some doubt too of the origin of the name alabaster. Maybe it was derived from the town of Alabastron in Egypt where the stone was first quarried and worked, or alternatively the name may well have received its genesis from the use made of this type of marble in making the slender narrow-necked vases or cruses without handles called 'alabastron'.

Colours

Normally the ground colour of these onyx marbles is white, but invariably they are veined by coloured fissures or in areas by the infiltration of metallic oxides. It is owing to their translucency and their soft delicate bands of colour in amber, orange and green, that these stalagmitic calcites have won such esteem with the makers of small objets d'art, and for fine quality clock cases and cigarette boxes, when the soft effect of the marble is offset by inlaying with other minerals which have a stronger or more contrasting colour.

Occurrences

Deposits of 'onyx marble' are widely distributed in almost every region of the world, but it is only in a few places that the deposits are of sufficient importance to be commercially worked. The most abundant supply of the marble comes from Algeria in North Africa, where it is found in quantity in the provinces of Oran and Constantine. The major quarries are situated close to Bon-Hanifa, a village about 10 miles north-east of the town of Mascara. Bon-Hanifa lies near to the ancient Roman town of Aquae Sirensis, which was noted for its hot springs, and it may well be that the deposits originated from these springs. The Constantine deposits lie about 10 miles from Constantine, the capital of the department of the same name, and much of the marble from this locality is bright red in colour. On the Moroccan side of the border with Algeria lies another deposit of stalagmitic marble, which may be considered an offshoot of the Algerian deposits. Like the Oran marble the colour of Moroccan marble is normally white with coloured veins, but material of a blue, grey, or pink colour mixed with green, as well as a bright red is found.

Deposits also occur in Egypt, where stalagmitic marble, in early times known as 'Egyptian alabaster', was found near the town of Alabastron. The Egyptian material, a translucent light amber rock marked with wavy bands (*Figure 15.3*), was formerly worked over a large area of the Nile Valley, but the little material quarried in recent years is obtained from workings on the lower flanks of the Asyut mountains, some 20 miles from the town of Asyut. During the nineteenth century some stalagmitic marble was obtained from the caves near Beni Suef in the Nile Valley, and material from this deposit was used for embellishing the famous alabaster mosque at Cairo.

About 300 miles south of San Diego lie the Pedrara quarries of Lower California, Mexico, where a deposit of stalagmitic marble is exposed on the surface or is not more than 8 or 10 ft. below ground. After mining, this white or green translucent rock veined with dark orange, amber or brown, and which is known as 'Pedrara onyx', is sent to San Diego for distribution. Other sources of onyx marble in Mexico are in the States of Puebla and Oaxaco. The 'Mexican onyx', as the marble is commonly called, is in America sometimes called Tecali marble, a name given to it by the Aztecs who deemed the stone too sacred for it to be used by the common people. The marble was almost solely devoted to the ornamentation of religious buildings or for the making of sacrificial vessels. Indeed 'Tecali' is but a corruption of the Aztec name Teocali given by the Mexican Indians

Figure 15.3. A stalagmitic marble with wavy bands

to their temples. It is from the Mexican localities that most of the onyx marbles used in England for ornamental pieces are derived.

The so-called 'Brazilian onyx' is a misnomer, for this material is found in the province of San Luis in the Argentine Republic. The marble from San Luis differs little in appearance from that found in Mexico. A similar marble is found and mined in Yavapai County, Arizona. This marble, commercially called 'Yava onyx', is found in irregular and somewhat lenticular layers from one inch to two feet in thickness interbedded with a coarse breccia formed of schistose and dioritic fragments in a sandy and calcareous matrix. Near Lehi, some 20 miles from Salt Lake City in Utah, occurs a vein of highly translucent stalagmitic marble of a bright lemon yellow colour traversed with orange-coloured sinuous veins. This 'Utah onyx', as it is called, is not an important source of marble.

Onyx marble is found near Laasee in the valley of the Vintschgau. It is slightly translucent with orange-coloured veins, is known as 'Tyrolese onyx' and is mainly worked in Vienna. The 'Stalagmite de Bédat' is found in the Haute-Pyrénées in caverns and grottoes on the banks of the river Ariège. Another deposit is found at Manère in the French Department of Pyrénées-Orientales.

Gibraltar stone is a stalagmitic deposit found in the caves which abound in the limestone rocks which form the Rock of Gibraltar (*Figure 15.4*). The material is a translucent travertine with brown and amber-coloured sinuous veins, and is used mainly for the production of small ornamental objects for sale to the tourists as souvenirs of their visit. 'Java onyx' is a stalagmitic marble usually dull white in colour or variegated with amber-coloured wavy banding. The rock, which is found around the town of Kediri (Wadjak) some 60 miles south-east of Surabaja (Surabaya) in the Toeloeng Agoeng district of Java, does not have the translucency of many other 'onyxes'. A beautiful translucent banded material of bright yellow colour comes from the Karibib district of South-West Africa. It is locally called 'aragonite' but is actually a stalagmitic calcite.

Figure 15.4. Gibraltar stone

A crystalline 'marble', which consists of fibrous crystals of calcite, is known as satin-spar (*see* gypsum). The material is found in veins and the fibrous crystals stretch across the vein from side to side. When polished with a flat surface the material shows a silky lustre. Calcite satin-spar—which occurs at Alston Moor in veins from 1 to 4 in. in thickness, at Glen Tilt, Perthshire and in several states in North America—is now scarce.

Some few years ago there were marketed, under the fanciful misnomers 'Imperial Mexican Jade' or just 'Mexican Jade', carved and fashioned pieces of a green material which were subsequently identified as calcite (marble). The colour was probably due to artificial staining.

LIMESTONES

Chemical and Physical Properties

Many of the architectural marbles, and some of these are used for small ornamental pieces, are simply limestones which owe their attraction to colour and to the patterning caused by included fossils. Unlike the marbles already mentioned, limestones are sedimentary rocks consisting mainly of calcium carbonate with varying amounts of impurities to which their colour may be due. They are sometimes laid down in layers, producing stratified rocks, although the stratification may be of any thickness from paper thin to layers so thick that no layering can be seen in pieces of average size. Indeed, in certain limestones stratification is entirely absent.

The deposition of lime rocks may occur through physico-chemical conditions, by the loss of carbon dioxide from bicarbonate rich waters, as in the formation of the stalagmitic marbles. Such occurrences may also happen with organic formation, which illustrates the difficulty, if not impossibility, of truly deciding the group to which a marble belongs.

Most limestones owe their origin to organic processes and these may be either biochemical or biomechanical. In the first of these are the vital activities of the organisms which promote a chemical condition favouring precipitation of lime; the bacterial limestones are of this type. Biomechanical deposits are due to the rock being formed from the detrital accumulation of organic materials, as in the case of coral, encrinital and shelly limestones. The grain-size of such mechanically formed rocks depends upon the initial sizes of the component organisms, or on the size of the fragments into which they naturally break. Such limestones may be heterogeneous in composition, consisting of a great variety of organic fragments embedded in a calcareous mud due to their comminution; one group of organisms often predominating to give character to the rock. Such rocks are the 'fossil marbles'.

Occurrences

Probably the most common marble is the so-called black marble which was so often used for casing clocks in the late Victorian and the Edwardian periods. These black marbles, often veined with white, are mostly obtained from the provinces of Hainault and Namur in Belgium. These marbles are known as the 'Noir Belge' (Belgian black) and are found along the Sambre and Meuse rivers. Much black marble is found in the Departments of Nord and Pas de Calais in northern France. That from Nord is known as 'Grande Antique' and that from Pas de Calais as 'Noir Français'. Other black marbles, for there are a number of localities which provide such marbles, are the 'Irish Black' found in County Carlow in Eire.

Many of the compact limestones are brightly coloured in reds, browns, yellows, and greens of varying tones and may be of variegated colours. There are so many of these marbles, often named from local quarries, that an attempt to name them would be confusing and have little value.

Fossil Marbles

The fossil marbles, owing to their obvious characteristics, do allow some grouping and description. The fossils visible in limestones may be either shelly (mainly the shells of the *Mollusca*), coralline (various corals), and encrinital (containing the remains of crinoids, or as they are sometimes known, sea lilies).

Shelly Marbles

The best known of the shelly marbles is the Purbeck marble, a blue-grey to reddish-brown marble made up of countless fossil shells of freshwater snails (*Paludina carinifera*) (*Figure 15.5*), hence the marble is sometimes known as Paludina limestone. The quarries supplying this marble stretch westwards from the Dorset town of Swanage for about five miles along the south coast of England. A similar marble is found near East Grinstead and Netherfield, near Battle, in Sussex. It is known as the Petworth marble or Bethersden marble, depending upon the locality where it was obtained, and, although resembling the Purbeck marble, the fossil shells are those of *Paludina fluviorum*, which is a larger species. A striking fossil marble is that which contains fossil ammonites on a dark brown groundmass (*Figure 15.6*). The Irish black marble—the Kilkenny black fossil marble—is picked out by white circles, which are abundant brachiopod shells.

Figure 15.5. Fossil marble: the Purbeck marble from Dorset

A most beautiful fossil marble is the so-called 'Fire marble', known also as lumachella, lumachelle or lumachello, a word which means little snail. This rather rare marble, which has been used for small ornamental pieces, is a dark brown marble marked throughout with small whitish shells which in certain parts exhibit iridescent colours rather like opal, and indeed the marble may be mistaken for opal in matrix. The marble is found in veins forming the roof of the lead mines at Bleiburg in Carinthia, Austria, and also in Astrakhan, in Russia.

Coralline Marbles

Fossil coral limestones (*Figure 15.7*) produce intriguing marbles, and the fossils can be of many diverse patterns. One such is the 'Red Ogwell

Marble' which contains the coral known as favosites (*Figure 15.8*). The so-called Petoskey stone from Michigan in the United States of America is a fossil coral limestone.

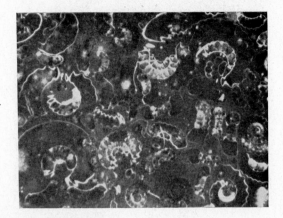

Figure 15.6. A fossil marble containing ammonite shells

Figure 15.7. A fossil coral
limestone. The fossil is Tham-
nastraea

Figure 15.8. A limestone containing the fossil coral Favosites cervicornis from Torquay,
Devon

Figure 15.9. Encrinital marble from Derbyshire

Encrinital Limestones

The encrinital limestones are usually fawn to reddish-brown in colour and are prettily marked by the broken stems of the crinoids (sea lilies). Such marbles are abundant in the Derbyshire quarries. The 'Hopton Wood marble' from Middleton and the 'Bird's-eye marble' from Ashford are examples of Derbyshire encrinital marbles (*Figure 15.9*) and many such fossil marbles are found elsewhere.

Other Marbles

The 'Landscape' or 'Cotham' marble is a light grey-coloured rock, having dark brown, nearly black, dendritic markings throughout, and which on polished surfaces of the rock frequently shows patterns which simulate trees and other vegetation. The marble is found at the base of the White Lias of the Rhaetic beds and is mined at Cotham, near Bristol. 'Florence marble', or as it is better known 'Ruin marble' is a calcareous marl of greyish-green colour which has suffered fracture in straight angular pieces (*Figure 15.10*).

Figure 15.10. Florence, or Ruin marble

Owing to infiltration of iron oxide a polished slice of the marble shows yellowish sections. The general picture appears like a panorama of ruined buildings and when viewed at a distance appears like a drawing in bistre. This rock occurs in the Val d'Arno, near Florence, in Italy.

The so-called 'lava cameos' which are occasionally met mounted in brooches or bracelets and are either of an opaque grey colour or brownish-yellow appear to be nearly always a fine-grained limestone, although sometimes they are just glass.

CALCITE

Chemical and Physical Properties

Pure calcite is water-white and the mineral, which is a calcium carbonate ($CaCO_3$), crystallizes in the rhombohedral system: the crystals have prismatic habit. The hardness of the pure calcite is 3, and is the standard 3 for Mohs's scale, but from the admixture of impurities marble may in some cases be slightly harder. The purest true marbles, such as the white statuary marbles from Carrara, break with a saccharoidal surface, while the fracture in limestones is usually much smoother. The refractive indices of calcite are 1·658 for the ordinary ray and 1·486 for the extraordinary ray, but in the compact and granular marbles the most pronounced edge seen in the refractometer is that of the extraordinary ray at 1·48, which can sometimes be seen to move upward on rotation of the specimen. The ordinary ray is seen with difficulty, much depending on the granular size of the calcite crystals. The limestones generally show an indistinct edge at about 1·50.

The density of pure calcite is 2·71, but in marbles and limestones there may be, and usually is, a lowering of the density due to the granular nature of the crystal aggregates; or the density may be raised owing to the inclusion of other minerals. It may be given that the range of density for marbles (and limestones) varies from 2·58 to 2·75.

Effects of Light

The absorption spectra and the fluorescence under ultra-violet light of marbles are too vague to be of value in identification. The luminescent glows exhibited under either wave-band of ultra-violet light, if any fluorescence is shown at all, is patchy, some of the veined material showing up the veins as a whitish glow. Some of the travertines, including Gibraltar stone, show a bright greenish-yellow glow and a strong phosphorescence under both wave-lengths of ultra-violet light. Under x-ray stimulation most true marbles and many limestones show the typical orange glow shown by calcite. As calcite is a carbonate a spot of acid placed on marble will produce an effervescence. This is a sure test for marble against some other, but not all, marble-like rocks.

Varieties of Calcite

A pink variety of calcite, cobalti-calcite, which owes its colour to cobalt, has been fashioned into cabochons as collectors' items. The true marble is a granular material and will be susceptible to staining; this is artificially carried out, usually by aniline dyes. Concretions of calcium carbonate with a pearly lustre which have been formed by the agency of water in limestone caves are called cave pearls. Despite its low hardness and strong cleavage a golden yellow calcite has been faceted for the whim of collectors.

CHAPTER 16

LESSER KNOWN ORNAMENTAL AND GEM MATERIALS

The following descriptions of the lesser known gemstones include those used for ornamental purposes, those rarer faceted stones occasionally met with in jewellery, and those which may be termed collectors items. All the minerals which have been known as fashioned pieces in collections are included, even if their use for pure ornamentation is, as in many cases, impracticable, since there is a possibility of such stones being released from collections and proceeding via trade channels to other collectors, or even to the jeweller's junk box. It seems a sounder treatment to give them a short notice than to omit them. The newly found mineral painite has been included in gem literature, despite only one crystal having been found, and this has not been cut into a gemstone. The descriptions of these stones are listed in alphabetical order, and no grouping is made. A division into the rarer faceted stones and the ornamental stones has little value, for so often one mineral will supply either transparent or translucent material suitable for faceting into stones, or translucent to opaque massive material which may be carved and polished into ornamental objects.

ALABASTER

The massive variety of the mineral gypsum is called alabaster, and is the variety of most importance in commercial gemmology, for the fully crystallized varieties have scant use in ornamentation.

Gypsum, a hydrous calcium sulphate ($CaSO_42H_2O$) when well crystallized produces excellent transparent monoclinic crystals, which are often twinned in swallow-tailed forms. These crystals, which are not used for purposes of ornamentation, are readily cleavable in one direction. Such crystals of gypsum are called selenite, for the crystals tend to show moon-like gleams from the cleavage surfaces.

A type of gypsum, generally white in colour, in which the mineral fills veins in rock formations with parallel fibrous crystals stretching across the vein from side to side, is known as satin spar (although a similar formation of calcite is also so-called). Satin spar is occasionally cut as polished slabs, cabochons or as beads. Pretty as they can be the low hardness—gypsum has a hardness of about 2 on Mohs's scale—precludes its use to any extent.

The massive rock-like variety of alabaster was known from the days of the Phoenicians, Assyrians and Egyptians, who made all kinds of beautiful vases and amphorae, and who were also the first to find out and use its beauty as a medium for direct and indirect lighting. The delicately wrought alabaster vases that were found in the tomb of Tutankamen were used to illuminate the temples in the land of the Pharaohs. Today the material is used not only for bowls for indirect electric lighting, but for small articles of utility, such as powder boxes, ash trays, clock cases, paper weights and other ornamental objects (*Figure 16.1*) (*see also* page 238).

Massive gypsum is usually deposited by the evaporation of an enclosed sea basin, or may be deposited from desert lakes. Gypsum is frequently formed in mineral veins where sulphuric acid, derived from the oxidation of pyrites and other sulphides, has acted upon limestone.

The purest form of alabaster is white and translucent but the material is often associated with a trace of ferric oxide which produces light brown and orange-coloured bands and veins, or with other impurities which colour the stone in yellows, browns and black in veins or patches of colour. The softness of the rock, especially when freshly quarried, enables it to be

Figure 16.1. Clock case in alabaster

carved easily. Indeed, alabaster can be scratched by a finger nail, but to a slight extent the mineral hardens after exposure to the air and will then take a good polish. Alabaster, too, is sufficiently porous to allow it to be stained and such artificial coloration is often produced.

The hardness of gypsum is given as 2 on Mohs's scale, but most alabaster is found to be harder than 2. The fractured surface is more finely granular than the saccharoidal fracture of marble. The translucency varies from highly translucent to practically opaque and the material has a glistening lustre. The refractive indices are 1·52–1·53, and in the case of the massive variety—alabaster—a shadow edge about this value is moderately clearly seen on the refractometer scale. The density of alabaster lies between 2·30 and 2·33. There is no absorption spectrum of value to be seen in alabaster, and the luminescence under ultra-violet light, usually a brownish shade of glow, gives little aid to distinction. Under x-rays the material is inert.

Massive gypsum is of world-wide occurrence, but only in relatively few localities are quarries worked for ornamental alabaster. One of the most important localities for alabaster is the quarries situated at Castellina, in the district of Volterra in Tuscany, Italy. The alabaster from this district is found in nodular masses embedded in limestone interstratified with marls. The mineral is mainly worked by mining through underground galleries.

The carving of Tuscan alabaster is carried out at Florence and Pisa and other cities of central Italy, and the industry dates from Etruscan times. The pure white Tuscan material is often carved into figurines having a religious significance. Some of this pure white material is, after carving, treated by immersion in cold water, which is then slowly raised to boiling point. The stone is allowed to cool very gradually and is afterwards thoroughly dried. This treatment is said to make the alabaster scarcely distinguishable from white marble. The material may be stained.

The most important quarries for ornamental alabaster in England are in the Counties of Derbyshire and Staffordshire. The Derbyshire quarries are in the neighbourhood of Chellaston, where the mineral is found in thick nodular beds or 'floors' and in small lenticular masses termed 'cakes'. These deposits are close to the surface and are worked by open pit mining. The major Staffordshire quarries are at Fauld near Hanbury, and near Weston, which lies close to the Derbyshire border. Occasional thin bands of fine granular gypsum of a pinkish colour are found along the coastal plains of Glamorgan in South Wales. It is known as 'Pink Welsh Alabaster' but is not commercially important.

The anhydrous calcium sulphate ($CaSO_4$) anhydrite has also been used as a gem material. The hardness of anhydrite is about 3 on Mohs's scale, the density is 2·9 and the refractive indices are 1·57 and 1·61 for the principal rays. The mineral, which crystallizes in the orthorhombic system, is usually white in colour, but may be blue, and is found at many different localities.

AMBLYGONITE

Occasionally clear transparent colourless or yellow crystals of amblygonite have been cut for those who covet the unusual. The mineral is a fluophosphate of aluminium and lithium ($LiAl(F,OH)PO_4$), a mineral which, like topaz, has the fluorine replaceable by the hydroxyl group. Amblygonite forms large but rough crystals of the triclinic system which have a tabular habit and a perfect basal cleavage. The hardness is 6 on Mohs's scale and for the gem material the density is between 3·015 and 3·033. The refractive indices for the cut stones so far examined approximate to 1·611 and 1·637 for the principal rays, the biaxial positive birefringence being 0·026. No clear absorption spectrum is seen with the yellow amblygonite and under the long-wave ultra-violet lamp the stones show a very weak greenish glow, but under x-rays the glow is a bright greenish-white. Apart from the physical and optical properties identifying amblygonite, microchemical tests will prove the phosphate content. Powder 'sneaked' from the edge of the stone will allow this to be done and will also allow flame tests to be carried out, for the powder introduced by means of a platinum wire into the colourless bunsen flame will colour the flame with the characteristic red of lithium.

The localities for amblygonite are Sao Paulo and Minas Gerais in Brazil—where most of the gem material is said to have emanated—and Pala, California and Maine in the United States of America. Saxony, France and Australia (Northern Territory) are other localities. Pale mauve amblygonite is found in the Karabib area of South-West Africa.

ANALCITE (Analcime)

At the whim of collectors some small colourless crystals of analcite have been cut. The mineral, which forms icositetrahedral crystals of the cubic system, is a hydrous sodium aluminium silicate with the formula $NaAlSi_2O_6H_2O$. The hardness is from 5 to $5\frac{1}{2}$ on Mohs's scale, the density is from 2·22 to 2·29 and the refractive index is 1·487. The mineral is a member of the zeolite group and is found in the United States of America, Czechoslovakia, Italy, Scotland, and in fine crystals from the Kerguelen Islands in the Indian Ocean. Australia and Japan are other localities for this mineral which may be said to have a world-wide occurrence.

ANATASE

One of the polymorphous forms of titanium oxide (TiO_2), rutile and brookite are the others, anatase is rarely cut as a gemstone. The mineral is brown or blue in colour and crystallizes in the tetragonal system, usually as bipyramids so that the form can be said to be octahedral. It is owing to this that the alternative name octahedrite is sometimes used for the mineral. Anatase has a hardness of $5\frac{1}{2}$–6 on Mohs's scale, a density which lies between 3·82 and 3·95 and refractive indices 2·493 for the extraordinary ray and 2·554 for the ordinary ray. The uniaxial negative birefringence is 0·061. Anatase shows no luminescence. The mineral results from the alteration of other titanium-bearing minerals and is also found in veins of hydrothermal origin. The localities for anatase are Isère in France and St. Gotthard and Binnenthal in Switzerland, in the Ural mountains of Russia and Minas Gerais in Brazil. Other localities are Massachusetts, North Carolina and Colorado in the United States of America, where blue crystals are found.

ANDALUSITE

Not commonly met with in jewellery, andalusite, which is named after the Spanish province of Andalusia where the mineral was first found, supplies stones of a greenish-brown, brownish-green to a rich green in colour, the stones owing much of their attractiveness to the extremely pronounced pleochroism which they exhibit. The mineral is an aluminium silicate corresponding to the formula Al_2SiO_5, and is therefore polymorphous (that is it has the same chemical composition) with the minerals kyanite and fibrolite. The crystals, belonging to the orthorhombic system, have a prismatic habit with vertically striated prisms which are nearly square in section and capped with pyramids, but much of the gem material is found as water-worn pebbles.

The hardness of andalusite is $7\frac{1}{2}$ on Mohs's scale and the specific gravity varies from 3·15 to 3·17. The least and greatest refractive indices vary from

1·634 to 1·641 and 1·644 to 1·648, the biaxial double refraction varying from 0·007 to 0·011. The sign is negative. The dispersion is approximately 0·016 between the B to G interval, and the three pleochroic colours of the stones are yellow, green and red which may be variable in intensity. The absorption spectrum of andalusite varies in that the deep green variety, believed to come from Brazil, shows a manganese spectrum, with an absorption band, graded in intensity, which ends in a knife-sharp edge at 5535 Å, and which is followed by fine lines at 5505, 5475 Å and fainter ones at 5180 and 4950 Å. There is a strong absorption in the blue and violet but a band at 4550 Å can just be seen. This has been noted in the normal types of gem andalusite and these stones, particularly those from Ceylon show this band to be accompanied by a narrow band at 4360 Å. These last two bands are probably due to iron. Andalusite exhibits no luminescence under the long-wave lamp, but the brownish-green stones from Brazil often show a dark green to yellowish-green glow under the short-wave ultra-violet lamp and a greenish-yellow glow under x-rays.

Andalusite of a dull green is found in the gem gravels of Ceylon, but Brazil is the more prolific source of the gem material, where the stones are found in secondary deposits, either in the stream beds or on the slopes of the hills under several yards of clay and gravel. This is in an area some 10 miles wide and 25 miles in length near the town of Santa Tereza in the State of Espirito Santo. Andalusite is also found at Minas Gerais in the State of Minas Gerais. The gem mineral is rarely found in crystals with good form and most of the gemmy material is found as water-worn pebbles. The Brazilian stones usually show a very strong flesh-red and olive green pleochroism, which is especially well brought out when the stones are cut with the table facet nearly at right angles to the vertical axis of the crystal. Such stones may closely resemble certain types of Brazilian tourmalines. A dark green andalusite is also found in Brazil, and so too are stones of a rose-red colour, although these are rare.

An impure opaque variety of andalusite in which the crystals contain carbonaceous inclusions with a cruciform arrangement is known as chiastolite (cross-stone). Sections of such crystals are cut and polished for amulets and charms in countries, particularly the Pyrénées, where the religious significance of the cross is profound. Owing to impurities chiastolite may have a lower hardness and density than for the transparent crystals. Chiastolite crystals are found in the Nerchinsk district of Transbaikalia in Siberia, at Sallas de Rohan near Brieux in Brittany and Mount Howden, north of Bimbowrie in South Australia. Other localities are at Hof in the Fichtelgebirge and in the slates around Skiddaw in Cumberland, but here the needle-like prisms are too slender for fashioning into gems. Sources in the United States of America are Arizona, Madera in Madera County, California. Other localities are in Maine, Connecticut, Massachusetts and New Mexico, and Fannin County, Georgia.

ANGLESITE

A stone only cut for collectors is the orthorhombic mineral anglesite, a lead sulphate, $PbSO_4$. Usually white in colour although shades of yellow, green or blue may be found, the mineral has a hardness of 3 on Mohs's scale, a density of 6·30–6·39 and refractive indices of α 1·877, β 1·882 and γ 1·894, biaxial and positive in sign with double refraction of 0·017. The lustre may be adamantine inclining to resinous or vitreous, and anglesite fluoresces with a weak yellow glow under short-wave ultra-violet light. The mineral has a world-wide occurrence and is found in large crystals at various places in the United States of America. Anglesite was originally found in the isle of Anglesey, hence the name, and fine crystals have been found in the Leadhill district of Scotland. Cuttable material comes from Bou Azzwr in Morocco.

APATITE

If apatite were not so soft, the mineral being the standard 5 on Mohs's scale, it would make a fine suite of gemstones as the colours range from white, yellow, green to blue and violet.

The mineral is a calcium phosphate, but there is always some fluorine or chlorine in the composition, hence the formula may best be written as $Ca(F,Cl)Ca_4(PO_4)_3$. In coarse non-gem quality crystals apatite reaches enormous sizes, often weighing hundredweights, but the clear crystals from which gemstones are cut are never large. The crystals belong to the hexagonal system and their habit is usually stumpy prismatic, or in some cases tabular.

Lovely blue stones are found in the Mogok Stone Tract of Upper Burma and in the gem gravels of Ceylon, some of which have a fibrous structure and when cut cabochon in the correct direction show a cat's-eye effect. Yellowish-green crystals found in the Spanish province of Murcia, probably in the Serra de Espuna, have been called 'asparagus stones', owing to their peculiar colour. From Arendal, in southern Norway, comes a beautiful bluish-green variety to which the name moroxite has been given. Well-formed prismatic crystals of yellow colour come from Cerro de Mercado, Durango in Mexico, and lovely violet-coloured stones are found in the Greifenstein in Saxony, Schlaggenwald in Bohemia and in the United States of America at Auburn, Maine and San Diego, California. Other localities are in Ajmer, Rajasthan and Devada, and Madras, in India, where sea-green material is obtained. A deep rich green apatite is found in Quebec and Ontario, Canada. There are many other sources of apatite, which is a widespread mineral, but the localities given are the better known places where gem material is found. Well-formed green crystals in an orange calcite come from Moçambique and form lovely mineral specimens, the apatite often being clear enough to produce cut stones. Yellow and green cat's-eye apatite has been seen and an intense sapphire blue coloured material comes from Minas Gerais, Brazil.

The density of apatite varies from 3·17 to 3·23, the blue stones generally being 3·18 and the yellow 3·22. The refractive indices are 1·63–1·64 with an exceptionally small negatively uniaxial birefringence of 0·002–0·004. The dichroism is usually feeble but distinct, except in the blue and some green stones. The blue stones show pronounced dichroism and the twin colours are blue for the extraordinary ray and pale yellow for the ordinary ray. The lustre is vitreous and the fire (0·013 B to G) is weak. Absorption

252

spectra of apatite can vary considerably; both blue and yellow stones show absorption spectra attributed to the rare earths, but the yellow-coloured stones show strongly two groups of closely spaced lines, one a group of about seven lines at about 5800 Å, which is just on the short-wave side of the D lines of sodium, and a group of about five closely spaced lines in the green of the spectrum at about 5200 Å. The blue-coloured apatites show rather broader bands, the strongest being at 5120, 4910 and 4640 Å. the last two being in the blue part of the spectrum. It is interesting to recall that the rare earth didymium is actually composite, containing the two elements praseodymium and neodymium, which are so often associated together. Thus the absorption spectrum will, in general, show bands due to the two elements, but the bands of one of the pair of elements may predominate. From the appearance of the absorption spectrum of yellow apatite, which is usually called a 'didymium spectrum', neodymium preponderates, while in blue apatite praseodymium is stronger.

The luminescence of apatite also varies. Results of the examination of a number of different coloured apatites are shown in Table 16.1.

TABLE 16.1

Colour	Long-wave ultra-violet light	Short-wave ultra-violet light	X-rays
Yellow	Lilac-pink	Weak lilac-pink	Pinkish-white to pinkish yellow and mauve
Blue	Bright dark violet-blue to sky-blue	Bright dark violet-blue to sky-blue	Very dim pinkish straw colour
Green	Greenish-mustard	Weak greenish-mustard	Yellowish-white to yellow
Violet	Greenish-yellow	Vague pale mauve	Very bright greenish-yellow with persistent phosphorescence

A massive sky-blue variety of apatite has been polished as an ornamental stone, and a variety with lapis from Siberia has been named lazurapatite.

APOPHYLLITE

Valued as a gemstone by collectors only, the hydrated potassium calcium silicate having the formula $KFCa_4(Si_2O_5)_4.8H_2O$, known as apophyllite, forms crystals of the tetragonal system with varied habit and which have a perfect basal cleavage. Apophyllite is usually colourless or it may have a pinkish, greenish or yellowish tint. The hardness of the mineral varies from $4\frac{1}{2}$ to 5 on Mohs's scale, and the density ranges from 2·30 to 2·50. The refractive indices are 1·535 and 1·537 and the small uniaxial birefringence may be either positive or negative in sign. The lustre is vitreous, although on the cleavage surfaces the lustre is pearly. There is no distinctive spectrum and normally the stones do not luminesce under ultra-violet light. A yellowish glow from apophyllite under short-wave ultra-violet light has been reported. Under x-rays the mineral shows either an orange or a weak bluish glow. Apophyllite is found in many places, particularly from the rocks of the Deccan trap of India. The mineral is also found at Guanajuato, Mexico (pink crystals on amethyst), Switzerland, Germany and a number of the states of North America.

ARANDISITE

An attractive apple-green material, arandisite is sometimes cut, together with the surrounding brown limonite. It is a basic silicate of tin but is considered to be a mixture of two constituents, perhaps colloidal and crystalline phases. The hardness is 5 on Mohs's scale; the density 4, but if with much limonite would be less, and the refractive index 1·70, but can be higher in parts. It is a rare mineral and is found only at the Arandis tin mine, north of Arandis, South-West Africa.

AUGELITE

Colourless crystals of this hydrated aluminium phosphate mineral which accords to the formula $2Al_2O_3.P_2O_5.3H_2O$ have been cut as gems for collectors. The monoclinic crystals have a tabular habit, a hardness of 5 on Mohs's scale and a density near to 2·7. The refractive indices are α 1·574, β 1·576 and γ 1·588. The mineral is biaxial and optically positive with a birefringence of 0·014. The stones have a vitreous lustre and do not exhibit luminescence under ultra-violet light. Augelite is found in the United States of America and Bolivia.

AXINITE

The broad acute-edged triclinic crystals of axinite, which form such attractive crystal groups, may be found large and clear enough to cut into gemstones for those who crave the unusual. Axinite, named after the axe-like shape of the crystals, is usually a typical clove-brown colour, or more rarely honey-yellow or plum-blue, and the stones are characterized by the strong dichroism they exhibit, the twin colours being olive-green, violet-blue and cinnamon-brown for the three principal directions. The indices of refraction, biaxial and negative in sign, are approximately 1·685 for the greatest and 1·675 for the least, the birefringence being 0·010–0·012. The hardness of axinite is 7 on Mohs's scale and the density varies from 3·27 to 3·29. The absorption spectrum of axinite shows three fairly obvious bands; a narrow band in the blue-green at 5120 Å and two broader bands at 4920 and 4660 Å in the blue. Other bands may be observed in some specimens; these are at 5320, 4440 and 4150 Å, the latter band being quite strong in some stones. No luminescence has been observed in gem axinite, but it has been reported that honey-yellow crystals from Franklin Furnace, New Jersey, U.S.A. may fluoresce red under short-wave ultra-violet radiations. This may well be due to included traces of manganese, as so many of the minerals from this noted zinc ore mining locality behave similarly.

Axinite is a complex calcium aluminium boro-silicate $(HMgCa_2.BAl(SiO_4)_3)$, but much variation of the composition occurs owing to the replacement of the calcium by iron, magnesium and manganese. The mineral occurs in cavities in granite or diabase and specially in the contact zones of these rocks. Axinite is found in magnificent crystal groups at St. Cristophe, near Bourg d'Oisans, Isère, France, from various localities in America and at the Botallack mine near St. Just, Cornwall, England. During 1964 a new source of gem quality axinite of reddish brown colour, and in quite large crystals, was discovered at Mina la Olivia in Baja California, Mexico.

AZURITE

The somewhat unstable basic copper carbonate $(Cu_3(OH)_2(CO_3)_2)$ is known as azurite from the typical azure-blue colour. Like malachite, to which mineral it slowly changes, azurite is a secondary ore of copper found in the oxidized portions of copper veins. It is found as prismatic monoclinic crystals of varied habit, often in spherical radiating groups, and as such is found at Chessy, near Lyons in France, hence the alternative name chessylite for the mineral. It is common in botryoidal or stalagmitic groups and massive in veins with malachite. Indeed it is rare to find azurite without its alteration product—malachite—and even the crystals become pseudomorphs of malachite after azurite.

The density of azurite lies between 3·77 and 3·89 and the principal refractive indices for the crystals are 1·73 and 1·84. The refraction is biaxial and positive in sign and the birefringence is 0·11, large by gem standards but small for a carbonate mineral. The hardness is $3\frac{1}{2}$–4 on Mohs's scale. Azurite needs little testing for the typical colour and its association with malachite makes distinction obvious. The two are so generally found together that pieces containing both the green and blue materials in bands is cut as an ornamental stone to which the name azurmalachite is given.

Azurite effervesces when touched with acid, and further will give a reaction for copper, thus if a fragment of a suspected specimen is moistened with hydrochloric acid and introduced into the edge of a Bunsen flame the flame will colour blue with the characteristic hue of the flame of copper chloride. Malachite behaves in similar manner.

Azurite is found at Chessy in France, Bannat in Romania, Tsumeb in South-West Africa, and Bisbee and Morenci in Arizona in the United States of America. The mineral is also found in New South Wales, Australia, and in Siberia. A rock-like mixture of azurite, malachite and cuprite is called burnite.

BARITE (Barytes)

The barium sulphate mineral $(BaSO_4)$ barite is also known as heavy spar. The mineral forms orthorhombic crystals which are white in colour and may be transparent to opaque. Crystals coloured yellow, green, red, blue or brown are sometimes found. The massive white material resembles marble. Barite is rarely cut as a gemstone, except for those who desire anything unusual, for the hardness is only 3 on Mohs's scale, which is too low for durability. There is, however, a stalagmitic variety of brown colour which shows a concentric structure when cut across the stalactite and such material has been polished as an ornamental stone. Barytes has a density of 4·3–4·6; for gemmy material the values are near 4·47, and refractive indices of α 1·636, β 1·637 and γ 1·648; the refraction is biaxial and positive in sign. The crystals show perfect cleavage in two directions. The mineral sometimes fluoresces and often phosphoresces with a faint blue or light green colour under ultra-violet light. Barytes has a world-wide occurrence.

BAYLDONITE

Found in mamillary concretions of fibrous crystals, probably of the monoclinic system, this greenish mineral has been reported as having been fashioned into gemstones. The composition is a complex hydrated lead copper arsenate—$(Pb,Cu)_3As_2O_8(Pb,Cu)(OH)_2H_2O$. The hardness is $4\frac{1}{2}$ on Mohs's scale, the density 4·35 and the three refractive indices are 1·95, 1·97 and 1·99, the refraction being biaxial and positive in sign. Bayldonite is found at Tsumeb in South-West Africa and in Cornwall.

BENITOITE

During the autumn of 1906 a prospector, J. M. Crouch, while searching for mercury and copper minerals in the area of the headwaters of the San Benito river of California, discovered in a vein of white natrolite some blue crystals. These were subsequently considered to be sapphire, but this notion was questioned by a Californian jeweller on account of the strong dichroism shown by the stones. The crystals were sent to Dr. G. D. Louderback, of the University of California, who identified them as a new mineral to which the name benitoite was given, after the locality in which they were discovered. That is one account of the finding of benitoite, but G. F. Kunz states that the crystals were found in 1907 by Hawkins and Edwin Sanders who were prospecting in the southern part of the Mount Diablo range near the San Benito–Fresno border, and that these crystals were brought to the attention of Dr. Louderback by Shreve and Company, a San Francisco firm who had purchased one of the cut stones from a lapidary, and who were later offered some of the rough material as sapphire.

Benitoite, a lovely sapphire-blue coloured stone, is unique in that it crystallizes in a class of the trigonal system which has a trigonal axis of symmetry and a plane of symmetry at right angles to it, a class known as the dihexagonal dipyramidal. It is a form that was mathematically considered possible in nature but not found until the discovery of benitoite which is, so far, the only example in nature.

The mineral is a barium titanium silicate with the formula $BaTiSi_3O_9$, and thus it has a chemical similarity to sphene. The density lies between 3·65 and 3·68, but the latter value is more common. The hardness is about $6\frac{1}{2}$ on Mohs's scale. The indices are 1·757 for the ordinary ray and 1·804 for the extraordinary ray, the refraction being uniaxial and positive in sign. The birefringence is strong, being 0·047. The pronounced dichroism shows twin colours of blue for the extraordinary ray and colourless for the ordinary ray, so that to obtain the best colour the table facet should be cut parallel to the vertical crystal axis, and as most of the crystals have a tabular habit this precludes the cutting of large stones. Benitoite has exceptionally strong fire, the colour dispersion for the B to G interval is 0·039 for the ordinary ray and 0·046 for the extraordinary ray (as measured by C. J. Payne). Thus the fire approximates to that found in diamond but the effect is masked by the body colour of the stone.

The lower density allows distinction from sapphire, but if the stone is set determination of this constant would not be possible and a refractometer reading would be necessary. Care is needed, however, in observing the shadow edges as the edge of the extraordinary ray at its highest is in the region of the shadow edge of the contact liquid (1·81) and may be missed unless its movement is carefully noted. The pronounced dichroism may also give information of value for there is no colourless ray in sapphire. What may be a simpler and more easily performed test is given by the bright blue fluorescent glow seen under short-wave (2537 Å) ultra-violet light, or under x-rays. This blue glow is not observed under the long-wave (3650 Å) radiation.

Benitoite has been found in only one locality, in the Diablo range of the Californian mountains in San Benito County, where the flattened triangular-shaped crystals, never of large size, are found in association with another rare titanium mineral—neptunite—in a matrix of white natrolite.

BERYLLONITE

A rare beryllium mineral—a beryllium-sodium phosphate, $NaBePO_4$— beryllonite is an interesting mineral found at Stoneham, Maine in the United States of America, in the company of phenakite and beryl. The crystals were usually considered to have orthorhombic symmetry, but have now been found to be monoclinic with pseudo-orthorhombic symmetry. As a gemstone this colourless mineral has only its rarity to recommend it. The indices of refraction are 1·553 and 1·562 for the principal rays thus the birefringence is 0·009, the refraction being biaxial and negative in sign. The lustre is vitreous, the hardness low, 5 on Mohs's scale, and the fire weak, the dispersion being only 0·010 for the B to G interval. The density varies from 2·80 to 2·85. The mineral is inert under ultra-violet light, but under x-rays there is a dark sky-blue fluorescence with a slight phosphorescence.

BORACITE

Some faceted stones of a pale green colour have been cut for collectors from the magnesium chloro-borate mineral known as boracite. The chemical formula for the mineral is $Mg_6Cl_2B_{14}O_{26}$, and it forms crystals of the cubic system with cubic, tetrahedral or dodecahedral habit. The hardness is 7 on Mohs's scale, the density is 2·96 and the refractive index is 1·661–1·671. The mineral is pseudo-isometric and may be orthorhombic so that some double refraction of positive sign may be apparent. The lustre is vitreous to adamantine and a very weak greenish fluorescence may be seen. The mineral is found in Germany, but it has been reported from the United States of America and Hanover district, Germany.

BRAZILIANITE

During the closing months of 1944 some yellowish-green crystals were found in a pegmatic dyke at a locality near Conselheira Pena in Minas Gerais, Brazil. When first found these crystals were thought to be chrysoberyl, to which they have some resemblance in colour but not in crystal form. Some of these crystals were shown by a dealer to F. H. Pough, then in Brazil, and he at once detected the differences in crystal form and that the hardness was lower than for chrysoberyl, but he could not recognize the crystals as being of any mineral that he knew. Later, in conjunction with E. P. Henderson, the crystals were found to be those of a completely new mineral to which the name brazilianite was given in honour of the country in which they were found. A specimen is shown in Plate XIV.

Brazilianite is a hydrous sodium aluminium phosphate and has the formula $Al_3Na(PO_4)_2(OH)_4$. Thus it has some degree of chemical affinity to turquoise and to amblygonite. The crystals, generally prismatic in form, are usually of fair size and belong to the monoclinic system of crystallization. The cleavage is perfect in one direction, which is parallel to one of the pinacoid faces. The material is brittle and shows a conchoidal fracture. The hardness is low, being $5\frac{1}{2}$ on Mohs's scale, and the density varies between 2·980 and 2·995. The optical properties show brazilianite to be biaxial positive with indices of refraction of α 1·603, β 1·612 and γ 1·623, giving a double refraction of 0·020. The dispersion is very low being only 0·014 for the B to G interval. There is no luminescence when the stone is bathed in ultra-violet light and no definite absorption spectrum has been noted. The dichroism is weak, merely a slight change of shade being noted.

Apart from the Brazilian locality already given, some crystals are said to have come from Corrego Frio, north of Sao Tome, which is also in the State of Minas Gerais. In 1947 another source of brazilianite was discovered at the Palermo mine, North Groton, in Grafton County, New Hampshire in the United States of America.

BROOKITE

One of the polymorphous forms of titanium dioxide (TiO_2), the others being rutile and anatase, brookite, which crystallizes in the orthorhombic system with varied habit, has scant use as a gemstone. The mineral is yellowish, hair-brown to reddish-brown in colour and has a hardness of $5\frac{1}{2}$–6 on Mohs's scale. The density varies from 3·87 to 4·08 and the refractive indices are near to 2·583 and 2·705 for the principal rays, the biaxial and optically positive double refraction being about 0·122, but it can reach to 0·157 for the index of the γ ray. The lustre of brookite is metallic adamantine. The mineral is found in France, Switzerland and the United States of America.

CANCRINITE

A semi-opaque yellow-coloured fibrous variety of cancrinite, a complex mineral with the approximate formula $3H_2O.4Na_2O.CaO.4Al_2O_3.9SiO_2$ $2CO_2$, has been cut as beads and as cabochons. The mineral is named after

Count Cancrin, Minister of Finance in Imperial Russia where the mineral was originally discovered. The mineral is occasionally found in crystals belonging to the hexagonal system which have a perfect prismatic cleavage, but is more often found massive. The hardness is between 5 and 6 on Mohs's scale and the refractive indices approximate to 1·50, which is all that would be expected to be seen on the ordinary refractometer with the massive gemmy material. The crystals of cancrinite have indices for the ordinary ray of 1·515–1·524 and for the extraordinary ray of 1·491–1·502, the double refraction of 0·022 being uniaxial and optically negative. The density varies from 2·42 to 2·50 (a specimen of the Canadian gem material gave a value of 2·435). The yellow gem cancrinite does not luminesce under ultra-violet light but an orange-yellow glow has been observed when the mineral is irradiated with x-rays. Cancrinite effervesces with acid. The mineral is found in many places, such as Russia, Transylvania, Norway and in Maine in the United States of America. The material reported as cut for gems comes from Bancroft and French river in Canada.

CASSITERITE

Cassiterite, tin oxide (SnO_2), is the principal ore of tin. Usually, owing to the presence of iron, the mineral is black and opaque, but occasionally crystals occur which are light reddish-brown in colour and sufficiently transparent to cut as faceted stones; their interest is for collectors only. The mineral crystallizes in the tetragonal system as square-section prismatic crystals capped by pyramids, and the crystals are often twinned with the twin plane parallel to one of the pyramid faces producing knee-shaped forms (geniculate twins). The crystals show only an indistinct cleavage.

Cassiterite has a hardness of about $6\frac{1}{2}$ on Mohs's scale and is characterized by having a high specific gravity of 6·95. The refraction, uniaxial positive, has indices of 2·003 for the ordinary ray and 2·101 for the extraordinary ray, thus the birefringence is 0·098. The dispersion is 0·071 between the B to G interval, and the lustre shown by the mineral is adamantine. Due probably to the iron content cassiterite does not show any luminescence and the stones show no distinctive absorption spectrum.

Cassiterite can be distinguished from brown diamond, brown zircon and sphene by the great density of the mineral, the absence of any typical absorption lines (from zircon), and from sphene by the absence or a much weaker dichroism, and from diamond by the double refraction.

The mineral is found in many places and particularly in the Malay peninsula. In Cornwall a source has been known since Roman times: in those days it was called the Cassiterides from the occurrence of the tin. Other localities are Mexico, Australia, Bolivia, Tasmania, Saxony, Indonesia and Spain where clear yellowish-red pieces suitable for cutting have been found, and at the Erongo tinfields, South-West Africa.

CELESTINE (Celestite)

The low hardness of $3\frac{1}{2}$ on Mohs's scale of celestine makes it a most undesirable gemstone. Celestite is a sulphate of strontium ($SrSO_4$) and crystallizes in the orthorhombic system with tabular habit. The crystals have at least two directions of cleavage and the rather uninteresting cut stones are fashioned from colourless or bluish crystals. The density lies between 3·97 and 4·00 and the refractive indices are given as α 1·623, β 1·624 and γ 1·633 with, therefore, a biaxial birefringence of 0·010 which is positive in sign. The gemmy material may have slightly higher values, for one specimen examined had values of 1·625 and 1·635 for the principal rays, the birefringence being in this case 0·010, and the density was found to be 3-997. A scraping taken from the girdle of a cut celestite and picked up on a platinum wire, will, when introduced into a colourless Bunsen flame colour it the rich red of strontium. A whitish or bluish-white glow is shown by celestite when under ultra-violet light.

Celestite occurs with sandstones or limestone and is often associated with sulphur, gypsum and colemanite at many different localities, particularly in Sicily, Switzerland, Italy and in south-western England. Many localities of the United States of America supply the mineral, but Tsumeb in South-West Africa is the locality from which most of the cut stones may have come. Orange crystals are found in Ontario, Canada.

CERUSSITE

Reported as having been cut for those who want the unusual is cerussite, a lead carbonate whose formula is $PbCO_3$. The mineral is usually white or grey in colour, but black, blue and green colours are known, these two latter owing their colour to copper. The hardness is only $3\frac{1}{2}$ on Mohs's scale and the density is near to 6·5 (6·46–6·57). The lustre is adamantine and the refractive indices are α 1·804, β 2·076 and γ 2·078. In common with carbonate minerals the double refraction is large in amount at 0·274, and is biaxial and negative in sign. The luminescence is variable but under the short-wave lamp it usually shows a pale blue or green glow. Some cerussite from Utah is said to show a bright orange under the long-wave lamp. The occurrences of the mineral are world-wide.

CHLORASTROLITE

Found as rolled pebbles which have weathered out from the basic igneous rocks which border the shores of Lake Superior in North America, chlorastrolite occurs as small spherical aggregates of greenish fibres. The mineral depends for its attractiveness upon its unique markings of white and green, the circular areas being caused by the radial groups of the fibrous crystals. Chlorastrolite is illustrated in Plate XIX, facing page 268. The material is not completely homogeneous but the main component is pumpellyite, a hydrated calcium aluminium silicate ($6CaO.3Al_2O_3.7SiO_2.4H_2O$), which forms narrow plates or fibrous crystals of the orthorhombic system. The hardness of chlorastrolite is from 5 to 6 on Mohs's scale, the density is between 3·1 and 3·5 and the mean refractive index, all that would be seen on a refractometer, is about 1·70. No luminescence is shown by the mineral under ultra-violet light. Chlorastrolite is usually cut in the cabochon style in order to bring out the beauty of the markings. The main source of the stones is along the shores of Isle Royale in Lake Superior and the shores of the Keweenaw peninsula on the Michigan side of the lake. Chlorastrolites are sometimes called 'green stones'.

CHONDRODITE

A member of the humite group of minerals, chondrodite is an unusual mineral cut for the whim of collectors. Of monoclinic symmetry the mineral is a magnesium silicate with fluorine and hydroxyl, and accords to the formula $2Mg_2SiO_4.Mg(F,OH)_2$. The colour of the mineral varies from yellow to garnet-red and brown; the hardness is $6\frac{1}{2}$ on Mohs's scale and the density varies from 3·1 to 3·2. The refraction is biaxial and positive in sign, the indices varying from 1·59 to 1·60 and from 1·62 to 1·64 for the principal rays. Some chondrodite shows a weak orange fluorescence under long-wave ultra-violet light and is inert under the short-wave lamp. The mineral (mostly honey-yellow in colour) is found at Pargas and Kafveltorp in Sweden and crystals of garnet-red colour are found in the Tilly Foster mine at Brewster, New York.

CHRYSOCOLLA

A cryptocrystalline mineral of mountain-green, bluish-green, sky-blue and turquoise-blue colour often with an opal or enamel-like texture, chrysocolla is a hydrous copper silicate ($CuSiO_32H_2O$), but the composition is somewhat variable. Indeed, through impurities such as free silica, alumina, black oxide of copper, limonitic oxide of iron and manganese oxide the colour can vary from those given above to brown and black. Much chrysocolla may be a mineral gel with copper oxide, silica, and water in varying proportions depending upon the conditions of formation. Thus, the constants of the mineral are variable. The mean refractive index is 1·50 (ω 1·46 and ϵ 1·57 have been determined in the case of microscopic acicular crystals from Mackay, Idaho). The hardness varies from 2 to 4 on Mohs's scale, rising to over 6 if much quartz be present, and the density varies between 2·00 and 2·45.

Chrysocolla is a mineral of secondary origin occurring in the oxidized zones of copper veins at widespread localities, particularly at Nevada, New Mexico and Arizona in the United States of America. Other localities are at Katanga in the Congo, in Russia and Chile. Much of the chrysocolla of jewellery consists of very attractive cabochons of green or blue and brown chrysocolla in botryoidal form embedded in rock crystal. Such material will have the hardness (7) and the refractive indices of quartz; the density may be slightly lower than the 2·65 for rock crystal owing to the slight lowering by the included chrysocolla.

It may be convenient to include in this section the stone called 'Eilat Stone', or 'Elath Stone', which is found near Eilat at the head of the Gulf of Aqaba on the Red Sea. It is said to come from the copper mines of King Solomon. The rock, which is usually cut into cabochons or 'tumbled', is a mixture of copper minerals. The constituents vary considerably, but include chrysocolla, turquoise and pseudomalachite, a copper phosphate mineral which accords to the formula $Cu_3P_2O_83Cu(OH)_2$ and resembles malachite in colour. Other copper minerals may be included, and in one case apatite was determined. The colour, which is variegated, is blue to green. The density, on specimens determined, varied from 2·8 to 3·2, and like most copper minerals, except turquoise itself, turns a spot of hydrochloric acid a yellow colour.

COLEMANITE

For the benefit of collectors who desire the curious the monoclinic mineral colemanite, a hydrous calcium borate $(Ca_2B_6O_{11}.5H_2O)$, has been fashioned. Most commonly colourless to milky white in colour, the mineral has a hardness of $4\frac{1}{2}$ on Mohs's scale, a density of 2·42 and is biaxial with positive sign. The refractive indices are α 1·586, β 1·592 and γ 1·614. Colemanite usually fluoresces whitish or green under ultra-violet light. The mineral is found mostly in the United States of America at Death Valley, California, and at Kern and Riverside Counties, California. It is also found at Clark County, Nevada.

CROCOITE

The bright hyacinth-red monoclinic crystals of the lead chromate $(PbCrO_4)$ mineral has been cut into cabochon stones at the whim of collectors. The low hardness of $2\frac{1}{2}$–3 on Mohs's scale and its distinct cleavage, contra-indicates its use as a gemstone despite its bright colour. The density of the mineral ranges from 5·9 to 6·1 and the refractive indices are well above the range of the refractometer: they are α 2·31, β 2·37 and γ 2·66, and the refraction is biaxial and positive. The absorption spectrum of crocoite, if in thick pieces, tends to cut off all the colours except the yellow, orange and red, but if in thinner section a distinct band is seen in the general absorption at about 5550 Å. Under ultra-violet light there may be seen a weak reddish or brownish glow which is probably more pronounced with the short-wave lamp. There is no fluorescence shown by the mineral when under x-rays. The mineral occurs in the Ural mountains of Russia, Rézbánya in Romania, Dundas in Tasmania, Ouro Preto in Brazil and in Arizona in the United States of America.

CUPRITE

The red oxide of copper (Cu_2O) forms red crystals of the cubic system and this mineral has been cut for collectors. The hardness of the mineral is 4 on Mohs's scale, and the density lies between 5·85 and 6·15. The refractive index of cuprite is 2·85 and the mineral has a widespread occurrence. When found the crystals often have the surface altered to the green basic carbon-ate, malachite. Only some crystals from Santa Rita, New Mexico, appear to have been cut, but the mineral has widespread occurrence.

DANBURITE

The calcium boro-silicate mineral which accords to the formula $CaB_2(SiO_4)_2$ and which is known as danburite has been fashioned into bright and attractive gemstones. It was first discovered at Danbury, Connecticut, U.S.A., from where the name danburite was derived, but the material from that source does not appear to have been cut. Gem quality material is found in the Mogok district of Upper Burma, from which source large wine-yellow and colourless stones have been produced. Stones of a good yellow colour have been cut from material found in Madagascar, and colourless crystals, from which faceted stones have been cut, emanate from Bungo, Japan. A danburite of light pink colour has been found at Charcas, San Luis Potosi, Mexico; colourless danburite has also been found in Mexico.

The crystals of danburite are orthorhombic and approximate in angles and habit to those of topaz. The hardness is 7 on Mohs's scale and the brilliant vitreous lustre enables the production of bright and durable gemstones from the crystals. The refraction is biaxial but the sign, owing to the angle between the optic axes being nearly a right angle, is negative for red to green light and positive for light of shorter wavelengths. The values of the least and greatest refractive indices are 1·630 and 1·636 with a double refraction of 0·006. The fire is small being only 0·017 for the B to G interval. The absorption spectrum shows, albeit very weakly, the rare earth spectrum of didymium (cf. yellow apatite). The density approximates to 3·00 and there is little variation from this value. Danburite will float in methylene iodide while the similarly coloured topaz will sink. In a similar manner danburite will sink in bromoform whilst the yellow quartz will float. Danburite fluoresces with a sky-blue glow when irradiated with ultra-violet light, and the mineral is said to phosphoresce with a reddish tint when heated. A danburite is shown in Plate XIV, facing page 130.

DATOLITE

A calcium boro-silicate mineral which accords to the formula $Ca(B,OH)SiO_4$ and is therefore near danburite in composition is datolite, which forms short prismatic monoclinic crystals of varied habit. Such transparent crystals, colourless, or with a pale tinge of yellow or green, are only cut for collectors; there is, however, a massive or granular type of milk-white to orange-brown colour which has been cut as cabochons. The hardness of datolite is near to 5 on Mohs's scale, the density varies from 2·90 to 3·00 and the principal indices of refraction are 1·625 and 1·669, the birefringence being 0·044, biaxial and negative in sign. The dispersion for the B to G interval is 0·016. The mineral sometimes fluoresces blue under ultra-violet light (said to be activated by europium), and sometimes a yellowish or pinkish white glow is seen under x-rays. The mineral is found at Habachtal near Salzburg in Austria, and at Springfield, Massachusetts and New Jersey in the U.S.A. The Alps of the Tyrol and the Lizard, Cornwall, England, are other sources of datolite. The massive variety is found, often with included copper, in the Lake Superior copper district and on Micopoten Island of Lake Superior.

DIOPSIDE

One of the pyroxene group of minerals which crystallizes in the monoclinic system with a perfect prismatic cleavage, diopside produces stones which are mostly bottle-green, although colourless, brownish and violet-blue stones are found, and some material is fibrous, producing cat's-eyes when cut cabochon. Diopside is a calcium magnesium silicate ($CaMg(SiO_3)_2$), but some of the magnesium is always replaced by iron which gives the green and brown colours to the stones. The iron may increase in quantity until the stones are so dark a green that they appear almost black and finally reach the calcium iron pyroxene hedenbergite which has the formula $CaFe(SiO_3)_2$. Some diopsides contain chromium and are then a much brighter and livelier green.

Diopside has a hardness of $5\frac{1}{2}$ on Mohs's scale, and the density varies little from 3·29 for the gem material but may reach higher values when the material is rich in iron and so dark as to be virtually hedenbergite. The biaxial double refraction is positive in sign and the refractive indices are 1·670–1·701, but may rise in the case of the material near hedenbergite in composition. The double refraction is 0·030, the lustre vitreous and the fire small in amount. The absorption spectrum of the chrome diopsides consists of two sharp lines at 5080 and 5050 Å in the green and a band at 4900 Å in the blue. There are rather woolly bands at 6350, 6550 and 6700 Å in the orange and red with a strong doublet at 6900 Å. The duller green diopsides do not show such a good spectrum but ill-defined bands may be seen at 5050, 4930 and 4460 Å. The luminescence shown by diopsides is somewhat variable. Under long-wave ultra-violet excitation some green stones glow with a green light, do not show any glow under the short-wave lamp and show a dull mustard-yellow glow under x-rays. A lighter green stone showed a mauve, an orange and a yellow glow under the three radiations, while a colourless stone showed mauve, a strong whitish-blue and a yellowish-lilac under similar radiations.

Beautiful chrome diopsides are found in the blue ground of the Kimberley diamond mines and in the Burma Stone Tract, the latter stones being chatoyant and producing attractive cat's-eyes. Diopsides of a more sombre green are found in the Ala Valley, Piedmont, Italy, and it is from this locality that the alternative name alalite is derived. The mineral is also found in the Zillerthal in the Austrian Tyrol, in the Ceylon gem gravels and in the State of Minas Gerais, Brazil. Material of a smoky yellow or brownish colour is found at Laurel and Three Rivers in Quebec, Canada, and small crystals of a bright green colour are found near to Georgetown in Eldorado County, California. Other North American sources are at St. Lawrence County, New York and at Crestmore, Riverside County, California. The green stones from Slyudyanka, Baikal, in Soviet Russia have been called Baikalite, and light-coloured diopside has been called by another alternative name, malacolite.

Violane, spelt violan in the United States of America, is a translucent to opaque dark violet-blue variety of diopside, which is usually found massive, but sometimes occurs crystalline. The material, which has a somewhat waxy lustre, takes an attractive polish and is worked into beads, but is mostly used for fancy articles and for inlay. The hardness of violane, which owes its name to its violet-blue colour, is 6 on Mohs's scale. The density is near to 3·23 and the index of refraction, as far as a blurred shadow edge can be read on the refractometer, is 1·69. Violane is found at Saint Marcel,

Piedmont, Italy. In recent years there has come from India a green to black star diopside showing a four-rayed star. These pieces have a density of 3·33.

DIOPTASE

The beautiful groups of emerald-green crystals of dioptase are of more importance and are lovelier than the small number of faceted or cabochon-cut stones which have been cut from them. Dioptase is a copper silicate and has a chemical likeness to chrysocolla. It accords to the formula $CuO.SiO_2H_2O$, and forms crystals of the trigonal system. The crystals have a hardness of 5 on Mohs's scale, which is too soft for effective use as a gemstone, moreover the green is too saturated and the stones are at best translucent only. The density ranges from 3·28 to 3·35 and the refractive indices are 1·644–1·658 for the ordinary ray and 1·697–1·709 for the extra-ordinary ray, the refraction is uniaxial and the sign positive. The double refraction approximates to 0·053 and the colour dispersion is 0·036 for the B to G interval, so that the stones have more fire than many gemstones, but this effect is masked by the rich body colour of the stone. The absorption spectrum shows only a broad band in the yellow and green centred at about 5500 Å and there is a strong absorption in the blue and violet. There is no luminescence induced in dioptase by ultra-violet light or x-rays. Some of the best crystallized specimens of dioptase are found near Altyn-Tübe in the Kirghiz Steppes of Russia; in the basin of the Niari river in the Republic of Congo; from the Katanga district of the Congo; the copper deposits of Atacama in Chile, and in Arizona and other localities in the United States of America.

DUMORTIERITE

Dumortierite is a basic aluminium boro-silicate, but until recently the formula had not been completely determined. This has now been carried out on a brown stone and will be referred to later. The mineral is normally found in violet and blue masses which when polished make attractive ornamental stones. The mineral crystallizes in the orthorhombic system but the crystals are usually fibrous or columnar aggregates producing a massive material without distinct form. With the massive material the refractive index would show as a blurred shadow edge on the refractometer at about 1·68. The density of the massive dumortierite varies from 3·26 to 3·41, the hardness is 7 on Mohs's scale and the lustre is vitreous. The individual fibres are strongly dichroic but in the mass the effect is not so evident. There is no diagnostic absorption spectrum and the luminescent phenomena are weak and variable.

In 1958 a red-brown faceted stone was reported as dumortierite. This stone, which came from Ceylon, had a density of 3·41 and the refractive indices were α 1·686, β 1·722 and γ 1·723. The biaxial double refraction, negative in sign, was therefore, 0·037. The pleochroic colours were black, deep red-brown and brown for the three directions. Careful chemical analysis produced a formula approximating to $4[(Al,Fe)_7BSi_3O_{18}]$. Rather surprisingly this stone was found to have a hardness of 8 on Mohs's scale.

Dumortierite is found near Lyons in the French Rhône valley, near Soavina, north of Ambatofinandrahana, Madagascar, and at Tvedestrand, Norway, but most of the gemmy material comes from Oreana, Humboldt County, Nevada (usually violet in colour). Dumortierite is also found in California, Washington and in Canada.

Much gem dumortierite, particularly from Arizona, is really dumortierite impregnating quartz. Such material will give a refractometer reading for quartz (1·54–1·55) with a density of about 2·8–2·9 although lower values have been found in specimens of, presumably, dumortierite in quartz which possibly emanated from India.

DURANGITE

Found as orange-red crystals of monoclinic symmetry, the fluo-arsenate of sodium and aluminium (Na(Al,F)AsO$_4$) mineral has been cut for collectors. The mineral has a hardness of 5 on Mohs's scale, a density which lies between 3·97 and 4·07 and the refractive indices are α 1·662, β 1·695 and γ 1·712. The biaxial negative refraction has a birefringence of 0·050. The stones are strongly trichroic in which two rays are almost colourless and the third is orange-yellow. Durangite is found at Durango, Mexico.

EKANITE

During 1953 a green translucent water-worn stone showing some asterism was found in a gravel pit in Ceylon by F. L. D. Ekanayake, who thought it to be a new mineral. Since that time further specimens, some exhibiting a four-rayed star, have come to light. It was not until early in 1961 that these stones were properly identified and found to be a new mineral. Ekanite is a metamict calcium thorium silicate having a hardness of 6 – 6½ on Mohs's scale, a refractive index of 1·5969 and a density of 3·28. The stones are markedly radioactive.

ENSTATITE

A member of the pyroxene group of minerals, enstatite is a magnesium-iron silicate with a formula (Mg,Fe) SiO$_3$, and crystallizes in the orthorhombic system. The crystals are usually green or brownish-green in colour and have two prismatic directions of cleavage. Most of the gem material is found as rolled pebbles. Some stones are chatoyant and a peculiar glassy grey variety has been cut cabochon in order to show this effect. An iron-rich type with a bronze-like lustre is known as bronzite.

The hardness of enstatite is 5½ on Mohs's scale and the density for the gemmy green stones lies between 3·26 and 3·28. The refractive indices for the green gem stones are 1·663 and 1·673 for the principal indices, the biaxial birefringence, which is positive in sign, is 0·010. With the increase of iron the indices rise. The dichroism is weak, the twin colours being green and yellowish-green. Enstatite is characterized by an absorption spectrum which has a sharp clear-cut single line at 5060 Å. There is no luminescence shown by the mineral.

266

With the increase of iron enstatite passes into hypersthene, which is a mineral too opaque for faceting but which often encloses minute tabular scales of what may probably be brookite, goethite or hematite, and such material cut as cabochons makes quite attractive stones. The density of hypersthene lies between 3·4 and 3·5, with the refractive indices ranging from 1·673 to 1·683 and from 1·715 to 1·731; the optical sign is negative. There is an attractive transparent brown intermediate hypersthene-enstatite found in Mysore, India, which has been faceted into gemstones. The refractive indices for these stones vary slightly around 1·669 and 1·680 for the least and greatest values. The optical sign is negative which suggests that the stone is nearer to hypersthene than to enstatite. The density is fairly constant at 3·3.

A leek green altered enstatite is known as bastite or schiller spar and is close to serpentine in composition. Bastite has a density of about 2·6, and a hardness of $3\frac{1}{2}$–4 on Mohs's scale. This material has been fashioned into cabochons. A six-rayed star enstatite has been reported which has a density varying from 3·30 to 3·41, and a refractive index about 1·68.

Enstatite of a good green colour is found with diamond in the blue ground of the South African mines, particularly the Kimberley mine, and brownish-green stones are found in the Mogok Stone Tract of Upper Burma. The chatoyant glassy greyish stones are said to come from Ceylon and bronzite is found at Styria in Austria. The mineral is found in the Fichtelgebirge in Bavaria and in the so-called olivine bombs of the Dreiser Weiher in the Eifel district of the German Rhineland. Enstatite is also found in Norway and California. Bastite comes from Baste near Harzburg in the Harz Mountains in Germany and from Burma. Hypersthene is more universal in its occurrence, but the material mainly comes from Norway, Greenland, Bavaria and the North American continent.

EPIDOTE

The dark brownish-green or pistachio green colour of epidote is characteristic of the mineral and gives to the mineral its alternative name of pistacite. Closely related to zoisite (which is orthorhombic) epidote is a calcium aluminium silicate with some iron, which accords to the formula $Ca_2(Al,OH)Al_2(SiO_4)_3$. The mineral crystallizes in the monoclinic system, usually as deep vertically striated prismatic crystals which seldom have distinct terminations. The crystals show a brilliant lustre and stones cut from them are a peculiar greenish-brown in colour which is darker the greater the percentage of iron they contain. The hardness is $6\frac{1}{2}$ on Mohs's scale, the density being about 3·4, and the principal refractive indices are 1·736 and 1·770 with a biaxial double refraction of 0·034 which is negative in sign. With less iron the refractive indices and the amount of double refraction can be lower than the values given above. The stones are strongly pleochroic, the twin colours being green, brown and yellow. The fire is moderate, the dispersion being 0·030, and the lustre is vitreous to metallic. The absorption spectrum shows a very intense band near 4550 Å in the α ray, is virtually absent in the γ ray, and in the β ray a second but much weaker line is seen at 4750 Å. Epidote shows no luminescence.

Clinozoisite is an epidote containing less than 10 per cent of the iron molecule and is usually a much lighter green in colour. The mineral is monoclinic and has a density near to 3·37, the refractive indices are α 1·724, β 1·729 and γ 1·734, with a birefringence of 0·010, which, however, is positive in sign. The absorption spectrum is similar to that of normal epidote.

When manganese is a replacing metal in the epidote composition the mineral piedmontite is produced, This is a red mineral which does not have a gem significance, but is the cause of the red colour in the red porphyry of Egypt. A chrome epidote or tawmawite is a deep green stone showing strong pleochroism (emerald-green and bright yellow) which is found at Tawmaw in the Kachin Hills of Upper Burma.

Epidote is a fairly common mineral and is found at many places in the alpine system of Austria, Switzerland and France. It is also found in Norway and there are a number of localities in the North American continent. Clinozoisite comes from Austria, Italy, Switzerland, Bohemia (Czechoslovakia) and Baja California, Mexico. A grey-green coloured clinozoisite is found in Kenya.

EUCLASE

A species which owes its name to the strong cleavage which makes the cutting of crystals such a hazardous matter and the cut stones so liable to fracture, euclase is a beryllium silicate ($Be(Al,OH)SiO_4$), and forms monoclinic crystals characterized by numerous smooth faces. The colour of the material is usually a pale aquamarine colour although stones with a strong greenish-blue colour have been encountered.

Like aquamarine in appearance, euclase may be distinguished by the positive biaxial optical character and the refractive indices are, for the principal rays, 1·652 and 1·672 with a birefringence of 0·020. The density is fairly constant at 3·10, and the hardness is $7\frac{1}{2}$ on Mohs's scale. The dispersion is 0·016 for the B to G interval, which is too weak for the stones to show much fire. The absorption spectrum is, in the case of the deeper coloured stones, characterized by two vague bands in the blue at 4680 and 4550 Å, and also lines in the red, due to chromium, which gives a strong doublet at 7050 Å. The luminescence, even under x-rays, is too feeble to be of value in distinction. Euclase shows a similarity to green spodumene both in colour and properties; spodumene, however, has less birefringence (0·015) and a slightly higher density (3·18). The principal localities for euclase are the Ouro Preto region of the Brazilian State of Minas Gerais. Some crystals come from near the Sanaka river in the Orenburg district of the southern Urals, and from the Morogoro district of Tanzania. Minor sources are from Bavaria and Austria in central Europe.

FIBROLITE (Sillimanite)

Sapphire-blue and chatoyant blue-green stones have occasionally been cut from the aluminium silicate mineral fibrolite (Al_2SiO_5) (Plate XIV) which is

PLATE XIX

Ornamental Minerals

Tugtupite

First discovered in Southern Greenland during 1960, tugtupite is a massive mineral of cyclamen-red colour which has been fashioned into cabochons and mounted in jewellery by the Danish Court Jeweller.

The mineral has tetragonal crystallization and is a sodium-aluminium beryllium silicate ($Na_8Al_2Be_2Si_8O_{24}$). The hardness is about 6 on Mohs's scale, the density is near 2·36 but may rise to 2·57 when other minerals are present. The refractive indices are $\omega = 1·496$ and $\epsilon = 1·502$. The stones fluoresce an apricot colour under long-wave ultra-violet light and a weaker salmon red in short-wave ultra-violet light. The effect under long-wave ultra-violet light is shown in the inset at lower left of colour plate.

Colour plate by courtesy of Ove Dragsted of Copenhagen

polymorphous with andalusite and kyanite, and crystallizes in the ortho-rhombic system. The crystals occur as long slender prisms without distinct terminations and are often in parallel groups. They have one direction of cleavage parallel to one pair of prism faces and are frequently fibrous, hence the name fibrolite. The alternative name is sillimanite (after B. Silliman, one-time professor at Yale University in the United States of America).

The hardness of fibrolite is, for the crystals, $7\frac{1}{2}$ on Mohs's scale, but for the compact material, owing to the fibrous nature, the hardness may vary from 6 to 7. The refraction is biaxial and positive in sign and the indices are 1·658 and 1·678, the birefringence being 0·020. The stones have little fire for the dispersion is only 0·015 between the B and G lines of the solar spectrum. The pleochroism is strong, the colours for the three principal optical directions being pale green, dark green and blue. The absorption spectrum is indistinct with bands at 4620, 4410 and 4100 Å. The density is 3·25. Fibrolite, which shows a very weak red fluorescence, at least in the transparent blue stones, is found in the Mogok Stone Tract of Burma, where some lovely violet-blue stones have been found, and in the Ceylon gem gravels where a greyish-green chatoyant fibrolite is obtained. A densely compact form of brownish or greenish colour which resembles jade is known. It has a density which lies between 3·14 and 3·18. Water-worn pebbles of a massive fibrous variety, usually called sillimanite, which are mostly fashioned as baroque stones by the tumbling process, are found in the valley of the Clearwater river in Idaho, U.S.A.

FLUORSPAR (Fluorite)

The beautiful cubic crystals of fluorspar, so many fine specimens of which grace our museums, are occasionally cut as gemstones, usually in the trap-cut style and mainly for collectors, for the hardness of fluorspar (fluorspar is the standard 4 on Mohs's scale) is far too low to resist the wear and tear encountered in jewellery. The range of colour shown by fluorspar is equalled by few other gemstones. The crystals may be colourless, yellow, brown, green, blue, violet and pink, but a true red is not known. An emerald-green fluorspar from Pforte in South-West Africa has been faceted and sold under the misnomer 'South African emerald'.

Blue John or Derbyshire Spar

More important ornamentally than the crystals is the massive crystalline variety known as Blue John or Derbyshire spar, a material which has been used since Roman times for vases and other decorative objects (*Figure 16.2*). Blue John is prettily patterned in curved bands of blue, violet and purple, the latter often so deep in colour as to be almost black, with often a reddish or colourless ground. The material is characterized by having only one source of supply, that is at Treak Cliff, an outlier of the Mam Tor range near Castleton in the Kinderscout district of Derbyshire, England, a source which is now said to be exhausted. The Blue John mine was driven for lead ore and consists of a number of workings opening out of a fine range of caverns where, often, the beautiful fluorite is not at first seen owing to the complete covering of the rock face by stalagmitic formations. The fluorspar occurs in nodular masses and veins in oölitic limestone (aggregates of little spherical deposits of carbonate of lime which has formed as concentric crusts around nuclei which may have been a grain of sand or a minute organism) and tends to be botryoidal in form with the typical radial and banded structure showing little trace of cubic structure. The amethystine colour of Blue John has been variously said to be due to traces of manganese, to impurities of vegetable origin or crude petroleum or both, and to physical disarrangement of the crystal lattice, possibly by radioactive emanations.

Figure 16.2. An exceptional vase of Blue John in the Geological Survey Museum at South Kensington, London

(By courtesy of the Controller of H.M. Stationery Office)

The most usual explanation of the colour is that a pulsatory flow of hydrocarbon-rich liquid caused the banded colour while the crystallization of the fluorite was taking place.

The fashioning of small objects of Blue John is carried out by first rough grinding the piece of spar to the requisite shape by the use of a foot lathe, a method which gives complete control through varying speeds. The roughly shaped piece is then finely surfaced by using a Water of Ayr stone, after which crocus powder (a coarse-grained iron oxide—a coarse rouge) on a revolving felt pad is applied to smooth the surfaces and to put on a semipolish. The final fine glaze polish is carried out with putty powder (tin oxide) on a power-driven lathe. For larger pieces, owing to the fact that the rock is chiefly composed of an aggregate of friable crystals, it is necessary to bond them after the piece has been cut to a suitable shape by an emery or carborundum powder-charged copper disc. The sawn piece is therefore heated in a natural resin which runs between the cracks of the aggregate of crystals thus effectively binding them. This bonding process needs to be repeated continuously as the process of turning on a lathe is carried out. The piece is cemented to a chuck and cut by the use of high-speed tools for the actual lathe shaping. The piece is then polished to produce the finished article. Care must be taken in the heating process, for overheating tends to lighten the colours, and while this may be desirable with dark coloured material it is disastrous in other cases.

Other Varieties of Fluorspar

Mention must be made of a massive fluorspar which does not exhibit the beautiful bands of colour shown by Blue John. Such material may be nearly colourless but veined with yellowish-brown markings, and there is a variety of strong violet-blue colour in which the aggregate nature of the crystals forming the piece are clearly seen. There is also the Yellow Ashover Spar, in which the colour is a full yellow and is obtained from the Ashover quarries in Derbyshire. A massive green fluorspar has a vogue for carved pieces and these may appear similar to massive green beryl. A hardness test on the base or other inconspicuous part will indicate the nature of the piece.

Occurrences

Apart from the localities already mentioned fluorspar is found, often in lovely crystal groups, at Weardale in Durham, Alston and Cleator Moor in Cumberland, in the lead mines of Derbyshire and in Cornwall, indeed it may be said that England provides the finest fluorite crystals. The Swiss source at Chamounix is notable for the pink octahedral crystals and fluorspar is also found at Brienz, Berne. The mineral is obtained from many localities in the United States of America, the more important being in the States of Illinois, New Hampshire and Missouri. There are other sources in Ontario, Canada, in Saxony, Bavaria and Baden in Germany, in Bohemia, Czechoslovakia and in Silesia, Poland. Italy and Norway also supply fluorspar.

Chemical and Physical Properties

Fluorspar is calcium fluoride (CaF_2) and crystallizes in the cubic system, most commonly as cubes and rarely as octahedra and dodecahedra. The cube forms are often bevelled at the edges by a form of a lower crystallographic index, and the cube faces often show very low pyramids (vicinal faces), which produce striations on the surface. Interpenetrant twinning is common and, due to parallel grouping of minute cubes, some crystals, particularly those of octahedral habit, exhibit faces with a drusy character. Many fluorspar crystals are coated with quartz or pyrites crystals, and some apparent fluorspar crystals are quartz or chalcedony pseudomorphs after fluorspar. *Figure 16.3* shows a group of fluorspar.

Fluorspar has an easy octahedral cleavage, but the cleavage surfaces are rarely perfect showing a stepped effect; it is this easy cleavage which makes the cutting of the crystals so difficult. The fracture, which is overshadowed by the easy cleavage, is flat conchoidal but in the compact types may be splintery.

The density of fluorspar is 3·18 and does not vary much from this figure in the case of crystals, but the massive types, owing to contamination

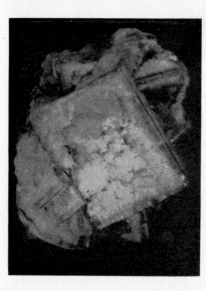

Figure 16.3. Crystals of fluorspar from Matlock in Derbyshire

with impurities, may vary between 3·00 and 3·25. The refractive index is 1·434 and the dispersion is very small (0·007 B to G). The absorption spectrum is generally vague and indecisive, but in the green variety weak bands occur at 6340, 6100, 5820 and 4450 Å, and there is also a strong broad band at 4270 Å which may be seen in sizeable pieces. Most fluorspar when excited by long-wave ultra-violet light exhibits a strong and often vivid sky-blue to violet-blue glow, said to be due to a trace of divalent europium. Some varieties show a green glow and this is ascribed to divalent ytterbium, and some, including the Blue John variety and many of the crystals from Illinois are inert. A brown luminescence has been recorded for fluorspar and the brown-coloured crystals from Clay Center, Ohio, show a white glow with a perceptible yellow afterglow. This is said to be due to the inclusion of petroleum or bituminous compounds. The fluorescence shown by fluorspar when under short-wave ultra-violet light is similar to that shown under the long-wave lamp, but very much weaker. Under x-radiation the glows induced are again similar, and in some cases glows may be induced even in Blue John. A persistent phosphorescence is generally prominent when fluorspar is bombarded with x-rays. Fluorspar has been made synthetically and some material (generally pink) has been cut and faceted for collectors.

FRIEDELITE

Faceted stones and cabochons of a rose-red to orange-red colour have been cut from the manganese silicate mineral friedelite, which has the formula $H_7(Mn,Cl)Mn_4Si_4O_{16}$, and which forms tabular crystals of the trigonal system. Most of the material is massive. The hardness is from 4 to 5 on Mohs's scale and the density is given as 3·07 (one specimen was found to have a density of 3·058). The refraction is uniaxial and negative in sign with indices for the ordinary ray of 1·66 and for the extraordinary ray of 1·63; the birefringence being, therefore, 0·030. The absorption spectrum shows a broad band centred at 5560 Å and a band about 4560 Å in the blue which is indistinct as there is a partial absorption in the blue and violet part of the spectrum. This absorption spectrum is not very diagnostic. A specimen of cut friedelite showed a red glow under ultra-violet light of both wavelengths. H. C. Dake mentions a bright yellow glow under long-wave ultraviolet light and a bright greenish glow under the short-wave rays for some friedelite. The localities for the mineral are France, Sweden and Franklin Furnace, New Jersey in the United States of America, the last named probably being the source of the gem material.

GAHNITE

The zinc-spinel gahnite ($ZnAl_2O_4$) which forms cubic crystals with octahedral habit is usually too dark a colour to cut into gemstones, however some stones of a tourmaline green colour have been found and cut. The hardness of gahnite is from $7\frac{1}{2}$ to 8 on Mohs's scale, the density is 4·40 and the refractive index is 1·805. Gahnite is found in zinc deposits at many different localities, but the locality of the green gemmy material is not known. Gahnite has been made synthetically.

HAMBERGITE

A beryllium borate ($Be_2(OH)BO_3$), hambergite forms colourless prismatic crystals belonging to the orthorhombic system. It was originally found in southern Norway in material of non-gem quality, but a discovery has now been made of large colourless crystals in central Madagascar. The mineral is characterized by its large double refraction which is biaxial and of positive sign, the indices ranging from 1·553 to 1·559 and from 1·625 to 1·631 for the principal rays; the birefringence being 0·072. The lustre is vitreous and the colour dispersion is small (0·015 B to G). In relation to the refractive indices the density of hambergite is remarkably low, being only 2·35. The hardness is $7\frac{1}{2}$ on Mohs's scale and no luminescence was shown by the specimens examined. Hambergite was named after Axel Hamberg.

HAÜYNITE (Haüyne)

More important as one of the constituents of lapis-lazuli, haüynite, named after the Abbé Haüy, is a complex sodium aluminium silicate with a formula $(Na,Ca)_{4-8}(Si_3,SO_2)_{1-2}(Al_6Si_6O_{24})$. Haüynite crystallizes in the cubic system and the translucent blue material has been cut as items of curiosity for collectors. The hardness is about 6 on Mohs's scale, the density is 2·4 and the refractive index is 1·496. There is usually no luminescence with the mineral but it has been reported that material from the Laacher See, Germany, may glow with an orange-red glow which is best seen under the long-wave lamp. The mineral, which is further discussed with lapis-lazuli in Chapter 11, is found at many places, particularly in Italy and the German Rhineland.

HERDERITE

Some greyish material of the mineral herderite has been fashioned for those who desire something different. A fluo-phosphate of beryllium and calcium $(CaBe(F,OH)PO_4)$ the mineral crystallizes in the monoclinic system. The hardness is 5 on Mohs's scale, the density is 3·00 and the negative biaxial refraction has indices of α 1·594, β 1·613 and γ 1·624, the double refraction being 0·030. The mineral fluoresces a pale greenish glow under both ranges of ultra-violet light and shows a strong orange glow with persistent phosphorescence under x-rays. Herderite is found in Saxony and at several places in the State of Maine, U.S.A.

HOWLITE

The massive variety of howlite, which is milk-white in colour and veined with black, has some use as an ornamental stone, despite its low hardness of $3\frac{1}{2}$ on Mohs's scale. The mineral is an aggregation of monoclinic (?) crystals and is a silico-borate of calcium $(8CaO5B_2O_36SiO_26H_2O)$. It has a density of 2·58 and the mean refractive index is 1·59. Howlite fluoresces a brownish-yellow by short-wave ultra-violet light and some Californian material is said to glow a deep orange with long waves and not to be responsive with the short-wave lamp. Howlite is found in large amounts in California in the United States of America. It is sometimes dyed blue.

IDOCRASE

The transparent varieties of idocrase, sometimes known under the name vesuvianite, are not often met in jewellery but more often in collections, despite the green and yellowish-brown stones having an attractiveness and sufficient hardness ($6\frac{1}{2}$ on Mohs's scale) to be suitable for some types of jewellery. What is more important as gem material is the massive green variety, called californite, which has some resemblance to the jades. Cyprine is a blue variety containing copper, and is so-called after Cyprus, which was the ancient source of copper. This variety is seldom met. A transparent yellowish-brown idocrase which is found at Amity, New York, has been called xanthite (after the Greek word for yellow).

Idocrase is a complex calcium aluminium silicate and accords to the formula $Ca_6Al(Al,OH)(SiO_4)_5$, in which some isomorphous replacement by iron of the aluminium, and the calcium by magnesium occurs. Titanium, fluorine, beryllium and boron may be present. It has been suggested that a tetragonal variation of the garnet type molecule is present in idocrase.

The tetragonal crystals of idocrase form square prisms capped with pyramids and are often terminated with the basal pinacoid, thus they have some similarity to the crystals of zircon, except that zircon rarely shows the basal pinacoid. Idocrase crystals often have the edges of the prism truncated by the second order prism producing an eight-sided form.

The density of idocrase ranges from 3·32 to 3·47—the golden brown stones from Canada were found to have a density of 3·38, a green specimen 3·42, but the massive green californite has a density somewhat lower, between 3·25 and 3·32. The refractive indices show some variation from ω 1·712 and ϵ 1·700 to ϵ 1·721 and ω 1·716, the optical sign changing from negative in the case of the lower values of refractive indices to positive for the stones having higher values. Idocrase has a vitreous lustre and shows only weak dichroism and little fire, the dispersion is 0·019 for the B to G interval. The absorption spectrum of idocrase consists of a strong band at 4610 Å and a weak band at 5285 Å. In the golden brown stones, however, the general absorption of the blue precludes observation of the 4610 Å band. Further, these brown stones (particularly those from Canada) sometimes show a rare-earth series of absorption bands, some six in all between 5910 and 5745 Å. The absorption band at 4610 Å is strongly seen in the californite variety and allows distinction of this stone from jadeite. This is of particular importance as the densities of these two minerals are near one another. Idocrase shows no luminescence. The stone is often found as an admixture with grossularite.

The localities for idocrase are the Ala valley, Piedmont, Italy, where green and brown crystals are found. Lake Baikal in Siberia, Zillertal in the Tyrol and Zermatt in Switzerland are other localities. The golden brown stones come from Laurel in the Laurentian mountains of eastern Canada. Californite, as its name implies, is found in Fresno, Butte and Siskiyou Counties of California, U.S.A., while the rare cyprine is found at Telemark in Norway. Some small crystals of a yellowish-green colour characterized by high pyramidal terminations with no basal pinacoid have been found near Quetta in West Pakistan.

IOLITE

Owing to the sapphire-blue colour of gem quality iolite, the material was in earlier days miscalled 'water sapphire'. Iolite is a complex silicate of magnesium and aluminium ($Mg_2Al_4Si_5O_{18}$) but replacement of part of the magnesium by ferrous iron and manganese, and the aluminium by ferric iron, often occurs. These replacements make the constants for iolite somewhat variable.

The name iolite is applied to the stone on account of the blue colour of the gem material, the name being derived from the Greek word for violet. Iolite, however, has other names applied to it, such as dichroite, from the strong pleochroism which is such a prominent feature with this species; and cordierite, a name given to the mineral in honour of the French geologist P. L. A. Cordier. The term cordierite is used for the mineral in mineralogy.

Iolite crystallizes in the orthorhombic system, the crystals are often found as short pseudo-hexagonal prismatic twins which to some extent resemble quartz. Most of the gem material is found in the gem gravels as water-worn pebbles. The mineral has a hardness of 7–7$\frac{1}{2}$ on Mohs's scale and the density may vary from 2·57 to 2·66, most gem material is, however, confined to the more restricted range of 2·57–2·61. The indices of refraction may vary within the limits of 1·53–1·54 to 1·54–1·55 and the amount of birefringence varies from 0·008 to 0·012. The sign of refraction is negative, but it has been reported as positive. Iolite has weak dispersion—the value being 0·017 in the B to G interval.

The pleochroism of iolite is particularly strong, the colours for the three principal directions being yellow, light blue, and dark violet-blue. The best blue colour is seen when the crystal is viewed down the length of the prism. The absorption spectrum of iolite resembles to some extent that of blue spinel in that the spectrum is due mainly to ferrous iron. The strong dichroism of iolite precludes any confusion with the singly refracting spinel. The absorption bands shown by iolite are not strong and are at 6450, 5930, 5850, 5350, 4920, 4560, 4360 and 4260 Å. The absorption spectrum varies with the direction, so that in the direction of the violet-blue colour the 6450 and 4260 Å bands are masked by the general absorption and appear as cut-offs which shorten the spectrum. Due probably to the iron content iolite does not luminesce under ultra-violet light.

The inclusions seen in iolite vary considerably, but one type seen in Ceylon stones is worthy of comment, for if profuse they tend to give the stone a red colour. These inclusions are thin hexagonal platelets of either hematite or goethite, which usually show a parallel orientation. Thus, if the stone is viewed when the thin tablets are broadside on the stone appears a good red colour, but if it is viewed so that the thin inclusions are edgewise on the red colour is not so pronounced, this effect giving a pseudo-dichroism. Such stones have been called 'Bloodshot iolite' and the inclusions seen in them are shown in *Figure 16.4*. Carved objects, said to be ancient Colombian and which had the appearance of grey jadeite, were found to be massive iolite.

The localities for iolite are the gem gravels of Ceylon and the Mogok Stone Tract of Upper Burma. Gem material is also found in Madagascar,

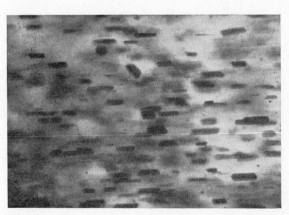

Figure 16.4. Hexagonal platelets of an iron mineral seen in 'Bloodshot iolite'

particularly from Mount Tsilaizina, and iolite is also found in the hills of Vizagapatam and the Trichinopoly and Coimbatore districts of Madras, India. Some iolite is found near the Great Slave Lake in the North-West Territories of Canada. Good iolite is found at Karasburg, South-West Africa.

KORNERUPINE

A rare magnesium iron aluminium boro-silicate, kornerupine has been faceted as gems, but its interest is mainly for collectors who crave the unusual. The mineral was first found at Fiskernaes in Greenland as material with a radiating columnar habit in translucent to transparent pieces of pale green to sage green colour. The mineral was reported upon in 1884 by J. Lorenzen who named it kornerupine in memory of A. N. Kornerup, a young Danish scientist. The material from Greenland is scarce and has no gem significance. In 1912 a pale sage green variety was discovered at Betroka, Madagascar, and later, in 1922, another deposit of similar coloured material was found at Itrongay in the same island. About 1936 some deep browny-green cut stones from the illam of Ceylon were identified as kornerupine and a number of such stones have since been found in parcels of Ceylon gravel. In 1952, although a similar but unidentified stone had been known for some time, a lovely green-coloured stone was identified as kornerupine, and there is little doubt that the stone came from the Mogok Stone Tract of Burma. It has been credibly reported that a star-kornerupine has been found at this locality. Other sources of kornerupine, but not necessarily of gem quality, are Waldheim in Saxony, where the mineral was first known as prismatine; some opaque material has been found at Port Shepstone in Natal, and material of two types, one a dark green and the other a yellow or greenish-yellow, comes from Lac Ste Marie, Gatineau, Quebec, Canada. Kornerupine cat's-eyes have been found.

Kornerupine has the formula $MgAl_2SiO_6$, with considerable replacement of the aluminium by iron and boron. The crystallization is orthorhombic, but the material, particularly that from Ceylon, is found as rolled pebbles. The hardness is $6\frac{1}{2}$ on Mohs's scale and the density varies from 3·27 to 3·45, the gem material having the more restricted range of 3·28–3·35. The indices of refraction approximate to α 1·665, β and γ 1·678 (Ceylon stones α 1·668, β and γ 1·680) with a negative biaxial birefringence of about 0·013. The gem varieties are pseudo-uniaxial. The stone has only moderate fire for the dispersion is 0·018 for the B to G interval, and shows pronounced dichroism with colours of green and yellow to reddish-brown, and is sufficiently strong as to be apparent to the eye. To obtain the best colour the stones need to be cut with the table facet parallel to the length of the crystal. The absorption spectrum shows several weak bands which are not easily observed, but a band at 5030 Å can usually be detected in most kornerupines. No fluorescence has been observed and this effect is probably due to the iron content poisoning the luminescence.

KYANITE

Characterized by having the same chemical composition as andalusite and fibrolite, that is aluminium silicate (Al_2SiO_5), kyanite forms flattened triclinic crystals with bladed habit, which are unique in having considerable differences in hardness in different directions. The Mohs's scale hardness being 7 across the crystal and 5 along the length. The name kyanite, or cyanite as it is spelt in older literature, indicates that the species is typically of a blue colour, which may be either a light or dark hue. The blue colour is almost always confined towards the centre of the crystal and tends to colourless towards the edges. The crystals display a marked cleavage parallel to the exceptionally large prism face, and this makes cutting hazardous. Chatoyant (cat's-eye) stones have been met.

The density of kyanite lies between 3·65 and 3·69, most gem material having the higher values of 3·68; the refractive indices for gem material approximates to α 1·715, β 1·726 and γ 1·732, the biaxial double refraction is 0·017 and is negative in sign. The dispersion between the B to G interval is 0·020. Kyanite shows pronounced pleochroism, the colours for the three principal directions are violet-blue, colourless and cobalt blue. The absorption spectrum shows a line in the deep red and two lines in the deep blue. The fluorescence shown by the mineral is variable but most stones show a dim red under the long-wave ultra-violet lamp, but this glow is more readily seen by the crossed filter method.

Gem quality kyanite is found in Burma, in Kashmir, Patiala and the Punjab in India, and Kenya. The mineral is found in Switzerland and in several states of America, particularly North Carolina. A white variety, found in the Pfitschtal district in Italy is called rhaetizite but this variety has no gem significance. A green coloured variety emanates from North Carolina. An alternative name for kyanite is disthene, a name meaning double strength and relates to the differential hardness of the mineral.

LAZULITE

The mineral lazulite is rarely met as fashioned stones or as ornamental material where the blue colour could be most effective. The mineral is an iron magnesium aluminium phosphate $(FeAl_2(OH)_2(PO_4)_2)$ which crystallizes in the monoclinic system. The hardness is $5\frac{1}{2}$ on Mohs's scale, the density is near to 3·1 and the mean refractive index is 1·62, a value which is near to turquoise and odontolite. Specimens from the Bhandara district of Central Provinces, India, gave a density of 3·17 and indices of refraction of α 1·615, β 1·635 and γ 1·645, the biaxial refraction being negative in sign. The lustre of lazulite is vitreous and stones show strong pleochroism; the two main colours are colourless and azure blue. The mineral, which is usually found in small pieces, comes from many localities, particularly from Minas Gerais, Brazil, Sweden, Austria, India and North Carolina, U.S.A. Lobito Bay, Angola is another source.

LEGRANDITE

A cut specimen of this rare mineral has been reported in literature. Legrandite is a hydrated zinc arsenate and is usually found in bundles of monoclinic crystals. The stone is transparent and of a bright yellow colour. The hardness is about 5 on Mohs's scale and the density varies from 3·98 to

4·04, and the refractive indices are α 1·675, β 1·690, and γ 1·735, thus the mineral has a birefringence of 0·060 and the refraction is positive in sign. The mineral is known only from Mexico.

LEPIDOLITE

The massive fine-grained rose-red granular lepidolite, or as it is sometimes called lithia mica, has been polished into slabs for ornamental purposes. The mineral has a hardness of $3\frac{1}{2}$ on Mohs's scale and the density lies between 2·8 and 2·9 for the massive material, although higher values up to 3·3 have been mentioned for lepidolite. The mean refractive index is 1·55. There is no distinctive absorption spectrum and no luminescence is shown by the mineral. Massive lepidolite is found in the Ural mountains of Russia, in Madagascar, in the States of Maine, California and Connecticut in the United States of America, and the Karibib district of S.W. Africa.

LEUCITE

For those who crave the curious, small colourless stones have been cut from the icositetrahedral crystals of leucite, mainly the crystals from the Italian volcanic rocks. Leucite is a potassium aluminium silicate $(KAl(SiO_3)_2)$ and crystallizes in the cubic system. The hardness of the mineral is $5\frac{1}{2}$–6 on Mohs's scale, the density varying from 2·45 to 2·50, being generally near to 2·48, and the refractive index is 1·51 but, although from its cubic crystallization the mineral is isotropic, specimens commonly show feeble double refraction between crossed nicols. Except under x-rays when a dull bluish glow may be seen, cut leucites show little luminescence. Leucite is found in the Alban Hills in Italy, in Germany and at a number of localities in the United States of America.

MAGNESITE

Transparent white crystals of magnesite, a magnesium carbonate $(MgCO_3)$ mineral which crystallizes in the trigonal system, have been cut as specimens for collectors. The hardness, about 4 on Mohs's scale, is too low for it to be a satisfactory gemstone. The density is 3·0–3·12 and the uniaxial refraction is optically negative with indices for the ordinary ray of 1·717 and for the extraordinary ray of 1·515; the birefringence is therefore 0·202. Much magnesite fluoresces with a blue, green or white glow, probably best under the short-wave lamp. A greenish phosphorescence is often seen. Magnesite will effervesce with warm acid. The clear gemmy crystals are said to come from Brazil, but the mineral has a world-wide occurrence.

MALACHITE

The agate-like banding of different shades of green readily distinguishes malachite from any other mineral (Plate XIX, facing page 268), except perhaps the much rarer pseudomalachite, or an opaque green aventurine quartz. Essentially a hydrated copper carbonate $(Cu_2(OH)_2CO_3)$ malachite is formed through the dissolving of copper ores and the subsequent deposition in rock cavities and veins as botryoidal, reniform or stalactitic masses.

The mineral is actually a compact mass of monoclinic crystals, at least so far as the material used for ornamental purposes is concerned. If the material shows crystal form these crystals are slender prisms in divergent arrangement and it is these prisms, as radial fibres closely packed together, which produce the botryoidal forms and the circular banding (*Figure 16.5*). The hardness of malachite is low at about 4 on Mohs's scale, and owing to the nature of its structure the mineral breaks easily, although with care it can be turned on a lathe. The density of the ornamental material has a mean value of 3·8 but varies somewhat according to the compactness. The mean refractive index, all that may be expected to be seen on a refractometer, is about 1·85, although for the fibres the values are α 1·655, β 1·875 and γ 1·909, the large birefringence being a common factor in carbonate minerals.

Figure 16.5. The circular banding seen in malachite

Malachite effervesces when touched with a spot of acid and if the acid is taken up by a platinum wire which is then introduced into a Bunsen flame the flame will be coloured green, if the acid used be nitric; if hydrochloric acid is used the colour will be blue. This indicates copper which is an essential part of malachite. The mineral does not show luminescence under ultra-violet light or x-rays.

The use of malachite in ornamentation is mostly in the guise of flat plates for inlay purposes, or as rather flat cabochons, or as beads. Malachite has a world-wide distribution, being a common ore of copper where it is found typically in the oxidation zone of copper deposits. Much of the malachite used for ornamentation in older days was obtained from the copper mines in the Ural mountains in Russia, the major mines being at Nizhne-Tagilsk, Bogoslovsk, and at Gumeshevsk and Mednorudiansk, where the best cutting material is found. Malachite suitable for cutting is obtained from Queensland, New South Wales and South Australia. The copper mines of Africa supply much malachite but little seems to be used for ornamental purposes, and the United States of America produces fine quality material at the copper mines of Arizona and elsewhere.

Malachite is often found together with the other copper carbonate azurite, and when the pieces are cut and polished a blue and green banded stone is produced to which the name azurmalachite is given. Malachite is also found in association with the copper silicate chrysocolla and they may be fashioned together. The opaque green aventurine quartz which looks so much like malachite may be distinguished from malachite by the red residual colour of the green quartz seen under the colour filter.

Pseudomalachite is a copper phosphate ($Cu_3P_2O_83Cu(OH)_2$) the monoclinic crystals of which form botryoidal structures similar both in colour and form to malachite. The hardness is $4\frac{1}{2}$ on Mohs's scale, the density is given as 3·6 and the mean refractive index is 1·80. The mineral is less common than malachite and is found at Rheinbreitbach in Germany, Nizhne-Tagilsk in Russia, and has been reported from Zambia and elsewhere.

MEERSCHAUM (Sepiolite)

Meerschaum, a word derived from the German meaning sea foam, is a hydrated magnesium silicate ($H_4Mg_2Si_3O_{10}$) and is a compact white mineral which is mostly used for the bowls of pipes. Microscopic examination has shown the mineral to be an intermediate mixture of a fine fibrous material and an amorphous substance of the same composition. The hardness is 2 on Mohs's scale, with a refractive index of about 1·53 which is only vaguely visible on the refractometer. The density is 2 but owing to the porosity of the dry material it will float on water. Meerschaum does not fluoresce. The mineral is found near Eski Shehr in Asia Minor in stratified earthy or alluvial deposits. Other sources are Moravia and near Thebes in Greece, in Spain and in the United States of America. Morocco was an early source of meerschaum, which was used in earlier times in place of soap and was known as Pierre de savon Maroc.

MELINOPHANE (Meliphanite)

Purely a collector's stone, melinophane is a fluo-silicate of beryllium, calcium and sodium with a formula $(Ca,Na)_2Be(Si,Al)_2(O,F)_7$, which forms yellow crystals of the tetragonal system. The hardness is just over 5 on Mohs's scale, the density is 3·0 and the uniaxial (sometimes biaxial) refraction of negative sign has indices of 1·612 for the ordinary ray and 1·593 for the extraordinary ray. The mineral is found in the Langesundfjord district of southern Norway.

MESOLITE

One of the zeolite group of minerals, mesolite is intermediate between natrolite ($Na_2Al_2Si_3O_{10}2H_2O$) and scolecite ($CaAl_2Si_3O_{10}3H_2O$), and the stone has been cut into cabochons which have a silky lustre. The fibrous crystals, white or colourless, are monoclinic in crystallization and packed closely together in the massive form produce the silky material. The hardness is 5 on Mohs's scale and the density of mesolite is 2·29, and the indices of refraction have a mean of 1·50. The mineral occurs in amygdaloidal basalt and similar rocks and is found in Sicily, Scotland, Ireland, Iceland, Greenland, India, Australia and the United States of America.

MICROLITE

A mineral rarely cut except for collectors, microlite—a calcium pyro-tantalate (Ca_2,Ta_2O_7)—is found in crystals of the cubic system which are of a brownish-green, yellowish-brown to hyacinth-red colour. The crystals are small and rarely large enough for cutting. The hardness is $5\frac{1}{2}$ on Mohs's scale, the density is 5·5 and the mineral has a refractive index of 1·93. Microlite occurs in Sweden, the island of Elba and at Maine, Virginia, and Massachusetts in the United States of America.

MILLERITE

Millerite, a nickel sulphide mineral which crystallizes in the trigonal system, usually found as brass- or bronze-yellow slender hair-like crystals, and hence sometimes known as capillary pyrites, seems unlikely as a gemstone. However, a stone of cloudy yellowish-green colour has been cut from material found at Rossing in South-West Africa. Millerite has a hardness of 3·00 to 3·50 on Mohs's scale and is said to have a density of 5·30 to 5·65. No refractive indices have been given for this mineral.

MIMETITE

Bright orange cabochons have been cut from mimetite found in Mexico. The mineral, which crystallizes in the hexagonal system, has a hardness of $3\frac{1}{2}$ on Mohs's scale and a density of about 7·1. It is only cut for collectors of the curious.

NATROLITE

A member of the zeolite family of minerals, natrolite is a sodium aluminium silicate with the formula $Na_2Al_2Si_3O_{10},2H_2O$. The massive material, white in colour, consists of orthorhombic fibrous crystals and is not very suitable for cutting purposes, but it has been fashioned for those who desire something different. The hardness is $5\frac{1}{2}$ on Mohs's scale, the density is from 2·20 to 2·25 and the refractive indices are α 1·480, β 1·482 and γ 1·493, the refraction being biaxial and positive in sign with the birefringence of 0·013. Norway and Scotland are two well-known localities for the mineral.

NEVADA WONDERSTONE

Used for ornamental objects and as baroque stones fashioned by the tumbling process, Nevada wonderstone is a volcanic rock which weathers into alternate stripes of red and buff, and which sometimes has grey patches. The material has a density of about 2·53. Nevada wonderstone is not to be confused with the dark grey pyrophyllite rock which has been called South African wonderstone, to which reference is made under Pyrophyllite.

ODONTOLITE

Variously known as 'bone turquoise' or 'fossil turquoise' but more correctly called odontolite—a word derived from two Greek words meaning tooth and stone—is a material which has a fine blue colour and simulates the true turquoise remarkably well. It is actually the fossilized bones, or more often the teeth, of extinct animals, particularly the mastodon and dinotherium, and perhaps other prehistoric beasts.

Odontolite has, therefore, an organic derivation, and specimens may still show this organic structure. The material has had the organic constituents completely, or in major part, replaced by another mineral, thus the mineral could vary in character between rather wide limits and this is particularly so with regard to density. Natural ivory (with about 40 per cent of organic material) has a density of about 1·80, and if the organic material is replaced by apatite (sp. gr. 3·2) the density would be much greater than for natural ivory. It has been found by x-ray powder photography that odontolite gives a typical apatite picture, so that apatite is a major replacing mineral in odontolite. There is, too, a certain amount of replacement by calcium carbonate, indicated by the effervescence shown when a spot of acid is placed on the specimen (a distinction from true turquoise). A further and more important replacement, or impregnation, is by the ferrous phosphate mineral known as vivianite ($H_{16}Fe_3P_2O_{11}$) to which the colour of odontolite is due. The colour of the material as mined is said to be a dingy greyish-blue and that the rich blue of the jewellery stones is said to have been brought out by subsequent heat treatment. The density of odontolite of a good blue colour is just over 3·00 and the refractive index varies from 1·57 to 1·63. The hardness is about 5 on Mohs's scale.

Odontolite is found at Simmore, near Auch in the Department of Gers in southern France, a locality which was known before the French Revolution as Languedoc, and for a time these deposits were systematically worked. An imitation odontolite has been made by calcining recent ivory and staining blue by soaking in a solution of copper sulphate. Experiment shows that such material does not differ in density from that of recent ivory, that is 1·8.

PAINITE

During 1957 a deep garnet-red crystal emanating from the Mogok gem gravels at Ohngaing village, Upper Burma, was identified as a new mineral, a mineral which could be cut as a gemstone. There may, therefore, be cut gemstones in existence which are at present unidentified. Painite, a calcium boro-silico aluminate, belongs to the hexagonal crystal system. The hardness of the mineral is $7\frac{1}{2}$ on Mohs's scale and the density is 4·01. The refractive indices are for the ordinary ray 1·816 and for the extraordinary ray 1·787, the mineral is therefore uniaxial and negative in sign and has a birefringence of 0·029. The dichroic colours are ruby-red and pale brownish-orange, the deeper colour being that of the ordinary ray. The absorption spectrum shows a faint chromium spectrum. The original specimen showed a red colour under crossed filters, a weak red glow under long-wave ultraviolet light and a stronger red glow under the short-wave lamp. Under x-rays the glow was a very dim bluish-yellow. The crystal showed feather-like sheets of minute cavities and inclusions of large hexagonal tabular crystals (*Figure 16.6*). The mineral was named after A. C. D. Pain who found the crystal about 1951.

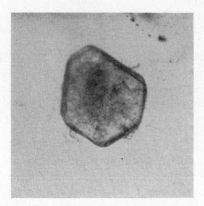

Figure 16.6. Inclusions in painite

PECTOLITE

Found in close aggregations of monoclinic acicular crystals, and of a white or greyish colour, pectolite has been fashioned into cabochons which have a silky lustre. The mineral is a sodium calcium silicate with the formula $HNaCa_2(SiO_3)_3$. Pectolite has a hardness of 5 on Mohs's scale, a density which varies from 2·74 to 2·88 and an optically positive biaxial refraction having indices of α 1·595, β 1·606 and γ 1·633, but only a vague reading of about 1·60 would be seen on the refractometer with the massive material. The mineral usually shows a yellow or orange glow under ultra-violet light (probably best under the short-wave lamp), and some phosphorescence, which may be strong, is often seen. The glows are said to be due to traces of manganese. Pectolite is one of the zeolites and is found in cavities in basalts and other volcanic rocks in Italy, Scotland and the United States of America.

PETALITE

Purely as collectors' pieces, colourless petalite, a lithium aluminium silicate $(Li_2O,Al_2O_3,8SiO_2)$, has been cut as faceted stones, but the gems have little merit owing to their glassy appearance. The mineral crystallizes in the monoclinic system but crystals are rare and the mineral is usually found massive. Petalite is cleavable and somewhat brittle and has a hardness of just over 6 on Mohs's scale. The density ranges from 2·39 to 2·46 and the refractive indices are α 1·504, β 1·510 and γ 1·516. However, a colourless stone of 2·17 carats gave values of α 1·5056, β 1·5122 and γ 1·5199, giving a positive biaxial double refraction of 0·014. The density was found to be 2·396. This stone showed a very weak and vague absorption spectrum showing a band at about 4540 Å, and under ultra-violet light showed a weak orange glow. Under x-rays a bright orange light was seen which had persistent phosphorescence. Petalite occurs in Sweden and in Massachusetts and Maine in the United States of America, and at Karabib, South-West Africa.

PHENAKITE (Phenacite)

A gemstone which has occasionally appeared in jewellery, phenakite resembles in appearance colourless quartz. Indeed, it was so often mistaken for quartz that the name phenakite is derived from the Greek for the word to cheat. Phenakite is a beryllium silicate (Be_2SiO_4) and is found in bright crystals of the trigonal system which may be either tabular or prismatic in habit. These crystals show no distinct cleavage. The refraction is uniaxial and positive in sign, the indices being 1·654 for the ordinary ray and 1·670 for the extraordinary ray, thus the double refraction approaches that of tourmaline, being 0·016. The stones have little fire for the dispersion is only 0·015 for the B to G interval, the bright vitreous lustre being their only saving grace. Phenakite is harder than quartz at $7\frac{1}{2}$–8 on Mohs's scale and the specific gravity varies between 2·95 and 2·97. There is no characteristic absorption spectrum and any luminescence under ultra-violet light is too weak to be of value—it may be pale greenish. Under x-rays the fluorescence is quite distinct and of a blue colour; there is no afterglow. Crystals of a bright wine-yellow and a pale rose-red, the latter said to emanate from Russia, are reported but such hues have not been met with in cut stones. During the early part of 1963 an emerald-cut phenakite of greenish-blue colour was reported. This stone, which had a density of 3·00 and refractive indices of 1·654 and 1·670, was noticeable for its strong dichroism ranging from a peacock-blue to violet-red. The stone fluoresced a light blue under ultra-violet light.

The usual occurrence of phenakite is most commonly in pegmatites, in granite druses and in mica schists. Crystals are found in the Tokawava river in the Ural mountains of Russia in association with emerald and chrysoberyl, and the Miask district in the Ilmen mountains are another Russian source. A prominent occurrence of large colourless crystals is at San Miguel di Piracicaba, Minas Gerais in Brazil. Other sources of phenakite are the Usugara district, Tanzania in East Africa, the States of Maine, New Hampshire and Colorado in the United States of America, Switzerland, and Alsace in France. Crystals of phenakite are found in the Klein Spitzkoppe in South-West Africa.

PHOSGENITE

Crystallizing in the tetragonal system, phosgenite is a chlorocarbonate of lead. With a hardness of about 3 it is only suitable for a collector's piece and its sole merit is the strong yellow fluorescence shown by the stone when under a beam of ultra-violet light. The density is about 6·2 and the indices of refraction are 2·114–2·140 with positive sign. The mineral is found in many places, including Sardinia, South-West Africa, Tasmania and New South Wales.

PHOSPHOPHYLLITE

In the Smithsonian Institute of America there is an emerald-cut specimen of phosphophyllite of bluish-green colour and weighing 5·04 carats. Phosphophyllite is essentially a zinc phosphate but is too low in hardness ($3\frac{1}{2}$

on Mohs's scale) for it to be an effective gemstone. The density is 3·1 and the refractive indices are 1·595–1·616 and positive in sign, the crystallization being monoclinic. The mineral shows a violet fluorescence under short-wave ultra-violet light. The source of the mineral is usually said to be in Bavaria, but the cut stone described is probably from Bolivia.

POLLUCITE

An extremely rare mineral, pollucite is a silicate of aluminium and caesium with the formula $H_2Cs_4Al_4(SiO_3)_9$, and is unique in containing the rare alkali metal caesium as an essential constituent. The mineral was first found in the granite pegmatites of the island of Elba. Breithaupt, in 1846, found pollucite in association with another rare mineral and he named them pollux and castor after the twin brothers of Helen of Troy in Greek mythology. Subsequently the name was modified to pollucite by attaching the usual mineralogical termination. Castor was proved later to be the mineral petalite.

Pollucite is a colourless or white mineral which has a vitreous lustre and is found in crystals of the cubic system, usually as cubes; it is often found massive. The hardness is $6\frac{1}{2}$ on Mohs's scale and the mineral has a density range between 2·85 and 2·94 (a colourless specimen weighing 1·725 carats was determined by L. J. Spencer as 2·86). The refractive index varies from about 1·517 to 1·525, the material from Maine having the higher index. The dispersion is low (0·012 for the B to G interval), and the luminescence under ultra-violet light or x-rays is usually orange or pink in colour.

Sources of the gem quality material (and the stone is only cut as collectors' pieces) are Newry, Oxford County, Maine and Middletown, Connecticut, U.S.A. Massive material has been found in the Black Hills of South Dakota, and a mauve-white massive pollucite has been found at Varuträsk, Västerbotten in Sweden. A cabochon-cut piece of this Swedish material was found to have an index of refraction of 1·518 and a density of 2·90.

PORPHYRIES

Porphyries are types of igneous rocks which show comparatively large and well-formed crystals embedded in a groundmass of much finer texture. The porphyritic structure is considered to be due to a two-stage crystallization, or solidification, of the igneous magma at the time of its intrusion into the surrounding rock or extrusion on to the earth's surface, when the magma contained already formed crystals enclosed in the molten liquid which subsequently solidified as a fine-grained groundmass. Porphyritic structure is common in rocks and it might be expected that a wide range of such a type of rock could well be used as an ornamental stone. This does not seem to be the case and the two porphyries first considered have more historical interest than as ornamental stones of modern application.

The first of these is the green porphyry found in the Province of Laconia in Greece, a rock with an olive-green groundmass with light green feldspar crystals sprinkled abundantly through it. The green colour is due to included epidote and chlorite throughout the rock, which was known in

classical times as Marmor Lacedaemonium Viride. It was later known as
Perfido serpentino, but the rock is not a serpentine. The quarries yielding
this rock lie between the towns of Sparta and Marathonisi.

The other, and perhaps more important porphyry is the famous red
porphyry of Egypt, Perfido Rosso Antico, which was known in classical
times as Porphyrites Leptosephos. This rock has a dark red groundmass,
the colour being due to included piedmontite, a manganese mineral. In
this groundmass is an abundance of small white and light pink feldspar
crystals. The rock is quarried from a dyke some 80–90 ft. in thickness on
the Jebel Dhokan mountain which lies some 25 miles inland from the
junction of the Red Sea with the Gulf of Suez and about 50 miles eastwards
from the Nile. It is doubtful whether the rock was known to the Egyptians
but probably it was discovered in the reign of Claudius by the Romans who
took it to Rome, where it was called Lapis porphyrites, and later 'The
Stone of Rome'. During the Roman occupation of Egypt thousands of
workmen were employed in the quarries and the stone was transported to
the Nile *en route* for the Imperial City of Rome. A carved head of the
Emperor Hadrian in Egyptian porphyry may be seen in the British
Museum at Bloomsbury, London. The head is said to have been made in
Egypt about A.D. 130 and the carving was carried out by using copper tools
fed with sand and emery.

Llanoite (or llanite) is a reddish porphyry which consists mainly of reddish microcline crystals in a dark brown matrix; but which also contains
small patches of quartz (?) which show bluish gleams. This rock is found
at Llano County, Texas, in the United States.

Although not strictly a porphyry, the rock called corsite, or sometimes
napoleonite, might conveniently be mentioned here. It is a greyish rock
containing lighter coloured oval rings showing some radial structure. The
material is an orbicular diorite or hornblende gabbro which occurs in the
island of Corsica. There are two fine examples of this material in the form
of vases in the Chateau de Malmaison outside Paris.

PREHNITE

Prehnite is an orthorhombic mineral, which is rarely found as distinct
crystals but forms aggregates with botryoidal habit in cavities in volcanic
rocks. It has been cut as cabochons or as carved pieces. The colour is
usually an oil-green but an attractive brown material is common, the green
material having some similarity to jade. Some translucent pale yellowish-
brown prehnite has been cut cabochon and such stones show a cat's-eye
effect.

Prehnite is a hydrated calcium aluminium silicate ($H_2Ca_2Al_2(SiO_4)_3$)
with a hardness of 6 on Mohs's scale. The density lies between 2·80 and
2·95, but for the gem material the range is much closer and lies between
2·88 and 2·94. The principal refractive indices are 1·61 and 1·64 with a
double refraction of 0·030. On the refractometer, owing to the massed
fibrous nature of the material only a vague shadow edge at about 1·63 will
be seen. No characteristic absorption spectrum is seen in prehnite and the
mineral does not normally exhibit luminescence, although the brownish-

yellow chatoyant stones may show a dull brownish-yellow glow under ultra-violet light and x-rays. Under the colour filter a weak reddish residual colour is seen.

Prehnite is found in China, New Jersey in the United States of America, at Bourg d'Oisans, south-east of Grenoble in France and the Cape Colony, from which place it was first brought over by Colonel von Prehn, hence the name. Attractive green and brown botryoidal masses are found at Prospect, near Sydney in New South Wales, Australia. Botryoidal groups of pale green prehnite are found at Renfrew, the Kilpatrick Hills, Dunbarton, the Campsie Hills, Stirling and elsewhere in Scotland. A mixture of chlorite and prehnite, often with inclusions of copper, occurs in the Lake Superior district and is said to produce attractive pink and green stones for which the name patricianite has been proposed.

PROUSTITE

The light red silver ore called proustite is more important for the lovely crystals of the trigonal system that it forms. Although the mineral has been cut for collectors it provides a most unsatisfactory gemstone for, not only is the hardness only $2\frac{1}{2}$ on Mohs's scale, but the glorious red colour rapidly darkens to a dark red to nearly black colour on exposure to light. The composition is silver sulphide ($3Ag_2S.As_2S_3$) and the mineral has a density varying from 5·57 to 5·64, the purer material having the lower values. The refractive indices, too high to be measured on the refractometer, are 2·7 for the extraordinary ray and 3·0 for the ordinary ray, the uniaxial negative birefringence being 0·3. Proustite is found as a primary silver mineral in silver deposits at Jachymov in Czechoslovakia, Freiberg in Saxony, Atacama in Chile, Alsace in France, at various places in Mexico, in Idaho, Colorado, Nevada in the United States of America and at Cobalt, Ontario in Canada.

PYROPHYLLITE

The compact massive variety of pyrophyllite, white, grey or greenish in colour, is in appearance like soapstone, and has, too, some similarity to massive talc in composition. It is an aluminium silicate with the formula $H_2Al_2(SiO_3)_4$ (soapstone has the formula $H_2Mg_3(SiO_3)_4$). The hardness is again similar to talc, that is about $1\frac{1}{2}$ on Mohs's scale, but the density is slightly higher at about 2·8. The refractive indices are 1·55 and 1·60, but these do not help very much with the massive material for only a vague shadow edge can be seen. Like soapstone, pyrophyllite has a greasy lustre and the two materials cannot be distinguished from each other by the eye alone. The higher density or a determination of the presence of aluminium will indicate which material is being handled. This may be carried out by a method commonly used by mineralogists. A fragment of the mineral is moistened with a solution of cobalt nitrate and then heated. If a blue colour results, aluminium is indicated and the material is probably pyrophyllite. On the other hand, if a pale red colour is produced magnesium is present and the mineral is probably soapstone. The method needs some practice before a positive result can be obtained with surety. In many localities pyrophyllite is often found in association with kyanite and andalusite. The material occurs in the Sverdlovsk (Ekaterinburg) district of the Ural mountains of Russia, in Scandinavia, in the region of Ouro Preto, Minas Gerais, Brazil, and in California, Georgia and Carolina in the United States of America. Much of the agalmatolite of China is pyrophyllite.

South African wonderstone, also known as Ottosdal G stone or Koranna stone, a dark grey slaty-looking rock, which is found near the village of Ottosdal in western Transvaal, has been used for ornamental objects. The stone occurs up to about 200 ft. in thickness in volcanic formations, the principal outcrop being at Gestoptefontein Hill. The composition is 89 per cent pyrophyllite with $9\frac{1}{2}$ per cent chloritoid or epidote and $1\frac{1}{2}$ per cent rutile. A specimen of this rock gave a vague refractive index of 1·58 and a density near to 2·72.

RHODIZITE

As the name indicates the rare potassium (caesium, rubidium) aluminium borate ($KAl_2B_3O_8$) mineral known as rhodizite is usually of a rose-red colour. When found as crystals the mineral forms dodecahedra of the cubic system, but there are grounds for doubt as to whether the crystals truly belong to the cubic system. The hardness of rhodizite is 8 on Mohs's scale, the density is 3·4 and the refractive index is 1·69. Specimens from Madagascar and the Urals were found to luminesce with a weak yellowish glow under ultra-violet light and to show a strong greenish or yellowish fluorescence, with perceptible phosphorescence, when irradiated with x-rays. Rhodizite was originally found in masses of a rose-red colour in the Ural mountains near Sverdlovsk, and crystals of yellowish and greenish hue have been found at Antandrokomby and Manjaka in Madagascar. Stones of this species are only fashioned for collectors.

RHODOCHROSITE

The massive rhodochrosite, for the mineral is also found as rhombohedral crystals of the trigonal system, and in granular masses, usually has a paler and more delicate rose-red colour than rhodonite. Rhodochrosite, the manganese carbonate ($MnCO_3$), as used as an ornamental stone, is characterized by the lovely pink shade of colour, which is variegated and in bands of different shades of pink. The material may be likened in its banding, but not in colour, with green malachite. Indeed, like malachite, the banding is due to stalagmitic formation, the prismatic crystals tending to a radial formation. Grey, fawn and brown colours are also found.

Although rhodochrosite is found in many different localities, only a few supply the compact material which is used as an ornamental stone, and its use as such began just before the commencement of World War II, when a quantity of this stalagmitic rose-coloured stone came from San Luis in Argentina. The deposit from which it came was said to have been found in a long-disused mine situated on a mountain fissure at a high altitude, which was said to have been worked by the Incas for silver and copper during the thirteenth century. It was owing to this connexion that the names

10+G.   289

'Rosinca' or 'Inca rose' were given to the stone. Colorado, Montana and other States of the North American continent are other sources of the mineral. Further localities are Romania, Hungary, the Central Provinces of India and Freiberg in Saxony, but these are unimportant as commercial sources for ornamental material.

The hardness of rhodochrosite is near to 4 on Mohs's scale and it is more easily scratched than is rhodonite. The density is rather variable and lies between 3·45 and 3·70, but the ornamental material has the smaller range of 3·5–3·65. The refractive indices are 1·820 for the ordinary ray and 1·600 for the extraordinary ray. The negative uniaxial double refraction of 0·220 is large in amount and characteristic of a carbonate mineral. These refractive indices can only be seen on stones cut from clear, nearly transparent, material (crystals), for in the ornamental rhodochrosite the crystalline aggregate precludes anything more than a diffuse shadow edge being seen on the refractometer. The absorption spectrum of the mineral shows a band at 5510 Å (and other vaguer lines), but the spectrum scarcely assists identification. A small clear crystal shows a band at 4150 Å, which could not be seen in the more opaque ornamental types. Under the stimulation of ultra-violet light a dull red glow was observed in samples of the mineral from Argentina and Colorado. The mineral effervesces with acid, but the test is not conclusive for rhodonite may contain some carbonate. A few small stones have been cut from the clearer crystals.

RHODONITE

Best known as an ornamental stone, translucent to opaque, and of a fine rose-red colour, rhodonite has at times been found sufficiently transparent to have been cut for collectors as faceted stones. Much translucent material is fashioned into beads and cabochons (Plate XIX, facing page 268), for ornamental articles and as an inlay, like rhodochrosite, to give colour contrast to the white variety of 'onyx marble'.

The mineral is a silicate of manganese ($MnSiO_3$) with some calcium usually present, and in the case of fowlerite from New Jersey, zinc is also present. When in crystals the stones are commonly large and rough and belong to the triclinic system, and according to some authorities the species is referred to the pyroxene group of minerals, but this is not universally agreed. The massive material is the most common and is found in the Urals in large masses resembling marble—a pink marble veined with black where the manganese has oxidized by weathering.

Rhodonite has a distinct cleavage and an uneven fracture and brittle nature; the lustre is vitreous to pearly on fractured surfaces. The mineral takes a good polish. The hardness is about 6 on Mohs's scale and the density varies between 3·40 and 3·70, but the more restricted range of 3·60–3·70 has been found for the gem quality material. The refractive index, as far as the vague shadow edge shown when the massive material is placed on the refractometer, is near to 1·73. The dichroism and absorption spectrum are not clearly defined in the massive material and rhodonite shows no luminescence under ultra-violet light or x-rays. An orange-red transparent cut stone, from Australian material, was found to have a density of 3·707 and refractive indices of 1·733 and 1·747 for the principal rays. The stone showed distinct dichroism with the twin colours orange-red and brownish-red, and the absorption spectrum showed a broad band centred at 5480 Å, a strong narrow line at 5030 Å and a weaker and more diffuse band at 4550 Å.

Rhodonite has a wide occurrence. The major localities are in the Sverdlovsk district of the Urals in Russia (mainly at Sedelnikovo, a village 25 km from Sverdlovsk), the Vermland district of Sweden, a number of localities in the United States of America, Mexico, the Broken Hill district of New South Wales, Australia, Southern Africa and in Cornwall, England.

RUTILE

Natural rutile is rarely encountered as a gemstone, for the material is very rarely transparent, and even if it were so the colour—red, brown or black—is too dark to produce attractive gems, although the black material has been used for mourning jewellery. Other colours, such as yellowish, bluish and violet have been reported, and extremely rarely a grass-green, but most of these are opaque and have not been met as cut stones.

The tetragonal crystals, which have vertically striated prisms capped with pyramids, are commonly twinned in knee-shaped forms (geniculate twins), and may even be so repeatedly twinned as to produce a closed ring. Acicular or hairlike crystals are common and when these are enclosed in rock crystal give rise to rutilated quartz, or as it is sometimes called Venus Hair Stone.

Rutile is titanium dioxide (TiO_2) and is polymorphous with anatase and brookite. The hardness of the mineral is $6-6\frac{1}{2}$ on Mohs's scale and the density is near to 4·2. The indices of refraction are 2·62 for the ordinary ray and 2·90 for the extraordinary ray, the positive birefringence being 0·287, thus cut stones show pronounced doubling of the back facets. The mineral is also exceptional in the degree of fire it displays, which is over six times that shown by diamond, but in the natural stones the effect is masked by the dark colour. The lustre of rutile is that known as adamantine-metallic and the dichroism is variable but usually strong. Rutile is widely distributed both in the localities where it is found and in the nature of the rocks in which it occurs. Of major gemmological importance is the synthetically produced rutile, which is discussed in the chapter on synthetic materials.

SCAPOLITE

The mineral scapolite is best explained as being part of an isomorphous series whose end members are marialite—$Na_4Cl(Al_3Si_9O_{24})$—and meionite —$Ca_6(SO_4CO_3)(Al_6Si_6O_{24})$—the whole group being the scapolite series; scapolite is therefore a silicate of aluminium with calcium and sodium. The mineral crystallizes in the tetragonal system with prismatic habit. The crystals, usually found in metamorphic rocks, are commonly coarse with large uneven faces. The crystals have three directions of easy cleavage parallel to the prism zone.

The gem material was first found about 1913 in the Mogok Stone Tract of Upper Burma as white, pink or violet stones, which are distinctly fibrous. When cut in the correct direction as cabochons these stones produce attractive cat's-eyes, the chatoyancy being due to the included parallel rod-like cavities. The pink stones of this type have been miscalled 'pink moonstone'. A clear yellow scapolite was found, about 1920, in Madagascar and 10 years later similar yellow material was found in the State of Espirito Santo, Brazil. Some yellow stones of this species have been found with the pink variety in Burma, and from Moçambique.

The hardness of scapolite is 6 on Mohs's scale and the density varies from 2·60 to 2·71. The refraction is uniaxial and negative in sign, with indices which rise from 1·540 for the extraordinary ray and 1·549 for the ordinary ray to 1·555 and 1·577 for the extraordinary and ordinary rays respectively, with increase of the meionite molecule. The pink and white stones have a density of 2·63, the refractive indices are ω 1·549 and ϵ 1·540, the double refraction being 0·009 (or 0·010 if the fourth place of decimals is taken into account). A violet scapolite cat's-eye reported upon had a density of 2·634 and refractive indices of 1·560 for the ordinary ray and 1·544 for the extraordinary ray, the birefringence being, therefore, 0·016. The constants of this variety shows that it conforms to an intermediate scapolite which has 50–80 per cent of the marialite molecule and 20–50 per cent of the meionite molecule. This intermediate scapolite has been called dipyrite or dipyre, but the name has been applied to common scapolite (which is also known as wernerite) which has 20–60 per cent of marialite and 40–80 per cent of meionite, or for another intermediate member of the family known as mizzonite. Much confusion occurs with these names in mineralogical texts. The clear yellow scapolite has the higher density of 2·70 and refractive indices of 1·568 and 1·548, the double refraction being 0·020.

The lustre of scapolite is vitreous inclining to resinous and the dispersion is weak, being 0·017 for the B to G interval. The dichroism of the pink and violet stones is strong, the twin colours being dark blue and lavender blue; the yellow stones show colourless or pale yellow and a yellow colour. The absorption spectrum of the pink and violet stones is characterized by bands in the red at 6630 and 6520 Å, with a strong absorption in the yellow; a spectrum ascribed to chromium. The scapolites from Burma show a yellow or orange fluorescence under long-wave ultra-violet light, and the spectrum of this glow, which is sometimes quite strong, exhibits the discrete structure due to uranium. Under the short-wave lamp the glow is more pinkish. The fluorescence under x-rays is much feebler and of a whitish to lilac colour and the stones quickly photocolour to a violet hue. The effect is, however, not permanent. The yellow transparent stones, particularly those from Burma, show a lilac or mauve fluorescence under ultra-violet light, a strong orange glow under x-rays and also photocolour to a violet shade.

An opaque massive yellow variety of scapolite found in Quebec and Ontario, Canada, which could be cut into effective cabochons, is characterized by the brilliant yellow fluorescence it emits when under long-wave ultra-violet light. Some material also phosphoresces with the same coloured glow. The spectrum of this glow shows the discrete spectrum of uranium.

SCHEELITE

Yellowish-white to brownish but sometimes almost an orange-yellow in colour, the calcium tungstate mineral scheelite ($CaWO_4$) has, despite its low hardness of $4\frac{1}{2}$–5 on Mohs's scale, been faceted as a gemstone for collectors. The crystals are of the tetragonal system and usually have a pyramidal habit. The density varies between 5·9 and 6·1 and the refractive indices are ω 1·918 and ϵ 1·934, the sign is positive and the birefringence 0·016. The lustre is vitreous inclined to adamantine and the absorption spectrum may show faintly the didymium rare earth spectrum of groups of lines in the yellow and green, the strongest of the yellow group being at 5840 Å. The most useful and striking feature of scheelite is the strong bright blue fluorescence shown by the mineral when it is bathed in short-wave ultra-violet light (2537 Å), in contradistinction to its lack of response to the long-wave ultra-violet lamp, under which it is practically inert. Scheelite is found in Czechoslovakia (in the old Bohemia), Saxony, Italy, Switzerland, Finland, France, England (Cumberland and Cornwall) and at Sonora in Mexico. In the United States of America it is found in South Dakota, Connecticut, Arizona and California. Much scheelite is obtained from Australia. Few of these localities produce material clear and transparent enough for cutting into faceted stones. In recent years scheelite of a fine yellow to orange colour has come from Santa Cruz, Sonora, Mexico from which stones over ten carats in weight have been cut. Good cuttable material is found in Arizona and California. The fine yellow coloured stones may resemble a coloured diamond but are easily differentiated by the strong double refraction of scheelite. Scheelite has been made synthetically.

SCORODITE

A mineral which has been reported from a gem laboratory is a variety of scorodite having an unusual blue colour with reddish overtones. Scorodite, which crystallizes in the orthorhombic system, is a hydrated zinc arsenate. The normal colour of the material is leek green to liver brown. The hardness of the mineral is 4 on Mohs's scale and it is soluble in hydrochloric acid, hence it would not in any way produce a durable stone. The density is 3·22, and the refractive indices vary between 1·74 and 1·81 and the stone shows pronounced pleochroism. The stone described came from Tsumeb, South-West Africa.

SERPENTINE

As an ornamental material serpentine is encountered in two main forms; as a hard massive variety known as bowenite and as the 'serpentine marble', which occurs as rock masses mixed with other minerals. The name serpentine is in some doubt, one version suggesting that the name arose from the ancient view that the mineral was a cure for a serpent's bite, and another, and perhaps better suggestion, that it was because of the resemblance of the dark green mottled variety to the skin of a serpent.

There can be many variations of the mineral and since the 19th century mineralogists have divided the serpentines into groups, and again into varieties, to some of which specific names have been applied. Most of these have no place in gemmology. A better division for gem purposes is: precious, or noble, serpentine comprising the purer translucent varieties having an oil-green colour; and the resinous-waxy yellow to yellow-green material called retinalite. The second type is the so called common serpentine which includes the rock-like types.

From x-ray studies G. Selfridge divided the serpentines into two groups, serpentine and antigorite, and he suggested the name serpentinite for the rock-like forms of serpentine, antigorite or a mixture of both. E. Whittacker and J. Zussman have more recently divided the serpentines into three groups: lizardite, antigorite and chrysotile.

Serpentine is a hydrated silicate of magnesium ($H_4Mg_3Si_2O_9$) and crystallizes in the monoclinic system, but the mineral is always massive and is never encountered as crystals. A number of different geological processes may produce the mineral by alteration of basic rocks of igneous origin or of metamorphic pyroxenes. Serpentine is soft, about $2\frac{1}{2}$ on Mohs's scale, except in the variety bowenite, which reaches 4 or more. The rock-like types may also vary in their hardness owing to the admixture of other minerals.

Most of the bowenite variety of serpentine used so much today for carvings and other articles of virtu is a translucent yellowish-green material, which often contains whitish cloudy patches. The density is 2·58–2·59 and the mean refractive index—all that is likely to be seen on a refractometer—is 1·56. The absorption spectrum shows bands at 4970 and 4640 Å but they have little diagnostic value. Owing to the iron content which in part gives the green colour to serpentine there is little, if any, luminescence under any excitation by ultra-violet light or x-rays. X-ray patterns have shown that bowenite belongs to the antigorite group of serpentines.

There is a translucent deep green or bluish-green variety of bowenite found in the South Island of New Zealand which was used by the Maoris, but little dark green bowenite is encountered today, nor is the rather coarser dark green bowenite from the Delaware river, Pennsylvania, and at Smithfield, Rhode Island, seemingly used. The density of a Maori earpendant in dark translucent bluish-green bowenite serpentine was found to be 2·617, slightly higher than the usual density for bowenite.

Much light yellowish-green bowenite, in the form of carved figurines has been exported from China to the Western World under the misnomer 'New Jade'. It is possible that this mineral has emanated from Tuoyuan in Hunan Province. Bowenite, known to the Persians as 'sang-i-yashm', is found in Afghanistan, and this material is utilized at Bhera in the Shahpur district of the Punjab for the manufacture of dagger hilts, knife handles, caskets, amulets and other articles. Afghan bowenite appears to occur in rock masses at the head of one of the mountain gorges that run down from the Safed Koh into the valley of the Kabul river. Bowenite, and other serpentines are found in South Africa.

A variety of serpentine called williamsite is a translucent stone of oil-green colour, often with whitish veins of brucite and cloudy patches; it also contains dark cubic or octahedral crystals which may be chromite or magnetite. Williamsite has a refractive index near to 1·57 and specimens were found to have a density near to 2·61. Under the long-wave ultra-violet lamp this variety of serpentine shows a weak whitish-green glow but is inert under the short-wave lamp and under x-rays. Some williamsite is found in the United States of America.

A deposit of serpentine, usually worked by native craftsmen, is found some 16,000 feet up in the Karakoram Mountains in Kashmir. The material was found to have a hardness of $2\frac{1}{2}$ on Mohs's scale; a density of 2·56 and an index of refraction of about 1·56. X-ray powder patterns showed that the material was lizardite with some brucite.

Two other varieties of serpentine should be mentioned. These are ricolite, which is a fine-grained serpentine occurring in curious coloured bands and is found at Rico in New Mexico; and satelite, a fibrous greyish to greenish-blue coloured material which produces a type of cat's-eye and comes from Maryland and California in the United States. It may be a variety of chrysotile.

The most notable source of the serpentine marble in classical times was the brecciated serpentine quarried at Casambala, a few miles north-east of Larissa in Thessaly, and known as Verde Antico; it was known to the Romans as Lapis Atracius for the quarries were near the ancient town of Atrax. It has been reported that the quarries were destroyed by the Germans during World War II. Some authorities class the Verde Antique with the ophicalcites. Much fine serpentine is found near Genoa and Levanto in Liguria, and near Prato in Tuscany. These Italian serpentines vary from green to brownish-red in colour and often the material is veined with white steatite.

In England the best known serpentine rock is that found on the southern promontory of the Lizard peninsula, Cornwall. The Cornish serpentines (the major quarries are at Kennack Cove, Kynance Cove, Spernic Cove and Carleon Cove) vary considerably in colour and texture and may be green, veined or spotted with red, brown or white, or may be red or purple to nearly black and relieved by coloured veining. The Lizard serpentine is usually fashioned locally into small wares suitable for the tourist. Serpentine marble is found at Rhoscolyn, Holy Island, which is off Anglesey, Wales. It is known locally as Mona marble. Another source of serpentine is at Portsoy, Banffshire, Scotland. Rock-like serpentines are found at St. Paul in the French Basses-Alpes, south of Innsbruck in the Austrian Tyrol, and at Hof Gastein in the province of Salzburg. A slightly banded material in two shades of green is found at the Congo Vaal mine near Carolina, Transvaal, South Africa, two pieces of which gave densities of 2·595 and 2·603. The material has been found to consist of antigorite with the lighter stripes of antigorite and calcite, to have a hardness of about $4\frac{1}{2}$ on Mohs's scale and therefore can be placed with the bowenites.

The density of serpentine marble varies somewhat, as might be expected in such an impure rock. The values between 2·5 and 2·7 are those most commonly found and in only a few cases have densities been recorded outside this range. Except for the hardness the other properties agree with those of bowenite. Serpentine has been stained to imitate jade.

Another variation of serpentine, which has been referred to earlier under 'Marble', is the serpentine mixed with more or less calcite, dolomite or

295

magnesite, producing a rock of clouded white to green which is called ophicalcite or ophicite. The best known of this material is that which comes from Connemara in Eire, and hence called 'Connemara marble' or 'Irish green marble'. The hardness of this material is about 3 on Mohs's scale and the index of refraction about 1·56. The density varies considerably and lies between 2·48 and 2·77. There is a strong absorption band at 4650 Å.

A variety of aluminous serpentine is pseudophite, or as it is often mis-called 'Styrian jade', a material which has been used to fashion small bowls and ornamental pieces. The material is found at Bernstein, Burgen-land, Austria, about 57 miles south of Vienna on the borders of Styria and Austria, a place which, before the Versailles Treaty, was in Hungary. Another material of similar appearance is found at Gurtipohl near St. Gallenkirche in Montafon Valley, Vorarlberg, a province of Austria which lies between the Tyrol and Liechtenstein. This material is worked as an ornamental stone under the name miskeyite. Pseudophite is soft, with a hardness of $2\frac{1}{2}$ on Mohs's scale, and the mineral is somewhat similar to the rock known as chlorite schist. The refractive index is about 1·57 and the density 2·69.

SHATTUCKITE (now PLANCHÉITE)

A hydrated copper silicate ($2CuSiO_3H_2O$) shattuckite is a compact granular or fibrous mineral of a blue colour, which may have an appearance like some turquoise or azurite. The fibres are of monoclinic symmetry but the material is massive and when cut is practically opaque. The density of the mineral is about 3·8 and the refractive indices are 1·752 and 1·815 for the principal directions, but only a vague reading of about 1·75 would be seen on a refractometer. Shattuckite is mainly found at the Shattuck mine, Bisbee, Arizona, where it forms pseudomorphs after malachite. Some material shows green patches, which may be malachite. The mineral has also been reported from Katanga in the Congo. The shattuckite which is fashioned, often by the tumbling process, is shattuckite in quartz or another mineral, and thus has a density which will not agree with shattuck-ite as a mineral. Densities of 2·84, 2·67 and as low as 2·53 have been recorded for this mixed material. Shattuckite has now been made synony-mous with planchéite, but the old name is kept here as being better known as a gem material.

SIDERITE (Chalybite)

A cut stone of this iron carbonate mineral has been reported, the specimen having a pistachio-brown colour. Siderite ($FeCO_3$) crystallizes in the tri-gonal system and is really too soft for a cut stone. The hardness is $3\frac{1}{2}$ to 4 on Mohs's scale; the density is 3·83 to 3·88, and the refractive indices $\omega = 1\cdot873$—$\varepsilon = 1\cdot633$; thus the birefringence is 0·240 and negative in sign. The cut stone reported is said to have come from Pinasquevia, Portugal.

SINHALITE

For a number of years a stone understood to be brown peridot has been known. The stone has refractive indices and other properties close to those of peridot, but has the somewhat higher density of 3·48, a discrepancy ascribed to an increase of unessential iron. In 1952 the nature of the stone was questioned and by means of x-ray crystallographic and chemical analysis the stone was found to be a completely new mineral species. It is a magnesium aluminium iron borate with the formula $Mg(Al,Fe)BO_4$ (peridot is $(Mg,Fe)SiO_4$). The colour of sinhalite varies from pale yellow-brown to golden or greenish-brown to black, the depth of colour being in relation to the iron content. The stones have a strong resemblance to brown chrysoberyl or brown zircon.

The crystallization of sinhalite is orthorhombic, but except for an isolated recovery of a good crystal from the Burma gem gravels, the material is found only as rolled pebbles from the gem gravels of Ceylon. Indeed, it is from Sinhala, the Sanskrit name for Ceylon, that the name of the species is derived. Sinhalite has been found in a contact metamorphic limestone in Warren County, New York, but this has no gem significance.

The hardness of sinhalite is $6\frac{1}{2}$ on Mohs's scale, the density lies between 3·47 and 3·49 and the refractive indices are 1·67 and 1·71 for the principal rays, the negative biaxial birefringence being 0·038. The pleochroism is distinct with the colours pale brown, greenish-brown and dark brown. The dispersion is 0·018 between the B and G interval, and the absorption spectrum is similar to that of peridot; the bands are at 4930, 4750, 4630 and 4520 Å, and there is a general absorption of the violet. Sinhalite does not luminesce.

SMITHSONITE

The bluish-green and green massive varieties of smithsonite, the zinc carbonate ($ZnCO_3$) which crystallizes in the trigonal system, have been cut as cabochon stones and mounted in jewellery under the name Bonamite, after the French for Goodfriend—Goodfriend Brothers first marketed the stones. The stones have a low hardness, 5 on Mohs's scale, but they are quickly identified by the high density which approximates to 4·3. The indices of refraction are 1·621 and 1·849, the refraction being uniaxial and negative in sign with double refraction of 0·228. As the material is usually massive these optical constants are not very helpful, as only a vague edge would be seen on the refractometer. Being a carbonate, smithsonite will effervesce when touched with acid and this may be used as a test if an inconspicuous part of the back is tested, for the acid will take away the polish. Apart from the green and greeny-blue material which is the common type used in jewellery, there is a pink smithsonite, due to cobalt, and a yellow variety which owes its colour to cadmium. Smithsonite is found at Laurium in Greece, Tsumeb in South-West Africa, Sardinia, Santander in Spain and New Mexico and Utah in the United States of America.

The zinc silicate mineral hemimorphite ($Zn_4(OH)Si_2O_7,H_2O$) is usually associated with smithsonite and massive material of blue or green colour, the colours often being banded, has been fashioned. The crystallization of the mineral is orthorhombic, the crystals when found doubly terminated show different inclinations of the faces at each end (hemimorphism) and hence the name of the mineral. The hardness is 5 on Mohs's scale, the principal refractive indices are 1·614 and 1·636. The density varies from 3·4 to 3·5. The localities for hemimorphite are similar to those for smithsonite.

SOAPSTONE

Soapstone is the massive variety of the mineral talc or steatite, an acid metasilicate of magnesium ($H_2Mg_3(SiO_3)_4$), and is used for carved ornaments. The mineral may be white to silvery-white, but because of impurities it may be green, brown, yellow or reddish, and often veined and mottled. The hardness of talc is 1 on Mohs's scale, but owing to the presence of impurities soapstone may be considerably harder, although it may usually be scratched by the finger-nail. The mineral is said to harden by the action of heat. Soapstone has a greasy feel and the density—which for pure talc is between 2·7 and 2·8—has a much greater variation and may be anything from 2·20 to 2·80. The refractive indices for talc are approximately 1·54 and 1·59 for the principal rays, but only a vague edge at about 1·54 would be seen on the refractometer in the case of the massive soapstone. The material does not luminesce. Soapstone is extensively carved into ornaments by the Chinese and the material had many uses in olden days, for the earliest scarabs of the Egyptians were of steatite and three-sided prism seals found at Knossos were of the same material. Steatite is of world-wide occurrence, and in some places forms extensive beds. The mineral is often associated with serpentine and with chlorite schists, and may be pseudomorphic after quartz. Notable localities are at the Limbue quarries, Lake Nyasa, central Africa, and in quarries at Kundol, Tdar State, Bombay Presidency, India. Some varieties of Indian steatite bear the name pratima culler or image stone. Some agalmatolite is steatite.

SODALITE

Best known as one of the components of lapis-lazuli, sodalite became of importance as an ornamental mineral on the discovery in Canada of masses of sodalite of a rich blue colour. Sodalite forms cubic crystals, usually of dodecahedral habit, which may be grey, greenish, yellowish, white, light red or blue in colour. It is only the blue-coloured massive variety which is used as an ornamental stone, a stone which in appearance may well be mistaken for lapis-lazuli.

In composition sodalite is a sodium aluminium silicate with sodium chloride ($3NaAlSiO_4.NaCl$) and the hardness of the mineral is $5\frac{1}{2}$–6 on Mohs's scale. The density varies from 2·15 to 2·35, but the value for the massive blue variety is near to 2·28. The refractive index is 1·48. Sodalite luminesces with patches of orange-coloured light when under ultra-violet light. The blue mineral has been found in the Langesundfjord district of southern Norway and also at Litchfield and West Gardner, Kennebec, Maine and at Salem, Essex County, Massachusetts in the United States of America. Another source is in the State of Rajputana (Rajasthan), India. The major commercial source is the massive royal blue material, often speckled with small spots of bright red, pink or orange, which may also include feldspar, which is found near Bancroft in the township of Dungannon, Hastings County, Ontario, where it occurs as segregations in a belt of nepheline syenite. Other Canadian localities are in the counties of Peterborough and Haliburton, Ontario, and in the rocks of Mount Royal in the City of Montreal.

Sodalite is also found in Bahia, Brazil; the Ice River, British Columbia, and very beautiful rich blue and more crystalline material comes from near Ohopoho in the northern region of South-West Africa.

Sodalite is fashioned as cabochons and beads, and is cut and polished into slabs for use as inlays in clock cases and cigarette boxes, when the lovely blue colour blends so admirably with the creamy-white 'onyx marbles'. The mineral was found in Canada at the time of a Royal visit and the blue sodalite was thus named 'Princess Blue'. In recent times the material used for inlay is termed in the trade by the names 'Canadian Blue Stone' or just 'Bluestone'.

Sodalite never reaches the beautiful ultramarine blue of true lapis-lazuli, the colour being more of a royal blue. Further, sodalite rarely contains the brassy specks of pyrites as is found in lapis, but it has been reported that pyrites has been seen in sodalite, so proof of lapis is not obtained by mere inspection. The density will provide a surer test, for the density of lapis is higher (2·75–2·95).

SPHENE

Sphene, which is either yellow, brown or green in gem quality material, is a very brilliant transparent stone with a resinous to adamantine lustre. It is named after the wedge-like shape of the monoclinic crystals, which are often twinned. The crystals are found in cavities in gneiss and granite, and also in such metamorphic rocks as schists and certain granular limestones.

Cut sphenes are characterized by having a pronounced fire, hence for the best effect the stones are always faceted in the brilliant or mixed cut styles and never in the cabochon form. Sphenes are magnificent stones when freshly cut, but the low hardness of $5\frac{1}{2}$ on Mohs's scale does not make the stones suitable for constant wear.

Sphene is a silicate of titanium and calcium ($CaTiSiO_5$) and it is from the titanium content that the alternative name for the species, titanite, is derived. The latter name, however, is more usually applied to the black or reddish-brown non-gem quality material. Some iron is always present in sphene and the rare-earths cerium and yttrium are commonly present. This trace of rare-earth impurity manifests itself in the absorption spectrum which generally shows, albeit weakly, the typical rare-earth spectrum of didymium.

The refraction of sphene is biaxial and positive in sign, the refractive indices varying from 1·885 and 1·990 to 1·915 and 2·050 for the two major directions. The double refraction likewise varies from 0·105 to 0·135, and thus exceeds in amount many other gemstones, so that the doubling of the back facets will be observed with ease. The stones show strong trichroism, the colours for the principal directions being greenish-yellow, reddish-yellow and nearly colourless, but the exact shades depend on the colour of the stone. The dispersion of sphene is 0·051 for the B to G interval, a fire greater than that of diamond. The density varies between 3·52 and 3·54 and sphene, probably owing to the presence of iron, does not exhibit luminescence. The stones are brittle and also have a weak cleavage.

The major localities for gem sphene are at Schwarzenstein and Rotenkopf in the Zillerthal of the Austrian Tyrol, in the St. Gotthard and the Grisons in Switzerland, in Renfrew County, Ontario, Canada, in Madagascar, and a very fine cut stone of 22·26 carats, which had a density of 3·542, and was an orange-brown colour came from the Burma Stone Tract. Both brown and green coloured sphenes are found at El Alamo, Pino Solo and San Quintin in Baja California. Brazil is another source.

STAUROLITE

Faceted gems of a deep brown colour have been cut from transparent crystals, but most staurolite is prized for the cross-shaped interpenetrant twin crystals which cross one another at nearly 90 degrees or 60 degrees (*Figure 16.7*). These crystals provide one of the so-called 'cross stones' (the

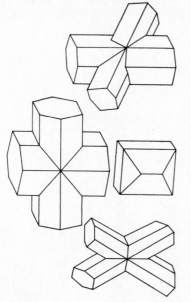

Figure 16.7. Typical crystals of staurolite

other being the chiastolite variety of andalusite) which are used as amulets and baptismal stones in Mediterranean countries. Staurolite is a hydrated aluminium silicate. A suggested formula is $2Al_2SiO_5Fe(OH)_2$, which shows the mineral to have a chemical relationship to kyanite. There may, however, be small scale isomorphous replacement by magnesium, manganese, cobalt or nickel. The crystals, which belong to the orthorhombic system, have a weak cleavage and show a conchoidal fracture. The hardness of staurolite is $7-7\frac{1}{2}$ on Mohs's scale, the density, which varies somewhat from 3·65 to 3·78, is generally just over 3·7. The refractive indices, biaxial and positive in sign, vary from 1·739 to 1·747 for the α ray, 1·744 to 1·754 for the β index, and 1·750 to 1·762 for the γ index; the birefringence varying from 0·011 to 0·015. The pleochroism is distinct but varies somewhat in the colours seen. These are usually colourless and some shade of yellow or red. The dispersion of staurolite is 0·023 for the B to G interval. The absorption spectrum shows a weak band at 5780 Å and a strong one at 4490 Å, but these are of no diagnostic importance. Staurolite does not show luminescence. The mineral occurs in crystalline schists and gneiss due to regional metamorphism and the crystals are often associated with garnet, fibrolite, and tourmaline. Staurolite is found in the Ticino and St. Gotthard districts of Switzerland, Finisterre and Morbihan in Brittany, France, Brazil, Russia, Scotland and several of the states of North America.

STIBIOTANTALITE

The transparent brownish-yellow niobate and tantalate of antimony ($SbO_2(Ta,Nb)_2O_6$), stibiotantalite, has been cut for collectors. To avoid confusion it may be mentioned that the earlier name for niobium (Nb) is columbium (Cb), the latter term being more commonly used in the United States of America for the element, and Cb is the symbol used in the Chart of the Periodic Systems used in this book. Stibiotantalite crystallizes in the orthorhombic system, has an adamantine to resinous lustre and one direction of distinct cleavage. The mineral has a decided resemblance to zinc blende. The hardness is $5\frac{1}{2}$–6 on Mohs's scale and the refractive indices are 2·46 and 2·39 for the greatest and least values respectively. The biaxial refraction is positive in sign. A specimen of the gemmy material, which comes mainly from Mesa Grande, San Diego County, California in the United States of America, was found to have a density of 7·46, but lower values for the mineral are given in mineralogical literature.

STICHTITE

A few cabochon stones of the rose-red or lilac-coloured mineral stichtite have been seen in collections of gem materials. Stichtite is a rather soft (hardness $2\frac{1}{2}$ on Mohs's scale) alteration product of serpentine and owes its red colour to the presence of chromium. In composition it is a hydrated carbonate-hydroxide of magnesium and chromium ($Mg_6Cr_2(OH)_{16}CO_3.4H_2O$), but the chromium is often replaced in part by iron. The mineral is opaque and often veined with green and is found massive as a matted aggregate of plates, fibres or micaceous scales which are small trigonal crystals, and which have a strong basal cleavage. By thin section mineralogical methods stichtite has been found to have uniaxial crystallization and to have refractive indices of 1·55 for the ordinary ray and 1·52 for the extraordinary ray, with a negative birefringence of 0·027. The fibres are pleochroic in shades of light and dark red, but this is not easily seen in the massive material. Likewise, in the mass only a blurred shadow edge will be seen in the refractometer at about 1·53. The material is rather friable and has a greasy, wax-like or pearly lustre, and the density has been found to range from 2·15 to 2·22 with South African material and 2·16 in material from Quebec. The absorption spectrum shown by stichtite is typically that of chromium, with three lines in the red at 6655 and 6300 Å and the third line approximately midway between. There are broad absorptions in the yellow-green and in the violet, the 'window' of blue light being centred at 5000 Å. No luminescence is shown by stichtite. First identified as a new material in 1910 from material found at Dundas in Tasmania, stichtite was also reported from the Black Lake district of Canada in 1918. In the same year the deposit in the Barberton district of Transvaal was mentioned although the material was first found here as early as 1883 but not reported upon. There is another occurrence in Algeria. The mineral was named after Robert Sticht of Tasmania.

TAAFFEITE

In 1945, Count Taaffe, a Dublin gemmologist, came across a pale mauve cut stone which had most of the characteristics of spinel but which showed distinct signs of double refraction. Investigation showed that the stone was a completely new mineral. This was followed by the finding of a second cut stone in 1949 and yet a third in the United States of America in 1957. These, and a stone of 5·34 carats found in 1967, are the sole representatives of the mineral species taaffeite, named after the finder of the first stone.

Taaffeite is a beryllium magnesium aluminate ($Be_4Mg_4Al_{16}O_{32}$) and seems to be the only known mineral having both beryllium and magnesium as essential constituents. The chemical composition indicates that the stone is intermediate between spinel and chrysoberyl. The system of crystallization is hexagonal and the habit is hexagonal prismatic as found in small crystals in rocks.

The hardness is 8 on Mohs's scale; the density is from 3·60 to 3·61 and the indices of refraction vary from 1·721 to 1·723 for the ordinary ray and from 1·717 to 1·718 for the extraordinary ray, the mineral having the small negative uniaxial birefringence of 0·004. The stones were too pale for the dichroism to be observed and the same reasoning applies to the absorption spectrum. However, in the original stone found by Count Taaffe a vague band in the blue was observed very near to and exactly like the band shown by blue spinel, a band due to ferrous iron, at 4580 Å. The fluorescence shown by these stones under ultra-violet light is a distinct green and this is more pronounced under x-rays, a luminescent glow similar to that shown by pale mauve spinels. The locality of taaffeite is unknown but the stones are believed to come from Ceylon.

THOMSONITE

Belonging to the zeolite family of minerals, thomsonite is a hydrated calcium sodium aluminium silicate—$(Ca,Na_2)Al_2Si_2O_8.H_2O$—which crystallizes in the orthorhombic system. The gem material is mostly columnar with a radial structure, or as radiated spherical aggregates or concretions, which are translucent and closely resemble agate. They may be milk-white, yellow, reddish, brownish and greenish, the fibres being arranged radially producing eye-like forms (Plate XIX, facing page 268).

Thomsonite has a hardness of about 5 on Mohs's scale; the density varies from 2·3 to 2·4, and the refractive indices are also variable and may have limits between 1·52 and 1·54, a vague shadow edge is all that would be seen on a refractometer. The lustre is porcellaneous and the stones take a good polish although they are somewhat brittle. Under ultra-violet light the luminescence seen is patchy with brownish and whitish glows.

The mineral occurs in cavities in lavas and other igneous rocks as a secondary mineral resulting from the alteration of feldspars and nephelite. The gemmy material is found on the shores of Lake Superior, particularly at Thomsonite Beach and the Isle Royale in the lake. A variety with a translucent olive-green colour, and which resembles some jadeite and is remarkably different from the usual 'eyed' thomsonite, is lintonite, which is found along the shores of Stockly Bay, Michigan, and near Grand Marais, Minnesota. A specimen of lintonite gave a density of 2·364 and refractive index of 1·53. A snow white variety of thomsonite from Arkansas is called ozarkite.

TREMOLITE

Tremolite (grammatite) is better known when in a compact mass of felted crystals as mutton-fat jade (nephrite). Two very dissimilar varieties of this monoclinic calcium magnesium silicate mineral need to be mentioned. The first is a greenish chatoyant variety which gives a good cat's-eye effect when cut cabochon and which comes from Ontario, Canada. The second is an attractive transparent lilac-pink variety (hexagonite) found at Fowler, St. Lawrence County, New York. A specimen of the cat's-eye type gave a density of 2·976 and a crystal of hexagonite a value of 2·980. The hardness of tremolite lies between $5\frac{1}{2}$ and 6 on Mohs's scale and the refractive indices are 1·60 and 1·62 for the least and the greatest indices. Hexagonite shows an orange fluorescence. An amphibole cat's-eye of tourmaline-green colour has come from Burma.

ULEXITE

Strictly not a gemstone, ulexite is included owing to its mention in gem literature for the curious optical effect which can be produced by the mineral. Ulexite is a hydrated borate of calcium and sodium ($NaCaB_5O_9.8H_2O$) and the mineral is made up of fine fibrous crystals of the monoclinic system. The hardness is 1 on Mohs's scale and the density is 1·65 or slightly higher. Specimens of the massive ulexite examined gave a hardness of 2, a density near 1·99 and the mean refractive index was found to be 1·51. The mineral is said to fluoresce blue and green under short-wave ultraviolet light and many specimens show phosphorescence.

The fibrous nature of the mineral allows cabochon stones to give an exceptionally good cat's-eye effect, but the material is far too soft and friable to be so used. The most interesting effect is seen when a slab of the mineral is cut and polished on both faces, so that the polished planes are at right angles to the direction of the fibres. It is seen then that the fibres are so straight and reflective that when newsprint is placed against one polished face it appears as if by magic, even with an inch or more of intervening mineral, on the opposite face. Such cut plates of ulexite have been called 'Television Stones'. The material emanates from the borax deposits of California, U.S.A.

UNAKITE

A variegated rock in red, pink and green colours used, particularly by amateur lapidaries, in the United States of America, is unakite. The material is a type of granite containing quartz, pink feldspar and green epidote and the rock owes its name to the source in the Unaka range of North Carolina, where it was first found. Other localities in the United States of America are said to produce the rock. The density of the material is variable depending upon the relative amounts of the heavier epidote and the lighter quartz and feldspar; values varying from 2·85 to 3·2 have been recorded. The refractive indices vary according to the areas examined and examination of one specimen showed that the pink areas gave an index of 1·52, the green areas 1·76 and the white parts 1·55. The material is prized simply for its mottled colouring and is usually fashioned in the cabochon form or tumbled baroques. Similar material comes from Rhodesia and from Galway Bay, Eire. The epidote of various colours found in the vicinity of Keimos, in Northern Cape, South Africa and sold as an ornamental stone under the name okkolite, may be a similar material.

VARISCITE

Despite its rich green to greenish-blue colour variscite has a limited use as a gem material. The mineral is a hydrous aluminium phosphate $(AlPO_4.2H_2O)$ but replacement of some of the aluminium by chromium and iron occurs, and to this the colour is due. The gem material is a massive variety composed of a compact mass of fibres of orthorhombic crystallization, which have biaxial negative birefringence; the principal refractive indices varying from 1·55 to 1·56 and from 1·58 to 1·59. A vague edge at 1·56 is all that would be seen in the case of the gemmy massive material. The hardness is 5 on Mohs's scale and the density varies from 2·4 to 2·6. The lustre is vitreous and the absorption spectrum shows a strong line at 6880 Å and a weaker line at 6500 Å; there is no luminescence shown by the mineral.

Variscite is found at Messbach in Saxon Voightland, sometime Variscia, and it is from this that the name of the mineral is derived. The most important source of gemmy material is the nodular masses called utahlite found in Tooele County, Utah. Banded material from Utah is known as sabalite or trainite, after the collector Percy Train of Manhattan. Ely in Nevada is another American source and much of the American material is concretions of variscite in quartz or chalcedony to which the name amatrice is given. A material which has the properties of variscite emanates from the top of a mountain near the town of Dayboro, about 40 miles north-west of Brisbane in Queensland, Australia. This material has been referred to as 'Australian turquoise' or 'Australian jade'.

VERDITE

A deep green ornamental stone often containing red or yellow spots was found in 1907 on the south bank of the Nord Kaap river, in the Barbeton district of Transvaal in South Africa, and from its colour the mineral was named verdite. Essentially a rock, it may be referred to as a massive muscovite rock coloured green by the chromiferous mica fuchsite. The material is rather soft, 3 on Mohs's scale, and the refractive index is about

1·58. The density varies between 2·80 and 2·99. The absorption spectrum shows three lines in the deep red and a vague line in the blue, a spectrum reminiscent of chromium coloured minerals. The rock does not exhibit luminescence. Similar material has been reported from the Piggs Peak mines, Swaziland, South Africa, and from the western slopes of the Green mountain range near Shrewsbury in Vermont, U.S.A. This latter material is known as the 'Green marble of Shrewsbury'. Somewhat similar material is found at Roeburne, Pilbara district, Western Australia, and probably in Venezuela and in the Canal Zone of Central America. There is a report extant that a vase found at Mohenjo-Dara, India, and reputed to be not later than 2750 B.C., is fashioned from a green mica rock, and may be nearly pure fuchsite.

Another rock of somewhat similar composition is selwynite. The material has been found to consist of chrome mica (fuchsite) with either diaspore or chlorite, and could be called an impure massive fuchsite. Specimens of this material gave a range of density of 2·79 to 3·11; the refractive index about 1·55. Vague chromium lines in the red end of the absorption spectrum could be seen. The rock comes from the Heathcote area of Victoria, Australia.

WARDITE

Found as bluish-green concretionary incrustations in cavities of nodular variscite at Cedar Valley, Utah, this mineral has some resemblance to turquoise. It is thought to be tetragonal in crystallization, has a hardness of 5 on Mohs's scale, a density of 2·81 and the refractive indices are 1·590 and 1·599. The mineral is a hydrous aluminium phosphate with the formula $Na_4CaAl_{12}(PO_4)_8(OH)_{18},6H_2O$. Sousmansite from Montebras in Sousmans, Creuse, France, may be identical with wardite.

WHEWELLITE

Clear colourless monoclinic crystals of the calcium oxalate mineral $(CaC_2O_4.H_2O)$ have been cut for collectors. With a hardness of only $2\frac{1}{2}$ on Mohs's scale such stones make unsatisfactory gems. The density is 2·23 and the biaxial optically positive refraction has indices α 1·490, β 1·555 and γ 1·650, thus the double refraction is large in amount at 0·160. The mineral has been reported from Saxony, Bohemia (Czechoslovakia) and Alsace, France.

WILLEMITE

Willemite, a zinc silicate (Zn_2SiO_4) which is chemically and crystallographically related to phenacite, is most important as an ore of zinc. The mineral is, however, occasionally found in transparent crystals of the trigonal system. It is from these crystals that a few greenish-yellow stones have been cut. The stones do not take a good polish, they have a somewhat resinous lustre, a low hardness ($5\frac{1}{2}$ on Mohs's scale) and a brittle nature with a conchoidal fracture. These preclude the stones from being cut into attractive gems. Some orange stones do, however, take a good polish.

The density of willemite varies between 3·89 and 4·18 and the refractive indices are 1·69 and 1·72, the uniaxial birefringence is 0·028 and is positive in sign. The dichroism is variable. The absorption spectrum shows several weak bands at 5830, 5400, 4900, 4420 and 4320 Å, and there is a strong band at 4210 Å. The yellow colour of the stone is due to iron, but much willemite contains traces of manganese to which is due the brilliant bright green fluorescence of the mineral when under the rays from an ultra-violet lamp or x-rays. Strong and persistent phosphorescence is often exhibited by willemite. The mineral, which is named after William I of the Nether-lands, is found in a number of localities, but the gemmy crystals mainly come from Franklin Furnace, New Jersey, the important zinc mining location of the United States of America.

WITHERITE

Translucent witherite of an off-white colour has been cut as collectors' pieces. Orthorhombic in crystallization, the mineral has the composition of barium carbonate ($BaCO_3$), a hardness near to $3\frac{1}{2}$ on Mohs's scale and a density which lies between 4·27 and 4·35. The refractive indices are α 1·532, β 1·678 and γ 1·680, the biaxial double refraction, negative in sign, is 0·148, which is large in amount and typical of a carbonate mineral. Witherite will effervesce with acid. The mineral is found in Cumberland and Northumber-land in England, in Japan, near Rosiclare, Illinois, U.S.A., and at Thunder Bay, Ontario, Canada.

WOLLASTONITE

A cabochon of white compact wollastonite, a calcium metasilicate ($CaSiO_3$), has been encountered. Wollastonite crystallizes in the monoclinic system and has a hardness of $4\frac{1}{2}$–5 on Mohs's scale. The density is from 2·8 to 2·9, and the optically negative biaxial refraction has values of 1·61 and 1·63 for the principal indices. The material when massive is identified with difficulty and may need an x-ray powder photograph to determine the mineral correctly. Wollastonite is found in Finland, Romania, Mexico, and in several of the states of North America. A compact variety is found on the Isle Royale in Lake Superior.

WULFENITE

More important for the beautiful crystal specimens which the mineral forms, wulfenite is found in tabular crystals of the tetragonal system which may be orange, yellow, green, grey or white in colour. The mineral is a lead molybdate ($PbMoO_4$), has a hardness of just below 3 on Mohs's scale, and a density varying from 6·7 to 7·0. The uniaxial birefringence is negative in sign, with indices of 2·402 for the ordinary ray and 2·304 for the extra-ordinary ray. Wulfenite is a secondary mineral found in lead and zinc deposits in Austria, Yugoslavia, Poland, Bohemia, Morocco, the Congo Republic, New South Wales, Mexico and the United States of America. The mineral is far too soft for use as a gemstone and is attractive only for its colour. It has apparently been cut for those who desire the unusual.

ZINC BLENDE (Sphalerite)

Often better known in its shortened form—blende—the mineral is a common and important ore of zinc. Usually the mineral is nearly black in colour, but occasionally it is found in transparent pieces of a yellowish-brown hue. It is from this latter material that the few faceted stones have been cut to satisfy those who prize the unusual. The low hardness, $3\frac{1}{2}$–4 on Mohs's scale, coupled with a perfect dodecahedral cleavage (6 directions) precludes zinc blende having much value as a gemstone. The density of the mineral is 4·09 and the refractive index is 2·37. Zinc blende has a large colour dispersion (0·156 for the B to G interval) which is over three times the fire shown by diamond. An absorption spectrum consisting of three bands in the red can sometimes be observed in zinc blende. They are at 6900 Å, 6670 Å, which is the strongest, and 6510 Å. Much zinc blende does not show these lines, which have been attributed to cadmium, but there is a danger that if they are present they may be mistaken for a zircon spectrum.

Blende, a zinc sulphide (ZnS), crystallizes in the cubic system, generally in tetrahedra, but often with cube, dodecahedral and trisoctahedral forms. Twins are common. The name zinc blende is derived from the German blenden (to deceive), because while resembling galena (lead sulphide) it yields no lead. In North American mineralogy the name sphalerite is used instead of zinc blende, and again this name is derived from the mining world—it means 'treacherous'. Zinc blende has been used for the 'dense-glass' prisms of refractometers.

The mineral has world-wide occurrence but the major localities for the transparent material are the Chivera mine, Cananea, Sonora, Mexico and Picos de Europa in the Cordillera Cantabrica, near Santander on the northern coast of Spain. An interesting variety, not of gem quality, is a massive granular variety from Tsumeb, north of Otavi in South-West Africa, which exhibits triboluminescence—that is, when struck or rubbed with a blade of a knife or wire brush, it emits showers of orange-coloured sparks. Except for this type, which also fluoresces orange under the influence of the ultra-violet lamp, zinc blende does not fluoresce.

ZINCITE

The red oxide of zinc (ZnO) has occasionally been found as irregular transparent pieces, but rarely as crystals, from which a few stones have been cut. The mineral crystallizes in the hexagonal system, is rather soft (4–$4\frac{1}{2}$ on Mohs's scale) and the density for gem quality material is near to 5·66. Owing to the high indices of refraction, 2·013 for the ordinary ray and 2·029 for the extraordinary ray, the lustre is adamantine. The uniaxial birefringence, which is positive in sign, is 0·016. Zincite, which if pure would be white in colour, owes its orange-yellow to deep red hue to traces of manganese oxide (MnO). The mineral does not fluoresce. The gem quality zincite is found in the famous zinc mines of Franklin Furnace, New Jersey in the United States of America.

ZOISITE

Before 1967 the only varieties of zoisite which had any pretensions as a gem material were the pink ornamental mineral known as thulite, and the green chrome-rich material with included black amphibole, which acts as the matrix for the large hexagonal crystals of ruby found in Tanzania. However, in 1967 beautiful transparent blue-violet crystals of zoisite were found in the Gilewy Hills in Tanga Province, Tanzania, and from these crystals amazingly attractive stones have been cut (see Plate XIV).

The cut stones, which are now being marketed under the name Tanzanite, are recovered from many deposits in the Umba valley. The crystals are found in various colours: blue, green, yellow, pink, brown and a peculiar colour which has been described as 'khaki'. All these shades of colour are said to turn to the favoured blue on careful heat treatment, and this is usually carried out. The heating is said to be carried out at 700°F (380°C) and any serious increase from this temperature is hazardous as at higher temperatures the stones tend to disintegrate.

Zoisite, which belongs to the epidote group of minerals, forms orthorhombic crystals and accords to the formula $Ca_2(Al.OH)Al_2(SiO_4)_3$. The hardness is just over 6 on Mohs's scale; the density 3·35 and the refractive indices are $\alpha = 1·692$, $\beta = 1·693$ and $\gamma = 1·700$ with positive birefringence of 0·0088. There is one perfect cleavage. The stone exhibits pronounced pleochroism; the colours respective to the three vibration directions are sapphire blue, purple and sage green. The absorption spectrum shows a broad absorption in the yellow-green near 5950 Å with two fainter bands, one in the green at 5280 Å and another in the blue at 4550 Å. There are several weak lines in the deep red. There is no noticeable luminescence under ultra-violet light. It has been suggested that the blue colour is due to vanadium.

Thulite, the massive pink variety, is named after Thule, the ancient name for Norway. The mineral is used as an ornamental stone as it has a pleasing pink colour which is often variegated with areas of white. The hardness is 6 and the density does not vary greatly from 3·10. The refractive index, at least so far as the vague shadow edge can be seen on the refractometer scale, is about 1·70. There is no typical absorption spectrum, and, except in the type from North Carolina which is said to glow orange-yellow under long-wave ultra-violet light, thulite does not fluoresce although a weak rose-coloured glow may be seen with x-rays. The mineral is found in the parish of Souland in Telemark; in Trondhjem and near Arendal in Norway. Other localities are in the Zillerthal in the Austrian Tyrol and in Mitchell County, North Carolina, and Western Australia.

The green zoisite with rubies from Tanzania, mentioned above, has been fashioned complete with the rubies as an ornamental stone for small objects, such as ashtrays, and has been named anyolite from anyoli the Masai name for green. Clinozoisite is a variety which has the chemical composition of zoisite but the crystal form of epidote and has been mentioned under that mineral. A massive greenish-grey variety of zoisite found in Wyoming is used for producing tumbled gems. This variety shows an absorption band at 4550 Å which is common to epidote.

CHAPTER 17

SYNTHETIC GEMSTONES

Since the advent during the nineteenth century of the more critical approach to the investigations of the occurrence and properties of minerals used for adornment, attempts have been made to produce exact copies of such minerals and crystals which are found in the earth.

For many years, unknown to the jeweller and layman, experiments on the synthesis of gemstones have been carried out in laboratories throughout the world. The majority of gemstones have been made synthetically, and some gemstones unknown to nature have been produced. To be of commercial importance the synthetic stones must be in crystals large enough to cut, and, further, must be cheaper than the mined stone.

What is a synthetic stone? Such a stone must not only have a chemical composition the same as the natural stone—this is true except for those synthetic gemstones which have no counterpart in nature—but it must also have crystallized as single crystals. Such crystals may have been grown by two major techniques. These are growth from a pure melt, of which the Verneuil and Czochralski methods need to be mentioned, and growth from a solution; they are covered here by descriptions of the hydrothermal and fluxed melt (melt diffusion) methods. The synthesis by high pressure and temperature mainly concerns the synthesis of diamond.

DIAMOND

Carbon

In view of its simple chemical composition, pure carbon, the synthesis of diamond should easily be achieved. Carbon when heated *in vacuo* volatilizes at a temperature of about 2,000°C (3,600°F), which is less than its melting point, and this vapour condenses back, not as diamond, but as the soft dimorphous form, hexagonal graphite, which is the stable form of carbon at ordinary temperature and pressure. Carbon does not dissolve in any ordinary solvent but does do so to some extent in molten iron. From the occurrence of diamond in iron-rich volcanic 'pipes', which suggests that pressure is also an essential condition of diamond formation, it might well be thought that under the right conditions of heat and pressure diamond might crystallize out from a carbon in iron solution. This was the basis of many earlier experiments on diamond synthesis, but according to theoretical thermodynamics such a synthesis appears to be impossible.

Of these earlier experiments those of Hannay and Moissan have been most discussed. In 1880 J. B. Hannay, a Glasgow chemist, published reports on the artificial production of diamonds based on the considerations that when a gas containing carbon and hydrogen is heated under pressure in the presence of lithium, potassium, sodium or magnesium, the hydrogen combines with the metal, and the carbon, in the nascent state, might well crystallize out as diamond. Using a wrought iron tube filled with reagents— light paraffin, bone oil and metallic lithium were used in the most successful experiments—he closed the ends by welding and then heated them to a dull red heat for some hours. Out of some 80 experiments only three or four of the tubes did not explode. In the most successful one some hard micro- scopic-size pieces were found and these pieces were identified, by the means then available, as diamond. Some of Hannay's pieces, mounted on a microscope slide, were placed in the care of the British Museum (Natural History) and have since been re-identified as diamond by F. A. Bannister and K. Lonsdale by the modern method of x-ray crystallography. Thus on the face of things the earliest experiment on diamond synthesis was successful. In view of recent work and certain other matters some authori- ties doubt whether Hannay did make diamonds.

Said to have been inspired by the news that diamond had been found in the Canon Diablo meteorite, the French chemist, Henri Moissan, as reported in 1896, dissolved sugar carbon in molten iron in his newly designed electric furnace to 4,000°F (2,200°C), and then chilled the mass suddenly in molten lead. The sudden cooling solidified the outer layer of iron and the slower cooling of the inner core set up enormous pressure as iron expands on cooling. After laboriously dissolving away the iron Moissan found small microscopic pieces which, following hardness and other tests, were acclaimed to be diamond. Moissan's minute pieces have been com- pletely lost so that the more modern techniques of identification cannot be applied.

S. R. Marsden had previously carried out a similar experiment to that of Moissan by dissolving sugar carbon in molten silver and cooling the melt slowly. Small pieces rescued from the residue were said to be diamond. Sir Charles Parsons and O. Ruff carried out extensive experiments using all the techniques which had been previously attempted by others, and finally concluded that diamond had not been made up to that time; a conclusion similarly and more recently reached by Geselle and others after their elaborate series of experiments. On the other hand, however, Sir William Crookes, in 1919, carried out similar experiments and is said to have confirmed Moissan's work.

During 1929, J. W. Hershey duplicated Moissan's experiment and was reported to have produced diamonds, but this was disputed and the claim died out. Friedlander was said to have stirred molten olivine with a carbon rod and to have produced minute hard pieces on the rod, but again nothing in the way of proof was forthcoming. A patent was applied for in 1950 to J. I. Marek and B. Salt for a modified process similar to that of Moissan's, but which differed in that the carbon was obtained from lignin and that the heating of the materials was carried out separately in a twin high-frequency induction furnace. The molten iron was then poured on to the pre-heated carbon and mixed. Black industrial-type diamonds were said to have been produced but nothing further has been heard of this. Many reports of diamond synthesis, and these are legion, have been based on a sort of fraud.

At the close of 1954 there was no real proof that diamond had been synthesized. As early as 1941 C. A. Nickle referred to experimental research on diamond synthesis at the Schenectady Laboratories of the General Electric Company. Little more was heard of these experiments until 1955 when the company published information on the synthesis of minute diamonds at Schenectady. One-carat synthetic diamonds are reported to have been made, but of industrial quality only.

Graphite

In 1947, P. W. Bridgman contributed valuable information on considerations of the thermodynamic equilibrium between graphite and diamond, and carried out considerable work on high pressures and temperatures.

Graphite is the stable form of carbon at normal temperatures and pressures up to 15,000 atmospheres (1 atmosphere equals 14·7 pounds per square inch); diamond is the high-pressure form of carbon, as shown by its higher density of 3·52 as against 2·25 for graphite. Diamond as we know it, is quite stable, but actually it is in the metastable condition as may be inferred by its change into graphite on heating to a temperature above 1,750°C (3,200°F) out of contact with air. In air, diamond commences to burn at a temperature of about 700°C (1,300°F) by combination with the oxygen of the atmosphere forming carbon dioxide. At the temperature of 1,750°C the thermal agitation of the atoms becomes so energetic that they swing loose from the diamond lattice and regroup into the more stable graphite lattice form.

Diamond being the high-temperature modification of carbon, it therefore needs high pressure to convert graphite into diamond. However, pressure alone is not enough, it also requires high temperature to allow sufficient agitation of the carbon atoms to shake themselves loose and become available for regrouping in the diamond crystal lattice form. In other words high temperature is needed as well as high pressure; there is also the question of the time factor, that is the reaction rate which is proportional to temperature and pressure.

Bridgman obtained high pressures in his experiments but found difficulty in obtaining high enough temperatures simultaneously with the pressure, and for a sufficient length of time. The success of the General Electric Company's team (F. P. Bandy, H. Tracy Hall, H. M. Strong and R. Wentorf) is due mainly to their overcoming this difficulty of obtaining high pressure and temperature simultaneously. By using a 1,000-ton press and special heat and pressure resisting chambers, pressures up to 1,500,000 pounds per square inch and temperatures up to 5,000°F (2,760°C) were produced. An undisclosed 'carbonaceous compound' was used to supply the carbon. Although the results of their experiments were only the production of minute crystals these are now made in such quantity that the product is now available commercially—its use is as diamond powder.

Since the announcement of the General Electric Company's successful synthesis there have been a number of other claims to such a successful synthesis of diamond. A Swiss biophysicist, D. L. Tomarkin, and a Puerto Rican chemist, M. Vilella, have patented a furnace which they have been operating at Spring Valley, New York. These workers have stated that their experiments, using a pressure of 250,000 pounds per square inch and a temperature of 6,000 (?°F), have produced small diamonds. The Swedish A.S.E.A. works claimed to have produced diamonds as early as February 1953 by a process discovered by Baltzar von Platen. Pressures of from 80,000 to 90,000 pounds per square inch and a temperature of 5,400°F (3,000°C) were used and stones up to 2 millimetres are said to have been made. The Dutch N. V. Bronswerk laboratory is reported to have produced diamonds in January 1955 in a manner similar to the General Electric Company's production, and in 1959 De Beers Consolidated Mines Ltd. announced the manufacture of synthetic diamonds in South Africa, and in 1961 by the National Physical Laboratory.

After the granting of independence to Congo, the main source of industrial grade diamonds, there were so many disturbances that there were engendered doubts as to the continuance of supply. It was this that led De Beers and the Société Minière du Beceka, the Congolese diamond mining company, to open, in 1963, a factory for the production of synthetic diamond operated by Ultra High Pressure Units Limited, at Shannon in Eire. This plant is said to have an output of 750,000 carats per annum. It has been further reported that synthetic diamonds are made in Japan.

The small synthetic diamond crystals, like fine sand, form as cubes, octahedra and dodecahedra which may depend on the temperature, a factor which may also influence the colour from black to white at the highest temperatures. It must be emphasized that so far there are no diamonds produced synthetically which are of sufficient size for gemstones to be cut from them; the few stones grown over a carat have been found to be multicrystalline. That in the future synthetic gem diamonds may well be produced cannot be denied, but such production is not feasible yet.

Nickel

It was found by J. Grenville Wells and K. Lonsdale that x-ray diffraction pictures of the American synthetic diamonds showed the presence of extra spots due to included nickel. This was confirmed by chemical analysis which demonstrated the presence of some 0·2 per cent of nickel. No reason has been advanced to account for this, but it well may be of catalytic value. No nickel has been found in Swedish synthetic diamonds. These nickel-rich American synthetic diamonds, as shown by B. W. Anderson, are often magnetic and *Figure 17.1* shows some of these pieces adhering to the pole of a small horseshoe magnet, a picture which also illustrates the small size of the pieces.

Boron Nitride

An interesting sequel to the General Electric Company's synthesis of diamond is the subsequent production by similar means, and by the same team of workers, of a cubic form of boron nitride (BN). The normal hexagonal boron nitride is a white powder, called 'white graphite'. It is apparently not found in nature although the occurrence of boric acid and ammonia in the Soffioni area of Tuscany has led to the suggestion that these two compounds are, in Tuscany, derived from the action of steam on subterranean boron nitride. The cubic form of boron nitride is produced, as in the synthetic diamond process, by high temperature with simultaneous high pressure, and the new synthetic material has been named borazon, from 'bor' (boron) and 'azon' from azo, a chemical term indicating nitrogen in the compound.

The material has a hardness comparable to diamond and the small crystals produced are generally black, brown or dark red, although milky-white, grey and yellow crystals have been produced. The density of borazon is said to be 3·45 and the crystals resist heat. While diamond burns at about 700°C (1,300°F) borazon is unchanged at a temperature of 1,800°C (3,500°F). Owing to its great hardness borazon could, if it can be produced at an economic price, be a substitute for diamond powder.

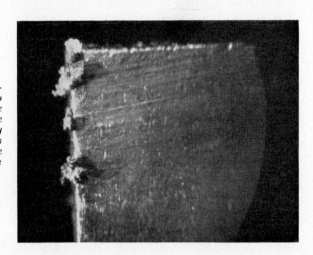

Figure 17.1. American synthetic diamonds adhering to the pole of a small horseshoe magnet. The edge of the magnet pole shown is only 6 mm in length, and this shows the very small size of the synthetic diamonds

RUBY AND SAPPHIRE

Ruby, the red variety of corundum, is a stone whose value is sufficiently high to warrant consideration of its synthesis. The earliest recorded experiments in this direction were those of Marc A. A. Gaudin, who produced a few tiny flakes of crystallized alumina by heating a previously ignited mixture of alum and a little potassium chromate covered with lamp black in a clay crucible. The experiment had no commercial significance, for although the globules were quite clear when molten they became opaque on cooling. Although many experiments were tried, in his last published notes, in 1869, Gaudin virtually admitted defeat. However, this was the beginning of the history of the synthetic stones now used in jewellery.

Reconstructed Stones

In 1885, or perhaps three years earlier, a number of rubies came on the gem market which were at first accepted as genuine. The genuineness of these stones was soon questioned and it transpired that they had been made by the direct fusion of small fragments of good colour natural ruby. These so-called reconstructed rubies were said to have been made by an enterprising priest in a small village near Geneva, hence they were known as 'Geneva rubies'.

The trouble that these stones caused at the time is well illustrated by the following abridged abstract from a trade paper of 1890.

A Berlin jeweller has just been the victim of a curious hoax. He recently received a circular from a Zurich firm offering rubies at remarkably cheap rates, and therefore entered into negotiation for the purchase of some. He bought 25 rubies for which he paid 4,500 marks (£225) receiving a guarantee from the firm that the stones were genuine. Shortly after, the jeweller heard that false rubies were being manufactured so cleverly as to deceive the connoisseur, and, becoming alarmed, sent those he had purchased to Paris to be examined by the Syndicate of Dealers in Precious Stones, who are considered unimpeachable authorities. They reported that the stones were not imitation, but were real rubies, which were small and consequently of little value, fastened together so cleverly as to render detection difficult. The jeweller then wrote to Zurich requesting the firm to take back the stones. This they refused to do on the ground that their guarantee only ensured the genuineness of the gems and contained no mention of their size.

Later, in 1895, the French chemist Michaud, developed a technique employing a fusion or sintering of poor quality Siamese rubies in a platinum crucible under an oxyhydrogen blowpipe, adding bichromate of potash to enhance the colour. As the process became well known and other people commenced making them, even in London's Hatton Garden, the price dropped so that their manufacture became uneconomic. With the introduction of Verneuil's method of ruby synthesis the reconstructed stones were no longer made, despite the fact that these crucible-made rubies, with their fine cracks and imperfections, which often appear like natural 'silk', have an appearance nearer to that of the natural ruby than the much cleaner modern synthetic. Only ruby has been produced by this method; the reconstruction process has not been applied to other colours of corundum. (Note: there is a recent suggestion that such rubies were never made.)

Fremy's Syntheses

During the time that the reconstructed ruby held sway the French chemists had not been idle. In 1877, E. Fremy in partnership with C. Feil worked on the problems of ruby synthesis and had successfully produced ruby and other colours of corundum. The synthesis was reported in the French scientific journal *Comptes Rendus des Séances*, and an abstract made in the *Mineralogical Magazine* of the Mineralogical Society of England for the year 1878, the revelant part of which is printed below.

Fremy and Feil have latterly succeeded in preparing artificially variously coloured crystallized corundum and emerald (? green sapphire) of such a size and transparency as to be suitable for the purposes of the jeweller and watchmaker. Several methods have been adopted, but that which is said to give the best results is to dissolve alumina in oxide of lead at high temperature in an earthenware crucible. After the solution is complete, the temperature is maintained for about 20 days. The silex of the crucible is gradually dissolved and by replacing the alumina causes it to crystallize out very slowly. The remarkable success obtained is mainly due to the authors having used as much material as 20 to 30 kilograms and having command of large furnaces. The various coloured specimens of corundum have the same specific gravity, hardness and crystalline form as the natural mineral. The artificial ruby was coloured, as in the natural ruby, by oxide of chromium, but the artificial sapphire was coloured by oxide of cobalt and they probably differ from the natural. Very blue sapphire does not give a spectrum at all like that due to cobalt. The true nature of the colouring substance is somewhat doubtful.

Later another French chemist, Auguste Verneuil, whose name has since become a byword in gemstone synthesis, joined as Fremy's partner in place of Feil. Their work progressed, and in a trade journal of 1890 was written the following.

> More valuable than mere theory was the fact that these chemists exhibited for the benefit of the Paris Academy of Sciences some hundreds of the specimens of the glittering red crystals they had succeeded in producing—the only regrettable part of the business is that owing to the high price of the chemicals required, and the difficulty of manipulation, the artificial rubies cannot be produced at a price cheaper than the natural precious stones.

In 1891 Fremy published an account of his synthesis in his book *Synthese du rubis*. Some of Fremy's rubies were used as watch jewels and a few were even cut as small gemstones. A year later, Moissan of synthetic diamond fame, published particulars of the process of fusing alumina in an electric furnace.

The Verneuil Furnace

The crucible method was never a success commercially, but Verneuil had learned much, and in 1891 he deposited with the Paris Academy of Sciences a sealed account of a new and revolutionary process of ruby synthesis; a process which he freely published to the world in November, 1902. In this paper of Verneuil's he told of the construction of an inverted oxyhydrogen blowpipe—his famous chalumeau—which in its essentials is still used today for the production of many types of synthetic stones.

The Verneuil inverted furnace (*Figure 17.2*) consists of two iron tubes (6) and (7). Tube (6) is widened into a circular chamber at the top, the lower and thinner end passing down the centre of the tube (7) into which it is tightly screwed so as to form a gas-tight joint. Both tubes are constricted to nozzles at the lower ends, that of (6) being situated close to but inside and above that of (7). Pure oxygen under pressure is admitted to the tube (6) through the pipe (10). Within the upper chamber of (6) is placed a small hopper (4) with a fine wire-mesh bottom (5) which is rigidly fixed to a metal rod which passes upwards through a block of resilient rubber (or a metal diaphragm) (3). At the top of this rod is an anvil head which is periodically struck by the hammer (1). This hammer, which is operated by an electromagnet or by a cam rotating on a shaft (not shown in the diagram), may be regulated so as to give a regular series of gentle taps. Hydrogen under pressure is admitted to the tube (7) by means of the pipe (11). This hydrogen meets and mixes with the oxygen at the orifice, where it is ignited.

Owing to the intense heat generated, some 2,000°C (3,600°F), it is necessary to protect the pipes against fusion and this is done by placing round them, just above the nozzles, a water jacket (9) with cold water continually running through it (with modern metals and construction this water jacket is sometimes omitted). Below the orifice is placed a fireclay support (16)

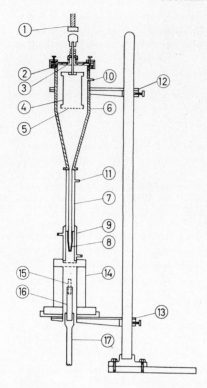

Figure 17.2. The Verneuil furnace. (1) Hammer, (2) Rubber gasket, (3) Corrugated metal diaphragm, (4) Powder hopper, (5) Sieve, (6) Main body of the furnace forming the expanded top of the inner tube, (7) Outer annular tube carrying the hydrogen, (8) Removable nozzle to inner tube, (9) Water jacket, (10) Oxygen inlet, (11) Hydrogen inlet, (12) and (13) Brackets for securing furnace to upright, (14) Divided fireclay chamber, (15) Window in fireclay chamber, (16) 'Candle' upon which the boule grows, (17) 'Candle' support connected to centring and raising and lowering adjustments (not shown)

(usually known as the 'candle') which is carried on an iron rod (17) connected to screw adjustments, whereby the candle may be centred below the orifice of the furnace; it may also be raised or lowered into or out of the flame, as the 'boule' grows. Boule is the name given to the pear-shaped single crystal which forms on the candle—the name is derived from the French word for ball, for the small specimens first made by Verneuil were ball-shaped. To protect the growing boule from cold draughts and to maintain a regular temperature around it, a divided fireclay chamber (14) is provided. This has a 'window' (15) in front of which is supported a coloured glass screen so that the growth of the boule can be watched without damage to the eyes.

Manufacture of Stones by Verneuil Process

In the manufacture of synthetic stones by the Verneuil process, or as it is sometimes called 'the flame fusion process' the gases and chemicals used must be of exceptional purity and have certain physical attributes. Today most factories manufacture their own gases and the chemical powders. To make the corundum gems—ruby, colourless, blue and fancy coloured sapphires—it is necessary to first prepare a fine powder of alumina as the feed powder. This is done by calcining crystals of ammonium alum in silica trays in a muffle furnace at 1,100°C for 2 hours. During decomposition, the noxious gases generated are carried off by high chimneys, the charge swells up spectacularly to a meringue-like cake. This is anhydrous (water-free) alumina in the so-called *gamma* form. These cakes are then ground down to a fine powder by a tumbling process.

This snow-white powder, which includes, if ruby is required, about 8 per cent chromic oxide added to the ammonium alum before calcining (producing a pale green powder), is placed in the hopper (4) at the top of the blowpipe. The bottom of this basket has a sieve with a 40–80 mesh through which the powder is shaken. The hydrogen gas is turned on and lit at the nozzle, and the oxygen is then admitted, which, with the already ignited hydrogen forms the intensely hot oxyhydrogen flame. The hammer (1) is then started, at about 80 taps per minute, causing the release of a sprinkling of the alumina powder at each tap. This powder travels down the oxygen stream and fuses as it passes through the hottest part of the flame, the melting point of alumina being 2,050°C.

The molten powder is caught on the top of the ceramic candle (16), which is about $\frac{3}{4}$–1 in. in diameter and is situated in the cooler part of the furnace. This fused alumina solidifies on the candle in the form of a small cone consisting of a number of small crystals of corundum. The tip of this cone remaining in the hotter part of the flame remains molten. By manipulation of the speed of tapping down of the powder, and the amount of powder delivered at each tap, which can be controlled by altering the distance the head of the peg is away from the hammer, and with control of the gas supply, a single central crystal grows upwards in stalagmitic fashion and opens out to mushroom shape, after which the speed of tapping is reduced in order to keep the boule diameter to about $\frac{3}{4}$ in. The rate of tapping, for ruby, is about 20 times per minute.

When the boule reaches a suitable size, about $2\frac{1}{2}$ in. (say 65 mm) in length for ruby, and weighs from 150 to 200 carats, the gas supply is cut off and the boule allowed to cool on the furnace. When cool it is removed from the furnace and broken away from the candle and from the fritted cone of crystal aggregates. The stem of the boule is nipped with a pair of pliers or given a slight tap with a hammer, which causes it to split into two nearly equal pieces, the faces of which are essentially plane (*Figure 17.3*).

Manufacturers employ slight differences in technique, but the essentials are the same, and little difference is to be noticed in the original blowpipe apparatus used by Verneuil to that used today, and even the arrangement of the banks of furnaces differs little. Quite recently, for a special purpose, an ingenious slow-motion drive to lower the growing boule (usually operated periodically by a hand wheel) and the rate of tapping, both of which are controlled by a photo-electric cell and an electronic circuit, have been constructed.

Without any addition to the pure alumina powder a clear water-white boule is produced—synthetic white sapphire—and such boules are made in considerable numbers for electric meter bearings, and for colourless gemstones. By the addition of suitable metallic oxides to the pure alumina powder a great number of other colours are produced in synthetic corundum.

It is reported that a French chemist who had learned Verneuil's process before leaving Europe, started making synthetic rubies at the small lumber camp of Hoquiam, Washington, in 1904. The capital for the project was supplied by two wealthy lumbermen, Polson and Ninemire. Small boules were produced but the location was too far away from jewel markets, and, further, the material produced was wont to crack-up, so the venture died. Ground up natural Montana sapphire has been experimentally used as the feed powder in the Verneuil process.

Sapphire

About the year 1907 attempts were made to grow blue sapphire boules but the initial experiments were somewhat of a failure. The true nature of the colouring in natural sapphire was still in doubt and the then logical use of cobalt was made. The boules produced from this alumina/cobalt oxide powder were found to be very patchy in colour, and they were at best a

Figure 17.3. Synthetic boules

Top row: (left) Ruby showing how the boule splits; (centre) White sapphire; (right) White sapphire boule showing the split plane

Bottom row: (left) Zircon-coloured synthetic spinel; (centre) Corundum boule experimentally coloured pink by manganese; (right) White spinel boule, showing the square form and the cone of small crystals from which it grew

poor imitation of sapphire blue. In order to overcome this patchiness of colour, the experimenters added magnesium oxide to act as a flux, and by this method produced a blue stone of uniform colour, but of a hue unlike that of natural sapphire. Such stones were cut and marketed and sold, under the fanciful name of 'Hope sapphire'. Examination of these stones showed that they had the characters of spinel and not those of corundum. It was this 'accident' which led to the production some 20 years later of the synthetic spinel which is now made in such lovely shades of colour.

When scientific investigation had clearly shown that the cause of the colour in natural sapphire was due to traces of titanium and iron, these trace elements, in the form of oxides, were employed with success in the synthetic manufacture of blue sapphire, which came out in 1910.

Colours of Transparent Synthetic Corundum

Table 17.1 gives a fairly complete list of the colours most commonly made in transparent synthetic corundum, complete with the manufacturers' trade names. In addition, some synthetic corundums have been made in America which are parti-coloured, such as blue sapphire one end and ruby the other.

TABLE 17.1

Colours of Transparent Synthetic Corundum

Colour	Manufacturers' trade name
Colourless	White sapphire
Red	Ruby
Dark red	Garnet colour
Deep pink	Rosaline
Pink	Pink sapphire
Lilac-pink	Rose de France
Orange	Padparadscha
Deep yellow	Danburite
Yellow	Topaz
Yellow-brown	Madeira topaz
Brown	Palmeira topaz
Green	Green sapphire
Pale green	Amaryl
Blue	Burma sapphire
Purple	Amethyst
Purple/green	Alexandrite

Asteriated Corundum

In 1947, by the introduction of a percentage of titanium oxide and subsequent heat treatment, asteriated corundum was made synthetically. These synthetic star-rubies and sapphires (other colours than blue and red have also been produced) are made by the normal Verneuil process, except that the alumina powder (plus the trace of colouring oxides) is intimately mixed with not less than 0·1 per cent and not more than 0·3 per cent of titanium oxide. The boules formed from this mixture are subsequently heated at a temperature above 1,100°C, which causes the precipitation of the titania as rutile needles along the prominent planes of the trigonal atomic lattice of the boule.

The synthetic star stones of early American manufacture had the artificial silk confined to the outside of the boule and the cabochon stones cut from them showed concentrations of silk at the upper two-thirds or three-quarters of the stone, the rest being clear and transparent and with all the characteristics of synthetic corundum. It is due to this silk that in the early stones of this type the arms of the star reach only three-quarters down the sides of the cabochon. More recently the American production has been of star stones which are much more opaque, so opaque that it is difficult to get light through them. All these American star stones show a star that is too bright and a body colour that is too strong, so that to a great extent they look unreal. Since then there has been a German production using a slightly different method, but still with a Verneuil process, in which a softer colour and more pleasing stars are seen.

Physical and Optical Properties

Inclusions

The physical and optical characteristics of synthetic corundums are those of natural stones, so neither density nor refractive index determinations will supply evidence of their synthetic nature. However, owing to

319

their mode of formation being so different to that in nature the internal inclusions differ from those of the natural stones in a sufficient number of respects clearly to identify them.

Synthetic rubies and sapphires, owing to the shape of the top of the boule and to the discontinuous feed of the powder—necessary in order that each increment of fused powder will have time to crystallize, and in conformity with the layer underneath it—show curved structure lines when

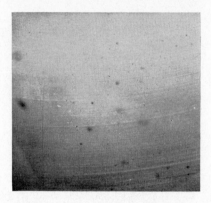

Figure 17.4. Curved lines and gas bubbles in a synthetic ruby

Figure 17.5. Curved bands and 'fire marks' in a synthetic blue sapphire

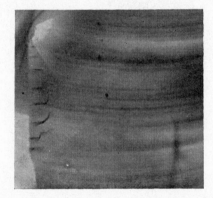

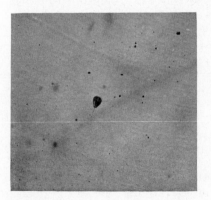

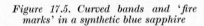

Figure 17.6. ' Tadpole-shaped' gas bubble and curved lines in a synthetic ruby

examined in the correct direction under a microscope. In the case of ruby these lines have been aptly likened to the grooves seen on a gramophone record (*Figure 17.4*). With blue sapphire the bands are wider and more diffuse (*Figure 17.5*) and these are often better seen if the stone is placed in a highly refractive oil in a white cell and the stone viewed in different directions, as under the microscope the bands may be so wide and diffuse that they may not be seen at all clearly.

Included gas bubbles, which may be round or take characteristic 'flask' or 'tadpole' shapes (*Figure 17.6*), are common and give positive evidence that the stone is synthetic. Clouds of very small bubbles, looking like black dots, are often seen and these sometimes tend to follow the direction of the curved bands of colour (*Figure 17.7*).

Figure 17.7. 'Flask-shaped' bubbles and a bubble cloud in a synthetic sapphire

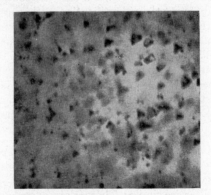

Figure 17.8. Bubble cloud and deceptive solid inclusions (probably undissolved alumina) in a synthetic ruby

Figure 17.9. Two-phase inclusions in a German synthetic star ruby

11 + G.

In natural rubies and sapphires the inclusions, as they are termed, are vastly different, so, unless the stone is so clean as not to show anything, the inclusions tell the trained worker whether the stone is made by nature or by man. Sometimes the inclusions in synthetic stones may be most deceptive, for undissolved alumina can produce natural looking inclusions (*Figure 17.8*) and in some cases triangular cavities containing a gas bubble may be observed (*Figure 17.9*). Careful observation will generally reveal that these deceptive inclusions are in conjunction with tell-tale normal gas bubbles and curved colour lines. Twinning lines in parallel planes usually indicate a natural stone, but these too have been seen, although rarely, in synthetic corundums. W. Plato has reported that under certain conditions some synthetic corundums show faint zonal lines with angles of 60° and 120°, but these lines are difficult to see and differ from the zonal lines observed in natural stones.

Absorption Spectrum

The absorption bands seen in synthetic ruby are the same as may be observed in natural ruby, so in the case of the prized red corundum the spectroscope will give no help in distinguishing between the two. With the blue sapphire the spectroscope does help, for in the natural stones the iron lines, a complex spectrum of three bands at 4500, 4600 and 4710 Å, are usually visible in the absorption spectrum. Sometimes only the 4500 Å line, as a fine but sharp line, may be seen in fine blue sapphires, while with the greenish-blue and green stones the three lines are strong. In the case of the synthetic blue sapphire this line at 4500 Å does not normally show, and although a weak smudgy line may sometimes be seen about this position, it is nothing like the sharp line of the natural stone. As iron is incorporated with titanium as the colouring agent in the synthetic blue sapphire, the absence of the strong 4500 Å absorption line poses a question. It may well be due to the evaporation of the iron in the heat of the furnace and it can therefore be assumed that titanium alone will give the lovely blue colour of the sapphire, the iron playing a very small part. The synthetic fancy-coloured sapphire which is made to imitate the alexandrite variety of chrysoberyl provides a case where the absorption spectrum is so markedly different that identification of the synthetic stone is easily accomplished by the spectroscope alone. In this synthetic, which is grey-green by daylight and purplish-red in artificial light, there is an absorption line in the blue at 4750 Å and there are no fine lines in the red as seen in the spectrum of the true alexandrite. This 4750 Å line which is ascribed to the element vanadium is only rarely seen in a natural corundum, and then the colour of the stone is different. The 4750 Å line has, however, been observed in a synthetic corundum of green colour. Some synthetic green sapphires show an absorption line at 6880 Å which may be due to nickel.

Colour Filter

The colour filter (Chelsea filter) gives little help in the identification of synthetic from natural rubies and sapphires for the effects seen through the filter are similar. There is one exception to this; that is in the synthetic green sapphire which shows reddish through the filter whereas the natural green sapphire shows dark.

Ultra-violet light

The luminescent effects shown by corundums when bathed in ultra-violet light are occasionally helpful as a means of identification. Synthetic rubies mixed in a parcel, or set with real rubies in a jewel, can sometimes be 'spotted' by their stronger glow. The short-wave lamp is probably the more helpful in this case. With synthetic blue sapphires the short-wave lamp very often induces a bluish-green glow in them, and, with care and turning the stone, the curved bands may be seen as bands of different intensity of light, in some cases where the bands have not been observed under lens or microscope examination. A low-power lens is useful when looking for the coloured fluorescent bands.

It has been found that synthetic corundums transmit ultra-violet light much more freely than do the natural corundums and proof of this effect may provide an ancillary method of identifying synthetic stones. The natural corundums usually absorb ultra-violet light below about 2900 Å, while the synthetic stones of this species generally transmit quite freely down to 2200 Å. With the aid of a spectrograph the absorption edge can be measured, but an easier and more practical method for identification purposes is to use a short-wave ultra-violet lamp which has its main emission at 2537 Å, which is between the absorption edges of the natural and the synthetic corundums, in conjunction with photographic paper. The suspected stone is placed, with other known stones as controls, on the bare surface of a slow photographic printing paper and these are immersed in a dish of water. A short exposure, some 5 sec, from the short-wave lamp held some 10 or 12 in. above is given and the paper then developed. As the ultra-violet rays will be transmitted through the synthetic corundums and not through the natural the paper will be darkened to some extent under where the synthetic stones have rested but not so under the natural stones. As the short-wave lamp emits some long-wave ultra-violet rays the exposure time is critical and must be gauged by the use of control stones. Particular care is needed with blue sapphires in which the method is not always certain. *Figure 17.10* shows the effects seen with different stones of the corundum species.

Identification and Detection of Difficult Corundums

The most difficult synthetic corundums to detect by the aid of the microscope, for they are usually very clean, are the pink, yellow, orange and brown stones. When irradiated by x-rays, if this facility is available, such stones, except the brown, in common with rubies, exhibit a pronounced afterglow (phosphorescence). Natural corundums do not show this afterglow, probably because they contain a trace of iron, for iron tends to quench the luminescence of minerals. Synthetic pink sapphires may be distinguished from natural pink sapphires in that the former glow violet under shortwave ultra-violet light and the latter crimson.

Another method which sometimes yields results in difficult cases is to immerse the stone in methylene iodide (refractive index 1·74, which is near to that of sapphire—1·76–1·77) in a glass cell and place this cell with liquid and stone on a piece of fine-grain photographic film. From a nearly parallel light source held some distance above (an enlarger with the lens stopped down makes an ideal source) a short exposure, about 15 sec., is given. On development of the film, curved lines may be visible, curved lines which do not reveal themselves by ordinary microscopic examination. This method may not always work, and further, it may be necessary to take the picture

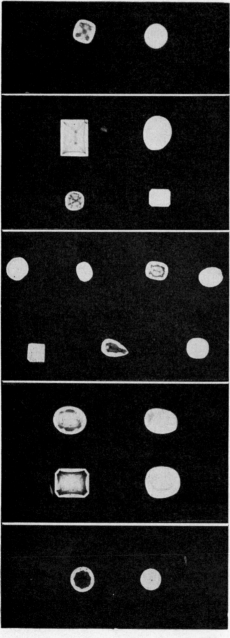

Figure 17.10. Effects of ultra-violet light on stones of the corundum species of various colours. The synthetic stones show a darkening of the film below the stones

with the stone in different positions, for one cannot tell the direction of the curved lines, but if results are obtained they are positive.

Recrystallized rubies

During 1958 the Bell Telephone Company of America experimented in the production of synthetic corundum, including the variety ruby, by a modification of the temperature-gradient method, but using higher temperatures and pressures. A silver-lined autoclave was used as it was found that ordinary iron autoclaves tended to produce a green colour in the crystals from iron contamination. The 'seeds' used in these experiments were cut from synthetic corundum of Verneuil flame-fusion make, and the resultant crystals were hexagonal prisms with tabular habit. While these Bell products had no commercial importance they have inspired Carroll Chatham and others to produce synthetic rubies by the hydrothermal method. The 'seeds' used are small water-worn Burma rubies (*Figure 17.11*) and the resulting crystals tend to show rhombohedral form. The hydrothermal rubies which have so far been examined, appear to fall into two types. One type has a dark red colour near to the hue of Siamese rubies, has veil-like twisting feathers reminiscent of the Chatham synthetic emerald, and such stones were found to show pronounced phosphorescence under x-rays. The second type is a Burmese ruby colour and very patchy in colouring. The inclusions are typically those of Burma rubies except that there are usually a number of circular exsolution feathers with a small crystal in the centre or at the edge—rather like some inclusions seen in Siamese stones. These synthetic rubies do not as a rule show phosphorescence under x-rays. In view of the difference in formation of these synthetic rubies to those made by the Verneuil process a suggestion is made that these stones should be called 're-crystallized rubies'. The hydrothermal technique is described under Quartz (page 334).

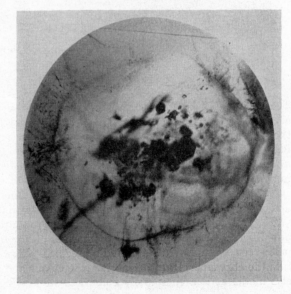

Figure 17.11. Hydrothermal grown synthetic ruby showing the natural ruby used as a 'seed'

Before 1961 a new method of making rubies was credibly reported. These synthetic ruby crystals are grown in the form of hexagonal plates 2–3 cm in diameter and up to 1 cm thick. The crystals are produced by a flux-melt method from a solution of aluminium oxide in lead fluoride contained in a platinum crucible which is heated in the ordinary laboratory furnace.

The crystals are grown for use as optical masers (microwave amplification by stimulated emission of radiation). This new scientific achievement, for which many revolutionary uses are envisaged, needs crystals having a greater homogeneity than can be obtained by the flame-fusion method. Like the Verneuil product, these maser rubies exhibit phosphorescence after bombardment with x-rays. Some may have been cut as gems.

Figure 17.12. A flux-melt furnace used for the experimental production of synthetic stones

(By courtesy of General Electric Company)

SPINEL

The 'accident' which led to the first synthetic spinel has been mentioned, and although L. Paris, a student of Verneuil's, carried out experiments on the making of synthetic spinel—he was credited with the production of a better blue stone by using calcium oxide instead of magnesia—it was not until the 1930s that this synthetically made species became of commercial importance.

Natural spinel, except for the red variety, has no great use in jewellery and a simple simulation of the natural spinel would have had no especial value. The synthetic spinel is therefore made to imitate stones of important but different species, such as aquamarine, blue zircon, green tourmaline, pale green Brazilian emerald, and a greenish-yellow shade which may imitate the chrysoberyl. An attractive rose colour and a royal blue shade are also made, as is a completely colourless stone which rivals the synthetic white sapphire in brilliance. When these colourless or white spinels as they are called were first marketed they were the subject of a silly scare when retailed by a jeweller and antique dealer with considerable Press ballyhoo as 'Jourado diamonds'. After many fruitless experiments a red synthetic spinel is now produced but this stone has properties slightly different from the usual run of the synthetic spinels of other colour. It will be mentioned later.

Physical and Optical Properties

Very rarely do the boules of synthetic corundum exhibit any crystal faces, but the spinel boules commonly show flat four-sided forms which indicate the cubic nature of the mineral, and unlike natural spinel synthetic spinel boules often show cubic cleavage cracks.

Normal natural spinel has the formula $MgO.Al_2O_3$ which implies equimolecular proportions of magnesia and alumina. It was found that equimolecular amounts of the two ingredients did not produce good boules, and the synthetic spinel as now made is usually in the proportion of 1 MgO to $2\frac{1}{2}$ Al_2O_3, the alumina remaining in the cubic (gamma) form. This extra alumina does slightly alter the physical and optical properties of the spinel and these differences provide a ready means of assessing the nature of the material. There is a difference in density from the value 3·60 of the normal natural spinel to 3·63 for the synthetic, and the refractive index is higher, from 1·72 (usually 1·718) for the natural to 1·73 (1·728) for the synthetic. The excess alumina in the synthetic spinel strains the crystal lattice and this is apparent when such stones are viewed between crossed nicols (polarized light) for a typical anomalous double refraction is seen, the stone extinguishing in stripes, and the effect, owing to its likeness to the stripes on a tabby cat, is called 'tabby extinction' (*Figure 17.13*). Further, many spinels show pseudo-interference figures when rotated between crossed nicols (*Figure 17.14*), and peculiar 'strain knots' may be observed (*Figure 17.15*). Also seen in synthetic spinels are worm-like gaseous tubes (*Figure 17.16*).

Colours of Synthetic Spinels

The blue colours of synthetic spinel are due to the addition of cobalt oxide sometimes modified with other metallic oxides. The yellow and yellowish green colours are due to a trace of manganese, and the dark green stones are coloured by chromium oxide, which in corundum gives a red colour, for at the temperature of the oxyhydrogen furnace the stable coloration of the (gamma) alumina and magnesia boules is green. A chromium-coloured red spinel is now marketed, but owing to the fracturing of the boules, only in small sizes. Recently, however, red spinels of larger size have been grown in the United States of America using the flame fusion method. Unlike the general run of synthetic spinels, these stones are made with equimolecular amounts of magnesia and alumina as in the case of natural spinels. Their density approximates to 3·60 and their refractive index from 1·722 to 1·725, the higher values, compared with those of the natural stones, being due to excess chromium.

Such red synthetic spinels vary somewhat in their internal structure, but

327

Figure 17.13. Anomalous double refraction (tabby extinction) in a synthetic spinel

Figure 17.14. Pseudo-interference figure shown by a synthetic spinel between crossed nicols

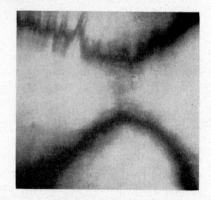

Figure 17.15. Strain knots in a synthetic spinel

as a rule show many gas bubbles and very pronounced curved colour lines. Sometimes, too, they may show straight lines rather like twin lines seen in some red and blue corundums of natural origin. The fluorescence spectrum differs from the 'organ-pipe' pattern as seen in the natural red spinel, for one fluorescent line near 6850 Å predominates markedly over the others.

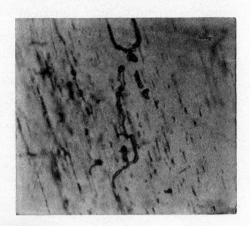

Figure 17.16. Worm-like distorted gaseous tubes in a synthetic spinel

(By courtesy of E. Gübelin)

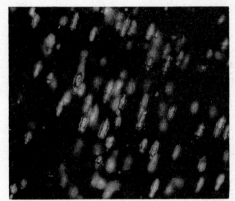

Figure 17.17. ' Profilated bubbles' in a synthetic spinel

(By courtesy of E. Gübelin)

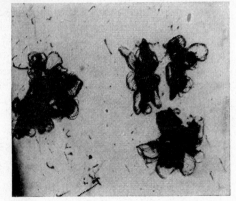

Figure 17.18. Solid crystals of alumina brought into being by exsolution. These are a disturbing kind of inclusion sometimes seen in synthetic spinel

(By courtesy of E. Gübelin)

The lovely pink coloured synthetic spinels which have been marketed for some years owe their colour to a trace of iron; a type with a colour change (being made to imitate the alexandrite) is, although rarely met, a better simulation than the much more common similarly coloured synthetic corundum.

A list of the usual colours of synthetic spinels and the trade names sometimes applied to them is given in Table 17.2.

TABLE 17.2
Colours of Synthetic Spinels

Colour	Manufacturers' trade name
Colourless	Synthetic white spinel
Blue	Hope sapphire
Blue (bright)	Azurite
Green-blue	Blue zircon
Pale blue	Aquamarine
Yellowish-green	Brazilian emerald
Dark green	Tourmaline green
Yellow green	Peridot
Pink	Synthetic pink spinel
Red	Synthetic red spinel
Green/red	Alexandrite

The terms erinite, erinide and emerala have been used for the yellow-green spinel.

About 1957 a new synthetic spinel appeared. This variety is made to imitate the moonstone, the schillerization probably being induced by some form of heat treatment of the synthetic white spinel. The rather bright blue-white fluorescence shown by these stones when irradiated with short-wave ultra-violet light (2537 Å) indicates their nature, for neither the 'heated quartz' imitation of moonstone, nor the true feldspar shows this type of luminescence. A blue schillerized synthetic spinel is known.

The synthesis of spinel is now also achieved by the flux-melt method and sizeable crystals have been produced which show good octahedral form. They are made in colours such as red, blue and yellow. Some are in crystal groups and have been mounted as such in jewellery.

Synthetic spinels rarely show curved colour bands or the structure lines as seen in the synthetic corundum. If bubbles are present they are sparse and may have a typical whorled or turned appearance with the end tending to show crystal form; they are termed 'profilated bubbles' (*Figure 17.17*). A disturbing kind of inclusion sometimes seen in synthetic spinel are solid crystals of alumina (*Figure 17.18*). The synthetic spinels may be distinguished by the unusual colour (for spinel), the refractive index and density, although there are certain zinc-rich spinels from Ceylon which have a higher refractive index than usual. They do not have the colour of the synthetic spinel, being mostly pale mauve to dark inky blue.

Absorption Spectrum

The blue colours of synthetic spinel show a distinctive absorption spectrum of three broad bands in the orange-red, yellow and green, the bands being centred at 6350, 5800 and 5400 Å, the latter being only about half the width of the first two. Cobalt does not produce a blue colour in natural minerals so this cobalt absorption spectrum will indicate that the stone is not natural. A blue glass coloured by cobalt exhibits a similar spectrum but in this case the bands are slightly wider apart and, further, it is the central band which is the narrowest. Such cobalt-coloured blue stones show a red or orange residual colour when viewed through the Chelsea colour filter, unlike sapphire, aquamarine and blue zircon which show a bluish-green through the filter. The synthetic spinel made to imitate the alexandrite also shows a cobalt absorption spectrum.

The yellow and greenish-yellow synthetic spinels show an absorption spectrum of two bands in the blue-violet at 4450 and 4220 Å due to manganese. In certain shades of pale-blue, the cobalt spectrum may be in association with the two bands due to manganese, and it sometimes occurs that the cobalt bands complete a spectrum which shows the bright fluorescence line of chromium.

Luminescence and Fluorescence

The luminescence of synthetic spinels has some diagnostic value. The synthetic white spinel shows only a faint misty glow under the long-wave lamp (3650 Å) but under short-wave rays (2537 Å) the glow is usually a bright bluish-white, although only a weak but distinct blue light may be seen in some white synthetic spinels. As the synthetic white sapphire shows a dull deep blue glow under short-wave excitation this provides a distinction between the two white synthetics. Synthetic white spinels emit an apple-green light when excited with x-rays, and with it a persistent afterglow. A few specimens have been found to give out a blue or greenish-blue light under x-rays. Synthetic white spinels quickly turn to a brown colour on irradiation with x-rays, but they may be decolorized by heating to about 250°C.

Most blue spinels show a red glow when under the long-wave ultra-violet lamp. Under the short-wave rays the glow seen may be either red, orange or bluish-white. The yellow, yellowish-blue and yellowish-green stones, those which show the manganese absorption spectrum, emit an apple-green glow with all radiations. The 'tourmaline green' colour of synthetic spinel shows a red glow under the long-wave lamp; a milky-greenish-white glow under the short-wave lamp, and usually a red colour under x-rays. The pink-coloured synthetic spinels are inert under any of the three radiations.

LAPIS-COLOURED SPINEL

Said to have been devised by a German dentist, a lapis-coloured synthetic spinel has been marketed since 1954. This is a coarse powder of synthetic spinel heavily charged with cobalt oxide which is sintered together in an electric furnace. Some specimens have bright specks of 'pyrites' so common in true lapis-lazuli, but in the case of the sintered spinel the specks are gold. These new synthetics show a brilliant red residual colour through the Chelsea colour filter and have a refractive index of 1·725, but the reading is

331

never as sharp as in transparent synthetic spinels of normal type. Sintered spinels have a hardness of 8, and a density of 3·52. The absorption spectrum may be observed quite clearly by light reflected from the surface of the specimen. It is a typical cobalt spectrum, although the distribution and strength of the bands are not quite the same as those shown by the blue spinels made by the Verneuil process. The three bands in this new spinel are at 6500 Å (broad and strong), 5800 Å (weak) and 4800 Å (strong).

RUTILE

A completely new synthetic gemstone came on the market in 1948, when synthetic rutile, a mineral long known in nature as black or dark red tetragonal crystals, made its appearance. These stones, which exhibit colours of pale yellow (this is nearly colourless), yellow, orange, red and sapphire blue, are grown as single crystals in boule form on a modified oxyhydrogen blowpipe. The feed powder used is a highly purified titanium dioxide (TiO_2).

Synthetic rutiles, sometimes called 'Titania', come from an American factory, but there are reports that such stones were made experimentally in Czechoslovakia during 1942. They are now said to be made in Japan.

It is known that rutile appears to lose oxygen when near its melting point, thus it is not possible to grow single rutile crystals on a normal blowpipe furnace. To overcome this difficulty an outer jet of oxygen is incorporated in the furnace to surround the normal lance of oxygen burning in an atmosphere of hydrogen. Further, it was found better to use a very sensitive hopper for the feed material to avoid cooling the flame. A vibrator is employed instead of the normal tapper. This is said to eliminate the usual layered (curved line) structure common with corundum synthetics. The lowering of the boule in the flame is arranged by worm-drive from a variable-speed motor and not by hand as in the manufacture of synthetic corundum and spinel.

Rutile boules are opaque black when they are taken from the furnace. The black material is heated in a stream of oxygen, when, as the treatment continues, the material changes from black to deep blue, light blue to green and then to pale yellow, though some turn to red, orange or deep yellow.

The most common variety of synthetic rutile met with in jewellery is the near colourless: other colours are rarely seen. Blue colours, it seems, are not now made commercially owing to their liability to chip at the facet edges. Rutile is rather too soft for a durable gemstone as the hardness is only 6–6½ on Mohs's scale. The density is 4·25 and the indices of refraction are, for the ordinary ray 2·62 and for the extraordinary ray 2·90. The large amount of double refraction, 0·287, strikingly shows in the cut stone by the exceptional separation of the rear facet edges when they are viewed through the stone. Another exceptional feature of rutile is the very large colour dispersion shown by the cut stones. This is about six times as great as that of diamond and gives to the stone a tremendous fire. The only noticeable feature in the absorption spectrum is an intense band in the violet causing a sharp cut-off at about 4300 Å. Synthetic rutile does not show luminescence, though some blue-coloured stones do exhibit electro-conductivity.

STRONTIUM TITANATE

A newer synthetic gemstone, again produced by the flame fusion process using an inverted oxyhydrogen blowpipe, was produced in America during 1955. This is strontium titanate ($SrTiO_3$) a compound not found as a natural mineral; perovskite, a calcium titanate ($CaTiO_3$) being the nearest to it in nature. Like the synthetic rutile boules the boules of strontium titanate are black when they come off the furnace and need to be heat treated in oxygen before decolorizing, which they do to a water-white, and are much more diamond-like than the synthetic rutile. The crystallization of strontium titanate is cubic, hence the material is isotropic and thus cut stones will show no doubling of the rear facet edges. The hardness is 6 on Mohs's scale, the refractive index is 2·41 and the density is 5·13, a value remarkably high for a transparent stone. The dispersion of strontium titanate is 0·19 (B to G), that is about four times the dispersion shown by diamond, thus the stone has less fire than rutile. The material is opaque to x-rays and displays no fluorescence under ultra-violet light, nor is there any typical absorption spectrum useful for identification. The stones have been sold under the names 'Fabulite' and 'Starilian'. The name strontium mesotitanate has been used by one advertiser for strontium titanate ('Fabulite'). Other titanates have been produced, such as barium titanate (density 5·90 and refractive index 2·40), zinc titanate, and calcium titanate, which has a density of 4·05 and refractive index of 2·40. This latter stone is of orthorhombic crystallization, but is near cubic.

SILICON CARBIDE ('Carborundum')

The well-known abrasive carborundum has been cut in faceted form for those who cherish a freak stone. Such cut stones are bluish-green in colour and resemble to some extent a 'bombarded' diamond. Carborundum is silicon carbide (SiC) and is manufactured by fusing 70 per cent of sand and 30 per cent of coke in an electric furnace, forming an iridescent dark porous mass which often shows, especially at the top of the crucible, well-defined hexagonal crystals with platy habit. The hardness of the material is $9\frac{1}{2}$ on Mohs's scale, the refractive indices being, for the ordinary ray 2·65, and for the extraordinary ray 2·69; the birefringence being 0·043. The dispersion is about twice that of diamond and the distinct dichroism provides a distinction from diamond. Carborundum often fluoresces with a dull orange-yellow light when under an ultra-violet lamp. The density of the material is 3·17. There are two modifications of silicon carbide, the alpha type, as above, and a beta type, which is isometric (cubic), but nothing seems to have been heard of this type, which can be colourless and would resemble diamond, as a gem material. Boron carbide, with a density of 2·51, has also been made and could be a possible gemstone.

QUARTZ

The synthesis of quartz has been accomplished in many academic experiments, but these had no value as a source of gem material for the natural crystals are so common and cheap that synthesis for gemstone purposes would be uneconomic. However, the synthetic production of quartz is interesting as it gives a guide to the undisclosed methods used in the growing of synthetic emerald crystals.

Synthetic colourless quartz grown in large crystals was an outcome of war-time necessity. Untwinned quartz crystals cut into thin plates of different crystal orientation and thickness are employed in a number of ways, utilizing the piezoelectric character of quartz, by the electronics industry. Natural untwinned crystals of quartz are not abundant in nature and are mined principally in Brazil, a locality which might well be denied to a belligerent, thus a synthetic production might well be a strategic necessity. Successful experiments were carried out by both sides during World War II.

Quartz, when fused in an electric arc or oxyhydrogen blowpipe does not recrystallize but solidifies to a silica glass, so that the flame-fusion method of Verneuil will not operate in the case of quartz, thus different methods of growing large quartz crystals became necessary.

Hydrothermal Process

The most successful method is a hydrothermal process and the present syntheses are derived from the experiments of G. Spezia during 1900 and 1909. Water is most effective in bringing many substances into solution, and in general hot water is better than cold. At atmospheric pressure (760 mm of mercury) water boils at 100°C (212°F), but if the water is under pressure the boiling point rises considerably, and this superheated water then becomes an even more powerful solvent and will bring into solution such materials as silica and the silicates. Any drop in the temperature, or the pressure, would leave a mineral-rich water in a state of supersaturation from which the mineral matter tends to separate out as well-formed crystals, or grow a 'seed' crystal suspended in the liquid to a much larger size.

Two methods have been used to grow crystals by the hydrothermal process, both of which use an autoclave—a thick-walled steel container which can be sealed to withstand high pressure and which can be heated either internally or externally (*Figure 17.19*).

In the first method, the so-called isothermal method, the 'seed' crystal is suspended in the autoclave with silica glass as a source material above it. The contained water, made alkaline with sodium carbonate, is kept at a constant temperature of 360°C (680°F). In this condition the silica glass dissolves and at this temperature remains in solution. Further glass dissolving causes SiO_2 in the form of quartz to be deposited on the seed crystal, growing it to a larger size.

The isothermal method was found to have defects and a second method, the temperature-gradient method, was found to be more satisfactory. In this method the seed, usually a plate cut from an untwinned quartz crystal, is again suspended in an alkaline solution in the 'bomb', as the autoclave is often called, crushed quartz being placed in the bottom of the autoclave as source material. In this method the temperature at the bottom of the autoclave is 400°C (750°F) and at the top 360°C (680°F). Thus the saturated hot liquid, as it rises, becomes supersaturated at the cooler top and deposits quartz on the seed growing it to a large crystal showing prominent faces.

There is a critical rate of growth which determines quality and freedom from flaws and twinning. The crystals themselves commonly show a faint iridescence on the faces, and on the basal faces attractive growth features, like slightly raised discs, are seen. The horizontal striations so commonly seen on the prism faces of natural quartz crystals are not apparent in the synthetic crystals.

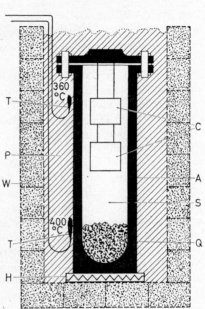

Figure 17.19. Diagrammatic sectional view of the autoclave (or bomb) used in the temperature-gradient method of growing large crystals of quartz. The silica-rich aqueous solution is at a temperature of 400°C at the bottom of the steel bomb and at 360°C at the top. The solution is under a pressure of 15 atmospheres. A. Steel autoclave or bomb. Q. Crushed quartz supplying silica to the high temperature water. S. Silica-rich aqueous solution. C. Seed plates. P. Heat resisting packing. H. Electric heater. W. Retaining walls. T. Thermocouples (pyrometers) for temperature recording

Cut Synthetic Quartz Stones

Cut stones of synthetic quartz are not commercially available, although there is a possibility that there are some faceted stones which have been cut for their interest as unique specimens. It is known that some specimens were cut, in this case coloured examples which owed their green colour to trace impurities derived from the metal of the autoclave, in order to illustrate a lecture and in 1969 some cut stones coloured blue by cobalt have been encountered. Whether the prized amethyst can be produced remains to be seen. The problem of the detection of such synthetic quartz has only been briefly touched upon and little is known. The blue fluorescence colour induced by x-rays has been suggested as a test for colourless synthetic quartz.

EMERALD

Early Experiments

The earliest well-recorded attempts on the synthesis of emerald were the experiments carried out by J. J. Ebelmen, one time Director of the Sèvres

Porcelain factory, who, in 1848, obtained very small crystals of emerald by heating powdered emerald with boric acid. This was rather a form of reconstruction than a true synthesis. Other workers using similar methods but different formulae also obtained limited success.

The experiments of P. G. Hautefeuille and A. Perrey carried out in 1888 produced small stones but far too small to cut into gemstones. The most successful experiment by these workers was when they used a mixture of alumina, beryllia, and silica, with a trace of chromic oxide, in the correct proportions for beryl. This was placed in a platinum crucible and covered with a layer of lithium molybdate. The charged crucible was then placed in an autoclave and the temperature raised to a dull red heat for some 24 hours, after which the temperature was raised to 800°C (1,480°F) and kept at that value for 15 days.

R. Nacken, in 1912, commenced experiments on the synthesizing of emerald and other minerals, including quartz, and in 1928 he successfully synthesized a number of minerals including emerald crystals up to one carat in weight. The method Nacken used was similar to the hydrothermal technique used for growing quartz crystals from a 'seed'. The autoclave was a thick-walled steel vessel, with a capacity of about 30 cubic centimetres, closed at one end with an internal screw plug. The solvent was water containing traces of a weak alkali and the raw material consisted of a mixture of beryllium oxide, alumina and silica in the correct proportions. This was raised to a temperature of about 370°–400°C (685°–750°F) for several days in the autoclave. The largest crystals grown were about 1 cm long and 2–3 mm wide. He also used the flux-melt method.

Resulting from experiments carried out by H. Espig and E. Jaeger at the North Bitterfeld factory of the German dyestuff combine, I.G. Farbenindustrie, a number of groups of emerald crystals were successfully produced in 1934. Groups of such crystals were shown at the Paris Exhibition in 1936 and a few cut stones were circulated, but mainly in scientific circles. These emeralds, which were called Igmeralds, from I.G. and emerald, were true synthetic emeralds.

Since the war synthetic emeralds, made in America, have entered the gemstone market. These are from the laboratory of Carroll F. Chatham at San Francisco, California, who, it is said, commenced his experiments earlier than 1930. Chatham says that his method is hydrothermal but discloses nothing of his techniques. He states that he uses crushed beryl as feed material and possibly a small natural crystal as 'seed'. At first these stones were called cultured emeralds, but this name was barred in the U.S.A. by legal process, the name 'created emeralds' being allowed. In England the stones should be called synthetic emeralds. The output from the San Francisco laboratories is said to be about 5,000 carats of crystals per month and about 12 months are needed to grow the crystals to suitable size.

Physical and Optical Properties

W. F. Eppler, after careful consideration of the differences in the inclusions seen in Nacken's synthetic emerald (*Figure 17.20*) and those seen in Igmerald and the Chatham syntheses, has concluded that the Nacken synthesis is probably hydrothermal and the Chatham synthesis is probably

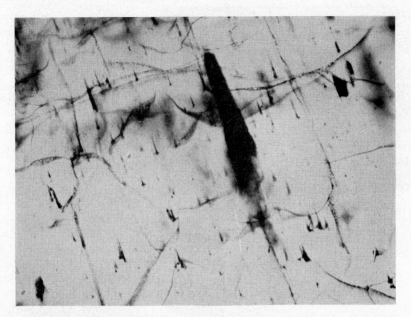

Figure 17.20. Inclusions in a Nacken synthetic emerald (circa 1926)

Figure 17.21. Feathers in an 'Igmerald' (1935)

(Photo: B. W. Anderson)

Figure 17.22. Parallel arrangement of feathers in an American emerald

Figure 17.23. Liquid-filled feather and zoning in an American synthetic emerald

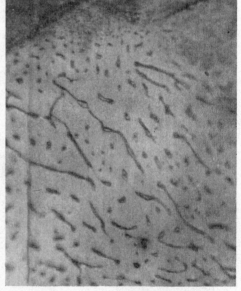

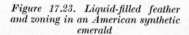

similar to or a modification of the Igmerald synthesis which Eppler suggests is a melt-diffusion method. It is now known that this is so.

Grown by a process which resembles to a great extent the method of formation in nature, synthetic emeralds do not exhibit the typical internal features of curved growth lines and included gas bubbles shown by the synthetic stones produced by the flame-fusion method of Verneuil. The synthetic emerald shows inclusions which are characteristic in themselves, but are remarkably like inclusions in natural stones. These inclusions are liquid filled feathers, usually two-phase, which assume veil-like formations and may be likened to curtains waving in a draught (*Figure 17.21*), or they may be in a series of parallel bands (*Figure 17.22*). Zoning is quite common and these zonal lines may be straight or angular in conformity to the hexagonal prism (*Figure 17.23*). Quite large crystals of phenakite may also be an inclusion, but three-phase inclusions, amphibole needles, mica plates and pyrite crystals, all of which are common inclusions in natural emerald are not seen in the synthetic stones.

The density of the synthetic emerald is perceptibly lower than the values found for natural emeralds. It is near 2·65, a value only just about that of quartz. Thus, in a bromoform/monobromonaphthalene mixture in which quartz just floats, a synthetic emerald will either remain freely suspended or just float. Natural emeralds will sink decisively in such a liquid. The refractive indices also differ perceptibly from those of natural emerald.

Figure 17.24. Feathers in a Zerfass (German) synthetic emerald

Again they are lower and are usually 1·563 for the ordinary ray and 1·560 for the extraordinary ray, the birefringence being approximately 0·003.

When viewed through the Chelsea colour filter the synthetic emeralds show a strong red residual colour which, while indicative, must not be taken as conclusive for some natural emeralds, particularly those from the El Chivor mine in Colombia also exhibit this strong red colour through the filter. This warning also applies to the fluorescent red glow shown by synthetic emeralds when they are bathed in invisible ultra-violet light, of which the radiations from the long-wave fluorescent ultra-violet lamp are the more diagnostic. It has been found that by the use of the short-wave lamp (2537 Å) the greater transparency to ultra-violet light of the synthetic emerald to the natural emerald may be demonstrated and used as a test (*Figure 17.25*). This greater transparency—down to 2300 Å in synthetic emeralds—may be ascribed to a greater purity and freedom from iron, the latter being such a common trace impurity in natural emerald, and may well be the cause of the absorption of the radiation below 3100 Å.

Carroll Chatham maintains that the synthetic crystals are free from impurities and strain so that they can be raised to an incipient white heat without damage, while the natural stone is destroyed far below the visible temperature range. Experiment has shown that there is some truth in this assertion. That synthetic emeralds are without strain is belied by the field shown when a synthetic emerald is examined in a polarized light when anomalous double refraction is clearly evident. Chatham reports that he can control the colour of his synthetic beryl crystals and has experimentally produced aquamarine and the pink variety of beryl called morganite.

During 1964 two new synthetic emeralds came on the market to vie with those grown by Carroll Chatham, which had held the monopoly for so

Figure 17.25. Differential transparency to ultra-violet light of synthetic and natural emeralds

long. These were the synthetic emeralds produced by Pierre Gilson of France and Zerfass of Germany. Both of these products appear to be grown by the flux-melt method and have similar range of density and refractive indices to those of Chatham's stones. The 'veil-like' feathers are also similar. The earlier Gilson stones do have one character different in that under the ultra-violet lamp they glow orange and not red, but recent products show red. The Zerfass stones show red.

About 1965 the American firm of Linde Air Products, the firm who first produced the star corundums, reported the production of a synthetic emerald grown by hydrothermal techniques. These Linde synthetic emeralds differ from those grown by Chatham, Gilson and Zerfass in that they have a higher density, 2·67, and higher values have been reported, and by their slightly higher indices of refraction and birefringence. One determination gave $\omega = 1 \cdot 572$ and $\varepsilon = 1 \cdot 567$; $\omega - \varepsilon = 0 \cdot 005$. The inclusions (*Figure 17.28*) are the usual 'veil-like' feathers, but often seen and more significant are the 'nail-like' inclusions formed by a dagger-like two-phased cavity 'crowned' by a small crystal or crystal group of phenakite crystals. These are similar to the 'nail-like' inclusions seen in the Nacken synthesis. The Linde stones exhibit a very strong crimson fluorescence and after bombardment with x-rays they show a strong 'after-glow' (phosphorescence). As far as is known the Linde stones are not freely marketed but are mounted into jewellery by a subsidiary firm of jewellery manufacturers set up specially for the purpose.

A group of Soviet scientists during 1963/4 experimented with the growing of beryl crystals 'doped', which is the scientists' term for artificially included trace elements, with vanadium, giving green stones; manganese,

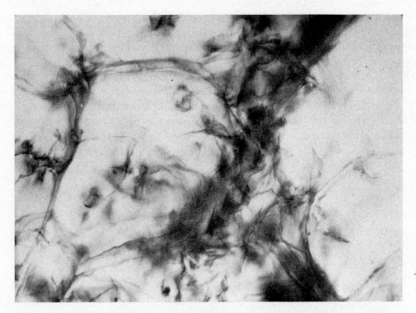

Figure 17.26. Feathers in a Gilson (French) synthetic emerald

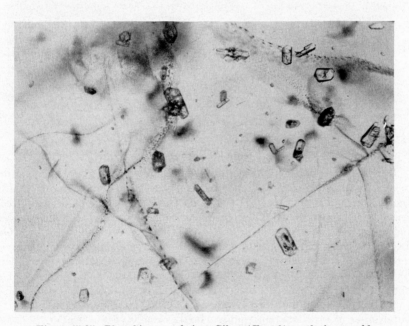

Figure 17.27. Phenakite crystals in a Gilson (French) synthetic emerald

which gave a grey-green colour; nickel, giving a light green; and cobalt, which gave a pinkish-brown tint. These experiments were only academic, but in 1967 green beryl crystals containing vanadium as a colouring agent were grown in Australia. It has been proposed to market such vanadium coloured beryls, and this will again pose a problem in nomenclature. In 1964 Hughes Aircraft Co. of America grew crystals of emerald by the flame-fusion Verneuil technique. The toxic nature of the chemicals used for this precluded the method, which was rapid in growth, from being a commercial way of producing gemstones. A high pressure technique has also been tried.

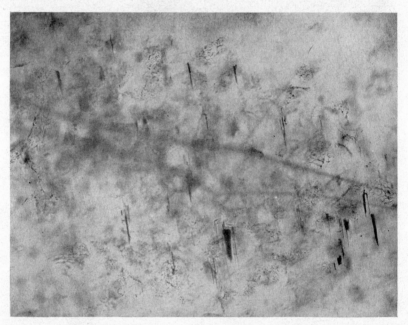

Figure 17.28. Feathers and needles in a Linde synthetic emerald

Synthetic emerald-coated Beryl ('Symerald', earlier 'Emerita')

During 1960 a new type of synthetic emerald, produced by J. Lechleitner of the Austrian Tyrol, was reported. In these stones, presumably hydrothermally made, the 'seed' is a faceted piece of colourless or pale green beryl over which the synthetic emerald is deposited as a layer, so that polishing alone is needed in order to produce the finished gemstone. The Lechleitner synthetic emerald-coated beryls have a density varying from 2·65 to 2·71, but generally about 2·69. The refractive indices approximate to 1·575 and 1·581, values which are comparable to natural emerald. It is characteristic of these stones that the edges show a network of cracks and a small facet is left unpolished (*Figure 17.29*). When immersed in liquid the outer layer of synthetic emerald is usually clearly visible. Under the long-wave fluorescent tube ultra-violet lamp the synthetic emerald coating will rim the stone with red fluorescent light. A similar stone, but made up as a multiple sandwich of white beryl and synthetic emerald, has been produced, but it is not common.

GARNET-TYPE SYNTHETIC STONES

Many of the newer synthetic stones which have entered the gem field are the outcome of the experiments aimed at the production of crystals for many modern scientific projects. The garnet-type stones are not in the true sense garnets for they have no silica, but they do have a garnet structure. The most important of these are the yttrium aluminium garnets ($Y_3Al_5O_{12}$), which are commonly colourless but owing to 'doping' may be coloured. An

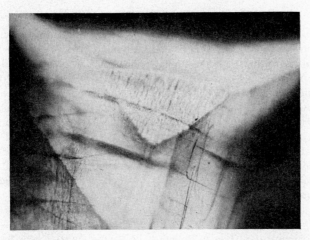

Figure 17.29. Synthetic emerald-coated beryl (Symerald) showing the reticulation of crack-like markings and one unpolished facet

example is a beautiful green stone coloured by chromium, sometimes with one of the didymium group of rare earths also, which vies with the demantoid garnet. These crystals are often denoted by the letters YAG. The stones are singly refractive for the crystallization is cubic, and they have a density of 4·6 and a refractive index of 1·83. The detection of the green stones is usually easy for the spectrum, whether it be that of chromium, didymium, or both, is sufficiently striking to more or less identify the gem as something out of the usual. Such garnets may be doped with other colouring ions so that all sorts of colours can be expected. The luminescence behaviour, too, can be unusual and informative, and this unusual behaviour also aids identification. Other synthetic stones of garnet type are grown such as, according to reports, yttrium gallium garnets (YGaG) and gallium aluminium garnets. An erbium garnet is produced, having the high density of 6·43. The yttrium iron garnet (YIG) is grown for its magnetic properties but has no place in gemmology, unless one needs an unusual black stone.

SCHEELITE

Scheelite, calcium tungstate ($CaWO_4$), is another mineral which has been extensively synthesized for its many uses in scientific apparatus. The growth of such crystals can be carried out by a number of crucible methods, but is now mostly grown by the 'pulling' technique devized by Czochralski in which a small 'seed' crystal is carefully lowered so as to just touch the surface of molten calcium tungstate. This 'seed' crystal is rotated and slowly raised producing a long rod-like crystal. Such crystals, which are colourless when pure, are 'doped' with various trace elements, such as neodymium which has produced a lavender coloured stone. But all sorts of colours may be predicted and the difficulty comes when such coloured synthetic material is grown in shades which are found in nature, such as brown. Identification may then be a problem. Colourless synthetic scheelite is another possible diamond simulant.

RARER SYNTHETIC CRYSTALS

Clear colourless synthetically produced periclase, magnesium oxide (MgO) has been cut as faceted gems for collectors of rarities. Periclase is a cubic mineral and is produced from a melt containing magnesium chloride and silica. The material has a hardness of 6 on Mohs's scale, a density of 3·59 and a refractive index of 1·738. Under the long-wave ultra-violet lamp the stones show a weak bluish glow which is stronger under the short-wave lamp, and under x-rays the glow seen is a strong mauve in colour.

Several colourless stones now being synthetically produced can, like strontium titanate (Fabulite), supply diamond simulants. One of these, lithium niobate ($LiNbO_3$), has, it is understood been marketed as a cut stone in North America under the name 'Linobate'. (This material has also been produced in other colours.) Lithium niobate has a hardness of about 6 on Mohs's scale; a density of 4·64 and refractive indices of 2·21–2·30 with a birefringence of 0·090. The dispersion is 0·13. Another stone is niobium 'doped' potassium tantalate, called KTN, which also has a hardness of about 6 on Mohs's scale, a density of 6·43 and a refractive index of 2·27. It is debatable whether this synthetic stone will be marketed.

Many other synthetic crystals have been grown and may conceivably come on the market at a later date. Among these may be mentioned the following: Gahnite ($ZnAl_2O_4$), which has a hardness of $7\frac{1}{2}$, a density of 4·6 and a refractive index of 1·82. The yellow crystals of the cadmium sulphide mineral called greenockite, even with their low hardness of $3\frac{1}{2}$ on Mohs's scale, may have a gem potential. They have a density of 4·82 with refractive indices of 2·506–2·529, the double refraction being 0·023. Colourless bromellite (Beryllium oxide = BeO) has been grown as small crystals. This material has a hardness of 5 on Mohs's scale, a density of 3·00 and refractive indices of 1·720–1·735, the birefringence being 0·015. Small crystals of chrysoberyl (including alexandrite), zircon, zincite and phenakite have been synthetically grown.

Fluorspar is another mineral which has been synthesized and often 'doped' to produce coloured material. The constants of fluorspar are 3·18 for the density and 1·43 for the index of refraction, the hardness being 4 on Mohs's scale. It must here be emphasized that the 'doping' of crystals grown synthetically may materially and strikingly alter the values of density and refractive index. A case which illustrates this is one reported in which a synthetically grown fluorspar crystal 'doped' with lanthanum had a density of 4·89 and refractive index of 1·47.

CHAPTER 18

IMITATION GEMSTONES

FAIENCE

The simulation of precious objects by substances of much less value reaches back to pre-history. According to A. Lucas an artificial blue frit composed of silica (quartz), copper (malachite), calcium carbonate and natron (sodium carbonate) had been carved into small objects as early as the 6th Dynasty (3503–3335 B.C.). It is, however, faience, a glazed siliceous ware made in Egypt as long ago as pre-dynastic times (before 4777 B.C.) which is the more important as a beginning of imitation gemstones.

Faience, which was used for beads, necklet pendants and rings, consisted of an inner core of gritty material, probably powdered quartz, and an outer coating of coloured vitreous glaze. Occasionally a thin middle layer was present between the core and the glaze which was apparently incorporated in order to enhance the glaze. Although glaze was used in Egypt so early in time, glass itself was not used before the 18th Dynasty (1587–1328 B.C.).

GLASS

The honour of the discovery of glass has been ascribed to several nations, but the oldest known specimens are Egyptian, and the material was successfully used by the Egyptian people to imitate such precious stones as emerald, turquoise, lapis-lazuli, jasper and onyx. Blue was the popular colour in those times and in this connexion it is interesting to note that the blue colour was obtained by the use of copper, cobalt and iron, metals, the oxides of which are used in a similar manner today. Glass, therefore, is the material that must be discussed first in any consideration of imitation gemstones.

Chemical and Physical Properties

Glass is a mixture of substances, or may be one only, which solidifies without crystallization on rapid cooling to produce a clear transparent solid. Unlike most substances which solidify from the liquid state to the solid state at a definite temperature, glass continuously increases in viscosity on cooling and there is no definite temperature at which glass can be said to solidify. For this reason glasses are often considered as 'supercooled' liquids.

The constituents of glasses are of two types; the glass formers, simple chemicals, mainly oxides, which can exist as glasses by themselves owing to the relative size of their atoms allowing the formation of a three-dimensional network structure. The other constituents, such as lime (calcium oxide) or lead oxide, which cannot form glasses by themselves, are used to thin out the network and produce a glass at a lower melting point.

The glass formers may be germanium oxide, beryllium oxide or phosphorous pentoxide, but supreme among them all, and incorporated in practically all glasses, is silica. Silica (SiO_2) actually becomes a silicate (SiO_4) in glass, each silicon atom grouping round itself four oxygen atoms in the shape of the regular tetrahedron, and each oxygen atom can hold two silicon atoms, the whole giving a certain flexibility to the complete structure.

The three-dimensional network of SiO_4 atoms can be broken up or thinned out by the inclusion of any substance soluble in the glass melt and which has no tendency to separate out on cooling. The most important of such substances are the oxides of the alkali metals—calcium, barium, lead and soda—and one effect of the inclusion of these extra constituents is to cause a lowering of the melting point of the glass.

The three-dimensional network of the glass formers is not symmetrical throughout the glass like the regular arrangement of the atoms in the crystal lattice. Further, the inclusion of the other constituents breaks up or thins out the SiO_4 tetrahedra in no regular manner. It is therefore impossible to picture the structure of glass, for the chains of atoms are twisted in all directions and the space given to each atom varies, the whole producing a random structure. This structure is common to all liquid substances and is one of the reasons why glass is termed a supercooled liquid, and to the gemmologist is known as an 'amorphous mixture of silicates'.

Before discussing the normal types of glass which are used to manufacture imitation gemstones, mention must be made of two glasses which have the composition of natural gemstones. The first of these is silica glass and may be considered as the connecting link between crystal and glass. If rock crystal (quartz) be heated in an oxyhydrogen blowpipe it melts at about 1,700°C (3,100°F) to a colourless glass—silica glass—a glass highly resistant to thermal change. The change of state from crystalline quartz to silica glass causes a drop in density from 2·651 to 2·21, and of refractive index from 1·544–1·553 to 1·46, the silica glass being isotropic.

Beryl, or a mixture having the same composition as beryl, has been fused (initially as an experiment to 'reconstruct' emerald) and found to form a beryl glass. Such beryl glasses have been faceted as gemstones when suitably coloured. An emerald-coloured beryl glass is produced by a trace of chromic oxide; a blue beryl glass by cobalt oxide and a pink colour by didymium oxide. These faceted beryl glasses are isotropic and therefore show no dichroism. Further they have a lower density and refractive index than for crystal beryl. The refractive index of these beryl glasses is about 1·52 and the density varies from 2·39 to 2·49, but is usually about 2·42. They have a hardness of 7 on Mohs's scale and usually contain many included gas bubbles.

Glass may be said to be a melt of an acidic oxide with a basic oxide at a high temperature, and which has been allowed to cool with sufficient rapidity to solidify without crystallization. It is a mixture and has no definite composition, therefore, as may be expected, the physical and optical characters vary within wide limits according to the type and composition of the glass.

Types of Glass

Glass is popularly divided into two main types; the crown glasses, consisting of silica, potash, soda and lime; and the flint glasses in which the lime of the crown glass is replaced by lead oxide.

The most common glass is that known as bottle, window or optical crown glass, which contains, besides the silica common to most glasses, lime, soda and potassium oxide. It is this type of glass which is used in making the cheap moulded imitation gems used in costume jewellery.

The second, and by far the more important so far as gemstone imitations are concerned, are the lead or optical flint glasses, which contain lead oxide, soda or potash, and sometimes thallium compounds, which, like lead, increases the dispersion and brilliancy.

Production of Glass Imitation Gemstones

The manufacture of glass consists of mixing the raw materials, including any colouring agent needed, to produce a mixture known as the 'batch', and melting them together in special crucibles called pots. The liquid glass produced by this melting, known as pot metal by the glass workers, is then used as required.

The actual methods used in the production of glass imitation gemstones from the pot metal may vary considerably. The glass imitation stones may be cut on a lap from sheet or rod (lapidary cut stones), but the most usual method is by moulding. The mould used is of iron and consists of two leaves, after the style of the culinary waffle iron; one half having the impressions of the crowns of the stones and the other half the pavilions. The mould is first oiled and then a layer of molten glass is spread upon the lower half and the mould closed. On cooling the mould is opened and the moulded stones removed and broken away from the thin 'flash' which connects them together at their girdles.

The cheapest glass imitation stones are made from crown glass and are sometimes finished by having the crown facets (or only the table facet) polished on a lap. Such a finish is termed 'half tin cut' (probably so named from the tin lap used and tin oxide being used as a polishing agent). If all the crown and pavilion facets are so polished the stones are then termed 'full tin cut'.

The backing of glass imitation stones by metal foil in order to give better reflection and brightness can be carried out by one of two methods: independent foiling and mirror foiling. In antique paste jewellery the foiling exists as an independent sheet of metal not in intimate contact with the stone. The upper surface of such colourless pastes may tarnish, and this by reflection from the foil of metal behind produces the agreeable yellow-bronze tinge which is so often seen in old paste jewellery. Mirror foiling, which started in about 1840, has the pavilion facets of the stone backed by a mirror in a similar way as are ordinary glass mirrors. This is produced by a mercury amalgam which is then coated with a gold-coloured lacquer to keep the mirror surface from damage. Such foiled stones are called chatons. A vacuum sputtering process has been experimented with in an endeavour to replace the mercury amalgamation for the foiling of paste stones. A

TABLE 18.1

Glass Colouring Agents

Colour	Agents
Reds	Copper oxide (a brilliant ruby under controlled reducing conditions) Gold compounds Purple of Cassius (a form of colloidal gold) Selenium (a ruby glass with an orange tint) Manganese oxide as free as possible from iron (violet-red) Iron oxides in the ferric state (brown-red) *N.B.—The purplish tinge of ruby golds may be counteracted by the addition of silver salts*
Pinks	Less concentrations of red colouring agents Selenium (under certain conditions) Neodymium in heavy lead glass (lilac-pink)
Orange	Combination of agents producing red and yellow colours Cadmium compounds
Yellow	Silver salts Antimony oxide Cadmium sulphide Iron and manganese (amber colours) Uranium trioxide Sodium di-uranate Carbon, alone or with a trace of manganese oxide Sulphur, alone or with carbon Titanium
Greens	Chromium oxide Uranium compounds (yellow-green) Iron in reducing conditions (blue-green) Iron in oxidizing conditions (yellow-green) Copper compounds (blue-green) Copper and chromium Cobalt oxide and red antimony Praseodymium (yellow-green)
Blues	Cobalt oxide Copper (pale blue) Cobalt oxide with manganese oxide (violet-blue)
Violets and Purples	Manganese oxide (purple in soda glass, violet in potash glass) Nickel oxide in potash glass
Browns	Sulphur with carbon Nickel in soda glass Iron compounds Uranium in quantity Iron with manganese
Smoke tints	Platinum Iridium
Opaque black	Large amount of tin oxide and remelting with manganese oxide and hammer slag from an iron works
Opaque white	Ordinary white (colourless) glass opacified by incorporating tin oxide, calcium phosphate or bone ashes. (This is an enamel and can suitably be coloured as for ordinary glass)

bright metal cone fitted to the bottom half of the pavilion of a colourless paste stone has been met.

The significance of the word 'paste' should be discussed. It is derived from the Italian 'pasta' which means dough or food and was formerly used exclusively for the cheapest types of glass imitation gems. Nowadays it is indiscriminately used for all glass imitations of gems, and often for imitations in plastic as well.

The better quality glass imitation gemstones are made of a highly dispersive glass containing lead or thallium. This glass is called strass, a name apparently derived from Josef Strass, an Austrian goldsmith—or by some accounts a chemist—who is said to have first used, if not to have discovered, this type of glass. Strass is a brilliant white paste, which can be suitably coloured. Its composition varies considerably, different makers having different recipes, but a general average composition approximates to 35 per cent silica, 50 per cent red lead oxide, 12 per cent potassium carbonate with traces of other substances, such as boron trioxide, alumina and arsenious oxide.

Coloured Glasses

To obtain coloured glasses traces of a colouring agent is mixed with the 'batch'. Such colouring agents are usually, but not always, metallic oxides. Table 18.1 lists many of the colouring agents used, but much depends upon the nature of the glass and the conditions of the melting.

Recently some coloured pastes for costume jewellery have been made from moulded and polished colourless glass, on the pavilion facets of which has been sprayed a pigment of suitable colour in an adhesive medium. When this has dried the pavilion is backed by silver or aluminium by a vacuum deposition technique. It has been suggested that a better range of colours can be obtained by this method, and that it obviates the need for the stocking of all sizes and all colours of ordinary pastes; only the different sizes in colourless pastes needing to be stocked and the colours produced as wanted. Many iridescent pastes appear to owe their iridescence to some form of vacuum sputtering, a technique commonly used in the blooming of camera lenses.

Determination of Glass Composition

In general practice the distinction between pastes and real stones presents no difficulty and for ordinary purposes it may seem unnecessary to proceed further in identification than to prove that the stone is an imitation. However true this may be in practice there will be cases where a fuller determination may be desirable or even necessary.

A mere determination whether the glass is crown or flint (lead), simple as it appears, is not so easy, for, although the two groups may be separated to some extent by their constants, the two types overlap, especially with the many newer types of glass in use today. Glasses could be identified and classified if a chemical analysis be made, but such time-consuming and exacting methods are outside the province of the gemmologist. However, F. A. Bannister ably showed that a fair determination of the type of glass could be ascertained by plotting the density and refractive index of the glass under test on a graph which he designed.

Bannister's graph (*Figure 18.1*) depends upon the relation of the constants of a given glass to that of silica glass. The formula is as follows:

$$\frac{\text{R.I. of specimen} - \text{R.I. of silica glass (1·46)}}{\text{Sp.Gr. of specimen} - \text{Sp.Gr. of silica glass (2·21)}}$$

plotted against the refractive index of the specimen. With the graph, however, it is only necessary to know the refractive index and density of the glass to find out with some degree of accuracy the type of glass.

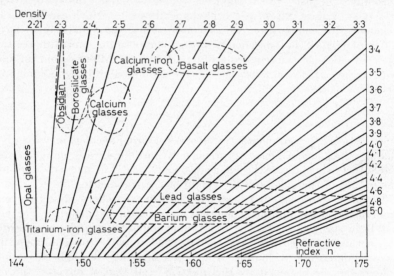

Figure 18.1. A chart for determining the composition of glass imitation gems. To ascertain the glass group draw a vertical line from the bottom edge at a point corresponding to the refractive index of the specimen. The point where this crosses the radial line representing the specific gravity of the specimen will show the group to which the glass belongs, since each type falls within limited areas which are clearly marked on the graph (after Bannister)

Density and Refraction

The density and refractive index of glass vary over a considerable range and in some cases overlap those of natural stones. Only in the range of beryl and topaz do glasses occur which have similar density and refractive index to the real stones, but in all natural stones about this range there are no singly refractive gems. The density of glass imitations may be said to extend from 2·00 to 4·20, and the refractive index from 1·44 to 1·70; however, a few freak stones have been found with a refractive index over 1·70 and below 1·49. Only the rare gems pollucite (1·51), rhodizite (1·69) and boracite (1·66), with perhaps the natural glass obsidian (1·50), are singly refractive natural stones between the range 1·50–1·70, so a singly refracting stone between these values suggests a paste. There is always the fear that an opal glass might imitate the fire opal, both in density and refractive index, but experience has shown that there are no commercial glass imitation stones simulating fire opal which have constants at all near those of the real stone.

Glass has a hardness of about 6 on Mohs's scale, but some boro-silicate glasses of the type used to produce the so-called 'mass-aqua' approach 7. On the other hand, the highly dispersive lead glasses are softer.

A crystal is a ready conductor of heat and hence feels cold to the touch, whilst glass imitations are characterized by their warmth to the touch. The test may be made by picking up the stone in tweezers, in order to avoid heat from the hand, and touching the stone with the tongue, which is the organ most sensitive to temperature.

Glass has a most pronounced conchoidal fracture, but this shell-like type of fracture is met with quite often in many real stones. It is unwise to accept such a type of fracture as conclusive evidence that the piece is glass. The lead-rich pastes, brilliant and fiery as they are, quickly deteriorate owing to the sulphur fumes in the atmosphere (particularly in industrial localities) interacting with the lead of the glass, producing lead sulphide which darkens the stones.

In many pastes it is often difficult, if not impossible, to obtain a satisfactory refractometer reading. This may be due to one of two causes; the first that the table facet is irregular and not truly flat, this being particularly evident in moulded stones where the centre of the large table facet is depressed owing to the shrinkage of the glass on cooling. The second reason is that some pastes are 'bloomed' like the camera lenses. This coating is a film of a substance with lower refractive index and is of such a thickness of approximately a quarter of a wavelength of light. The principle behind the process is to lower the surface reflectivity and let more light into the body of the stone. The value of the method, and it has been applied to real stones too, is debatable. The only effect of such a film is that there is sometimes a tarnish seen on the facets and that it most effectively precludes the taking of a refractometer reading unless the film be first removed. This can be done by rubbing with a rouged leather.

When testing paste imitation gemstones on an ordinary standard refractometer with a highly dispersive glass prism, the shadow edges seen are

Figure 18.2. Swirl striae in a paste

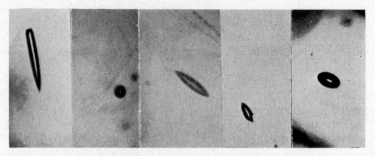

Figure 18.3. Typical bubbles in glass

usually sharper than the edges seen with real stones. Conversely, the shadow edges seen when paste stones are examined on a refractometer having a prism of synthetic spinel are a pronounced and wide spectrum edge in striking contrast to the sharp edges shown by real stones on this instrument.

Inclusions

Microscopic examination of the internal structure of glass imitations shows that the material can vary considerably. The best lead-glass pastes are usually very clean but may contain sparse gas bubbles. The cheaper quality pastes usually show bubbles, and these may be quite large. 'Swirl' or 'cooling' striae, sweeping curved lines which may be likened to the effect seen when treacle is stirred, are commonly present (*Figure 18.2*).

Figure 18.4. 'Breadcrumb' inclusions in an emerald-coloured paste

352

Bubbles in glass generally assume characteristic forms. These may be round, oval or elliptical, bullet or torpedo (cigar) shapes, and the smaller round bubbles may congregate into strings like necklaces. Sometimes sheets of small bubbles form feathers, and these are common in emerald-coloured glasses and then simulate the mossy inclusions so often seen in real emerald. *Figure 18.3* shows some of the shapes assumed by bubbles in glass. Bubbles drawn out into fine long tubes are sometimes encountered, and when these are fine such a glass will produce a cat's-eye effect. A convincing cat's-eye so produced in silica glass of a greyish colour is marketed. Extraneous matter, like breadcrumbs, have been seen in green pastes which simulate emerald (*Figure 18.4*).

Figure 18.5. Aventurine glass (goldstone) showing the copper crystals

Many of the semi-translucent pastes which are made to represent the chalcedonies and other ornamental stones, have the opacifying medium and colour in swathes. Such stones are usually full of bubbles, some of which seem to be filled with solid matter and appear opaque. The so-called aventurine glass, or goldstone as it is commonly known, is a soda-lime glass coloured reddish-brown by cuprous oxide which by subsequent treatment crystallizes out as masses of thin triangular or hexagonal plates of crystallized copper. Under a lens or microscope these copper crystals clearly show as polygonal spangles in a clear glassy base (*Figure 18.5*). Despite the copper content of this glass the density of goldstone is remarkably low, values between 2·50 and 2·80 being recorded, while the refractive index is 1·53. One stage in the preparation of this aventurine glass is the formation of a dark red glass called haematinon or purpurine, a glass which was known to the ancients. A goldstone with a blue ground is now produced.

Glass always tends to crystallize out, and such incipient crystallization, termed devitrification, often shows itself by the formation of groups of radiating crystals. Such devitrified glass has been used for ornamentation, particularly so if the glass is coloured and the crystal sheaves are another colour. One of the purpurines, a glass already mentioned, resembles a red opaque enamel and when examined under a microscope shows a structure resembling myriads of fern leaves randomly arranged and of different sizes. One such piece was found to have a refractive index of 1·64 and a density of 3·77.

The semi-opaque pastes which imitate turquoise, jade, lapis-lazuli and other ornamental stones, may often show on the surface little pits where included bubbles have been cut through in the polishing. It is generally possible to see a little way into the stone and there below the surface small bubbles may be seen, thus enabling the stone to be identified as glass.

Glass is isotropic and thus can show no dichroism. When rotated between crossed nicols in a polarizing apparatus glass stones should, in theory, show a dark field in all positions, but most pastes show some degree of strain, and this is evident by the anomalous extinction shown by the paste stones. This indicates an anomalous birefringence which is not regularly positioned. Indeed, D. Brewster showed that while well-annealed glass is isotropic, glass under stress behaves like a uniaxial negative crystal and shows bi-refringence, the amount being proportional to the stress.

Pastes

Colour filter

Many blue pastes owe their colour to cobalt and show, when viewed through the Chelsea colour filter, a red residual colour. There are, however, a number of blue pastes which owe their colour to other agents, such as copper, and these do not show the residual red through the filter. Unlike ruby, red pastes do not show the bright red glow when seen through the filter, but this effect does not distinguish pastes from garnets.

Absorption spectrum

Except in the case of the cobalt-coloured blue pastes the absorption spectra of glass imitation stones are not very distinctive. The cobalt-blue glasses show a typical absorption spectrum of three bands, one in the orange-red, one in the yellow, and the third in the green, a spectrum similar to that shown by blue synthetic spinel. There is a striking difference between the two, however, for in the cobalt spectrum of blue glass it is the centre band which is the narrowest, whereas in spinel it is the band in the green which is the narrower. Red coloured pastes vary somewhat in their absorption spectra; many act as a 'colour filter' and pass only a wide band of red light with the rest of the spectrum absorbed. Others show a wide and strong absorption band blotting out the yellow and green. Such a spectrum may indicate selenium as the colouring agent. Some rose-red pastes show the rare-earth lines in the yellow and green as are seen in yellow apatite, and these are due to didymium. Green pastes generally show a strong band (or cut off) in the red and absorption in the violet. Other coloured pastes, including the blues coloured by copper or iron, show no distinctive spectra.

Fluorescence

The fluorescent effects shown by pastes when bathed in ultra-violet light vary considerably. The best effect is seen under the short-wave lamp (2537 Å) when the glows vary from weak greenish-white to a bright bluish-white, for under the long-wave lamp (3650 Å) glass is usually only weakly fluorescent. In general the fluorescence of pastes is not too helpful and may even, if care is not taken, lead to a wrong assumption. The pastes coloured by uranium compounds fluoresce a very bright apple-green and if this glow is examined spectroscopically the typical discrete spectrum of uranium may be seen.

Rhinestone and Diamanté

It may be useful to mention the term rhinestone, a name which is often used as a sales aid. The origin of the term seems to be in doubt, but it may well have originated as a name for the quartz gems which were found near, and worked upon, in the twin towns of Idar and Oberstein. Later the term seems to have been used for the variegated multicoloured glass stones which had a vogue for some time. The term seems now to be used for any type of coloured glass imitation gemstone. Diamanté is the term used for the bright colourless pastes used to decorate fabric, but is now also used for the jewellery set with glass imitation stones.

PORCELAIN

Porcelain has occasionally been used for the production of some semi-opaque imitation gemstones. Porcelain, or pottery, is simply a baked uniformly fine clay and the frits and faiences mentioned at the beginning of the chapter are a type of porcelain. The material is not as a rule cut and polished, but moulded and then glazed with a glassy coating; thus the refractive index will be of little assistance in its identification. On the other hand the specific gravity is fairly constant at 2·3 and this will give an indication of the nature of such material, for, with the exception of a few minerals like sodalite and thomsonite, this value is not common to ornamental gem materials.

HEMATINE

Hematine, or 'scientific hematite', a metallic composition—probably a stainless steel containing chromium and nickel or some sort of sulphide mixture—is made to imitate the true hematite. The imitation hematite is readily distinguished from the true mineral by its attraction to a magnet, for true hematite is not magnetic. This imitation gives a streak somewhat like true hematite and the material is mostly met as intaglios of a Greek or Roman warrior's head. Some real hematite is however so carved.

PLASTICS

It is necessary in this section to discuss the more modern materials known by the collective name of plastics, an omnibus term for a vast number of artificially produced materials now used for the purposes of utility and decoration.

The rigid plastics with which we are concerned are usually the final stage

355

in the polymerization of comparatively large molecules formed by the condensation of simpler organic substances, for example

$$\text{(benzene ring)} \quad \text{plus } CH_2{=}CH_2 \rightarrow \quad \text{(benzene ring)}\ CH_2CH_3 \quad \rightarrow \quad \text{(benzene ring)}\ CH{=}CH_2$$

which polymerizes to form

$$CH_2CH_2{-\!-\!-}\left[\underset{C_6H_5}{\overset{|}{CH.CH_2}}\right]_n{-\!-\!-}\underset{C_6H_5}{\overset{|}{C}}{=}CH_2$$
$$\underset{C_6H_5}{\overset{|}{}}$$

polystyrene—Distrene (Great Britain) or Victron (U.S.A.).

Celluloid

The earliest known plastic was celluloid which is a mixture of the lower nitrates of cellulose and camphor heated to 110°C under pressure. The starting point of this earlier plastic was cotton linters. These by carefully controlled nitration give a long-chain tough structure which, with the addition of camphor produces the tough and elastic doyen of all plastics. The material, which is extremely inflammable, has a density for the purer material of 1·35, but may rise to 1·80 or over when containing 'fillers', and these high values are very evident in the imitation ivories made of this material. The refractive index is between 1·495 and 1·520, and the readily sectile material has a low hardness, about 2 on Mohs's scale. A useful test for celluloid, which tests for the nitro group, is to use a 5 per cent solution of diphenylamine in concentrated sulphuric acid. Sufficient quantity of this reagent may be made by dissolving 0·5 g (2·5 carats) of the solid diphenyl-amine in 10 ml (10 c.c.) of sulphuric acid. The reagent is best when freshly made and a spot of this liquid placed on a specimen of celluloid will turn deep blue.

The inflammability of celluloid acted as a spur to the production of a similar plastic without this dangerous property. By substituting the nitrat-ing process used in the making of true celluloid by an acetylation—the cellulose being treated with acetic acid instead of nitric acid—safety celluloid or cellulose acetate is produced. This material burns with a quiet and easily extinguishable flame giving off a vinegary smell. The density is 1·29 for the purer material, and this again may be increased with 'fillers'. The range of the refractive index is from 1·49 to 1·51, and like celluloid it is sectile.

Many modifications of cellulose are made in plastic form by using the esters, ethyl cellulose, methyl cellulose, and benzyl cellulose, but these are not at the moment important to this study.

On the addition of formaldehyde, casein—the protein part of milk—is converted into a hard insoluble plastic, and such material is occasionally met in the form of beads or small carved pieces. This 'protein plastic' has a density restricted to the range 1·32–1·39, but most specimens are constant at 1·33. The refractive index is 1·55. A spot of concentrated nitric acid placed on an inconspicuous part will stain the piece yellow, due to the formation of xanthoproteic acid, as this acid does with any protein. A peeling heated on a knife blade will char and give off the smell of burnt milk. Casein plastic may be semi-transparent to opaque.

Bakelite

The normal type of phenolic resin, so well known as bakelite and commonly used for articles of utility, is also made in a clear glass-like type which may be dyed in various colours. Bakelite is only moderately tough in this clear form and has the disadvantage of yellowing with age, therefore it is not very suitable for simulating clear-coloured stones but it does make a very effective 'amber'. This clear type of bakelite has a density of 1·25–1·30, and a rather high refractive index varying between 1·61 and 1·66. The material is tougher and slightly harder than the celluloids.

In the case of bakelite, if the density and refractive index tests are not possible for a given piece under examination, the following chemical test may be performed with advantage. A few chips or flakes scraped from the specimen are placed in a small test tube and covered with distilled water. After boiling the water with the scrapings in it, a very small pinch of the yellow powder 2·6 dibromoquinonechlorimide is added. The liquid is allowed to cool and a drop of very dilute alkali (caustic soda solution) is introduced. The production of a blue colour (bromchlorphenol blue) shows the presence of phenol indicating the piece to be bakelite. It must be realized that this blue is an extremely sensitive pH indicator and very easily discoloured by too much caustic soda ($NaOH$) which should be added in an extremely weak solution drop by drop.

A modification of the phenol bakelite is known as the amino plastic. In this material, which is translucent and is dyed in various delicate shades of colour, urea replaces the phenol in bakelite. The density is about 1·50 and the hardness near to 2 on Mohs's scale. The refractive index varies from 1·55 to 1·62.

Perspex

Better known under the name Perspex is the acrylic resin (a polymethylmethacrylate) which is normally a clear glass-like material which can be suitably coloured. Perspex has been used for the production of moulded faceted imitation gemstones, and for the cores of solid bead imitation pearls. The material is characterized by the low density of 1·18, and it has a refractive index of 1·50.

Polystyrene

Comparative newcomers to the range of plastics are the styrene resins, of which polystyrene is the best known and one which has been used to produce faceted stones by the injection moulding process. Polystyrene (polyvinyl benzene) has the low density of 1·05 and an index of refraction of 1·59. The material is sectile and is readily dissolved by such liquids as toluene, amyl acetate (but not acetone), bromoform, monobromonaphthalene and methylene iodide.

Other Plastics

Tables 18.2 and 18.3 give information on the more important materials covered by the omnibus term 'plastics'.

Plastic	Chemical Composition	Identification
BAKELITE Phenol formaldehyde	(structure: phenol-formaldehyde network with OH, CH₂ groups)	Characteristic group— Phenol
BEETLE Urea formaldehyde	$OC\begin{smallmatrix}N=CH_2\\N=CH_2\end{smallmatrix}$	Smell on heating— Organic nitrogen
BEETLE MELAMINE Melamine formaldehyde	(melamine triazine ring with $N(CH_2OH)_2$, $(OHCH_2)_2N-C$, $C-N(CH_2OH)_2$)	Smell on heating— Organic nitrogen
GLYPTALS OR **ALKYDS** Condensation of Phthalic anhydride with Polyhydric alcohol	(structure with COO, COOCH₂—C—CH₂COO, COOCH₂—CHCH₂—COO, OOC, CH₂, COO—CH, COO·CH₂OOC)	Phthalic anhydride Derivatives with resorci or phenol
NYLON Polyamide	$-\overset{O}{C}(CH_2)_4\overset{O}{C}NH(CH_2)_6NH\overset{O}{C}(CH_2)_4\overset{O}{C}NH(CH_2)_6NH-$	Organic nitrogen
POLYSTYRENE Styrene polymer	$CH=CH_2$ → $CH_2-CH_2\left[CH-CH_2\right]C-CH_2$ with C_6H_5 groups, subscript n	Characteristic group— Styrene Smell on heating
EPOXY-ESTERS Epichlorhydrin derivatives	$CH_2-CH-CH_2\left[O-R-O-G\right]_n O-R-O-CH_2-CH-CH_2$ with O epoxide rings and OH	Characteristic groups— (G) (R)
PERSPEX Methyl methacrylate Polymer	$\left[CH_2-\underset{COOCH_3}{\overset{CH_3}{C}}-CH_2-\underset{COOCH_3}{\overset{CH_3}{C}}\right]_n CH=\underset{COOCH_3}{\overset{CH_3}{C}}$	Characteristic groups— Methacrylic acid $CH_2=CH_3COOH$

lastics

Method of Testing

ent: 2.6-Dibromo-*p*-benzoquinone-4-chlorimide
y milligrams of the substance are boiled for several minutes in distilled water. The clear solution is decanted from the due and to it is added a small portion of the reagent, dry, or preferably a few drops of dilute alcoholic solution. The xture is then made slightly alkaline with dilute sodium hydroxide solution. A blue coloration indicates PHENOL.

these resins have very characteristic smell when heated
or organic nitrogen: (*a*) Lime mixture: 20 parts calcium oxide/1 part manganese dioxide; (*b*) Neutral solution, manganese rate/silver nitrate. A small quantity of the substance is mixed with 2 to 3 times as much lime mixture and slowly heated to ness in micro test-tube over the mouth of which is a paper spotted with manganese/silver solution. Dark stain indicates ROGEN. If stain spotted with benzidine acetate turns dark blue.

plastics gently heated in dry micro test-tube give sublimate on cooler part of the tube. This may appear as feathery cry-ls on wall of tube or cotton-wool like crystals across the tube. This is characteristic but if styrene or oil is present the limate may be in the form of a drop of viscous liquid. (If styrene present, smell characteristic.) In each case presence of halic anhydride may be confirmed by forming derivative: (*a*) With resorcinol to produce fluorescein—yellow solution with en fluorescence, (*b*) with phenol to produce phenolphthalein—colourless in acid solution, pink in alkaline solution. In h case sublimate heated with twice the amount of reagent and drop of conc. sulphuric acid, smelt washed out into small ker and sodium hydroxide added dropwise till alkaline (melt best made *in situ* in original tube).

very slight smell on heating nylon in dry tube (difference from Beetle or Beetle Melamine)
for organic nitrogen as given above for Beetle and Beetle Melamine

ed in dry tube Polystyrene very readily de-polymerized giving styrene, volatile with strong characteristic smell, irritat-; and reminiscent of gas works

xy esters including Araldite commonly used as adhesive for joining stones and fastening pearls, etc., in jewellery. Dissolve conc. sulphuric acid. This solution applied to filter paper gradually turns a cherry red colour, definitely confirmed by adding rops formalin and pouring into small quantity of water. Green coloration confirms EPOXY-ESTER.

ed in dry tube Perspex de-polymerizes rapidly on reaching temperature of about 300°C, the monomer condensing on the oler part of the tube. If tube allowed to cool and then slightly heated monomer rapidly boils about 100°C giving charac-ristic smell.

Other glass-like plastics have been produced from a number of starting groups varying considerably in qualities, particularly hardness, according to other groups with which they are condensed. For example, ethylene is readily converted into polythene a flexible waxy solid, but with the phenyl compound, phenyl ethylene produces the glass-like polystyrene mentioned above. An exceedingly large number of such plastics can be obtained varying over a wide range of hardness and so on as a result of similar modification. Alkyd or allyl compounds are starting points of many of these.

TABLE 18.3

Properties and Uses of Plastics

Plastic	Properties	Uses
Bakelite	Hard clear plastic, very pale at first, gradually darkening through pink to brown	Can be used for stage purposes, takes good polish and stands up to rough handling In jewellery makes very good simulant for amber. Low gravity very suitable Used in clear tints and filled to simulate semi-opaque and opaque stones, also woods Often used in bijouterie and trinkets
Beetle	Hard clear plastic Clear and remains so	As for Bakelite but could also be used for the paler stones such as rose quartz, pink beryl, etc.
Beetle melamine	As Beetle in general properties but superior in hardness, durability and finish	Can be used with advantage wherever Beetle is used
Glyptals or Alkyds	Good bonding agent, particularly if modified with styrene Not used as aggregate of stone	Commonly used bonding agent for various types of simulants— Reconstructed stones from powdered actual material of the natural stone Simulants bonded from aggregate of suitably coloured materials, not, or only partly, natural (A number of turquoise simulants of both the above types have been examined)
Nylon	Encountered in two main forms, as fibre or thread or in the solid form Exceedingly tough and hard wearing	As thread—pearl stringing, etc. —for bunch jewellery In solid form could be encountered as simulant of almost any stone, particularly such as agates, jasper, chalcedony
Polystyrene	Clear colourless plastic moderately resistant to surface wear	As for Perspex Dyed in various colours
Epoxy-ester	Reactive, Cold setting Usually supplied in two-pack form	Could be used as actual plastic in simulants of various stones but far more commonly used as a cement, for which purpose it is exceedingly strong and permanent under very adverse conditions —soudé and other cemented stones —cementing pearls, etc., in jewellery
Perspex	Water-white plastic Moderately hard but fairly easily scratched, marring surface	Main use in bijouterie and trinkets Can be made to imitate almost any stone or wood. Good finish and permanent if not subjected to undue surface wear.

CHAPTER 19

COMPOSITE AND ARTIFICIALLY COLOURED STONES

DOUBLETS

Unlike most of the natural gemstones the glass imitation stones are soft and will not resist the attack of a common file. Either to overcome this lack of durability, or to produce a larger stone from two smaller pieces of real stone, the various types of composite stones were devised. These are called doublets, or when constructed of three pieces or layers, triplets; the latter name, at least in Europe, seems to be dying out and all composite stones are called doublets.

The true doublets are made of two pieces of real stone of the same species cemented together and so faceted that the plane of joining lies along the girdle (*Figure 19.1a*). Such stones are not obvious when in a setting, but they are rarely encountered. Microscopic examination of such a stone will show that it is made of two parts, as the cement layer can usually be seen. Further any 'feathers' or other inclusions will not be continuous from one part to the other, and as the two parts will rarely be oriented correctly to each other examination in polarized light will show the stone to have optical anomalies.

A doublet made with the crown of the stone composed of a piece of real stone of the species simulated cemented on to a pavilion of material of lesser value (*Figure 19.1b*) is not frequently met. The most deceiving type of such composite stones are the diamond doublets, made with a crown of real diamond cemented on to a base of any suitable colourless material, such as rock crystal, synthetic white sapphire or spinel, or even glass. Such stones even if not made for fraudulent purposes are prone to fraudulent use. Diamond doublets are easily spotted providing the observer knows what to look for. Apart from the possibility of the presence of coloured rings due to deterioration of the cement layer, or an unnatural 'feather' in one plane due to the same cause, the double nature of the stone can be seen by observing the reflection of the edge of the table facet on the cement layer. If the stone is held in a good light and viewed in different directions oblique to the table facet, the plane of joining will behave as a reflecting surface reflecting the edge of the table facet (*Figure 19.2*).

Garnet-topped doublets

The most common doublet is the garnet-topped doublet which consists of a piece of almandine garnet forming the crown of the stone with a suitably coloured glass for the pavilion (*Figure 19.1c*). These composite stones are made by fusing almandine garnet—one of the few natural minerals which will fuse to glass—on to a 'button' of glass having the desired colour.

12* 361

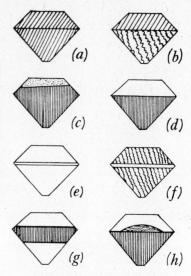

Figure 19.1. Types of doublets. (a) True doublet with top and base of genuine stone of the species simulated. (b) Real stone top and inferior stone base. (c) Garnet top and glass base. (d) Rock crystal top and glass base. (e) Soudé emerald. Rock crystal top and base with coloured layer between. (f) 'Soudé sur spinel'. As for (e) but synthetic white spinel substituted for the rock crystal. (g) Triplet with coloured glass centre section and rock crystal or some other real stone, such as sapphire, for the crown top and for the pavilion base. (h) The hollow doublet in which the lower side of the crown is hollowed out to contain a coloured liquid

The colour of the glass controls the colour of the completed stone, for the thin piece of red garnet plays little part in the selective absorption of the light. Such colours as red, pink, blue, green, peridot colour and aquamarine colour are commonly encountered. If the garnet top is thin and is cemented to a colourless glass base, a colourless doublet is produced. After the garnet is fused on to the glass button a stone is cut from the composite mass, and as little care is taken in orienting the piece, the line of joining of the garnet and glass may not, and rarely does, coincide with the plane of the girdle.

Unset garnet-topped doublets if placed table facet downwards on a sheet of white paper usually show a red ring round the girdle (except in the case of the red colours). Owing to the fusion of the garnet and glass the junction commonly contains a great number of bubbles in the one plane, and possibly

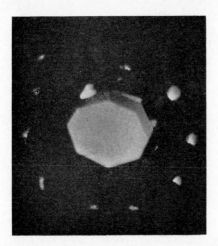

Figure 19.2. The reflection of the edge of the table facet on the cement layer, and ' Newton's rings' where the cement has deteriorated, seen in a diamond doublet

(By courtesy of the *Journal of Gemmology*)

crystal or needle inclusions in the garnet top, a completely anomalous effect which indicates the nature of the stone (*Figure 19.3*). Placed in a dish of highly refractive liquid the difference in relief of the top and bottom will show the stone to be composite.

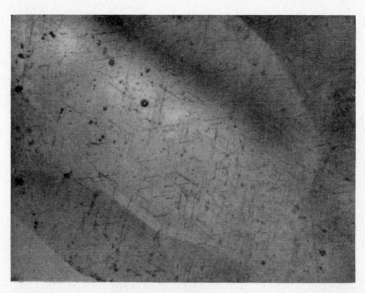

Figure 19.3. Needle inclusions in the top and a layer of bubbles in one plane seen in a garnet-topped doublet. The difference in relief of the garnet top can also be seen

Soudé Emeralds

The so-called soudé emeralds as originally made were constructed with a crown and pavilion of two pieces of colourless quartz (rock crystal) cemented together with a thin layer of green gelatine between (*Figure 19.1e*). The quartz soudé emeralds have the density and refractive index of quartz (2·65 and 1·54–1·55 respectively) but they suffered from the disadvantage that after a time the green colour of the gelatine turned to yellow. The rock crystal used for the two parts was selected for the inclusions it had in it for these natural inclusions made the 'emerald' more deceptive. These stones had a good emerald-green colour and, owing to the dyestuff used, they showed a red colour through the Chelsea colour filter like that of real emerald. When immersed in water in a white cell (eggcup or teacup) and viewed sideways these soudé emeralds show clearly the colourless top and base with the green layer between. Thus when they are unset detection is easy. Similar quartz soudées have been found where the gelatine layer is of other colour than green, and one strange variety was seen which exhibited a colour change to imitate the alexandrite.

A more common type of soudé emerald is made by a similar construction using two pieces of quartz, but with a different type of green layer, which is probably a metallo-organic substance containing copper. An unusual factor with these stones is their high density, near 2·8, which is ascribed to the nature of the green layer.

Recently a newer type of soudé emerald has entered the market. It is made similarly to the quartz type just mentioned except that the crown and pavilion are made of synthetic white spinel. Thus the refractive index of such stones will be 1·73 and the density, again slightly higher than for synthetic spinel, varies from 3·66 to 3·69. Owing to the refractive index being higher than the quartz types it is better, in the case of these soudé spinels, to use methylene iodide for immersion in order to see the clear white parts and the green central layer (*Figure 19.4*). These 'spinel emerald doublets' as they are sometimes called are made in quite large sizes and also in small trap-cut stones of calibre sizes. This type has been made in other colours, including black, a rich yellow and an amethyst colour. In

Figure 19.4. A spinel soudé emerald immersed in methylene iodide and viewed through the side clearly shows the colourless top and bottom and the line of green colour

the United States of America the soudé emeralds are known as triplets. Although a soudé emerald constructed with two pieces of beryl, instead of quartz, was known earlier than 1930, such composite stones were rare. However, in 1966 a firm in Idar-Oberstein marketed such a type of soudé in which the layer joining the two pieces of beryl consisted of a green coloured duroplastic cement. These stones are known under the name 'smaryll', and may be detected by the woolly bands in the red part of the absorption spectrum, apart from the pale top and bottom showing up when a sideways view of the stone is taken when immersed in water. Colourless sapphire has been used for the two pieces of soudé type stones.

Quartz Doublets

Variations of the quartz doublets are where the crown of the stone is colourless quartz while the base is made of a suitably coloured glass which usually has an index of refraction of 1·51 and a density between 2·55 and 2·61. Another type encountered consisted of a crown of yellow quartz cemented to a base of rock crystal, while a less interesting type had a crown and base of glass with a coloured layer between.

An unusual type of doublet, or triplet, consisted of a crown of rock crystal, the underside of which was hollowed out to take a coloured liquid or paste, the base being finished with a pavilion of glass cemented to the top portion. A triplet, as its name suggests, is made of three pieces. They are not common, but when found usually have a crown of quartz, the centre part being coloured glass and the base completed with a second piece of quartz. Other types of doublet encountered were a composite stone consisting of a crown of synthetic white spinel and a base of strontium titanate ('fabulite'); and a pale emerald cemented to a base of green aventurine quartz.

Star Stones

An ingenious composite stone is the so-called star quartz doublet and is made to resemble the star-sapphire. The star of these doublets is shown by transmitted light, for the natural star in rose quartz, which is the type used, only shows the star by light which has passed through it (diasterism), whereas in the true star stones the star is seen by light reflected from canals inside the stone (epiasterism). These star doublets are made with a cabochon of star rose quartz cut in the correct optical direction, to the back of which is cemented a blue glass and a mirror, or else a mirror incorporating a blue dye, which masks the pale pink of the quartz and gives a bluish hue to the completed stone. Star quartz doublets are easily detected if the stone is examined under an electric light, as, unlike the natural star stones, the image of the electric light bulb will be seen at the crossing of the arms of the star, and this image increases in size the nearer the stone is brought to the lamp.

Some imitation star stones have been produced by ruling fine lines, in three directions at 60 degrees to each other, across the back of a cabochon which has been cut from suitably coloured glass or synthetic corundum. A composite cat's-eye has been reported which was made of two pieces of synthetic yellow corundum with a layer of fibrous material between.

Opal

Opal doublets are thin slices of precious opal cemented on to a piece of opal matrix or a special black glass called opalite. This method allows a thin seam of quality opal, which would otherwise be wasted, to be used as a gemstone, but the value of these doublets is considerably lower than for a homogeneous opal. Difficulty may be experienced in detecting the opal/opal matrix doublet from a stone consisting of a seam of opal naturally occurring on the matrix, especially when mounted in a setting. A new composite opal, originating from Australia, is an opal doublet of normal type to which a concave-convex 'cap' of rock crystal is cemented over the top of the opal, thus forming an opal triplet: the stones are aptly marketed under the name 'Triplex opals'.

A new opal imitation is one made of a cabochon of rock crystal, or of glass, which has been backed with a slice of iridescent mother-of-pearl from the pearl oyster or from the colourful shell of the abalone.

Jadeite

Doublets, or more correctly triplets, have been produced in jadeite. They are constructed of a hollow cabochon of translucent pale grey jadeite into which is inserted an accurately fitting kernel of the same material, this kernel being cemented in with a cement impregnated with an organic green dyestuff which gives to the whole piece the colour of 'Imperial jade'. The base is completed by a third piece of jadeite. When unset the join between the pieces is readily seen at the edge of the stone, but when concealed by the setting the cabochon may be most deceptive. Such pieces, set or unset, are easily detected by the abnormal absorption spectrum caused by the dyestuff used, and this spectrum is similar to that seen in the case of the dyed jadeite mentioned later.

Cameo and Intaglio Doublets

Cameo and intaglio doublets are numerous. Usually the carved (or moulded) front is glass and the back is chalcedony, but some have the base also of glass and the cornelian colour is produced by the cement which joins the two pieces.

METHODS OF CHANGING COLOURS OF STONES

Pale emeralds and even colourless quartz may be mounted in a closed setting which contains a green-coloured foil either to enhance or to give colour to the stones. This green foil may cause the stones to show red through the Chelsea colour filter, an effect which, according to M. D. S. Lewis, is due to selective reflection. Thus care must be taken in using the filter, especially with 'emeralds' in old jewellery, for much Victorian jewellery had the stones foiled, for example, ruby, sapphire, and particularly topaz and amethyst. Another process sometimes used with stones in closed-back settings is to paint the rear facets with suitable colour, and this is sometimes done when the stones are open set. Mexican water opals are sometimes painted black on the back of the stone, or a piece of purple material is placed in the setting behind them. This is said to be legitimate for trade purposes.

A method of painting used by the unscrupulous to 'correct' the yellowish colour of off-colour diamonds is by coating the pavilion facets with a tinge of violet dye, a colour complementary to yellow. This treatment does not last and may be detected, sometimes by the accumulation of dye on the unpolished girdle edge, or better by washing the stone in hot water, or alcohol, which will remove the dye and leave the stone in its true colour. A method used in the United States of America to tint the stone (an undisclosed method but possibly a sputtering technique) is more dangerous as it needs the use of acids to remove the colour.

Iris quartz is a rock crystal with naturally ocurring thin air-filled cracks which produce iridescent colours. The effect can sometimes be produced by heating the quartz and rapidly cooling it in water, and if the water is coloured by a dye the dye will dry out in the cracks and colour them. Such treated stones are known as firestones, and when the dye is a green colour this cracked quartz has been marketed under the misnomer 'Indian emerald'. Quartzite, a rock made up of grains of quartz is carved into beads and dyed; the stain penetrating between the grains. Such stones are often dyed red and have been sold as red jade or tourmaline.

A number of gem species change colour on heating or by bombardment with particles of atomic size. Quartz, topaz, beryl and zircon are the species most commonly heat treated, while diamond is the stone treated by atomic bombardment. This aspect is discussed more fully in the chapter on colour, and is mentioned when the stones so affected are described.

Materials which are in any way porous may be artificially stained, and the staining of agate (chalcedony) is a major industry at Idar-Oberstein in Germany. The methods of staining depend upon the use of an aniline dye in which the material is soaked, or the formation of coloured chemical precipitates in the pores of the stone. Aniline dyes are not used to any extent for they tend to fade, chemical precipitation being the most common method for the staining of agate.

Black onyx is produced by boiling slabs of greyish chalcedony in a solution of sugar which enters the pores between the sub-microcrystallites. The slab is then treated by soaking in sulphuric acid. Sugar has the chemical formula $C_{12}H_{22}O_{11}$. The final treatment with sulphuric acid with its great affinity for water, abstracts the eleven molecules of water, $H_{22}O_{11}$, leaving C_{12}, which is black carbon in a finely divided form, in the interstices. A blue colour is produced by soaking the stone in potassium ferrocyanide and then in a solution of ferrous sulphate. When impure quartz (jasper) is so treated the imitation known as 'Swiss lapis' is produced. A red colour is obtained by soaking the stone in iron nitrate, or ferrous sulphate, and subsequently heating to red heat. This turns the iron compound into ferric oxide which remains in the interstices and gives an artificial cornealian colour, or if banded, where some bands of the agate do not take dye, sardonyx. Green colours are produced by nickel salts (rarely used) or chromium salts (more generally used) to give 'chrysoprase'. Hydrochloric acid will give a yellow colour. A pale blue dyed chalcedony, resembling to some extent the turquoise, may be coloured by a cobalt compound and show weakly the typical cobalt absorption bands.

Turquoise is said to be dyed to improve the colour but often the only treatment is to wax the stones, usually by soaking in paraffin wax. Such waxed stones appear to be acceptable for trade purposes. More is told of the treatments used on turquoise in the description of that stone (Chapter 11). Greyish-white jadeite is stained to an 'Imperial jade' colour by the use of a combination of two organic dyes; a yellow dyestuff and a blue one. Such dyed jadeite is very convincing when fresh but fades after some months, even in the dark. The artificial nature of the colour in such pieces may be detected by the colour concentrating along cracks, and better by the abnormal absorption spectrum shown by them. This is due to the absorption bands of the dyestuffs which give a wide band in the orange-red at 6500 Å and a narrower band at 6020 Å. Further, the jadeite line at 4370 Å is often obscured by the general absorption of the blue-violet produced by the dyestuffs. White jadeite is also stained to a strong mauve colour which is much deeper in hue than any natural mauve jadeite. This coloration is said not to fade.

A type of serpentine, probably near bowenite, is also stained to an Imperial jade colour, and possibly by a similar combination of dyes as used for the jadeite staining. Here again the spectrum is apparent. Alabaster is also dyed various shades and so is the stalagmitic calcite from Mexico, this latter material when dyed green has been marketed under the misnomer 'Mexican jade'. A reddish-violet dyed beryl has been reported from South America. Aventurine quartz has been dyed red and has been marketed as 'red jade' or 'topaz'.

CHAPTER 20

THE FASHIONING OF GEMSTONES

The bright faces seen on the more regularly formed crystals and the crude polish given to water-worn pebbles by being rubbed against one another in running water, may well have been the incentive to produce a polish on other brightly coloured minerals used by early man for utility and decoration. Who first learned to polish the rough surfaces of these hard substances is lost in the mists of pre-history, but these early attempts may have been to give a sort of polish to the irregular surfaces by rubbing one stone against another. Grinding the stone to symmetrical shape did not come until much later, indeed, shaping was most probably first carried out to give an edge to stone tools and weapons rather than to give symmetry to ornaments.

The earliest styles of fashioning were those which produced a curved surface, a style now perpetuated by the cabochons, or simply a flat surface upon which the worker could engrave. Curiously the engraving of gems was carried out in times far earlier than the fashioning with symmetrically arranged flat facets as in the styles in common use today.

The beautifully symmetrical and highly polished gemstone of modern production may be said to emanate from the original work of the lapidaries and diamond polishers of mediaeval times, and these crafts have altered very little from those early days. The diamond polisher cuts diamonds only and is simply and explicitly called a diamond polisher, whereas the craftsman who cuts the other and softer gemstones is known as a lapidary. This is because, for reasons which will be outlined later, the methods of operation have certain differences.

STYLES OF CUTTING

Cabochon Cut

The earliest form of cutting simply gave a curved surface to the stone, and, collectively known as the cabochon cut, there are four types of this style (*Figure 20.1*). These are the simple cabochon which has a convex (dome-shaped) upper surface and a flat base; the double cabochon in which the base also is convex, but less steep than the top; the third type is known as the hollow cabochon in which the underside is hollowed out to form a concave depression making a concavo-convex form. A very low domed simple cabochon is known as tallow-topped owing to its resemblance to a drop of candle grease.

In stones cut *en cabochon*, as the French term it, the outline of the setting edge may be circular, oval, polygonal or of a fancy shape; a common fancy outline being a heart shape. The cut is used for those stones which are translucent or opaque, such as turquoise and jade. Stones showing optical effects as asterism and chatoyancy must be so cut to bring out to the full the star and cat's-eye effects. The play of colour in opal and the adularescence of moonstone are best shown by this style of cutting. Deep coloured almandines are often cut as hollow cabochons in order that the depth of colour may be lightened, and in some cases the hollowed back is foiled to make the stone appear more brilliant. Such hollow cabochons of almandine garnet are called carbuncles, a name used since ancient times for cabochon-cut red stones, but now usually restricted to the almandine garnet.

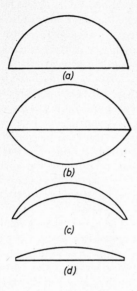

(a)

(b)

(c)

(d)

Figure 20.1. The cabochon cuts: (a) simple cabochon, (b) double cabochon, (c) hollow cabochon, (d) tallow-topped cabochon

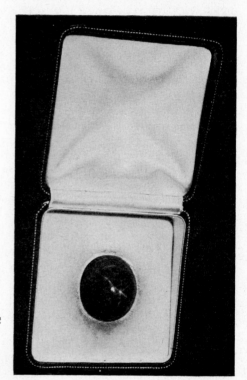

Figure 20.2 A large star sapphire cut in the cabochon style

Some badly flawed and poor quality sapphires are cut in the double cabochon style, and such stones are sometimes set with the flatter side uppermost as this gives a better colour and lustre. Star corundums and chrysoberyl cat's-eyes are set with the steeper dome to the front while the curved back of the stone is usually left unpolished. *Figure 20.2* shows a star sapphire cut in the cabochon style.

Rose Cut

The first of the styles of cutting which employ flat facets is that known as the rose cut or rosette, a name derived from a fanciful resemblance in the arrangement of the facets to the petals of an opening rosebud. The origin of the style is not known with any surety but it developed sometime before the sixteenth century. The rose cut consists of an upper portion only, the underside being just a single large flat base. The upper portion takes the form of a pyramid with three-sided facets meeting at the apex at a more or less steep angle. The rose cut is mostly used for diamonds owing to its economy in material allowing small cleavage fragments and macles to

Top plan

Figure 20.3. The round rose style of cutting

Side elevation

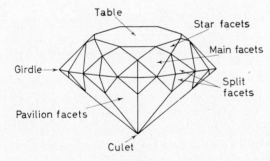

Figure 20.4. The facet names of a cut stone

be used up. In Victorian jewellery the then popular bright blood-red pyrope garnets from Bohemia were cut in this style.

There are variations in the disposition of the facets in the rose cuts, and, if one excepts the small chips of diamond cut with irregular triangular facets and a flat base, called senaille, which are used in the cheaper jewellery, the most common form is the round rose. In its most usual form the facets are arranged in multiples of six and in two groups, the upper six facets constituting the crown or star while the lower facets are the cross facets, or as they are often known, the teeth or dentelle (*Figure 20.3*).

In the Dutch or crowned rose the height of the pyramid from the base is usually equal to half the diameter of the stone, and the distance from the base to the crown is three-fifths of the total height; the diameter of the crown being three-quarters that of the base which may be round or oval. The Brabant or Antwerp rose is similar to the Dutch rose except that the pyramid is more flattened. The distribution of the facets is the same in each of these three types. The cross rose and the rose recoupée are modifications of the facets and are shown in *Figures 20.5* and *20.6*.

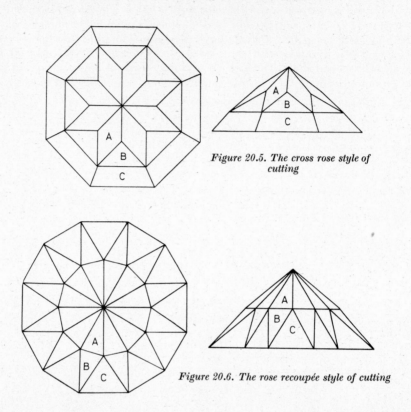

Figure 20.5. The cross rose style of
cutting

Figure 20.6. The rose recoupée style of cutting

The rosette has a crown of the normal six triangular facets, but the dentelle of the round rose is replaced by six rectangular facets; it is a simpler form. The double rose may be described as two roses joined together base to base, but in certain cases the heights of each may not be equal, and if the top half of the double rose is excessively elongated a drop-shaped form, termed a briolette (*Figure 20.7*), is produced, but such a stone can be faceted with rectangular facets in place of the triangular facets.

Figure 20.7. The briolette

Table Cut

What was probably the first advance from the mere polishing of the diamond octahedron—termed 'point stones'—was the table cut (*Figure 20.8*). This cut was produced by truncating one of the corners of a diamond octahedron until a face about equal to half the width of the stone was secured. The opposite corner was then removed in the same way leaving a face about a quarter the width of the stone. The whole of the faces were then polished. The table cut, a style extensively used by the ancient Indian

Figure 20.8. The table cut

cutters, may have many variations both in the depth of the stone and in the outline of the setting edge. Such table-cut diamonds are usually encountered only in old Indian jewellery, but a similar cut was used by the Nuremberg diamond polishers in 1373. One modification of this cut is made very thin and acts as a window or coverglass for small miniatures set in rings. Such stones are usually known as portrait stones.

Trap Cut

The table cut may well be said to have been the forerunner of the trap cut which is so popularly used at the present time for important diamonds and coloured gems. This cut, sometimes called the step cut, has the large table facet surrounded by a series of strip-like rectangular facets which increase in steepness towards the setting edge (the girdle); the lower half of the stone (the pavilion) having similarly arranged rectangular facets decreasing in steepness towards the basal facet at the point (*Figure 20.9*).

Base plan   Top plan

Figure 20.9. The trap or step cut

The outline of such stones can take many forms. They may be square, rectangular, triangular, kite-shaped, keystone-shaped and lozenge-shaped, and other polygonal forms. The rectangular form with the corners truncated, producing an eight-sided outline, is often called the emerald cut on account of its extensive use in cutting emerald (*Figure 20.10*). Small trap-cut stones of a long rectangular shape are known as baguettes and are considerably used as supporting stones on the shoulders of the so-called single-stone rings, and are used in designed pieces of jewellery. The term calibré is applied to small trap-cut stones, usually of square outline which are cut to special sizes to fit channelled settings in designed jewellery, in fact they are 'tailored to fit' and that is literally the meaning of the name. Some of these small calibré stones, although trap cut, do sometimes deviate

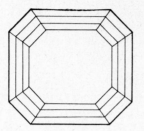

Figure 20.10. The emerald cut

from the true definition in that the outline may be curved forcing curvature on some of the facets, but these facets are still strip-like. Such are the marquise or navette (boat-like) and half-moon (lunette) shapes. A common modification of the trap cut is the cross cut, or scissors cut as it is sometimes called. Here the side facets consist of four triangular facets corresponding in each of the rectangular facets of the regular trap cut (*Figure 20.11*). The double scissors cut has a double set of these triangular facets on each side facet.

Figure 20.11. The scissors cut or cross cut

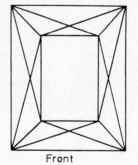
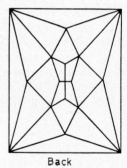

Front   Back

Brilliant Cut for Diamonds

The most common cut for diamond is the brilliant cut; it was said to have been devised by a Venetian cutter named Vicenzio Peruzzi at the end of the seventeenth century. The brilliant cut is the style most suitable for the diamond, for when correctly cut it not only produces the greatest amount of fire and brilliancy, it also enables the best use to be made of the octahedral form of the diamond crystals. The style has become so universally used for diamond that the name 'brilliant' is now synonymous for diamond.

The standard brilliant cut (*Figure 20.12*) consists of 58 facets, 33 on the top or crown of the stone, and 25 on the base or pavilion. The crown has a large eight-sided central facet called the table which is surrounded by 8 triangular star facets. These in turn are surrounded by 8 quadrilateral facets,

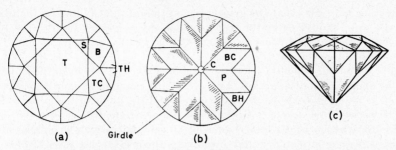

Figure 20.12. The brilliant cut: (a), T, table eight sides; S, star facets (8) three sides; B, bezel or top main facets (4) four sides*; TC, top corner facets (4) four sides*; TH, top half or break facets (16) three sides: (b) BH, bottom half or break facets (16) three sides; BC, bottom corner facets (4), four sides*; P, pavilion or bottom main facets (4) five sides*, and C, culet (1) eight sides

called bezels (four of these are called quoins and the other four templets); the significance of these latter names will be more apparent when the methods of cutting diamonds are discussed. Surrounding the bezels and meeting the edge of the girdle, or setting edge of the stone, are 16 triangular facets which are variously known as skill facets, cross facets, break facets, or halves.

The back portion of the stone, or pavilion as it is called, has 8 long five-sided facets called the pavilions which are symmetrical with the 8 bezels

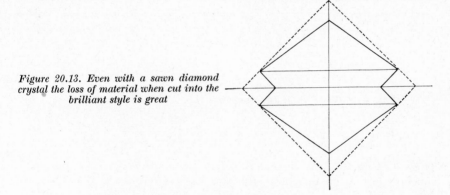

Figure 20.13. Even with a sawn diamond crystal the loss of material when cut into the brilliant style is great

on the crown of the stone. Corresponding to those on the front of the stone there are 16 skill facets just below the girdle and joining up with the pavilions. At the point of the stone where the pavilions meet at the bottom there is usually ground on a small facet parallel to the table facet of the crown. This culet as it is called, put on to prevent splintering, is sometimes omitted in small stones.

In cutting diamonds, or indeed other stones which owe their beauty to dispersion of light and to fire and not wholly to their body colour, it is

* It should be observed that the difference between these two facets is only that they are differently orientated to the shape and, therefore, require polishing in different directions.

necessary to ensure that the greater proportion of light falling on the front of the stone should strike the rear facets at angles greater than the critical angle for the mineral concerned, and thus be totally reflected back to the eye of the observer.

For diamond, which has a critical angle of 24° 26′, the back facets need to be at an angle of approximately 41° to the plane of the girdle, and the angle between the side facets of the crown and the plane of the girdle needs to be between 35° and 37°. As the angle of the octahedron is 54° 44′ a considerable wastage of material—some 50–60 per cent—occurs in cutting such a stone from a diamond crystal; even when the crystals are sawn the loss is great (*Figure 20.13*).

Modifications of Brilliant Cut

There are many modifications of the brilliant cut, both in outline and in the number of facets. Marquise (*Figure 20.14*) is the name used when the

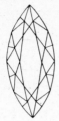

Figure 20.14. The marquise or navette

outline is boat-shaped, although navette is used in a similar connexion. A pear-shaped outline is called a pendeloque (*Figure 20.15*), and an outline which tends to be squarish with rounded corners is termed cushion-shaped

Figure 20.15. The pendoloque

(*Figure 20.16*). Many of the old Brazilian diamonds were so cut, for not so much is lost in cutting, but with this cut the brilliancy is not so well brought out. For small diamonds the single cut, or eight cut may be used in which there are only 8 facets surrounding the table and 8 pavilion facets below the girdle (*Figure 20.17a*). The Swiss cut has 17 facets on the crown,

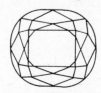

Figure 20.16. The cushion-shaped brilliant

the table being surrounded by 8 large triangular star facets, the points of which reach the girdle (*Figure 20.17b*). On the pavilion there are 8 large skill

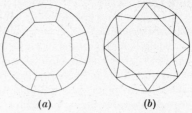

Figure 20.17. (a) The eight cut, (b) the Swiss cut

(a)   (b)

facets whose points reach half-way down the pavilion facets, thus there are 16 facets on the base making 33 facets (34 if there be a culet) in the completed stone. The zircon cut (used extensively for zircon) is characterized by a second set of facets surrounding the culet (*Figure 20.18*).

Figure 20.18. The zircon cut

For large stones a greater number of facets than the 58 of a standard brilliant may be put on but they will still conform to the general symmetry. More elaborate modifications of the brilliant cut are the king cut which has a twelve-sided table with 48 surrounding facets to form the crown of the stone, and 37 facets, including the culet, on the pavilion, that is 86 facets

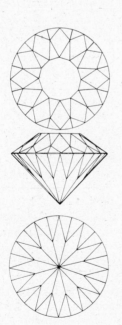

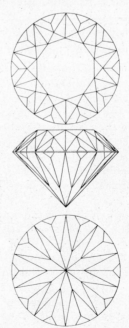

Figure 20.19. The king cut   Figure 20.20. The magna cut

in all (*Figure 20.19*). The magna cut has a ten-sided table facet surrounded by 60 facets on the crown and 41 facets on the pavilion, making 102 facets in all (*Figure 20.20*).

Whatever the type of stone, one which is well cut is preferable to one which is badly fashioned. Perfection in cutting, which is sometimes called the 'make' of the stone, is much more important in the case of diamonds than in other stones, for faults and imperfections adversely affect the value of the diamond. Such faults can be bad proportions; unsymmetrical outlines or large culets, as common in the old Brazilian stones, which are visible through the table facet. Overthick or irregular girdles and, perhaps, 'naturals' on the girdle may be a disadvantage. Another imperfection, thought to be due to too rapid bruting of the crystal, is the defect known as 'bearded girdles', which are many fine lines on or just within the girdle. Polishing marks on some of the facets, and extra facets put on to remove a flaw, are also detrimental to the value of the diamond.

Other Cuts

There are many other styles of cutting used for stones other than diamond, the most common of which is the mixed cut. This has a brilliant cut top and a step cut base. Some cuts such as the Portuguese cut and the Scotch cut, which are often used for yellow and brown quartz, have over 200 facets. The lens cut is a style in which the front of the stone is cut with a series of long parallel facets forming a cylindrical dome-shaped top, the base being step cut. The buff top is similar except that there are only three parallel facets which run across the width of the stone and not along the length as in the lens cut. An alternative to these is that the top is just a cylindrical dome. If the stone is rather soft, as in fire opal, the table facet may be domed, and a domed table may be seen in some peridots and amethysts.

Variations in Diamond Cuts

During the later months of 1961 a new and revolutionary technique for the fashioning of diamonds was introduced. This is the Profile cut (*Figure 20.21*) brought out by Arpad Nagy. Economy of diamond material is the basic idea behind the technique, for in the new cut the diamond thickness is no more than 1·5 mm. Stones of various shapes, such as heart-shaped, square, rectangular, lozenge and other fancy outlines, can be cut to standardized dimensions. The stones can therefore be bought by size which makes interchangeability easy for the jewellery manufacturer.

The diamond crystal is first sliced into plates of the desired thickness by means of ganged diamond saws. Each plate is then given the profile desired and the top polished to provide a table facet. The bottom is then shaped and polished into a series of V-grooves which have the correct angle to give total internal reflection. The cutting of the grooves is performed by polishing the stone on a special lap machined with negative serrations.

The Profile cut allows considerably greater area of visible diamond than a brilliant cut of similar size. Viewed from above a Profile cut diamond resembles a row of baguettes joined by a common table facet; or if two sets of grooves are cut across at right angles to each other the resemblance is to a number of small square trap-cut stones with a common table facet. This cut was earlier known as the Princess cut.

The girdles of faceted stones are usually left unpolished, and even in diamond the girdle is the only surface of the brilliant which remains in the bruted condition. It is kept as thin as possible so as to be hardly visible. Despite this, attempts have been made with some success to polish the girdle edge of diamonds with a view to improving the refractive properties. L. H. Roselaar in America produced the 'Multi-facet cut' which had the girdle of the diamonds polished with 40 small rectangular facets—making a stone having 98 facets.

The firm of Monnickendam of Portslade, Sussex, England, have experimented with the cylindrical polishing of the girdle of diamonds by using special machinery—probably identical or similar to the machine perfected

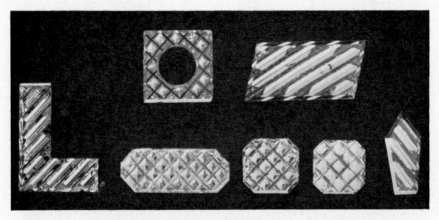

Figure 20.21. Different cuts in the Profile diamond

by F. C. Jearum of Surrey, England. The apparatus consists of a double dolly bar fitted across one headstock of a special lathe. The bars carry at the centre the diamond which is to have its girdle polished. The diamond is clamped against the two centre ends of the double dolly bar by the crown and culet, thus allowing the girdle to be exposed. The fitting is rotated by the lathe head, and by an arrangement of gears the diamond is simultaneously rotated in the axis of the dolly bars. Opposite this headstock is another live head which carries a scaife rotating in a vertical plane. When the girdle of the diamond is in contact with the scaife the double rotatory movement of the diamond against the spinning scaife, which is charged with diamond powder, polishes the edge of the girdle.

Intaglios and Cameos

Gemstones are also carved. Flawed, translucent and opaque gemstones may be carved in the shape of leaves, flowers or stylized designs. Intaglios (*Figure 20.22*) are incised carvings for the purposes of use as seals, while cameos (*Figures 20.23 and 20.24*) have the carving above the surface. In both cameos and intaglios a layered material having two distinct colours is often used, in particular banded agates and shells of the Giant Conch and the Helmet shell.

Mosaics

The fitting together of small pieces of coloured ornamental stones to form a pattern or picture is called a mosaic or inlay and may be either of two types. The first of these is the Florentine mosaic, which is sometimes known under the names intasia or pietra dura (*Figure 20.25*). The pattern is made up of suitably shaped pieces of coloured stone—marbles, coral, malachite, opal, lapis lazuli and turquoise are often used—cemented into a recess

Figure 20.23. Shell cameo

Figure 20.22. Intaglio carved in
an amethyst

Figure 20.24. A fine stone cameo (white on a greyish-brown background) being a carved copy by R. Hahn of Idar-Oberstein of the Tazza Farnese. Actual size about eight inches

cut into, usually, a black marble slab which forms the background. Parquetry is somewhat similar except that the pieces of stone are cut in geometrical shapes and then set in a metal mount. Some Scotch agate brooches are built on this style. The second type, the Roman or Byzantine mosaic (*Figures 20.25 and 20.27*) is not made of natural minerals but of small pieces of coloured glass rods of uniform length cemented in an upright position to a recess in usually, a glass frame. The patterns depicted are often those of ancient ruins.

Figure 20.25. A Florentine (intasia or pietra dura) mosaic

Figure 20.26. Roman mosaics

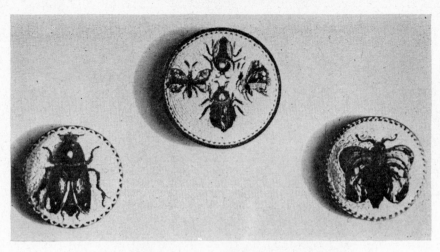

Figure 20.27. Roman mosaic

POLISHING

The older conception of the polish of a material was that it was simply one of superfine grinding so that the hills and the dales of the uneven surface were ground finer until any scratches thereon were too small to be visible. The work of G. Beilby during the early part of the twentieth century showed that this was not so, except in a small number of cases. Beilby found evidence that in polishing there is an actual flow of the solid surface with the formation of a liquid-like layer. This layer, termed the Beilby layer, lies like a coat of varnish over the underlying scratches. That the scratches are only varnished over by the layer may be demonstrated by etching with acid when they are revealed again.

In 1937 G. I. Finch experimented with the new technique of electron diffraction, which reveals the structure of the surface layer of a solid. He substantiated and extended Beilby's findings. Briefly put, Finch found that there are four different types of polish layer in minerals. They are as follows:

(1) No Beilby layer as the melting point of the material is too high for the necessary local fusion. In this case, therefore, the polishing is just a fine abrasion. Such is the polish surface of diamond and graphite.

(2) A Beilby layer forms but immediately recrystallizes in conformity with the underlying structure. This is what occurs when corundum and quartz are polished.

(3) The Beilby layer forms but remains amorphous except parallel to important crystal planes, or on long heating. Calcite and kyanite are examples.

(4) In this case the Beilby layer remains amorphous on all surfaces. This occurs with zircon and spinel.

The existence of the Beilby layer, a layer too thin to give a reading on a refractometer, for the shadow edge shown is that of the underlying solid, explains to some extent the reason for the differences in the techniques in the polishing of diamond and those used for the polishing of stones of other species.

Diamonds

The polishing of diamonds was first practised about the beginning of the fourteenth century on Indian stones, many of which were polished with small facets all over the surface by means of leather laps or 'mills'. Probably at the end of the same century, Loderwyck Van Bergen (Louis van Berquen) a Belgian, is said to have discovered the principles of polishing diamonds by using diamond powder, although they may have been known earlier.

The craft of the diamond polisher differs in certain essentials from that of the lapidary who cuts the other gemstones. The rough diamonds received by the diamond polishing works may be crystals having excellent form, or they may be very distorted and rough with little outward sign of crystallization. Thus the first task is to examine thoroughly the rough stone, both as to the surface and the internal features, for the stone may contain inclusions in the form of black spots (carbons), or various other included minerals, as well as cleavage cracks and splits, called by the polishers by the term 'gles'.

Methods of Separation

In the case of large rough diamonds, and in any diamond containing flaws, advantage is taken of the strong octahedral cleavage of diamond to separate the stone into smaller pieces. This is done so that pieces of a more workable size may be obtained, and to remove flawed parts, so that the maximum yield and purity is assured.

The separation of diamonds by the use of the cleavage direction is the job of the cleaver who, with the aid of a sharp-edged piece of diamond set in a holder, cuts a small groove or 'kerf' in the cleavage direction (*Figure 20.28*). For this operation the stone to be cleaved is set into a holder, and when the groove has been cut to a sufficient depth, this holder with the stone mounted on it is placed in a lead support attached to the bench. A blunt steel knife is then inserted into the groove with the blade parallel to the cleavage direction. A sharp steady blow is then struck on the back of the blade with a steel hammer, when the stone, if correctly grooved and the blade set right, will split into two pieces (*Figure 20.29*)

A more modern method (invented in 1905) for separating diamonds into two pieces is by sawing the stones. Well-formed octahedral crystals are commonly sawn in two. The sawing is carried out by the use of a rapidly revolving diamond-charged phosphor-bronze disc, and the stone to be sawn is first marked out in Indian ink to show the direction in which it is to be sawn. The stone is then set between two metal 'dops', which are fixed to a counterpoised movable arm on the sawing machine. The diamond is suspended above the diamond saw, and by manipulating adjusting screws can be moved laterally for centring over the saw. The phosphor-bronze disc is about 3 in. (7·5 cm) in diameter and has a thickness of 0·06 mm, and is run at a speed of approximately 6,000 r.p.m. The edge of the saw is impregnated with diamond powder mixed with olive oil by a hand roller,

Figure 20.28. Grinding the groove to take the blade preparatory to cleaving the diamond

(By courtesy of Shell Petroleum Company Limited)

which not only forces the diamond powder into the edge of the disc but also spreads this edge to give a 'set' so that the saw will not bind in the cut (*Figure 20.30*).

The diamond is then gently lowered on to the edge of the revolving saw, starting the cut at a corner of the crystal (*Figure 20.31*). It is also necessary to ensure that the sawing will be across the 'grain', that is across the traces of the cleavage edges. While the cutting process is proceeding the saw needs constant replenishment with the diamond powder and olive oil, for if the

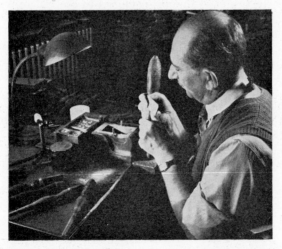

Figure 20.29. The cleaving blade in position ready for the blow which will cause the diamond to split in two

(By courtesy of Shell Petroleum Company Limited)

384

Figure 20.30. Charging the sawing disc with diamond powder

(By courtesy of Shell Petroleum Company Limited)

disc runs dry it is likely to be torn and the stone broken. One operator, the sawyer, deals with this and may look after a battery of as many as 40 saws (*Figure 20.32*). It takes up to 8 hours to cut a crystal weighing 1 carat. The cut, in the case of well-formed octahedral crystals, is made through the thickest part so as to produce two equal halves.

Grinding

The next process is to grind the stone into a truncated double cone

Figure 20.31. A close-up of a diamond saw cutting through a diamond crystal

(By courtesy of Shell Petroleum Company Limited)

Figure 20.32. A battery of diamond saws

(By courtesy of Shell Petroleum Company Limited)

(*Figure 20.33*). Previously carried out by a laborious method of hand grinding by working two diamonds one against the other, grinding is now done mechanically. This grinding, termed 'bruting' or 'girdling', is carried out by mounting one stone on the headstock of a special lathe. Another diamond, selected for its sharp edges, is mounted at the end of a long holder which the bruter or grinder holds firmly under his arm. He grinds one stone against the other until both are the required shape, a double cone with one end, where the table facet will be placed flatter than the other. The roughly rounded edge, called the rondist, will become the girdle in the case of brilliant-cut stones, for bruting is not done in the case of emerald-cut stones and rarely for baguette shapes.

From the bruter the stone goes to the polishers who grind on the facets to complete the finished product. As a stone cannot be polished except

Figure 20.33. The diamond in the chuck is ground to circular shape by the other diamond in the stick which is held by the grinder

(By courtesy of Shell Petroleum Company Limited)

across a 'grain' it is necessary for these directions to be known (*Figures 20.34* and *20.35*). A certain nomenclature is used in describing the grain. Stones which have been sawn are said to be '4-point', for the table facet will be parallel to a cube face—a face of fourfold symmetry—and will have two directions of cleavage traces.

'Three-point' stones are those which have the table facet parallel to an octahedral face, a face of trigonal symmetry. Along this direction the stone can only be cleaved and cannot be sawn; further, polishing such a surface is difficult and slow. Only cleavages and 'spinel-twins', the so-called macles, are in this category. Macles are disliked by the diamond polisher owing to

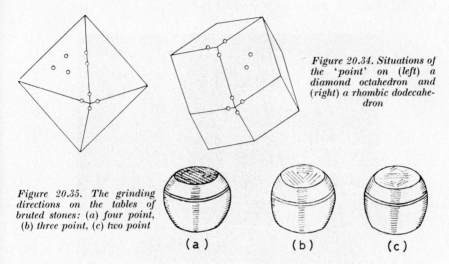

Figure 20.34. Situations of the 'point' on (left) a diamond octahedron and (right) a rhombic dodecahedron

Figure 20.35. The grinding directions on the tables of bruted stones: (a) four point, (b) three point, (c) two point

(a)   **(b)**   **(c)**

the twin-plane, or naat, which gives the stone a cross grain. 'Two-point' stones have the table facet parallel to a dodecahedral face and give two directions for polishing.

Technique of Faceting and Polishing

Polishing operations are usually divided into two groups and it is usual for the craftsmen to specialize on one group. These are the cross worker (kruisworker) who cuts the table facet and four main side facets, and the corresponding four back facets and the culet. Care must be taken at this stage to ensure the correctness of the angle of these facets from the girdle, a gauge being used to check them. From the cross worker the stone goes to the brillianteerder who puts on all the remaining facets.

The cutting of the facets and the polishing are carried out in one operation. This is performed on a revolving horizontal 'lap' or 'scaife' (*Figure 20.36*), a cast iron lap about half to three-quarters of an inch in thickness and having a diameter of about 12 in. (30 cm). The scaife is most carefully balanced so as to run perfectly true on the spindle, and the scaife, after the scouring of the surface with sandstone blocks, is charged with diamond powder and olive oil. The speed of rotation used is between 2,400 and 3,000 r.p.m.

The diamond to be polished is mounted in a 'dop' (*Figure 20.37*) which consists of a brass cup with a soft copper tail. The dop is filled with soft solder into which the diamond to be polished is mounted whilst the solder is still pasty. In modern practice a mechanical dop, which came out between the two World wars, is extensively used (*Figure 20.38*), but for some cuts the older solder dop is still the best. The copper tail of the dop is gripped in a movable bench clamp called a 'tong' or 'tang', which with its two feet on the bench and the dop set with the diamond resting on the scaife, forms a tripod.

One or two stops fixed to the bench, which is called the mill, prevent the tong being carried round by the motion of the lap, and, in order to give

Figure 20.36. The diamond being polished on the scaife
(By courtesy of Shell Petroleum Company Limited)

added pressure, lead weights are loaded on to the arm of the tong. The operator can feel whether he is polishing the stone in the correct direction for the grain. Moving the angle of the tong in relation to the scaife will enable the best polishing position to be found. By bending the copper stalk of the dop most of the side facets can be polished on, and the stone may only need resetting when the rear facets are to be polished. Constant inspection is made as the work of polishing proceeds as all facets must be symmetrical and of uniform size for the group. On completion the stone is cleaned in acid and methylated spirits, after which it is passed to the sorting rooms for grading into size and quality.

Other Gems

The methods used by the lapidary for the cutting of stones other than diamond, although similar in many respects, differ in that there are two distinct processes, a definite cutting where the facets are ground on leaving a finish like ground-glass, and a final polishing of these facets.

As most of these softer gems depend on colour for their beauty, and in the case of doubly refractive stones may have a certain direction giving

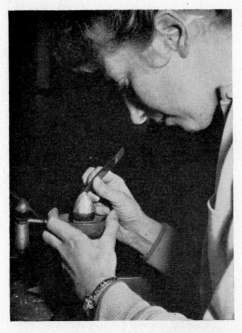

Figure 20.37. Mounting the diamond in the solder dop in preparation for cutting

(By courtesy of Shell Petroleum Company Limited)

the best colour, the lapidary faces different problems to those of the diamond polisher. Therefore the initial examination of the rough material will be to determine the best position for the table facet in relation to the optical effects, and to cut as large a stone as possible which is free from flaws.

Cutting

The rough material is first sawn to the required size, slitting as it is

Figure 20.38. Diamonds being polished on the scaife by using mechanical dops

(By courtesy of Shell Petroleum Company Limited)

termed. The sawing, which is carried out very much more rapidly than in sawing the much harder diamond, is usually done on a vertical diamond-charged disc for the harder minerals such as ruby, sapphire and emerald, while a softer mineral may be slit on a 'mud saw'. This is a metal disc with its lower edge dipping into a 'mud' of abrasive and water. In either case the rough crystal is just held in the hand and pressed against the periphery of the saw. Larger pieces may be held in a clamp which allows the rough to be fed against the saw.

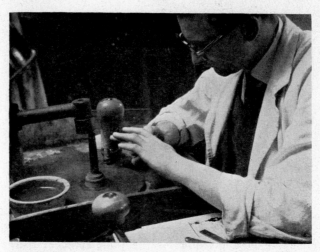

Figure 20.39. The lapidary's cutting lap showing the 'jamb peg' behind the lapidary's hand and the hand crank for driving the 'mill' in the foreground

Grinding

The cutter grinds on the facets using a horizontal lap made of iron, copper or gunmetal (*Figure 20.39*). The grinding agent may be diamond powder, carborundum or emery powder, water being used as a lubricant except in the case of diamond powder. On the cutter lies the responsibility of ensuring the shape of the stone, the correct optical directions for best colour, and the symmetry of the facets, besides getting the most weight out of the rough piece without detriment to the other properties.

To grind the stone the cutter first mounts it with cement on to the end of a 'gem stick' (*Figure 20.40*), a tool looking like an overgrown penholder, so that the direction in which it is proposed to grind the table facet is at right angles to the gem stick. Then giving a turn or two to the driving crank of the lap, for it is usually hand driven, as motor drives do not allow the control needed for best work, the cutter, holding the gem stick in his hand, brings the stone down on the rotating lap, which has already been charged with abrasive and water applied with a brush. For the table facet the gem stick is held vertically and it is remarkable how quickly the facet is ground on.

To grind the side facets the cutter uses the 'jamb peg', a vertical metal rod fixed to one side of the cutting bench carrying a pear-shaped piece of hard wood, or an oblong board, pierced with a number of holes. Into one of these holes is placed the pointed end of the gem stick so that it makes the required angle with the lap. In this way the angles of the facets are regulated and purely by hand pressure they are ground to correct size and symmetry.

When the facets of the crown are completed the stone is unset and re-cemented on to the gem stick the reverse way up—this is termed 'sticking it back upwards'—and from this position the back facets are ground on. The stone is then removed from the gem stick and thoroughly cleaned in order to remove all traces of abrasive.

Figure 20.40. Polishing a side facet on a stone. The lapidary is holding the 'gem stick' which he has engaged in a suitable hole in the 'jamb peg'

Polishing Powder

The shaped stone now looking like a piece of ground glass, goes to the polisher who polishes each facet, taking care not to enlarge their sizes. This is carried out in a similar way as for the initial cutting except that the lap may be copper, pewter or wood and may be motor driven. The polishing powder is finely ground and may be either rouge (iron oxide), green rouge (chromium oxide), putty powder (tin oxide), cerium oxide, or one of the forms of silica known as tripoli or rotten-stone. After all the facets have been polished the stone is thoroughly cleaned.

TOOLS USED FOR GEMSTONE CUTTING AND POLISHING

In some modern cutting works, particularly where only low priced material such as synthetic stones are cut, use is made of a mechanical faceting head which accurately regulates the spacing and angles of the facets. For fine gems the use of such a tool would be prone to cause a loss of weight in the finished stone, a most important factor in the case of valuable material. In America, where there is a considerable vogue in gem cutting by amateurs, elaborate machinery is marketed, mostly as self-contained units with mechanical faceting heads.

Although the horizontal lap is almost universally used for faceted gems, for agates and other ornamental stones, and even for some transparent quartz, vertical sandstone grinding wheels are used. In the Nahe valley around Idar-Oberstein in the German Rhineland such types of large sandstone wheels were formerly driven by water-wheels and the grinder

Figure 20.41. A magnificent carving in rock crystal by the German carver Martin Seitz

lay prone on a low stool fashioning the agate by pressing it against the rotating grindstone. The polishing was then done on beechwood drums which were also driven by the water mill. Today, water has given way to electric power and smaller grinding wheels before which the grinder can sit comfortably at his work. The agate is first cut to rough size by a circular saw charged with diamond powder; it is then shaped by grinding on carborundum or sandstone wheels and finally polished on beechwood drums or leaded discs with rotten-stone as a polishing agent.

The carving and engraving of gemstones (*Figure 20.41*) is carried out by the use of fine burrs like dentists' drills. These may be made of carborundum or more commonly of hardened steel which are charged with diamond dust in olive oil. The worker has before him a number of these burrs of different shapes and sizes. Such tools are driven from a fixed headstock by electric motor, a suitable burr being screwed into the chuck for the work in hand. The art of gem carving embraces not only the cutting of cameos and intaglios but quite large carvings in hardstone. The hollows of agate cups and ashtrays are cut by a similar headstock fitted with a larger burr called a cupping tool.

Cabochon-cut stones are first 'roughed-up' on a carborundum wheel, which is often worn into grooves to assist in giving the rounded outline to the stone. The final grinding and polishing being carried out on either vertical wheels and buffs or on horizontal laps.

The drilling of the string holes of stone beads and the holes for the loops of stone pendants is still carried out by using the age-old bow-drill. The drills used are iron or steel shafts, one end of which is pointed to fit into the upper bearing of the drill framework, and the other end split to take a suitably sized piece of carbonado or diamond bort. Tightly fitted to the centre of the drill shaft is a long wooden bobbin around which runs the string of the fiddle bow. The beads to be drilled are cemented in lines on a board which is then placed under the drilling frame. This frame consists of two wooden uprights between the top of which is pivoted a long wooden arm carrying a metal bearing to take the pivot of the drill. The free end of this arm is held by the driller under his left armpit; a turn of the bowstring is put round the bobbin, the pivot of the drill placed in the upper bearing and the diamond point on the centre of the bead to be drilled. Then by a to and fro motion of the bow held in the worker's right hand the bead is drilled straight through from top to bottom. The control of the drilling pressure needed is supplied by the driller's armpit pressing on the arm. It is said that this method is more efficient than can be obtained by the use of modern mechanical drills. Tube drills have been used for hardstone drilling and some of the ancient Oriental jades have been drilled by using as a tube drill bamboo rods charged with emery or sand.

The production of baroque-shaped gems by the tumbling process (*Figure 20.42*) is carried out by 'churning' the stones with an abrasive agent, and then with a polishing compound, in a rotating drum. The process takes some considerable time but large quantities of material, depending upon the size of the container, can be tumbled at one time. Although the method is not new (it was said to have been carried out in Cornwall, England, many years ago) it now has a considerable vogue in the United States of America and in Germany.

Fire-marks, sometimes called chatter-marks, are crack-like markings seen near the facet edges of corundums. They are caused by local overheating during polishing producing incipient parting cracks. They are more common in synthetic corundum than in natural corundum as less care is taken in the polishing process. It is a characteristic of corundum only.

WEIGHTS AND MEASURES

The price of a finished gemstone depends upon the quality, perfection of cutting, and the weight. The unit of weight used almost exclusively for gemstones is the metric carat of 200 mg ($\frac{1}{5}$ g), a unit which is of comparatively recent derivation.

A carat weight has been used for the weighing of gold and gemstones since ancient times, but the derivation of the weight is obscure. Seeds which have a fairly constant weight were used as 'weights', indeed the English grain was derived from the use of a seed of wheat taken from a well-ripened ear, and the carat weight was said to have been derived from the weight of a seed of the carob or locust tree, whose seeds are remarkably constant in weight whether taken from the centre or the ends of the pod. The seeds of the carob tree (*Ceratonia siliqua*) are chocolate-brown and are of a flattened pear-shaped form. According to L. J. Spencer the seeds have an average weight of 0·197 g. The same author refers to the Greek weight ceratium, and also the Roman siliqua, as being equivalent to $\frac{1}{144}$ oz., or $3\frac{1}{3}$ gr., which is only slightly more than the $3\frac{1}{6}$ gr. of the old English carat.

Also claimed as the origin of the carat weight are the orange kidney-shaped seeds with a black spot at one end obtained from the coral tree (*Erythrina corallodendron*). These have an average weight of 0·197 g, but

Figure 20.42. Machine for tumbling gems

are not so constant as the seeds of the carob tree. Kuara, the African name for one species of the coral tree has been suggested as the origin of the name carat, but the most likely origin of the carat, both in name and weight, is from the *Ceratonia siliqua*.

The carat weight, often divided into 4 diamond grains, varied considerably in different parts of the world. At one time this difference was from 0·1885 g to 0·2135 g. The English carat was approximately 0·205409 g, but even so often varied from that value. A. Church pointed out that the English carat weighs 3·1683 gr. which makes the carat in grammes to be 0·205304. This value of 0·205304 g was the weight defined for the carat by the Standards Department of the Board of Trade and reported in the proceedings of the Weights and Measures Acts of 1878, 1888 and 1889, but the old English carat was never a legal weight.

The old English carat had the subdivisions as fractions, from $\frac{1}{2}$ to $\frac{1}{64}$, and the weight was expressed as a series, namely, 1, $\frac{1}{2}$, $\frac{1}{4}$, $\frac{1}{32}$, and rarely as a unit and an unreduced fraction, that is $1\frac{50}{64}$. The diamond grain (4 diamond grains to a carat) is often used when referring to a diamond, a three-quarter carat diamond being spoken of as a three-grainer, but the grain was rarely ever used as weight.

The international aspect of trading in gemstones called for an international standard. In 1871 an attempt was made by Paris gem merchants to standardize the carat at 0·205 g and this was approved in 1877, but contrary to their hopes, it did not gain international recognition. In 1907 Paris again took the lead in a second attempt to obtain world standardization. The Comité International des Poids et Mesures proposed a metric carat of 200 mg, a weight approximately $2\frac{1}{2}$ per cent less than the old English carat weight. This proposal was accepted by the Quatrième Conference Generale des Poids et Mesures in Paris, and they approached through diplomatic channels those other countries who would be interested. Even-

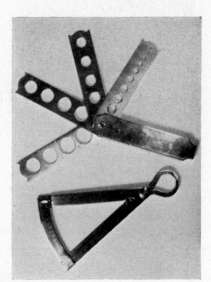

Figure 20.43a. Diamond gauges: top—stencil gauge; bottom—caliper gauge

tually practically all countries legalized the position and the metric carat is now universally standard.

In England, as the Weights and Measures (Metric system) Act of 1897 more or less covered the metric carat, the inclusion of the metric carat as a unit of weight in the Act was put through by an Order in Council, which legalized the new unit, 1 metric carat equals 0·200 g, as from April 1, 1914. This legalization does not make the use of the metric carat compulsory and the older weights may still be used, but the confusion to the user is sufficient to discourage their use.

The denominations of the legal metric carat weights are 500, 200, 100, 50, 20, 10, 5, 2, 1, 0·5, 0·2, 0·1, 0·05, 0·02, 0·01, 0·005. It is the trade practice, however, to weigh to the second place of decimals only and to ignore the third figure. Diamonds under one carat in weight are often referred to as being so many points, a point being $\frac{1}{100}$ part of a carat, and therefore 0·01 carat. A half carat stone is 0·50 carat and hence a fifty pointer.

When the stone is set and therefore only an estimation of the weight can be accomplished, use is made of a stencil gauge, a metal or plastic plate

Figure 20.43b. Leveridge's caliper gauge

cut with circular or cushion-shaped holes having diameters corresponding to the girdle diameters of correctly proportioned diamonds of various sizes. The stencil is placed over the stone and different sized holes tried, the hole which just outlines the girdle of the stone gives the approximate weight of the diamond. More efficient are the so-called caliper type gauges, such as the Moe, Rayner (*Figure 20.43a*) and Leveridge (*Figure 20.43b*). Such instruments measure the girdle diameter and the depth of the stone from table to culet, usually in millimetres. Referring these measurements to the tables supplied with the gauge, a close approximation, often less than 5 per cent in error, may quickly be obtained. The Leveridge gauge, which shows the measurements on a dial, is a particularly useful tool, as the weights of

Figure 20.44. A modern balance for weighing gemstones

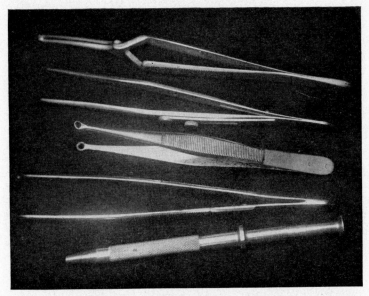

Figure 20.45. Various types of stone tong

fancy-cut diamonds can be assessed as well as stones of other species than diamond. A modern balance for weighing gems is illustrated in *Figure 22.44*.

Some of the cheaper stones are not sold by the carat but by the gram, the ounce or the pennyweight. Some stones, particularly the synthetic stones, are not sold by weight but by size, the millimetre being used for the synthetic stones and the centimetre for ornamental stones. Paste stones are sold by size, the millimetre again being the unit, although the 'Paris plate', a stencil gauge marked with arbitrary numbers is sometimes used.

For the handling of gemstones, tongs, also called tweezers or 'corn-tongs' (the origin of the name being uncertain), are used (*Figure 20.45*). There are various types now available, including some which have a locking device so that the stone is held firmly when the finger pressure is removed. One type is spring loaded so that on pressure on the plunger three wire prongs project with which the stone may be gripped. At one time tongs were made with small ring ends for the express purpose of holding pearls. The springiness and the width of the points of tongs can vary greatly and the individual worker should select a pair most suitable to himself. Minia-ture scoops or shovels are used for picking up groups of stones from the table so that they may be transferred to the balance pan for weighing, or to a stone packet. Such packets, in which stocks of gemstones are kept, may be purchased from jewellers' material shops. These packets usually have folded in them a tough internal lining tissue which to some extent prevents the stones piercing through the outer packet. It is often ad-vantageous to place a fold of lint or cotton wool in the packet to act as a bed for the stones and in order to prevent them rubbing together which will often cause the facet edges to become chipped, an effect called 'paper wearing'. In the case of zircons, in which this so easily happens each individual stone is separately wrapped in a twist of tissue paper.

CHAPTER 21

PEARL—ITS CULTIVATION AND IMITATION

THE ORGANIC GEMS

The gem materials which have been discussed have dealt almost entirely with those substances which owe their genesis to Mother Earth, or to the activities of mankind in laboratories throughout the world. A number of gem materials are formed by biological processes, among which is the lovely pearl, and the story of these gems is told in the following pages.

NATURAL PEARL

There are few lovelier gems than fine pearls, and, like their much harder sisters, diamond, ruby, sapphire and emerald, pearls have been held in high esteem throughout the ages.

The discoverer of the decorative beauty of pearls is lost in the mists of pre-history; it may well be that pearls were the earliest gems known to mankind, gems which need no treatment by lapidary or artist to enhance their native beauty. Some savage, dwelling by the seashore or river bank in mankind's early days on this earth, feeding upon those shellfish which produce pearls, may well have been the first to have found them.

That pearls are obtained from oysters is a general conception, and, indeed, the shell of the pearl oyster resembles strongly that of the true oyster, but the oyster which produces the pearl so prized in jewellery comes from another soft-bodied animal which has more affinity zoologically to the scallop than to the true edible oyster. The pearl oyster belongs to a group of molluscs popularly known as bivalves (animals with a double shell), and the scientific name for the class of these animals is *Lamellibranchia*.

Nature and Formation

Any shelled mollusc can produce a pearl of sorts, but only those animals which have a shell with a pearly (nacreous) lining can form lustrous pearls worthy of use in ornamentation. The formation of a pearl is an abnormal case of the normal biological processes which build up the shell forming the protective covering of the animal. To understand the nature and formation of pearls some knowledge of the anatomy of the animal and the structure of the shell is necessary.

Anatomy of the Mollusc

One of the more rudimentary forms of animal life, the mollusc consists of a soft visceral mass enclosed between two valves of shell which are hinged together. The animal has a heart, a mouth and alimentary system, but has no head. There are two large abductor muscles attached to the two parts of the shells (the valves); these muscles serve to pull the shells together so as to close the animal in. On the ventral side of the abductor muscles are two plate-like gills, rather like curtains. Near the mouth, which is adjacent to the hinge line of the shells, is the foot, and from a gland in a small pit near the base of the foot is secreted a substance which forms into a number of fibres, called the byssus, which serves to attach the animal to the rocks and debris of the sea floor.

The most important part of the animal, in regard to pearl formation, is the fold of epithelial tissue which covers the animal loosely beneath and above, the two halves being joined to one another along the hinge line of the shells. This double flap of skin is termed the mantle and is responsible for the formation of the shell.

The abductor muscles, by relaxing, allow the shells to open by virtue of a black inanimate elastic ligament near the hinge which is compressed when the valves are closed. This opening of the valves, termed gaping, allows sea-water to enter, and this flow of water carries with it the microscopic animal life from which the mollusc obtains its sustenance, these minute organisms being driven by hair-like processes, or cilia, on the gills, their wave-like motion wafting the food-laden water towards the mouth. It is this circulating water which supplies the life-giving oxygen.

The mantle is bounded on its outermost faces by a layer of secretory cells—the ectoderm—and from these cells is secreted the shell-forming substance. The shell is composed of three layers, although a fourth layer occurs at places where the abductor muscles are attached. These three main layers are a dark horny outside layer composed of the organic substance conchiolin ($C_{32}H_{48}N_2O_{11}$), a scleroprotein of keratin type—this layer is called the periostracum. The second layer is shelly and is made up of prismatic columns of crystalline calcium carbonate, usually in the form of calcite. The prisms of this layer are arranged at right angles to the surface of the shell and are held together by a 'mortar' of conchiolin—this layer is aptly termed the prismatic layer. These two layers are secreted by the cells at the edge of the mantle and once formed cannot increase in thickness. The third, or inner, layer forms the internal surface of the shell and this is normally secreted by the entire surface of the mantle and increases in thickness during the whole of the animal's life. It is this layer which provides the commercially important mother-of-pearl, and is known as the nacreous layer. This nacre is built up of overlapping platelets of crystalline calcium carbonate in the form of aragonite, and the principal crystal axes of these platy crystals are for practical purposes at right angles to the shell surface. Where the abductor muscle is attached to the shell another layer similar to the prismatic layer is formed, a layer which is known as the hypostracum, but this has little importance in our study.

Blister Pearls

The shell is a natural arrangement to protect the animal, and the nacreous inner surface of the shell provides a smooth cover for the soft mantle to bear against. Should, therefore, a sharp piece of grit, such as a grain of sand, a piece of broken shell, or even the intrusion of a shell-boring animal, get between the shell and the mantle, irritation would be set up and this the animal would attempt to ease. This it does by secreting nacre over the irritant and cementing it to the shell. This smooth bulge, or blister as it is called, can occasionally be removed from the shell and used as a jewel, such objects being termed blister pearls. They may be almost regular hemispheres or of a very irregular shape, and the non-nacreous base where it has been cut from the shell—a part usually concealed by the setting if the blister is mounted—clearly shows that it has been removed from the shell and is not a true pearl. Blister pearls are sometimes called chicot pearls.

Encystation

The highly prized whole pearls which are so important in jewellery are formed by another method, that of encystation, and such pearls are often termed 'cyst' pearls. The irritant in the case of these pearls is usually a minute parasite, which may be a trematode or a cestode worm. These minute wriggling intruders do not allow the oyster to cement them down on to the shell to form a blister so another type of action is taken. The mollusc immobilizes such a lively irritant by first forming a depression in the mantle

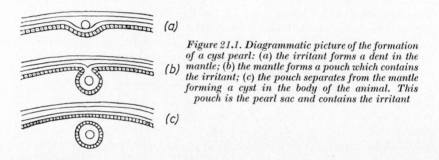

Figure 21.1. Diagrammatic picture of the formation of a cyst pearl: (a) the irritant forms a dent in the mantle; (b) the mantle forms a pouch which contains the irritant; (c) the pouch separates from the mantle forming a cyst in the body of the animal. This pouch is the pearl sac and contains the irritant

into which the worm is trapped. By successive stages this depression deepens until a sac-like pouch is formed, this eventually joins at the neck producing a hollow sac of invaginated mantle tissue completely inside the connective tissues of the body of the oyster and quite separate from the mantle of which it was a part. The wound in the mantle coalesces (*Figure 21.1*). This sac containing the irritant, now most probably dead, is called the pearl sac, and is essential for the formation of a pearl. The nacre-secreting cells of the pearl sac are now on the inside surface; they are still living cells and go on secreting nacre over the irritant building up a usually spherical mass of nacre which is a pearl. There are other theories given to account for the formation of the pearl sac but the outline given above is the most generally accepted, although in a minor way and in other molluscs it is considered that different causes promote the occurrence.

The deposition of the pearly substance around the irritant in the pearl sac is arranged in layers, thus giving to the pearl a concentric structure. These layers are built up, like the nacre of the shell, of minute platy crystals of calcium carbonate in a network of the organic substance conchiolin, the crystals being so arranged that their principal axes are at right angles to the surface of the layers, thus giving a radial structure to the pearl (*Figure 21.2*). The fact that pearls have this concentric and radial structure has an importance in their testing. The calcium carbonate in gem pearls is practically always in the form of aragonite, and only in some freshwater pearls are the prismatic layers of calcite prisms found at all. The layers are seasonal growth and may be likened to the growth rings of trees, but unlike trees the age of the pearl cannot be assessed from the rings for, due to various causes, the deposition is often irregular and varies also in thickness.

Nomenclature

These 'free pearls', free because they are not attached to the shell, are termed 'cyst' or 'mantle' pearls when found in the connective tissue. Near

Figure 21.2. A thin section of a natural pearl photographed in polarized light. This clearly shows the concentric structure and the dark cross, the so-called 'extinction cross' confirms the radial arrangement of the crystallites

the margins of the mantle 'hem pearls' of a rather dark colour may be found. Pearls found in the neighbourhood of the abductor muscle are termed 'muscle pearls' and are usually of fairly good colour, and near the ligament at the hinge of the valves are found dark brown conchiolin-rich pearls called 'ligament pearls'.

Chemical Properties

The chemical composition of pearl is about 82–86 per cent calcium carbonate (as aragonite); 10–14 per cent conchiolin, and 2–4 per cent water. The density of aragonite is 2·93, therefore, pearls would have a density lower than this value owing to the other lighter constituents; conchiolin having a density of 1·34 and water 1. The density of pearls ranges from 2·60 to 2·78 (the non-nacreous pearls from the giant conch and the giant clam are over 2·8) and to some extent the pearls from different sources conform to narrower ranges. Table 21.1 gives a general idea of the value of density for the more important pearl types.

The beautiful lustre of pearls is known as the orient of pearl and is due to a combination of two optical effects. These are the breaking up of light into minute spectra by diffraction caused by the irregular edges of the overlapping crystal plates of aragonite (*Figure 21.3*), and by the interference of light at thin films given by these same platelets. It is the edges of these overlapping platelets which cause the pearl to feel rough when the surface

TABLE 21.1

Pearl Density

Locality	Mollusc	Colour of pearl	Range of specific gravity
Persian Gulf	*Pinctada vulgaris*	Creamy-white	2·68–2·74
Gulf of Manaar	*Pinctada vulgaris*	Pale cream-white	2·68–2·74
North coast of Australia	*Pinctada margaritifera*	Silver-white	2·68–2·78
North-west coast of Australia	*Pinctada maxima*	Silver-white	2·67–2·78
Shark Bay, W. Australia	*Pinctada carcharium*	Yellow	
Venezuela	*Pinctada radiata*	White	2·65–2·75
Japan (natural)	*Pinctada martensi*	White, with greenish tinge	2·66–2·76
Florida, and Gulf of California	*Strombus gigas* (the great conch)	Pink	2·85
	Haliotidae (the abalone)	Greens, yellows, blues, etc.	
Gulf of California		Black	2·61–2·69
Freshwater pearls North America	*Unio*	White	2·66 to over 2·78
Europe	*Unio margaritifera*	White	
Cultured pearls Japan	*Pinctada martensi*	White	2·72–2·78
Non-nucleated cultured pearls Japan	*Hyriopsis schlegeli*	White	2·67–2·70
Australia	*Pinctada margaritifera or maxima*	White	about 2·70

is drawn over the teeth; a useful test for pearl against imitation pearls, which are smooth to the teeth. It is no test for cultured pearls which have a true nacreous outer skin and feel rough like real pearls. The cause of the delicate shades of colour, such as that prized pinkish tone termed rosée, is unknown. These colour nuances are so minute and subtle as to be distin-

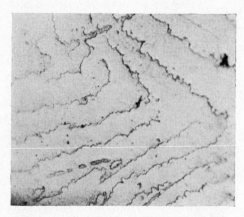

Figure 21.3. A magnified photograph of the ridges of the overlapping plates as seen on the surface of the pearl (× 180, reduced by half in reproduction)

(By courtesy of V. G. Hinton)

guished only by experienced persons. Likewise the cause of the colour of nacreous pearls showing pronounced colour, such as golden-yellow, yellow, pink, blue, grey, gunmetal, bronze and black, is not clearly known, but it often has some affinity with the colour of the shell, and, to some extent, to the position of the pearl in the oyster. The nature of the water which the animal inhabits has been proposed as a reason for some of the colours.

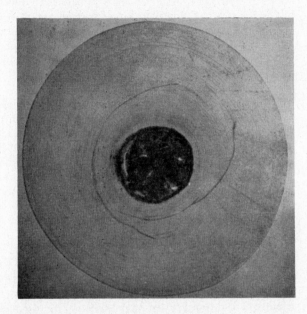

Figure 21.4. A photograph of a thin section of a natural pearl with a con-chiolin-rich centre

The so-called 'blue pearls', pearls of a leaden-grey colour, possess a broad conchiolin layer lying near the surface, or have a 'mud centre', that is a central core rich in conchiolin (*Figure 21.4*). It is this dark coloured organic substance showing through the translucent layers of aragonite crystals which give such pearls the dark appearance.

Pearl-producing Animals

The animals which produce the pearls so prized in jewellery belong to the second order (Filibranchia) of the class known as Lamellibranchia. The generic name is Pinctada, although in previous years the name employed was either Margaritifera, or Pteria, and earlier still the term Meleagrina was used. Various species of Pinctada produce pearls and to some extent these species live in well-defined localities. This being so, the different species will be mentioned when the various fisheries are discussed. All Pinctada are sea-water animals: there are other sea-water shell fish which also produce pearls and which have been found useful in decorative jewellery. Such animals include the giant conch and the giant clam, and the haliotis with its highly coloured nacreous shell. Other pearls are found in fresh-water molluscs, particularly the mussels (Unio). Such animals and their pearl production will be discussed later.

Life History of Pearl Oyster

The life history of the pearl oyster begins with the shedding of the ova or spermatozoa into the sea according to the sex of the animal. In the pearl oyster the sexes are separate although cases of sex reversal are not unknown. Oysters are gregarious animals and therefore the ova and spermatozoa are ejected in localized waters making the chances of fertilization great. After about 24 hours the fertilized egg commences to develop a tiny bivalve shell but remains a free-floating animal carried about at the whim of the ocean currents. After about a week the animal, if not carried out to parts where the sea bed is unsuitable, or if not a victim to larger predatory animals, attaches itself by the thread-like byssus to hard objects or seaweed fronds on the sea bottom. These youngsters are at this stage about 0·1 mm in diameter and are termed spat.

It is clear then that the nature of the sea bed has much to do with the formation of colonies of oysters, and suitable conditions of depth and temperature of the water are necessary factors. The dead coral, rocks and shells on the sea bed to which the oysters attach themselves is collectively known as culch, and artificial culching of the sea bed is sometimes carried out.

The oyster grows rapidly for the first two years of its life and for the first five years has to battle with its enemies—the starfish, skates and rays, filefishes, the boring molluscs and sponges. The size of the full-grown oyster depends upon its species and upon the conditions in which it lives.

Natural Pearl Fisheries

The finest pearls are those which the jewellery trade term oriental and these are confined to the fisheries in the Persian Gulf, which extend from Kuwait in the north to the Trucial coastal waters in the south: those off the islands of Bahrain are the best known. The other fishery is in the Gulf of Manaar which separates Ceylon from India. Perhaps the somewhat unimportant fishery in the Red Sea may also be included as supplying oriental pearls.

Persian Gulf

The beautiful pearls fished in the Persian Gulf, a fishery which has been known since 300 B.C., are never very large, usually being under one grain in size: pearls over 12 grains are rare. The pearl oyster which lives in these waters is the *Pinctada vulgaris*, a small oyster with a shell about 6 cm ($2\frac{1}{2}$ in.) in diameter and which is fished solely for the pearls which may be found in it, for the shell is too small to have any commercial value itself.

The diving season in the Persian Gulf lasts from about the middle of May until the end of September, and it is during this period that the teakwood sailing dhows, which are sometimes equipped with auxiliary motors, sail out to the limestone reefs where the pearl oysters abound. During the interwar years as many as 600 dhows, some so large that they carried 100 men, left for the fishing grounds, but since World War II the scale of the fisheries has decreased till now only a small number of boats operate the fishery. The finding, refining and export of oil in Bahrain and on the mainland has materially altered the status of the labour market, with the subsequent trend for the worker to take employment with the oil firms rather than to engage in the more precarious pearl fishing. Whether the residues from the refineries and leakage from the tankers will have a deleterious effect on the life of the pearl oyster has yet to be seen.

The manner of diving employed by the Arabs in the Persian Gulf fisheries has scarcely altered since the time of the Arab historian Ibn Batuta in the fourteenth century, and indeed perhaps has not changed for the past two thousand years.

When the fishing grounds are reached the crew of the dhows extend their square-bladed oars out from the side of the vessels in order to steady the craft and to provide a place of attachment for the descending ropes (*Figure 21.5*). Two ropes are employed, one of which is fixed to a stone of about 50 pounds weight upon which the diver stands when he is ready to descend. The diver is naked except for a loin cloth, for modern diving dresses with their attendant pumps are not used. On his fingers and big toes he wears protective sheaths, and either carried in his hand or slung round his neck is a

Figure 21.5. Pearl fishing dhow in the Persian Gulf

string bag to which is attached the second rope. This rope is used to haul him to the surface on completion of his dive.

When ready to submerge the diver takes a deep breath and fixes on his nose a leather clip, rather like a clothes peg, then pulling free the slip-knot of the rope holding the stone, the weight of which rapidly takes him to the bottom. Reaching the sea bed the diver steps off the stone and plucks as many oysters as he can from the immediate vicinity, placing them in the string bag. The divers, thin and wiry individuals whose age may be anything from 20 to 70 years, make about thirty dives of approximately one and a half minutes' duration each day, going to a depth which varies from 5 to 15 fathoms (30–90 ft.); but depths much above 8 fathoms are not common. When ready to ascend the diver jerks on the rope attached to the basket. This is the signal to the crewmen to haul him up, but meanwhile he may start climbing hand over hand up the rope in order to reach the surface and fresh air all the quicker.

Each diver and crewman receive a share of the profits. The men who work the ropes and do not dive get only half the amount of that received by the diver, as their work is less arduous. The men are given two advances of pay during the year, one at the beginning of the season and the other half-way through the off season, these being intended to maintain the diver's family whilst he is away at sea and during the time he is not working. It is these advances of pay which had, prior to 1923, been the cause of much abuse. In that year Shaikh Hamad bin Isa al Khalifah, the then deputy ruler, instituted reforms which have made the lot of the divers much better.

Gulf of Manaar

The celebrated fisheries located in the Gulf of Manaar, an arm of the Indian Ocean which, with Palk Strait, separates Ceylon from the southern tip of India, have been known for some 2,500 years. In this fishery the conditions needed for the well-being and growth of the pearl oysters are only found on the patches of rock, termed paars, which lie within a half mile to 18 miles from the shore and at a depth of not more than 15 fathoms (90 ft.). Either through becoming exhausted, or being covered by shifting sand, the fishing is now only of sporadic occurrence.

Figure 21.6. Pearl fishing in the Gulf of Manaar. The pennant is on one of the marker buoys

The oyster found in these fisheries is the same species as that fished in the Persian Gulf—the small mollusc *Pinctada vulgaris*—and the method of fishing is also by naked diving.

In recent years motor boats and dredges have been used, which, to some extent, has replaced the old practice of diving for oysters. The method is, however, said to have its disadvantages.

Before the formation of India and Ceylon as separate countries the working of the Gulf of Manaar fisheries was carried out by state control from Ceylon, and the fishing boats operated from the temporary hutted town of Marichchikkaddi on the north-east coast of the island, Indian people being permitted to join the camp only through certain indicated routes. The only fishery operated since the partition of the two countries from direct British rule was that of 1955, and this was from Tuticorin on the Indian side of the Gulf.

At the commencement of the fisheries an inspection of the fishing grounds is made and the fishing areas marked out by flagged buoys (*Figure 21.6*). Divers are sent down to take samples of the oysters from the various paars within the buoyed areas and from the data so obtained by this survey a plan is made for the guidance of the pearl fishers, and to ensure that the areas are not overfished.

After this preliminary Governmental survey has been made an advertisement is published in various languages in a number of local and world newspapers. This advertisement gives the date the fishery is to be commenced, the location of the paars to be fished and the estimate of the likely production, and finally the method of payment, for the Government puts up the oysters in lots as deemed expedient. It is this advertisement which attracts the divers, gem buyers and small merchants, with many Indian and Sinhalese coolies to the fisheries.

The divers, or the ship masters (Tindals) provide the sailing vessels and the gear necessary for the actual fishing while the Government sees to the shore buildings and much of the shore labour. The buildings, comprising those for administration and social services, and sites are leased out for

Figure 21.7. Gulf of Manaar pearl fishery. Auctioning the oysters

the period of the fishery to dealers and merchants who usually sit on a mat before open-fronted stalls.

After the day's fishing the anchors are weighed and the ruddy-hued sails hoisted for the run home. On the arrival at Marichchikkaddi the catch is unloaded and separated into three piles; two are selected for the Government and the third divided among the divers and crew who may sell them as they will.

The oysters selected by the Government are counted and auctioned in lots of 1,000 or in multiples of that number (*Figure 21.7*). The balance unsold at the end of the day is disposed of privately on the following day.

The recovery of the pearls from the oysters is carried out by simply

leaving them to rot, assisted by the maggots from the blowflies which
infest the area. The rotten mass is subsequently searched through by hand
for the larger pearls; and the smaller ones are recovered by washing in
ballams, which are simply dug-out canoes. The mass of decomposed oyster
and shells is placed in these dug-outs and covered by water, the floating
scum being skimmed off, and one by one the shells are removed and examined for any pearls and blister pearls. By constant changing of the water
the bulk of the filth remaining is washed over the edge of the ballam and
finally the remaining debris known as 'sarraku' is carefully searched,
usually by women, for any remaining small pearls.

The pearls recovered are then sold to the numerous buyers who congregate
at the fisheries. The pearls usually go to Bombay for drilling.

Red Sea

The Red Sea fisheries, which flourished at the time of the Ptolemies, is
not now of great importance, but some fishing takes place on the 'banks'
along the Arabian shore between Jidda, which was once the pearl centre,
and the Farasan Islands; and also along the opposite African shore near
Massawa. The oysters fished are the small *Pinctada vulgaris* of the Persian
Gulf and Ceylon fisheries, but the pearls found are said to be whiter than
those from the other oriental sources. They were previously marketed
through Alexandria and have, from this connexion, been known as 'Egyptians'. The somewhat larger oyster *Pinctada margaritifera* has also been
fished from the Red Sea locality, but for the value of the shell only.

Figure 21.8. An early photograph of the Shark Bay pearl fishery

Minor Fisheries

A minor fishery is in the Arabian Sea off the cost of Bombay around the mouths of the Indus, south of Karachi.

There are oyster beds off the Mergui archipelago, a group of islands in the Andaman Sea which lie just off the west coast of Lower Burma. These beds, indeed, stretch southwards to the Malacca Strait and may be said to be the northern section of the fisheries of the Malay archipelago and northern Australia. Here the oyster is the *Pinctada margaritifera* (the black-lipped oyster) and the shell has considerable commercial value, any pearls found being rather in the nature of a 'bonus'.

Australia

The pearl fisheries of Australia extend from Shark Bay on the west coast (*Figure 21.8*), right round the north-west and northern coasts, through the Torres Strait which separates the tip of Cape York peninsula of northern Queensland from Papua, and thence to the fishing area of the Coral Sea.

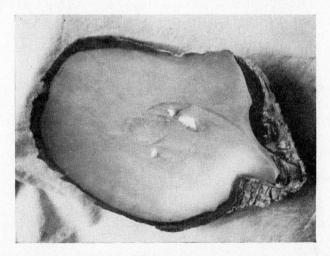

Figure 21.9. Gold-lip shell (Pinctada maxima) *with blister pearls from the Thursday Island fishery*

Adjacent, and one may say part of the Australian fisheries, are the Aru Islands in the Arafura Sea south of Indonesia where Dobo is the pearling centre and pearls from this locality are sometimes called 'Dobo pearls'. The Sulu Sea and the littorals of the Philippine Islands are also fishing grounds.

Thursday Island is the main centre of fishing but the luggers are mostly based on Broome on the north-west coast of Australia. In these waters naked diving has practically disappeared, except for some goggle diving in shallow waters of the tropical islands. The modern armoured diving suit is now used in fishing for the large oyster *Pinctada maxima*, the gold-lipped or silver-lipped oyster (*Figure 21.9*), which may measure up to 12 in. in diameter, the pair of valves weighing as much as 12 lb. The fishing in these tropical waters is mainly for the shell, which forms a more commercially important industry, than for the, often large, white Australian pearls which may be found in the oysters. The pearls are recovered by a similar method as used in the Ceylon fisheries, that is by allowing putrification in 'poogie' tubs.

The small fishery at Shark Bay produces from the *Pinctada cacharium* a small oyster some 3–4 in. in diameter, pearls of a yellowish or straw colour, often with an attractive golden tinge, and often up to 20 grains in weight.

South Sea Fisheries

The fisheries, mainly run by native fishers, in the numerous islands of Micronesia and Polynesia, produce from the *Pinctada maxima* pearls similar to those found in Australian waters. These pearls are often large and of good shape—round, drop and button-shaped—and may sometimes weigh to over 100 grains. The most important centre of the South Sea fisheries is Tahiti in the Society Islands, but most of the pearls are fished from the Tuamoto archipelago. The more northern fisheries in Micronesia are allied to the Australian fisheries. Note may be made of the fisheries around the Sulu Sea, where the oysters are often dredged by the use of rakes having curved prongs which are slowly drawn along by boats. The waters around the Palau Islands just north of Papua were, when under Japanese control, used for the cultivation of pearls from the large oysters *Pinctada margaritifera* and *Pinctada maxima.*

Japan

The fisheries in Japanese waters, where the oyster is the small *Pinctada martensi*, are now unimportant owing to the cultivation of cultured pearls in the east coast inlets. Any natural pearls found in Japanese waters would be suspect.

New World Fisheries

Turning to the seas of the New World the first to consider are the fisheries of the coastal waters of Venezuela. These fisheries were known to the natives long before Columbus visited the South American continent in the sixteenth century. Under the Spaniards the fisheries flourished, but the enterprise failed at the turn of that century owing to the acts of cruelty and oppression which caused the natives to turn against the settlers. The fisheries were abandoned and not restarted until the nineteenth century.

The Venezuelan fisheries are centred mainly around the islands of Margarita and Cuagua. The oyster found in these waters is the small mollusc *Pinctada radiata*, an animal similar in size to the Ceylon pearl oyster. The pearls from these oysters are never of large size and vary in colour from white to bronze or even black, and the white pearls from Venezuelan waters are often so extremely translucent as to be almost glassy.

The Gulf of Mexico is often mentioned as an area for pearl fishery, and admittedly there is an unimportant fishery off the Marquesas which lie off the western tip of Florida keys. The important Mexican fisheries are situated on the western coastline of the country. These fisheries have been known to the Old World since the conquests by Cortes in the sixteenth century. The fishing waters extend from the apex of the Gulf of California, all round the littorals of Baja California, and along the Pacific coast of Mexico proper. The oyster fished is a greenish-edged variety of *Pinctada margaritifera* (*mazatlanica*), and the fishing was originally carried out by nude diving, but in more recent years armoured diving suits have been used. The chief trading centre for the Mexican fisheries is at La Paz. The Gulf of California is the locality which supplies many of the black and gunmetal-coloured pearls.

In the Gulf of Panama along the northern shores of Colombia light yellowish and silvery-grey pearls are found in the thin-shelled oyster *Pinctada squamulosa*, but this fishery has little importance.

Other Pearl-producing Molluscs

Salt Water

Other members of the mollusca which live in salt water also produce pearls, and in this connexion three of these animals need to be mentioned.

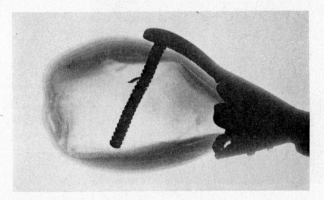

Figure 21.10. X-radiograph of a Haliotis pearl showing the hollow centre of such a pearl

The first of these is the abalone of American waters (the haliotis), which in New Zealand is the Paua shell prized for its highly iridescent mother-of-pearl. The Japanese call the abalone 'Awabi'. Such shellfish are univalves (single-shelled creatures) and may produce rather baroque pearls which are, like the shell, highly coloured and iridescent. Such pearls are often hollow inside (*Figure 21.10*) but their highly coloured iridescence serves to prevent confusion with any other pearl. An abalone pearl of reddish colour is found in the *Haliotis rufrescens*. The ormer shells (*Haliotis tuberculata*) which abound in the shallow waters off the Channel Islands produce pearls of sorts, but rarely have they been worthy for use in ornamentation.

The second, and much more commercially important type of fancy pearl is that produced by the giant conch (*Strombus gigas*), the shell of which is used for the making of cameos. The pink or white pearls from this animal, the so-called conch pearls, are non-nacreous and have a porcelain-like surface with a peculiar appearance and a sheen like watered silk; the markings have been likened to 'flames' (*Figure 21.11*). It is by this surface structure that the pearls are distinguished from coral. The density of these conch pearls is higher than for the nacreous pearls from the pearl oyster and ranges from 2·81 to 2·87. The giant clam (*Tridacna gigas*), another large mollusc, also produces a similar type of pearl, white in colour, having similar characteristics to those of the conch pearl.

Other members of the mollusca which occasionally give pearls, but have little commercial importance are the pinna, the placenta, the mytilus, the cassis, the venus which gives the porcellaneous black and dark purple clam pearls, the trochus, the xancus, and the turbo marmoratus, the central column of the latter shell often being turned into beads for necklets. The malleus, found on the Pacific coast of America produces a brass-coloured or black pearl having no iridescence. The density of black clam pearls has been found to lie between 2·21 to 2·66.

Figure 21.11. 'Flame' markings seen on the surface of conch pearls

Fresh Water

The pearl-producing mollusca so far discussed have been those which live in salt water, but a number of freshwater shellfish produce nacreous pearls of varying degrees of beauty. The best of these river pearls are found in the mussel (Unio), which inhabits the rivers of Europe and America. The pearls from this mollusc have a nacreous lustre and, although never having the lovely orient of the pearls from the pearl oyster, can at times be of exquisite beauty. Such pearls are found, as they have been for some 2,000 years, in the rivers of Scotland, when they are known as 'Scotch pearls' and in North Wales and Ireland. Scotch pearls are found in the Tay, Earn and Teith in Perthshire and many rivers in Aberdeenshire and Inverness-shire. The Doon and Nith of southern Scotland are other rivers where the pearl-producing mussel is found.

The method of fishing in Scotland is for the fisherman to wade into the river and search the bottom with a glass-bottomed bucket through which he is able to peer below the surface of the water (*Figure 21.12*). He uses a cleft stick to bring up the mussels and these he puts into a string bag after which he returns to the bank and opens the mussels, searching the soft flesh for any pearls it may contain.

The river Conway in north Wales and many streams of Ireland are fished in a similar manner. Many freshwater pearls are in the regalia of England, Scotland and Ireland, and some are quite beautiful.

The historical fishery of the Vologne river of the French Department of the Vosges seems not now to be fished, and the same may be said of other French rivers which are inhabited by the pearl mussel. The German and Austrian rivers, particularly the Bavarian streams are haunts of the Unio, and the Bavarian river Ilz produces pearls which are fished and marketed today. The others, including the streams on Luneburg Heath, are now unimportant, and the same may be said of the Russian and Scandinavian rivers.

River pearls have long been known from the North American continent, particularly in the streams of the Mississippi valley. Such pearls are often coloured, are rarely spherical and often assume various baroque forms

Figure 21.12. Fishing for pearl mussels in a Scottish river

in the shape of wings, dog's teeth, petals and other bizarre forms, shapes which lend themselves to the production of 'flowers' in jewellery. Although pearls are found in the freshwater mussel (Unio) in American rivers, many of the pearls are obtained from the niggerhead (*Quadrula ebena*), the three-ridge (*Quadrula undulata* or *Quadrula plicata*), the bullhead (*Pleurobema oesopus*), the buckhorn (*Tritogonia verrucosa*), and a number of other genera of shellfish.

Freshwater pearls are found in the rivers of the Amazon basin and in the rivers of Canada, where in the Nova Scotia district they are obtained from a bivalve named *Alasmodon margaritifera*. The *Cristaria plicata* of Chinese rivers is of more interest in the production of cultured blister pearls and for the nacre covering of metal images, than for the few pearls they may contain. Rather attractive freshwater pearls of pinkish colour are obtained from the rivers of East Pakistan.

The freshwater pearls rarely have as fine an orient as the oriental pearls, but they do have a soft pleasing appearance. The better quality freshwater pearls are, like their salt-water sisters, mainly aragonite, although those from the Alasmodon are generally made up of the calcite prismatic structure. Freshwater pearls usually fluoresce strongly when bathed in a beam of x·rays, probably due to a trace of manganese, while natural sea-pearls do not; this tends to invalidate the fluorescence test for cultured pearls.

Grading and Shape

Pearls are graded according to colour and shape. The colour grading in the best pearls depends upon delicate tinges of colour, which may be apparent only to the most experienced eye. Such nuances are termed rosée when showing a delicate shade of pink; silvery and white are other classifications. There is a subtle yellow tinge in pearls, a colour nuance which is more appreciated by the darker skinned ladies of Latin countries. Fancy coloured pearls are those which have a decided colour and can be yellow. bronze, gunmetal, black, rose-pink, green and blue.

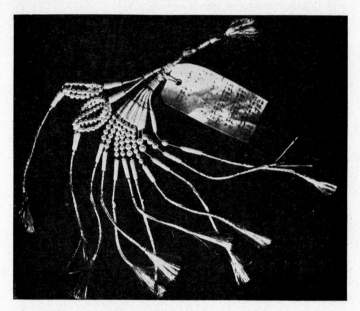

Figure 21.13. A 'Bombay bunch'

The shapes of pearls vary greatly, the perfectly spherical pearls mostly being used for necklets. Pear-shaped or the so-called drop pearls are used for ear-rings and pendants, while those with a button shape (with one side somewhat flattened), sometimes called boutons, are suitable for ear-studs, dress studs and for rings. Irregularly shaped pearls are called baroque pearls (barroks), and very small pearls are seed pearls.

Drilling

The drilling of pearls, generally carried out in Bombay in the case of oriental pearls, is done by using a bow drill with a needle bit which has the end flattened to a spade point. The pearl is drilled from each end, calipers being used to ensure the centring, and the freshly drilled pearl has a very straight hole 0·3–0·4 mm in diameter. This is, of course, for pearls selected for necklets, for the drop and button pearls are only partly drilled so as to be cemented on to a metal peg. Sometimes, in the case of these partly drilled pearls, a groove is cut in the side of the hole, and at the end the hole is enlarged by the aid of a 'dog-leg' cutter; the metal peg of the mount is then made with a key-shaped end and this is slid down the groove and rotated at the bottom so that it cannot be pulled out. The peg in all cases is cemented with the aid of a pearl cement; the best being a special cement rather like white sealing wax, and slight heat is necessary in order to soften it.

The oriental pearls which are drilled completely through so as to be used for necklets are usually sorted into quality and size at Bombay. These are prepared for marketing by stringing each size on silk; a number of sizes suitable for a necklet are then held together and finished off by tassels of silver wire and blue silk. Such a bunch of pearls is known as a 'Bombay bunch' (*Figure 21.13*) and is usually provided with a pearl statement (*see below*) on an attached label. Sometimes drop and button pearls are drilled across the top of the drop or across the low back of the button pearl so that they may be sewn on to material. Such pearls are known as 'Chinese drilled'; they have less value than pearls drilled normally.

Price Calculation

The calculation of the price of pearls is based upon the pearl grain, of which there are four to the metric carat, and therefore a quarter of a carat (0·25 carat). The pearl grain (not to be confused with the troy grain) is not an official weight and pearls are always weighed in metric carats, but this weight is converted into pearl grains (multiply by four) for the purposes of price calculation.

The formula for the finding of the price of a single pearl depends upon squaring the weight in grains and then multiplying the result by the 'base' price. The base price is that value decided upon by the dealer who takes into consideration the shape, colour, orient and cleanness from blemishes of the pearl. For example: a pearl weighing 8·4 grains gives (8·4 × 8·4) which is 70·56, at 1s. base, or, as the trade term it, 'once the weight'. This value (at 1s. base) is then multiplied by the base price, say 3s. 3d. in this instance. Therefore 70·56s. × 3s 3d. (or in metric 3·25s.) will give 229·32s., or when worked out to pounds, shillings and pence, gives £11 9s. 4d. (to the nearest penny) as the price of the pearl.

In the case of pearl necklets, which are usually composed of pearls of different sizes and in graduated arrangement, a slightly different method of price calculation is adopted. The base value having been decided on, the pearls are then weighed in groups and the average weight of the pearls in each group found. The price of each group at 'once the weight' (1s. base) is calculated by multiplying the average weight by the total weight of the group in grains. The price at 'once the weight' of each group is then added together and the total so obtained multiplied by the base price to obtain the total price of the necklet. This last working is generally set out as a final 'pearl statement'. It is a trade usage to carry out all calculations to the second place of decimals only, even should the third figure be a nine. An example of the method of calculating the value of a pearl necklet is shown below.

The calculation of the value of a necklet of pearls in five sizes at 4s. 9d. base.

(*a*) 1 pearl weighing 7·32 grains
(*b*) 2 pearls weighing 12·24 grains
(*c*) 8 pearls weighing 30·84 grains
(*d*) 36 pearls weighing 54·32 grains
(*e*) 74 pearls weighing 46·24 grains

The calculation necessary to obtain the value of each group at 'once the weight' (1s. base) would be as follows:

(*a*) 7·32 × 7·32 which gives 53·58s.
(*b*) 12·24 × (12·24 ÷ 2), that is 12·24 × 6·12 giving 74·90s.
(*c*) 30·84 × (30·84 ÷ 8), that is 30·84 × 3·85 giving 118·73s.
(*d*) 54·32 × (54·32 ÷ 36), that is 54·32 × 1·50 giving 81·48s.
(*e*) 46·24 × (46·24 ÷ 74), that is 46·24 × 0·62 giving 28·66s.

This is set out as a pearl statement as under:

 1 pearl weighing 7·32 grains average 7·32 at 1s. base   53·58s.
 2 pearls weighing 12·24 grains average 6·12 at 1s. base   74·90s.
 8 pearls weighing 30·84 grains average 3·85 at 1s. base 118·73s.
36 pearls weighing 54·32 grains average 1·50 at 1s. base   81·48s.
74 pearls weighing 46·24 grains average 0·62 at 1s. base   28·66s.

121   150·96 grains   357·35s.

The value of the necklet at 4s. 9d. (4·75s.) will be:

357·35s. multiplied by 4·75s. which gives:
1,690·27s., or £88 10s. 3d. (to nearest penny).

Seed pearls are generally sold by the ounce.

Treatment

The 'doctoring' of pearls by 'skinning' has often been mentioned. The notion is that by removing a bad-coloured or blemished outer layer, a more attractive, although smaller, pearl could be obtained. The layer is removed by careful filing of the surface, or by the use of abrasive emery paper. There are, however, very few people who are experienced in this exacting work, and in any case the result is problematical.

Cracks in the surface of pearls are sometimes 'cured' by soaking them in warm olive oil, but such improving methods, called decraqueler, are fraught with danger, for at quite a low temperature—about 150°C (300°F)—the pearls tend to turn to a brown colour and then lose their value.

Protection

Pearls will last for centuries provided normal care is used in protecting them. The loss of lustre and the cracking of pearls are due to one of two things: (1) to the drying out of the organic constituent—the conchiolin—so that too dry an atmosphere is detrimental to pearls: (2) the facility of the mineral part—calcium carbonate—to be dissolved away by weak acids. This is manifest in the formation of a barrel shape assumed by well-worn old pearls in necklets (*Figure 21.14*). This effect is particularly evident in the pearls near the snap end where the necklet lies close to the neck and where the pearls are close to the skin, the erosion being due to the acid nature of exudations from the skin. Keeping pearls in cotton-wool may also be detrimental for much cotton-wool is not acid free.

Modern cosmetics which seep into the string canal may penetrate into the layers of the pearl and cause deterioration; they may also rot the string causing it to break. Thus, pearls should be cleaned periodically, and this is best done when the necklets are restrung. Such restringing and cleaning should be carried out at intervals of not longer than six months, and should be carried out only by a competent pearl stringer who will know the correct way to clean the pearls and the correct silk to use for the stringing. The best necklets should be strung so that there is a knot between each pearl, then, should the necklet be accidentally broken only one pearl at most would be lost. Many insurance companies make it a condition of the policy that pearl necklets are cleaned and restrung at prescribed intervals.

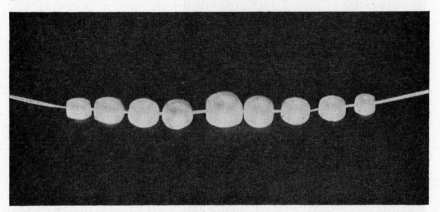

Figure 21.14. A pearl necklet showing many of the pearls to have worn barrel shaped

Staining

The staining of pearls is sometimes carried out. This may be to induce the delicate rosée tint, but such a staining is not very successful; methods to induce a black colour are quite often employed with dark coloured pearls which are not acceptable for jewellery. The most common method is to soak the pearls in a weak solution of silver nitrate and then expose them to sunlight or ultra-violet rays. This treatment causes the silver to be reduced (by the action of the organic constituent) to a finely divided condition: this powder is black in colour, and gives that hue to the pearl, which is 'buffed up' to give a lustrous finish.

Such 'treated' pearls are not commercially acceptable, but the identification of such artificial coloration is not easy. X-rays may give an answer owing to the 'reduced silver' being congregated in the conchiolin-rich layers. This causes an opacity to the rays instead of a transparency. On the film, therefore, such organically rich areas will show light and not dark as in untreated pearls. Such a test is more effective in the case of cultured pearls so stained than with stained natural pearls. Alternatively, some powder scraped from the string canal may prove this silver coloration by showing the characteristic lines of silver in the spectrum. It has been found that naturally coloured black pearls show a dim reddish glow when examined by light passed through a copper sulphate solution and the pearls viewed through a red filter. Pearls stained black artificially do not show this dim red glow.

CULTURED PEARLS

With the popularity of pearls it is not surprising that experiments have been made to stimulate the pearl-forming shellfish to produce objects of this nature. Indeed, such experiments are centuries old, for the covering with nacre of objects inserted between the shell and the mantle of pearl-producing molluscs is attributed by the Chinese to a native of Hou-Tcheon-Fou who

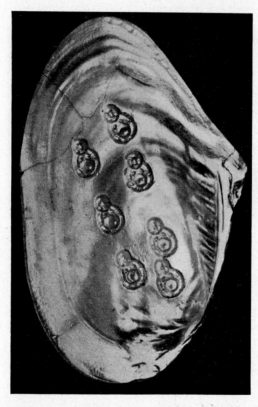

Figure 21.15. Pearl covered Buddhas on Chinese freshwater mussel (Cristaria plicata)

lived in the thirteenth century. For centuries the Chinese have inserted objects, particularly metal figures of Buddha, between the shell and the mantle of the Chinese freshwater mussel (*Cristaria plicata*) (*Figure 21.15*).

History of Early Experiments

The Swedish naturalist, Carl V. Linne, tried experiments for the making of pearls using a freshwater mussel. This was during the eighteenth century. The method Linne employed was to bore a small hole through the shell of the mollusc and insert in the hole a fine silver wire bearing on its end a rough fragment of limestone. This artificial nucleus was placed near the ends of the shell to avoid too much irritation of the animal's body and to avoid connecting the nucleus to the shell—in order to avoid producing a blister pearl—and the nucleus was kept away by the wire. The results were not encouraging and had no commercial significance.

During the last decade of the nineteenth century the Japanese Kokichi Mikimoto, an itinerant peddler of noodles who became interested in pearls, commenced experimental production of the cultured semi-spherical or blister pearl (*Figure 21.16*). In 1896 he patented the process used and such objects were commercially produced.

The method used was to force open the valves of a pearl oyster and cement to the nacreous internal surface of the shell a spherical bead of mother-of-pearl. The jaws were released and the animal returned to the water, when after a few years the oyster was found to have coated the bead

Figure 21.16. X-ray picture of a pair of ear-rings set with cultured blister pearls (Mabe pearls)

with nacre, which seems to have been deposited with greater rapidity than for the deposition in the case of oysters forming a blister pearl naturally. As nacre cannot be deposited on the cemented side of the bead this needs to be ground off and is usually replaced by a piece of mother-of-pearl which is ground symmetrically to shape. This non-nacreous base is covered by a closed-back setting when mounted in jewellery. There appear to be variations of this type of cultured pearl in that the mother-of-pearl base may be pegged into the bead nucleus, or may be just cemented on to the flat surface of the bead. Most commonly the original bead nucleus is removed and after the inside of the shell of nacre has been polished, and may be tinted, the empty recess is refilled by a new bead and backing which is cemented in by the use of a white cement. Such an object makes a striking picture when photographed by x-rays. Such pearls are called 'Mabe' pearls. A cultured blister pearl, probably of Mabe type, in which the bead was made of half a nut, probably an areca nut, has been met.

It is said that Mikimoto first marketed the fully spherical cultured pearls during 1913, but it was 1921 before the whole cultured pearl came upon the general market to any extent. This was the outcome of many years of experiment, which contrary to general belief was not the brain child of Mikimoto, who, however, had much to do with the subsequent commercial marketing of these cultured pearls. There is still some doubt as to who first produced a whole cultured pearl, but the most successful experiments were essentially those of Japanese workers. The history is vague, but investigation has shown that it was in all probability Tatsuhei Mise, a carpenter who became interested in pearls because of his stepfather who had been on an oyster prospecting trip to Australia. He had no scientific training, but working on an idea of his own he produced at his home in Watakano-shima in Matoya-wan (wan means bay) a whole cultured pearl. The pearl was developed in the Japanese pearl oyster (*Pinctada martensi*) by a tissue graft around a tiny lead nucleus. The exact date is unknown but it was prior to 1904. In 1907 Mise applied for a patent on his process but was refused such protection on the ground of Mikimoto's early patent and another patent by one Nishikawa, which in point of fact was five months later. Mise was, however, granted a patent on the needle he used in his method, and this was the first patent issued in respect of whole cultured pearls. Mise left no published record of his work.

The first person to produce whole cultured pearls from planned scientific experiments was Tokichi Nishikawa, who until 1905 was a technologist in the Japanese Bureau of Fisheries. In this year he resigned to take up research on pearls. The method used by Nishikawa was in essentials similar to that of Mise except that tiny gold and silver nuclei were used. Nishikawa applied for a patent on October 23, 1907, five months after Mise's application, and, the patent office accepting the claim made by Nishikawa that he had completed his invention as early as 1899, granted him protection, but even so this was not until 1916, and when Mise's earlier application had been ruled out as an infringement. In 1908, however, Nishikawa and Mise signed an agreement of joint ownership of the Mise/Nishikawa method: this seemed to indicate the priority of Mise's discovery. Nishikawa died in 1909.

In 1914 Mikimoto again came on the scene when he applied for a patent for his own method of spherical pearl culture, and this was granted in 1916, 50 days before the Nishikawa patent was granted, a patent applied for seven years earlier than Mikimoto's. Mikimoto did not invent the method he patented, the inventor being Otokichi Kuwabara, a great friend of Mikimoto, whose previous profession was that of a dentist. This Kuwabara/Mikimoto method is the so-called 'all-lapped' system, by which a bead nucleus was wrapped and tied with fine silk thread in a sac made from the mantle of an oyster, this being inserted into the body of another oyster where it was attached 'by pressing'. Today it is the Mise/Nishikawa method which is extensively used, as the Mikimoto method was found to be too delicate and wasteful. Subsequent intermarriage of the principal families gave rise to some sort of unified organization presided over by Kokichi Mikimoto until his death in 1955 at the age of 96.

Australian Cultivation Farms

The modern production of cultured pearls has been brought to a fine art in Japan, and also in certain islands of the Equatorial Pacific Ocean, such as the Palau group, which were under Japanese mandate during the years between World Wars I and II. Except for an abortive attempt to cultivate pearls in Australian waters during 1907, Japan has been the only source of cultured pearls. However, after 35 years' embargo on the cultivation of pearls by the Government of Western Australia, the State, during 1956, granted a licence for 3 years for an Australian company, to grow cultured pearls in a prescribed area in Brecknock Harbour which lies between Augustus Island and the mainland of Western Australia. In a bay here, now called Kuri Bay, cultivation has been carried out by the company using Japanese technicians, with the large oyster *Pinctada maxima*. Cultured blister pearls of large size have been successfully produced, which after removal from the shell, are sent to Japan to have the nucleus removed, the inside of the blister polished and if required tinted, and the empty recess refilled with a fresh mother-of-pearl bead and a backing which is cemented in by a special white cement. Whole culture pearls are also produced in Australian waters and these pearls are of large size, some being over 100 grains in weight. These cultured blister and cultured whole pearls were seen on the European market during the autumn of 1958, which indicates a faster rate of growth when the large oyster is used. Some experiments with the production of non-nucleated pearls have also been carried out in these waters but the pearls formed were usually baroque. It has been reported that cultivation has been restarted in the Palau group and has started in the Mergui peninsula and possibly around Hong Kong, Korea and certain Pacific islands.

An Australian firm has started banks of oysters at Port Moresby in New Guinea, and Friday, Banks and Thursday Islands in the Torres Straights.

Japanese Cultivation Farms

The pearl-producing mollusc which lives in Japanese waters is the small oyster *Pinctada martensi* (*Figure 21.17*), which at maturity is not more than about 8 cm (3 in.) in length. The centre of the pearl culture carried out in

Figure 21.17. The Japanese pearl oyster Pinctada martensi, *showing the size at various stages of growth from three weeks*

421

Japanese waters is in Ago-wan, a bay which is situated near the Shima Hanto (hanto means peninsula) which itself forms the greater part of the Ise-shima National Park at the south-eastern end of Mie Prefecture. Other nearby bays—Gokasho-wan; Matoya-wan; Kagamiura-wan and Nie-wan, all of which, like Ago-wan, lie on the eastern coastline of the main Japanese island of Honshu—are also used for oyster farms. There have been attempts to develop the industry in other parts of Japan, such as the Omura-wan in Kyushu, and the Tsushima islands and Tosa-wan in Shikoku. Recently a new strain of *Pinctada martensi* has been bred which grows to double the size of the same species grown in Ago Bay. These larger oysters allow pearls of up to 12 mm diameter to be produced as against the maximum of 10 mm obtainable with the Ago Bay strain.

Figure 21.18. Amas, diving girls, collecting oysters
(By courtesy, the Cultured Pearl Company Ltd.)

The geographic and climatic conditions in the Ago-wan area are perfect for the production and growth of pearl oysters which demand water of a uniform shallow depth never falling below 10°C. These small bays along the peninsula provide protected water in which permanent oyster beds may be safely laid.

The pearl fisheries (farms) start with the collection of naturally grown oysters common to the area, or more usually now, oysters raised from cultivated 'spat'. Motor launches, or fishing skiffs, with a crew of four or five, two or three being divers, go out to collect these oysters.

Figure 21.19. Girls diving for virgin oysters
(By courtesy, the Cultured Pearl Company Ltd.)

Figure 21.20. General view of rafts in pearl cultivating area
(By courtesy, the Cultured Pearl Company Ltd.)

423

Diving Techniques

The divers are mostly women, for it is said that these Japanese women have more endurance and can hold their breath longer than men whilst under water. These sturdy, picturesque divers, known as amas, in former days dived practically nude, but today they are clothed in short white sarongs and long-sleeved white shirts which cover them from throat to knees. They bind their hair and cover their heads with white cotton kerchiefs, and their faces are protected with wide glass-fronted face masks which cover all except the mouth and chin (*Figure 21.18*).

When the floor of the bay is less than 5 m (16 ft.) deep the only kit taken is a small hand-net about 25 cm (10 in.) in diameter, a 3-cm mesh cotton netting bag some half a metre in depth, and a large wooden bucket about 50 cm deep and 60 cm in diameter (20 × 24 in.) which is attached to the diver's waist by a stout cord (*Figure 21.19*). The ama gives a powerful kick as she dives below the surface, then gropes along the dark sea floor. On each dive she collects, according to the skill of the diver, from 1 to 10 oysters which she puts into her hand-net and transfers to the wooden tub on surfacing. Each dive lasts for about 25–40 sec; the constant holding of the breath causes the amas to breathe with a peculiar whistling sound when they come up from a dive.

In deeper water, up to 8 m (25 ft.), the amas operate directly from the sides of the boat, using a heavy stone or weight on a rope which passes over a davit on the boat's gunwale, just aft of amidships. Taking a deep breath the diver, with another rope round her waist, grasps the rope with the weight, and on release of this rope, sinks quickly to the bottom. On the diver's signal the crew in the tender pass the lifeline over the davit and haul the girl up to the boat, into which she empties her net containing the oysters she has gathered. She rests on the deck for about two minutes while the weight on its rope is raised. The divers work for two $2\frac{1}{2}$-hour periods each day, and during the non-working period rest on the shore before open fires. The active figures of these industrious women add colour to the enchanting scenery of the Shima peninsula (*Figure 21.20*) and attract thousands of sightseers every year.

Sorting of Collected Oysters

The oysters collected by the divers are taken to the sorting tables at the shore base. Here the unsatisfactory shells are discarded, and the 2-year oysters are separated by their size from the 3–4-year-old individuals. The catch is weighed in order to credit the diver who receives a rate of pay per kan (about $8\frac{1}{4}$ pounds), representing about 100 oysters. The 3–4-year-old oysters are taken to the 'farms' and distributed over previously cleaned moderately rocky bottoms of shallow water. These remain undisturbed until the next April or May, when divers again collect the oysters for them to be taken to the laboratory for nucleus insertion.

Cultivation of the Spat

The principle of the cultivation of 'spat' had long been understood and methods had been devised for such cultivation in the case of edible oysters.

The earliest method employed consisted in the collection of 'spat' by allowing them to settle on submerged stones, or pieces of bamboo, and then removing them to more sheltered waters where their growth could more easily be observed. It was later discovered that the free-swimming 'spat' develops, just before settling, a marked aversion to light, and to avoid this special cages were developed by Mikimoto. These cages, some $84 \times 54 \times 20$ cm (approximately $2\frac{3}{4} \times 1\frac{3}{4} \times \frac{3}{4}$ ft.), are formed by covering a heavy galvanized wire frame of 2 cm wire mesh, and having seven horizontal wire mesh shelves and provided with a door at the foot of the cage. Black painted boards are fastened to the sides and bottom which provide a darkened area attractive to the 'spat'. The cages are, before attachment of the boards, dropped into hot tar and then into a sand and cement mixture to provide an excellent base upon which the larvae can settle. Some 50 cages are suspended, at a depth of 6 m (about 20 ft.) from large frame rafts supported by empty oil drums or barrels. In 1947 a simplified and inexpensive 'spat' collector was designed. It consists of a bamboo raft frame from which is suspended a series of 40 straw ropes strung with discarded shells of the oyster, abalone or turbo.

These rafts are set out in July, the oyster spawning season being from July to September, and are anchored in suitable waters in a series of 5 or 10 lashed together end to end. The cages remain in place until late November, by which time the young oysters are 1·5 cm long (just over a half-inch). They are then transferred to rearing cages which resemble in many details the collecting cages, except that the size of the covering mesh is smaller, 1 cm, or cotton mesh may be used, and the internal divisions are slightly different. These cages are either distributed over the sea bottom in sheltered waters or suspended from rafts, the nature of the cages providing suitable protection to the young oysters from predatory natural enemies. The cages, however, do not protect the oysters from the damage caused by the so-called 'red tides' a poisonous form of plankton which chokes the oysters. The young oysters are allowed to remain undisturbed until they are a year old and some $2\frac{1}{2}$ cms (1 in.) in diameter. These oysters are then sown in shallow water, 3–5 m deep (10–16 ft.), which has a rough rocky bottom, and here the oysters are allowed to remain undisturbed for about 2 years.

From June to August the oysters, now 3 years old, are collected by women divers and brought to cleaning barges—large fully decked pontoon-like structures with a simple sloping roof—which has been towed to the collecting site by motor launches. The shells are there cleaned from adhering incrustations and seaweed by scraping with a blunt knife. Distorted and old shells are discarded and undersized shells returned to the growing beds for another year. The cleaned shells are then placed in culture cages in shallow water for 10 days for acclimatization to their new environment and to recover from the shock of cleaning.

After the period of acclimatization the oysters are taken up from the cages and prepared for the operation of nucleus insertion. One of three methods is used to induce the partial opening of the valves (shells). The oysters may be placed in shallow trays with the hinge of the shell downwards and then covered with seawater, when, in a minute or two the valves 'gape'

Figure 21.21. Opening the oysters and inserting pegs

and are then forced about 1 cm apart by the use of opening forceps, called the 'shell speculum', inserted between the shells at the antero-ventral region sufficiently enough to allow a bamboo wedge, or 'key', to be inserted at the postero-ventral region and at about 45 degrees to the hinge line (*Figure 21.21*).

An alternative to this 'stagnant water method' is the 'running water technique', and this differs solely by the fact that the trays are supplied with constant running water. In a third method, the 'dry method', the host oysters are brought in baskets to the station wharf about 24 hours before the nucleus insertion. The baskets meanwhile are hung from nearby rafts, and some 30 min. before the technicians are ready to carry out the operation the oysters are dumped on to the wharf, and shortly after about

426

25 per cent of the oysters begin to 'gape'. These are selected for immediate operation and the bamboo wedge is inserted; this must not be kept in for more than 2 hours before the operation for the insertion of the nucleus is performed.

The oysters which do not 'gape' within the time are returned to the water for another 4 hours and again taken to the wharf for testing, The 'gaping' of the valves indicates that the oyster is healthy and vigorous enough to withstand the operation, which is best carried out only 20 min. after the 'keying' of the oyster. This 'keying' itself needs care, for should the edge of the shell be broken, the animal first repairs this damage to the detriment of the formation of the pearl sac and the quality of the resultant pearl.

While the pegging or keying of the oysters is carried out the technicians who do the actual operation prepare their desks and apparatus, and also a supply of mother-of-pearl beads used for the nucleus.

Nucleus Operation

Preparation of Nuclei

The best material for the nucleus is a substance which is not foreign to the oyster; a spherical bead of mother-of-pearl is eminently suitable and is consistently used. As these nuclei range in diameter to more than 6 mm for *Pinctada martensi* to as much as 13 mm for pearls cultured in *Pinctada maxima*, a solid heavy shell from which they are to be cut must be obtained. Before China's embargo on trade, the shell for the beads of cultured pearls were obtained from the Gamanose clam shell from the Yangtse river. Since then shell from the pig-toe mussel found in the Mississippi valley is used. In some cases sea-water Trocus shell has been used.

The American shells are shipped to Japan for processing. This is carried out by cutting the shells into small cubes of the required general size. They are then placed between iron sheets, the upper one being revolved, and by the general rubbing of the cubes between these plates they attain a roughly spherical shape. The beads are then placed in cotton bags and subjected to a further grinding treatment. This may be followed by placing powdered talc or jeweller's rouge in the bag to impart a polish to the surface, although a polished surface is not essential.

The finished beads are then graded to size: for *Pinctada martensi* they are from 1·2 mm to 6·6 mm in diameter, each group being 0·3 mm larger with individual variation within the groups of less than 0·05 mm. Larger nuclei up to 13·2 mm are prepared for *Pinctada maxima*, and beads between 6·3–6·6 mm are used for *Pinctada margaritifera*. Experiments with plastic beads as a substitute for the nucleus showed the material to be unsatisfactory, but marble mechanically prefabricated into spherical beads has been used experimentally. This marble has been obtained from Shikoku and Gifu Prefecture; but from experiments on cultured pearls which have been found to have an unusual nucleus it is conjectured whether the material is a marble or a banded talc.

Preparation of Graft Tissue from Oyster

The technicians first prepare the graft tissue from the frilled mantle edge of a living oyster. A selected oyster is carefully opened by inserting the blade of a knife between the valves and the abductor muscle is then cut from its attachment to one shell. With the blunt edge of a scalpel all extraneous matter is scraped out and then a strip of living tissue, about 0·75 cm wide and 7 cm long is cut from the mantle edge. This is smoothed out on a wet graft trimming block—a soft wooden disc some 2 cm thick and 8 cm in diameter made from the crape myrtle or magnolia—and the adhering slime wiped off with a viscose sponge. The piece is first cut into strips 2–3 mm in width, and then transversely into tiny squares, the size of which is determined by the size of the nucleus employed. It must be of such a size as to cover one-third of the nucleus. The whole block, with the cut tissue adhering, is then dipped in a beaker of seawater, the tissue remaining alive for about 2 hours if kept wet and at a temperature of 17°–22° C. There is a report that to obtain a better rate of production and a higher quality of pearls, both the pearls and the instruments used are dipped into a solution of an antibiotic such as aureomycin.

Insertion of Nucleus

With the nuclei and the grafts prepared all is ready to perform the operation of nucleus insertion. Taking one of the partly opened 'pegged' oysters, the technicians—these are usually women—place it in the desk clamp. This is a specially designed brass spring clamp for holding the oyster in position without lateral movement and without damaging the shell. The clamp is mounted on a telescopic column which has an adjustable tilting head, the whole being mounted on a heavy wooden base.

With the aid of a spatula the operator smooths back the mantle folds exposing the body and foot of the animal, holding the latter down and slightly extending it with an instrument called the retractor hook. This is to prevent muscular action. With a flat probe a small cut is made in the epithelium of the foot, and this is enlarged into a slender channel into the main mass of the tissue. Along this channel is passed a piece of the graft tissue to the site selected for the nucleus. A mother-of-pearl nucleus is then picked up with the moistened end of the nucleus lifter—a special probe with a cup-shaped end—and with this instrument is inserted down the channel into the body of the oyster so that it is just above the previously introduced graft tissue. The channel is carefully closed by gently smoothing back the foot mass (*Figure 21.22*).

Culturing of the Pearls

Unless a second, or possibly a third nucleus is to be inserted, the foot is released from the retractor and the plug removed from between the valves, whereupon the oyster closes. It is then returned to the holding tray and subsequently to the culture cages in sheltered waters for a period of 4–6 weeks in order that they may convalesce. After this time they are inspected, dead shells removed and the remainder transferred to permanent culture rafts by motor boats or barges. In restricted waters a newer method is employed. As the rafts take considerable space a modern innovation, the 'straw code' or 'bamboo pole' method, is used. These entail the fastening of the oysters round a piece of straw code or a bamboo pole which are then hung vertically in the water. This uses a greater depth of water but less area than the cages.

Some 60 cages, holding over 3,000 oysters, are suspended at a depth of 2–3 m. (7–10 ft.) from the permanent culture rafts. They are periodically inspected, usually three times a year and the oysters cleaned from encrusting growths. Dead oysters are removed, and a few opened in order to

Figure 21.22. Inserting the dice of mantle in culturing pearls

determine the growth rate of the pearls. There is a report that the pearls are examined by weak x-rays to detect whether the oyster has ejected the bead nucleus as a large percentage of the larger beads are aborted (spat out) within the first year. After a period of from 3 to 6 years (usually $3\frac{1}{2}$ years) the oysters are recovered and taken to the laboratory where the shells are opened and the cultured pearls removed—and also any natural pearls which may have formed. The pearls are then washed free from slime and carefully dried (*Figure 21.23*). Cultured pearls of dark colour, and most of them show a greenish tinge, are 'bleached' by placing them in a warm weak solution of hydrogen peroxide which lightens the dark conchiolin causing the unattractive shade of colour.

Grading

The pearls are then graded into size by the use of sieves with different size holes: it is at this time that all deformed pearls are removed. The next operation is to count the pearls and this is done by sliding into the container of pearls a paddle-like plastic plate having ten rows of ten holes. On withdrawing the paddle and seeing that all the holes are occupied a quick count of 100 pearls is made.

Figure 21.23. Removing the cultured pearls

After counting, the pearls are graded for quality. There are three main grades: A—good, B—medium and C—poor. These gradings are then divided into three subdivisions, taking into consideration the form, colour, lustre and the perfection of surface. This work is carried out by valuers who subsequently place the market price on the necklets, pairs or single pearls as is considered most suitable.

Drilling

The drilling of pearls for necklets, and their stringing, is carried out at the fishery estate. Any blemish on the pearl to be drilled is marked with an ink spot and the drilling commenced at this point. The drilling itself is carried out by using a mild steel wire 0·75 mm in diameter with its end ground to a triangular point. This is held in a small chuck directly driven by a fractional horse-power motor. In line with the chuck is a movable tailstock with a small brass chuck into which the pearl to be drilled is fixed. This tailstock is capable of being moved along the drill bed and when this is moved forward to the pearl the motor is automatically started and the pearl drilled more than half-way through. The pearl is then removed and a sliver of bamboo is passed into a centring hole in the back of the tailstock chuck. The drill is restarted and the hole drilled from the opposite side. A vertical drill is sometimes used, in which case the pearl is held by two side chucks. Some modern drills are double and simultaneously drill from each end to the centre. Some are so arranged that when one drill reaches a certain distance it 'backs off' to allow the opposite drill to carry through without touching the first. In theory this method should produce a straight canal, but x-ray pictures show that the two drillings are rarely joined straight. This is considered to be due to the straight layers in the mother-of-pearl bead causing the drill to run in line with the layers and to go off course. X-ray pictures have revealed extra drill holes which are at an

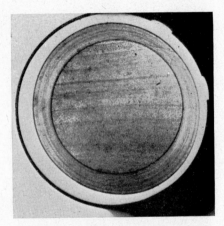

Figure 21.24. A photograph of a thin section of a cultured pearl showing the large bead nucleus with parallel layers surrounded by the comparatively thin layer of true nacre

angle and travel nearly to the outside of the pearl. It is suggested that these are made to allow the weak dye used for tinting to be directed to the discontinuation layer of conchiolin surrounding the bead nucleus.

Weight of cultured Pearls

The pearls are then graduated into necklets, a grooved tray being used for the purpose, as is used for genuine pearls. After graduation they are strung on silk, the ends being tied with enough silk left over for the snap to be attached. The rows are passed for inspection, weighed and recorded. Finally 100 necklets are tied together and the total weight found.

The unit of weight for cultured pearls from Japan is the momme, which equals 3·75 g or 18·75 carats. The base method is not used for cultured pearls, a parcel of a number of necklets being sold as 'so much' per momme.

Composition of Whole-cultured Pearl

A whole-cultured pearl consists of a large bead nucleus of mother-of-pearl surrounded by a thin layer of true nacre usually between half a millimetre and one millimetre in thickness, which has been secreted around the nucleus by the oyster. As the nucleus consists of a bead cut from a shell, the layers conform to the surface of the shell, and are in general parallel and straight; never concentric. Hence the bead shows directional properties of which advantage is taken in the testing of cultured pearls (*Figure 21.24*).

Non-nucleated Pearl Production

Attempts have been made to produce a cultured pearl without a nucleus and some success has been attained by workers using the freshwater mussel *Hyriopsis schlegeli* (*Figure 21.25*), which abounds in the freshwater Biwa-ko (ko means lake) in Shiga Province of Honshu. This mussel, locally called ike-chogai, is a large bivalve with a greenish-black periostracum and an internal nacre of fine colour and lustre. It is a slow-growing mollusc, which takes some 7 years to attain operable age for culture, and does not reach maturity until it is 10–13 years old. This animal has an internal anatomy

Figure 21.25. Shell of the Hyriopsis schlegeli

complicated by a long twisting intestine leaving little space in the connective tissue useful for nucleus insertion, and experiments using nuclei of any size caused either a high mortality rate or produced bad coloured pearls.

To overcome this a system of grafting by pieces of epithelial tissue is employed. The pieces are cut from the mantle of a mussel in a similar manner as for normal pearl culture. This graft tissue is inserted alone into the body of the mussel, no bead nucleus being used. From 6 to 10 grafts used to be inserted into the gonads (sex organs) by means of a special type of forceps which simply intrudes the graft into place without any incision being made.

The pearls produced were baroque in shape and poorly coloured. Later, it was found that if the dice of mantle be inserted into incisions made in the edge of the mantle, pearls of better shape and quality could be produced.

Hyriopsis schlegeli are not, so far, propagated artificially, as sufficient natural clams are available in the lake to satisfy present needs. The clams spawn in June and July and the eggs attach themselves to fish, but they later fall to the lake bed. The clams, which are three-quarters buried in the mud of the lake, are recovered by local fishermen, who drag a trawl net fitted with rakes, the prongs of which are spaced so that only mature clams are caught. They are then kept in pens until needed for the operation.

The operating procedure consists of the removal of the clams from the retaining pens to a building where trained girls peg the shells open and expose the mantle. Ten incisions are made in each half of the mantle and into each is pressed a piece cut from the mantle of another clam. After the operation the clams are placed in plastic baskets which are then suspended about three feet below the lake surface for three years. They are then removed and any pearls carefully removed with tweezers.

The recovery rate of these Biwa pearls is good as about 60 per cent of the mussels operated on produce pearls, and nearly 100 per cent of these bear the full twenty pearls. At full growth the clam reaches nine inches and the animal lives for about thirteen years. If the animal is returned to the water after the removal of the crop of pearls, a second crop of pearls may adventitiously form. The Biwa lake non-nucleated cultured pearls, sometimes called tissue-graft cultured pearls, are a bright white in colour and are usually 'bun' shaped and run to about 7·5 mm in diameter.

The cultivation of non-nucleated pearls has been accomplished in Australian waters using the large oyster *Pinctada maxima*. Quite large pearls, often difficult to detect, are produced.

Treatment

Preservation

It will be realized that cultured pearls consist of some 80 per cent non-pearly material, that is the large mother-of-pearl bead, and the comparatively thin outer layer of true nacre. Such pearls cannot in any way be described as natural pearls, and moreover, although they are serviceable and beautiful they are never quite comparable to the pearls formed by natural processes throughout. Cultured pearls often show a greenish tinge and subcutaneous markings, rather like varicose veins, and, if the skin is thin, the sheen of the mother-of-pearl bead may show as a gleam when the pearls are rotated. Just as much care, perhaps even more, should be taken with cultured pearls, particularly when strung into necklets, for grease from the skin and cosmetics tends to enter the discontinuation layer between the bead nucleus and the outer nacreous layer. This grease is usually dirty, for it picks up dirt remarkably quickly, and shows through the thin pearly outer layer and gives the pearls an unhealthy appearance. Cultured pearl necklets should therefore be cleaned just as frequently as the real pearl necklets. The formation of a barrel shape to the pearls at the back of the necklet is just as likely with cultured pearls as it is for real pearls, but the effect is even more serious for the periphery of the pearl may have the nacre completely worn away leaving two 'caps' of nacre at either end.

Some cultured pearls have been found unaccountably to darken, and this has been attributed to the action of sulphur on a trace metal in the pearl causing the formation of a dark sulphide which gives to the pearl a blackish colour. Soaking in hydrogen peroxide (normal 10 or 20 volumes solution) for a few days may clear this and give a great improvement in colour. The use of hydrogen peroxide is not advised except in such cases, for indiscriminate use may cause pearls, real or cultured, to assume a chalky appearance.

Staining

Cultured pearls may be stained rosée by first bleaching in hydrogen peroxide for several hours and then immersing in a dye made up of vegetable oil, or alcohol, and eosin and letting the pearl soak for 1–24 hours according to the depth of colour required. A black colour is induced in cultured pearls by the use of silver nitrate, as described for the blackening of real pearls. Pearls have been turned to a black colour by exposing them to 100,000 roentgens of *gamma* rays from cobalt 60 for approximately 16 hours. This treatment has been carried out in Japan on cultured pearls. L. B. Benson investigated the staining of cultured pearls and found that there were two other types, one of which had the bead nucleus coloured before nucleation and the other surface dyed. Surface dyed pearls, either natural or cultured, could be identified by swabbing with a minute pad of cotton wool moistened with a very weak solution of hydrochloric acid, which removes some of the dye giving a brown stain on the cotton wool.

THE DETECTION OF CULTURED PEARLS

When the whole-cultured pearl first came on the European market during 1921 it was quickly seen that some means of detection was imperative if the value of real pearls was not to suffer. These early cultured pearls, seen in necklets, studs, pins, rings and brooches, were of good quality, a quality better than many of the cultured pearls marketed today. With no previous experience to rely upon the jeweller was mostly at a loss over these pearls.

Many ideas and suggestions for the detection of these new pearls were considered and tested with experimental apparatus. The story of these endeavours, which have led up to the present methods allowing undeniable proof as to whether a pearl is cultured or real, needs to be told, for this history shows how the scientist and the gemmologist have solved one of their most difficult problems.

X-ray and Ultra-violet Tests

It should be clear from what has been told before that the difference in structure of the layered nature of the bead nucleus of a cultured pearl as against the concentric structure of the real pearl, would provide distinction if some satisfactory method could be evolved to show this difference, or if any other test would conclusively prove that there was a bead inside the pearl. Initial experiments by G. F. Herbert Smith and E. Hopkins were by the use of fluorescence under long-wave ultra-violet light, and these workers considered, at the time, that the greenish-yellow glow shown by the cultured pearl was so markedly different from the sky-blue effect exhibited by oriental pearls that they could be distinguished by that means, apart from the peculiar greenish tinge and other surface markings as seen in ordinary light. It was later found that this green fluorescence was common to some natural pearls, particularly those from adjacent waters, and also was not so pronounced in some pearls as in others: this method did not provide the clear-cut answer required.

About the same time the employment of x-rays was mooted as a possibility that the rays might reveal the presence of the bead, as the bones are revealed in the flesh. The ordinary radiographic technique as known in those days proved unsuccessful as a means of spotting the bead core. Nor could the genuineness of the real pearl be proved by x-rays. As will be seen later, differences in technique now allow this method to be used with some degree of success.

As early as 1922, the question of the greater density of cultured pearls to real pearls was described as a test. A mixture of methylene iodide and benzene was the liquid used for this 'heavy liquid' determinative method. It was not wholly successful, for, although it was found at the time that oriental pearls had a density of about 2·68, Australian pearls from 2·70 to 2·79 and cultured pearls about 2·75, there was too much overlap. P. Kerr and B. W. Anderson independently worked on these lines much later and found that while most oriental pearls floated and most cultured pearls sank in a heavy liquid made up to suspend freely a piece of Iceland spar (calcite —sp. gr. 2·71), the experiment could only be a guide.

The Lucidoscope

M. B. Szillard described an apparatus which he named the lucidoscope, which depended upon the transparency of the layers of the mother-of-pearl bead nucleus of a cultured pearl when they are oriented parallel to a beam of strong light. The apparatus consisted of a powerful light source, in the base of the instrument, directed upwards through a system of condensing lenses on to the glass base of a receptacle which contained the pearl to be tested. The pearl rested on a centrally perforated and concave diaphragm placed in the receptacle which was filled with a liquid having an index of refraction near to that of the pearl (*Figure 21.26*). Above was a low-power microscope to observe the effect, and this could be changed to a camera in order to record the result photographically. In some cases the microscope was dispensed with and the observation made with a binocular head loupe. On switching on the light and turning the pearl round in the liquid with the aid of a pair of eyed tongs the layered structure, if the pearl is cultured, usually shows up as light and dark stripes when the layers are parallel to the light beam (*Figure 21.27*). The method, which is suitable for undrilled and part-drilled pearls as well as for drilled pearls, is specific for cultured pearls as long as the stripes can be seen. The effect can fail with thick-skinned cultured pearls and by this method pearls cannot be proved to be real.

Quick proof of thin-skinned cultured pearls may be carried out in the lucidoscopic way by employing the microscope with a powerful light source and immersing the pearl in a highly refractive liquid in a glass cell, a diaphragm being used upon which to rest the pearl and to limit the light to the central portion of the cell. Strung necklets of thin-skinned cultured pearls can be examined dry in the beam of a strong light, such as the beam emerging from the socket of an endoscope (described later) when the needle is not in position. Each pearl in turn is held in the beam of light and rotated to see if the tell-tale stripes are present. Such a method is termed 'candling' in the United States of America. Experiments by Leroux-Raub-Frohlich showed that if a beam of long-wave ultra-violet light be passed through a correctly oriented cultured pearl resting on a piece of bare film the 'stripy' pattern will be seen on development.

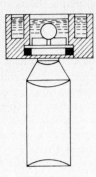

Figure 21.26. Principle of the lucidoscope

Pearl Compass

An interesting piece of apparatus devised by Professor R. Nacken for the detection of cultured from real pearls is the pearl compass. The principle of the instrument is that a crystalline substance will take a certain position according to its crystallographic structure when brought into a magnetic field. The apparatus (*Figure 21.28*) consists of a powerful electromagnet, between the poles of which is set the pearl to be tested. The pearl is cemented, centrally to the end of a glass rod which is suspended by a silk or quartz thread from the adjustable head of the upright glass tube. When the pearl is correctly oriented between the pole pieces the current is switched on and any movement of an indicating bristle or vane observed. The mother-of-pearl core of a cultured pearl causes the pearl to turn, except if the layers of the core are already parallel to the lines of force of the magnetic field. If

436

Figure 21.27. The layered structure seen in a cultured pearl on examination with a lucidoscope

they are not parallel then they are pulled round under the influence of the magnetic force to such a position (*Figure 21.29b*). The radial and concentric structure of a real pearl causes no turning movement and the pearl remains stationary (*Figure 21.29a*). It is clear that as there is one position where a cultured pearl will not turn under the magnetic influence it is necessary to take two observations when the pearl does not turn; this is done by rotating the pearl through 90 degrees by the use of the adjusting head. The reliability of the method is weak, and it is only recommended for perfectly round pearls. Unsymmetrical mounting, metal in the drill hole and odd-shaped pearls will give spurious results.

Pearl Microscope

Examination of the walls of the string canal in drilled pearls by the use of a microscope with a special mounting for the pearl opens up another

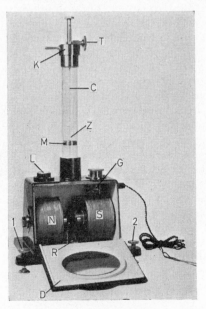

Figure 21.28. The pearl compass: (C) quartz torsion fibre; (D) front cover; (G) lamp for internal lighting; (K) rotatable head; (L) spirit level; (M) graduated indicating ring; (N) and (S) magnet coils; (R) steadying platform; (T) height adjusting screw; (Z) indicating fly; (1, 2) levelling screws

437

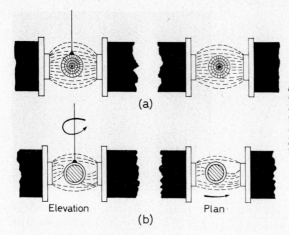

(a)

Elevation   Plan

(b)

Figure 21.29. Schematic diagram of the action of the pearl compass. (a) The magnetic field has no turning action on a natural pearl; (b) the straight layers of the bead in a cultured pearl tend to orient themselves in line with the magnetic field and the pearl moves

profitable line of inquiry. The 'pearlometer' (*Figure 21.30*) devised by H. Michel and G. Riedl is such an instrument that will illustrate the method and the apparatus. The microscope itself is a normal instrument, either monocular or binocular, which contains a built-in light source below the stage, and a subsidiary adjustable lamp which throws a strong beam of light illuminating the pearl from the front or sides. The essential accessory for the pearl-testing microscope is the so-called cardiometer (*Figure 21.31*). This is a special stage-support for the pearl and has a very thin needle, with the end polished to a mirror finish, and which is inserted into the string hole of the pearl.

The mirror end of the needle when in the string canal of the pearl is examined by the microscope and, by reflection shows the nature of the canal walls. The needle can be raised and lowered by adjustment of the graduated ring of the cardiometer and measurements of one-thousandth of a millimetre may be made of the rise or fall of the needle in the drill hole of the pearl. Thus, the thickness of the layers of a real pearl, or the thickness of the nacreous 'skin' of a cultured pearl may be measured. Therefore, by observing the reflection of the canal wall in the mirror of the needle whilst it is raised or lowered in the string hole, it may be seen whether the pearl has a concentric structure throughout, or has a bead nucleus of a cultured pearl.

A similar idea was employed in the apparatus designed by J. Galibourg and F. Ryziger who, instead of employing a fine needle with a polished end, arranged for the pearl to be mounted on a holder which allowed a thread of mercury to be squeezed up, from a container below, into the string canal. By varying the pressure on the container by a screw and pressure plate the thread of mercury may be allowed to ascend or descend in the drill hole. The brilliant reflecting surface of the meniscus of the mercury providing a convex mirror reflecting the surface of the canal walls. A simplified arrangement devised by G. O. Wild and H. Biegel is said to be more convenient in use. More successful than some other methods which have been suggested, the examination of the canal walls by the microscope and reflecting needle method does suffer, however, from the time-consuming 'setting-up'.

Figure 21.30. The pearl microscope: (1) light switches, (2) microscope focusing adjustment, (3) binocular microscope, (4) lamp for side lighting, (5) the cardiometer, (6) substage lighting

The Endoscope

During 1926, C. Chilowski and A. Perrin brought out the endoscope for the examination of drilled pearls, it being modified a year later by René and Simon Bloch. The endoscope is recognized as being the most satisfactory instrument for the positive identification of both genuine and cultured drilled pearls.

The endoscope (*Figure 21.32*) consists of a powerful source of light in a suitable housing, the source being either an arc-lamp or a 'Pointolite' lamp. The beam of this light is passed through a system of condensing lenses and then through a fine hollow needle which has at its end two polished mirrors at 45 degrees in opposite senses. The first, or interior mirror

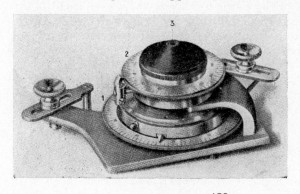

Figure 21.31. The cardiometer: (1), (2) calibrated adjustments for the rise and fall of the mirror/needle, (3) aperture for the needle

439

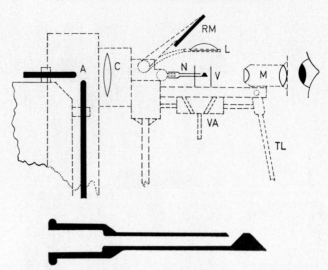

Figure 21.32. Schematic diagram of the endoscope: A, Arc-light; C,
Condenser; RM, Reflecting mirror to show surface of pearl; L, Lens
to enlarge surface of pearl; N, Needle; V, Vice to hold pearl; M,
Microscope to view end of needle; VA, Vice adjustment; TL,
Traversing lever to move pearl along needle. Below: Enlarged section
of needle

causes the beam of light to reflect upwards and out of a small aperture cut
in the top of the tube: the exterior mirror forms the end of the tube. The
surface of this end-mirror is viewed by a small low-powered microscope
which is capable of being directed vertically and horizontally small distances
and of being focused on to the needle end. Above the optical system is
arranged a low-powered bi-convex lens which allows the operator, while
seated before the instrument, to see the surface of the pearl whilst it is on
the needle.

When the needle, of which there are three sizes (0·3, 0·4 and 0·5 mm in
outer diameter) is placed on the instrument and the arc lit, a fine beam of
bright light is seen directed up through the aperture in the top of the needle.
If, however, a natural pearl is first placed on the needle, this upward beam
of light will enter one of the concentric layers and travel round it by a
process of total reflection. This totally reflected beam will be 'lost' (*Figure
21.33a*) except when the needle is at the centre of the pearl, when the reflected beam will strike the end-mirror of the needle and be reflected out
through the drill hole where it will be seen as a brilliant reflection through
the microscope eyepiece (*Figure 21.33b*). In practice the pearl is passed back
and forth along the needle while observing the end-mirror through the
microscope. When the centre of the pearl passes across the mirrors of the
needle a flash of light is seen which proves without doubt that the pearl is
concentric throughout and therefore real.

A cultured pearl with its layered structure cannot return the light reflected from the first mirror of the needle to the end-mirror, hence, no
'flash' will be seen when the pearl is drawn back and forth along the

needle. In this case the beam of light entering the pearl travels along the straight layers of the mother-of-pearl core and will be seen as a cat's-eye streak on the outside of the pearl (*Figure 21.33c*). Should the layers of the bead nucleus be parallel to the needle and horizontal to the base of the instrument no streak will be seen on the outside of the pearl; rotation of the pearl on the needle will bring the layers vertical and show the streak from front to rear over the top of the pearl. In practice it is usual always to rotate the pearl so that the streak moves, as it is more apparent in certain positions.

Some genuine pearls have a conchiolin-rich core and this may preclude the reflection of the light, and hence give no flash. In such cases the charac-

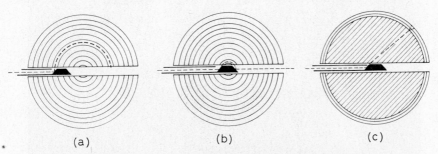

(a)   (b)   (c)

Figure 21.33. Paths of light rays from an endoscope needle when a natural or cultured pearl is mounted on it: (a) a natural pearl not central on the needle showing the light 'lost'; (b) a natural pearl when central on the needle showing the ray reflected from the end-mirror out through the drill hole; (c) a cultured pearl, which has straight layers in the core, cannot return the light ray to the end-mirror but directs the light up through the layers to the outside of the pearl

teristic 'cut-off' of the general illumination shown by the pearl as seen from the top lens as the needle passes into the dark core is indicative. Examination by a hand lens of the structure seen down the drill canal will show the dark centre and the reason for the lack of result.

The vice which holds the pearl on the endoscope is connected to the traversing lever which moves the pearl along the needle, and the end of this traversing lever travels over a scale marked with a zero when the lever is vertical and therefore the mirrors of the needle are central in the pearl. The divisions, marked one to five, on each side of the zero mark are centimetres and are divided into millimetres. As the lever is so designed to move the pearl one-tenth the distance of the sweep of the lever over the scale, the movement of the arm of the lever over 1 cm of the scale indicates 1 mm movement of the pearl; thus, as the scale is marked in millimetres, one-tenth of a millimetre may be measured. This enables the reflections from the concentric layer edges of a real pearl to be measured, and also the thickness of the nacreous outer layer of a cultured pearl.

Despite the layered structure of the bead of mother-of-pearl which forms the nucleus of cultured pearls, this structure does not show as lines on the wall of the string canal, and the surface, as seen in the endoscope needle, is uniform. With part-drilled genuine pearls the endoscope will be of little use, but a cultured pearl may show the 'streak' when the needle is able to penetrate the pearl only a short distance. With experience and constant practice, and when the pearls are clean and 'easy', some 200 pearls an hour can be tested on the endoscope, which in competent hands gives infallible results (*Figure 21.34*).

Figure 21.34. The endoscope in use

Lauegrams

Methods involving examination of the structure of the walls of the string canal cannot, of course, be utilized when the pearl is undrilled; there is also difficulty when the pearl is only partly drilled. In 1924 the Frenchman, Dauvillier, and later in collaboration with Shaxby, considered the effect of taking lauegrams by x-rays of natural and cultured pearls which, according to known experiments should give a different pattern in one direction with cultured pearls, whereas with the radial structure of the crystallites of real pearls a similar pattern should be obtained from whatever direction the narrow beam of x-rays passed through the centre of the pearl. This method was put on a firm basis by Galibourg and Ryziger in 1926.

The production of lauegrams will be referred to in the chapter on x-rays in gem testing, but for completeness may be briefly described here. A narrow beam of x-rays passed along the symmetry axis of a crystal will produce on a suitably placed photographic plate a pattern of spots indicative of that symmetry (*Figure 21.35*). This method provides the most conclusive identification of undrilled or partly drilled pearls.

This is due to the fact that the aragonite crystallites which, common to a number of minerals which crystallize in the rhombic system, form 'cyclic twins' having a pseudo-hexagonal symmetry, are radially arranged in natural pearl and are not so arranged in cultured pearl. Thus in a real pearl a narrow beam of x-rays passed through the centre of the pearl must travel along the vertical axes of the aragonite crystallites whatever be the orientation of the pearl, and this will produce a lauegram having a pseudo-hexagonal system of spots.

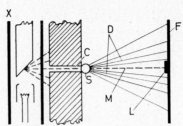

Figure 21.35. Schematic diagram of the lauegram method: X, x-ray tube; C, collimator or diaphragm; S, pearl; M, main trace of the x-ray beam; D, diffracted rays; L, lead disc to cut out heavy spot of main trace (not usually employed in pearl testing); F, film

In the case of cultured pearls the picture varies with the orientation of the bead nucleus; from that of the 'genuine' picture (*Figure 21.36*) to a picture showing a rectangular system of four spots, sometimes termed the Maltese Cross pattern (*Figure 21.37*). This occurs because the bead nucleus is made from mother-of-pearl having straight layers to which the aragonite crystallites are arranged perpendicularly. Thus, a narrow beam of x-rays passing through the pearl at right angles to the layers (*b* in *Figure 21.38*) will be travelling along the vertical axes of the crystallites and will give a hexagonal spot pattern as in a genuine pearl. At right angles to this direction the x-ray beam is travelling across the prisms of the crystallites and this is a direction of fourfold symmetry, and the characteristic four-spot pattern is produced.

Experiment has shown that the hexagonal pattern will persist even if the pearl is up to 30 degrees from the vertical to the plane of the layers. Beyond this the picture becomes distorted and a kite-shaped pattern occurs, and then the four-spot pattern becomes increasingly evident (*Figure 21.39*). It will be seen therefore, that the hexagonal picture by itself does not give

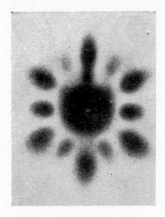

Figure 21.36. Lauegram of genuine pearl

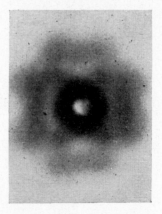

Figure 21.37. Lauegram of cultured pearl

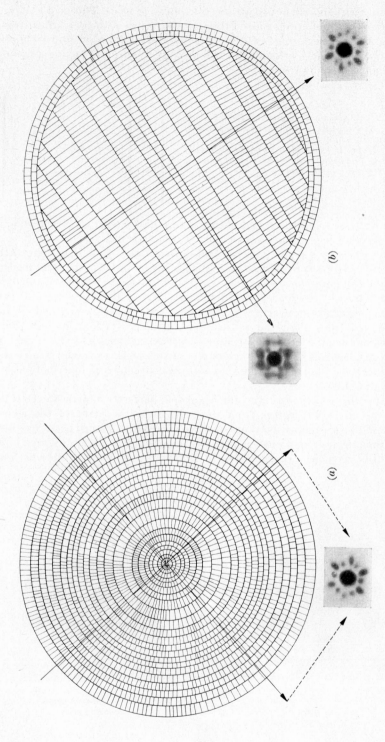

Figure 21.38. Schematic diagram of the lauegram method for identifying pearls by x-rays

a true indication of the nature of the pearl. If a hexagonal picture is first obtained nothing is proved, but on turning the pearl through an angle of 90 degrees and taking another picture, then, if this is also a hexagon, the pearl is real, for proof has been made that the pearl structure is radial. If the first picture shows a Maltese Cross pattern then the pearl is cultured and no further test need be made.

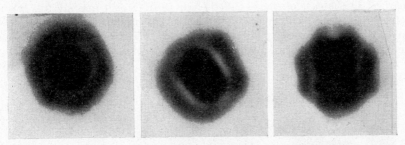

Figure 21.39. Showing the change of lauegram spot pattern from the position where a nearly perfect hexagon is produced (left), to the pattern obtained at 45 degrees, the so-called kite pattern (centre), to the Maltese Cross pattern (right)

It may be of interest to mention that button-shaped pearls when taken with the x-ray beam traversing the short axis will not give a hexagon but will show a circular ring, usually termed the halo pattern. Even the hexagonal spot pattern can vary considerably in its appearance, from a pattern where the spots are developed into spokes, the spoke pattern, or the spots may be joined together producing a closed hexagon.

Exposure Time for Lauegrams

All lauegram work needs lengthy exposure times and therefore the x-ray tubes used must have some cooling arrangement—water-cooling is commonly used. Absence of cooling need not preclude lauegrammatic work, for lengthy exposures can be carried out with intermittent exposures of short duration, but this is time-consuming. For satisfactory work and for readable spot pictures the collimator which narrows the x-ray beam needs to be no more than 1·5 mm in diameter, and the distance from the pearl to the film cassette about 7·5 cm, for with this size of collimating tube and subject/film distance the heavy 'main trace' of the undeviated x-ray beam seen in the centre of the spot picture will not mask the outer spot pattern, and shielding off this central main beam is unnecessary. A fast double-coated film is used and placed in cassettes fitted with intensifying screens in order to give a stronger picture and lessen the exposure time.

Shadowgraph or Skiagram

The shadowgraph method, also known as the direct or skiagram method, which was such a failure during the initial early experiments, has now been found by a difference in technique to be of definite value and is now being increasingly used in laboratories throughout the world for the rapid testing of pearls. The comparative ease with which necklets of pearls may be examined makes the method seem more attractive than is actually the case. Taking the picture presents few problems providing certain factors are

taken into consideration, but interpretation of the picture may need considerable skill and can only be confidently carried out by workers who have
had much experience.

The method depends upon the differences in x-ray transparency of the
conchiolin to that of the calcium carbonate which make up the composition
of the pearl. The conchiolin in natural pearls may fill the centre of the
pearl, as in the case of the so-called 'blue pearls', or it may fill fine layers
between the concentric layers of the aragonite crystals, and if these show
up on the x-ray picture as circles or arcs near the centre of the pearl then
that pearl can be assumed genuine (*Figure 21.40*).

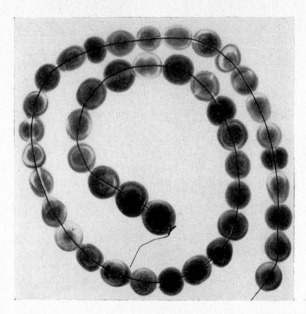

*Figure 21.40. Direct x-ray
picture of a natural pearl
necklet (positive print)*

In the case of cultured pearls the effect is that normally the oyster does
not like the job of coating with nacre the large bead nucleus placed in its
body and first coats the bead with a layer of conchiolin, which is in some
cases irregularly deposited. The transradiancy of this layer of conchiolin
produces in an x-ray direct picture an outline of the bead nucleus, which
itself is usually somewhat more opaque to the rays than the outer rim of
nacre (*Figure 21.41*). Further, if the cultured pearl happens to be so oriented
that the straight bands of the mother-of-pearl nucleus are perpendicular to
the surface of the film, that is parallel to the x-ray beam, they may show on
the picture as weak stripes across the bead due to the slightly different
radiability of the layers. This is a similar effect to that seen in one of the
oldest methods of pearl testing, that is by the lucidoscope. The detection of
the non-nucleated pearls by x-ray shadowgraph method is less easy for
there is no bead nucleus to show up. What is seen is either a large cavity or
a fine vermiform patch, which may not even be at the centre of the pearl.
However, this, with the strong fluorescence shown by Biwa pearls under
x-rays, is conclusive evidence of this cultivation.

Exposure times

The structures seen in an x-ray photograph of pearls are as a rule very fine and the photographic technique therefore needs the use of a very fine grain film. Such fine grain films are slow and need long exposures; the best type of film to use and the exposure times needed can only be worked out by experience.

(a)

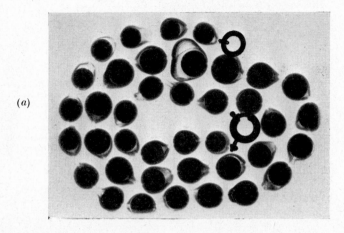

(b)

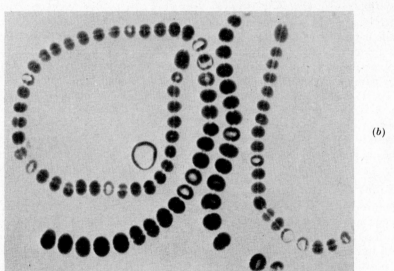

Figure 21.41. Direct x-ray picture of (a) nucleated and (b) non-nucleated cultivated pearl necklet (positive prints)

Pearls, being spherical bodies, necessitate the x-rays having different thicknesses to travel; a large distance at the centre of the pearl and grading to relatively nothing at the edges. Hence the edges tend to be overexposed and may mask the structure, such as the division between the bead and outer layer in thin-skinned cultured pearls. A. E. Alexander devised a

447

method to get over this differential exposure by placing the pearls to be tested in a plastic dish which rests upon the paper-covered film. Into this dish is poured carbon tetrachloride, which has a similar radiability to pearl, until the pearls are immersed up to their greatest diameter; this to some extent equalizes the pearls' thickness and also helps to absorb the scattered x-rays secondarily produced when the primary beam strikes solid bodies, in this case the pearls (*Figure 21.42*).

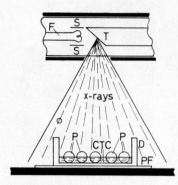

Figure 21.42. Schematic diagram of the method of taking direct x-ray pictures with pearls immersed in carbon tetrachloride: T, target of x-ray tube; F, filament of x-ray tube; S, shields to focus cathode rays; P, pearls; D, plastic dish containing carbon tetrachloride; PF, photographic film; CTC, carbon tetrachloride

Anchoring of Pearls for Photography

With loose pearls which might 'run about' in the tray, a system of nylon threads netted across a suitable frame will anchor them, the pearls resting in the interstices of the net from which they may readily be identified as to their position on the film. Alternatively a layer of Plasticine can be spread on the paper covering of the film and the pearls pressed into it. After exposure the Plasticine and the pearls adhering to it may be stripped off the paper and their position maintained. In this case the pearls are not immersed in carbon tetrachloride (Carbonyl in the U.S.A.) as the Plasticine seems to function as an anti-scatter stop, even if not wholly as an equalizer of the unequal thickness of the pearls.

Processing of Film

The processing of the film is a normal photographic job, and there may be some advantage in overexposure and underdevelopment. The interpretation of the picture is always made from the negative, which is translucent and will always show more of the tones and detail than can be seen on a positive print, the negative is best viewed, if a proper viewing box is not available, by holding the film up to a 40 or 60 watt pearl or opal bulb electric lamp. With all precautions taken it is rarely that a 100 per cent result can be obtained with pearl necklets by the direct x-ray method or with cultured pearl necklets which are normally easier to interpret. Care must be taken not to misinterpret a picture when the bead nucleus is not spherical. Drop and oval-shaped nuclei have been encountered in cultured pearls, but they are rare as it is said that the mortality of the oysters is greater when nuclei of other than spherical shape are used.

Fluorescence

The fluorescent glows shown by pearls under ultra-violet light are not discriminative, and this applies whether the radiations are long-wave (3650 Å) or short-wave (2537 Å). Under the influence of x-rays, however, genuine pearls rarely show any glow, but cultured pearls glow with a greenish-yellow light. This is much weaker in intensity than the bluish-white glow shown by all pearls under ultra-violet light. Thus this glow under x-rays, which needs to be viewed in total darkness, may give some indication as to whether the pearl is cultured. The glow in cultured pearls is derived from the bead core of mother-of-pearl which contains a trace of manganese. The test is not conclusive, for all freshwater pearls and some seawater pearls from Australian waters show a similar fluorescence. G. O. Wild has suggested a variation of the method which is carried out by examining the fluorescence of the bead induced by x-rays through the drill canal using a low-powered microscope for the observation. A further method suggested by this worker is to mount the pearl on a micrometer stand and gradually raise the pearl into a narrow beam of x-rays limited by a lead conduit 1 mm wide. This beam strikes a suitably placed fluorescent screen and when the edge of the pearl reaches the beam a shadow in the form of an arc is shown on the screen. When the pearl is raised farther, if it is cultured, a sudden flash of light is seen when the x-rays strike the bead core. Genuine pearls do not show this effect. Non-nucleated cultured pearls from Biwa Lake, Japan, show a strong greenish-yellow glow under x-rays, but the non-nucleated pearls cultured in salt water areas, such as Australia, do not show this glow.

Core Scraping Test

A. E. Alexander has suggested that scrapings from the core of a pearl by the aid of a suitable wire, show, when examined microscopically, a typical block-like pattern if the pearl is cultured. Further, if the scrapings are tested for manganese and a positive result obtained the pearl must be cultured. These tests are far too delicate for general testing.

IMITATION PEARLS

Fish-scale Essence

The popularity of pearls for adornment led to their imitation, and today the manufacture of imitation pearls has become a world-wide industry. In 1656 a French rosary maker, Jonquin, produced imitation pearls at Passy on the outskirts of Paris. Jonquin had noticed that water in which small fish had been washed contained a highly lustrous substance, which when concentrated and applied to small beads produced a remarkably good imitation of pearls. Jonquin's pearls were small hollow spheres made from an opalescent and easily fusible glass, the inside of which was lined with parchment size which 'fixed' the fish-scale essence giving the pearly appearance. The interior of the bead was finally filled with wax in order to increase the solidity of the bead (*Figure 21.43*). These beads, often known as 'Roman pearls', are not commonly encountered today as they have been superseded by a type using a solid glass bead upon the outside of which is applied the pearly coating. Thus imitation pearls have at least two parts—a material producing the pearly coating and the rigid base.

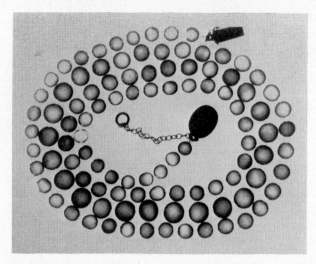

Figure 21.43. An x-ray picture of an early type (wax-filled) imitation pearl necklace

Quite early it was discovered that the iridescent lustre of fish scales was not part of the scales themselves, but was created by tiny crystals embedded in the skin attached to them, and it is suspensions of these minute crystals in a suitable vehicle which produces the 'essence d'orient', a term which may have been derived from the possibility that the Chinese knew of the material long before Jonquin's discovery. Others at the time, a period before the art of chemical analysis was commonplace, believed the crystallites to be silver and called the material 'fish silver'. When careful purification and analysis became possible the crystallites were found to be the organic chemical compound guanine.

Guanine ($C_5H_5ON_5$) is a derivative of purin and belongs to the group known as the purin bases, and is a decomposition product of the nucleins. Guanine is actually a waste material secreted by the fish and is closely allied to uric acid. The guanine has a density of 1·6 and forms colourless needles or lath-shaped crystals which are not decomposed by heat under 360°C, are insoluble in neutral solvents, are non-toxic, non-corrosive and are chemically inert.

Until 1919 the manufacture of essence d'orient was principally a French industry, the scales of the bleak (*Alburnus lucidus*) being used for the purpose. These small fish are found in the Seine and other European rivers; at one period when the French manufacture was at its height a million francs' worth of bleak scales were exported annually from the Thames. In 1919 it was discovered that the sardine herring caught in Norwegian waters produced a superior quality of pearl essence. A French company exploited the discovery, erected a factory in Norway, employed trained chemists, and constantly strove to improve the purity and quality of their pearl essence. Until the outbreak of World War II the company prospered, but in 1939 the business ceased and the process was taken to America. About 1943 experiments were made with the herring from British Columbian waters, but this was not commercially successful. Since the end of the war the

Norwegian herring industry has returned to the manufacture of fish scale essence, and South Africa is producing its own essence from the scales of fish caught off the coasts of South and South-West Africa. In 1949 some experiments on similar lines were carried out by the Scottish herring industry, but little has since been heard of this endeavour.

The best fish scales are obtained from the herring fisheries of the Bay of Fundy, an inlet which practically divides Nova Scotia from New Brunswick in North America. Here the tides range from 30 to 60 ft. and literally boil-up the ocean floor liberating a steady supply of fish food which attracts countless schools of herring. The fish are trapped in weirs, caught in seine nets, and loaded into crates on the scale boats—these boats, or dorys have slatted false bottoms. As the fish flop round in the crates they lose their scales which drop through the slats in the crate, and through the false floor to the bottom of the boat. The scales are then scooped into baskets and hurried to the factory, which is situated at Maine on the American side of the bay, where, because of the numbing cold of the Fundy region the scales arrive perfectly preserved.

As soon as the scales are brought to the factory they are put into mixers or churns with a suitable cleansing mixture. The movement of the churns causes the scales to rub together releasing the tiny and delicate guanine crystals which are embedded in the rough fatty tissue attached to the fish scales. These crystalloids, as they are termed, are strained away from the scales which are discarded. The final purification and suspension of the crystals is then made in a special solvent, which may be an ether/amyl acetate solution. This aggregate of guanine crystals in viscous liquid is then added as required to the vehicle, usually a nitrocellulose lacquer, which forms the final 'paint' employed for covering the modern imitation (mock) pearls. A dyestuff is incorporated in the lacquer if coloured finishes are needed.

Glass and Plastic Beads

The beads of the modern imitation pearls, or as they are sometimes called, simulated pearls, usually consist of glass beads formed on an iron or copper wire in a blow-torch flame (*Figure 21.44*). Subsequent treatment in acid dissolves away the wire and leaves a cavity forming the string canal. The glass used is a special opalescent type termed 'Alabaster' (not to be confused with the massive variety of gypsum). Moulded plastics, such as Perspex or polystyrene are often used for the cheap types of imitation pearls, but they are too light in weight to hang well when strung into necklets. Further, these plastic beads often show a ridge where the 'flash' escapes from the junction of the two halves of the mould, for these plastic beads are moulded. Vegetable ivory beads have been used as the core for imitation pearls but they are too opaque to give the finished pearl the desired lustre. During 1922 some imitation pearls consisting of a mother-of-pearl bead coated with pearl essence were subject of a celebrated Court case. Such imitation pearls did not seem to appear again until about 1950 when a few were seen. Today one firm does make and market such pearls. They have been variously called 'imitation cultured pearls' or 'shell-based imitation pearls'.

451

The beads are coated with the pearl essence, either by spraying or dipping, dipping usually being preferable. The dipping is carried out by mounting some 500 beads on special dipping boards. These boards bristle with 'tooth-picks' upon which the pearls are threaded: they are mounted in

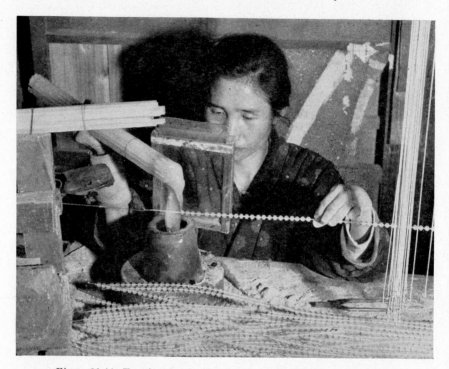

Figure 21.44. Forming the glass beads from easily fusible glass in Japan

pairs and with the beads on the underside are gently lowered into the pearling solution until all the beads are submerged. After removal the boards are mounted in a machine which rotates them slowly so as to ensure an even coat while drying (*Figure 21.45*). The drying room needs to be air-conditioned and dust free, each dip taking from 1 to $2\frac{1}{2}$ hours to dry. Successive coats up to ten may be put on, but usually not less than five are given so as to build up the bead to a lustrous 'pearl'. The finished pearls are graded, matched and threaded on nylon or double cotton. Imitation pearls used for ear-rings, brooches or pendants may have only a half hole, or none at all. Such pearls are usually cemented into the settings.

Identification

Imitation pearls are easily identified by examination of the surface with a hand lens. The surface, looking like blotting paper, does not have the fine serrated structure of a real pearl, and at the string canal the surface of the pearl essence usually shows a wearing away from attrition with the adjacent bead. Most imitation pearls feel smooth when rubbed against the teeth, unlike the effect with natural or cultured pearls which feel chalky or

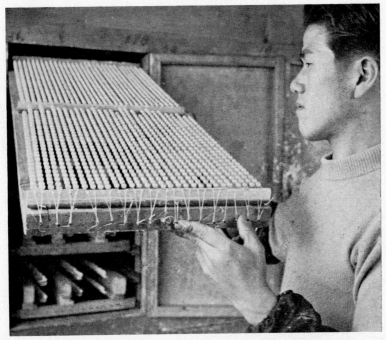

Figure 21.45. Drying the coated beads producing imitation pearls

gritty. It has been noted, however, that some recent imitation pearls have been found to give this gritty feeling. A pin pressed into the surface of a coated pearl will scratch or indent it, whereas it will not do so with a nacreous pearl; nor with the hollow glass bead type of imitation. These earlier types of imitation pearls—with a hollow glass envelope—will reveal their nature by lens examination which shows a jagged edge to the string canal, bubbles in the glass envelope, and if a spot of ink is placed upon the surface it will appear doubled owing to the reflection from the internal surface of the glass shell.

Owing to their opacity to x-rays the glass beads of the modern imitation pearl show up white on the negative (or solid black on a positive print made from it). In the x-ray picture in *Figure 21.46* the nine pearls on each end of the necklet of otherwise cultured pearls, and the one 'intruder' in the body of the necklet, stand out vividly.

An extremely good imitation of natural pearl essence is now made by purely synthetic methods. To the practised eye, however, the colour is slightly less 'warm' and all the samples so far tested gave a reaction with sodium sulphide and the material gradually blackens in an impure atmosphere. The fish scale essence usually gives a reaction for nitrocellulose.

Density

The density of imitation pearls varies with the type and with the material from which the core is made. The earlier hollow glass bead type has a density usually below 1·55. With the solid bead type of coated glass the density is usually higher than for the natural or cultured pearl, being between 2·85 and 3·18, the higher values, over 3, being the most common. Just after World War II some of the glass bead imitation pearls were found to have densities of 2·3 and about 2·56. The use of these low-density glasses was considered to be due to the difficulty of obtaining the correct type of glass at this time. However, recent reports suggest that such a glass (density 2·53) is even now being used in America.

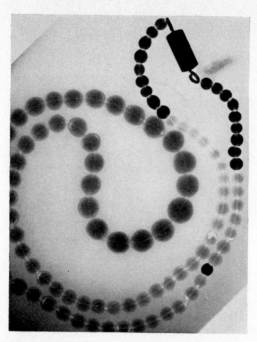

Figure 21.46. X-ray picture showing imitation pearls appearing black in a necklet of otherwise cultured pearls

Simulation

An unusual type of 'blister pearl' has been encountered which was constructed by covering a bead of mother-of-pearl with an envelope, so thick as to be loose and not adhering to the base, and the 'pearl' completed with an outer skin of glass. Black pearls have been imitated by polished spheres of hematite. Such fakes can easily be identified by the much greater density of hematite, just over 5, and by the red streak shown by the mineral when it is rubbed across a piece of white unglazed porcelain. The pink conch pearl is simulated by coral, among other substances, but the typical 'flame' markings on the surface shown by the pink conch pearl serves to identify the true from the false. A 'pink pearl' made of suitably coloured glass, which even had imitation flame markings has been met. Examination of this piece, however, showed bubbles in the glass.

CHAPTER 22

CORAL, SHELL AND OPERCULUM

CORAL

The name coral brings to mind the atolls of the South Seas, those narrow reefs surrounding the beautiful transparent waters of the central lagoon. Lovely as they are these atolls do not supply the precious coral so well known in the jewellery of many ages, for there are many corals and the one which supplies the lovely red and pink coral so prized for ornamentation is not a reef builder.

There is much misconception concerning the formation of coral, particularly that of the noble coral used in jewels, a coral scientifically known as *Corallium nobile* or *Corallium rubrum*. Generally expressed as being the axial skeleton of the coral polyp, which gives the impression of being an internal skeleton, similar to the bones of our bodies, coral is better described as being a scaffolding upon the surface of which the boneless animals live as a colony.

The Coral Polyp

The coral polyp, a primitive type of plant-like animal called a zoophyte, is a small whitish creature about a fifteenth of an inch in diameter. It has a tube-like body from the upper rim of which project eight tentacles surrounding the 'mouth', this top portion being known as the oral zone. Thus the animal tends to resemble a sea anemone in miniature.

At the base of the tube-like body is the basal disc, which, in the case of colonies is connected by a layer of communicating canals of living tissue, called the hydrorhiza, to the enteron, or stomach, of each individual member of the colony. The hydrorhiza are embedded in a gelatinous mass, termed the coenosarc, and which itself is covered by a skin-like membrane called the perisarc. Thus the whole colony forms a single entity, and it is from the lower surface of the coenosarc, and from the base of the polyp, that the coral is formed.

Reproduction may be sexually from ova and sperm, or by budding. In the colonies themselves there is always rigorous segregation of the sexes. Usually a colony consists of individuals of one sex only, and if a colony is bisexual it is found that the sexes occupy separate branches. The male individual discharges his fertilizing cells into the water, some of which find their way into the body of a female and penetrate the eggs already prepared for fertilization.

The fertilized eggs of microscopic size are ejected into the water by the female and they subsequently develop into free-swimming medusal forms. The surviving medusal forms, for mortality is high, sink and attach themselves by their convex surfaces to a stone, rock, crab, bottle, but never bare metal. Once the swimming form has attached itself securely to its new home, a knob appears on its free end which quickly enlarges and it soon becomes a fully developed polyp. Calcium carbonate is secreted around the point of attachment forming the nucleus of the coral structure, and of a new colony. The coenosarc grows over the calcareous deposit and the second stage of reproduction commences. This is by a species of budding or self-germination of the polyp itself within the coenosarc—a knob-like protuberance forming and then developing into a polyp. Thus the newly formed colony is gradually populated. As the colony continues to grow the coenosarc spreads to accommodate the new inhabitants, and in order to provide living room for them is continually separating calcium carbonate from the seawater, and redepositing the mineral in the form of spicules of calcite as coral.

At first this deposition of lime is confined to the point of attachment of the original polyp and then the skeleton commences to extend into a column upon which a number of secondary polyps form. Some of these lateral

Figure 22.1. Growth of coral and showing the way beads are cut from the 'tree'

polyps also start to shoot out sideways and this produces a branch-like form to the whole colony. The branches spread out as widely as possible and are haphazardly arranged, but no two branches spring from the same point of incidence. These branches may be more or less straight or may twist and turn about in an irregular manner; they may also produce secondary branches and so on. Each branch becomes smaller than its parent and terminates with a rounded blunt point covered by a very sensitive layer of coenosarc which projects beyond the end of the branch itself (*Figure 22.1*).

Geographical Locations of Coral

The polyps of *Corallium rubrum* are very sensitive to changes of temperature, preferring waters between 13°C and 16°C, and which are comparatively still and clear; muddy water being fatal to the growth of the coral colonies. Such requirements limit the geographical distribution to certain well-defined areas, which may be said to stretch from southern Ireland through the Bay of Biscay to Madeira, the Canaries and the Cape Verde islands; thence through the Mediterranean, the Red Sea, Mauritius, the

Malay archipelago and Japanese waters. The actual fisheries are those of the Malay and Japanese waters, and most important of all, the waters of the Mediterranean. The best red coral is fished off Algiers and Tunis on the African side, while on the European side the waters off the coasts of Sicily, Calabria, Naples, Sardinia, Corsica, and parts of the French and Spanish seaboard provide good material.

Method of Dredging

The actual 'fishing', carried out mostly by Italian fishers for some 6 months of the year, is usually performed by dredging. Divers have been employed but are not so satisfactory as the dredging method. A special net called 'ingegno' is employed for securing the coral. It consists of a heavy wooden cross or beam weighted in order to make it sink. To this are attached some 20–30 coarse rope nets, weighted tassels or tufts of horse hair and about a similar number of smaller bags made of ordinary fishing net. The whole contraption is dragged across the bed of the sea by a rope from a fairly large sailing vessel and the coarse nets become entangled with the coral growths and tear them from their seatings, the coral being collected when the dredge is drawn to the surface.

Fashioning

Most of the fashioning of Mediterranean coral is an Italian industry, being carried out at Torre del Grecco near Naples. The coral is first sorted into various grades of colour to which typical Italian names are applied (Table 22.1).

TABLE 22.1

Coral Names and Colour

Name	Colour
Bianco	Pure white
Pelle d'angelo	Pale flesh pink (angel's skin)
Rose pallido	Pale rose
Rosa vivo	Bright rose
Secondo coloro	Salmon colour (second colour)
Rosso	Red
Rosso scuro	Dark red
Arciscuro or Carbonetto	Very dark red (ox-blood red)

After sorting the coral is passed on to the workers, the majority of whom are women. Only primitive tools are used, even beads being roughly shaped with a knife and finally ground to shape on a grindstone. Sometimes a crude form of lathe is used and the drilling is done by a bow-driven hand-drill. Coral is mostly fashioned into beads, small carved objects and cameos. The plain polished pieces of coral in natural shape and about half to three-quarters of an inch long, bored crossways through the centre, are known as 'Arabian beads'. Much of the worked coral from Italy is sent to the Orient, the peoples of India and China favouring the material for ornamental and ritual purposes. Coral contrasts well with turquoise and the Arabians and North African natives used the two gems in combination for the ornamentation of camel trappings and other articles.

Chemical and Physical Properties

The composition of coral is almost wholly calcium carbonate ($CaCO_3$) with about 3 per cent of magnesium carbonate ($MgCO_3$), and possibly a trace of iron oxide and some $1\frac{1}{2}$–4 per cent of organic matter of indeterminate composition. J. Walton, working with thin sections of coral found dark red radii passing from the centre to the outside surface, and these radial colour bands are seen on a longitudinal section as lines of pigment running parallel to the length of the section. Indeed, these colour bands are clearly visible on the surface of much coral by the eye alone, when the effect is reminiscent of the structure seen on polished longitudinal faces of ivory.

The hardness of coral is about $3\frac{1}{2}$ on Mohs's scale and the material is easily broken, producing a hackly type of fracture. Coral has a density of between 2·6 and 2·7. Although the refractive indices have little value in the testing of coral it is interesting to record that J. Walton obtained on specially polished specimens indices of 1·65 and 1·49, which are those of calcite. Therefore the calcium carbonate in coral is in the form of calcite. A spot of acid placed on the surface of coral will cause effervescence owing to the rapid formation of carbonic acid gas—a useful test for coral against certain of its imitations.

The cause of the colour of red and pink coral is not fully understood. Iron has been suggested but another theory is that the colour is mainly dependent on the organic part. R. Pearl has said that oil of turpentine removes the red colour of coral, and this, if true, would tend to indicate an organic cause of coloration, but there is always the fear that the piece or pieces worked upon have been intensified in colour by artificial means and it is this colour that has been removed by the organic solvent.

There may be seen in a thin section of red coral an absorption band in the blue-green at about 4940 Å, but this has little value in testing. Under ultra-violet light coral is only weakly responsive, and any glow seen is a pale violet or a dull purplish-red. While this has little value for identification it should be noted that some glass imitations of coral are made of uranium glass and show the characteristic strong green fluorescence, and some plastic imitations show an orange-red glow.

Besides the white to red coral of *Corallium rubrum*, a white coral, *Oculinacea vaseuclosa*, has been fashioned for ornamentation. A black coral, known as 'Akabar' or 'King's coral' (*Antipathes spiralis*), and a blue coral known as 'Akori' coral (*Allopara subirolcea*) has been fished from off the Cameroon coast. Both these types are horny in nature. A specimen of black coral was found to have a density of 1·34, and a vague refractive index of 1·56. This indicates that the material is organic and may be conchiolin. Unlike true precious coral this type does not effervesce with acid. Some black coral from Hawaii has been carved and mounted in jewellery.

Syntheses and Simulation

Coral is extensively imitated and by many materials. What is probably the most attractive counterfeit of coral is a suitably stained vegetable ivory, but this may be identified by the dot-like cell structure seen when the surface is examined by a lens. Mixtures of rubber and gypsum, powdered marble mixed with isinglass and coloured red with cinnabar or red lead, stained calcined bone, coral dust suitably bonded together, or even plain sealing wax have all been used in the simulation of precious coral. Today the most common substitutes are glass, porcelain, and the various plastics.

SHELL

The calcareous armour of many of the shellfish which inhabit the shores of tropical seas have a use in personal decoration. This is particularly so in the case of those shells which have an iridescent lustre, and the most prized of these are the large pearl oysters (*Pinctada maxima* and *Pinctada margaritifera*) from the waters of northern Australia and the Torres Strait, and these form an important and major export in Western Australian economy.

Methods of Fishing

The discovery of pearl shell in north-western Australian waters was made in 1861, at Nickol Bay, and later the fisheries extended from Exmouth

Figure 22.2. Torres Strait pearling lugger. Note the look-outs at the main mast head

Gulf, south of Onslow, to the Torres Strait and out to the Great Barrier Reef. In the early days of the pearl shell fisheries, skin divers (naked divers) searched for the shells, but quite soon the influence of the European brought the introduction of the armoured diving dress which is now used almost exclusively. The large shells are fished from sailing luggers (*Figure 22.2*), one or two masted craft of about 8–10 tons, and sailed by a crew of 6 or 7 including the diver. With the era of the pearling fleets came the birth of the township of Broome which is the centre of the pearling industry in these waters.

The luggers sail out with a store of provisions to last for a six-week trip, and on reaching a likely spot, reef the sails and drop anchor. The diver

Figure 22.3. Pearl shell divers in Australian waters

dresses in his suit and when ready goes over the side (*Figure 22.3*). He may go down for about an hour, filling his basket or bag with the shells, and on a signal to the boat crew given on his life-line is hauled up to the surface and climbs back into the lugger.

The shells which have been brought up are opened by the use of a broad flat-bladed knife and the fleshy oyster, the meat as it is termed, is removed and searched for any pearls that may be present (*Figure 22.4*). The edges of the shells are trimmed and they are then stacked in boxes which have stretcher-like carrying handles to enable them to be taken through the surf to the shore station (*Figure 22.5*). There the shell is sorted into qualities and boxed for transit to Europe and the United States of America, the latter being the chief consumer of pearl shell. Manilla shell is the name given to the pearl shell obtained from the Philippines and Burmese shell to that from the waters around the Mergui archipelago.

Ornamental Use

The shell is used for making mother-of-pearl buttons, knife handles, inlay and other ornaments. Some dark-coloured shell from the black-lip

Figure 22.4. Opening Australian pearl shell

Figure 22.5. Carrying
the shell ashore

pearl oyster suitably cut, produces a cat's-eye effect and these are used as
buttons and even mounted in jewellery. Mother-of-pearl carving has been a
staple industry of Bethlehem in Palestine (Israel) since the middle of the
eighteenth century. Carved mother-of-pearl in leaf and other designs is a
prominent feature of costume jewellery, and necklets made of the lustrous
small topshells which have had their dark outer periostracum removed are
also produced.

The shells with brightly coloured blue and green nacre, termed Paua
shells (*Figure 22.6*) in New Zealand and Abalones in American waters, are
fished for their beautiful mother-of-pearl. These shells belong to the family
Haliotis, and are larger brothers to the earshells of the Channel Islands.
These big colourful shells, which sometimes produce pearls, are found along
the Great Barrier Reef off the eastern shore of Queensland, the waters of
New Zealand and the coasts of California and Florida.

The larger members of the Trocus, the topshells, are also fished for the
value of their shell, and sometimes the thick column of the shell is turned
into beads and strung as necklets.

Figure 22.6. The Paua
shell or Abalone (Haliotis)

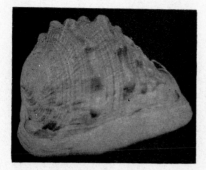

Figure 22.7. The helmet shell found in the warm waters of the West Indies

Two of the largest and most beautiful shells in the world are used for the carving of cameos, which often rely on the different colour shown by the material when cut to different depths. The shell most commonly used for cameo cutting is the Helmet shell (*Cassis madagascariensis*) (*Figure 22.7*) which is found in the warm waters of the West Indies. Cameos cut from this shell stand out in white bas-relief against a brown background (*Figure 22.8*), the shells from Madagascar being sent to Italy for carving. The giant, or Queen, conch (*Figure 22.9*) (*Strombus gigas*) which produces the pink conch pearls, is another inhabitant of the West Indies and Florida coast, and is used for cameo carving. With this shell the carving is white on a rose-coloured background, or vice versa. The pink colour unfortunately tends to fade on too great exposure to light.

A type of pearl sometimes used in jewellery is cut from suitable pieces of the shell of the sea snail (Turbo). Such a pearl is distinguished by the pearly top surface and the yellowish non-nacreous back. These objects are known as Antilles pearls or oil pearls. The so-called *coque de perle* is cut from the central whorl of the nautilus shell and resembles to some extent a blister pearl. It has, however, a thinner skin and is much more hollow inside and is usually filled in with wax or cement. The inner septa (*Figure 22.10*) which divide the nautilus shell up into chambers, are used for inlay work.

Figure 22.8. Cameo cut in a Helmet shell

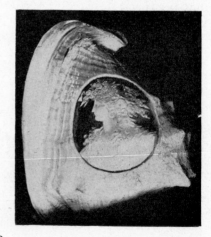

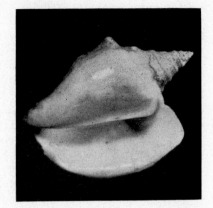

Figure 22.9. The giant or Queen conch shell

OPERCULUM

Occasionally the gemmologist meets with unusual objects mounted in jewellery, and one such object is the so-called 'shell' or 'Chinese' cat's-eye, which is more correctly known as operculum. These cat's-eyes have no optical effect and they owe their popular name solely to their eye-like markings and circular form. They are the lid, or door, which shuts in certain types of shellfish when they retire into their shell, hence the name operculum, which is derived from the Latin and means a lid or cover.

An operculum is common to many of the univalve shellfish and may be well explained by considering the better known and analogous member of the Mollusca, the edible winkle (periwinkle—*Littorina littorea*). The horny plate found attached to the animal is this winkle's trap-door or operculum, and the trap-door of another mollusc, the gastropod *Turbo petholatus* supplies the calcareous operculum employed in jewellery.

The animal *Turbo petholatus* of the order Aspidobrachia, is like a large

Figure 22.10. An x-ray picture of a nautilus shell showing the septa and the syphuncle, a tube connecting each chamber

463

snail in appearance. Its shell, also, resembles the shell carried by the periwinkle, but is larger and has more rounded whorls and a taller spire (*Figure 22.11*). Beyond this the resemblance ceases, for the shell is nacreous within and the porcelain-like periostracum is prettily coloured a medium to light brown with a cream or white mottling.

These animals haunt the tangled masses of seaweed on the shores of the tropic seas of Oceania, Melanesia and Polynesia, specimens having been obtained from Darwin, north Australia, Papua (New Guinea), Indo-China, the Moluccas, Fiji Islands, Tahiti and Samoa. They were extensively collected for their opercula by the fighting forces engaged against the Japanese in World War II.

The operculum, generally round or slightly oval, varies in size from a quarter of an inch to 3 in. in diameter but is generally between one-half and 1 in. (12–25 mm). Its convex upper surface has the appearance of porcelain with the apex of the dome coloured green and verging to yellow and white on one side, and through reddish brown to dark brown on the other (Plate XIX). The reverse or base is flat and shows spiral lines of growth and a

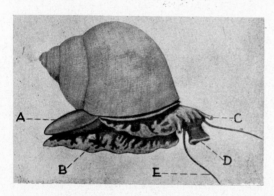

Figure 22.11. *Turbo petholatus—*
A, operculum; B, foot; C, eye;
D, proboscis; E, tentacles

deep dextral spiral cut conforming to the direction of growth from the original point of beginning or nucleus which is rather eccentric to the true centre of the piece. The base, which is the side of attachment to the animal, is covered with a brownish skin of conchiolin.

The operculum is a cuticular development of calcareous and organic substances secreted from a group of cells situated on the dorsal side of the foot of the animal. It is so placed that it acts as a door to the aperture of the shell when the animal retires within, and rests on the animal's back behind the shell when the animal is crawling.

The composition of these pieces is mainly calcareous, with some horny organic matter and water. The density lies between the limits 2·70 and 2·76 and the hardness is about $3\frac{1}{2}$.

In New Ireland, on the Bismarck archipelago, these pieces have been used as the 'eyes' for the grotesque and gaudily painted images or idols found in the temples. In beautiful Stewart Island opercula are used for money.

A similarly calcareous operculum from another mollusc is coloured white with a central eye of red colour, and in some cases the surface is covered with raised 'pimples'. These types have also been encountered in jewellery.

The use of fossil ammonites in jewellery may briefly be mentioned. These fossil ammonites, molluscs resembling in many ways the nautilus, flourished in the Mesozoic era about 150 million years ago. They have a coiled shell and consist of a series of chambers which are often indicated on the outside by a convoluted line. The fossils are actually mineralized, often being calcite

Figure 22.12. Ammonites from the Oxford clay

casts of the interior of the ammonite shell, although some have the shell replaced by iron pyrites and the inside filled with greenish calcite (*Figure 22.12*).

Vast numbers of these fossils are found in the Lias of Dorset, and some of these, particularly the small ammonite promicroceras, have been mounted in gold and silver. It was quite an industry before 1914 but very little mounting is now carried out and only older pieces are available.

A number of ammonites found in the Western States of America, and elsewhere, have the septa filled with crystals and the smaller specimens of these are split in two and the cut surfaces polished to produce articles of jewellery.

CHAPTER 23

AMBER AND JET

AMBER

Chemical and Physical Properties

A time-hardened resin which exuded from certain pine trees, particularly *Pinus succinifera*, which flourished in Oligocene times just before the great Ice Age, that is more than 30 million years ago, amber is in composition a complex mixture of several resins, succinic acid and a volatile oil. It accords to the general expression $C_{10}H_{16}O$, but also contains a certain amount of hydrogen sulphide (H_2S).

Amber is transparent to translucent and has a greasy lustre. The colour is normally yellow or brown, but may be reddish or whitish; it is often clouded and sometimes fluorescent. The hardness is slightly above 2 on Mohs's scale, and the fractured surface usually shows a conchoidal type of break. The material begins to soften at 150°C and finally melts at 250°–300°C. The refractive index is 1·54 and the specific gravity approximates to 1·08

Most amber shows a bluish-white fluorescence, which is brighter on freshly broken surfaces, when exposed to radiations from the long-wave ultra-violet lamp. Under stimulation from the short-wave ultra-violet lamp the fluorescence is a mustard-green colour, although some Burmese amber shows a blue glow under such excitation. Under bombardment by x-rays amber is inert.

Occurrences

The principal source of amber is along the shores of the Samland coast of East Prussia, near Koenigsberg, which is now incorporated into the U.S.S.R. and renamed Kaliningrad. The amber from this locality is called succinite. There are two sources of amber in the district, the sea amber, which has been washed up on the shore by wave action; and the pit amber obtained by open-pit mining for the amber drops (block amber) in the Oligocene deposits of glauconite sand. This sand consists of grains of the hydrous potassium-iron silicate mineral called glauconite, and owing to its greeny-blue colour is known as the 'blue earth'. The sea amber, which has been washed out from the sea bed, is, owing to the low density of the material, carried by tides and currents for considerable distances. Such amber may therefore be found on all the shores of the Baltic Sea, and may even be found on the shores of Norway and Denmark. It has even drifted on to the shores of the English east coast and as far south as the Isle of Thanet.

Treatment

This pit amber, the main pit being at Palmnicken, is obtained by digging out the blue earth with steam shovels and dredges, after a sufficient area of overburden has been cleared. The blue earth is then taken to the washing plant where, by means of powerful streams of water, the amber is separated from the sand, washed and sized, and finally graded. The amber may be clear and transparent, when it is known as clear; slightly turbid, due to a number of contained gas bubbles and then resembling goose fat, and hence termed fatty, or by the Germans flohmig. A variety containing a vast number of bubbles making the material quite cloudy is called bastard, while bony or osseous amber has the appearance of dried bone. The foamy or frothy type is chalky in appearance. The small pieces not of gem quality are treated by heat in large retorts in order to produce succinic acid, amber oil and colophony, the latter being used for the preparation of varnish.

Figure 23.1. Pendant of 'sun spangled' (stress figured) amber

Small pieces which are clear enough for gem use are pressed together under gentle heat in order to produce pieces of a size suitable for working—a true reconstruction. This pressed amber, or ambroid, as it is called, was a process first carried out in Vienna; the small pieces of amber (which softens at about 180°C) are welded together under a pressure said to be 120,000 pounds per square inch. Such pressed material may be identified by the margins of different clarity and by the elongation of the bubbles due to the flow under pressure. Cloudy material may be clarified to some extent by careful heating in rape seed oil (colza oil), which penetrates and enters the air spaces causing the cloudiness. This clarified amber, unless great care is taken in the operation, will often exhibit crack-like marks which resemble nasturtium leaves. These are known to the amber workers as 'sun spangles' and are possibly due to stresses set up in the amber, or release of such stresses (*Figure 23.1*). A number of amber ornaments have been marketed which show rather large nasturtium leaves and which appear to have been artificially induced and coloured. Staining, too, is carried out, sometimes to redden the yellowish-brown colour in order to simulate the so-called 'aged' colour of amber, or to produce other colours, particularly green.

Inclusions

Inclusions in amber have a special appeal—who has not heard of the 'fly in the amber'? (*Figure 23.2*). These occur through the resin exuding from pine trees catching up insects, pieces of moss, lichens and pine needles. A clear piece of amber enclosing a perfect insect is a most prized possession, not only to the layman, but to the zoologist and geologist, to whom such

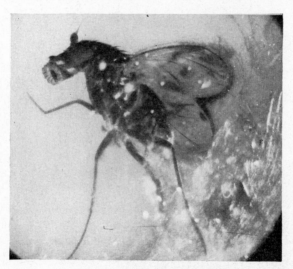

Figure 23.2. Fly in amber

pieces are as an open book showing the flora and insect life of those bygone days. Not all inclusions of amber are organic, for amongst other inorganic inclusions, perfectly formed crystals of pyrites have been observed.

Nomenclature

The Germans call amber by the name Bernstein, a name of comparatively ancient date, for in the early Middle Ages powdered amber was much prized in Germany as an aromatic incense. The name Bernstein is derived from the Low German bernen (to burn), for amber burns quite readily with a sweet smell. The Greek name for amber was electron, from its property of attracting light articles when it is rubbed, for rubbing produces a charge of negative electricity on the amber.

Occurrences of Materials Similar to Amber

Although most of the commercial amber comes from the Baltic deposits, there are other sources of similar material though often of a slightly different chemical composition. Probably the most important of these is the Burmese variety, or burmite as it is usually known. This amber is very much redder in colour than the Baltic variety; it is found near Myitkyina in the valley of the Hukong, a tributary of the Chindwin river, and not far from the jadeite mines. This amber differs from succinite (the Baltic variety) in being harder and denser and is often found to contain included calcite. The Burma amber is obtained from a clayey soil and is mined by the Maingthas, the peoples of the Bhamo district, during the season from March to May. Several shafts are sunk close together for a depth of about 45 ft., three men working each pit, one below and two above; the 'twinlon' method of basket, hooked bamboo pole and bamboo shear legs (similar to the method used in ruby mining) being used to bring up the soil, from which the amber pieces are washed out. The cleaned pieces are sent to Mandalay for disposal, most of the material going to China.

Along the Simeto river, near Catania in Sicily, is found an amber of a reddish-brown colour and fluorescent in appearance. Sicilian amber is called simetite, after the name of the river along whose banks and mouth the material is found. At several places in Romania is found an amber, named appropriately roumanite, which is said to contain less succinic acid and more hydrogen sulphide. The occurrences are somewhat widespread in the country, the most important localities being in the province of Muntenia near Buzau. This amber has a density between 1·05 and 1·12, a hardness of 2–2½ on Mohs's scale, varies in colour between yellow, brownish-green, brown, green and blue, and shows a striking fluorescence. Other places in this state where amber is found are Ramnicul-Serat and Prahova. In the province of Dobrogea, along the shores of the Black Sea, near Valzea in the province of Oltenia and at Bacau, Neamt, Putna and Sucava in Moldavia are deposits of amber, but, particularly in the last-named locality, the amber is often of a dark to blackish-green colour, or may be bluish. Amber varying between brown-yellow and wax to honey-yellow is found near Sibiu and Alba in Transylvania in the central part of the country.

Gedanite is a softer and lighter variety of amber, with a hardness of 1½–2 on Mohs's scale and a density near to 1·02. The name is derived from Gedanum, an old name for Danzig, the north German town, near which is found this variety of amber. Gedanite contains little succinic acid, or none at all. Amber has been found in small quantities in a number of different places, none of which are of great importance, but mention may be made of deposits in the north American continent. A variety called chemawinite is found around the south-western margin of Cedar Lake, Manitoba, Canada; and there is a small deposit recorded from the Eocene beds on the north-east side of the Simi Valley in Ventura County, California.

Amber has also been found in Pitt County, North Carolina, Coffee Bluff on Tennessee river in northern Hardin County, near Gifford, Hot Springs County, Arkansas, Wando river, South Carolina, and at several places in Maryland, New Jersey, New York, Massachusetts, Mississippi, Wyoming and Colorado.

Synthesis and Simulation

Copal

Amber is simulated by many substances, both natural and artificially produced. Copal resin, a recent fossil resin, is the most important of the natural amber imitations. It is the exudation from various trees, and may come from many parts of the world, particularly from the West Indian locust tree from South America, from trees in West, Central and East Africa, and from New Zealand. The most important are those pieces which have been buried for some considerable time in the earth. This is particularly so with the New Zealand variety, a copal from the kauri pine (*Agathis australis*), hence termed 'kauri gum'. The physical and optical properties of these copal resins do not differ very much from those of true amber, but, owing to the more recent hardening of the copal resins, they are more susceptible to attack by solvents than is the case with amber. A spot of ether (methylated ether obtainable from any chemist will be suitable) placed on the surface of copal will quickly produce a sticky patch, whereas in true amber there is no action. Under ultra-violet light, particularly the short-wave lamp, copals show a whiter fluorescence than does amber.

Plastics

Bakelite—Probably the most important imitation of amber is the plastic known as phenol formaldehyde (Bakelite). This material has a greater density than amber, averaging 1·26, so that such imitations will sink in a solution of salt in water which will float amber. The refractive index is also higher, averaging 1·66. However, both of these factors may not be determined conveniently in many cases, such as with carved pieces or mounted specimens, but the problem may be overcome by boiling a peeling in about 2 ml of distilled water and afterwards testing the water for phenol which tends slightly to dissolve out in the hot water. This may be done by adding to the water in which the peeling has been boiled a small pinch of 2·6 dibromoquinonechlorimide and then adding a very small drop of caustic soda solution from the end of a glass rod. The formation of a blue colour in the water indicates phenol and therefore phenolic resin. Bakelite imitations of amber are, in general, inert under ultra-violet rays or x-rays; if there is any glow at all it is usually a brown fluorescence quite unlike that given by true amber.

Celluloid can also be used as an amber imitation. This material has a refractive index of 1·50 and a density about 1·38, but the material may easily be identified by the blue colour induced in a spot of 5 per cent solution of diphenylamine in sulphuric acid placed on the surface of the specimen. Celluloid shows a yellowish-white fluorescence under ultra-violet rays and x-rays.

Casein, the hardened milk plastic, does not appear to be used very much as an amber imitation despite the fact that material of clear amber colour can be produced. The material seems to be met with in the cruder 'filled' form as cheap beads. Casein may be identified by the density and refractive index, 1·33 and 1·55 respectively. Under both long-wave and short-wave ultra-violet light the material fluoresces with a white glow, but, in contra-distinction to celluloid, casein is inert under x-rays. If a drop of nitric acid be placed on an inconspicuous surface a bright yellow spot is left. This is conclusive, but the effect may be masked by the body colour.

Urea-formaldehyde resin, the amino-plastic, can make a passable imitation of amber, but as yet does not appear to be used. The density of this plastic is about 1·50 and the refractive index is usually greater than 1·55, generally near to 1·60.

Perspex, the polymethylmethacrylate resin, is another plastic which has great possibilities as an amber imitation. It is easily recognized by its rather characteristic density of 1·18; identification may be carried out by using a salt solution made up by putting 10 level teaspoonfuls of common salt in an ordinary tumbler of water. Such a solution has a density of between 1·12 and 1·14, so that amber will float and Perspex will sink in such a saline solution. However, care must be taken for if too much salt is put in a saturated solution will be obtained and as this has a density of 1·20, then the Perspex will float also. Control specimens added will ensure that this does not occur.

Polystyrene—The comparatively new plastic, polystyrene, is finding increasing use as a medium for the production of fancy costume jewellery owing to its ready flow in injection moulding techniques. The density of this material is 1·05, just lower than for most amber, a fact that may appear to make distinction a little hard. The identification of this plastic is, however, quite easy, for it dissolves readily in benzene or toluene. In fact, it dissolves in most hydrocarbon liquids. The refractive index is about 1·50. There is a vast number of polymerized organic compounds now made for the plastics industry, many of which, suitably coloured, could supply an amber imitation, but those mentioned are the most likely.

Two new amber imitations of German origin are 'polybern', which consists of small pieces of real amber in a coloured polyester resin; and 'bernat', which is a plastic which has a similar refractive index to amber but the higher density of about 1·23. This latter imitation is sometimes sold with pieces of plants and insects embedded in it.

Fly in Amber

It used to be said that a fly in amber was a sure proof that the piece was amber. This is not true today for 'amber' with flies, beetles, and even moths and butterflies has been produced and mounted in jewellery. These are usually obvious as the plastic 'tomb' is too clear and the animal or insect too big, also they show no signs of having been embedded alive, as is the case of the insects caught by the true amber as it trickles down from the pine tree engulfing the small insects, which struggle in their death throes producing swirls in the then viscous resin. There is a record of a fly in amber doublet; a piece of real amber formed the base upon which was placed an insect which was enclosed by a 'lid' of a material which was possibly copal resin. It is understandable that insects can be caught up by copal resin and one case is known where a small scorpion was entombed in kauri gum.

Glass

Glass imitations of amber have a much higher density and are cold to the touch, whereas amber feels warm. The hardness of glass is greater. Quite a number of yellow glasses are coloured by uranium oxide and hence show a brilliant yellow-green fluorescence under the ultra-violet lamp. Other glasses not containing uranium may contain manganese and this gives a dull greenish glow which is entirely different from the glows shown by amber under the ultra-violet lamps.

Tests for Amber

A most useful test for amber, providing that care is used in its application, is to apply the blade of a knife to an inconspicuous spot and test for the sectility. Amber, pressed amber and the copal resins break away in powdery splinters or chips. Glass is not touched unless a great deal of pressure be applied. Bakelite is resistant to the blade but will tend to peel off in rather large chips, while the other plastics peel easily. Except for glass, which does

Figure 23.3. A cross in carved jet

not peel anyway, such peelings, resting on the knife blade and introduced into a flame, will give characteristic reactions. Amber and copal will burn with an aromatic smell: Bakelite and casein will only char, the first tending to give off a carbolic smell and the second that of burnt milk. Celluloid will burn readily, while the safety celluloid (cellulose acetate resin) will burn less readily and give off a vinegary smell.

JET

A gem popular in Victorian times, jet, with its intense black colour and capacity for taking a high polish, was pre-eminent for certain types of jewellery, particularly those of an ecclesiastical nature (*Figure 23.3*) and mourning jewellery. Indeed 'Whitby jet' is known far and wide, and Whitby—an ancient seaport town of Yorkshire—derived its chief industrial fame from its jet industry, an industry which had flourished since Roman times, which reached its peak during the middle of the nineteenth century and lasted until the beginning of the twentieth century, when the wheel of fashion turned and jet became more the symbol of Victorianism and less desired.

Jet was known in England before the advent of the Romans; even before recorded history, for jet beads, pendants and charms have been found in early burial mounds in widely scattered parts of the British Isles. True, it is questioned whether all this material came from the Whitby area but undoubtedly a great deal did. There is evidence that jet was mined as early as 1500–1400 B.C. During the Roman occupation of Britain the jet mines were opened up and jet shipped to Rome. Written records have traced down through the ages Yorkshire jet and the Whitby jet workers.

The name jet has been derived from the old French jyet or jaiet, which was itself derived from the Latin gagates, either directly or through the German gagat. The word was apparently first obtained from the Greeks and derived from Gagee or Gagas, a place on the Mediterranean coast of Asia Minor, from where the Romans obtained their jet.

Chemical and Physical Properties

Jet is a fossil wood allied to brown coal, and is derived from driftwood which has been subjected to chemical action in stagnant water and subsequently flattened by great pressures. The material is soft, about $2\frac{1}{2}$ on Mohs's scale, but may reach as high as 4 in some cases. It breaks with a lustrous conchoidal fracture. The density approximates to 1·33 (1·30–1·35) and when a flat surface is tested on the refractometer a vague blurred edge at about 1·66 is seen. Jet shows no luminescence under ultra-violet light or x-rays.

The material burns like coal, of which it is really a variety, and when rubbed is said to give off a strong odour, an effect remarked upon by the Roman writer Pliny. Friction is said to develop electricity in jet just as it does in amber, but different pieces of jet may vary considerably in their power to induce frictional electricity, some being quite inert in this respect. It is owing to this effect that jet has been called 'black amber'.

Occurrences

Jet is found in the Upper Lias of the Yorkshire coast, in the neighbouring dales of Rosedale and Bilsdale and at Great Ayton and Oakham Wood near Hawsker, which is one of the earliest known workings. One of the richest deposits is at Robin Hood's Bay, 4 miles south-east of Whitby town. The jet rock is a lias shale, dark blue to black in colour, dense in texture, and smelling strongly of oil when freshly broken. The 'jet rock' which gives the best 'hard' jet is extracted from the lower bed of the Upper Lias—the *Ammonites serpentinus* zone.

The jet, which is found in horizontal seams from 1 to 6 in. thick, and usually of a wedge shape, is mined by tunnelling into the sea cliffs, or the

Cleveland hills. The material is also found amongst the debris from the cliff falls along the shore; such pieces are water-worn and are very useful to carve and work.

Jet is found in a number of other parts of the world, particularly at Villaviciosa in the province of Asturias in Spain. Such material is worked at Oviedo, but during the hey-day of the Whitby jet industry much Spanish jet was imported and worked at Whitby. Another source of jet is in the Department of Aude, France, where the material, like that of Spain, is found in irregular veins in the lower marls or greensands of the cretaceous series corresponding to the Sussex gault. Other deposits are in the United States of America, particularly from the Henry mountains of Utah, at Württemberg in Germany and in Russia. None of these appear to be systematically worked.

Simulation

Scotch cannel, and similar material from the coal measures at Newcastle, have been used as a substitute for jet, but they are more brittle. In the same way Pennsylvanian anthracite has been so used.

Imitations of jet are furnished by vulcanite—the hard vulcanized rubber—by glass, by obsidian and by black stained chalcedony—the so-called 'black onyx'. The plastics, too, may now be said to provide an imitation of jet. 'Paris jet' is a black glass.

If a heated needle is pressed into a suspected piece of jet it will melt and give off the typical fumes of burning coal should the specimen be jet or cannel coal, but if vulcanite the smell will be of burning rubber. Such treatment will show up glass, obsidian or stained agate for the needle will have no effect on these materials. With Bakelite any fumes would smell of phenol (carbolic acid), with celluloid the piece would probably take fire, with casein a smell of burnt milk and with Perspex or polystyrene typical aromatic or fetid odours will be produced.

Jet-like in appearance and a material which has been used for carvings is albertite, a mixture of hydrocarbons, which is a mineral asphalt with a glistening black pitch-like lustre. Unlike most mineral asphalts, albertite is moderately insoluble in organic solvents, the density is fairly constant at about 1·097, hardness is near to $2\frac{1}{2}$ on Mohs's scale and on the refractometer an edge is seen at about 1·55.

CHAPTER 24

IVORY AND TORTOISE-SHELL

IVORY

The soft mellow beauty of ivory has been used as a medium of artistic expression from the dawn of history; indeed, pre-history, for some of the earliest examples of man's experiments in art, or picture writing, are the crude carvings on mammoth ivory found in the caves in Périgord, France, and on similar pieces from the Swiss Lake Dwellings. Throughout all great civilizations, Egyptian, Assyrian, Mycenean, Greek, Etruscan and Roman, the fine texture and rich creamy colour of ivory has inspired those ancient masters of the glyptic art.

The rudely scratched pieces from the Dordogne caves, the small carved head made from mammoth ivory which was found at Vestonie and estimated to be 30,000 years old, the gold-encrusted 'Snake Goddess of Knossos', or the ivory treasures of Tut-ankh-amen's tomb, are ivory pieces which form the pages of history before the written word was known. From Classical times, the early Christian era, the mediaeval period until the present day, ivory has assumed an increasing importance as a medium for the artist craftsman.

The thirteenth century saw the zenith of ivory carving in Europe, and that same century also saw the formation, during the Yuan dynasty, of a department of ivory workers in the Palace of Pekin. At first the Chinese produced only pieces having a purely domestic or utilitarian object, such as the vase-like brush holders called 'Pei-Tung', for which the hollow portion of the ivory tusks was so suitable. During the later Ming period the Chinese produced work of a more ornamental nature which, in the seventeenth century, reached the elaboration of the 'two-stage' and 'three-stage' work, work which shows two or three distinct layers of carvings cut one behind the other in the thickness of the ivory (*Figure 24.1*), and so well finished that the backs of the small figures are carved with the same care as is used for their fronts. During the nineteenth century the art of ivory carving in China became more commercialized and repetition for export became a large well-organized trade.

In Japan, ivory is regarded as a precious material and, as in China, tradition demands that, however odd the original shape of the piece of ivory, the carved piece must conform to the original shape (*Figure 24.2*). Utilizing Japanese legends and stories, the carvers produced in fine sculpture scenes from folklore, birds, flowers, animals and children, besides mythological creatures of wild imagination. The curious 'netsukes', so commonly seen in ivory, are typically Japanese; they are merely buttons as the very name netsuke tells, for the word means 'a root to suspend something on'. Primitive Japanese hunters suspended their arms and belongings from

Figure 24.2. Female immortal carved in a single piece of ivory (it is nearly 3 ft. high)

Figure 24.1. A fossil ivory vase with 'stage' work

their belt by means of a button or a lump of material, and it is easily understood how such a lump would be roughly cut or carved till, with the development of artistic feeling, the elaborate carved netsuke came into being.

In the present century ivory has been used less for the glyptic artist than as a decorative material for small articles of utility and personal adornment. The use of ivory for handles, where often the small tips of tusks, termed 'points', are employed, gives grace to fine cutlery, and the exquisite softness and the excellent polish exhibited by ivory lends itself admirably

476

to those aristocrats of the dressing table, ivory-backed hair brushes, mirrors and their accessories. The almost perfect elasticity of ivory has made this material the ideal medium for billiard balls and for fine-toothed combs, and it is invaluable in the production of precision scales and rulers.

Types of Ivory

What is ivory? Ivory, or more correctly dentine, is a substance common to the teeth of all mammals, and provided the teeth, or teeth modifications such as tusks, are sufficiently large to supply material suitable for fashioning these may be the source of the ivory of commerce. They comprise the tusks of the elephant, both recent and fossil, the teeth of the hippopotamus, the tusks of the walrus and the narwhal, and to a lesser extent the tusks of the boar and the teeth of the cachalot whale.

Elephant

Of prime importance are the elephants, the tusks of which are the upper incisor teeth of the animal, and, unlike human teeth, continue to grow through life. The teeth or tusks not being subjected to habitual attrition from an opposed tooth grow to an extraordinary length following a curve originally impressed upon them by the form of the socket. The tusk gradually widens from the projecting apex to that part which is embedded in the bone sockets of the skull and is hollow, in a conical form, for about a third of its length. This cavity, or 'nerve' as it is sometimes called, continues as a narrow canal, towards the point of the tusk, which consists of ivory only, with just a small patch of enamel on the tip of young teeth.

The African elephant (*Elephas africanus*), a giant which roams the forests of central Africa supplies most of the commercial ivory. The tusks average about 15–16 pounds in weight, although in exceptional cases tusks of around 70 pounds are obtained. Very heavy tusks, over 200 pounds in weight, have been found but are extremely rare. The best African ivory has a warm transparent mellow tint with little grain or mottling. The Cameroons supply the best material, while Loango, Congo, Gabon and Ambriz produce the next best quality, and this is followed by ivory from Ghana (Gold Coast) and Sierra Leone. The ivory from the Sudan is always 'ringy', that is with alternate dark and light coloured concentric rings. Angola and Ambriz ivory is generally 'hard', while Zanzibar and Moçambique ivory is usually 'soft'. Hard and soft are terms applied in commerce, but the characters are difficult to define. The hard, or bright ivory is distinctly harder to cut and is, as it were, more 'glassy', while soft ivory will stand differences of temperature better and does not crack so easily. Abyssinian ivory is soft with a rather thick 'bark'—the outside or skin portion of the tusk. Egyptian ivory, so-called because it is imported over the borders of Egypt and then taken across the continent by desert caravans, may be either the hard or soft type, but owing to the extremes of temperature reached during the trek across the desert this transported ivory is very liable to develop cracks.

The Asiatic elephant (*Elephas maximus*) inhabits Burma, Siam (Thailand),

Cochin China and India, and is often called the Indian elephant. These animals have smaller tusks than their African cousins; indeed the elephants from Ceylon have no tusks at all, while, unlike the African elephant, the female, or cow, Indian elephant is also tuskless. Asiatic ivory is more of a denser white, more open in texture, softer to work and yellows more easily. Ivory from Siam is usually soft. It may approach an intermediate type termed 'bastard', but on the whole is considered the best type for working and appearance. It has been suggested that much Indian ivory is in reality African which has reached India by way of Zanzibar and Moçambique.

Fossil ivory—The so-called fossil, or mammoth, ivory is in general obtained from the remains of an early elephant, the woolly mammoth (*Elephas primigenius*) which roamed the northern hemisphere during the geological period known as the Pleistocene, some 200,000 years ago. Many of these great beasts with their inordinately long, spirally curved and divergent tusks, were overwhelmed by ice during the great Ice Ages which devastated much of northern Europe, Asia and America in that geological epoch.

This fossil ivory is not a true fossil, for the tusks have not been altered by mineralization; it is a true ivory, sometimes showing little loss of beauty, despite the countless years the tusks have been preserved in ice below the arctic ground. It is in Siberia that most of these refrigerated tusks are found, and they are particularly abundant in the neighbourhood of the Lena river, and other rivers which discharge into the Arctic Ocean. An earlier elephant, the mastodon of Miocene times, is sometimes found in the icy ground of Alaska around the Yukon river. Much of this material is darkly stained and unusable, but at least one carver works in the small amount of mastodon ivory still sound and of a sufficiently good colour to cut into brooches and pendants.

Hippopotamus

Both the incisor and canine teeth of the hippopotamus (*Hippopotamus amphibius*), a genus of pachydermatous (thick skinned) quadrupeds which inhabit the rivers of central Africa, supply an ivory which is denser and of finer grain than the ivory of the elephant. These teeth, known as 'sea-horse teeth', for the animal is sometimes known as the sea-horse or river-horse, weigh from 1 pound to 6 pounds or more and are characterized by their thick layer of enamel.

Walrus

The walrus (*Odobaenus rosmarus*), sometimes called the morse, is an amphibious mammal of the seal family which has an enormous development of the canine teeth of the upper jaw, and a tumid appearance of the muzzle caused by the magnitude of their sockets and by the thickness of the upper lip. These great canines, often two or three feet in length and of a flattened 'trefoil' section, form two tusks directed downwards. The lower jaw which possesses no canines becomes narrow in front so as to pass between them.

Walrus ivory is less dense and rather coarser than either of the ivories from the elephant and hippopotamus. The exterior possesses a much finer texture and grain than the core which in appearance and properties bears a resemblance to ordinary bone and which extends a long way up the tooth. The walrus, the name is derived from the Scandinavian 'val-ros' (whale-horse), inhabits the Arctic seas and the colder parts of the north temperate zone.

Narwhal

A species of whale inhabiting the Arctic seas, the narwhal is seldom seen south of the Shetland islands, or roughly south of latitude 65°. The 'horn' of the animal is really an incisor tooth, but it projects straight out from the front of the head on the left side, for the narwhal possesses two teeth only, the left one developed to an extraordinary length while the right one is rudimentary and projects only a few inches. The female of the species has only rudimentary teeth and they are concealed in the bone like the right tooth of the male. In some rare cases the male has been found with two long tusks, both of which are spirally twisted in the same direction, and they are slightly hollow. Narwhal tusks may reach to about 10 ft. in length and produce a rather coarse ivory which in olden days was sold as 'the horn of the unicorn'.

Hog and Cachalot Whale

The strong curved teeth of the hogs, particularly the boar and the wart-hog, and other members of the swine family (Suidea) supply an ivory suitable for small articles. It is used similarly, but to a lesser extent, to the recurved conical teeth of the cachalot, or sperm, whale which is abundant in southern and northern waters, and which swims in schools between the Arctic and Antarctic circles. The ivory from both these animals is coarse and at times has more of the consistency of bone than of true ivory.

Elephant Teeth and Rhinoceros Horn

An unusual ivory is that which is cut from the molar teeth of the elephant. Any cross-section of these teeth shows a characteristic mottled or banded appearance made up by fawn, brown and cream tints. This characteristic structure is due to the teeth being composed of vertical plates of dentine separately enveloped with enamel and cemented together by the cement. As the surface of the tooth is worn down by mastication, the harder enamel is exposed in elevated ridges, thus forming a grinding mill, which crushes and grinds the vegetable food, the sole source of nutriment of the elephant. This molar ivory often shows cracks along the division of the enamel and the cement which produces a weakness in the material. There are definite differences in the arrangement of the enamel in Asiatic elephant molars to those of the African beast; the patterns are elongated ovals and lozenge-shaped areas respectively and this allows distinction to be made. Such ivory is sometimes used for the production of knife handles and often forms the base plate of small models of elephants carved in ivory. The horn of the rhinoceros has been used for ivory in China, but the horn of this animal is not ivory for it consists of a closely packed mass of hairs or horny fibres growing from the skin of the animal. These horns may be up to a foot in length, and the material has a low hardness and a density of 1·29.

Chemical and Physical Properties

In all teeth the ivory or dentine forms the main mass of the tooth. On the wearing face this is covered by a layer of enamel which is the hardest substance of the body structures of all mammals. The 'fang' or root end—that part of the tooth which fits into the bony socket of the skull or jaw—is covered by a layer of cement, the crusta petrosa as it is called. The centre of the tooth is in general hollow, the pulp cavity, which in life contains the tooth pulp which forms the new dentine. Neither the enamel, which is generally absent altogether in elephant tusks, nor the cement, has any importance as an ivory.

The ivory from elephants—the Proboscidea—shows in transverse sections, striae of different shades of cream proceeding in the arc of a circle and forming by their decussations minute curvilinear lozenge-shaped spaces which appear like an engine-turning (*Figure 24.3*). These 'lines of Retzius', as they are called, are seen only in ivory from the elephants, and are not apparent in ivory from the other animals. Much ivory shows a grained

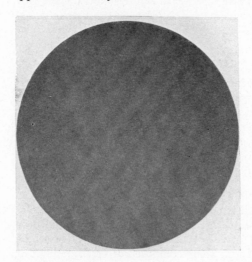

Figure 24.3. The 'engine-turning' or lines of Retzius seen on elephant ivory

appearance along directions parallel to the length of the tusk; but such a striation may be well reproduced in the celluloid imitations of ivory. The engine-turning is not seen in the imitations and provides a certain check on the piece being ivory. The lines of Retzius, or engine-turning, are due to the dentine being permeated with fine thread-like canals filled with a brownish gelatinous substance, which in life conducts the delicate nerve fibrils. These fine canals extend outward from the pulp cavity of the tusk in flattened spirals of opposite hands, and it is these dense pores with their gelatinous content which give to ivory its beautiful polish and exceptional elasticity.

Examination of a thin peeling of ivory by a low-powered microscope, preferably with the peeling immersed in an oil of similar refractive index—such as clove oil (n—1·54)—reveals fine fibrils undulating across the field, with, if the peeling is at all thick, darker grain lines crossing at right angles to the 'wave-like' canals (*Figure 24.4*). There is one direction in which the canals can be viewed end-on, and they will then appear as dots; even in this position, however, there will still be seen a wave-like formation made up of the dots. In hippopotamus ivory the undulating pattern is much finer, while in walrus and narwhal ivory it is much coarser with more ramification of the canals. In boar and whale teeth the canals appear straighter and are somewhat radial from the centrum of the tooth.

The chemical composition of ivory is mainly calcium phosphate, and is near to hydroxyl apatite which has the formula $(Ca_3OH)_2(PO_4)_6Ca_4$, with some organic matter, mainly collogen with a trace of elastin. The percentages of mineral matter to organic matter vary considerably; in elephant ivory they are about 65 per cent and 35 per cent respectively. The density of elephant ivory varies between 1·70 and 1·90, the lower values being for

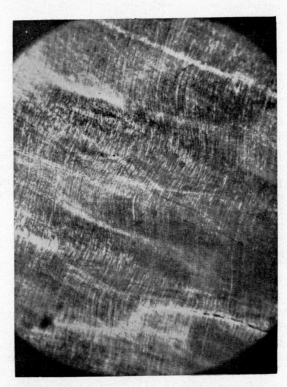

Figure 24.4. Undulating fibrils seen in a magnified thin section of ivory

the soft ivory and the higher values for the hard type. Hippopotamus ivory is usually denser, at a little over 1·90, and walrus and narwhal ivory is somewhat higher still, being over 1·95. Unless the ivory has a 'bony' structure the value rarely reaches 2. The refractive index is 1·54 and the hardness varies between $2\frac{1}{4}$ and $2\frac{3}{4}$ on Mohs's scale.

Ivory is not resistant to chemical action; nitric acid and phosphoric acid soften it, the latter chemical being used to soften ivory which has been spirally peeled off as sheets from the tusk, a technique employed for obtaining large sheets for paintings. Should the ivory be damaged in any way during life the repair is effected by natural processes, but the repair material is a bony type of ivory termed osteodentine. When irradiated with

16+G.

ultra-violet light ivories fluoresce with a bluish light varying from a whitish-blue to a deep violet blue, the deeper shades being given by the more coarse ivories of the boar. Irradiation by x-rays does not induce a luminescent glow in ivory, an effect common with many organic substances.

Fashioning and Preservation

Ivory, unlike bone, requires no preparation before fashioning, the shaping being carried out by the use of band saws or circular saws, drilling machines and lathe turning operations. Carving is done by the use of ordinary carving chisels as used for wood carving. The fashioned ivory articles are finished by polishing and burnishing, the work being carried out by the use of rotating wheels dressed with 'sea-horse' hide (hippopotamus skin) using tripoli or pumice as a polishing medium, the final polish being given with fine pumice and oil. The scrap pieces, and ivory dust, are sold to manufacturers of pigments who burn it to produce ivory black.

The tendency for ivory to turn yellow has been ascribed to atmospheric action under certain conditions, and, in the case of carvings this mellowing with age is a quality considered more beautiful. In the case of ivory articles subject to handling, the absorbent nature of ivory will cause it to take up the fatty acids and oil from the skin once the high polish and finish have worn off. Ivory may be bleached to some extent by exposing to sunlight, preferably under a glass shade, to prevent cracking by the heat of the sun's rays; likewise, ivory should never be dried before a fire or radiator. To preserve the tint of ivory, the surface may be wiped from time to time with a cloth damped with methylated spirits and ordinary whiting, which not only maintains the polish but cleans the surface of acids which in the course of time cause a discoloration of the surface. The stains of perfume, or other toilet preparations, are more difficult to remove and need the attention of a skilled ivory worker.

Simulation
Bone

There are many imitations of ivory, both natural and artificial. Bone, which has a composition very similar to that of ivory, may be distinguished by the very different structure, and to some extent by its slightly higher density—approximately 2·00, at least for the compact type used in the arts. This material is usually obtained from the long-bones of the ox, although many fine carved pieces have been produced from the hard bone of the mandible of the large whales. Containing rather more organic content, particularly of a fatty nature, than ivory, bone requires certain preparation, termed degreasing, before use. Steeping in brine for some days and subsequently simmering in hot water for about 6 hours in order to remove the fatty matter is carried out.

Bone has a hardness of about $2\frac{1}{2}$ on Mohs's scale and a refractive index near to 1·54. When a peeling is microscopically examined the structure is seen to be completely dissimilar to that of ivory, and, moreover, shows a marked difference when the sections are transverse and when they are parallel to the length of the bone. The material is characterized by the presence of canals which permeate the bone in a longitudinal direction, canals which in life pipe the vital fluids. When a transverse section of bone is examined with low magnification the field is seen to be pierced with oval or circular cavities surrounded with small dot-like or seed-like spaces, called lacunae, in concentric arrangement. These are known as the Haversian systems. The remainder of the field is made up of less distinctly oriented lacunae and fine canals, called canaliculi, which link up the main Haversian canals (*Figure 24.5*). When a longitudinal section of bone is examined it is seen that the 'pipes' will be cut so as to produce long cavities depending

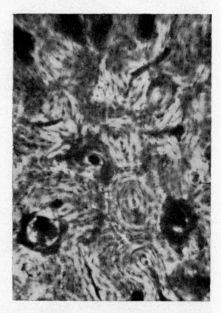

Figure 24.5. Photomicrograph of a transverse thin section of bone

upon how nearly to parallel the run of the tubes is to that of the section. Dot-like lacunae and canaliculi complete the remainder of the field (*Figure 24.6*).

The surface of any piece of worked bone when examined with a lens will show short dark lines or dots. These are the cut Haversian canals into which dirt has infiltrated. It is thus evident that bone can be stained to any colour and perhaps more easily than ivory; staining is often carried out. The fluorescence of bone under ultra-violet light is markedly similar to that shown by ivory, and although it is possibly a whiter blue than the usual fluorescence of ivory, this is insufficient to provide a clear diagnosis. Like ivory, bone does not fluoresce under x-rays.

Deer-horn

A substance near to bone which has been used for small carvings, and particularly for inlays, is that from the antler of the deer (Cervus). This horn is a deciduous bony structure crowning the head of stags. It is a type of bone characterized by extreme rapidity of growth and is derived from the distal point of a pedicle of bone projecting from the frontal bones of the skull. Deer-horn, or stag-horn, as it is more commonly called, shows a good resemblance to bone, but is usually more brown in tint. The hardness is $2\frac{1}{2}$ on Mohs's scale, the density lies between 1·70 and 1·85 and the index of refraction is approximately 1·56. A thin peeling when microscopically examined shows a structure similar to that of bone, but the Haversian canals are less prominent. In Germany stag-horn has been much used for inlay and there are many fine specimens of sixteenth and seventeenth century firearms so decorated. The material has been used in Japan for small carvings and netsukes, and many fine pieces of Sheffield cutlery are handled with horn from the Axis deer (*Cervus axis*) from Asia.

Figure 24.6. Photomicrograph of a longitudinal section of bone

Vegetable Ivory

Ivory palm—Used as an imitation of ivory are the hard seeds, or nuts, of certain palm trees. The most important of these is the Ivory palm (*Phytelephas macrocarpa*), a native of the Andean plains of Peru, where it is known as Homero or Pullipunta. It is also found along the Coast of Darien (known there as Anti), and along the Magdalina river in Colombia where the name Tagua is applied. This tree is one of the most beautiful of the palm family. It grows in damp localities and is characterized by a short and procumbent stem. Proceeding from its crown is a magnificent tuft of light green pinnated leaves of extraordinary size and beauty rising to 30 or 40 ft. in height (*Figure 24.7*). The flowers are on a crowded spadix and have neither calyx nor corolla. The fruit, weighing 20–25 pounds, which is as large as a man's head, consists of six or seven 4-celled drupes aggregated together, and contains from six to nine nuts of somewhat triangular form and reminiscent of a fattened kernel of a Brazil nut, each nut being about as large as a hen's egg. They are commercially known as Corozo nuts (*Figure 24.8*).

These seeds, in the very young state, contain a clear insipid fluid which travellers can drink. As the nuts become older the fluid becomes milky and of a sweet taste. It gradually continues to change until it becomes exceedingly hard and so white as to resemble ivory so completely that few names have ever been better applied than that of 'Vegetable ivory'.

Figure 24.7. Ivory nut palm

The composition of vegetable ivory is nearly pure cellulose, a resistant carbohydrate ($C_6H_{10}O_5$), which is the fundamental constitution of the cell walls of plants, and therefore forms the framework of vegetable tissues. The hardness is about $2\frac{1}{2}$ on Mohs's scale and the refractive index about 1·54, a value so commonly found in organic substances. The specific gravity varies from about 1·40 to 1·43, and the fluorescence effect seen under ultraviolet light is similar, but weaker, than the glow shown by ivory, with which it agrees in being inert under x-rays.

A thin peeling (vegetable ivory is very slightly more sectile than true ivory) shows under magnification a pattern quite dissimilar to that shown

Figure 24.8. Ivory palm nuts
(Corozo nuts)

by either ivory or bone, in that it consists of a great number of torpedo-shaped cells running in roughly parallel lines (*Figure 24.9*). If higher magnification is used these long cells are seen to have sideshoots which terminate in clubbed ends, the complete cell appearing like some grotesque insect of the centipede class. The appearance of these cells will naturally differ, being long-shaped if the section be cut parallel to them, oval if cut obliquely, and dot-like if the cells are cut transversely, a position rarely obtained with a random cut.

Doom palm—There is another type of palm nut which may have a

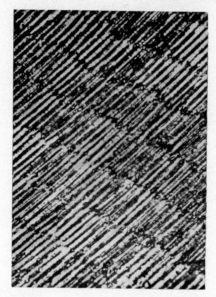

Figure 24.9. Photomicrograph of a thin section of vegetable ivory

value as an ivory imitation. This is the Doom palm (Doum palm) nut of the Borasseae tribe of palms. This Doum palm tree (*Hyphaene thebaica*) is remarkable as the single instance of branching in the palm family (*Figure 24.10*), and grows in north and central Africa, where, with its fan-shaped leaves, it is in some instances most plentiful and sometimes grows amidst the very sands of the desert.

Figure 24.10. Doom palm

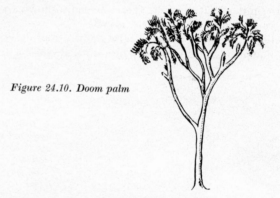

The fruit of the Doom palm is irregular, not unlike a quince, and has a reddish-brown outer skin which may be compared to that of a pomegranate. When the skin is peeled off, a considerable thickness of spongy dry substance is found within it which has an insipid sweetness and a remarkable resemblance to gingerbread. Indeed, this 'fruit' is used as an article of food, and an infusion of it as a beverage; hence the palm is often called the 'gingerbread palm'.

In the centre of the fruit is the one seed or nut which supplies the vegetable ivory material. The shape of the nut is rather like that of a fig and when cut open the hard white and translucent kernel is seen to have a large central cavity conforming to the outside of the nut (*Figure 24.11*).

The density of the Doom palm vegetable ivory is between 1·38 and 1·40, just below that of the Corozo nuts; the hardness is also slightly lower. The refractive index at 1·54 and the whitish-blue fluorescence under ultra-violet light and absence of any glow under x-rays are again similar to Corozo nut ivory.

Examined microscopically a thin peeling of Doom palm ivory shows structural similarity to that of the ivory nut palm, with, occasionally, an end-on view showing a polygonal outline to the cells which resembles greatly the structure seen in a leaf.

Vegetable ivory, which like true ivory, needs no pretreatment before fashioning, will take stain well, and when a red or pink tint is induced on rounded beads, may be mistaken for and has been sold as coral. However, these vegetable ivory imitations do not effervesce with acid as do the true corals.

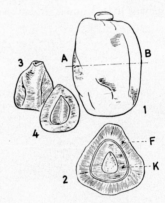

Figure 24.11. Doom palm nuts. 1, Fruit; 2, section across AB; F, fleshy part; K, kernel (nut); 3, nut removed from fleshy part; 4, section through nut

Tests

From the foregoing it will be seen that the most effective test for these different ivories is to examine a small peeling, which can usually be removed from an inconspicuous part of the object, by microscopically observing the structure. A drop of oil placed on the peeling after it has been pressed flat by a knife blade on to the glass microscope slip will facilitate viewing the interior.

Plastic and Fictile Ivory

Regarding manufactured material, the most usual and effective ivory imitation is celluloid, which is 'filled' to give the desired opacity, and some-times to give the correct density. By pressure bonding a number of sheets of the plastic together a grained effect is produced. The tests previously mentioned for the detection of celluloid will supply the necessary proof of the material, which, when a peeling (and the material is very sectile) is examined microscopically, shows a fine grained structure. Other types of plastics do not make such a convincing ivory imitation as celluloid, but they may be met.

The so-called 'fictile ivories', usually copies or reproductions of artistic ivories, are simply castings made in fine plaster of Paris tinted with yellow ochre, with the surface subsequently treated with a mixture of wax, spermaceti or stearine. These are obvious from mere inspection.

TORTOISE-SHELL

Tortoise-shell, with its beautiful mottled colour and semi-transparency, is not, as its name would lead to believe, obtained from the tortoise. The material is obtained from the carapace or shield of a sea turtle, the Hawks-bill turtle (*Chelone imbricata*) which is found in most tropical and subtropical seas, particularly the Malay archipelago, the West Indies and Brazil. The most highly prized shell, with a rich brown mottling on a warm translucent yellow background is obtained from the turtles which inhabit the Moluccas and the Island of Celebes, now renamed Sulawesi, in the East Indies.

Tortoise-shell is so-called because formerly the order of animals to which it belongs was little known, and all were confused under the general name of

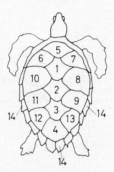

Figure 24.12. The Hawks-bill turtle showing the blades of tortoise shell: 1, 2, 3, 4, cross-backs; 5, 6, 7, shoulder plates; 8, 9, 10, 11, main plates; 12, 13, tail plates; 14, hoof

tortoises. The name Hawks-bill is derived from the horny beak-like covering of the upper jaw, and imbricata from the remarkable peculiarity in this species of the arrangement of the 13 plates forming the carapace, which, instead of being joined together by their edges so as to make one piece, are thinned off at their edges and overlap each other like the tiles of a roof.

The 13 plates, or blades as they are called, which form the main part of the carapace, are collectively known as the heart, and names are given to the respective plates (*Figure 24.12*); while the 24 small marginal plates, variously called hoofs, claws, feet or noses, have little or no value as tortoise-shell. The carapace, usually about 2 ft. to 2 ft. 6 in. in length, weighs from 5 to 8 pounds. The separate blades, usually measuring about 8 by 6 in., although they may reach 13 by 8 in., are about an eighth of an inch thick, and weigh up to 9 oz. for the larger sizes.

The plates are separated from the bony skeleton of the animal by heat. At one time the shell was obtained by cruelly suspending the living creatures over a fire until the dorsal shields separated from the bone. Today the turtles are killed first. Care is needed in all the operations needing heat, for if it is excessive the colour of the shell tends to darken.

Fashioning

When received by the tortoise-shell worker the plates are curved and ridged and their first process is to flatten them by the application of low heat and pressure and the removal of the ridges by scraping and rasping. The tortoise-shell is then trimmed and shaped by the same fine saws that are used to work ivory. The extreme thermoplasticity of tortoise-shell, which softens in boiling water, is taken advantage of in the production of larger sheets. In this case the two edges to be joined are bevelled, scraped clean, and after being placed closely together are put in a press which is then immersed in boiling water. Sometimes common salt is added to prevent change of colour, but this tends to make the tortoise-shell somewhat brittle. Likewise thicker pieces may be similarly built-up by pressing together several sheets whilst heated to a temperature of boiling water; small boxes are produced by moulding a sheet under such conditions. The shell being fairly expensive, chips, and even dust, of tortoise-shell are softened and moulded together in a manner analogous to the production of pressed amber. The resulting material, often artificially coloured at the same time, is darker and has little of the pleasing coloration of the true material.

Tortoise-shell is polished by first smoothing the surface by the use of charcoal dust, whiting or rotten-stone with water and finally finishing with a soft leather and oil, or by the use of a mechanically operated 'dolly' wheel. Broken pieces of tortoise-shell may be repaired by joining the fractured ends by the use of solid Canada balsam applied to the broken edges and the pieces tightly wired together and left for about 24 hours, the excess Canada balsam being removed with a knife. The inlaying of gold, silver or mother-of-pearl into tortoise-shell is carried out by arranging the pieces on the shell and pressing them in by the aid of hot water, after which the piece is quickly submerged into cold water with the further application of pressure.

Blond shell, which is now receiving some popularity, is a plain orangy-yellow coloured shell and has no mottling. It is material obtained from the plastron, or belly shield, of the Hawks-bill turtle. In the trade it is called yellow belly.

Chemical and Physical Properties

Tortoise-shell is similar to those other horny tissues which make up horns, claws and nails, and consists of a protein (keratin) of very complex composition, but approximates to 55 per cent carbon, 20 per cent oxygen, 16 per cent nitrogen, 6 per cent hydrogen and 2 per cent sulphur. The hardness is about $2\frac{1}{2}$ on Mohs's scale and the specific gravity is fairly constant at 1·29. The refractive index is 1·55 and the material is readily sectile. If examined microscopically, the mottling of tortoise-shell is seen to be made up of spherical spots of colour—the closer together the spots the deeper the colour, rather like the effect seen in screen printing (*Figure 24.13*). In the case of imitations of tortoise-shell—the plastics celluloid, casein, Bakelite and some others make excellent imitations—the colour is shown to be in patches or swathes and there is no dot-like or disc-like structure seen when microscopically examined (*Figure 24.14*). An imitation some-

16* 489

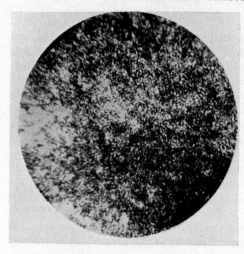

Figure 24.13. The colour in tortoise-shell is made up of small dot-like patches as shown by this photo-micrograph

times met with consists of a thin veneer of real tortoise-shell cemented to a base of suitable plastic.

Under the ultra-violet lamp the clearer and yellower portions fluoresce with a bluish-white colour; as does the blond shell. Both are inert under x-rays in common with most organic substances. The imitations of tortoise-shell behave variously under the rays from an ultra-violet lamp, but in a number of cases the glow seen is yellow.

Use of Preservatives

From Roman times tortoise-shell has been used as an inlay for furniture, and the material was increasingly used by Boule, the cabinet maker to Louis XIV of France, who employed dark-coloured shell inlaid with brass in his so-called 'Buhl' furniture. The tortoise-shell objects inlaid with small pin-head dots of silver, called piqué work, has lost favour and is not now made.

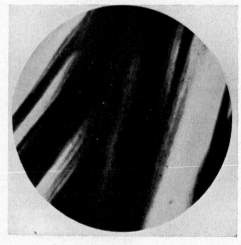

Figure 24.14. The colour in plastic imitations of tortoise-shell is in swathes

A tortoise-shell article needs very little care to preserve its beauty, but such articles should be kept away from heat and damp. The high polish can be maintained by periodic application of a drop of olive oil to which a little rouge may be mixed, on a soft cloth. Tortoise-shell-backed brushes should be washed in luke-warm water, for hot water tends to bring the shell up in fine ridges, and they should be dried naturally. Tortoise-shell articles which have suffered damage should be returned to the makers, who will repolish the surface by scraping it flat and repolishing by the use of a mechanical mop. Broken articles can be repaired by them using the well-known thermoplastic properties of the material.

Ivory and tortoise-shell are usually a trade combination, the ivory worker also working in tortoise-shell, a combination all the more romantic because in one of the oldest Indian legends the unstable nature of the world is symbolized by the elephant standing on the back of the humble, patient tortoise.

CHAPTER 25

HOW GEMSTONES ARE IDENTIFIED

METHODS IN COMMON USE

The identification of gem materials depends to some extent on whether they are in the rough state or whether they are cut and polished, and even on the manner in which they are fashioned. Further, if the stone is set in jewellery certain tests cannot be used and reliance must then be placed on other methods. Indeed, ingenuity is quite often needed in order to find the best method of approach and the best tests to apply in order to 'pin down' the nature of the stone.

Many gem minerals are found as crystals and from a knowledge of their crystal forms, or more elaborately by the measurement of the angles between their natural faces, they may often be clearly identified. Certain physical properties, particularly the optical characters of a mineral, will aid such an identification just as they will in cut stones. The modern method of x-ray crystallography will give a positive result, but such a method is outside the scope of the ordinary gemmologist, jeweller or connoisseur. Simply applied chemical tests may well assist in the identification of rough material, and in either cut or rough material the behaviour under ultra-violet light may help.

Only occasionally is the jeweller confronted with natural crystals and rough minerals. When he is the specimens are generally found to be nothing more than quartz crystals or pebbles of topaz of little value, which the customer usually thinks, or hopes, are diamond. Every jeweller should aim at a general knowledge of the natural appearance and crystal forms met with in minerals from the lowly quartz to the valuable 'gem' stones, even to diamond, for they are now often mounted in the rough state.

Probably more important is the identification of cut gemstones. With so many divers minerals now cut and polished, the vast numbers of synthetically produced gems and the modern artificial products which simulate precious stones, the jeweller has had perforce to call scientific methods to his aid. The rough and ready method of hardness testing by the use of a file, so common a test at the turn of the century, has now little value and much risk when applied to many of the gem minerals which may be encountered today.

It is true that the intrinsic colour of a stone will often tell the experienced jeweller what a stone is. The lustre and nuances of diamond, the characteristic colour of an emerald, a sapphire or a ruby, tell him much, and in earlier days he was rarely wrong. Today, however, with all the new stones, synthetics and other simulants, it is less easy to be sure and the only accurate identification is that made by scientific methods.

INSTRUMENTS

In the following pages the methods used in such scientific identification and the instruments which are employed in this work will be described. However, like all such studies, much basic elementary knowledge is necessary for the understanding of the working of the instruments themselves and how they may be used to produce the evidence required in order to identify a stone. Thus, as the behaviour of light in a crystal varies with the type of crystal it is necessary to understand something of the various crystal types. Chapter 26 will give sufficient of this elaborate subject, called crystallography, for a general idea to be obtained of gem crystals and their forms.

Except for the determination of specific gravity (i.e. relation of the weight to the volume) most of the instruments used in gem testing function by light rays. This is true whether the instrument is a microscope, a refractometer, or a spectroscope. The latter has been found over the past few years to be a potent weapon in the armoury of the gemmologist. It is therefore necessary to discuss in an elementary way something of the physics of light, without which any observation would be meaningless.

The study of the features of a stone by such a simple piece of apparatus as a hand lens, or a colour filter—which can be carried in a waistcoat pocket—can often tell the worker the nature of the stone, provided that he knows what to look for, or in other words sensibly applies the principles learnt from the following pages.

CHAPTER 26

CRYSTALS

The descriptions of the gem minerals will have shown that many are found as crystals, homogeneous bodies which have plane and often lustrous faces and which show a regularity in their arrangement. Such forms are an outward expression of an inner orderly arrangement of the atoms which make up the mineral. Some gem materials are found as irregular pieces which, by optical means, can be shown to be crystalline in structure; while others, such as opal (a hardened gel) and the natural glasses, do not have this regularity of internal structure even if the chemical composition is similar to that of a crystalline mineral (*Figure 26.1*). The artificial glasses and plastic imitations are similarly non-crystalline substances, but the synthetic gemstones are truly crystalline.

INTERNAL STRUCTURE

The Atom

To obtain an understanding of the structure of crystals it is necessary to know something of the atom itself. An atom may be said to be the smallest part of an element, giving the term element the meaning more commonly assigned to it in practical chemistry. However, each atom is now known to be a complex system consisting of planetary particles, each with unit negative electrical charge and which are called electrons, surrounding a heavy nucleus containing a number of positively charged particles called protons. There are a similar number of protons to electrons so producing, by balancing the positive and negative charges, an electrically neutral atom. Except for the hydrogen atom all the nuclei of atoms also contain a number of uncharged particles called neutrons, whose possible function is to act as a 'cement' against the repulsive action of the positively charged protons to each other.

Thus an atom contains three elementary particles, two of which, the proton and the neutron, have approximately equal weight (mass), while the electron has a mass much smaller, weighing only 1/1840 that of a proton. The structure of atoms is shown in *Figure 26.2*. An atom may be considered as consisting of a core—small and compact—surrounded by a 'cloud' of electrons describing orbits which may be circular or of varying ellipticity. The electrons, the protons and the neutrons spin on their own axes, so that the atom is a highly dynamic system. The positive electron, the positron and the mesons, so often referred to in atomic physics have no importance in the discussion of crystals and will receive no further mention.

Atomic Weight

Each of the chemical elements is made of like atoms, atoms which have the same nuclear charge, or as it is better known, atomic number; that is,

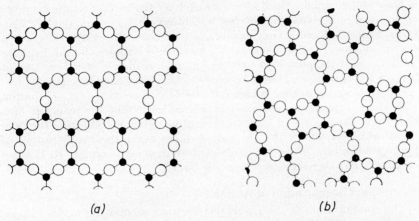

Figure 26.1. (a) A two-dimensional representation of crystal form with high degree of geo-metric order and (b) a glass of the same composition with less orderly arrangement of the atoms
(After W. H. Zachariasen)

they have the same number of protons. Commencing with hydrogen (atomic number 1) which has one proton and one planetary electron, each succeeding atom contains one more proton and electron. Thus helium has two protons and two electrons and has atomic number 2, while uranium, the heaviest atom, if the laboratory-produced transuranic elements are disregarded, has 92 protons and the same number of electrons.

However, this does not complete the picture, since, except for hydrogen, all the nuclei of the other atoms contain neutrons, varying from two in the case of helium to 146 in the uranium atom. The atomic weight of an element is the weight of the protons and neutrons which form the nucleus of the atom, the planetary electrons having so little mass (weight) that for practical purposes their weight may be neglected. While the number of protons determines the nature of an atom not all the atoms of a given element possess the same number of neutrons, therefore such atoms will vary

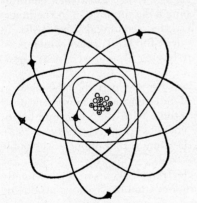

Figure 26.2. Stylized diagram of the structure of an atom. In the core or nucleus the circles with a cross represent the protons, the plain circles are the neutrons and the full black discs with cross bars are the electrons

**Carbon atom
atomic weight 12**

in their atomic weight. Such atoms which have the nuclear charge (number of protons) of a given element but which have different numbers of neutrons, hence different atomic weights, are termed isotopes. An element, as described above, usually consists of a mixture of isotopes and this explains the reason for the published values of atomic weights of the elements not being a whole number. It may be conveniently mentioned here that hydrogen may have an isotope which consists of one neutron and one proton with the one planetary electron. It will be clear that the inclusion of a neutron in the nucleus of the hydrogen atom, while not affecting the electrical neutrality will double the weight of the atom; this heavy isotope of hydrogen has been given the name deuterium and the symbol D. Further comments on this isotope will be made later.

Electronic Configuration of Atoms

The configuration of the planetary electrons around the nucleus is important, for the chemical properties of an element, chemical compounds, and the formation of crystals depend a great deal upon the disposition of the electrons. The electrons circle the nucleus in all directions as a 'cloud' in

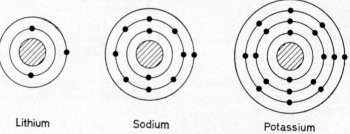

Lithium   Sodium   Potassium

Figure 26.3. Electronic configuration of atoms having similar chemical characters

given orbits which may be described as the average of their movements, the radius of which defines a 'shell' or 'energy level'. Each shell contains only a given number of electrons, there being a maximum of 2 in the innermost shell (known as the K shell), 8 each in the second and third shells, 18 each in the next two shells and 32 in the next full shell, above which is an unfinished shell starting with the element having atomic weight 87 (francium).

Strikingly apparent is the connexion between the periodic classification of the chemical elements devised by D. I. Mendeleeff and the aforementioned electronic structure of the atoms. Thus atoms with the same number of electrons in the outer shell have similar chemical properties (*Figure 26.3*). When the outer shell is completely filled the atom is that of one of the noble gases which are chemically inert (*Figure 26.4*).

If the atom gains or loses one or more electrons it ceases to be electrically neutral and becomes what is known as an ion. Gain of electrons producing negatively charged ions called anions, and loss must produce positive ions called cations. It will be seen that if the hydrogen atom is ionized by removal of its sole electron the resulting ion is the proton. Likewise the removal of the two electrons from the helium atom will leave the nucleus consisting of two protons and two neutrons. This is the *alpha* particle. Removal of the one electron from the hydrogen isotope deuterium will leave the nucleus of one proton and one neutron producing the deuteron. These are mentioned here for all of these particles have been used in the artificial coloration of diamond.

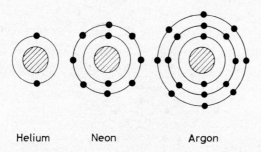

Helium   Neon   Argon

Figure 26.4. Electronic configuration of atoms of the noble gases

The characteristic orderly arrangement of the constituent atoms in a crystal can now be efficiently studied by means of x-rays. This, however, is the work of the crystallographer and has little part in normal gem identification. Some further remarks on the subject will be given in the chapter 'X-rays in Gem Testing'.

Atomic Bonding

Ionic Bond

The atomic bonding of atoms producing a solid substance is essentially a pattern which is repeated at regular intervals in all three dimensions. This atomic bonding can be accomplished in four different ways. The most important is the ionic bond in which the atoms are in the ionized state and the forces holding the structure together are due to electrical attraction between the ions. This may be illustrated by the structure of common salt (NaCl) where the sodium atom has one electron in its outer shell while the chlorine atom has one electron deficient from the full number needed to complete the shell. By transference of the outer electron of the sodium atom to the chlorine atom each form a stable gas structure, but they are now charged ions and produce a strong electrostatic attraction, the two forming a molecule of sodium chloride (*Figure 26.5*).

The description given above tends to imply that only two ions are electrically connected, whereas all the ions of an ionic structure suffer electronic attraction producing a solid structure. This may be illustrated by considering the distribution of ions in the unit cell, the smallest complete unit of pattern in a crystal, in the case of a crystal of sodium chloride (the mineral halite) (*Figure 26.6*). It may be advantageous to mention here that the array of points (atomic positions) in space at which the pattern repeats itself is called the space lattice, of which there are only 14 variations possible.

Ionic bonding may not be confined to ions with one electric charge, for two or three interchanges of electrons can occur. Thus, for example, atoms

497

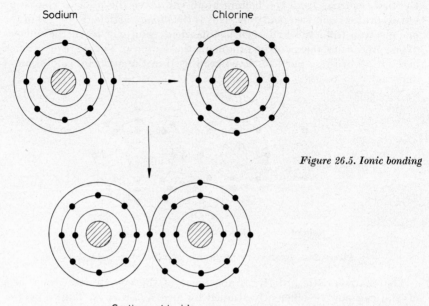

Sodium   Chlorine

Figure 26.5. Ionic bonding

Sodium chloride

with three electrons in the outer shell can combine with three atoms requiring one electron each to form the noble gas structure. It is this which explains the chemical valency and may be illustrated by lithium fluoride LiF), lithia (Li_2O) and lithium nitride (Li_3N), for fluorine is *monovalent*, oxygen is *divalent* and nitrogen is *trivalent*.

Homopolar Bond

The second type of bonding is the co-valent, or homopolar bond, in which atoms share electrons to form an electron pair; each atom sharing its electron with the other and so approaching a noble gas structure. Thus, two

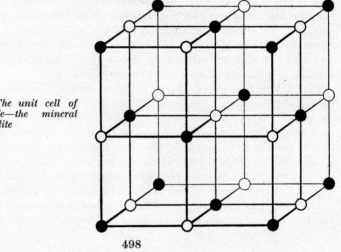

Figure 26.6. The unit cell of sodium chloride—the mineral halite

498

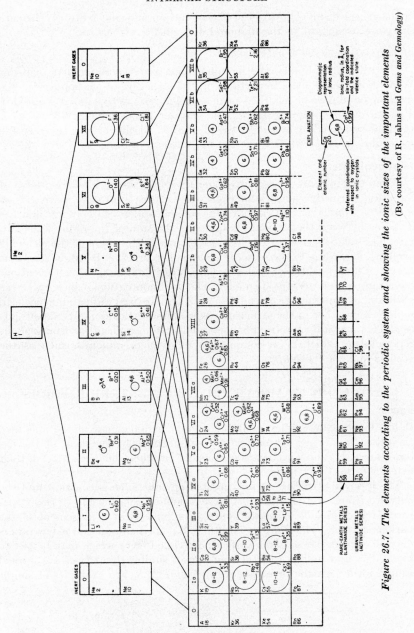

Figure 26.7. The elements according to the periodic system and showing the ionic sizes of the important elements

(By courtesy of R. Jahns and Gems and Gemology)

hydrogen atoms may share their single electrons producing a molecule of hydrogen, a molecule being the smallest discrete unit which can exist. A molecule of Al_2O_3 is, therefore, the smallest unit which will have the character of alumina, but it must be pointed out that this is not true of corundum (ruby and sapphire), for corundum is crystallized Al_2O_3 and the smallest unit of a crystal which can remain alone is the unit cell. Co-valent

499

bonds are most important in the case of carbon and silicon atoms; they are therefore important in the diamond and silicate structures.

Metallic and van der Waals Bonds

The other two bonds, the metallic bond and the residual or van der Waals bond, have little importance in the structure of gem minerals. The metallic bond may be regarded as an aggregate of positive ions immersed in a gas or cloud of free electrons. The van der Waals bond is a very weak residual force holding molecules together when all direct bonds between the molecules are satisfied. It is present to some extent in nearly all crystals.

Isomorphism

When two ions are brought together there is a distance where a force of repulsion abruptly sets in and resists any closer approach. With this in mind it is convenient to consider the ions as spheres in contact, and the distance between their centres is taken as the sum of the radii of the two ions. The relative sizes of the ions are shown in the chart of the elements arranged according to the periodic system (*Figure 26.7*). It will be seen that the anions, such as the oxygen ion, have large ionic radii, while the cations have radii which are much smaller. The common cations which enter the structure of minerals are often those with similar sized radii and, hence, can replace each other in the structure without unduly straining the space lattice. This accounts for the phenomenon of isomorphism, or isomorphous replacement, which is so common in many gem minerals, such as the garnets and the feldspars.

SYMMETRICAL ARRANGEMENT OF EXTERIOR FORMS

Faces

It has been made evident that the regular arrangement of the ions in a crystal is the inward reason for the symmetrical arrangement of the exterior faces. It is now necessary to consider crystals from the aspect of their exterior forms.

The internal structure of any crystalline substance is constant and the outward shape of a crystal must have a definite relationship to this structure. Hence, ideally, a crystal shows a symmetrical arrangement of the various surfaces which are usually flat, but in diamond and a few others may be curved. These plane surfaces are called faces which may be of two kinds, like and unlike. Crystal made up of similar (like) faces are termed simple forms, a cube or octahedron (*Figure 26.8*) are examples of simple

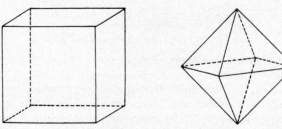

Figure 26.8. The cube and the octahedron

PLATE XX

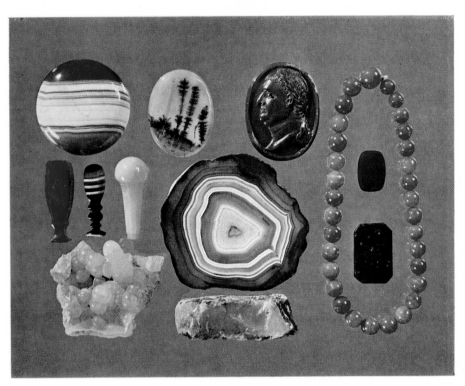

Gemstones in their natural form

Rough and Fashioned Specimens of the Silica Group

Agate	Moss agate	Prase	Cornelian bead necklet
Cornelian Agate Chrysoprase	Agate		(*inside*)
Botryoidal chalcedony	Chrysoprase seam		Sard; Bloodstone

forms, while a crystal which consists of two or more simple forms is termed a combination of forms (*Figure 26.9*). A form which is made up entirely of similar and interchangeable faces is termed a closed form (*Figure 26.10*), but others which do not enclose space unless in combination with other forms are called open forms. Thus, the hexagonal prismatic crystal of emerald is made up of two open forms, that of the six equal four-sided faces of

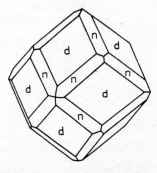

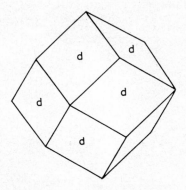

Figure 26.9. Combination of forms. The faces of the dodecahedron have their edges truncated by the faces of another form. In this case by the icositetrahedron, a 24-faced form. Such a combination of forms is common in garnet

Figure 26.10 The dodecahedron with twelve four-sided faces is a closed form. This is a common form in which garnet crystallizes

the hexagonal prism which is closed by the six-sided faces which form the top and bottom of the crystal (*Figure 26.11*). The intersection of any two adjacent faces is called the edge, and the junction of three or more faces is known as a solid angle (*Figure 26.12*). A zone is a series of faces on a crystal which have their edges mutually parallel to each other and to a common line through the centre of the crystal which is called the zone axis (*Figure 26.13*).

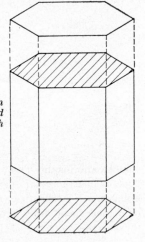

Figure 26.11. Two types of faces are needed to enclose space in the hexagonal emerald crystal. They are the six four-sided faces which form the prism and the two six-sided faces which close the top and bottom. Both of these are open forms

Angles

The angles formed by the inclination of two corresponding faces of crystals of the same substance are constant and, as mentioned earlier, may provide means of identifying crystals, even if the crystals are of widely different shapes and sizes, or are of abnormal growth so common in natural crystals. The measurements may be carried out only if the crystal faces are

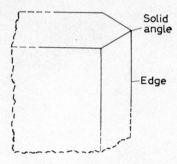

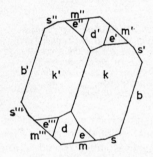

Figure 26.12. An edge and a solid angle on a crystal

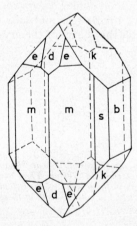

Figure 26.13. Zones of faces on a crystal of peridot. The faces m, s, b, form a zone, and another zone is formed by the faces b and k

(After E. S. Dana)

smooth and bright. The instruments used are either a contact goniometer, a type of protractor at the centre of which is pivoted a straight-edged movable arm; or a reflecting goniometer or spectrometer, an instrument which is described more fully later with reference to its use in refractive index measurements. In crystallography the interfacial angles are by convention the angles between the normals (perpendiculars) to the two faces and not the outside angle formed by them (*Figure 26.14*). The measurement of interfacial angles plays little part in gem testing but may be of value in the case of some natural crystals met with.

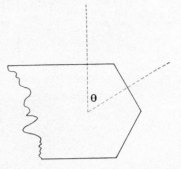

Figure 26.14. Interfacial angles are measured from the perpendiculars of the two faces and not the angle made by the two faces. The interfacial angle is θ in the illustration

Planes of Symmetry

The regular faces of crystals are arranged according to certain laws of symmetry which form the basis of a classification into 32 mathematically possible classes and into seven crystal systems. There are three kinds of symmetry which need concern the reader. They are a plane of symmetry, an axis of symmetry and a centre of symmetry. A plane of symmetry is an imaginary plane which divides a perfectly shaped crystal into two parts, one of which is the mirror image of the other. Thus in a brick, which has three pairs of dissimilar faces, there will be three planes of symmetry (*Figure 26.15*); and in the case of a cube there will be nine planes, for planes from one edge to a diagonally opposite edge are possible.

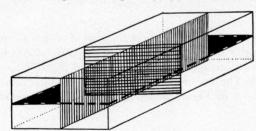

Figure 26.15. The planes of symmetry in a brick. This is the basic form of the orthorhombic system

The second kind of symmetry is the symmetry axis, an axis about which a crystal when rotated comes to occupy the same position in space more than once during a complete revolution of 360 degrees. Depending upon the symmetry a crystal may occupy the same position twice (twofold, diad or digonal axis), three times (threefold, triad or trigonal axis), four times (fourfold, tetrad or tetragonal axis) or six times (sixfold, hexad or hexagonal axis) during a complete rotation about a symmetry axis. The axes of symmetry of a cube are shown in *Figure 26.16*. The centre of symmetry, the third type of symmetry, is only possible when like faces and edges occupy corresponding positions on opposite sides of a central point, therefore a brick or cube has such a centre but a tetrahedron, a solid with four triangular faces, cannot have a centre (*Figure 26.17*).

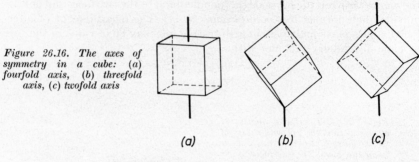

Figure 26.16. The axes of symmetry in a cube: (a) fourfold axis, (b) threefold axis, (c) twofold axis

(a)   *(b)*   *(c)*

Figure 26.17. The crystal illustrated on the left has a centre of symmetry, but the tetrahedron on the right cannot have one

Crystallographic Axes

Crystals are further divided into seven systems. In describing crystals it is convenient to assume certain lines passing through the centre of an ideal crystal as axes of reference. These imaginary lines, called crystallographic axes, intersect at the centre of the crystal, called the origin, and in most crystals are parallel to symmetry axes or normal to symmetry planes. Every face of a given 'form' must have similar intercepts with the crystal axes, for example, each face of an octahedron intercepts each of the three crystal axes at an equal distance from the origin. The seven systems with their axes and maximum symmetry (for each system has several classes with lower symmetry) are as follows.

Cubic System

The cubic, regular or isometric system has three axes all of which are of equal length and at right angles to one another. There are nine planes of symmetry and thirteen axes (3 tetragonal, 4 trigonal and 6 digonal) and there is a centre of symmetry. The axes in a cube and examples of crystals of the cubic system are shown in *Figure 26.18*. Diamond, garnet, spinel,

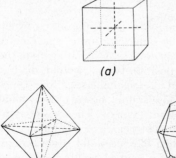

(a)

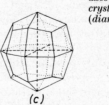

(b)   *(c)*

Figure 26.18. The crystallographic axes in a cube and examples of cubic crystals: (a) cube, (b) octahedron (diamond), and (c) icositetrahedron (garnet)

fluorspar, zinc blende, and pyrites crystallize in the cubic system, but the two minerals mentioned last do not have the full symmetry of the system.

Tetragonal System

The tetragonal system has three axes all of which are at right angles to one another and which have the two horizontal axes (the lateral axes) of equal length, but the vertical or principal axes are either longer or shorter than the lateral axes. There are five planes of symmetry, and five axes of symmetry (1 tetragonal and 4 digonal) and there is a centre of symmetry. The crystallographic axes in a tetragonal prism and examples of crystals belonging to this system are shown in *Figure 26.19*. Zircon, idocrase, rutile

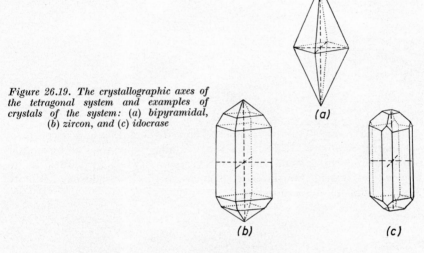

Figure 26.19. The crystallographic axes of the tetragonal system and examples of crystals of the system: (a) bipyramidal, (b) zircon, and (c) idocrase

and cassiterite form crystals having the full symmetry of this system, while the gem scapolite belongs to this system but has modified symmetry.

Orthorhombic System

The orthorhombic system has three axes which are all at right angles to one another but all of which have different lengths. The principal axis or vertical axis is either longer or shorter than the lateral axes—the longest of the lateral axes is known as the macro axis, and the shorter the brachy axis. There are three planes of symmetry, three digonal axes and a centre of symmetry. *Figure 26.20* shows the axes in a stylized orthorhombic crystal and examples of crystals of the system. Topaz, chrysoberyl, peridot, iolite, andalusite, danburite, kornerupine and enstatite are some of the minerals which crystallize in the orthorhombic system.

Monoclinic System

The monoclinic or oblique system has three axes of unequal length, two of which are at right angles to each other, and the third, the clino axis, is inclined at an angle to the plane which contains the other two. Such

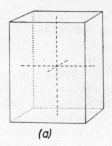

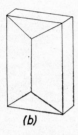

(a)

Figure 26.20. The crystallographic axes
of the orthorhombic system and examples
of crystals of this system: (a) fundamental
form with axes, (b) staurolite crystal,
and (c) topaz crystal

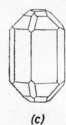

(b)

(c)

crystals have one plane of symmetry, one digonal axis and a centre of
symmetry. *Figure 26.21* illustrates the crystallographic axes and examples
of crystals of the system. Important gemstones which crystallize in the
monoclinic system are kunzite, sphene, orthoclase feldspar, epidote,
diopside, brazilianite and datolite.

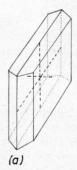

Figure 26.21. The crystallographic
axes and examples of crystals of the
monoclinic system: (a) gypsum (selenite) crystal with axes, (b) orthoclase feldspar crystal, and (c) epidote
crystal

(a)

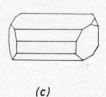

(b)

(c)

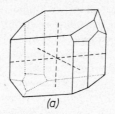

(a)

*Figure 26.22. The crystallographic axes
and examples of crystals of the triclinic
system: (a) axinite crystal with axes,
(b) albite feldspar crystal, and (c)
rhodonite crystal*

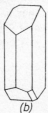

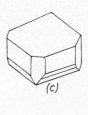

(c)

(b)

Triclinic System

The triclinic or anorthic system has three axes which are all of unequal length and which are all inclined to each other. There is a centre of symmetry but no symmetry planes or axes. *Figure 26.22* shows crystals of this system. Axinite, rhodonite, the plagioclase feldspars and turquoise crystallize in the triclinic system.

Hexagonal System

The hexagonal system has four axes, three of which are lateral axes of equal length which intersect at 60 degrees to each other, while the fourth,

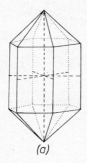

(a)

*Figure 26.23. The crystallographic
axes and examples of crystals of the
hexagonal system: (a) crystal with
axes, (b) apatite crystal, and (c)
beryl crystal*

(b)

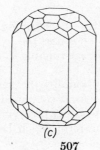

(c)

507

the vertical axis is either longer or shorter than the lateral axes and is at right angles to the plane containing them. There are seven planes of symmetry and seven axes of symmetry (1 hexagonal and 6 digonal) and there is a centre of symmetry. *Figure 26.23* shows the axes of the hexagonal system and shows crystals of emerald and apatite which crystallize in the system, the latter having lower symmetry.

Rhombohedral (or Trigonal) System

The rhombohedral or trigonal system has similar axes to that of the hexagonal system, indeed, many crystallographers incorporate the rhombohedral and hexagonal systems together to form two divisions. The rhombohedral system has only three planes of symmetry (1 trigonal and 3 digonal axes). In this system the main axis is one of threefold symmetry and not

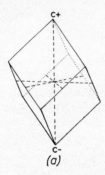

(a)

Figure 26.24. The crystal axes and some common forms of the trigonal system: (a) rhombohedron with axes, (b) tourmaline crystal, and (c) corundum crystal

(b)

(c)

sixfold as in the hexagonal system. There is a centre of symmetry. *Figure 26.24* shows the axes and examples of crystals of the rhombohedral system. The important gems ruby, sapphire and tourmaline, as well as such rarer gems as benitoite and phenakite crystallize in the rhombohedral system.

Lettering of Crystallographic Axes

There is a convention regarding the lettering of the crystallographic axes in which the vertical axis is known as the 'c' axis, that running from right to left is the 'b' axis, and the one running from front to back is the 'a' axis. The forms of many crystals have special names applied to them. These are the prism whose faces parallel the vertical axis and intersect two lateral axes. The pinacoid: a form composed of two faces which are parallel to two (in the hexagonal system three) crystallographic axes. The pyramid: the name given to the form which has the faces intersecting three axes, while a dome has faces which intersect the vertical axis and one other and is parallel to a third (*Figure 26.25*).

The crystallographer has special notations to describe the faces on a crystal with reference to the crystallographic axes, the most used being the three-figure index method devised by W. H. Miller, hence known as Miller indices, in which the numerals represent the reciprocal of the intercepts which the face in question makes with the crystal axes. Thus the octahedral face, which cuts each of the three axes 'a', 'b' and 'c' at equal distances from the origin has the symbol 111, and the cube face which cuts only one axis and is parallel to the other two has the symbol 100. In the case of the hexagonal system the pinacoid face has a four-figure symbol as it cuts the

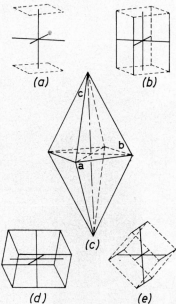

Figure 26.25. The forms of crystals: (a) basal pinacoid, (b) the prism, (c) the pyramid, (d) and (e) are dome forms

vertical axis and is parallel to the three lateral axes. This is therefore the 0001 face. These symbols will not be discussed further for they are an aspect of pure crystallography rather than gemmology.

DISTORTED CRYSTALS

Most of the crystals found in nature have not grown under ideal conditions. Although the angles between like faces of these 'distorted' crystals are constant for the mineral, owing to some faces having grown at the expense of others, their aspect appears very different from the ideal crystal and can appear to have the symmetry of another crystal system. *Figure 26.26* illustrates how quartz crystals can show distorted growth.

A crystal having the full symmetry of the system is termed a holohedral, or holosymmetrical, crystal. Some crystals, however, possess only half the number of faces required by the symmetry of the system to which they belong and such crystals are termed hemihedral crystals. Crystals which exhibit different forms at either end of the crystal are termed hemimorphic crystals, and such 'polar' crystals are said to show hemimorphism. Crystals showing good faces are said to be euhedral and those which do not as anhedral.

Crystals may occur in groups which are commonly irregularly related to one another, but sometimes the faces and edges of the crystals are in parallel arrangement with other crystals in the group and usually joined to them. Such crystals are said to show parallel growth, or parallel grouping (*Figure 26.27*).

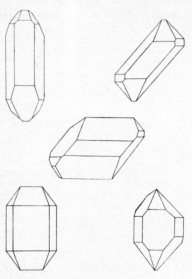

Figure 26.26. Distorted quartz crystals

Figure 26.27. A tourmaline crystal showing parallel growth

Twin Crystals

Many crystals are 'twinned', that is they are composed of two individuals in such a way that one half is in reverse position to the other and could be brought to parallel position by rotation through 180 degrees. The plane dividing the twin crystal is called the twin plane and the axis about which rotation is necessary to produce parallel position is termed the twin axis and this is usually perpendicular to the twin plane. The twin crystal has from the commencement of its growth been a twin and physical rotation of the two parts has not occurred.

There are various types of twin crystals, such as the simple, or contact twin, the most important of which is the spinel twin where one half of the octahedron is in reverse position producing the flattened star-shaped or triangular crystals which are called macles in diamond nomenclature. Some types of twinning, particularly in the tetragonal system show geniculate (knee-shaped) forms. In interpenetrate twins the crystals have grown so

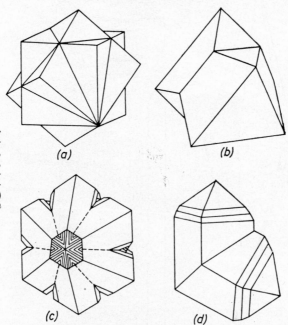

Figure 26.28. Some examples of twin crystals: (a) interpenetrate twin of fluorite, (b) contact twin of spinel, (c) pseudo-hexagonal trilling of three rhombic crystals of alexandrite, (d) geniculate twin of zircon

mixed together that they cannot be divided into two halves; such a twinning is common in fluorspar. Repeated twinning occurs when the twins repeat three times (trillings), four times (fourlings) or six times (sixlings). Such types of repeated twinning often causes the crystal to appear to have a higher symmetry than it actually has. An example is the trilling of alexandrite. Repeated twinning of thin lamellar crystals often shows as parallel striations on a face or cleavage. This polysynthetic twinning is well shown by the plagioclase feldspars and is illustrated in *Figure 9.5*. Most twin crystals are characterized by their having re-entrant angles. *Figure 26.28* illustrates some types of twin crystals.

HABIT

The characteristic shape of a crystal is known as its habit (*Figure 26.29*). While the interfacial angles are always the same for crystals of the same mineral, the forms of crystals can differ greatly, and for reasons which are not clearly understood. In gem minerals it has been noticed that a different habit can occur in crystals of the same mineral which come from different localities, or are of a different colour. Sapphire crystals from Ceylon take the habit of a bipyramid while others from Montana are short prismatic in habit. Aquamarine is usually found as long prismatic crystals, while pink beryl (morganite) usually forms crystals which are short and tabular. Other types of habit are octahedral (diamond and spinel), dodecahedral (garnet), bladed as in kyanite and acicular, in slender needle-like crystals such as are found in rutilated quartz.

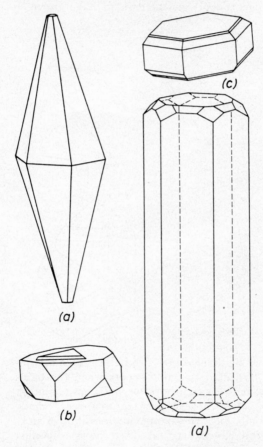

Figure 26.29. Habit in crystals: (a) Ceylon sapphire, (b) Montana sapphire, (c) pink beryl, (d) aquamarine

PITS AND STRIATIONS

Many crystals exhibit small pits (etch marks) (*Figure 26.30*) or striations on their faces and such marks are useful in showing whether the faces belong to the same form. They may also give an indication of the symmetry, a triangular pit for instance indicates a threefold symmetry at right angles to the face on which it occurs. The striations are due to an entirely different cause. In this case the markings are the result of oscillation between two

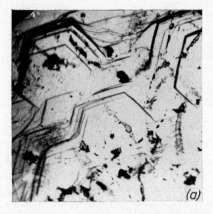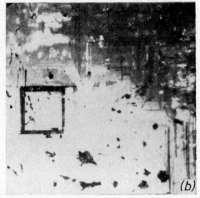

Figure 26.30. Etch marks on the faces of a beryl crystal: (a) hexagonal markings on the basal pinacoid, (b) rectangular markings on the prism face

(By courtesy of B. W. Anderson)

forms, thus the horizontal striations on the prism faces of a quartz crystal are the result of oscillation between the prism face and the rhombohedral face. Likewise the striations in alternate directions on the faces of a pyrites cube, which illustrates the lower symmetry, are due to similar oscillations between the cube face and the edges of the pyritohedron (*Figure 26.31*).

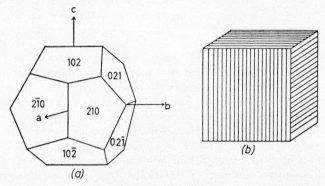

Figure 26.31. The pyritohedron and the cube are two common forms in which iron pyrites crystallize. The striations in alternate directions on adjacent faces of the cube are the traces of the edges of the faces of the pyritohedron which, as shown by the protruding axes (arrows), are at right angles to the crystal axes

POLYMORPHISM

When a mineral has a chemical composition the same as another mineral but crystallizes in a different system or class, the effect is termed dimorphism, or collectively polymorphism. For example diamond and graphite are both carbon but crystallize in the cubic and hexagonal system respectively and the rhombohedral calcite has the same chemical make-up as the orthorhombic aragonite.

17+G.

CHAPTER 27

HARDNESS, CLEAVAGE AND FRACTURE

HARDNESS

Bound up with the atomic bonding of a substance are the properties of hardness, cleavage and fracture. A high degree of hardness in a precious stone is necessary for only hard substances can take and retain a good polish. Though it may seem absurd to say that a stone 'looks hard' it is in fact true that an experienced eye can judge to some extent the hardness of a cut stone by the quality of the polish on its facets, as hardness and refractive index are the two factors which govern the lustre of a stone.

Although the general meaning of hardness is well enough understood it is less easy to define the term, since there are at least two types of hardness; that measured by the metallurgist, who presses some kind of indenter on to the surface, and the mineralogist's hardness, which is assessed by the resistance of a mineral to scratching or abrasion. What is probably the best definition is that given by Osmond: 'Hardness is that property possessed by solid bodies in varying degree to defend the integrity of their form against causes of permanent deformation and the integrity of their surface against causes of division'. This still gets no nearer, however, to expressing hardness in numerical terms.

Mohs's Scale

Probably the first to describe and use a method of measuring hardness was Réaumur who, in 1722, investigated the results of pressing together the edges of two right-angled prisms made of the substances to be compared. A far more practical means of assessing hardness was proposed by the German mineralogist Friedrich Mohs who, in 1822, after extensive experiments, chose ten well known and easily procurable minerals and arranged them in order of their 'scratch hardness' to serve as standards of comparison. Although the numbers of Mohs's list have no quantitive meaning, it is commonly known as Mohs's scale, and still forms the universally accepted standard of hardness amongst mineralogists and gemmologists. Mohs's scale is as follows:

10. Diamond	5. Apatite
9. Sapphire	4. Fluorspar
8. Topaz	3. Calcite
7. Quartz	2. Gypsum
6. Orthoclase feldspar	1. Talc

The numbers on Mohs's list are not quantities, they represent an order only. Diamond is enormously harder than any other mineral, and the gap between 10 and 9 on the list is far greater than that between any other of the numbers. The only substances with hardness between 9 and 10 are the artificially prepared abrasives carborundum (silicon carbide) and boron carbide, to which must now be added borazon (boron nitride) which is said to have a hardness near to that of diamond.

The number 7 on Mohs's scale is an important one, as any gemstone must be at least as hard as this if it is to withstand the action of grit in the air or on clothes, since this grit consists largely of particles of sand, that is, quartz. Stones such as peridot, the resplendent sphene, and the beautiful green demantoid garnet which do not reach this standard of hardness are thus only suitable for occasional wear in brooches, pendants and the like. Worn every day (in a ring, for instance) they would soon lose their lustre. Opal, and still more, pearl, coral and amber, are also relatively soft, and yet much worn in jewellery. Here, however, the case is somewhat different, for such stones are fashioned with curved surfaces and faint scratches are less of a blemish than where highly polished facets are concerned.

Brittleness

A hard stone is not necessarily a tough stone: despite its tremendous hardness, even diamond is rather brittle, and would certainly not withstand a heavy blow on the anvil as legend would suggest. Zircon is notoriously brittle, at least so far as the surface is concerned, for the facet edges chip badly. Unmounted zircons should always be kept in a case where there is no danger of the stones touching one another, or if in a packet each stone should be separately wrapped in a screw of tissue paper.

By special techniques, metals can be grown as single crystals, and a piece of metal of this kind is found to be so weak that it can easily be torn asunder in the fingers. However, if the test piece is gently worked to and fro, it is found to become rapidly harder and tougher and stronger, as the result of the formation of a polycrystalline mass in place of the single crystal with its planes of weakness at the mercy of any sudden stress. Another analogy that can be used to illustrate the same point is plywood, which in quite thin sheets is remarkably strong and resistant to any attempt to split it, whereas the individual sheets of which it is composed are flexible and easily broken.

Thus it is that substances such as the jade minerals and agate are among the toughest minerals known, while the black microcrystalline form of diamond known as carbonado combines the hardness of diamond with the toughness that single crystals of diamond cannot attain, and are thus very highly valued for industrial purposes.

Scratch Hardness Tests

For the gemmologist, scratch hardness, based on the standard minerals in Mohs's list, is the only practical basis for experiment, and can, for all its crudities, occasionally be very useful. The most popular way of applying hardness tests on minerals, apart from the indiscriminate use of a file, has been by means of hardness 'points' or 'pencils'. In these, suitable sharp fragments of the standard minerals on Mohs's scale are mounted in wooden or metal holders. Such implements are certainly convenient, and allow good control when applying the point to the mineral to be tested. With rough gemstones indeed, unless they are fine crystal specimens, there is nothing to be said against their use. The hardness point should be applied firmly but not forcibly to some inconspicuous part of the stone to be tested. The 'feel' of the point as it is drawn a short way along the specimen will at once reveal to an experienced worker whether the stone tested is harder or softer than the point—that is, whether it grips or 'skids'. The whole thing should be done on quite a small scale; a large scratch is a sign of careless work. Any mark produced should be rubbed with the moistened finger and examined with a lens to ensure that it is a true scratch and not powder from the point itself ground off by the harder specimen.

Lacking these special hardness points a small, hard, triangular file, hardness about $6\frac{1}{2}$, can be used. A good penknife or needle has a hardness about 6, while window glass may be reckoned as 5–$5\frac{1}{2}$, and a finger-nail as $2\frac{1}{2}$ on Mohs's scale.

If it really seems necessary to apply a hardness point or file to a faceted stone, never scratch the table or culet, as any mark here will be immediately visible—even a paste has some beauty and value, and should not be spoiled in the testing. Work therefore as near to the girdle as possible, or on the girdle itself if the stone be unmounted. When testing faceted stones, however, it is far better to work the other way round, that is, to let the specimen to be tested act as the 'hardness point' against polished plates of standard substances, such as sapphire (synthetic or natural), topaz, and quartz. Pieces of these can be obtained from a lapidary, and should cost very little, as they need not be of gem quality. Failing this source of supply, the smoother parts of a sapphire boule, a cleavage surface of white or yellow topaz, and the smooth face on a quartz crystal will serve perfectly well, and window glass, of course, is universally available.

Sclerometer

One of the earliest attempts to measure hardness in terms of relative numerical values was by means of an instrument termed a sclerometer. In one form of this, the surface to be tested was fixed horizontally on a small carriage, which could be moved by means of a string passing over a pulley. A steel or diamond point attached to a lever was allowed to rest upon the surface of the specimen. A hardness value was obtained either by determining the load which must be applied to the point in order to produce a visible scratch when the carriage was moved, or by finding what load must be added to the string passing over the pulley in order to move the carriage and produce a scratch when the point was subjected to a standard load. This method produces fairly consistent results with minerals of no great hardness, and serves to demonstrate very clearly the way in which scratch hardness varies according to the direction on the crystal in which the scratch was made. This can best be done by carrying out the tests on a well-developed crystal face, and turning the carriage into a number of different orientations. If now a drawing is made of the face in question and from the central point a number of lines are drawn of lengths corresponding to the hardness found in each direction, a perimeter drawn round the ends of these lines will show a pattern related to the symmetry of the face in question.

Variations in Hardness

Structure

Testing cut gemstones by such a method as the above would be quite impracticable, but it is mentioned here in order to show one way in which the variations in hardness in a crystal can be demonstrated under controlled conditions, and to drive home the point that the symmetry of crystals is a fundamental thing and not merely a matter of geometry. When it is said that the six faces of a cube are identical, this may be manifestly untrue so far as size goes in an actual specimen owing to accidents of growth, since crystals are seldom formed under 'ideal' conditions. However, the properties of the faces are identical, so that not only the hardness curve described above is the same on each, but curves showing heat conduction, elasticity and so on, will also be the same, as will be their reaction to chemical solvents, in which pittings and markings again revealing the underlying symmetry will be produced.

Though variations in hardness with crystal direction do exist, such differences are usually not very great, and would not be noticeable when carrying out the ordinary scratch tests used in practical testing. One mineral, kyanite, an aluminium silicate, occurs in pale blue bladed crystals which are occasionally cut as a gem. Parallel to the length of the blades, on the prominently developed pinacoid faces, it will be found that the crystal is easily scratched by the point of a knife blade whereas at right angles to this the knife blade will make no impression. In terms of Mohs's scale the hardness may be said to vary from $4\frac{1}{2}$ to 7.

Diamond is a mineral in which the variations in hardness, though not perhaps very great, are of high practical importance. It has already been stressed that diamond is harder than any other substance. To grind and polish diamond, therefore, the only possible abrasive is diamond itself; and it is only because one can abrade diamond along its softer directions by the action of its harder surfaces that cutting and polishing of the stone becomes commercially feasible. It has been found by x-ray study and in practice by diamond cutters that directions parallel to the crystal axes are those of least hardness. On a cube face there are thus two optimum polishing directions; on a rhombic dodecahedron there is one (parallel to the short diagonal), while faces of the octahedron are inclined equally to all three axes, and are thus the hardest and most intractable for working.

Locality and Colour

Variations in hardness due to crystal structure are to be expected, and can readily be explained. More difficult to understand are the variations according to locality and according to colour in the same species. Colour differences do, it is true, indicate slight differences in composition; enough perhaps to affect the hardness of the stone to some degree. Lapidaries maintain that ruby is 'softer on the wheel' than sapphire, and W. F. Eppler found that, in grinding, ruby was about 25 per cent softer than colourless sapphire. In sawing or drilling, ruby has proved itself at least as hard as sapphire, which shows how complex a property, or mixture of properties, 'hardness' is and how difficult to classify and measure.

The difference in the hardness of diamond according to its provenance is almost certainly not a true hardness difference, but a variation in what might be termed 'cuttability' due to stones from certain localities, such as Australia and Borneo, having irregularities in their texture. In grinding and polishing diamond it is essential for the craftsman to know and feel the direction of the cutting 'grain'. Where the rough crystal is twinned or several crystals have grown in together the cutter encounters resistant patches, which he terms a 'nart'; the result is as disconcerting to him as a knot in the even grain of a piece of wood is to the carpenter. Where a locality abounds in such stones they naturally gain an evil reputation among diamond manufacturers and are said to be too hard to cut. That there are no fundamental differences in the hardness of diamond (other than the hardness according to crystal direction already discussed) has been proved by quantitative tests with diamond powder derived from crystals from different localities, in which the powder from reputedly 'soft' diamonds such as those from the Congo has proved itself as efficient an abrasive as that derived from crystals from other districts.

Indenter Tests

When a reliable measurement of hardness is needed, as, for example, on a new or unknown gem mineral, perhaps the best method available today is a micro-indentation test of the 'Knoop' type, or the double-cone indenter developed by P. Grodzinski. The marks made in these tests are so small as to be invisible except under the microscope, and the long narrow shape of the indenter ensures that there is little risk of shattering the surface. The procedure in these tests is, however, too elaborate to be quickly undertaken, and the stone needs to be unmounted.

CLEAVAGE

One of the peculiarities of crystals is the tendency to break or split parallel to certain definite directions. This property of cleavage, as it is called, is one of the many consequences of that regular internal arrangement of the atoms which distinguishes crystals from amorphous solids. Some atomic layers, usually those representing an important face in the crystal, are strongly coherent, but are attached to the neighbouring layers above and below by relatively weak forces. Where such a condition exists there will naturally be a direction of weakness parallel to these layers which would constitute at least potential cleavage planes. In confirmation of this simplified version of the underlying causes of cleavage, it is in fact found that cleavage planes in any mineral are always parallel to a possible crystal face in that mineral. The word possible is used to indicate that the crystal face to which the cleavage is parallel is not necessarily actually present in each specimen, but is one which, by the laws of crystal symmetry might properly be formed in that mineral. For example, fluorspar is almost always found crystallized in the form of simple cubes, whereas the cleavage planes are parallel to the octahedral faces (*Figure 27.1*).

Types of Cleavage Surface

Cleavage surfaces can be highly perfect, as in mica, topaz, or calcite, or imperfect as in fluorspar. Again, in some minerals the cleavage is readily developed (calcite) in which case the term easy cleavage can be applied, or much less readily—difficult—as in peridot. By the use of these four adjectives an adequate description of any cleavage can be given. Thus fluorspar can be said to have an easy but imperfect octahedral cleavage, while the octahedral cleavage of diamond could be termed perfect but rather difficult. Calcite's rhombohedral cleavage is an example of 'easy and perfect' and the rather obscure basal cleavage of beryl fulfils the conditions for 'difficult and imperfect'. The popular term 'strong' cleavage might well be avoided as it is a most inappropriate adjective for a plane of weakness.

Cleavage surfaces are seldom entirely on the same level; there are usually some minutely 'stepped' places when underlying layers are exposed. The surface will often show a slightly pearly lustre due to its laminated nature and perhaps some iridescent colours where a thin film of air has penetrated some underlying layers of incipient cleavage. There is no pattern or structure to be seen in reflected light, unless it be the stepped effect already referred to, but modern interferometry has shown that even if a cleavage surface is quite perfect to the eye, steps of molecular dimensions occur at intervals. On crystal faces, however, no matter how perfect they may

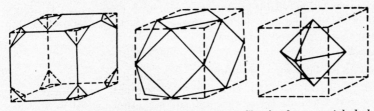

Figure 27.1. The cleavage directions of fluorspar. Showing how an octahedral form can be cleaved out of a cube crystal

seem, there is always some faint signs, in lines of growth, striations, etchings or other marks which distinguish them from either cleavage planes or polished flats. Such polished surfaces are seldom truly flat, which gives them an insipid look, and parallel and slightly curved polishing marks, due to the action of the polishing wheel, may often be detected.

Obviously, too easy a cleavage is not a desirable quality in a precious stone. It is a nuisance to the lapidary, since under the stresses, vibrations, and sudden changes of temperature inseparable from the grinding and polishing processes, flaws due to incipient cleavage are very likely to develop, or the stone may actually part along a cleavage plane. A further drawback in cutting stones with pronounced cleavage is the fact that a mineral cannot properly be polished along a cleavage plane (a fact well known to the diamond cutter) which adds a further complication to the cutting process. On the other hand, diamond cutters make good use of the octahedral cleavage of diamond in the preliminary shaping or trimming of stones of awkward shape before the grinding process begins, with great saving of time and labour.

Of the well-known gemstones, topaz has perhaps the most easy and perfect cleavage—parallel in this case to the basal plane of the crystal. A sudden shock, such as a fall on to the glass top of a dressing table, may well cause a topaz to snap in two, especially if it is in an elongated form, such as a drop-shaped ear pendant. The beautiful lilac-coloured kunzite is another gem with a notoriously easy cleavage, making cutting difficult; while the very name of the rare mineral euclase refers to its extreme readiness to part along the cleavage planes.

Parting

There is another effect akin to cleavage, but due to a different cause—in this case a tendency to split parallel to planes of weakness due to lamellar twinning. This phenomenon is known as parting, and the separation here can only occur at intervals dictated by the thickness of the twin layers instead of between any adjacent atomic planes parallel to the cleavage direction. Corundum is usually cited as a mineral which has well-developed parting parallel to the basal plane, and a less pronounced effect parallel to the rhombohedral faces. These are undoubtedly planes of weakness in the mineral but whether they are parting planes or true cleavages seems to be a moot point. The planes left by the parting are sometimes extremely perfect, and may be found in synthetic stones where there is no sign of lamellar twinning visible under the polarizing microscope. However, the point is chiefly one of academic interest, since the effects of parting and cleavage are very much the same.

Cleavage as Test for Gemstones

One can hardly say that cleavage forms a useful 'test' for certain gemstones, but a knowledge of cleavage can sometimes assist in arriving at a conclusion as to the nature of a gemstone. For example an 'aquamarine' showing two cleavage cracks at right angles to one another can be condemned at once as a synthetic spinel (which has cubic cleavage); and careful scrutiny of the girdle of a diamond under a lens or microscope will often reveal small chips of which the sides are composed of two of the four directions of the cleavage.

Direction of Cleavage

Where a mineral possesses a very easy cleavage, particularly if this is parallel to three or more directions so that the solid shapes bounded by cleavage planes can be induced, it may be quite difficult to break the stone in any other directions. If a crystal or cleavage rhomb of calcite is struck with a hammer or even pounded in a mortar, and the fragments studied, practically every tiny piece will be seen to be bounded by cleavage planes forming little rectangular blocks in which the interfacial angles are identical. Again, in the case of diamond powder, the grains when examined under the microscope will be found to be angular and bounded by cleavage surfaces, and it is these sharply angled fragments that make this material so efficient as an abrasive, in addition, of course, to its superlative hardness.

Quartz, spinel (natural) and garnet are amongst the gemstones which show practically no sign of cleavage.

TABLE 27.1
Minerals Showing Pronounced Cleavage

Mineral	No. of directions	Parallel to
Topaz	1	Basal pinacoid
Apophyllite	1	Basal pinacoid
Orthoclase	2	Basal and clino pinacoids
Euclase	1	Clinopinacoid
Fibrolite	1	Clinopinacoid
Epidote	1	Basal pinacoid
Kyanite	1	Macropinacoid
Spodumene	2	Prism
Diamond	4	Octahedron
Fluorspar	4	Octahedron
Calcite	3	Rhombohedron
Dioptase	3	Rhombohedron
Synthetic spinel	3	Cube
Blende	6	Dodecahedron

FRACTURES

Even in minerals which have easy cleavage, more random breakage can occur, and in minerals like quartz which have no pronounced cleavage such fractures as they are called are the rule rather than the exception. Many different terms have been used to describe the various types of fracture found in different minerals, but only two are sufficiently distinctive and frequent to be worth describing. The first of these, the shell-like conchoidal fracture, will be familiar as it is well shown by chipped glass (*Figure 27.2*).

Figure 27.2. Conchoidal fracture in the natural glass obsidian

This is the natural type of fracture to be expected when an amorphous substance (or indeed any substance with no pronounced plane of weakness) is struck a sharp blow at some definite point. A series of shock waves travel from the point of impact in the form of a cone, with this point as the apex. Under ideal conditions a form like a limpet (bulb of percussion) is produced, and this can be demonstrated by tapping sharply with a small hammer on a flat surface of flint. Conchoidal fracture is very typical in glass; where it is developed on a large scale in a gemstone it should certainly give rise to suspicion. However, it must be remembered that quartz, beryl, corundum or in fact any mineral, can on occasion show this type of fracture. The other type of fracture which should be mentioned is the hackly or splintery fracture found in tough, fibrous minerals such as nephrite jade.

CHAPTER 28

SPECIFIC GRAVITY

HISTORICAL ASPECTS

The differing degrees of 'heaviness' found in solids must have been recognized even by primitive man in handling implements of wood and stone, and later, of metal. In comparing the density of substances it is the weight of equal volumes, of course, that must be considered. The contrast between a bucketful of feathers, for instance, and a bucketful of lead would indeed be pretty striking; the one easily portable by a child and the other weighing nearly two hundredweight.

Equal volumes of liquids are easy to obtain for comparison, but how can one measure the volume of an irregular solid? Aristotle, as early as the fourth century B.C., saw that the answer could lie in measuring the amount of water it displaces when immersed, but it was the great mathematician Archimedes, in the following century, who first used displacement methods in practice, and we still speak of 'Archimedes' Principle' in this connexion. Another curious method of comparing densities used by the ancients was to make a copy of the object in wax and compare the actual weight with that of the wax model; a most time-consuming business.

The first actual density figures that have come down to us are due to an Arabian scientist, al Biruni, who lived about A.D. 1000, who actually evolved a crude form of 'specific gravity bottle' (*see* later). Some of al Biruni's results were very good. In more recent times, the most complete series of specific gravity figures ever compiled by one man from his own determinations is that given by M. J. Brisson in his book *Pésanteur spécifique des Corps* published in 1787, two years before the French Revolution. Brisson had access to the King's cabinet of minerals and gemstones, and the measurements, weight and specific gravity of such famous stones as the 'Pitt' or 'Regent' diamond are given in the work. Working with two accurate balances, weighing his specimens in air and either distilled water or pure rainwater at a temperature of 14° Réaumur—that is 17½°C—Brisson's results, when very large, pure specimens were available, were very good indeed.

NOMENCLATURE

Before considering the various methods by which the density of gemstones can best be measured, it will be as well to give the definitions of the terms used. The specific gravity of a substance is its weight compared with that of an equal volume of pure water at a temperature of 4°C. The density of a substance is its weight per unit volume, and its numerical value will of course depend upon the system of measures used. Density can be expressed,

522

for instance, in pounds per cubic foot. However, in scientific work density is always given in grammes per cubic centimetre, and since the gramme is fixed as being the weight of one cubic centimetre of pure water at 4°C, the density of a body has the same numerical value in these units as the specific gravity, and the terms can be used alternatively. The temperature of 4°C is chosen because this is the critical point at which water is at its most dense. In practice water at this temperature is never used. For very accurate work, a temperature correction can be applied from tables, but since only the third place of decimals is usually affected no temperature correction at all is needed for determinative purposes.

The abbreviation 'sp. gr.' is commonly used for specific gravity, while in scientific publications 'd' is used for density, often with an indication of the temperature of the experiment and the temperature of the water to which the comparison is referred. Thus d^{18}_4 would mean the density of the mineral at 18°C referred to water at 4°C. The coefficient of expansion of solids is in general far lower than for liquids, so that the density hardly varies measurably within the range of room temperatures.

One condition, unfortunately, is essential before the specific gravity (density) of a stone can be measured, that is it must be free from its setting. This is perhaps the main reason why this important determinative method has been so disregarded by jewellers. There are two main methods, although there are many modifications of each; they are known as the hydrostatic method and the heavy liquid method. The hydrostatic method is probably the best means for getting accurate results on fairly large individual specimens, but it needs a sensitive balance, some calculation, and 15 min or more of time for each determination. Heavy liquids, on the other hand, are rapid in action where only an approximate result is needed (for instance, to find out whether a cat's-eye is a chrysoberyl or a quartz). They need no calculation, no balance, and give just as good results with tiny specimens as with large ones. Flotation methods also hold the advantage where fine comparisons between stones of very similar density are concerned (for example between natural and synthetic emeralds), and for the rapid sorting of whole parcels of stones according to their densities. Heavy liquids will be discussed first.

HEAVY LIQUID METHOD OF MEASURING SPECIFIC GRAVITY

If a stone is placed in a liquid of lower density than itself it will naturally sink: but if it is placed in a liquid of greater density than itself it will float at the surface. In a liquid of the same density it will remain freely suspended in any position, neither rising or falling. All that is needed then to assess the density of an unknown stone, is to slip it into a series of tubes containing liquids of known density, and observe whether it rises or falls. In theory the method is simplicity itself and in practice too it is undoubtedly the most useful of all methods, though there are snags. One of these is the difficulty of finding liquids dense enough to float the stones of high specific gravity, and for the upper values it is necessary to use a solution which is both poisonous and expensive.

Types of Liquids

A large number of liquids have been recommended from time to time, but three are all that are needed to cover the range from 1·0 to 4·15; intermediate values being obtainable as required by dilution. The three liquids are bromoform, methylene iodide, and an aqueous solution of thallium salts, conveniently known as Clerici solution. To these may be added acetylene tetrabromide as a possible alternative to bromoform, and another lighter liquid would be needed to dilute these if lower densities are needed. A detailed account of the properties of these liquids is given below.

Bromoform

Bromoform ($CHBr_3$) has a composition analogous to the well-known anaesthetic, chloroform ($CHCl_3$), and has a rather similar ethereal smell and sweetish taste. Bromoform when pure is a colourless, mobile fluid, having a density of 2·90 at 15°C, and with a refractive index of 1·598 at 19°C. The freezing and boiling points are 6°C and 149°C respectively. This liquid should be protected from the action of light, as also should methylene iodide and in fact all organic compounds where a halogen replaces the hydrogen in the molecule. Keeping a piece of copper foil or a few copper turnings in the liquid will to some extent avoid this darkening and may after a time clear darkened liquid. The liquids are best kept in dark bottles in a dark cupboard. The density of bromoform as supplied is apt to vary somewhat between 2·85 and 2·90, but this slight difference is not very important so far as gemstones are concerned. In ordering bromoform from any supplier it is wise to stipulate on a pure bromoform with a density of 2·90, as there is a pharmaceutical product containing alcohol which has too low a density to be useful.

Acetylene Tetrabromide

Acetylene tetrabromide, or Sym.-tetrabromoethane as the chemist may prefer to call it, has the formula $CHBr_2 . CHBr_2$. It is a nearly colourless liquid when fresh, and has a density of 2·96 and a refractive index of 1·638 at room temperature. Though it has a slightly higher density than bromoform it does not form such clear and stable solutions, and is thus less in favour

Methylene Iodide

Methylene iodide (CH_2I_2) is undoubtedly the most useful of all liquids to the gemmologist. Not only does it have a higher density than most other pure liquids (between 3·32 and 3·33 at room temperature) but it also has a very high refractive index (1·745 at 18°C) which gives it great value in both these important fields. When fresh, it is a pale yellowish-brown fluid, freezing at 5°–6°C, and boiling at 180°C. It is volatile, and has a distinctive smell. It has a marked tendency to turn brown or black if exposed to light, due to decomposition with release of free iodine. This can readily be checked by keeping pieces of copper strip in the bottle containing the fluid, and a badly affected sample can be cleaned by degrees in similar manner, though shaking with mercury is quicker.

It will be seen from the formulae of these compounds that they are essentially substituted hydrocarbons which are compounds of carbon and hydrogen only and as such are not generally miscible with water. Fortunately, however, for the gemmologist's purpose they are miscible over a wide range with many hydrocarbons such as benzene, toluene, and so on, all of which are of much lower specific gravity rendering the production of liquids of special density easily accomplished. Care must be taken to see that no water, water-wet stones or tongs, come into contact with them, as the result will be a messy emulsion.

Clerici Solution

Just the reverse is true of the last heavy liquid to be mentioned—the Clerici solution. This is a concentrated solution in water of two very soluble thallium salts—the formate and malonate—in equimolecular proportions. It is named after the Italian chemist who first proposed its use in 1907. Being an aqueous solution, it must be diluted with distilled water only, and any tongs or specimens placed in the solution should be cleaned carefully so as to be free from traces of organic fluids adhering from previous tests. The actual density of Clerici solution will of course vary with its saturation, and the amount of salts in the solution at saturation point will in turn vary with the temperature to considerable degree. At room temperatures in warm weather a stable liquid of density about 4·2 can be obtained, but with a liquid of this strength some of the salts will crystallize out in cold weather.

While it is convenient to have some concentrated Clerici solution in stock for rapidly 'gingering up' a sample which has become too dilute for the purpose in hand, in practice Clerici solution slightly diluted to a density of 4·0 is the highest density liquid likely to be needed, and this, in a tightly closed bottle, should hold its density indefinitely. Clerici solution is practically colourless when fresh, becoming a little yellowish in time. It is far more viscous than the other liquids, is poisonous, and attacks the skin in a rather unpleasant manner. It is very slow to filter and is rather a messy substance to handle. It is also rather expensive. Much, however, can be forgiven a liquid that can float corundum at room temperatures; and being an aqueous solution it has the advantage that it may be re-concentrated by simple evaporation without loss of the essential thallium salts, while to recover the other 'organic' heavy liquids in a pure state usually means a distillation process.

Lower Density Liquids

A few other liquids, useful in the lower density ranges, may conveniently be mentioned here. Ethylene dibromide ($C_2H_4Br_2$) is a volatile colourless liquid with an ethereal odour, which has a density of 2·18–2·19 at room temperatures. The chief use of ethylene dibromide is in hydrostatic weighing as described later. Carbon tetrachloride (CCl_4) is a very volatile liquid boiling at 76°C. It has a peculiar smell, a low surface tension and is non-inflammable. It is a powerful solvent for fats and is extensively used as a 'dry' cleaner for clothes. It has a low refractive index (1·44) and a rather high density (1·59), and on occasion has been used as a medium for hydrostatic weighing. Its heavy vapour, however, copiously given off even at room temperatures, is apt to vitiate the true swing of the balance and is therefore not recommended. Monobromonaphthalene exists in two forms, according to the position of the bromine in the molecule. It is the liquid *alpha* form, a rather oily fluid, smelling somewhat like its parent naphthalene, which is variously used as an immersion medium, as a refractometer contact liquid, and as a diluent for heavy liquids. Its formula is $C_{10}H_7Br$ and it boils at 279°C. The refractive index is 1·66 and the density is 1·49. It is not very volatile, and is not easily removed from glass dishes, stones or hands.

Benzene and Toluene

To complete the list of useful liquids are the two common aromatic hydrocarbons benzene (C_6H_6), which has a boiling point of 80°C, a density of 0·88 and a refractive index of 1·50, and toluene ($C_6H_5 . CH_3$) which boils at 111°C, has a density of 0·87, and a refractive index of 1·49. Benzene is highly inflammable and is chiefly useful as a cleaning agent and as a temporary diluent for heavy liquids. Toluene (often known as toluol) is not quite so volatile or odorous. It is a good medium for hydrostatic weighing.

Method of Using Liquids

Liquid Containers

Having enumerated the most important liquids, it remains to describe how best they may be used. This must depend very largely, of course, on the stones most frequently tested by the user, how often the tests are needed and how accurately he wishes to assess the density of his stones. The nature and size of the containers will be contingent on these factors and also on the dimensions of the stones likely to be tested. As the liquids are all somewhat costly economy is essential, therefore the containers should be as small as possible consistent with their having wide enough mouths to allow the free entry of tongs for introducing and recovering the specimens, and a sufficient depth to give a column of liquid in which the rate of rise or fall of the specimens tested can be fairly judged.

The small wide-mouthed bottles with Bakelite screw caps, mainly used for solid chemicals, are well suited for the job, and are inexpensive, although Bakelite is rendered brittle by the vapour of many of these liquids. Weighing bottles with ground-glass stoppers are more attractive, have a better depth in proportion to their width, and enable the behaviour of the specimens to be observed more easily, but they are more expensive and rather fragile. Corked specimen tubes about $2\frac{1}{2}$ in. deep by $\frac{3}{4}$ in. wide, are quite effective, they are cheap and have a flat base so will stand upright on a plane surface. It is a wise plan when using weighing bottles or specimen tubes to house them up to about three-quarters of their depth in holes bored in a heavy block of wood, in which the tubes fit snugly when not actually in use, secure from damage and shielded from the light. Each tube should have a label near the top showing clearly its approximate density, and the cork or stopper should preferably be labelled also. Stock bottles of the pure liquids should be kept in reserve in a dark cupboard.

Density Range

So much for the housing of the heavy liquids: now as to their density range. An imposing array of tubes containing liquids with closely graded density values have little value for general work. It is better to limit the stock of ready-mixed liquids to two or three preferred values—using pure liquids where possible, as these have densities which are invariable apart from temperature fluctuations—and mixing a special liquid to solve any particular problem which may require measurement of a density not very close to any of the standard set. An advantage of using pure bromoform or methylene iodide (apart from knowing their density to be reliable) is that one can pour them out when a test is needed into a container suitable for the occasion, and need not be too stingy with the quantity. After the test is finished, the liquid can be filtered back into the stock bottle, thus keeping it in a clean state.

A suitable range of density liquids which time has found to be most convenient are as follows:

(1) Bromoform, diluted with toluene or monobromonaphthalene to the density of quartz—sp. gr. 2·65.

(2) Pure bromoform—sp. gr. 2·90 (usually 2·86).

(3) Methylene iodide, diluted with toluene, bromoform or monobromonaphthalene to match pink tourmaline—sp. gr. 3·06.

(4) Pure methylene iodide—sp. gr. 3·32.

(5) Clerici solution diluted with distilled water to match sapphire—sp. gr. 3·99.

Another Clerici solution diluted to match diamond (sp. gr. 3·52) might be quite useful and a diluted bromoform liquid in which calcite slowly sinks (sp. gr. 2·70) is useful for testing emerald.

It should always be a rigid rule to clean both specimen and tongs before placing them into any of the liquids. In the case of the Clerici solution a beaker of water should be handy in which to rinse the stone and tongs after immersion. With the other liquids which are more volatile, thorough wiping with a dry cloth is usually sufficient; if a cleaning fluid is needed this should on no account be water (with which they are immiscible) but should be benzene, toluene or lighter petrol.

Formerly it was the fashion to keep a check on the density of the mixed solutions by using two stones of established density to act as 'indicators'. Thus a bromoform solution might have as indicators quartz (floating) and aquamarine (sinking to the bottom), serving to show the density of the liquid to lie between the values of 2·65 and 2·70. This is a fairly practical method where, as in the instance given, the indicators have specific gravity values fairly close to one another. A more accurate and simpler plan is to use only one indicator, and to choose one which has the density you wish the liquid to be. Slight departure from the ideal of exact suspension of such an indicator will not usually matter, and a more serious rise or fall can be rectified quite easily by further dilution or addition of pure liquid as the case may need.

With practice a close approximation to the density of a stone can be obtained by watching its speed of rise or fall in a known liquid, provided that this has a density not too far removed from that of the stone—say ±0·10. Even a very rapid rise or fall will give a clue. It is unwise to test porous stones in heavy liquids, as their colour may be affected; turquoise is the chief stone to be careful about in this connexion. Provided that clean bromoform solutions are used, and the immersion is not prolonged, pearls do not seem to be adversely affected by tests in heavy fluid.

So far, heavy liquids have been considered in their most usual function of providing an approximate density value for gemstones, but it must always be remembered that these liquids, within their range, provide perhaps the most accurate of all methods for obtaining the exact density of an immersed solid, for by careful dilution of the heavier liquid a point can be reached whereat the stone remains exactly suspended in the fluid, neither rising nor falling wherever it is placed. This matching process, adding the diluent drop by drop, and stirring thoroughly after each addition to ensure a homogeneous fluid, requires a good deal of patience; there is a tendency to overshoot the mark in a desire to speed up the experiment. When an exact match has been obtained, it will only remain a match for that particular temperature, the slightest warming with the hand, for instance, will cause the specimen to sink owing to the slight lowering of the density of the liquid as it expands on warming. Thus for really accurate work some form of temperature control is needed, more particularly in the subsequent task of finding the exact density of the liquid, which now remains to be done.

Methods of Finding the Density of Liquids

There are a number of ways of finding the density of the liquid and these will now be outlined.

Pycnometer method—A pycnometer or 'specific gravity bottle' (*Figure 28.1*) in its simplest form is just a nicely made little bottle with an accurately

Figure 28.1. The pycnometer or 'specific gravity bottle'

ground-in glass stopper pierced with a capillary opening. The weight of water contained in the bottle when completely filled at a stated temperature is engraved on the vessel, and may be 5, 10, 25, or 50 g. Although usually very accurately made, it is wise to check this figure by weighing the bottle empty and dry and then when filled completely with distilled water at a known temperature. The pycnometer is filled and the stopper is then carefully slid into position and gently pressed home. This will cause an overflow of water through the capillary opening. The bottle should then be wiped dry with a clean cloth or duster, taking care that the heat of the hands does not affect it. The bottle should also be examined to make sure that no air bubbles have become entrapped when the stopper was introduced. The dry weight of the bottle subtracted from the weight when filled with water will then give the weight of the enclosed water at the temperature of the experiment. If this temperature is not indicated by the maker, a comparison can still be made by reference to tables giving the density of water at all room temperatures.

The pycnometer having been calibrated (preferably on some earlier occasion, since it is essential that it is now quite dry) the 'unknown' heavy liquid should now be run in through a small funnel as quickly as possible, filling it to the brim, inserting the stopper, and wiping away the slopover as in the case of water. To avoid mess, this operation should be done on a saucer or some form of dish. As soon as the flask has been dried, it should be weighed. The weight of the fluid contained compared with that of the water gives an accurate measure of its density. The process is not a very difficult one where mixtures of bromoform or of methylene iodide are concerned. With Clerici solution it is far less easy and pleasant, owing to the difficulty of removing the overflowed liquid, which cannot just be wiped off, but needs to be rinsed off by means of a jet from a wash-bottle. Since one does not want to use more liquid than necessary the smaller sizes of pycnometer (5 or 10 ml) are the best, though they are less easy to obtain.

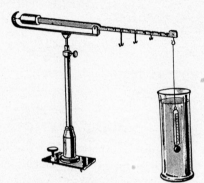

Figure 28.2. The Westphal balance

Modification of pycnometer method—What amounts to a rapid variation of the above is to withdraw 5 ml of the solution by means of a pipette (which is a tube with a small bulb in the middle and a tapered outlet, marked in its upper part with a ring up to which the liquid must be sucked) and discharging the contents of the pipette into a weighed beaker, which is then immediately reweighed and the increase noted.

The Westphal balance—This is an efficient though simple balance, with one long arm marked at equal distances from the pivot with nine notches and with a hook on the end. The other arm is simply a short counterpoise. A standard plunger, which is also a thermometer, is suspended from the hook and is exactly balanced by the counterpoise (*Figure 28.2*). If the plunger is immersed in a narrow cylinder of water, a wire rider of unit value must be added to the hook to restore the balance. In order for this to happen, the makers have chosen as their unit a rider having a weight that is exactly equal to that of the water displaced by the standard plunger. If a liquid of density 2·0 were substituted for the water, two such weights would be needed to produce an even balance. With pure bromoform of density 2·9, a third weight of the same value would have to be placed on the ninth notch in addition to the two unit weights at the end. With a sample of methylene iodide which has a density of 3·324, three unit weights would be needed from the end hook, one unit weight on the third notch, one tenth-unit weight on the second notch, and one hundredth-unit weight on the fourth notch. From this it can be seen how by immersing the plunger to standard depth in a liquid of unknown density, this density can be determined quite quickly and without calculation by finding the number, denomination and position on the balance arm of the weights needed to bring the apparatus to an even balance. The appropriate rider-type weights representing the various decimal values are provided with the balance. The chief fault of the balance is that a considerable quantity of liquid is required.

By substituting a pan and clip, in which specimens can be held, in place of the normal plunger, the Westphal balance can be adapted to determine

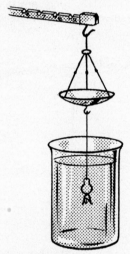

Figure 28.3. A modification of the Westphal balance

the density of solids if these are not large (*Figure 28.3*). With the pan suspended from the hook at the end of the graduated arm, and the clip below it immersed in water, it will be found necessary to add rider weights to the arm to achieve a counterpoise. Let the reading of these (using the decimal notation as outlined above according to their positions on the arm) be A. Clear these weights, place the stone to be tested in the pan, and again add weights to obtain a counterpoise. Let these weights total B. Finally, the process is repeated with the stone held in the clip, immersed in water below the pan. If the weights added on this occasion total C, then the specific gravity of the specimen is given by $(A - B)/(C - B)$. This is, of course, only one form of hydrostatic weighing which will be discussed later in this chapter.

The hydrometer method—A hydrometer is a convenient instrument for measuring quickly the density of a liquid. It usually consists of a glass bulb loaded with shot or mercury, with a narrow stem above it marked with a

density scale (*Figure 28.4*). The instrument is so calibrated that, when immersed in a fluid, it takes up a level such that the correct density is read off
from that part of the stem at the surface of the liquid. With a long stem and
widely spaced scale, such an instrument can give an accurate reading to
three places of decimals in a matter of seconds, but the range of so accurate
a hydrometer would be very limited, and it would require an inordinately
great amount of liquid to float it. A convenient compromise is to have several
quite small hydrometers, each of which cover a limited range of densities.
Such instruments, covering the ranges 2·5–3·0, 3·0–3·5 and 3·5–4·0,
would fulfil most practical needs. Such instruments are not obtainable from
stock but they could be made at no great cost by hydrometer manufacturers.

Refractive index method—The liquid density can also be found by taking
the refractive index of the solution. The fact that Clerici solution is rather
viscous, poisonous and expensive and can be used only in small quantities,

Figure 28.4. The hydrometer

makes the above four methods not very suitable for this liquid. With the
method about to be described, however, the reverse is true, since Clerici
solution is well adapted for measurement by this technique.

Where two liquids are completely miscible, and one liquid has a higher
refractive index and density than the other, both the refractive index and
the density of any mixture of the two will depend upon the proportion in
which they are mixed, and there is a direct connexion between the density
and the refractive index of such mixtures. In the case of Clerici solution,
the addition of water, which has a refractive index of only 1·334, to the
concentrated solution, which has an index over 1·67, has the effect of lowering both the density and refractive index very drastically. By carefully
diluting a sample of Clerici solution so that three indicators of different
known densities are in turn caused to suspend in a solution, and checking
the refractive index at each stage on a refractometer, a graph showing the
relation between the refractive index and density of the sample of Clerici
solution for any intermediate point can be prepared, for the 'plot' of the
three indicators should lie in a straight line. Samples of Clerici solution do
not vary greatly in this matter and the graph (*Figure 28.5*) will serve fairly
well. In any case the slope of the line will be the same for every sample of
Clerici solution, so that if, in the case of any particular specimen, the
result obtained from the use of the graph is known to be, say, 0·03 too high,

the same correction should apply to a specimen of any other density. The method is extremely rapid once a graph is available, and has the advantage that small quantities of liquid are needed. If great accuracy is aimed at, a very careful matching of specimen and liquid is necessary, and the refractive index must then be taken quickly and accurately, using sodium light, and estimating as closely as possible to three decimal places.

Mixtures of bromoform and methylene iodide, between which there is a good range both of density and refractive index, can also be utilized effectively by this general method. Where only an occasional experiment of this kind is carried out, there is no need to go to the trouble of making a graph, since the density can be calculated by simple proportion. For example, pure methylene iodide with a density of 3·324 and a refractive index

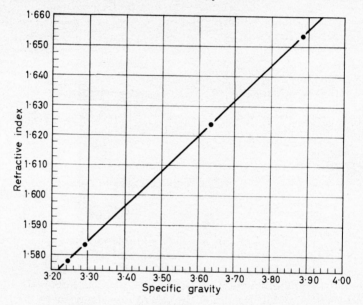

Figure 28.5. Graph of density/refractive index of Clerici solution
(After Payne, Franklin and Anderson)

of 1·745, was carefully diluted with bromoform—density 2·895 and refractive index 1·598—until the yellow stone under test remained suspended in the stirred mixture. The refractive index of the mixture was found to be 1·697. In using these two liquids a density difference of (3·324 − 2·895) 0·429 corresponded with a refractive index difference of (1·745 − 1·698) 0·147. The critical mixture showed a lowering of refractive index from that of pure methylene iodide of (1·745 − 1·697) 0·048. If the corresponding drop in density be denoted by x, the formula should read

$$\frac{0\cdot429}{0\cdot147} = \frac{x}{0\cdot048}$$

Therefore x equals (0·048 × 0·429)/0·147, which works out at 0·140. The density of the mixture (and of the specimen) will thus be (3·324 − 0·140) 3·184.

Indicator method—If a complete range of indicators, differing in density in steps of only 0·01 or 0·02, were available for the required range, this would provide a rapid and sure means of obtaining an estimate, sufficiently close for all practical purposes, of the density of any heavy liquid. Such a comprehensive set of indicators could be made from glasses but would be expensive. An indicator set, far less comprehensive but nonetheless most useful, is marketed by the Gemmological Association. The indicators are made of optical glass and the density value is engraved on each. Aside from this, there is a good range of minerals which can act as indicators, and by intelligent use, if necessary by including pieces of non-gem minerals, it is usually possible to make a close estimate of the density of an unknown stone suspended in a specially made heavy liquid mixture. Clear pieces of orthoclase (2·56), quartz (2·65), calcite (2·71), fluorspar (3·18), green peridot (3·34), white topaz (3·56), chrysoberyl (3·72) and natural or synthetic sapphire (3·99) are easily obtainable and can be relied upon to have densities of the values stated.

One other very accurate method of measuring the density of a liquid will be described a little later, when discussing the use of ethylene dibromide in hydrostatic weighing.

HYDROSTATIC WEIGHING

Water

Despite its slowness and certain other disadvantages, hydrostatic weighing remains the most practical method for accurate density determinations, provided the specimen tested is not too small. The chief requirements are a good balance, a metal or wooden bridge to straddle the left-hand pan of the balance, a beaker of about a 100 ml size, and some fine and coarse wire for suspending the stone in the liquid. A glass thermometer reading to 50°C or 100°C is also needed for accurate work.

Either a chemical or a diamond balance can be used. The former will probably be the more sensitive, the latter the more stable and rapid in use. For laboratory work, one of the new types of aperiodic balance is ideal, since it combines accuracy with speed of weighing, and obviates the use of small weights.

First weigh the stone as accurately as possible. It does not matter whether the weights used are carats or grammes, since both are based on the metric system, which makes calculation easy. Estimate to 0·005 carat or to 1 mg, according to the weights used. Place the bridge over the left-hand pan in such a way as not to impede the free swing of the balance. Fill the beaker three-quarters full of distilled or boiled water and place it on the bridge. Avoid using water direct from the tap, not because of the impurities it contains, which will not appreciably affect the density, but because it contains a lot of air, and tenacious air-bubbles will form on the stone and wire cage and falsify the result unless prevented or removed.

A spiral wire cage, formed from fairly thick copper or brass wire and capable of holding a stone of from 1 to 50 carats should have been previously prepared, and provided with the finest possible suspending wire consistent with strength. The suspending wire should end in a generous loop which can slip over the lower hook at the left-hand end of the balance arm. The wire should be made of such a length that when in position the cage is immersed completely, but does not touch the bottom of the beaker (*Figure 28.6*).

The cage should now be suspended from the balance arm, with the spiral immersed in the beaker of water. Any bubbles seen should be removed with a camel's-hair brush (previously well wetted) and the empty cage then carefully weighed. Since this weight will vary only very slightly in subsequent experiments (owing to different temperatures, different amount of water in the beaker, and so on) it will save time to have a note of it in the weight box or some other handy place, though for work of any accuracy its exact weight must be checked on each occasion. An alternative method is to counterpoise the empty cage with a piece of wire cut to the appropriate weight, which can be hung from the hook of the opposite balance arm. If this is successfully done, no allowance for the weight of the cage need of course be made. To get an exact counterpoise for each occasion is, however, a

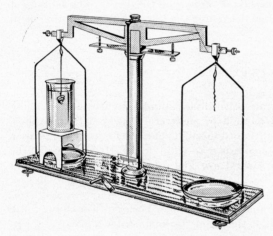

Figure 28.6. The balance set up for hydrostatic weighing

tricky business, and on the whole to subtract the weight of the cage each time is more to be recommended.

At this stage, it is usually best to grip the beaker with the left hand and the suspending wire with the right, and remove them both clear of the balance. The specimen to be tested can now be safely ensconced in the cage and freed from any bubbles before replacing the whole contraption and proceeding to weigh the stone in water.

This done, the necessary figures are to hand: it now remains to apply the formula. The calculation is simple, but it is surprising how often errors are made at this stage. First, subtract the weight of the empty cage from that of the stone and cage weighed together. This will give the weight of the stone alone in water W. Subtract this from the weight in air A, and divide the result into the weight in air. Thus, sp. gr. $= A/(A-W)$. For example:

Weight of stone in air . . . 8·405 carats
Weight of spiral in water . . 15·760 carats
Weight of spiral and stone in water . 22·145 carats

Thus, weight of stone in water equals (22·145 − 15·760) equals 6·385 carats. Therefore

$$\text{sp. gr.} = \frac{8 \cdot 405}{8 \cdot 405 - 6 \cdot 385} = 4 \cdot 161$$

Other things being equal, the accuracy of the method depends upon how large the stone is. One says 'large' advisedly, because it is not the weight but the volume that matters, since upon this depends the amount of water displaced, that is the 'loss in weight'. When this figure is large, a small error in weighing, say 0·01 carat, makes very little difference to the final answer, but with small stones, the error becomes serious and the results unreliable. With a ruby weighing 2 carats an error of 0·01 carat in the water weighing will lead to an error of eight in the second decimal place of the density, which is quite serious. Even with an accurate balance, the method of hydrostatic weighing is hardly worth using with stones of a carat or under, and heavy liquids have to be pressed into service.

Other Liquids

Greater accuracy with small stones can be obtained by using certain other liquids in place of water, since this has the grave disadvantage of a high surface tension. At the surface of all liquids there is a sort of 'skin' effect, owing to the attraction of the molecules below the surface, and this is called surface tension, and is measured in terms of force (dynes) across a linear centimetre of the surface film. In water this figure is 73, whereas in ethyl alcohol it is only 23 and in toluene it is 28. Thus, if one of these organic fluids are used—or carbon tetrachloride or ethylene dibromide, which are denser but also have a low surface tension—a much freer swing of the balance will be obtained when the wire is dipping into the liquid. Also the 'wetting' properties of the liquid give less tendency to bubble formation than when using water.

Water has a density practically equal to unity at room temperatures, so that by simply dividing the weight of the stone by its loss in weight in water the density can be obtained. When liquids other than water are used correction must be made for the difference in density from that of water. All that is required however is to multiply the result obtained by the simple formula given above by the density of the liquid used at the temperature at the time of the experiment, L. The formula then becomes $[A/(A − W)] \times L$.

The densities of the commercial samples of these low surface tension liquids can hardly be relied upon beyond the second place of decimals, and moreover the change of density of each with temperature is too large to be ignored if one is bent on accurate work. A good stock of a chosen liquid (say 500 g, which should be kept in a well-stoppered bottle) should be obtained and calibrated at a known temperature, and the variation with temperature of each liquid can be taken without question from the literature. To calibrate a sample a careful hydrostatic determination on two or more pieces of pure quartz (rock crystal) weighing 50 carats or more is carried out. The density of the liquid is then given by the equation:

$$\text{Density of liquid} = \frac{2 \cdot 6508 \times \text{loss of weight in liquid}}{\text{Weight of stone}}$$

The known and very constant density of quartz is 2·6508; if concordant results are obtained with several experiments, it can confidently be taken that the value obtained is correct. The temperature of the liquid must be taken carefully during, or immediately after the experiment in each case (a thermometer which will read to a tenth of a degree C is needed). Having now established the density of the sample for a particular temperature, the densities of the sample for all temperatures likely to be encountered, say from 10°C to 25°C, which is equivalent to 50°–77°F, can be calculated and kept on record. Tables of the densities for toluene and ethylene dibromide at different temperatures are given at the end of the book.

The actual values determined by experiment on the purchased sample of liquid will probably be found not to agree exactly with the figures given. This does not matter in the least (providing that the experiments have been accurately carried out), as the necessary adjustment is easily made by adding or subtracting from the temperature when each experiment is carried out just so many degrees as to bring that particular sample of liquid in line with the table. For example, supposing a sample of ethylene dibromide was calibrated at 18·0°C, and found to have a density of 2·18175 using one piece of quartz, and 2·18183 using another. On the standard table, these densities would be appropriate for 19·0°C, so that all that is necessary when using that sample of liquid in future determinations is to add 1·0°C to the observed temperature before reading from the table.

An exactly similar procedure can be carried out with toluene, which is also an excellent liquid for hydrostatic weighing, and has the advantage of being cheaper than ethylene dibromide. The latter is more accurate in use, simply because of its higher density, which gives a greater loss in weight for a given volume, so that the inevitable small errors in weighing have a less serious effect on the answer.

A mixture of alcohol and sodium carbonate which, in the correct proportions, make a solution of density equal to that of water, but with better wetting properties and lower surface tension, has been suggested as a hydrostatic liquid, but simpler and probably as effective is a drop of Teepol or Wettol or other photographic wetting agent poured on the top of the water in the beaker. A far more important point is to realize that difficulty of testing is more often than not the result of attempting to work with dirty stones. Such stones should be washed in carbon tetrachloride, or other grease remover, and rinsed in alcohol (methylated spirit) before a density determination, or indeed any other test.

DECIMAL PLACES IN DENSITY FIGURES

In recording density figures it is seldom desirable to quote more than two decimal places, for, except with very large stones and most careful work, this is the best accuracy that can be attained. It is scientifically bad to give a whole string of decimal figures which have no meaning. Significant figures are all that matter, therefore some knowledge of the third decimal place is chiefly useful in acting as a guide to which second figure is the true one. For example, an andalusite giving on calculation a density of 3·147 would be quoted as 3·15, while one calculated as 3·142 would be given as 3·14.

WEIGHING LARGE MATERIAL

It is often required to obtain the specific gravity of large pieces of material, the size of which is beyond the capacity of the ordinary balance. For this purpose the Walker balance will be found useful.

The balance (*Figure 28.7*) consists of a graduated brass beam (A) about 20 in. long engraved with a millimetre scale. About 6 in. from the end is a hardened steel knife-edge (B), which rests on supports on a heavy standard (C) and allows the beam to swing freely. From the shorter arm is suspended a heavy counterweight (D) which can be moved to any position on the (usually) notched shorter arm of the steelyard. A second and lighter standard (E) is provided with a slot through which the long arm of the steelyard is passed, an arrow head (or the top of the beam) coinciding with the zero on the vertical scale (F) when the beam is level.

The specimen (G) to be weighed is securely bound round with thin wire or string (cotton thread) and is suspended from a loop of fine wire (H) passed

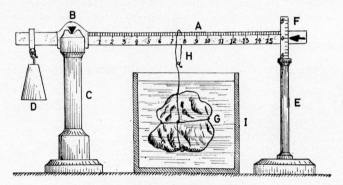

Figure 28.7. The Walker balance

over the beam. This loop is moved along the beam until a position is found where the weight of the specimen and the counterpoise counterbalance each other, and the balance is in equilibrium, with the arrow head pointing to zero. This gives the reading *a*. The specimen is then completely immersed in water contained in a large glass or tin vessel (I) and moved along the beam until again balanced and a second reading *b* is obtained. The readings *a* and *b* are inversely proportional to the weights of the body in air and water respectively. Hence the density is given by dividing the second reading by the difference between the second and first readings or

$$\text{sp. gr.} = \frac{b}{b-a}$$

Several counterweights will be found necessary to deal with specimens of different weights, but only one must be used for each determination.

An ordinary spring balance, such as that used for weighing silver may, in an emergency, be used for determining the density of large carvings and so forth. The specimen is suspended by a wire from the hook of the balance and the weight noted, then the specimen is immersed in water (dangled in a bucket of water whilst suspended from the balance), a camera tripod makes a useful support for the spring balance, and the new weight noted. Then, as for normal hydrostatic weighing, the weight in air divided by the loss of weight will give the density. While not particularly accurate such a determination may be all that is needed to identify a specimen.

Even without actual measurement, the density of a stone may help in its identification. What the Americans call the 'heft' of a stone, that is the feeling of weightiness or lightness when balanced in the hand, can often serve as a valuable guide, and the faculty of judging density by this method can be developed considerably by practice.

The jeweller must take notice of the density of stones when he is asked to estimate for the replacement of stones of another species. Stones which must be of the same size in order to fit the setting. A striking example of this is given where the replacement of a diamond by a strontium titanate ('Fabulite') is requested. If the diamond (density = 3·52) weighs 2·00 carats, then the 'Fabulite' (density = 5·13) will weigh nearly half as much again—actually 2·91 carats. If this effect be not taken into account there may be considerable error in estimating the cost of the alteration. The difference in weight of two stones of the same size but of different species may be ascertained by using the following formula:

$$\frac{\text{Density of the stone required} \times \text{Weight of the original stone}}{\text{Density of the original stone}}$$

A table of specific gravities is given in the Identification Tables.

CHAPTER 29

LIGHT AND OPTICAL EFFECTS

EARLY INVESTIGATIONS INTO LAWS OF LIGHT

It is only natural that speculation as to the nature and investigation into the laws of light should have begun very early. The most reasonable of the early theories was that of Pythagoras (about 550 B.C.), who considered the sensation of sight to be caused by particles continuously shot out from luminous surfaces and entering the pupil of the eye. The school of Plato maintained that the sensation of sight was caused by the union of three ocular beams. The first was a stream of 'divine fire' emanating from the eye itself, the second something emanating from the object seen, and the third that of the light of the sun, but the whole idea was extremely nebulous. However, the Platonists knew two very fundamental laws of light: (1) that light travelled in straight lines when it travelled in a homogeneous medium, and (2) that when a ray of light was reflected at any surface the angle between the incident ray and the surface was equal to the angle made by the reflected ray.

The Egyptian astronomer Ptolemy, about A.D. 150, made an investigation of the bending of light when it passed into glass and into water, but although he measured and tabulated the angles the incident ray makes with the surface, and the angles the refracted ray in the second medium makes with the surface, he did not succeed in seeing what laws connected them. In 1621, W. Snell, a professor of mathematics at Leiden, discovered the laws of refraction which Ptolemy failed to deduce from his experiments. Snell died in 1626 without publishing his results, and René Descartes, who had perused Snell's papers, published them as his own discovery a few years later.

The seventeenth century produced many advances and discoveries in the theories of light. Grimaldi, in 1665, gave an interesting account of experiments on 'diffraction', which is the name he gave to the small spreading out of light in every direction upon its admission into a darkened room through a small aperture: an experiment that showed that light bends round corners in the same way as sound does, but to a very much smaller extent. A year later Sir Isaac Newton discovered that light could be separated into its component colours when it was passed through a prism of glass, and he developed the idea that light consists of exceedingly minute particles shot out from a luminous body which caused the sensation of sight when they impinged upon the retina. This emission or corpuscular theory was indeed similar to that proposed by Pythagoras some 2,000 years earlier. Newton's masterly handling of the theory and his authority in the world of science combined to retard for nearly 200 years the development of the wave theory expounded by the Dutch physicist Christian Huygens in 1678

Erasmus Bartholinus, in 1669, discovered double refraction and polarization, but the phenomena were not explained until the work of Fresnel some 144 years later. In 1676 Olaus Römer, the Danish astronomer, by observing apparent irregularities in the time of rotation of Jupiter's satellites, demonstrated that light travels with a definite speed through space, and he estimated the speed of light to be about 192,000 miles per sec. Two years later Huygens formulated the first clear statement of the wave theory, which supposes light to consist of waves of some sort emanating from a luminous surface, and he showed how reflection and refraction follow normally from such a theory, but he was unable to show why light bends round corners so little.

It was about 130 years later that Thomas Young discovered the principle of interference and showed how a beam of light may be divided into two portions, which under certain conditions will produce darkness when both portions illuminate the same point. This follows quite naturally from any wave theory but would not be possible with a corpuscular theory such as that postulated by Newton. Young had in mind longitudinal waves such as may be demonstrated by the transmission of compression along a spiral spring, and it was left to Fresnel in 1814, by introducing a happy guess made by Robert Hooke in 1672, to propose that the waves were transverse, that is the individual particles in the path of the wave vibrate perpendicularly to the direction in which the wave is travelling, in the manner of the waves produced on the surface when a stone falls vertically into calm water.

Fresnel by assuming the transverse character of the waves was further able to explain the polarization of light.

WAVE THEORY OF LIGHT

The wave theory of light postulates that it must travel in some sort of medium, a medium which fills all space, and to account for this there was assumed the existence of a hypothetical medium, elastic and weightless, which was termed the ether, and which pervades all space and all material bodies. The theory supposes that wave-motion is propagated by successive parts of the ether setting each other in motion by mutually attractive forces.

In 1873 the wave conception was modified by the introduction of the electromagnetic theory of James Clerk Maxwell who, following Michael Faraday's work on electromagnetism, suggested that the vibrations were due to periodic alterations in the electrical and magnetic condition of the ether. Maxwell showed mathematically that the ether which was required for the conveyance of light was the same as was required for the transmission of electric and magnetic actions, and the known laws governing these would lead to electromagnetic waves which have all the characteristics of light. Twenty years later H. Hertz proved experimentally the existence of electric waves, confirming Maxwell's theoretical reasoning.

The electromagnetic wave theory shows light to be a form of radiant energy, which, as it has particles which have mass as well as wave form, is of dual nature. Whilst most of the characters of light may be explained by the wave theory, in the detailed explanation of the emission and absorption of light, and of fluorescence, it has been found necessary to use another theory, the quantum theory of Max Planck. This theory states that light energy can only be emitted or absorbed in small 'packets' of definite size, called quanta or photons. Modern physicists use both theories and the two have not been completely unified. As the work of the gemmologist mainly concerns the behaviour of the light rays through crystals and optical instruments his prime interest lies in the wave theory.

Formation of the Wave-Front

According to the wave theory of Huygens each point in a luminous surface is vibrating and sending out spherical waves into the ether. Each vibrating point in the wave-front is the source of a secondary wavelet, and at any instant the surface which touches all the secondary wavelets is the new wave-front. In *Figure 29.1*, O is a luminous point and PQ a portion of

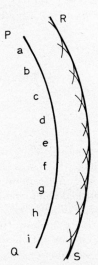

Figure 29.1. The formation of a wave-front and a secondary wave-front

the spherical wave-front. The neighbouring points a–i will all be vibrating in unison and each of these may be considered as the centre of a new disturbance sending out its own spherical wavelet. At a certain instant these wavelets are represented by the arcs of circles which have a–i as their centres, and it is evident that the position RS of another sphere with O as its centre envelops the secondary wavelets and forms the new wave-front. If the point O is a great distance away PQ becomes a straight line and the wave-front becomes a plane wave-front and the secondary wave-front is also plane (*Figure 29.2*).

The Wave Form

The generalized idea of a wave form is shown in *Figure 29.3*. The length of the nearest distance measured between two particles on the wave surface in identically the same position and travelling in the same direction is the wavelength and is usually designated by the Greek lower case *lambda* (λ). The intensity of the energy (light) is determined by the amplitude which is shown by the distance of the top of the wave curve from the mean level.

The intensity of the light is proportional to the square of the amplitude, and inversely proportional to the square of the distance from the source. The path travelled by the wave between one wavelength constitutes one cycle and the number of these cycles completed each second is the frequency, which may be expressed as the speed of light in air (strictly, a

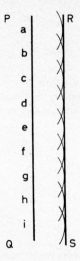

Figure 29.2. The formation of a plane wave-front and a secondary plane wave-front

vacuum) divided by the wavelength. The frequency remains constant regardless of the medium through which it passes. However, the distance travelled or the speed of travel does not remain constant from one medium to another, for on entering an optically denser medium there is a resistance to the transmission and the wavelength for the given form of energy changes. On emerging from the dense medium the wave assumes its original shape and original speed. This change in wavelength can be likened to a person walking at a constant number of steps per second (frequency). The speed or distance travelled in a given second will be determined by the length of step which may be long or short depending upon the type of ground over which he is travelling.

ELECTROMAGNETIC SPECTRUM

Visible light forms only a small part of the electromagnetic spectrum known to science and stretches from the high frequency (short wavelength)

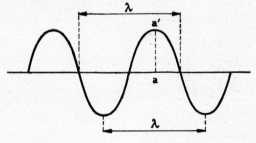

Figure 29.3. Wave form. λ indicates wavelength and a–a' the amplitude

gamma rays to the long radio waves, and beyond (*Figure 29.4*). Besides the visible spectrum other ranges of the long electromagnetic spectrum, such as x-rays, *gamma* rays, and ultra-violet light, and maybe infra-red rays, have an importance in the study of gemmology. The convention used in *Figure 29.4* is that most commonly adopted by physicists, that is with the shorter wavelengths on the left and increasing length of wave to the right. In the discussion, in a later chapter, of the absorption spectra of gemstones it will be seen that this is reversed and the long wavelengths are on the left. From the beginning of the use of the absorption spectra as an aid to gem testing it has been the convention to have 'red on the left'. It matters not one whit which convention is used.

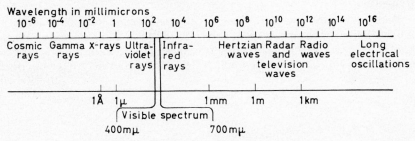

Figure 29.4. The electromagnetic spectrum

MEASUREMENT AND SPEED OF LIGHT

There are various units of measurements used for the shorter wavelengths, the most usual being the Ångstrom unit or tenth metre, a unit suggested by the Swedish physicist A. J. Ångstrom in 1868, which has a measurement of one ten-millionth of a millimetre (10^{-7} mm). This unit is variously indicated by the letters Å.U. or more commonly just Å. Other measurements are the millimicron or micromillimetre ($m\mu$ or $\mu\mu$), which has a length of one millionth of a millimetre (10^{-6} mm), or the micron (μ), which measures a thousandth of a millimetre (10^{-3} mm). Thus the mean wavelength of sodium light is 5893 Å, 589·3 mμ, or 0·5893 μ, according to the unit it is expressed in. The range which constitutes visible light is usually given as between 4000 Å and 7000 Å, but much depends upon the acuity of the eye, which varies between different people, some being able to see farther into the 'invisible' ultra-violet and infra-red than can others.

During the nineteenth and twentieth centuries a number of determinations of the velocity of light in air or vacuum were made, and the speed, for practical purposes, was found to be 300,000 km/sec (186,000 miles per sec). The results of all recent experiments are consistent with giving a velocity of light *in vacuo*, usually denoted by the symbol *c*, as 299,776 ± 4 km/sec.

LIGHT TRANSMISSION

Transparency

The ability of a material, such as a gemstone, to transmit light is termed transparency and a rough classification into degrees of transparency may be made as follows:

(1) Transparent—when an object viewed through the material shows clear and distinct.

(2) Semi-transparent—considerable light penetrates the material but the object seen through would appear blurred.

(3) Translucent—some light passes through but no object can be seen.

(4) Semi-translucent—slight transmission of light through thin edges of the material.

(5) Opaque—no light passes through the material.

These descriptions are considered to refer to specimens of ordinary thickness, for in thin section most 'opaque' substances transmit some light.

Reflection

More important considerations are the behaviour of light when it is returned from the surface or is transmitted through a substance. When light falls on any surface separating two media (the term medium is used to express any substance through which light passes and may refer to either

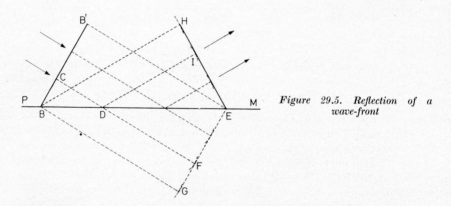

Figure 29.5. Reflection of a wave-front

solids, liquids or gases) part of it is always reflected back into the first medium and part refracted into the second.

A wave-front impinging on a plane surface is returned at a similar but opposite angle (*Figure 29.5*). PM is the reflecting surface and BB' a wave-front. As soon as the wave-front strikes the surface a secondary wave is sent out from B, and each point on the wave-front, such as C, gives rise to a secondary wave when it reaches the surface, as at D, and at the instant at which reflection is complete a secondary wave is about to start from E. If reflection had not occurred the point D on the wave-front would have reached F; instead a secondary wave of radius DI equal to DF has developed and similarly the reflected wave at B gives rise to a secondary wave of radius BH equals BG. The straight line joining the apices of these radii with E forms the new wave-front.

A simpler manner of expressing the laws of reflection is by indicating the wave by a straight line (*Figure 29.6*), where the incident ray IO falling on a reflecting surface PM at O (called the point of incidence) is returned along OR. NO is termed the normal at the point of incidence, the normal being an imaginary line at right angles to the surface separating the two media at the point of incidence. The angle ION is the angle of incidence (i) and the angle NOR is the angle of reflection (r). The laws of reflection are therefore: (1) the angle of incidence (i) is equal to the angle of reflection (r); (2) the incident ray, the normal and the reflected ray are all in the same plane.

Figure 29.6. A simple illustration of the laws of reflection

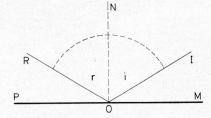

Refraction

When light enters the second medium refraction occurs and the light is bent away from the original direction of travel. If the ray is travelling from an optically rarer medium to an optically denser medium the ray is slowed-up and is bent towards the normal. Should, however, the ray be travelling from an optically denser to an optically rarer medium the ray is bent away from the normal. Refraction may be illustrated by the analogy of a column of soldiers being slowed-up and deviated when marching from open ground into a dense wheatfield and out again into open ground (*Figure 29.7*).

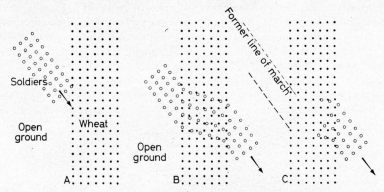

Figure 29.7. A column of soldiers deviated when passing through a dense wheatfield

The refraction of a wave-front when it meets the surface separating a rarer and a denser medium is shown geometrically in *Figure 29.8*. In this diagram RS is the surface separating the two media and AB the advancing wave-front. Assuming the denser medium to be twice as optically dense as the first medium the light advancing from A will be slowed up to half the speed it had whilst travelling through the first medium, hence the wave will only travel half the distance as the ray travelling along AB. Therefore, if there is described in the denser medium an arc of a circle with centre A and radius half BC, a tangent drawn from this arc to C will be the new wave-front.

18+G.   545

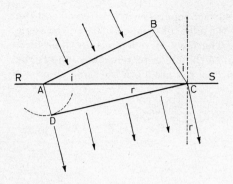

Figure 29.8. Refraction of a wave-front

Refractive Index

For any two media in optical contact Snell found the following laws of refraction to be true.

(1) The sine of the angle of incidence bears to the sine of the angle of refraction a definite ratio which depends only upon the two media in contact and the nature (colour) of the light: that is (sine i)/(sine r) is a constant.

(2) The incident ray, the normal at the point of incidence and the refracted ray are all in the same plane.

When the optically rarer medium is used as a standard, and air (strictly, a vacuum) is universally so used, the ratio (sine i)/(sine r), when light passes into the second medium, is known as its refractive index. However, as the refractive index of a medium differs for different coloured light rays, that is for different wavelengths, it is usual to use the yellow light of sodium vapour which is a nearly monochromatic light having a mean wavelength of 5893 Å. Reference to *Figure 29.8* shows that the angle BAC equals (i), and the angle ACD equals (r). Thus (sine i)/(sine r)=(BC/CA)/(AB/AC)=2·00, proving that the sine rule and the velocity relationship are equivalent.

A simpler geometrical exposition of the refractive index is by indicating the light rays as straight lines (*Figure 29.9*). The incident ray IO strikes the

Figure 29.9. The geometry of refractive index

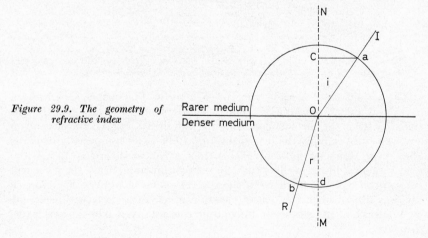

surface of the two media at the point of incidence O and is refracted along OR. The normal is shown as NM. The angle of incidence (i) ION is clearly seen to be greater than the angle of refraction (r) ROM. Any increase or decrease in the angle of incidence will cause an increase or decrease in the angle of refraction, and this will be in some definite proportion relating to the sine law. If a circle (*Figure 29.9*) is described with its centre at O and with any radius which cuts the incident and refracted rays at (a) and (b) respectively, and perpendiculars (ca) and (bd) dropped on to the normal, there are produced two right-angled triangles whose hypotenuses are the incident and refracted rays enclosed by the circle. In a right-angled triangle the sine of an angle is the ratio between the side opposite the angle and the hypotenuse (the hypotenuse is the side opposite the right angle). As the hypotenuses in both triangles have the same length, being the radii of the same circle, the refraction could be measured by the ratio of the lengths of (ac) and (bd), and if the upper medium is air this ratio will be the refractive index. It will be shown later, when the measurement of refractive index is discussed, that this geometrical method may be used to obtain a rough idea of the paths of rays when the refractive indices of the two media are known. In practice, the trigonometrical ratios of the sine of the angles as given by Snell's law are used, for the angles of light rays can by suitable instruments be measured accurately.

Critical Angle and Total Internal Reflection

Light is reversible, hence a ray can pass from a denser to a rarer medium, in which case, as already mentioned, the refracted ray bends away from the normal; that is the incident ray (now in the denser medium) makes a smaller angle with the normal than does the refracted ray. Therefore, when the angle of incidence is progressively increased there must be an incident ray which refracts out of the first and into the second medium so that the refracted ray makes an angle with the normal of 90 degrees, that is the ray just grazes the surface of the two media in contact. Any further increase of the angle of incidence will require the ray to turn back into the first (denser) medium where it obeys the laws of reflection and not the laws of refraction. The angle of incidence which gives an angle of refraction of 90 degrees is termed the critical angle, and the effect where the ray is turned back into the first medium is termed the total internal reflection of light. The connexion between refractive index and critical angle is expressed by the formula sine $i = 1/n$, where i is the critical angle and n the index of refraction. Hence, it follows, if air is the rarer medium, that the higher the refractive index of the denser medium the smaller will be the critical angle.

The critical angle and the total internal reflection of light is illustrated by *Figure 29.10*, where IO2 is the angle of incidence which gives a refracted ray, OR2, of 90 degrees, that is the critical angle, and IO3, a ray which is greater than the critical angle, is totally reflected along OR3. Total internal reflection is an important property of which advantage is taken in the construction of many optical instruments, including the refractometer, and to it the brilliancy of diamond and other stones of high refraction is in part due.

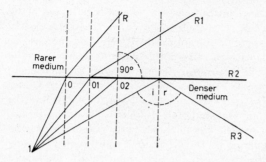

Figure 29.10. Total internal reflection of light and the critical angle

COLOUR DISPERSION

In the descriptions of light rays just given a single wavelength (colour) of light has been assumed, but white light, as Newton found, is composite. A medium has a different refractive index for each wavelength (colour of light), hence, a beam of white light which is incident at an angle and then passes through the transparent medium with parallel sides emerges laterally displaced but parallel to the incident rays (*Figure 29.11*). The emergent rays are uncoloured for the difference in the angles of refraction of the various coloured rays refracted into the parallel plate are countered by the similar, but opposite, angles of refraction on their emergence into the air again, and are thus recombined into white light.

Figure 29.11. Paths of rays through a parallel sided plate

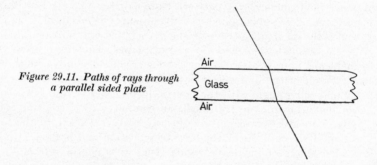

If a beam of white light passes through a transparent medium with two inclined faces, such as a glass prism, the rays fan out into the familiar colours of the rainbow, as each colour is deviated still farther on emergence and cannot recombine. The longer waves (red light) are bent or deviated least, and the shorter waves (violet light) are bent more, or are said to be more refrangible (*Figure 29.12*). This 'analysis' of white light is termed colour dispersion and is the cause of the chromatic effect seen in gemstones which is called fire.

Colour dispersion, usually shortened to dispersion, is strong in diamond, synthetic rutile, white zircon, and in the synthetic strontium titanate, while in such coloured stones as demantoid garnet and sphene the dispersion though also strong is in these cases masked by the colour. Dispersion is measured by the difference between the refractive index of the medium

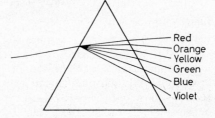

Figure 29.12. Colour dispersion of white light on passing through a prism

for the red ray and for the violet ray. As there are many red rays and many violet rays (wavelengths which cover these two colours) it is usual to measure the refractive index of the medium for the Fraunhofer B line of the solar spectrum (6870 Å in the red) and the G line (4308 Å in the blue-violet). Subtracting the value of the refractive index of the B ray from the index of the G ray the dispersion of the medium for the B to G interval is found. For some purposes, specially in the case of optical glasses, the smaller interval between the Fraunhofer C line (6563 Å in the orange-red) and the F line (4861 Å in the blue) is used. Table 29.1 illustrates the refractive indices of diamond for different colours of the spectrum.

TABLE 29.1

Refractive Index—Wavelength Values of Diamond

Colour	Wavelength	Refractive index
Red	6870 Å	2·407
Yellow	5890 Å	2·417
Green	5270 Å	2·427
Violet	3970 Å	2·465

Therefore the dispersion between these red and violet wavelengths gives the dispersion of diamond as 0·058, but between the more restricted B to G range (which is for practical purposes universally adopted) the value of dispersion for diamond is 0·044, and between the C and F lines is 0·026.

Plotted on a graph with the refractive indices as ordinates and the wavelengths as abscissae the resultant 'curve' is found not to be a straight line but a curve with varying curvature. This is more prominent in some stones and occurs because the refractive index increases strongly on the long-wave side of an absorption band. This is shown by Table 29.1 there being, in the case of diamond, an absorption band in the ultra-violet. The dispersion of light through glass prisms is made use of in the spectroscope, an extremely valuable instrument for the identification of gemstones by their absorption spectra, a subject which is discussed in a later chapter.

Accurate measurements of the dispersion of gemstones are made by obtaining the refractive indices of the stone for red and blue light (the difference between the two measurements giving the dispersion) by using the method of minimum deviation (discussed later). A good approximation may be made by using an ordinary refractometer with red and blue coloured light sources, or by using similar coloured filters placed before the white light source, or even over the eyepiece.

OPTICAL EFFECTS

Lustre and Sheen

Certain characters of gemstones are due to reflection and refraction of light. Of these fire has already been referred to, but the surface brilliancy of a gemstone, known as the lustre, depends upon the quality and quantity of the reflected light, and this depends in turn upon the refractive index of the substance and the perfection of its polish. Since the perfection of polish depends largely on hardness, this also has a marked effect on the brilliancy of a stone. Among opaque substances metals have the highest lustre. In addition many sulphides (such as pyrites) and oxides (such as hematite) have a metallic or submetallic lustre. The majority of gemstones, however, have an index of refraction similar to that of ordinary glass, and hence, are said to have a glassy, or vitreous lustre. There is a division into other types which are listed in Table 29.2.

TABLE 29.2

Lustre	Mineral
Metallic	Silver
Adamantine	Diamond
Subadamantine	Demantoid garnet
Resinous adamantine	Certain zircons
Vitreous	Quartz
Resinous	Amber
Silky	Fibrous minerals such as satin-spar
Pearly	Usually seen only on cleavage surfaces
Waxy	Turquoise

Lustre is, therefore, a reflective effect from the surface of the stone, but reflection can occur at surfaces of differing refractive index within the stone, and such an effect is termed sheen. The most common of these is the whitish or bluish sheen, or schiller, seen in the moonstone variety of feldspar, which is termed adularescence, and is due to an intergrowth of albite and orthoclase feldspars in alternate layers. The silvery sheen seen in silver obsidian is likewise due to reflections from microscopic needles (microlites) due to incipient crystallization in the natural glass. The flashes of colour so prominent in labradorite feldspar, known as labradorescence, may be, in part a sheen effect; but is more probably due to an interference effect at thin films; a phenomenon discussed later in the chapter.

Chatoyancy and Asterism

Other optical effects which are due to reflection within the stone are those due to reflections from numerous parallel cavities or fine fibrous inclusions regularly oriented in accordance with the symmetry of the crystal. Of these, the cat's-eye effect, termed chatoyancy, is one of the more important. This effect has been amply explained when the most important cat's-eye chrysoberyl was discussed. Other species producing cat's-eyes include quartz, tourmaline, beryl, scapolite, diopside and apatite.

When the cavities or fine needle-like inclusions are parallel to more than one crystal face a star-stone is produced when the stone is cut cabochon with the apex of the dome perpendicular to the plane of the included structures. The star is in general best seen by a single reflected light, and the effect is then known as epiasterism. When light is transmitted through the stone the effect is termed diasterism and this is common in rose quartz; the effect in this mineral is made use of in constructing a composite stone which produces an imitation of star sapphire. The best star-stones are produced by rubies and sapphires which show three bright rays crossing each other at 60 degrees at the centre and thus producing a six-pointed star. Occasionally a six-rayed (12-pointed) star is seen which is due to a second set of needles oriented on the second order prism. A feeble star effect is sometimes seen in spinel and garnet, which may give a four-pointed star, or if the needles are oriented parallel to the faces of the dodecahedron a three-rayed (six-pointed) star is produced. Beryl is sometimes found with a star effect but this is usually very weak.

Opalescence

Another optical effect due to internal reflection is the scattering of light by particles of matter in the path of the light, making a visible 'beam' or 'cloud' such as is caused by a ray of light illuminating particles of dust floating in the air of a room. This is the so-called Tyndall effect and is the cause of the milky opalescence in some opal, and in opalescent glasses and some pastes. It also causes in part the optical effect in moonstone.

PHENOMENON OF INTERFERENCE

If light waves from a single source are split into two rays and then recombined after one of the parts has travelled a short extra distance, the two rays may be out of phase with one another, that is the crests of the two sets of waves are not accurately superimposed, hence the phenomenon of interference occurs.

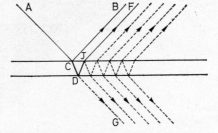

Figure 29.13. Diagram explaining the interference of light at thin films of differing refractive index

The iridescent colours which are exhibited by thin films of transparent substances are caused by this type of interference and may be explained by *Figure 29.13*. AC represents a ray of light incident on the thin film—magnified greatly in the diagram—at C. Part of this ray is reflected along CB and the other part refracted along CD. At D part of the ray is reflected along DJ and the other part is transmitted along DG. Of the ray DJ part is reflected, and the other part is refracted along JF. The two parallel rays CB and JF interfere when they are brought to a focus at the same place by any lens such as that in the eye. For the reflected ray at C has only to travel along CB whilst the ray CDJ has to travel the distance CD and DJ in the film. Therefore, there is a path difference between the two rays which is greater the greater the thickness of the film and the greater the obliquity of the ray. With monochromatic light (light of a single wavelength) reinforcement or darkness will occur according to whether the path difference is a whole number of wavelengths or an odd number of half-wavelengths. Since in white light the different colours of the spectrum are merely waves of different lengths the different colours will be reinforced with different thicknesses of film and with different obliquities. This is the explanation of the colours in a soap bubble and those seen on an oil film on a pool of muddy water. It is also a cause of the play of colour seen in opal, and similar flashes in labradorite feldspar, and in part the bluish schiller of moonstone.

DOUBLE REFRACTION AND POLARIZATION

In treating with the reflection and refraction of light it has been assumed that the light travels through the medium as one ray. This is true in the

Figure 29.14. The doubling of print as seen through a rhomb of Iceland spar

case of singly refractive substances, termed isotropic media, such as glass, resins, gels, and minerals which crystallize in the cubic system. However, in the case of the crystals belonging to the remaining six crystal systems the light rays do not behave in such a simple manner, for on entering such media the rays divide into two parts, each of which, in general, travels with a different speed and hence has a different index of refraction. Such material is known as doubly refractive or anisotropic media.

552

This splitting of a ray into two rays causes an object which is viewed through the medium to appear to have doubled edges, the amount of separation varying with the amount of the double refraction; the strength of the double refraction being the difference between the refractive indices of the two rays along the viewing direction. This doubling effect is particularly well seen in the case of the clear colourless variety of calcite called Iceland spar (*Figure 29.14*) and may be seen in most doubly refractive gemstones which will show the rear facet edges doubled when they are viewed through the stone with the aid of a lens or microscope (*Figure 29.15*).

Ordinary light radiation from a luminous source consists of an amazing mixture of vibrations lying at all possible directions at right angles to the direction of travel of the ray of light. Such light is said to be unpolarized.

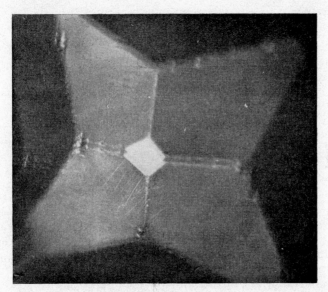

Figure 29.15. The doubling of the back facets as seen through a tourmaline by the use of a microscope or lens

When, due to some cause or another, vibrations in one direction predominate over those in the other directions, the light is partially or completely plane polarized, that is the transverse waves are vibrating in one plane only (*Figure 29.16*). As has already been shown, when a dot is viewed through a piece of Iceland spar two dots are seen side by side. Then, if another piece of Iceland spar be rotated over the first piece of spar the two images of the spots disappear and reappear alternately, showing that the rays have attained a one-sided nature, in fact they are plane-polarized at right angles to each other. This polarization of the two rays in doubly refractive stones is of considerable importance in gem testing.

OPTIC AXES

In crystals belonging to the tetragonal, hexagonal and trigonal systems there is one direction, that parallel to the vertical crystal axis, in which light behaves as if the crystal were singly refracting. Such a direction of single refraction in a doubly refracting crystal is known as an optic axis, and as there is one such axis in crystals of these three systems such crystals are termed uniaxial crystals. In any other direction in the crystal the ray is split into two rays with maximum divergence when the ray is travelling perpendicular to the optic axis. One of the rays obeys Snell's law, has a constant index of refraction which is denoted by the symbol ω, and is called the ordinary ray; this ray always vibrates at right angles to the optic axis. Depending upon the direction the other ray takes within the crystal the speed of the ray varies, that is the refractive index varies between that of the ordinary ray (ω) to a second limiting value, hence this ray is known as the extraordinary ray and is denoted by ϵ. In directions parallel to the optic

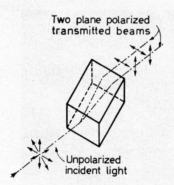

Two plane polarized transmitted beams

Unpolarized incident light

Figure 29.16. Double refraction and polarization

axis only the ordinary ray is seen; in all other directions the extraordinary ray is also found, varying in its refractive index, and when it reaches its fullest divergence the ray vibrates parallel to the optic axis. The arithmetical difference between the refractive index of the ordinary ray and that of the extraordinary ray at its maximum divergence gives the birefringence (double refraction), and, further, the speed of the extraordinary ray (ϵ) may be either slower or faster than the ordinary ray (ω); if it is faster, that is it has a lower refractive index than that of the ordinary ray, the crystal is said to be optically negative, and if slower to be optically positive, that is when the extraordinary ray has a higher index of refraction than that of the ordinary ray.

The optics of the other three systems, the orthorhombic, monoclinic and triclinic systems, are much more complex, for there are three optical directions and two optic axes in such crystals, which are hence termed biaxial crystals. The three mutually perpendicular critical vibration directions, to each of which belongs a definite refractive index, correspond to the maximum, intermediate and minimum light velocities. They are designated α, β and γ respectively, but β is not the arithmetical mean between α and γ, for the β refractive index is sometimes nearer to α than to γ, when the crystal is said to be optically positive; or is nearer to γ than to α, when the optical sign is negative. Further consideration is given to these optical directions in the chapter on the measurement of refractive indices.

CHAPTER 30

COLOUR IN GEMSTONES

Colour is of supreme importance to the lover of precious stones and forms the most important single guide to the identity of a gem so far as the eye is concerned. The subject of colour is a vast and complex one, and in these pages only certain aspects of it can be dealt with at all fully. Colour is the specific response of the eye and its attendant nervous mechanisms to certain kinds of light and, therefore, may be said to come under the category of psychology; it can thus be described and discussed without any reference to energy, wavelength or other physical concepts. Since physical phenomena are susceptible to exact measurement, it is the physical basis for colour sensations that can be studied with the greatest profit by the gemmologist. Colour as a sensation and the part played by the human eye will only be briefly dealt with in this work, and the physical and chemical aspects of the subject given greater detail.

TERMS AND THEIR INTERPRETATION

Colours differ from one another in three ways, so far as their appearance goes; in their hue, their tone or brilliance, and in their intensity or saturation. By hue is meant that attribute by which a colour can be described as red, or green, or blue. Tone is that quality of brightness which, in the case of neutral greys, approaches white at one end of the scale and black at the other, while the term intensity refers to the vividness of the colour—that is the degree to which it differs from a grey of the same tone. A study of the 'colour cone' (*Figure 30.1*) should assist the reader to comprehend the meaning of these somewhat confusing terms and their relationships.

The terms tone, saturation and so on, are more useful in discussing the colours of paints and dyestuffs than in gemmology, where hue (usually simply called colour) is the main criterion. Ideally gemstones should have either no trace of colour at all or else a full-blooded (that is, saturated) colour to give true satisfaction to the eye; tints and shades, which are admirable for distempered walls and textiles, have an insipid effect when seen in transparent material, although in translucent stones such as jade and chalcedony they may be quite pleasing.

The sensation of hue, which is the psychological effect produced by physiological reactions to light, is closely connected with the wavelength of light—thus entering the realm of physics. White light from the sun, or from any other solid incandescent source at a comparable temperature of 6,000°C or so, consists of light of a vast number of wavelengths within the visible range, although the actual radiation from the sun extends far beyond the visible range at either end of the spectrum. This range of visible light extends from about 7800 Å to about 3800 Å; the longer waves represent red light and the shortest visible rays are violet, while in between are the range of spectrum colours orange, yellow, green and blue—shading imperceptibly into one another. The limits for the visual range given above are not sharp, but depend upon the individual observer and upon the conditions under which the light is presented to the eye; the limits given have been greatly exceeded when powerful emission lines have been received by a dark-adapted eye. On the other hand, the sensitivity of the eye to waves at the ends of the spectrum is so low (*Figure 30.2*) that the importance of the

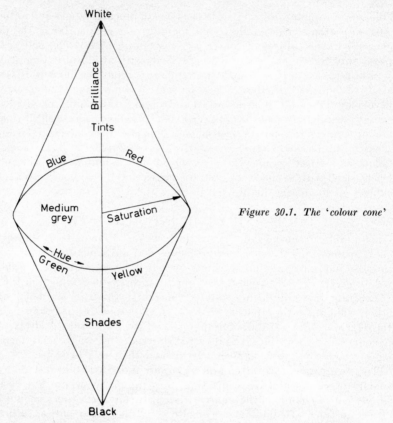

Figure 30.1. The 'colour cone'

extreme wavelengths from the colour point of view is entirely negligible. It is more convenient and practical to consider the range of visible light to extend from 7000 to 4000 Å.

It has already been explained that by passing a narrow beam of white light through a glass prism it can be spread out into a whole series of spectrum colours according to their wavelength. Although there are only six main colour names (or seven if one includes indigo) yet these can readily be subdivided by using such terms as 'orange-yellow', 'yellow-green' and so on, for intermediate hues. The systematic use of these colour terms is recommended by American gemmologists. In actual fact, by comparing small portions of the spectrum with one another, a trained eye can distinguish over a hundred pure hues which are perceptibly different from one another, although when variations in tones and intensities are also considered there are said to be over a million perceptibly different 'colours'.

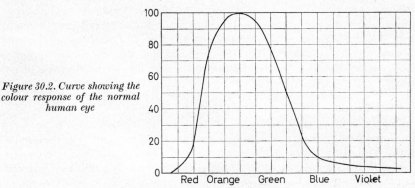

Figure 30.2. Curve showing the colour response of the normal human eye

LIGHT

There are three main factors which determine the colour of an object. The light by which it is viewed, the object itself, and the whole of that delicate receiving apparatus which for the sake of brevity may be called the eye.

Standard Source of Light

The standard source of light by which all colours are judged directly or indirectly, is the mixed light from the sun which we call 'white', and artificial light which is mostly from an incandescent source and approximates fairly closely to sunlight. In darkness there can be no colour as there can be no vision of any kind, and in dim light colour vision is defective as can be demonstrated by looking at coloured objects in bright moonlight. The golden glare of sodium-vapour street lamps drastically affects the appearance of coloured objects for their light consists virtually of one wavelength only; they are thus monochromatic, that is of one colour. Under such lighting objects can only appear yellow, or grey or black, according to how much of the yellow rays they reflect or absorb. A coloured object is simply one which absorbs certain colours (wavelengths) selectively from white light, transmitting or reflecting the other coloured rays more or less strongly. The combined effect of the residual rays is called the 'colour' of the object.

Residual Colour

As shown by Newton, white light is composed of all the colours of the rainbow intermingled. Therefore, when white light, for example, passes through a sheet of signal red glass, the glass absorbs practically all the blue, green and yellow rays, but transmits the red rays freely. Thus, the only sensation transmitted through the eye to the brain is red, and such a glass is spoken of as red. Similarly, if the light reflected from the cover of a book consists mainly of blue rays we speak of the book as blue. All coloured objects, in fact, derive their colour from the light falling upon them or transmitted through them; it is the rays they absorb and which we do not see which determines the rays that we do see; that is the residual colour.

It is for this reason that a diamond dealer prefers to work by a north light, or south light if south of the equator, for by this cold and constant light, little influenced by the position of the sun, he can exercise those delicate perceptions and comparisons of colour by which he is enabled to grade his diamonds correctly. The difference between reflected sunlight from the northern (or southern) sky and the direct rays of the sun is quite considerable, the 'cooler' light from the sky is due to the preferential scattering of the blue portion of the sun's rays by particles in the atmosphere.

Artificial Light

Electric lamps near to sunlight in spectral distribution have been marketed for the colour matching of textiles and attempts have been made in the United States of America by the Gemological Institute of America, and by E. Gübelin of Switzerland, to provide a carefully calibrated artificial source of white light which can serve as a standard illumination in all countries for the judging of shades of colour in diamond. Such a light is intended to be used in connexion with a standard set of diamond samples, carefully graded colorimetrically, which serve for comparison. Quite recently an improved colorimeter for diamonds has been produced in the United States of America, by the Gemological Institute of America, whereby the diamond colour is computed electronically, thus to some extent avoiding any psychological or physical variation in eyesight.

THE EYE AND COLOUR VISION

Before treating with the causes of colour absorption in gemstones a few words may be said about the human eye—the only real arbiter of colour effects. The eye consists essentially of a flexible lens of variable focal length, limited by a diaphragm (the iris), through which light is focused to form an inverted image of the object viewed on the sensitive surface of the membrane known as the retina, which lines the back wall of the eye. The retina is connected with the brain (where all messages of light and colour are translated into sensations) by the optic nerve. The sensory layer of the retina consists of small rod-like structures interspersed with shorter conical bodies, which are known respectively as rods and cones. Only the cones are thought to be sensitive to colours and only the cones are capable of acute vision. A small central area known as the yellow spot near the emergence of the optic nerve contains cones only, and it is here that the image of an object is focused for the clearest possible vision.

The rods, on the other hand, are the structures which enable us to see to some extent in a dim light; for this reason they are the chief feature in the retina of a nocturnal animal. The rods contain a reddish substance (rhodopsin), commonly called the visual purple, which is rapidly bleached on exposure to light. The visual purple can thus only begin to form in the dark, and its presence can make the sensitivity of the eye several thousand times greater than it is in bright light—hence the power of the dark-adapted eye to see objects which would be quite invisible before this transformation has had time to take place.

There have been many theories of colour vision, and a final answer to all the problems connected with this intricate subject is still to be found. For most practical purposes, however, the 'three colour' theories, particularly the Young-Helmholtz theory, serves very well. According to the simplest form of this theory, the human retina contains three varieties of cone, which are sensitive to the red-yellow, green, and blue-violet parts of the spectrum, respectively. It is assumed that three light-sensitive chemical compounds are present in these different groups of cones, each of which undergoes a breakdown when exposed to light of the appropriate wavelengths, transmitting messages to the brain. The spectral regions where these receptors are active overlap considerably. Thus in the central part of the spectrum all three will be functioning, though the green receptors will be much more active than the other two, which will function alone at the extreme ends of the spectrum. The action of these three receptors in varying strengths permits all the familiar sensations of colour by persons of normal vision. More recent work seems to indicate the presence of not merely three but as many as seven different types of receptors. About 10 per cent of men and less than 1 per cent of women are in some measure colour-defective, or are colour-blind. In such persons it is supposed that one or more of the red, green or violet-sensitive colour receptors is not functioning, thus limiting and distorting to a lesser or greater degree the perception of hue.

COLOURING METALS OF GEMSTONES

Allochromatic and Idiochromatic Minerals

The majority of gemstones would be colourless if they were chemically pure —that is if they contained only those elements ascribed to the species in its ideal chemical formula. Diamond, corundum, beryl, topaz, spinel, chrysoberyl, zircon, quartz and many others are examples of minerals which are colourless in the 'pure' state. The very fact that each of the above can be found in a colourless state and in a wide variety of colours is a sign that they have no characteristic colour of their own. Such minerals are known as allochromatic to distinguish them from the smaller group of idiochromatic or self-coloured minerals, in which the colour can be ascribed to an element which forms an essential part of their structure. For this reason idiochromatic minerals can show little variation in hue.

Examples of idiochromatic minerals, together with their chemical formulae and the element to which the colour may be ascribed are given in Table 30.1.

From Table 30.1 it will be noticed that colouring propensities are ascribed to atoms or ions of copper, iron, manganese and chromium. There are several other elements closely related to these in their electronic structure which are also known to give rise to coloured salts and to cause colour in allochromatic minerals when they enter these as 'impurities'. These are nickel, cobalt, vanadium and titanium. Of all the 92 elements it is these eight which are most noticeable for the effect they have on colour. They occupy consecutive positions in the periodic table of the elements, with atomic numbers 22 (titanium) to 29 (copper). They are known as transitional or transition elements, because in them the regular process of adding one electron to the outer shell for each increase in atomic number is

TABLE 30.1

Colouring Metals of Idiochromatic Minerals

Mineral	Colour	Composition	Colouring metal
Malachite	Green	$CuCO_3 . Cu(OH)_2$	Copper
Azurite	Blue	$2CuCO_3 . Cu(OH)_2$	Copper
Chrysocolla	Greenish-blue	Hydrous copper silicate	Copper
Dioptase	Green	H_2CuSiO_4	Copper
Turquoise	Sky-blue	Aluminium Cu phosphate	Copper
Almandine	Red	$Fe_3Al_2(SiO_4)_3$	Iron
Peridot	Green	$(Mg,Fe)_2SiO_4$	Iron
Rhodonite	Rose-red	$MnSiO_3$	Manganese
Rhodochrosite	Rose-red	$MnCO_3$	Manganese
Spessartite	Orange	$Mn_3Al_2(SiO_4)_3$	Manganese
Uvarovite	Green	$Ca_3Cr_2(SiO_4)_3$	Chromium

interrupted, and the extra electron is accommodated in the next shell, nearer the nucleus. It so happens that, when surrounded by the electrical forces existing in most ionic crystals, the electronic structure of these elements becomes 'tuned in' to the electromagnetic vibrations of particular frequencies in visible light, and absorb energy from the light rays as they pass through the crystal. This gives rise to absorption bands, and thus to colour in the residual rays.

Chromium

It is to chromium that the finest colours amongst the gemstones are mainly due. Why a chromium green or red should be brighter and clearer than the best colours that iron, shall we say, can produce, is something of a puzzle. The answer lies, without much doubt, in the intense and clear-cut nature of the absorption bands to which the chromium ion gives rise. This means that the colours which are not absorbed are left at almost full intensity. In the case of iron this is not so. There are here so many possible electronic transitions that there is some absorption at almost all frequencies, with the result that there is a general greying, or saddening as the dyer would call it, of the residual shade.

It is to chromium, then, that the magnificent crimson-red of ruby and the hardly less rich red of spinel is due, although only some 1–2 per cent is present in the stone, taking the place of alumina in the crystal lattice. Pyrope garnets contain enough of the almandine molecule to assume a faint purplish-red when iron is the only colorant, but when chromium enters the molecule the finest blood-red pyropes are produced. The influence of the surrounding atomic field on the particular wavelengths absorbed by an ion is well shown here, since uvarovite—the garnet-containing essential chromium—is bright green in colour and not red. Green is in fact the most usual colour produced by chromic oxide in crystals. The incomparable colour of emerald and the lovely green shades seen in jadeite are chromium colours. Demantoid garnet, enstatite chrome-diopside, and euclase are other examples of green stones where this element plays an important role as a colorant.

Unless some inhibiting factor, such as the presence of iron, is operative, minerals coloured by chromic oxide tend to show a red fluorescence under ultra-violet light and x-rays. In the case of ruby a bright red fluorescence is produced in sunlight or intense artificial light, and this adds appreciably to the fine colour effect of the stone. Another feature of the colour-absorption in many chromium compounds is the extreme transparency in the deep red, even where the coloured mineral is green. This transparency to red light is found, for example, in emerald, and causes this chrome-coloured variety of beryl to appear red when viewed through a suitable colour filter—this will be described later. Alexandrite is also transparent in the red; a fact which contributes to its colour-change in artificial light. Alexandrite is an instance where the red and green colours produced by chromium are almost evenly balanced. In daylight the stone should have an almost emerald green colour, while in ordinary electric light, which is richer in red and poorer in blue and violet light, it appears raspberry red. This extreme colour-change is seen only in fine Siberian specimens; in those from Ceylon it is usually not so pronounced.

Chrome alum, incidentally, displays a rather similar balance between green and red. Here, one gets the curious effect that strong solutions of the salt, seen in depth, appear purplish-red, while more dilute solutions or thinner samples appear green. The reason is that the salt is very transparent to deep red rays, and somewhat less so to green rays. The eye is more sensitive to the green rays, so that in fairly thin or dilute solutions it is the green colour which impresses the eye. In greater concentration the green rays are all absorbed, and the red rays, which still suffer hardly any absorption, are then visible, since they are the only ones which remain. This curious phenomenon is sometimes referred to as dichroism, but it must not be confused with the mineralogist's use of the word, about which more will be said later. The effect is correctly called dichromatism.

Iron

The second of the colouring metals to consider is iron, which is the most ubiquitous colorant in nature. The yellows and browns of rocks and sands are largely ascribable to iron. It is present to greater or less extent in many of the gemstones, giving green, yellow, brown and even red colorations, according to its state of oxidation and the forces acting upon its ions in each medium. As remarked earlier, the colours due to iron are not so brilliant as those caused by chromium, but some of them, nonetheless, are very fine.

Ferric iron (Fe_2O_3) is the basis for the yellow and green tints seen in chrysoberyl, the green in green sapphire, the blue or bluish-green of aquamarine, and the yellow in orthoclase, andradite and spodumene. Ferrous iron (FeO) takes credit for such varied colours as the blue of blue spinel, the purplish-red of almandine garnet and the lovely yellowish-green of peridot. The influence of iron is seen in many other minerals not listed above, such as tourmaline of green or brown colour, epidote, nephrite jadeite and many others.

Cobalt

Cobalt is usually associated in the mind with the colour blue—yet minerals containing cobalt, and most cobalt salts, are not blue but pink. The explanation of this apparent anomaly will be discussed later in the chapter; at the moment it can be remarked that, though no natural gemstone is coloured blue with cobalt, gemmologists are familiar enough with cobalt blue in synthetic spinel, ranging from the pale blue of aquamarine or zircon to royal blue stones which are intended to represent sapphire. Blue pastes are often coloured by cobalt, and the blue glass bases of some garnet-topped doublets are similarly coloured.

Vanadium

Vanadium, like cobalt, is another of the transition elements which has no place as a colorant among the natural gems. True, its presence in minute traces in some emeralds has been held by some to influence the colour; but it is certain that chromium plays the major role. In rare cases a natural 'alexandrite' sapphire, containing vanadium, has been found. The colouring action of vanadium is seen, however, in the curious type of synthetic sapphire which is extensively used to imitate alexandrite. The actual colour of this material is difficult to describe; it is a curious slaty-greenish-purple in daylight, while in electric light it is a rich purplish-red.

Titanium

The influence of titanium in colouring the gem minerals is difficult to trace, but it plays an undoubted part in the colouring of blue sapphire, and surely too in the rare gem benitoite. Traces of titanium and small amounts of iron are found in natural blue sapphires. These elements are included in the alumina powder used to produce synthetic blue sapphire by the Verneuil process. Curiously enough the iron seems to evaporate or otherwise disappear during the flame-fusion process as no sign of the iron absorption bands seen in native sapphires can be detected in their synthetic counterparts, and this forms a useful aid to distinction.

Nickel

Nickel forms many coloured salts, but does not commonly occur in gemstones. True, chrysoprase and green opal from Silesia owe their pleasant shade of apple green to this element. Chalcedony of neutral tints is often stained green to represent chrysoprase, but here chromium salts and not nickel are normally used.

Copper

Copper is the only metal not yet mentioned in this brief survey of the influence as colouring agents of the transition elements. Actually, though copper plays a prominent role among the idiochromatic minerals, it does not appear as a colorant among the allochromatic gemstones.

LIGHT ABSORPTION BY TRANSITION ELEMENTS

The way in which the transition elements absorb light is often very characteristic, so that by noting the nature and position of the absorption bands with a spectroscope one can with confidence name the element giving rise to the absorption, and hence to the colour of the mineral. In other cases the absorption causing the colour is too vague and generalized to yield this information. Details of absorption bands are given in a later chapter. Here a broad summary may be given.

Chromium gives rise to fine absorption lines which have no influence on colour and to clear-cut absorption maxima in the yellow-green and violet regions of the spectrum, with free transmission in the deep red. The position, intensity and breadth of the yellow-green band determines whether the stone acting as host to the chromic ions appears red or green or 'alexandrite colour'.

Iron absorbs to some extent throughout the whole spectrum, but absorption bands are most marked in the blue and violet, giving rise to brown, green or yellow colorations. In nickel there is also an overall absorption, but with no clear-cut bands. The red is absorbed, but there is good transmission in the violet and beyond, so that cobalt-nickel 'black glass' is used with mercury vapour lamps to isolate ultra-violet light for the study of luminescence.

The absorption due to vanadium is rather similar to that of chromium, but has fewer fine lines and less emphatic broad bands. Titanium in some way resembles iron but produces no clear absorption bands in the visible region. With manganese are found bands of increasing sharpness and intensity from the blue down to the violet and beyond, producing pink, orange or red colorations; while the absorption of the blue cobalt compounds is peculiarly distinctive, with their three strong, broad bands in the orange-red, yellow and green, and free transmission in the deep red.

COLOUR CHANGES PRODUCED BY HEAT AND RADIATION

The colours produced by the transition elements just discussed are for the most part stable to heat, light and other radiations, since the elements concerned have entered the lattice of the host mineral, even if this may have entailed some distortion. Moreover, the presence of these foreign elements has a slight but measurable effect on the physical properties of the mineral concerned; more particularly on the refractive index, which is especially sensitive to such intrusions and can be measured with great accuracy. A number of the coloured gemstones, however, do not belong to this category. Their colours are not so stable to heat or radiations, and their colouring agents are present in such minute quantity that their nature is difficult to establish with any certainty, and seem to have very little influence on their properties.

Heat Treatment

Quartz, topaz and zircon are the most prominent examples of this type of coloration. Each of these minerals is colourless when pure; each displays an imposing variety of colour in nature; and in each the colour can be altered, in suitable specimens, by heat treatment or by radiation. In some cases, blue zircon for example, the resulting colour is not matched by any of the naturally occurring varieties of the species. If the colour is indeed due to the presence of foreign atoms, these must be present in extremely small concentration; too small to be estimated by the methods of ordinary chemical analysis.

Since the 'burning' of certain types of quartz and topaz gives rise to stones in which the colour is both attractive and permanent, it is understandable that this practice is considered legitimate in the gem trade— especially as it is hallowed by long custom. In the case or zircon, the method by which sky-blue or greenish-blue stones can be produced from reddish-brown rough is of fairly recent origin. A considerable percentage of the treated stones are by no means stable in colour, but the spectacular beauty and consequent saleability of the stones is such that this disadvantage is condoned, and the stones are an undoubted commercial success.

Quartz in nature is usually colourless and water-clear, or is milky-white. Of the coloured varieties, amethyst is the most famous and may vary in tint from the merest blush of pinkish-violet to a deep violet of tremendous intensity. The colour used to be ascribed to the presence of manganese for no very sufficient reason—possibly because of a certain similarity in hue to dilute solutions of potassium permanganate. More recently iron and also titanium have been suggested as colorants for amethyst. Other theories have been mentioned in the chapter on quartz, but as yet there is no final proof.

Much amethyst is 'burnt' to produce the fine yellow, brown or reddish-brown stones. It has often been stated that smoky quartz can be used to produce similar stones, but according to G. O. Wild this is not so. Smoky quartz and citrine both remain completely clear up to 1,000°C and over (the 'smokiness' of the former disappearing above 250°C), while when amethyst is heated above 500°C a slight cloudiness appears which becomes very marked above the inversion point of *alpha*-quartz at 575°C, resulting in stones which have almost the schiller of moonstone. The problem is complicated further by the fact that some amethyst turns green on heating, such as the prasiolita from Montezuma in Brazil. In the Zambezi escarpment of Zambia amethyst is found which is parti-coloured green and purple, the green colour, it is suggested, might be due to heating by tropical conditions over long periods of time. Wild maintains that the cause of colour cannot be the same for amethyst as for the natural brown or yellow quartz called citrine. He also was the first to note that the yellow stones produced by the heat treatment of amethyst are virtually non-dichroic, while in true citrine or smoky quartz the dichroism is quite distinct.

The heat treatment of amethystine quartz must be carried out under carefully controlled conditions if the desired colour is to be obtained, and the same is true for topaz; here the nature of the raw material is also very important. Only the yellowish-brown topaz crystals from the Ouro Preto district of Brazil have the curious property of becoming rose-pink when carefully heated at a dull red heat (300°–450°C). It is remarkable that these 'pinked' stones reveal a fluorescence and absorption doublet in the red end of the spectrum at 6820 Å, albeit very faintly. This is undoubtedly due to the presence of traces of chromic oxide, to which the colour may also be ascribed. Apparently the heat treatment allows the chromic ion to take up its position in the lattice and thus exert its influence on the light absorption in a manner not possible when scattered colloidally in the original sherry-brown coloured crystal.

The colour changes in zircon under the influence of heat are still more complicated and puzzling; here, not only the nature of the rough and the degree of heating, but also the oxidizing or reducing nature of the surrounding atmosphere modify greatly the nature of the colours obtained. Fuller information on the native methods of 'cooking' zircons has been given in the chapter on zircon. Other gemstones which are commercially heat treated are the greenish aquamarine (or some brown beryls) which turn to a beautiful sky-blue when heated to between 300°C and 400°C; and the dark green tourmalines from South-West Africa which turn to an emerald green hue. Violet sapphires, which are probably a mixture of ruby and blue sapphire, turn to a pink colour on heating, which probably decolorizes the blue colour and leaves the red or pink.

Radium-treated Stones

A number of cases are known where specimens of the gem minerals having an attractive hue when first recovered are found to fade on exposure to strong light: this largely prohibits their use in commercial jewellery. On the other hand, colour may be induced in many of the gem minerals by exposing them to x-rays or to the rays emanating from radium or other radioactive substances. Natural white or pale yellow sapphires assume a rich topaz-yellow tint when treated with x-rays for only a few minutes. The value of the stones could be greatly enhanced by this method were it not that the induced colour fades again when the stone is exposed to strong sunlight, or is heated to about 230°C. The kunzite variety of spodumene provides another example of a stone which changes colour rapidly under x-rays; in this case the resultant colour is green. Several other examples might be quoted of these induced colorations, but they are of more scientific than practical interest.

COLOUR CHANGES IN DIAMOND

Exposure to Radium

Much more permanent alterations in colour can be produced in diamond, either by exposing the stones to the action of radium salts or radium emanation, or to bombardment by various atomic particles of high energy. Broadly speaking, the result of prolonged treatment of this kind is to induce in diamond a tourmaline-green colour. Beginning in 1904, Sir William Crookes carried out many thorough experiments on the action of radium on diamond, and he found that it was the so-called *alpha*-particles (that is helium nuclei) emitted by radium which caused diamond to change gradually to green. He also found that the treated diamonds are strongly radioactive and that the radioactivity, like the colour, persisted for an indefinite number of years. The most vigorous chemical treatment had no effect, or only a temporary one, on the strength of the radioactivity, and none whatsoever on the colour. An octahedron of diamond 'greened' by Crookes was presented by him to the British Museum (Natural History) in 1914, and has retained its colour, and radioactivity, to the present day.

Later work by the American workers S. C. Lind and D. C. Bardwell showed that heating radium-treated diamonds at a dull red heat (450°C) for several hours had the effect of destroying both colour and radioactivity: this was in addition to the method which Crookes had found effective— repolishing the stone. The later workers also found that the gas radon (radium emanation) acted more quickly than the salts of radium itself in inducing the green tint in diamond. Ten days in a tube of the gas produced a change of colour which it would have taken several months to effect by radium bromide.

The green tint produced is more attractive when it is not too pronounced for when the diamond is overexposed the tint tends to be a blackish-green rather akin to that seen in some tourmalines. It is not at all like the apple-green tint seen in the very rare natural green diamonds. Nor has any marked radioactivity been observed in any untreated diamond of any colour. This fact suggests easy and certain methods whereby the laboratory worker can detect that suspected diamonds have been radium treated. Leaving the diamond in contact with a photographic film or plate overnight in a light-tight box will cause a marked blackening of the emulsion on

Figure 30.3. An autoradiograph of a radium-treated diamond

development of the film, the resultant autoradiograph often showing the shape of the stone and a curious echo of the facet pattern beyond the borders of the stone (*Figure 30.3*). Heavily treated stones may even glow in the dark. Scintillations can also be seen when a radioactive diamond is placed on a zinc-sulphide screen in a dark-room, and the screen near the stone examined with a lens after the eye has become thoroughly dark-adapted. These scintillations are very beautiful and impressive, each tiny splash of light representing the effects of one *alpha*-particle striking the zinc-sulphide screen. There are countless numbers of such flashes in every second, and the fact that this could continue for years without any measurable diminution of the weight of the stone gives some inkling of the tiny proportions of an atom and the myriads that go to make the smallest appreciable speck of matter. A radium-treated diamond will also discharge an electroscope in a few minutes, providing the most sensitive test available, aside from a Geiger counter.

The mystery of how a radioactive layer can become so strongly attached· to the surface of a diamond as to defy removal save by abrasion or strong heating has never been satisfactorily solved, and even the nature of the radioactive atoms does not seem to have been properly investigated. A measurement of the range in air of the *alpha*-particles emitted by a treated diamond was carried out some years ago by L. V. Grimmett, and was found to correspond with the range characteristics of polonium, a radioactive element with a half-life period of some 200 days, which is the last stage in the chain of radioactive decay in the radium series before reverting to the inactive element, lead. Polonium, however, only emits *alpha*-particles, and since treated diamonds are capable of fogging a photographic film through black paper and, to a lesser degree, through a sheet of aluminium, it is evident that there must be other atoms concerned, capable of sending out *beta* and *gamma* rays also.

Radium is a fabulously rare and fabulously expensive substance, as well as being very dangerous to handle. Most of the world's supplies are locked up in lead-lined safes in hospitals and institutions. Thus the opportunity for the radium-treatment of diamonds is limited. Nevertheless, a score or more 'radium-greened' diamonds are known to be on the market, and a demand by a collector for a fancy green diamond may result in some of these stones being hopefully offered. Always they are condemned by a laboratory test, their characters having already been recorded years before in the laboratory archives, and they are withdrawn again into retirement to await a later opportunity. The physiological danger of wearing a radium-treated diamond cannot be great, for one such diamond tested by a Geiger counter revealed that the radiation was no greater than that given off by a radium-dial wrist watch.

As a process the radium treatment of diamond is already assuming an old-fashioned air, for this is an atomic age and man is no longer content to wait upon the natural disintegrations of certain rare atoms, but is able to produce streams of atomic and subatomic particles by means of an ingenious automatic acceleration system in the cyclotron. The Van de Graaf generator, and now fast neutrons from an atomic reactor (atomic pile) have been used for the artificial coloration of diamonds. Each of these processes gives a slightly different result, hence, it will be better to discuss them separately.

Cyclotron-treated Diamonds

Cyclotroned diamonds are coloured by bombardment with fast moving protons, deutrons or *alpha*-particles and the colour produced is, like radium-treated stones, a green colour, or if overexposed black. For treatment the diamonds are mounted on a long probe which is inserted into the vacuum chamber of the cyclotron (in some types of apparatus), or on special holders, usually made of aluminium, for those cyclotrons which can produce external beams. The heat generated when the atomic particles hit the target, in this case the diamonds and the holder, is intense and some means of cooling must be used. The probe or holder is usually water-cooled and further cooling is carried out by a jet of liquid helium. If the cooling is not efficient and the stone heats the resulting colour is brown and not green. Further, 'cyclotroned green diamonds' may be turned to a golden-brown or yellow colour by subsequent heat treatment at about 800°C. In the short exposures used the coloration is only skin deep and disappears on recutting. In all cases, whatever the type of bombardment used, bombarded diamonds are intensely radioactive for some hours after treatment, but this dies out and the stones cease to be radioactive. The colour, however, remains and so far as is known, this colour is permanent.

A careful examination of cyclotroned stones will reveal a series of reflections of triangular cubist patterns that show varying intensity of green, and a stone which has been treated through the table will, when examined with the pavilion up, show a dark ring around the girdle. A diamond treated through the pavilion will show a light ring round the girdle, and when viewed through the table will show a 'watermark' rather like an opened umbrella surrounding the culet (*Figure 30.4*). It is said that

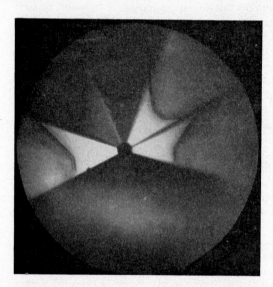

Figure 30.4. The 'umbrella' seen around the culet in a bottom-treated cyclotroned diamond

by irradiating the diamond through the side these tell-tale markings can be eliminated. In such a case the only distinction is by the unnatural green colour of the stone. With the brown colours, as G. R. Crowningshield has pointed out, there is always a narrow absorption line at 5940 Å in the treated yellow and brown stones, whereas this line is absent in natural yellow and brown diamonds. It has been further reported that irradiated diamonds of a brownish-pink colour show absorption lines at 6370 Å and a pair of lines at 6200 and 6100 Å in conjunction with the 5940 Å line.

Pile-treated Diamonds

A similar state of affairs occurs with the pile-treated diamonds, in which neutrons are the particles, but here the coloration is throughout the stone. The colours produced are, like the cyclotroned diamonds, green, brown and yellow, the brown and yellow stones are obtained after heat treatment. The diamonds when they come from the pile are intensely radioactive and dark green in colour. The radioactivity quickly dies out, and by subsequent controlled heat treatment any of the colours named may be obtained. There are no characteristic markings to be seen in pile-treated diamonds and with the green-coloured stones the unnatural colour is the main guide, but with the brown stones the 5940 Å absorption line is present and gives conclusive evidence of treatment.

Electron Accelerator Treated Diamonds

By the use of fast moving electrons from an accelerator, such as a Van de Graaf generator, diamonds have been coloured a pale aquamarine blue to greenish-blue hues. Such stones are not easy to detect, but the treatment is not extensively carried out. It is known that all natural blue diamonds are of type II; these are transparent much farther down in the ultra-violet than are the Cape stones which are normally used for coloration experiments, and, further, the natural blue diamonds are electroconducting. Therefore, if it can be proved that a blue diamond conducts electricity and is transparent to ultra-violet to 2200 Å, then the colour is natural and not artificially produced. Bombardment with *gamma*-rays will also induce a bluish-green colour in diamond. This method is not commonly used.

Absorption Spectra and Fluorescence Changes Accompanying Colour Change

It will be seen from the above that the changes in colour of bombarded diamonds are accompanied by changes in absorption spectra, and indeed changes in fluorescence, and both may be modified by subsequent heat treatment. It was found by R. A. Dugdale that diamonds pile treated with from 1 to 10 units of neutrons (1 unit equals 5×10^{16} neutrons) turned black and showed no fluorescence, but when subsequently heated in controlled stages, paler shades of green and brown were produced. It was also found that when the stones were heated to 350°C for some time there was a strong development of the 5040 Å line and they gave a green fluorescence. On slight further heating to about 400°C, both the absorption and the fluorescence disappeared. It is clear that the colour changes cannot be explained on the old 'colouring oxide' type of theory; but a general explanation is possible on the lines of the more recent hypotheses which will be discussed a little later in this chapter. We are dealing with actual defects in the crystal lattice produced by intensive bombardment, and the absorption of light is always attendant on such defects, as seen also in synthetic rutile, for example.

CAUSES OF COLOUR IN INORGANIC SUBSTANCES

The reasons for the appearance of colour in organic molecules such as those of the dyestuffs have been fairly well understood, in terms of composition and molecular structure, for many years. Chemists have been able to predict with some certainty the types of synthetic compounds which will produce brilliant and fast dyes. Colours in inorganic substances have not proved so susceptible to logical treatment; but, beginning in the 1920s, fruitful lines of thought on this complex subject have been increasingly explored and expanded. K. Fajans and his school were the foremost pioneers in promulgating these new ideas and carrying out experiments to prove their validity. More recently the American chemist W. A. Weyl has made outstanding contributions to the subject on the same general basis. Reports on these researches have been widely scattered in the literature, but the main ideas have been assembled by Weyl in his monograph on *Coloured Glasses*. An attempt will be made here to summarize some of the more important findings of Fajans, Weyl and others working on the new lines, since they illuminate so helpfully many of the completely inexplicable features of inorganic colour phenomena.

Colour in solids is due to (a) the nature of the atoms involved and (b) the chemical and electrical forces acting between them. In organic chemistry, where compounds consist chiefly of carbon, hydrogen and oxygen, the factor (b) is by far the most important, but in inorganic compounds (a) plays an important part. Though there is no sharp demarcation between coloured and colourless atoms or ions, since the same element often forms both colourless and coloured ions under different conditions of combination or of valency, nonetheless, Piccard and Thomas in 1923 suggested that the following three groups could be formulated.

(1) Coloured ions, such as those of the transition elements chromium, cobalt, iron and so on, already discussed.

(2) Latently coloured ions, such as those of arsenic, antimony, cadmium, iodine and sulphur, which on occasion form brightly coloured compounds of which CdS, HgI_2, and As_2S_3 are examples.

(3) Colourless ions, like those of aluminium, barium, calcium, and the alkali metals.

Just as, in organic compounds, colour is found to result where there are fields of chemical or electrical force which are unsaturated or unbalanced, so, in inorganic compounds, unsaturated valencies or weak bonds favour the absorption of light and deepen the colour. On the other hand, complete saturation of the chemical valencies and strong binding forces favour light transmission. Another recognized fact is that where a compound contains the same element in two states of valency there is a deepening of colour. Well-known examples of this are ferrous and ferric iron in gall ink, and the complex cyanides of iron such as Prussian blue, which is ferric ferrocyanide.

Colour or light absorption is also intensified where valency forces are not uniformly distributed. A good instance of this is graphite, which has strong linkages within the planes of carbon atoms but only feeble forces between them. Diamond, on the other hand, has a highly symmetrical and powerful distribution of valency and electrostatic forces, and is normally extremely transparent. The dark colour of certain diamonds is almost certainly due to imperfections in the crystal lattice, and it is by 'knocking holes in the lattice' that bombardment by atomic particles causes diamonds to change to green, or brown or black.

Prolonged heating allows these defects to 'heal', and the stone resumes its normal transparency and colour. Similar phenomena have been found to operate in synthetic rutile prepared by the flame-fusion process. Titanium dioxide, of which rutile is the naturally occurring tetragonal form, is pure white and is used in the paint industry. In nature it is commonly a deep brownish-red or black, and as prepared in the Verneuil furnace it is also dark and opaque unless precautions are taken. The cause for this is a tendency for the material to crystallize with a deficiency of oxygen in the lattice, leaving gaps which act as electron traps. By reheating the crystal in the presence of oxygen transparent, almost colourless, boules are obtained. By controlling the oxygen content, orange, brown, blue and other colours can be obtained, none of which are due to 'impurities' in the general sense.

The optical properties of an ion—that is, its refractivity, its light absorption and emission—are functions of its own electronic configuration and its environment, which may modify the arrangement of its outer electrons. The electric fields of the neighbouring ions exert a polarizing (that is deforming) influence on the electron orbits of the absorption centre. Thus the nature of its closest neighbours, their numbers (that is what is known as the co-ordination number of the atom) and their geometrical arrangement in space (crystal symmetry) are equally important for its colour and fluorescence. It is these facts that account for the difference between the optical properties of an ion in its gaseous state and the same ion in a condensed system (solid or liquid). For instance, the electron configurations of the transition elements in their gaseous state do not permit absorption of visible light quanta; but under the polarizing influence of large and polarizable anions their ions are able to cause absorption.

Large anions are more polarizable than smaller ones; thus bromides and iodides are likely to be more coloured than fluorides or chlorides of the same element (for example the halides of nickel). Further, an ion surrounded by a symmetrical series of atoms, to each of which it is equally bound, is unlikely to be coloured. Examples are NaCl, in which each sodium is equally linked to six chlorine atoms, and CaO, MgO, SrO, BaO, in each of which the metal ion is surrounded symmetrically by six oxygen atoms. In contrast to these, the reddish-yellow oxide PbO, known as the mineral massicot, or the commercial product litharge, is coloured, according to Weyl's hypothesis, precisely because the lead ion is not in the centre of the group of eight oxygen atoms with which it is co-ordinated; being closer to one group of four than to the other. Weyl was able to substantiate this idea by preparing mixed crystals of SrO (which has a sodium chloride structure) containing up to 16 mols per cent of PbO. The resultant crystals are white; x-ray analysis showed that in these crystals the Pb ions are symmetrically surrounded by six oxygens as in the NaCl structure.

As has already been stated, it is difficult to account for the strong colorations in some varieties of quartz, zircon and so on in terms of the usual 'colouring oxides' hypothesis, since no other substances seem to be present in analysable quantity. Moreover, the effect of heat and radiation in altering or destroying the colour remains unexplained. Weyl makes the following suggestion in connexion with amethyst and rose quartz. First, he points out, even if a crystal is 99·999 per cent pure, there will still be 0·001 per cent of impurity amounting to 10^{16} foreign atoms in each cubic centimetre of the crystal. Density, refractive index, or thermal expansion will not be affected by such traces of impurity, but other properties such as fluorescence and colour may be greatly influenced.

Tetravalent titanium is extremely widespread in nature; it is therefore likely that in minute concentration these atoms can squeeze into the quartz lattice, though they are really too large for the structure. Each titanium atom thus represents a flaw or centre of distortion. Under the influence of radioactive radiations these flaws in a crystal are liable to participate in an electron transfer process. The addition of an electron to a tetravalent titanium ion results in its reduction to a trivalent state—which makes it even larger than before and causes it to become strongly deformed by its environment, and liable to cause absorption of light, producing an amethystine colour.

The intense violet colorations produced by exposing certain kinds of glass to the sun's rays is thought to be due to a similar process, though the colour in solutions and glasses are never as intense for a given concentration as in crystals, there being less rigidity in the environment and therefore less distortion.

Though it is still not certain what causes the colours in quartz, topaz and zircon, or the mechanism by which they change colour when heated or irradiated, these ideas of Weyl give a fresh line of approach and are likely to lead to an eventual explanation.

CHAPTER 31

THE MEASUREMENT OF
REFRACTIVE INDEX

It has been explained that when a ray of light passes obliquely from a transparent medium to another of lower optical density the ray is refracted away from the normal, and, as the angle of the incident ray is increased there is reached an angle where the refracted ray just grazes the surface of the two media in contact. This particular angle, where the refracted ray makes an angle of 90 degrees with the normal, is known as the critical angle. Any further increase in the angle of incidence will cause the ray to be reflected into the first medium, that is it is totally internally reflected. Upon this optical effect is based the principle of the jeweller's refractometer.

REFRACTOMETER METHODS

Types of Refractometer

W. H. Wollaston was the first to suggest that if the critical angle of a substance in optical contact with a block of glass having a higher index be measured, the refractivity of the substance of lower index could be assessed. This is the principle of the elaborate and very accurate Abbe-Pulfrich refractometer used in many laboratories (*Figure 31.1*). These instruments make possible accurate measurements of the critical angles but the result is only obtained after trigonometrical computation.

The first direct reading instrument was that designed by Professor Bertrand in 1885 (*Figures 31.2* and *31.3*). The optical system of the Bertrand instrument left much to be desired and the readings made by it were not entirely reliable. In 1905 G. F. Herbert Smith designed a more efficient instrument, but as in the Bertrand refractometer the scale was marked in arbitrary numbers and each instrument needed an individual card with the refractive index of each scale number marked upon it, further, in the original instrument the highest index which could be read was 1·76. Two years later the improved Herbert Smith refractometer (*Figure 31.4*), in which the scale was calibrated in indices of refraction and could be read to 1·80, was produced and is still commercially available.

Since this time many other makes of refractometer have been placed on the market in England and abroad. Among these are the American Gem Refractometer which uses a section of a half cylinder of glass for the 'dense glass' and mirrors instead of lenses for the transmission of the light rays to the eyepiece. The Rayner instrument (*Figure 31.5*) uses a small prism of glass instead of the truncated glass hemisphere as used in the Herbert Smith instrument; this instrument makes use of prisms of such small

Figure 31.1. The Abbe-Pulfrich refracto-
meter in use

dimensions as to enable prisms of other singly refractive materials to be used, such as zinc blende and even diamond, thus extending the range of the refractometer. Synthetic colourless spinel, although it will only read to 1·68, has the property of showing the two shadow edges of doubly refractive stones much more clearly defined than does glass when white light is used. The reason for this will be explained later.

Function of the Refractometer

The function of the refractometer is to project on to a suitable scale a shadow of the critical angle formed by two media in contact. As the dense glass has an invariable refractive index, the critical angle will alter in conformity with the second medium in contact with it, hence, a suitably calibrated scale will allow the measurement of the critical angle in terms of

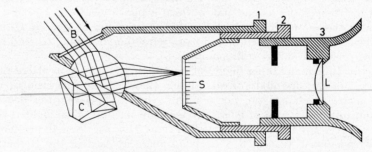

Figure 31.2. Diagram of the optical system of the Bertrand refractometer

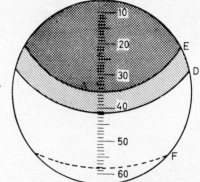

Figure 31.3. The scale of the Bertrand refractometer

refractive index of the second medium. The critical angle of a ray of light passing from a dense medium into air is smaller the higher the refractive index of the dense medium (*Figure 31.6*). When two media with different refractive indices are in contact, such as a gemstone on a highly refractive glass, the critical angle is greater when the index of the second medium is higher than for another medium of lower index in contact with the same first medium (*Figure 31.7*).

From the previous discussion it will be clear that all the incident rays between the normal, N' and I (*Figure 31.8*) will be refracted out through the

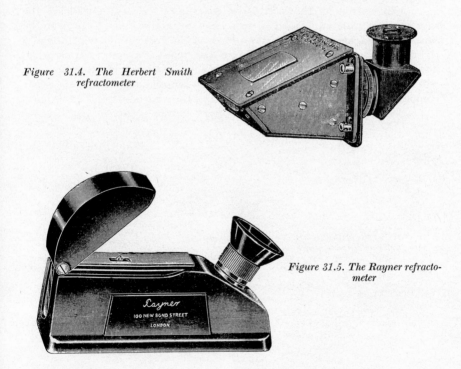

Figure 31.4. The Herbert Smith
refractometer

Figure 31.5. The Rayner refractometer

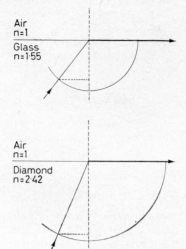

Figure 31.6. When the ray is passing from a dense medium into air the critical angle is smaller the higher the index of the medium

stone, except for some reflected light which always occurs at refracting surfaces. Between I and A all the incident rays are totally reflected, hence, the area BR will be brightly illuminated, while between R and N′ the illumination will be dim for it will be illuminated solely by the residual reflection of the refracted rays.

The dense glass is the essential part of the refractometer and the remaining optical system of the instrument consists of lenses to parallelize the rays on to a scale calibrated in indices of refraction, and to project the image of the scale (and the shadow edges of the critical angles), through a right-angled totally reflecting prism on to a focusing eyepiece. Thus, when a stone of lower refractive index than the dense glass is in position the scale will be divided into two parts, one of which is brilliantly lit and the other comparatively dark; therefore the position of the edge between the two parts

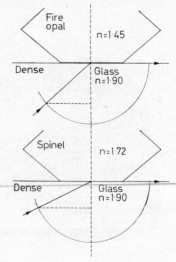

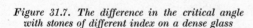

Figure 31.7. The difference in the critical angle with stones of different index on a dense glass

crossing the scale is a measure of the refractive index of the stone under test.

When white light is used, owing to the difference in dispersion between the highly dispersive lead glass of the refractometer prism or hemisphere and that of the stone, the shadow edge is a small spectrum whose width depends upon the difference in the dispersion between the stone and prism. The nearer the dispersions are to each other the sharper will be the shadow edge. This accounts for the ability of those instruments which have a synthetic spinel prism to show clearly the two edges in doubly refractive stones, since the spinel has a dispersion similar to those of the stones tested. To obtain a similar result with instruments having a standard glass prism would need the use of monochromatic light (usually that of sodium vapour). The measurement of the refractive indices of doubly refractive stones will be discussed later.

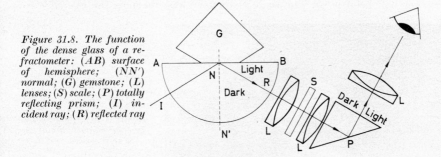

Figure 31.8. The function of the dense glass of a refractometer: (AB) surface of hemisphere; (NN') normal; (G) gemstone; (L) lenses; (S) scale; (P) totally reflecting prism; (I) incident ray; (R) reflected ray

Contact Liquids used in Refractometer

If the stone to be tested is placed directly on to the dense glass of the refractometer no reading will be obtained, for the two media are not in optical contact owing to a thin film of air which separates them; this air cannot be manually displaced unless such an excessive pressure is applied as will damage the instrument. This problem is surmounted quite easily by interposing between the stone under test and the dense glass a liquid with a higher refractive index than the stone, and which will 'wet' the surfaces. For practical purposes a liquid having as high a refractive index as the dense glass (most dense glasses used for refractometers have an index greater than 1·86) would be the most convenient. However, liquids of very high refraction are difficult to prepare, are usually corrosive and are noxious to use.

The standard liquid now used as a contact liquid for refractometers is that devised by B. W. Anderson and C. J. Payne, which is non-harmful and has a constant refractive index of 1·81. The liquid consists of sulphur-saturated methylene iodide to which is added 18 per cent of yellow crystalline tetraiodoethylene. In the case of the spinel refractometer pure methylene iodide will provide a less expensive liquid, for the refractive index (1·74) is higher than that of the spinel which forms the prism. With instruments which have zinc blende or diamond prism readings higher than 1·81 and up to about 2·00 can be obtained by using either West's solution (which is made by dissolving yellow phosphorus and sulphur in methylene iodide in the proportions 8:1:1, and which has an index of refraction of 2·05), or selenium bromide in methylene iodide, which is less difficult to prepare than West's solution. (*Caution:* West's solution and selenium bromide are dangerous liquids, and should only be used under laboratory conditions. The first is spontaneously inflammable and the second has a staining action on the skin.)

Preparation of Refractometer for Use

To prepare the refractometer for use the instrument should be arranged in front of the light source (white light or a monochromatic source as necessary), and if a desk lamp is used it may be an advantage to stand the instrument on the closed box in which the refractometer is normally kept. The surface of the prism should be clean and an occasional rub with a rouged leather will keep it so. The scale is then viewed through the eyepiece to

Figure 31.9. Applying the spot of contact liquid to the refractometer prism

see that it is evenly illuminated, the instrument being adjusted in its position before the lamp until this is so. The scale should then be put into correct focus by adjustment of the rotatable eyepiece. On completion of this the figures and divisions of the scale should be clear and the whole scale have a uniform intensity of light. A small drop of the contact liquid supplied with the instrument should then be applied to the centre of the glass prism (*Figure 31.9*) and the stone to be tested, which should first be cleaned, carefully placed table facet down on to the centre of the prism. If possible the hinged lid of the refractometer should be lowered in order to exclude any top light. On looking down the eyepiece (*Figure 31.10*) the scale will be found to be divided into two portions, the top part (except in the Tully refractometer in which the scale is erect) being a dark greenish colour and the bottom part quite bright. The division between the two parts will appear as a colour fringe (when white light is used with a standard instrument) and the value of the refractive indices will be in this fringe where the green and yellow meet. For the best results the eye should be kept close and central to the eyepiece.

In the standard refractometers which have a prism or hemisphere of dense glass, the glass used is very soft. It is certainly far softer than the hard gemstones which are placed upon it, hence, it is essential to ensure that the polished surface of the prism is not scratched by careless placing of the stone on it, for an instrument with a scratched surface can never give good readings. After use the contact liquid should be removed by absorbing it with blotting paper or wiping with a soft cloth, and if the instrument is only occasionally used a smear of Vaseline over the dense glass will be an advantage, but this needs to be thoroughly cleaned away before the refractometer is used again.

Figure 31.10. Observing the shadow edge with the refractometer (the lid has been left up for photographic purposes)

Source of Light

Even singly refractive substances have an indefinite number of indices according to the wavelength of the light used, hence the spectral edge seen when white light is the source. It is usual, therefore, when accurate readings are needed and in order to observe the two shadow edges in birefringent stones to use a light source which is, so far as is practicable, monochromatic, *i.e.* consisting of light of one wavelength only. For example, sodium vapour which consists of light of wavelengths, 5890 and 5896 Å, which for our purpose may be considered as being monochromatic and on which the standard tables for refractive indices are usually based.

Such a source may be produced by means of a gas or spirit flame in which an asbestos wick saturated with a sodium salt (washing soda or common salt) is inserted. A much more efficient and bright source is that from a lamp generating light by an electric discharge through sodium vapour. These lamps, so much more practical and cleaner, are made in small sizes suitable for use with refractometers. The makers of the Rayner refractometer supply a dark orange colour-filter which, if used with a bright light source such as a tungsten incandescent lamp of 100 watts or more, will sharpen the shadow edges sufficiently for the separation of the two edges in most doubly refractive stones to be seen.

Distant Vision Technique

From the foregoing it is assumed that a flat facet on the stone to be tested is essential for a refractometer reading of the shadow edges. This is perfectly true if accurate readings to the third place of decimals are to be made. It has, however, been found that by a special technique the refractive indices of stones with curved surfaces, such as cabochon cut or carved stones, may be measured with some degree of accuracy.

This method, devised by Lester B. Benson of America, is variously termed the 'spot contact' or 'distant vision' method. It is more easily carried out with refractometers in which the optical train is simple and in which the eyepiece can be removed, as is the case with some American refractometers. However, the method can still be carried out with success with those instruments in which the eyepiece is fixed, as is the case of the Rayner refractometer. The scheme is to apply the smallest drop of contact liquid to the centre of the dense glass, then the curved surface of the piece to be tested is gently placed on the surface of the dense glass on this spot of liquid. On looking through the eyepiece—not in the normal way, but with the eye withdrawn to about 15 in. away from the eyepiece—a small disc will be seen. When the eye is slowly moved in an up-and-down direction the small disc is seen to change from being fully dark in the low index part of the scale and completely light in the high index region. At some point between these two there will be a position, if the stone has a refractive index between the two points, where the disc is bisected by a line of shadow. When this position is found it must be carried mentally for an instant while the eye is lowered so that the scale of the refractometer, which was previously out of focus, can be read.

Practice will beget proficiency in this method, which is usually sufficiently accurate for the discrimination of stones of similar appearance but which have dissimilar refractive indices. There are special auxiliary lenses available which help to make the refractometer scale and the disc to be focused more easily at the same time. With this method the measurement obtained is often found to be one or two digits low in the second place of decimals. The distant vision technique is also useful in the case of tiny faceted stones which give too faint an edge when the refractometer is used in the ordinary way.

Colour Fringe

The refractometer with a synthetic spinel prism will, owing to the similarity of dispersion of the prism to those of the gemstones which can be measured by such an instrument, show sharp shadow edges in white light. However, paste stones are usually made of glass with a high dispersion and are at once noticeable for their strong and wide colour-fringed shadow edges. Thus most pastes may be identified easily by their colour fringe when a spinel refractometer is used. Another advantage of the spinel instrument is that owing to the restricted range of the scale, the divisions are more open and estimation of the third place of decimals is more easily made.

In the standard refractometer careful observation of the sharpness or otherwise of the coloured fringe of the shadow edge in white light will give some idea of the dispersive power of the stone under test and this may give useful confirmatory information.

Bright Line Readings

Occasionally stones, especially pastes, do not give a shadow edge. This is sometimes due to surface tarnish or to the sputtering of 'coated' stones. If the film of tarnish or the film due to sputtering is removed by rubbing the stone with a rouged leather it may then be possible to obtain a refractive index measurement. Sometimes the cause is more obscure and the trouble persists. In many of these awkward cases a measurement of the refractive index may be obtained from 'bright line' readings obtained by the method of grazing incidence.

This is accomplished, with the Rayner instrument, by removing the covering shield of the dense glass. This cover has two pins which fit into sockets on the instrument and allows the cover easily to be pulled off or replaced. The window through which the light normally enters the instrument is blocked up, a process which can easily be carried out by placing a matchbox before the opening. A matchbox when on its side completely covers the refractometer window. A suitable lamp is then arranged at a level slightly above the level of the dense glass of the refractometer and the contact liquid and stone is placed on the glass prism. On observing the scale through the eyepiece a bright line, or lines in birefringent stones, will be seen crossing the practically dark scale at the position of the refractive indices of the stone. The best results are with trap-cut stones.

Effect of Shadow on Refractometer

So far it has not been clearly explained that the stone under test needs to be rotated on the dense glass to ascertain whether the shadow edge is a

Figure 31.11. The Rotagem

single edge or may become a double line (in the case of birefringent stones). To rotate the stone entails careful control with the fingers if the stone is not to be tilted with resultant damage to the soft dense glass of the instrument by the sharp and hard facet edges of the stone. In the early 1930s J. F. Halford Watkins designed a spring-holder which fitted on to the Herbert Smith refractometer and by gripping the stone allowed it to be turned without tilting by the manipulation of a knob. So far as is known this was never commercially marketed. In 1954, D. S. M. Field of Canada designed a fitting to take the place of the cover of a Rayner refractometer. This accessory, known as the Rotagem (*Figure 31.11*), held the stone on to the dense glass by a rubber pad on the end of a rotatable stem fitted with a control knob.

Isotropic materials including stones belonging to the cubic system of crystallization—amorphous materials, such as glass (pastes), resins (amber), and gels (opal)—have only one index of refraction, that is they only show one shadow edge whatever the orientation of the stone on the dense glass, since in this case light is refracted equally in all directions and polarization does not take place. In doubly refractive stones there are two edges to be seen and the behaviour of these edges on the refractometer when the stone is rotated on the dense glass can give diagnostic information, for the full double refraction of such a stone can be measured on any facet. These effects will now be considered.

Uniaxial Stones

It has already been explained that in uniaxial stones there are two indices of refraction, the ordinary ray which gives a shadow edge which is invariable in position, and the extraordinary ray which, in general, will be seen to yield a shadow edge moving to another limiting position when the stone is turned. If the moving edge has the higher index the sign of refraction is said to be positive; if it is the lower edge which moves the sign is

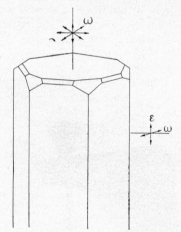

Figure 31.12. *The vibration directions in a uniaxial crystal*

negative. The refractometer, although ingeniously projecting the shadow edge of the critical angle for the two media, the dense glass and the stone under test on to a scale giving direct reading of refractive indices, these will only be those in the plane of the facet lying on the dense glass. The refractive index or indices seen on the scale will depend on the vibration directions in this particular facet. In uniaxial stones the vibration directions of the ordinary ray are at right angles to the optic axis (the direction of single refraction), while in directions within the crystal at right angles to the optic axis there are two vibration directions for any one ray; one at right angles to the optic axis (ordinary ray) and one parallel to the optic axis (extraordinary ray), these are thus vibrating at right angles to each other (*Figure 31.12*).

A uniaxial stone cut with its table facet parallel to the optic axis will show the extraordinary ray to move from the position of greatest birefringence to the position of the ordinary ray. Thus, such a stone placed on the dense glass of the refractometer will, when the direction of the vertical crystal axis—which is also the direction of the optic axis—is parallel to a line drawn from the window of the instrument to the eyepiece, show a single edge due to the vibrations of the ordinary ray. When the stone is turned the extraordinary ray will be seen to separate until, when the angle turned is 90 degrees, the maximum separation of the two shadow edges is obtained. Careful measurement of these shadow edges at their maximum separation and the subtraction of the lowest numerical reading from the greatest will give the value of the birefringence of the stone.

If the facet tested is cut perpendicular to the optic axis the vibrations of both the ordinary ray and the extraordinary ray will be present and the full double refraction will be seen at all positions during a complete rotation of the stone; a test on another facet would be necessary before the optic sign could be determined. If the table facet does not lie in either of these planes, it will be seen that on turning the stone on the refractometer there will be the stationary shadow edge of the ordinary ray and that the extraordinary ray will move from some position between that of the ordinary ray and that of the full divergence of the extraordinary ray, but that the extraordinary ray will not at any time coincide with the ordinary ray.

Biaxial Stones

In biaxial stones there are two directions of single refraction (optic axes) and three critical refractive indices, α, β and γ, as explained earlier. Although there can be only two polarized rays passing along any one direction in the crystal the three refractive indices correspond to rays vibrating in three mutually perpendicular directions. One of these, α, has the lowest refractive index and consists of rays vibrating parallel to the acute bisectrix in optically negative crystals, and parallel to the obtuse bisectrix in positive crystals. Another ray, γ, has the highest refractive index and is vibrating parallel to the obtuse and the acute bisectrix respectively in the two instances mentioned. The third ray, β, has an intermediate index and consists of light vibrating at right angles to the plane of the optic axes, that is at right angles to α and γ. *Figure 31.13* illustrates the vibration directions in a biaxial crystal.

The behaviour of the shadow edges on the refractometer is more complicated in the case of biaxial stones for, in general, both the shadow edges seen on the refractometer scale move and are thus both 'extraordinary'. The question of the β ray and the sign of refraction also needs comment. When the angle between the optic axes is small, either the shadow edge with the higher index, or that with the lower index will move very little, then it will be easy to see whether the sign is positive (β nearer to α) or negative. When the facet tested happens to be cut at right angles to the vibration direction of one of the critical rays, this ray will be seen as an invariable edge when the stone is rotated on the refractometer. When this direction is β there will be four positions during a rotation of the stone through a full circle, where the moving edge crosses over the invariable β

position giving at four points a single edge—that of β. A table facet cut so that it is oriented haphazardly to the main optical directions, as is the case in most gemstones, will give readings much more difficult to interpret. Each of the principle refractive indices will be reached by one or other of the shadow edges at different positions of the stone. Both shadow edges move and it is a matter of taking the lowest reading reached by the lower

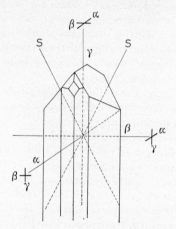

Figure 31.13. The principal vibration directions in a positive biaxial crystal. SS are the optic axes

and the highest reached by the higher edge to determine the full birefringence of the stone. The determination of β is difficult to determine in such cases, but generally the optic sign may be obtained by noting which of the two shadow edges passes the half-way mark between the highest and lowest readings. If it is the upper one the stone is positive, and if the lower it is negative.

Monochromatic light

The shadow edges seen in a refractometer when monochromatic light is used are sharp but may not be obvious. These edges may quite easily be missed if the observer has no notion where they should be. Therefore it is better first to use white light in order to find out more easily where the edges are, and then to use monochromatic light to see the two edges and to read their indices. A polaroid disc rotated over the eyepiece will select each edge in turn and may help in the reading of weak shadow edges.

HIGH REFRACTIVE LIQUID METHODS

The refractometer provides the most convenient method for the measurement of the refractive indices of gemstones, but the constant can be measured, either accurately or approximately by a number of other methods and these will be discussed now. The methods depending upon the behaviour of gemstones in liquids of high refraction have some importance and will be dealt with first. When a transparent stone is immersed in a liquid of the same refractive index it becomes virtually invisible, as, for example, does ice in water, and this gives a simple and effective method of gauging the refractive index of gemstones whether they are rough or cut.

The stones are immersed in liquids of known refractive index contained in suitable glass vessels, and the stones will have a refractive index near to that of the liquid in which they most completely disappear. The method is most useful in the detection of 'intruders' in a parcel of small stones, for if a liquid matching the bulk of the stones is chosen any stones of a different species will show up by their different relief. This method is particularly useful for a multi-stone diamond brooch in which some synthetic white sapphires or spinels are suspected. In methylene iodide, such stones would show up by their low relief against the high relief shown by the diamonds (*Figure 31.14*). The method is less satisfactory with white zircon, synthetic

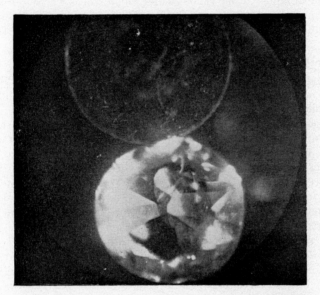

Figure 31.14. *Difference in relief of gemstones in a highly refractive liquid*

rutile or synthetic strontium titanate which have refractive indices near to that of diamond.

Becke Line Method

The above method is capable of greater refinement, when small fragments of the material, or even cut stones, are immersed in liquid and examined microscopically. The method, known as the Becke line method, needs considerable operational practice in order to obtain good results. An edge of the stone is sharply focused and when the focus is raised or lowered a bright rim of light will be seen passing from the stone into the liquid, or vice versa, according to which has the higher refractive index. Trial with several liquids will give a pair, one of which has a higher and one a lower refractive index than the stone; therefore the index of the stone must lie somewhere between the indices of the two liquids. The closer together the differences in refractive indices of the two liquids the more accurate the final determination of the index of the stone will be. In white light the edges of the specimen appear coloured when a near match is obtained, but for accurate results monochromatic light should be used. The rule for the Becke line is simple and may be expressed as follows.

(1) On lowering the focus the line of light passes into the substance of lower refractive index.

(2) On raising the focus the line of light passes into the substance of higher refractive index.

The best results are obtained with the Becke method when small fragments scraped from a specimen are used, for much depends upon the shape of the piece examined. Hence the method is particularly useful in the testing of amber, stone carvings and rough stones where a tiny splinter can be removed and immersed in a pool of liquid on a glass microscope slide for examination.

Plato Method

First described by W. Plato the method is a variation of the Becke line test. The method depends on the difference in behaviour of the light effects of the shadow edges of stones immersed in liquid as seen through the microscope. Briefly, when a stone is immersed in a liquid of a higher refractive index than that of the stone and the focus is in the liquid above the stone, the facet edges appear black; when the focus is lowered into the stone the appearance of the facet edges is white. This determines that the stone has a lower index than that of the liquid. Conversely, if the stone has a higher index than the liquid the effect is reversed, the facet edges appearing white when the focus is in the liquid, and black when in the stone. In bire-fringent stones it is the greater refractive index which seems to be the effective one, but Plato found that by using a polarizing plate the two edges of a doubly refractive stone could be measured. With this method the best results are obtained when the sub-stage diaphragm is partially closed; there may be some advantage in removing the sub-stage condenser, but not, of course, the partially closed diaphragm.

Immersion Contrast Method

A much simpler method of refractive index measurement by immersion in liquids has been worked out by B. W. Anderson. Actually a modification of the Becke line test, this immersion contrast method, however, needs no microscope. The stones to be tested are placed in a glass dish and immersed in a suitable fluid. The cell with the stones in liquid is placed on a ground-glass sheet which is so placed that an underside view can conveniently be seen in a mirror. The stones in the cell are illuminated by a single overhead light and on examining the stones through the underneath mirror striking differences are seen in accordance with their refractive indices, in relation to the refractive index of the liquid in which they are immersed (*Figure 31.15*). Stones with a higher index than that of the liquid show a dark border and the facet edges appear as white lines. In stones with an index lower than that of the liquid this effect is reversed, the borders being white and the facet edges appearing as black lines. Further, a good indication of the degree to which the index of the stone and liquid differs can be obtained by noting the width of the dark or pale border and of the lines denoting the facet edges. When a near match exists between the stone and the fluid these signs almost disappear and spectrum colours are seen at the margin of the stone, due to the higher dispersion of the fluid, unless monochromatic light is used.

The effect can be obtained photographically, giving a permanent record, by placing a piece of slow film or bromide paper under the dish and exposing to an overhead light for a second or so before developing in the usual manner. The negative so obtained will be in reverse, that is the darks and lights

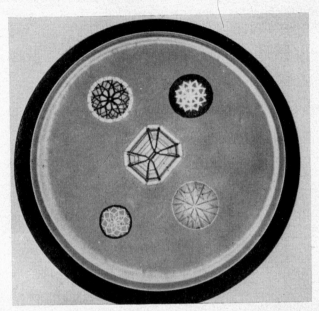

Figure 31.15. The effect of immersion contrast
(By courtesy of B. W. Anderson)

will be reversed. This is important if bromide paper is used, but in the case of film, this will normally be printed on to paper afterwards, which corrects the effect to normal.

The immersion contrast method may be used for cabochon stones as well as for faceted stones. In some cases the method has been found to show up the curved structure lines in synthetic corundum which could not be seen during ordinary microscopic examination. If the refractive index of the immersion liquid is near to that of the stone the picture will produce a 'life-size' reproduction of the stone, showing clearly the symmetry and distribution of the facets, and any outstanding internal structures and zoning. Such a picture may be of considerable value in cases needing future identification of the stone. Photographic emulsions are more sensitive to blue than to yellow light and the refractive index of the liquid will be higher for the blue rays. This must be remembered when stones having an index of refraction near to that of the liquid are examined.

Shadow Methods

Similar in operation are various tests known as the shadow methods. The set-up is again similar. The specimen is immersed in oils of different refractive indices and, according to a method devised by G. O. Wild, the microscope can be dispensed with. The cell of liquid and stone is held over a bright surface, such as white blotting paper, with sufficient room below for a piece of black card with a straight edge to be passed from one side. When the stone and liquid match in index there is no deviation of the light rays (*Figure 31.16a*), but when the liquid in which the stone is immersed has the higher index the edge of the black card will advance into the stone (*Figure 31.16b*), or if the liquid is of lower refractive index the stone will cut into the edge of the card (*Figure 31.16c*).

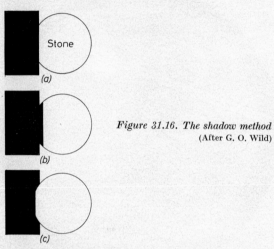

Figure 31.16. The shadow method
(After G. O. Wild)

The reason for this is explained by W. F. Eppler (*Figure 31.17*). Shown in vertical section is the corner outline of an aquamarine (n—1·57) immersed in methylene iodide. On looking at the specimen vertically from above the only light from the card edge that can reach the eye is that which follows the indicated line. The light enters the eye from farther 'into' the specimen, on the right side of the view straight through the stone. This is shown as a

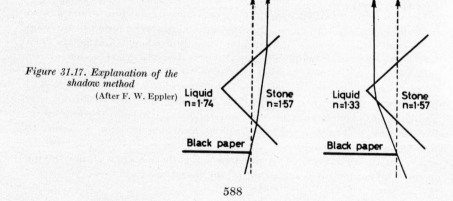

Figure 31.17. Explanation of the shadow method
(After F. W. Eppler)

dotted line. The black card thus seems to have proceeded into the stone. When the stone is immersed in water (n—1·33) the edge of the card is visible on the left of the view straight through the stone and seems to have travelled out of the specimen.

Suitable Liquids for Immersion Methods

The following liquids are suitable for use with the immersion methods of measuring the refractive index.

Water	1·33	Clove oil	1·54	Carbon disulphide	1·63
Alcohol	1·36	Ethylene dibromide	1·54	Acetylene	
Amyl acetate	1·37	Nitrobenzene	1·55	tetrabromide	1·63
Chloroform	1·45	Brom-toluene	1·55	Monobromo-	
Petroleum	1·45	Dimethylaniline	1·56	naphthalene	1·66
Carbon tetrachloride	1·46	Benzyl benzoate	1·56	Monoiodo-	
Turpentine	1·47	Monobromo-		naphthalene	1·70
Olive oil	1·47	benzene	1·56	Methylene iodide	1·74
Glycerine	1·47	Orthotoluidine	1·57	Methylene iodide	
Castor Oil	1·48	Aniline	1·58	and sulphur	1·78
Xylene	1·49	Cinnamon oil	1·59	Methylene iodide,	
Toluene	1·49	Bromoform	1·59	S & C_2I_4	1·81
Benzene	1·50	Cassia oil	1·60	Phenyldi-	
Cedar wood oil	1·51	Monoiodobenzene	1·62	iodoarsine	1·85
Monochlorbenzene	1·53	Monochlor-		West's solution	2·05
Canada balsam	1·53	naphthalene	1·63		

Slight differences in the purity of these oils and liquids occur in the commercial state and it is advisable to check these values on a refractometer if accurate work is contemplated. For usual routine operations these values may be accepted.

A number of these liquids are deleterious to the human system and they should not be inhaled, but for the short period during which they would be used they would not be harmful. The two last mentioned fluids are dangerous and should not be allowed to get on to the skin or blistering will occur.

LIGHT RAY DEVIATION METHOD

Direct Measurement Method

The following three methods of refractive index measurement depend upon the amount of bending of a ray of light passing from one medium to another of greater optical density. The first of these, called the direct measurement method, or de Chaulnes method, depends upon the change of focus caused by placing a plate of the substance whose refractive index is required to be found over an object in the focus of a microscope (*Figure 31.18*). Two parallel surfaces of the medium are needed, such as the table and culet of a diamond, or the two parallel faces of an octahedral crystal. By using the calibrated fine adjustment of the microscope, or better by using a microscope fitted with a scale and vernier on the body tube, the real and apparent depth of the stone may be measured. The microscope is first focused on to a mark on the top facet and the vernier reading noted (A), and then a mark below the stone on the surface of the glass slide upon which the specimen is resting is now focused through the stone and a second vernier reading

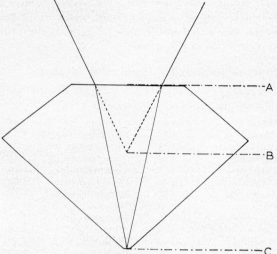

Figure 31.18. The principle of the direct measurement method of refractive index determination

taken (B). Finally a third reading is taken (C) when the microscope is focused on to the surface of the bare glass slide. As the refractive index of the medium depends on the ratio of real depth of the specimen and the apparent depth when seen through the specimen then:

$$\frac{\text{Real depth}}{\text{Apparent depth}} = \frac{C-A}{B-A} = \text{Refractive index}$$

The method is not very accurate but it can be useful with stones having a higher refractive index than can be measured on the refractometer.

Brewster's Angle

Having no great accuracy and being rather difficult to carry out is the method known as Brewster's angle. It may on occasion serve to distinguish between stones of similar appearance when the difference in the refractive index is considerable, such as demantoid garnet and peridot or black diamond and black spinel. David Brewster found that when light was reflected from a transparent surface, the maximum degree of polarization in the reflected light was attained when the reflected and refracted rays were at 90 degrees (*Figure 31.19*), and that the refractive index of the medium equals tan i, where i is the angle of maximum polarization. To carry out the measurement some form of optical angle measuring apparatus fitted with a

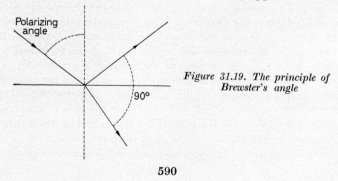

Polarizing angle

90°

Figure 31.19. The principle of Brewster's angle

polarizer is needed. This may be a spectrometer, as described in the following pages, which is fitted with a polaroid plate or nicol prism in the eyepiece, so turned that its vibration direction is at right angles to those of the reflected rays. Measurement of the angle where the reflected ray of a source of light incident on the surface of the stone is found to be nearly polarized will, on computation, give the refractive index.

Minimum Deviation Method

The most accurate method of refractive index measurement is by the method of minimum deviation, a method which can be applied to any unmounted transparent stone which has well-cut facets. The method, however, needs rather elaborate apparatus, a spectrometer, and a great deal of skill and calculation before a result can be obtained. It is, however, the best method for obtaining accurate values of dispersion, but unless the stone is specially oriented the full double refraction cannot be measured. The table spectrometer (*Figure 31.20*), which is normally used for this method, will be first discussed as an instrument using a glass prism, and then when the glass prism is replaced by a gemstone of which the index of refraction is required.

Table Spectrometer and use with Glass Prism

The table spectrometer consists essentially of a collimator, fixed rigidly. This has an adjustable slit at one end to control the amount of light needed; immediately behind the slit is a tube containing an optical system so arranged that the slit is placed exactly at the principal focus, ensuring that all the light transmitted is rendered parallel. This parallel light then falls on the prism and is refracted as already explained.

The prism is supported on a table which can be rotated, surrounded by a rigid graduated circle; a telescope, held by an arm rotating round the circle, gathers the light from the prism, revealing the spectrum.

In all this, so far, there is nothing radically different from hand spectroscopes. The real difference lies in the graduated circle, divided into degrees,

Figure 31.20. The table spectrometer

591

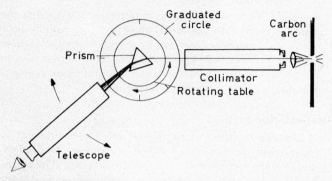

Figure 31.21. Diagram of the spectrometer fitted with a glass prism

half degrees or even quarter degrees. A vernier is attached to the arm of the telescope and angles can be measured on the circle to the nearest minute or half-minute (*Figure 31.21*).

It remains to describe the adaptation of this instrument for measurement of refractive indices, known variously as the minimum deviation, prism or goniometric method, and consisting of a measurement of the angle of the prism and the angle of deviation of the spectrum, and a calculation based on a formula.

For the initial experiment it is best to use the prism provided with the instrument. As already stated, this is of optical flint glass and has optically flat faces, giving an angle of 60 degrees (approximately). It is, in fact, from every point of view, the ideal object to measure; no stone that the author has ever measured is so perfectly suited to this purpose.

If the prism is adjusted so that spectrum is visible it can be seen, by rotating the prism on the supporting table, that there is a position beyond which the rays forming the spectrum will not pass, whichever way the prism is turned. This is called the position of minimum deviation (where the spectrum is least deviated from the original path of the light). This is the position of symmetry where the angle of entry into the prism is equal to the angle of emergence: at all other positions the deviation will be greater. In the following argument it will be advisable to consider the light as being monochromatic (that is, of one wavelength).

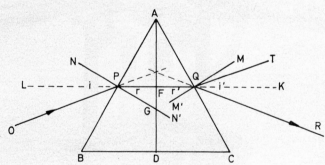

Figure 31.22. The principle of the minimum deviation method of refractive index measurement

In *Figure 31.22* let ABC be the prism, BAC being the refracting angle, OP the path of incident ray, PQ of the refracted ray and QR of the emergent ray, NN' and MM' the normals to the prism faces AB and AC at P and Q respectively. Let AD be the bisectrix of BAC cutting PQ normally at F and cutting NN' at G. Let LK be the projection at either end of PQ.

Then in the triangles APG and PFG, APG = PFG (since they are both right angles), AGP is common, therefore FPG = PAG; but FPG is the angle of refraction (*r*) and PAG is half the prism angle BAC, so that the angle of refraction is equal to half the prism angle.

Now OPN is the angle of incidence and is composed of LPO and NPL, but NPL = FPG (angle of refraction *r*) = half prism angle BAC.

If QT is drawn parallel to OP (the incident ray), then TOK = LPO by construction; but LPO = RQK, therefore LPO = half TQR, but TQR is, equal to the angle of minimum deviation (*d*), since TQ is parallel to OP, therefore LPO = half angle of deviation *d*. Thus the angle of incidence OPN = half BAC + half TQR.

Thus if the prism angle is called A and the deviation angle is called D, we have

$$\text{the refractive index} = \frac{\sin i}{\sin r}$$

but $i = \frac{1}{2}A + \frac{1}{2}D$ and $r = \frac{1}{2}A$, therefore

$$\text{the refractive index} = \frac{\sin \frac{1}{2}(A+D)}{\sin \frac{1}{2}A}$$

From this it is obvious that if it is possible to measure the deviation and the prism angle, the refractive index may readily be calculated by means of mathematical tables.

The prism angle is turned toward the collimator and the reflections of the slit are measured on either side, according to the laws of reflection (angle of incidence = angle of reflection); the angle subtended by these two reflections is equal to twice the angle of the prism (*Figure 31.23*).

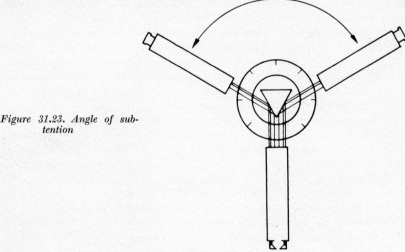

*Figure 31.23. Angle of sub-
    tention*

593

Great care should be taken to be absolutely sure of this angle. The measurements should be repeated several times until agreement is reached. It follows from this that if the reflection angle be measured to the nearest minute the angle of the prism can be calculated to the nearest half-minute.

The deviation angle should be measured on both sides and the mean of the two angles taken. It is perhaps enough to measure the angle subtended by the spectrum on both sides and halve the result. Deviation should be at its minimum.

The simple case has been presented of a glass prism using monochromatic light. The most useful light source is the carbon arc, which gives a strong, continuous spectrum in addition to the sodium emission lines (5893 Å). Lithium (6708 Å) and thallium (5349 Å) can readily be introduced into the arc. In fact, all metallic emission spectra can be so introduced.

By measuring the deviations of various lines in the visible spectrum the dispersion can be calculated. It should be remembered that the prism has to be adjusted to minimum deviation for every line measured.

The dispersion of a substance is sometimes given as the difference in refractive index for the B and G lines of the solar spectrum. A more favourite range is hydrogen (6563 Å) and hydrogen (4341 Å), while lithium (6708 Å) to calcium (4227 Å) is sometimes used.

Table Spectrometer and use with Gemstones

It is obvious that the glass prism can be replaced by a prism of another substance, and in applying this method to the study of gemstones it will be realized that it is possible to find two facets of a cut stone which together will form a prism suitable for the purpose. It is at this stage that the first trouble occurs. With the single exception of diamond very few stones are well enough cut to give good reflection images and, as a direct result, they yield poor spectra. The prism angle also is important. The glass prism has an angle of about 60 degrees, this is the desirable angle, but such angles, unfortunately, are not always obtainable. (The larger the angle the greater the deviation, and consequently greater accuracy in the result.)

If the prism angle is too great there is total internal reflection at the second prism face, and consequently no spectrum can be seen. The rule governing this limit is that the prism angle must not exceed twice the critical angle. The only gemstones in which the prism angles are thus seriously limited are diamond and blende (critical angle 24 degrees). Zircon has a critical angle of $30\frac{1}{2}$ degrees and demantoid 32 degrees for sodium light.

It is necessary to adjust the prism so that both faces are in zone. In the case of the glass prism this can be achieved by means of the screws attached to the rotatable table for that purpose. A gemstone should be fixed on wax and is not so readily adjustable. It is convenient to obtain the spectrum first by naked eye; this will generally be found to be slanting when the sodium line is seen through the telescope. The stone should be tilted until the spectrum moves horizontally when the stone is turned, not rising or falling; in this position the reflections of the slit can be brought into view by turning the stone to the required angle. Final adjustments can be made and the stone is then in position for the measurements.

The question now arises as to the optical nature of the stones. With cubic minerals such as diamond, blende, garnet, spinel, and fluorspar there is only one index of refraction, and in consequence any suitable pair of facets will suffice; the mineral has the same refractive index in any direction.

With doubly refracting stones complications arise. In uniaxial minerals (tetragonal, hexagonal and trigonal), the optic axis coincides with the principal crystallographic axis. Uniaxial stones have two indices; the ordinary ray has the same refractive index in any direction, the extra-ordinary ray is at its maximum (positive) or minimum (negative) in directions perpendicular to the optic axis. In practice this means that any prism will give the refractive index of the ordinary ray, but unless the prism is cut so that the direction of the light is normal to the optic axis, the maximum double refraction will not be obtained.

Actually very few species of gemstones are cut to obtain maximum double refraction. Tourmaline is an exception, since (especially in the green varieties) the ordinary ray is too strongly absorbed, and so the stone is cut with the table facet parallel to the crystallographic axis, the shape of the crystal guiding the lapidary's hand. It follows that a prism formed by the table facet and a back facet will have its edge (if projected) parallel to the optic axis, and so the beam of light will be normal to the axis, complete double refraction resulting. Quartz, owing to its natural crystal habit, is sometimes cut with the table facet parallel to the optic axis.

With corundum, however, the ordinary ray has a richer colour than the extraordinary ray in all colour varieties, so that the ideal cutting is with the table facet normal to the optic axis; since rubies and sapphires are usually rather shallow cut stones it is impossible to use two of the back facets as a prism, and consequently the full double refraction is never obtainable unless the stone is specially cut for this purpose (in which case it would be less desirable as a gemstone). A curious fact about this valuable and highly prized species is that the facets, even the table (which is naturally the best polished), are rarely polished flat enough for the purpose.

Zircons are usually brilliant-cut, with the table facet more or less parallel to the optic axis; a suitable pavilion facet may be found that will yield very nearly the full double refraction in conjunction with the table. The double refraction, however, is so large (0·058 to 0·059) that the orientation of the prism needs to be exactly perpendicular to the optic axis to obtain its maximum.

The case of biaxial stones is almost hopeless with normally cut gemstones, since there is no ordinary ray with a constant refractive index. In ortho-rhombic crystals, the plane of the optic axes is parallel to two of the crystallographic axes and normal to the third; that is, it can be parallel to any one of the three planes of orthorhombic symmetry. The optic axes are, of course, directions of single refraction, in this case the mean refractive index β, which can also be obtained in any direction parallel to the plane of the two optic axes; the direction of the acute bisectrix of the optic axes gives α and β (positive) or β and γ (negative), the obtuse bisectrix β and γ (positive) and α and β (negative). The optic normal, that is the direction normal to the optic axial plane, gives α and γ, the full double refraction. Unfortunately, stones are rarely cut so as to yield prisms oriented for any of these directions.

In monoclinic crystals the plane of the optic axes is related only to the ortho axis b; it must either be parallel or normal to b, so that the optic axes bear only a slight relationship to the external crystal symmetry.

Here again suitable cut stones are very rare, since the same rule concerning the indices and their directions applies as in orthorhombic crystals.

Triclinic minerals having no axis or plane of symmetry, may have optic axial planes in any direction. Fortunately this, the lowest system of crystal symmetry, is very rare in gemstones. among transparent stones only the rarely cut axinite and kyanite being triclinic.

MEASUREMENTS AND CALCULATIONS

The following two cases are actual examples of measurements and calculations made by C. J. Payne.

The first example is a diamond, chosen since this species is beyond the range of any refractometer, the second is a tourmaline, chosen as an example of the measurement of double refraction (for the left readings 360 degrees are added for convenience). All values are for the sodium D lines (5893 Å).

I. Silver-cape diamond, emerald cut, weight $3\frac{3}{4}$ carats (approximately). Readings for prism angle:

Left	=	$403°55'$	$395°24'$	$404°18\frac{1}{2}'$	$403°56\frac{1}{2}'$
Right	=	$315°47\frac{1}{2}'$	$307°15\frac{1}{2}'$	$316°11'$	$315°49'$
2A	=	$88°7\frac{1}{2}'$	$88°8\frac{1}{2}'$	$88°7\frac{1}{2}'$	$88°7\frac{1}{2}'$
A	=	$44°3\frac{3}{4}'$	$44°4\frac{1}{4}'$	$44°3\frac{3}{4}'$	$44°3\frac{3}{4}'$

The best value appears to be A $= 44°3\frac{3}{4}'$

Readings for deviation angle:

$$446°2'$$
$$273°44'$$

$$2D = 172°18' \text{ therefore } D = 86°9'$$

Refraction index $= \dfrac{\sin \frac{1}{2}(A+D)}{\sin \frac{1}{2}A} = \dfrac{\sin \frac{1}{2}(44°3\frac{3}{4}' + 86°9')}{\sin \frac{1}{2}(44°3\frac{3}{4}')} = \dfrac{\sin 65°6\frac{3}{8}'}{\sin 22°1\frac{7}{8}'}$

$$\text{log. } \sin 65°6\frac{3}{8}' = 1·95766$$
$$\text{log. } \sin 22°1\frac{7}{8}' = 1·57416$$

$$\text{log. } 0·38350 = 2·4183$$

II. Pale pink tourmaline, optic axis parallel to length of stone, $d = 3·055$. Readings for prism angle:

Left	=	$424°37\frac{1}{2}'$	$424°5'$	$424°43\frac{1}{2}'$	$425°18'$
Right	=	$295°9'$	$294°36\frac{1}{2}'$	$295°14\frac{1}{2}'$	$295°49\frac{1}{2}'$
2A	=	$129°28\frac{1}{2}'$	$129°28\frac{1}{2}'$	$129°29'$	$129°28\frac{1}{2}'$
A	=	$64°44\frac{1}{4}'$	$64°44\frac{1}{4}'$	$64°44\frac{1}{2}'$	$64°44\frac{1}{4}'$

The best value appears to be A $= 64°44\frac{1}{4}'$

Readings for the deviation angle:

$$
\begin{array}{ccc}
 & \omega & \epsilon \\
\text{Left} = & 418°10' & 415°47' \\
\text{Right} = & 301°45' & 304°11' \\
\hline
2D = & 116°25' & 111°36' \\
\text{therefore } D = & 58°12\tfrac{1}{2}' & 55°48'
\end{array}
$$

$$
\text{Refraction index} = \frac{\sin \tfrac{1}{2}(64°44\tfrac{1}{4}' + 58°12\tfrac{1}{2}')}{\sin \tfrac{1}{2}(64°44\tfrac{1}{4}')} \qquad \frac{\sin \tfrac{1}{2}(64°44\tfrac{1}{4}' + 55°48')}{\sin \tfrac{1}{2}(64°44\tfrac{1}{4}')}
$$

$$
= \frac{\sin 61°28\tfrac{3}{8}'}{\sin 32°22\tfrac{1}{8}'} \qquad \frac{\sin 60°16\tfrac{1}{8}'}{\sin 32°22\tfrac{1}{8}'}
$$

$$
\begin{aligned}
\log.\sin 61°28\tfrac{3}{8}' &= \text{I.94379} & \log.\sin 60°16\tfrac{1}{8}' &= \text{I.93870} \\
\log.\sin 32°22\tfrac{1}{8}' &= \text{I.72865} & \log.\sin 32°22\tfrac{1}{8}' &= \text{I.72865}
\end{aligned}
$$

$$
\log. 0{\cdot}21515 = 1{\cdot}6411 \qquad\qquad \log. 0{\cdot}21005 = 1{\cdot}6220
$$

Double refraction $\omega - \epsilon$ since tourmaline is negative is $0{\cdot}0191$.

CHAPTER 32

COLOUR IN GEM-TESTING

FILTERS

However exactly two colours may match one another to the unaided eye, there is still a strong possibility that so far as their spectral composition is concerned they are vastly different. This is certain to be the case if the colours belong to two gemstones of different species, or to a real and to an imitation stone made to resemble it. The simplest way in which differences in the spectral composition of two similar colours can be revealed is by using a suitable colour filter. A colour filter is a piece of coloured glass or gelatine, or in some cases a coloured solution, which filters light of mixed wavelengths passing through it. A filter allows certain colours to pass, others it absorbs. Any coloured transparent substance is in one sense a colour filter, but those most sought after, because they are most efficient for their purpose, are those which have sharp, well-defined absorption bands and relatively narrow regions in which they transmit.

Colour filters are much used in photography; a wide range is available from both Kodak and Ilford. One series represents an attempt to provide approximately monochromatic light in each of the main spectral regions by means of filters of almost pure colours. These are 'spectrum red', 'spectrum yellow' and so on, and transmission curves are provided by the makers showing the wavelength of the peak transmission and the rapidity with which this falls away on the long-wave and short-wave side. Another useful series is designed for use in conjunction with a mercury lamp. Mercury vapour emits light of only a few wavelengths in the visible spectrum, namely in the orange-red at 6234 and 6152 Å, a yellow doublet at 5790 and 5770 Å, a green line at 5461 Å, a blue doublet at 4359 and 4348 Å, and violet lines at 4078 and 4047 Å. Filters are provided which transmit each of these but cut out all the others. Thus a 'mercury yellow' filter transmits only the yellow mercury doublet. Combined with a mercury lamp, these filters thus provide a much more efficient monochromatic source in the various regions of the spectrum indicated than can be expected with the more general type of filter designed for use with white light.

Chelsea Filter

The most generally useful filter for gemmological purposes, however, is not a monochromatic but a dichromatic type—that is one transmitting narrow bands of light in the two chosen regions of the spectrum. The most efficient of these so far produced is known as the Chelsea filter (*Figure 32.1*), which was originally devised in the laboratory of the London Chamber of Commerce, in 1934, and marketed shortly afterwards by the Gemmological

Association. This transmits in the deep red near 6900 Å and in the yellow-green near 5400 Å. Through such a filter substances can only appear red or green or a brownish tint resulting from a mixture of the two. It so happens that emerald, though a green stone, absorbs considerably in the yellow-green region transmitted by the Chelsea filter and transmits freely

Figure 32.1. The Chelsea colour filter

in the deep red. Thus, through this filter, a typical emerald of good commercial quality (Colombian or Siberian) will appear decidedly red—almost a ruby red in favourable cases. The result is most striking when the stone is held close to an ordinary electric light and viewed through the filter held close to the eye (*Figure 32.2*). All green pastes, most soudé emeralds, green sapphire and most tourmalines show no red through the filter. On the other hand, green fluorspar, green zircon and demantoid garnet do show a pinkish appearance under the filter, though not the decided red of a good-class emerald.

Figure 32.2. Using the colour filter

Since neither South African nor Indian emeralds show a change to red the filter must be used with care and discretion if mistaken judgments are not to be made. In the hands of an experienced user it can undoubtedly be a most useful gadget where more precise tests cannot be applied. It may be of value also in arousing suspicion where synthetic emeralds are concerned, since these, with their colour entirely due to chromium, are remarkable for the tremendously strong ruby-red seen through the Chelsea filter.

Another series of colours which appear unexpectedly red through this same filter are the blue colours due to cobalt—whether in synthetic blue spinel, blue cobalt glass, or a doublet with the latter as a base. Cobalt in this form gives rise to three massive absorption bands, one of which covers the green transmission region of the filter, while on the other hand, deep red is freely transmitted. Thus, the Chelsea filter provides a quick means of checking the presence of those common fakes, the pale blue synthetic spinels which represent aquamarine and blue zircon. The genuine aquamarine and blue zircon cut out practically all the red from the spectrum, and thus through the filter have a distinctive green appearance, while the spinel imitation is either a bright red or a peculiar orange-brown colour. Unfortunately, natural blue spinel can appear reddish through the filter and so can a Ceylon sapphire containing a touch of chromium—that is a mauve or slightly purplish sapphire.

Other Filters

The Chelsea filter was by no means the first to be applied to the detection of emerald imitations—there were many such 'emerald loupes' issued on the Continent, mostly making use of cobalt glass as a basis. In none of these, however, were the regions of transmission so clearly cut, and many were so dark as to be nearly opaque.

Attempts have also been made to extend the filter technique to cover a wide range of stones. In Michel's 'Detectoscope' a whole series of filters could be turned into position in a viewing instrument with a built-in light, and, by studying long lists of the reactions to be expected in each case with each of the well-known coloured stones, many of these could be identified with some degree of certainty. More recently, L. Trumper has had some success along similar lines, and has had the ingenious idea of using a slab of synthetic ruby as part of one of his filters. Although the results obtained by these means can be most interesting, so far as the accurate identification of gemstones is concerned more definite tests are desirable.

DICHROISM AND PLEOCHROISM

A far more important form of colour analysis is possible in most doubly refractive transparent stones. A beam of light reaching the eye after passing through a doubly refractive crystal, as has been explained, consists in general not of one ray but of two, each of which is polarized and vibrating in a plane at right angles to each other. If the crystal is coloured, each of the rays will usually undergo a different degree or type of colour absorption in its passage through the stone, and will thus emerge differently coloured. It is not possible for the unaided eye to separate the two rays, which reach it simultaneously and are following an identical path, but by quite simple polarizing apparatus the two rays can be observed separately, or, better still, side by side.

What the unaided eye can do, however, is to notice a change in colour or in depth of colour as the stone is viewed from different directions. This change in colour with direction is known as dichroism (two-colour effect), or by the more general term pleochroism (many-coloured effect). If dichroism can be detected it is a sure sign that the stone concerned is birefringent. By this means, therefore, ruby can quickly be distinguished from spinel or garnet of similar colour, since the latter are cubic minerals, and therefore singly refractive and non-dichroic. The absence of detectable dichroism does not necessarily mean that the stone is singly refractive, nor does the strength of the dichroism bear any relation to the extent of the birefringence. Thus the mineral zircon, despite its notable double refraction, is practically non-dichroic in its natural state, while blue apatite, aquamarine and iolite, none of which has strong double refraction, are all markedly dichroic stones.

Uniaxial Stones

The influence of the crystal direction upon colour is not merely of importance from the diagnostic point of view; it also greatly concerns the lapidary, though he may not think of it in scientific terms. For example, ruby is a colour variety of corundum—a uniaxial mineral—which means that along the optic axis there is one ray only, the ordinary ray, which always vibrates at right angles to the optic axis. In all other directions the ordinary ray is mingled with the extraordinary ray, although only in light travelling at right angles to the optic axis does this attain its maximum difference in refractive index and in colour from the ordinary ray. From a colour point of view, therefore, it is vitally important that, in a dichroic mineral, the better colour should be that belonging to the ordinary ray. In both ruby and sapphire this is so, and the lapidary gets his best effects where he can cut the table facet of the stone at right angles to the optic axis, so that the observer looking down at the stone is looking along the optic axis and receiving, undiluted, the fine colour of the ordinary ray.

In ruby, the ordinary ray is a fine crimson, while the extraordinary ray has a less pleasing yellowish tinge. In sapphire the ordinary ray is deep blue, the extraordinary ray a paler and more greenish or yellowish blue. The peculiar appearance of synthetic ruby and sapphire is partly due at least to the fact that they have been wrongly oriented when cutting. In most natural rubies the optic axis will be found nearly perpendicular to the table: the lapidary is guided in his choice not only by the run of the colour but by the squat habit of the crystals. The presence of strong dichroism through the table facet (as seen with a dichroscope) is at least an indication that the ruby may be synthetic. In sapphire the colour is seldom homogeneous, occurring in bands, patches and zones, and the distribution of these rather than the optical direction will determine the lapidary's choice of cutting.

Not all uniaxial gems are so obliging as to show their best colour along the optic axis. In both aquamarine and blue apatite, for instance, the ordinary ray is a feeble tint compared with the fine blue of the extraordinary ray. Since the ordinary ray must always be present to at least 50 per cent in terms of colour, this means that the best one can do in these cases is to cut the stone with its table facet parallel to the optic axis, and be content to see the blue of the extraordinary ray at half strength.

Even within one species, the strength of the dichroism varies considerably. Tourmaline is a good example of this. Tourmaline is often quoted as an extreme case of dichroism, and it is stated that the ordinary ray is almost completely absorbed. This is actually only true of the dark brown and dark green varieties; in the red, pink, yellow and paler green stones the dichroism is not nearly so intense. Thus, while with a dark green tourmaline crystal the lapidary is bound to make his table facet parallel to the crystal and the optic axis if he is to get any light and colour in the stone at all, in pink and other pale coloured tourmalines he will want the deepest colour possible, and will get a better coloured stone if the table facet can be oriented at right angles to the optic axis.

Biaxial Stones

In biaxial stones the matter is more complex. Although there can still only be two polarized rays passing along any one direction in the crystal, there are three critical refractive indices corresponding to rays vibrating in the three mutually perpendicular directions.

In a coloured biaxial crystal there will generally be a particular colour or shade of colour associated with each of these critical vibration directions. Rays travelling and vibrating in random directions will have refractive indices and colours intermediate between those belonging to the principal directions. Coloured biaxial stones, therefore, are pleochroic or trichroic rather than dichroic, though the last expression is still commonly used for them.

Perhaps the most startling case of pleochroism is with the gem mineral iolite. The three colours in this attractive species are α, pale brownish yellow, β, pale blue, and γ, deep violet blue. Stones cut parallel to the prism edge show a fine sapphire blue when viewed through the table, while at right angles to this it appears to be almost colourless. A gemstone of much greater commercial importance which also shows remarkable pleochroism is the chrome-rich type of chrysoberyl known as alexandrite. In fine Siberian specimens of this rare gemstone there are three contrasted colours belonging to the principal rays, the hues belonging to the least, mean, and greatest indices being raspberry-red, orange, and an almost emerald green. In the larger and usually more flawless alexandrites from Ceylon there is less chromium, therefore the above colours are thus far less pronounced. The lapidary has to take great care to cut the stone so that the reddish appearance can be seen through the table in artificial light. Another pleochroic stone in which red and green rays are often intermingled to give an interesting and elusive colour effect is andalusite, while in the variety of spodumene known as kunzite the rather insipid pink seen at right angles to the prisms of the crystal is replaced by a wonderful deep lilac colour when one looks down its length—a colour not quite equalled by any other gemstone.

The Dichroscope

When a dichroic stone is rotated under a polarizing prism or polaroid sheet, in orientations where the vibration-direction of one of the coloured rays corresponds with that of the polarizer, the colour of this ray only will be visible. Thus a change of colour will be noticeable if the stone or polarizer be turned. It is usually more convenient, if it can be arranged, to view side by side both the coloured rays reaching the eye along any one direction. This can conveniently be done with the aid of a dichroscope (*Figures 32.3, 32.4*). This is a simple little instrument consisting essentially of a metal tube

Figure 32.3. The optical system of a dichroscope: (A) sliding metal tube carrying the endplate (B) with rectangular aperture (C); (D) inner tube carrying the optical calcite (E), to the ends of which are cemented glass prisms (F) (these are not always present but do produce clearer images); (G) packing, usually of cork, to hold the doubly refracting rhomb in the tube; (H) the eye lens

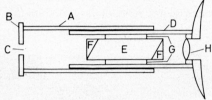

Figure 32.4. Using the dichroscope

with a small rectangular window at one end and an eyepiece at the other. Within the tube is mounted a piece of optical calcite (Iceland spar) of sufficient size to present, by virtue of its strong double refraction, a doubled image of the window of the instrument, which in a properly made and adjusted dichroscope are contiguous but not overlapping.

In most commercial dichroscopes an attachment for holding and rotating the stone in front of the window of the instrument is fixed to the tube (*Figure 32.5*). This is convenient but not really necessary, since with practice the stone can easily be held in tongs, or if large in the fingers, and manipulated as desired. Most instrument work in gemmology can be carried out at least as well in artificial light as in daylight; but for the observation of dichroism, bright sunlight is undoubtedly superior.

It is absolutely essential that the stone be turned into different positions to obtain the fullest dichroic or pleochroic effects. Not only must it be remembered that there can be no dichroism visible in the direction of an optic axis, but also it should be realized that only when the vibration-directions of the light forming the images of the dichroscope window correspond exactly with those of the two dichroic rays can these be seen in their proper colours. In other orientations, part of each is resolved into each dichroscope image, and when the rays are at 45 degrees to those of the dichroscope, both dichroscope images will be of identical colour.

Figure 32.5. Dichroscope by J. H. Steward with arrangement for holding the stone during observation of dichroism

Dichroscopes making use of polaroid have been constructed. In the first of these, designed by Thibaut, four sectors of polaroid were cut and mounted at one end of the dichroscope tube. Opposite sectors were made to have identical vibration-directions, perpendicular to those of light passing through the other two.

When the dichroic effect is exceedingly feeble no matter which way the stone is turned, it is better to disregard it, since it is very easy to imagine such effects and draw false conclusions. Light from the sky, or light reflected from any non-metallic surface is to some extent polarized and will cause one image of the dichroscope to appear darker than the other; this again may be misleading on occasion.

For all its importance, dichroism is very seldom of great diagnostic value, that is, it will not by itself enable one to identify with complete certainty any particular gem.

SPECTRUM ANALYSIS

A more searching analysis of colour is made possible by using the spectroscope, which owed its beginning to the genius of Isaac Newton who, as told earlier in the book, analysed sunlight with the aid of a glass prism, producing the well-known series of rainbow colours known as the solar spectrum. Josef Fraunhofer (independently of Wollaston), at the beginning of the nineteenth century, first observed and mapped the dark lines which cross the spectrum of the sun, the principal members of which he labelled A, B, C, D and so on—Fraunhofer line symbols which are used to this day. Some 15 years later David Brewster suggested that these dark lines in the sun's spectrum were due to absorption of light in the vapours surrounding the sun, but it was left to R. W. Bunsen and G. R. Kirchhoff to first prove that the bright yellow double line seen in a spectrum when the glowing vapour of a sodium compound was examined are the same lines, seen in reverse, as the Fraunhofer D lines. The experiments of many other workers further contributed to the knowledge of spectra, and the study of the various types of spectra have led to great advances in the understanding of the physics of the atom, and in astronomy, medicine and in the qualitative and quantitative analysis of the composition of materials. Through the work of Arthur Church, E. T. Wherry, B. W. Anderson and C. J. Payne, the examination of the absorption and fluorescence spectra of gemstones has now become a powerful method of gem-testing.

Bright-line Spectrum

A beam of white light from an oil, gas or ordinary electric lamp produces, when passed across a prism—as previously explained under dispersion—a ribbon of rainbow colours from red to violet. This type of emission spectrum, is called a Newtonian or continuous spectrum, and is produced by incandescent solids. A similar spectrum from the light of the sun, which as mentioned above is crossed with dark lines, is known as the Fraunhofer or solar

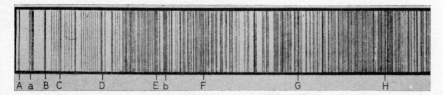

Figure 32.6. One of Josef Fraunhofer's drawings of the solar spectrum

spectrum. One of Fraunhofer's drawings of the solar spectrum is shown in *Figure 32.6.* In 1834 W. H. Fox-Talbot, chiefly remembered as a pioneer of photography, found that he could distinguish the red flames given by lithium and strontium salts by observing them through a prism and noting the very different bright-line spectrum given by each. It is the differences in the position of the bright lines in the spectrum produced by different elements, either pure or in combination, when they are volatilized in a flame, electric arc or electric spark, which provides the basis of the spectrum analysis of materials.

Such a bright-line emission spectrum is due to electronic disturbances within the atom. With incandescent vapours of compounds, a band spectrum may occur: this is a curious banded or fluted formation, each band consisting of a group of very fine lines, comparatively wide apart at one end and crowded closer and closer together at the other until the last are so close as to appear to be one dense line at the 'head'. Band spectra refer to spectra in the molecular state; they are sometimes known as Swan spectra. It must not be taken as implied that the bright-line spectra are confined to the visible part of the electromagnetic spectrum, this is of course not so: the 'bright lines' extending right down through the ultra-violet.

Flame Spectra

Emission spectra of the alkali metals and the alkaline earths, and many rare-earth elements, which may be volatilized by the heat of the Bunsen flame, may be identified by the bright lines seen in the visible spectrum. Such flame spectra are illustrated in *Figure 32.7*. In carrying out flame analysis with a direct-vision spectroscope a short length of platinum wire mounted on a piece of glass rod may be used, after it has first been cleaned by immersion in hydrochloric acid and heated. This cleaned wire is used to take up a small quantity of powder from the specimen which has been moistened with hydrochloric acid. The charged wire is then inserted into the cool part of the Bunsen flame and brought up into the hotter part (*Figure 32.8*) while the flame is examined spectroscopically. In this connexion it must be mentioned that the yellow doublet of sodium inevitably appears— for one part in 40 million in any sample will produce the yellow lines—and these should be disregarded unless the flame is coloured strongly yellow and the yellow doublet appears in strength. Flame spectra have little value

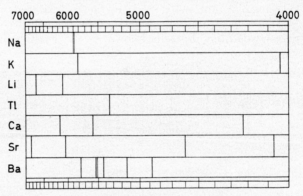

Figure 32.7. Flame spectra of the three commoner alkali metals and the alkaline earths and thallium

in gem determination, although, in some cases powder 'sneaked' from the girdle of a stone may be so analysed and information gained. Thus a flame test for lithium may be found useful in checking the identity of the rare mineral amblygonite—a fluophosphate of aluminium and lithium. As lithium is such a rare constituent in gem minerals proof of its presence has real significance.

Visual Examination with Spectrometer

Visual examination of the emission spectra, and the measurement of the wavelengths of the lines, can be carried out by the aid of a spectrometer, such as the instrument described for the method of refractive index measurement by the minimum deviation method. The use of such an instrument enables the higher temperature of the electric arc using purified carbons, upon the lower one of which a sample of the substance to be analysed is placed, to be conveniently carried out, and thus allow less easily volatilized substances to be examined for their bright lines.

With the spectrometer, measurement of the wavelength of the lines is made possible by reference to a graph prepared for the glass prism used. The graph is made by plotting as a curve the angular readings of the telescope for a number of different bright lines of known wavelengths of various elements, and plotting them on the graph which has the angular measurements as abscissae (horizontal line) and wavelengths as ordinates (vertical line). The wavelength of any unknown line can then be found from its angular measurement by reference to the graph. The element to which that wavelength agrees is found by reference to published tables of wavelengths, such as D. M. Smith's *Visual Lines for Spectrum Analysis*, or *Wavelength Tables for Spectrum Analysis* by Twyman and Smith. Larger dispersions, hence greater accuracy, may be obtained by using a hollow prism filled

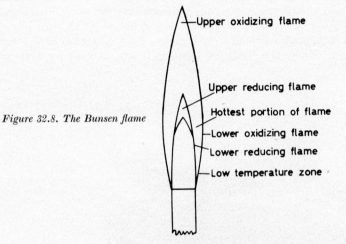

Figure 32.8. The Bunsen flame

Upper oxidizing flame

Upper reducing flame

Hottest portion of flame

Lower oxidizing flame

Lower reducing flame

Low temperature zone

with carbon disulphide or cinnamic aldehyde, or by a diffraction grating, the latter giving an even dispersion throughout the whole range of wavelengths. The diffraction grating will be discussed at greater length later in the chapter.

In the ultra-violet region lie the more diagnostic spectral lines which are so useful in spectrum analysis. A spectrometer with a glass prism is of little use in spectrum analysis in the ultra-violet, for the ultra-violet lines are not visible to the eye. Even if a camera were arranged to photograph the lines, owing to the strong absorption of the glass for wavelengths below 3000 Å, half of the ultra-violet spectrum would be lost.

The Spectrograph

Spectrum analysis by the production of bright-line spectra, usually called line spectra, is carried out by means of a spectrograph using quartz (pure rock crystal) prisms and lenses, a material which transmits ultra-violet light down to well below 2000 Å. Such instruments record the lines photographically, and if 'long-range spectrum plates', which have an emulsion which responds from the near infra-red right down to the shorter ultra-violet are used, a very complete spectrum can be obtained. Spectrographs are totally enclosed and consist of an adjustable slit for the light to enter, and a collimating lens system to parallelize the rays from the slit on to the quartz prism which disperses the light. The dispersed rays, or really images of the slit, are then focused by a lens system (the camera lens) on to the photographic plate which is carried in a dark slide (cassette). The instruments are 'dog-leg' in shape if the bend due to the deviation of the rays through the prism is in a horizontal plane, but if in a vertical plane the bend is entirely enclosed within the instrument. The quartz prism, owing to the fact that quartz is not only birefringent but also has the power of rotating the plane of polarized light in the direction of its optic axis, is made in two halves, one of right-hand and one of left-handed rotation, each cut so that the rays pass along the optic axis. These two halves are cemented together so as to produce a 60 degree prism. The slit needs to be made accurately and the lenses carefully computed and designed. Finally, the plate holder must be oriented accurately to the beam of the rays.

Spectrum analysis using a quartz spectrograph is a laboratory technique and some experience is needed to carry it out successfully. Only the bare

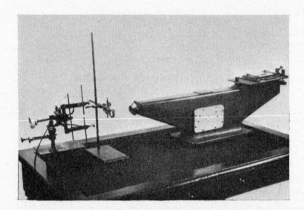

Figure 32.9. A quartz spectrograph set up for spectrum analysis

outlines of the method can be given in this résumé. The choice of electrodes for the arc will depend upon the electric current available and the nature of the work to be done. Pure carbons must be used if alternating current is the only source of electricity available. If direct current, either from the mains or through a suitable rectifier, is available metal electrodes may be used, the most useful being those of pure copper or the non-metal graphite.

It is necessary to ensure that the arc and the quartz condensing lens used to focus the light of the arc on to the slit are both correctly aligned with the optical system of the spectrograph, and that a photographic plate in its cassette is in position. *Figure 32.9* shows how a quartz spectrograph is set up. A photograph of the spectrum of the pure electrodes is then made by striking the arc with, of course, the dark slide of the cassette open. The plate is then readjusted and a small quantity of the powdered substance to be analysed is then placed in a shallow depression in the lower of the vertical electrodes and the arc struck again. The width of the slit and the exposure time, say 5–10 sec, need to be found by experience. From three to six spectra can be accommodated on each plate, depending upon the length of the slit, which may be adjusted by a sliding V-shaped diaphragm.

On development of the plate a series of black lines will be seen which, due to the optical system of the spectrograph, are usually slightly curved. The measurement of the spectral lines is carried out by identifying certain lines of the spectrum of the pure electrodes and using these as 'fixed points' from which the unknown lines in the spectrum of the substance analysed, which is superimposed on that of the electrodes, can be determined by interpolation; a measuring microscope is often used for such a purpose. In some large spectrographs a wavelength scale is provided which is printed on to the spectrum plate photographically. The wavelength of the lines determined from the spectrum plate are then looked up in a table of wavelengths of the elements, and the elements in the sample thus found. For practical purposes the easiest and safest procedure is to rely on comparison with known spectra. Standard plates are taken of the elements most commonly encountered and these can be juxtaposed with the unknown spectrum. From this the presence or absence of each element can be systematically established. Such comparison spectra can, of course, be photographed on one plate if only certain elements are to be searched for. A variation of the above method is to use a high tension electric spark in place of the arc.

Ultimate Lines

W. N. Hartley, and later A. de Gramont, found that it was not always the strongest spectral line of an element which is the most persistent when the substance is present in diminishing amount. Hartley's persistent lines were termed *raies sensibles* by de Gramont who gave the name *raies ultimes* for those which remained last when the quantity of the element was decreased almost to vanishing point. The raies ultimes lie mostly in the ultra-violet region, while the raies sensibles are more often found in the visible part of the spectrum and enable very small quantities of the elements concerned to be detected by quite simple apparatus. The strength of the lines, usually marked from 1 to 10, are given in the wavelength tables, both for arc and spark spectra, the two of which need be in no way identical. The most persistent lines being marked by special symbols. Thus, if the raies ultimes of an element are missing the element is not present and this simplifies the search.

Fluorescence Spectrum

A number of substances which glow with a fluorescent light when irradiated with blue light, ultra-violet rays, x-rays or cathode rays, may, when examined with a spectroscope show this fluorescent light to be made up of bright and discrete bands. Such a fluorescence spectrum has a value in the distinction of ruby from red spinel and for some diamonds. More will be said of this when discussing the luminescent characteristic of gemstones.

ABSORPTION SPECTRA

From the point of view of gemstone identification the absorption spectrum is the most important. When discussing colour it was mentioned that the absorption of light by a substance determines the residual colour. In many cases the colour absorption can only be interpreted by a curve produced from data obtained by the use of an elaborate instrument called a spectrophotometer. Such an instrument is not used in general gem-testing, despite the valuable information that may be obtained with it. More often the absorption, particularly of coloured stones, is in well-marked bands or finer dark lines which cross the otherwise continuous spectrum, obliterating certain colours or wavelengths when white light is transmitted through or reflected from the stone. The distribution of these dark bands or lines provide, often without measurement, partial or complete identification of the gemstone.

Spectroscopes

A small hand spectroscope is the only additional instrument needed for this powerful method of gem identification to be carried out. The spectroscopes and the techniques of their use need to be discussed before telling of the absorption spectra themselves.

Direct-vision Spectroscopes

There are two distinct types of hand, or as they are more often called direct-vision, spectroscopes available for use. The first of these is the prism

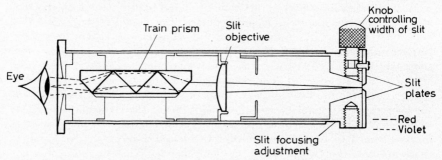

Figure 32.10. The construction of the direct-vision prism spectroscope made by R. & J. Beck (No. 2458)

type which operates by dispersing the light through a train of glass prisms. In the second type of instrument the spectrum is produced by diffraction of light from a finely ruled grating. The direct-vision prism instruments are the more commonly used for the spectrum produced is clearer and brighter, but the instrument must be carefully chosen, since, if the dispersion is too small, the bands in the red region are too cramped for the details to be seen. Owing to the unequal dispersion of the prism for the different wavelengths the spectrum produced by these instruments is closed up at the red end and expanded in the blue and violet end. Thus the absorption lines in the red end of the spectrum are sharper while the bands in the blue are more diffuse.

There are many different makes and design of direct-vision spectroscopes (*Figure 32.10*), but all operate on the same principle. Prism spectroscopes are available in which a wavelength scale can be seen projected above the coloured spectrum (*Figure 32.11*), but such instruments have the disadvantage that some provision must be made for illuminating the scale in the accessory tube, and sometimes the scale is not quite accurate for all parts of the spectrum, especially when the focus is altered. A built in spectroscope made to the design of E. Gübelin (*Figure 32.12*) has internal lighting and scale illumination. Arranged in the form of a microscope stand, the instrument has spring tongs for holding the stone under test and a number of other refinements. The firm of Rayner supply a spectroscope to fit their gemmological microscope, but in practice it is found that these 'fixed' instruments lack the flexibility for examining mounted specimens, opaque specimens by reflected light, or under the different types of illumination sometimes useful, that the simple hand-held spectroscope is so well adapted.

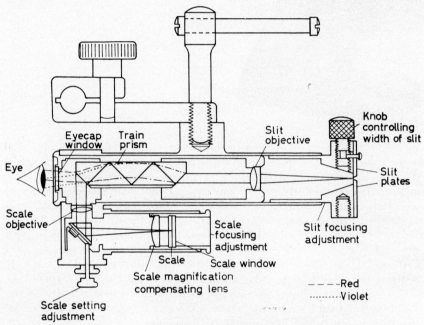

Figure 32.11. The construction of the wavelength direct-vision spectroscope made by R. & J. Beck (No. 2522)

Diffraction Grating Spectroscopes

The diffraction grating spectroscopes produce their spectra by diffraction and interference of the incident light rays by a finely ruled grating of about 14,000 lines to the inch. Such gratings are ruled on glass with a diamond point by the use of an accurate dividing engine. The resulting effect is a number of opaque lines, where the diamond has scratched the glass, with fine transparent spaces between each ruled line. As such glass gratings are expensive to produce celluloid casts, or replicas, are made and used for most of the commercial spectroscopes.

A diffraction grating consists of a number of equally spaced opaque lines ruled on a transparent substance (some gratings are ruled on metal and the

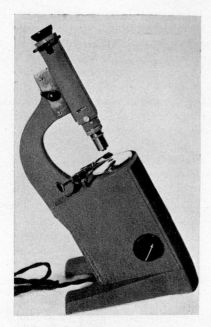

Figure 32.12. The Gübelin spectroscope

spectral effect produced by reflected rays), the width of each line being equal to the space between two adjacent lines. If A_1A_2 (*Figure 32.13*), the width of the combined line and space, is d, and a plane wave with wavelength λ is incident perpendicularly on the grating, all the clear spaces will act as secondary sources and emit rays in all directions. If all the rays making an angle θ with the normal are considered, then all the rays from each space can be replaced by a resultant coming from the mid-point of that space, and the problem reduces to that of compounding a number of parallel rays C_1D_1, C_2D_2, and so on, from a number of equidistant points C_1C_2. If C_2K is drawn perpendicular to C_1D_1, then the common difference of these rays is C_1K equals $C_1C_2 \sin C_1C_2K$ equal to $d \sin \theta$, and the rays reinforce in the direction θ if $d \sin \theta$ equals $n\lambda$, where n has any integral value, positive or negative, and a bright line is seen at this angle.

Figure 32.13. The principle of the diffraction grating

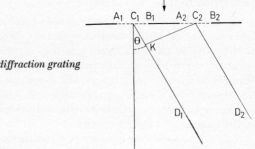

As reinforcement occurs when $n\lambda$ equals $d \sin \theta$, when n equals 0, $\sin \theta$ equals 0, thus for all values of λ this will be a maximum, so the centre of the pattern, the direct image, is white with white light. If n equals 1, 2, 3 and so on, $\sin \theta$ is proportional to λ, so that with white light, spectra—called spectra of the first, second, third order—are formed. The first order images form two first order spectra, one on each side of the direct image. The second order and third order pairs of spectra are still farther away from the direct image, but these two pairs overlap each other. It is one of the first order spectra which is used as the spectrum in diffraction grating spectroscopes, and this explains why the spectrum can never be so bright as that seen in a prism instrument, for only a portion of the incident light forms this one spectrum.

In a grating spectrum the red end is more open than in prism instruments while the blue and violet end is relatively more closed up. Hence a diffraction spectroscope is sometimes better for observation in the blue end, provided that sufficient light is transmitted.

Figure 32.14. A direct-vision diffraction spectroscope made by R. & J. Beck (No. 2447)

A direct-vision diffraction spectroscope (*Figure 32.14*) is usually shorter in length than the corresponding prism instrument. Further, the diffraction instrument is often more suitable for the addition of measuring fitments. One such instrument is the Beck wavelength grating spectroscope (*Figure 32.15*) which despite its awkward 'dog-leg' shape can measure wavelengths to an accuracy of about 5–10 Å, the bands to be measured being moved into coincidence with fine cross-hairs in the eyepiece by means of a calibrated drum.

Technique

The observation of the dark absorption lines in gemstones needs some practice and attention to a number of details. First, the parallel-jawed slit must be adjusted—in most of the spectroscopes used in gem-testing the width of the slit may be narrowed or widened by means of an adjusting screw. When there is plenty of light the slit needs to be as narrow as possible, but open just enough to clear the horizontal streaks caused by the touching parts of the slit jaws or minute dust particles closing the gap. Heavy streaks are the sign of a dirty slit, and this should be corrected by opening the jaws widely and rubbing them gently with the wedge-shaped end of an orange stick or a sharpened match-stick. With dark stones which are not passing very much light the slit needs to be opened wider.

Another important factor is the focusing of the slit, spectroscopes have a sliding inner tube enabling this to be accomplished, for without proper focusing the finer lines to be seen in the spectrum may well be missed. With prism instruments the focus is not necessarily the same for the red end as for the violet end of the spectrum and the instrument needs slight re-focusing for the best viewing at either end of the spectrum. The suitability and adjustment of a spectroscope may conveniently be done by observing the Fraunhofer lines of the sun's spectrum which may be seen in the spectroscope from any part of the day sky. These Fraunhofer lines may also be seen, and used for focusing a spectroscope, from the light of the moon, in which case the instrument should be directed at the moon itself. The focus

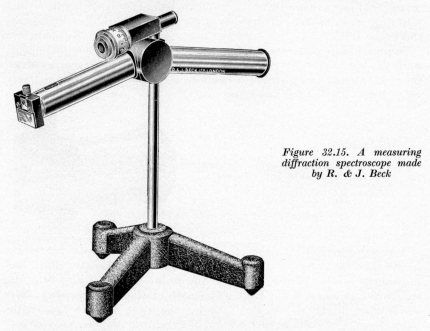

Figure 32.15. A measuring diffraction spectroscope made by R. & J. Beck

and slit width of the instrument should be adjusted until the dark lines are clearly and distinctly seen. The bright-line spectrum underlying the continuous spectrum of the fluorescent tube electric light is also useful for the adjustment of a spectroscope, and a good zircon will also provide suitable lines upon which to set the slit and focus of an instrument.

In English gemmology it is the convention to observe the spectrum with the red on the left, and all the illustrations of gem absorption spectra in this book are so drawn. Modern physics now usually postulates that spectra be viewed and illustrated with the wavelengths increasing in length from left to right, that is red on the right. In most American gem literature this system, which is the reverse to that used in England, is the convention which is used, and drawings need to be turned round (upside down) to bring the lay-out into the English convention.

Illumination of Specimen to be Examined

Most important in the examination of the absorption spectra of gemstones is the illumination of the gem specimen to be tested. There are two techniques, the transmitted light method and the reflected light method, both needing a powerful source of light if the best results are to be obtained. Such a source is a 300 or a 500 watt projection lamp suitably screened with asbestos lined box fitted with ventilation louvres, or other suitable cover to prevent glare to the eyes and to allow the light to pass only in the required direction. Alternatively, a microscope intensity lamp, although not so powerful, will provide a useful source.

Microscope Method

It is then necessary to transmit a concentrated beam of this light through the specimen and to project it evenly on to the slit of the spectroscope. The most satisfactory method is to make use of a microscope placed before the lamp, with the body tube in a vertical position and a $1\frac{1}{2}$-in. objective fitted.

Figure 32.16. Using the spectroscope by the microscope method

The eyepiece is removed and the stone to be tested is placed on a glass slide on the stage of the microscope. If the stone is small it may be an advantage to place it on a small metal diaphragm which has a small central aperture. The light from the lamp is concentrated on to the microscope mirror by a bull's-eye condenser, the stone itself and the focus of the microscope are both adjusted until the microscope tube is filled with light which has passed through the stone. A piece of ground glass placed on top of the microscope tube during this operation will prevent glare and enable the finding of the optimum position. The spectroscope, held in the hand, is then rested lightly on the top of the microscope tube in place of the eyepiece and an excellent streak-free spectrum may then be observed.

With stones of moderate refractive index enough light may be transmitted when they are placed table facet downwards on the glass slide.

Diamond and other highly refractive stones may not allow this, but more light may be transmitted if they are rested on their pavilion facets which are nearly parallel to the corresponding crown facets. A ball of wax or Plasticine placed on the glass slip into which the edge of the stone may be pressed will often help to hold it in the best position for light transmission. *Figure 32.16* illustrates such a set-up.

In place of a bull's-eye condenser the light from the lamp may be concentrated on to the microscope mirror by a 500 or 600 ml flat-bottomed round flask filled with water, this forming a 'lens' which has great light-gathering power and which also filters out the heat rays from the lamp which might otherwise damage the stone. A similar flask filled with a strong filtered solution of copper sulphate will be found valuable for facilitating observations in the blue and violet parts of the spectrum, and for observing fluorescent lines in the red. The use of the copper sulphate condensing filter does not allow the yellow and red parts of the spectrum to be seen for the copper sulphate solution passes only blue and violet. The value of the filter lies in the fact that the absorption bands in the blue and violet can then be seen without the glare from the brighter colours of the spectrum to which the eye is more sensitive. Hence, too, any bright lines due to fluorescence will appear on a black background and be seen more readily. The blue filter should only be used after a preliminary observation of the spectrum has been made in ordinary light, for a misidentification has been known to occur owing to the dark bands in the red being obscured by the blue filter and not being observed.

Reflected Light Method

Stones with weak spectra or translucent and opaque stones may be examined for their absorption spectrum by reflected, or scattered, light. In this case the stone is placed, for preference on a black cloth, in the pool of light condensed by the bull's-eye condenser from the strong light source (an intensity lamp is quite efficient in this method). The spectroscope is held at an angle of about 45 degrees with the slit an inch or two from the stone. Such a technique is particularly useful for the heat-treated zircons and for jade and turquoise. R. K. Mitchell has devised a stand to hold the spectroscope in order to simplify this form of observation (*Figure 32.17*).

Effect of Strength of Absorption Spectrum

Variations in the strength of the absorption spectrum dependent upon the depth of the transmission may to some extent alter the appearance of the spectrum by causing adjacent bands to coalesce when they are intense. More important is the fact that there may be important differences due to dichroism or pleochroism, and in such cases the absorption will differ along different directions. Such differences, however, seldom interfere with the recognition of the spectrum and may even need the aid of a piece of polaroid or a nicol prism to isolate the vibration directions for the differences to be seen. A weak absorption spectrum may often be seen more clearly by introducing over the microscope eyepiece a piece of polaroid turned into the optimum position.

616

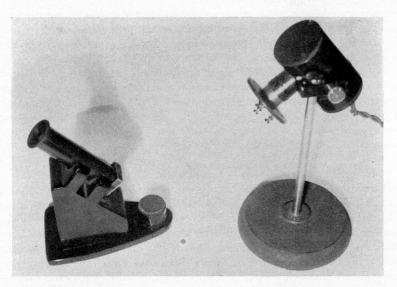

Figure 32.17. The reflected light method of observing absorption spectra using the Beck prism spectroscope on a Mitchell stand and an intensity lamp as the light source

ELEMENTS DETERMINING COLOUR OF GEMSTONES

In the descriptions of gemstones in earlier chapters the absorption spectra for each species and variety has been given. The measurements of the various lines and bands being given in Ångstrom units, but such a method of identifying spectra by measurement is not easy and certainly not practical. The visual arrangement of the bands is usually sufficient to identify or to aid in the identification of a great number of the gems, and in only a few cases would recourse be needed to measuring apparatus. Plates XXI and XXII show some of the absorption spectra of gemstones as seen through a diffraction grating spectroscope, and in the appendices a fuller range of spectra, in black and white and drawn as seen through a prism spectroscope are shown.

In a number of cases the element to which the gemstone owes its colour may be shown by the type of absorption spectrum produced. Thus chromium, which gives to ruby and spinel a red colour, and to emerald and alexandrite a green colour, shows a typical absorption spectrum consisting of fine lines, including a strong doublet, in the red part; a broad absorption of varying width and intensity in the yellow and green. There may be lines in the blue and the violet part of the spectrum is invariably absorbed. There are, however, significant differences in the absorption spectra of these different stones which are sufficient to aid in their identification.

Chromium

Chromium usually enters the crystal lattice in minerals by small-scale isomorphous replacement of aluminium oxide, thus the presence of a chromium spectrum suggests a mineral containing aluminium. Another distinctive and remarkable phenomenon connected with chromium spectra is the 'reversibility' of the narrow lines in the red; these can be seen as bright emission lines due to fluorescence or as dark absorption lines, according to the conditions. The presence of iron is apt to mask the effect, and so can an excess of chromium. Gems which show chromium spectra apart from the four mentioned above are pyrope garnet, pink topaz, jadeite, demantoid garnet, nephrite, diopside, hiddenite, uvarovite garnet, enstatite, euclase, kyanite, some peridot, green-stained chalcedony and some green glass, but in many of these cases the chromium spectrum is accompanied by that due to some other element.

Iron

The absorption spectra due to iron can be divided into two groups; the 'ferrous' iron due to divalent or ferrous oxide (FeO), which often replaces magnesia, and the trivalent 'ferric' iron corresponding to ferric oxide (Fe_2O_3) which replaces alumina. Divalent iron produces red, green or blue coloured stones and the absorption bands are in the green and blue of the spectrum. Examples of stones coloured by ferrous iron are almandine garnet, peridot, sinhalite, blue spinel, diopside, kornerupine, axinite, iolite and idocrase. The gemstones which owe their colour to ferric iron are usually yellow, blue or green in colour and the bands in the absorption spectra are of shorter wavelength than those due to ferrous iron. They are found in the 4500 Å region where the blue merges into the violet. Stones showing absorption spectra due to ferric iron are yellow-green, green and blue natural sapphires, brown and yellow chrysoberyl, aquamarine, yellow orthoclase and the similar coloured spodumene, jadeite, demantoid garnet and epidote.

Manganese

The absorption spectra due to manganese, which gives a rose pink or aurora-red colour to rhodonite, rhodochrosite and spessartite garnet, consist mainly of bands in the green, centred about 5500 Å, and in the blue, the latter being in the general absorption of the short-wave end of the spectrum and being seen with difficulty. The absorption spectrum is not sufficient to separate rhodonite from rhodochrosite, but that of spessartite garnet is sufficiently distinctive, although usually accompanied by the almandine spectrum, to separate it from almandine, and certainly enough to separate the stone from the similarly coloured hessonite garnet. There is some support for the contention that pink and red tourmalines owe their colour chiefly to manganese, but the absorption spectrum of these stones— usually very weak, but particularly strong in the brownish-red or violet-red variety—shows little in common with manganese spectra. Of diagnostic importance are the two narrow bands situated at 4485 and 4230 Å in the violet, which are seen in the manganese-coloured yellow and greenish-yellow and greenish-blue synthetic spinels. These bands are, in the blue-toned stones, present in conjunction with the bands due to cobalt.

Cobalt

Cobalt, which produces a red colour in natural minerals, gives to some glass, plastics and synthetic spinel a blue colour. The presence of cobalt in

PLATE XXI

ANGSTROM UNITS

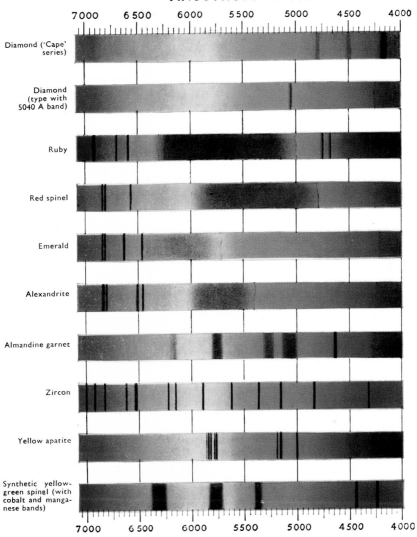

Absorption spectra of gemstones.

Note that the scales are shown linear, as with a diffraction grating
spectroscope.

these blue stones produces a striking and diagnostic spectrum of three bands centred in the orange, yellow and green, but these bands, although they have a general similarity, differ slightly in their arrangement in the three materials. In synthetic blue spinel the bands are centred at 6300, 5800 and 5430 Å, and there is a much weaker band at 4780 Å. In this spectrum the central band appears widest and the band in the green the narrowest. In blue glass the bands are centred at 6560, 5900 and 5380 Å, and there is a vague line at 4950 Å. In cobalt blue glass it is the central band which is the narrowest. A specimen of cobalt blue polystyrene plastic showed the centres of the bands to be at 6520, 6100 and 5660 Å. The cobalt absorption bands have been discussed in more detail because they show the presence of cobalt, which at once proves the stone to be counterfeit for no natural gemstone is coloured by cobalt, and, further, the distribution of the bands will tell the nature of the material. In the case of a blue glass-based garnet-topped doublet it must be remembered that the almandine spectrum may also appear in conjunction with the cobalt bands shown by the glass. The rarely met synthetic spinel showing a colour change that imitates the alexandrite shows a cobalt spectrum.

Vanadium

The more popular alexandrite imitation, that is synthetic corundum, owes its colour to vanadium. In this stone the absorption spectrum is nearly unique and certainly diagnostic for this variety of synthetic sapphire, for in the bright blue there is an exceptionally clear and sharp, although not always strong, line at 4750 Å. In only one type of natural stone has this line ever appeared, that is in a very rare type of colour-change natural sapphire from Burma, but in this stone the colour is decidedly different from either true alexandrite or the synthetic sapphire made to imitate it.

Copper

Copper, which in the monovalent state (cuprous) produces a red colour, and in the divalent state (cupric) gives a blue or green colour, has an importance as far as absorption spectra are concerned only with turquoise, for azurite and malachite do not show any distinct absorption bands. The bands in turquoise are a broad but faint absorption band centred at 4600 Å, a strong band in the violet at 4320 Å and another in the obscurity of the violet at 4200 Å, which can rarely be seen by the eye. It is the 4320 and 4600 Å bands which provide the diagnostic spectrum, and which can be seen by light reflected from the surface of the stone, helped by the use of the copper sulphate filter before the light source. It must be mentioned that none of the usual turquoise imitations show these bands, but the plastic bonded turquoise marketed in the United States of America will show the absorption bands.

Selenium

Selenium, probably in conjunction with cadmium sulphide, gives a red colour to glass and these red glasses show a broad absorption band in the green. Bands centred at 5320, 5370, 5400 and 5600 Å have been measured in red glasses, from which it seems unlikely that all red glasses owe their colour to the same cause.

Uranium

The striking absorption spectrum of zircon was first noted (with that of almandine garnet) by Arthur Church in 1866, and these observations were the beginning of the study of the absorption spectra of gemstones. The absorption spectrum of zircon, ascribed to uranous uranium, consists of a number of sharp lines and bands distributed throughout the spectrum, and is a most convincing absorption spectrum when fully developed. Even so, the spectrum can vary considerably in the number of lines which can be seen. Burma zircons show the greatest number of bands, while the Ceylon zircons rarely show more than about 14. In the untreated reddish-brown zircons from Indo-China the lines are difficult to detect, but in the colourless, blue and golden yellow stones produced by heating this rough, the strongest line at 6535 Å, usually accompanied by the weaker, 6605 Å line, may be seen, thus identifying the stone. These fine lines are best seen by the reflected light method. The low-type (metamict) green zircons show only the 6535 Å line, but in this case not as a sharp line but as a rather diffuse band, a sign of depreciation of crystal structure.

Rare Earth Spectra

The 'rare earth' spectra consist of fine lines whose wavelength is very little affected by the nature of the host crystal. This is due to the fact that the transition from one element to the next involves no change in the outer electron shell, but instead there is a steady 'filling up' of a deeper lying electron group. Thus the outer electrons are not involved in these absorption processes, but do act as a screen behind which the electron shifts, allowing absorption and fluorescence to take place relatively undisturbed. The most important rare earth spectrum is that of didymium (a mixture of the absorption bands of praseodymium and neodymium) and which consists of a group of fine lines in the yellow and a weaker group in the green. This spectrum is seen most strongly in the yellow apatite and may serve to identify the mineral. The spectrum may, however, be observed, but usually very weakly, in green and colourless apatite, danburite, sphene, idocrase, scheelite, calcite and fluorite; in fact all minerals which have calcium as an ingredient. A case is recorded where a strong didymium spectrum has been observed in emerald, but this was found to be due to the spectrum from an inclusion of the mineral parasite in the emerald. Blue apatite shows a different rare earth spectrum which has bands in the orange, green and blue. The 'rare earth' spectrum shown by the bright green andalusite from Brazil is now known to be due to manganese.

Diamond

The absorption spectra of diamond are not now believed to be due to trace elements but are dependent upon the structure of the diamond crystal itself, and indeed, many complex features are revealed by the study of the absorption spectra of diamond. As noted in the chapter on diamond

Plate XXII

ANGSTROM UNITS

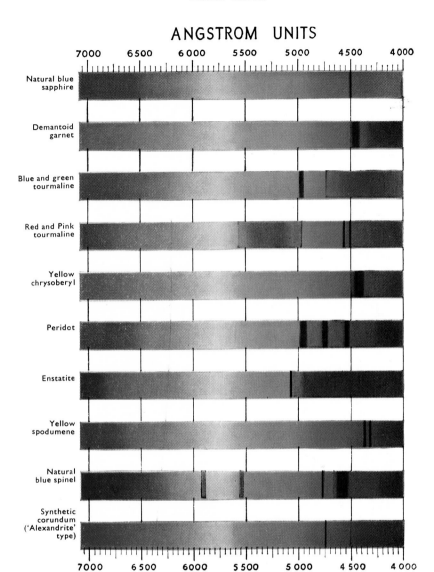

Absorption spectra of gemstones.

The scales here are linear, not condensed towards the red end as with a
prism type spectroscope.

(Chapter 2) the absorption characters can be linked up with those of luminescence to produce three groups. Most gem diamonds, particularly those of the 'Cape' series show a strong band in the obscurity of the violet at 4155 Å. Brown diamonds and other naturally tinted diamonds usually show a sharp band at 5040 Å. This line, and one at 5940 Å, have importance with other characters in the identification of artificially coloured diamonds.

Miscellaneous Spectra

There are a few miscellaneous spectra which deserve mention. Zinc blende shows narrow absorption bands in the red end of the spectrum. There is in this stone a narrow band at 6650 Å, which may be intense, very weak or even not observable. There is a feebler narrow band at 6510 Å and a broader band at 6920 Å. The blue mineral sodalite may show a strong and rather broad band at 6800 Å and weaker bands at 5950 and 5400 Å. Bands at 4410 and 4100 Å and a weaker band at 4620 Å have been observed in fibrolite: these may be due to iron. Synthetic rutile shows a band at about 4230 Å beyond which there is practically no transmission.

Neither the quartz gems nor topaz, except the pink stones, exhibit any absorption bands of diagnostic value, and tourmaline is most uncertain in its display of absorption bands. Synthetic blue sapphires at best show only a very weak and vague smudge at about 4500 Å, which is totally unlike the line in the natural blue sapphire. Natural yellow sapphires from Siam and Australia show the full 4500 Å complex strongly, while the similar coloured sapphires from Ceylon do not (they fluoresce strongly with an apricot coloured light under ultra-violet light). The synthetic yellow sapphire only shows a vague smudge of the 4500 Å line and in the brownish-yellow types there is a strong absorption from 4500 Å downwards into the violet. Natural green sapphires show the 4500 Å complex strongly while the synthetic green corundum does not show a distinctive spectrum. No spectrum of diagnostic value has been observed in the synthetic strontium titanate.

Canary or uranium glass, which is sometimes used as an imitation stone show vague bands in the blue and violet at 4950, 4600 and 4300 Å which often appears as a cut-off to the violet. Orange glasses often show an abrupt cut-off near 5900 Å beyond which they are nearly opaque, and are in fact a 'colour filter'. Fire opal, which resembles these orange glasses in colour, usually has a rather less defined cut-off and may transmit light down to 5750 or even to 5550 Å according to the depth of tint. The chromium bands in green glasses are much more diffuse than the chromium lines in minerals. These bands are usually at 6820, 6610 and 6340 Å. Pink glasses owing their tint to didymium are sometimes cut as gems (the rare earth spectrum is sometimes in association with the selenium band in deeper pinkish-red glasses). It will be prudent to mention here that the anti-glare glass—known as Crookes glass and used in spectacles—is tinted by didymium and will show the didymium rare earth spectrum. Students who customarily wear Crookes lenses and who have not realized their peculiar absorption properties, have sometimes been sorely puzzled by the persistent absorption band in the yellow which they notice in all stones which they examine with the spectroscope, for these bands will show up even if the glass is on the eyepiece side of the spectroscope.

CHAPTER 33

THE MICROSCOPE

One of the most useful pieces of apparatus for the study and identification of gemstones is the microscope. Indeed with a suitably designed microscope nearly every necessary test can be accomplished, although many of them may be more conveniently carried out by the use of other instruments.

The microscope, as usually understood, consists mainly of a tube containing a number of lenses, but a simple microscope consists of one lens only—a lens consisting of a piece of glass or other colourless transparent material having curved surfaces. Such a simple lens is the ordinary magnifying glass.

LENSES AND THEIR FUNCTION

No full understanding of the microscope can be obtained without considering the function of lenses and their behaviour to rays of light. The surfaces of lenses may be of two types—convex or concave. Convex lenses, in which the thickness is greater at the centre, cause a pencil of light rays to converge towards a point, while the opposite type, concave lenses, cause divergence of a pencil of rays away from the axis of the lens. Convex lenses are the most important in the production of a magnifying system, but concave lenses are often used in intimate contact with them in order to rectify certain optical defects.

Focus

The convergence or divergence of light rays through a lens is due to refraction, and the action of the two types of lens may best be explained by consideration of the geometrical representation of the paths of light through them. Beams of parallel rays striking the lens surface parallel to its axis (the straight line joining the centres of curvature of its surfaces) are bent by refraction of the rays by the denser medium of the lens. After passing through a convex lens (*Figure 33.1*) the rays meet at a point, called the focus of the lens; after passing through a concave lens (*Figure 33.2*) the rays diverge, but these divergent rays if produced backwards meet at a focus.

Where the incident light is parallel to the optical axis the distance from centre to focus is the focal length of the lens, and is generally denoted by the symbol f. The convention is that if the focal length, as measured from the lens, is in the same direction as that in which the incident light is proceeding, the lens is positive; whereas if it is measured in the opposite direction to the incident light, the lens is negative. It is for the above reasons that convex lenses are sometimes called positive lenses, while concave lenses are called negative.

As concave lenses play no part in magnifying instruments, except in combination, they need not be further mentioned and consideration is given to convex lenses only. When light rays from a distant object, such as the sun, are incident on a converging lens, they are brought to a focus, the principal focus, at some distance on the other side of the lens. It is also true that if a well-illuminated object is placed on one side of a convex lens, but at a greater distance than the principal focus, a real but inverted image of the object will be found focused at some point on the other side of the lens.

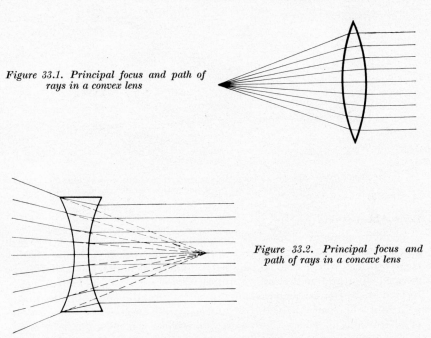

Figure 33.1. Principal focus and path of rays in a convex lens

Figure 33.2. Principal focus and path of rays in a concave lens

These two focal points, that where the object is positioned and that where the image of the object is formed on the other side of the lens, are interchangeable and are called the conjugate foci. Since any luminous body is a collection of luminous points, the action of a lens on the light from such a body is to form a collection of images, the total result being the image of the body. *Figure 33.3* illustrates the formation of a real image and also the effect when the image is not in focus.

When an object is placed at a considerable distance on one side of a convex lens, the image formed on the other side is small and at the focus; advancing the object to a position nearer to the lens causes the image to be farther away and to be larger, and if brought still closer so as to near the principal focus of the lens the image is still farther away and is magnified several times (this is the principle of the magic lantern or slide projector).

If the object is brought nearer to the lens than the principal focus no real image is formed, a virtual image being formed on the object side, and the principal focus is the focus at infinity. What happens now is that the real image is lost; the virtual image then appears on the opposite side of the lens. The image no longer actually exists in space, it cannot be demonstrated by means of a screen, it is magnified and erect and from observation one cannot tell that this so-called virtual image is not a real object. This is the principle of the magnifying glass and may be better understood by reference to *Figure 33.4*.

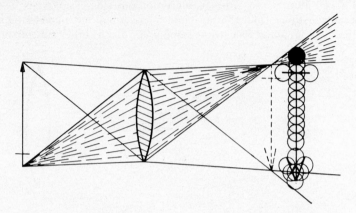

Figure 33.3. The formation of a real image by a convex lens and the cause of the 'out of focus' effect if the image is not at the conjugate focus

Lens Aberrations

It might be inferred from the foregoing remarks that a single lens will give a perfect image of an object, but this is not the case. Even a highly corrected lens will not do so completely; the reasons for this can only be grasped by a profound study of optics. There are many defects in lenses, termed aberrations, which preclude the ideal formation of an image; that is a faithful and clearly defined copy of the object. There are two major types of aberrations in lenses; chromatic aberration, which is due principally to the material of the lens, and spherical aberration, which is due to the form of the lens. There are other defects of a lesser nature, but these need not concern an elementary exposition as is intended here.

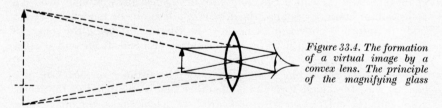

Figure 33.4. The formation of a virtual image by a convex lens. The principle of the magnifying glass

Chromatic Aberration

The most important of the single-lens defects is that of chromatic aberration. Refracting substances vary in their effects on light of different colours, refracting short wavelengths such as violet more than long wavelengths such as red. This is the effect known as dispersion or fire and has been explained in the chapter on light. As the power of a lens is due to its refraction of light rays, and thus depends upon the refractive index of the lens material, an axial object point emitting white light will be imaged as a short spectrum lying along the axis, the violet being focused nearer to the lens and the red farther away (*Figure 33.5*). This aberration can largely be

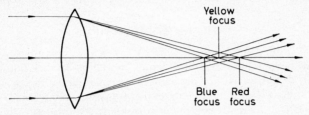

Figure 33.5. How chromatic aberration occurs

corrected by combining a positive and a negative lens of suitable powers and made of different types of glass, having different dispersions, which combined together bring rays of two different colours, usually blue-violet and orange-red, to a uniform focus. Such composite lenses are termed achromatic lenses (*Figure 33.6*).

Figure 33.6. Principal sections of achromatic lenses

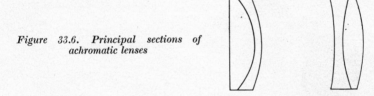

Achromatic lenses do not correct for all the colours and therefore have a small colour fringe which is known as the secondary spectrum. With certain special types of glass, in combination with fluorspar or a glass near to this in optical property, it is possible to produce a lens which will focus three colours in the same plane; the residual error is then extremely small. Such lenses are called apochromatic and are used in the highest class of instruments, but they require the use of compensating eyepieces.

Spherical Aberrations

A spherical surface focuses the light which passes through the margin of the lens to a different focus from that passing through its centre (*Figure 33.7*). As every point source in the object is focused, therefore, not to a

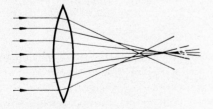

Figure 33.7. Spherical aberration

625

point but to a fuzzy disc, only an indistinct and badly defined image is formed. This effect is known as spherical aberration; it is corrected to a large extent by using combinations of lenses with surfaces of different curvatures, and often by limiting the aperture of the lens to the central part only by the use of a diaphragm, thus using only those rays which travel through the central part of the lens where the effect is not so pronounced.

SIMPLE MICROSCOPES

It is now possible to discuss the various types of simple microscopes, such as the ordinary magnifiers with which jewellers are so familiar. These magnifiers, or loupes as they are sometimes called, must be considered with two points of view in mind. The greater the power of such lenses the more pronounced the aberrations (unless corrected) and also the shorter is the focus (and working distance), hence, a watchmaker's eyeglass cannot usefully be more powerful than that giving four times the enlargement of the actual object; such a lens having a working distance of about $2\frac{1}{2}$ in. which allows space for the use of tools.

For the inspection of a surface or for the observation of inclusions inside a gemstone, working distance does not become so important and more

Figure 33.8. The aplanatic magnifier

powerful lenses may be used in such cases. The low-price folding magnifiers with from one to three single lenses, each of which may be folded in or out of the case and used separately, or in conjunction, to give various magnifications, can be useful but suffer from the usual defects of uncorrected lenses. For the study of gemstones the best type of hand lens is the aplanatic magnifier (*Figure 33.8*) which consists of a double-convex crown-glass lens cemented between meniscus lenses of flint glass. Such corrected lenses have a flat field, that is they have a good definition over the whole field which is usually free from colour. Such a lens of $10 \times$ magnification is recommended for use by gemmologists. As a lens is simply an adjunct to the eye to obtain the greatest field of view it should be held as close to the eye as possible. Care should be taken that the lens surfaces are not scratched, for scratches impair the visibility and may lead to an incorrect interpretation of the image seen.

Magnification of a Lens

The magnification of a lens depends upon the ratio of the size of the image to the size of the object when seen by the eye alone, but an object held at arm's length and observed by the eye appears to be much larger than the same object much farther away, hence it is necessary to have a standard.

The nearer the object is brought to the eye the larger is the image on the retina of the eye and the more visible the fine detail becomes, until a point is reached where the internal lens of the eye, which adjusts itself for objects at different distances, is at its extreme limit. If the object is brought nearer such a position, the eye either cannot focus it or has to make an exertion to see it distinctly, therefore the gain in size is counterbalanced by the loss of definition. This near-point or least distance of distinct vision, as it is termed, differs with different people, but for the greater part of adult life this distance measured from the eye to the near-point is 10 in. (250 mm). This distance is therefore taken as the standard of comparison and is generally denoted as Dv.

If the magnified image can be thrown on to a screen, as in the case of the real image produced by a magic lantern, both the object and the image can be measured and the magnification computed, but in the case of a magnifying lens the image is virtual, just a 'ghost' and cannot be measured. The

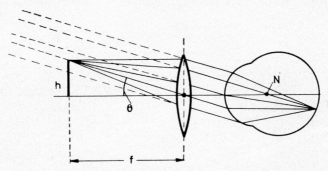

Figure 33.9. Principle of magnification. N, nodal point or optical centre of the eye; f, focal length of lens; h, height of object above centre line; θ, visual angle

magnification in the case of a simple lens is defined as the ratio between the angle subtended at the eye by the virtual image and the angle subtended by the object at the least distance of distinct vision.

Figure 33.9 shows the principle more clearly; the parallel bundles of rays leave the lens to enter the eye at an inclination θ to the axis. This is known as the visual angle. Now the inclination is dependent upon h and f and therefore the visual angle is h/f, which is the tangent of θ, that is, tan θ equals h/f. The magnification may be expressed therefore as

$$\frac{\text{Visual angle of image seen with lens}}{\text{Visual angle of object seen at near point with the unaided eye}}$$

When the angles are small, this can also be expressed as h/f divided by h/Dv which can be further reduced to Dv/f, but f is the focal length of the lens so that if this focal length be divided into the least distance of distinct vision the magnifying power of the lens is obtained. For example, a lens of 25 mm focal length has a magnifying power 250/25 and gives a magnification of 10 times.

A lens of 2-in. focal length will have a magnifying power of 5 for 10/2 equals 5. Therefore, to find the magnifying power of a lens all that is required to know is the focal length, because the least distance of distinct vision is standardized (10 in. or 250 mm). The focal length of a positive (convex) lens may be ascertained by holding the lens at right angles to a beam of sunlight—parallel light—and finding the sharp focus of the beam on the other side by a piece of white paper. The distance of the paper to the centre of the lens is the focal length.

The magnification is always expressed by linear diameters; by the relative lengths of object and image and not by their relative areas or cubic capacities. Magnification is usually represented by the multiplication sign and the number of diameters.

COMPOUND MICROSCOPE

The simple microscope—the hand lens—has the limitation that it can only satisfactorily be used for low powers, and in order to obtain greater magnifi-

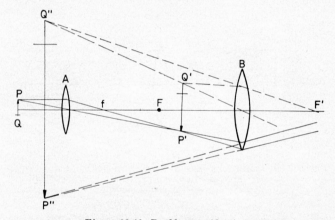

Figure 33.10. Double magnification

cation it becomes necessary to employ the compound microscope. This instrument carries out the process of magnification in two stages; first by the object glass (or as it is more often known—the objective) situated at the lower end of the microscope tube, a lens which forms a real image of the object near the top of the tube. This image produced by the objective is then further magnified by the eye lens (known as the ocular) which is situated at the top of the tube, a lens which, acting as a simple magnifier, gives a much larger virtual image of the real image produced by the object glass.

This double magnification is illustrated in a simple manner by *Figure 33.10.* The lens A, or objective, is of short focal length, and is so placed that the object PQ is just beyond its principal focus, so that a real inverted and slightly magnified image is produced P'Q'. The second lens, or eyepiece, B, is placed at such a distance from the objective that the image formed by the latter is just inside the principal focus F, and hence the eyepiece, acting as a simple microscope, gives a virtual and magnified image P"Q". In practice, in order to correct the various aberrations, both the objective and ocular consist of combinations or trains of lenses. This is well shown by *Figure 33.11* which illustrates a modern microscope in section.

Compound microscopes, although fundamentally similar in that they are constructed to produce an uncoloured and undistorted enlarged image of an object, may vary considerably in design and equipment.

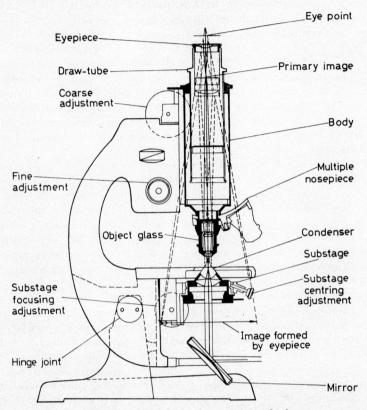

Figure 33.11. The parts of an ordinary compound microscope

Special types of instruments are built for the specialist sciences of petrology, metallurgy and biology, and although gemmology is not very exacting in its demands on the microscope—in general a comparatively low-power instrument is all that is needed—special instruments have been designed in order to facilitate the examination of gemstones. It is in binocular vision and in the special techniques required to illuminate the specimen in order to investigate the internal structure, and not in high magnification, that the microscopes built entirely for gemmological use are characterized.

PARTS OF THE MICROSCOPE

The instrument may be divided into two sections; the optical system, the fundamental principles of which, except for the substage condenser, have been discussed, and the mechanical side, the so-called stand. The more important parts of the microscope (*see Figure 33.11*) are the foot or base of the instrument, which is usually of a horse-shoe shape or of a tripod form. It is essential that the foot has sufficient size and weight to give good stability to the limb which is hinged to it. The limb, which is usually constructed to accommodate the hand for carrying the microscope, carries at its upper and lower ends the working-parts of the instrument.

At the top of the limb are the coarse and fine adjustments, knurled wheels for turning the pinion which engages with the rack on the body tube. The body tube, which carries the optical system, has a dove-tail beam sliding in a similarly shaped recess in the body which comprises the head of the limb. The rack is also incorporated in this slide and together they allow the body tube to be raised or lowered under the action of the coarse adjustment pinion. The body tube may have fitted in to it with a smooth sliding fit, a draw tube, which is the means of producing a change in separation between the objective and the eyepiece sometimes necessary when certain compensations are needed.

The upper end of the draw tube carries the ocular, or eyepiece, which should fit smoothly into the draw tube which has an internal diameter of 23·30 mm (0·9175 in.), a standard laid down by the Royal Microscopical Society in 1899. This, one of four standard sizes, is known as the small size R.M.S. standard eyepiece, or the No. 1, and is the only one in general use today. The lower end of the body tube is made to take the screw fitting of the objective; the screw thread is also an R.M.S. standard and conforms to a Whitworth pattern screw with 36 threads to the inch with a diameter of 0·800 in.

The fine adjustment produces the very slow motion required when focusing high-power objectives, and such fine adjustments are often supplied with a graduated drum or scale so that depth measurements may be taken.

At the lower end of the limb is mounted the rigid platform upon which the object to be examined is placed. This platform is known as the stage, and may be square or circular (in which case it is often rotatable) and has a central aperture to allow the light from the reflecting mirror placed below it to illuminate the object. The stage may be fitted with clips to hold the glass slide upon which the object is placed or mounted, or it may have a mechanical stage, which allows the slide to be moved slowly across the stage in two directions. Such a mechanical stage, which in some microscopes is built in the stage, has little application in gemmological practice.

Below the stage is the substage mount, a circular fitment, standardized with an internal diameter of 1·527 in. (38·786 mm), into which may be fitted various accessories; such as a plane or iris diaphragm, a short focus condensing lens or an aplanatic combination of such lenses, polarizing apparatus or light filters.

Many substages are made so that they can be raised or lowered by rack and pinion movement and also swung out and clear of the optical axis of the microscope.

Below the substage and fixed in gimbals attached to the tailpiece of the limb is the mirror, which, in general, has a concave mirror on one face and a plane mirror on the other, although in some cases the concave mirror is replaced by a white opal glass giving a scattered light reflection. Some microscopes are fitted with a multiple nosepiece into which may be screwed two or three objectives of different powers which may be clicked into position into the optical axis as required. A more modern practice is to screw each objective into special quick change mounts having spring clips and these may be quickly slipped into a special fitting mounted on the lower end of the body tube. Such an arrangement provides better centring of the objective than is usual in the multiple nosepieces. In the best instruments the objectives are computed and mounted so that when a higher or lower power is put into position little refocusing is necessary. That is, they are said to be parfocal.

The function of the objective, sometimes called the object glass, is to produce the primary magnified image with as little distortion as possible.

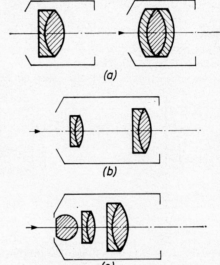

Figure 33.12. Arrangement of lenses in object glasses of various powers. (a)— low powers 3 and 2 in. (b)—medium, $1\frac{1}{2}$, 1 and $\frac{2}{3}$ in. (c)—high, $\frac{1}{2}$, $\frac{1}{4}$ and $\frac{1}{6}$ in.

They are made with composite lenses, or a series of such lenses, and of various focal lengths of powers (*Figure 33.12*). The range of powers in which objectives can be obtained are tabulated below; they are given in inches and in millimetres, for the Continental measurements are now increasingly used.

3 in.	75 mm	$\frac{1}{3}$ in.	8 mm
2 in.	50 mm	$\frac{1}{4}$ in.	6 mm
$1\frac{1}{2}$ in.	35 or 32 mm	$\frac{1}{6}$ in.	4 mm
1 in.	25 mm	$\frac{1}{8}$ in.	3 mm
$\frac{2}{3}$ in.	16 mm	$\frac{1}{12}$ in.	2 mm
$\frac{1}{2}$ in.	12 mm	$\frac{1}{16}$ in.	1·5 mm

The metric measurements do not completely agree with the English values, but are sufficiently near for general purposes. Most manufacturers employ their 32 mm object glasses for the $1\frac{1}{2}$ in.

It must clearly be understood that the focal length given above does not imply that this is the distance between the front lens of the objective and the object focused on. Apart from other optical considerations, it must be remembered that the focus of a lens system is taken from the centre of that system; thus the working distance in normal lenses is less than the focal length.

The gemmologist must have a sensibly large working distance, for he rarely works on thin sections and his objects are gemstones (often in settings) which have considerable depth, and it is also necessary to see a fair amount of the specimen at once; that is to have a good field of view. Neither of these factors can be obtained if high powers are used. In practice it is found that the $1\frac{1}{2}$ in. and the 1 in. glasses are those most commonly used, with higher powers up to $\frac{2}{3}$ in. for special work.

It will be seen from the foregoing that the duty of the ocular is to produce an enlarged virtual image of the primary image formed by the objective. We have considered the eyepiece as a single lens, but for many reasons a single lens is impracticable. Hence the oculars of modern microscopes are made up of two positive (plano-convex) lenses; the first, termed the field lens, and the second, nearer the eye, the eye lens.

EYEPIECES

There are two chief forms of eyepieces used in microscopes, the most commonly used being the Huygenian (*Figure 33.13*) which consists of two plano-convex lenses placed with their curved surfaces towards the incident light.

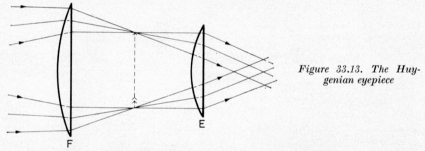

Figure 33.13. The Huygenian eyepiece

They are separated by a distance equal to half the sum of their focal lengths, a condition which is only approximately fulfilled in practice. The ratio of the focal lengths of the field lens to the eye lens is usually about 2:1, but may vary somewhat from this value. It will be seen that the image formed by the objective is situated between the lenses of the eyepiece, and at this focal plane is placed a diaphragm. The Huygenian eyepiece which is practically achromatic, can only be used as a magnifier if used the reverse way up, that is with the field lens used as an eye lens. This type is sometimes called a negative eyepiece.

The Ramsden eyepiece throws the eyepoint farther out. This type consists of two plano-convex lenses of the same focal length and the same material, placed at a distance from each other equal to two-thirds the focal length of either. In theory, this distance should be one-half of the focal length, but this brings the field lens into the focal plane, and any dirt or imperfection on this lens would then be sharply focused. In the Ramsden eyepiece the curved faces of the lenses are towards one another; the focal plane is in front of the field lens (*Figure 33.14*). As the pair can be used as a separate magnifier this is sometimes termed a positive lens.

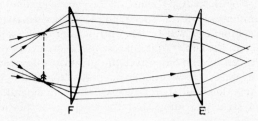

Figure 33.14. The Ramsden eye-piece

An inclined eyepiece is available which may replace the normal ocular; such an accessory permits observation to be made while sitting down despite the microscope being in the vertical position, this also prevents much eyestrain (*Figure 33.15*).

Figure 33.15. An inclined binocular eyepiece

Most oculars are marked either with the focal length, a code letter or number, or their magnification. Table 33.1 will give some idea of the power of such eyepieces if they are marked.

TABLE 33.1

Old notation	Numbered notation	Focal length in millimetres	Magnification*
A	1	50	5 ×
B	2	42	6 ×
C	3	30	8 ×
D	4	25	10 ×
E	5	20	12 ×
F	6	17	15 ×

* The magnification power is that for distance of distinct vision, namely 250 mm. 6 ×, 8 ×, and 10 × are most useful.

The substage condenser is a system of lenses fitted below the stage, often in a focusing mounting, which is employed to converge the light received from the mirror on to the object being examined. There are several types of such lens systems, some of which are corrected for aberration, but this is not so important as in the case of objectives. The most useful type is that known as the Abbe substage condenser combined with an iris diaphragm

(*Figure 33.16*). The use of the substage condenser is bound up with the illumination of the specimen, therefore further consideration of its use in gemmology will be left until a later discussion.

In the compound microscope, there are two separate magnifications; that given by the objective, the primary magnification; and that given by the eyepiece, the secondary magnification. These two magnifications multiplied together will therefore give the full magnification of the compound lens system providing that the eyepiece is placed at the distance of distinct

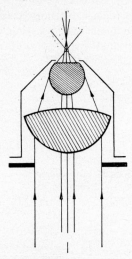

Figure 33.16. The Abbe condenser

vision (10 in.) from the objective. For example, a 1-in. objective, magnifying approximately 10 ×, in conjunction with an ocular (say No. 2) magnifying 6 × would give a total magnification of 60 × providing the distance between the eyepiece and objective is 10 in.

The earlier microscopes were constructed on this principle which accounts for the long tube length of such instruments. Modern microscopes have a tube length of approximately $6\frac{1}{2}$ in., or two-thirds of the standard, which greatly lessens the magnification as computed by the multiplication of the primary and secondary magnifications. It is therefore necessary if a shorter (or longer) tube length than 10 in. is used to calculate the difference, or proportion of 10 in., so that instead of multiplying the primary magnification by 10 it is necessary to multiply by a fraction of which 10 is made the denominator and the actual tube length the numerator. For example, with a 1 in. (10 ×) objective and a No. 2 eyepiece (6 ×) separated by a tube length of $6\frac{1}{2}$ in. the magnification would work out as follows:

$$60 \times \frac{6\frac{1}{2}}{10} \text{ or } 60 \times \frac{6\cdot5}{10}$$

which gives 39 ×.

For all ordinary purposes the tube length may be reckoned from the two ends of the adjustable tube into one end of which the objective screws and upon the other the eyepiece rests, and, indeed, it must be understood that magnification calculated on the above method is only approximately correct as there are other factors which play a part: these have not been considered. Calculation by the formula given will, however, give a satis-factory estimate of the magnification. It is of course assumed that the magnification of both the objective and the ocular are known, and this is generally the case, as manufacturers either mark their lens systems or give the required information in their literature.

Magnification, so often considered to be the primary criterion of a micro-scope, is in reality only of secondary importance, for the reason that the image of a point depicted by any optical system is not a point but a disc. Owing to the wave nature of light, a lens cannot produce a point image of a point object, but produces instead a bright spot of light surrounded by diffraction rings (the diffraction pattern or 'antipoint'), an effect known as the Airy disc. Therefore if, for example, two points in the object are so close together that in the image their diffraction discs overlap, the two points will no longer appear separate, but rather as one, and no amount of magni-fication will pull them apart. The power to define fine detail is termed the resolving power.

With the microscopes used in gemmology, the finer points of resolution and magnification are of no great consequence, for, owing to the depth of the specimens required to be examined, a long working distance is necessary and comparatively low powers are used. Indeed, even if high powers could be employed, the field of view would be so small that much of the structural appearance necessary for diagnosis would be missed.

INSTRUMENTS FOR THE EXAMINATION OF INTERNAL FEATURES OF GEMSTONES

The most common use of the microscope in gemmology is to examine the internal features in a gemstone. For such work a simple type of low power instrument is satisfactory providing the optical system is good (*Figure 33.17*).

Figure 33.17. A general purpose type of microscope suitable for gem-testing

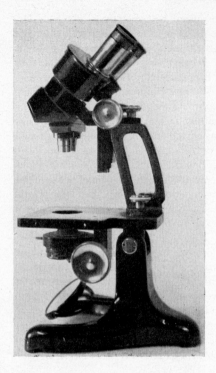

Figure 33.18. The Greenough binocular microscope

Figure 33.19. The Gemological Institute of America's 'Custom Mark V "A" Gemolite', a microscope incorporating a zoom lens and provision for light and dark field illumination, as well as top lighting

Should much work of a continuous nature be contemplated a Greenough type binocular microscope with paired objectives and inclined eyepieces (*Figure 33.18*) is most valuable as it gives colour-free stereoscopic vision and an erect image and not one that is reversed left to right and upside down as in an ordinary monocular microscope. Further, the use of both eyes serves to avoid strain. Certain microscopes, such as the American 'Gemolite' (*Figure 33.19*), and similar Swiss instruments, are built solely for gemmological requirements. These instruments have a built-in light source which gives both direct and 'dark field' (this will be mentioned later) illumination, and are fitted with special gem holders. A horizontal type of microscope with a special stone holder is in use in Germany and appears to be most efficient and these, like some others, are fitted with dichroscopes and spectroscopes which may replace the eyepiece.

POLARIZED LIGHT

When polarized light is to be used in testing stones some form of polarizer to produce such light is necessary as an adjunct to the microscope; and another is needed to analyse the polarized light. Such polarizers may be the prism invented by W. Nicol in 1828, or a disc of the new material known as 'Polaroid'. The nicol prism depends upon the fact that the two rays in a doubly refractive crystal are plane-polarized in directions at right angles to one another. Therefore, if one of the rays is eliminated the other passing through will emerge from the crystal vibrating in one plane only.

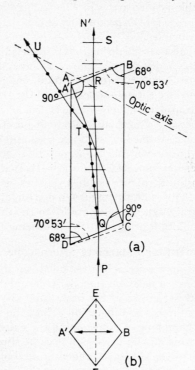

Figure 33.20. The nicol prism

Prisms

These nicol prisms, or 'nicols' as they are called, consist of a cleavage rhomb of Iceland spar (calcite) suitably divided and re-cemented. A clear flawless cleavage rhombohedron of the spar, about three times as long as it is broad, is selected, ABCD in *Figure 33.20(a)*. By grinding and polishing, the inclination of the end faces AB and CD is altered to A′B and C′D which then make an angle of 68 degrees with the edges BC and AD respectively, the angle made by the natural faces being 70 degrees 53 minutes. The prism is then cut diagonally along plane A′C′, perpendicular to the faces A′B and C′D and parallel to the longer diagonals of these faces, that is EF in *Figure 33.20(b)*, which shows a view of the upper face of the prism. After polishing the cut surfaces the halves are cemented together in their original positions with Canada balsam.

When a ray of ordinary light PQ (*Figure (33.20a)*), enters the prism in a direction parallel, or nearly parallel, to its length, the extraordinary ray, QRS, has a refractive index very close to that of the balsam film A′C′ and consequently passes out through it and emerges at the other end of the prism. The ordinary ray, QT, however, has a much higher index than the balsam film and strikes it at an angle beyond the critical angle; it is therefore totally reflected at the film and passes out through the side of the prism along TU, where it may be absorbed by the non-reflecting mounting of the prism. The only light transmitted by the prism is the extraordinary ray which vibrates parallel to the shorter diagonal of the prism, indicated by the double-headed arrow in *Figure 33.20(b)*. There are certain other types of prisms made for the production of polarized light but they all operate on the same principle.

The material called Polaroid is made from a vast number of small crystals of quinine iodosulphate, known as herapathite, held in uniform alignment in a plastic base to produce a film, the polarizing effect being due to the complete absorption of one ray and the transmission of the other with very little absorptive effect—in fact, the phenomenon of extreme dichroism. More recently a method of producing a polarizing film has been evolved, in which no re-formed crystals are used and the polarizing action based upon a careful linear control of the molecular structure of the plastic, forming a homogeneous and haze-free sheet. Its manufacture entails the formation of a brush-like structure inside a sheet of clear tough plastic called polyvinyl-alcohol. This is first stretched in one direction so that the long tangled molecules straighten out, all parallel to the direction of the stretch. A dip into iodine solution brings out the polarizing properties.

Equipment for Polarizing Microscope

To equip a microscope for polarized light observation it is necessary to incorporate a polarizer (nicol or polaroid disc) below the stage; and another, the analyser either in the body tube above the objective or over the eyepiece. A further consideration is that the stage should be rotatable. For the simple technique of determining the existence of double refraction all that is needed is a polarizer which may be slipped into position below the stage in place of the substage condenser, and an analyser to fit over the eyepiece or to screw into the lower end of the body tube in place of the objective, which is then screwed into the lower end of the analyser fitting. At least one of the nicols or polaroids should be capable of rotation. Some sort of rotatable stage can be extemporized by turning a metal disc, so that a projecting rim bounding a central aperture fits snugly into the aperture of the stage where it acts as a bearing. *Figure 33.21* shows such a made-up rotating stage and *Figure 33.22* shows types of accessory polarizing fittings. *Figure 33.23* shows a simple microscope fitted with polarizing equipment and the extempore rotating stage.

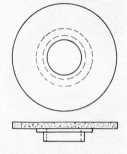

Figure 33.21. A made-up rotating stage to fit into the stage aperture of an ordinary microscope. It may be turned-up from any non-ferrous metal or plastic

Petrological Microscope

The most complete microscope for polarized light observations is the instrument used by scientists for the study of rocks in thin section—the so-called petrological microscope (*Figures 33.24* and *33.25*). These instruments incorporate the nicol prisms (or polaroid discs), a built-in rotating stage which is divided into degrees on the edge and can be read to minutes of arc by vernier, and a substage condenser, which, like the lower nicol, can be swung in or out of the optical axis of the instrument. The analyser is usually fitted into a box which can be slid in or out of the body tube, or in some cases into a hinged box which can be turned over the eyepiece. Another addition is a Bertrand lens which can be pushed in or out of the optical axis; this is used to bring the focal plane in correct position with regard to

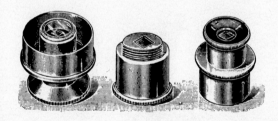

(a)

Figure 33.22. Auxiliary polarizing equipment: (a) substage polarizer, analyser to screw in above the objective and analyser to fit over the eyepiece, (b) substage polariser and eyepiece analyser by Beck

(b)

Figure 33.23. A simple fixed-stand microscope (the Beck, London No. 10) fitted with polarizing equipment and an extemporized rotating stage

the ocular when interference figures (to be discussed later) are to be obtained by the use of convergent polarized light. The oculars of petrological micro-scopes are fitted with cross-wires arranged parallel to the vibration direc-tions of the polarizer and analyser. As only the lower polarizer is rotatable, it is usually so arranged as to click into the crossed position.

Figure 33.24. The petrological microscope

640

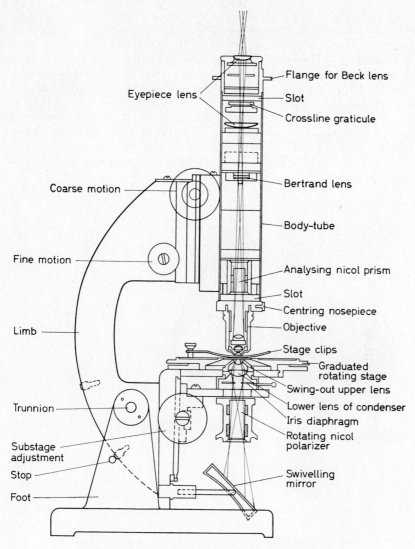

Flange for Beck lens
Eyepiece lens
Slot
Crossline graticule
Coarse motion
Bertrand lens
Body-tube
Fine motion
Analysing nicol prism
Slot
Centring nosepiece
Limb
Objective
Stage clips
Graduated rotating stage
Swing-out upper lens
Trunnion
Lower lens of condenser
Iris diaphragm
Rotating nicol polarizer
Substage adjustment
Stop
Swivelling mirror
Foot

Figure 33.25. The optical system of the petrological microscope

TECHNIQUE OF FOCUSING MICROSCOPE

In use the microscope is set up about 8 in. in front of a good light (*Figure 33.26*), after having screwed a suitable objective into the bottom of the body tube and slipped the necessary ocular into the top. Set a specimen slide on the stage with the object over the stage aperture—for practice a prepared slide of an insect or botanical specimen is convenient. Direct light on the object from the mirror. It will be assumed that no substage condenser is to be used for this experiment but only a rotating or iris diaphragm below the stage.

21+G.   641

It now only remains to focus the microscope. Preliminary investigation will have shown that the movement of either the coarse or the fine adjustment in a clockwise direction will bring the body tube nearer the stage. It will therefore be thought that the best method of focusing would be to rack down. This should not be done, for it leads to disaster; it is only too easy to overshoot the focus, or to have started below the focus, with the consequence that the objective is pushed right through the slide which is irreparably smashed, and with possible damage to the expensive objective. The correct method is to start with the tube racked down until the objective nearly touches the slide (observing from the side, not through the eyepiece while racking down). Then, looking through the eyepiece, rack the body tube upwards until the object is in sharp focus.

Figure 33.26. The microscope set-up

If, when racked up, the microscope does not focus on to the object, generally owing to missing the focus or to the object not being centred below the objective, begin again from the start and watch out for any specks to come into focus. These specks are dust or slight defects on the slide and will indicate that the object is not in centre and that the slide requires to be moved along. Alternatively, if the object cannot be located easily, the eyepiece may be removed and the object observed, and centred, by looking through the back lens of the objective.

The mirror should then be adjusted so that the light reflected up the tube travels coaxially through the objective of the microscope. To check this, rack up slightly; if the light is central the magnified object will remain stationary, but if oblique the object will appear to travel in the direction of the light. The centring of the light beam may be accomplished by removing the eyepiece and inspecting the rear lens of the objective while tilting the mirror until the light source appears central. At the same time, the diaphragm should be adjusted until about two-thirds of the area of the back lens of the objective remains clear. Replace the eyepiece and view the specimen. If the light is too bright, move the light source farther away or find other means of dimming it. A ground-glass screen is effective for this. Do not use the iris or disc diaphragm to moderate the light. The function of the diaphragm is to govern resolving power not to diminish intensity.

When using the Abbe substage condenser and plane mirror, it is necessary to ensure that the lens system is central in the optical axis of the microscope, and, what is even more important, that it is correctly focused. The centring of the condenser can be checked and adjusted by closing the iris diaphragm as far as possible and focusing on the central spot of light.

Following the rules outlined above will allow the worker continually to obtain images of good quality consistent with the limitations of the instrument. When using a monocular microscope learn to keep both eyes open. Learn to disregard the image produced by the unused eye, for eyestrain is practically non-existent if both eyes are kept open. If possible—it is not easy—use the eyes alternatively to exercise both.

CARE AND CLEANING OF INSTRUMENTS

Elementary as it may seem, some hints on the care and cleaning of instruments are called for. When not in use the microscope should be kept under cover, or in its case. A bell-glass cover is useful, but a clean cloth draped over it, or the modern polythene bags, are much better than leaving the instrument open. Even if the instrument is left for a short time, cover it up, for dust is the major cause of all troubles. To clean the adjustments use paraffin oil on a clean rag and finally grease with a good quality grease. The coarse adjustment is best cleaned by removing the body tube completely from the body by racking up the tube until out of the bearings.

It is sometimes found that the coarse adjustment becomes loose and the tube tends to rack down under its own weight. To cure this it is necessary to tighten either one or two screws on the top or at the rear of the limb carrying the pinion (different manufacturers place these screws in different positions). To get at the fine adjustment it may be necessary to remove the screws from the cover-plate—much care is required here, as there is generally an actuating spring bearing against the plate which will tend to fly out when the screws are loosened. The worker doubtful of his mechanical ability had far better let the manufacturer recondition the microscope.

Dust on the lenses is a common trouble and show as specks in the field of view. First ascertain on which lens system, eyepiece, objective, condenser, or even the mirror, these specks are. This may conveniently be found by rotating the eyepiece and seeing whether the specks move; if they do then this is the offending part. Likewise by slightly unscrewing the objective, or by lowering and raising the condenser, or by slightly tilting the mirror, movement of the specks will indicate on which of the parts dust has collected.

To clean lenses, use a very soft, well-washed cotton handkerchief kept in a dust-proof box, sparsely moistened if necessary with xylol or alcohol (methylated spirits), or use the soft 'lens paper' sold by all optical dealers. It is permissible to unscrew the top and bottom lenses of the ocular to clean the internal surfaces, but care must be taken to replace them at the correct ends of the ocular tube. It is inadvisable to take the objective apart—leave that job to the manufacturer's technician. An eyepiece should always be left in the draw tube, so that dust will not collect on the sides of the tube nor fall down on to the back lens of the objective.

EXAMINATION OF INTERNAL STRUCTURE OF GEMSTONES

When examining the internal structure of gemstones there are two funda-mental differences to consider as against the examination of a prepared thin section on a slide. The first is the much greater thickness of the specimen which necessitates the use of comparatively low-powered objectives in order to have a sufficiently large working distance below the objective. The second important point is that for light to pass evenly through the specimen it should be a parallel-sided plate. In the case of gemstones, except between the table facet and the culet (if one is present), there is no position where this

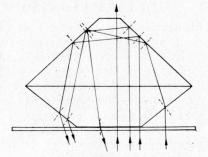

Figure 33.27. The paths of parallel light rays from the microscope mirror through a corundum resting table facet down on a glass slide (re-fractive index of corundum is 1·77; the critical angle 34·5 degrees)

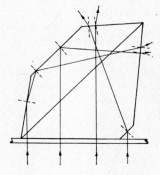

Figure 33.28. The paths of parallel light rays from the microscope mirror through a corundum resting pavilion facet down on a glass slide (refractive index of corundum is 1·77; the critical angle 34·5 degrees)

Figure 33.29. The paths of parallel light rays from the microscope mirror through a rock crystal resting table facet down on a glass slide (refractive index of quartz is 1·55; the critical angle just over 40 degrees)

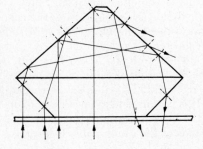

can occur in a faceted stone. Light rays from the mirror of the microscope (parallel light rays being assumed for this initial discussion—that is the plane side of the mirror with a distant source of light, such as daylight, and that the substage condenser is not being used) are reflected from the steep rear facets by total internal reflection (*Figure 33.27*). The same stone resting on a pavilion facet (*Figure 33.28*) does pass more light yet still leaves much of the interior of the stone in darkness. The greater the refractive index of the stone the greater is the total internal reflection, and naturally the converse is true. Compare *Figure 33.29* with *Figure 33.27*, yet even with the greater escape of light in the case of rock crystal, it is still difficult to see into the interior of the stone. Mounting the stone on the glass slide with a little Plasticine, so that it is table facet uppermost, or even with a little practice holding the stone in that position, may allow better inspection of the internal features.

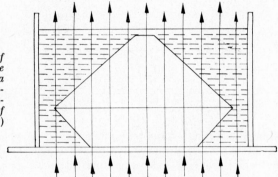

Figure 33.30. The paths of parallel light rays from the microscope mirror through a yellow apatite which is immersed in acetylene tetrabromide (refractive index of both stone and liquid is 1·63)

Liquid Immersion

It is clear from the foregoing that some other method must be used if the worker is to 'get into' the stone to make a thorough examination of the internal structure. It has been remarked that the optimum condition is a parallel-sided plate, therefore, if the stone could be embedded in a substance having the same refractive index as the stone under test and the sides made parallel, it should be possible to see clearly all the interior of the stone.

Can this be done? In some cases the optimum condition can be obtained quite simply—that is by immersing the stone in a liquid of the same refractive index as that of the stone; such as, beryl in *o*-tuluidine (refractive index 1·575); white topaz in iodobenzene (refractive index 1·62) or hessonite garnet in methylene iodide (refractive index 1·74), to quote a few. Further, as a liquid in a flat-bottomed cell has a horizontal surface, the second requirement is met—that of a parallel-sided plate. This is illustrated in *Figure 33.30*.

In practice it is not at all necessary to use a liquid of exactly the same refractive index as that of the stone being tested. A liquid having a refractive index comparatively near will suffice; as corundum gems are those most constantly requiring examination, owing to the synthesis of that species, methylene iodide (refractive index 1·74) will be the most useful. However, the cheaper, although less refractive, liquid α-monobromonaphthalene (refractive index 1·66) is now more commonly used and is nearly as effective as the more expensive methylene iodide. *Figure 33.31* illustrates this quite clearly. In the absence of the more highly refractive liquids, cigarette lighter petrol (refractive index 1·49) or even water (refractive index 1·33) might be better than nothing at all.

One of the objections to the use of the liquids normally used, apart from the extra work involved in setting-up and in the added equipment needed, is that the stone requires cleaning from the liquids used after the examination is made. This is particularly a nuisance when examination is made of a

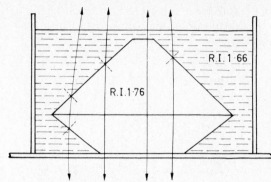

Figure 33.31. The paths of parallel light rays from the microscope mirror through a ruby which is immersed in monobromonaphthalene (refractive index of stone is 1·76 and that of the liquid 1·66)

stone in a setting—monobromonaphthalene is worse than methylene iodide in this respect. A liquid which has been suggested as an immersion liquid and which leaves the stone in a perfectly clean condition is ethylene glycol mono-ethyl ether, which is sold under the names 'cellosolve' and 'oxitol'. The low refractive index of 1·408 does not seem to be detrimental.

Lighter fluid (petrol), or a weak solution of a wetting agent or one of the modern detergents may be used as a cleaning agent. The final drying may best be carried out by the well-known method of placing the wet piece of jewellery in warm box-dust (fine sawdust) which dries up the moisture by absorption. This leaves the back of the stone, usually difficult to reach by ordinary drying methods, mirror-clean; a necessary attribute if the stone is to show its maximum brilliancy.

Monobromonaphthalene has a marked affinity for dust particles which cannot be removed from it except by constant filtering. Such dust particles can look very much like minute bubbles which are so often seen in synthetic gems (or even like natural inclusions), and thus lead to a wrong conclusion. Quite large air bubbles often tend to cling to the surface of the stone when immersed in liquid, and a hasty worker may well accept these as bubbles inside the stone and arrive at an incorrect decision that a genuine stone is synthetic, or vice versa.

Dry Examination

To avoid, so far as possible, encountering such difficulties, modern usage suggests that the initial examination should be made dry, and the use of liquid resorted to only in difficult cases. How may this be done? It has already been stated that you cannot 'get into' a stone when not immersed in liquid; true, but in the cases considered, parallel light rays from the microscope mirror were postulated. If the light rays impinging on the stone are oblique, say convergent, the position is much improved. This may be effected by the use of a substage condenser which 'throws' the light into the stone in such directions that the beams meet the pavilion facets at angles less than the critical angle of total reflection. The effect is shown by *Figure 33.32*.

It can be seen from this illustration that if the condenser is adjusted the whole stone will be evenly illuminated and with the rays refracted out through the pavilion facets. Further, it will be found, rarely, that, as depicted in the drawing, the stone would be relatively so large compared with the lens of the substage condenser. There are, however, great variations in the size of condensers fitted to microscopes.

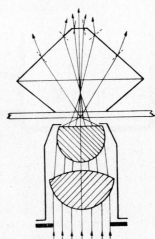

Figure 33.32. The path of light rays through a ruby after the parallel rays from the microscope mirror have been converged by the substage condenser. The Abbe substage condenser is not compensated, therefore the rays from the edge of the lens do not come to a focus at the same point as the rays through the centre of the lens. It will readily be seen that if the condenser is adjusted the whole stone will be illuminated

Glass Cells for Holding Immersion Oil

The selection of the glass cell to contain the immersion oil calls for some comment. Probably the best obtainable are those made from a glass ring fused to a plate of optical glass. These are somewhat expensive and are usually rather small, being mounted on a 3 × 1 glass microscope slide. Larger cells of this type are sold. Such cells are quite suitable for loose stones but are far too small to accommodate mounted specimens, especially brooches and pendants.

The large thin glass dishes, such as are used for certain chemical experiments, are quite useful as they take a sufficient depth of liquid to enable the pieces of jewellery to be kept immersed whilst being turned to allow observation to be made along different directions. The so-called Petri dishes used for bacteria culture are also useful, or, in fact, any glass dish with a tolerably flat base may be employed.

There is usually, however, a major defect inherent in these makeshift 'cells', in that they are rarely if ever made of optically clean glass, and therefore often exhibit the 'swirlmarks' and bubbles typical of the lower qualities of glass. When in use, if the focus of the microscope is lowered so that the base of the cell is in view, these defects become apparent and the inexperienced worker may well accept such structures as being within the stone, thus leading to a wrong diagnosis.

A second point, that of viewing the stone along different directions, may cause some difficulty. If the stone is loose this can be accomplished quite easily by turning it while holding it with corn-tongs (tweezers) in the liquid —the free hand being used to make the small adjustments of focus necessary. Likewise, pieces of jewellery may be similarly held and turned, but, as mentioned above, a deep cell and a depth of liquid is necessary.

Many attempts have been made to produce a cell with an arrangement whereby the stone may be turned whilst immersed in liquid, and these are at best only suitable for unmounted stones. Such cells have never been wholly successful for several reasons. Rotation along two axes, necessary for complete examination is difficult to attain; and should the arrangement

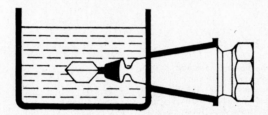

Figure 33.33. A glass cell with stopper arranged to carry the stone about one axis. Devised by G. O. Wild

employ, as they mostly do, a control rod passing through the side of the cell, a liquid-tight fitting is required. The holding of the stone also presents some difficulty—wax, used in many cases, tends to deteriorate rapidly through contact with the immersion liquid; if metal grips are employed the liquid tends to corrode them.

An interesting type of glass cell seen by the author, is one devised by G. O. Wild. Essentially it is a fairly deep glass cell fitted with a neck at one side which is closed by an accurately fitted ground-glass stopper. The stone is held by wax to the inner end of the stopper and may be rotated around one axis only by rotation of the stopper itself, which is sufficiently tight fitting to prevent leakage of the immersion liquid (*Figure 33.33*). A type of cell marketed by the Gemological Institute of America known as the Shipley universal immersion stage, allows turning through two axes at right angles. It consists of a cell mounted on a glass base; a rod passing through the side is rotated by the external handle of dial form marked in degrees. Internally this rod engages a ring fitting which has a second ring rotatable on its inner circumference. To this inner ring, which is also graduated, is fixed the projecting stone-holder which carries the specimen at the centre of the two rotating axes.

Immersion Sphere

An ingenious device for viewing immersed stones from different directions, devised by Dr. Gübelin, employs a hollow glass sphere filled with liquid having the same refractive index as the glass and into which is inserted the stone fixed to a closely fitting stopper. The sphere is then placed on a wooden ring on the microscope stage so that it may easily be rotated. The prime advantage of this accessory is in the observation of interference figures and therefore will be further discussed when polarized light effects are considered. A similar type of spherical stone-holder is the *Interference figure bulb* marketed by the Gemological Institute of America. A more elaborate, but similar type of apparatus, made by the firm of E. Leitz to the design of C. Klein and K. Schlossmacher is shown in *Figure 33.34.*

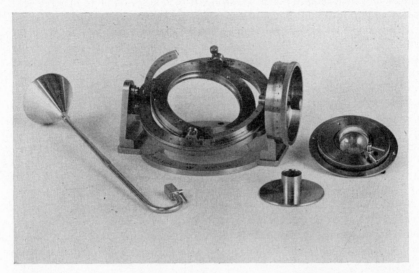

Figure 33.34. Klein and Schlossmacher's immersion sphere made by Leitz of Germany

There seems to be little added merit in employing the substage condenser in combination with immersion in highly refractive liquid. For convenience in those instruments where the substage condenser is not easily removable from the optical axis of the microscope, it can be well left in. If the condenser has an easy focusing adjustment (rise and fall), some adjustment of this may well be useful in picking up indistinct curved lines or fine 'silk'.

DARK-FIELD ILLUMINATION

So far it has been assumed that the specimen under examination is illuminated by light passing directly from the mirror of the microscope, or through the substage condenser. This is the method of observation by transmitted light and is the usual method adopted in Great Britain. In the United States of America and on the Continent an indirect method of illuminating the specimen is often favoured. This is by lateral illumination, or as it is termed dark-ground or dark-field illumination.

To explain adequately the use and effect of dark-ground illumination it must be recognized that microscopic vision depends upon resolution and visibility—and visibility depends upon contrast. It is well known that a dark object, say a dark blue sapphire, is less visible when placed on a piece of black velvet, than is, say a ruby on a green background. In fact, there is little contrast in the first example and much in the second. It is common knowledge that the web of the spider is quite invisible against the bright sky, but if the gossamer web is illuminated by the sun and seen against a dark background, such as a bush, it is clearly seen as shining bright lines. It is upon this effect that dark-ground illumination owes its value. Therefore, if we can observe inclusions in gemstones as bright points of light (the inclusions being lit up by the lateral rays making them self-luminous) on the darker field of the rest of the stone, it may be possible to observe structures which would not be apparent when the stone is fully illuminated.

How may this dark-field illumination be obtained and what is its precise value in gem-testing? The necessary requirement is to cut out the central beams of light from the microscope mirror, allowing only oblique rays in the form of a hollow cone which do not enter the objective directly, but only when reflected from inclusions making these appear self-luminous. This is usually carried out by placing a dark 'stop' or 'patch' centrally and below the substage condenser (*Figure 33.35*). Many forms of dark-ground illuminators are available. When special microscopes with self-contained lighting are employed, the method becomes most effective and useful. Such internal illumination of the substage fitments is the basis of the special gemmological microscopes. Generally speaking dark-ground illumination yields more striking pictures as the contrast of a white pattern on a dark ground is always more arresting. However, one cannot easily generalize on the subject, whether to choose transmitted light or dark-field illumination, since both need to be given serious consideration. In most cases it is an advantage to use dark-ground illumination when 'silk' is present, and liquid inclusions

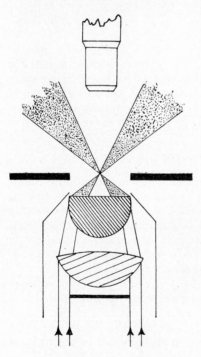

Figure 33.35. Arrangement for the production of dark-ground illumination. Only the lateral rays which do not enter the objective are transmitted through the substage condenser

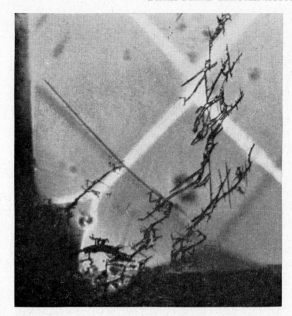

Figure 33.36. Dendritic figures of liquid-filled fissures in a Montana sapphire as seen by transmitted light
(By courtesy of E. Gübelin)

may produce more striking effects in this type of lighting—fine patterns being generally more conspicuous, while coarse patterns are better seen in transmitted light (*Figures 33.36* and *33.37*).

In most cases, dark-ground illumination gives better results with included crystals, whether transparent or opaque, colourless or coloured, as transmitted light causes the crystal to appear as a coal-black blob, while dark-ground illumination may well bring out the beauty of the crystal's

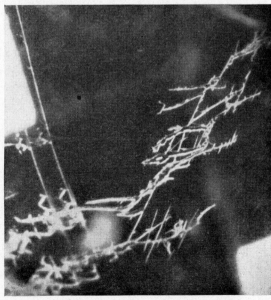

Figure 33.37. The same inclusions as seen in Figure 33.36, but seen in dark-ground illumination
(By courtesy of E. Gübelin)

habit, especially when the dark-field illumination is so constructed that the intensity can be varied on different sides.

A modified dark-ground, actually a mixture of the two types of illumination, is obtained when the mirror of the microscope is adjusted so that the reflected beam is 'off-centre' from the optical axis—the correct position for ordinary illumination. Experiment shows that such adjustment of the mirror will often bring out fine detail, especially is this so in the case of the very pale and indistinct curved striations of synthetic corundums. Movement of the mirror—wobbling it about—whilst observing the specimen often enables the worker to 'pick-up' fine structure which would most likely be missed. When the substage condenser is in the optical train, lowering it will often perform a similar service.

It was found by F. Zernike in 1932 that differences in optical path, causing what are generally referred to as phase differences, could be made visible in transmitted light microscopy as differences in intensity. By its use many fine structures are made more easily visible. Although this phase contrast method has recently been applied to mineralogy and to advanced techniques in gemmology, the difficulty and expense of modifying the polarizing microscope for phase contrast work precludes the general use of the method which will not be further discussed.

It has been found of value, especially when diamond is to be examined, that if it is suitably held on the stage of the microscope, and a strong and narrow beam of light from an intensity lamp is directed on to the stone from the front or side of the stage, the interior of the gem may be examined with ease. This is always difficult to attain when ordinary lighting is used for stones of high refraction.

The observation of the surface structure of a specimen, whether it is transparent or opaque, is sometimes called for. It is rarely necessary in such cases where 'top-lighting' is required to employ anything more complicated than a desk lamp arranged to throw light down on to the surface, aided, perhaps, by the 'bull's-eye' stand condenser. There are various types of reflectors made to fit on the stage, or over the objective; and for metallurgical investigations vertical illumination through the objective itself is used. These have no employment in gemmological techniques.

METHODS OF INDICATING INCLUSION POSITIONS

It may not be out of place to mention the usual methods of indication to another person where, in the field of the microscope, a particular inclusion is situated. There are special indicating eyepieces obtainable, either single or double, whereby two workers can observe the same field at the same time. These eyepieces are fitted with a movable pointer which may be turned to indicate the position.

There are two usual methods of indicating the position of a point in the field of a microscope. Probably the best known is the clock-face method. The field is looked upon as the face of a clock and the indication given by naming the hour at which the inclusion is situated (*Figure 33.38*). The second method is more often used in the case of polarizing microscopes, which generally have cross-hairs set in the ocular. This is the compass indication;

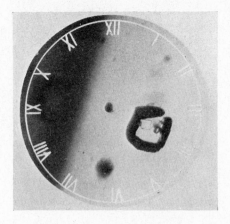

Figure 33.38. The clock-face method of indicating position. The three-phase inclusion in the South American emerald is situated at 4 o'clock

the vertical hair being designated as north-south and the horizontal hair as east-west. Indication being given as north-west, south-east and so forth (*Figure 33.39.*)

POLARIZING MICROSCOPE

Arrangement of Optical and Polarizing Apparatus

In the case of the polarizing microscope the general principle of setting-up is the same as for a normal instrument. It is in the arrangement of the optical and polarizing apparatus that differences occur, and there are three such arrangements which may be used in gem distinction.

The first of these is when one nicol only is in the optical train of the microscope. The second arrangement, the most useful in gem-testing, has both nicols in the optical train; these are in the crossed position, but the substage condenser is usually removed from the microscope. Such an arrangement uses what is known as parallel polarized light. The third method is similar, with both the nicols in the train and in the crossed position, but in this case a short focus substage condenser is also placed in the train. This

Figure 33.39. Using the cross-hairs as position indicators. The vertical hair is designated north-south, and the horizontal hair as east-west. The large zircon inclusion in a yellow sapphire is situated in the south-east quarter

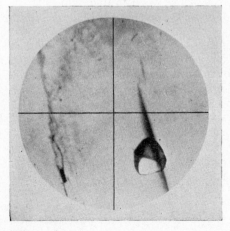

653

produces what is known as convergent polarized light and is used for the production of interference figures. In the best polarizing microscopes a subsidiary magnifier, known as the Bertrand lens, may be placed in the axis of the microscope in order to focus the first image in the correct plane for it to be picked up by the ocular.

When one nicol only is used—either the polarizer or the analyser (usually the polarizer)—and a coloured anisotropic stone is placed on the stage, the vibration direction of the nicol will 'select' the vibration directions of the stone. Therefore, upon rotating the stage with the stone upon it, the field may vary in colour every 90 degrees, due to the differential selective absorption of each of the two rays of the doubly refractive stone. Hence, such an arrangement allows pleochroism to be observed, much in the same way as with a dichroscope except that the twin-colours are not viewed side by side. Thus, there will be no doubt when the dichroism is moderate to strong, but if it is weak it may be missed, for the eye cannot 'carry' the colour; in such cases the direct comparison, as in the dichroscope, is much to be preferred.

Crossed Nicols

To examine stones in parallel polarized light, both nicols must be in the optical axis, and be 'crossed' to one another. In the standard petrological microscopes the polarizer clicks into position when the crossed position is attained. In the 'built-up' instruments the crossed position must be found by trial, that is by rotating either the polarizer or analyser until it is seen that the field is dark.

This 'crossing' and the dark field it gives may be explained as follows: light transmitted by the polarizer is, say, vibrating only parallel to an east-west direction, but the analyser has its vibration direction parallel to north-south. Thus the emerging extraordinary ray of the polarizer now becomes the ordinary ray of the analyser and is totally reflected by the film of balsam and absorbed by the casing (or totally absorbed by the material if polaroid discs are used). Consequently the light does not reach the eye and therefore the field is dark.

When a singly refracting stone, say a piece of glass or any isotropic mineral is placed on the stage, that is, interposed between the crossed nicols, no alteration of the conditions are produced, as such substances have no power to change the vibration direction of the entering light. Therefore, if any stone belonging to the cubic system, or any amorphous substance, is examined between crossed nicols, it will give a dark field at all positions during a complete rotation of the stage.

In all experiments using polarized light the best results are obtained when the stone is immersed in a highly refractive liquid, such as monobromonaphthalene. This is in order to avoid surface reflections from the inclined facets of exterior light. True, if there are two parallel facets, such as table and culet, any effects can be observed at the top face, but immersion in liquid is safest.

When an anisotropic stone is examined between crossed nicols, the field does not remain dark during a complete rotation of the stage carrying the stone, except when the direction of observation is parallel to an optic axis.

In all other directions the field becomes four times light and four times dark during a rotation of the stage through a full circle, that is, it will become dark, or extinguish, in four positions at intervals of 90 degrees, and between those positions of darkness the field is illuminated; being at its brightest at 45 degrees from the dark position. Extinction occurs when the vibration directions of the stone are parallel to the vibration directions of the nicols; for in such positions light from the polarizer is not resolved by the stone but passes on to the analyser as if the stage was empty. Hence darkness results.

In the foregoing remarks it may be assumed that a clear-cut decision as to whether a stone is singly or doubly refracting may be made by the simple observation of the effect between crossed nicols. Although this is generally true there are many occasions when the results, unless the worker has had considerable experience, are not so clear. Many isotropic substances are under a state of strain, either wholly or more usually in patches, and thus do not exhibit a completely dark field during a complete rotation of the specimen through 360 degrees, but show a light and dark patchiness over the whole field. This effect is termed anomalous double refraction.

Anomalous Double Refraction

Such anomalies should not worry any worker who has had some experience of polarizing effects, but they do in many cases cause trouble to the tyro. The characteristic difference in the extinction shown by true doubly refracting materials and the anomalous extinction shown by materials in strain is as follows. In true double refraction the extinction, that is the cut-off of the light, occurs regularly at every quarter of the circle of rotation (at every 90 degrees), and is quite sharp. The pattern due to anomalous double refraction is patchy, the whole field being made up of light and dark patches or stripes which may move across the field as the stage is rotated, but, in general, have no relation to any orientation at 90 degree intervals. This last observation may not be true in the case of some garnets, which do show a very good approximation to four times light and four times dark during a complete rotation of the stage. This effect has been remarked upon during the description of garnets.

The strain causing this anomalous effect may be set-up by a number of causes, such as that due to the rapid cooling of glass; hence some pastes may exhibit the phenomenon. It is, however, in the case of synthetic spinel that the effect has most importance in diagnosis. Due to the excess of alumina present in the synthetic spinel the crystal lattice is in the state of some strain. This is shown by the characteristic anomalous double refraction; a field crossed with alternate light and dark stripes. This pattern has been likened to the stripes on a tabby cat, and the name 'tabby extinction' has been applied to it (*Figure 33.40*). The anomalous doubly refractive effect in the case of garnet has already been mentioned.

Several other effects of a minor nature, but disconcerting to the student, may with advantage be mentioned. As this method for the detection of double refraction is very critical, any double refractive inclusion in a singly refractive medium, for example a zircon or diopside crystal in a garnet, will

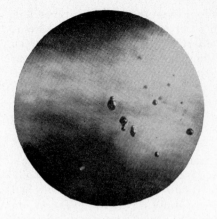

Figure 33.40. 'Tabby extinction' and 'profilated' gas bubbles in a synthetic spinel

tend to show up as a bright spot of light. Likewise, dust particles (often quartz grains) floating in the immersion liquid will also give bright spots of light. Practice soon begets proficiency in evaluating the various polarization effects. In certain cases, notably in some corundums, twin-planes which are evanescent when observed in ordinary light are much more prominent when viewed between crossed nicols, and this is true for a number of other inclusions.

Although polarizing microscopes have been postulated, polarizing apparatus need not necessarily have a lens system. Two polaroids arranged in the crossed position and held over a light source, providing that an arrangement for rotating the specimen between them is incorporated, is all that may be required in order to detect double refraction. Indeed, small polarizers of this type have been designed by R. Shipley, J. Walton and E. Rutland. The small Rutland polariscope is little larger than a pocket lens and has been proved quite efficient (*Figure 33.41*). A useful polariscope is one based on the Meakin strain viewer, in which a circle of polaroid about 2 in. in diameter fills an aperture in the base of the instrument which contains a low voltage electric lamp. An arm above this carries another polaroid disc which is in the crossed position to the lower polar. There is space between the upper and lower polars to comfortably hold and rotate the specimen under test. There is also room to place a lens over the specimen whereby it is often possible to observe the interference figure.

Figure 33.41. The Rutland polariscope

INTERFERENCE FIGURES

The use of convergent polarized light for the production of interference figures needs the microscope to be set up with the nicols crossed and a strongly convergent lens placed in the substage fitting. If the microscope is provided with a Bertrand lens a $\frac{1}{4}$-in. objective is inserted and the eyepiece retained. If, however, there is no Bertrand lens a 1-in. objective is preferable and the eyepiece must be removed. Those microscopes which have a Bertrand lens and $\frac{1}{4}$-in. and 1-in. objectives (all good petrological microscopes should have them) give the choice of either optical system. The former gives larger figures, while the latter, though yielding small figures, gives sharper definition; most workers prefer the Bertrand lens. When all these conditions have been observed the microscope is set for the experiment.

Technique for Obtaining Interference Figures

The stone should be immersed in a liquid of approximately its own refractive index; the liquid should be contained in a small glass dish and the stone held in a pair of tongs. On turning the stone in the liquid, the interference figure will appear. The beginner may experience a little difficulty at this stage. The stone should be turned until interference colours appear; when this occurs the focus should be lowered until the objective nearly touches the stone and the interference figure will emerge. The best results are usually obtained when the objective is actually immersed in the oil.

The most suitable liquid for general purposes is monobromonaphthalene (refractive index 1·66), which is suitable for topaz, tourmaline, andalusite, peridot, enstatite, spodumene, euclase, fibrolite, apatite, danburite, and so on. It can be diluted with toluene or benzene (refractive index 1·50) for quartz, beryl, iolite, felspar and scapolite, among others. For stones of higher refractive index, methylene iodide is suitable, while for stones such as zircon, sphene and cassiterite, the only possible liquid so far known is a mixture of white phosphorus, sulphur and methylene iodide (refractive index up to 2·05), discovered by C. D. West. This is rather an unpleasant liquid and is not recommended to beginners.

The Interference Phenomena

The figures occur only in crystals that are birefringent, and are caused by the interference of converging rays of the same wavelength when travelling out of phase as a result of their differing velocities within the crystal medium.

In the case of uniaxial crystals (tetragonal, hexagonal, and trigonal) the figure consists of a series of coloured rings intersected by a black cross (*Figure 33.42*).

Biaxial crystals (orthorhombic, monoclinic and triclinic) give a pattern as shown in *Figures 33.43* and *33.44*. In this case, however, there are variations depending on the nature of the refractive indices. Biaxial minerals have three indices of refraction, α, β, γ. Where β approximates closely to either α or γ, the 'brushes' (or isogyres, as they are called) are close together, as represented in *Figures 33.43* and *33.44*. Where β is about the mean of α and γ, the isogyres are widely separated and only one can be seen in the field at a time (*Figure 33.45*).

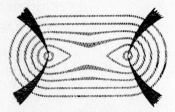

Figure 33.43. Biaxial in 45 degree
position

Figure 33.42. Uniaxial

In cases where β nearly coincides with α or γ, the figure appears to be uniaxial, distinction appearing on rotation. True uniaxial figures do not alter, whereas pseudo-uniaxial figures show a separation of the isogyres. Biotite (brown mica) is an excellent example of a pseudo-uniaxial mineral; this phenomenon is rare amongst gemstones.

In biaxial minerals the acute bisectrix is equidistant from the two eyes of the figure and is normal to a line joining them. The eyes or melatopes represent the emergence of the optic axes; the angles subtended by these axes and the acute bisectrix are invariably denoted by the symbol V; thus, the angle subtended by the two axes, that is, the optic axial angle, is $2V$. This angle can be measured if the stone is rotated on a spindle attached to a graduated circle; it is sufficient to measure it to the nearest degree. The greatest angle to be seen in the field of vision is about 30 degrees—when $2V$ is greater than this, only one isogyre is visible at one time (*Figure 33.45*).

Unlike uniaxial figures, biaxial figures rotate when the stone is rotated; the 'straight' or extinction position is shown in *Figure 33.44* while *Figure 33.43* shows the 45 degree position.

In addition to the information that the stone is uniaxial or biaxial, the optical sign can be deduced from these figures. Various plates can be obtained for this purpose—the quartz wedge, the gypsum plate and the mica plate. Of these the mica plate is the easiest to use and is recommended to beginners.

It consists of a thin sheet of mica, cut in such a way as to retard light by one quarter of a wavelength ($\frac{1}{4}\lambda$), This is inserted in the tube of the microscope in a slot provided for it immediately above the objective. (If there is no slot, it should be held at an angle of 45 degrees just below the objective.)

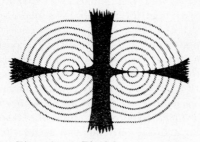

Figure 33.44. Biaxial straight position

Figure 33.45. Biaxial large 2V

In the case of a uniaxial mineral, the cross in the centre of the figure disappears, and two short bars or lenticular spots appear in its place. If the slow direction of the plate is lengthwise, and the slot is north-east–south-west, the bars will be seen disposed as in *Figure 33.46* for positive, and *Figure 33.47* for negative minerals. It will be noticed that the dark spots appear in the enlarged quadrants.

In the case of quartz these quadrants are the only guide, since quartz has the peculiar property of rotating the polarization of light, with the result that the cross does not appear in the inner ring, nor any dark spots with the mica plate, since the spots are merely parts of the displaced cross.

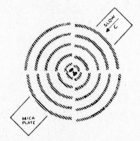

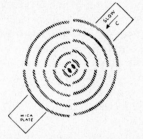

Figure 33.46. Positive uniaxial   *Figure 33.47. Negative uniaxial*

In the case of biaxial figures the detection of the optical sign is more complicated. The figure has to be rotated into the straight or extinction position (*Figure 33.44*). When the mica plate is inserted the whole figure appears to divide along the horizontal axis, one half of each set of rings increasing in size and the other half decreasing; the process is reversed for either set. A black spot will appear in the centre of the enlarged half of either set of rings, adjacent to the dividing line. If the black spot is above the line on the left and below on the right, the optical sign is positive (*Figure 33.48*); if the spot is below on the left and above on the right it is negative (*Figure 33.49*). In cases where $2V$ is large and only one isogyre and set of rings appear in the field of vision the nature of the isogyre denotes whether it is the left or right part of the figure. The stone should be rotated first to the 45 degree position, when the isogyre will be curved into a hyperbola. *Figure 33.43* shows the relation of the isogyres in the 45 degree position. It can be seen that the optical sign is determinable from one set of rings provided it is known which set of rings is under observation.

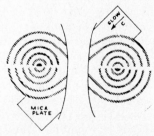

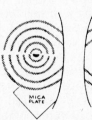

Figure 33.48. Biaxial positive   *Figure 33.49. Biaxial negative*

In extreme cases, where $2V$ approximates to 90 degrees, the isogyres will be straight in any position, so that the mica plate is of no use for determining the optical sign unless $2V$ is accurately measured beforehand. In such cases the mineral can be only weakly positive or negative, and to the ordinary student determination of its optical sign will not be of great assistance in determining the nature of the stone. Quartz wedges are used by experts in deciding the sign in such cases, but the technique is too complicated to be described here.

If monochromatic light is used instead of white light, the interference figure will be much sharper and clearer since it will consist of the colour of the source contrasted with black. In biaxial stones the optic angle, $2V$, varies according to the wavelength of light. In some cases this difference is very considerable, and is clearly discernible if red and blue colour filters are interposed. In extreme cases such as danburite, which has a large $2V$, the optical sign is negative for the red ray and positive for the violet, that is, the acute bisectrix becomes the obtuse. In this particular case the optic angle for red is less than for violet, this property being denoted in tables of optical constants as $r < v$. The effect is due to differences in dispersion of α, β and γ. In many minerals it is slight but in a few cases it is strong enough to be distinctive.

The size of interference figures is controlled by two factors—birefringence and thickness. The shallower the stone or the lower the birefringence, the larger the rings. This can be demonstrated with the white mica, muscovite, which, having a perfect cleavage, can be reduced to any required thickness, while a comparison of calcite (double refraction 0·172) and apatite (double refraction 0·004) of the same depth will demonstrate the influence of the other factor.

The value of these phenomena for purposes of identification is considerable in certain cases where the standard tests of specific gravity and refractive index are either inapplicable or inconclusive. As examples, on the one hand may be mentioned stones cut *en cabochon* and in settings as well as in the rough, and on the other hand species such as andalusite and tourmaline, the physical properties of which are similar; but—being orthorhombic and trigonal respectively—they yield biaxial and uniaxial figures.

DRAWINGS FROM THE MICROSCOPE

It is clear that with a petrological microscope, complete with graduated rotating stage and with cross-hairs in the ocular, measurement of the angles between the facets of a cut stone, between the cleavage directions, or between crystal faces of well-formed inclusions, may often be obtained. Such work can often provide useful additional information and can be carried out if necessary with an ordinary monocular microscope to which is fitted a goniometric ocular. Such a fitting consists of a Ramsden ocular, in the focus of which are cross-hairs which rotate about a divided circle, and which reads by means of a vernier to 5 min of arc (*Figure 33.50*). Any ocular fitted with cross-hairs has an added value in that the webs act as comparisons for straightness or curvature of fine striae, such as may be found in natural or synthetic corundum.

Figure 33.50. The goniometric ocular

The inclusions seen in many gemstones when viewed by a microscope often invite a permanent record. Particularly is this so in those, often beautiful, patterns which indicate the provenance of the gem, or are typical of the species. Such pictorial representation provides a far better reference than the memory.

It is often suggested to the student that he draws on paper the picture he sees through the eyepiece of his instrument. Much can be learnt by this method, which has the advantage that a composite picture may be built up showing a number of typical inclusions of stones of one species, or of one locality (*Figure 33.51*). A simple aid to accurate drawing is to use a paper ruled with lines in squares in conjunction with a graticule with square rulings. Such graticules can be obtained as discs which can be placed in the ocular so that it rests on the stop between the field lens and the eye lens. At this position it will be in focus, or if it is not sharp it can easily be brought into sharp focus by slightly unscrewing the eye lens—this has to be unscrewed in the first place to allow the graticule disc to be dropped into position.

Objects sketched in this manner using the guide squares in the ocular to act as guides to the squares on the paper may also be measured by reference

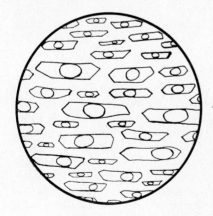

Figure 33.51. A drawing of the two-phase inclusions seen in smoky quartz

to a stage micrometer. This is a 3×1 glass slip with lines ruled on it at 1/10th mm and 1/100th mm intervals (or 1/100 in. and 1/1000 in.). If the micrometer is placed on the stage of the microscope and viewed under the same conditions as the object that has been drawn by means of the squared paper, it is easy to see how many tenths or hundredths of a millimetre (or fractions of an inch) are included in each square. This can be noted on the drawing and the dimensions of the objects may then be obtained by measuring the drawing.

Camera Lucida

A difficulty with drawing from the microscope is that the eye must of necessity be taken from the eyepoint above the ocular to see the paper upon

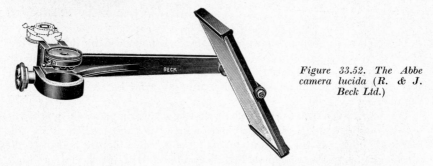

Figure 33.52. The Abbe camera lucida (R. & J. Beck Ltd.)

which the picture is to be drawn. In consequence of the difficulty in keeping the image in mind, loss of detail, accuracy of dimensions and relative position may suffer. To overcome this, various pieces of ancillary apparatus have been devised. One such fitting is the Abbe camera lucida (*Figure 33.52*). It consists of a prism which is silvered and has a small clear aperture at its centre. This fits over the ocular and has a large mirror placed a few inches from it. The paper upon which the drawing is to be made is reflected by the mirror into the prism, and in turn by the silvered surface, into the eye. At the same time the object is seen through the clear aperture in the prism. Thus the image is seen superimposed on the paper and can readily be drawn. This type of camera lucida is best used with the microscope in the upright position, a position which is always necessary when a stone is being examined.

PHOTOMICROGRAPHY

The most effective and fascinating type of reproduction is undoubtedly that of photographing the picture seen through the eyepiece. Photography through a microscope is correctly called photomicrography. It should not be called microphotography, which is the production of a very small picture, much smaller than the object and which has considerable use as 'microfilm recording' of documents. The art of photomicrography calls for some slight knowledge and a certain amount of ancillary apparatus. The 'camera' may be completely incorporated in the microscope, as in the very fine, but expensive, instruments specially built for visual and photomicrographic purposes, or the camera may be just a home-made arrangement which can be constructed by any enthusiastic amateur.

Camera and Camera Method of Taking Film

All that is actually needed for photomicrography is a suitable rigid and light-tight box or 'camera' to carry the photographic film or plate at a convenient distance from the eyepiece of the microscope and at right angles to the optical axis. The camera requires no lenses, for the optical system of the microscope performs the duties of the lenses in an ordinary camera. The

Figure 33.53. Microscope camera (R. & J. Beck Ltd.)

only other requirement needed is for the box to be arranged to carry a viewing screen of fine ground-glass for focusing the image, and which may be removed easily and replaced by the plate holder (dark slide).

Commercial microscope cameras may be just a conical or tapered metal box which fits over the eyepiece and clamps on to the draw tube of the microscope (*Figure 33.53*). The upper face of the box is fitted with a frame which carries a focusing screen which can be replaced by a plate holder (they usually take quarter plate or larger size; some the $3\frac{1}{4}$ in. $\times 3\frac{1}{4}$ in. lantern plate size, but most popular is the $3\frac{1}{2}$ in. $\times 2\frac{1}{2}$ in.). The lower end of the box contains a shutter which is operated by a lever or by a cable release. A similar, but more elaborate type of microscope camera, has a separate ocular fitted to it so that the image of the subject can be observed up to and during the time of exposure. The ocular contains hair-lines which are focused by the eye lens, and when this is done the image seen in the ocular is focused by the microscope focusing adjustments. The image is then in focus in the correct plane of the photographic plate. A ground-glass screen is also provided so that the focus can be checked before the exposure, and to see the amount of light reaching the plate (*Figure 33.54*). Similar cameras may be obtained which take pictures on standard 35 mm film, in which case the

Figure 33.54. Eyepiece microscope camera fitted to petrological microscope

carrier allows transport of the film, as in the ordinary miniature camera; there is no ground-glass viewing screen in such cameras. Many of the modern 35 mm single lens reflex cameras are eminently suitable for photomicrograhy as special fitments are obtainable to go in place of the camera lens, which in this case is removed as the microscope optics act as the camera lens system. These fittings are made to clamp on to the draw tube of the microscope and the focusing can then be carried out through the reflex viewer.

It is perfectly possible to use an ordinary hand camera to take pictures through the microscope. All that is needed is to construct a stand which will hold the camera steady so that the lens mount rests squarely on the eyepiece. Some miniature (35 mm) cameras may sit fairly steadily on the microscope ocular, or a tube support may be made in which the lens mount of the camera rests (*Figure 33.55*). It should be noted that when a hand camera is used the ocular is left in position. In this method the microscope is first focused as for the ordinary observation and then the camera is mounted on the eyepiece. The camera having been first adjusted with the range scale at infinity, the aperture fully open and the shutter set to time or bulb, if the exposure needed is greater than allowed for by the shutter's slowest speed.

The Gemological Institute of America have found a method of adapting the Polaroid Land Automatic 100 camera so that it can be used with a binocular microscope. This Land camera has a shutter which on being opened by the operator is closed electronically when the photocell beside the lens records enough light to correctly expose the film. The modifications made so that the camera can be used with a binocular microscope are an adaptor to carry the camera lens snugly over one eyepiece, and a 'lightwire' (made up of bundles of light transmitting fibres) one end of which is in an adaptor holding it central over the other eyepiece. The other end of the

Figure 33.55. Miniature camera (35 mm) used for photomicrography. The camera is resting on a special fitment

'lightwire' fits over the light cell aperture of the camera. In general this set-up will ensure correctly exposed negatives, but some adjustment can be made if necessary.

In the plate type of microscope cameras with eyepiece focusing, the focusing is done through that and then checked by examining the image on the ground-glass screen. With the simple type of microscope camera the focusing must be carried out by examining the image formed on the ground-glass screen, for the focus is not the same as when looking down the eyepiece of the microscope when the camera is not in position. The use of a clear spot in the centre of the ground-glass screen is often valuable in focusing. This clear area may be made by smearing a little Vaseline on the ground side of the glass, and final sharpness of focus can be determined better if the image is examined with a low power lens. When the focus is satisfactory the viewing screen is replaced by a charged plate holder and, when ready, the dark slide of this carrier slid open and the exposure made by either operating the cable release or simply by operating the electric light switch. After the exposure has been made the dark slide is closed over the plate and the plate carrier removed to the dark-room for processing.

Film Taking with Microscope Tube Eyepiece Removed

A method sometimes favoured is to dispense with the camera completely and to take the picture of the real image formed by the objective. For this method the eyepiece is removed and a ground-glass screen laid across the top of the microscope tube, with the ground side facing the objective. The image of the object to be photographed is then formed on the glass by the ordinary method of focusing the microscope with the coarse and fine adjustments. The ground-glass is then removed and a piece of bare film substituted for it, being held down on to the top of the tube by a flat opaque object, This must of course be carried out in darkness or in the feeble light of a red dark-room lamp (with slow 'line' film a yellow light may be used, but if panchromatic material is used a green light is necessary or complete darkness). The exposure is made by switching on the light for the time previously decided. This method can give very sharp pictures but the image is very small and needs to be enlarged by projection printing (by an ordinary enlarger). *Figure 33.56* shows a photomicrograph taken by this method, an enlargement of it, and a similar picture taken with an eyepiece microscope camera.

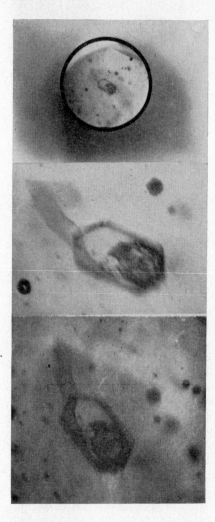

Figure 33.56. A photomicrograph taken on a piece of film placed over the microscope tube with the eyepiece removed, with below it an enlargement of the same negative. At the bottom is a picture of the same inclusion taken by the conventional microscope camera. The inclusion is an orthorhombic crystal in a blue apatite

Illumination

In general the stronger the source of light used to illuminate the object to be photographed the better, for the stronger the light the shorter the exposure needed. This can be of some consequence if the microscope set-up is not too rigid and liable to suffer from the effects of surrounding movement, and it is certainly of importance if liquid is used to immerse the stone, for ripples are easily set up by vibration. If some vibration cannot be avoided the use of more viscous immersion liquids, such as glycerol (glycerine), may be used in the case of stones of low refractive index, but care must be exercised that bubbles are cleared away.

The use of the substage condenser is of considerable value as much may be achieved in 'sharpening' the image by lowering or raising the substage lens system. Likewise, considerable improvement may be made by adjusting the iris diaphragm to different apertures. The value of dark-ground illumination versus transmitted light depends considerably upon the nature of the inclusion requiring to be photographed. Sometimes dark-ground illumination gives more spectacular effects (*Figure 33.57 a, b*), but this is not always so (*Figure 33.58 a, b*). Often a combination of dark-ground illumination and transmitted light is of advantage (*Figure 33.59*).

Exposure

Having selected the inclusion, or feature, of the stone it is wished to photograph by examination under the microscope, the camera is fixed in position (it may be mentioned here that the use of the eyepiece is not essential but its employment is more common as it gives a wider field). The image is now focused for the camera and the substage equipment is adjusted to give the best conditions of sharpness. Consideration is now given to the time of exposure required.

The exposure needed depends on the brightness of the field as seen in the ground-glass screen, and on the type of film or plate used. The use of a photoelectric exposure meter is not completely successful, for the small area of light coming from the objective is not sufficient to fill the grid of the meter. The best type of exposure meter to use is probably the extinction type, such as the Practos (*Figure 33.60*). Even with these meters, unless some time is allowed for the eye to become accommodated, overexposure is probable. Experience will show how the meter can be calibrated so as to give a fair estimate of the exposure needed. The exposure can range from $\frac{1}{25}$ sec to 30 min or more for very dark images and slow film. This is particularly so when the picture is taken in polarized light. With long exposures it is purely trial and error plus experience, for the exposure meters do not read beyond 4 or 5 min. The recently produced CdS electric exposure meter has a much smaller 'grid' and such an instrument has been found

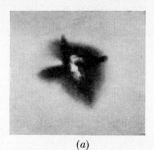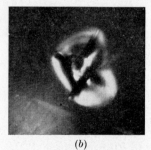

(a)   (b)

Figure 33.57. Zircon crystal surrounded with a halo in a Ceylon sapphire:
(a) in transmitted light, (b) in dark-ground illumination

(By courtesy of E. Gübelin)

667

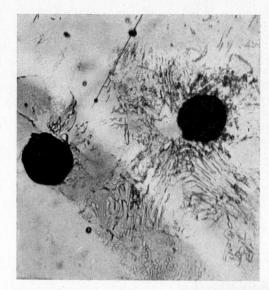

Figure 33.58a. Typical inclusion picture of a Montana sapphire. Black opaque crystals surrounded by flat films of shredded liquid drops. The crystals do not appear interesting while the liquid film betrays its curious pattern

(By courtesy of E. Gübelin)

Figure 33.58b. The same inclusions as in Figure 33.58a but photographed in dark-ground illumination show more clearly the characteristics of the crystals while the fine droplets hardly show

(By courtesy of E. Gübelin)

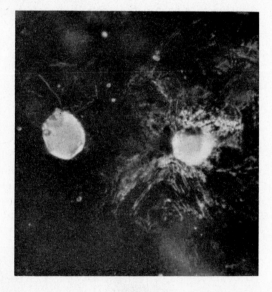

useful for estimation of the exposures for photomicrography provided the exposure time required is not outside the range of the instrument. Some calibration is needed to ascertain the '*f* number' of the microscope eyepiece, for there is no camera iris diaphragm when the lens system of the camera is removed.

Variety of Film or Plate

The best type of film or plate to use depends upon the subject and upon the facilities available to the worker for processing. A rapid panchromatic

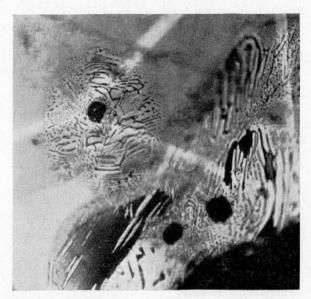

Figure 33.59. Inclusions in a Montana sapphire taken in combined transmitted and dark-ground illumination
(By courtesy of E. Gübelin)

plate is probably the most suitable for all-round work, despite that the changing of the dark slides and the development must be carried out in darkness or with a dark green safe-light. For those who have no effective dark-room, orthochromatic emulsions are more suitable and for the photography of inclusions are quite satisfactory. Such materials need only a red safe-light when charging cassettes (dark slides) and when developing. For fine detail a non-colour-sensitive film or plate, such as the 'Line' film used for copying drawings, is very suitable, especially when processed with a fine-grain developer. Such material needs about five times the exposure as ordinary 'ortho' film but has so great a latitude that small errors in exposure are of little consequence.

There are occasions when it is not felt justified to make a plate or film record of an inclusion but a record would make a useful addition to the

Figure 33.60. An extinction exposure meter, the Practos

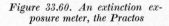

669

'library'. This may be carried out quite simply by using a suitable sized piece of bromide paper in place of the film—the bromide paper acting similarly to a film and, of course, needs similar development as for a film. Such a method saves expensive film, but, of course, cannot be reproduced by printing—the fact that it is, strictly speaking, a negative does not always matter (*Figure 33.61*).

Figure 33.61. Photomicrograph taken on bromide paper of two-phase inclusions in a white topaz

Colour films are applicable to photomicrography, and although colour prints from them are somewhat expensive and lose much detail, the 35 mm reversal colour films (Kodachrome, Ektachrome, Gevacolor, Agfacolor, Ferraniacolor, etc.) produce transparencies which, when mounted as 2 in. × 2 in. slides, make most interesting subjects for projection. Even 35 mm negatives in black and white may easily be contact printed on to another film to make positives for projection.

Magnification

To ascertain the magnification of a photomicrograph when using the plate microscope camera, all that is necessary is to place on the stage of the microscope a finely divided scale (for the average magnifications used in gemmology an ordinary celluloid scale graduated in fractions of an inch or in millimetres is sufficient). Focus this scale on the ground-glass screen of the camera and measure with a similar scale the distance between the two marks (units) of the magnified image of the lower scale. For example, a millimetre scale is projected on to the ground glass and the image is measured with a millimetre scale; the distance between the two marks representing 1 mm is found to be 25 mm. Therefore the magnification is × 25. In the case of the closed cameras, such as the 35 mm miniature cameras, the image on the negative is smaller than the image seen through the eyepiece of the microscope by direct observation. It is quite feasible to open the back of the camera, hold the shutter in the open position, and by placing a piece of ground-glass across the negative track to see the image produced and then measure the image as already detailed. Such a technique is not easy in miniature cameras. A far better procedure is to take a

670

series of photomicrographs with the camera of a stage micrometer scale placed on the microscope stage. A picture of this scale is taken with each combination of ocular and objective and unchanged drawtube extension. The negatives, or prints taken from them, may be used to measure the magnification of any combination of objectives and oculars (using, of course, the same camera) by reference to the scale on the stage micrometer.

CHAPTER 34

INCLUSIONS IN GEMSTONES

INCLUSIONS IN IDENTIFICATION AND PROVENANCE

The microscope is the best means of observing the small inclusions seen in gemstones, so that it is fitting that notes on these included structures should follow the description of that instrument. In earlier chapters it has been shown by text and illustrations that these enclosures, better known as inclusions, provide a means of establishing whether a stone is of natural origin or whether it has been synthetically or artificially made. There is, however, much more to the study of inclusions than that, for not only may the included structures give some information as to the species of the stone (*Figure 34.1*), but in many cases the country of its origin (*Figure 34.2*) is also discovered. Through the investigations of H. Michel, E. Gübelin and W. F. Eppler, among others, inclusions have been found to supply considerable information concerning the genesis of gemstones.

The round or elliptical bubbles and irregular swirl marks so characteristic of glass imitation stones (*Figure 34.3*) and the round, tadpole-shaped, or flask-shaped or bomb-shaped (profilated) bubbles of synthetic stones (*Figure 34.4*) give conclusive evidence of the nature of the stone. The typical picture of profuse crystals with a 'fused' look in conjunction with the swirls of colour so aptly called 'treacle' seen in the orange-brown hessonite garnets (*Figure 34.5*), the 'horsetail' asbestos fibres in demantoid garnet, the rows of octahedral crystals in natural spinel and the peculiar stress cracks seen in moonstone are examples of inclusions which identify the stone.

The following can be quoted as examples of inclusions which reveal the provenance of a gemstone. The typical three-phase inclusions of the emerald from Colombia, the actinolite blades of the Russian emeralds and the profuse mica plates seen in the emerald from South Africa. The typical large, clear, rounded crystals with 'silk' and 'treacle' seen in the rubies from Burma, and the feathers with script-like design, often with a black crystal at the centre or towards the margin of the feather, which are characteristic of Siamese corundums.

CLASSIFICATION

Gübelin has divided gemstone inclusions into three main groups. The first group, termed the pre-temporary or pre-existing inclusions, consist mostly of solid crystals or earthy or amorphous matter which were present before the gem crystal formed and which were enveloped in the new growth. The second group, the con-temporary inclusions, are those formed at the same time as the host mineral. They may be due to drops of the mother-liquor, or rising gas bubbles which were surrounded by the growing gem crystal; or

Figure 34.1. Asbestos fibres in radial or horsetail arrangement seen in a green stone betoken a demantoid garnet

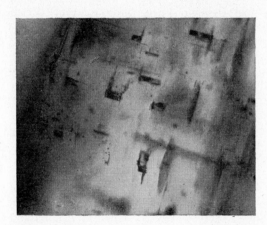

Figure 34.2. Comma-like inclusions typical of an Indian emerald

Figure 34.3. 'Feather' of bubbles in a green paste

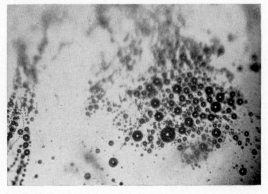

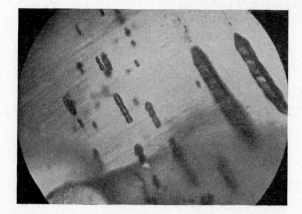

*Figure 34.4. Profilated bub-
bles and curved striae in a
synthetic ruby bead*

maybe crystals of the same or another species which grew at the same time
and became enveloped in the larger host crystal. It seems at first sight
inexplicable that inclusions can develop after the formation of the
crystal, but this can occur and produces what are known as post-temporary
or post-formed inclusions. Such an occurrence happens when certain areas
in the crystal recrystallize by chemical alteration. The formation of such
inclusions by the combination of independent elements not forming the
basic composition of the host crystal, and which is termed exsolution, may
be caused by natural heat treatment after the host crystal has formed.
The infiltration of liquid impurities into cracks and fissures following the
formation of the gem may crystallize out and 'heal' the cracks, forming
the so-called healing feathers which appear as flat fluid films or as irregular
liquid shreds or as drops (*Figure 34.6*).

A different classification of the inclusions seen in gemstones might be
made by dividing them into two main classes, as primary inclusions and
secondary inclusions. Primary inclusions may then be divided into autogenetic inclusions, which originate from the mother-liquor or magma and
are caused by peculiarities of growth, and xenogenetic inclusions which are
foreign substances enclosed within the crystal at the time of growth.

*Figure 34.5. Crystals and swirls in a hessonite
garnet. Swirls are primary autogenetic inhomo-
geneities and the foreign crystals of zircon are
primary xenogenetic inclusions*
(By courtesy of E. Gübelin)

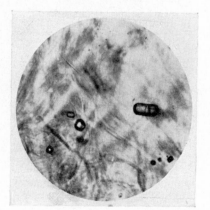

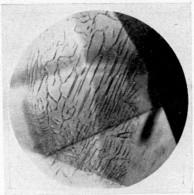

Figure 34.6. Healing feather in a Ceylon sapphire
(By courtesy of E. Gübelin)

Secondary inclusions may be divided into healing fissures, or inclusions formed by exsolution.

Again, a division into four groups may be made: (1) solid inclusions which may be of the same material as the host or one completely foreign to it; (2) internal cavities containing liquid or gas or both, and even solids in the form of one or more small crystals; (3) cracks and fissures filled with gas or liquid which are termed flags or feathers; and (4) growth phenomena which includes zonal structures and irregular distribution of colour.

SOLID INCLUSIONS

Examples of solid inclusions, either of the same mineral as the host or of a species foreign to it, are coarse or slender crystals of rutile, tablets of mica, zircon crystals with haloes and well-developed crystals of many other species (*Figure 34.7*), including rhombohedral crystals of Iceland spar or precipitations of platy crystals of calcite, and dendritic inclusions of chlorite, manganese and iron oxides.

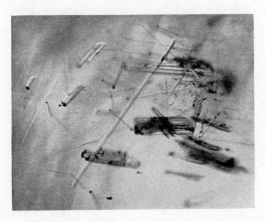

Figure 34.7. Solid inclusions consisting of long and short tremolite needles in a Rhodesian (Sandawana) emerald

GAS AND LIQUID

Internal cavities may be liquid or gas filled, the first named may include those cracks filled with solution from which the gem was formed, with water, carbonic acid and other liquids. The cavities in such cases obey the crystallographic laws of the host crystal and are termed negative crystals (*Figure 34.8*), but these cavities may not necessarily have the outline of the

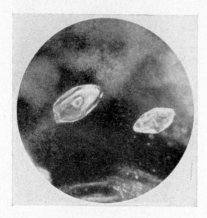

Figure 34.8. Negative crystals in a Ceylon sapphire. A typical example of primary autogenetic inclusions

(By courtesy of E. Gübelin)

crystal forms. These cavities sometimes contain a bubble of gas in the liquid, sometimes called a libella in liquid inclusions, giving what is known as a two-phase inclusion, that is two phases of matter. A still higher development is where the filling consists of three states of matter. In these three-phase inclusions one or more gas bubbles and one or more crystals are bedded in the liquid which fills the rest of the cavity (*Figure 34.9*).

Gaseous inclusions occur as bubbles in natural glasses, such as moldavite and billitonite, and in synthetic stones, as well as in the cement layer of doublets, and in paste and imitation stones.

Figure 34.9. Cavities with libella overlying a feather and with zonal 'silk' in a sapphire. Small triangular markings may be pits in the surface wall of the cavity, or may be tetrahedral crystals, in which case the whole inclusion should be termed a three-phase inclusion

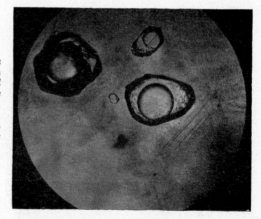

Figure 34.10. Liquid-filled feather or healing feather in a Ceylon sapphire. This is a secondary inclusion

By courtesy of E. Gübelin)

Internal cracks or fissures are usually classed as inclusions, especially when liquid or gas has entered the crack which may alter the chemical composition or molecular arrangement within the stone and form inclusions. Liquid, when present in the crack, is often distributed in small drops of bizarre shapes producing hieroglyphic or mesh-like patterns forming flags or feathers which have some similarity to the wings of insects (*Figures 34.10* and *34.11*). The liquid drops which make up such feathers are, on

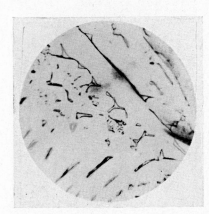

Figure 34.11. Almost completely healed crack with residual, bizarre-shaped droplets in a Ceylon sapphire

(By courtesy of E. Gübelin)

higher magnification, seen to contain a libella (gas bubble). Cracks which contain only fine films of air or liquid if examined under the microscope from above them—looking perpendicularly through them—show only the delicate borders of the film, but on viewing the film obliquely a brownish hue may be seen, and in some positions the flag may appear dark owing to the total internal reflection of light.

GROWTH PHENOMENA

Phenomena due to growth include the fine parallel lines due to repeated twinning (*Figure 34.12*), and zoning, which may be inferred as being due to interruptions or slight changes of composition of the mother-liquid (*Figure 34.13*). Such zoning may show as slight differences in the colour of the neighbouring layers, or it may be marked out by layers of small primary xenogenetic crystals (*Figures 34.14* and *34.15*). Interrupted growth, which in natural species forms straight and angular striations, also causes the curved bands and lines in synthetic corundums, for the periodic accretion of material is made on the slightly arched dome of the boule.

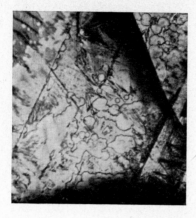

Figure 34.12. *A practically healed crack which has run across various twin lines in a Burma sapphire*

(By courtesy of E. Gübelin)

Figure 34.13. *Hexagonal zoning. A primary autogenetic feature in a Burma sapphire*

(By courtesy of E. Gübelin)

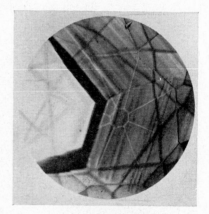

Figure 34.14. *Zonal concentration of rutile needles marking previous phases of crystal growth. These are primary xenogenetic inclusions and in this case are in a Ceylon ruby*

(By courtesy of E. Gübelin)

Figure 34.15. Primary xenogenetic inclusions formed by foreign liquid drops which adhered to previous crystal faces. Later on tiny microlites crystallized by extracting their ingredients from the drops. The haloes are residual liquid. A sapphire from Thailand

(By courtesy of E. Gübelin)

HEAT EFFECT ON BUBBLE INCLUSION

It often surprises observers to find that a bubble in an inclusion diminishes in size on warming the stone and finally disappears. This effect can occur in cavities containing only one bubble or in those where there are two immiscible liquids, in which case only one bubble will disappear. This effect is

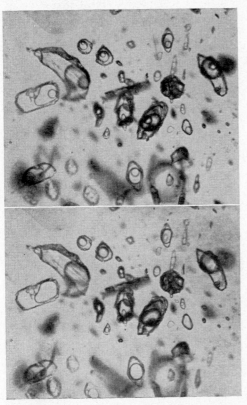

Figure 34.16. The disappearance of a gas bubble on warming in a cavity containing two immiscible liquids. Yellow beryl from Madagascar

due to the fact that the surrounding liquid is carbonic acid which has a critical point of temperature of 31·1°C, and when the heat of the microscope lamp warms the stone to that temperature the liquid surrounding the bubble becomes gaseous. *Figure 34.16* shows this effect in a yellow beryl.

ZIRCON HALO INCLUSION

The so-called zircon halo inclusion which consists of brownish 'wings' surrounding a small zircon crystal (*Figure 34.17*) needs comment. The haloes

Figure 34.17. Zircon haloes inclusion in an almandine garnet

round the small crystal were first thought to be due to local alteration of the substance of the host mineral by radioactivity from the included zircon. This notion is not now thought to be the true cause and the view is taken that the brownish marks are simply stress cracks caused by unequal thermal expansion of the zircon and the host mineral. R. K. Mitchell has suggested that the expansion may not be thermal but due to increase in size of the included zircon crystal which has degenerated to the metamict type.

CHAPTER 35

LUMINESCENCE

EMISSION OF VISIBLE LIGHT

The emission of visible light from a substance at room temperature has intrigued mankind from the earliest times, and is a phenomenon which today has many applications in art and industry. In the study of gemstones these various coloured glows may give useful diagnostic information, the value of which is increasingly being appreciated.

There are various types of this 'cold light', all of which depend upon the stimulation of the atoms of the substance by the reception of some form of energy. What may well have been the earliest observations of this phenomenon were of the luminous glow produced by fire-flies, glowworms and by decayed organic matter. This bioluminescence depends upon the oxidation of the chemical make-up of the substance, and is simply one manifestation of chemiluminescence, which is so well illustrated by the glow given off by oxidizing phosphorus, and hence the effect was known under the name phosphorescence, a term now restricted to the 'after-glow' which is a light emission after previous exposure of the substance to radiation.

A luminescence may be induced in some substances by rubbing. Termed triboluminescence, this effect has been known for countless years. S. H. Ball mentions in his work on gems and ornamental stones of American Indians: 'The Pueblo Indians of the upper Rio Grande during their rain ceremonies, beat the drum to imitate thunder and rubbed together pieces of white quartz to produce an incandescent glow simulating lightning'. At Mecos, New Mexico, a cylinder was found, set in a rectangle with a shallow groove into which the cylinder exactly fitted, both of white vein quartz. The cylinder is about 3 in. long and $\frac{1}{2}$ in. in diameter. Knowing that 'lightning sets' were still used in religious ceremonies at San Ildefonsa, experiment was made of rubbing the cylinder in the groove and finally the stones became visible in a strange pale glow which flickered and died for all the world like distant lightning. Here we have a perfected machine perhaps 700 years old. The first Indian to observe the luminescence of quartz must have done so centuries earlier.

Sugar will give a similar effect if crushed by a spoon against the side of a basin and the luminescence observed in complete darkness. The dull, cinder-like variety of zinc blende from Tsumeb, South-West Africa, exhibits orange-coloured 'sparks' if lightly rubbed or scratched by another mineral or metal blade.

Diamonds emit light when rubbed as was discovered by Robert Boyle in 1663, and G. F. Kunz found that all the diamonds he tested exhibited the phenomenon after being rubbed on wood, wool or some metals. The effect was most markedly seen on rubbing against wood in a direction against the grain. Some materials exhibit luminescence on heating below the temperature of incandescence. This thermoluminescence, as it is termed, will be further mentioned when photoluminescence is discussed, for the effects have much in common.

Photoluminescence, the type of luminescence most useful to the gemmologist, is excited by an incident radiation of short wavelength, such as ultra-violet light and x-rays, the latter is sometimes termed röntgenoluminescence, causing the emission of light in the visible range during the period of irradiation. This effect being known as fluorescence, from the mineral fluorspar, which shows, as a rule, the phenomenon quite strongly. In many cases the emission of a visible glow continues for some time after the exciting radiation has been cut off. This after-glow is called phosphorescence.

Historically, the earliest observation of this type of luminescence was probably the fluorescence seen in aqueous extracts from woods which were employed in early pharmacy.

The beginning of the recognition of these effects in solid substances was the experiments of one Vicencio Casciarola, a bootmaker and some-time alchemist of Bologna. Casciarola, in 1602, calcined the mineral barium sulphate, which probably owing to the impurities present, produced a phosphorescent alkaline earth sulphide. This was known as Bologna stone.

The first really scientific investigation of the phenomenon of photoluminescence was carried out by A. E. Becquerel about 1859, who studied the luminescence of such materials as fluorspar, calcite, ruby and diamond. Other work was carried on about this time by J. Herschel and Sir David Brewster. Later, A. Verneuil, of synthetics fame, and P. Lenard made further contributions to the knowledge of photoluminescence.

Right up to the time of Herschel the opinion was that fluorescence was nothing but diffusion or dispersion of the incident radiation. G. G. Stokes thought otherwise, and suggested that the light was a new creation due to the absorption of the more refrangible radiations. Experiment proved that the incident light once having excited fluorescence was unable to excite further fluorescence in a similar substance. Stokes from this, inferred that the rays which provoked the fluorescence were absorbed by the fluorescing material, and he established the general law, known as Stokes law, that the fluorescent glow always has a longer wavelength than the exciting radiations.

In the closing decades of the nineteenth century, Sir William Crookes carried out a number of important observations, particularly with diamond, in which experimentation he used cathode rays as a means of excitation. Luminescence developed by such means is termed cathodo-luminescence, and such luminescence was investigated by Lecoq de Boisbaudran in France.

The absorption spectra of gemstones are well understood as a ready means of distinguishing some gemstones. These absorbed wavelengths of light represent an apparent loss of energy, but in nature, nothing is ever lost, so what has become of the energy? Careful scientific study has shown that this absorbed energy becomes converted into heat rays and thus agrees with Stokes theory that the absorbed light is re-emitted as radiation of longer wavelength. Stokes law has been found to be not strictly true for all cases, but the 'anti-Stokes' effect need not be considered in detail for general purposes.

So far we have examined the absorption in the visible part of the spectrum, but the same effect can be found to apply to those parts of the long magnetic spectrum above and below the visible red and violet. Thus, if absorption takes place in the invisible part of the spectrum below the visible range it could be expected that any emission may be in the visible spectrum and produce a coloured glow. Such an effect does occur and is fluorescence.

QUANTUM THEORY

In the general understanding of light phenomena the gemmologist has confined himself to the wave theory of light propagation, which answers most of the problems he encounters. To understand fluorescence, it is necessary to refer to the more modern concepts of M. Planck and A. Einstein —the so-called 'quantum' theory. This theory postulates that though the wave character of light has to be maintained, the energy which is carried by these waves has a corpuscular nature in which light is assumed to be composed of units called 'photons' or 'quanta'. Further, an atom can only absorb or emit a definite quantity of light, this quantity being one photon of a given frequency (wavelength).

This principle was further developed by Niels Bohr, who stated that an atom can only exist in certain energy states (or levels). The lowest of these is termed the 'ground state', and those of higher energy 'excited states'. Further, these energy levels are discrete and the atom can only absorb, or emit, light of certain discrete wavelengths.

An absorption of energy which transposes an electron from the inner stable orbit round the nucleus of the atom (ground state) to an outer orbit (excited state) will, in the case of fluorescence, spontaneously return to ground level with the emission of light. In the case of phosphorescence some of the excited electrons do not immediately return to ground level, but pass into a 'metastable' level of somewhat smaller energy. In this metastable position the electron is 'trapped' until further energy is imparted to it— generally by heat movement in the surrounding medium—which allows a return to the initial excited state from which a return to ground level with the emission of light is possible (*see Figure 35.1*).

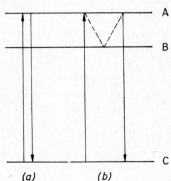

Figure 35.1. (a) Fluorescence. An electron taking energy from the incident ultra-violet light (or x-radiation) jumps from the stable orbit (C) to the excited state (A) from which it immediately returns to the stable orbit with the emission of light. (b) Phosphorescence. An electron taking energy from the incident ultra-violet light (or x-radiation) jumps from the stable orbit (C) to the excited state (A), but does not return to the stable orbit at once. The electron drops into a metastable level (B) from which it can only return to stable level after again taking energy from the surrounding medium, which allows it to get back to the excited state from which it can return directly to the stable level with emission of light

683

ULTRA-VIOLET LIGHT

Photoluminescence may be stimulated by ultra-violet light, x-rays and by the so-called Grenz rays, which are soft x-rays of long wavelength—about 5–10 Å—and are rays which are sometimes called infra-röntgen rays. Cathode rays (streams of electrons), as mentioned earlier will also induce fluorescence, and considerable work has been carried out on gemstones by W. Crookes and by H. Michel using these rays.

For practical purposes, owing to the ease of their production and their isolation from other rays, those wavelengths which comprise ultra-violet light are the most suitable. It is these rays, their production and their effects which will be principally considered in this chapter.

Ultra-violet light may be said to cover the wave bands from 4000 Å (that is at the end of the visible violet) down to 100 Å, which may be said to be the commencement of x-rays. However, below 2000 Å the rays are useless for practical purposes for they are intensely absorbed by air and any work with them needs to be done in a vacuum.

The region from 4000 to 2000 Å is the practically usable range of wavelengths, and this region is divided into three zones, which are the long-wave or near ultra-violet and extends from 4000 to 3150 Å. Below this comes the medium band comprising the wavelengths between 3150 and 2800 Å. The third zone is the short-wave or far ultra-violet which extends from 2800 to 2000 Å. (These divisions were defined at the Congress held in Copenhagen in 1932.) The most spectacular effects are undoubtedly induced by the near ultra-violet zone, but the short-wave ultra-violet light may in certain cases be the more diagnostic.

Ultra-violet rays are produced by solar emission, but owing to atmospheric absorption no rays below 2950 Å reach the earth. The rays are also produced by an electric arc set up between iron or carbon electrodes, or an arc by an electric discharge through mercury vapour. Electric discharges through hydrogen, argon, xenon or mercury vapour at low pressure also emit ultra-violet light, but all sources emit considerable visible light which masks any luminescent glow from a fluorescent substance. To overcome this a screen or filter, which will cut out the visible light but allow the required wave-band to pass, must be interposed between the light source and the specimen to be irradiated; the specimen being in darkness with the invisible ultra-violet rays impinging upon it.

Wood's Glass Filter

The filter most commonly used to cut out the visible light from a radiating source, and yet pass the long-wave ultra-violet light, is a cobalt glass with about 4 per cent of nickel oxide. This filter, devised by R. W. Wood and usually known as Wood's glass, passes the wavelengths between 4000 and 3000 Å, with the maximum transmission at 3050 Å (*Figure 35.2*).

One of the simplest methods of observing long-wave ultra-violet luminescence can be carried out by screening a suitable source of radiation by a 'window' of Wood's glass, and allowing the transmitted ultra-violet rays to impinge on the specimen which is itself in darkness. Thus a suitable dark box in which to view the specimen may be fitted with a Wood's glass window, which, when directed to a ray of sunlight, will give some fluorescent effects, but they are weak.

An inexpensive piece of apparatus for observing long-wave ultra-violet luminescent effects is a box-like structure made in two sections, in one of which a photo-flood is enclosed. This supplies a moderate intensity ultra-violet source. The other section consists of the viewing box which is separated from the other by a window of Wood's glass, which screens the visible rays but allows the long ultra-violet rays to pass.

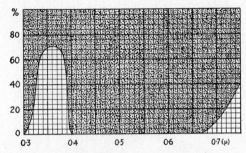

Figure 35.2. OX1 ultra-violet filter (Wood's glass filter). Integrated visible transmission 0·02 per cent

Long-wave Medium Pressure Mercury Lamps

A more powerful source of ultra-violet emission is that given by an electric arc employing special 'cored' carbon electrodes, or iron electrodes, the latter, however, suffering from the defect that direct current is required for their operation.

What is probably the best and most easily controlled source of ultra-violet light is that produced by a medium pressure mercury arc, having a pressure of 1–10 atm., generated between solid electrodes by a high tension current, the electrodes and mercury being enclosed in a tube of fused silica. This is housed in a suitable reflector to the front of which is fitted a light-tight cover containing a window of Wood's glass or other suitable filter. The electrical equipment—the transformer and starting gear—being housed in the stand portion of the lamp (*Figure 35.3*).

The mercury arc produces an emission spectrum having strong lines in the visible part of the spectrum at 5790, 5770, 5460, 4358 and 4046 Å, that is in the yellow, green, blue and violet which account for the greenish-blue colour of the light emitted by the unshielded mercury arc lamp. In the invisible ultra-violet there is an exceptionally strong line at 3650 Å with weaker lines at 3984, 3906, 3654, 3341, 3131 and 3125 Å. It is these lines which are passed by the Wood's glass filter and supply the long-wave ultra-violet light. Below 3000 Å the only strong line is at wavelength 2537 Å which is the resonance line of mercury. *Figure 35.4* shows the energy distribution of the various lines in a medium pressure mercury arc.

Another type of ultra-violet lamp is the so-called 'black-lamp'. This in appearance is similar to a 150 W ordinary gas-filled electric light bulb, except that the glass bulb is black in colour—actually, it is made of Wood's glass. The light source inside the bulb consists of a short quartz glass tube in which a mercury arc is generated between two electrodes, the necessary starting being attained by a fine wire auxiliary electrode adjacent to one electrode and coupled to the other by a high resistance which is housed in the bayonet type 3-pin cap.

Such a lamp cannot be connected directly to the 200–240 V a.c. mains but requires to be fed through a choke; it is for this reason that a 3-pin bayonet cap is employed in order that the bulb cannot be inserted into an ordinary light holder.

This lamp gives a large spread of ultra-violet light, but owing to the thinness of the Wood's glass bulb transmits rather more of the deep red and violet visible light than is convenient for analytical employment. It is

Figure 35.3. A medium pressure quartz-mercury lamp with Wood's glass filter. The Hanovia lamp No. 11

suggested that for the more accurate use of such a lamp, a subsidiary Wood's glass screen be interposed between the lamp and the article being examined. Further, in all cases, the employment of a quartz or quartz glass lens to concentrate the ultra-violet light on to the subject is of great advantage. This is particularly so when the fluorescing article is on the stage of a microscope and the luminescence observed through the microscope—a technique which is of value in certain cases.

Medium pressure mercury-vapour lamps take from 2 to 5 min after switching on before they attain full brightness, and if switched off, or if the electric supply is interrupted, they must cool down before they will re-light, but if they are left switched on re-lighting takes place automatically when they are sufficiently cool.

Fluorescent Tube Lamp

A long-wave ultra-violet lamp which has been found to be of value in the detection of synthetic emeralds, and to a slight extent synthetic rubies, is a modification of the fluorescent tubes so commonly used for office and workshop lighting. Such a lamp generates the bright visible light by an electrical discharge through mercury vapour at low pressure. This emits short-wave ultra-violet light which causes a highly fluorescing powder coated on the inside of the tube to glow with a bright light. The glass of the tube is of such a type that the harmful short-wave rays are not transmitted. The lamp for ultra-violet emission has as its internal coating a compound which luminesces

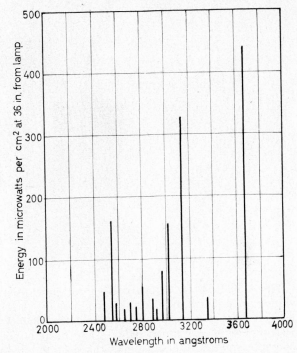

Figure 35.4. Energy distribution in the various lines of the spectrum of a typical medium pressure quartz mercury arc

with only ultra-violet light and some violet light, and again the glass does not transmit the short waves and much of the visible light. The range emitted by this lamp is from about 4100 to 3000 Å. Such a lamp is illustrated in *Figure 35.5*.

Short-wave Filter

The medium ultra-violet wave band, that from 3150 to 2800 Å, is not important from a gemmological point of view, but the short-wave band from 2800 to 2000 Å may be found to be of considerable value in gem diagnosis.

A priori it might be thought that a suitable filter to isolate the strong mercury resonance line at 2537 Å from the mercury arc produced in the medium pressure lamp would provide the required source of short-wave ultra-violet light. If such a filter were available this may well be done, but such a filter does not exist commercially. Therefore some sort of a compromise is needed. Such a compromise is a filter which passes as much of the 2537 Å line as possible and as little as possible of the 3650 Å band and visible light, combined with a lamp which will not emit so much visible glow or long-wave ultra-violet light.

Figure 35.5. The Allen long-wave fluorescent ultra-violet lamp. This lamp produces violet and ultra-violet radiation which is continuous from about 4100Å to about 3000Å

This is effected by using an electrical glow discharge through mercury vapour, in a quartz tube, at a low pressure of 1 or 2 mm, in which case the 2537 Å line is more pronounced and the 3650 Å band much less. The visible glow is very much reduced and bluer in colour. Further the tube operates practically cold, unlike the medium pressure lamp which gives off considerable heat. This is important because the Wood's glass filter can be made of heat-resisting glass whereas the filter used for short-wave operating cannot, and thus tends to crack easily. Thus, the short-wave filter, such as the OX7 filter made by Chance Bros., becomes a much more efficient separator of the short-wave radiation when the low pressure tube is used. The transmission of the OX7 filter is shown by *Figure 35.6.*

Figure 35.6. OX7 ultra-violet filter

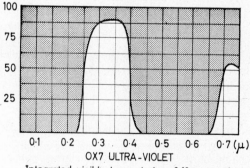

OX7 ULTRA-VIOLET

Integrated visible transmission 0·10 per cent

Short-wave Lamps

A number of models of short-wave ultra-violet lamps are made in Great Britain, in Germany and in the United States of America, where probably more advanced designs are produced, including many which are battery operated and of sufficiently small size to be portable. *Figure 35.7* shows a commercially produced short-wave ultra-violet lamp made by Hanovia. The

Figure 35.7. A commercial short-wave ultra-violet lamp. The 'chromatolite' by Hanovia Ltd.

need for ballast, choke or capacitor in the lamps used off the domestic electricity supply tends to make the lamps rather expensive. Even the battery operated American lamps have accessory electrical equipment fitted in the lamp housing.

The comparatively inexpensive germicidal lamp made by Philips Electrical Company, which consumes only 7 W, has an envelope which will pass ultra-violet light down to 1850 Å. Such a lamp, owing to its richness in the 2537 Å line, its lower intensity of the 3650 Å band and low emission of luminous glow (*Figure 35.8*), can be an efficient and comparatively inexpensive source of short-wave ultra-violet light in conjunction with an OX7 filter. *Figure 35.9* shows the make up of the lamp itself which operates

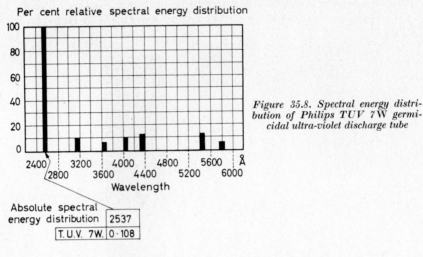

Per cent relative spectral energy distribution

Figure 35.8. Spectral energy distribution of Philips TUV 7W germicidal ultra-violet discharge tube

directly off the 200–250 V a.c. mains. The initial starting is brought about by a trace of neon which has no appreciable effect on the luminosity except for an orange glow surrounding the electrodes, the remaining visible light being the blue glowing column of light between the two electrodes due to the mercury vapour. It is a simple job to make a light-tight housing for such a lamp, with an aperture fitted with an OX7 filter which should be placed as near as possible to the lamp itself. A reflector made of polished aluminium, which is the most efficient reflector of ultra-violet, may be incorporated. The ranges of ultra-violet emission of the three types of ultra-violet lamps is shown by the spectrograms in *Figure 35.10*.

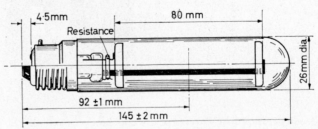

Figure 35.9. The Philips TUV 7W germicidal ultra-violet discharge tube

Argon Lamp

The small argon lamp, in which a glass bulb fitted with two electrodes is filled with the inert gas argon, has the gas excited by the passage of an electric current. Such a lamp has been used for the observation of some

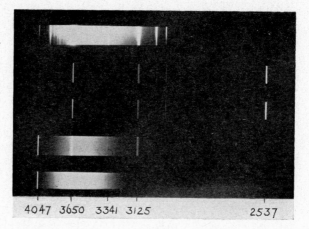

Figure 35.10. Spectrograms showing the emission of the three types of ultra-violet lamps discussed in the text. (1) Hanovia long-wave lamp with Wood's glass filter; (2) Philips TUV 7 short-wave lamp with Chance OX7 filter; (3) American Mineralight short-wave lamp; (4) English Longlamp extra-long-wave ultra-violet lamp; (5) American Burton extra-long-wave ultra-violet lamp

4047 3650 3341 3125 2537

luminescent effects although it has a low emission of ultra-violet and according to J. De Ment gives no radiation of utility below 3900 Å. The argon lamp, which plugs into an ordinary electric lamp-holder and consumes so little current that it scarcely turns the house meter, has a value in the observation of phosphorescence in some materials. The very low visible violet light given off by the argon bulb would mask weak fluorescence but when turned off will show any phosphorescence—providing the room is in darkness.

Fluograms

A novel method of examining phosphorescence, mentioned by Dake, is to employ an unscreened photoflash lamp. Such bulbs give a momentary 'burst' of light often over 300,000 candle-power in intensity after which the phosphorescence of the specimen irradiated may be seen. The presence of weak phosphorescence (but, of course, not its colour) may be ascertained by placing the specimen on a photographic film in a dark-room and keeping for a few hours in a light-tight box. On developing the film a darkening showing the outline of the stone will be seen if the stone phosphoresces.

These have been termed fluograms or luminograms (*Figure 35.11*). Indeed,

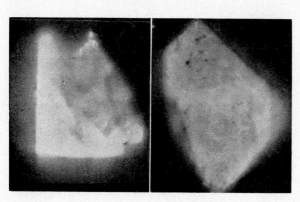

Figure 35.11. Fluograms of fluorspar

should the emitted radiations be in the ultra-violet instead of the visible region such a method will detect this ultra-violet phosphorescent response.

Photographing Fluorescence

The fluorescence of materials may be photographed by their own luminous glow by the use of an ordinary hand camera provided that a filter which stops all the reflected ultra-violet rays is placed over the lens. Such filters are the 'Wratten 2B' or Ilford 'Q' filters. Ultra-violet absorbing filters may be constructed by employing certain solutions in glass cells. Such solutions are a 1 per cent solution of cerium ammonium sulphate, or 2 per cent solution of sodium nitrate. Panchromatic plates or films should be used for the actual photography.

Precautions in Use of Ultra-violet Equipment

A word of warning is necessary regarding the use of any ultra-violet equipment, particularly short-wave equipment. The human eye is vulnerable to ultra-violet, and exposure can cause a burning and subsequent scarring of the epithelial layers of the cornea, also some inflammation (conjunctivitis) may be felt some hours after irradiation. Longer exposures

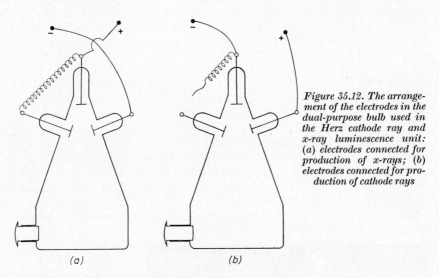

Figure 35.12. The arrangement of the electrodes in the dual-purpose bulb used in the Herz cathode ray and x-ray luminescence unit: (a) electrodes connected for production of x-rays; (b) electrodes connected for production of cathode rays

(a)   (b)

may also produce erythema (skin reddening) similar to the initial stages of sunburn, this may cause discomfort without the benefit of a lasting skin tan. This effect does not appear until an hour or so after the exposure and may then last for hours or even days.

The above observations are included for general guidance but the worker need not be apprehensive of danger. It is not necessary to look directly at the ultra-violet source, even so it is not dangerous to look directly at the beam from a long-wave ultra-violet lamp (providing that the Wood's glass filter is in position). True, in such a case the eyeballs tend to fluoresce and make everything appear misty. Do not, however, look directly at a medium pressure mercury arc lamp (or an arc lamp) without the filter on, for there is nothing then to stop the physiologically dangerous rays of short wavelength (around 2537 Å). Thus, never look directly at a lamp passing these short-wave ultra-violet rays unless wearing glasses, which, even if made of ordinary plain glass, will stop the 2537 Å radiation. They also afford a great measure of protection from direct rays and from rays scattered from the object and surrounding surfaces.

CATHODE RAYS AND X-RAYS

The excitation of luminescence by cathode rays (cathodo-luminescence) requires the use of special apparatus which is not readily available. During the 1920s H. Michel and G. Riedl of Vienna had made, by the firm of G. L. Herz, apparatus for the production of cathode rays and x-rays for the study of gemstone luminescence by these rays. The specimen to be irradiated was placed in the glass bulb and the air in this was subsequently evacuated by a mercury pump. The evacuated bulb contained three electrodes, which by altering the outer connexions could be arranged to produce either cathode rays or x-rays at will. *Figure 35.12* shows how this is done. The whole equipment, the cathode ray bulb, the x-ray bulb, the mercury pump and the

Figure 35.13. The complete unit for the production of cathode rays and x-rays as made by C. L. Herz of Vienna

induction coil and battery for the generation of the high-tension current, was housed in a portable cabinet (*Figure 35.13*). Michel and Riedl carried out a considerable amount of work on the luminescence of gemstones by this type of apparatus. An investigation of the cathodo-luminescence of natural and synthetic sapphire was carried out by B. W. St. Clair, using the cathode ray tubes designed by W. W. Coolidge. This worker found that synthetic sapphires phosphoresced while the natural stones did not, and, further, that synthetic stones turned decidedly brown when placed in a beam of cathode rays whereas the natural stones did not.

Precautions in the Use of X-rays

The apparatus needed to generate x-rays is fully discussed in the following chapter. The only precautions required to be taken when luminescence
effects are to be seen is to mask the light from the filament in the case of
hot cathode tubes with a glass window, or to mask completely the fluorescence from the glass of the tube in gas-tubes. As most of the modern tubes
are completely shielded, with the exception of the window through which
the x-rays are directed, all that is necessary is to fit a cork into this aperture
to stop the light coming through.

With those tubes which have a window of beryllium, no such precautions
are necessary. In all observations of luminescence a dark-room, or dark-
box, is necessary in order to see the, sometimes weak, luminescent effect.

The physiological dangers by radiation damage through x-rays are real,
but if care is taken not to expose the eyes or body to the direct x-ray beam
—any observation of luminescence being studied through a thick lead glass
window—no harm will come to the operator. Modern x-ray sets are well
shielded.

COLOUR FILTERS

It is interesting to recall that Riedl and Michel have used various colour
filters to separate the components in a mixed colour fluorescence. Further,
the red glow seen with minerals which owe their colour to chromium may
conveniently be observed when screened between suitable crossed filters.
This method, first devised by Stokes, consists of a bright source of white
light before which is placed a filter (a saturated solution of copper sulphate)
which passes only blue and green light. The specimen is placed in this beam
of coloured light and is observed through a filter passing red light only.
Any red fluorescent glow of the mineral will be seen against a dead black
background; thus even very weak effects can be detected by this arrangement, whereas these might be masked by the residual reddish tinge transmitted by the normal ultra-violet filters.

CHARACTERISTIC GLOWS OF STONES UNDER RADIATION

Distinction of Synthetic from Natural Stones

The use of luminescent effects in gem-testing is based on the characteristic
glows given by the stone under radiations of different wavelength, for the
response may not be the same for different ranges of radiation. In general,
the long-wave lamp gives the more spectacular results so far as the production of visible light in luminescent substances is concerned, but often the
usually much weaker glows induced by the short-wave lamp may be more
diagnostic, and so may be the glows induced by x-rays.

While the glow emitted by the stone while under one type of radiation
can aid diagnosis, the comparison of the results shown by the stone under
two, or maybe even three, types of radiation can greatly increase the value
of luminescence as a diagnostic method. Thus diamond, which usually gives
a blue or violet glow of variable intensity under long-wave ultra-violet
light, responds weakly to the short-wave ultra-violet rays, while under
x-rays the stones fluoresce with a bright violet-light or whitish-blue light.

Further, diamonds which glow with a strong blue light under the long-wave lamp are found to show an afterglow (phosphorescence) of yellow colour.

Synthetic white sapphires and spinels, and white pastes, all stones which if small and mounted in jewellery can be difficult to determine, show only a weak response, if any, to radiations from the long-wave ultra-violet lamp. Synthetic white spinels and some pastes show a bluish-white glow under the short-wave lamp while the synthetic white sapphire usually responds with a rather dim deep blue glow. Under x-rays the synthetic white sapphires may show a red glow and the white spinels a green or blue glow.

Stones, such as ruby, red spinel, alexandrite and emerald, which owe their colour to the chromium ion, should fluoresce with a strong red glow. Indeed the ruby, spinel and alexandrite do so, but under the long-wave lamp emerald usually shows a green light, the reason for which is not understood. The synthetic green (tourmaline green) spinel which is coloured by chromium also shows the red glow under the long-wave ultra-violet lamp, but under the short-wave radiations the glow is the whitish-blue common to most synthetic spinels, this glow in the case of coloured synthetic spinels is often modified by the body colour of the stone. The strong crimson glow shown by rubies and red spinels when under any of the radiation wavebands is of value in separating those stones from other stones of red or pink colour. In the case of ruby, x-rays will assist in determining the synthetic from the natural stones, for the synthetic stones, which are probably purer and do not contain any appreciable iron as do the natural rubies, show a perceptible afterglow, whereas the natural rubies do not. The same effect cannot be said to hold true for the new synthetic red spinels.

Ultra-violet Rays

The use of ultra-violet rays as a means of identifying the synthetic from the natural emerald needs to be discussed, for the fluorescence method of detection has been widely publicized. The luminescent effects shown by natural and synthetic emeralds under the various types of radiation are shown in Table 35.1.

It is well known that the chromium phosphor is strongly activated by blue and violet light, and that it is the long wavelengths of the near ultra-violet and the visible violet light emitted by the 'fluorescent type' lamp which causes the strong fluorescence in synthetic emerald. The Wood's glass

TABLE 35.1

Luminescent Effect of Natural and Synthetic Emeralds

Radiation	Natural	Synthetic
Long-wave lamp (3650 Å)	Usually green, but in rare cases crimson (Chivor stones)	Reddish gleams with green
Short-wave lamp (2537 Å)	As above but usually weaker	As above but usually stronger reddish gleams
X-rays	Crimson	Crimson
Ultra-long-wave—'fluorescent tube' lamp (4100–3100 Å)	Greenish or dark	Strong crimson

filter in the normal long-wave ultra-violet lamp does not pass these longer wavelengths and such lamps are less useful for the distinguishing of synthetic emerald. That such a crimson glow is not given off by the natural emeralds may be accounted for by a trace of iron as an impurity which 'poisons' the fluorescence.

Benitoite, scheelite, and most synthetic spinels, except the red synthetic spinel, glow with a blue light when irradiated with the short-wave ultra-violet rays (2537 Å) but do not luminesce under the long-wave lamp (3650 Å). Thus, benitoite can quickly be distinguished from blue sapphire which it so resembles. Synthetic blue sapphires can be detected, or at least suspected, by the stronger dull but deep green glow they show under the short-wave lamp since the natural blue sapphires are usually inert. In some cases it will be found that the glow shown by synthetic blue sapphires is banded in conformity with the curved bands of colour typical of synthetic sapphires, and these curved bands can often be seen better under fluorescence conditions than by ordinary observation.

Under the long-wave lamp the yellow sapphires from Ceylon exhibit an apricot coloured glow, and these stones do not show a characteristic absorption spectrum. The yellow sapphires from Australia and Siam are rich in iron and, hence, do not luminesce, but these stones show strongly the 4500 Å complex in their absorption spectrum. The synthetic yellow sapphires are usually inert under the long-wave lamp, but may fluoresce with a reddish-orange light which is rather different to the apricot glow given by Ceylon yellow sapphires. These synthetic yellow sapphires do not show a characteristic absorption spectrum.

Fluorescence Spectrum

When the light from a fluorescing substance is examined by a spectroscope, the fluorescence spectrum may show in some cases that the emitted

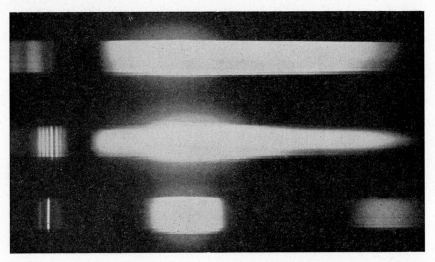

Figure 35.14. Fluorescence spectra of synthetic emerald (top), natural red spinel (centre), and ruby (bottom), excited by photoflood lamp and filtered through weak copper sulphate solution

(By courtesy of B. W. Anderson)

light is in discrete bands. This effect occurs particularly in substances which are activated by uranium, by chromium, or, as in diamond, by lattice defects. The effect is most important in distinguishing between the chromium coloured ruby and red spinel. The ruby shows the strong doublet at 6935 Å as a strong bright line, with a broader and more diffuse brightish band on the shorter wavelength side. The natural red spinel shows a group of bright lines at 6800 Å (the strongest being at 6750 and 6860 Å). These lines have aptly been called the 'organ pipe' lines. The new synthetic red spinels show only a single strong line at 6860 Å. *Figure 35.14* shows the fluorescence spectra of ruby, natural red spinel and synthetic emerald, and the picture illustrates that the emission in the case of the synthetic emerald is much farther into the deep red. These chromium fluorescence spectra can most easily be examined by illuminating the specimen with a strong light, before which is placed a flask containing a saturated solution of copper sulphate. The bright fluorescent lines are then seen against a black background.

Infra-red Filter

R. K. Mitchell has shown that if natural and synthetic emeralds are placed in a pool of blue light, formed by a strong light source which has

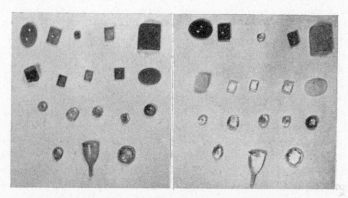

Figure 35.15. Infra-red photograph of gemstones. Top row, natural emeralds; second row, synthetic emeralds; third row, natural rubies; bottom row, synthetic rubies. Left, Ilford HP3 film; right, Gevaert infra-red film

passed through a copper sulphate filter, and the stones viewed through an infra-red filter (as used for infra-red photography), the synthetic emeralds will show up a brilliant red while the natural emeralds will scarcely show. It is probably the same effect which is the major cause of the differential effect seen when emeralds are photographed on an infra-red film with an infra-red filter over the camera lens (*Figure 35.15*).

A list of the important fluorescent colours given by gem materials under the different ranges of radiation is given in the Appendices.

CHAPTER 36

X-RAYS IN GEM-TESTING

HISTORY AND NATURE OF X-RAYS

The momentous discovery by the German physicist W. K. Röntgen in the year 1895, of a type of radiation which passed through material opaque to ordinary light, supplied the key which opened the door to vast advances in science and industry.

Until 1912 the nature of these rays, usually known as x-rays, remained in doubt, a doubt which stimulated many inquiries and which ultimately led to one of the most profound and fundamental experiments of the present century. This experiment, carried out by Max von Laue and his assistants Friedrich and Knipping, undeniably proved the rays to be 'light' of very short wavelength, and at the same time proved the regular arrangement of the atoms in crystals. More of this anon, for upon this experiment depends a number of methods which have been, and are, used for the determination of gem materials and pearls.

As a preliminary it may be as well to discuss in an elementary manner something of the history which led up to the discovery of x-rays and the apparatus used for their production, before considering the use of the rays as a gem-testing tool.

During the latter half of the nineteenth century many experiments were carried out on the character of high tension electrical discharges through gases at pressures of 2 or 3 atm to a nearly complete vacuum. Much experimental work on these discharges was carried out by Geissler, Lenard, and Hertz, whose work on the longer 'Hertzian-waves' led to the discovery by Marconi of 'wireless'. In Great Britain, Sir William Crookes, as well as Professor Herbert Jackson of King's College, for whom it has been claimed that he discovered x-rays almost at the same time as Röntgen, were pioneers in these experiments.

When a high-tension electric current from an induction coil or a transformer is discharged between two separated metal rods, termed electrodes, at atmospheric pressure, it takes well-known forms. With the electrodes so far separated that no actual spark may pass, thin tree-like streaks of a purple colour proceed from them. These streaks branch out in all directions, while from the tips of the 'branches' straight and very fine blue lines seem to stick out like hairs of a brush, producing the so-called brush discharge. This phenomenon is exemplified in nature by 'St. Elmo's Fire'.

On reducing the amount of separation of the electrodes there comes a distance where the discharge becomes a long purple thread-like spark with tree-like branches leaving it at different points along its track. These subdivide into finer and finer streaks until they are lost to sight and reach their destination as silent discharges. At still shorter separation of the electrodes the spark is bright blue, wavy and free from ramifications and is accompanied by a loud 'snap'; and with nearer approximation of the electrodes to one another the discharge is reminiscent of the well-known low-voltage arc formed between carbons.

For those experiments requiring a gas pressure less than that of the atmosphere, a glass bulb fitted with either fixed or adjustable electrodes and capable of being exhausted to any practicable extent is used. With the pressure only slightly below that of the atmosphere a spark discharge still occurs, quieter and more thread-like, even when the electrodes are separated three or four times their normal sparking distance in air.

At a pressure of about 10 mm of mercury the discharge broadens out until it takes the form of a thick purplish glow, known as the positive column, which swells in the middle and falls away until it is quite narrow near the electrodes. This glow fades to nothing near the cathode (the electrode at negative potential), which is tipped with a violet light known as the negative glow, while the ill-defined non-luminous region between them is termed the Faraday dark space.

A very small electromotive force (voltage) is now necessary to maintain the discharge as the conductivity rises to a high value. Geissler tubes are simple tubes of this nature with constricted portions to concentrate the discharge and make it brighter, or twisted into fantastic shapes and made of fluorescent glass so as to give pretty colour effects.

At a still lower pressure the positive column first expands until it occupies the whole bulb, the negative glow at the same time increasing to form a sheath of violet light round the cathode and the Faraday dark space enlarges. Further decrease in gas pressure shows the positive column to break up into a series of fluctuating nebulous striae of glowing gas separated by dark spaces, with further enlargement of the Faraday dark space and increase in brightness of the negative glow. At the same time the conductivity decreases and ultra-violet light is strongly emitted.

When the pressure is down to about $\frac{1}{2}$ mm of mercury the negative glow detaches itself, leaving a dark space between itself and the cathode (*Figure 36.1*). This is known as the Crookes dark space, which, as the exhaustion is

Figure 36.1. Appearance of a discharge tube at a pressure of about $\frac{1}{2}$ mm of mercury: A. Crookes dark space; B. negative glow; C. Faraday dark space; D. positive column luminous

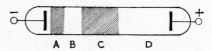

carried further, lengthens, pushing the negative glow and the Faraday dark space before it, until when the pressure is down to about $\frac{1}{50}$ mm of mercury, the whole tube is completely filled with the dark space and the walls of the tube fluoresce brightly. On further exhaustion the fluorescence dies out and the current stops altogether.

The fluorescence on the walls of a tube so exhausted that the Crookes dark space fills the whole of the tube—such a tube being called a Crookes tube—was early recognized as being due to a radiation emanating from the negative electrode. This radiation, discovered by T. Plücker in 1859, was named cathode rays by Goldstein in 1876.

Crookes carried out a number of experiments with these rays and found that they travelled in straight lines normal to the surface of the cathode whatever the position of the anode (the positive electrode) in the tube, that they were deflected by a magnetic field, possessed momentum and carried an electric charge. Crookes suggested that the rays were a 'fourth state of matter'—an ultra-gaseous state called by him radiant matter. British physicists tended to agree with Crookes while the German school contended that the rays were some form of light—a wave motion in ether.

In 1897, Professor J. J. Thomson proved by a series of elegant experiments that radiant matter or cathode rays are a stream of negatively charged particles which have been formed by the disintegration of atoms of gas in the·vacuum tube. These particles, or corpuscles as Thomson called them, are now known as electrons and are not molecules or atoms, but something much smaller with a mass equal to $\frac{1}{1840}$ of the mass of the hydrogen atom and having a velocity which varies from $\frac{1}{30}$ to $\frac{1}{3}$ the speed of light. They are one of the constituents out of which atoms are built and are the particles which form the planetary outer negative sheath surrounding the positive nucleus of the atom.

Röntgen's Experiment

The discovery of x-rays was purely the result of an accidental or casual observation of something which had no bearing on the experiment being carried out. Röntgen was experimenting with the passage through gases of an electric current, for which purpose he was using a highly exhausted Hittorf tube, a type of vacuum tube where the cathode faces an enlarged end of the main tube, while the anode is situated in a side 'annex' tube (*Figure 36.2*).

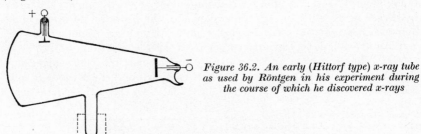

Figure 36.2. An early (Hittorf type) x-ray tube as used by Röntgen in his experiment during the course of which he discovered x-rays

The tube at the time of the experiment was completely covered with black paper. Hanging on a wall some distance away was a paper screen coated with barium platino-cyanide which had been used in other experiments. To Röntgen's surprise this fluorescent screen shone brightly when the Hittorf tube was switched on, and, like Fleming in the case of the discovery of penicillin, Röntgen turned from his original experiment to investigate something for which there was no apparent cause.

When objects were placed between the tube and the screen, shadows were cast, hence the effect was due to some radiation coming from the tube, a radiation which was able to pass through black paper, a thing ultra-violet light could not do, and further, the radiations acted on a photographic plate even when the plate was shielded from ordinary and ultra-violet light.

Röntgen called these radiations x-rays because their nature was then unknown, and, although they were officially called Röntgen rays after their discoverer, x-rays remains the ever popular term.

Relationship with Atomic Weight

Further experiments showed that the invisible radiations travelled in straight lines. They were, unlike ordinary light, not refracted by prisms or lenses nor were they affected by a magnetic field, but could ionize gases. It was quickly noticed that the greater the atomic weight of a substance the greater its opacity to the rays; in other words the absorptive power of a material to x-rays is a function of the atomic weight, for example carbon, oxygen, nitrogen and hydrogen have low atomic weights and are therefore readily 'radiable' (the term used for the degree of transparency to x-rays);

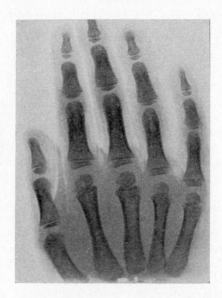

Figure 36.3. Radiograph of a child's hand showing the differ- ence in transparency (radia- bility) of the flesh and bones

while iron, lead, gold and platinum are elements with high atomic weights and are much less transparent to the rays.

The flesh, made of the light-weight atoms of carbon, oxygen, nitrogen and hydrogen, is much more transparent to x-rays than the bones which contain the heavier calcium and phosphorus atoms, so, by their aid we can see the bones through the flesh when the effect of the radiations is made visible by a fluorescent screen or a photographic plate (*Figure 36.3*). Medical science was quick to realize the importance of the penetrating power of x-rays, and within a few months of Röntgen's discovery they were put to use in the location of a bullet.

Cathode Ray Experiments

When a stream of fast moving electrons—cathode rays—in a highly exhausted tube carrying a high-tension current greater than 30,000 V strike a solid object, whether it be the glass walls of the tube or a subsidiary metallic electrode within the vacuum tube, x-rays are produced by the destruction of the cathode rays.

It may therefore appear strange that x-rays remained undiscovered for so long with all the experimental work with discharge tubes going on. Indeed, it was said that Sir William Crookes on one occasion sent back to the makers some photographic plates with the complaint that they were faulty, for when developed they had shadows on them. They had been on a bench and were actually the first x-ray pictures and were of his own fingers. Why these shadows were not recognized for what they were was, probably, not only due to another superimposed picture, but also from the large area from which the x-rays were generated, that is the glass of the tube, producing not only the true shadow but a wide and overlapping penumbra as well. Professor Lenard also missed discovering the rays solely because he used in his cathode ray experiments fluorescence screens made of an organic compound which, brightly fluorescent when irradiated with ultra-violet light or cathode rays, were inert when x-rays are used, an effect common with organic materials.

Crystals and X-rays

Quite early on Röntgen thought that x-rays were some form of light but no verification of the fact could at that time be found. The whole subject was the cause of much controversy which lasted for many years. It was not until 1912 that proof of the nature of x-rays was accomplished. In that year, Max von Laue, an assistant lecturer at Munich, having been approached by a student with a question on crystal optics, was reminded that the then general conception of the structure of a crystal was that it had a regular arrangement of its atomic constituents, and with a linear distance between them of one or two Ångstrom units. He also knew that if x-rays were electromagnetic waves, they would probably be of the short wavelength of about one Ångstrom unit, a length far too short to be diffracted by any ruled grating as may be used to diffract visible light.

Laue realized that if a crystal was as so described it would act as a natural grating, and would, if x-rays are short wavelength light, diffract a narrow beam, or rather, as he was inclined to suspect, scatter the x-rays. C. G. Barkla, in 1906, had discovered that matter containing 'heavy' atoms 'scattered' an x-ray beam producing 'characteristic x-rays', characteristic of the heavy atoms. Laue thought this scattering might produce diffraction patterns from a crystal. More will be said about these characteristic rays at a later stage—for the present it may be told that Laue's assumption was incorrect, and the proof he wanted did not come from scattered rays, but from rays transmitted through the crystal.

Two research students, Friedrich and Knipping, who had studied under Röntgen, co-operated in carrying out the experiments. A crystal of copper sulphate was used in the preliminary experiments, copper sulphate is of triclinic symmetry and complex structure. It was possibly the worst type of crystal that could have been chosen, and the fact that their first experiments were arranged to receive scattered radiation, with their photographic plates either between the source of the x-rays and the crystal or at the side and parallel to the narrow beam of x-rays, precluded any success from their initial trials.

Friedrich and Knipping then set up their apparatus so that an extremely narrow beam of x-rays, the beam being limited by a collimating tube of lead, was directed on to the face of the crystal and a photographic plate set up behind it, a position adopted in order to try out every avenue after the failure of the initial experiments. On developing the plate a pattern of spots surrounding the heavy central spot due to the undeviated main beam were seen to have been produced. They were unsymmetrical but clearly proved the possibility of diffraction of x-rays by crystals.

Further experiments, in which crystals of high symmetry, such as zinc blende, copper oxide, fluorspar and halite (salt), and in one experiment a diamond was employed, supplied further proof of the nature of x-rays. Thus, in one classic experiment sufficient proof was obtained to substantiate the theory that x-rays were 'light' of short wavelength, and that crystals did have a regular atomic arrangement as suggested by theory, and set the scene for the modern methods of x-ray crystallography with which the name of the Braggs is so intimately associated.

APPARATUS FOR PRODUCTION OF X-RAYS

Transformers

Apparatus for the production of x-rays consists of two essential parts—equipment for producing the high-tension current necessary, and the vacuum tube in which the rays are generated.

The high-tension generator in the early days was a simple induction coil—the so-called Ruhmkorff coil—which is just a modification of the common medical shocking coil. Such coils, sometimes alluded to as 'open core' transformers, normally required direct current for their operation. Modern high-tension generators employ a 'closed core' transformer—bigger brothers to the small transformers used in wireless receiving sets. These operate on alternating current only.

The transformer type of apparatus may have many different modifications and ancilliary apparatus can be incorporated for smoothing and rectifying the current. The transformer itself, may, in the case of modern tubes, have separate tappings to give a low voltage supply for the heating of the filament—this will be discussed later. All modern high-tension generators are 'built-in', and, so far as that part of the equipment is concerned, are robust and foolproof. Any electrical defects in any part of the x-ray equipment are jobs for the professional electrical engineers.

Most modern sets are equipped with a control panel which contains all or some of the following control knobs, meters and switches: a mains 'on' and 'off' switch, a high-tension 'on' and 'off' switch which starts and stops the machine actually delivering x-rays and which may be in the form of a hand or clock time-switch. Such a timer may give an exposure time of from $\frac{1}{10}$ to 10 sec (hand timer), or from 10 sec to even several hours: this being done by a special clock. The meters incorporated are a voltmeter to indicate the potential difference between the anode and the cathode of the

703

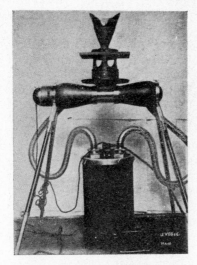

Figure 36.4. The Metalix pearl-testing apparatus

tube; and a milliammeter which measures the current passed by the tube. As will be discussed later these measurements give some indication of the quality and quantity of the x-rays produced.

Knobs to give variable control of the voltage and current are usually provided. As with ordinary wireless sets for the reception of radio broadcast, each make of set has a different layout of the control panel. They may have a greater or less number of controls than indicated above. In the case of the Metalix pearl-testing set (*Figure 36.4*) there may be none except an 'on' and 'off' switch. A general purpose set built specially for gem-testing is shown in *Figure 36.5*.

Figure 36.5. General purpose x-ray set for gem-testing. The central observation window at the top is for viewing luminescent effects through a lead glass window. The meter on the left indicates the high-tension voltage and that on the right shows the current in milliamperes. These are mounted on the lid which is raised in order to adjust the tube and set the specimens. Below are two swing doors and a lower drop door. On each side of this lower door is a control panel. That on the left has a red pilot light; the wheel controlling the sliding resistance which controls the input voltage to the tube; and the 'on' and 'off' contactor button. To the right is the milliampere (current) control and a 30 min timing clock. Inset is shown the tube and setting accessories

Vacuum Tubes

Focus Tube

The early tubes, as used by Röntgen (*see Figure 36.2*) generated x-rays by the impact of the accelerated electron stream on the glass walls of the tube. This gave a large area of surface giving off x-rays of low concentration. In 1896, the 'focus tube' was introduced almost simultaneously by several workers, particularly by Jackson, and was for some time known in Great Britain by his name as the *Jackson tube*.

The main feature of the focus tube is that the aluminium cathode is made concave with a curvature such that the electrons, which leave it normal to the surface, produce a cone of rays meeting at a point some distance greater than the geometrical focus, due to the mutual repulsion of the fast travelling electrons. The focal point of this cathode ray stream is so arranged that it impinges on the anode, usually termed the 'target' or the 'anticathode', from which x-rays are generated. These travel radially outwards in all directions as shown diagrammatically in *Figure 36.6*.

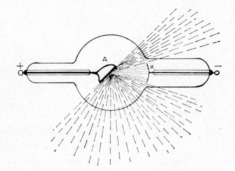

Figure 36.6. The Jackson tube with concave cathode. Directions of the cathode stream (electrons) shown with dashes. Note: The x-rays pass through the space occupied by the cathode stream and have only been omitted here to avoid confusion

In the more modern version of this tube the target is made of heavy metal of high melting point. This is necessary owing to the fact that only about one per cent of the electron energy is used in producing x-rays while 99 per cent simply heats up the target: this heating must be minimized by various methods, such as a large mass of metal of high melting point, cooling fins, and even a system of water cooling has been employed in these 'gas tubes'.

There is an auxiliary anode, usually coupled externally to the target, which makes for smoother running. As these so-called gas tubes, for their action depends upon the residual gas in the evacuated tube, 'harden' with use, that is the gas in the tube becomes more rarefied (a hard tube offers more resistance to the current than a softer tube), the tubes are fitted with an arrangement to allow a very small quantity of air or gas to enter them. *Figure 36.7* illustrates such a gas tube with a softening device containing absorbent material which will let some of its absorbed gas into the tube when the high-tension current is passed through it by means of the adjustable side wires. Today gas tubes are used solely for special purposes.

Hot-cathode Tube

An important advance in x-ray tube design was made by the introduction, in 1913, of the 'hot-cathode' type of tube which was brought out by the American W. D. Coolidge. The fundamental phenomenon upon which the hot-cathode tube depends is that a heated metal emits electrons—the so-called 'thermionic effect'. It is this effect which is the basis for most of the electronic devices, such as the wireless valve, the television screen, radar and the modern x-ray tube.

The fact that air in the neighbourhood of hot metals became electrically conducting was known to early workers, including Edison, and was for some time called the 'Edison effect'. In 1880 Geitel and Elster in Germany investigated the problem more thoroughly, but for nearly 20 years the reason for the effect remained a mystery. There were two possible explanations; that the charged particles were emitted from the hot body, or that the neighbouring gas or air molecules had become ionized.

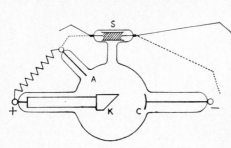

Figure 36.7. A diagrammatic representation of a gas x-ray tube with softening device. A, the positive electrode or anode, which is coupled externally to the massive anticathode or as it is more commonly known, the target. K, the anticathode or target. C, the negative electrode or cathode, which is made concave in order to bring the cathode rays (electrons), which are emitted from the surface in a direction at right angles to it, to a focus on the target. S, the softening device employed to let a small quantity of gas into the tube should it harden. This sometimes occurs after prolonged running

In 1899 Professor J. J. Thomson measured the ratio of the charge to the mass of the particles carrying electricity near a hot carbon filament. He found that they had the same value as have cathode rays and were the same fundamental particles that are now called electrons. Thomson also found that these electrons were emitted from the hot cathode and were not due to ionization of the surrounding gas molecules by the hot filament.

A later improvement came about when it was found, actually by Wehnelt in 1904, that a filament coated with an alkaline earth oxide, such as calcium oxide or barium oxide, would give a much greater emission of electrons than would an ordinary carbon or metal filament. Today most apparatus used in 'electronics' have such 'coated' filaments.

A hot-cathode tube, often known as a Coolidge tube, does not depend upon the ionization of the residual gas in the tube, but upon the supply of electrons emitted from the heated filament, hence, the highest possible vacuum is necessary for these tubes. In Coolidge tubes the control of intensity of the x-radiation, determined by the number of electrons emitted, is simply carried out by adjustment of the filament current which alters the temperature of the filament hence the increase or decrease of the number of electrons emitted.

The quality of the radiation is altered by the adjustment of the high-tension voltage—the positive potential applied to the anode which accelerates the electrons. A further advantage in these hot-cathode tubes is that control of focus of the electron stream on to a small area of the target is readily arranged by an accessory electrode, or metal shield, surrounding the filament and maintained at a negative potential, which, in some sets can be adjusted by alteration of this 'bias' voltage. *Figure 36.8* shows in schematic fashion a hot-cathode tube.

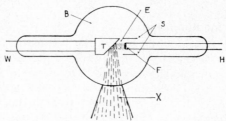

Figure 36.8. Schematic diagram of a Coolidge type hot-cathode x-ray tube. B, evacuated glass bulb. F, filament. E, electron stream. T, target (anti-cathode). X, x-ray beam. S, shielding device focusing the electron stream. W, water cooling and electrical con-nexions. H, low voltage filament current and high voltage electrical connexions

Shielding of Tubes

Modern improvements consist of a complete shielding of the x-ray tube in order to prevent stray radiation from reaching the operator, for the physiological effect of long or frequent exposure to x-rays (for the dosage is cumulative) results in grave degeneration of blood and tissue.

In such shielded tubes the aperture through which the rays are directed is a 'window' of Lindemann glass—so-called after its inventor, Professor Lindemann—which is a glass incorporating lithium, beryllium and boron. In recent tubes aluminium or, better, beryllium in thin sheet forms the window of the tube.

PRODUCTION OF X-RAYS

Continuous Radiation

In many modern tubes, and specially for those tubes used for special pur-poses, such as for crystal diffraction, it is now the more general practice to mount the target so that its surface is at right angles to the cathode stream, and not at an angle of 45 degrees as was formerly universal.

When electrons, accelerated to a high velocity by the positive charge on the target or any positive anode, strike the surface of a solid body, x-rays are produced. If the electron is stopped without making any direct collision with an atom in the target the violent deceleration is enough to produce a pulse of radiation. This is in accordance with the 'classical' theory of electromagnetic waves. The x-rays so produced form a continuous band of wavelengths whose lower limit is equal to 12·35 divided by the voltage (reckoned in kilovolts), thus the greater the high-tension supplied to the tube the shorter is the minimum wavelength produced. This continuous, 'general' or 'white' x-radiation is analogous to white light of the visible spectrum in being a mixture of all wavelengths, of course down to but not below the shortest wavelength permitted by the impressed voltage.

The intensity of the continuous radiation, which in theory extends to the ultra-violet region (the longest x-rays which reach up to the shortest ultra-violet radiations are termed Grenz rays, after the German word for threshold) increases as the high-tension voltage increases, and has a maximum or 'hump' just before the minimum wavelength is reached. That is when the bombarding electrons have given up all their kinetic energy in the production of x-rays. Intensity, that is the amplitude of the wave-form, is very much a function of the current, in milliamperes, passing across the tube.

Line Radiation

When the energy of the bombarding electrons is powerful enough to ionize the atoms of the target material radiation of discrete wavelengths is produced. This so-called 'line spectrum', for it is analogous to the 'line' or emission spectrum of ordinary light rays, is known as the 'characteristic radiation', for it is characteristic of the element of the target, is caused by ionization by removal of one of the inner electrons which is replaced by an electron from a state of higher energy. Such a mechanism also operates, as Barkla found in 1906, when a beam of x-rays falls upon any material. For, provided that the wavelength of the x-rays incident upon the body are shorter than the characteristic wavelength of the element bombarded, these 'fluorescent' characteristic rays will be emitted. Such induced radiation may provide some of the so-called 'scattered' rays which can be a nuisance when x-rays are employed in certain forms of work.

Filters

It is now seen that x-rays may be produced by two different processes, a continuous band of wavelengths, and a 'line' spectrum. This may be better understood by reference to *Figure 36.9*. Further, it is possible to

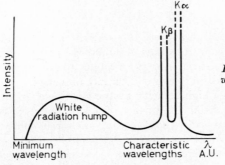

Figure 36.9. Continuous x-ray spectrum with characteristic line spectrum. Shortest wavelength on the left

obtain a near approach to monochromatic x-rays (x-rays of one wavelength only) by the insertion of suitable filters. Such filters are very thin sheets of elements, usually metallic, which have an atomic number one or two lower than the atomic number of the metal of the target. For example: a copper target (atomic No. 29) is filtered by a screen of nickel (atomic No. 28), or a molybdenum target (atomic No. 42) by a zirconium (atomic No. 40) filter. The reasons for selective filtering are rather outside the scope of this work and the reader is referred to the many excellent technical books on x-rays for the explanation.

USE OF X-RAYS IN GEM-TESTING

The uses to which x-rays may be employed in gem-testing depend first upon the fluorescent visible light induced in certain materials by the rays, secondly, upon the variable transparency of different materials to the rays, and lastly, to the effects of diffraction of the rays from the atomic planes of the material.

Fluorescence

The first of these, that of fluorescence, has pride of place in being the phenomenon which led to the discovery by Röntgen of these very rays. Some gemstones and pearls show a typical fluorescence when bombarded by x-rays—it being necessary to view the effects in a darkened room and to ensure that the visible light from the tube filament is obscured. It is only in recent years that much attention has been paid to the various 'glows' that emanate from a substance which is irradiated with invisible light, of which fluorescence by x-rays is but one example, and is coupled up with the similar phenomena induced by other forms of radiation. This aspect has been discussed in the chapter on the luminescence of gemstones.

Transparency

The difference in transparency to x-rays of different substances has been remarked upon, and it has been told that the radiability depends to a great extent upon the atomic weight of the element or elements forming the substance. The greater the atomic weight the more opaque is the substance to the rays, thus, diamond (atomic No. of carbon is 6) would be expected to be most transparent, and zircon, containing the heavier zirconium atom (atomic No. of Zr. is 40), or the lead-glass imitations having the heavy lead atom with an atomic number of 82, to be comparatively opaque to the rays. This is borne out by experiment and is illustrated in *Figure 36.10*. It

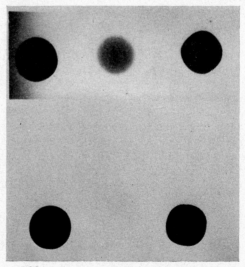

Figure 36.10. In these two radiographs of a zircon (left), a diamond (centre) and a glass imitation gemstone with a refractive index of 1·63 (right) is shown the opacity to the rays of the zircon and the paste; while the diamond is transradiant. The upper picture was taken on a very slow 'line' film (7 sec exposure), while in the case of the bottom picture there was a 5 sec exposure but fast x-ray film was used, and in this case the diamond was shown to be completely transradiant

709

must be understood that for comparable results the operating conditions, that is, the voltage and current, the exposure time and the metal of the x-ray tube's target must be the same.

The German scientist C. A. Doelter carried out a number of experiments on the transparency of gemstones to x-rays. He found that amber, diamond, phenacite and jet were quite transparent to x-rays, and corundum nearly so. Chrysoberyl, opal, andalusite and kyanite less so, while topaz, feldspar, diopside, spodumene and quartz were translucent. Spinel, fluorspar and hessonite garnet Doelter found to be semi-translucent and tourmaline, turquoise, peridot and sphene to be nearly opaque. Almandine garnet, zircon, rutile, epidote, and surprisingly, beryl, were found to be practically opaque to x-rays. The lustrous lead-glass imitations of diamond are very opaque to the rays, but it must not be assumed that all glass imitations are, for some glasses are moderately transradiant.

Comparative tests for the radiability of a substance to x-rays can have a great value when the difference is very great, for example, diamond and zircon and especially when taken together on one film at the same time. In

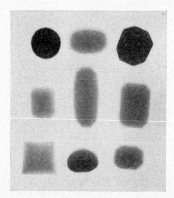

Figure 36.11. Comparison of the radiability of some equal sized gemstones to x-rays. Top row (reading from the left): zircon, aquamarine, almandine. Centre row: citrine, topaz, tourmaline. Bottom row: phenacite, corundum, chrysoberyl

Doelter's list there seem to be several inconsistencies, particularly is this so in the case of beryl, which, taking into consideration the atomic numbers of the constituent elements, should have a pronounced transparency to the rays. An experimental radiograph of some gem stones, illustrated in *Figure 36.11* shows a strong disagreement with Doelter's results with regard to beryl, which in the photograph approaches more nearly to the transparency expected. Corundum also shows a departure from its position in the table, in being less transradiant than expected, both from Doelter's work and from the low atomic numbers of its constituents.

Although differences in the target material of the x-ray tube used, and in operating conditions, may cause spectacular differences, the occurrence of trace elements, such as caesium (atomic No. 55) in beryl, and titanium (atomic No. 22), chromium (atomic No. 24) and iron (atomic No. 26) may, in the case of corundum, have a bearing on the inconsistencies, also the close atomic packing of the latter species may have a bearing, as it does on the density, 3·99, which is higher than expected from its composition.

The difference in the composition of the various parts of composite stones may well be shown by the difference in radiability of the two, or more, parts. This is clearly illustrated in the radiograph of a diamond doublet (*Figure 36.11*). The stone had a diamond crown and a synthetic white sapphire pavilion.

This differential transmission of x-rays through materials which have a complex or irregular structure is used to produce the direct x-ray picture

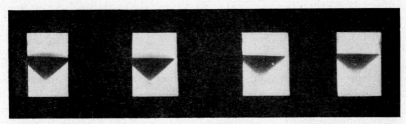

Figure 36.12. Radiographs of a diamond doublet. Diamond top and synthetic white sapphire base. These are four different exposures

or skiagram, as it is sometimes called. This method has some value in the testing of pearls and the special x-ray technique used in such work was discussed when dealing with pearl testing in the section on organic gems.

Diffraction

Laue Method of Diffraction

The diffraction techniques, which are simply the original method as used by Laue and his co-workers, or some modification of it, must now be considered. The most important from the gemmologist's point of view are the straight lauegram method; the x-ray 'powder' photograph and the back-reflection methods.

In all these cases it is necessary to limit the normal cone of x-rays to a very narrow beam. This is done by using a pin-hole (approximately 0·5 mm in diameter) collimating system of metal discs pierced with the pin-holes mounted in a metal tube so arranged as to be in perfect alignment with the focal spot on the target. Alternatively, just a lead block pierced with a fine hole will serve for most diagnostic work, and is the type used for pearl testing by the lauegram method, when an aperture of not more than 1·5 mm is usually employed. The narrow beam is passed into the stone or pearl which is suitably mounted on the end of the orifice from which the x-ray beam emerges.

At some distance from the specimen, approximately 7·5 cm in the case of pearls, and about 3 cm for diffraction pictures of crystals or stones, in which case a much smaller aperture is employed, is placed a film to receive the diffracted rays (*Figure 36.13*). As the diffracted beams are only a very small part of the main narrow beam of x-rays, which itself produces a heavy overexposed spot on the film, generally known as the main trace, their photographic intensity is not very great.

In order to avoid a very long exposure time, one or two intensifying screens are employed in conjunction with a fast single-or double-coated x-ray film. The function of these intensifying screens, which are simply cardboard coated with an x-ray fluorescent compound, is to enhance the weak photographic effect on the light-sensitive chemicals of the emulsion by the actinic action from the visible bluish light induced on the screen by the x-rays which have been transmitted through the specimen. With double-coated x-ray film it is practical to employ two screens, one on the tube side of the film and one on the back. The screen on the tube side has little absorptive effect on the rays which pass through it causing fluorescence on the coated side.

It must be clear that care is necessary to ensure that the coated side of the screens are facing the film, and, of course, the film must be bare against the intensifying screens, for, if covered by paper wrapping, none of the fluorescent light from the screens would be able to affect the emulsion and no amplification of intensity could occur. Indeed, the paper would tend to absorb the radiations and the weak beams of diffracted rays made weaker still. Loading the cassettes, as the film holders are called, with film must be done in a dark-room, for naked film must be employed, and if single-coated film is employed with the one screen necessary, it must be ensured that the emulsion side is against the screen.

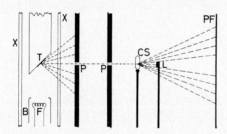

Figure 36.13. Schematic diagram of the Laue method of x-ray diffraction. X, x-ray tube; T, target; F, filament; B, bias shield; P, pinhole system; CS, crystal specimen; L, lead stop to limit central beam; PF, photographic film

When a crystal is so arranged that the narrow cylindrical beam of x-rays travels along, or parallel to, an axis of symmetry, the beam is reflected off the internal atomic planes and produces on a suitably placed film a series of symmetrically arranged spots surrounding the heavy main trace. This heavy central overexposed spot is generally 'stopped-off' with a lead disc. These atomic planes act towards x-radiation in the same way as visible light is affected by diffraction gratings, except that with x-rays the planes behave as semi-transparent reflectors. Thus, a certain number of parallel planes makes an additive contribution to the total reflection obtained and hence the general optical law of interference operates, that is as in the interference of light at thin films which gives to opal its wonderful play of colour. *Figure 36.14* is a diagrammatic representation of this.

When radiation from a source S is reflected from the planes that are d apart, the distances between the different reflected rays SXR, SX_1R, and so on are an exact multiple of the wavelength λ. The difference between SXR and SX_1R equals XY plus XZ and the angles YXX_1 and ZXX_1 are equal. Hence YX_1 equals ZX_1 equals $d \sin \theta$, or YX_1 plus ZX_1 equals $2d \sin \theta$. Hence $N\lambda$ equals $2d \sin \theta$, where N is the number of wavelengths of the radiations in Ångstrom units and θ the angle of incidence of the rays. Thus, from this formula known as Bragg's law, which is the basis of all x-ray crystal analysis, when two of the factors λ, d, and θ are known, the third is calculable.

Figure 36.14. Diagrammatic representation of x-ray beams reflected off the internal atomic planes of a crystal that is so arranged that the narrow cylindrical beam of x-rays travels along or parallel to an axis of symmetry

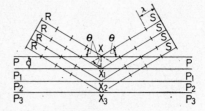

Laue Diffraction Patterns

For the production of spot diffraction Laue patterns, ordinary white radiation is suitable. This technique is employed for most gem-testing by x-rays. In Laue diffraction x-ray work it must clearly be understood that the pattern of spots is influenced by the direction in which the x-ray beam passes through a crystal. Indeed what the lauegram, as the spot pattern is called, tells, is the symmetry of the crystal along a given direction by the symmetry of the spot pattern. The symmetry of the crystal is only shown perfectly when the narrow x-ray beam travels through the crystal parallel to an axis of symmetry, and it should therefore be clear to the reader that the spot pattern will differ when the beam passes down the vertical crystal axis of a beryl crystal—a direction of sixfold symmetry (*Figure 36.15*)—

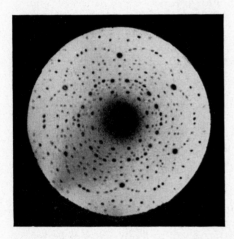

Figure 36.15 Laue diffraction pattern taken down the c axis of a beryl crystal. The sixfold symmetry of this direction is shown by the arrangement of the spots

from a pattern which is obtained from an x-ray beam which enters a diamond crystal at right angles to the octahedral face—a direction of trigonal symmetry (*Figure 36.16*).

The use of the lauegram method in the testing of pearls is more fully discussed in the section giving the modern gem-testing operations.

Powder Diffraction

Laue pictures of a gemstone will only give information of the crystallographic symmetry of the crystal structure. There is, however, another method, of which there are several variations. This is the powder method. Some powder scraped from the specimen to be examined is placed in a capillary tube of Lindemann glass, plastics, or even rolled on to an oil-covered

23*   713

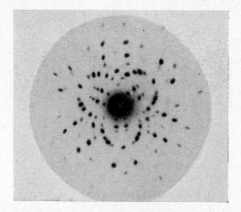

Figure 36.16. A lauegram taken down a trigonal axis of symmetry of a crystal

hair. The specimen is then placed in front of the collimating tube as for an ordinary lauegram. Indeed, it is similar in every way to the lauegram technique except that the specimen is in powder form instead of a complete individual crystal.

A picture taken in this manner shows, as the particles of the powder are minute crystal particles in disorientation, a series of rings instead of a series of symmetrical spots. The strength and distance apart of these rings is characteristic for each substance and differs from others, so that if a 'control' picture is taken of a known substance (mineral), another specimen expected to be the same will give a similar picture provided that the specimen film distance is the same. *Figure 36.17* shows a powder photograph of a diamond.

This is an elementary exposition of the powder photograph method, which requires, if very serious work is to be done, a 'catalogue' of pictures of all minerals in order to make the comparison with that of an unknown specimen. A 'filing system' is necessary in order to find quickly the control picture. This may sometimes be done by referring to the distance from the centre of the stronger lines and a catalogue made up on that scheme.

Certain modifications of this method, commonly utilized today, employ a 'circular camera' with a strip film arranged around the circumference, while the powder specimen is centrally placed in respect to the circularly arranged film, and, further, the powder specimen may be rotated during the exposure. This method, ascribed to Debye and Scherrer, is

Figure 36.17. Powder diffraction photograph of diamond

considerably employed in mineralogy and metallurgy, and is only one of somewhat similar modifications used today.

Back Reflection Method

At the close of 1946, Holmes and Switzer, of the Gemological Institute of America, devised apparatus to give a rotating powder photograph from a crystal or gemstone. The method is a variation of the back reflection method ascribed to Sachs. The gemstone is mounted on a special holder so constructed that the specimen is rotated about one axis and oscillated about another at 90 degrees to the first; the specimen being in the path of a narrow beam of x-rays. Secondary beams of x-rays are generated by reflection of the primary beam from planes of atoms within the specimen to produce an x-ray diffraction pattern of circles by back reflection. Like all pictures of this nature control pictures are necessary. Although little has been heard of the value of the method, the preliminary reports stated that good results had been obtained from it, both from single crystals, that is ruby, spinel, and so on, and from crystalline aggregates, such as onyx, lapis, and also turquoise, a material often difficult to test, and for which the method could have considerable value.

COLOUR CHANGE FOLLOWING X-RAY BOMBARDMENT

Finally, a word of warning to those having access to x-ray equipment. X-rays may in certain cases alter the colour of stones bombarded by them. This induced coloration may be, and generally is, only temporary, but may require heat or some other form of light radiation to correct the colour to the original hue.

In some cases the change of colour is most spectacular. This is so in the case of kunzite which changes from the lovely lilac pink to an attractive green. In the weak yellow sapphires from Ceylon a good and better yellow, quite like the yellow of Brazilian topaz, can be induced by x-ray bombardment, and remains for some time if the stone is not exposed to heat or sunlight. Such coloured stones usually revert to their original colour (cases have occurred where the new colour is not the same as the original) after a few minutes' heating at 230°C (446°F) or in about 3 hours' exposure to strong sunlight. This is the test for such 'artificially coloured' stones.

CHAPTER 37

ELECTRICAL AND MAGNETIC
PHENOMENA OF GEMSTONES

ELECTRICITY

When the electrical nature of the atom is considered it will not be surprising that more tangible electrical effects may be induced in material structures, and this is true of gem materials. Such manifestations are those of frictional electricity, pyro-electricity, piezo-electricity and electroconductivity.

Frictional Electricity

In many substances an electric charge can be induced by rubbing—this is frictional electricity. It is best known in the case of amber, for as early as 600 B.C. Thales knew that when amber was rubbed with silk it acquired the property of attracting light articles. W. Gilbert in the sixteenth century found that this property was shared by other substances and he named the effect 'electrification' after electron the Greek word for amber. Thus the effect shown so well by amber of picking up small pieces of paper is no sure test, for some amber substitutes may behave similarly.

The production of electricity by friction lies in the ability of the rubber or the rubbed to part with some of the outer electrons of the surface atoms. The electrons which have parted from one of the two substances attach themselves to the other substance, or it may be said that the surface atoms of the two substances become ionized. Thus both of the materials, the rubber and the rubbed, become electrically charged. It is well known in electrostatics that like charges repel and unlike charges attract. All uncharged bodies contain atoms with equal charges of positive and negative electricity, but if a charged body, for example one with a positive charge, is brought near it attracts the negative charge within the uncharged body and repels the positive one. Hence, the end of the previously uncharged body nearest the charged body acquires a negative charge. The negative charged surface being nearer to the positive charged body its attraction is greater than the repulsion of the positive charge in the same (uncharged) body. Thus an uncharged body is attracted towards a charged one.

When a body is electrified by friction the nature of the charge produced depends upon the substance with which it is rubbed. Thus glass becomes negatively electrified when rubbed with flannel, but positively when rubbed with silk. When briskly rubbed with a cloth, such stones as diamond, tourmaline and topaz exhibit positive electricity. The electrical sign of a charged body can be ascertained by the use of an electroscope but the methods of determining this need not be gone into here. Frictional electricity is of scant importance in gemmology.

Pyro-electricity

When certain crystals are heated electrical charges are developed at polar positions. This effect, termed pyro-electricity, is common in some tourmaline crystals but apparently not in the black variety—schorl—and in untwinned quartz crystals. When such crystals are suspended over an asbestos mat heated from below to about 200°C, they will, on cooling, show particular regions of the quartz and the ends of the tourmaline crystals to be oppositely electrically charged. That such a warmed crystal possesses electric charges may be demonstrated by the experiment devised by A. E. Kundt. A finely powdered mixture of red lead oxide and sulphur is blown through a muslin mesh, whereby the particles become electrically charged by friction—the sulphur negatively and the red lead positively—and will settle on the faces or regions of the crystal of opposite electrical sign. Thus on opposite ends of the tourmaline crystal one end will collect the yellow sulphur and the other the red lead; and on alternate corners of the quartz crystal there will be either red lead or yellow sulphur. It is this pyro-electric effect of tourmaline which causes tourmalines on display in a jeweller's window to attract dust so readily. The heat of the window casement warms the stones so that an electric charge develops.

Piezo-electric Effect

During 1880 a phenomenon was observed and studied by the brothers Pierre and Jacques Curie in that some crystals when subjected to mechanical compression in particular directions develop electric charges on certain regions. This is known as the piezo-electric effect, a term introduced by W. G. Hankel of Leipzig who derived the term from the Greek piezein which means 'to press'. The effect is found to occur in hemihedral crystals, the most important of which are rock crystal and tourmaline. Others, but less hard and durable, are boracite (chloromagnesium borate), and Rochelle salt (sodium potassium tartrate), the last named showing the effect to a greater extent than any other crystal.

Of great importance is the 'converse effect', first predicted by G. Lippman of Paris in 1881, and later verified by the Curies. Reverse effect occurs when a difference of potential (voltage) is applied across opposite faces of a suitably cut plate of a piezo-electric crystal and there arises mechanical stresses which produce in the dimensions of the plate changes in the thickness and length. The length diminishes and the thickness increases when the electric field is in one direction, the thickness decreasing giving increased length when the field is applied in the opposite direction. The dimensional change is proportional to the magnitude of the applied potential difference. No change occurs along the direction of the optic axis in doubly refracting crystals.

Early in 1917, P. Langevin of France applied the piezo-electric properties of quartz to the transmission of ultrasonic waves under water. Later, during the latter part of 1917 and early 1918, W. G. Cady, whilst with a group working on piezo-electric crystals for submarine detection on behalf of the Navy of the United States of America, investigated the erratic electrical behaviour of the crystals and discovered that this peculiar behaviour

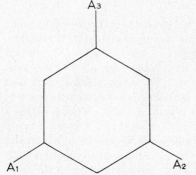

Figure 37.1. The electric axes in a quartz crystal

(After G. O. Wild)

when understood could be controlled and turned to good account. In 1922 Cady took out patents on electrically vibrating quartz crystals as a method for measuring and controlling frequencies in radio broadcasting.

If an alternating potential difference is applied to a plate cut from a quartz crystal it will be subject to a series of alternating extensions and contractions of the same frequency as the alternating current supply. In other words the crystal plate will undergo forced vibrations. These vibrations are normally very small, but if the frequency of the applied voltage is varied, a resonance effect is obtained, there being one particular point at which the vibration becomes very large and appreciable energy is absorbed. This resonance is exceedingly sharp and occurs over a frequency variation of a few parts in a million, so that it forms an ideal control for an oscillator.

G. O. Wild has explained how electric charges can be released by a suitably cut plate of quartz. The configuration of silicon and oxygen atoms in the unit cell of the quartz crystal consists of six negative oxygen atoms combined with three positive silicon atoms in such a manner that two oxygen atoms compensate one silicon atom at the termination of the electric axes, of which there are three in the unit cell (*Figure 37.1*). The drawing (*Figure 37.2*) which shows only three oxygen atoms, while in fact there are

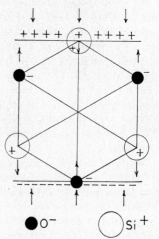

Figure 37.2. Diagrammatic representation of the piezo-electric effect. The arrows denote the direction of pressure

(After G. O. Wild)

two in each case with their centres at equal distance from the plane of the drawing, above and below, illustrates the piezo-electric effect. When pressure is exerted on the face which is normal to the electric axis the O (negative) atoms move towards one face while the Si (positive) atoms move towards the other, thus binding opposite charges, so that a positive charge appears near the O (negative) atoms and a negative one near the Si (positive) atoms.

Quartz Oscillator Frequency

The actual frequency at which a crystal operates depends upon the manner in which the slice is cut from the whole crystal. The two most common types of slice are the X-cut in which the width of the slice is at right angles to the prism face of the quartz crystal, and the Y-cut in which the width is parallel to the prism face of the crystal (*Figure 37.3*). It is the thickness of the slice, however, which controls the actual frequency of the quartz

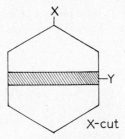

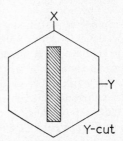

Figure 37.3. The directions of the X-cut and Y-cut slices of quartz for oscillator plates

oscillator. Another complication with the normal X-cut and Y-cut is that the temperature can affect the frequency; this defect has been to a great extent overcome by slices cut from quartz crystals at different orientations. Indeed, a quartz crystal can be sliced at many different angles to produce oscillating plates of different characteristics. Untwinned quartz is essential for the production of such oscillator plates; it was owing to the possible need of these for war potential during World War II that the synthesis of quartz was encouraged.

A simple oscillator circuit controlled by quartz crystal is shown in *Figure 37.4* (Pierce-Miller oscillators). Electrical oscillations of the tuned circuit LC induce mechanical oscillations in the quartz (Q). The electric charges thus set free react with the LC circuit through the grid of the thermionic

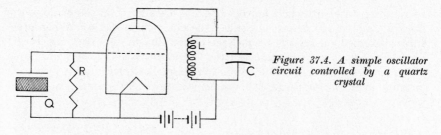

Figure 37.4. A simple oscillator circuit controlled by a quartz crystal

valve and keep the LC circuit exactly on the frequency of the quartz crystal plate.

The controlling influence of a quartz piezo-electric crystal has been used, not only to control the radiating frequency of radio transmitters, including radar, but is made use of in many other electronic devices, including the quartz clock. Further, quartz crystal oscillators can be used to produce ultrasonic (supersonic) waves, above 20,000 vibrations per sec, which is the limit that the human ear can register. These waves, which can be produced in air and liquid, have been found to be of considerable value in science and medicine, and for some industrial requirements.

Electroconductivity

The conduction of electricity through a metal occurs because metallic atoms possess one or more outer electrons which are easily removed from their orbits, leaving positive ions. A metal then may be considered as a closely packed collection of positive ions with 'clouds' of migratory free electrons. The application of a potential difference (voltage) between the ends of a piece of metal, say a wire, will cause these free electrons to travel to the positive end of potential difference leaving a low electron density at the other end which is filled up by electrons from the negative pole. Thus there is a continuous flow of electrons as long as the potential difference is applied. An insulator is a substance through which it is impossible to pass an electric current for such substances, such as glass and porcelain, possess no free electrons. Hence, no movement of electrons occurs when a potential difference is applied to their ends.

Electroconductivity is of interest to the gemmologist in the exceptional case of certain diamonds. Diamonds are normally good insulators, but in certain types, named by J. F. H. Custers as Type IIb, there are lattice imperfections with loose electrons. A potential difference applied to such a diamond will cause a migration of electrons to the positive pole. This flow of electric current is small at first, only a few milliamperes, but the flow tends to heat up the crystal which liberates more and more electrons from the atoms and the current increases rapidly to several amperes; the diamond will get red hot if the current is not turned off.

It is known that all natural blue diamonds are of this Type IIb and are electroconductive, while the artificially coloured blue diamonds treated by electron bombardment are of a type which is not electroconducting. Therefore proof of electroconductivity could be a means of testing for artificial coloration of blue diamonds. All that is necessary for this test is a simple circuit consisting of a source of current, a voltmeter and two electrodes between which the diamond is held. These are connected in series. Alternatively, a neon lamp circuit tester (usually sold in the form of a screwdriver) may be used. In use the stone to be tested is placed on an electrode which is connected to the line side of an alternating current supply (90–450 V). When the screwdriver blade is touched on the stone and the button at the end of the handle touched with the finger the neon lamp in the handle will, if the stone is conducting, light up.

Some Type IIb diamonds are said to be semi-conductors and are becoming of increasing importance in certain types of electronic apparatus, and they can also be used as counters of *gamma*-rays.

MAGNETISM

It has long been known that an almandine garnet will affect a delicately poised magnetic needle and be attracted by a powerful electromagnet. Although the separation of mineral grains by magnetic methods has been used to a considerable extent, the magnetic susceptibilities of gemstones have not been investigated to any great extent.

There are two main types of magnetism. Paramagnetism is when the material becomes magnetized by induction, or is said to possess induced magnetism. Only a few substances, iron, steel, nickel, cobalt and certain alloys, exhibit to a marked degree the phenomenon of paramagnetism, and such strongly magnetic substances are termed ferromagnetic substances. The facility with which iron nails and steel needles may be picked up by an ordinary horse-shoe magnet is obvious proof of the intense magnetic action of such substances.

However, when iron-rich minerals are considered there is less obvious co-relation. True, magnetite (lodestone) is strongly attracted to a magnet, whereas both pyrites and hematite, with 46 and 70 per cent of iron respectively, are not affected by an ordinary hand magnet. In this connexion reference can be made to the so-called 'hematine', which is used as an imitation of real hematite, for this material is attracted to a hand magnet and may be distinguished from the true hematite which is not attracted.

The other type of magnetism, diamagnetism, shows the opposite effect, that is the substance is repelled by a magnet; bismuth is the type example of this effect. In any case these effects, except in the ferromagnetic substances, are small and of little importance in gem-testing techniques. However, B. W. Anderson found that by the use of a sensitive aperiodic balance and a small powerful hand magnet some assessment could be made of paramagnetism.

The experimental procedure is to assess the magnetic 'pull' exerted on a specimen by noting its loss of weight when it is attracted by a magnet held closely above it. The aperiodic type of balance is used since the magnetic attraction exerted on the stone can be followed as it takes place and the weight read off directly on the scale, which is the projection of a transparent graticle attached to the pointer of the balance. As the metal of the balance pan may be found to exert a slight magnetic pull a large cork of known

721

weight is placed on the pan and the stone to be tested placed on this cork pedestal. The cork and stone are then weighed together in the usual manner and are left on poise. The magnet is then held immediately above the stone and lowered slowly and steadily. When the poles have approached to within a quarter of an inch or so of the upper surface of the specimen, if the latter has any magnetic susceptibility, the scale will begin to record a marked loss in weight. The minimum weight which could be 'held' by the magnet is then taken as the required reading. The difference between this 'held' weight and the true weight of the specimen and cork is recorded. The mean of at least three readings being taken.

From the experiments it became clear that the size of the stone played a very important role, and that the smaller stones were 'saturated' with magnetic lines of force, while with a big stone much of the material would be outside the strongest field of attraction. To 'iron out' irregularities due to size, Anderson, used the entirely empirical formula

$$\text{Pull} = \frac{\text{Magnetic loss} \times 100}{\sqrt{\text{Weight}}} \text{ (in milligrams)}$$

From the results obtained by these experiments, iron-containing gem-stones are the most strongly magnetic, but the mere percentage of iron in a mineral, as mentioned earlier in the case of pyrites, does not necessarily give a clue to the magnetic susceptibility; the nature of the other elements present and the structure of the crystal playing an important part. The other strongly magnetic stones were found to be those which contain manganese. The results found by Anderson are given in Table 37.1.

TABLE 37.1
Magnetic Determinations

Magnetism	Stone	Pull (formula)
Strong	Almandine*	290–410
	Spessartite	250–360
	Rhodochrosite	270 +
	Rhodonite	280–370
	Hematite	220–310
Moderate	Demantoid	120–200
	Epidote	100 +
	Pleonaste	80–130
	Peridot	50– 75
	Pyrope*	40– 75
	Dark green tourmaline	50– 70
	Hessonite	40 +
	Indicolite	40 +
Weak	Brown sinhalite	
	Green tourmaline	

* The term 'almandine' is confined to stones with a refractive index of 1·79 and over, while 'pyrope' are those stones with an index below 1·75. Intermediate members of the pyrope/almandine series give intermediate magnetic values

As with care and patience an ordinary balance could be used for the magnetic determinations, a worker having no other apparatus than a good balance and a small magnet could differentiate between the following stones: the more magnetic of the two is mentioned first.

Demantoid	from Green zircon, sphene or diamond
Pyrope	from Ruby or spinel
Hematite	from Black pearl or black diamond
Spessartite	from Hessonite or zircon
Rhodonite or rhodochroisite	from Thulite
Brown peridot	from Sinhalite
Stainless steel	from Marcasite (pyrites)
Hematine	from Hematite

The last pair can, however, be distinguished simply by the attraction by an ordinary magnet, for hematine is ferromagnetic.

CHAPTER 38

CHEMISTRY AND GEMSTONES

Chemistry is a subject of only occasional application by the practical gemmologist, but some idea of the scope of the science in relation to gem materials is both interesting and useful. It throws light on the one hand on the suitability of the various gem materials for certain uses and on the other provides that knowledge of the principles of chemical reactions, which is necessary if incorrect deductions are to be avoided on those occasions when the gemmologist does find it necessary to apply those simple tests called upon from time to time.

CHEMICAL COMPOUNDS

All existing material, tangible or intangible, whether existing as solid, liquid or gas, is to the chemist built up of simpler units. These, in fact, may in themselves be quite simple as the metals, small groups as in the case of most inorganic compounds, or exceedingly complex units which go to build up many of the organic compounds.

The pure metals are built up of one type of matter only, referred to by the chemist as elements, for example copper, silver or gold. Inorganic compounds are built up of two or more dissimilar elements—quartz = silicon oxide (SiO_2), two elements; calcite = calcium carbonate ($CaCO_3$), three elements; and so on to complex materials such as tourmaline which has a great number of elements present.

Organic compounds, on the contrary, are very often 'heavy' compounds composed of few different elements but combined in various groupings and quantities resulting in some very complex compounds. In these compounds carbon is the essential element and may be in combination with varying quantities of hydrogen, oxygen, nitrogen and so on, joined in a very diverse number of ways. Organic compounds are, in fact, innumerable but here again the gemmologist is concerned with very few. These include certain materials of animal origin (actually these are usually mixtures of organic and inorganic compounds) several products of vegetable life, and a number of synthetic compounds which are basically wholly organic and of a definite composition. In the first class are the ivories (dentine); fossil ivory—not greatly different in composition; bone where the organic and inorganic parts, though arranged in an orderly structure, are intimately dispersed; and what is probably the most interesting of all, pearls, which are built up of concentrically arranged 'shells' of the inorganic compound aragonite (calcium carbonate) and the organic compound conchiolin (a scleroprotein), the proportion being in round figures about 7 to 1, a small amount of water also being present. The second class is probably best represented by the so-called 'vegetable ivory' (the corozo nut which is substantially albumen)

724

and the fossilized plant product, amber, which are entirely organic in composition. There are also other resins not fossilized or only partly so. The last class is in the main made up of the synthetic resins and plastics. These are dealt with more fully in a separate item.

NOMENCLATURE

It will be appreciated that to investigate the compounds mentioned above, covering only those in which the gemmologist is directly interested, some knowledge of the language of the chemist and the nomenclature he uses in identifying and referring to the various compounds is necessary. It is not intended here to go deeply into those natural laws governing the manner and proportions in which the various elements combine to produce the compounds enumerated. It will be sufficient if it is realized that the chemist's formula is not merely a 'shorthand', but that every formula not only indicates the ingredient elements but also is a definite statement of the proportions of each and in many formulae the precise way in which the elements are connected.

The smallest unit of a chemical compound is called a molecule, an example of which is sodium chloride (common salt), a molecule consisting of one atom of sodium (Na) united to one atom of chlorine (Cl). Each atom is given a chemical symbol which consists of one or two letters derived from the usually Latin name of the element. This symbol, in addition to acting as an abbreviation, stands for one atom of the element and enables chemical formulae to be written which give at a glance the exact chemical composition of any pure substance. Thus, one atom of zinc (Zn) combined with one atom of sulphur (S) will form zinc sulphide, which when crystallized is the mineral zinc blende, with the formula ZnS.

In the greater number of cases the formula indicates that more than one atom of a given element is in the compound. In the formula this is indicated by small subscript numbers written after the symbol. Such a formula is that of alumina, which when crystallized is corundum—ruby and sapphire. The formula for this pure substance is Al_2O_3 which means that the compound has a molecule consisting of two atoms of aluminium (Al) and three atoms of oxygen (O).

Such chemical formulae based on the use of letter symbols indicating atoms are empirical, giving only the relative numbers of atoms present in the compound and do not represent the actual constitution. While it is unnecessary to go into details of structural formulae, it is often of value to employ the 'rational' system. Thus, while the formula for spinel can be written as $MgAl_2O_4$, it may be more enlightening to see the same formula as magnesia and alumina, that is $MgO\,Al_2O_3$. This type of formula is specially useful in the case of synthetic spinel which has extra alumina, for this could not be expressed clearly with the normal formula, but a better idea can be gained by the rational formula: for example $MgO\,2\frac{1}{2}Al_2O_3$.

Another variation in formula occurs when a chemical group has a value more than unity. This is exemplified by the formula for almandine garnet, the iron aluminium silicate, which is expressed as $Fe_3Al_2(SiO_4)_3$. The silica group, SiO_4, as indicated by the brackets and the subscript number outside

725

the brackets, has three times the number of atoms given by the symbols in the brackets, for example three atoms of silicon and 12 atoms of oxygen, The composition of almandine garnet could be expressed, perhaps better, by the rational formula as $3FeO\ Al_2O_3\ 3SiO_2$.

The use of brackets in formulae can have another significance. In this case two or more symbols in the brackets indicate that the elements are interchangeable in variable amounts. An example of this is in the formula for topaz, which is written as $Al_2(F,OH)_2SiO_4$, where the fluorine (F) and the hydroxyl (OH) radical (to be discussed later), are interchangeable to a more or less greater extent.

It must be pointed out that the molecule, say of Al_2O_3, while being the smallest part of alumina which can remain alone, is not the smallest part of a crystal of corundum, for the smallest part of such a crystal is the unit cell, which contains Al_4O_6 in the trigonal unit.

ATOMIC WEIGHT

The relative weights of all atoms are accurately known, and these atomic weights are the weights of various atoms relative to oxygen which equals 16·00. Thus, calcium, a metallic element (symbol Ca) has the atomic weight of 40·08; carbon, a non-metallic element, has the atomic weight of 12·01. Combined in certain proportions according to the formula $CaCO_3$ these elements form calcium carbonate, which in the crystalline form may be either calcite or aragonite. From the formula, therefore, calcium carbonate consists of

1 calcium	40·08
1 carbon	12·01
3 oxygen (16×3)	48·00
	100·09

The total gives the molecular weight. As the molecular weight in this case happens to approximate to 100 the other figures in this case give the approximate percentage composition of each element. If the composition does not work out to 100, then to find the percentage of any element in the compound it is necessary to divide the weight of the element with the weight of the entire molecule and multiply the result by 100. Table 16 gives the accepted symbols, the atomic number and the atomic weights of the important elements.

ELEMENT GROUPS AND PERIODIC CLASSIFICATION

Elements in general naturally fall into two groups, metals and non-metals, while a few possess one or more properties common to both groups, for example arsenic occurring in realgar and there showing the properties of a metal, and in smaltite where it takes the place usually associated with a non-metallic radical. Metals usually, but not always, play the part of the basic or positive element in a simple compound, while non-metals play the negative or acidic part. Therefore elements can be divided into electro-positive or electro-negative elements, depending on whether they ionize with a deficiency of electrons (positive) or an excess of electrons (negative).

TABLE 38.1

The Chemical Elements with their Symbols, Atomic Numbers and Approximate Atomic Weights

	Symbol	At. No.	Approx. At. Wt.		Symbol	At. No.	Approx. At. Wt.
Aluminium	Al	13	27·0	Molybdenum	Mo	42	95·9
Antimony	Sb	51	121·8	Neodymium	Nd	60	144·3
Argon	A	18	39·9	Neon	Ne	10	20·2
Arsenic	As	33	74·9	Nickel	Ni	28	58·7
Barium	Ba	56	137·4	Niobium	Nb	41	92·9
Beryllium	Be	4	9·0	Nitrogen	N	7	14·0
Bismuth	Bi	83	209·0	Osmium	Os	76	190·2
Boron	B	5	10·8	Oxygen	O	8	16·0
Bromine	Br	35	79·9	Palladium	Pd	46	106·7
Cadmium	Cd	48	112·4	Phosphorus	P	15	31·0
Caesium	Cs	55	132·9	Platinum	Pt	78	195·2
Calcium	Ca	20	40·1	Potassium	K	19	39·1
Carbon	C	6	12·0	Praseodymium	Pr	59	140·9
[Cassiopaeum = Lutecium]				Protoactinium	Pa	91	231·0
Cerium	Ce	58	140·1	Radium	Ra	88	226·0
Chlorine	Cl	17	35·5	Radon	Rn	86	222·0
Chromium	Cr	24	52·0	Rhenium	Re	75	186·3
Cobalt	Co	27	58·9	Rhodium	Rh	45	102·9
[Columbium = Niobium]				Rubidium	Rb	37	85·5
Copper	Cu	29	63·5	Ruthenium	Ru	44	101·7
Dysprosium	Dy	66	162·5	Samarium	Sm	62	150·4
Erbium	Er	68	167·2	Scandium	Sc	21	45·1
Europium	Eu	63	152·0	Selenium	Se	34	79·0
Fluorine	F	9	19·0	Silicon	Si	14	28·1
Gadolinium	Gd	64	156·9	Silver	Ag	47	107·9
Gallium	Ga	31	69·7	Sodium	Na	11	23·0
Germanium	Ge	32	72·6	Strontium	Sr	38	87·6
Gold	Au	79	197·2	Sulphur	S	16	32·1
Hafnium	Hf	72	178·6	Tantalum	Ta	73	180·9
Helium	He	2	4·0	Tellarium	Te	52	127·6
Holmium	Ho	67	164·9	Terbium	Tb	65	159·2
Hydrogen	H	1	1·0	Thallium	Tl	81	204·4
Indium	In	49	114·8	Thorium	Th	90	232·1
Iodine	I	53	126·9	Thulium	Tm	69	169·4
Iridium	Ir	77	193·0	Tin	Sn	50	118·7
Iron	Fe	26	55·8	Titanium	Ti	22	47·9
Krypton	Kr	36	83·7	Uranium	U	92	238·0
Lanthanum	La	57	138·9	Vanadium	V	23	50·9
Lead	Pb	82	207·2	Wolfram	W	74	183·9
Lithium	Li	3	6·9	Xenon	Xe	54	131·3
Lutecium	Lu	71	175·0	Ytterbium	Yb	70	173·0
Magnesium	Mg	12	24·3	Yttrium	Y	39	88·9
Manganese	Mn	25	54·9	Zinc	Zn	30	65·4
Mercury	Hg	80	200·6	Zirconium	Zr	40	91·2

D. Mendeléeff, in 1869, enunciated a periodic classification of the elements based on the order of their atomic weights in which at regular stages elements of similar nature occur and thus form well-defined groups. It is now known that a more fundamental order than atomic weights is the atomic number which represents the positive charge on the nucleus of the atom of each element, neutralized by an equal number of planetary electrons in the normal atom. This and the periodic table have been mentioned in the discussion on crystals.

VALENCY

The capacity of an element to combine with or replace atoms of a unit element, such as hydrogen, is termed the valency of the atom, and the explanation of this lies in the electronic structure of the atom; this also was explained when dealing with crystals.

Valency is often graphically shown by linkages from the symbol of the element. Hydrogen is monovalent (univalent) hence will be shown as

Water	Ammonia	Methane
	H H	H
	\ /	|
H—O—H	N	H—C—H
	|	|
	H	H
Oxygen is	Nitrogen is	Carbon is
divalent	trivalent	tetravalent

Such a compound with all the bonds satisfied is termed a saturated compound. If, however, one or more bonds is left unsatisfied, it confers a tendency to unite with other atoms or groups whereby this odd linkage will be satisfied, for example, the so-called hydroxyl (OH) is a common radical with a valency of one (univalent), for one bond is left free or unsatisfied. Another example which might be met in gemmology is CaF, that is in apatite.

Certain elements as a rule confer certain properties when combined with other elements: hydrogen confers acidity, as in hydrochloric acid (HCl), sulphuric acid (H_2SO_4); whereas metals in general confer basic, or sometimes alkaline, properties: sodium hydroxide (NaOH), magnesium hydroxide ($Mg(OH)_2$). Those compounds formed from a base or a metal with an acid are called salts. Where a multivalent acid is involved one or more of the hydrogens might be replaced by the metal giving acidic salts, but if the entire hydrogen valencies are satisfied the salt is neutral, for example NaH_2PO_4 (sodium dihydrogen phosphate) very acid, Na_2HPO_4 (disodium hydrogen phosphate) less acid, Na_3PO_4 (tri-sodium phosphate) neutral. Again, the different hydrogen atoms may be replaced with one, two or three elements; $LiAlPO_4$ with (F,OH), that is amblygonite.

CHEMICAL REACTION

Two chemical substances when in solution and brought together may, in many cases, suffer an exchange of radicals forming entirely new compounds. This is a chemical reaction. Sodium chloride and silver nitrate react together to form silver chloride and sodium nitrate. This is expressed as a chemical equation as $NaCl + AgNO_3 = AgCl + NaNO_3$. Such an equation shows that equal weights are involved before and after the reaction.

The chemical compounds which have a similar composition and a closely related crystal form are said to be isomorphous, and a series of these an isomorphous series. Such isomorphous series are common in gem minerals and are particularly important in the garnets and feldspars as has been discussed in the description of those gems. The isomorphous replacement of one element by another in the composition depends upon the comparable size of the replacing ions.

It has already been shown that the 'empirical' method of writing a chemical formula, though neater in form and usually simpler, does not give nearly so much information about a compound as does the 'rational' formula. This is the case to an even much greater degree in organic compounds than in the inorganic compounds. For instance, the formula C_2H_6O tells little about the compound except that it contains carbon, hydrogen and oxygen and has a molecular weight of 46. It does in fact represent at least two compounds: (a) C_2H_5OH, alcohol (actually ethyl alcohol) and (b)$(CH_3)_2O$, ether (actually dimethyl ether). These may be written in a still more informative manner

$$\begin{array}{cc} \overset{H}{\underset{H}{H-C}}\overset{H}{\underset{H}{-C}}-OH & \text{and} & \overset{H}{\underset{H}{H-C}}-O-\overset{H}{\underset{H}{C}}-H \end{array}$$

or to quote another example C_6H_6 may not necessarily always be benzene. $HC{\equiv}C-CH_2-CH_2-C{\equiv}CH$ is a diacetylene compound (Dipropargyl), and, benzene which can only rationally be expressed in another graphic way as a cyclic compound

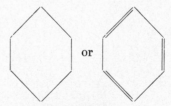

which is of so common occurrence in organic chemistry as to be understood in the shortened versions

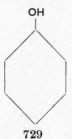

or

phenol, C_6H_5OH being usually written

OH

729

A chemist would in fact use these varying types of formula as convenient so long as they indicated what he requires to convey, for example he may write: 'the glass-like synthetic resin Distrene is in fact polystyrene prepared from styrene which is vinyl benzene

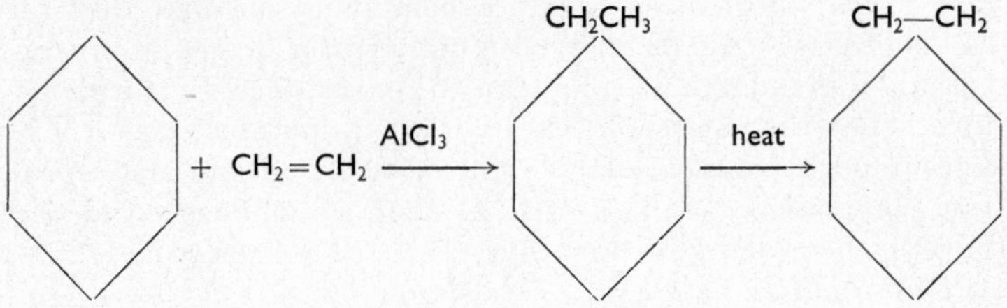

and polymerized to

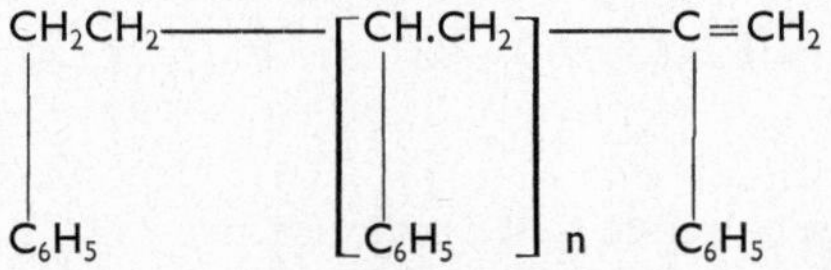

and from this would tell where the linkages are, where there are single and double bonds and generally the qualities of the compound'.

The above reaction does indeed introduce the reader to those important chemical reactions by which simple compounds may be converted into those widely utilized large molecular compounds—the plastics. In these the molecule may be either a long thin chain-like structure, for example the polyamides of which Nylon, one of the best known, is

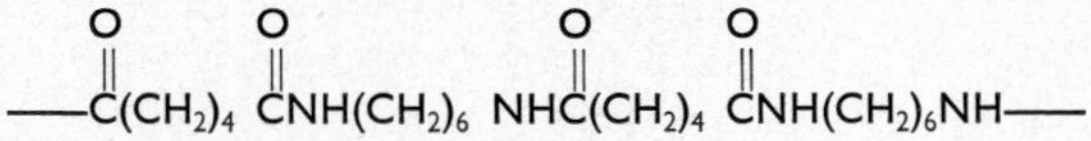

various net-like molecules mainly of interest in the coating industry, and the skeleton solids (three-dimensional), one of the earliest and best known being Bakelite

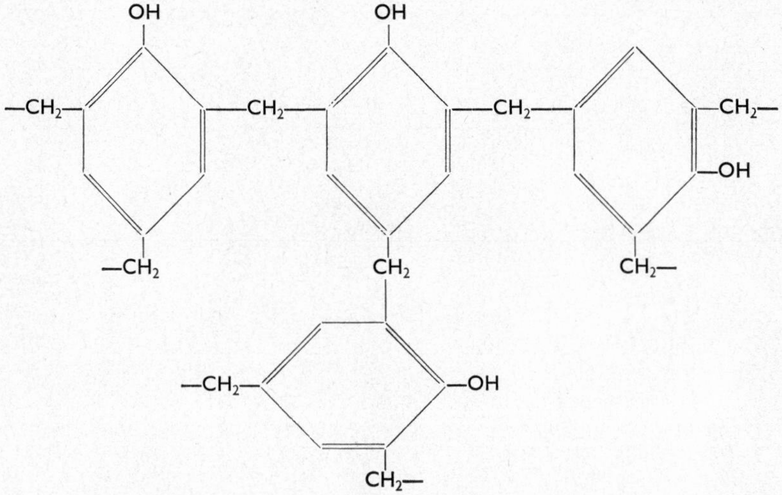

730

CHEMICAL TESTS

In those rare occasions when a chemical test is an advantage in order to give added information for the identification of a gem material all that is generally needed is to determine the presence or otherwise of a certain element or radical. Such tests may often be carried out by the use of very small quantities of the substance and reagents, and using a lens or microscope to watch the behaviour of the reacting substances.

The most useful and easy test that can be applied to a gem material is to observe the behaviour of a spot of acid, usually dilute hydrochloric or nitric, when it is placed on the specimen. Some of these reactions to acid have already been mentioned, such as those given for some turquoise imitations and that for the protein plastic—casein.

That a mineral contains a carbonate is usually evident by the effervescence seen when a spot of acid is placed upon it. This is due to the rapid evolution of the gas carbon dioxide (carbonic acid gas). As there may be

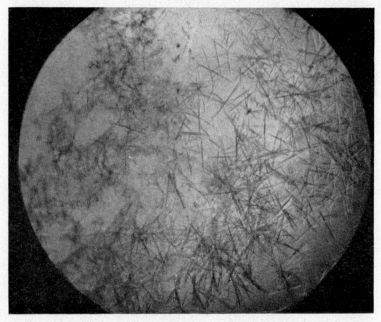

Figure 38.1. Chemical test for calcium. Calcium sulphate crystals produced by the test

cases where minerals other than a carbonate may 'fizz' with acid, a confirmatory test for carbon dioxide may be made by holding above the spot of acid on the specimen a glass rod which has at its end a drop of lime water. This will turn milky if the gas coming off is carbon dioxide.

This test, which may be carried out under the microscope on scrapings from the specimen, is useful in detecting odontolite from turquoise, coral from its usual imitations, but not from pink pearl. Smithsonite and malachite fizz and so does rhodochrosite, but here it may be unsatisfactory

731

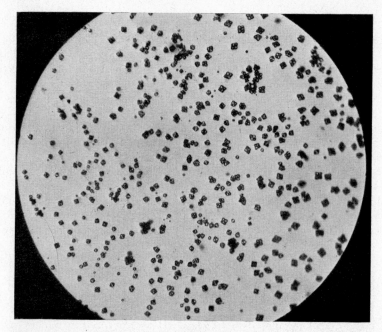

Figure 38.2. Ammonium-phospho molybdate crystals resulting from the test for phosphate

as a test against rhodonite, the manganese silicate, as the latter mineral often contains some carbonate.

The detection of calcium is sometimes of value, and this can effectively be carried out if the substance can be brought into solution. This test is usually best carried out microscopically on scrapings removed from the specimen which are immersed in a drop of hydrochloric acid on a glass slide. After a few minutes a drop of dilute sulphuric acid is introduced into the pool of hydrochloric acid on the slide. If calcium is present radiating groups of needle-shaped crystals of calcium sulphate are formed (*Figure 38.1*).

Substances containing phosphate can be identified by the bright yellow precipitate produced in a solution of the substance in a drop of strong nitric acid on the addition of an excess of ammonium molybdate accelerated by gentle warming of the slide. Again, this test is more conveniently carried out under the microscope, when the bright yellow precipitate is seen to be aggregates of yellow crystals with octahedral form (*Figure 38.2*). The test for phosphate in conjunction with that for calcium may be of value in the separation of shell from ivory or bone, as well as being helpful in identifying phosphate minerals. A warning here: arsenate minerals will give a similar reaction.

Chemical tests are very useful in identifying plastics, and certain tests were mentioned when these synthetic resins were discussed.

IDENTIFICATION TABLES

TABLE 1

Identification table of the refractive indices, optical characters, hardness and densities of the gem materials. For ease of reference the values are tabled in groups.

Refractive indices are the most important testing factor, so the values given for these are printed in ascending order. The density values, rather less used in gem-testing, in most cases increase with increasing refractive index and they thus fall within limits to defined groups, and therefore may be readily found in the table. Any constants outside the given range, or which may not easily be found within that range, are printed in italics and are repeated in ordinary type in their correct places. The word 'to' between figures implies variation in range, while '—' indicates the greatest and least readings in doubly refractive stones. 'I' means isotropic, 'U' uniaxial, and 'B' biaxial. The names of liquids are printed in italics.

Glass imitation stones may be said to have refractive indices which lie between 1·50 and 1·70, and such stones are rarely found outside these limits. So, as there are few natural singly refractive stones which lie between these values an isotropic stone having any refractive index between 1·50 and 1·70 may be suspected to be a paste.

Refractive index	Birefringence	Optic sign	Optical character	Hardness	Density	Name
1·3					**1·0**	
1·334	—	—	—	—	1·00	*Water*
1·36	—	—	—	—	*0·79*	*Alcohol*
1·37	—	—	—	—	*0·88*	*Amyl acetate*
1·4						
1·408	—	—	—	—	*0·936*	Cellosolve
1·54	—	—	I	2 to 2½	1·03 to 1·10	Amber
1·54	—	—	I	2	1·03 to 1·10	Copal resin
1·59	—	—	I	2¼	1·05	Polystyrene
1·53 (mean)	—	—	—	2	1·00 to *2·00*	Meerschaum
1·64 to 1·68	—	—	I	2½ to 4	1·10 to 1·40 usually 1·30 to 1·35	Jet
1·434	—	—	I	4	*3·18*	Fluorspar
1·44 to 1·46	—	—	I	5½ to 6	1·98 to 2·20	Opal
1·435 to 1·455					1·97 to *2·06*	Fire opal
1·60 to 1·63	—	—	I	2	1·15 to 1·20	Vulcanite (hard rubber)
1·50	—	—	I	2	1·18 to 1·19	Perspex
1·45	—	—	—	—	*mean 0·85*	*Petroleum*
1·45	—	—	—	—	1·498	*Chloroform*
1·46	—	—	I	6	*2·21*	Silica glass
1·47	—	—	—	—	1·26	*Glycerol at 20°C (glycerine)*
1·61 to 1·66	—	—	—	2¼	1·25 to *2·00* usually 1·26 to 1·30	Bakelite
1·47	—	—	—	—	*0·87*	*Turpentine*
1·47	—	—	—	—	*0·91*	*Olive oil*
1·47	—	—	—	—	*approx. 0·95*	*Castor oil*
1·48	—	—	I	5½ to 6	2·15 to 2·35 usually 2·25 to 2·30	Sodalite

Table 1—(cont.)

Refractive index	Birefringence	Optic sign	Optical character	Hardness	Density	Name
1·487	—	—	—	5 to 5½	2·22 to 2·29	Analcite
1·480–1·493	0·013	Positive	B	5½	2·20 to 2·25	Natrolite
1·48 to 1·50	—	—	I	5½	2·34 to 2·39	Moldavite
1·48 to 1·51	—	—		5	2·33 to 2·42	Obsidian
1·486–1·658	—	—	—	3	2·71	Calcite (marble)
1·54	—	—	—	2½	1·26 to 1·35	Tortoise-shell
1·49	—	—	—	—	0·87	Toluene
1·49	—	—	—	—	0·87	Xylene
1·490 to 1·505	—	—	I	1½	1·26 to 1·80 usually 1·29 to 1·40	Cellulose acetate plastic
1·55 to 1·56	—	—	I	2¼	1·32 to 1·34	Casein (protein plastic)
1·495 to 1·510	—	—	I	1½	1·36 to 1·80 usually 1·36 to 1·42	Celluloid
1·54	—	—	—	2½	1·38 to 1·42	Vegetable ivory
1·49 to 1·53	—	—	I	5	2·36 to 2·51	Tektites
1·490–1·650	0·160	Positive	B	2½	2·23	Whewellite
1·496	—	—	I	5½ to 6½	2·4	Hauynite
1·56	—	—	—	2½	1·60 to 1·85	Deer horn
1·54	—	—	—	2¼ to 2½	1·70 to 1·98 / 1·70 to 1·85 / 1·85 to 1·98	Dentine ivory Elephant Hippopotamus, Walrus and Narwhal

1·5   **2·0**

Refractive index	Birefringence	Optic sign	Optical character	Hardness	Density	Name
1·45	—	—	I	5½ to 6	2·00 (mean)	Opal
1·50	—	—	—	—	0·89	Benzene
1·54	—	—	—	2½	2·00	Bone
1·54	—	—	—		2·19	Ethylene dibromide
1·50 (mean)	0·011	Positive	U	2 to 4	2·00 to 2·45	Chrysocolla
1·48	—	—	I	5½ to 6	2·15 to 2·35 usually 2·25 to 2·30	Sodalite
1·50 (mean)	—	—	I	5½	2·70 to 2·90	Lapis-lazuli
1·50	—	—	I	2	1·18 to 1·19	Perspex
1·495–1·505	—	—	—	1½	1·29 to 1·40	Cellulose acetate
1·487	—	—	I	5 to 5½	2·20 to 2·29	Analcite
1·480–1·493	0·013	Positive	B	5½	2·20 to 2·25	Natrolite
1·46	—	—	I	6	2·21	Silica glass
1·50 (mean)	0·001	Positive	B	5	2·29	Mesolite
—	—	—	—	4 approx. unglazed	2·3	Porcelain
1·490–1·650	0·160	Positive	B	2½	2·23	Whewellite
1·48 to 1·50	—	—	I	5½	2·34 to 2·39	Moldavite
1·48 to 1·51	—	—	I	5	2·33 to 2·42	Obsidian
1·504–1·516	0·012	Positive	B	6 to 6½	2·39 to 2·46	Petalite
1·495–1·510	—	—	I	1½	1·36 to 1·42	Celluloid
1·496	—	—	I	5½ to 6½	2·4	Hauynite
1·51	—	—	—	—	approx. 0·95	Cedar wood oil (microscope objective immersion oil)
1·51 (mean)	0·020	Positive	B	1	1·65 to 2·00	Ulexite
1·51	—	—	I	5½ to 6	2·45 to 2·50	Leucite
1·517 to 1·525	—	—	I	6½	2·85 to 2·94	Pollucite
1·51 (mean)	0·022	Negative	U	6	2·42 to 2·50	Cancrinite
1·515–1·717	0·202	Negative	U	3½ to 4½	3·00 to 3·12	Magnesite

Refractive index	Birefrin- gence	Optic sign	Optical character	Hardness	Density	Name
_1·49_ to 1·53	—	—	I	5	2·36 to 2·51	Tektites
1·52–1·53	0·010	Positive	B	1½ to 2	2·30 to 2·33	Gypsum (ala- baster)
1·52–1·55	0·027	Negative	U	2½	2·15 to 2·22	Stichtite
1·52–1·54	0·028	Positive	B	5 to 5½	2·3 to 2·4	Thomsonite
1·52–1·53 to 1·53–1·54	0·008	Negative	B	6	2·56 to 2·59	Orthoclase feld- spar (moon- stone)
1·522–1·527	0·005	Negative	B	6	2·56	Yellow ortho- clase feldspar
1·522–1·530	0·008	Negative	B	6½	2·56 to 2·58	Microcline feld- spar
1·553–_1·625_ to 1·559–_1·631_	0·072	Positive	B	7½	2·35	Hambergite
1·586–_1·614_	0·028	Positive	B	4½	2·42	Colemanite
1·53	—	—	—	—	—	_Canada balsam_
1·53	—	—	—	—	_1·106_	_Monochlor- benzene_
1·535–1·537	0·002	Pos/Neg	U	4½ to 5	2·30 to 2·50	Apophyllite
—	—	—	—	6 to 6½	approx. 2·5	Nevada wonder stone
1·530 to 1·539	0·004 (?)	Negative	B	7	2·58 to 2·62	Chalcedony
1·53 (mean)	—	—	—	2	_1·00_ to 2·00	Meerschaum
1·53–1·54 to 1·54–1·55	0·008 to 0·012	Negative	B	7	2·57 to 2·66 us- ually 2·57 to 2·61	Iolite
1·530–1·556	0·026	Negative	B	3½ to 4	2·80 to _3·30_ us- ually 2·8 to 2·9	Lepidolite
1·532–_1·680_	0·148	Negative	B	3½	_4·27_ to _4·35_	Witherite
1·54	—	—	—	—	2·19	_Ethylene di- bromide_
1·54	—	—	—	—	_1·08_	_Clove oil_
1·54	—	—	—	2½	_1·38_ to _1·42_	Vegetable ivory
1·54	—	—	—	2½	2·00	Bone
1·54	—	—	—	2½ to 2⅔	_1·70_ to _1·98_	Dentine ivory
1·54	—	—	I	2 to 2½	_1·03_ to _1·10_	Amber
1·54	—	—	I	2	_1·03_ to _1·08_	Copal resin
—	—	—	—	3½	2·6 to 2·7	Coral
1·54 approx.	—	—	—	7	2·58 to 2·91	Jasper
1·54 approx.	0·011	Positive	B	6 to 6½	2·62	Albite feldspar (peristerite)
1·54 approx.	—	—	B	1 to 2	2·7 to 2·8	Soapstone
—	—	—	—	3½ to 4	2·20 to 2·78	Pearl
					2·69 to 2·73	Fine pearl
					2·40 to 2·65	Blue pearl
					2·67 to 2·78	Australian pearl
					2·70 to 2·78	Cultured pearl
					2·20 to 2·66	Black clam pearl
1·542–1·549	0·007	Negative	B	6 to 6½	2·62 to 2·65	Oligoclase feld- spar (sunstone)
1·544–1·553	0·009	Positive	U	7	2·65	Quartz
1·544–1·560	0·016	Negative	U	6	2·63	Scapolite (pink and white)
1·548–1·568	0·020	Negative	U	6	2·71	Scapolite (yel- low)
1·55	—	—	—	—	_1·198_	_Nitrobenzene_
1·55	—	—	—	—	_1·42_	_Bromotoluene_
1·55	—	—	—	2½	_1·26_ to _1·35_	Tortoise-shell
1·553–1·562	0·009	Negative	B	5½ to 6	2·80 to 2·85	Beryllonite

Table 1—*(cont.)*

Refractive index	Birefrin- gence	Optic sign	Optical character	Hardness	Density	Name
1·553–*1·625* to 1·559–*1·631*	0·072	Positive	B	7½	2·35	Hambergite
1·55 to 1·56	—	—	I	2¼	*1·32 to 1·34*	Casein plastic
1·55–*1·60*	—	—	—	1½	2·8	Pyrophyllite
1·56	—	—	—	—	*0·99*	*Dimethylaniline*
1·56	—	—	—	—	*1·12*	*Benzyl benzoate*
1·56	—	—	—	—	*1·499*	*Bromobenzene*
1·56	—	—	—	2½	*1·60 to 1·85*	Deer horn
1·56 (mean)	—	Negative	B	5	2·4 to 2·6	Variscite
1·560–1·568 1·565–1·573 (yellow)	0·008	Positive	B	6 to 6½	2·68 to 2·69	Labradorite feld- spar
1·56	—	Negative	B	2½ 4	2·5 to 2·7 2·58 to 2·62	Serpentine (bow- enite)
1·560–1·563	0·003	Negative	U	7½	2·65	Synthetic emer- ald
1·56–1·57 to 1·58–1·59	0·006 to 0·007	Negative	U	7½	2·69 to 2·75	Emerald
1·571–1·577	0·006				2·69	Colombia (Chivor)
1·578–1·584	0·006				2·71	Colombia (Muzo)
1·566–1·571	0·005				2·69	Brazil
1·581–1·588	0·007				2·73	Russia
1·587–1·593	0·007				2·75	Transvaal
1·585–1·592	0·007				2·75	Rhodesia
1·583–1·590	0·007				2·73 to 2·74	India
1·584–1·591	0·007				2·74	Habachtal
1·588–1·594	0·006				2·76	Pakistan
1·567–1·576	0·009	Negative	B	6 to 6½	2·73	Bytownite feldspar
—	—	—	—	2½	2·60 to 2·85	Pinite
1·57	—	—	—	—	*1·004*	*Orthotoluidine*
1·57	0·003	Pos/Neg	B	2½	2·60 to 2·85	Pseudophite
1·57	—	Negative	B	2½	2·61	Serpentine (var, williamsite)
1·57 approx.	—	—	—	3 to 4	2·7 approx.	Ophicalcite (Con- nemara marble)
1·486–1·658	0·172	Negative	U	3	2·71 2·5 to 2·6	Calcite marble
1·570–1·575 to 1·580–1·586	0·005 to 0·006	Negative	U	7½	2·68 to 2·73	Aquamarine; yel- low and some pink beryls
1·571–*1·614*	0·043	Positive	B	3 to 3½	2·90 to 2·98	Anhydrite
1·574–1·588	0·014	Positive	B	5	2·7	Augelite
1·57 to 1·58	—	Negative	B	3½ to 4	2·5 to 2·7	Bastite
1·57–*1·63*	—	—	—	5	*3·00 to 3·10*	Odontolite
1·58	—	—	—	—	*1·022*	*Aniline*
1·50	—	—	I	5½	2·70 to 2·90	Lapis-lazuli
1·58 (mean)	—	—	—	3	2·80 to 2·99	Verdite
1·58–1·59 to 1·59–*1·60*	0·008 to 0·009	Negative	U	7½	2·80 to 2·90	Some white and pink beryls
1·586–*1·614*	0·028	Positive	B	4½	2·42	Colemanite
1·59	—	—	—	—	2·86 (2·90 pure)	*Bromoform*
1·59	—	—	—	—	*approx. 1·05*	*Cinnamon oil*
1·59 (mean)	0·020	Negative	B	3¼	2·58	Howlite
1·59	—	—	I	2¼	*1·05*	Polystyrene
1·595 (mean)	0·009	Positive	U	5	2·81	Wardite
1·593–1·612	0·019	Negative	U	3½	*3·00*	Melinophane
1·595–*1·616*	0·021	Positive	B	3½	*3·1*	Phosphophyllite

Refractive index	Birefringence	Optic sign	Optical character	Hardness	Density	Name
1·595–1·633	0·038	Positive	B	5	2·74 to 2·88	Pectolite
—	—	—	—	3½ to 4	approx. 2·8	Mollusc shell
—	—	—	—	3½ to 4	2·84 to 2·89	Conch pearl
1·61–1·64	0·030	Positive	B	6	2·80 to 2·95 usually 2·88 to 2·94	Prehnite
1·61–1·65	0·040	Positive	B	5½ to 6	2·6 to 2·85 approx. 2·6 approx. 2·8	Turquoise American Persian and Egyptian
1·603–1·623	0·020	Positive	B	5½	2·980 to 2·995	Brazilianite
1·616–1·631	0·015	Negative	B	4½ to 5	2·8 to 2·9	Wollastonite
1·517 to 1·525	—	—	I	6½	2·85 to 2·94	Pollucite
—	—	—	—	6 to 7	2·85 to 3·20	Unakite
1·63	—	—	—	—	2·95	Tetrabromethane
1·66 to 1·67	—	—	I	7	2·96	Boracite
1·654–1·670	0·016	Positive	U	7½ to 8	2·95 to 2·97	Phenacite
1·60–1·62	0·02	Negative	B	5½ to 6	2·98	Tremolite
1·625–1·669	0·044	Negative	B	5	2·90–3·00	Datolite
1·62 (mean)	0·027	Negative	B	6½	2·90 to 3·02	Nephrite

1·6   3·0

Refractive index	Birefringence	Optic sign	Optical character	Hardness	Density	Name
1·60	—	—	I	6 to 6½	3·28	Ekanite
1·60	—	—	—	—	1·05	Cassia oil
1·60 (mean)	—	Positive	B	6½	3·1 to 3·2	Chondrodite
1·58–1·59 to 1·59–1·60	0·008 to 0·009	Negative	U	7½	2·80 to 2·90	Some white and pink beryls
1·603–1·623	0·020	Positive	B	5½	2·980 to 2·995	Brazilianite
1·593–1·614	0·019	Negative	U	3½	3·00	Melinophane
1·586–1·614	0·028	Positive	B	4½	2·42	Colemanite
1·595–1·616	0·021	Positive	B	3½	3·1	Phosphophyllite
1·60–1·62	0·02	Negative	B	5½ to 6	2·98	Tremolite
1·60 to 1·63	—	—	—	2	1·15 to 1·20	Vulcanite (hard rubber)
1·60–1·63 to 1·62–1·65 mean 1·62	0·027	Negative	B	6½	2·90 to 3·02	Nephrite
1·57 to 1·63	—	—	—	5	3·00 to 3·10	Odontolite
1·595–1·633	0·038	Positive	B	5	2·74 to 2·88	Pectolite
1·600–1·820	0·220	Negative	U	4	3·45 to 3·70 usually 3·50 to 3·65	Rhodochrosite
1·61 (mean)	0·030	Positive	B	5	3·00	Herderite
1·610–1·620	0·010	Positive	B	8	3·56	Topaz (white and blue)
1·571–1·614	0·043	Positive	B	3 to 3½	2·90 to 2·98	Anhydrite
1·616–1·634 to 1·630–1·652	0·014 to 0·022	Negative	U	7 to 7½	3·00 to 3·12	Tourmaline
1·553–1·625 to 1·559–1·631	0·072	Positive	B	7½	2·35	Hambergite
1·616–1·631	0·015	Negative	B	4½ to 5	2·8 to 2·9	Wollastonite
1·61–1·64	0·030	Positive	B	6	2·8 to 2·95 usually 2·88 to 2·94	Prehnite
1·61–1·65	0·040	Positive	B	5½ to 6	2·6 to 2·85	Turquoise
1·611–1·637	0·026	Positive	B	6	3·01 to 3·03	Amblygonite
1·615–1·645	0·036	Negative	B	5½	3·1	Lazulite
1·70 (mean)	—	—	B	5 to 6	3·1 to 3·5	Chlorastrolite
1·61 to 1·66	—	—	—	2½	1·25 to 1·30 (higher if filled)	Bakelite

Table 1—(*cont.*)

Refractive index	Birefringence	Optic sign	Optical character	Hardness	Density	Name
1·62	—	—	—	—	*1·83*	*Iodobenzene*
—	—	—	—	6 to 7	2·85 to 3·20	Unakite
1·625–1·669	0·044	Negative	B	5	2·9 to 3·00	Datolite
1·625–1·635	0·010	Positive	B	3½	3·97 *to* 3·99	Celestine
1·62–*1·85*	0·230	Negative	U	5	4·30 to 4·35	Smithsonite
1·63	—	—	—	—	*1·26*	*Carbon disulphide*
1·63	—	—	—	—	*1·93*	*Monochlornaphthalene*
1·63	—	—	—	—	2·95	Tetrabromethane
1·630–1·636	0·006	Negative	B	7	3·00	Danburite
1·630–1·638	0·008	Positive	B	8	3·53	Topaz (brown and pink)
1·63–1·64	0·002 to 0·004	Negative	U	5	3·17 to 3·23	Apatite
1·634–1·644 to 1·641–1·648	0·007 to 0·011	Negative	B	7¼	3·15 to 3·17	Andalusite
1·63–1·66	0·030	Negative	U	4 to 5	3·05 to 3·07	Friedelite
1·700–1·706	0·006	Negative	B	6	3·09 to 3·12	Thulite (zoisite)
1·434	—	—	I	4	3·18	Fluorspar
1·633–*1·873*	0·240	Negative	U	3½ to 4	3·83 to 3·88	Siderite
1·636–1·648	0·012	Positive	B	3	*4·3 to 4·6*	Barytes (barite)
2·65–2·69	0·043	Positive	U	9¼	3·17	Carborundum
1·74 to 1·81	—	Neg/Pos	B	4	3·22	Scorodite
1·64 to 1·68	—	—	—	2½ to 4	usually *1·20 to 1·30*	Jet
1·644–1·697 to 1·658–*1·709*	0·053	Positive	U	5	3·28 to 3·35	Dioptase
1·70	—	—	—	6½	3·0 to 3·4	Saussurite
—	—	—	—	5 to 5½	3·25	Smaragdite
1·486–1·658	0·172	Negative	U	3	2·71	Calcite
1·490–1·650	0·160	Positive	B	2½	*2·23*	Whewellite
1·652–1·672	0·020	Positive	B	7½	3·10	Euclase
1·654–1·667 mean 1·66	0·013	Positive	B	7	3·30 to 3·36	Jadeite
1·654–1·670	0·016	Positive	U	7½ to 8	2·95 to 2·97	Phenacite
1·654–1·689	0·036	Positive	B	6½	3·34	Peridot
1·658–1·678	0·020	Positive	B	6½ to 7	3·25	Fibrolite
1·65–*1·90*	0·25	Negative	B	4	3·74 to 3·95 usually 3·8	Malachite
1·66	—	—	—	—	*1·49*	*Monobromonaphthalene*
1·66 to 1·67	—	—	I	7	2·96	Boracite
1·660–1·675	0·015	Positive	B	7	3·17 to 3·19	Spodumene
1·662–*1·712*	0·050	Negative	B	5	3·94 *to* 4·07	Durangite
1·663–1·673	0·010	Positive	B	5½	3·26 to 3·28	Enstatite
1·665–1·678 to 1·668–1·680	0·013	Negative	B	6½	3·28 to 3·35	Kornerupine
1·67–*1·70*	0·030	Positive	B	5½	3·29 3·23	Diopside Violane
1·67–*1·71*	0·038	Negative	B	6½	3·47 to 3·49	Sinhalite
1·675–1·685	0·010	Negative	B	7	3·27 to 3·29	Axinite
—	—	—	—	—	3·28	*Klein's solution*
1·68 (mean)	—	—	B	7	3·26 to 3·41	Dumortierite
1·74	—	—	—	—	3·32	*Methylene iodide*
1·532–1·680	0·148	Negative	B	3½	4·27 *to* 4·35	Witherite
1·67–1·68 to *1·71–1·73*	0·010 to 0·020	Negative	B	5 to 6	3·4 to 3·5	Hypersthene
1·69	—	—	I	8	3·4	Rhodizite
1·69–*1·72*	0·028	Positive	U	5½	3·89 *to* 4·18	Willemite
1·692–*1·700*	0·008	Positive	B	6	3·35	Zoisite

Refractive index	Birefringence	Optic sign	Optical character	Hardness	Density	Name
1·700–1·712	0·005 (mean)	Neg/Pos	U	6½	3·32 to 3·47 3·25 to 3·32	Idocrase Californite
1·72	—	—	I	7¼	3·36 to 3·55	Massive grossular garnet
1·736–1·770	0·034	Negative	B	6½	3·25 to 3·50 usually 3·4	Epidote
1·72–1·73	0·010	Positive	B	6 to 6½	3·37 approx.	Clinozoisite
1·73	0·010	Positive	B	6	3·40 to 3·70 usually 3·6 to 3·7	Rhodonite
2·42	—		I	10	3·52	Diamond
1·885–1·990 to 1·915–2·050	0·105 to 0·135	Positive	B	5½	3·52 to 3·54	Sphene
1·630–1·638	0·008	Positive	B	8	3·53	Topaz (brown and pink)
1·610–1·620	0·010	Positive	B	8	3·56	Topaz (white and blue)
—	—	—	—	—	3·58	*Rohrbach's solution*
1·72 usually	—	—	I	8	3·58 to 3·61	Spinel
1·738	—	—	I	6	3·59	Periclase (synthetic)
—	—	—	—	—	3·60	*Methylene iodide with iodine and iodoform*
1·718–1·722	0·004	Negative	U	8	3·60 to 3·61	Taaffeite
1·724 to 1·729	—	—	I	8	3·61 to 3·65	Spinel (synthetic)
1·77 to 1·80	—	—	I	8	3·63 to 3·90	Spinel (Ceylonite)
1·742 to 1·748	—	—	I	7¼	3·65	Hessonite garnet
1·757–1·804	0·047	Positive	U	6½	3·65 to 3·68	Benitoite
1·715–1·732	0·017	Negative	B	5 to 7 directional	3·65 to 3·68	Kyanite
1·739–1·750 to 1·747–1·762	0·011 to 0·015	Positive	B	7 to 7½	3·65 to 3·78	Staurolite
1·73 to 1·75	—	—	I	7¼	3·65 to 3·70	Pyrope garnet
1·75 to 1·78	—	—	I	7½	3·70 to 3·95	Pyrope/almandine series garnet
1·75–1·76	0·008 to 0·010	Positive	B	8½	3·71 to 3·72	Chrysoberyl
1·65–1·90	0·25	Negative	B	4	3·74 to 3·95 usually 3·8	Malachite
1·74 (mean)	—	—	I	8	3·75 (mean)	Gahnospinel
1·87	—	—	I	7¼	3·77	Uvarovite garnet
1·73–1·84	0·110	Positive	B	3½ to 4	3·77 to 3·89	Azurite
1·752–1·815	—	—	—	6	3·8	Shattuckite
1·89	—	—	I	6½	3·82 to 3·85	Demantoid garnet
1·69–1·72	0·028	Positive	U	5½	3·89 to 4·18	Willemite
2·493–2·554	0·061	Negative	U	5½ to 6	3·82 to 3·95	Anatase
1·633–1·873	0·240	Negative	U	3½ to 4	3·83 to 3·88	Siderite
2·583–2·705	0·122	Positive	B	5½ to 6	3·87 to 4·08	Brookite
1·760–1·768 to 1·770–1·779	0·008 to 0·010	Negative	U	9	3·90 to 4·00	Corundum
1·78 to 1·81	—	—	I	6	3·90 to 4·10	Zircon (low type)
1·78 to 1·81	—	—	I	7½	3·95 to 4·20	Almandine garnet
1·625–1·635	0·010	Positive	B	3½	3·97 to 3·99	Celestine
1·662–1·712	0·050	Negative	B	5	3·97 to 4·07	Durangite
1·675–1·735	0·060	Positive	B	5	3·98 to 4·04	Legrandite
1·7					**4.0**	
1·704	—	—	—	—	—	*Iodonaphthalene*

Table 1—(*cont.*)

Refractive index	Birefrin-gence	Optic sign	Optical character	Hardness	Density	Name
1·70 approx.	—	—	—	5	4·00	Arandisite
1·70 approx.	—	—	—	5 to 5½	3·25	Smaragdite
1·70 (mean)	—	—	B	5 to 6	3·1 to 3·5	Chlorastrolite
1·700–1·706	0·006	Negative	B	6	3·09 to 3·12	Thulite (zoisite)
1·700–1·712	0·005	Neg/Pos	U	6½	3·32 to 3·47 3·25 to 3·32	Idocrase Californite
1·662–1·712	0·050	Negative	B	5	3·97 to 4·07	Durangite
1·64–1·69 to *1·66–1·71*	0·053	Positive	U	5	3·28 to 3·35	Dioptase
1·67–1·70	0·030	Positive	B	5½	3·29	Diopside
1·67–1·71	0·038	Negative	B	6½	3·47 to 3·49	Sinhalite
1·715–1·732	0·017	Negative	B	5 to 7 direc-tional	3·65 to 3·68	Kyanite
1·67–1·68 to *1·71–1·73*	0·010 to 0·020	Negative	B	5 to 6	3·4 to 3·5	Hypersthene
1·69–1·72	0·028	Positive	U	5½	3·89 to 4·18	Willemite
1·718–1·722	0·004	Negative	U	8	3·60 to 3·61	Taaffeite
1·714 to 1·736	—	—	I	8	3·58 to 3·64	Spinel
1·724 to 1·729	—	—	I	8	3·61 to 3·65	Synthetic spinel
1·72	—	—	I	7¼	3·36 to 3·55	Massive grossular garnet
1·72–1·73	0·010	Positive	B	6 to 6½	3·37	Clinozoisite
1·73	0·010	Positive	B	6	3·6 to 3·7	Rhodonite
1·675–1·735	0·060	Positive	B	5	3·98–4·04	Legrandite
1·738	—	—	I	6	3·59	Periclase (synthetic)
1·73 to 1·75	—	—	I	7¼	3·65 to 3·80	Pyrope garnet
1·73–1·84	0·110	Positive	B	3½ to 4	3·77 to 3·89	Azurite
1·739–1·750 to 1·747–1·762	0·011 to 0·015	Positive	B	7 to 7½	3·65 to 3·78	Staurolite
1·736–1·770	0·034	Negative	B	6½	3·25 to 3·50 usually 3·4	Epidote
1·74	—	—	—	—	3·32	*Methylene iodide*
1·74 (mean)	—	—	I	8	3·75 (mean)	Gahnospinel
1·74 to *1·81*	—	Neg/Pos	B	4	3·22	Scorodite
1·742 to 1·748	—	—	I	7¼	3·65	Hessonite garnet
1·75–1·76	—	Positive	B	8½	3·71 to 3·72	Chrysoberyl
1·75 to 1·78	0·008 to 0·010	—	I	7½	3·80 to 3·95	Almandine/ pyrope garnet
1·752–1·815	—	—	—	6	3·8	Shattuckite
1·757–1·804	0·047	Positive	U	6½	3·65 to 3·68	Benitoite
1·760–1·768 to 1·770–1·779	0·008 to 0·009	Negative	U	9	3·90 to 4·00	Corundum
1·77 to *1·80*	—	—	I	8	3·63 to 3·90	Spinel (Ceylonite)
1·78 to *1·81*	—	—	I	7½	3·95 to 4·20	Almandine garnet
1·787–1·816	0·029	Negative	U	7½	4·01	Painite
1·78 to *1·81*	—	—	I	6	3·90 to 4·10	Zircon (low type)
1·79	—	—	—	—	—	*Methylene iodide with sulphur*
1·79 to *1·81*	—	—	I	7¼	4·12 to 4·20	Spessartite garnet
2·583–2·705	0·122	Positive	B	5½ to 6	3·87 to 4·08	Brookite
2·368 to 2·371	—	—	I	3½ to 4	4·08 to 4·10	Zinc blende
1·68	—	—	—	—	4·15	*Clerici's solution*
2·1	—	—	I	5½	4·1 to 4·9	Chromite
2·21	—	—	B	5 to 6	4·1 to 6·2	Samarskite
2·62–2·90	0·287	Positive	U	6 to 6½	4·2	Rutile (natural and synthetic)

Refractive index	Birefrin-gence	Optic sign	Optical character	Hardness	Density	Name
—	—	—	—	$3\frac{1}{2}$ to 4	4·2 approx.	Chalcopyrite
1·532–1·680	0·148	Negative	B	$3\frac{1}{2}$	4·27 to 4·35	Witherite
1·62–1·85	0·23	Negative	U	5	4·30 to 4·35	Smithsonite
1·636–1·648	0·012	Positive	B	3	4·3 to 4·6	Barytes
1·95–1·99	0·020	Positive	B	$4\frac{1}{2}$	4·35	Bayldonite
—	—	—	—	7	4·35 approx	Psilomelane
1·80	—	—	—	$7\frac{1}{2}$ to 8	4·40	Gahnite
—	—	—	—	—	4·6	*Retger's salt*
1·83	—	—	—	$7\frac{1}{2}$	4·6	Yttrium alumin-ium garnet
2·21–2·30	0·090	—	—	6	4·64	Lithium niobate
1·925–1·984	0·059	Positive	U	7 to $7\frac{1}{2}$	4·67 to 4·70	Zircon (high type)
2·06 to 2·26	—	—	—	$6\frac{1}{2}$	4·7 to 5·0	Euxenite
—	—	—	—	6 to $6\frac{1}{2}$	4·85 to 4·90	Marcasite
—	—	—	—	3	4·9 to 5·4	Bornite
—	—	—	—	$6\frac{1}{2}$	4·95 to 5·10	Pyrites
2·94–3·22	—	—	U	$6\frac{1}{2}$	4·95 to 5·16	Hematite
1·8					**5·0**	
—	—	—	—	$3\frac{1}{2}$ to 4	5·0	Pentlandite
1·80	—	—	I	$7\frac{1}{2}$ to 8	4·40	Gahnite
1·77–1·80	—	—	I	8	3·63 to 3·90	Spinel (Ceylonite)
1·757–1·804	0·047	Positive	U	$6\frac{1}{2}$	3·65 to 3·68	Benitoite
1·804–2·078	0·274	Negative	B	3 to $3\frac{1}{2}$	6·46 to 6·57	Cerussite
1·81	—	—	—	—	—	*Methylene iodide with sulphur and tetraiodo-ethylene*
1·74 to 1·81	—	Neg/Pos	B	4	3·22	Scorodite
1·78 to 1·81	—	—	I	$7\frac{1}{2}$	3·95 to 4·20	Almandine garnet
1·752–1·815	—	—	—	6	3·8	Shattuckite
1·787–1·816	0·029	Negative	U	$7\frac{1}{2}$	4·01	Painite
1·79 to 1·81	—	—	I	$7\frac{1}{4}$	4·12 to 4·20	Spessartite garnet
1·79 to 1·81	—	—	I	6	3·90 to 4·10	Zircon (low type)
1·60–1·82	0·220	Negative	U	4	3·50 to 3·65	Rhodochrosite
1·83	—	—	—	$7\frac{1}{2}$	4·6	Yttrium alumin-ium garnet
1·73–1·84	0·110	Positive	B	$3\frac{1}{2}$ to 4	3·77 to 3·89	Azurite
1·85	—	—	—	—	—	*Phenyl di-iodo-arsine*
1·62–1·85	0·23	Negative	U	5	4·30 to 4·35	Smithsonite
1·87	—	—	I	$7\frac{1}{2}$	3·77	Uvarovite garnet
1·633–1·873	0·240	Negative	U	$3\frac{1}{2}$ to $4\frac{1}{2}$	3·83 to 3·88	Siderite
1·877–1·894	0·017	Positive	B	$2\frac{3}{4}$ to 3	6·30 to 6·39	Anglesite
1·88–1·99	0·105	Positive	B	$5\frac{1}{2}$	3·52 to 3·54	Sphene
1·89	—	—	I	$6\frac{1}{2}$	3·82 to 3·85	Demantoid garnet
2·41	—	—	I	6	5·13	Strontium titan-ate
—	—	—	—	3 to $3\frac{1}{2}$	5·3 to 5·65	Millerite
1·93	—	—	I	$5\frac{1}{2}$	5·5	Microlite
2·7 to 3·0	0·300	Negative	U	2 to $2\frac{1}{2}$	5·57 to 5·64	Proustite
2·013–2·029	0·016	Positive	U	4 to $4\frac{1}{2}$	5·66	Zincite
2·85	—	—	I	$3\frac{1}{2}$ to 4	5·86 to 6·15	Cuprite
1·918–1·934	0·016	Positive	U	$4\frac{1}{2}$ to 5	5·9 to 6·1	Scheelite
2·31–2·66	0·35	Positive	B	$2\frac{1}{2}$ to 3	5·9 to 6·1	Crocoite
1·9					**6·0**	
1·91–2·05	0·135	Positive	B	$5\frac{1}{2}$	3·52 to 3·54	Sphene
1·65–1·90	0·25	Negative	B	4	3·74 to 3·95 usually 3·8	Malachite

Table 1—(*cont.*)

Refractive index	Birefrin-gence	Optic sign	Optical character	Hardness	Density	Name
1·918–1·934	0·016	Positive	U	4½ to 5	*5·9 to 6·1*	Scheelite
1·925–1·984	0·059	Positive	U	7 to 7½	*4·67 to 4·70*	Zircon (high type)
1·93	—	—	I	5½	*5·5*	Microlite
1·95–1·99	0·020	Positive	B	4½	*4·35*	Bayldonite
2·85	—	—	I	3½ to 4	*5·86 to 6·15*	Cuprite
2·36–2·66	0·35	Positive	B	2½ to 3	*5·9 to 6·1*	Crocoite
—	—	—	I	5½	*6·0 to 6·3*	Cobaltite
2·114–2·140	0·026	Positive	U	3	*6·2*	Phosgenite
2·21	—	—	B	5 to 6	*4·1 to 6·2*	Samarskite
1·877–1·894	0·017	Positive	B	2¾ to 3	*6·30 to 6·39*	Anglesite
1·804–2·078	0·274	Negative	B	3 to 3½	*6·45 to 6·57*	Cerussite
2·304–2·402	0·098	Negative	U	2¾ to 3	*6·7 to 7*	Wulfenite
2·003–2·101	0·098	Positive	U	6½	*6·8 to 7*	Cassiterite

2·0 and over   7·0

Refractive index	Birefrin-gence	Optic sign	Optical character	Hardness	Density	Name
2·003–2·101	0·098	Positive	U	6½	*6·95*	Cassiterite
2·013–2·029	0·016	Positive	U	4 to 4½	*5·66*	Zincite
1·915–2·050	0·135	Positive	B	5½	*3·52 to 3·54*	Sphene
2·05	—	—	—			*West's solution*
1·804–2·078	0·274	Negative	B	3 to 3½	*6·45 to 6·57*	Cerussite
2·06 to 2·26	—	—	—	6½	*4·7 to 5·0*	Euxenite
2·1	—	—	I	5½	*4·1 to 4·9*	Chromite
2·114–2·140	0·026	Positive	U	3	*6·2*	Phosgenite
2·120–2·135	0·015	Negative	U	3½	*7·0 to 7·25*	Mimetite
2·21	—	—	B	5 to 6	*4·1 to 6·2*	Samarskite
2·21–2·30	0·090	—	—	6	*4·64*	Lithium niobate
2·304–2·402	0·098	Negative	U	2½ to 3	*6·7 to 7*	Wulfenite
2·31–2·66	0·35	Positive	B	2½ to 3	*5·9 to 6·1*	Crocoite
2·39–2·46	0·07	Positive	B	5½ to 6	*7·46*	Stibiotantalite
2·368–2·371	—	—	I	3½ to 4	*4·08 to 4·10*	Zinc blende
—	—	—	—	4½ to 5	*7·54*	Breithauptite
2·41	—	—	I	6	*5·13*	Strontium titanate
2·42	—	—	I	10	*3·52*	Diamond
2·493–2·554	0·061	Negative	U	5½ to 6	*3·82 to 3·95*	Anatase
2·583–2·705	0·122	Positive	B	5½ to 6	*3·87 to 4·08*	Brookite
2·62–2·90	0·287	Positive	U	6 to 6½	*4·2*	Rutile
2·65–2·69	0·043	Positive	U	9¼	*3·17*	Carborundum
2·7–3·0	0·30	Negative	U	2 to 2½	*5·57 to 5·64*	Proustite
2·85	—	—	I	3½ to 4	*5·85 to 6·15*	Cuprite
2·94–3·22	—	—	U	6½	*4·95 to 5·16*	Hematite
—	—	—	U	5 to 5½	*7·33 to 7·67*	Niccolite
—	—	—	—	3½	*7·2 to 7·9*	Domeykite
—	—	—	—	3½	*8·38*	Algodonite

The optical properties of gem materials are explained by the following short table

TABLE OF OPTICAL PROPERTIES

Single refracting or isotropic	{ Amorphous substances and cubic crystals } one index of refraction, n

| Doubly refracting or anisotropic | Hexagonal, Trigonal, Tetragonal } Uniaxial { two indices of refraction, ω and ϵ; positive, ω less than ϵ; negative, ϵ less than ω |
| | Rhombic, Monoclinic, Triclinic } Biaxial { three indices of refraction, α, β and γ; positive, $\alpha\beta$—γ; negative, α—$\beta\gamma$ |

When the intermediate index of refraction β is nearer to α = positive, when nearer to γ = negative

TABLE 2

REFRACTIVE INDICES

Water	1·334	Scapolite	1·55–1·56
Alcohol	1·36	*Nitrobenzene*	1·55
Amyl acetate	1·37	*Bromotoluene*	1·55
Cellosolve	1·408	Tortoise-shell	1·54
Fluorspar	1·434	Beryllonite	1·553–1·562
Opal	1·44 to 1·46	Hambergite	1·553–1·625
Petroleum	1·45	Casein	1·55 to 1·56
Chloroform	1·45	Pyrophyllite	1·56–1·60
Silica glass	1·46	*Dimethylaniline*	1·56
Glycerol	1·47	*Bromobenzene*	1·56
Turpentine	1·47	*Benzyl benzoate*	1·56
Olive oil	1·47	Deerhorn	1·56
Castor oil	1·47	Variscite	1·56 (mean)
Sodalite	1·48	Bowenite serpentine	1·56
Analcite	1·487	Labradorite feldspar	1·56–1·57
Natrolite	1·480–1·493	Synthetic emerald	1·560–1·563
Moldavite	1·48 to 1·50	*Orthotoluidine*	1·57
Obsidian	1·48 to 1·51	Pseudophite	1·57
Calcite	1·486–1·658	Williamsite serpentine	1·57
Toluene	1·49	Ophicalcite	1·57 (mean)
Xylene	1·49	Bastite	1·57–1·58
Celluloid	1·495 to 1·505	Bytownite feldspar	1·57–1·58
Tektites	1·49 to 1·53	Natural emerald	1·57–1·58
Whewellite	1·49–1·605	Aquamarine	1·57 to 1·60
Hauynite	1·496	Anhydrite	1·571–1·614
Benzene	1·50	Augelite	1·574–1·588
Chrysocolla	1·50 (mean)	Odontolite	1·57 to 1·63
Lapis lazuli	1·50 (mean)	*Aniline*	1·58
Perspex	1·50	Verdite	1·58 (mean)
Mesolite	1·50	Colemanite	1·586–1·614
Petalite	1·504–1·516	*Bromoform*	1·59
Cedar wood oil	1·51	*Cinnamon oil*	1·59
Ulexite	1·51 (mean)	Howlite	1·59 (mean)
Leucite	1·51	Polystyrene	1·59
Cancrinite	1·51 (mean)	Wardite	1·595 (mean)
Magnesite	1·515–1·717	Melinophane	1·593–1·612
Pollucite	1·517–1·525	Pectolite	1·595–1·633
Gypsum	1·52–1·53	Phosphophyllite	1·595–1·616
Orthoclase feldspar	1·52–1·53	*Cassia oil*	1·60
Microcline feldspar	1·52–1·53	Ekanite	1·60
Thomsonite	1·52–1·54	Chondrodite	1·60 (mean)
Stichtite	1·52–1·55	Brazilianite	1·603–1·623
Canada balsam	1·53	Tremolite	1·60–1·62
Monochlorbenzene	1·53	Vulcanite	1·60 to 1·63
Chalcedony	1·530–1·539	Rhodochrosite	1·600–1·820
Iolite	1·53–1·54	Nephrite	1·61 (mean)
Lepidolite	1·530–1·556	Herderite	1·61 (mean)
Meerschaum	1·53	Topaz (white and blue)	1·610–1·620
Witherite	1·532–1·680	Prehnite	1·61–1·64
Apophyllite	1·535–1·537	Wollastonite	1·616–1·631
Ethylene dibromide	1·54	Turquoise	1·61–1·65
Bone	1·54	Amblygonite	1·611–1·637
Vegetable ivory	1·54	Lazulite	1·615–1·645
Clove oil	1·54	Bakelite	1·61 to 1·66
Ivory (dentine)	1·54	*Iodobenzene*	1·62
Amber	1·54	Tourmaline	1·62–1·64 (mean)
Copal resin	1·54	Celestine	1·625–1·635
Jasper	1·54	Datolite	1·625–1·669
Albite feldspar	1·54 (mean)	Smithsonite	1·62–1·85
Soapstone	1·54 approx.	*Carbon disulphide*	1·63
Oligoclase feldspar	1·542–1·549	*Monochlornaphthalene*	1·63
Quartz	1·544–1·553	*Acetylene tetrabromide*	1·63

24*

Table 2—(*cont.*)

Danburite	1·630–1·636	Staurolite	1·74–1·75 (mean)
Topaz (brown and		Scorodite	1·74 to 1·81
pink)	1·630–1·638	Chrysoberyl	1·75–1·76
Apatite	1·63–1·64	Almandine/pyrope	
Friedelite	1·63–1·66	garnet	1·75 to 1·78
Barytes	1·636–1·648	Shattuckite	1·75 to 1·81
Jet	1·64 to 1·68	Benitoite	1·757–1·804
Andalusite	1·64–1·65 (mean)	Corundum	1·76–1·77
Siderite	1·633–1·873	Ceylonite spinel	1·77 to 1·80
Euclase	1·652–1·672	Almandine garnet	1·78 to 1·81
Phenakite	1·654–1·670	Painite	1·787–1·816
Peridot	1·654–1·689	Zircon (low type)	1·78 to 1·81
Fibrolite	1·658–1·678	*Methylene iodide with*	
Malachite	1·65–1·90	*sulphur*	1·79
Monobromonaphthalene	1·66	Spessartite garnet	1·79 to 1·81
Jadeite	1·66	Gahnite	1·80
Boracite	1·66 to 1·67	Cerussite	1·804–2·078
Spodumene	1·660–1·675	*Methylene iodide with*	
Durangite	1·662–1·712	*sulphur and*	
Dioptase	1·66–1·70 (mean)	*tetraiodoethylene*	1·81
Enstatite	1·663–1·673	Yttrium al. garnet	1·83
Kornerupine	1·670–1·685	*Phenyl di-iodoarsine*	1·85
	(mean)	Uvarovite garnet	1·87
Diopside	1·67–1·70	Anglesite	1·877–1·94
Sinhalite	1·67–1·71	Demantoid garnet	1·89
Axinite	1·675–1·685	Sphene	1·9 to 2·0
Legrandite	1·675–1·735	Scheelite	1·918–1·934
Dumortierite	1·68 (mean)	Zircon (high type)	1·925–1·984
Rhodizite	1·69	Microlite	1·93
Willemite	1·69–1·72	Bayldonite	1·95–1·99
Zoisite	1·692–1·700	Cassiterite	2·003–2·101
Arandisite	1·70 (mean)	Zincite	2·013–2·029
Iodonaphthalene	1·70	*West's solution*	2·05
Smaragdite	1·70 (approx.)	Euxenite	2·06 to 2·26
Chlorastrolite	1·70 (mean)	Chromite	2·1
Thulite	1·70	Phosgenite	2·114–2·140
Hypersthene	1·70–1·71 (mean)	Mimetite	2·120–2·135
Idocrase	1·700–1·712	Samarskite	2·21
Spinel	1·714 to 1·736	Lithium niobate	2·21–2·30
Kyanite	1·715–1·732	Wulfenite	2·304–2·402
Taaffeite	1·718–1·722	Crocoite	2·31–2·66
Hydrogrossular garnet	1·72	Stibiotantalite	2·39–2·46
Synthetic spinel	1·724 to 1·729	Zinc blende	2·368–2·371
Clinozoisite	1·72–1·73	Strontium titanate	2·41
Periclase (synthetic)	1·738	Diamond	2·42
Rhodonite	1·73	Anatase	2·493–2·554
Pyrope garnet	1·73 to 1·75	Brookite	2·583–2·705
Azurite	1·73–1·84	Rutile	2·62–2·90
Epidote	1·736–1·770	Carborundum	2·65–2·69
Methylene iodide	1·74	Proustite	2·7–3·0
Gahnospinel	1·74 (mean)	Cuprite	2·85
Hessonite garnet	1·742 to 1·748	Hematite	2·94–3·22

TABLE 3

SPECIFIC GRAVITIES

Meerschaum	1·00 to 2·00	Perspex	1·18 to 1·19
Amber	1·03 to 1·10	Jet	1·20 to 1·30
Copal resin	1·03 to 1·10	Bakelite	1·25 to 1·30
Polystyrene	1·05	Tortoise-shell	1·26 to 1·35
Benzyl benzoate	1·12	Cellulose acetate	1·29 to 1·40
Vulcanite	1·15 to 1·20	Casein	1·32 to 1·34

Table 3—(*cont.*)

Celluloid	1·36 to 1·42	Bytownite feldspar	2·73
Vegetable ivory	1·38 to 1·42	Pectolite	2·77 to 2·88
Monobromonaphthalene	1·49	Pyrophyllite	2·8
Deer horn	1·60 to 1·85	Mollusc shell	2·8
Ivory (dentine)	1·70 to 1·98	Beryllonite	2·80 to 2·85
Opal	1·98 to 2·20	Lepidolite	2·8 to 2·9
Ulexite	1·99	Wollastonite	2·8 to 2·9
Bone	2·00	Verdite	2·80 to 2·99
Chrysocolla	2·00 to 2·45	Wardite	2·81
Stichtite	2·15 to 2·22	Conch shell	2·84 to 2·89
Ethylene dibromide	2·19	Pollucite	2·85 to 2·94
Natrolite	2·20 to 2·25	Unakite	2·85 to 3·20
Analcite	2·20 to 2·29	*Bromoform*	2·86
Black clam pearls	2·20 to 2·66	Prehnite	2·88 to 2·94
Silica glass	2·21	Datolite	2·90 to 3·00
Whewellite	2·23	Nephrite	2·90 to 3·02
Sodalite	2·25 to 2·30	*Tetrabromethane*	2·95
Mesolite	2·29	Phenacite	2·95 to 2·97
Porcelain	2·30	Boracite	2·96
Albaster	2·30 to 2·33	Tremolite	2·98
Thomsonite	2·3 to 2·4	Brazilianite	2·980 to 2·995
Apophyllite	2·3 to 2·5		
Obsidian	2·33 to 2·42	Melinophane	3·00
Moldavite	2·34 to 2·39	Herderite	3·00
Hambergite	2·35	Danburite	3·00
Tektites	2·36 to 2·51	Odontolite	3·00 to 3·10
Petalite	2·39 to 2·46	Tourmaline	3·00 to 3·12
Hauynite	2·4	Saussurite	3·00 to 3·4
Blue pearls	2·40 to 2·65	Amblygonite	3·01 to 3·03
Variscite	2·40 to 2·60	Friedelite	3·05 to 3·07
Colemanite	2·42	Thulite	3·09 to 3·12
Cancrinite	2·42 to 2·50	Phosphophyllite	3·1
Leucite	2·45 to 2·50	Lazulite	3·1
Rhyolite (Nevada wonderstone)	2·5 (about)	Euclase	3·10
		Chondrodite	3·1 to 3·2
Marble	2·5 to 2·6	Chlorastrolite	3·1 to 3·5
Bastite	2·5 to 2·7	Andalusite	3·15 to 3·17
Yellow orthoclase feldspar	2·56	Carborundum	3·17
Microcline feldspar	2·56 to 2·58	Spodumene	3·17 to 3·19
Moonstone feldspar	2·56 to 2·59	Apatite	3·17 to 3·23
Iolite	2·57 to 2·66	Fluorspar	3·18
Howlite	2·58	Scorodite	3·22
Chalcedony	2·58 to 2·62	Diopside	3·23 to 3·29
Bowenite serpentine	2·58 to 2·62	Fibrolite	3·25
Jasper	2·58 to 2·91	Smaragdite	3·25
Coral	2·6 to 2·7	Californite	3·25 to 3·32
Pinite	2·60 to 2·85	Epidote	3·25 to 3·50
Pseudophite	2·60 to 2·85	Enstatite	3·26 to 3·28
Turquoise	2·60 to 2·85	Dumortierite	3·26 to 3·41
Williamsite serpentine	2·61	Axinite	3·27 to 3·29
Albite feldspar	2·62	*Klein's solution*	3·28
Oligoclase feldspar	2·62 to 2·65	Ekanite	3·28
Scapolite	2·63 to 2·71	Dioptase	3·28 to 3·35
Quartz	2·65	Kornerupine	3·28 to 3·35
Synthetic emerald	2·66	Jadeite	3·30 to 3·36
Pearl	2·67 to 2·78	*Methylene iodide*	3·32
Labradorite feldspar	2·68 to 2·69	Idocrase	3·32 to 3·47
Beryl	2·68 to 2·90	Peridot	3·34
Natural emerald	2·69 to 2·76	Zoisite	3·35
Augelite	2·7	Hydrogrossular garnet	3·36 to 3·55
Ophicalcite	2·7	Clinozoisite	3·37
Lepidolite	2·7 to 2·8	Rhodizite	3·4
Lapis lazuli	2·70 to 2·90	Rhodonite	3·40 to 3·70
Calcite	2·71	Hypersthene	3·4 to 3·5

Table 3—(cont.)

Sinhalite	3·47 to 3·48	*Clerici's solution*	4·15
Rhodochrosite	3·50 to 3·65	Rutile	4·2
Diamond	3·52	Chalcopyrite	4·2
Sphene	3·52 to 3·54	Witherite	4·27 to 4·35
Topaz	3·53 to 3·56	Smithsonite	4·30 to 4·35
Rohrbach's solution	3·58	Barytes	4·3 to 4·6
Spinel (natural)	3·58 to 3·61	Bayldonite	4·35
Periclase	3·59	Psilomelane	4·35
Taaffeite	3·60 to 3·61	Gahnite	4·40
Spinel (synthetic)	3·61 to 3·65	*Retger's salt*	4·6
Ceylonite	3·63 to 3·90	Yttrium al. garnet	4·6
Hessonite garnet	3·65	Lithium niobate	4·64
Benitoite	3·65 to 3·68	Zircon (high type)	4·67 to 4·70
Kyanite	3·65 to 3·68	Euxenite	4·7 to 5·0
Pyrope garnet	3·65 to 3·70	Marcasite	4·85 to 4·90
Staurolite	3·65 to 3·78	Bornite	4·9 to 5·4
Almandine/pyrope garnets	3·70 to 3·95	Pyrites	4·95 to 5·10
Chrysoberyl	3·71 to 3·72	Hematite	4·95 to 5·16
Malachite	3·74 to 3·95	Pentlandite	5·0
Gahnospinel	3·75	Strontium titanate	
Uvarovite garnet	3·77	(Fabulite)	5·13
Azurite	3·77 to 3·89	Millerite	5·3 to 5·65
Shattuckite	3·8	Microlite	5·5
Demantoid garnet	3·82 to 3·85	Proustite	5·57 to 5·64
Anatase	3·82 to 3·95	Zincite	5·66
Siderite	3·83 to 3·88	Cuprite	5·85 to 6·15
Brookite	3·87 to 4·08	Crocoite	5·9 to 6·1
Willemite	3·89 to 4·18	Cobaltite	6·0 to 6·3
Corundum	3·90 to 4·00	Phosgenite	6·2
Zircon (low type)	3·90 to 4·10	Anglesite	6·30 to 6·39
Almandine garnet	3·95 to 4·20	Cerussite	6·45 to 6·57
Celestine	3·97 to 3·99	Wulfenite	6·7 to 7·0
Durangite	3·97 to 4·07	Cassiterite	6·8 to 7·0
Legrandite	3·98 to 4·04	Mimetite	7·0 to 7·25
Painite	4·01	Domeykite	7·2 to 7·9
Zinc blende (sphalerite)	4·08 to 4·10	Niccolite	7·33 to 7·67
Chromite	4·1 to 4·9	Stibiotantalite	7·46
Samarskite	4·1 to 6·2	Breithauptite	7·54
Spessartite garnet	4·12 to 4·20	Algodonite	8·00 to 8·39

TABLE 4

COLOUR DISPERSIONS OF GEMSTONES

Rutile	0·28	Spessartite garnet	0·027
Anatase	0·213†	Willemite	0·027
	0·259‡	Almandine garnet	0·027
Siderite	0·240	Staurolite	0·023
Strontium titanate	0·19	Pyrope garnet	0·022
Zinc blende	0·156	Kyanite	0·020
Lithium niobate	0·13	Spinel (natural and synthetic)	0·020
Cassiterite	0·071	Peridot	0·020
Demantoid garnet	0·057	Taaffeite	0·019
Sphene	0·051	Idocrase	0·019
Anglesite	0·044	Sinhalite	0·018
Diamond	0·044	Kornerupine	0·018
Benitoite	0·044	Corundum	0·018
Flint glass	0·041*	Scapolite	0·017
Zircon	0·039	Iolite	0·017
Dioptase	0·028†	Spodumene	0·017
	0·036‡	Tourmaline	0·017
Epidote	0·030	Danburite	0·017
Hessonite garnet	0·027	Crown glass	0·016*

Table 4—*(cont.)*

Datolite	0·016	Quartz	0·013
Euclase	0·016	Apatite	0·013
Andalusite	0·016	Feldspar	0·012
Fibrolite	0·015	Pollucite	0·012
Chrysoberyl	0·015	Beryllonite	0·010
Phenacite	0·015	Cancrinite	0·010
Hambergite	0·015	Leucite	0·010
Smithsonite	0·014†	Silica glass	0·010
	0·031‡	Calcite	0·008‡
Topaz	0·014		0·017†
Brazilianite	0·014	Fluorite	0·007
Beryl	0·014		

* These are mean values for glasses of these two types. The dispersion of glasses can vary considerably
† Ordinary ray.   ‡ Extraordinary ray

The values given in Table 4 are the differences between the refractive indices of the stones for the Fraunhofer B line, a red ray at 6870 Å, and the G line, a blue ray at 4308 Å. Except where stated the values given are for the ordinary ray in uniaxial stones and the *alpha* direction in biaxial stones, for as indicated, the dispersion is in some cases considerably different for the different rays in doubly refractive stones.

TABLE 5

HARDNESS

Mohs's scale	
1 Talc	6 Orthoclase feldspar
2 Gypsum	7 Rock crystal
3 Calcite	8 Topaz
4 Fluorspar	9 Corundum
5 Apatite	10 Diamond

Finger nail is about 2½, Copper coin is about 3, Window glass is about 5½, Knife blade is about 6, Steel file is about 6½

Gemstones in the order of their hardness according to Mohs's scale

10	{ Diamond { Borazon (?)*		{ Almandine garnet Andalusite Beryl
9½	Boron carbide*	7½	{ Euclase Fibrolite
9¼ 9	Carborundum* Corundum		Hambergite Painite { Uvarovite garnet
8½	Chrysoberyl		{ Hessonite garnet
		7¼	Pyrope garnet
8	{ Rhodizite Spinel Taaffeite Topaz		{ Rhodolite garnet Spessartite garnet
		7 to 7½	{ Iolite Staurolite
7½ to 8	{ Gahnite Phenacite		{ Tourmaline Zircon

* Synthetically produced abrasives

Table 5—(cont.)

Gemstones in the order of their hardness according to Mohs's scale

7	Axinite Boracite Danburite Dumortierite Jadeite Quartz Spodumene	5½	Brazilianite Chromite Cobaltite Diopside Enstatite Lazulite Lazurite (lapis-lazuli) Microlite Moldavite Natrolite Smaltite Sphene Willemite
6½	Benitoite Cassiterite Chalcedony Chondrodite Demantoid garnet Epidote Euxenite Hematite Idocrase Kornerupine Nephrite Peridot Pollucite Sinhalite Zircon (low type)	5 to 7	Kyanite (varies with direction)
		5 to 6	Chlorastrolite Glass (normally) Hypersthene Samarskite
		5 to 5½	Analcite Datolite Niccolite Thomsonite
6 to 6½	Ekanite Marcasite Microcline feldspar Petalite Plagioclase feldspar Pyrites Rutile	5	Apatite Augelite Beryllonite Dioptase Durangite Herderite Legrandite Mesolite Obsidian Odontolite Pectolite Smithsonite Variscite Wardite
6	Amblygonite Cancrinite Columbite Lithium niobate Orthoclase feldspar Periclase Prehnite Rhodonite Scapolite Silica glass Strontium titanate Zoisite	4½ to 5	Apophyllite Breithauptite Scheelite Wollastonite
5½ to 6½	Hauynite Opal Psilomelane	4½	Bayldonite Colemanite Pseudomalachite
		4 to 5	Bowenite serpentine Friedelite
5½ to 6	Anatase Brookite Leucite Melinophane Sodalite Stibiotantalite Tremolite Turquoise	4 to 4½	Zincite
		4	Cuprite Fluorite Malachite Rhodochrosite Scorodite

Table 5—(*cont.*)

3½ to 4	⎰ Algodonite Azurite Bastite Chalcopyrite Domeykite Magnesite Marble Pentlandite Siderite Zinc blende	2½ to 3½	Pearl
		2½ to 3	⎰ Crocoite Wulfenite
3½	Celestine Cerussite Coral Howlite Lepidolite Millerite Mimetite Phosphophyllite Witherite	2½	Albertite Ivory Proustite Pseudophite Stichtite Tortoise-shell Vegetable ivory Whewellite
		2 to 4	Chrysocolla
3	Anglesite Anhydrite Barite Bornite Phosgenite Verdite	2 to 3	⎰ Bone Plastics
		2 to 2½	Amber Meerschaum Alabaster (gypsum)
		1½ to 2	Gedanite Pyrophyllite Soapstone
2½ to 4	⎰ Jet Serpentine	1	Ulexite

TABLE 6

GEMSTONES IN ORDER OF THEIR CRYSTAL SYSTEMS

Cubic	Tetragonal—(cont.)	Trigonal
Analcite	Apophyllite	Benitoite
Boracite	Cassiterite	Calcite (marble)
Bornite	Chalcopyrite	Corundum
Chromite	Idocrase	Dioptase
Cobaltite	Melinophane	Friedelite
Cuprite	Phosgenite	Hematite
Diamond	Rutile	Magnesite
Fluorite	Scapolite	Millerite
Gahnite	Scheelite	Phenacite
Garnet	Wardite (?)	Proustite
Hauynite	Wulfenite	Quartz
Lazurite (lapis-lazuli)	Zircon	Rhodochrosite
Leucite		Siderite
Microlite		Smithsonite
Pentlandite		Stichtite
Pollucite	*Hexagonal*	Tourmaline
Pyrites	Algodonite	Willemite
Rhodizite	Apatite	
Smaltite	Beryl	
Sodalite	Breithauptite	*Orthorhombic*
Spinel	Cancrinite	Andalusite
Strontium titanate	Mimetite	Anglesite
Zinc blende	Niccolite	Aragonite
	Painite	Barite
Tetragonal	Taaffeite	Bronzite
Anatase	Zincite	Brookite

Table 6—*(cont.)*

Orthorhombic—(cont.)	*Monoclinic—(cont.)*	*Monoclinic—(cont.)*
Celestine	Azurite	Tremolite
Cerussite	Bayldonite (?)	Ulexite
Chlorastrolite	Beryllonite	Whewellite
Chrysoberyl	Brazilianite	Wollastonite
Columbite	Chondrodite	
Danburite	Colemanite	*Triclinic*
Dumortierite	Crocoite	
Enstatite	Datolite	Amblygonite
Fibrolite	Diopside	Axinite
Hambergite	Durangite	Kyanite
Hypersthene	Epidote	Microcline feldspar
Iolite	Euclase	Plagioclase feldspar
Kornerupine	Gypsum	Rhodonite
Marcasite	Herderite	Turquoise
Natrolite	Howlite (?)	
Peridot	Jadeite	
Prehnite	Lazulite	*Amorphous*
Pyrophyllite	Legrandite	Amber
Samarskite	Lepidolite	Billitonite
Scorodite	Malachite	Chrysocolla (?)
Sinhalite	Meerschaum (?)	Copal resin
Staurolite	Mesolite	Ekanite
Stibiotantalite	Nephrite	Glass
Thomsonite	Orthoclase feldspar	Ivory
Topaz	Pectolite	Jet
Variscite	Petalite	Moldavite
Witherite	Phosphophyllite	Obsidian
Zoisite	Pseudomalachite	Odontolite (?)
	Serpentine	Opal
	Shattuckite	Plastics
Monoclinic	Sphene	Silica glass
Anhydrite	Spodumene	Tortoise-shell
Augelite	Talc (soapstone)	Vegetable ivory

TABLE 7

GEM MATERIALS ACCORDING TO COLOUR

Colourless	*Colourless—(cont.)*
Amblygonite (Tr)	Magnesite (Tr)
Analcite (Tr)	Petalite (Tr)
Anglesite (Tr)	Phenacite (Tr)
Apatite (Tr)	Pollucite (Tr)
Apophyllite (Tr)	Quartz (Tr)
Augelite (Tr)	Rutile (synthetic) (Tr)
Barite (Tr)	Spinel (synthetic) (Tr)
Beryl (Tr)	Spodumene (Tr)
Beryllonite (Tr)	Strontium titanate (Tr)
Celestine (Tr)	Topaz (Tr)
Chrysoberyl (Tr)	Tourmaline (Tr)
Colemanite (Tr)	Whewellite (Tr)
Corundum (Tr)	Zircon (Tr)
Danburite (Tr)	
Datolite (Tr)	*Yellow and orange*
Diamond (Tr)	Amber (Tr and Tl)
Diopside (Tr)	Amblygonite (Tr)
Euclase (Tr)	Anglesite (Tr)
Feldspar var; orthoclase (Tr)	Apatite (Tr)
Fluorspar (Tr)	Axinite (Tr)
Hambergite (Tr)	Barite (Tr)
Leucite (Tr)	Beryl (Tr)
Lithium niobate (Tr)	Beryllonite (Tr)

Table 7—(cont.)

Yellow and orange—(cont.)

Brazilianite (Tr)
Cancrinite (Tl to Op)
Cassiterite (Tr)
Chalcedony (Tl to Op)
Chrondrodite (Tr)
Chrysoberyl (Tr)
Copal resin (Tr)
Corundum (Tr)
Danburite (Tr)
Datolite (Tl to Op)
Diamond (Tr)
Feldspar var; orthoclase (Tr), var; sunstone (Tr to Tl)
Fluorspar (Tr to Tl)
Garnet vars; hessonite, spessartite and topazolite (Tr)
Idocrase (Tr)
Jadeite (Tl)
Legrandite (Tr)
Marble (Tl to Op)
Melinophane (Tr)
Millerite (Tl)
Mimetite (Tl)
Opal var; fire opal (Tr to Tl)
Ophicalcite (Tl to OP)
Phenacite (Tr)
Phosgenite (Tl)
Quartz (Tr)
Rutile (synthetic) (Tr)
Scapolite (Tr)
Scheelite (Tr to Tl)
Silica glass (Tr)
Sinhalite (Tr)
Smithsonite (Op)
Soapstone (Op)
Sphene (Tr)
Spinel (Tr)
Spodumene (Tr)
Staurolite (Op)
Stibiotantalite (Tr)
Thomsonite (Op)
Topaz (Tr)
Tourmaline (Tr)
Willemite (Tr)
Wulfenite (Tr to Tl)
Zinc blende (Tr)
Zircon (Tr)

Brown

Amber (Tr to Tl)
Anatase (Tr)
Andalusite (Tr)
Axinite (Tr)
Barite (Tr to Op)
Beryl (Tr)
Brookite (Tl)
Cassiterite (Tr)
Chalcedony (Tl to Op)
Chondrondite (Tr to Tl)
Chrysoberyl (Tr)
Corundum (Tr)
Datolite (Tl to Op)
Diamond (Tr)

Brown—(cont.)

Epidote (Tr)
Fibrolite (Op)
Fluorspar (Tr)
Garnet var; hessonite and spessartite (Tr)
Hypersthene (Tl to Op)
Idocrase (Tr)
Jadeite (Tl to Op)
Kornerupine (Tr)
Marble (Op)
Microlite (Tr to Tl)
Moldavite (Tr)
Obsidian (Tr to Tl)
Peridot (Tr)
Prehnite (Tl)
Quartz (Tr)
Rhodochrosite (Tl to Op)
Rutile (synthetic) (Tr)
Scheelite (Tr)
Serpentine (Op)
Siderite (Tl)
Sinhalite (Tr)
Soapstone (Op)
Sphene (Tr)
Staurolite (Op)
Stibiotantalite (Tr)
Thomsonite (Op)
Topaz (Tr)
Tourmaline (Tr)
Willemite (Tr)
Zinc blende (Tr)
Zircon (Tr)

Red and pink

Amber (Tr to Tl)
Andalusite (Tr)
Barite (Tr)
Beryl (Tr)
Cassiterite (Tr)
Chalcedony (Tl to Op)
Chrondrodite (Tr to Tl)
Coral (Tl to Op)
Corundum (Tr)
Crocoite (Tr to Tl)
Cuprite (Tr)
Danburite (Tr)
Datolite (Tl to Op)
Diamond (Tr)
Durangite (Tr to Tl)
Fluorspar (Tr)
Friedelite (Tr to Tl)
Garnet var; pyrope and almandine (Tr)
Jadeite (Tl to Op)
Marble (Op)
Microlite (Tr to Tl)
Opal (fire opal) (Tr to Tl)
Painite (Tr)
Pearl (Tl to Op)
Phenakite (Tr)
Quartz var; rose quartz (Tr to Tl)
Rhodizite (Tr)
Rhodochrosite (Tl to Op)
Rhodonite (Tl to Op)
Rutile (Tr)

Table 7—(cont.)

Red and pink—(cont.)
Scapolite (Tr to Tl)
Smithsonite (Tl)
Spinel (Tr)
Spodumene (Tr)
Staurolite (Op)
Stichtite (Op)
Thomsonite (Op)
Thulite (Op)
Topaz (Tr)
Tourmaline (Tr)
Tremolite (Tr)
Wulfenite (Tl)
Zincite (Tr)
Zircon (Tr)
Zoisite (Tl to Op)

Purple and violet
Apatite (Tr)
Axinite (Tr)
Beryl (Tr)
Corundum (Tr)
Diopside var; violane (Op)
Dumortierite (Op)
Fibrolite (Tr)
Fluorspar (Tr to Tl)
Garnet var; almandine and rhodolite (Tr)
Jadeite (Tl)
Lepidolite (Op)
Marble (Op)
Quartz (Tr to Tl)
Scapolite (Tr to Tl)
Spinel (Tr)
Spodumene (Tr)
Stichtite (Op)
Taaffeite (Tr)
Tourmaline (Tr)
Zircon (Tr)

Blue
Anhydrite (Tr to Tl)
Apatite (Tr to Tl)
Anatase (Tr to Tl)
Anglesite (Tr)
Azurite (Op)
Barite (Tr to Tl)
Benitoite (Tr)
Beryl (Tr)
Celestine (Tr)
Cerussite (Tl)
Chalcedony (Tl to Op)
Chrysocolla (Tl to Op)
Corundum (Tr)
Diamond (Tr)
Diopside var; violane (Op)
Dumortierite (Op)
Euclase (Tr)
Fibrolite (Tr)
Fluorspar (Tr)
Hauynite (Tl to Op)
Idocrase var; cyprine (Tl to Op)
Iolite (Tr)
Jadeite (Tl to Op)
Kyanite (Tr)
Lapis-lazuli (Op)

Blue—(cont.)
Lazulite (Op)
Odontolite (Op)
Pearl (Op)
Quartz var; crocidolite (Op)
Rutile (synthetic) (Tr)
Scapolite (Tr to Tl)
Scorodite (Tr to Tl)
Shattuckite (Op)
Smithsonite (Tl to Op)
Sodalite (Op)
Spinel (Tr)
Topaz (Tr)
Tourmaline (Tr)
Turquoise (Op)
Wardite (Op)
Zircon (Tr)
Zoisite (Tr)

Green
Andalusite (Tr)
Anglesite (Tr)
Apatite (Tr)
Bayldonite (Tl to Op)
Bastite (Op)
Beryl (Tr)
Boracite (Tr)
Cerussite (Tl)
Chalcedony (Tl to Op)
Chlorastrolite (Op)
Chrysoberyl (Tr)
Chrysocolla (Tl to Op)
Corundum (Tr)
Datolite (Tr to Op)
Diamond (Tr)
Diopside (Tr)
Dioptase (Tr to Tl)
Ekanite (Tl)
Enstatite (Tr)
Epidote (Tr)
Euclase (Tr)
Feldspar var; microcline (Tl to Op)
Fibrolite (Tr)
Fluorspar (Tr to Tl)
Gahnite (Tr)
Garnet var; demantoid and uvarovite (Tr)
Garnet var; massive grossular (Tl to Op)
Idocrase (Tr) var; californite (Tl to Op)
Jadeite (Tl to Op)
Kornerupine (Tr)
Kyanite (Tr)
Malachite (Op)
Marble (Op)
Moldavite (Tr)
Nephrite (Tl to Op)
Ophicalcite (Tl to Op)
Peridot (Tr)
Phosphophyllite (Tr)
Prehnite (Tl to Op)
Pyrophyllite (Op)
Pseudomalachite (Op)
Pseudophite (Op)
Quartz (Tr)

Table 7—*(cont.)*

Green—(cont.)

Rhodizite (Tr)
Serpentine (Tl to Op)
Smaragdite (Op)
Smithsonite (Tl to Op)
Soapstone (Op)
Sphene (Tr)
Spodumene (Tr)
Thomsonite (Op)
Topaz (rare) (Tr)
Tourmaline (Tr)
Tremolite (Tl)
Turquoise (Op)
Variscite (Op)
Verdite (Op)
Willemite (Tr to Op)
Wulfenite (Tl)
Zircon (Tr)

White

Alabaster (Tl to Op)
Anhydrite (Tr to Tl)
Amber (Tl to Op)
Barite (Tl)
Bone (Op)
Cerussite (Tl)
Chalcedony (Tl to Op)
Colemanite (Tl)
Coral (Tl to Op)
Datolite (Tl to Op)
Gypsum var; satin spar (Tl)
Howlite (Tl to Op)
Ivory (Tl to Op)
Jadeite (Tl to Op)
Marble (Op)
Meerschaum (Op)
Mesolite (Tl)
Nephrite (Tl to Op)
Opal (Tl to Op)
Pearl (Tl to Op)
Pectolite (Tl)
Pyrophyllite (Tl to Op)
Quartz var; milky (Tl to Op)
Scapolite (Tr to Tl)
Thomsonite (Op)
Ulexite (Tl)
Witherite (Tl to Op)
Wollastonite (Tl to Op)
Wulfenite (Tl to Op)

Grey

Apophyllite (Tl)
Cerussite (Tl)
Chalcedony (Tl)
Diamond (Tr to Tl)
Feldspar var; labradorite (Op)
Herderite (Tl to Op)
Marble (Op)
Obsidian (Tl to Op)
Pectolite (Tl to Op)
Pyrophyllite (Tl to Op)

Black

Amber (Op)
Anatase (Op)
Cassiterite (Op)
Chalcedony (stained) (Op)
Coral (Op)
Diamond (Op)
Garnet (Op)
Jadeite (Op)
Jet (Op)
Marble (Op)
Obsidian (Op)
Opal (with play of colour) (Tl to Op)
Pearl (Op)
Quartz var; morion (Op)
Rutile (Op)
Spinel (Op)
Tourmaline var; schorl (Op)

Metallic colours

White	Cobaltite
Tin white to steel grey	Algodonite
Tin white to steel grey	Domeykite
Tin white to steel grey	Smaltite
Brass yellow	Pyrites
Bronze yellow	Pentlandite
Golden yellow	Chalcopyrite
Grey yellow	Marcasite
Copper red	Breithaup-tite
Pale copper red	Niccolite
Brownish-black	Euxenite
Black	Columbite
Black	Tantalite
Iron black	Chromite
Brilliant black	Hematite
Brilliant black	Psilomelane

Tr transparent: Tl translucent: Op opaque

TABLE 8

THE PLEOCHROIC COLOURS OF THE PRINCIPAL GEMSTONES

Anatase (distinct)	Pale blue or yellowish; dark blue or orange
Andalusite (strong)	Yellow; green; red
Apatite (weak except in Burma stones)	
Yellow (asparagus stone)	Golden yellow; greenish-yellow
Blue green (moroxite)	Pale yellow; sapphire-blue
Axinite (strong)	Violet; brown; green
Benitoite (strong)	Colourless; greenish to indigo-blue

Table 8—(cont.)

Beryl (distinct)	
Green (emerald)	Yellowish-green; bluish-green
Greenish-blue (aquamarine)	Colourless to pale yellowish-green; pale bluish-green
Blue (aquamarine)	Colourless; sky-blue
Pink (morganite)	Pale rose; bluish-rose
Yellow (heliodor)	Pale yellowish-green; pale bluish-green
Violet	Violet; colourless
Chrysoberyl (strong in deep colours)	
Yellow	Colourless; pale yellow; lemon yellow
(Cat's-eye)	Reddish-yellow; greenish-yellow; green
Green (alexandrite)	
Natural light	Emerald-green; yellowish; columbine-red
Artificial light	Emerald-green; reddish-yellow; red
Corundum (strong)	
Red (ruby)	Pale yellowish-red; deep red
Blue (sapphire)	Pale greenish-blue; deep blue
Green	Yellowish-green; green
Violet	Yellowish-red; violet-red
Yellow	Imperceptible
Corundum synthetic (*alexandrite type*)	
In natural light	Pale brownish-green; deep mauve
In artificial light	Brownish-yellow; deep mauve

Other synthetic corundums show dichroic tints in general agreement with the natural corundums of similar colour

Danburite (very weak)	Pale yellow; very pale yellow; pale yellow
Dioptase (weak)	Dark green; light green
Enstatite (distinct)	Green; yellowish-green; brownish-green
Epidote (strong)	Green; yellowish-green; yellow
Euclase (distinct)	Colourless; pale green; green
Fibrolite (distinct)	Colourless; pale yellow; sapphire-blue
Iolite (strong)	Pale blue; pale yellow; dark violet-blue
Kyanite (distinct)	Pale blue; blue; dark blue
Peridot (distinct)	Yellow-green; green
Quartz (weak)	
Yellow (citrine)	Yellow; slightly paler yellow
Violet (amethyst)	Purple; reddish-purple
Smoky quartz	Brown; reddish-brown
Rose quartz	Pink; pale pink
Heat treated amethyst 'topaz' colour	Imperceptible
Sphene (*titanite*) (strong)	Colourless; yellow; reddish-yellow
Spodumene (strong)	
Pink (kunzite)	Colourless; pink; violet
Green (hiddenite)	Bluish-green; grass-green; yellowish-green
Yellow	Pale yellow; deep yellow; yellow
Staurolite (distinct)	Red; brown; yellow
Topaz (distinct)	
Yellow	Honey-yellow; straw-yellow; pinkish-yellow
Blue	Colourless; pale pink; blue
Pink	Colourless; very pale pink; pink
Green	Pale green; bluish-green; colourless
Tourmaline (strong)	
Red (rubellite)	Pink; dark red
Blue (indicolite)	Light blue; dark blue
Green	Pale green; dark green
Brown	Yellowish-brown; deep brown
Zircon (weak except in blue)	
Red	Columbine-red; clove-brown
Blue	Colourless; sky-blue
Green	Brownish-green; green
Yellow	Brownish-yellow; honey-yellow
Brown	Yellowish-brown; reddish-brown

TABLE 9

COLOUR FILTER

A table of the effects seen when the stone is viewed through a dichromatic filter, such as the Chelsea colour filter, which transmits a band of green and a band of red light. The residual colour will be more intense the stronger is the body colour of the stone. The best results are seen when the stone is illuminated with light from a tungsten electric lamp (desk lamp) and the filter held close to the eye.

Green stones

Alexandrite	red
Aquamarine	distinctively green
Aventurine quartz	reddish
Chrome chalcedony	red
Chrysoprase	green
Demantoid garnet	reddish
Emerald	pink to red

(Some emeralds from South Africa and India may not show a red hue, but remain greenish)

Enstatite	green
Fluorspar	reddish
Glass (pastes)	green
Hiddenite	slight pink
Jadeite	green
Peridot	green
Sapphire	green
Soudé emerald	green

(The old type soudé emerald may show red)

Stained bowenite	red
Stained chalcedony	red
Stained jadeite	red
Synthetic corundum (alexandrite colour)	red
Synthetic emerald	strong red
Synthetic sapphire	red
Synthetic spinel	red
(Some old types may show green)	
Tourmaline	green

(Certain anomalous green tourmalines have been found to show red)

Zircon	reddish

Red stones

Garnets	dark red (no fluorescence)
Garnet-topped doublets	dark red (no fluorescence)
Glass (pastes)	dark red (no fluorescence)

Red stones—(cont.)

Ruby (natural and synthetic)	strong fluorescent red
Spinel	fluorescent red
Spinel (synthetic)	fluorescent red

(The pink synthetic spinel does not show a red colour through the filter)

Blue stones

Aquamarine	distinctive green
Garnet-topped doublets	greenish-blue
Glass (pastes)	
Dark blue	red
Light blue	greenish
Lapis-lazuli	weak brownish-red
Sapphire	blackish-green

(The blue sapphire which shows a purple colour under artificial light usually shows red under the filter)

Sodalite	slightly brownish
Spinel	reddish
'Swiss lapis'	greenish-blue
Synthetic sapphire	dark greenish-blue

(The natural and synthetic sapphire are indistinguishable under the colour filter)

Synthetic spinel	
Dark blue	red
Light blue	orange
'Zircon' colour	orange to red
'Lapis-lazuli colour'	bright red
Zircon	greenish

Purple stones

Amethyst	reddish
Violet sapphire	bright red

TABLE 10

THE LIGHT SPECTRUM

	Ångstrom units
Ultra-violet	1000 to 3900
Violet	3900 to 4300
Blue	4300 to 4900
Blue-green	4900 to 5100
Green	5100 to 5500
Yellow-green	5500 to 5750
Yellow	5750 to 5900
Orange	5900 to 6300
Orange-red	6300 to 6500
Red	6500 to 7000
Deep red	7000 to 7800
Infra-red	7800 to 10,000,000

An Ångstrom unit is one ten-millionth of a millimetre, or 0.0000001 (10^{-7}) millimetre

THE MAJOR FRAUNHOFER LINES

		Ångstrom units
A	oxygen	7593·8
B	oxygen	6867·2
C	hydrogen	6563
D1	sodium	5895·9
D2	sodium	5890·0
E	iron	5269·5
F	hydrogen	4861·5
G	iron	4307·9
H	calcium	3968·5
K	calcium	3933·7

THE PRINCIPAL EMISSION LINES USEFUL FOR CALIBRATION

Element	Lines	Notes
Barium	5881 (yellow) 5778 (yellow) 5536 (yellow-green) 5519 (yellow-green) 5425 (green) 5137 (green) 4937 (blue-green) 4874 (blue) 4554 (blue)	Barium lines are better produced by arc than by Bunsen flame
Calcium	6162 (orange) 5590 (yellow-green) 4227 (violet)	Calcium lines can usually be obtained by inserting a calcium compound in the Bunsen flame
Copper	5218 (green) 5153 (green) 5106 (green)	Copper lines are best produced by arc excitation
Lithium	6708 (red) 6103 (orange)	Given by lithium compound in Bunsen flame. Red line is strong, orange line is weak
Mercury	6234 (orange) 6152 (orange) 5790 (yellow) 5770 (yellow 5461 (green) 4359 (blue) 4348 (blue) 4078 (violet) 4047 (violet)	The mercury lines are best obtained from a mercury vapour electric discharge lamp. The lines may be picked up underlying the continuous spectrum of a fluorescent lighting tube

Table 10—(*cont.*)

Potassium	7669 (deep red) 7665 (deep red) 4047 (violet) 4044 (violet)	Can be induced by potassium compound in Bunsen flame
Sodium	5890 (yellow) 5895 (yellow)	Sodium compound in Bunsen flame
Strontium	6870 (red) 6060 (orange) 4607 (blue) 4078 (violet)	Strontium compound in Bunsen flame
Thallium	5350 (green)	Thallium compound (Clerici's solution) in Bunsen flame

Modern scientific literature uses wave frequencies rather than wavelengths and this may be puzzling to students of gemmology. The table below will illustrate the relation between these different types of notation.

INTERCONVERSION OF ÅNGSTROM UNITS, WAVE NUMBERS (cm⁻¹), AND ELECTRON VOLTS

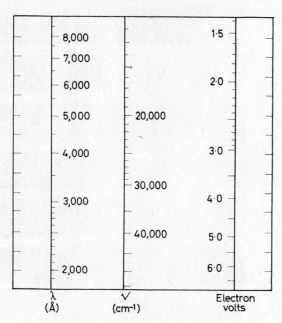

1 electron volt (eV) equals 8,066 cm⁻¹ (v)
cm⁻¹ equals number of waves in a centimetre

A straight edge placed horizontally across the diagram, using the two outer scales as guides, will give interconversion between the different energies

TABLE 11

THE ABSORPTION SPECTRA OF GEMSTONES

The following spectrum plates are drawn as seen through a prism type spectroscope.

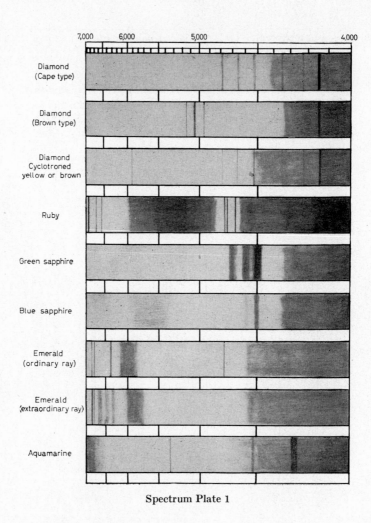

Spectrum Plate 1

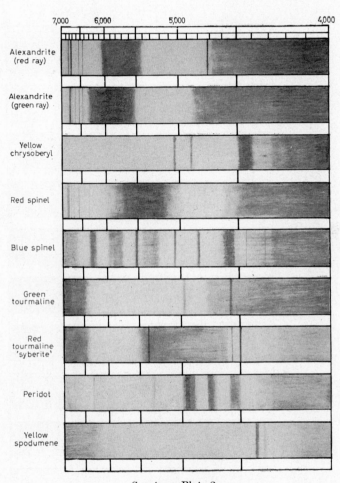

Spectrum Plate 2

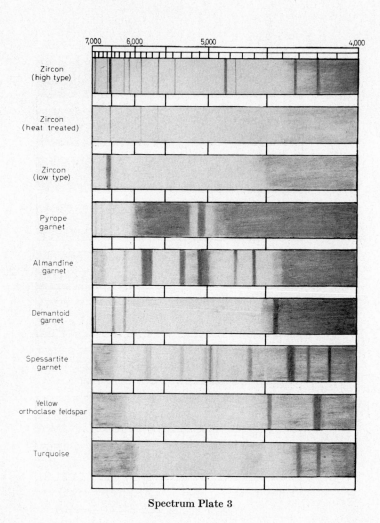

Spectrum Plate 3

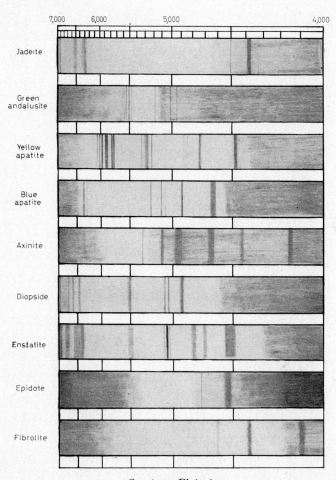

Spectrum Plate 4

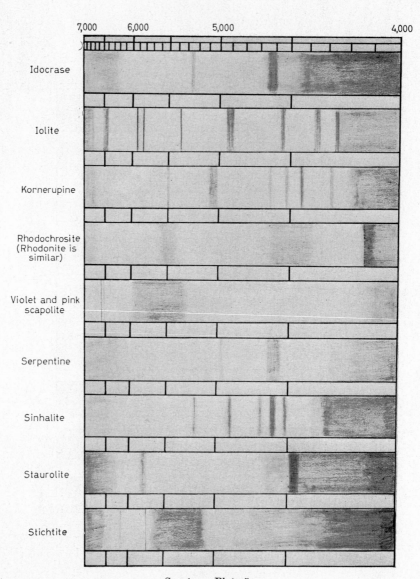

Spectrum Plate 5

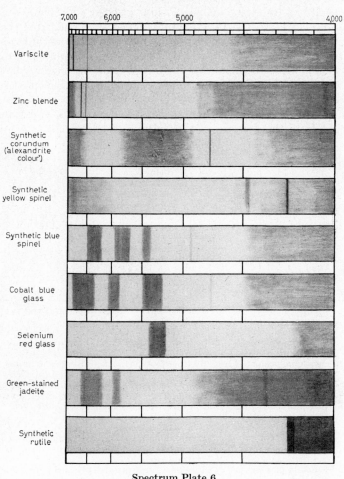

Spectrum Plate 6

TABLE 12

THE FLUORESCENT COLOURS OF GEMSTONES

The following table gives the more common luminescent colours shown by gem materials under each of the three types of radiation—long-wave ultra-violet, short-wave ultra-violet and x-rays. As it is extremely difficult to analyse the shades of colour in the various groups, the wide division into the six colours of the Newtonian spectrum, with the addition of white, has therefore been adopted. It must be understood that under *red* the shade may vary from deep plum red, through crimson, to rose and pink; and *blue*, from a rich dark blue to a bright whitish-blue. Some attempt has been made to indicate the depth of colour and the intensity of the glow by placing the names of the stones in descending order. The lilac-coloured glow is listed under violet. In the case of synthetic emerald the red glow is much stronger when the stones are irradiated with extra long-wave ultra-violet and near violet light from the fluorescent type ultra-violet lamp.

Colour	Long-wave ultra-violet light (3650 Å)	Short-wave ultra-violet light (2537 Å)	X-rays (mean 1 Ångstrom)
White	Ivory Casein Copal resin Amber Tortoise-shell Opal	Synthetic white spinel Paste (some) Ivory Casein Copal resin Amber Tortoise-shell Opal	Diamond Scapolite
Red	Synthetic ruby Natural ruby Natural and synthetic pink sapphire Red spinel Synthetic orange sapphire Alexandrite Synthetic (alexandrite) sapphire Synthetic green sapphire Synthetic blue spinel Ceylon blue sapphire Synthetic emerald Emerald (some) Calcite (some) Kyanite Fire opal (brownish-red)	Natural and synthetic ruby Natural pink sapphire Red spinel Synthetic orange sapphire Calcite (some) Alexandrite Synthetic (alexandrite) sapphire Synthetic emerald Ceylon blue sapphire Diamond Natural emerald (some) Fire opal (brownish-red)	Natural and synthetic ruby Natural and synthetic pink sapphire Red spinel Synthetic orange sapphire Ceylon blue sapphire Synthetic (alexandrite) sapphire Synthetic blue spinel (some) Synthetic green spinel Synthetic emerald Morganite Natural emerald Thulite
Orange	Kunzite Ceylon yellow sapphire Scapolite Diamond Ceylon blue sapphire Synthetic (alexandrite) sapphire	Ceylon yellow sapphire Scapolite Diamond Ceylon blue sapphire Synthetic orange sapphire	Kunzite Ceylon yellow sapphire Calcite (including marble) Scapolite Synthetic white sapphire

Table 12—(*cont.*)

Colour	Long-wave ultra-violet light (3650 Å)	Short-wave ultra-violet light (2537 Å)	X-rays (mean 1 Ångstrom)

Orange	Natural white sapphire
	Synthetic green sapphire
	Synthetic orange
	  sapphire
	Natural mauve spinel
	  (some)
	Topaz (some)
	Sodalite (orange spots)
	Lapis-lazuli (orange
	  spots)
		Synthetic green
		  sapphire (brownish-
		  orange)
		Natural white sapphire
		Synthetic (alexandrite)
		  sapphire
			Synthetic (alexandrite)
			  sapphire
			Synthetic green
			  sapphire
			Massive green garnet
			  ('Transvaal jade')
			Petalite
			Pale yellow sinhalite
			Topaz (some)

Yellow	Diamond Amber Apatite Zircon Topaz Fire opal (brownish) Paste	Diamond Zircon Amber	Diamond Zircon Cassiterite Cultured pearl Freshwater pearl Rhodizite Diopside Lapis Sodalite (yellow spots)

Green	Synthetic yellow spinel
	Synthetic yellow-green
	  spinel
	Willemite
	Opal (some)
	Diamond
	Pale blue natural
	  spinels (some)
	Emerald (some)
	Apatite
	Paste (some)
	Amber
	Synthetic white spinel
	  and sapphire (very
	  weakly)
		Synthetic yellow and
		  green spinels
		Willemite
		Opal (some)
		Synthetic green spinel
		Diamond
		Amber
		Paste
			Synthetic yellow spinel
			Synthetic yellow-green
			  spinel
			Willemite
			Synthetic white spinel
			Diamond
			Paste
			Opal (some)
			Natural spinels (some)
			Taaffeite
			Rhodizite
			Amblygonite
			Topaz

Blue	Diamond Danburite Fluorite Paste Pearl Casein Ivory Amber Moonstone	Benitoite Scheelite Fluorite Danburite Diamond Synthetic blue spinel Synthetic blue sapphire Paste (some) Ivory Amber Copal	Fluorite Benitoite Beryllonite Diamond Scheelite Synthetic blue sapphire Kyanite Phenakite Synthetic white spinel (some) Synthetic blue spinel Paste (some) Lapis-lazuli Sodalite Topaz Zircon Moonstone

Violet	Fluorite
	Diamond
	Apatite
	Scapolite
	Morganite
	Diopside
		Fluorite
		Diamond
		Morganite
		Synthetic pink sapphire
			Fluorite
			Danburite
			Synthetic yellow
			  sapphires (some)
			Synthetic white
			  sapphires (some)
			Scapolite
			Pink tourmaline
			Zircon

TABLE 13
THE CHEMICAL COMPOSITION OF GEMSTONES

Elements

Diamond	C

Haloids

Fluorite	CaF_2

Sulphides

Bornite	Cu_5FeS_4
Chalcopyrite	$CuFeS_2$
Cobaltite	CoAsS
Marcasite	FeS_2
Millerite	NiS
Pentlandite	(Fe,Ni)S
Proustite	$3Ag_2S\ As_2S_3$
Pyrites	FeS_2
Zinc blende	ZnS

Oxides

Anatase	TiO_2
Brookite	TiO_2
Cassiterite	SnO_2
Chalcedony	SiO_2
Chromite	$FeCr_2O_4$
Chrysoberyl	$BeAl_2O_4$
Corundum	Al_2O_3
Crocoite	$PbCrO_4$
Cuprite	Cu_2O
Gahnite	$ZnAl_2O_4$
Hematite	Fe_2O_3
Microlite	$Ca_2Ta_2O_7$
Opal	$SiO_2\ nH_2O$
Painite	CaBoro-silico aluminate
Periclase	MgO
Psilomelane	MnO_2 (Colloidal)
Quartz	SiO_2
Rutile	TiO_2
Samarskite	NiTa oxide with rare earths
Scheelite	$CaWO_4$
Spinel	$MgAl_2O_4$
Strontium titanate	$SrTiO_3$
Taaffeite	$Be_4Mg_4Al_{16}O_{32}$
Wulfenite	$PbMoO_4$
Zincite	ZnO

Carbonates

Azurite	$Cu_3(OH)_2(CO_3)_2$
Calcite (marble)	$CaCO_3$
Cerussite	$PbCO_3$
Magnesite	$MgCO_3$
Malachite	$Cu_2(OH)_2CO_3$
Phosgenite	$(Pb, Cl)_2CO_3$
Rhodochrosite	$MnCO_3$
Siderite	$FeCO_3$
Smithsonite	$ZnCO_3$
Stichtite	$Mg_6Cr_2(OH)_{16}CO_34H_2O$

Silicates

Analcite	$NaAlSi_2O_6H_2O$
Andalusite	Al_2SiO_5
Apophyllite	$KFCa_4(Si_2O_5)_48H_2O$
Axinite	$HMgCa_2BAl_2(SiO_4)_4$
Benitoite	$BaTiSi_3O_9$
Beryl	$Be_3Al_2(SiO_3)_6$
Cancrinite	$3H_2O4Na_2OCaO4Al_2O39SiO_22CO_2$ approx.
Chrysocolla	$CuSiO_32H_2O$
Chlorastrolite	$6CaO3Al_2O37SiO_24H_2O$
Chondrodite	$2Mg_2SiO_4Mg(F, OH)_2$
Danburite	$CaB_2(SiO_4)_2$

Silicates—(cont.)

Datolite	$Ca(B, OH)SiO_4$
Diopside	$CaMg(SiO_3)_2$
Dioptase	$CuOSiO_2H_2O$
Dumorticrite	$4(AlFe)_7BSi_3O_{18}$
Enstatite	$(Mg, Fe)SiO_3$
Epidote	$Ca_2(AL, OH)Al_2(SiO_4)_3$
Euclase	$Be(Al, OH)SiO_4$
Feldspar group	
Orthoclase	$KAlSi_3O_8$
Microcline	$KAlSi_3O_8$
Albite	$NaAlSi_3O_8$
Anorthite	$CaAl_2Si_2O_8$
Fibrolite	Al_2SiO_5
Friedelite	$H_7(Mn, Cl)Mn_4Si_4O_{16}$
Garnet group	
Almandine	$Fe_3Al_2(SiO_4)_3$
Andradite	$Ca_3Fe_2(SiO_4)_3$
Grossular	$Ca_3Al_2(SiO_4)_3$
Pyrope	$Mg_3Al_2(SiO_4)_3$
Spessartite	$Mn_3Al_2(SiO_4)_3$
Uvarovite	$Ca_3Cr_2(SiO_4)_3$
Hauynite	$(Na, Cl)_{4-8}(SiO_3SO_2)_{1-2}(Al_6Si_6O_{24})$
Howlite	$8CaO5B_2O_36SiO_26H_2O$
Hypersthene	$(Fe, Mg)SiO_3$
Idocrase	$Ca_6Al(Al, OH)(SiO_4)_5$
Iolite	$Mg_2Al_4Si_5O_{18}$
Jadeite	$NaAl(SiO_3)_2$
Kornerupine	$MgAl_2SiO_6$
Kyanite	Al_2SiO_5
Lepidolite	$H_4K_2Li_2Al_4Si_6O_{22}$
Leucite	$KAl(SiO_3)_2$
Meerschaum	$H_4Mg_2Si_3O_{10}$
Melinophane	$(Ca, Na)_2Be(Si, Al)_2(O, F)_7$
Mesolite	$(Ca, Na_2)Al_2Si_3O_{10}(H_2O)_{2-3}$
Natrolite	$Na_2Al_2Si_3O_{10}2H_2O$
Nephrite	$Ca_2(Mg, Fe)_5(OH)_2(Si_4O_{11})_2$
Pectolite	$HNaCa_2(SiO_3)_3$
Petalite	$Li_2OAl_2O_38SiO_2$
Peridot	$(Mg, Fe)_2SiO_4$
Phenacite	Be_2SiO_4
Pollucite	$H_2Cs_4Al_4(SiO_3)_9$
Prehnite	$H_2Ca_2Al_2(SiO_4)_3$
Pyrophyllite	$H_2Al_2(SiO_3)_4$
Rhodonite	$MnSiO_3$
Scapolite	
Marialite	$Na_4Cl(Al_3Si_9O_{24})$
Meionite	$Ca_6(SO_4CO_3)(Al_6SI_6O_{24})$
Serpentine	$H_4Mg_3Si_2O_9$
Shattuckite	$2CuSiO_3H_2O$
Sodalite	$3NaAlSiO_4NaCl$
Sphene	$CaTiSiO_5$
Spodumene	$LiAl(SiO_3)_2$
Staurolite	$2Al_2SiO_5Fe(OH)_2$
Steatite	$H_2Mg_3(SiO_3)_4$
Thomsonite	$3(Ca, Na_2)Al_2Si_2O_8H_2O$
Topaz	$Al_2(F, OH)_2SiO_4$
Tourmaline	$(NaCa)(LiMgFeAl)_9B_3Si_6(O, OH)_{31}$
Tremolite	$CaMg_3Si_4O_{12}$
Willemite	Zn_2SiO_4
Wollastonite	$CaSiO_3$
Zircon	$ZrSiO_4$
Zoisite	$Ca_2(Al,OH)Al_2(SiO_4)_3$

Sulphates

Anglesite	$PbSO_4$
Anhydrite	$CaSO_4$

25+G.

Table 13—*(cont.)*

Sulphates—(cont.)

Barytes	$BaSO_4$
Celestine	$SrSO_4$
Gypsum	$CaSO_42H_2O$

Phosphates

Amblygonite	$LiAl(F, OH)PO_4$
Apatite	$Ca(F, Cl)Ca_4(PO_4)_3$
Augelite	$2Al_2O_3P_2O_53H_2O$
Beryllonite	$NaBePO_4$
Brazilianite	$Al_3Na(PO_4)_2(OH)_4$
Herderite	$CaBe(F, OH)PO_4$
Lazulite	$FeAl_2(OH)_2(PO_4)_2$
Phosphophyllite	$Zn_3(PO_4)_24H_2O$
Turquoise	$CuAl_6(PO_4)_4(OH)_85H_2O$
Variscite	$AlPO_42H_2O$
Wardite	$Na_4CaAl_{12}(PO_4)_8(OH)_{18}6H_2O$

Borates

Boracite	$Mg_6Cl_2B_{14}O_{26}$
Colemanite	$Ca_2B_6O_{11}5H_2O$
Hambergite	$Be_2(OH)BO_3$
Rhodizite	$KAl_2B_3O_8$
Sinhalite	$Mg(Al, Fe)BO_4$
Ulexite	$NaCaB_5O_9$

Arsenates

Bayldonite	$(Pb, Cu)_3As_2O_8(Pb, Cu)(OH)_2H_2O$
Durangite	$Na(Al, F)AsO_4$
Legrandite	$Zn_{14}(AsO_4)_9OH12H_2O$
Mimetite	$(PbCl)Pb_4(AsO_4)_3$

Oxalate

Whewellite	$CaC_2O_4H_2O$

Arsenides

Algodonite	Cu_6As
Domeykite	Cu_3As
Niccolite	$NiAs$
Smaltite	$CoAs_3$

Niobates and Tantalates

Columbite	$(Fe, Mn)(Nb, Ta)_2O_6$
Euxenite	$(Y, Ce, Er, U)(Nb, Ti)O$
Lithium niobate	LiO_3
Samarskite	$(Fe, Ca, UO_2)_2(Ce, Y)(Nb, Ta)_6O_{21}$
Stibiotantalite	$SbO_2(Ta, Nb)_2O_6$

Antimonides

Breithauptite	$NiSb$

TABLE 14

DENSITY CORRECTION TABLES FOR TOLUENE AND ETHYLENE DIBROMIDE

Note:—Commercial samples of toluene and more particularly of ethylene dibromide may vary appreciably in density from the figures given below. For really accurate determinations, therefore, it is wise to purchase a fair quantity (say 1 lb.) which can then be calibrated and will last for years if kept in a stoppered bottle.

A convenient method of calibrating a sample is to carry out a hydrostatic determination with a large piece of pure quartz (say 50 carats) and to work 'backwards,' assuming the density of quartz to be 2·651. Supposing the density of a sample of toluene at 11·3°C is found on calibration to be 0·8734 —a figure corresponding to a temperature of 10·3°C in the tables, the worker will know that it is necessary to subtract 1°C from his actual temperature in all future experiments before referring to the table.

DENSITIES OF TOLUENE FROM 5°C TO 25°C

°C	Density	°C	Density	°C	Density	°C	Density
5·0	0·8787	11·2	0·8725	17·4	0·8663	23·6	0·8601
5·1	0·8786	11·3	0·8724	17·5	0·8662	23·7	0·8600
5·2	0·8785	11·4	0·8723	17·6	0·8661	23·8	0·8599
5·3	0·8784	11·5	0·8722	17·7	0·8660	23·9	0·8598
5·4	0·8783	11·6	0·8721	17·8	0·8659	24·0	0·8597
5·5	0·8782	11·7	0·8720	17·9	0·8658	24·1	0·8596
5·6	0·8781	11·8	0·8719	18·0	0·8657	24·2	0·8595
5·7	0·8780	11·9	0·8718	18·1	0·8656	24·3	0·8594
5·8	0·8779	12·0	0·8717	18·2	0·8655	24·4	0·8593
5·9	0·8778	12·1	0·8716	18·3	0·8654	24·5	0·8592
6·0	0·8777	12·2	0·8715	18·4	0·8653	24·6	0·8591
6·1	0·8776	12·3	0·8714	18·5	0·8652	24·7	0·8590
6·2	0·8775	12·4	0·8713	18·6	0·8651	24·8	0·8589
6·3	0·8774	12·5	0·8712	18·7	0·8650	24·9	0·8588
6·4	0·8773	12·6	0·8711	18·8	0·8649	25·0	0·8587
6·5	0·8772	12·7	0·8710	18·9	0·8648		
6·6	0·8771	12·8	0·8709	19·0	0·8647		
6·7	0·8770	12·9	0·8708	19·1	0·8646		
6·8	0·8769	13·0	0·8707	19·2	0·8645		
6·9	0·8768	13·1	0·8706	19·3	0·8644		
7·0	0·8767	13·2	0·8705	19·4	0·8643		
7·1	0·8766	13·3	0·8704	19·5	0·8642		
7·2	0·8765	13·4	0·8703	19·6	0·8641		
7·3	0·8764	13·5	0·8702	19·7	0·8640		
7·4	0·8763	13·6	0·8701	19·8	0·8639		
7·5	0·8762	13·7	0·8700	19·9	0·8638		
7·6	0·8761	13·8	0·8699	20·0	0·8637		
7·7	0·8760	13·9	0·8698	20·1	0·8636		
7·8	0·8759	14·0	0·8697	20·2	0·8635		
7·9	0·8758	14·1	0·8696	20·3	0·8634		
8·0	0·8757	14·2	0·8695	20·4	0·8633		
8·1	0·8756	14·3	0·8694	20·5	0·8632		
8·2	0·8755	14·4	0·8693	20·6	0·8631		
8·3	0·8754	14·5	0·8692	20·7	0·8630		
8·4	0·8753	14·6	0·8691	20·8	0·8629		
8·5	0·8752	14·7	0·8690	20·9	0·8628		
8·6	0·8751	14·8	0·8689	21·0	0·8627		
8·7	0·8750	14·9	0·8688	21·1	0·8626		
8·8	0·8749	15·0	0·8687	21·2	0·8625		
8·9	0·8748	15·1	0·8686	21·3	0·8624		
9·0	0·8747	15·2	0·8685	21·4	0·8623		
9·1	0·8746	15·3	0·8684	21·5	0·8622		
9·2	0·8745	15·4	0·8683	21·6	0·8621		
9·3	0·8744	15·5	0·8682	21·7	0·8620		
9·4	0·8743	15·6	0·8681	21·8	0·8619		
9·5	0·8742	15·7	0·8680	21·9	0·8618		
9·6	0·8741	15·8	0·8679	22·0	0·8617		
9·7	0·8740	15·9	0·8678	22·1	0·8616		
9·8	0·8739	16·0	0·8677	22·2	0·8615		
9·9	0·8738	16·1	0·8676	22·3	0·8614		
10·0	0·8737	16·2	0·8675	22·4	0·8613		
10·1	0·8736	16·3	0·8674	22·5	0·8612		
10·2	0·8735	16·4	0·8673	22·6	0·8611		
10·3	0·8734	16·5	0·8672	22·7	0·8610		
10·4	0·8733	16·6	0·8671	22·8	0·8609		
10·5	0·8732	16·7	0·8670	22·9	0·8608		
10·6	0·8731	16·8	0·8669	23·0	0·8607		
10·7	0·8730	16·9	0·8668	23·1	0·8606		
10·8	0·8729	17·0	0·8667	23·2	0·8605		
10·9	0·8728	17·1	0·8666	23·3	0·8604		
11·0	0·8727	17·2	0·8665	23·4	0·8603		
11·1	0·8726	17·3	0·8664	23·5	0·8602		

Table 14—(cont.)

DENSITIES OF ETHYLENE DIBROMIDE FROM 10°C TO 20°C

°C	Density	°C	Density	°C	Density	°C	Density
10·0	2·1998	12·6	2·1946	15·2	2·1894	17·8	2·1842
10·1	2·1996	12·7	2·1944	15·3	2·1892	17·9	2·1840
10·2	2·1994	12·8	2·1942	15·4	2·1890	18·0	2·1838
10·3	2·1992	12·9	2·1940	15·5	2·1888	18·1	2·1836
10·4	2·1990	13·0	2·1938	15·6	2·1886	18·2	2·1834
10·5	2·1988	13·1	2·1936	15·7	2·1884	18·3	2·1832
10·6	2·1986	13·2	2·1934	15·8	2·1882	18·4	2·1830
10·7	2·1984	13·3	2·1932	15·9	2·1880	18·5	2·1828
10·8	2·1982	13·4	2·1930	16·0	2·1878	18·6	2·1826
10·9	2·1980	13·5	2·1928	16·1	2·1876	18·7	2·1824
11·0	2·1978	13·6	2·1926	16·2	2·1874	18·8	2·1822
11·1	2·1976	13·7	2·1924	16·3	2·1872	18·9	2·1820
11·2	2·1974	13·8	2·1922	16·4	2·1870	19·0	2·1818
11·3	2·1972	13·9	2·1920	16·5	2·1868	19·1	2·1816
11·4	2·1970	14·0	2·1918	16·6	2·1866	19·2	2·1814
11·5	2·1968	14·1	2·1916	16·7	2·1864	19·3	2·1812
11·6	2·1966	14·2	2·1914	16·8	2·1862	19·4	2·1810
11·7	2·1964	14·3	2·1912	16·9	2·1860	19·5	2·1808
11·8	2·1962	14·4	2·1910	17·0	2·1858	19·6	2·1806
11·9	2·1960	14·5	2·1908	17·1	2·1856	19·7	2·1804
12·0	2·1958	14·6	2·1906	17·2	2·1854	19·8	2·1802
12·1	2·1956	14·7	2·1904	17·3	2·1852	19·9	2·1800
12·2	2·1954	14·8	2·1902	17·4	2·1850	20·0	2·1798
12·3	2·1952	14·9	2·1900	17·5	2·1848		
12·4	2·1950	15·0	2·1898	17·6	2·1846		
12·5	2·1948	15·1	2·1896	17·7	2·1844		

THE RELATION BETWEEN REFRACTIVE INDEX AND DENSITY OF CLERICI SOLUTION AND METHYLENE IODIDE WITH SUITABLE DILUTANTS

If a specimen under test is found to be freely suspended in the liquid the density of that liquid may be ascertained from its index of refraction.

Clerici Solution: Water

Refractive index	Density	Refractive index	Density	Refractive index	Density	Refractive index	Density
1·500	2·584	1·550	3·008	1·600	3·432	1·650	3·854
1·510	2·669	1·560	3·093	1·610	3·517	1·660	3·939
1·520	2·753	1·570	3·178	1·620	3·601	1·670	4·023
1·530	2·838	1·580	3·263	1·630	3·685		
1·540	2·923	1·590	3·348	1·640	3·770		

The above table is based on the work of Anderson, Payne and Franklin

Methylene Iodide: Toluene

Refractive index	Density	Refractive index	Density	Refractive index	Density	Refractive index	Density
1·610	2·007	1·650	2·403	1·690	2·809	1·730	3·205
1·620	2·106	1·660	2·502	1·700	2·908	1·740	3·394
1·630	2·205	1·670	2·601	1·710	3·007		
1·640	2·304	1·680	2·710	1·720	3·106		

TABLE 15

WEIGHTS AND MEASURES

The unit of weight used for the weighing of gemstones is the *metric carat*.

The metric carat is one-fifth of a gramme (0·200 gramme) and is equal to 3·08647 Troy grains.

The *diamond grain*, not so often used as formerly, is one-fourth of a carat, that is 4 diamond grains to a carat.

A diamond weighing less than a carat, that is a decimal part of a carat, is often spoken of as a so many pointer or weighing so many points. Thus a diamond weighing 0·65 carat is said to be a 65 pointer.

Pearls are usually weighed in carats but the weight is then converted to pearl grains, which like the diamond grains are a quarter of a carat. Thus a 1 carat pearl is a 4 grain pearl.

The pearl and diamond grain is not a weight in the general sense but, especially in the case of pearls, is used owing to the calculation of price by the 'base' system.

Cultured pearls are sold in Japan by the Japanese weight called the momme: 1 momme equals 3·75 g, or 18·75 carats, or 75 pearl grains.

Some of the ornamental types of stones are sold by the gramme, the Troy ounce or even the Avoirdupois pound and ounce.

The metric weight with the gramme as unit is:

1 milligram which is one thousandth of a gramme
1 gramme
1 kilogram which is a thousand grammes

1 gramme (1000 milligrams)	=	5 metric carats
500 milligrams	=	2·5 metric carats
200 milligrams	=	1 carat
100 milligrams (0·10 gramme)	=	0·50 carat
50 milligrams	=	0·25 carat
20 milligrams	=	0·10 carat
10 milligrams (0·010 gramme)	=	0·05 carat
5 milligrams	=	0·025 carat
2 milligrams	=	0·010 carat
1 milligram	=	0·005 carat

The Troy weight is sometimes used instead of the metric weight for weighing large quantities of rough and ornamental stones. The Troy weight is also used for precious metals.

The unit is the Troy ounce and the complete table is shown under:

24 grains (gr.)	=	1 pennyweight (dwt.)
20 pennyweights (480 gr.)	=	1 ounce (oz.)
12 ounces (5760 gr.)	=	1 pound (lb.)

The pound Troy is now no longer legal and the Troy ounce divided into decimal parts is the legal Troy weight. The pennyweight is now rarely used.

The ordinary weights used for general merchandise, the Avoirdupois weight, may be used, in the absence of the correct Troy or carat weights, and the resulting weighing converted into the system of weights required. The Avoirdupois weights are given overleaf.

Table 15—(*cont.*)

16 drams (drs)	=	1 ounce (oz.)
16 ounces (437½ grains)	=	1 pound (lb.) (7000 grains)
14 pounds	=	1 stone
28 pounds	=	1 quarter (qr.)
4 quarters, or 112 pounds	=	1 hundredweight (cwt.)
20 hundredweights	=	1 ton

It is only the ounces and pounds which are likely to be used.

The Troy grain and the Avoirdupois grain are equal to one another, but the weight of the respective pounds and ounces are not the same.

Synthetic stones and glass imitation stones are usually sold by the size in millimetres, and not by weight. Thus round stones will be the length of the diameter in millimetres, while oblong or oval shaped stones will be designated by the two dimensions, the width and the length; for example, an oblong trap-cut stone 14 × 20 mm.

Conversion Factors

Grains to grammes	×	0·0648
Grammes to grains	×	15·4324
Pennyweights to grammes	×	1·5552
Grammes to pennyweights	×	0·6430
Ounces (Troy) to grammes	×	31·1035
Grammes to ounces (Troy)	×	0·03215
Ounces (Troy) to ounces (Avoirdupois)	×	1·09714
Ounces (Avoirdupois) to ounces (Troy)	×	0·91146
Ounces (Avoirdupois) to grammes	×	28·3495
Grammes to ounces (Avoirdupois)	×	0·03527
Pounds (Avoirdupois) to ounces (Troy)	×	14·5833
Ounces (Troy) to metric carats	×	155·517
Ounces (Avoirdupois) to metric carats	×	141·7475
Pennyweights to metric carats	×	7·77
Inches to millimetres	×	25·400
Inches to centimetres	×	2·540

Although the metric carat is now almost universally used, some of the undermentioned foreign weights may occasionally be encountered.

Indian
A rati is equal to 0·91 carat
A tola is equal to 58·18 carats. (By physical weighing of a known weight.)
A mangelin is equal to 1·75 carats
64 ratis equal 1 tola
To convert ratis to carats multiply by 10 and divide by 11

Burmese
A rati is equal to 0·91 carat
A bali is equal to 58·18 carats (64 ratis)
A tickal is equal to 80 carats (88 ratis)
A viss is equal to 880 carats
A lathi is equal to 1·75 carats

Ceylonese
A chevvü, chow or tank is equal to 21·84 carats (24 ratis)
A manchadi is equal to 1·15 carats

Thai (Siamese)
A catty is equal to approximately 3015 carats

Iranian (Persian)
A miscal is equal to 36·40 carats (40 ratis)
2 miscals equal 1 Dirhem

Turkish
A checky is equal to 1600 carats (320 grammes)

Brazilian
An oitava (octavo) is equal to approximately 17·5 carats

APPENDICES

FAMOUS DIAMONDS AND THOSE LARGE DIAMONDS TO WHICH NAMES HAVE BEEN APPLIED

Name	Locality	Weight (rough)	Weight (cut)
Akbar Shah	India	116 cts.	71·70 M. cts.
Arc	South Africa	381 cts.	
Arkansas	United States of America	27·21 M. cts.	
Austrian yellow	India		137·27 M. cts.

Reported as now recut to a stone of 100 cts.

Name	Locality	Weight (rough)	Weight (cut)
Barkly breakwater	South Africa	109¼ cts.	
Beaumont	South Africa	273 cts.	
Beau Sancy	India (?)		34 cts.
Blue Tavenier	India	112½ cts.	
Bob Grove	South Africa	337 cts.	
Brady	South Africa	330 cts.	
Braganza	Probably a topaz of 1680 cts.		
Broderick	South Africa	412½ cts.	
Brunswick blue	?		13¼ cts.
Burgess	South Africa	220 cts.	
Carns	South Africa	107 cts.	
Colenso	South Africa	133·145 M. cts.	
Coromandel	Brazil	400·65 M. cts.	
Cuban Capitol	South Africa	23 cts.	
Cullinan	South Africa	3106 M. cts.	
Cumberland	India		32 cts.
Darcy Vargas	Brazil	460 M. cts.	
Dary-i-noor	India		186 cts. *Major part of Great Table*
Dewey	United States of America	23·75 M. cts.	
Dresden green	India		41 M. cts.
Dresden white	*See Saxon white*		
Dresden yellow	India	*(Four brilliant cut stones, largest weighing 38 M. cts.)*	
Dudley	*See Star of South Africa*		
Empress Eugenie	India		51 cts.

One version gives the Empress Eugenie as a Brazilian stone weighing 52·27 M. cts.

Name	Locality	Weight (rough)	Weight (cut)
English Dresden	Brazil	119½ cts.	76½ cts. pendeloque
Eugenie	*See Empress Eugenie*		
Eureka	South Africa	21·25 M. cts.	10·73 M. cts.
Excelsior	South Africa	995·2 M. cts.	21 brilliants. Largest 69·68 M. cts.
Fineberg Jones	South Africa	206½ cts.	
Florentine yellow	*See Austrian yellow*		
Fly	South Africa	60 cts.	
Governader Valadares	Brazil	108·30 M. cts.	
Great Mogul	India	787½ cts.	280 cts.

The Koh-i-nûr and the Orloff have both been identified with this stone

Name	Locality	Weight (rough)	Weight (cut)
Great Star of Africa	South Africa	Part of the Cullinan diamond	530·2 M. cts. pendeloque

This is the largest cut diamond in the world and is set in the sceptre of the British Regalia

Name	Locality	Weight (rough)	Weight (cut)
Great Table	A legendary stone supposedly of 242 cts.—See Dary-i-noor		
Great White	*See Imperial diamond*		
Harvey Young	South Africa	269½ cts.	
Hope blue	India		44·4 M. ct

This stone is probably part of the Blue Tavenier
The Hope diamond is now in the Smithsonian Institute

Name	Locality	Weight (rough)	Weight (cut)
Idol's Eye	India	—	70·20 M. cts.
Imperial	South Africa	468·9 M. cts.	184.5 M. cts. oval brilliant and a 20 ct. stone
Jagersfontein	South Africa	215 M. cts.	
Jahan Akbar Shah	*See Akbar Shah*		
Jehangir	India		83·03 M. cts. Drop-shape engraved
Jonker	South Africa	726 M. cts	Largest stone 125·65 M. cts., and 11 others
Jubilee	South Africa	650·8 M. cts.	245·35 M. ct brilliant
Julius Pam	South Africa	248 M. cts.	123 M. cts.
Koh-i-noor or Koh-i-nûr	India	Said to be 800 carats	191 M. cts. recut to 108·93 M. cts
Lethoso	Lethoso	601·25 M. cts.	
Libertador (Liberator)	Venezuela	155 cts.	3 stones, 39·80 cts. 18·12 cts. and 8·93 cts.
Litkie	South Africa	205½ cts.	
Matan or *Mattan*	Probably a quartz of about 367 cts.		
Minas Gerais	Brazil	172·5 M. cts.	
Moon			183 cts.
Moon of the Mountains	India	(legendary)	

There is an unsubstantiated suggestion that the Moon diamond is the recut Moon of the Mountains

Nassak	India	89¾ cts.	80·3 M. cts. recut to 43·38 M. cts.
New Star of the South	Brazil	140 cts.	
Niarchos	South Africa	426·5	130
Nizam	India	340 cts.	277 cts.
O'Reilly	South Africa	21¼ cts.	
Orloff	India	about 300 cts.	199·6 M. cts.
Orpen-Palmer	South Africa	117¾ cts.	
Otto Borgstrom	South Africa	121½ cts.	
Pam	South Africa	115 M. cts.	56·6 M. cts.
Pasha of Egypt	India		40 cts.
Paul 1	India		10 cts.

Claimed as a red diamond, but is pink and probably foiled

Paulo de Frontin	Brazil	49·5 M. cts.	
Peace	India		12·25 cts. heart shape
Pitt	*See Regent diamond*		
Pigott	India		Estimated 49 cts. Now destroyed
Polar Star	India		Approx. 40 cts. cushion brilliant
Porter-Rhodes	South Africa	153·5 M. cts.	56·60 Emerald cut stone
Presidente Vargas	Brazil	726·6 M. cts.	Largest cut stone 48·26 M. cts.
'Punch' Jones	United States of America	34·46 cts.	
Red Cross (canary yellow)	South Africa	about 370 cts.	205 cts. square brilliant
Regent	India	410 cts.	140·5 M. cts. cushion brilliant

Name	Locality	Weight (rough)	Weight (cut)
Reitz	*See Jubilee diamond*		
Sancy	India		55 M. cts.

The Sancy has been confused with a similarly shaped stone weighing 60·40 M. cts.

Name	Locality	Weight (rough)	Weight (cut)
Saxon white	India		49·71 cts.
Shah	India		88·7 M. cts.
Southern Cross	Brazil	118 cts.	
Spaulding	*See Stewart*		
Star of Africa	*See Great Star of Africa*		
Star of Africa No. 2	South Africa		317·4 M. cts. cushion
Star of Africa No. 3	South Africa		94·45 M. cts. pendeloque
Star of Africa No. 4	South Africa		63·65 M. cts. square brilliant

The Stars of Africa were cut from the Cullinan diamond

Name	Locality	Weight (rough)	Weight (cut)
Star of Este	India		26·16 M. cts.
Star of Egypt	Brazil		106·75 M. cts. emerald cut
Star of Minas	Brazil	179·38 M. cts.	
Star of South Africa	South Africa	83·50 M. cts.	47·75 M. cts. pendeloque
Star of the South	Brazil	261·88 M. cts.	128·8 M. cts. brilliant
Stewart	South Africa	296 M. cts.	123 M. cts. brilliant
Taj-i-mah	India		146 cts.
Tennant	South Africa	112 cts.	68 cts. brilliant
Tiger-eye (amber coloured)	South Africa	178½ cts.	61½ cts. brilliant
Tiffany yellow	South Africa	287·42 M. cts.	128·51 M. cts. brilliant
Van Zyl	South Africa	229¼ cts.	
Vargas	*See Presidente Vargas*		
Venter	South Africa	511 cts. octahedron	
Victoria	*See Imperial*		
Victory	Sierra Leone	770 M. cts.	
Webster kopje	South Africa	124 cts.	
Williamson pink	Tanganyika	54 M. cts.	23·60 M. cts. brilliant
Wittelsbach blue	India (?)		35·32 M. cts. brilliant
Woyie river	Sierra Leone	770 M. cts.	30 stones largest 31·35 M. cts.

M. cts.—Metric carats   Cts.—Old carats

BIBLIOGRAPHY

From the extensive literature on gem materials which has been published since very early times the undermentioned works have been selected. Some attempt has been made to include works of the various Continental countries and important works of America. Under the heading of 'General', the works listed include those on gem-testing and the fashioning of gemstones. The second group includes those works which deal with individual gem materials. The bibliography concludes with a list of the periodicals dealing with gemstones, or have sections dealing with gems. Latest editions only are given.

GENERAL

Anderson, B. W. (1964). *Gem Testing*. London. German translation by W. F. Eppler (1955), Stuttgart

Anon (1934). *Gemstones*. London; Handbook of the Imperial Institute

Axon, G. V. (1967). *The Wonderful World of Gems*. New York

Ball, S. H. (1951). *A Roman Book on Precious Stones*. Los Angeles

Bauer, M. H. (1896). *Edelsteinkunde*. Leipzig. 3rd ed. by K. Schlossmacher. (1932), Leipzig. English ed. by L. J. Spencer (1904), London

Blakemore, K. (1966). *Collecting Gems and Ornamental Stones*. London

Boardman, J. (1968). *Engraved Gems*. London

Bolman, J. (1950). *Welke edelsteen is dit?* Leiden

Cavenago-Bignami, S. (1965). *Gemmologia*. Milan

Chalmers, R. O. (1966). *Australian Rocks, Minerals and Gemstones*. Sydney

Chudoba, K. F. and Gübelin, E. J. (1966). *Edelsteinkundliches Handbuch*. Bonn

— — (1956). *Echt oder synthetisch?* Stuttgart

Church, A. H. (1924). *Precious Stones*. London

Cooper, C. W. (1924). *The Precious Stones of the Bible*. London

Cooper, L. and Cooper, R. (1966). *New Zealand Gemstones*. Wellington

Curran, M. (1961). *Jewels and Gems*. London

Dake, H. C. (1957). *The Art of Gem Cutting*. Portland, Oregon

Detter, T. (1951). *Adelstenar och Pärlor*. Stockholm

Doelter, C. A. (1893). *Edelsteinkunde*. Leipzig

— (1915). *Die Farben der Mineralien inbesondere der Edelsteine*. Braunschweig

Dragsted, A. (1933). *De aedle stene og deres mystik*. Copenhagen

Dragsted, O. (1953). *Guld & Aedle Stene*. Copenhagen

Eppler, W. F. (1934). *Edelsteine und Schmuckstein*. Leipzig

Fisher, P. J. (1965). *Jewels*. London

— (1966). *The Science of Gems*. New York

Franco, R. R. and Campos, J. E. de S. (1965). *As Pedras Preciosas*. San Paulo, Brazil

Gübelin, E. J. (1953). *Inclusions as a Means of Gemstone Identification*. Los Angeles

— (1968). *Die Edelsteine de Insel Ceylon*. Privately printed. Montreux

Hammes, J. (1962). *Edelsteinen*. Zeist, Holland

Holstein, O. (1936). *Fachkunde des Diamantschleifers*. Idar-Oberstein

Howard, J. H. (1946). *Revised Lapidary Handbook*. Greenville

Iyer, L. A. N. (1948). *A Handbook of Precious Stones*. Calcutta

Kraus, E. H. and Slawson, C. B. (1947). *Gems and Gem Materials*. New York

Kunz, G. F. (1915). *The Curious Lore of Precious Stones*. Philadelphia and London

Liddicoat, R. T. (1962). *Handbook of Gem Identification*. Los Angeles

McCallien, W. J. (1965). *Scottish Gem Stones*. London
McIver, J. R. (1966). *Gems, Minerals and Rocks of Southern Africa*. London
McLintock, W. F. P. and Sabine, P. A. (1951). *A Guide to the Collection of Gemstones in the Geological Museum*. London
Michel, H. (1926). *Die Kunstlichen Edelsteine*. Leipzig
Parsons, C. J. and Soukop, E. J. (1961). *Gems and Gemology*. California
Pearl, R. M. (1948). *Popular Gemology*. New York and London
Perry, N. and Perry, R. (1967). *Australian Gemstones in Colour*. Sydney
Schlossmacher, K. (1965). *Edelsteine und Perlen*. Stuttgart
Schubnel, H-J. (1968). *Les Pierres Précieuses*. Vendome
— (1968). *Pietre Preziose Gemme E Pietre Dure*. Novara, Italy
Shipley, R. M. (1951). *Dictionary of Gems and Gemology*. Los Angeles
Sinkankas, J. (1961). *Gemstones and Minerals*. New York
— (1962). *Gemstones of North America*. Princeton, New Jersey
— (1963). *Gem Cutting*. New Jersey
— (1968). *Van Nostrand's Standard Catalog of Gems*. Princeton, New Jersey
Sitwell, H. D. W. (1953). *The Crown Jewels*. London
Smith, G. F. H. and Phillips, F. C. (1958). *Gemstones*. London
Spencer, L. J. (1946). *A Key to Precious Stones*. London
Sperisen, F. J. (1961). *The Art of the Lapidary*. Milwaukee
Tardy, M. (1965). *Les Pierres et les Perles*. Paris
Terpstra, P. (1949). *Edelstenen*. Den Haag
Walton, J. (1954). *Physical Gemmology*. London
— (1954). *A Pocket Chart of Ornamental and Gem Stones*. London. German translation by W. F. Eppler (1957), Stuttgart
Webster, R. (1964). *The Gemmologist's Compendium*. London
— (1966). *Practical Gemmology*. London
Weinstein, M. (1958). *The World's Jewel Stones*. New York
Wild, G. O. (1936). *Praktikum der Edelsteinkunde*. Stuttgart
— and Biegel, K. H. (1950). *Kleiner Wegweiser zum Bestimmen von Edelsteinen*. Stuttgart
Willemse, A. (1935). *De Edelsteenen*. Eeckeren

BOOKS ON INDIVIDUAL GEM MATERIALS

Diamond
Anon. (1960). *The Diamond Dictionary*. Los Angeles
Argenzio, V. (1966). *The Fascination of Diamonds*. New York
Austin, A. C. and Mercer, M. (1941). *The Story of Diamonds*. Los Angeles
Balfour, I. (1963). *Famous Diamonds*. London
Bruet, E. (1952). *Le diamant*. Paris
Bruton, E. (1961). *The True Book about Diamonds*. London
Cattelle, W. R. (1911). *The Diamond*. London and New York
Champion, F. C. (1963). *Electronic Properties of Diamonds*. London
Copeland, L. L. (1966). *Diamonds; Famous, Notable and Unique*. Los Angeles
Crookes, W. (1909). *Diamonds*. London and New York
Dickenson, J. W. (1966). *The Book of Diamonds*. London
Doughty, O. (1963). *Early Diamond Days: The Opening of the Diamond Fields of South Africa*. London
Eppler, W. F. (1933). *Der Diamant und seine Bearbeitung*. Leipzig
Fersman, A. and Goldschmidt, V. (1911). *Der Diamant*. Heidelberg
Grodzinski, P. (1953). *Diamond Technology*. London
Hahn, E. (1956). *Diamonds*. London

Diamond—(cont.)

Hermann, F. (1948). *Diamanten*. Vienna
Lensen, G. (1966). *Produktions—und Handelgeschichte des Diamenten*. Berlin
Shipley, R. M. (1948). *Famous Diamonds of the World*. New York
Streeter, E. W. (1882). *The Great Diamonds of the World*. London
Sutton, J. R. (1928). *Diamond; a Descriptive Treatise*. London
Tolansky, S. (1955). *The Microstructures of Diamond Surfaces*. London
— (1962). *The History and Use of Diamond*. London
Wade, F. B. (1916). *Diamonds. A Study of the Factors Which Govern Their Value*.
    New York
Williams, A. F. (1923). *The Genesis of the Diamond* (2 vols). London
Williams, G. F. (1906). *The Diamond Mines of South Africa* (2 vols). New York

The silica group

Dake, H. C., Fleener, F. L. and Wilson, B. H. (1938). *Quartz Family Minerals*.
    New York and London
Idriess, I. (1968). *Opals and Sapphires*. London
Leechman, F. (1961). *The Opal Book*. Sydney
Liesegang, R. E. (1915). *Die Achate*. Dresden and Leipzig
Quick, L. (1963). *The Book of Agates*. London
Wollaston, J. C. (1924). *Opal; the Gem of the Never Never*. London

Jade

Bishop, H. R. (1906). *Investigations and Studies in Jade* (2 vols). New York
Goette, J. (1937). *Jade Lore*. New York
Hansford, S. H. (1950). *Chinese Jade Carving*. London
— (1968). *Chinese Carved Jades*. London
Hardinge, C. (1961). *Jade; Fact and Fable*. London
Nott, S. C. (1937). *Chinese Jade Throughout the Ages*. London
Palmer, J. P. (1967). *Jade*. London
Ruff, E. (1950). *Jade of the Maori*. London
Whitlock, H. P. and Ehrmann, M. L. (1949). *Story of Jade*. New York

Turquoise

Pogue, J. E. (1915). *The Turquoise*. Washington, D.C.

Pearl

Bolman, J. (1941). *The Mystery of the Pearl*. Leiden
Boutan, L. (1925). *La Perle*. Paris
Cahn, A. R. (1949). *Pearl Culture in Japan*. Washington, D.C.
Cattelle, W. R. (1907). *The Pearl, its Story, Charm and Value*. Philadelphia and
    London
Dakin, W. J. (1913). *Pearls*. New York
Kunz, G. F. and Stevenson, C. H. (1908). *The Book of the Pearl; the History, Art,
    Science, and Industry of the Queen of Gems*. London
Michel, H. (1940). *Perlen und Kulturperlen*. Leipzig
Mikimoto, K. (1920). *The Story of the Pearl*. Tokyo, Osaka and London
Parkert, O. W. (1925). *Die Perle*. Leipzig
Reece, N. C. (1958). *The cultured pearl*. Tokio

Amber

Bachofen-Echt, A. (1949). *Der Bernstein und seine Einschlüsse*. Vienna
Buffum, W. A. (1898). *The Tears of the Heliades or Amber as a Gem*. London

Amber—(cont.)

Farrington, O. C. (1923). *Amber; its Physical Properties and Geological Occurrence.*
Chicago
Schmid, L. (1931). *Bernstein.* Dresden and Leipzig
Williamson, C. G. (1932). *The Book of Amber.* London

Ivory

Williamson, C. G. (1938). *The Book of Ivory.* London

PERIODICALS

The Gemmologist. Monthly, 1931–1963. London
Gems and Gemology. Quarterly, since 1934. Los Angeles. (Official journal of the
Gemological Institute of America)
The Journal of Gemmology. Quarterly, since 1947. London. (Official journal of the
Gemmological Association of Great Britain.) Previously monthly as *Gem-*
mological News and *Journal of Gemmology*
Zeitschrift der Deutschen Gesellschaft für Edelsteinkunde. Quarterly, since 1952.
Idar-Oberstein. Formerly *Achat.* (Official journal of German gemmology)
The Australian Gemmologist. Monthly, since 1958. Melbourne. (Official journal of
the Australian Gemmological Association)
Bulletin Association Français de Gemmologie, Paris

The undermentioned periodicals contain a section on gem materials, or occasional
articles of gemmological interest.

Rocks & Minerals. Monthly, Peekshill, New York, U.S.A.
Gems and Minerals. Monthly. Mentone, California, U.S.A.
Diamant. Monthly. Antwerp, Belgium
The Lapidary Journal. Monthly, Del Mar, California, U.S.A.

The following textbooks are useful additions.

Dana's Textbook of Mineralogy by W. E. Ford. 4th ed. 1932. New York and London
Rutley's Mineralogy by H. H. Read. 24th ed. 1947. London
A Field Guide to Rocks and Minerals by F. H. Pough. Profusely illustrated with
many plates in full colour. 1955. Cambridge, Mass., U.S.A.
Tables of Physical and Chemical Constants by G. W. C. Kaye and T. H. Laby.
13th ed. 1967. London, New York and Toronto, Longmans

BIRTHSTONES

Official list issued by the National Association of Goldsmiths of Great Britain and Ireland

Month	Colour	Official stone
January	Dark red	Garnet
February	Purple	Amethyst
March	Pale blue	Aquamarine
April	White (transparent)	Diamond
May	Bright green	Emerald
June	Cream	Pearl
July	Red	Ruby
August	Pale green	Peridot
September	Deep blue	Sapphire
October	Variegated	Opal
November	Yellow	Topaz
December	Sky-blue	Turquoise

GEMSTONES FOR THE DAYS OF THE WEEK

Day	Stone
Sunday	Topaz or diamond
Monday	Pearl or crystal
Tuesday	Emerald or ruby
Wednesday	Amethyst or loadstone
Thursday	Carnelian or sapphire
Friday	Emerald or catseye
Saturday	Diamond or turquoise

EMBLEMS OF THE TWELVE APOSTLES

Apostle	Stone
Andrew	Blue sapphire
Bartholemew	Red carnelian
James	White chalcedony
James-the-less	Topaz
John	Emerald
Matthew	Amethyst
Matthias	Chrysolite
Peter	Jasper
Philip	Sardonyx
Simeon	Pink hyacinth
Thaddeus	Chrysoprase
Thomas	Beryl

SUGGESTED LIST OF PERMISSIBLE NAMES FOR GEMSTONES

The inception of the Trade Descriptions Act of 1968 has presented problems in nomenclature. Although careful consideration has been given in the text of this book, a number of names are mentioned which under the Act may be open to objection; only the Courts in their wisdom can resolve these. In an endeavour to give some guide to this problem there is now appended a list of suggested permissible names for gemstones (with some modifications made by the author) which was originally produced by the National Association of Goldsmiths of Great Britain and Ireland and the Gemmological Association of Great Britain[1]. It must be pointed out that this list was prepared for English usage; in the United States of America there are some differences as there well may be in other countries.

The nomenclature given in this list is not exhaustive and some of the rarer gemstones and gem materials are not tabulated.

Under the Act, the name 'cairngorm', traditionally used for brown quartz, might well be suspect since very little, if any, brown quartz is now mined at the Cairngorm Mountains in Scotland which is the origin of the name of the stone. Most of the material now comes from other countries. Although the name 'cairngorm', applied to such stones, is of *trade usage*, it has been decided that such usage does not constitute a defence in law against a prosecution under the Act.

The addition of the place of origin to the designations given in the nomenclature list may only be given if there is no doubt as to its accuracy, or if its accuracy can be proved.

The terms 'Brazilian-', 'Mexican-', 'Algerian-' or 'Italian onyx' for the stalagmitic calcites should not be used. The term 'onyx-marble' has been held to be not allowable and it is considered that the material should be called just 'marble', the basis for this argument being that two mineral names—onyx and marble—are involved, assuming that 'onyx' is the name for a definite mineral (of the silica group). The author does not wholly agree with this, because the name 'onyx' has been used from time immemorial for both the chalcedony and for the stalagmitic calcite. Such border-line cases will not be completely resolved until tested by the Courts.

NOMENCLATURE FOR GEMSTONES AND PEARLS

AMBER

Species	Colour	Recommended trade name
Amber	All colours	Amber, with or without appropriate colour description

ANDALUSITE

Andalusite	Green, red, brown	Andalusite, with or without appropriate colour description

---

[1] *Code of Trading*, National Association of Goldsmiths of Great Britain and Ireland, London, 1967

BERYL

Species	Colour	Recommended trade name
Emerald	Bright green*	Emerald
Aquamarine	Pale blue, pale greenish-blue	Aquamarine
Beryl	White	White beryl
	Green†	Green beryl
	Golden, yellow	Golden or yellow beryl
	Pink	Pink beryl, Morganite

* *Colour due to chromium*
† *Colour not due to chromium*

CHRYSOBERYL

Chrysoberyl	Yellow, yellowish-green, yellowish-brown, brown	Chrysoberyl
Chatoyant Chrysoberyl	Translucent yellow to greenish or brownish—showing chatoyancy	Chrysoberyl cat's-eye
Alexandrite	Green to greenish brown by daylight, red to reddish brown by artificial (tungsten) light	Alexandrite

CORAL

Coral	Red, pink, white, sometimes black	Coral, with or without appropriate colour description

CORUNDUM

Ruby	Red	Ruby
	Red, with star effect	Star-ruby
Sapphire	Blue	Sapphire
	Blue, grey, etc., with star effect	Star-sapphire
	All colours other than the above	Yellow sapphire, green s., pink s., mauve s., etc.

DIAMOND

Diamond	White, yellowish white, yellow, brown, green, pink, red, mauve, blue, black	Diamond

EMERALD—See Beryl

FELDSPAR

Orthoclase	White	Adularia
	Yellow	Orthoclase
Moonstone	Whitish with bluish shimmer of light	Moonstone
Microcline, Amazonite	Opaque green	Amazonite or Amazon stone
Oligoclase and Orthoclase	Whitish-red-brown—flecked with golden particles	Sunstone Aventurine feldspar
Labradorite	Ashen grey with bluish or reddish or yellowish or green gleams	Labradorite

FLUORITE, FLUORSPAR

Species	Colour	Recommended trade name
Fluorite, Fluorspar	Green, yellow, red, blue, violet, etc.	Fluorspar, Fluorite, with or without appropriate colour description
	Banded blue and other colours	Fluorspar or Blue John

GARNET

Species	Colour	Recommended trade name
Garnet	All colours	Garnet
Almandine	Violet-red	Almandine or almandine garnet
Pyrope	Red to crimson	Pyrope or pyrope garnet
	Pale violet	Rhodolite or rhodolite garnet
Spessartite	Brownish-red, orange-red	Spessartite or spessartite garnet (or spessartine if preferred)
Grossularite	Pale green and other colours (translucent)	Grossularite, grossular garnet or massive grossular garnet
	Transparent	Grossular garnet
	Orange—yellowish-red, Orange—reddish-brown	Hessonite or hessonite garnet
Andradite	Yellow	Andradite or andradite garnet
	Green, yellowish-green	Andradite or Demantoid or demantoid garnet
	Black	Melanite garnet

IOLITE

Species	Colour	Recommended trade name
Iolite Cordierite	Blue and dingy brown	Iolite or Cordierite

JADE (PYROXENE)

Species	Colour	Recommended trade name
Jadeite	Green, whitish with emerald green flecks, mauve, brown, orange, opaque to translucent	Jadeite, or Jade
Chloromelanite	Dark green or nearly black, with white flecks, opaque to translucent	Chloromelanite, or Jade

JADE (AMPHIBOLE)

Species	Colour	Recommended trade name
Nephrite	Green, white, single coloured and flecked, opaque to translucent	Nephrite, or Jade

LAPIS-LAZULI

Species	Colour	Recommended trade name
Lapis-lazuli	Blue (opaque) often with brassy specks of pyrite; opaque whitish-light blue	Lapis-lazuli

MALACHITE

Species	Colour	Recommended trade name
Malachite	Green veined, banded	Malachite

MARCASITE—See PYRITE

OPAL

Species	Colour	Recommended trade name
Opal	Milky with quickly shimmering rainbow-like play of colours	Opal or white opal
	The same on dark background	Opal or black opal
	Transparent straw-coloured or colourless, iridescent	Opal or water opal
Fire Opal	Fiery red to browny-red	Opal or fire opal
Matrix Opal	Flecks of opal in matrix	Opal matrix

PEARL

Pearl	All colours	Pearl, with or without appropriate colour description

PEARL (CONCH)

Conch Pearl	Pink, white (no pearly lustre)	Conch pearl, with or without appropriate colour description

PERIDOT, OLIVINE

Olivine	Yellowish-green, olive green, brown	Peridot

PYRITE AND MARCASITE

Pyrite Marcasite	Brassy-grey with metallic sheen	Pyrite or Marcasite

QUARTZ

Rock crystal	Colourless	Quartz or rock crystal
Amethyst (*natural colour*)	Light to dark violet	Amethyst
Amethyst (*heat-treated*)	Yellowish, brownish-yellow	Citrine or golden or yellow quartz
	Reddish, reddish-brown reddish-yellow	Quartz with or without appropriate colour description
	Green	Green quartz
Citrine	Yellow, brownish-yellow	Citrine or golden or yellow quartz
Smoky Quartz	Smoky or brownish yellow to black—when brownish yellow to brown or smoky brown	Smoky quartz
		Brown quartz
Rose-quartz	Milky rose-pink	Rose-quartz

QUARTZ (with inclusions)

Species	Colour	Recommended trade name
Prase	Leek-green	Prase
Chatoyant Quartz	Whitish-grey, greyish green, greenish-yellow, blue, with shimmering streaks of light	Quartz cat's-eye
Crocidolite (pseudomorph)	Yellowish-brown, brownish golden yellow with shimmering streaks of light	Tiger's-eye
Crocidolite (pseudomorph)	Like tiger's-eye but greyish blue	Hawk's-eye
Aventurine Quartz	Yellowish-browny-red, yellow, brown, red, or green, with small flakes of mica	Aventurine quartz

QUARTZ (Cryptocrystalline) CHALCEDONY GROUP

Chalcedony (*translucent*)	Grey to bluish and green*	Chalcedony
Chrysoprase	Apple-green and light green	Chrysoprase
Cornelian	Red in various shades	Cornelian
Heliotrope	Dark green with red spots	Bloodstone Heliotrope
Jasper	Whitish, yellow, red, green, brown, etc.	Jasper
Plasma	Leek-green	Plasma
Agate	Banded in various colours, white, yellow, grey, red, brown, blue, black, etc.	Agate, onyx sardonyx, etc., as appropriate
	Milky with green or rust-coloured moss-like inclusions	Moss-agate

* Colour due to chromium

RUBY AND SAPPHIRE—See CORUNDUM

SERPENTINE

Serpentine	Translucent green	Bowenite
	Emerald-green with black spots	Williamsite
	Green, grey-green, whitish and reddish-brown rock	Serpentine

SPHENE

Sphene	Yellow, green, brown and grey	Sphene, with or without appropriate colour description

SPINEL

Spinel	All colours	Spinel; or red s., pink s. orange s., etc., respectively

SPODUMENE

Species	Colour	Recommended trade name
Spodumene	Yellowish-green, brownish-green, pale yellow	Spodumene
Hiddenite	Bright green*	Hiddenite
Kunzite	Rose-pink, lilac, violet	Kunzite

* Colour due to chromium

TOURMALINE

Tourmaline	All colours	Tourmaline; or red t., green t., parti-coloured t., etc., respectively

TOPAZ

Topaz	All colours	Topaz; or white t., pink t., blue t., etc., respectively

TURQUOISE

Turquoise	Sky blue, blue, bluish-green, greenish;	Turquoise
Turquoise matrix	Flecks of turquoise in matrix	Turquoise matrix

ZIRCON

Zircon	All colours	Zircon; or blue z., red z., etc., respectively

ZOISITE

Zoisite	Blue, violet and brown	Zoisite (with colour as prefix)

GLOSSARY OF UNUSUAL NAMES

This list includes alternative or disused gem names, misnomers and trade names. Misnomers are printed within inverted commas and trade names in italics.

Accarbaar (Akabar)	Black coral
Accidental pearl	Natural pearl
Achrite	Dioptase
Adamantine spar	Silky brown sapphire
Adamite	Artificial corundum powder
'Adelaide ruby'	Red South African garnet
Adinol	A silicified porphyry or diabase
Aeroides	Pale sky-blue aquamarine
'African emerald'	Green fluorspar
'African jade'	Massive green grossular garnet
Agalmatolite	Steatite; pyrophyllite or pinite
Agaphite	Vitreous variety of Persian turquoise
Agstein	Jet
'Alabandine ruby'	Almandine garnet
Alalite	Diopside
'Alexandrite', or	Synthetic change colour sapphire or spinel
'Alexandrine'	
'Almandite'	Synthetic spinel
'Alaska black diamond'	Hematite
'Alaska diamond'	Rock crystal
Alasmoden pearls	Freshwater pearls
'Alencon diamond'	Rock crystal
Allepo stone	Eye agate
'Almandine spinel'	Natural violet spinel
Almaschite	Romanian amber
Alomite	Sodalite
Aloxite	Aluminium oxide powder
'Alpine diamond'	Pyrites
Alshedite	Sphene
Alundum	Aluminium oxide powder
Amarillo stone	Figured chalcedony (Texas)
Amaryl	Light green synthetic corundum
Amatrix (Amatrice)	Mixture of variscite, chalcedony and quartz
Amause	Glass (strass)
'Amazon jade'	Green microcline feldspar
'Amberine'	Yellowish-green moss agate
'America jade'	Californite (idocrase)
'American ruby'	(1) Pyrope garnet
	(2) Rose quartz
Ampullar pearl	Pearl from the epidermis of the oyster
'Ancona ruby'	Rose quartz
'Andalusite'	Brown tourmaline
Aphrizite	Black tourmaline
Apricotine	Apricot-coloured garnets from New Jersey
Apyrite	Peach-coloured tourmaline
Aquagem	Light blue synthetic spinel
'Arabian diamond'	Rock crystal
'Arabian magic diamond'	Synthetic colourless or yellow sapphire
Argillite	A slate-like rock from British Columbia
'Arizona ruby'	Pyrope garnet
'Arizona spinel'	Garnet
'Arkansas diamond'	Rock crystal
Arkansite	Transparent brookite
Armenian stone	Lapis-lazuli
Asparagus stone	Yellow-green apatite
'Atlas pearls'	Beads of white satin spar
'Australian ruby'	Garnet
Australite	Tektite
Awabi pearl	Abalone pearl (Japanese)

Axe stone	Nephrite
Aztec stone	Smithsonite
Azules opal	Water opal with red and green flecks with bluish haze
'*Azurite*'	Sky-blue smithsonite
Azurlite	Pale blue chalcedony
Bacalite	Amber from Lower California
'Baffa diamond'	Rock crystal
'Balas ruby'	Red spinel
Bamboo pearl	Tabasheer
Baroda gem	Foiled back colourless glass
'Bastard emerald'	Peridot
Bayate	Ferruginous jasper (Cuba)
Beekite	Agatized coral
Beccarite	Green zircon
Bell pearl	Drop pearl
Belomorite	Moonstone (Russia)
'Bengal amethyst'	Purple sapphire
Berigem	Synthetic greenish-yellow spinel
Binghamite	Chatoyant quartz with goethite inclusions
Bird's eye pearl	Freshwater pearl with dark rings
Bird's eye quartz	Jasper with colourless spherulites
Bishop's stone	Amethyst
'Black amber'	Jet
'Black diamond'	Hematite
Black moonstone	Labradorite feldspar
Blackmorite	Reddish-yellow common opal from Montana
'Blue alexandrite'	Change colour sapphire
Blue chrysoprase	Chalcedony with included chrysocolla
'Blue opal'	Lazulite
Blue point pearl	Pearls from the *Quadrula undulata*
Boakite	Brecciated green and red jasper
Bobrowka garnet	Demantoid garnet
'Bohemian chrysolite'	Moldavite
'Bohemian diamond'	Rock crystal
'Bohemian ruby'	(1) Pyrope garnet
	(2) Rose quartz
'Bohemian topaz'	Citrine
Boke	Rose coloured coral (Japanese)
'Bone turquoise'	Odontolite
'Bornholm diamonds'	Rock crystal
Bourguignon pearls	Wax-filled imitation pearls
'Brazilian aquamarine'	Blue topaz
'Brazilian diamond'	Rock crystal
'Brazilian emerald'	Green tourmaline
'Brazilian peridot'	Light green tourmaline
'Brazilian ruby'	Red or pink topaz
'Brazilian sapphire'	Blue tourmaline
'Briancon diamond'	Rock crystal
'Brighton diamond'	Rock crystal
'Brighton emerald'	Green glass
'Bristol diamond'	Rock crystal
Brown pearl	Conchiolin rich pearls of low value
Burnt amethyst	Heat treated yellow quartz
'Buxton diamond'	Rock crystal
Byewater	A colour grade of yellowish diamond
Cabra stone	Fluorite
Cacholong	Porcelaneous common opal
Calaite (Kalaite)	Turquoise
Calbenite	Myrickite
Chalcomalachite	Mixture of malachite, calcite and gypsum
Californian tiger's eye	Chatoyant bastite (serpentine)
Californian iris	Kunzite
'California jade'	Californite (idocrase)
'California moonstone'	Chalcedony
'California onyx'	Banded stalagmitic calcite and aragonite
'California ruby'	Garnet
'California turquoise'	Variscite

Cambay stone	Indian carnelian
Canada moonstone	Peristerite feldspar
Callainite	Near turquoise (Brittany)
Canary stone	Yellow carnelian
Canary diamond	Yellow diamond
Cand (Cann)	Fluorspar (Cornwall)
Candite	Blue spinel
'Cape chrysolite'	Prehnite
'Cape emerald'	Prehnite
'Cape ruby'	Pyrope garnet
Carneol	Pink-dyed chalcedony
Catalin	Phenolic resin plastic
Catalinaite	Jasper from Catalina Island
Cateye	Operculum
Catlinite	A clay-like mineral used by early American Indians
Cat's eye opal	Harlequin opal showing a streak of light
Cedarite	Amber from Manitoba, Canada
Celestial stone	Turquoise
Cellon	Cellulose acetate plastic
Ceragate	Waxy yellow-coloured chalcedony
Cerulene	Calcite coloured green and blue by malachite and azurite
'Ceylon chrysolite'	Yellow-green tourmaline
'Ceylon diamond'	Colourless zircon
'Ceylon opal'	Moonstone
'Ceylon peridot'	Yellow-green tourmaline
Chalchihuiti	Mexican name for jade or other green stone
Chalcomalachite	Malachite-calcite mixture
Chalmeleonite	Change colour tourmaline
Chank pearl	Pearl from the *Turbinella scolymas*
Cherry opal	Red coloured common opal
Chicken bone jade	Yellowish burned or buried jade
Chicot pearl	Natural blister pearl
Chi Ku Pai jade	Chicken bone jade
'Chinese cat's eye'	Shell cat's eye
Chinese jade	Jadeite
'Chinese turquoise'	Mixture of calcite, quartz and soapstone dyed blue
Ch'iung Yü	Red jadeite
Chloropal	(1) Green common opal
	(2) An opal-like hydrous silicate of iron
Chlorophane	Fluorite which fluoresces on heating
Chlorospinel	Green spinel
Chlor-utalite	Variscite
Chrome idocrase	Emerald-green idocrase
Chromepidote	Chrome-rich epidote from Burma also known as Tawmawite
Chrysanthemum stone	A radial aggregate of xenotime and zircon (Japan)
'Chrysoberyllus'	Greenish-yellow beryl
Chrysocarmen	Red to brown copper-bearing stone with blue or green spots
Chrysolite	Undesirable name for yellow-green chrysoberyl or for peridot, etcetera
Chrysolithus	Yellow beryl
Chrysopal	Green common opal
Chrysophrase	Green dyed chalcedony
Chrysoquartz	Green aventurine quartz
Cinnabar matrix	Quartz with red cinnabar inclusions
Cinnamon stone	Hessonite garnet
Ciro pearl	Imitation pearl
Cleiophane	Zinc blende
Cloud agate	Agate with dark cloud-like markings
Coconut pearl	Pearls from the clam of Singapore
'Coconut pearl'	Round concretions found in coconuts. Of no value
'Colorado diamond'	Transparent smoky quartz
Colorado goldstone	Aventurine quartz
'Colorado jade'	Green microcline feldspar
'Colorado ruby'	Pyrope garnet

'Colorado topaz'	Yellow quartz
Coltstone	Acrylic resin plastic
Common opal	Opal without play of colour (may be coloured)
Comptonite	Variety of thomsonite
'Congo emerald'	Dioptase
'Copper emerald'	Dioptase
'Copper lapis'	Azurite
Coral agate	Agate with a coral-like design, or agate pseudo-morphous after coral
'Coralline'	Red dyed chalcedony
Coro pearl	Imitation pearl
'Cornish diamond'	Rock crystal
Corsican green	Serpentine-bastite with schiller
Corundolite	Synthetic white spinel
Cotterite	Quartz with inclusions of white clay
Craquelées	Crackled rock crystal (fire-stones)
Creolin	Brecciated jasper
Creolite	Red and white banded jasper (California)
Crispite	Quartz or agate with green hair-like needles
Crocidolite opal	Opal with included crocidolite (an opal cat's eye)
Crop pearl	Baroque pearl
Cross-grained stones	Irregularly shaped and intergrown diamond crystals
Cross stone	(1) Staurolite twin crystals
	(2) Chiastolite (andalusite)
Crusite	Chiastolite
Crysiolon	Carborundum powder
Cymophane	Chrysoberyl cat's eye
Cyst pearl	Natural whole pearl
Dallasite	A green and white rock from Vancouver Island, British Columbia
Damburite	Synthetic light red corundum
Daourite	Red tourmaline
Darwin glass	Tektite
'Dauphiné diamond'	Rock crystal
Davidsonite	Yellow-green beryl
Dear pearl	Lustreless natural pearl
Dekorite	Phenolic plastic
De la Mar pearl	Imitation pearl
Delatynite	Romanian amber
Delawarite	Aventurine feldspar
Delta pearls	Imitation pearls
Demidovite	Blue compact chrysocolla
'Desert amethyst'	Solarized glass
Desert glass	Obsidian or moldavite
Diakon	Acrylic resin plastic
Diamantine	Crystallized boron abrasive powder
Diaspore	Hydrous aluminium oxide mineral
Dirigem	Synthetic green spinel
Disthene	Kyanite
Distrene	Polystyrene resin plastic
Ditroite	Sodalite
Dragomite	Rock crystal (Galicia)
Duluth agate	Agate from Lake Superior
Durosol	Aluminium oxide abrasive powder
Dust pearls	Very small seed pearls
Earth stone	Mined amber
Ebonite	Vulcanized india rubber
Eclogite	Pyroxene garnet rock in South African diamond pipes
Edinite	Prase
Egeran	Idocrase
Egg pearl	Natural egg-shaped pearl
Elbaite	Pink tourmaline (Elba)
Elco pearls	Imitation pearls
Eldoradoite	Blue chalcedony
El Doradoite	Yellowish quartz (California)
'Electric emerald'	Green glass
'Elie ruby'	Pyrope garnet

Elite pearls	Imitation pearls
Elixirite	Banded rhyolite from New Mexico
Ellandra pearls	Imitation pearls
Emeralda	Synthetic yellow-green spinel
'Emerald malachite'	Dioptase
'Emerald matrix'	Green fluorspar
Emeraldine	Dyed green chalcedony
'Emeraldite' or 'Emeralite'	Pale green tourmaline
'Emeraudine'	Dioptase
Emildine (Emilite)	Spessartite garnet (South Africa)
Empirite	Name for tektites found in Georgia
'*Endura emerald*'	Green glass
Enhydros	Chalcedony nodules partly filled with water
Epidosite	Epidote
Erinide	Yellowish-green synthetic spinel
Erinoid	Casein plastic
'Esmeralda'	Green tourmaline
Essonite	Hessonite garnet
'Evening emerald'	Peridot
Eye agate	Banded agate with cutting so that bands are concentric
Eye diamond	Fish-eye diamond
Eye stone	Thomsonite
Fairburnite	Fortification agate (South Dakota)
Fairy stone	Staurolite crystal (twinned) or an imitation of same
Falcon's eye	Silica pseudomorph of blue crocidolite
Fales	Any stone with differently coloured layers
'False amethyst'	Purple fluorite
'False chrysolite'	Moldavite
'False emerald'	Green fluorite
'False lapis'	Lazulite, or dyed jasper
'False topaz'	Citrine or yellow fluorite
Falun brilliants	Lead glass imitation stones
Fancy pearls	Coloured natural nacreous pearls
'Fashoda garnet'	Pyrope garnet
Feather gypsum	Satin spar
Fei-ts'ui	Jade
'Feldspar-apyre'	Andalusite (French)
'*Ferrers (Ferros) emerald*'	Green glass
Ferrolite	Black iron slag proposed for use as a gem
'*Fire pearl*'	Billitonite
Flame spinel	Orange-red natural spinel
Flash opal	Opal with a single-hued flash of colour
Fleches d'amour	Rutilated (sagenitic) quartz
'Flinder's diamond'	White topaz
Flohmig amber	Fatty amber, full of bubbles
Flower agate	Chalcedony with flower-like inclusions
Foil back	Chatons
Forcherite	Orange-yellow opal coloured by orpiment
Fossil pineapple	Opal pseudomorph after crystals of glauberite, gay lussite, or gypsum
Fowlerite	Rhodonite
Framesite	An aggregate of diamond, bort and carbon from Premier mine
French colour rubies	Light red rubies
Frost agate (Frost stone)	Agate with white markings
Fuh yu	Abalone shell and pearl
'Fukien jade'	Soapstone
Futuran	Phenolic resin plastic
Gegat	Jet
Galalith	Casein plastic
'Garnet jade'	Massive green grossular garnet
Geneva ruby	Reconstructed ruby
'German diamond'	Rock crystal
'German lapis'	Blue dyed jasper
German mocoas	Imitation moss agate
Gibsonite	Pink thomsonite

'Gibsonville emerald'	Greenish quartz
Giguku	Jade (Japanese)
Giogetto	Black coral
Girasol	(1) Fire opal
	(2) A type of water opal
	(3) Moonstone, etcetera
Girasol pearl	Imitation pearl
Girasol sapphire	Sapphire cat's eye
'Glass agate'	Obsidian
Glass lava	Obsidian
Glass meteorite	Moldavite
Glass opal	Hyalite
Glass stone	Axinite
Gles	Small cleavage cracks in diamond
Gold fluss	Aventurine glass
Gold opal	Fire opal
Gold quartz	(1) Small particles of gold in quartz or quartzite
	(2) Golden coloured crystal quartz
'Gold sapphire'	Lapis-lazuli
Goldstone	Aventurine glass
'Gold topaz'	Golden quartz
Goodletite	Marble forming the matrix of rubies (Burma)
Green ear	Ear-shaped freshwater pearls
'Green garnet'	Enstatite
Green John	Massive green fluorite
'Green onyx'	Stained green chalcedony
'Green quartz'	Fluorite
Green starstone	Chlorastrolite
Greenstone	(1) Nephrite
	(2) Chlorastrolite
Grenalite	Staurolite
Griqualandite	Crocidolite (Tiger's eye)
Guadalcanal cat's eye	Operculum
Guarnaccino	Yellowish-red garnet
Gum animé	Copal resin
Haida slate	Argillite
Hair amethyst	Sagenitic amethyst
Hairstone	Sagenitic quartz
Hakik	Agate (Indian)
Hammer pearls	Baroque (hammer-head shaped) pearls
Hard mass	Imitation gems in hard glass
'Hawaiian diamonds'	Rock crystal
Hawaiite	Peridot (Hawaii)
Haystack pearl	Natural high domed button pearl
Heliolite	Aventurine feldspar
Heliotrope	Bloodstone (quartz)
Hematine	Imitation hematite
Hematite garnet	A synthetic iron-rich garnet
'Herkimer diamond'	Rock crystal
Herrerite	Blue and green smithsonite
Hinge pearls	Elongated baroque pearls from the hinge of the fresh-water mussel
'Hinjosa topaz'	Yellow quartz
Holstein	Fossil wood
'Honan jade'	Soapstone (agalmatolite)
'Hope sapphire'	Synthetic sapphire blue spinel
'Horatio diamond'	Rock crystal
Horn coral	Black coral
'Hot Springs diamond'	Rock crystal
Hsi jade	Clear water or clear black jade
Hsieh jade	Ink black jade
Hsiu Yen	Green and white jasper
Hungarian cat's eye	Quartz cat's eye
Hyacinth	(1) Orange-brown zircon
	(2) Hessonite garnet
Hyacinth of Compostella	Reddish iron-rich quartz
Hyaline	Opalescent milky quartz

Hyalite	Clear colourless opal
Hyalithe	Red, brown, green or black opaque glass
'Iceland agate'	Obsidian
Image stone	Agalmatolite
Imperial jade	Fine green Chinese jade
Imperial Yu stone	Green aventurine quartz
Inanga	Grey nephrite
Inca emerald	Emerald from Equador
Inca stone	Pyrites
Indian agate	Moss agate
Indian cat's eye	Chrysoberyl cat's eye
'Indian emerald'	Green stained crackled quartz
'Indian jade'	Green aventurine quartz
'Indian topaz'	Yellow sapphire
Invelite	Phenolic resin plastic
Iolanthite	Banded reddish jasper
'Irish diamonds'	Rock crystal
Iron opal	Red or yellow common opal
Iserine (Iserite)	Black iron mineral used to imitate hematite
'Isle of Wight diamond'	Rock crystal
Isle Royale greenstone	Chlorastrolite
Italian chrysolite	Idocrase
'Italian lapis'	Stained jasper
Itatli	Aztec name for obsidian
'Ivory turquoise'	Odontolite
Jacinth	(1) Red-brown zircon
	(2) Hessonite garnet
Jadeolite	Green syenite resembling jade, possibly pseudojadeite
'Jade Tenace'	Saussurite
'*Jadine*'	Australian chrysoprase
Japan pearl	Old name for cultured blister pearl
Japanese coral	Dark red coral with white core
Jargoon	Colourless or pale coloured zircon
Jasp agate	Intermediate between jasper and agate
Jaspe fleuri	Jasp agate
Jasperine	Banded jasper
'Jasper jade'	Green jasper, serpentine, etcetera
Jaspillite	Banded hematite and jasper
Jasponyx	Banded jasp agate
Jaspopal	Intermediate jasper and opal
Jet stone	Black tourmaline (schorl)
Johannes gem	Synthetic rutile
Johnite	Vitreous and scaly turquoise
'*Jourado diamond*'	Synthetic colourless spinel
Kahurangi	Pale green translucent nephrite
Kalmuck agate (opal)	Cacholong
'Kandy spinel'	Almandine garnet
Kan Huang jade	Light yellowish jade
Kaolite	Moulded imitation cameos, etcetera, in baked clay
Karlsbad Spring stone	Banded gypsum used for carvings
Kashgar jade	Inferior nephrite
Kawakawa	Nephrite (Maori)
Kenya gem	Synthetic rutile
Keweenaw agate	Agate from Lake Superior
Keystoneite	Chalcedony coloured blue by chrysocolla
'Khoton jade'	Inferior nephrite
'Kidney stone'	Nephrite
Kikukwaseki	A radial aggregate of zircon and xenotime (chrysanthemum stone)
'Killiecrankie diamond'	Colourless topaz
Kimpi	Red or brown jadeite
Kingfisher jade	Bluish-green jadeite
'King topaz'	Natural yellow sapphire
Kinradite	Orbicular jasper
Kismet pearls	Imitation pearls
Kollin garnet	Almandine garnet
'Korea jade'	Bowenite serpentine

Kyauk-ame	Black jadeite
Kyauk-atha	White translucent jadeite
La Beau pearls	Imitation pearls
Labrador moonstone	Labradorite feldspar
Lactoid	Casein plastic
Laguna pearls	Imitation pearls
'Lake George diamonds'	Rock crystal
'Lake Superior agate'	Thomsonite, or correctly agate
'Lake Superior fire agate'	Glass imitation of opal
Lake Superior greenstone	Chlorastrolite
Lao Kan C'hing jade	Bluish jade
La Paz pearls	Mostly grey and bronze pearls from the Gulf of California; or for coloured pearls from the hammer-head clam
Lapis crucifer	Staurolite crystals
Lardite	Agalmatolite
La Tausca pearls	Imitation pearls
Lat yay	Clouded jadeite
Laurelite	Idocrase
Lavendrine	Amethyst quartz
Lazurfeldspar	Bluish orthoclase (Siberia)
Lazurquartz	Blue quartz (chalcedony)
Lechosos opal	Opal with deep green and red flashes of colour
Leonite	Tibet stone (eosite)
Leuco-sapphire	Colourless sapphire
Ligament pearl	Hinge pearl
Lingah pearl (shell)	Pearls (shell) from Persian Gulf
Lintonite	Variety of thomsonite
'Lithia amethyst'	Kunzite
'Lithia emerald'	Hiddenite
Lithoxyle (Lithoxylite)	Opalized wood
Litoslazuli	Massive purple fluorspar
Liver opal	Menilite (impure opal)
Lluvisnando opal	Yellowish water opal with pronounced flames
Love arrows	Sagenitic quartz
Love stone	Aventurine quartz
Lucinite	Variscite
'Lux sapphire'	Iolite
Lynx eye	Labradorite with green flash
'Lynx sapphire'	Iolite
Maiden pearl	Newly fished pearl
Malacon	Glassy brown variety of zircon
'Manchurian jade'	Soapstone
Manganese spar	Rhodochrosite
Man Yu	Jade of blood red colour
Maori stone (jade)	Nephrite
'Mari diamond'	Rock crystal
Mariposite	A foliated rock with bright green streaks of mica
'Marmarosch diamond'	Rock crystal
'Marmora diamond'	Rock crystal
Marvella pearls	Imitation pearls
'*Mascot emerald*'	Soudé emerald
'Mass aqua'	Hard glass imitation
Mass opal	Opal matrix
'Matara (Matura) diamond'	Colourless zircon
Maxixe aquamarine	Boron-rich deep blue aquamarine (easily fades)
Mayaite	Diopside jadeite (Central America)
Mecca stone	Cornelian
Medfordite	A type of moss agate
'*Medina emerald*'	Green glass
Melanite	Black andradite garnet
Melichrysos	Yellow zircon
Menilite	Banded grey and brown common opal
'Mexican agate'	Banded calcite or aragonite
'Mexican diamond'	Rock crystal
'Mexican jade'	Green dyed stalagmitic calcite
'Mexican onyx'	Stalagmitic calcite

Micatite	Phenolic resin plastic
Midge stone	Moss agate
Milhama pebbles	Jasper pebbles
Milk opal	Milky white common opal
Mixte	Composite stone, half real and half imitation
Mock pearl	Imitation pearl
'Mogok diamond'	White topaz
Molochites	Green jasper
'Montana jet'	Obsidian
'Montana ruby'	Red garnet
'Mont Blanc ruby'	Rose quartz
Morion	Dark brown quartz
Moro	Blood red coral (Japanese)
Moroxite	Greenish-blue apatite
'Mother of emerald'	Prase
Mountain crystal	Rock crystal
'Mountain jet'	Obsidian
'Mountain ruby'	Red garnet
Mozarkite	A chert or flint
Muller's glass	Hyalite glassy opal
Muscle pearls	Small distorted pearls found near the muscle of the oyster
Mussel egg	Freshwater pearl
Mussite	Diopside
'Mutzschen diamond'	Rock crystal
Mya yay	Best quality green jadeite
Nassau pearl	Pink conch pearl
Nautilus pearl	Oval section of Indian nautilus (Coq de pearl)
Needle stone	Sagenitic quartz
'Nerchinsk aquamarine'	Blue topaz
'Nevada diamond'	Obsidian
'Nevada topaz'	Obsidian
'Nevada turquoise'	Variscite
New Zealand greenstone	Nephrite
Nicolo	Black or dark brown onyx with thin bluish-white layer
'Night emerald'	Peridot
Nigrine	Black rutile
Nixonoid	Cellulosic plastic
Noble opal	Precious opal
Norbide	Boron carbide abrasive
Occidental agate	Poor quality agate
Occidental amethyst	Real amethyst (violet quartz)
Occidental cat's eye	Quartz cat's eye
Occidental chalcedony	Poor quality chalcedony
Occidental cornelian	Poor quality cornelian
'Occidental diamond'	Rock crystal
'Occidental topaz'	Citrine
'Occidental turquoise'	Odontolite
Oeil de boeuf	Ox eye labradorite feldspar
'Olivene (olivine)'	Demantoid garnet
Onegite	Amethyst with needle-like inclusions
'Onyx obsidian'	Parallel banded obsidian
'Onyx opal'	Banded opal
Opal agate	Alternate bands of opal and chalcedony
Opalite	Impure common opal, or Chert from Lander Co., Nevada
'Orange topaz'	Brownish-yellow quartz
'Oregon jade'	Dark green jasper
'Oregon moonstone'	Chalcedony
Oriental agate	Good quality agate
'Oriental alabaster'	Stalagmitic calcite
'Oriental almandine'	Purple-red sapphire
'Oriental amethyst'	Violet sapphire
'Oriental aquamarine'	Aquamarine coloured sapphire
'Oriental cat's eye'	Girasol sapphire
Oriental cat's eye	Chrysoberyl cat's eye
Oriental chalcedony	Good quality chalcedony
'Oriental chrysoberyl'	Yellowish-green sapphire

'Oriental chrysolite'	Greenish-yellow chrysoberyl or sapphire
Oriental cornelian	Deep coloured cornelian
'Oriental emerald'	Green sapphire
'Oriental topaz'	Yellow sapphire
Orletz	Russian name for rhodolite
'Osmenda pearl'	Same as Coq de perle
Owl eye	Eye agate with two similar eyes
Ox-eye	Labradorite feldspar
Ox-eye agate	Similar to owl eye
Ozakite	Thomsonite
Pacific cat's eye	Operculum
Padparadscha (h)	Synthetic orange sapphire
Pai Yu (Pao Yu)	White jadeite or nephrite
Pagoda stone (Pagodite)	(1) Agalmatolite
	(2) Fossil limestone
	(3) Translucent agate with pagoda-like markings
Panabase	Copper ore, properly tetrahedrite but often copper pyrites in a quartz base.
Panama pearls	Slate blue to black pearls from the Gulf of Mexico
Pantha	White translucent jadeite
'Paphros diamond'	Rock crystal
Paredrite	One of the 'favas' of the Brazilian diamondiferous gravels (TiO_2 plus H_2O)
Paragon pearls	Round pearls of large size
Paragon pearls	Imitation pearls
Paris pearls	Imitation pearls
Passau pearl	Freshwater pearl from Central Europe
Paste	Glass imitation stones
Pate de riz	Glass imitation of jade
Patona pearls	Imitation pearls
Patricia pearls	Imitation pearls
Paulite	Nearly black hypersthene with coppery inclusions
Peacock stone	Malachite
Pearl doublet	Cultured blister pearl
Pearl opal	Cacholong
'Pecos diamonds'	Rock crystal
'Pectolite jade'	Pectolite
Peganite	Variscite
Peiping (Pekin) jade	Any true jade but usually nephrite
Pelhamine	Precious serpentine
'Pennsylvania diamond'	Pyrites
Peredell topaz	Greenish topaz
Perigem	Synthetic light yellow-green spinel
Petal pearls	Distorted flattened pearls
Petosky stone (agate)	Fossil limestone (Michigan)
Picotite	Black spinel
Picrolite	Serpentine
Pigeon blood agate	Cornelian
Pingoes d'agoa	Colourless water-worn pebbles (Brazil)
'Pink moonstone'	Scapolite
Pinna pearls	Pearls from the Pinna mussel
Pin fire opal	Precious opal with play of colour in small patches
Pipe stone	A red siliceous clay (Catalinite)
Pistacite	Epidote
Pi Yu	Jadeite or nephrite with a vegetable green colour
Plexiglas	Acrylic resin plastic
Plume agate	Moss agate (flower agate)
Point chalcedony	Grey chalcedony with red spots
Polka dot agate	Translucent chalcedony with small red, brown or yellow dots
Polyphant stone	Serpentine diabase (Cornwall)
'Pomegranate ruby'	Red spinel
Pompadour pearls	Imitation pearls
Poppy stone	Orbicular jasper
Porcelainite	Metamorphosed baked clay
Potch	Miners term for opal which is colourful but 'dead'
Prasemalachite	Chalcedony filled with malachite

Prase opal	Nickel stained green opal
'Prismatic moonstone'	Chalcedony
'Prismatic quartz'	Iolite
'Pseudochrysolite'	Moldavite
Pseudojadeite	Probably a green albite feldspar
Pudding stone jade	Lighter coloured nodules of nephrite cemented by darker material
Pyralin	Cellulosic plastic
Pyralmandite	Name suggested for the intermediate garnets of the Py/Al series
Pyrandine	Alternative to Pyralmandite
'Pyroemerald'	Green fluorite
'Quartz topaz'	Citrine
'Quebec diamond'	Rock crystal
Quetzalztli	Translucent green jade (Mexico)
Quincite (Quinzite)	(1) Pink sepiolite
	(2) Pink common opal
Radient	Synthetic white spinel
'Radium diamond'	Smoky quartz
Rainbow agate (chalcedony)	Iridescent agate
Rainbow obsidian	Iridescent obsidian
Rainbow quartz	Iris quartz
Raspberry spar	Rhodochrosite
Redmanol	Phenolic resin plastic
'Red Sea pearls'	Coral beads
Resinoid	Phenolic resin plastic
Retinalite	Honey yellow serpentine
'Rhine diamond'	Rock crystal
Rhodoid	Cellulose acetate plastic
Riband agate	Banded agate
Riband (Ribbon) jasper	Jasper with stripes of alternating colour
Richlieu pearls	Imitation pearls
Ricolite	Banded serpentine
Ripe pearls	Pearls with good orient
River agate	Water-worn moss agate pebbles
River pearls	Freshwater pearls
Rock glass	Obsidian
'Rock (Rocky mountain) ruby'	Pyrope garnet
Rogueite	Greenish jasper (Oregon)
Roman pearls	Imitation pearls
Romanzovite	Dark brown grossular garnet
Rosaline	Thulite
Rose garnet	Xalostocite, or incorrectly for rhodonite
Roseki	Agalmatolite
'*Rose kunzite*'	Synthetic pink sapphire
Roselite (Rosolite)	Xalostocite
'Rose moonstone'	Pink scapolite
Rosterite	Rose red beryl (Elba)
Rothoffite	Yellow to brown andradite garnet
Royalite	Purplish-red glass
Royal topaz	Blue topaz
Rozircon	Pink synthetic spinel
Rubace (*Rubasse*)	Red stained crackled quartz
Rubasse	Quartz coloured red by scales of iron oxide
Rubicelle	Orange-red spinel
Rubolite	Red coloured common opal
'Ruby balas'	Red spinel
'Ruby spinel'	Red spinel
Ruin agate	Brecciated agate or agate with patterns of ruins
Sabalite	Banded green variscite
Safirina	Blue spinel or blue quartz
Safranite (*Saffronite*)	Citrine
Sagenite	Quartz with needle-like inclusions
'Salamanca topaz'	Fiery coloured citrine
'San Diego ruby'	Red tourmaline
Sang-i-yeshan	Dark green bowenite serpentine

Saphir d'eau	Iolite
'Sapphire quartz'	Blue chalcedony, also blue silicified crocidolite
'Sapphire spinel'	Blue spinel
Sapphirine	Correct for a non-gem Mg.Al silicate mineral. Used also for (1) Blue chalcedony, (2) Blue spinel (3) Blue glass
Sard	Translucent brown to reddish chalcedony
Sardium	Artificially coloured sard
Satelite	Fibrous serpentine
'Saxon chrysolite'	Topaz
'Saxon diamond'	Topaz
'Saxon topaz'	Yellow quartz
'Schaumberg diamond'	Rock crystal
Schiller spar	Bastite
Schmelze	Glass
Schnide	Blue glassy common opal
Schorl	Black tourmaline
'Scientific brilliant'	Synthetic white sapphire
'Scientific emerald'	Green beryl glass
'Scientific topaz'	Synthetic pink corundum
'Scotch (Scottish) topaz'	Yellowish-brown quartz
Seed pearls	Small pearls less that $\frac{1}{4}$ grain
Serra stone	Brazilian agate
Shell marble	Lumachella
'*Siam aquamarine*'	Blue zircon
'Siberian chrysolite'	Demantoid garnet
'Siberian ruby'	Red tourmaline
Siderite	Blue quartz
Siliciophite	Chrysotile in common opal
'Silver Peak jade'	Malachite
Sioux Falls jasper	Quartzite (South Dakota)
'Sinopal or sinople'	Reddish aventurine quartz
Sira	Abrasive aluminium oxide
Smaragdite	Green zoisite type of rock resembling jade
Smaragdolin	Green beryl glass
Sobrisky opal	Opal from Death Valley, California
Soldered emerald	Soudé emerald (composite stone)
Soldier's stone	Amethyst
'Soochow jade'	Bowenite serpentine or soapstone
'South African jade'	Massive green grossular garnet
Spalmandite (spandite)	Names suggested for intermediate almandine-spessartite garnets
'Spanish emerald'	Green glass
'Spanish lazulite'	Iolite
'Spanish topaz'	Yellowish-brown quartz
Sparklite	Colourless zircon
Spessartine	Spessartite garnet
Sphalerite	Zinc blende
Spinach jade	Nephrite
'Spinel ruby'	Red spinel
St. Stephen's stone	Red-spotted white chalcedony
Starlite	Blue zircon
Starolite	Star rose quartz doublet
'Star topaz'	Yellow star sapphire
'Stolberg diamonds'	Rock crystal
Strawberry pearl	Pink coloured baroque freshwater pearl with a pimply surface
'Styrian jade'	Pseudophite
Sugar stone	Pink datolite (Michigan)
Sun opal	Fire opal
Sweetwater agate	Fluorescent moss agate from Wyoming
Sweetwater pearls	Freshwater pearls
'Swiss jade'	Green dyed jasper
'Swiss lapis'	Blue dyed jasper
'*Synthetic alexandrite*'	Synthetic corundum or spinel
'*Synthetic aquamarine*'	Synthetic corundum or spinel
'*Synthetic turquoise*'	An imitation turquoise

Syntholite	Synthetic corundum imitating the alexandrite
Syriam (Syrian or Suriam) garnet	Almandine garnet
Tabasheer	Amorphous opal-like silica found in the joints of some types of bamboo
Takin	Engraved emerald (India)
Taltalite	Green tourmaline (Brazil)
Tama	Jade (Japanese)
Tangiwai(te)	Bowenite (New Zealand)
'Tasmanian diamond'	Rock crystal
Tauridian topaz	Blue topaz
Tawmawite	Massive chrome-rich epidote
Taxoite	Green serpentine (Pennsylvania)
Tecla pearls	Imitation pearls
Tibet stone	Mixture of aventurine quartz and quartz porphyry (Eosite)
Tigerite	Tiger eye
Tokay lux sapphire	Hungarian obsidian
Tomb jade	Buried jade which has turned to a red or brown colour
'Tooth turquoise'	Odontolite
'Topaz cat's eye'	Chatoyant yellow sapphire
Topazolite	Greenish-yellow to yellow andradite garnet
'Topaz quartz'	Brownish-yellow quartz
'Topaz saffronite'	Brownish-yellow quartz
Tosa coral	Japanese coral
Trainite	A type of banded variscite
Traversellite	Green diopside
Tree stone (tree agate)	Mocha stone (moss agate)
'Trenton diamond'	Rock crystal
Tripletine	Emerald-coloured beryl triplet
Turkey fat ore	Cadmium-coloured yellow smithsonite
Turtle back	(1) Chlorastrolite
	(2) Turquoise or variscite matrix
Turtle-back pearl	Oval natural blister pearl with a fairly high dome
Tuxtlite	Sodium/magnesium pyroxene, the principal constituent of mayaite
Uigite	Chlorastrolite from Skye
Ultralite	Red-violet synthetic sapphire
Unionite	Pink zoisite (thulite)
Unripe pearls	Poor quality pearls
'Ural chrysolite (emerald or olivine)'	Demantoid garnet
'Uralian sapphire'	Blue tourmaline
'Utah turquoise'	Variscite
Utahlite	Variscite
Vabanite	Brown-red jasper specked with yellow (California)
Valencianite	Adularia feldspar
'Vallum diamond'	Rock crystal
Variolite	Dark green orthoclase with lighter coloured globules
Vashegyrite	An aluminium phosphate mineral, said to be like variscite, but may be yellow or brown
Verde de Corsica	Green dialage and labradorite
'Vermeil', 'Vermeille'	Orange-red stones, may be zircons, garnets or spinels
Vermilite	Cinnabar in opal
'Vesuvian garnet'	Leucite
'Vesuvianite jade'	Californite
'Vienna (Viennese) turquoise'	A turquoise imitation
Vigorite	Phenolic resin plastic
Viluite	Idocrase
Vinegar spinel	Yellowish-orange spinel
Violan(e)	Violet massive diopside
Violet stone	Iolite
Violite	Purple synthetic sapphire
Viscoloid	Cellulosic plastic
'Volcanic chrysolite'	Idocrase
Volcanic glass	Obsidian

Vorobievite	Pink beryl
Vulcanite	Hard black rubber
Walderite	Synthetic white sapphire
Wart pearl	Baroque pearl
'Washita diamond'	Rock crystal
'Water sapphire'	Iolite
Water stone	Glassy orthoclase, or hyalite opal
Wax agate	Yellow to yellowish-red agate with waxy lustre
Wax opal	Yellowish opal with waxy lustre
'White garnet'	Leucite
Wilconite	Purplish-red scapolite
Wild pearl	Natural pearl
Wilsonite	Purplish-red scapolite
Wiluite	Idocrase
Winchellite	Lintonite (thomsonite)
Wing pearl	Baroque pearl shaped like a wing
Wisconsin pearls	Fine coloured freshwater pearls from the Unio of the Mississippi
Wolf's eye	(1) Moonstone
	(2) Tiger's eye
Wood agate	Agate pseudomorph after wood
Wood opal	Opal pseudomorph after wood
Wood stone	Fossil wood
Xihuitl	Turquoise (Aztec)
Xyloid jasper	Jasperized wood
Xylonite	Cellulosic plastic
Xylopal	Opalized wood
Yanolite	Violet axinite
'Yaqui onyx'	'Onyx marble' from Baja California
Yu	Jade
Yui ko lu jade	Tomb jade coloured green from bronze objects buried near it
'Zabeltitzten diamond'	Rock crystal
Zarafina	Blue spinel or blue chalcedony
Zeasite	Wood opal
Zebra stone (jasper)	Limonite with lighter brown layers of shell material
Zenithite	Strontium titanate
Zeuxite	Green tourmaline (Brazilian)
Zircolite	Synthetic white sapphire
'Zircon spinel'	Synthetic pale blue spinel
Zirctone	Synthetic bluish-green sapphire
Zonite	Chert or jasper (Arizona)
Zonochlorite	Near chlorastrolite
Zylonite	Cellulosic plastic

INDEX

To avoid unnecessary duplication the terms given in the glossary of unusual names are not repeated in the index below. This glossary—on pages 791–804—should be consulted if the required name is not found in the general index.

Abalone pearls, 411
Abalone shells, 411, 461
Abbe condenser, 634, 647
Aberrations of lenses, 624–626
Absorption spectra, 609, 621
  alexandrite, 97, 98
  almandine garnet, 139
  aquamarine, 91, 92
  chromium, 617
  chrysoberyl, 97, 98
  cobalt, 331, 354, 619
  coloured plates of, facing pages 618, 620
  copper, 619
  demantoid garnet, 147
  diamond, 46, 620
  emerald, 89
  grossular garnet, 146
  iron, 619
  manganese, 331, 618
  miscellaneous, 621
  monochrome illustrations of, 760–765
  orthoclase, 152
  peridot, 128
  pyrope garnet, 137
  rare earth, 354, 620
  ruby, 69
  sapphire, 69
  selenium, 354, 619
  spessartite garnet, 142
  spinel, 104
  synthetic stones, 322
  topaz, 110
  tourmaline, 116
  uranium, 620
  vanadium, 322, 619
  zircon, 122, 123
Acetylene tetrabromide, 524
Achroite, 114
Achromatic lenses, 625
Actinolite, 180, 211, **214**
Adamas, 13
Adorno, A. D., 83
Adularescence, 149, 370, 550
Adularia, 149
Afghanistan,
  lapis lazuli in, 207
  rubies in, 66
  spinel in, 106
Agalmatolite, 219, 289, 298

Agate, 180–185
  coloured plate, facing page 268
  fossil, 181
  grinding, 392
  iris, 183
  moss, 180
  nodules, 10
  occurrences, 184
  staining, 176, 178, 367
  theories of formation, 182, 183
  water, 185
Agatized coral, 182
Agatized wood, 181
Ago wan, 422
Airy disc, 635
Akabar coral, 458
Akori coral, 458
Alabaster, 238, **247**, 367
  Egyptian, 238
  pink welsh, 249
'Alabaster', 451
'Alabaster onyx', 238
Alalite, 264
Alasmoden pearls, 413
Albertite, 474
al Biruni, 522
Albite feldspar, 149, 150, 154, **156**
Albite/oligoclase, 156
Alderton, R. W., 79, 82
Alexander, A. E., 447, 449
Alexander II, 100
Alexandrite, **96**, 344
  absorption spectrum, 97
  coloured plates, facing pages 98, 500
  luminescence, 98
  occurrences, 100
  simulation of, 101
Algeria,
  beryl in, 88
  onyx marble in, 238
Algodonite, 226
Alibert, J. P., 213
Allen ultra-violet lamp, 688
Allochromatic coloration, 559
Alluvial deposits, **5**, 15, 17, 18, 19, 22
Almandine garnet, 134–136, **139**, 370
  coloured plates, facing pages 140, 500
alpha particles, 121, 497, 565–567
Amas, 424
Amatrice, 304
'Amazon jade', 218

Amazonstone (amazonite), 11, 149, **153**
  coloured plates, facing pages 268, 500
  jade imitation, as, 218
Amber, **466–472**, 725
  flies in, 471
  imitations of, 470
  inclusions in, 468
  localities, 469
  occurrences, 466
  properties, 466
  stained, 468
  sun spangled, 467, 468
  test for, 472
  transparency to x-rays, 710
Amber oil, 467
Amblygonite, 249
Ambroid, 467
Amethyst, 133, 152, 160, 167, **168**, 378
  coloration of, 168, 564
  coloured plate, facing page 168
  geodes, in, 10
  heat treatment of, 169
  inclusions in, 170, 171
  occurrences, 171
Amino plastic, 357, 358, 360, 471
Ammonites, 465
Amphibole, 211, 219, 303
Amygdales, 10
Amygdaloidal cavities, 10
Analcite, 250
Anatase, **250**, 258, 291
Andalusite, **250**, 269, 289, 300, 710
Anderson, B. W., 46, 103, 104, 138, 312, 435, 577, 586, 605, 721
Andesine feldspar, 154, **157**
Andradite garnet, 134, 135, **146**
  formation of, 9
Anglesite, 251
Angola,
  diamonds in, 28, 30, 31
  lapis lazuli in, 208
Ångström, A. J., 543
Ångström unit, 43, **543**, 759
Anhedral crystals, 510
Anions, 496, 500
Anomalous double refraction, 655
  garnet, in, 136
  glass, in, 354
  synthetic spinel, in, 327, 328, 655, 656
Anorthite feldspar, 149, 154, 155, **159**
Anthracite, 474
Antigorite, 294, 295
Antilles pearls, 462
Antwerp rose cut, 372
Anyolite, 308
Apache tears, 227, 229
Apatite, 99, **252**, 262, 283
Aperiodic balance, 533
Apophyllite, 253

Aquamarine, 76, **91**, 113, 340
  coloured plate, facing pages 94, 500
  cutting of, 95
  inclusions in, 95
  occurrences, 92
'Arabian beads' (coral), 457
Aragonite, 401, 403, 413, 442, 443, 728
'Aragonite', 240
Arandisite, 254
Archimedes, 522
Argentina,
  garnet in, 138
  onyx marble in, 239
  rhodochrosite in, 289
Argon lamp, 690
Aristotle, 522
Arizona, garnet in, 137, 148
Artificial coloration of diamond, 49, 565–569
Artificial pearl essence, 453
A.S.E.A. (Sweden), 312
Ashover spar, 271
Asparagus stone, 252
Asterias, 74, 75, 94, 95, 102, 106, 140, 173, 265, 267, 277, 319, 365, 370, 551
Asterism, 550
Astridite, 219
Atherston, D. G., 20
Atom, 494–497
Atomic bonding, 497
Atomic number, 494
Atomic reactor (pile), 49, 567
Atomic weight, 494, 496, 726
Augelite, 254
Augite, 206
Australia,
  diamond in, 19
  emerald in, 84
  garnet in, 134, 143
  malachite in, 280
  opal in, 192–196
  peridot in, 129
  quartz in, 166, 168, 172, 173
  sapphire in, 65
  spinel in, 106
  topaz in, 112
  zircon in, 125
'Australian jade', 304
'Australian turquoise', 304
Australites, 231
Austria,
  emerald in, 77
  garnet in, 142
Autoclave, 334–336
Autoradiography, 121, 566
Aventurine glass, 353
Aventurine quartz, 7, **175**, 219, 279, 281, 368
Avoirdupois (weight), 773, 774

Axes,
brachy, 505
clino, 505
crystallographic, 504
lateral, 505, 508
macro, 505
optic, 553, 554, 583, 584
principal, 505
symmetry, of, 503, 504
vertical, 505, 508
Axestone, 213
Axinite, 254
Azurite, 200, **255**, 281, 296
Azurmalachite, 255, 281
coloured plate, facing page 268

Baguette cut, 373, 386
Baikalite, 264
Bakelite, **357**, 358, 360, 470, 472, 474, 730
Balances, 396, 397
aperiodic, 533
chemical, 533
gemstone, 396
spring, 537
Walker, 537
Westphal, 529, 530
'Balas ruby', 102
Bali (weight), 774
Ball, S. H., 681
Ballams, 408
Ballas, 43
Band spectra, 605
Banded agate, 182, 379
Bandy, F. P., 311
Bannister, F. A., 310, 349
Bannister's graph, 350
Bardwell, D. C., 566
Barite (barytes), 255
Barkla, C. G., 702, 708
Barnato, B., 22–24
Barnato Brothers, 24
Baroque pearls, 414
Barrok pearls, 414
Bartholinus, E., 540
Barysphere, 1
Barytes (Barite), 255
Basalt glass, 229
Basanite, 186
Base system (for pearls), 415, 773
Bastard amber, 467
Bastard ivory, 478
Bastite, 267
Basutoland (Lesotho), diamonds in, 37
Batchelor, H. H., 85
Batea, 18
Batuta, Ibn, 405
Bauer, M., 85

Bavaria, garnets in, 143
Bayldonite, 256
Bead nuclei, 427
'Bearded girdles', 378
Beck, R. and J., 610, 611, 613, 614, 662, 663
Becke line, 585
Becquerel, A. E., 682
Beers, de, 20
Beilby, G., 382
Beilby layer, 382
Beit, A., 24
Belgian black marble, 241
Bell Telephone Company, 325
Belonites, 228
Benitoite, 75, 256
Benson, Lester B., 102, 434, 580
Benzene, 525, 526
'Bernat', 471
Bernstein, 468
Berquen (Bergen), L. van, 383
Bertrand lens, 639, 654, 657
Bertrand, Professor, 573
Beryl, **76–95**, 346, 368
coloured plates, facing pages 94, 500
inclusions in, 94, 95
star, 94
transparency to x-rays, 710
Beryl glass, 346
Beryllonite, 257
Beryl Mining Company, 85
beta-rays, 567
Bethersden marble, 242
Bezel facets, 375
Biaxial stones (crystals), 554, 583, 602, 657
Bibliography, 780–783
Biegel, H., 438
di Billi, F. O. D., 199
Billitonite, 231, 232
Bingley, W., 67
Bioluminescence, 681
Biotite, 3
Bird's-eye marble, 244
Birefringence, 554
Birthstone table, 784
Biruni, al, 522
Biwa pearls, 432, 446
Bixbite, 93
'Black amber' (jet), 473
Black dyed opal, 188
Blackfellow's buttons, 232
Black marble, 381
Black moonstone, 158
coloured plate, facing page 268
Black onyx, 367, 474
Black opal, 187
'Black Prince's ruby', 75, 102
Bleaching pearls, 429
Blende, 307

Blister pearls,
  cultured, 419
  natural, 399
Bloch, R. and S., 439
Block amber, 466
Block caving (diamond mining), 25, 26
Blond shell, 489
'Bloodshot iolite', 276
Bloodstone, 180
  coloured plate, facing page 268
  hematite, 233
Blooming (lenses and pastes), 349, 351
Blue earth, 466, 467
Blue frit, 345
Blue ground, 22, 23, 25, 26
Blue John, 269, 271, 272
'Blue moonstone', 180
Blue pearls, 403, 445
Bluestone, 299
Blue-white, 41
Boar ivory, 477, 479, 482
Bohemia, garnets in, 137
Bohr, N., 683
Boisbaudran, L. de, 682
Bolivia, diamonds in, 38
Bologna stone, 682
'Bombay bunch', 414, 415
Bonamite, 218, 297
Bonded turquoise, 204
Bone, 482
Bone turquoise, 203, 282
Bony amber, 469
Boracite, **257**, 350
Borazon, 43, 52, 313, 515
Borneo,
  diamonds in, 16
  sapphires in, 66
Bornite, 226
Boron carbide, 52, 333, 515
Boron nitride, 312, 515
Bort (boart; bortz), 42, 393
Bottlestone, 231
Boules, synthetic, 316, 317, 319, 327, 332, 333
Bouteillenstein, 231
Bouton pearls, 414
Bowenite serpentine, 218, 220, **294**, 295, 367
Boyle, R., 681
Brabant rose cut, 372
Brackett, R. N., 18
Bragg, W. and I., 703
Bragg's law, 712, 713
Branner, J. C., 18
Brauns, R., 140
Brazil,
  beryl in, 92, 94
  chalcedony in, 178, 179, 180, 184, 185
  chrysoberyl in, 101
  diamonds in, 16, 376

Brazil—*Contd.*
  feldspar in, 153
  garnet in, 138, 141, 143, 144
  quartz in, 166, 168, 169, 172, 173, 174
  spinel in, 106
  spodumene in, 133
  topaz in, 107, 108, 110, 112
  tourmaline in, 118
Brazilianite, 258
  coloured plate, facing page 130
'Brazilian onyx', 239
Break facets, 375
Breccia, 5
Brecciated agate, 5, 186
Brecciated jasper, 5, 186
Breithauptite, 226
Brewster, D., 354, 590, 604, 682
Brewster's angle, 590
Bridgman, P. W., 311
Bright line spectra, 605
Brilliant cut, 42, 374, 386
  cushion-shaped, 376
  marquise-shaped, 376
  pendeloque-shaped, 376
Brillianteerder, 387
Briolette, 372
Brisson, M. J., 522
British Isles,
  agate in, 184
  amber in, 466
  amethyst in, 172
  beryl in, 92
  cornelian in, 179
  hematite in, 244
  jet in, 473
  moss agate in, 181
  serpentine marble in, 236
  topaz in, 112
  turquoise in, 202
British Guiana (Guyana), diamonds in, 37
British Museum (Bloomsbury), porphyries in, 287
British Museum (Natural History),
  'greened' diamond in, 565
  synthetic diamond in, 310
Brittleness, 515
Bromellite, 344
Bromoform, 524, 527
Bronzite, 266, 276
Brookite, 250, **258**, 267, 291
Brown, J. C., 87
Brown quartz, 167
Brucite, 294, 295
Bruting diamonds, 386
Bubbles,
  glass, in, 352, 353, 454
  synthetic corundum, in, 320, 321
  synthetic spinel, in, 329, 330
Buddstone, 180

Buff-top cut, 378
Bull's-eye condenser, 652
Bultfontein diamond mine, 20, 24, 25
Bunsen, R. W., 605
'Buried' jade, 211
Burma Ruby Mines Company, 58, 59
Burma Stone Tract, 11, 12, 300
    amber in, 469
    chrysoberyl in, 101
    corundum in, 57, 70, 71
    feldspar in, 151
    garnet in, 138, 143, 145
    jadeite in, 216
    lapis lazuli in, 208
    peridot in, 129
    quartz in, 166, 172
    spinel in, 103, 106
    spodumene in, 133
    topaz in, 122
    zircon in, 122, 125
Burmese shell, 460
Burmite, 469
'Burnite', 469
Button pearls, 414, 415
Byon, 60, 62, 63
Byssus, 399
Bytownite feldspar, 154, **159**
Byzantine mosaic, 381

Cabochon cuts, 369, 393
Cacholong, 190
Cacoxenite, 166
Cady, W. G., 165, 717
Cailliaud, F., 77
Cairngorm, 160, 167, 785
Calcite, 1, 7, 10, 190, 206, **245**, 252, 295
    satin spar, 240
    stalagmitic, 237
Calcium, test for, 732
Calcium titanate, 333
Calibre stones, 374
Californite, 218, 274, 275
Callainite, 203
Cameo doublets, 366
Cameos, 180, 379, 392, 411, 457, 462
Camera lucida, 662
Cameras for photomicrography, 662–665
Canada,
    feldspar in, 154, 156, 158
    garnet in, 142, 144, 145, 148
    lapis lazuli in, 208
    nephrite in, 213
    quartz in, 172
    sodalite in, 298
Canadian bluestone, 299
Canary glass, 621
Cancrin, Count, 259
Cancrinite, 258

Candle, 316
'Candling', 436
Cannel coal, 474
Canutilos, 79
Cao, M., 83
Capes (diamonds), 40, 46, 49
Carat weight, 393, 415, 773
Carbon, 309
Carbonado (carbons), 18, 43, 393
Carbonate, test for, 731
'carbons', 43, 383
Carbon tetrachloride, 525, 535
Carborundum, 52, **333**, 392, 515
Carborundum wheel, 393
Carbuncles, 134, 139, 370
Cardiometer (pearl), 438, 439
Care of pearls, 416
Carnelian, 179
Carob tree, 393, 394
Carvalho, M., 82
Carving of gemstones, 392
Carystus, marble of, 237
Cascalho, 17
Casciarola, V., 682
Casein, 356, 470, 472, 474
Cassiterite, 259
Catalyst, 22
Catherine the Great sapphire, 75
Cathode rays, 684, 693, 701
Cathodoluminescence, 693
Cations, 496, 500
Cat's-eyes, 370
    amphibole, 303
    apatite, 99, 252, 550
    beryl, 550
    chrysoberyl, 96, 99, 174, 370, 550
    diopside, 99, 264, 550
    feldspar, 153
    kornerupine, 277
    kyanite, 277
    prehnite, 102, 287
    quartz, 99, 102, 174, 550
    satelite, 295
    scapolite, 99, 292, 550
    tourmaline, 99, 102, 114, 550
    tremolite, 303
Catty (weight), 774
'Cave pearls', 246
Celestine (celestite), 259
'Cellosolve', 646
Cells for liquid, 647, 648
Celluloid, **356**, 470, 472, 474, 487
    amber imitations of, 470, 472
    safety, 356
Celsian, 149
Central African Republic, diamonds in, 34–36
Cerium oxide, 391
Cerkonier, 120
Cerussite, 260

Cestode worms, 400
Ceylon,
  chrysoberyl in, 100
  corundum in, 64, 71, 73
  feldspar in, 151
  garnet in, 138, 141, 143
  spinel in, 106
  tourmaline in, 117
  zircon in, 123, 125
Ceylonite, 102, 104, 106
Chalcedony, 147, 152, **176**, 177, 194,
    219, 238, 478
  chrome, 178
  staining of, 180, 367
Chalcopyrite, 225
Chalumeau, 315
Chalybite, 296
Chance Brothers, 688
Characteristic x-rays, 708
Charles II sapphire, 75
Chatham, C., 325, 336, 340
Chatham synthetic emerald, 336
Chatons, 347
Chatoyancy, 550
Chatter marks, 393
Chaulnes, de, refractive index method,
    589
Checky (weight), 774
Chelsea colour filter, 88, 90, 92, 110,
    126, 147, 170, 175, 178, 215, 322,
    331, 339, 354, 363, 366, **598**
  table of effects under, 757
Chemawinite, 469
Chemical composition of gems, table of,
    768–770
Chemical compounds, 724
Chemical formulae, 725, 726, 729, 730
Chemical nomenclature, 725
Chemical reactions, 728
Chemical tests for calcium, carbonate
    and phosphate, 731, 732
Chemical valency, 728
Chemiluminescence, 681
Chert, 186
Chessylite, 255
Chevee, 224
Chevvu (weight), 774
Chhatrapati Manick ruby, 74
Chiastolite, 251, 300
Chiastolite slate, 8
Chicot pearls, 400
Chile,
  aventurine quartz in, 175
  lapis lazuli in, 207
  turquoise in, 202
Chilowski, C., 439
China,
  amethyst in, 173
  bowenite serpentine in, 218, 294
  chalcedony in, 179

China—*Contd.*
  diamonds in, 40
  jadeite in, 216
  nephrite in, 213
  turquoise in, 199
Chinese cat's-eye, 463
Chinese drilling (pearls), 415
Chinese freshwater mussel, 413, 432
Chinese jade, 210
Chivor mines, 89, 339
Chivor Mining Company, 79
Chlorastrolite, 260
  coloured plate, facing page 268
Chloromelanite, 215, 219
Chlorite, 165, 180
Chondrodite, 261
Chow (weight), 774
Chromatic aberration, 624
Chrome chalcedony, 178
Chrome diopside, 264
Chrome epidote, 268
Chrome tourmaline, 118
Chromite, 225, **226**, 294
Chromium coloration, 560
Chromium oxide, 391
Chrysoberyl, **96–102**, 344
  absorption spectra of, 97, 98
  cat's-eyes, 66, 98, 99, 174, 370, 550
  coloured plates, facing pages 98, 500
  cutting, 101
  inclusions in, 100
  localities of, 100, 101
  luminescence of, 98
  optical characters of, 97
  transparency to x-rays of, 710
Chrysocolla, 165, 180, 200, **261**
  in quartz, 165, 180
'Chrysolite', 96, 127
Chrysoprase, 178
  coloured plate, facing page 268
  jade imitation, as, 219
Chrysotile, 294, 295
Chudoba, K. F., 120
Church, A., 122, 139, 232, 394, 605
Cinnabar, 180
Cinnamon stones, 144
Cipollino marble, 236, 237
Circular polarization, 162, 163
Citrine, 160, 168
  coloured plate, facing page 168
Clam pearls, 403, 412
Clarke, V., 74
Classification of diamonds, 40
Cleavage, **518–521**
  in diamond, 44, 383
  in topaz, 109
Cleaving diamonds, 383, 384
Cleopatra's emerald mines, 77
Clerici's solution, 524, **525**, 527
Clinozoisite, **268**, 308

Closed forms (crystals), 501
Coal, 4
Coated beryl, 342
Coated diamonds, 40
Cobalt coloration, 561
Cobalti-calcite, 245
Cobaltite, 225
Cobra Emerald Ltd., 86
Cobra Emerald Mining Company, 86
Coenosarc, 455, 456
Coggin Brown, J., 61, 87
Cohen, L., 24
Colemanite, 260, **262**
Colesberg kopje, 20, 23
Colombia,
  chalcedony in, 179
  emerald in, 78
  ruby in, 66
  sapphire in, 66
Colombian Emerald Development Cor-
  poration, 79
Colombian Emerald Syndicate Ltd.,
  79
Colophony, 467
Colour, **555–572**
  causes of, 569
  changes, 366–368
    aquamarine, in, 91, 565
    corundum, in, 565
    diamond, in, 49, 565–569
    heat, by, 367, 563
    quartz, in, 169, 170, 367, 565, 564
    radiation, by, 565
    topaz, in, 110, 111, 367, 563, 566
    tourmaline, in, 117, 565
    zircon, in, 123–125, 367, 563–565
  cone, 555, 556
  filters, 598–600
    separating fluorescence by, 694
    table of effects under, 757
  grading of diamonds, 40
  inorganic substances, in, 569
  pearls, of, 403, 413, 414
  residual, 557
  table of dispersions, 748, 749
  table of gemstones, 752–755
  terms, 555
  theories as to causes, 569–572
  vision, 558
Coloured diamonds, 41
Coloured pearls, 403, 413, 414
Colouring metals in gemstones, 560–
  562, 617–620
Columbite, 225, **226**
Combination of forms (crystals), 501
Composite stones, 101, 102, **361–366**,
  710
Composition of pearls, 401
Compound microscope, 628, 629
Comptes Rendus des Séances, 314

Conch,
  giant, 379, 462, 463
  pearls, 403, 411, 412, 462
Conchiolin, 399–403, 446, 724
Conchoidal fracture, 521
Condenser, substage, 633, 634
Conglomerate, 5
Congo,
  diamonds in, 30, 31
  garnet in, 148
  peridot in, 129
Connemara marble, 219, 236, 296
Consolidated African Selection Trust
  Ltd., 32
Consolidated Mines of South-west
  Africa Ltd., 28, 29, 30
Contact liquid (refractometer), 577
Contact metamorphism, 7, 8
Continuous spectrum, 605
Conversion factors (weights), 774
Coolidge tube, 693, 706
Copal resin, 470, 471, 472
Copper coloration, 562
Coque de perle, 462
Coral, 380, 411, **455–459**
  imitation of pink pearl, 454
  localities of, 456, 457
  names of colours, 457
  polyp, 456
Coralline marbles, 242
Coral tree, 394
Cordierite, 275
Cordier, P. L. A., 275
Cornelian (carnelian), 179, 367
Corn tongs, 397
Corozo nuts, 485, 724
Corrombe, 17
Corsite, 287
Corundum, **54–75**, 382, 393
  coloured plates, facing pages 54, 62,
    72, 500
  localities of, 66
  synthetic, 75, 101, 113, 129, 173, 318
  transparency to x-rays, 710
Cotham marble, 244
Counting diamonds, 43
Coutinho, M. de A., 83
Co-valent bonding, 498
Crackled quartz, 91, 166
Crater glass, 232
'Created emeralds', 336
Crinkles (diamond), 13
Cristobalite, 160, 234
Critical angle, 376, 547, 548, 573, 575,
  576
Crocidolite, 174
  coloured plate, facing page 268
Crocoite, 262
Crookes, W., 310, 565, 566, 682, 684,
  698, 699, 700, 702

Crookes dark space, 699
Crookes glass, 621
Crookes tube, 699
Cross cut, 374
Cross facets, 375
Cross rose cut, 372
Cross stone,
    chiastolite, 251
    staurolite, 300
Cross worker (diamond cutting), 387
Crossed filter techniques, 98
Crossed nicols (polars), 654
Crouch, J. M., 256
Crown (of faceted stone), 374
Crowningshield, G. R., 568
Crusta petrosa, 480
Crystal, 492, **494–513**
    angles of, 501, 502, 503
    axes of, 504–509
    colour plates, facing pages 16, 22, 500
    distorted, 509, 510
    faces, 500
    habit, 55, 511, 512
    Hemihedral, 510
    holohedral, 509
    internal structure of, 494
    systems, 504–508
    table of gems by systems, 751, 752
    twinned, 510, 511
Cube (as crystal), 504
Culet, 375
Culch (pearl fisheries), 404
Cullinan diamond, 20
Cultured pearls, 402, 414, **418–449**
    blister, 419
    composition of, 431
    density of, 435
    detection of, 434–454
    drilling, 430
    early experiments on, 418–420
    farming, 421–429
    fisheries,
        Australia, 420
        Hong Kong, 421
        Japan, 420
        Mergui archipelago, 421
        Palau Islands, 420
    grading, 430
    non-nucleated, 432
    nucleating operation, 427
    nuclei for, 427
    surface structure of, 433
    testing, 434–449
Cupid's darts, 165
Cupping tool, 392
Cuprite, 262
Curie, P. and J., 165, 717
Curvette (style of cutting), 224
Cushion-shaped brilliant, 376
Custers, J. F. H., 720

Cutting, 389
    beryls, 95
    chrysoberyls, 101
    emerald, 89, 390
    hematite, 224
    jade, 217
    kunzite, 133
    lapis lazuli, 208
    peridot, 129
    pyrites, 222
    quartz, 142
    ruby, 390
    sapphire, 390
    spinel, 106
    topaz, 113
    tourmaline, 119
    zircon, 126
Cyclotron, 49
Cyclotroned diamonds, 49, 567
Cyprine, 274, 275
Cyst pearls, 400, 401
Czechoslovakia,
    corundum in, 66
    garnet in, 137
    moldavite in, 230
    opal in, 190
Czochralski 'pulling' method, 309, 344

Dake, H. C., 273, 691
Danburite, 113, **262**
    coloured plate, facing page 130
Dark field (dark ground) illumination,
    649–652
Darwin glass, 233
Das, S. C., 199
Datolite, 263
Dauvillier's method for lauegrams, 442
David, Professor, 84
De Beers, 312
De Beers Consolidated Mines Ltd., 24,
    312
De Beers diamond mine, 20
De Beers Mining Company, 24
Debye, 714
Decraqueler, treatment of pearls, 416
Deer horn, 483
Demantoid garnet, 127, 134, 146,
    147
    coloured plate, facing page 140
De Ment, J., 691
Density of pearls, 401, 402, 412, 435,
    453
Density/refractive index relation, 531,
    532
Density tables, 735–744, 746–748
Dentelle (teeth), in cutting, 371, 372
Denudation of rocks, 4
Derbyshire spar, 269
Descartes, R., 539

INDEX

'Detectoscope', 600
Detritus, 5
Deuterium (deuterons), 49, 496, 567
Devitrification of glass, 353, 354
Dewey diamond, 18
Diamagnetism, 721
Diamanté, 355
Diamond, 13–51, 309, 382
  absorption spectra of, 46, 47
  artificial coloration of, 49, 565–569
  atomic structure of, 43, 44
  cape, 40
  cleavage in, 43, 44, 383
  coated, 40
  colour grading of, 40
  coloured, 40
  coloured plates, frontispiece and
    facing pages, 22, 34, 42, 500
  composition of, 13
  counting, 43
  crystal forms of, 13, 14
  cutting,
    bruting, 386
    cleaving, 383, 384
    girdle polishing, 379
    girdling, 386
    grinding, 384, 385
    lap, 387
    mill, 388
    polishing, 369
    sawing, 383, 385, 386, 387
    scaife, 387
  doublets, 50, 51, 52, 711
  dust, 42
  electroconducting, 333, 369, 716,
    720, 721
  first water, 41
  flat, 40
  flaws in, 48
  fluorescence of, 46
  gauges, 395
  genesis of, 22
  glassy, 33
  grading, 40
  grain, 387, 514
  grain (weight), 394
  hardness tester, 43
  industrial uses of, 42
  laxey, 15
  localities of,
    Angola, 30, 31
    Australia, 19
    Bolivia, 38
    Borneo, 16
    Botswana (Bechuanaland), 21
    Brazil, 16
    Central African Republic, 34, 35,
      36
    China, 40
    Congo, 30, 31

Diamond—*Contd.*
  localities of—*Contd.*
    Equatorial Africa, 33
    Ghana (Gold Coast), 31, 32
    Guyana (British Guiana), 37
    Guinea, 33
    India, 13
    Indonesia, 16
    Ivory Coast, 32
    Lesotho (Basutoland), 21, 37
    North America, 18
    Rhodesia, 27
    Russia, 38
    Sahara, 37
    Sierra Leone, 32
    South Africa, 19
    South-west Africa, 28
    Tanzania (Tanganyika), 35
    Venezuela, 38
    West Africa, 33
    Witwatersrand, 37
  macles, 13, 40
  mêlée, 40
  mines,
    Aichal, 39
    Bultfontein, 20, 24, 25
    De Beers, 20
    Dutoitspan, 20, 24
    Finsch, 21
    Griqualand, 24
    Jagersfontein, 20, 43
    Kimberley, 20, 23
    Koffyfontein, 20
    Majgawan, 15
    Mir, 39
    Premier, 20, 21, 43
    Wesselton, 20
    Williamson, 36, 37
  mining, 17, 22, 24, 28, 31
  naats, 19
  naturals on, 50
  neutroned, 49
  notable,
    Cullinan, 20
    Dewey, 18
    Dudley, 20
    Hope, 15
    Jehangir, 13, 15
    Koh-i-nûr, 13, 15
    Presidente Vargas, 18
    Punch Jones, 18
    Star of South Africa, 20
    table of, 777–779
    Woyie river, 33
  optical properties of, 44
  origin of, 22
  painted, 49
  phosphorescence of, 47
  physical properties of, 43
  piggy-back, 50

813

Diamond—*Contd.*
pipes, 15, 20–25, 35, 39
'points' (for cutting directions), 387
point stones (style of cutting), 373
powder, 42, 392
recovery by x-ray fluorescence, 39, 53
radiation counters, 43
sand, 40
scientific uses of, 42
simulants, 49, 50
sorting, 40
synthesis, 50, 309–311
transparency to x-rays, 48, 709, 710
turning tools, 43
types of, 47, 48
vitriers, 43
wire drawing dies, 43
world production of, 39
writing pencils, 43
Diamond Trading Company, 40, 41
Diamond Treasury (Moscow), 127
Diamondiferous formations, 21
Diasterism, 173, 365, 551
Dichroism, 561, 600–604
Dichroite, 275
Dichromatism, 561
Dichroscope, 602–604
Diffraction grating, principle of, 612
Diffraction patterns by x-ray,
crystals, 711–715
pearls, 442–445
Dimorphism, 513
Dinny bone, 186
Dinosaur bone, 186
Diopside, 99, 206, 214, 236, **263**
transparency to x-rays, 710
Dioptase, 265
Direct method of refractive index measurement, 589, 590
Dirhem (weight), 774
Dispersion, colour, 548, 549
measurement of, 549
table of, 748, 749
Distant vision technique of refractive index measurement, 580
Disthene, 278
Distorted crystals, 509, 510
Distrene, 356
Dobo pearls, 409
'Doctoring' pearls, 416
Doelter, C. A., 710
Dolomite, 295
Dome faces (crystals), 509
Domed table facet, 378
Domeykite, 226
Doom (Doum) palm, 485–487
Dop used in polishing, 383, 388
'Doped' synthetic crystals, 340, 344

Double refraction, 552
anomalous, 327, 328, 354, 655
Doublets, 101, 102, 188, 206, **361–365**
cameo, 366
diamond, 50, 51, 52, 361, 362
garnet-topped, 75, 361–363
intaglio, 366
jadeite, 365, 366
opal, 188, 190, 365
star rose quartz, 365, 551
synthetic spinel, 363, 364
true, 361
types of, 361–366
Dravite, 114
Drawing from the microscope, 660–662
Drilling,
beads and hardstones, 393
pearls, 414, 430
Drills, bow, 393
Drop-shaped pearls, 414, 415
Drusy cavity, 10
Dry diggings, diamond, 20, 21, 22
Dugdale, R. A., 569
Dullam, 65
Dumelle's heat treatment of topaz, 111
Dumortierite, 165, 180, **265**
Durangite, 266
Durr-i-Dauran, Shah, 102
Dutch N.V. Bronswerk laboratory, The, 312
Dutch rose cut, 371, 372
Dutoitspan diamond mine, 20, 24
Dyed stones, 367, 368

Ebelmen, J. J., 335
Ectoderm, 399
Edges, crystal, 501, 502
Edison effect, 706
Edwardes ruby, 74
Egypt,
agate in, 184
emerald in, 77
onyx marble in, 238
peridot in, 128
silica glass in, 233
turquoise in, 199
'Egyptian alabaster', 238
Egyptian pebbles, 185
Eight-cut of diamond, 377
Eilat stone, 261
Einstein, A., 683
Ekanayake, F. L. D., 266
Ekanite, 266
Elath stone, 261
Electricity,
frictional, 716
pyro, 716, 717
piezo, 716–719

Electroconductivity, 333, 569, 716, 720, 721
Electromagnetic spectrum, 542, 543
Electron treated diamonds, 49, 569
Electron volts, 759
Electrons, 49, 494, 495, 497, 498, 683, 706, 726
Electropositive and negative elements, 726
Elephant ivory, 477
Elephant teeth, 479
Elster, x-ray experiments by, 706
'Emerala', 330
Emerald, **76–91**
  absorption spectrum of, 89
  coloured plate, facing page 84
  cut used for, 42, 373, 374
  cutting, 89, 390
  fluorescence spectrum of, 89, 696
  inclusions in, 80, 81, 84, 87, 88
  luminescence of, 89, 695
  mines,
    Algeria (?), 88
    Australia, 84
    Austria, 77
    Brazil, 82
    Chivor, 78
    Colombia, 78
    Cosquez, 78, 80
    Egypt, 77
    Habachthal, 77
    India, 86
    Kenya, 88
    Moçambique, 88
    Muzo, 78, 80
    Nemoncón, 78
    Norway, 88
    Pakistan, 87
    Rhodesia, 86
    Russia, 84, 100
    Somondoco, 78, 79
    South Africa, 85
    Transvaal, 85
    United States of America, 88
  simulation of, 90
  soudé, 90, 164, 363, 364
  synthetic, 90
  trapiche, 82
Emerald-coated beryl, 342
Emerald-cut, 42, **373**, 374, 386
Emerald Proprietary Mines, 84, 85
Emerita (symerald), 342
Emission lines, table of principal, 758, 759
Emission spectra, 605
Emmanuel, H., 17
Enantiomorphism, 162
Encrinital marbles, 6, 7, 244
Encystation (pearls), 400
Endoscope, 439

Energy states (levels), 496, 683
England,
  alabaster in, 249
  amber in, 466
  fluorspar in, 269
  hematite in, 224
  jet in, 473
  'marbles' in, 244
  quartz in, 172
  turquoise in, 202
Engraved gems, 369, 379, 380, 392
Engraving tools, 392
Enhydros, 185
Enstatite, 214, **266**
Eosite, 175
Epiasterism, 173, 365, 551
Epidote, **267**, 308
  transparency to x-rays, 710
Eppler, W. F., 117, 176, 177, 336, 338, 517, 588, 672
Equatorial Africa, diamonds in, 33
Erbium garnet, 343
'Erinide', 330
Espig, H., 336
Espinoso, B., 82
Essence d'orient, 450
Essonite garnet, 143
Ethylene dibromide, 525, 535
  table of density correction for, 770–772
Euclase, 268
Euhedral crystals, 149, **510**
Euxenite, 225, **226**
Exposure meters, 667, 669
Eye agate, 184
Eye, colour and vision response of, 557, 558
Eyeglass, watchmaker's, 626
Eyepieces (oculars),
  binocular, 633
  goniometric, 660, 661
  Huygenian, 632
  indicating, 652
  microscope, 632
  Ramsden, 632, 633, 660

Fabulite, 50, **333**, 344
Faces, crystal, 450
Faceting heads, mechanical, 392
Faience, 203, 345
Fajans, K., 569, 570
False cleavage (parting), 68, 520
Famous diamonds,
  Cullinan, 20
  Dewey, 18
  Dudley, 20
  Hope, 15
  Jehangir, 13, 15
  Koh-i-nûr, 13, 15

Famous diamonds—*Contd.*
Presidente Vargas, 18
Punch Jones, 18
Star of South Africa, 20
Woyie river, 33
table of, 777–779
Faraday dark space, 699
Faraday, M., 540
Farming cultured pearls, 421–429
Fashioning gemstones, 369–394
Fatty amber, 467
Favas, 18
Fayalite, 127
Feil, C., 314, 315
Feldspar (felspar),
albite, 154, 156
amazonite, 153
andesine, 152, 157
anorthite, 154, 159
bytownite, 154, 159
coloured plates, facing pages 130, 268
labradorite, 154, 157
microcline, 153
oligoclase, 154, 156
orthoclase, 149
peristerite, 156
perthite, 154
plagioclase, 154–159
sunstone, 155, 156
transparency to x-rays, 710
Fermor, L., 138
Ferrer's 'emerald', 90
Fersman, A. E., 207
Fibrolite, 268
colour plate, facing page 130
Fictile ivories, 488
Field, D. S. M., 581
Figure stone, 219
Filters, 598–600
Chelsea, 589
colour, 589
infra-red, 697
ultra-violet,
absorbing, 692
long-wave (Wood's glass), 684,
685, 688, 692
short-wave, 687
x-ray, 708
Finch, G. I., 382
Finland,
feldspar in, 158
star corundum in, 66
Finsch mine, 21
Fire (in gemstones), 45, 51, 548
Fire marble, 242
Fire marks, 320, 393
Fire opal, 187, 189, 350, 378
Firestones, 166, 366
'First water' diamonds, 41
Fish scale essence, 450

Fisheries, pearl, 404–414
Flame-fusion process, 316
Flame spectra, 606
Flèches d'amour, 165
Flohmig amber, 467
Florence marble, 244
Florentine mosaic, 380, 381
Flowering obsidian, 227
Fluograms, 691
Fluorescence, 682, 683
by x-rays, 709
colours of gems, table of, 766, 767
diamond, of, 46, 47, 694, 695
emerald, of, 89, 695
glass, of, 354, 355
pearl, of, 413
ruby, of, 70, 695
sapphire, of, 71, 695
spectra, 609, 696
spinel, of, 104, 695
synthetic stones, of, 323, 331, 695
Fluorspar (fluorite), 269
colour plate, facing page 500
cutting, 270
synthetic, 344
transparency to x-rays, 710
Flux melt process, 309, 326, 330, 336,
340
Focal length of lenses, 622–624
Focus tube (x-ray), 705
Foiled stones, 347
'Fool's gold', 222
Form birefringence, 174
Formation of pearls, 400
Formosa (Taiwan), nephrite in, 214
Forms, crystal, 501, 504
Forsterite, 127
Fortification agate, 184
Fossil,
agate, 181
coral, 182
dinosaur bone, 186
ivory, 478, 724
limestone, 6, 7
marble, 241, 244
opal, 189
turquoise, 282
wood, 186
Fox, J. J., 47
Fox Talbot, W. H., 605
Fractures in stones, 521
France,
garnet in, 147, 148
odontolite in, 283
onyx marble in, 240
zircon in, 122, 125
Fraunhofer, J., 604, 605
Fraunhofer lines, 604, 605, 614
table of the major, 758
Free pearls, 401

Fremy, E., 314, 315
Freshwater pearls, 412, 414
Fresnel, 540
Frictional electricity, 473, 716
Friedelite, 273
Friedlander, 310
Friedrich (x-ray lauegrams), 698, 702, 703
Frit, 203, 345
Frohlich, 436
Fuchsite, 175, 219, 304, 305
Fulgarites, 233
Furnace slag, 234
Fused-sand glass, 233

Gahnite, 273, (synthetic) 344
Gahnospinel, 103, 104
Galena, 307
Galibourg, J., 438, 442
Gallium aluminium garnets, 343
Gamma rays, 543, 567, 569, 721
Garnet, 134–148
  almandine, 139, 170
  andradite, 146
  coloured plates, facing pages 140, 500
  demantoid, 147
  formation of, 7–9
  grossular, 143
  hessonite, 143
  pyrope, 136, 371
  pyrope/almandine, 138
  rhodolite, 138
  spessartite, 142
  transparency to x-rays, 710
  uvarovite, 148
Garnet-topped doublets, 75, 90, 92, 93, 129, 361–363
Garnet type synthetic stones, 343
Gaudin, M. A. A., 313
Gedanite, 469
Geiger counter, 566, 567
Geissler, 698
Geissler tubes, 699
Geitel, 706
Gem belts, 11
Gem stick, 390
Gemmological Association, 533, 589, 599, 785
Gemolite microscope, 636
Gemological Institute of America, 41, 42, 558, 648, 649, 664, 715
General Electric Company (diamond synthesis), 22, 311, 312
'Geneva rubies', 313
Geniculate twins (crystals), 511
Geodes, 10
Geological Museum, London, 127
German lapis, 208

Germany,
  nephrite in, 207
  quartz in, 172, 174, 179, 184
  spessartite garnet in, 143
  topaz in, 111, 112
Geselle, 310
Ghana (Gold Coast), diamonds in, 32
Giant conch, 379
Gibraltar stone, 240, 245
Gidgee opal, 190
Gilbert, W., 716
Gilson, P., 340
Girdle, of cut stones, 371, 379
Girdling diamonds, 386
Glass, 345–355, 451–471, 474
  absorption spectra of, 354
  aventurine, 353
  beryl, 346
  bottle, 347
  coloured, 349
  colouring agents of, 348
  crown, 347
  densities of, 350
  determination of composition of, 349
  devitrification of, 353, 354
  flint, 347
  fluorescence of, 354, 355
  for cores of imitation pearls, 451
  haematinon, 353
  imitation amber, 471, 472
  inclusions in, 352
  natural, 227–234
  purpurine, 353, 354
  refractive indices of, 350
  silica, 334, 346
  transparency to x-rays of, 710
  types of, 347
Glassy diamonds (glassies), 33
Glassy ivory, 477
Gles (in diamonds), 383
Globulites, 228
Glossary of unusual names, 791–804
Gneiss, 7
Goethite, 165, 267, 276
Gold Coast (Ghana) diamonds, 31, 32
Golden quartz, 169
Gold in quartz, 167
Goldstein, 699
Goldstone, 208, 353
Goniometer (contact and reflecting), 502
Goniometric ocular, 660, 661
Goor, J., 33
Goshenite, 76, 91
Goutte d'eau (topaz), 109
Grading diamonds, 40
Grading pearls, 414
Graft tissue (cultured pearls), 427

Grain (weight),
  diamond, 394, 773
  pearl, 773
Gram(me), 773
Gramont, A. de, 609
Grande antique marble, 241
Granite, 2, 3, 9, 160
Granulite, 7
Graphite, 13, 22, **311**, 389
Grease table, 26, 27
'Green marble of Shrewsbury', 305
Greenockite, 344
Greenough microscope, 636
Green Pigeon Emerald Mine, 86
Green rouge (chromium oxide), 391
Greenstones, 261
Grenville Wells, J., 312
Grenz rays, 684, 707
Grimaldi's theories of light, 539
Grimmett, L. V., 567
Grinding,
  in diamond cutting, 385
  in lapidary work, 390
Griotte marble, 237
Griqualand West Diamond Mine, 24
Grodzinski, P., 518
Grossular garnet, 134, 135, 139, 142,
  143, 236
  as jade imitations, 218
  coloured plates, facing pages 140, 268
  localities for, 144, 145
Guanine, 450, 451
Guatemala, jadeite in, 216
Gübelin, E. J., 48, 71, 88, 137, 140, 144,
  216, 588, 648, 672
Guinea, diamonds in, 33
Guyana, diamonds in, 37, 38
Gypsum, 247
  alabaster, 247–249
  formation of, 4
  satin spar, 247
Gypsum plate, 658

Habit (crystals), 54, 55, 511, 512
Haematinon glass, 353
Halford Watkins, J. F., 106, 581
Haliotis, 403, 411, 461
Hall, A. L., 144
Halves (facets), 375
Hamberg, A., 273
Hambergite, 273
Hankel, W. G., 717
Hannay, J. B., 309
Hanovia Ltd. (ultra-violet lamps), 686,
  689, 691
Hansford, H. S., 210
Hard ivory, 477
Hardness, 514–518
  indenter tests, 518

Hardness—*Contd.*
  points, 515, 516
  scale (Mohs), 514
  table of, 749–751
  tests, 515, 516
  variations in, 517
Hartley, W. N., 609
Hautefeuille, P. G., 236
Haüy, Abbé, 273
Haüynite (haüyne), 206, 273
Haversian systems, 483
Hawaii,
  coral in, 458
  obsidian in, 229
  peridot in, 129
Hawk's bill turtle, 488
Hawk's eye, 174
Heat treatment,
  aquamarine, 91
  beryl, 367
  quartz, 169, 367
  spodumene, 133
  topaz, 110, 367
  tourmaline, 117
  zircon, 123, 367
  zoisite, 308
Heavy liquids, 523–528
  determining the density of, 528–533
Heavy media separation for diamond
  recovery, 26, 27
Heavy spar, 255
Hedenbergite, 264
'Heft', 538
Heliodor, 76, 91, 93
  colour plate, facing page 94
Heliotrope, 180
Helmet shell, 379, 462
'Hematine', 355, 721
Hematite, **223**, 276, 355
  as black pearl imitation, 454
  'scientific', 355
Hemihedral crystals, 510
Hemimorphism, 114, 510
Hemimorphite, 297
Hem pearls, 401
Henckel, 107
Henderson, E. P., 258
Henwoodite, 202
Herbert Smith, G. F., 434, 573
Herderite, 274
Herschel, J., 682
Hershey, J. W., 310
Hertfordshire pudding stone, 5
Hertz, H., 540, 698
Herz, G. L., 692, 693
Hessonite garnet, 142, **143**
  coloured plate, facing page 140
  transparency to x-rays, 710
Hexagonite, 303
Hidden, A. E., 130

Hiddenite, 130–132
Hippopotamus ivory, 478, 481
Hittorf tube (x-ray), 700
Hmyawdwin, 61
Hobbs, W. H., 18
Holmes powder diffraction method, 715
Holohedral crystals, 509
Holosymmetrical crystals, 509
Homopolar bond, 498
Honduras, opal in, 191
Hooke, R., 540
Hope diamond, 15
'Hope sapphire', 318
Hopkins, E., 434
Hopton Wood marble, 244
Hornblende, 3, 206
Hot cathode tube (x-ray), 706
Howlite, 206, **274**
Hue (colour), 555
Hughes Aircraft Company, 342
Huygenian eyepiece, 632
Huygens, C., 539, 540, 541
Hyalite, 190
Hydrogrossular garnet, **144**, 218
Hydrometer for specific gravity measurement, 530
Hydrophane, 190
Hydrostatic weighing, 523, 533–538
Hydrothermal crystal growth, 309, 325, 334, 336
Hydrothermal rubies, 325
Hypersthene-enstatite, 267
Hypostracum, 399

'Iceland agate', 229
Iceland spar, 553
Icositetrahedron, 501, 504
Identification of gemstones, 492, 493
Identification tables, 735, 772
Idiochromatic colour, 127, 559
Idocrase, 136, 218, **274**
I.G. Farbenindustrie, 336
Igmerald, 336, 337, 338
Igneous rocks, 1, 2, 6
Ike-chogai, 432
Ilford Ltd. (colour filters), 598
Illam, 64
Image stone, 298
Imitation coral, 458, 459
'Imitation cultured pearls', 451
Imitation gemstones, 345–360
Imitation pearls, 402, **449–454**
density of, 453
identification of, 452, 453
Immersion contrast method of refractive index measurement, 586, 587
Immersion sphere, 648
'Imperial Mexican jade', 240
Inca rose, 290

Inclusions in gemstones, 672–680
agate (moss), 181
almandine garnet, 139–141
amethyst, 170, 171
apatite, 666
aquamarine, 94, 95
beryl, 94, 679
chrysoberyl, 99, 100
classification of, 672
corundum (ruby and sapphire), 71–73, 668, 669, 675–679
demantoid garnet, 147, 673
diamond, 48
disappearing bubble, 679
emerald, 80, 81, 84, 87, 88, 673, 675
examination of, 644–648
gas and liquid, 676
glass, 351–353, 673
growth phenomena, 677
hessonite, 144, 145, 674
iolite, 276
labradorite, 158
liquid and gas, 676
moldavite, 231
moonstone, 150–152
obsidian, 228, 229
painite, 284
peridot, 128, 129
pyrope garnet, 137
rock crystal, 165, 166
silica glass, 234
solid, 675
spessartite garnet, 143
spinel, 105
sunstone, 157
synthetic stones, 320, 321, 325, 329, 337–342, 674
topaz, 111, 112, 670
tourmaline, 117
zircon, 125
zircon haloes, 73, 139, 667, 680
Indenter tests for hardness, 518
India,
aquamarine in, 92
chalcedony in, 179–181, 184
corundum in, 66
diamond in, 13
emerald in, 86
feldspar in, 151, 153, 156
garnet in, 140
jasper in, 186
quartz in, 172, 174, 175
turquoise in, 199
'Indian emerald', 91, 366
'Indian jade', 219
Indicating eyepiece, 652
Indication of position in microscope field, 652, 653
Indicators for heavy liquids, 527, 533
Indicolite, 114

Indo-China, zircon in, 122-126
Indonesia, diamonds in, **16**
Industrial diamonds, **40**
Infra-red filter and photography, 697
Inorganic substances, colours in, 569
Intaglio doublets, 366
Intaglios, 180, 379, 392
Intasia, 380, 381
Interfacial angles (crystals), 502, 503
Interference figures, 657–660
Interference of light, 551
Iolite, 11, **275**
Iona stone, 236
Ionic bonding, 497, 498
Ionic radii, 499, 500
Ions, 496, 500, 570, 571, 729
Iran (Persia), turquoise in, 198
Iris agate, 183
Iris quartz, 166, 366
Irish black marble, 241, 242
Irish green marble, 236, 296
Iron coloration, 561
Iron oxide, 391
Iron roses, 224
Isaacs, Barnet, 24
Isaacs, Henry, 24
Isogyres, 657–659
Isomorphism, 108, 136, 500
Isomorphous replacement, 500, 728
Isotopes, 496, 497
Italy,
    alabaster in, 249
    garnet in, 143, 147
    marble in, 235, 245
Ivory, 283, **475–488**, 724
    bastard, 478
    boar, 477, 479, 482
    care of, 482
    composition of, 480, 481
    density of, 481
    elephant, 477
    fashioning of, 482
    fictile, 488
    fossil, 478, 724
    glassy, 477
    hard, 477
    hippopotamus, 478, 481
    imitation, 482, 488
    mammoth, 478
    morse, 478
    narwhal, 479, 481
    nature of, 480
    properties of, 480–482
    ringy, 477
    river horse, 478
    sea horse, 478, 482
    soft, 477, 478, 481
    structure of, 480, 481
    types of, 477
    vegetable, 458, 484–487

Ivory—*Contd.*
    walrus, 478, 481
    whale, 479
Ivory Coast, diamonds in, 32
Ivory palm, 484

Jackson, H., 698, 705
Jackson tube (x-ray), 705
Jacobs finds South African diamond, 19, 20
Jade, 210–220
    coloured plates, facing pages 212, 218
    imitations of, 218–220
    mutton fat, 211
    New Zealand, 213
Jade albite, 216
Jadeite, **214–220**, 275, 276, 303
    coloured plate, facing page 218
    cutting, 217
    occurrences, 216
    staining of, 219, 367
    triplets, 220, 365, 366
'Jade matrix', 214
Jaeger, E., 336
Jagersfontein diamond mine, 20, 43
Jahanger, Shah, 102
Jamb peg, 390
James Bay Syndicate, 18
Japan,
    cultured pearls in, 421
    jadeite in, 216
    obsidian in, 229
    quartz in, 166, 172, 174, 179
    topaz in, 107, 112
Japanese Bureau of Fisheries, 420
Jargoon, 120
Jasp-agate, 186, 187
Jasp-opal, 190
'Java onyx', 240
Jayaraman, A., 168
Jearum, F. C., 379
Jehangir diamond, 13, 15
Jet, 4, **472–474**
    occurrences, 473
    properties of, 473
    transparency to x-rays, 710
Jonquin, 449, 450
'Jourado diamonds', 327

Kan (weight), 424
Kashmir, sapphires in, 64, 73
Kauri gum, 470, 471
Kenya,
    emeralds in, 88
    feldspar in, 156, 157
Kerf (separation of diamond), 383
Kerr, P., 435
Keying oysters for culturing, 427

Khalifah, Shaikh, 406
Kilkenny black fossil marble, 242
Kimberley Central Diamond Mining Company, 24
Kimberley diamond mine, 20, 23, 28
Kimberlite, 22, 25, 26
King cut, 377
King's coral, 458
Kirchoff, G. R., 605
Kirsten, F., 26
Klein, C., 649
Klein, F., 79
Klerk, de, 20
Knipping, 698, 702, 703
Knoop indenter hardness tester, 518
Kobin (in ruby mining), 60
Kodak Ltd. (colour filters), 598
Koh-i-nûr diamond, 13, 15
Kopje walloping, 24
Koranna stone, 289
'Korea jade', 218
Kornerup, A. N., 277
Kornerupine, 277
Krassov, 39
Kruisworker, 387
KTN, 344
Kundt, A. E., 717
Kunz, G. F., 130, 256, 681
Kunzite, 11, 93, **130–133**
    colour change by x-rays, 715
    colour plates, facing pages 130, 500
    occurrences, 131
Kuri Bay, Australia, 421
Kuwabara, O., 420
Kyanite, 269, **277**, 289
    transparency to x-rays, 710
    cat's-eyes, 277

Labradorescence, 550
Labradorite feldspar, 154, **157**
    coloured plate, facing page 268
Landerite, 146, 236
Landers, C. F. de, 146
Landscape agate, 181
Landscape marble, 244
Langevin, P., 717
Lap, 387, 392
Lapidary, 369, 389
Lapidary work, 369–389
Lapis-coloured synthetic spinel, 208, 331
Lapis lazuli, **206–209**, 299, 380
    coloured plate, facing page 268
    imitation of, 208
    occurrences of, 207
    properties of, 206
Lathi (weight), 774
Laue, Max v., 698, 702, 711
Lauegrams of pearls, 442, 445

Laufer, B., 199
Lauvikite, 159
Lava cameos, 245
Lavras series, 17
Laws of light,
    reflection, 545
    refraction, 546
Laxey diamonds, 15
Lazulite, 203, 278
Lazurapatite, 253
Lazurite, 206
Lebin (in ruby mining), 60
Lechatelierite, 233
Lechleitner, J., 342
Lechleitner synthetic emerald, 342, 343
Legrandite, 278
Leiper, H., 110
Leitz, E., 649
Leme, F. P., 83
Lenard, P., 682, 698, 702
Lens cut, 378
Lenses, 622–628
    aberrations of, 624–626
    achromatic, 625
    Bertrand, 639, 654, 657
    focus of, 622–624
    magnification of, 626–628
Lepidolite, 279
Leroux, 436
Leschot, Professor, 42
Lesotho (Basutoland), diamonds in, 37
Leucite, 279
Leveridge gauge, 396
Lewis, M. D. S., 366
Liesegang, R. E., 183
Ligament pearls, 401
Light,
    early notions of, 539, 540
    interference of, 551
    polarization of, 552, 553
    reflection of, 544
    refraction of, 545, 552, 553
    sources for,
        absorption spectroscopy, 614
        microscope, 641, 649
        refractometer, 578, 579
        spectroscope, 614–617
    speed of, 543
    table of spectrum, 758
    total internal reflection of, 547, 548
    transparency to, 543, 544
    wave form of, 541, 542
    wave theory of, 540
Lightwire, 664, 665
Lignite, 4
Limestone, 4, 6, 7, 9, 11, 206, 240–244
Limonite, 174, 179
Lind, S. C., 566
Linde Air Products, 340

Lindemann glass, 707, 713
Lindemann, Professor, 717
Linne, C. V., 418
'Linobate', 344
Lintonite, 303
Lippman, G., 717
Liquid immersion (microscope), 645
Liquids for immersion methods, 589
Lithia emerald, 130
Lithia mica, 279
Lithium niobate, 344
Lithosphere, 1, 2
Lizardite, 294, 295
Llanoite (llanite), 287
Lobo, B. F., 17
Lodes, 9
London Chamber of Commerce, 598
Lonsdale, K., 310, 312
Lorenzen, J., 277
Louderback, G. D., 256
Loupes (lenses), 626
Lucas, A., 345
Lucidoscope, 435–437
Lumachella(e), 242
Luminescence, 681–697
    alexandrite, 98, 99, 695
    benitoite, 696
    diamond, 46, 47, 694, 697
    emerald, 89, 695
    gemstones, 681–697
    glass, 354, 355
    moonstone, 153
    ruby, 70, 695–697
    sapphire, 71, 695
    spinel, 104, 105, 695, 697
    spodumene, 131
    synthetic stones, 323, 331, 696, 697
    topaz, 110
    tourmaline, 116
    x-rays, by, 665, 709
Luminograms, 691
Lunette, 374
Lustre, 13, 69, 540
Lydian stone, 186

Mabe pearls, 419
Mackowsky, M.-T., 134
Macles, 13, 40, 387
Madagascar (Malagasy),
    beryl in, 93
    chrysoberyl in, 101
    feldspar in, 151, 152, 154, 158
    garnet in, 141, 143
    quartz in, 166, 172, 174
    ruby in, 66
    sapphire in, 66
    spodumene in, 132
    topaz in, 112
    tourmaline in, 118

'Madeira topaz', 169
Magma, 1–3
Magna cut, 377,378
Magnesite, 279, 295
Magnetism, 721
Magnetite, 105, 294
Magnification,
    lenses, of, 625, 627, 628
    photomicrographs, of, 670
Magnifiers, 622, 623, 626
Make (of cut stone), 378
Malachite, 175, 200, 203, 204, 255, 262,
    279, 289, 296, 345, 390
    coloured plate, facing page 268
Malacolite, 264
Malawi (Nyasaland), corundum in, 66
Mammoth ivory, 478
Manchadi (weight), 774
Mangelin (weight), 774
Manilla shell, 460
Mantle (of oyster), 401
Mantle pearls, 401
Maori stone, 213, 294
Marble, 1, 4, 6, 7, 235–246, 380, 427
Marble of Carystus, 237
Marcasite, 221
Marco Polo, 57, 199, 207
Marek, J. I., 310
Marekanite, 227
Margarites, 228
Marialite, 291, 292
Marine Diamond Corporation, 30
Marquise cut, 374, 376
Marsden, S. R., 310
Martin, A. E., 47
Masers, 326
'Mass-aqua', 351
'Matara diamonds', 120
Maw-sit-sit, 216
Maxixe beryl, 92
Maxwell, J. C., 540
Measurement of refractive index, 573–
    597
Measurements of stones, 397
Mechanical dop, 388
Mechanical faceting head, 392
Meerschaum, 281
Meionite, 291, 292
Melanite garnet, 135, 146
Mêlée, 40
Melinophane (Meliphanite), 281
Melt diffusion method (crystal grow-
    ing), 309
Mendeleeff, D. I., 496, 727
Mendoza, F. M., 78
Menilite, 190
Ment, J. de, 691
Mesolite, 281
Mesons, 494
Metalix x-ray apparatus, 704

Metallic bonds, 450
Metamict stones, 121, 123, 266
Metamorphic rocks, 1, 6
Metamorphism, 6, 7, 8
Meteorites, 230
Methylene iodide, **524**, 527, 585, 645
'Mexican emeralds', 78
'Mexican jade', 240, 368
'Mexican onyx', 239
Mexico,
    garnet in, 141
    jadeite in, 216
    nephrite in, 214
    obsidian in, 229
    onyx marble in, 239
    opal in, 191, 192
    quartz in, 172
    topaz in, 112
Miarolite cavities, 3
Mica plate, 658
Michaud (synthetic ruby), 314
Michel, H., 98, 438, 600, 672, 684, 693, 694
Microcline feldspar, 149, **153**
    as jade imitation, 218
Microlite, 282, 550
Micron, 543
Microscope,
    care and cleaning of, 643
    compound, 628, 629
    drawing from, 660–662
    eyepieces, 632
    focusing, 641
    Gemolite, 636, 637
    Greenough binocular, 636
    magnification of, 634, 635
    objectives, 631, 632
    oculars, 632
    parts of, 629, 631
    pearl, 437, 439
    petrological, 639, 641
    polarizing, 638, 639
    Rayner gemmological, 637
    simple (lens), 626
Midnight Star sapphire, 75
Mikimoto, K., 419, 420, 425
Milky quartz, 166
Mill, diamond, 388
Miller, W. H., 509
Miller indices, 509
Millerite, 282
Millimicron (unit of measurement), 543
Mimetite, 282
Minas series, 17
Mineralogical Magazine, 314
Mingaye (Australian opal), 192
Minimum deviation method, 591–597
Mining,
    diamond, 17, 22, 31
    emeralds, 79, 86

Mining—*Contd.*
    methods, 12
    opal, 195
    ruby and sapphire, 59–64
Miscal (weight), 774
Mise, T., 420
Miskeyite, 296
Mitchell, R. K., 616, 617, 680
Mizzonite, 292
Moçambique,
    emerald in, 88
    star beryl in, 95
    tourmaline in, 118
Mocha stone, 181
Moe diamond gauge, 396
Mogok, 11, 59, 277, 292
Mohs, F., 68, 514
Mohs's scale, 514
Moissan, H., 19, 309, 310, 315
Moldavite, 230, 231
Molina rosa marble, 23
Momme (weight), 413,
Mona marble, 295
Monitor jets, 12
Monnickendam, A., 379
Monobromonapthalene, **525**, 527, 646
Monochromatic light, 579, 584
Montana sapphires, 55, **66**, 73, 318
Montana Sapphire Syndicate, 85
Moonstone, **149–152**, 158, 330
    coloured plate, facing page 268
Moralla, 79
Morgan, J. P., 93
Morganite, 76, **93**, 340
    coloured plate, facing page 94
Morion, 167
Morocco, onyx marble in, 238
Moroxite, 252
Morse ivory, 478
Mosaics, 380–382
Moss agate, 180, 181
Mother-of-pearl, 399, 419, 427, 428, 431, 443, 451, 454, 460, 461
Mountain mahogany, 227
Mud saw, 390
Müllers glass, 190
Multi-facet cut, 379
Muscle pearls, 401
Mussel pearls, 418, 432
Mussels, 412, 413, 418, 432
Mutton fat jade, 211, 213, 303
Myrickite, 180

Naats, 19, 387
Nacken, R., 336, 340, 436
Nacre, 399, 431
Nacreous layer (pearl shell), 398, 399
Nagy, A., 378
Napoleonite, 287

Narwhal ivory, 479, 481
National Association of Goldsmiths, 785
National Physical Laboratory, 312
Natrolite, 281, **282**
  relation to mesolite, 281
Natural glasses, 227–234
'Naturals', 50
Nautilus, 463
Navette cut, 374, 376
Neolith, 204
Nephrite, 145, **210–214**, 217, 303
  coloured plate, facing page 212
Netsukes, 475, 476
Neutroned diamonds, 49
Neutrons, 49, 494, 497, 567, 568

7
773

C. A., 310
Nicol prism, 637, 638
Nicol, W., 637
Nicols (polars), crossed, 654
Niekerk, S. van, 20
Nigeria, topaz in, 111, 113
Ninemire, 318
Nishikawa, T., 420
Nobbies, 193
Nodules, 10
Noir Belge marble, 241
Noir Français marble, 241
Non-nucleated cultured pearls, 402, 431, **432**, 446
North America,
  beryl in, 88, 92, 93, 94
  chalcedony (and agate) in, 177–184
  corundum in, 55, 66, 73
  diamonds in, 18
  feldspar in, 152, 153, 156–159
  jade in, 213, 214, 216
  jasper in, 186
  lapis lazuli in, 208
  onyx marble in, 239
  opal in, 196
  peridot in, 129
  quartz in, 166, 167, 170, 172, 177–179
  sodalite in, 298
  spodumene in, 130–132
  topaz in, 107, 109, 112
  tourmaline in, 117–119
  turquoise in, 197, 198, 201, 204
Norway,
  corundum in, 66

Norway—*Contd.*
  emerald in, 88
  feldspar in, 156, 159
  garnet in, 143
  peridot in, 129
  zircon in, 125
Noselite, 206
Nuclear charge, 496
Nucleus operation on cultured pearl, 427
N.V. Bronswerk (Holland), 312
Nyasaland (see Malawi)
Nyf, 13
Nylon, 358, 360, 730

Objectives, microscope, 631, 632
3, 160, **227–229**, 350, 474
  lal fracture in, 521
, 231
n, 13, 44, 500, 504
32
tric, 660, 661
an, 632
g, 652
pe, 632
1, 632, 633, 660
203, **282**
chem   distinction, 731
Oil pear 462
Oitava (ight), 774
Okkolite, 04
Oligoclase eldspar, 154, **156**
Olivine, 1, 126
'Once the weight', 415
Onyx, 180
'Onyx-alabaster' (oriental), 237, 238
Onyx-marble, 10, 180, 208, 235, **237**, 238, 290, 299, 785
  formation of, 10
Opal, **187–196**, 380
  doublets, 188, 190, 365
  imitations, 365
  transparency to x-rays, 710
  wood, 6, 189
Opalescence, 189, 551
Opalite, 190, 365
Open forms of crystals, 501
Operculum, 463
  coloured plate, facing page 268
Ophicalcite, 236, 295, 296
Optic axial angle, 658–660
Optic axis, 553, 554, 583, 584
Optic sign, 582, 583, 584, 658
Optical properties, table of, 744
Optical separation of diamond (mining), 27
Orbicular jasper, 185, 186
'Oregon jade', 180
O'Reilly, J. R., 20

Orient of pearl, 401, 413
'Oriental alabaster', 237
Ormer shells, 411
Ornamental stones, 247–308
    coloured plate, facing page 268
Orthoclase feldspar, **149**, 150, 152
    coloured plate, facing page 130
Oscillators, quartz, 719, 720
Osmond, 514
Osseous amber, 467
Osteodentine, 481
Ottosdal G stone, 289
Ounce (weight), 773, 774
'Oxitol', 646
Ozarkite, 303

Paars (oyster beds), 406
Padparadscha, 54
    colour plate, facing page 72
Pagoda stone, 184
Pain, A. C. D., 283
Painite, 283, 284
'Painted' diamonds, 366
Painted stones, 90, 366
Pakistan,
    emerald in, 87
    garnet in, 145, 146
    lapis lazuli in, 208
    pearls in, 413
'Palmyra topaz', 169
Paludina limestone (marble), 242
Panna Diamond Mining Syndicate,
    15
Paper wearing, 121, 397
Parallel grouping (crystals), 510
Paramagnetism, 721
Paris Academy of Sciences, 315
'Paris jet', 474
Paris, L., 326
Parsons, C., 310
Parting (false cleavage), 68, 520
Paste, 349
Paua shell, 411, 461
Pavilion facets, 375
Pavonazzo marble, 237
Payne, C. J., 103, 577, 596, 605
Peace ruby, 74
Pearl, J., 82
Pearl, R., 143, 458
Pearl, 398–454
    composition of, 401
    orient of, 401
    structure of, 401, 431
Pearl,
    cardiometer, 438, 439
    compass, 436–438
    endoscope, 439
    essence, 449
        imitation, 453

Pearl—*Contd.*
    fisheries,
        salt water,
            Australian, 402, 409, 420, 421
            cultured, 402, 410, 420–422
            Gulf of California, 402, 410, 411
            Gulf of Manaar, 402, 404, 406
            Gulf of Mexico, 410
            Gulf of Panama, 411
            Indian, 409
            Japanese, 402, 410, 420–422
            Mergui archipelago, 409
            Persian Gulf, 402, 404
            Red Sea, 404, 408
            Shark Bay, 402, 408, 410
            South Sea Islands, 409, 410, 420
            Venezuela, 402, 410
        fresh water,
            Amazon Basin, 413
            Bavaria, 402, 413
            Canada, 402
            China, 418
            Eire (Ireland), 412
            France, 402, 413
            Pakistan, 413
            Russia, 402, 413
            Scandinavia, 402, 413
            Scotland, 402, 412, 413
            United States of America, 402,
                413
            Wales, 402, 412, 413
    grain (weight), 415, 773
    lauegrams, 442
    lucidoscope, 435–437
    microscope, 437, 439
    mussels, 403
    oysters, 398, 399
    sac, 400
    statement, 415
    stringing, 415
Pearlometer, 438
Pearls,
    alasmodon, 413
    antilles, 462
    baroque, 414
    barrok, 414
    Biwa, 432, 446
    bleaching of, 429
    blister, 399, 419, 421
    blue, 403, 446
    Bombay bunch of, 414, 415
    bouton, 414
    button, 414, 415
    'candling', 436
    care of, 416, 433
    chicot, 400
    Chinese drilled, 415
    clam, 403, 412
    coloured, 403, 413, 414
    conch, 403, 411, 412, 462

Pearls—*Contd.*
cultured, 402, 414, 418–449
cyst, 400, 401
density of, 401, 402, 412, 435, 453
Dobo, 409
doctoring, 416
drilling, 414, 430
drop-shaped, 414, 415
fluorescence of, 413, 446, 449
free, 401
grading, 414, 430
haliotis, 411
hem, 401
imitation, 402, 449–454
ligament, 401
mabe, 419
mantle, 401
muscle, 401
mussel, 418
natural formation of, 400
non-nucleated cultured, 402, 421, 432, 446
oil, 462
pear-shaped, 414
price calculation of, 415
river, 412
roman, 449
rosée, 402, 414, 417
Scotch, 412
seed, 414, 416
shapes of, 414
skinning, 416
staining, 417, 434
surface structure of, 402
testing, 434–449
treatment of, 416, 433
Pectolite, 284
'Pedrara onyx', 239
Pegmatites, 3, 12
Pei-Tung, 475
Pendoloque, 376
Pentlandite, 226
Pentelicum marble, 235
Perfido rosso antico, 287
Perfido serpentine, 3, 287
Periclase (synthetic), 344
Peridot, **126–130**, 296, 378
coloured plates, facing pages 108, 500
transparency to x-rays, 710
Perisarc, 455
Peridotite, 22
Periodic classification of the elements, 499, 726
Periodic system, 499
Periostracum, 399, 461, 464
Peristerite feldspar, 156
Permissible names, list of, 785–790
Perovskite, 333
Perrey, A., 336
Perrin, A., 439

Persia (Iran), turquoise in, 198
Persistent lines of emission spectra, 609
Perspex, as imitation gemstones, 357, 451, 471, 474
Perthite feldspar, 154
Peruzzi, V., 374
Petalite, **284**, 286
Petoskey stone, 243
Petri dishes, 647
Petrified dinosaur bone, 186
Petrified wood, 186, 189
Petrological microscope, 639–641
Petworth marble, 242
Phantom crystals, 162
Phase-difference microscopy, 652
Phenakite (phenacite), 100, **285**, 338, 344
transparency to x-rays, 710
Philips Electrical Company Ltd., 689
germicidal lamp of, 689–691
Phosgenite, 285
Phosphate, test for, 732
Phosphophyllite, 285
Phosphorescence, 681–683
diamond, of, 47, 695
Photography,
films (plates) for, 669, 670
fluorescence, 692
infra-red, 697
micrography, 662–671
Photoluminescence, 682, 684
Photons, 541, 683
Piccard, 570
Piedmontite, 268
Pierre des Incas, 221
Pieters, S., 175
Pietersite, 175
Pietra dura, 380, 381
Piezoelectric effect, 717
Piezoelectricity, 716–719
quartz, in, 164, 165
tourmaline, in, 115
Pigeon stone, 156
Piggy-back diamond, 50
Pile, atomic, 49, 567
Pile treated diamonds, 49, 568
Pinacoid, 508, 509
Pineapple opal, 190
Pingo d'agoa, 109
Pinite, 219
'Pink moonstone', 292
Pink Welsh alabaster, 249
Pipes, diamond, 15, 20–25, 309
Piqué work, 490
Pistacite, 267
Pit amber, 466
Pit glass, 232
Pits (in crystals), 512, 513
Placer deposits, 5
Plagioclase feldspars, 149, 150, **154–159**